ISBN 978-0-266-96402-5
PIBN 10916416

TENTH ISSUE.

A STATISTICAL ACCOUNT

OF

AUSTRALIA

AND

NEW ZEALAND

1902-3

BY

T. A. COGHLAN.

PUBLISHED BY AUTHORITY OF THE GOVERNMENT OF THE STATE OF NEW SOUTH WALES
AND OF THE COMMONWEALTH OF AUSTRALIA.

1904

SYDNEY: W. A. GULLICK, GOVERNMENT PRINTER.

PREFACE.

The general plan adopted in previous issues has been followed on the present occasion, but additional chapters have been added, giving a general and physical description of each State and of New Zealand, and the scope of several others has been greatly enlarged. In order to make space for the new matter, the historical sketches appearing in the last two issues have been omitted. Owing to the necessity for printing off the chapters as they were compiled, no attempt has been made to arrange them in their natural order of sequence, but the voluminous index provided will save the reader inconvenience on this score.

In all cases the figures have been revised to accord with the latest information, and as a rule they refer either to the year 1902 or to the year 1903; in some instances, however, owing to the undue delay in publishing the official statistics, I have been compelled to use figures relating to 1901, but the instances where this was necessary were neither many nor important.

Care has been taken to correct errors which have escaped notice in previous editions, and to keep this edition free from them. Should any such have remained undetected, as in the multitude of references is quite possible, it would be deemed a favour if their nature and position were pointed out.

I desire to return thanks to the Statisticians of the States and New Zealand, and to the various officers of the Commonwealth and of the States who have so readily on all occasions supplied me with information asked for.

The issues of this work for past years appeared under the title of "The Seven Colonies of Australasia." It will be noticed that the present edition is entitled "A Statistical Account of Australia and New Zealand."

T. A. COGHLAN.

Statistician's Office,
Sydney, 27th January, 1904.

CONTENTS.

AREA AND PHYSICAL CONFIGURATION.

THE Australasian colonies comprise the continent of Australia, the adjacent island of Tasmania, and the islands of New Zealand. The group was formerly subdivided politically into seven colonies; but on the 1st January, 1901, the five mainland states and Tasmania became the Commonwealth of Australia, New Zealand retaining its position as a separate colony. The respective areas of the six states and New Zealand are as follow:—

State.	Area in acres.	Area in square miles.
New South Wales	198,848,000	310,700
Victoria	56,245,760	87,884
Queensland	427,838,080	668,497
South Australia	578,361,600	903,690
Western Australia	624,588,800	975,920
Tasmania	16,778,000	26,215
Commonwealth of Australia	1,902,660,240	2,972,906
New Zealand	66,861,440	104,471
Australasia	1,969,521,680	3,077,377

To the area of the Commonwealth shown in the table might be added that of New Guinea, comprising 90,000 square miles. This would bring the area of territory controlled by the Commonwealth to 3,062,906 square miles, and the total area of British Australasia to 3,167,377 square miles.

The British Empire, exclusive of territories under protectorates and spheres of influence, extends over an area of 8,856,000 square miles, so that about 35 per cent. of its area lies within the limits of Australia and New Zealand. Australasia is more than twenty-six times as large as the United Kingdom; more than fifteen times as large as France; more than half as large again as Russia in Europe; and almost equal in extent to the continent of Europe or to the United States of America.

A

AUSTRALIA.

THE sea-girt continent of Australia is situated in the Southern Hemisphere, between the Indian and Pacific Oceans, and lies in that portion of the globe extending from lat. 10° 39′ S. to lat. 39° 11′ S., and from long. 113° 5′ E. to long. 153° 16′ E. On the north it is bounded by the Timor Sea, the Arafura Sea, and Torres Strait; on the east by the Pacific Ocean; on the south by Bass Strait and the Southern Ocean; and on the west by the Indian Ocean. From north to south the greatest length measures 1,971 miles, and the greatest breadth east and west is about 2,400 miles. Its superficial area is approximately 2,946,691 square miles, with a coast-line measuring about 8,850 miles. The coastal perimeter is equal to 1 mile for every 333 square miles of area—the smallest proportion shown by any of the continents. The Tropic of Capricorn divides Australia into two unequal parts, and in its vast area the continent contains every variety of climate from temperate to tropical.

As regards the general appearance of its land surface, Australia may be described as a plateau, fringed by a low-lying well-watered coast, with a depressed and, for the most part, arid interior. In its mean height, the land mass of the continent rises to a less elevation than that of any other of the continental surfaces of the globe. Fully 500,000 square miles of the area of Australia consist of a great central plain, the vast bulk of which is situated to the south of the 22nd degree; but portions of it stretch upward to the low-lying country in the region south of the Gulf of Carpentaria.

The vast cordillera of the Great Dividing Range originates in the south-eastern corner of the continent, and runs parallel with and close to the eastern shore, through the states of Victoria and New South Wales, right up to the far-distant York Peninsula of Queensland. In Victoria the greatest elevation is reached in the peaks of Mount Hotham and Mount Smyth, each over 6,000 feet in height, with various other summits exceeding 5,000 feet. The loftiest portion of the range is in the region near the confines of Victoria and New South Wales, where Mount Kosciusko reaches an altitude of over 7,000 feet. The Dividing Range, with its lateral spurs, receives various sectional names in the states through which it passes. More detailed reference to these will be found in the chapters dealing with the physical characteristics of particular states. The seaward slope of the range is generally sharp and precipitous, and in places marked by chasms and precipices unequalled in grandeur in any other part of the world. On the western side, the descent is more gradual, the table-land merging by easy degrees into the great plain region towards the centre of the continent. In Victoria, the mountain range known as the Grampians commences near the south coast at Portland Bay, and runs in a north and south direction connecting with the Dividing Range by the Pyrenees and Australian Alps. In South Australia, a chain of mountains of no great elevation runs northward from Cape Jervis to the region occupied by Lake Torrens and other salt-water lakes. The plateau in Western Australia is traversed by ranges in various localities, and these, while of no great altitude, possess a certain grandeur in some instances, from the fact that their rugged masses rise abruptly from a level plain. Little accurate knowledge is at present possessed of the mountainous region in the "Nor'-west" district of Western Australia, and in the Northern Territory of South Australia.

The continent possesses no mountains clothed with perpetual snow, nor are there any active volcanoes on its surface. More or less conclusive signs of past glacial action have been reported from the Southern States, and there is also evidence of convulsive volcanic movements in some regions. In Victoria certain peaks in the western district have been in eruption posterior to the arrival of the aboriginal. Perfectly shaped cones may be seen, together with beds of ash and scoriæ little affected by denuding agencies. In the Mount Gambier district of South Australia there are some beautiful little crater lakes occupying the crater hollows of extinct volcanoes. Considerable outpourings of lava took place in late Tertiary times from many points in the Great Dividing Range of Eastern Australia. In the Illawarra district of New South Wales the irruption of an igneous dyke turned portion of the coal seams into a natural coke, the article being largely used on the old metropolitan steam trams. The sandstone in the vicinity of Sydney has in places been hardened by similar means. It is noticeable, however, that all recent volcanic action was confined to the coastal area, no evidence of late lava flows being met with in the plain district of the interior. For a long time Mount Wingen in New South Wales was looked upon as a volcano, but the fires of this burning mountain result from the slow combustion of coal seams in its interior, probably ignited in the first instance by the agency of lightning.

It has been customary to regard the central portion of the continent as being a vast desert, but later knowledge has caused a considerable modification of this idea. There is undoubtedly a large area occupied by barren sandhills, or covered for miles with deposits of peculiar rounded boulders. Then there is the spinifex country, which looks fair enough from a distance, but is actually more hopeless for settlement purposes than what is sometimes called the "Stony Desert," which in good seasons is covered with fine pasturage, and has been occupied for pastoral purposes.

Although there are numerous spacious harbours on the coast of Australia, the shore line, generally speaking, is broken by few remarkable indentations, the most extensive being the Gulf of Carpentaria on the north, which extends inland for a distance of 650 miles, with a breadth of 400 miles, and Spencer's Gulf on the south, penetrating inland for 180 miles, with a breadth varying from 10 to 80 miles. On the north-west coast there are some fine inlets, but none reaches the dimensions of the smaller of the gulfs just mentioned.

Geological research seems to show that Australia is one of the oldest existing land surfaces, and the remarkable character of its fauna and flora as compared with those of other lands is due to this great antiquity

A peculiar feature in the physical aspect of Australia is the absence of rivers connecting the coast-line with the interior, and in keeping with this is the solid outline of the shore generally. From the appearance on the map of the concourse of streams comprised in the Murray and Darling systems, the idea of a well-watered country might be inferred. Many of the tributary streams, however, have running water only after periods of heavy rainfall, and generally fail to reach the main drainage line. The Darling is reckoned amongst the longest rivers in the world, for in certain seasons it is navigable from Walgett to its confluence with the Murray, a distance of 1,758 miles, and thence downward to the sea, a further 587 miles, making a total navigable extent of 2,345 miles. This by no means conveys a true idea of the river, for in dry seasons it can hardly be said to drain its own watershed, and gives water to, rather than receives it from, the surrounding country. In flood-time these rivers spread out over an immense extent of territory, but with the cessation of the rainfall the waters speedily drain off, and the flow is confined to the river beds. Another system of inland drainage comprises the streams which terminate in Lake Eyre, in South Australia. These include all the channels which lead south from the northern watershed, and from the MacDonnell Range, an isolated mass of eruptive granite in the centre of the continent. Such are the Barcoo, Thomson, Diamantina, Cooper's Creek, and several others. They are all absorbed in the saline swamp of Lake Eyre, and some of them, in dry periods, do not reach so far, but sink their scanty contents into the sands.

A large portion of the southern district of West Australia, and part of the western district of South Australia, is destitute of running streams. Indeed over a considerable extent of the coast line in the Great Australian Bight there is no break in the continuity of the bare and precipitous cliffs. Inland from the Bight the aspect is sterile and forbidding, but here and there patches of good country may be found, needing only the presence of permanent water to make them fit for occupation.

In the western half of Australia there are no river systems except upon the coast, and the desert indications begin on the crest of the table-land. In the Kimberley district there are some fine streams which penetrate some distance inland, but this portion of the continent has yet to be thoroughly explored.

The absence of lakes of any considerable size or permanence is another characteristic of the physical features of Australia. As marked on some maps, the inland lakes of South Australia appear to possess a considerable size, but they are mostly shallow salt marshes, their area depending entirely on the rainfall. Lake Eyre is 39 feet below sea-level, and although in the wet seasons it receives a vast volume of water, it shrinks in periods of drought into a mere salt bog. Lake Torrens is 100 feet above sea-level, and lies between Lake Eyre and the sea. Lake Amadeus is a salt marsh in the interior of the continent, which receives the western drainage of the MacDonnell Range. Much of the drainage received by these lakes passes off by evaporation, but a large volume sinks into the earth, finding its way to the sea by subterranean channels, or else helping to swell the store of artesian water in the reservoirs hidden deep below the surface of the soil.

It will not be necessary here to refer further to the physical features of the country, as these are described with some detail in the following pages dealing with the characteristics of the various states.

NEW SOUTH WALES.

Area and Boundaries.

THE State of New South Wales lies almost entirely between the 29th and 36th parallels of south latitude, and between the 141st and 153rd meridians east of Greenwich. It is bounded on the east by the Pacific Ocean, to which it presents a coast-line extending over 700 miles, from Point Danger at its north-eastern extremity to Cape Howe at the south-east. From the point last mentioned, which is also the north-east limit of the state of Victoria, it is bounded by an imaginary line, running in a north-westerly direction to the source of the Indi, a stream rising at the foot of Forest Hill, a few miles south of the Pilot Mountain, one of the most conspicuous peaks of the Australian Alps. The southern boundary of the state follows the course of the Indi, and afterwards of the Murray, into which the first-named stream ultimately merges, as far as the 141st meridian of east longitude. The intersection of the Murray with this meridian forms a common point of the three states of New South Wales, Victoria, and South Australia.

On the west, the state is separated from South Australia by the line of the 141st meridian, as far as its intersection with the 29th parallel of south latitude, at which point New South Wales, South Australia, and Queensland touch. Commencing at this point, the northern boundary of the state follows the 29th degree of latitude, till it is crossed by the Macintyre River, one of the upper branches of the Darling, not far from the 149th meridian. Thence it follows the course of the Macintyre upward, to the junction of its tributary, the Dumaresq; leaving the Macintyre, it follows the tributary stream till it meets a spur extending from the Main Dividing Range to the junction of Tenterfield Creek and the Dumaresq. The boundary runs along this spur until it joins the main range, thence, almost parallel to the coast, it follows the Dividing Range to Wilson's Peak, where the Macpherson Range branches eastward. Following the last-named range, the northern boundary reaches the coast at Point Danger.

The area comprised within these limits is estimated at 310,700 square miles. The length of the state, from Point Danger on the north to Cape Howe on the south, is 680 miles. From east to west, along the 29th parallel, the breadth is 760 miles, while diagonally from the south-west corner, where the Murray passes into South Australia, to Point Danger, the length reaches 850 miles.

Coastal Features.

The coast-line of New South Wales, while not deeply indented, is by no means monotonous in outline. Rugged and precipitous cliffs alternate with long stretches of silver or golden sands, varied by curving bays and wide river estuaries. In places the coast-range approaches so close to the shore that the mountains appear to rise sheer out of the ocean. In no instance do the capes project very far out from the mainland, and the coast is singularly free from dangerous reefs or shoals, while lighthouses have been erected at various prominent points. The general trend of the shore-line is from north-east to south-west through about four degrees of longitude, from Point Danger on the north in longitude 154 degrees E. (about) to Cape Howe on the south in longitude 150 degrees E.

Commencing on the north, the principal indentations are as follow :—

Byron Bay, inside the cape of the same name offers shelter, in all but north-east weather, to vessels trading to Queensland. A large pier has been constructed, by means of which the produce of the neighbouring districts of the Brunswick and Tweed may be shipped when an entrance to these rivers is impracticable.

At Shoal Bay, the entrance to the Clarence, the anchorage is safe and commodious, and when the works designed for improving the river entrance are completed, it promises to be one of the best ports on the coast.

Trial Bay, at the mouth of the Macleay, Port Macquarie, at the mouth of the Hastings, and the harbour at Forster, near Cape Hawke, afford good anchorage. Port Stephens, a little farther south, is a safe and commodious port, and the scenery of its shores is remarkably beautiful. At present this harbour is little used, owing to its proximity to Newcastle and the sparseness of the population in its immediate neighbourhood.

Twenty miles farther south is Port Hunter, at the mouth of the river of that name. When first used, the harbour was inconvenient and dangerous; but this has been altered entirely by the breakwaters and training-walls which have been constructed. Newcastle harbour is now safe and roomy, with shipping facilities equal to those found in any other Australian port.

A few miles farther south is Lake Macquarie, in the centre of the coal-field of the Newcastle district, and covering an area of 44 square miles. The great drawback to the lake as a shipping port has been the shallowness of its entrance; but extensive dykes and training-walls have been commenced, which have already increased the draught of water in the channel.

Broken Bay, 15 miles north of Port Jackson, forms the mouth of the River Hawkesbury. It has a bold entrance, and on Barranjoey, the southern headland, a fine lighthouse has been erected. The bay has three branches, Brisbane Water being the northern, the Hawkesbury mouth the centre, and Pittwater the southern arm. The first-named opens out into a series of lakes, and the town of Gosford, standing at the head of one of them—the Broadwater—is the centre of an important district. The scenery at and around Broken Bay is characteristically Australian, and in natural beauty rivals even Sydney Harbour. South of Broken Bay the coast-line is a succession of high cliffs and sandy beaches.

The entrance to Port Jackson lies between perpendicular cliffs of sandstone several hundred feet high, and only 74 chains, or nearly one mile, apart. Sydney Harbour has been too often described to require a lengthy reference here. It holds the first place amongst the harbours of the world for convenience of entrance, depth of water, and natural shipping facilities. Its natural beauties charm all who visit its shores, and in the quiet waters of its numerous bays and coves the navies of the world might securely rest. The area of water surface of the harbour proper is 15 square miles, and the shore-line is 165 miles in circuit. At the South Head is erected a splendid lighthouse, fitted with an electric arc light, visible at a distance of 25 miles. On the shores of Port Jackson stands Sydney, the capital of New South Wales and the mother city of the Australias.

Botany Bay, the first port entered by Captain Cook, lies a few miles south of Sydney. It covers an area of 24 square miles, and receives the waters of several small rivers. The bay has very little trade; but it is frequented by craft in search of shelter during stress of weather.

Wollongong, Kiama, and Ulladulla are small harbours which have been snatched, as it were, from the sea, and are important shipping places.

About 80 miles to the south of Sydney the coast is broken by an important inlet called Jervis Bay. Its entrance is 2 miles wide, and on its bosom safe anchorage may be found in any part. It is surrounded by rich agricultural and mineral country.

Bateman's Bay, at the entrance to the Clyde, is an inlet of some importance, and coastal steamers also load produce at the mouths of the Moruya, Tuross, and Bega Rivers.

Twofold Bay is a magnificent sheet of water, near the southern limit of the state. Formerly it was the seat of a large whaling trade, which is now, however, all but extinct. It is well sheltered, and a fine jetty affords ample shipping facilities. Its trade is chiefly with the neighbouring states, in produce and live stock, the bay being the nearest outlet on the sea-coast for the rich district of Monaro. A railway is planned to connect the port with the table-land and the metropolis, and Twofold Bay promises to become a considerable shipping place in the near future. On its shores is situated the town of Eden.

No islands of any note belong geographically to New South Wales. The Broughton Islands, lying a few miles northward of the Heads of Port Stephens, are the largest in extent. Solitary Island, situated near the northern part of the coast, between the Bellinger and Clarence Rivers, and Montagu Island, 18 miles south-east of the Moruya River estuary, have been selected as sites for lighthouses, but are not otherwise important. Norfolk Island, having an area of 8,607 acres, has recently been placed under the administration of the New South Wales Government; and Lord Howe Island, 3,220 acres in extent, and lying some 360 miles off the coast, in the latitude of Port Macquarie, belongs politically to the state.

General Physical Characteristics.

The surface of New South Wales is divided naturally into three distinct zones, each widely differing in general character and physical aspect, and clearly defined by the Main Dividing Range, which traverses the country from north to south. The table-land, which forms the summit of this range, comprises one of these zones, and marks the division between the coastal region, forming the eastern watershed, and the great plain district of the interior.

The tableland district is divided into two sections, a northern and a southern, and these are traversed by the vast cordillera known as the Great Dividing Range. The width and altitude of the tableland are the greatest in the south-eastern portion of the State, which has the appearance of having been convulsed in past ages by some tremendous plutonic force. In the Muniong Range, the southernmost section of the cordillera, are found the loftiest peaks in Australia—Mount Kosciusko and Mount Townsend rising to a height of 7,328 and 7,260 feet respectively. The former is interesting, from the fact that it is probably one of the oldest land surfaces in the world. It has now the appearance of being the denuded remnant of a much higher peak—probably of volcanic origin—and must have stood out as a prominent landmark at the time when the sea extended through Central Australia, and washed the foothills of the Eastern ranges, when Tasmania was but a peninsula of the mainland, and when the Alps and the Himalayas were lying fathoms deep beneath the waters of the ocean. For six months of the year snow may be seen on the high peaks of the Muniong Range, and although Kosciusko is 700 feet below the snow line, heavy snowfalls have been known to occur even in the middle of summer. The Monaro Range, as the next northern section of the Dividing Chain is called, averages about 2,000 feet in height, although the head of the Kybeyan River reaches an altitude of over 4,000 feet. This range encloses on the south the rich and beautiful pastoral and agricultural district known as the Monaro Plains. As the tableland runs northward, it decreases in height and width, until it narrows to a few miles only, with an elevation of scarcely 1,500 feet. Further north the plateau widens again, and also increases in altitude, although the average height of the Main Range is inconsiderable, compared with that of its principal lateral spurs. The Blue Mountains district is the best known portion of this division. It extends eastward from the Main Range, and is bounded on the north by the Colo River; on the south and south-west by Cox's River, and on the east by the Nepean-Hawkesbury Valley. Its chief peaks are Mount Clarence (4,000 feet); Mount Victoria (3,525 feet), and Mount Hay (3,270 feet). These ranges for long offered an inaccessible barrier to the first settlers in New South Wales, and it was not until 1813 that they were successfully crossed by Messrs. Wentworth, Lawson, and Blaxland, and the way opened to the rich plains of the west. The Blue Mountain scenery possesses a charm, which is peculiarly and distinctively Australian. Seen from the plains, the mountains appear tame and insignificant; but the first view from some point on the edge of the tableland into the depths below, leaves a never-to-be-forgotten impression on the memory of the beholder. The mind here recoils with awe at the sight of the majestically stupendous scale on which Nature has worked. In many places, cliffs of bare sandstone, stained with various shades of brown and grey, rise almost perpendicularly to a height of 2,000 feet from the valley below. The hoary antiquity of these silent ranges appeals strongly to the mind of the scientific inquirer, for examination shows that these awe-inspiring precipices and stupendous gorges have not been caused by violent volcanic upheaval, but have been carved out by the slow but irresistible erosive agency of running water. On clear days the distances are softened by a curtain of delicate blue haze, a fact that has earned for the ranges their appellation of Blue Mountains. The prevailing Australian gum tree gives a somewhat monotonous aspect to the tableland, but in the valleys and on the mountain sides the wealth of beautiful ferns and characteristic Australian flowers lends a charming diversity to the scene.

The Dividing Range gradually decreases north of the Blue Mountains until as a narrow ridge it divides the waters of the Goulburn and Hunter on the east from those of the Namoi and Castlereagh on the west. The mass widens out once more in the Liverpool Ranges, where Mount Oxley rises to a height of 4,500 feet, and farther north in the New England Range, the highest peak of which, Ben Lomond, reaches an elevation of 5,000 feet. The average height of the northern tableland is between 2,500 and 3,000 feet. Mount Wingen, situated in a spur of the Liverpool Range, and close to the town of Scone, is one of the natural curiosities of Australia. It is a burning mountain. Its fires, however, are not volcanic, but result from the combustion of seams of coal some distance underground, and geologists have estimated that the burning has been going on for at least 800 years.

The main range throws off many spurs towards the sea on the eastern slope. These divide the waters of the numerous rivers which flow into the Pacific Ocean, but the ranges in the coastal district, as a rule, run parallel with the tableland, of which in some places they form the eastern edge.

The North Coast Range runs from north to south from Mount Marsh in the Richmond Range to the Hastings River district, at an average distance of 35 miles from the coast. It is not of great altitude, the average elevation being about 2,000 feet. The Illawarra Range forms the western boundary of the Illawarra district. It commences at Clifton, on the sea coast, and gradually recedes inland, although its average distance from the ocean is only about five miles. As it approaches the north bank of the Shoalhaven it becomes locally known as the Cambewarra Range. Valuable coal seams occur on the seaward face of the Illawarra Range, and these are profitably worked at Clifton, Bulli, Corrimal, Mount Keira, and Mount Kembla. The Currockbilly Range commences near Marulan, on the south bank of the Shoalhaven, and terminates on the north bank of the Moruya, about eight miles from the ocean. Its chief elevations are Budawang (3,630 feet), Currockbilly (3,619 feet), and Pigeon House (2,398 feet). Throughout a large portion of its course, the range forms the eastern fringe of the southern tableland. The South Coast Range is a spur from the Monaro Range running in a southerly direction towards the Victorian border, on nearing which it deflects to the westward, and terminates on the left bank of the Snowy River. Its highest peak in New South Wales is Coolangubra (3,712 feet).

In addition to the above, there are various isolated peaks standing out as prominent landmarks in the coastal district. Mount Warning, so named by Captain Cook, is situated near the head of the Tweed River, and in clear weather is visible 60 miles away. Mount Wohiman, or Clarence Peak, lies to the south of Shoal Bay, and is about 1,200 feet in height. Mount Seaview, 3,100 feet in height, is about eight miles south of the Hastings Range and 40 miles from the coast. The Brothers are three conspicuous peaks, 1,700, 1,650, and 1,910 feet high respectively, situated near Camden Haven. They were so named by Captain Cook. Jellore, seven miles north-east of Mittagong, and 2,372 feet in height, may occasionally be seen from Sydney, 70 miles distant. Coolangatta, near the mouth of the Shoalhaven, is 1,000 feet in height. Dromedary, so named by Captain Cook, is a prominent landmark, south of the Tuross River, about 2,700 feet in height.

The western slope of the cordillera is entirely different from the eastern just described. Numerous ramifications of the general mountain system are thrown off, but all slope gently towards the great central plain of the interior. So gentle, indeed, is the declivity that the dividing lines of the various watersheds as they extend westward are scarcely visible, being only indicated by a succession of low ridges and isolated elevations.

In the extreme west of the state, verging on South Australia, another mountain system exists, forming the western edge of an immense depression, through which the largest rivers of the Australian Continent hold their devious course. The Barrier and the Grey Ranges are part of this system. They consist of low hills, hardly rising to the dignity of mountains, and culminating in a few solitary peaks, such as Mount Arrowsmith and Mount Lyell, which attain an elevation of only 2,000 feet above sea-level.

Traces have been found of the existence at some earlier period of a range of primary rocks, extending from Orange to Cobar and Wilcannia, and forming the watershed between the Lachlan and part of the basin of the Darling. The range no longer exists as a landmark, for owing to denudation it has almost entirely disappeared.

The main range already described, traversing the country from north to south, gives rise to numerous rivers flowing into the South Pacific.

In the extreme north of the state, the Tweed and Brunswick Rivers flow through a rich country of semi-tropical aspect. Their courses are short, and bar-entrances render them navigable only for small craft.

A few miles south of the Brunswick, the Richmond descends from the heights of the Macpherson Range, on the slope of Mount Lindsay, one of the highest peaks of the northern table-land. The river has three branches, and is navigable on the main arm as far as Casino, 62 miles, and on Wilson's Creek to Lismore, 60 miles from the sea. The Richmond drains an area of about 2,400 square miles of country, rugged in its upper basin and heavily timbered, and in its lower course flowing through rich alluvial land, where the produce of semi-tropical climes grows luxuriantly.

Immediately south of the last-named stream is the Clarence—the largest river on the eastern watershed. It takes its rise in a spur of the Main Dividing Range, and runs in a south-easterly direction for 240 miles, carrying a considerable body of water through one of the richest districts of the state, and emptying itself into the Pacific at Shoal Bay. The upper part of its basin is very rugged, so much so that its principal tributaries, the Mitchell, Nymboi, Timbarra, and Orara Rivers, rising in the New England table-land, between Armidale and Tenterfield, all flow in an opposite direction to the course of the main stream, generally trending to the north-east, and even, in the case of the Orara and the Nymboi, to the north-west. The Lower Clarence is a magnificent stream, averaging half-a-mile in width, from its mouth upwards, for nearly 50 miles, and it is navigable for 67 miles, as far as Copmanhurst. Ocean-going steamers of large tonnage ascend the river as far as Grafton, 42 miles from the sea. The area of country drained by the Clarence is over 8,000 square miles, or nearly half as large again as the basin of the Thames, whose course, although about as long as that of the Clarence, is navigable for only 60 miles.

Two short rivers, the Bellinger and the Nambucca, both navigable for some distance by small craft, enter the Pacific between the Clarence and Trial Bay.

Into Trial Bay, the Macleay, one of the principal rivers of the coast, discharges, after a course of 200 miles from its source near Ben Lomond. With its principal feeders, the Guyra, the Apsley, and the Chandler, the Macleay drains an area of 4,800 square miles of country, the upper part of which, especially that portion through which the Apsley flows, is extremely rugged and precipitous. Series of waterfalls, some of which have a perpendicular descent of over 200 feet, mark the course of this stream, as it runs through narrow gorges whose sides rise in places to a height of about 2,000 feet; in its lower course the valley widens very considerably into magnificent alluvial plains. The Macleay is navigable for more than 30 miles, as far as the town of Greenhills, a few miles above Kempsey. The country through which it flows is for the most part thickly timbered.

The Hastings is the next stream met with, and empties itself into the sea at Port Macquarie. The country which it drains is rich, undulating, and densely wooded, and the area within its watershed is 1,400 square miles. Its chief arm is formed by the Wilson and Maria Rivers, on the left bank, the latter joining the main stream a few miles above Port Macquarie.

The Manning rises in the Main Dividing Range, and flows almost due east. The valley through which it flows is densely wooded, and the agricultural land on both sides of the river is unsurpassed for fertility. The Manning has a length of 100 miles, and, like most of the rivers of the seaboard, its course lies through undulating country, broken in the upper portion, but widening out as it nears the sea. Its chief tributary is the Barrington, on the right bank; on the left, it receives the Barnard River, the Dawson, the Lansdowne, the Nowendoc, Rowley's River, and other small streams. The Manning is navigable for ocean-going vessels as far as Wingham, about 20 miles from its mouth.

Before reaching the Hunter, several small streams are met with, amongst which may be mentioned the Wollomba and Maclean, falling into Wallis Lake; the Myall, which empties into Myall Lake; and the Karuah, which reaches the ocean at Port Stephens.

The Hunter is one of the chief rivers of the state, and has its source in the Liverpool Range. It flows first in a southerly direction until its confluence with the Goulburn; thence it takes an easterly course, and reaches the sea at Port Hunter, on the shores of which is situated the city of Newcastle. The Hunter receives numerous tributaries. The chief of these, in addition to the Goulburn, already mentioned, are the Wollombi, the Paterson, and the Williams. With its tributaries, the Hunter drains a country extending over 11,000 square miles—an area more than twice as large as the basin of the Thames. The river is navigable for ocean-going vessels as far as Morpeth, 34 miles from the sea; whilst the Paterson and the Williams are both navigable, the one for a distance of 18 miles, and the other for 20 miles. The upper courses of the main river and its branches are through hilly, if not mountainous districts; but its lower course is mainly through rich, sandy, alluvial flats. Through its lower course, the river drains the largest and most important coal-field in Australia. The length of the Hunter is over 200 miles.

Though less important than the Hunter, from a commercial point of view, the Hawkesbury, which reaches the sea at Broken Bay, is none the less one of the finest rivers of the eastern seaboard. It is formed by the united waters of many streams, each of considerable local importance. Its chief tributaries come from the table-land or gorges of the Blue Mountains, but the principal branch of the river itself rises in the main range, farther south. The range forming the watershed between the Hawkesbury and the streams flowing eastward, leaves the main range near Lake Bathurst, runs north-easterly, and terminates at the sea near Coalcliff.

Under the name of the Wollondilly, the Hawkesbury has its source not many miles from Goulburn. Flowing past that town, it proceeds in a northerly direction until it receives the waters of the Cox River, which come from the Blue Mountains, after passing through wild gorges, wherein may be found some of the most magnificent scenery in Australia. From the junction of the Cox River the stream is known as the Warragamba, which name it retains until its junction with the Nepean. Though smaller than the Warragamba, the Nepean gives its name to the united waters of the two streams. After receiving the Nepean, the river flows along the foot of the Blue Mountains, through a rich valley highly cultivated. From the Blue Mountains it is augmented by the waters of two streams, the Grose and the Colo, and from the junction of the latter the river is called the Hawkesbury. Still running northward, it is joined by the Macdonald, an important stream, navigable for some distance above its confluence with the Hawkesbury. The Macdonald comes from the north, and joins the river on the left bank. After turning to the east, the Hawkesbury holds its course through broken country, the scenery of which has been pronounced equal to any other river scenery in the world, and finally reaches the sea at Broken Bay. Its course extends over 330 miles, and the drainage area may be set down as 8,000 square miles. Navigation is possible as far as Windsor, 70 miles from the mouth, and a little dredging would enable sea-going vessels to reach that town.

In the neighbourhood of Sydney, some small streams fall into Botany Bay. Two of these, the Woronora and George's River, have their sources on the eastern slope of the ranges in which the Nepean, Cordeaux, and Cataract rise, and after rapid courses unite their waters before falling into the bay.

Generally speaking, the rivers south of Sydney are of less importance than those to the north, as the width of the coastal strip narrows considerably. The Shoalhaven, nevertheless, merits more than passing notice. Rising in the coastal range and following the direction of the coast, it flows northerly through deep gullies, marked by magnificent scenery peculiarly Australian ; then turning sharply to the east, it enters the alluvial plains, which are counted amongst the richest and most productive in the country. The Shoalhaven is 260 miles in length, but is navigable only for a few miles, and drains a district 3,300 miles in area. Farther south, in the narrow belt between the ranges and the sea, flow the Clyde, Moruya, Tuross, and Bega Rivers. They all pass through rich, undulating, agricultural country, and each has an average length of 60 to 70 miles. The Towamba River, at the extreme south of the state, empties itself into the Pacific at Twofold Bay.

The physical aspect of the eastern rivers is much the same, their upper courses being amidst broken and mountainous districts, and their lower waters flowing through undulating country with rich alluvial flats along their banks, for the most part highly cultivated. Where uncultivated, the country is densely covered with timber, some of which attains a magnificent growth, yielding the finest hardwood, and, in the north, cedar and pine.

Though belonging to another river system, the upper basin of the Snowy River is situated in New South Wales. This river receives the snow-fed streams rising on the southern slopes of the Monaro Range, its principal tributaries being the Bombala and the Eucumbene. The Snowy River and its tributaries water a considerable portion of the highest table-land of the state, between the mountain ranges of which are found large tracts of arable land. After leaving New South Wales, the Snowy has a rapid and tortuous course, and finally enters the sea between Cape Howe and Bass Straits, in the state of Victoria. The area of its watershed in New South Wales is about 2,800 square miles.

The western watershed of the state is, in its physical features and geographical character, the antithesis of the eastern. Instead of a narrow strip of country shut in by the sea and mountains, and intersected by numerous short rivers with a rapid flow, the western watershed forms a vast basin through which the quiet waters of a few great rivers have their long though uncertain courses. The rivers of the western region all belong to the fluvial system of the Murray, which carries to the Southern Ocean, through the state of South Australia, the drainage of a watershed immense in extent, embracing the northern portion of Victoria and the western and larger part of New South Wales, and reaching almost to the centre of Queensland.

The Murray, or Hume, the southern branch of this vast river system, rises in the Snowy Mountains, from which its three principal sources, the Hume, the Tooma, and the Indi descend. The first two of these streams rise on the northern and western slopes of Mount Kosciusko; the Indi, which is really the main river, has a longer course, rising in a gully near the Pilot Mountain, at an elevation of 5,000 feet above the sea. From the confluence of these rivers the Murray rapidly descends towards the plains below Albury, where it is only 490 feet above sea level, with a course of 1,439 miles still to run. From Albury downwards the river receives many tributaries on both banks, those from New South Wales being the most important. Above Albury the tributaries are for the most part mountain torrents, carrying to the main stream the melted snows of the Australian Alps. In its lower course, however, the Murray is augmented, through the Murrumbidgee and the Darling, by the waters of secondary systems as important as its own.

Before being joined by the Murrumbidgee, the Murray receives, from a series of ana-branches, the drainage of a large portion of the country lying between the two main streams. The Billabong Creek runs almost through the centre of the plain spreading between the Murray and Murrumbidgee; in the middle of its course it communicates with the latter river, through Colombo and Yanko Creeks, whilst on the south it feeds the Murray by the channel of the Edward River. The Edward itself is an important stream. With the Wakool, Tupal, and Bullatale Creeks, and many other smaller and less important water-courses, it forms a fluvial system, interlacing the whole country from Tocumwal to the Murrumbidgee junction, which has been aptly named Riverina. From its farthest source at the foot of the Pilot Mountain to the town of Albury, the Murray has a length of 280 miles; thence to the Darling River junction its course is 852 miles; and from that point to the sea, below Lake Alexandrina, it is 587 miles in length. The river has thus a total course of 1,719 miles, of which 1,250 are between the states of Victoria and New South Wales. It has been navigated as far as the Ournie gold-field, about 150 miles above Albury, and 1,590 miles from its mouth.

The Murrumbidgee has its source at the foot of a hill overlooking the Coolamon Plains, at a height of nearly 5,000 feet above the sea. Its course first shapes itself southward, but near the town of Cooma it takes a sharp curve and runs in a northerly direction until it approaches Yass. Here it curves again, trending to the west in a line parallel to the Murray; but turning south-west on receiving the Lachlan, it finally joins the main river after a course of 1,350 miles. The area drained by the Murrumbidgee is estimated at 15,400 square miles. In the upper part of its course it receives from both sides numerous rivers and creeks, the most important of which are the Umaralla, Molonglo, and Yass Rivers on its right, and the Goodradigbee and Tumut Rivers on its left bank. All these flow through mountainous country over a series of plateaux, which from the Coolamon and Coorangorambula Plains to the plains round Gundagai and Wagga successively diminish in height from 5,000 feet to 720 feet and 607 feet above the sea.

The chief tributary of the Murrumbidgee is the Lachlan, rising in the Main Dividing Range, where its principal feeders also have their source. These are the Boorowa, Crookwell, Abercrombie, and Belubula—all rapid streams, occasionally swollen by melted snows from the table-land. After receiving the Boorowa, the Lachlan flows to the Murrumbidgee, through 500 miles of plain country, without receiving any tributary of a permanent character. The water-courses which carry off the surplus water from the plains on each side of the river, only reach it in time of flood. The total length of the stream is 700 miles, and its basin has an area of 13,500 square miles. The lines of demarcation between the Lachlan basin and that of the Murrumbidgee on the south and of the Darling on the north-west, are hardly perceptible on the ground, so flat is the country through which these great rivers flow.

Of all the tributaries of the Murray, the Darling drains the largest area, extending as it does over the greater portion of the western district of New South Wales, and embracing nearly all Southern Queensland. From its confluence with the Murray at Wentworth up to its junction with the Culgoa a few miles above Bourke, the Darling receives only two tributaries, the Paroo and the Warrego, both intermittent, though of vast size in times of flood. For over 1,000 miles this great river holds its solitary course, Nile-like, feeding the thirsty plains of the south with water falling many hundred miles distant on the downs of Queensland. The course of the river is tortuous in the extreme: in many places a narrow neck of land, a mile or two across, separates parts of the river 20 miles distant if the stream were followed. The Darling presents the phenomenon, not uncommon in Australian rivers, of banks much higher than the plain behind; indeed, the river bed itself, though from 30 to 40 feet beneath the bank, is in some places but little below the general level of the country. Successive floods have added to the height of the banks, and have raised the bed of the stream correspondingly.

The Darling has no source under that name, which applies only to that part of the river as far as the Bogan junction. Above this point it takes the name of the Barwon, until its confluence with the Gwydir; then it is known as the Macintyre, and afterwards the main branch receives the name of the Dumaresq. The last-named stream has its source in the Dividing Range, on the summit of the table-land at the extreme north-east of the state, not far from the head of the Richmond. The Dumaresq, Macintyre, and Barwon form, however, what might really be called the Upper Darling, and this appellation would be geographically accurate. The variety of names by which, not only the Darling, but many other Australian rivers are known, is due to the fact that they were discovered in sections, the identity of which was not established until years afterwards, and the sectional names have survived.

The Darling receives, in its upper course, many tributaries, which drain the southern portion of Queensland, but these rivers only flow for a short part of their courses in New South Wales. Chief among them are the Mooni, Narran, Bokhara, Culgoa, Warrego, and Paroo. The principal affluents of the Darling within the boundaries of New South Wales are on the left bank. The Gwydir, Namoi, Castlereagh, Macquarie, and Bogan are the most important. These streams are all of considerable length and similar in character; their upper valleys are on the table-lands, and their lower courses lie through alluvial plains and good pastoral country. The Darling is navigable, in times of freshets, as far as the township of Walgett, 1,758 miles from its confluence with the Murray; thence to the sea the distance is 587 miles, making a total length of navigable water from Walgett to the sea of 2,345 miles, and it therefore ranks high amongst the rivers of the world, as estimated by navigable length. Unfortunately, however, its upper course is open only during part of the year.

Here and there along the course of the western rivers are found lakes, sometimes of considerable dimensions. These lakes are in reality shallow depressions, receiving water from the overflow of the rivers in times of flood, and in return feeding them when the floods have subsided. Lake Urana is the most important in the Murray and Murrumbidgee basin, and Lakes Cowal, Cudgellico, and Waljeers, in that of the Lachlan. Along the Darling are Lakes Poopelloe and Gunyulka on the left bank, and Laidley's Ponds and Lakes Pammaroo, Tandou, and Cawndilla on the right, near Menindie. On the South Australian frontier are Lake Victoria, formed by the overflow of the Murray, and others of less importance. The area of these lakes is undefined, as they vary in size according to the rainfall, sometimes covering a vast extent of country, and at other times being reduced to the proportions of mere waterholes, whilst in seasons of great drought they are absolutely dry.

On the summit of the Main Dividing Range, and within a few miles of the inland towns of Goulburn, Queanbeyan, and Braidwood, two of the principal lakes of the state are situated. Lake George is 16 miles in length and 6 miles in width, draining a basin whose area is about 490 square miles. It is situated at an elevation of 2,200 feet above the sea, and the scenery around it is very beautiful. This lake exhibits the phenomenon of a large drainage area without a visible outlet, for though it receives many small water-courses, no stream leaves it. Lake Bathurst, a few miles east of Lake George, is another depression on the summit of the Dividing Range, and covers in ordinary seasons an area of about 15 square miles. It is similar in character to Lake George, having no outlet to the sea. Both lakes, in periods of great drought, shrink considerably in area; but Lake George in most seasons is a fine sheet of water.

VICTORIA.

Area and Boundaries.

VICTORIA is situated in the south-eastern portion of the continent of Australia, and lies between the parallels of 34° and 39° south latitude, and the meridians of 141° and 150° east longitude. The greatest length east and west is about 480 miles, and the greatest width, in the west, about 250 miles. The surface area of the state is 87,884 square miles. Roughly speaking, the country has the shape of a scalene triangle, of which the vertex is at Cape Howe. On the north and north-east Victoria is bounded by the River Murray and a surveyed line running from Forest Hill, near the head waters of the stream, to Cape Howe. The southern boundary is formed by the Southern Ocean and Bass Strait, the Pacific forming the south-eastern boundary. On the west, the state is bounded by South Australia, the dividing line being about 242 geographical miles in length, and approximating to the position of the 141st meridian of east longitude.

Coastal Features.

The total length of the coast line is about 750 miles. A reference to the map shows that there are three prominent projections on the south; terminating respectively in Cape Nelson, Cape Otway, and Wilson's Promontory. The last-mentioned projection is the southmost point on the continent of Australia, and is situated in latitude 39° 8′ south, longitude 146° 26′ east. The most western point on the coast, at the termination of the frontier line, is in latitude 38° 4′ south. Proceeding thence eastward from the head of Discovery Bay, the coast begins with a succession of sandstone cliffs backed by grassy undulating country extending for some distance inland. Between Discovery Bay and Portland Bay there is a well-wooded peninsula broken by expanses of grassy meadow, Capes Bridgewater and Nelson lying at the extremities of small projections. Portland Bay is a crescent-shaped inlet with stretches of sandy beach backed by granite cliffs. Farther round are Port Fairy and Warrnambool Bay. From this point downwards to Cape Otway there is a series of precipitous cliffs; Cape Otway itself is a bluff headland at the extremity of a range of coastal mountains. It is provided with a lighthouse at an elevation of 300 feet above sea-level, and the beams from its powerful lantern are visible many miles out at sea. From this point the coast takes a decided sweep to the north-east to the head of Port Phillip through about a degree of latitude. Between Cape Otway and the Barwon Heads, close to the entrance of Port

Phillip, the coast is rugged, and along the whole extent of this shore line there are only two places where a landing can be effected—at Apollo Bay and Loutit Bay—and these are difficult of approach in south-easterly weather. Point Lonsdale and Point Nepean are the headlands marking the entrance to Port Phillip Bay, the largest inlet on the coast of Victoria. The bay is a land-locked inland sea, having an extreme length of 30 geographical miles from north to south, and a breadth from east to west of about 35 miles. The entrance is about 2 miles across, and a short distance within there were originally numerous sandbanks and shoals impeding navigation; these have been so dealt with that they do not now offer any serious hindrances to navigation, as the channels are well-defined and lighted. The western arm of Port Phillip, known as Corio Bay, forms the harbour at Geelong, and Hobson's Bay at the northern extremity is the port of Melbourne. At Queenscliff, just within the heads, there is a lighthouse at a height of 109 feet above sea-level. Cape Schank is an imposing headland on the peninsula between Port Phillip and Western Port, and is provided with a lighthouse 278 feet above sea-level. The greater part of Western Port is shallow and unfit for navigation, but good anchorage may be found with shelter in all winds. The shores of the inlet are generally flat, and in some places swampy, but there is some excellent land in the surrounding district. Cape Liptrap is a narrow point on the western shore of Waratah Bay, and culminates a short distance inland in an eminence rising to a height of over 500 feet and constituting a prominent landmark. Wilson's Promontory, the southmost point of Australia, is a towering granitic mass connected with the mainland by a narrow sandy isthmus, and is a prominent turning-point for vessels from the westward bound for the east coast of Australia. The headland is provided with a lighthouse at an elevation of 383 feet above sea-level. Lying off its extremity are several rocky islets, whose granitic sides rise steeply out of the long rolling waves of the Southern Ocean. Rounding the promontory, the next important indentation is Corner Inlet, protected at its entrance by numerous islands, of which the largest is Snake Island. The inlet is not of much account for navigation purposes, as it is very shallow, portions of it being quite dry at low tide. From this point onward the coast trends north by east, and the greater part of it right up to Cape Howe is low and sandy. Here is situated the Ninety-mile Beach, consisting of an unbroken line of sandy shore, whose monotony is hardly relieved by a background of low sandy dunes. The length of this stretch of coast-line is, moreover, considerably in excess of 90 miles. Towards the eastern portion the sand dunes are backed by a succession of lakes, in places communicating with the sea by narrow channels. Farther on, where the shore line sweeps round to the east, the elevation increases, occasionally rising into bluff eminences. The principal headlands in this portion of the coast are Cape Conran, Cape Everard, and Ram Head. Cape Everard is supposed to have been the first portion of the coast seen by Captain Cook, and the projection was named by him Point Hicks. Cape Howe, the eastern extremity of the state, lies in latitude 37° 31′ south and longitude 149° 59′ east.

The largest island possessed by Victoria is French Island, situated in Western Port, but a considerable portion of its area consists of mud-flats and swamps, so that it is but scantily peopled. Phillip Island, also situated in Western Port, has a population of about 400. Snake Island and Sunday Island, lying off Port Albert, are both low and swampy. Gabo Island, about 5 miles south-west of Cape Howe is provided with a lighthouse and signalling station.

General Physical Characteristics.

The southward projection of the Great Dividing Range of Australia traverses the state from east to west at a distance varying from 60 to 70 miles from the coast. There are thus, roughly speaking, three great surface divisions—the plain sloping from the mountains southwards to the sea, the elevated table-land country traversed by the Dividing Range, and the plain region sloping from the mountains northward to the Murray River.

The eastern portion of the Great Dividing Range is known as the Australian Alps, and the range terminates to the west in the Pyrenees and Grampians. There are at least six peaks in the cordillera exceeding 6,000 feet in height, and a considerable number between 5,000 and 6,000 feet, the principal being Mount Bogong, 6,508 feet; Mount Feathertop, 6,303 feet; Mount Hotham, 6,100 feet; Mount Cobberas, 6,025 feet; Mount Gibbs, 5,764 feet; and Benambra, 4,840 feet. The average elevation of the Victorian mountains is, however, only about 3,000 feet. Snow lies on the higher portions of the Dividing Range during several months of the year. Below the winter snow-line the mountains are generally well wooded, some of the trees reaching gigantic proportions; but the peaks above this line are bare, or partially covered with stunted trees and shrubs. The scenery in some of the mountain ranges, and particularly in the Bogong Mountains, makes a deep impression on all beholders, and, as in New South Wales, the characteristics are such as are not found in any other part of the world. The first impression left on the mind at sight of these examples of Nature's handiwork is one of stupendous power, coupled with a feeling of weirdness and utter loneliness. The absolute stillness is rarely broken by the song of birds, the whirring of wings, or the cry of wild animals. Parts of these primeval ranges have never been trodden by the foot of white man, and, it is believed, were inaccessible even to the aboriginal native. Geologists affirm that the mountain ranges here belong to the very dawn of time, and, indeed, the tremendous proportions of the giant trees found in the valleys are silent witnesses to a great antiquity. Under different atmospheric conditions, the mountains present many beautiful gradations of colouring, ranging at times from deep purple to delicate blue. On clear days the distant summits stand sharply outlined against the sky, while at other times looming through a wreath of mist and cloud, the mighty mass of the nearer elevations is strangely intensified.

The surface of Victoria is drained by two fluvial systems, the one consisting of streams which have their sources on the northward slope of the Dividing Range and flow towards the Murray, the other comprising the watercourses which have their origin on the seaward slope of the mountains and which drain into the Southern Ocean. Of the rivers comprised in the first category, the most important are as follows. The Goulburn, which has a total length of 345 miles, rises in the vicinity of Mount Matlock, and its course lies through some most picturesque country; in its upper portion it winds in and out through labyrinthine ranges whose sides are in places heavily timbered, while in others steep and bare precipices rise abruptly from the channel of the stream. Lower down it passes through stretches of rich agricultural land. Its tributaries, the Jamieson, Howqua, Seven Creeks, and Broken River all drain country possessing somewhat similar characteristics. The Loddon (225 miles) enters the Murray near Swan Hill. The Campaspe (150 miles) rises near Mount Macedon, and, after receiving the waters of the Coliban, drains some excellent agricultural land, and enters the Murray at Echuca. The Ovens has a course of 140 miles from its source in the vicinity of St. Bernard Mount till it gives up its waters to the Murray near Bundalong; its lower course runs through splendid pastoral country. Between the King River, which joins the Ovens at Wangaratta and the main stream, are situated the fertile Oxley Plains. The Mitta Mitta rises in the Bogong district at an altitude of over 2,000 feet, and after a course of 175 miles joins the Murray a few miles to the east of Albury. During its course the stream receives several tributaries, of which the most noteworthy are the Dark River on the right, and the Victoria, Bundarrah, and Big Rivers on the left bank. Much of the country drained by this river is mountainous, and contains some very wild and picturesque scenery. The Avoca (163 miles) and the Wimmera (228 miles) both fail to reach the Murray, the lower courses of the rivers terminating in salt lakes or marshes.

The Snowy is the longest of the coastal rivers, and after a course of 300 miles, only 120 of which, however, are in Victoria, enters the sea near Point Ricardo. The country passed through in Victoria is wild and almost wholly unoccupied. West of the Snowy River the Tambo, Mitchell, and Latrobe drain into the lakes in the Gippsland district. The Yarra rises near Mount Baw Baw, and after a course of 150 miles enters the sea at Port Phillip. The name of the river is an aboriginal term, signifying everflowing. Its upper course lies through rough mountain country, clothed in places with magnificent forests of beech. After receiving the waters of Badger Creek, the stream emerges into a more open region, where it is joined by the river Watts. In the country drained by these tributaries there are some densely-covered forest areas, containing magnificent specimens of eucalyptus amygdalina. Some of these giants of the bush reach a height of over 400 feet; in one specimen that was measured the distance from the ground to the first branch, where the tree had a diameter of 4 feet, was no less than 295 feet. Other trees measured close to the ground had a circumference of 130 feet. The leaves of the E. amygdalina, as well as of the E. globulus, which abounds in the district, yield on distillation a valuable medicinal oil. Near the sea, where the city of Melbourne stands, the stream widens considerably, and the channel has been deepened to afford increased facilities for navigation. The Hopkins (155 miles) rises in the southern slopes of the Pyrenees, and after draining some excellent pastoral country, and in addition the fertile Warrnambool district, enters the ocean near the town of Warrnambool. The Glenelg, which has a length of 280 miles, is one of the most tortuous rivers in the state; its basin contains fine pastoral country.

The lakes in the north-western district are indeterminate as to area, their size depending on the rainfall. Lake Hindmarsh in some seasons has an area of 30,000 acres, and Lake Albacuyta of 13,000 acres. These depend for their supplies on the expansion of the Wimmera River; Lake Tyrrell, 60 miles north-west of Lake Albacuyta, also owes its existence to a stream flowing into it from the south; but it has no ascertained outlet. In seasons of drought its waters dwindle considerably, and this applies also to Lake Buloke, 50 miles south of Lake Tyrrell, which has an area of 11,000 acres. On the southern side of the Dividing Range, and due north from Cape Otway, are situated Lakes Corangamite and Colac. The waters of Lake Corangamite, which is situated at an elevation of 380 feet above sea-level, are salt, and cover an area of 90 square miles. The lake is 16 miles long, and has a breadth of 8 miles in its widest part. Lake Colac, with an area of 10 square miles, is fresh. The soil in the districts surrounding these lakes is extremely fertile, and shares with the Gippsland district the claim to be considered as the garden of Victoria.

The Gippsland Lakes lie immediately to the rear of the Ninety-mile Beach, and are separated from the ocean by a narrow belt of sand interspersed with chains of salt-water lagoons. In places the lakes communicate with the sea by narrow shifting channels, and, to obviate this disability to navigation, the Victorian Government went to considerable expense in the construction of a permanent entrance. The most important of the lakes are Lake Wellington, Lake Victoria, and Lake King. Farther east is Lake Tyers, a beautiful expanse, the scenery surrounding which has been compared to that of Port Jackson and Port Stephens in New South Wales. The principal lakes, which receive the drainage of several rivers and creeks, are fresh water; they are visited by large numbers of tourists, to whom they offer many attractions. The Gippsland district is famed for its fertility, and is the home of a prosperous agricultural and pastoral population.

QUEENSLAND.

Areas and Boundaries.

THE State of Queensland occupies the north-eastern portion of the continent of Australia, and embraces within its limits an area of 668,497 square miles. It is bounded on the north by the Gulf of Carpentaria and Torres Strait, on the east by the Pacific Ocean, on the south by the State of New South Wales, and on the west by South Australia and the Northern Territory of that State.

Coastal Features.

Queensland has a coast line measuring 3,000 miles, well marked and lighted throughout, and portions of it, particularly in the north after leaving Keppel Bay, are remarkable for the beauty of their scenery. From Mackay northwards towards Bowen, the Whitsunday Passage offers magnificent views of mountains rising abruptly from the margin of the ocean, together with many picturesque islands, whose densely-wooded sides dip down to waters of the deepest blue. The Hinchinbrook Passage is especially noted for the grandeur of its scenery, particularly in autumn, when the wild mountain sides next the sea are brightened by the presence of numerous flashing cascades. In addition to the hosts of islands off the east coast, the presence of the Great Barrier Reef tends to break the force of the waves, and affords a comparatively smooth passage up or down the coast. This vast natural breakwater, built up by the tireless energy of the coral polyp, lies at a distance of from 10 to 150 miles from the shore, and the long voyage from Torres Strait on the north, as far down as Cape Capricorn, may be performed entirely within the sheltered channel thus formed. There are numerous openings by means of which vessels sailing in the open ocean may pass through to the calmer waters between the reef and the shore, but these passages require very skilful negotiation. Captain Cook's vessel, the "Endeavour," had the misfortune to strike on the reef in 1770, and but for the fact that a portion of the coral came away when the ship floated off, and helped to block up the rent in her timbers, the historic voyage would have had a disastrous ending. Cook appropriately named the headland near by Cape Tribulation, and the stream at the mouth of which he careened and repaired his vessel the Endeavour River. The point in the reef where his mishap took place has been located, and a gun and various other relics are stated to have been recovered therefrom.

Proceeding northwards from Point Danger, the northernmost point of New South Wales, there is a stretch of rather uninteresting coastline, the first important headland being Lookout Point, on the extreme end of Stradbroke Island. The projection on the north-western corner of the island is known as Amity Point. Cape Moreton, on Moreton Island, is a rocky promontory, on which a lighthouse has been erected. The next important projection is Double Island Point, on the southern crescent of Wide Bay. Here a lighthouse has been erected at a height of 315 feet above the level of the sea. From this point northward the coastline takes a decided sweep to the west, through about 11 degrees of longitude. Bustard Head stands at the entrance to Port Curtis. The bluff promontory on the north-eastern end of Curtis Island was named Cape Capricorn by Captain Cook, because it lies almost precisely under the tropic line. A lighthouse stands on the headland at a height of 316 feet above the sea. Continuing northward past Cape Manifold and Cape Townsend, shoals of small islands are passed through. Cape Conway lies at the northern end of Repulse Bay, and the passage north wards from this point is thickly studded with islands, the scenery in the neighbourhood being strikingly picturesque. Cape Bowling Green, on the southern part of the bay of the same name, is provided with a lighthouse. Near Cape Cleveland the coastal scenery for miles is dominated by Mount Elliott, which rises to the height of 4,000 feet. From Cape Grafton northwards the coastline offers much grand and striking scenery. At times the mountain sides rise directly out of the ocean, at others retreating inland, many charming vistas of wooded plain and rugged height are disclosed. Cape Tribulation, named by Captain Cook, is about 30 miles south of Cooktown, while 30 miles northward is the projection known as Cape Flattery. The Great Barrier Reef is here fairly close to the shore, and there are numerous subsidiary reefs and islets. Farther north Cape Melville stands at the entrance to Bathurst Bay. Higher up on Cape York Peninsula are the headlands named Cape Direction and Cape Grenville. Cape York, the most northern point of Queensland and of the Australian continent, is situated in latitude 10° 40″. Rounding Cape York and turning southward into the Gulf of Carpentaria, the scenery undergoes a complete change. Instead of the lofty precipices and richly-wooded heights and islands of the eastern coast, the Gulf shore for many miles consists of monotonously low swampy ground and dismal clumps of mangrove. The only noteworthy projections on the eastern side are Duyfken Point (erroneously spelled on the map as "Duyfhen") and Cape Keerweer, both reminiscent of the early Dutch visitors to these localities. On the southern shore are Points Tarrant and Bayly.

The eastern coast of Queensland, from Point Danger right up to Cape York, is diversified by numerous indentations, but the contour of the shore line in the Gulf of Carpentaria is more or less regular and unbroken. Commencing from the south, the first noteworthy indentation is Moreton Bay, the entrance to which is protected by Moreton and Stradbroke Islands. The bay, which receives the drainage of the Brisbane River, is shallow, and navigation is rendered difficult by the presence of numerous flats and banks. The channel, however, is well lighted, and the more troublesome obstacles are being removed by constant dredging. Wide Bay is situated at the mouth of the Mary River, between Fraser or Great Sandy Island and the mainland. A dangerous shifting bar obstructs the entrance. Hervey Bay is protected by the northern end of Great Sandy Island. Higher up is Port Curtis, with Facing Island opposite it. Keppel Bay is a large inlet, on which the town of Rockhampton is situated, Curtis Island lying at the south. Broadsound is a considerable inlet situated in latitude 22°, the sea near its entrance being dotted with numerous small islands. Port Denison is the harbour of Bowen, and possesses excellent anchorage of from three to five fathoms. Cleveland Bay, on which Townsville is situated, is protected on the south by Cape Cleveland, and on the north by Magnetic Island. The approach is well marked and lighted. Rockingham Bay is a large inlet in latitude 18°, Hinchinbrook Island lying at its southern extremity. Mourilyan Harbour, north of Double Point, has a narrow entrance, but affords excellent anchorage of from four to twelve fathoms. Cooktown is situated on the Endeavour River, and while the entrance to the bay is narrow the port is easily negotiated. Princess Charlotte Bay is a large inlet situated in latitude 14°. Near the head of Cape York Peninsula is situated the harbour of Port Albany. The fortified harbour of Thursday Island, an important place of call for steamers trading to China and Japan, is situated in Torres Strait. In the Gulf of Carpentaria there is a fine harbour at the mouth of the Batavia River, named Port Musgrave. The best anchorage at the head of the Gulf is the Investigator Road.

General Physical Characteristics.

As is the case in New South Wales, the main features in the relief of Queensland are a coastal belt, a table-land region, and a great interior plain district.

The Great Dividing Range extending northwards from New South Wales enters Queensland territory at Wallangarra. Proceeding northwards to Maryland the range divides, the Herries Range branching off to the north-west, and the Main Range continuing to the north-east for about 40 miles. Here another bifurcation takes place, the Macpherson Range stretching to the sea coast, where it terminates at Point Danger, and the Main Range extending in a general north-westerly and westerly direction for about 35 miles. Another spur here branches off in a seaward direction, while the Main Range extends westerly and then northerly, and with many twists and turns traverses the entire length of the State. Grey Range enters the State at the 142° meridian, and extends northward to Gowan's Range, the Cheviot Range branching off to the westward. In the central districts are the Drummond, Peak and Denham Ranges. Clarke's Range and Leichhardt Range extend northwards in the northern districts nearly parallel to each other. The Boomer Mountains, Broadsound Ranges, and Connor's Range form the coast range nearly to Mackay. From Townsville, northwards, the coast range is in close proximity to the sea, and is rugged and picturesque in character, while some of the peaks reach a considerable elevation. In the southern coastal district much of the land between the mountains and the sea is very suitable for farming purposes, most of the rivers and creeks running through alluvial soil of great richness. The highest peak in Queensland is Mount Bartle Frere, 5,438 feet. Mount Roberts in the Central district is 4,350 feet in height, and Mount Barney in the Macpherson Range reaches 4,300 feet. In the Coast Ranges the highest points are Wooroonooran, 5,400 feet, in the Bellenden Ker Range, and Mount Dalrymple, 4,200 feet, in the Mackay Range.

The rivers of Queensland may be classified into four distinct systems:—1. Those flowing eastward into the Pacific. 2. Those which form the head waters of the Darling and its tributaries. 3. Those flowing westward from the Great Dividing Range. 4. Those flowing into the Gulf of Carpentaria. As in the case of New South Wales, the coastal rivers of Queensland flowing into the Pacific Ocean have short rapid courses, and in periods of excessive rainfall are liable to floods. The entrances also are sometimes difficult to negotiate, on account of the presence of sandbars and shoals. Much has been accomplished in the way of getting rid of these disabilities by persistent dredging, and the channels have been artificially deepened; nevertheless, it is only in the tidal waters of these rivers that navigation is possible for ocean-going steamers. In Southern Queensland the principal coastal rivers are the Logan, Brisbane, and Pine, which drain into Moreton Bay; the Caboolture, flowing into Deception Bay; the Mary and Burrum, entering Wide Bay; and the Burnett, Kolan, and Elliott Rivers, which debouch into Hervey Bay. In Central Queensland the Calliope and Boyne Rivers drain into Port Curtis. The Fitzroy River is the second in point of size on the eastern coast, and is navigable by deep-sea vessels as far as Rockhampton. The river enters the sea at Keppel Bay, and during its course receives several tributary streams, the principal of which are the Dee, Dawson, Mackenzie, and Isaac Rivers, the total area of its basin being about 55,600 square miles. In Northern Queensland the chief coastal rivers are the Pioneer, entering the sea at Mackay; the Don at Bowen. The Burdekin, which debouches into Upstart Bay, is the finest of Queensland's coastal rivers. Its drainage area covers 53,500 square miles. Numerous tributaries discharge into the main stream, the most important being the Boyne, Bogie, Belyando, Suttor, Cope, Campaspie, Basalt, Clarke, and Star Rivers. Even in the driest seasons the stream, within a few miles of its outlet, carries a large body of fresh water, and this probably prevents the formation of a defined bar close to its mouth. Farther north, the Ross River falls into Cleveland Bay; the Herbert enters the sea at Lucinda Point; the Tully flows into Kennedy Bay; the Moresby into Mourilyan Harbour; the Russell and Mulgrave at Bramston Point; the Barron near Cairns; the Endeavour at Cooktown; the Mosman and Daintree near Port Douglas; the Bloomfield into Weary Bay; the Endeavour at Cooktown; the Normanby into Princess Charlotte Bay; and various small streams higher up in Yorke's Peninsula. The celebrated Barron Falls are situated on the Barron River, at the point where the stream descends from the table-land and leaps down a distance of 830 feet to the valley below. The main fall is 370 feet in height.

The rivers rising in the western slopes of the Dividing Range include the Macintyre or Barwon, which receives the Macintyre Brook, and the Dumaresq or Severn, and after crossing the New South Wales border, unites with the Moonie River. The Condamine, or Balonne, rises near Warwick, and after being joined by the Maranoa River, separates into branches, which all become united with the western fluvial system of New South Wales. The Warrego rises in the Warrego Range, and, flowing southerly, joins the Darling. The Paroo and the Bulloo, or Corni Paroo, lie between the Grey Range and the Warrego. These are in reality depressions, along which in seasons of exceptional rainfall a large body of water finds its way into New South Wales southwards towards the Darling. Further west the Victoria, or Barcoo, flows under the name of Cooper's Creek into Lake Eyre, while the Diamantina loses itself in the stony desert to the north-east of that lake.

Several fine navigable streams fall into the Gulf of Carpentaria; but as the northern country round the Gulf is only in the initial stages of development, their capabilities, with the exception of the Norman and Albert Rivers, remain unutilised. Amongst the principal streams debouching into the Gulf are the following:—Batavia, Archer, Colman, Mitchell, Staaten, and Gilbert on the eastern shore; and the Norman, Flinders, Leichhardt, Albert, and Gregory on the southern shore. Much of the country through which these rivers flow is excellently adapted for pastoral purposes, while the mountains in which they have their sources contain mineral treasures, as yet only partially developed.

The only lakes worthy of mention in Queensland are Lake Galilee, or Jochimo, and Lake Buchanan. These are situated in Central Queensland, and are both salt. Some of the western rivers flow into salt lakes, but their area is indeterminate, as their volume depends on the rainfall.

For general purposes the State has been divided into twelve districts. A brief description of the characteristics of each division may not be without interest.

The Moreton District occupies the south-eastern portion of the State immediately to the north of New South Wales, and extends inland to the Dividing Range. It is a fertile, well-watered district, drained by the Brisbane, Bremer, and Logan Rivers. Sugar cane and maize are grown and thrive luxuriantly, coal occurs in several localities on the Bremer, and gold is found in the Enoggera Ranges, west of Brisbane.

The Darling Downs District lies immediately to the west of the Moreton District, in the table-land region, and forms one of the richest pastoral and agricultural areas of the State. The southern portion is the great wheat-growing district of the State, and at Stanthorpe, near the New South Wales border, large deposits of tin have been found. North of the Moreton District is the Burnett or Wide Bay District. The rich alluvial soil in this division is especially suitable for the growth of sugar, cotton, arrowroot, ginger, and other tropical productions. In the Gympie district rich deposits of gold have been found, while coal is worked on the Burrum River.

Port Curtis District lies to the north of the Burnett division, and is watered by the Dawson, Fitzroy, Calliope, and Boyne Rivers. This area is rich in mineral wealth, gold being found at the Calliope River, the Boyne, Fitzroy, and at Mount Morgan.

The Leichhardt District is a fine pastoral area west of the Port Curtis Division, and is watered by various tributaries of the Fitzroy. Copper, gold, coal, and other minerals are also found.

The Maranoa District consists of table-land and downs, and lies west of the Darling Downs and south of the Leichhardt District. It is watered by the Maranoa, Culgoa, Balonne, and Moonie Rivers. Much excellent pastoral country is found throughout, while in the Roma district the soil is well adapted for wheat.

The Warrego District lies westward of the Maranoa, and is almost exclusively pastoral in character. The rainfall is intermittent, and the water supply in many places is obtained from bores, which have generally yielded very successful results.

The Kennedy District occupies the middle coastal portion of the state, and is well watered by the Burdekin and other streams. The country round Mackay produces a large quantity of sugar. In this division also is situated the Charters Towers Goldfield, one of the richest in the State.

The Burke District lies west of the Kennedy division, and extends to the southern portion of the Gulf of Carpentaria. Much of this area is under occupation for pastoral purposes, but a large extent of country is yet undeveloped. At Croydon are situated the well-known goldfields of that name, while at Cloncurry, in addition to gold, there are rich deposits of copper.

The Mitchell District lies to the westward of the South Kennedy division. It is watered by the Barcoo and Thompson Rivers, and is entirely pastoral.

The Gregory District lies between the Mitchell, Burke, and Warrego Districts and the South Australian boundary. It is watered by the Diamantina, Herbert, Wilson, and Mulligan Rivers, and traversed by Cooper's Creek and other watercourses. The district is almost entirely given over to pastoral pursuits. Opals have been found in various places throughout the area. Its south-eastern boundary is formed by the Grey and Cheviot Ranges; other ranges in the south are the Coleman, Cameron, and Macgregor Mountains.

SOUTH AUSTRALIA.

Area and Boundaries.

THE State of South Australia occupies a position midway between the other four provinces on the Australian mainland, and embraces within its limits a total area of 903,690 square miles. As originally constituted by the Imperial Statute 4 and 5 William IV, cap. 95, the 132nd meridian of east longitude formed the western boundary, and the 141st meridian the eastern limit. From north to south the province extended from the 26th parallel of south latitude to the Southern Ocean. The area of territory comprised within these boundaries was about 300,000 square miles. By fixing the western boundary at the 132nd meridian, a strip of country about 90 miles in width was left intervening between that meridian and the eastern frontier of Western Australia, and this region, containing an area of over 80,000 square miles, was added to South Australia in 1861. Two years later, a further accession was made by including within the confines of the State all the country stretching northward from the 26th parallel of south latitude to the Indian Ocean, in addition to the territory lying between the meridians of 129° and 138° east longitude. The area of the state was thus brought up to its present large proportions, next to Western Australia the province being the most extensive of the group. The portion of the state to the north of the 26th parallel, known as the Northern Territory, is so dissimilar, as regards climate and resources, to the southern division, that it may almost be looked upon as a separate possession.

Coastal Features.

The coast line on the south, with the exception of the large inlets of Spencer Gulf and St. Vincent's Gulf, is not diversified by any very remarkable indentations. From west to east the shore line has a general downward trend through about six degrees. Commencing from the western extremity, there is a vast crescent-shaped curve terminating at Cape Catastrophe, and forming the eastern portion of the Great Australian Bight. For the first 120 miles from the western boundary the shore is backed by precipitous limestone ridges, varying in height from 400 to 600 feet. Passing the head of the Bight, the first noteworthy headland is Cape Nuyts, a lofty promontory a little to the eastward of longitude 132°. Rounding this point, Fowler's Bay opens out, and thence, after passing through the cluster of islets known as Nuyts Archipelago, Streaky Bay is entered, one of the finest harbors in this portion of the coast. The northern headland is named Point Brown, while Cape Bauer lies at the south. Farther down is Cape Radstock a well-known landmark for mariners sailing to the east. Then comes Anxious Bay, which affords good anchorage but is unsafe during the prevalence of certain winds. Off Cape Finniss lies Flinders Island and the Investigator Group, the names being reminiscent of the explorer of earlier days. Coffin's Bay, to the eastward of Point Sir Isaac, offers excellent shelter from westerly or southerly gales. Sleaford Bay, between Cape Wiles and Cape Catastrophe, is a fine inlet with deep water in various parts. Spencer's Gulf is the largest inlet on the south coast of Australia; its entrance lies between Cape Catastrophe at the western extremity, and Cape Spencer at the foot of Yorke's Peninsula on the eastern side, and is 47 miles wide. Port Augusta at the head of the Gulf is distant 180 miles from the entrance. The inlet has a shore line of about 400 miles and offers everywhere excellent facilities for navigation to vessels of the greatest burden. Spencer's Gulf is separated from the next large inlet, called St. Vincent's Gulf, by Yorke's Peninsula. St. Vincent's Gulf has a width at the entrance of thirty-four miles, and a length of about eighty miles. Port Adelaide is situated on its eastern shore, and is the principal harbor of the State. The entrance to St. Vincent's Gulf is protected on the south by Kangaroo Island, one of the largest islands on the Australian Coast. It measures eighty miles east and west, and has an average width of about twenty miles. Cape Borda, a well-defined headland, is situated on its western side, and Cape de Couedie and Cape Gantheaume on the south. The passage between the island and Yorke's Peninsula is called Investigator's Strait, and that between the eastern portion and the mainland, Backstairs Passage. From Encounter Bay to the eastern boundary of the state the coast is generally low and flat. Between Cape Jaffa, at the southern extremity of Lacepede Bay, and Rivoli Bay, the presence of numerous reefs and shoals, in some cases extending out for many miles from the shore, necessitates extreme caution on the part of navigators. After leaving Rivoli Bay the next important headland is Cape Banks, conspicuous by a white sand hummock near its extremity. Cape Northumberland is the last projection on the eastward portion of the coast, and is a prominent elevation capped by the McDonnell Lighthouse. Generally speaking, the south coast, which has a total length of upwards of 1,600 miles, is well-marked and lighted.

The northern coast, which embraces the shore line of Arnhem Land with the western portion of the Gulf of Carpentaria, is more broken and irregular than the south coast. Here, too, are the estuaries of several fine rivers, while, with the exception of the Murray, there is hardly a river worthy of mention that reaches the Southern Ocean. Commencing on the western boundary, the chief inlets are Queen's

Channel and Keys Inlet. Passing the headlands of Cape Hay and Cape Scott, Anson Bay is entered, the Peron Islands lying at the northern entrance. After threading through several small islets, the entrance to Port Darwin opens out. This fine harbour was named after Dr. Darwin, who accompanied King on his surveys of the north coast (1818–1822), and is remarkable for its magnitude and security, as well as for the beauty of its scenery. Situated in latitude 12° 28′ 22″ south and longitude 130° 50′ 26″ east, the harbour has an entrance two miles in width, with a depth of water of about 15 fathoms. Within there is unlimited accommodation for all classes of vessels, the depth ranging from 4 to 15 fathoms, with good anchorage close up to the shore. The chief drawback to the many natural advantages of the port is the extraordinary rise and fall of the tide, the spring tides rising to from 16 to 24 feet, and the neaps from 2 to 12 feet. This disadvantage has, however, been combated by the erection of a splendid jetty, provided with every convenience for mooring. A peculiar feature of the harbour is the presence of a natural dock, formed by a sloping sand bank at the foot of Fort Hill, where vessels may be safely stranded at spring tides, repaired at low-water, and re-floated on the next recurring high tide. The town of Palmerston is situated on a plateau-like expanse 60 feet above the level of the sea, and occupies a commanding position near the entrance. Opposite Port Darwin, and to the westward of the large inlet of Van Diemen's Gulf, are the two large islands called Melville and Bathurst Islands. The former is 75 miles long and 38 broad, and is fertile and well watered. A military station at one time existed at Port Dundas, but since its abandonment in 1840 the island has been given over to the almost exclusive possession of the blacks. Between the Coburg Peninsula, enclosing the western portion of Van Diemen's Gulf and Melville Islands, the passage is known as Dundas Strait. Rounding the peninsula numerous groups of islands are passed through, the chief of those which have received names being the Goulburn, Crocodile, Elcho, and Wessel Islands, but none of them has any commercial importance, and indeed they are rarely visited, except perhaps by the proas of the Malay traders. In the Gulf of Carpentaria, the principal inlet is Blue Mud Bay, off which there are numerous islands, the largest bearing the Dutch name of Groote Eylandt.

General Physical Characteristics.

As previously stated, the only river of importance discharging into the Southern Ocean is the Murray, which flows through South Australian territory from the 141st meridian of east longitude, and debouches into Lake Alexandrina, and thence into the sea at Encounter Bay. The entrance is dangerous during the prevalence of certain winds, but much has been done in the way of deepening and improving the channel. Proceeding westward from the Murray, two small rivers, the Hindmarsh and the Inman, empty into the bay, but their mouths are obstructed by sand bars and reefs. The Torrens rises in the Mount Lofty Ranges, and, after many twists and turns in a westerly direction, reaches the Torrens Gorge, whence it emerges from the hills and drains the fertile Adelaide Plains. After separating North Adelaide from the southern portion of the city, it spreads its waters over a vast tract of swampy land at a short distance from the coast. Ten miles north of Port Adelaide, the Gawler flows into St. Vincent's Gulf at Port Gawler. Farther west there are no streams of importance, the country surrounding the Bight in particular being destitute of streams of any magnitude.

In the Northern Territory, however, there are several fine navigable rivers, and with the further development of this portion of South Australia they are certain to assume considerable importance. The McArthur flows into the Gulf of Carpentaria opposite the Sir Edward Pellew Islands, and is navigable for small vessels for a distance of 50 miles. Much of the basin drained by this stream consists of good pastoral lands. The Roper, which debouches into the Gulf at Limmen's Bight, is navigable for about 90 miles. This is the best known river on the northern coast, and much of the country surrounding it has been taken up for pastoral purposes. The Goyder flows into Castlereagh Bay, and is navigable for 13 miles, but the lower course of the stream is lined by dense and impenetrable mangrove jungles. The Blyth enters Boucaut Bay, and is navigable for a distance of 18 miles. Into Van Diemen's Gulf flow the three Alligator Rivers, discovered by King in 1820, and named respectively the East, West, and South Alligator. They are all navigable for some distance from their mouths. The Adelaide discharges into Adam Bay, after draining a large extent of good pastoral country, It is accessible to vessels drawing from 10 to 12 feet, and has been navigated for a distance of 80 miles. The Daly River debouches into Anson Bay, and is navigable for vessels of light draught for 60 miles. In spite of the fact that there is only about 3 feet of water on the bar at low tide, the rise of tide, being from 18 to 24 feet, permits the largest vessels to negotiate the entrance with safety. Good agricultural land is found on its banks, and deposits of copper also occur within its basin. The Victoria, discovered by Stokes in 1839, is the finest river on the northen coast. Between Turtle and Pierce Points the entrance is 20 miles wide, and the stream is navigable by vessels of the heaviest burthen for 50 miles from its mouth. The area of the basin of the Victoria has been computed as, approximately, 90,000 square miles. Little is known of the major portion of its watershed, but extensive tracts have been occupied for pastoral purposes.

Many watercourses are found in the interior, and some of them extend for hundreds of miles, but their volume varies with the season. Cooper's Creek, the Diamantina, and other streams from South-Western Queensland at times inundate the country for thousands of square miles, at others dwindle to mere chains of pools. The Todd, the Finke, and the Macumba either sink into the plains or, in favourable seasons, reach the inland lakes.

A reference to the map will make it appear as if South Australia were well provided with lakes, some of them being of considerable extent. These expanses of water are, however, mostly salt and useless for purposes of navigation.

The largest group of salt lakes is found to the north of Spencer's Gulf, and includes Lake Eyre, the surface of which is 39 feet below sea-level, Lake Torrens, Lake Gairdner and Lake Frome. The largest of these occasionally exceed 100 miles in length, but in periods of drought they dwindle into comparative insignificance and at times become quite dry. Their sites are then marked by expanses of black mud with saline incrustations, and the earlier explorers who attempted to cross these hideous bogs had to turn back repeatedly in despair. Farther to the north, and towards the centre of the continent, is the salt morass called Lake Amadeus.

Several lakes are situated close to the south coast between Cape Banks and Guichen Bay. Lake Bonney is fresh and has a length of 25 miles by a breadth of 2 miles in its widest part. Its waters are, however, shallow, although it is surrounded by fairly high banks. Lake George is about 10 miles long by 5 in width at the broadest part. Lake St. Clair is a much smaller expanse, and is salt and shallow. The morass called Lake Hawdon lies north and east of Lake Eliza, and is 40 miles long by 8 wide. The Coorong, 40 miles west of Lake Hawdon, has an opening to the sea near the mouth of the Murray. It is about 70 miles long and 4 wide. Lakes Alexandrina and Albert are situated at the mouth of the Murray and are joined by a narrow channel. From their appearance, it seems a likely assumption that they were originally arms of the sea, and that their coastal banks have resulted from upheaval. Lake Alexandrina is 24 miles long and 14 miles wide, and is generally shallow. Lake Albert is 14 miles long by about 8 in breadth at its widest part.

In the Mount Gambier region several remarkable lakes are found occupying the craters of extinct volcanoes. The most celebrated of these is the Blue Lake, which is irregularly circular in shape and about a mile in diameter. The sides of the lakes which are several hundreds of feet in height, descend precipitously to the water and are agreeably diversified by charming verdure. Soundings have proved the depth of the lake to be about 240 feet, and on clear days its waters are of a most beautiful deep blue.

The general physical contour of the surface of South Australia in no way resembles that of the eastern states already described. In those States the general trend of the mountains is parallel to the shore, and there are the three more or less well-defined zones of coastal district, tableland, and interior plain. But in South Australia the mountains pierce the interior and end abruptly amongst the inland salt lakes and swamps. North of Lake Torrens no well-defined system of mountains exists. The first group of mountains is that of the Adelaide Chain, which commences at Cape Jervis and penetrates in a northerly direction to Lake Frome, a distance of 350 miles. The range attains its greatest elevation in the Mount Lofty and Barossa districts, the highest points being Mount Lofty, 2,334 feet, and Razorback, 2,834 feet. Its course is interrupted here and there by a few narrow gorges, through which flow the small streams discharging into St. Vincent's Gulf. The Flinders Range commences in the conspicuous landmarks called the Hummocks, at the head of St. Vincent's Gulf, and pursues a northerly direction to the head of Lake Torrens. The highest points in this range are the Bluff, 2,404 feet, and Mount Remarkable and Mount Brown, each about 3,000 feet. On the west side of the Adelaide Chain are the fertile and extensive Adelaide Plains, one of the finest wheat-growing districts in the world. Plains of similar fertility, but of less extent, are found between the longitudinal ridges of the Flinders Range and the northern prolongation of the Adelaide Range. On the eastern side of the Adelaide chain stretches the plain of the south-east, towards the western boundary of which the Murray flows. From north to south this plain is 290 miles in width, and about 100 miles from east to west. A vast plain district also stretches north and west from Lake Torrens. The Gawler Range originates in Eyre Peninsula, on the western side of Spencer Gulf, and, reaching an elevation of 2000 feet, extends to the southern shores of Lakes Everard and Gairdner. The Warburton and Stewart Ranges lie west and north of these ranges, and where the province adjoins the boundary of the northern territory the country rises to the McDonnell Ranges, the highest elevation between the northern and southern watersheds. Respecting the mountains in the Northern Territory, little can be said, as they have not, up to the present, received any detailed examination.

In the south-eastern portion of the province are situated Mount Gambier, Mount Schanck, Mount Terrible, and several other isolated peaks, which were formerly volcanoes, the craters being now occupied by fresh-water lakes. The best known of these, the Blue Lake of Mount Gambier, has already been alluded to.

For a long time it was supposed that the interior of South Australia was a barren desert, the home of the hot blasts that periodically visit the south. Although a large portion of the territory is admittedly arid and inhospitable, in many places near perennial waters the soil is of surprising richness. With the further exploitation of the large stores of artesian water underlying the country, much of the seemingly hopeless wilderness will, in time to come, be made to "blossom as the rose."

WESTERN AUSTRALIA.

Area and Boundaries.

THE state of Western Australia, as its name implies, occupies the western portion of the Australian continent, and is by far the largest of the states, containing within its confines an area of no less than 975,920 square miles. On its eastern boundary it is separated from South Australia by the 129th meridian; the Indian Ocean washes its northern and western shores; and the southern boundary is formed by the Great Southern Ocean. The greatest length of the territory, from Cape Londonderry on the north to Peak Head on the south, is 1,480 miles, and the greatest breadth, from Steep Point on the west to the meridian on the east, is about 1,000 miles.

Coastal Features.

With the exception of that portion to the northward of the 18th parallel, the coast line of Western Australia is singularly regular and unbroken, so that the total estimated length, 5,200 miles, is small when compared with the area of the state. On the southern coast, a long unbroken rampart of limestone cliffs stretches from Eucla, on the eastern boundary, round the western horn of the Great Australian Bight to Cape Arid. No river or creek pierces these frowning precipices, nor is there refuge of any kind for the storm-beaten vessel. Westward from Cape Arid, Esperance Bay and Doubtful Island Bay afford safe anchorage, but they are difficult of access during the prevalence of certain winds. King George's Sound is one of the most important inlets on the south coast The entrance is between two bluff headlands, named respectively Cape Vancouver and Bald Head, and the harbour, which extends inland for some 10 miles, is well sheltered from all but south-westerly gales. An inner sheet of water, called Oyster Bay, is connected by a narrow channel with the Sound. Three miles southward another break in the shore line of the Sound leads into Princess Royal Harbour, on the northern shore of which the town of Albany is located—once an important place of call for the mail steamers. Situated as it is, the Sound is an important strategic naval position, and this fact has been recognised by the authorities, who have taken steps to fortify it. The country round the shores of the Sound is celebrated for the variety and profusion of the wild flowers flourishing there, amongst which the sweet-scented boronia is especially remarkable. From King George's Sound round to Cape Leeuwin the coast is fringed by rugged granitic masses, and is broken by several small streams flowing into the sea. Cape Leeuwin is situated in the south-western corner of the continent, where the Indian and Southern Oceans meet, and is a prominent landmark for vessels voyaging to Australia. On calm, bright days the view from the lighthouse on the point, 700 feet above the sea, discloses enchanting vistas of Hamelin Bay, the mouth of the Blackwood River, and numerous islets and reefs flashing gaily in the sunlight; but when the wind blows strongly from the west, the Lioness quivers as the thunderous waves dash at her feet, while the swirling spray is borne by the blasts for a long distance inland. Passing the Leeuwin, and sailing northwards, the next important point is Cape Naturaliste, at the entrance to Geographe Bay, on the shores of which stands the town of Busselton, the outlet of a thriving timber and dairying district. Leaving Cape Bouvard, 40 miles to the south of Perth, the low, scrub-covered Garden Island, sheltering Cockburn Sound, comes into view. Near by is Rottnest Island, on which the Governor's marine residence is situated, and the site also of a native prison. Between the two islands, vessels from the south approach the port of Fremantle on the Swan River. Two hundred miles further up the coast is the port of Geraldton, off which lie the dangerous Houtman's Abrolhos, the scene of many a wreck when the Dutch vessels in times gone by were wont to visit this portion of the continent. The Abrolhos have for ages been the resort of countless numbers of sea fowl, and rich deposits of guano are obtained on several of the islands in the group. Shark's Bay is an extensive inlet in latitude 26°, Dirk Hartog Island lying to the westward. Valuable deposits of pearlshell have been obtained from the shallow banks in this bay. Steep Point, on the west, is the most westerly point of the continent. North of this bay is situated Exmouth Gulf, a capacious inlet, with North-west Cape at its outer extremity. From the Leeuwin up to this point, the shore-line has had a north-westerly sweep, but from this onward the general trend is to the north-east. Cossack Harbour is the port of the magnificent pastoral district known as the "Nor' West," lying between the Ashburton and De Grey Rivers. Higher up is Roebuck Bay, on which the township of Broome is situated. King Sound is an extensive indentation, on the western extremity of which is situated the important headland of Cape Leveque. The inlet is the centre of the shipping trade of the great West Kimberley district, and the harbour offers excellent facilities for shipping. At the entrance to the Sound is the cluster of rocky islets known as the Buccaneer Archipelago. Between King Sound and Cambridge Gulf, the coast is deeply indented, the principal inlets being Collier Bay, Brunswick Sound, York Sound, Montague Sound, and Admiralty Gulf. Cambridge Gulf is a fine inlet, offering excellent anchorage for vessels of every class. The township of Wyndham, at the head of the gulf, is the business centre of the whole of the East Kimberley district, and is the north-eastern terminus of the West Australian system of telegraphs. A large volume of trade is carried on with the southern ports, and also with Port Darwin, in the northern territory of South Australia. Numerous islands lie off the coast between King Sound and the Gulf, the most important being Augustus Island, near Camden Sound, and Bigge Island, north of York Sound. None of these islands has been very carefully examined, but they appear to be of the same rugged sandstone formation as the adjoining coast. Dampier's Archipelago, Barrow Island, and numerous others lie north-east of the North-west Cape. They are chiefly of granite formation, and some of them are well-grassed.

General Physical Characteristics.

The whole of the interior of Western Australia, embracing the country between the 19th and 31st parallels of latitude, and 121st and 129th meridians of longitude, consists of a vast tableland between one and two thousand feet above the level of the sea. Of this immense stretch of territory, the greater portion consists of sand dunes and stony ridges, with here and there areas of clayey soil. Except in connection with the development of its mineral resources, it is believed that little of this portion of the state will ever be available for settlement. The lakes found in this district, except in periods of heavy rainfall, are merely salt marshes of greater or less extent, and sometimes become dry clay-pans. North of the 19th parallel the country consists of alternately high and low-lying expanses of tableland, intersected by several ranges of mountains. The Kimberley portion of this district contains several fine rivers. Much of the south-western and southern sea boards is of a flat, sandy character, and is covered in parts with vast forests, containing jarrah, karri, white and red gum, and many other timbers of great commercial value. In the limestone region north of the Great Australian Bight there are some fine stretches of grass country, needing only a permanent water supply to make them rank amongst the productive divisions of the state.

As previously stated, there are no streams of much importance flowing into the Southern Ocean; indeed, on the shores of the Bight there is a stretch of country, 300 miles in length, unpierced by any watercourse. The Blackwood, Warren, Kalgan, and Phillips enter the sea west of the Bight, towards Cape Leeuwin, some magnificent forest country being found in the basin of these streams. Flowing into the Indian Ocean, on the west coast, are the Preston, Collie, Swan, Greenough, Murchison, and Gascoyne. The Swan, upon which Perth, the capital of the State, is situated, receives the name of Avon above the tidal waters. On the north-west are the Ashburton, Oakover, Fortescue, and Fitzroy. The Kimberley district is watered by the Fitzroy, Ord, Pentecost, Durack, Drysdale, &c. Pastoral occupation is rapidly spreading in the districts traversed by these streams, while the rich auriferous discoveries have also conferred an added importance on the territory.

In the southern portion of the State the Stirling Range, situated about 40 miles to the north-east of Albany, attains its highest elevation in Mount Toolbrunup, which reaches an altitude of about 3,000 feet. The range possesses a certain grandeur from the fact of its being perfectly isolated and rising abruptly from a level plain. In the south-western district the Darling Range runs north and south from Yatheroo to Point D'Entrecasteaux on the south coast. From its proximity to the western seaboard, this range exercises a great influence over the climate of the State in its most populous area. The highest point is Mount William, 1,700 feet in altitude, situated in the Murray district. Between the Fortescue and Ashburton Rivers is the Hamersley Range, in which Mount Bruce rises to a height of 3,800 feet, and is supposed to be the loftiest peak in the State. In the Kimberley district is situated the Princess May Range, running in an easterly direction from York Sound, the highest point in which, called Mount York, is probably 3,000 feet high. Mount Hann, in the same range, reaches an elevation of 2,000 feet. The King Leopold Range stretches south-easterly from Collier Bay, but no point in the chain exceeds an elevation of 2,400 feet. In the south-western district, between Cape Naturaliste and the Leeuwin, an interesting series of limestone caves is found in undulating country at a distance of from 1 to 3 miles from the coast. For beauty and picturesqueness these caves rival those in the Jenolan district of New South Wales, and in some respects are unsurpassed anywhere in the world.

TASMANIA.

Area and Boundaries.

THE island State of Tasmania is the smallest in the Federation, and contains an area of 26,215 square miles. On the north it is separated from the mainland of Australia by Bass Strait, a broad channel of from 80 to 150 miles in width. The Tasman Sea forms its eastern boundary, and its southern and western shores are washed by the waters of the Great Southern Ocean. From north to south the island is about 200 miles long, and the breadth from east to west in its widest part is about the same distance.

Coastal Features.

The southern portion of the eastern shore of the island is rich in picturesque inlets and bold headlands. Hobart, the capital of the state, is beautifully situated on the river Derwent, which debouches into Storm Bay. Behind the city, the cone of Mount Wellington rises to a height of over 4,000 feet. The bay is protected on its eastern side by Tasman's Peninsula, the extremities of which are guarded by the bluff headlands of Cape Pillar and Cape Raoul. These two headlands are composed of masses of columnar basalt rising to a height of several hundreds of feet. Some of the pillars stand as outliers to the main body, the intervening softer mass having been detached by the combined action of wind and sea. For ages the waves of the Southern Ocean have been relentlessly beating at these lofty promontories, and at times large portions of the mighty mass, undermined by the ceaseless erosive agency of the salt water, topple over and sink heavily into the ocean. Tasman's Peninsula is connected with Forestier's Peninsula, lying to the northward, by the narrow isthmus of Eagle Hawk Neck. The land-locked harbour, enclosed by these two peninsulas, is called Norfolk Bay. On the north-eastern portion of Forestier's Peninsula lies North Bay. Sailing northwards from this inlet for about 10 miles the beautiful and peculiarly-shaped Maria Island is reached, supposed to have been named by Tasman after the daughter of his patron, Antony Van Diemen. The island, on the northern side of which cliffs of basalt rise to a height of over 2,000 feet, is almost severed in twain by the deep indentations of Oyster Bay and Reidle Bay, situated respectively on the western and eastern sides, and joined by a narrow neck of land. Higher up on the mainland is another large inlet named

Oyster Bay, with Freycinet's Peninsula on its eastern flank. Schouten Island lies off the extremity of this peninsula, being separated from it by the narrow passage called Geographe Strait. Proceeding southward from Tasman's Peninsula, the two large islands called North and South Bruni are found lying to the east of the D'Entrecasteaux Channel. These two islands, which are joined by a narrow sand spit, contain an area of 90,000 acres. Opposite South Bruni is the estuary of the Huon River. The channel is here bordered by numbers of beautiful bays with well-wooded slopes. Between the South-East and South-West Capes there are several small islands and reefs requiring very skilful navigation. From the South-West Cape the coast trends northward again, and after passing Hilliard Head the fine harbour of Port Davey opens out. Thence the most conspicuous headlands are Rocky Point, Point Hibbs, and Cape Sorell; the latter standing at the entrance to the splendid expanse of water known as Macquarie Harbour. North ward of this inlet the most prominent headlands are—Sandy Cape, Bluff Point, and Cape Grim. Opposite the western apex of the State are situated Hunter's Island, the Three Hummocks Islands, and Robbin's Island. Circular Head is one of the most remarkable projections on the northern coast. It consists of a narrow peninsula running out from the mainland for a distance of about six miles, and terminating in a rocky bluff about 400 feet high. This point is a prominent landmark for vessels sailing from Victoria to Tasmania. Amongst the chief indentations on the north coast are Port Frederick, Port Sorell, and Port Dalrymple, the latter receiving the drainage of the Tamar River on which is situated the town of Launceston. There are several islands off the eastern apex of the state, the most important being Clarke Island, Cape Barren Island, and Flinders Island. The last mentioned is the largest island dependency of the State, and contains an area of 513,000 acres.

General Physical Characteristics.

It is believed that Tasmania originally constituted a southward prolongation of the mainland of Australia, and the continuation of the Great Dividing Range, lying near the eastern seaboard of the continent may be traced through the Furneaux and Kent's group across to the island state. From the central range, traversing the country from north-west to south, various lateral spurs diverge, further ramifications from which branch away in all directions. The centre of the island is occupied by an extensive plateau, with an elevation on the northern side, of between three and four thousand feet above the level of the sea. This table-land district extends from Dry's Bluff in the north-west to the Denison Range in the south-west, and although it recedes here and there at the sources of the chief rivers, presents a precipitous slope to the north, west, and east. Several fine fresh water lakes are situated on the comparatively level stretches on the summit, and these in some instances act as feeders to the streams which reach the coast. The plateau determines the northern, western, and southern drainage slopes of the island and maintains its general elevation from Dry's Bluff at an altitude of 4,257 feet on the north to Cradle Mountain, 5,069 feet in the north-west, a distance of nearly 50 miles; from the Bluff south-west to the Denison Range, for over 60 miles; and from the same point in a southerly direction to Table Mountain, 3,596 feet, a distance of about 43 miles. Below this central plateau there is a second table-land region at a lower elevation, maintaining an altitude of between 1,200 and 2,000 feet. This division stretches westward, including the Middlesex Plains, the Hampshire Hills, and the Emu Plains, and its limits follow the coast line more or less closely, the space between it and the ocean in some localities widening out into low lying expanses raised very little above sea level. At intervals, rising abruptly from this region, various isolated peaks are to be seen, the chief being Mount Bischoff, 2,598 feet, Valentine's Peak, 3,637 feet, Mount Tor, and Mount Pearse, 3,800 feet. In addition there are, round the coast, ridges and plateaus more or less elevated such as Ben Lomond on the north-east, 5,010 feet, Mount Wellington, near Hobart, 4,166 feet, and the Frenchman's Cap, near Macquarie Harbour, 4,756 feet. It has been principally among the plains and lower levels of the North-western, Midland, and Southern portions of the island that settlement has taken place, chiefly in the geological areas of Tertiary and Mesozoic age. Here, in the recent Tertiary period, the soil of the plains and valleys has been enriched by extensive outbursts of basalt with accompanying tuffs. There is evidence to show that these basaltic sheets, which cover large areas in the Midland, North-western, and North-eastern districts, are invariably associated with the ancient Tertiary lake systems. It is from these volcanic rocks that the rich chocolate soils have been produced, and but for their agency a large portion of what is now the most fertile area of the State would have been comparatively poor or perhaps hopelessly barren.

Tasmania is well supplied with rivers, some of them of considerable volume, flowing through fine scenery and magnificent forests, and in some instances adorned with picturesque waterfalls. The largest is the Derwent, which rises in the central plateau, and enters the sea at Storm Bay. In the lower portion of its course, the river widens out into a magnificent estuary on which the capital city, Hobart, is situated. The Derwent receives numerous tributaries, of which the chief are the Nive, Dee, Ouse, Clyde, and Jordan from the north, and the Florentine, Russell, Styx, and Plenty from the south. The Huon issues from Lake Edgar, and after flowing through a heavily-timbered, rich, fruit-growing district, debouches into the D'Entrecasteaux Channel. The Coal River takes its rise in the eastern mountains and falls into the sea at Pittwater, near Hobart. On the north, the Tamar flows into Bass Strait, and after passing Launceston forms a fine estuary with excellent facilities for navigation. The river is formed by the confluence of the North and South Esk at the city, and is fed by numerous tributaries higher up. The Mersey, on which the town of Latrobe is situated, enters the sea at Port Frederick. On the west and south-west the following streams flow into Macquarie Harbour:—The Gordon, which emerges from Lake Richmond, and receives in its course the Wedge, Denison, Serpentine, and Franklin, and the King River, with its affluents the Queen and the Eldon. In the north-west are the Pieman and Arthur rivers. On the east, the watershed approaches very close to the shore and there are no streams of any great importance. Two short rivers, the Swan and the Swanport, discharge into Oyster Bay.

Several large freshwater lakes are situated on the central table-land. Of these the most extensive are the Great Lake, 13 miles long by a maximum width of 8 miles, and with an area of 28,000 acres; Lakes Sorell and Crescent, 17,000 acres; Lake St. Clair, 10,000 acres; and Lakes Arthur and Echo, each about 8,000 acres. These lakes serve as natural reservoirs for the supply of numerous rivers flowing chiefly to the southward. Most of them are very deep and owe their origin to the same causes which have produced the beautiful lakes of Scotland and Wales. In addition to those mentioned there are numerous lagoons and mountain tarns.

NEW GUINEA.

THE island of New Guinea lies close to the northern extremity of Queensland, being separated from the mainland by Torres Strait. Excluding Australia itself, New Guinea is the largest island in the world, and lies between the equator and 12° south, and between 130° 50′ and 134° 30′ east longitude. Its greatest length is 1,490 miles, and its maximum breadth 430 miles, its area being about 234,770 square miles. It is occupied by British, Dutch, and German colonists; the British portion includes the south-east of the island, with an area of 90,540 square miles, of which 87,786 are on the mainland, and 2,754 square miles comprise various groups of islands. The eastern end of the possession is very mountainous; moving westward, the various chains unite to form a great central cordillera, which attains its highest point in the Owen Stanley Range, where Mount Victoria rises to a height of 13,200 feet above sea-level. Conspicuous also in the eastern portion of the island are Mount Suckling (12,228 feet), Mount Obree (10,246 feet), Mount Yule (10,046 feet), and Mount Brown (7,940 feet). The mountains follow the coast, and are distant from it about 20 to 50 miles; at the head of the Gulf of Papua the ranges become broken and considerably reduced in height, as well as further removed from the seaboard. The western portion of the possession may be generally described as low and swampy, densely clothed with forest; dense forest growth is also characteristic of the mountains. New Guinea is a well-watered country; its two largest rivers are the Fly River, with its tributary (the Strickland), and the Purari. The Fly River has a total length of 600 miles, but some portion of its upper course lies within Dutch territory. The river has been navigated for a great distance, and it is said that small steamers of fair draught can ascend over 500 miles. The Purari rises in German territory, and is navigable for a considerable distance from its mouth. There are many other rivers, but, as they have not been explored, no detailed description of them can be given. The southern and south-east coast-line is well indented, and several fair harbours exist.

Lying as it does just under the equator, the climate of New Guinea is very warm, but as no extensive range of observations has been made, the maximum and minimum temperature cannot be definitely stated. At Port Moresby the average shade temperature at 9 a.m. is 81·6° Fahrenheit, with a maximum of 94°; this would argue very high maximum daily temperature, but not greater than along some portions of the northern coast of Australia. The rainfall varies greatly in different parts of the island; at Port Moresby the quantity recorded in 1901 was 54 inches, but this was probably in excess of the average; at Dogura on the north-east coast, on the opposite side of the island, the average is 59 inches; but at Samarai, at the south-east end of the island, the rainfall registers between 120 and 130 inches per annum. At Daru, in the west of the possession, the average is about 85 inches, but a fall of nearly 150 inches has been registered, and it is probable that equally great rainfall is experienced in the central mountains.

NEW ZEALAND.

Area and Boundaries.

THE Colony of New Zealand consists of the three main islands named respectively North Island, Middle Island, and Stewart Island, together with the numerous subsidiary islands which from time to time have been added to the territory by proclamation. The group is situated in the South Pacific Ocean about 1,200 miles to the south-east of Australia. That portion of the Southern Ocean which lies between the Australian Coast and New Zealand is now distinguished as the Tasman Sea, in honor of the first discoverer of New Zealand and Tasmania. Including outlying islands, the total area embraced within the limits of the Colony is 104,471 square miles, of which the North Island with adjacent islets constitutes 44,468 square miles, the Middle Island with adjacent islets 58,525 square miles, and Stewart Island with adjacent islets 665 square miles.

The North Island.

Coastal Features.

This island is, as its name implies, the northernmost of the group, and is separated from the Middle Island by Cook Strait. In shape it is peculiar, consisting of a roughly square main body, with projections stretching from each corner, the longest being to the north-west. This remarkable northward peninsula is about 280 miles long, and from 53 to 8 miles in breadth, and is almost cut in two by the Hauraki Gulf on the eastern side, and the Manukau Harbour on the west. On the narrow isthmus intervening, the town of Auckland has been built. At the extremity of the peninsula lies the headland of Cape Reinga, from which, according to Maori legend the souls of the dead were plunged into the abode of departed spirits. A little to the eastward is North Cape, and to the west Cape Maria Van Diemen. Off the point lie the rocky islets known as the Three Kings, the scene of several disastrous shipwrecks. Proceeding down the western coast from Cape Maria Van Diemen, the first inlet of importance is Ahipara Bay, with Reef Point at its southern entrance. Next come Kiapara Harbour and Manukau Harbour. Lower down is Kawhia Harbour, with Albatross Point on the southward entrance. Here the coast takes a westerly sweep and forms the North Taranaki Bight. On the extremity of the western projection of the island is situated Cape Egmont, with the prominent landmark of Mount Egmont standing a little distance inland. Sweeping round to the south the coast line forms the capacious South Taranaki Bight. Port Nicholson and Palliser Bay are situated in the southern prolongation of the island. Rounding Cape Palliser a long stretch of unindented coast line leads up to Kidnapper's Point at the southern entrance to Hawke Bay. Passing Poverty Bay and East Cape and turning westward the Bay of Plenty is entered. Next comes the Hauraki Gulf, off which are situated the Barrier Islands, with Aiguilles Point on the extremity of the Great Barrier. The eastward coast line of the northern peninsula possesses numerous indentations, the most remarkable of which is the Bay of Islands with Cape Brett at its southern entrance. This inlet is one of the finest harbours in New Zealand, being superior to that of Auckland as regards facility of entrance, and possessing deep water and good anchorage in almost every part. As the name implies, the surface of the bay is diversified by numerous small islands, and these, with their verdurous slopes and lustrous beaches, together with the many beautiful bays and headlands on the mainland, constitute a scene which, for charm, stands almost unrivalled.

General Physical Characteristics.

The main body of the North Island is mountainous, although there are some extensive stretches of plain country, portions of which are of surprising richness and fertility. In the northern peninsula the ranges do not rise to any great altitude, Tutanoe, the highest point, having an elevation of 2,570 feet. Southward from East Cape the highest summit is Hikurangi, which reaches 5,530 feet. On the west coast, south of Whaingaroa Harbour, are Mount Karehoe and Mount Pironghia, reaching an altitude, respectively, of 2,370 and 2,800 feet. The volcanic summits to the south reach a much greater elevation. One of the most remarkable is Mount Egmont, in the New Plymouth District. This is an extinct volcanic cone, 8,260 feet in height, and the summit is clothed with perpetual snow. Rising abruptly from the plain, it presents a sublime spectacle, the cone being one of the most perfect in the world. Tarawera is the well-known volcanic summit in the celebrated Lake District, and rises to a height of 3,600 feet. Farther down are the Te Whaiti Range leading to Kaimanawha, near Hawkes' Bay, and the prolongations to Kaweka and the Ruahine Range, ending in the Tararua and Haurangi at Cape Palliser, these successive ranges forming the backbone of the island to Cook's Strait. The Tongariro Mountain in the Lake Taupo District consists of the united outflow of lava from several distinct cones. Ngauruhoe, the highest of these, reaches 7,515 feet. From Nguaurhoe, the Red Crater, and Te Mari discharges of lava took place as recently as 1868, and steam and vapours are still given off from various vents, accompanied by considerable noise. Ruapehu lies south of the Tongariro group, and reaches an elevation of 9,008 feet, being in part above the line of perpetual snow. This mountain is in the solfatara stage, and possesses a crater-lake which occasionally is troubled by slight eruptions giving rise to large volumes of steam. In March, 1895, an eruption took place, when several hot springs were formed, while the heat of the lake increased. The sides of the depression occupied by the lake are covered with ice and snow, and the water, which is 300 feet below the surrounding crater rims, is inaccessible except with the use of ropes and ladders. This area and the three craters on Tongariro are situated in a straight line which if produced would pass through the boiling springs of Tokaanu on the southern edge of Lake Taupo, the volcanic country north-east of the lake, and White Island, an active volcano in the Bay of Plenty, about 27 miles from the mainland.

The district occupied by the hot springs constitutes one of the most remarkable and interesting features of the North Island. They are found over a large extent of country from Tongariro, south of Lake Taupo, to Ohaeawai in the extreme north, a distance of about 300 miles, but it is in the neighbourhood of Lake Rotorua, about 40 miles north-east of Lake Taupo, that the principal seat of hydrothermal action is encountered. Many of the hot springs have been proved to possess remarkable curative powers in certain complaints, and the Government has taken considerable pains to render them accessible to the visitor in search of health. The beautiful Pink and White Terraces in this district were almost completely destroyed by the eruption of Mount Tarawera in 1886, but it is stated that natural agencies are at work which will in time renew them. Some of the hot springs assume the form of geysers, and eject boiling water, fragments of rock, mud, &c., to a considerable height.

Of the plains, the principal are those in the Hawke's Bay District; the Wairarapa Plain in the Wellington District; the West-Coast Plain, stretching from near Wellington to some distance north of New Plymouth; and the Kaingaroa Plain, which stretches in a north-easterly direction from Lake Taupo to the Bay of Plenty. A great portion of the last-mentioned is, however, covered with pumice sand and is unfit for agricultural or pastoral occupation.

The principal river in the North Island is the Waikato. Rising in the Central Range, near Ruapehu, it flows into Lake Taupo, thence flowing north-westward it enters the ocean a short distance to the south of Manukau Harbour. The river is navigable for 100 miles from its mouth by small vessels. The Thames rises in the high land near the Lake District, and after a course of 100 miles enters the sea at the Firth of Thames. Several small streams, including the Tarawera, drain into the Bay of Plenty. The Wairoa, Waikari, and Mohaka fall into Hawke Bay. The Wanganui flows into the South Taranaki Bight, and the Hutt into Port Nicholson.

A large number of streams drain the Auckland peninsula, their courses necessarily being very short. There is, indeed, little of the North Island that can be passed over without meeting a stream of ever-running water.

The Middle Island.

Coastal Features.

The Middle or South Island, as it is sometimes called, is much more compact in shape than the North Island, from which it is separated by Cook Strait, the passage being about 90 miles across in its widest part, and 16 at the narrowest. From Jackson's Head, in Cook Strait, to Puysegur Point, at the extreme south-west, the length of the island is about 525 miles, the greatest breadth, in the Otago District, being about 180 miles. Sailing across from Wellington, in the North Island, the first port of call in the Middle Island would, probably, be Picton on the opposite shore of the strait, at its narrowest part. Here is the beautiful inlet called Queen Charlotte Sound, which Captain Cook described as a collection of the finest harbours in the world. The immense bays in this fine stretch of water were much frequented by whalers in the early days. Westward lies another capacious inlet called Pelorus Sound. The approach to Tasman or Blind Bay, the next important indentation on the north, lies through a narrow but deep channel, between D'Urville Island and the mainland, called French Pass. Shut in by high precipitous hills, the scenery in this passage, with its swift-running current, is remarkably imposing. At the head of the bay is the township of Nelson, encircled by a background of lofty hills, and a few miles eastward is the village of Whakapuaka, where the cable from Australia reaches the land. Golden or Massacre Bay, at the extreme left of the northern shore, was the scene of the murder by the natives of an entire boat's crew belonging to the company of the explorer Tasman. Rounding Cape Farewell, the upper portion of the western coast will be found somewhat deficient in noteworthy indentations. Westport, on the southern shore of the Karamea Bight, possesses a good harbour. At Greymouth, lower down, large sums of money have been spent on the improvement of facilities for shipping, the port being the outlet for a rich mineral and agricultural district. Thence southward the coast line presents no important indentations until the wonderful inlets of the western Otago district are reached. Here, between the parallels of 44° and 46°, the rock-bound coast rises in places sheer from the ocean depths to a height of 5,000 or 6,000 feet, and is pierced by numerous sounds or fiords, which penetrate inland for distances ranging from 6 to 20 miles. These inlets are narrow and very deep. Milford Sound, the finest example, has a depth in its upper part of no less than 1,270 feet. It is surrounded by mountains, which, with the exception of Mount Cook, are the highest on the south coast, and its narrow entrance appears still more restricted from the height of the gigantic precipices on either side. Within the sound, a sublime spectacle opens out, towering mountains rising on both sides of the narrow channel, clothed with verdure at their base, and with magnificent waterfalls tumbling down their flanks. Here and there the cold blue mass of the glacier protrudes itself, while, far above, the mist-wreathed snow-clad cones rear their heads in silent majesty to the skies. The great Sutherland Waterfall, in the vicinity of the Sound, is stated to be 1,904 feet in height. Of the other inlets of this class to the south of Milford Sound, the chief are George Sound. Doubtful Inlet, Daggs Sound, Breaksea Sound, Chalky Inlet, and Preservation Inlet.

The southern and eastern shores of the Middle Island do not offer any noteworthy indentations. Close to Invercargill is the Bluff Harbour, a well known port of call for vessels trading to the south. On the east coast the principal harbours are Otago Harbour, at the head of which Dunedin is situated; Oamaru, the outlet for the district of the same name; Timaru, at the elbow of Canterbury Bight; and Akaroa and Lyttelton Harbours, on Banks Peninsula.

General Physical Characteristics.

The inland physical features of the Middle Island are particularly striking. Almost throughout its entire length the island is traversed by a range of mountains called the Southern Alps, which throws off numerous lateral spurs towards the east and west. In the south, a network of ranges spread out over the Otago district. In the east, towards the centre of the island, are the Malvern Hills and Hunter's Hills, and the ranges occupying the greater portion of Banks Peninsula. The Kaikoura Range runs between Cook's Strait and Banks Peninsula. South of Nelson, the Spenser and St. Arnaud Mountains break off towards the east. The highest peak in the Southern Alps is Mount Cook, situated about the centre of the range, and rising to a height of 12,349 feet. This mountain was called by the natives Ao Rangi, or the Cloud-Piercer. Other notable peaks are Mount Stokes, 12,200 feet, and Mount Aspiring, 9,940 feet. In the southern system are Earnslaw, 9,165 feet; Double Cone, 7,688 feet; and Mount St. Bathans, 6,600 feet.

In point of beauty and sublimity of scenery, the Southern Alps compare favourably with the Alps of Switzerland, while as regards variety they are superior to the European range. The snow line in New Zealand is below that of Switzerland, so that the mountains, while not quite so high as the Swiss Alps, nevertheless present all the varied features of the Alpine uplands. On both sides of the range there are extensive glaciers, those on the western side descending in places to within 700 feet of the sea level into the midst of evergreen forests, and most of them are easily accessible. The Tasman Glacier, on the eastern slope, has an area of 13,664 acres, with a length of 18 miles and an average width of over a mile, and as regards length and width is superior to the famous Alletsch Glacier of Switzerland. The Murchison Glacier contains 5,800 acres, and is 10 miles long and over three-quarters of a mile in average width; and the Godley Glacier, 8 miles long and over a mile wide, has an area of 5,312 acres. In addition to these, there are numerous others of smaller extent, all of them possessing features of great beauty and interest. The waters produced by the melting of the snowfields and glaciers give rise to numerous rivers, nearly all of which flow through the fertile plains of the east.

The Middle Island possesses numerous lakes, many of which are of great beauty, and some of them are situated at a considerable elevation above the level of the sea. Lake Tekapo, in the Canterbury district, is 2,468 feet above the sea-level, and is 15 miles long by about 3 broad. Thirty miles distant, towards the south, is Lake Pukaki, one of the most picturesque Alpine lakes in the island. It lies at an elevation of 1,746 feet above sea-level, and, like similar lakes in this and other Alpine regions, has probably been formed by the retreat of an immense glacier. Close to the lake, the majestic cone of Mount Cook, crowned with snow and ice, is a conspicuous feature in the landscape. Lake Ohau, near Pukaki, is 12 miles long and 2½ miles in width, and its waters are less turbid than those of its larger neighbours. Several fine lakes are found in the Otago district. Lake Manapouri covers an area of 50 square miles, and is nearly surrounded by beautifully-wooded snow-capped mountains. Te Anau is the largest lake in New Zealand. It is 38 miles long, and from 1 to 6 miles in width, and has an area of 132 square miles. Wakatipu is 52 miles long, and from 1 to 3 miles broad, with an area of 114 square miles. The lake is situated at an elevation of 1,070 feet above the level of the sea, and, as its depth has been proved by soundings in various places to be from 1,170 to 1,240 feet, a large portion of its bed is considerably below sea-level. Wanaka and Hawea are two beautiful little lakes in the northern Otago district. From what has already been said, it will have been concluded that a great portion of the surface of the Middle island is mountainous; nevertheless there are several fairly extensive plain districts, particularly on the eastern side of the main range. Of these, the most noteworthy are the Canterbury Plains, with a length of about 130 miles, and a width varying from 30 miles north of the Rangitata to very narrow limits further south. In the north are the Karamea Plains, the Waimea Plains, the Fairfield Downs, the Wairau Plains, the Hanmer Plains, and the Amuri Plains, lying between Cook Strait and the Hurunui River. In the Southern district are the Oamaru Downs, Moraki Downs, and the Mataura Plains.

The Middle Island is well provided with rivers, but, for the most part, they are merely mountain torrents, fed by the snows and ice-fields of the ranges. At times, when there is a more excessive melting of the snows than usual, they are liable to rise in flood, and, where not confined by precipitous rocky walls, form beds of varying width, frequently strewn with enormous deposits of shingle. The Clutha is the largest river in New Zealand as regards volume of water. It drains an extensive area of the southern mountain region, and after a course of 154 miles enters the sea about 60 miles south of Dunedin. It is navigable for small vessels for about 30 miles from its mouth. From the proximity of the mountains to the shore, the streams on the western coast have short rapid courses. The Buller, Grey, and Hokitika are navigable for a few miles, but great expense had to be incurred in connection with the removal of the obstructing sand-bars at their mouths. The Grey and Buller possess special importance from the fact that they are the chief ports of shipment in connection with the coal export trade of the west. On the eastern slope there are hundreds of small streams along the whole extent of the island.

Stewart Island.

This small island, which embraces an area of about 425,000 acres, is the southernmost of the group. It is separated from Middle Island by the passage called Foveaux Strait, and is distant 25 miles from the Bluff on the south of the Middle Island. The greater portion of Stewart Island is rugged and forest clad; but, although lying so far to the south, the climate is mild, and the soil when cleared of the thick undergrowth is very fertile. Mount Anglem and Mount Rakeahua are the highest peaks, the former reaching an elevation of 3,200 feet, and the latter 2,110 feet. The coast line possesses numerous attractive bays and fiords. Half-Moon Bay is the principal port, and near by is situated a beautiful sheet of water, about 10 miles by 4 miles in extent, called Paterson Inlet. Port Pegasus is a fine land-locked harbour, 8 miles long and about 1½ mile wide. Fish and game are abundant, while the oysters are of fine size and flavour, and have achieved an Australasian reputation.

The Outlying Islands.

Of the outlying islands, the principal are the Chatham Islands, the Kermadecs, the Auckland Islands, and the Cook Group. The Chathams lie 480 miles east-south-east from Wellington. The largest island of the group has an area of about 222,500 acres, of which an irregularly-shaped lagoon in the interior contains 45,960 acres. A fourth of the entire area is clothed with forest, but there is good pastoral country in the remainder. Pitt Island has an area of 15,530 acres. In addition to these, there are several smaller, unimportant islands. Sheep-raising is the principal industry in the group.

The four Kermadecs are named, respectively, Raoul or Sunday Island, Macaulay Island, Curtis Island, and L'Espérance or French Rock. Sunday Island contains 7,200 acres, Macaulay Island 764 acres, Curtis Island 128 acres, and L'Espérance 12 acres. Sunday Island is 20 miles in circumference, and its highest point reaches an elevation above sea-level of 1,723 feet. The surface is rugged, and almost the whole area is covered by a dense forest. Throughout the island the soil is exceedingly fertile, resulting from the decomposition of volcanic lavas and tuff. There are three fresh-water lakes in the interior, but they are so difficult of approach as to be practically useless.

The Auckland Islands are situated 290 miles to the southward of the Bluff Harbour. The largest of the group is 27 miles long, with a breadth of about 15 miles, and in its highest part is 2,000 feet above sea-level. There are some fine harbours in this island, Port Ross being considered one of the best harbours of refuge in the world. A depôt for the use of shipwrecked mariners is maintained on the island by the Government of New Zealand.

The Cook Group contains several beautiful and fertile islands. Rarotonga rises to a height of 3,000 feet above the level of the sea, and its fertile soil is covered with rich vegetation right to the summits of the mountains. The island is well-watered, but is deficient in good harbourage. Aitutaki has a circumference of 18 miles, and contains some splendid groves of cocoanut trees on the level lands near the coast with fine pasturage inland.

Palmerston Island is about 220 miles from the nearest island in the Cook Group, and contains areas of good soil with some fine hardwood timber. The island is remarkable as being the "San Pablo" of Magellan.

Penrhyn Island is about 1,200 miles east of Samoa, and is one of the most famous pearling islands of the Pacific. It possesses a splendid harbour, capable of accommodating the largest vessels.

Suwarrow lies about 500 miles to the eastward of Apia in the Samoan Islands. It is a coral atoll, 50 miles in circumference, with a reef enclosing a land-locked lagoon about 12 miles long and 8 miles wide. The entrance is half a mile in width, and there is unlimited anchorage with depths of from 3 to 30 fathoms. Situated out of the path of the hurricanes, the island, which is uninhabited, is sufficiently fertile to support a small population, and would form a valuable trading depôt for the various islands in the neighbouring Pacific.

CLIMATE.

THE Tropic of Capricorn divides Australia into two parts. Of these, the northern or inter-tropical portion contains 1,145,000 square miles, comprising half of Queensland, the Northern Territory of South Australia, and the north-western divisions of Western Australia. The whole of New South Wales, Victoria, New Zealand, Tasmania, and South Australia proper, half of Queensland, and more than half of Western Australia, comprising 1,932,000 square miles, are without the tropics. In a region so extensive, very great varieties of climate are naturally to be expected, but it may be stated as a general law that the climate of Australasia is milder than that of corresponding lands in the Northern Hemisphere. During July, which is the coldest month in southern latitudes, one half of Australasia has a mean temperature ranging from 40° to 64°, and the other half from 64° to 80°. The following are the areas subject to the various average temperatures during the month referred to:—

Temperature, Fahr.	Area in sq. miles.
35° — 40°	300
40° — 45°	39,700
45° — 50°	88,000
50° — 55°	617,800
55° — 60°	681,800
60° — 65°	834,400
65° — 70°	515,000
70° — 75°	275,900
75° — 80°	24,500

The temperature during December ranges from 50° to above 95° Fahr., half of Australasia having a mean temperature below 83°. Dividing the land into zones of average summer temperature, the following are the areas which would fall to each:—

Temperature, Fahr.	Area in sq. miles.
50° — 55°	300
55° — 60°	66,300
60° — 65°	111,300
65° — 70°	74,300
70° — 75°	362,300
75° — 80°	439,200
80° — 85°	733,600
85° — 90°	570,600
90° — 95°	584,100
95° and over	135,400

Judging from the figures just given, it must be conceded that a considerable area of the continent is not adapted for colonisation by European races. The region with a mean summer temperature in excess of 95° Fahr. is the interior of the Northern Territory of South Australia north of the 20th parallel; and the whole of the country, excepting the seaboard, lying between the meridians of 120° and 140° and north of the 25th parallel, has a mean temperature in excess of 90° Fahr.

Climatically, as well as geographically, New South Wales is divided into three marked divisions. The coastal region, which lies between the parallels of 28° and 37° south latitude, has an average summer temperature ranging from 78° in the north to 67° in the south, with a winter temperature of from 59° to 52°. Taking the district generally, the difference between the mean summer and mean winter temperature may be set down as averaging not more than 20°, a range smaller than is found in most other parts of the world. The famed resorts on the Mediterranean seaboard bear no comparison with the Pacific slopes of New South Wales, either for natural salubrity or for the comparative mildness of the summer and winter.

Sydney, situated as it is midway between the extreme points of the state, in latitude 33° 51′ S., has a mean temperature of 63°, corresponding with that of Barcelona, the great maritime city of Spain, and of Toulon, in France; the former being in latitude 41° 22′ N., and the latter in 43° 7′ N. At Sydney the mean summer temperature is 70·8°, and that of winter 53·9°. The range is thus 16·9° Fahr. At Naples, where the mean temperature for the year is about the same as at Sydney, the summer temperature reaches a mean of 74·4°, and the mean of winter is 47·6°, with a range of 26·8°. Thus the summer is warmer, and the winter much colder, than at Sydney. The highest temperature in the shade experienced in Sydney was 109°, and the lowest winter temperature 36°, giving a range of 73°. At Naples the range has been as great as 81°, the winter minimum falling sometimes below the freezing-point. The mean temperature of Sydney for a long series of years was—spring 62°, summer 71°, autumn 64°, and winter 54°.

Passing from the coast to the table-land, a distinct climatic region is entered. Cooma, with a mean summer temperature of 65·4° and a mean winter temperature of 41·4°, may be taken as illustrative of the climate of the southern table-land, and Armidale of the northern. The first-named town stands in the centre of the Monaro plains, at an elevation of 2,637 feet above sea-level, and enjoys a summer as mild as either London or Paris, while its winters are far less severe. On the New England table-land, the climate of Armidale and other towns may be considered as nearly perfect as can be found. The yearly average temperature is scarcely 56·5°, while the summer only reaches 67·7°, and the winter falls to 44·4°, a range of temperature approximating closely to that of the famous health-resorts in the south of France.

The climatic conditions of the western districts of the state are entirely different from those of the other two regions, and have often been cited as disagreeable. Compared with the equable temperature of the coastal district or of the table-land, there may appear some justification for such a reputation, but only by comparison. The climate of the great plains, in spite of the heat of part of the summer, is very healthy. The town of Bourke may be taken as an example. Seated in the midst of the great plain of the interior, it illustrates peculiarly well the defects as well as the excellences of the climate of the whole region. Bourke has exactly the same latitude as Cairo, yet its mean summer temperature is 1·3° less, and its mean annual temperature 4° less than that of the Egyptian city. New Orleans also lies on the same parallel, but the American city is 4° hotter in summer. As regards winter temperature, Bourke leaves little to be desired. The mean winter reading of the thermometer is 54·7°, and accompanied as this is by clear skies and an absence of snow, the season is both refreshing and enjoyable.

The rainfall of New South Wales ranges from an annual average of 64 inches at Port Macquarie, on the northern coast, and Kiandra, in the Monaro district, to 9 inches at Milparinka, in the Trans-Darling country. The coastal districts average about 42 inches of rain per annum; on the table-land the mean rainfall is 32 inches, but in the western interior it is as low as 20 inches, while at the ten stations in the far west the average was only 14 inches. The average rainfall of Sydney during forty-two years was 50 inches, while during 1902 a fall of 43·07 inches was recorded.

The climate of Victoria does not differ greatly from that of New South Wales; the heat, however, is generally less intense in summer and the cold greater in winter. Melbourne, which stands in latitude 37° 50′ S., has a mean temperature of 57·3°, and therefore corresponds with Bathurst in New South Wales, Washington in the United States, Madrid, Lisbon, and Messina. The difference between summer and winter is, however, less at Melbourne than at any of the places mentioned. The mean temperature is 6° less than that of Sydney and 7° less than that of Adelaide—the result of a long series of observations being:—Spring, 57°; summer, 65·3°; autumn, 58·7°; winter, 49·2°. The highest recorded temperature in the shade at Melbourne was 110·7°, and the lowest, 27°; but it is rare for the summer heat to exceed 85°, or the winter temperature in the day time to fall below 40°.

Ballarat, the second city of Victoria, about 100 miles west from Melbourne, and situated at a height of about 1,400 feet above sea-level, has a minimum temperature of 29°, and a maximum of 104·5°, the average yearly mean being 54·1°. Bendigo, which is about 100 miles north of Melbourne, and 700 feet above the level of the sea, has a rather higher average temperature, ranging from a minimum of 31·2° to a maximum of 106·4°, the average yearly mean being 59·4°. At Wilson's Promontory, the most southerly point of Australia, the minimum heat is 38·6°, and the maximum 96·4°, the average yearly mean being 56·7°.

During the year 1902 the rainfall at Melbourne amounted to 23·98 inches; while for a long series of years it averaged 25·58 inches, with an average of 131 days during the year on which rain fell. At Echuca, during 1902, 9·91 inches fell, and 28·05 at Portland. At Wilson's Promontory the rainfall was 35·29 inches.

As about one-half of the state of Queensland lies within the tropics, it is but natural to expect that the climate should be very warm. The temperature, however, has a daily range less than that of other countries under the same isothermal lines. This circumstance is due to the sea-breezes, which blow with great regularity, and temper what would otherwise be an excessive heat. The hot winds which prevail during the summer in some of the other colonies are unknown in Queensland. Of course, in a territory of such large extent there are many varieties of climate, and the heat is greater along the coast than on the elevated lands of the interior. In the northern parts of the state the high temperature is very trying to persons of European descent.

The mean temperature at Brisbane, during December, January, and February, is about 76°, while during the months of June, July, and August it averages about 60°. Brisbane, however, is situated near the extreme southern end of the colony, and its average temperature is considerably less than that of many of the towns farther north. Thus the winter in Rockhampton averages nearly 65°, while the summer heat rises almost to 85°; and at Townsville and Normanton the average temperature is still higher.

The average rainfall of Queensland is high, especially along the northern coast, where it ranges from 60 to 70 inches per annum. At Brisbane 50·01 inches is the average of thirty-five years, and even on the plains of the interior from 20 to 30 inches usually fall every year. During 1902, 16·03 inches of rain fell in Brisbane, the number of wet days being 86.

South Australia, extending as it does over about 26 degrees of latitude, naturally presents considerable variations of climate. The southern portions have a climate greatly resembling that of the coast of Italy. The coldest months are June, July, and August, during which the temperature is very agreeable, averaging for a series of years 53·6°, 51·7°, and 54° for those months respectively. On the plains slight frosts occasionally occur, and ice is sometimes seen on the highlands. The summer is the only really disagreeable portion of the year. The sun at that season has great power, and the temperature frequently reaches 100° in the shade, with hot winds blowing from the interior. The weather on the whole is remarkably dry. At Adelaide there are on an average 120 rainy days per annum; during the last sixty years the mean rainfall has been 20·88 inches per annum, while farther north the quantity recorded was considerably less. The country is naturally very healthful, and in evidence of this it may be mentioned that no great epidemic has ever visited the state.

The climate of the Northern Territory of South Australia is extremely hot, except on the elevated table-lands. Altogether, the temperature of this part of the state is very similar to that of Northern Queensland, and the climate is equally unfavourable to Europeans. It is a fact worthy of notice that the malarial fevers which are so troublesome to the pioneers of the northern parts of Australia almost, and in some cases entirely, disappear after the land has been settled and consolidated by stock. The rainfall in the extreme north, especially in January and February, is exceedingly heavy. The average yearly rainfall in the coast districts is about 63 inches.

Western Australia has practically only two seasons—the winter, or wet season, which commences in April and ends in October; and the summer, or dry season, which comprises the remainder of the year. During the wet season frequent and heavy rains fall, and thunderstorms with sharp showers occur in the summer. The extremes of drought and flood experienced in the other states are almost unknown in Western Australia, but during the summer months the north-west coast is sometimes visited by hurricanes of great violence. In the southern and early-settled parts of the state the mean temperature is about 64°; but in the more northern portions the heat is excessive, though the dryness of the atmosphere makes it preferable to most tropical climates. At Perth, in 1902, the mean temperature was 63·6°, the maximum being 103·7° and the minimum 38·5°; and the rainfall for the same year was 27·06 inches, rain having fallen on 93 days. Observations extending over a period of twenty-two years show the average rainfall at Perth as 33 inches. Although the heat is very great during three months of the year, the nights and mornings are almost always cool, and camping out is not attended with danger owing to there being so little moisture in the air.

Tasmania, protected as it is by its geographical position and by the tempering influence of the surrounding ocean from extremes of heat or cold, enjoys an exceedingly genial climate. The greater part of the island in the settled regions is characterised by a mild and equable temperature, ranging between the extremes of 20° to 44° in winter and 78° to 96° in summer. Spring and autumn are the most pleasant seasons of the year, especially the latter, when the mean reading of the thermometer is about 57°. The mean temperature of Hobart for the last fifty years has been 55°. The richness of its flora is an evidence of the genial nature of the climate of the state, while the purity of its atmosphere is proved by the small proportion of zymotic diseases recorded in the bills of mortality. The hot winds of the continent of Australia are felt in the northern parts of the island only, and even there they are greatly reduced in temperature by their passage across Bass Straits. Generally speaking, all through the summer months there are alternate land and sea breezes which tend to cool the atmosphere even on the hottest days. The climate is fresh and invigorating, and is much recommended as a restorative for those whose constitutions have been enfeebled by residence in hotter climes. Large numbers of tourists in search of health visit the island every summer. The rainfall, except in the mountain districts, is moderate and regular. The average downfall at Hobart for a long series of years was 25·10 inches, with 167 wet days per annum. In 1902 rain fell on 140 days, the total recorded for the year being 21·90 inches.

The climate of New Zealand is in some respects similar to that of Tasmania, but the changes of weather and temperature are often very sudden. As the colony extends over more than 10 degrees of latitude, its climate is very varied. That of the North Island is somewhat similar to the climate of Rome, Montpellier, and Milan; while the Middle or Southern Island more resembles Jersey, in the Channel Islands. The mean annual temperature of the North Island is 57°, and of the Middle Island 52°, while the yearly average of the whole colony for each season is as follows:—Spring, 55°; summer, 63°; autumn, 57°; and winter, 48°. The mean temperature of New Zealand is lower than that of similar latitudes in Europe, though higher than is experienced in America on corresponding parallels. The mean temperature of the South or Middle Island is less by about 5° than that of the North Island. Snow very seldom lies on the ground at the sea-level in the North Island, and only occasionally in the South Island. The summits of Ruapehu, the highest mountain in the North Island, and of the great mountain chain in the South Island, are covered with perpetual snow from an altitude of 7,500 feet above the level of the sea. Ice is occasionally seen in winter-time in all parts of New Zealand. The whole colony is subject to strong breezes, which frequently culminate in gales. The rainfall during 1902 varied very much at the several observing stations. At Auckland it amounted to 38·28 inches, while at Wellington there was a fall of 38·75 inches. At Rotorua, in the North Island, 48·72 inches fell during the year, and at New Plymouth, on the west coast, 52·04 inches were recorded. At Dunedin, on the east coast of the Middle Island, the rainfall amounted to 53·56 inches, while at Hokitika, on the west coast, no less than 96·07 inches fell during the year. Periods of lasting drought are almost unknown in the colony; indeed, it is very seldom that the records of any station show the lapse of a whole month without rain. The number of days in the year on which rain fell varied from 120 at Rotorua to 245 at New Plymouth.

The following table shows the distribution of rainfall area in Australasia:—

Rainfall.	Rainfall area in square miles.			
	Australia.	Tasmania.	New Zealand.	Australasia.
Under 10 inches ...	1,219,600	....	....	1,219,600
10 to 20 „ ...	843,100	9,440	....	852,540
20 to 30 „ ...	399,900	....	69,650	469,550
30 to 40 „ ...	225,700	8,380	17,410	251,490
40 to 50 „ ...	140,300	8,380	17,410	166,090
50 to 60 „ ...	47,900	....	....	47,900
60 to 70 „ ...	56,100	....	....	56,100
Above 70 „ ...	14,100	....	....	14,100
Total.........	2,946,700	26,200	104,470	3,077,370

THE DISCOVERY OF AUSTRALIA AND NEW ZEALAND.

IT is impossible to say who were the first discoverers of Australia, although there is evidence that the Chinese had some knowledge of the continent so far back as the Thirteenth Century. The Malays, also, would seem to have been acquainted with the northern coast; while Marco Polo, who visited the East at the close of the Thirteenth Century, makes reference to the reputed existence of a great southern continent. There is in existence a map, dedicated to Henry the Eighth of England, on which a large southern land is shown, and the tradition of a Terra Australis appears to have been current for a long period before it enters into authentic history.

In 1503, a French navigator named Binot Paulmyer, Sieur de Gonneville, was blown out of his course, and landed on a large island, which was claimed to be the great southern land of tradition, although Flinders and other authorities are inclined to think that it must have been Madagascar. Some French authorities confidently put forward a claim that Guillaume le Testu, of Provence, sighted the continent in 1531. The Portuguese also advance claims to be the first discoverers of Australia, but so far the evidence cannot be said to establish their pretensions. As early as 1597, the Dutch historian, Wytfliet describes the Australis Terra as the most southern of all lands, and proceeds to give some circumstantial particulars respecting its geographical relation to New Guinea, venturing the opinion that, were it thoroughly explored, it would be regarded as a fifth part of the world.

Early in the Seventeenth Century, Philip the Third of Spain sent out an expedition from Callao, in Peru, for the purpose of searching for a southern continent. The little fleet comprised three vessels, with the Portuguese pilot, De Quiros, as navigator, and De Torres as admiral, or military commander. They left Callao on the 21st December, 1605, and in the following year discovered the island now known as Espiritu Santo, one of the New Hebrides Group, which De Quiros, under the impression that it was indeed the land of which he was in search, named "*La Austrialia del Espiritu Santo.*" Sickness and discontent led to a mutiny on De Quiros' vessel, and the crew, overpowering their officers during the night, forced the captain to navigate his ship to Mexico. Thus abandoned by his consort, De Torres, compelled to bear up for the Philippines to refit, discovered and sailed through the strait that bears his name, and may even have caught a glimpse of the northern coast of the Australian Continent. His discovery was not, however, made known until 1792, when Dalrymple rescued his name from oblivion, bestowing it upon the passage which separates New Guinea from Australia. De Quiros returned to Spain to re-engage in the work of petitioning the king to despatch an expedition for the purpose of prosecuting the discovery of the Terra Australis. He was finally successful in his petitions, but died before accomplishing his work, and was buried in an unknown grave in Panama, never being privileged to set his foot upon the continent the discovery of which was the inspiration of his life.

During the same year in which De Torres sailed through the strait destined to make him famous, a little Dutch vessel called the "Duyfken," or "Dove," set sail from Bantam, in Java, on a voyage of discovery. This ship entered the Gulf of Carpentaria, and sailed south as far as Cape Keerweer, or Turn-again. Here some of the crew landed, but being attacked by natives, made no attempt to explore the country. In 1616, Dirk Hartog discovered the island bearing his name. In 1622 the "Leeuwin," or "Lioness," made some discoveries on the south-west coast; and during the following year the yachts Pera and Arnhem explored the shores of the Gulf of Carpentaria. Arnhem Land, a portion of the Northern Territory, still appears on many maps as a memento of this voyage. Among other early Dutch discoverers were Van Edels; Poel, in 1629, in the Gulf of Carpentaria; Nuijts, in the "Gulden Zeepaard," along the southern coast, which he called, after himself, Nuijts Land; De Witt; and Pelsaert, in the "Batavia." Pelsaert was wrecked on Houtman's Abrolhos; his crew mutinied, and he and his party suffered greatly from want of water. The record of his voyage is interesting from the fact that he was the first to carry back to Europe an authentic account of the western coast of Australia, which he described in any but favourable terms. It is to Dutch navigators in the early portion of the Seventeenth Century that we owe the first really authentic accounts of the western coast and adjacent islands, and in many instances the names given by these mariners to prominent physical features are still retained. By 1665 the Dutch possessed rough charts of almost the whole of the western littoral, while to the mainland itself they had given the name of New Holland. Of the Dutch discoverers, Pelsaert was the only one who made any detailed observations of the character of the country inland, and it may here be remarked that his journal contains the first notice and description of the kangaroo that has come down to us.

In 1642, Abel Janszoon Tasman sailed on a voyage of discovery from Batavia, the head-quarters of the Governor and Council of the Dutch East Indies, under whose auspices the expedition was undertaken. He was furnished with a yacht, the "Heemskirk," and a fly-boat, the "Zeehaen" (or "Sea Hen"), under the command of Captain Jerrit Jansen. He left Batavia on what has been designated by Dutch historians the "Happy Voyage," on the 14th August, 1642. After a visit to the Mauritius, then a Dutch possession, Tasman bore away to the south-east, and, on the 24th November, sighted the western coast of the land which he named Van Diemen's Land, in honor of the Governor under whose directions he was acting. The honor was later transferred to the discoverer himself, and the island is now known as Tasmania. Tasman doubled the southern extremity of Van Diemen's Land and explored the east coast for some distance. The ceremony of hoisting a flag and taking possession of the country in the name of the Government of the Netherlands was actually performed, but the description of the wildness of the country, and of the fabulous giants by which Tasman's sailors believed it to be inhabited, deterred the Dutch from occupying the island, and by the international principle of "non-user" it passed from their hands. Resuming his voyage in an easterly direction, Tasman sighted the west coast of the South Island of New Zealand on the 13th December of the same year, and describes the coast line as consisting of "high mountainous country."

Tasman was under the belief that the land he saw was part of a great polar continent discovered some years before by Schouten and Le Maire, to which the name of Staaten Land had been given. He, therefore, duplicated the designation; but within three months afterwards Schouten's "Staaten Land" was found to be merely an inconsiderable island. Tasman's discovery thereupon received the name of New Zealand, on account of a fancied likeness to a province of Holland to which it bears not the least resemblance, and by this name it has been known ever since. Tasman sailed along the coast to a bay, and there he anchored. This inlet is known as Golden or Massacre Bay, called by Tasman, Murderer's Bay. Here an unprovoked attack by the Maoris on a boat's crew resulted in the death of four of Tasman's sailors. Leaving Murderer's Bay, Tasman steered along the west coast of North Island. Vainly seeking a passage to the east, he passed and named Cape Maria Van Diemen, finally taking leave of New Zealand at North Cape. At the Three Kings Islands he made an attempt to land, but the ferocious aspect of the natives terrified his boat's crew, and the voyage was resumed. Tasman left New Zealand with a most unfavourable impression of its inhabitants. He had been off the coast for some three weeks without landing or planting the flag of his country thereon, and more than a century and a quarter elapsed before another European is known to have visited New Zealand.

The first English navigator to sight the Australian continent was William Dampier, who made a visit to these shores in 1688, as supercargo of the "Cygnet," a trader, whose crew had turned buccaneers. On his return to England he published an account of his voyage, which resulted in his being sent out in the "Roebuck" in 1699 to further prosecute his discoveries. To him we owe the exploration of the coast for about 900 miles—from Shark Bay to Dampier's Archipelago, and thence to Roebuck Bay. He appears to have landed in several places in search of water. His account of the country was quite as unfavourable as Pelsaert's. He described it as barren and sterile, and almost devoid of animals, the only one of any importance somewhat resembling a racoon—a strange creature, which advanced by great bounds or leaps instead of walking, using only its hind legs, and covering 12 or 15 feet at a time. The reference is, of course, to the kangaroo, which Pelsaert had also remarked and quaintly described some 60 years previously.

During the interval elapsing between Dampier's two voyages, an accident led to the closer examination of the coasts of Western Australia by the Dutch. In 1684 a vessel had sailed from Holland for the Dutch possessions in the East Indies, and after rounding the Cape of Good Hope, she was never again heard of. Some twelve years afterwards the East India Company fitted out an expedition under the leadership of Commander William de Vlamingh, with the object of searching for any traces of the lost vessel on the western shores of New Holland. Towards the close of the year 1696 this expedition reached the island of Rottnest which was thoroughly explored, and early the following year a landing party discovered and named the Swan River. The vessels then proceeded northward without finding any traces of the object of their search, but, at the same time, making fairly accurate charts of the coast line.

The great voyage of Captain James Cook, in 1769-70, was primarily undertaken for the purpose of observing the transit of Venus, but he was also expressly commissioned to ascertain "whether the unexplored part of the Southern Hemisphere be only an immense mass of water, or contain another continent." H.M.S. "Endeavour," the vessel fitted out for the voyage, was a small craft of 370 tons, carrying twenty-two guns, and built originally for a collier, with a view rather to strength than to speed. Chosen by Cook himself, she was renamed the "Endeavour," in allusion to the great work which her commander was setting out to achieve. Mr. Charles Green was commissioned to conduct the astronomical observations, and Sir Joseph Banks and Dr. Solander were appointed botanists to the expedition. After successfully observing the transit from the island of Tahiti, or Otaheite, as Cook wrote it, the Endeavour's head was turned south, and then north-west, beating about the Pacific in search of the eastern coast of the great continent whose western shores had been so long known to the Dutch. On the 6th October, 1769, the coast of New Zealand was sighted, and two days later Cook cast anchor in Poverty Bay, so named from the inhospitality and hostility of the natives.

The expedition had thus far been sailing southward. Dissatisfied with the results, and finding it difficult to procure water in sufficient quantities, Cook put about, determining to follow the coast to the northward. He named a promontory in the neighbourhood Cape Turnagain. Another promontory more to the north, where a huge canoe made a hasty retreat, he called Cape Runaway. In the month of November he touched at a point on the coast, where he landed and erected an observatory for the purpose of observing the transit of Mercury—one of the chief objects of his expedition on that occasion. A signal station was erected on the headland from which Cook took his observation, and which is now known as Shakespeare's Head. On the 9th of November the transit of Mercury was successfully observed, and the name Mercury Bay was given to the inlet where the observation was made. Two localities, for reasons which will be obvious, were called Oyster Bay and Mangrove River. Before leaving Mercury Bay, Cook caused to be cut upon one of the trees near the watering-place the ship's name and his own, with the date of arrival there, and, after displaying the English colours, took formal possession of it in the name of His Britannic Majesty King George the Third. It is noteworthy that Cook always managed to obtain wood and water wherever wood and water were to be had, no matter whether his intercourse with the natives were friendly or otherwise. He also contrived to carry on his surveys in spite of all opposition with such accuracy and deliberation that they remained the standard authority on the outlines of the islands for some seventy years or more. He was, moreover, a benefactor in no mean degree to the natives, who seldom knew the meaning of meat, save at a cannibal feast after a tribal victory. He not only improved their vegetables by giving them seed potatoes, but he turned loose fowls and pigs to supply their flesh larder. To the time of writing, the wild pigs which haunt the forests and the mountain gorges are called after Captain Cook, and they furnish many a solitary shepherd, miner, farmer, and gum-digger with excellent meat. Cook was, perhaps, either more prudent, or more successful than Captain Tobias Furneaux, of the consort "Adventure," who, in a subsequent voyage to New Zealand, lost an entire boat's crew of nine men, who were captured or killed, and duly cooked and eaten by the Maoris.

On the 17th December, the "Endeavour" doubled North Cape, which is the northern extremity of North Island, and began the descent of its western side. The weather now become stormy, and with a repetition of Tasman's experience from an opposite course on the same coast, very dangerous. Often was the vessel compelled to stand off in great distress, and intercourse with the natives was considerably interrupted. At one point, however, the English mariners satisfied themselves that the inhabitants ate human flesh—the flesh, at least, of enemies who had been killed in battle. On January 30th, 1770, Cook erected a flagpost on the summit of a hill in Queen Charlotte's Sound, where he again hoisted the Union Jack, and, after naming the bay where the ship was at anchor after the Queen, took formal possession of the South Island in the name of His Majesty King George the Third.

Cook crossed the waters of Doubtless Bay on the same day that the French Captain, De Surville, in the "St. Jean Baptiste," was approaching the land at Mangonui. A few hours afterwards, and totally ignorant of Cook's presence in New Zealand waters, the Frenchman anchored in this very inlet and named it Lauriston Bay. This navigator was sent out by his Government, who believed that the English had found "an island of gold" in the South Seas, and sailed post haste from India to see if he could not participate in the exploitation of the precious metal. He was received by the natives with great hospitality; but, finding nothing more valuable than spars for his ship, he proceeded to South America, carrying away in irons the Rarawa chief, Ngakinui, who had entertained him and his sick seamen with great hospitality while on shore. Ngakinui pined on ship-board for his native food, and died some eighty days after his seizure. De Surville, only eleven days after the death of this unfortunate Maori chief, was drowned in the surf at Callao.

After voyaging westward for nearly three weeks Cook, on the 19th April, 1770, sighted the eastern coast of Australia at a point which he named after his lieutenant, who discovered it, Point Hicks, and which modern geographers identify with Cape Everard.

The "Endeavour" then coasted northward, and after passing and naming Mount Dromedary, the Pigeon House, Point Upright, Cape St. George, and Red Point, Botany Bay was discovered on the 28th April, 1770, and as it appeared to offer a suitable anchorage, the "Endeavour" entered the bay and dropped anchor. The ship brought-to opposite a group of natives, who were cooking over a fire. The great navigator and his crew, unacquainted with the character of the Australian aborigines, were not a little astonished that these natives took no notice of them or their proceedings. Even the splash of the anchor in the water, and the noise of the cable running out through the hawse hole, in no way disturbed them at their occupation, or caused them to evince the slightest curiosity. But as the captain of the "Endeavour" ordered out the pinnace and prepared to land, the natives threw off their nonchalance; for on the boat approaching the shore, two men, each armed with a bundle of spears, presented themselves on a projecting rock and made threatening signs to the strangers. It is interesting to note that the ingenious "wommera," or throwing-stick, which is peculiar to Australia, was first observed on this occasion. As the men were evidently determined to oppose any attempt at landing, a musket was discharged between them, in the hope that they would be frightened by the noise, but it produced no effect beyond causing one of them to drop his bundle of spears, of which, however, he immediately repossessed himself, and with his comrade resumed the same menacing attitude. At last one cast a stone towards the boat, which earned him a charge of small shot in the leg. Nothing daunted, the two ran back into the bush, and presently returned furnished with shields made of bark, with which to protect themselves from the firearms of the crew. Such intrepidity is certainly worthy of passing notice. Unlike the American Indians, who supposed Columbus and his crew to be supernatural beings, and their ships in some way endowed with life, and who were thrown into convulsions of terror by the first discharge of firearms which they witnessed, these Australians were neither excited to wonder by the ship, nor overawed by the superior number and unknown weapons of the strangers. Cook examined the bay in the pinnace, and landed several times; but by no endeavour could he induce the natives to hold any friendly communication with him. The well-known circumstance of the great variety of new plants here obtained, from which Botany Bay derives its name, should not be passed over. Before quitting the bay the ceremony was performed of hoisting the Union Jack, first on the south shore, and then near the north head, formal possession of the territory being thus taken for the British Crown. During the sojourn in Botany Bay the crew had to perform the painful duty of burying a comrade—a seaman named Forby Sutherland, who was in all probability the first British subject whose body was committed to Australian soil.

After leaving Botany Bay, Cook sailed northward. He saw and named Port Jackson, but forebore to enter the finest natural harbour in Australia. Broken Bay and other inlets, and several headlands, were also seen and named, but the vessel did not come to an anchor till Moreton Bay was reached, although the wind prevented Cook from entering this harbour. Still sailing northward, taking notes as he proceeded for a rough chart of the coast, and landing at Bustard and Keppel Bays and the Bay of Inlets, Cook passed over 1,300 miles without the occurrence of any event worthy of being chronicled, till suddenly one night at 10 o'clock the water was found to shoal, without any sign of breakers or land. While Cook was speculating on the cause of this phenomenon, and was in the act of ordering out the boats to take soundings, the "Endeavour" struck heavily, and fell over so much that the guns, spare cables, and other heavy gear had at once to be thrown overboard to lighten the ship. As day broke, attempts were made to float the vessel off with the morning tide; but these were unsuccessful. The water was rising so rapidly in the hold that with four pumps constantly going the crew could hardly keep it in check. At length one of the midshipmen suggested the device of "fothering," which he had seen practised in the West Indies. This consists in passing a sail, attached to cords, and charged with oakum, wool, and other materials, under the vessel's keel, in such a manner that the suction of the leak may draw the canvas into the aperture, and thus partially stop the vent. This was performed with great success, and the vessel was floated off with the evening tide. The land was soon after made near the mouth of a small stream, which Cook called, after the ship, the Endeavour River. A headland close by he named Cape Tribulation. The ship was steered into the river, and there careened and thoroughly repaired. Cook having completed the survey of the east coast, to which he gave the name of New South Wales, sighted and named Cape York, the northernmost point of Australia, and took final possession of his discoveries northward from latitude 38° south to latitude 10½° south, on a spot which he named Possession Island, thence returning to England by way of Torres Straits and the Indian Ocean.

The great navigator's second voyage, undertaken in 1772, with the "Resolution" and the "Adventure" is of less importance. The vessels became separated, and both at different times visited New Zealand. Captain Tobias Furneaux, in the "Adventure," also found his way to Storm Bay in Tasmania. In 1777, while on his way to search for a north-east passage between the Atlantic and Pacific Oceans, Cook again touched at the coast of Tasmania and New Zealand.

On his return to England, Cook gave a most graphic description of New Zealand and its people. Men engaged in commerce became impressed with the value of the various articles which New Zealand produced, and hence of its importance as a market for manufactured goods; while the savant and the scientist regarded with great interest the information recently published respecting a race of people who, while having a real though hitherto undescribed form of civilisation, were yet greedy eaters of human flesh. Cook's report of the genial climate, the fertile soil, and the evergreen forests of the new archipelago, not only excited considerable interest in England, but so captivated the eminently practical mind of Benjamin Franklin that the American philosopher published a proposal for its immediate colonisation.

Meanwhile, in 1772, Captain Marion du Fresne anchored his two ships, the "Marquis de Castries" and the "Mascarin," in the Bay of Islands. These vessels formed a French expedition of discovery. Sailing from Nantes, on the Loire, Lieutenant Crozet, in command of the King's sloop "Mascarin," had lost his masts, and the two ships put into the Bay of Islands to refit. Du Fresne was frequently on shore during his stay, and habits of intimacy begat in the mind of the French Commander confidence in the friendship of the natives. Both races lived in harmony for several weeks. "They treated us," says Crozet, "with every show of friendship for thirty-three days, with the intention of eating us on the thirty-fourth." The Maori version, given by Dr. Thompson, is: "We treated Marion's party with every kindness for thirty days, and on the thirty-first they put two of our chiefs in irons, and burned our sacred places." It matters little whether the Maoris had any valid excuse for eating their guests or not, the fact remains that an attack was made on the French, when twenty-eight of their party and the commander were killed and eaten. Crozet, who had a party of men engaged in getting spars on the Kawakawa River, was also in danger of being trapped by the treacherous savages; but being forewarned, he was enabled to punish those who had killed his comrades and sought his own destruction. Before leaving the river he refitted the two vessels, and, after a stay of sixty-four days in the Bay of Islands, continued his voyage.

On his first voyage, in 1770, Cook had some grounds for the belief that Van Diemen's Land, as Tasmania was then called, was a separate island. The observations of Captain Furneaux, however, did not strengthen this belief, and when making his final voyage, the great navigator appears to have definitely concluded that it was part of the mainland of Australia. This continued to be the opinion of geographers until 1798, when Bass discovered the strait which bears his name. The next recorded expedition is a memorable one in the annals of Australian History—the despatch of a British colony to the shores of Botany Bay. The fleet sailed in May, 1787, and arrived off the Australian coast early in the following January. The history of the British settlements in the Southern Seas has been given with considerable detail in the last issue of this volume, and it has not been considered necessary to reproduce it; in order, however, to assist the reader in his study of Australian affairs the following tables have been compiled; they show the principal occurrences in Australia and New Zealand, arranged in chronological sequence from the arrival of Captain Phillip to the present time.

CHRONOLOGICAL TABLE FOR AUSTRALIA AND TASMANIA.

DATES of events following the establishment of a settlement in New South Wales :—

1788	N.S.W.	First fleet arrives at Botany Bay.—Formal possession taken of Sydney Cove.—Proclamation of the Colony by Governor Phillip.—Settlement founded at Norfolk Island; expedition sent by Phillip.—La Perouse visits Botany Bay.
	Tas.	Bligh visits Van Diemen's Land in the "Bounty."
1789	N.S.W.	Discovery of Hawkesbury River.
	Tas.	Cox discovers Oyster Bay.
1790	N.S.W.	Second fleet arrives with the New South Wales Corps.
1791	W.A.	Vancouver's explorations.—Discovery of King George's Sound.
1792	N.S.W.	Resignation of Governor Phillip.
	S.A.	D'Entrecasteaux visits Fowler's Bay.
	Tas.	D'Entrecasteaux explores the north-east coast.
	W.A.	D'Entrecasteaux explores the south-west coast.
1793	N.S.W.	Arrival of the "Bellona" with first free immigrants.
1794	Tas.	Captain Hayes enters and names the Derwent.
1795	N.S.W.	Settlement of the Hawkesbury.—Arrival of Captain Hunter.
1796	N.S.W.	Bass and Flinders explore Port Hacking.
1797	N.S.W.	Discovery of coal at Illawarra and on the Hunter (or Coal) River.
1798	Vic.	Discovery of Bass' Strait by Bass and Flinders.—Bass visits Western Port.
	Tas.	Circumnavigation of Van Diemen's Land by Flinders.
1799	N.S.W.	Flinders explores the north coast.—Wilson penetrates to the Lachlan River
	Q'ld.	Flinders makes explorations on the east coast.
1800	N.S.W.	Governor Hunter recalled, superseded by Philip Gidley King.
	Vic.	Lieutenant Grant explores the coast.
	S.A.	Lieutenant Grant sights Cape Northumberland.
1801-2	W.A.	The whole of the western coast examined by Baudin.
1801-3	......	Survey of Australian coasts by Flinders.
1801	W.A.	Flinders examines the south coast.
1802	Vic.	Discovery of Port Phillip by Murray.—Exploration of Port Phillip by Flinders.
	S.A.	Flinders explores Spencer's and St. Vincent's Gulfs, and meets Baudin at Encounter Bay.
	Tas.	Baudin surveys the east coast.
1803	N.S.W.	First wool sent to England.—Cayley's attempt to cross the Blue Mountains.
	Vic.	Lieut.-Colonel David Collins founds a settlement at Port Phillip.
	Tas.	Bowen lands at Risdon.
1804	N.S.W.	The Castle Hill convict insurrection.—Abandonment of Norfolk Island ordered by British Government.
	Vic.	Collins abandons Port Phillip.
	Tas.	Foundation of the Van Diemen's Land colonies.—Collins founds Hobart Town and Paterson founds York Town.—The assignment system established by Governor King.—Fifty friendly blacks massacred at Risdon, through a mistake of Lieutenant Moore.

1805	N.S.W.	Macarthur starts extensive sheep farming at Camden.
	Tas.	Norfolk Island colonists settled at New Norfolk, Norfolk Plains, etc.
1806	N.S.W.	Severe floods in the Hunter.—Governor King retires and is succeeded by Captain Bligh.
	Tas.	Launceston founded.
1807	N.S.W.	Orders given for final shipment of convicts from Norfolk Island.
	Tas.	Laycock's overland expedition from Launceston to Hobart.
1808	N.S.W.	Deposition of Governor Bligh.
	Tas.	254 settlers from Norfolk Island receive grants of land.
1809	N.S.W.	Arrival of Colonel Lachlan Macquarie.
1810	Tas.	Death of Collins.—Extreme scarcity of provisions; prisoners released and permitted to roam in search of food.
	W.A.	Captain de Freycinet explores the western and north-western coasts.
1811	Tas.	Governor Macquarie visits Van Diemen's Land.—Hobart Town laid out.—Lieut.-Colonel Davey appointed Governor.—Van Diemen's Land made a single colony.
1812	N.S.W.	Creation of Supreme Court.
1813	N.S.W.	Passage across Blue Mountains discovered by Blaxland, Wentworth, and Lawson.
1814	......	The name of "Australia" given, on the recommendation of Flinders, to the great southern continent hitherto known as "New Holland."
	N.S.W.	Creation of Civil Courts.—Hamilton Hume discovers the Berrima and Goulburn districts.
	Tas.	First Law Courts established; jurisdiction limited to personal matters under the value of £50.—Outrages by bushrangers.
1815	N.S.W.	Governor Macquarie lays out the town of Bathurst.—Captain Evans discovers the Macquarie River.
	Tas.	Arrival of first immigrant ship with free settlers.—Coastal explorations of Captain James Kelly.—First exportation of wheat to Sydney.
1816	N.S.W.	Establishment of Bank of New South Wales.
1817	N.S.W.	Oxley explores the interior.—Meehan and Hume discover Lake George, Lake Bathurst, and Goulburn Plains.
	Q'ld.	Lieutenant King surveys the eastern coast.
	Tas.	Lieutenant-Governor Davey retires, and Colonel William Sorell appointed.
1818–22	W.A.	Lieutenant King surveys the whole western coast.
1818	N.S.W.	Free immigration stopped.
1819	N.S.W.	Commissioner Bigge inquires into the condition of the colony.
1820	Tas.	Colonel Paterson introduces 300 pure Merino sheep from McArthur's flock.
1821	N.S.W.	Governor Macquarie recalled.—Sir Thomas Brisbane appointed.
	Tas.	Governor Macquarie visits Hobart Town.
1823	N.S.W.	The first Australian Constitution.—Explorations by Cunningham.—John Dunmore Lang arrives in Sydney.—Oxley discovers the Tweed River.
	Q'ld.	The Brisbane River discovered by Surveyor Oxley.—Cunningham discovers Pandora Pass.
	Tas.	Partial separation from New South Wales.
1824	N.S.W.	Freedom of the Press proclaimed.—Trial by jury introduced.—First Land Regulations.—Hume and Hovell explore southward.
	Vic.	Hume and Hovell travel overland from Sydney to Port Phillip.
	Q'ld.	Expedition to prepare Moreton Bay for the establishment of a penal settlement.

Year	Colony	Event
1824	Tas.	Outbreak of convicts at Macquarie Harbour.—Governor Sorell succeeded by Lieut.-Colonel George Arthur.
1825	N.S.W.	Sir Ralph Darling succeeds Governor Brisbane.—Formation of Australian Agricultural Company.
	Q'ld.	Captain Logan appointed Superintendent of Moreton Bay.—Lockyer explores the Brisbane River.
	Tas.	Formation of the Van Diemen's Land Company and the Van Diemen's Land Establishment.—Van Diemen's Land declared a separate colony.—Initiation of campaign against bushrangers.
	W.A.	Military station established at King George's Sound.
1826	N.S.W.	Darling River discovered by Sturt.—Explorations by Cunningham.
	Vic.	Fort Dumaresq founded at Western Port.
	Q'ld.	Official establishment of penal settlement at Moreton Bay.—Governor Brisbane visits the settlement.
1827	N.S.W.	The colony becomes self-supporting.—Feverish speculation in land and stock.
	Q'ld.	Cunningham discovers the Darling Downs.—Governor Darling visits Moreton Bay.
	Tas.	Explorations of Henry Hellyer.
1828–30	N.S.W.	Severe droughts.
1828	N.S.W.	Second Constitution.
	Vic.	The Western Port settlers return to Sydney.
	Q'ld.	Cunningham discovers a route from Moreton Bay to the Darling Downs, and explores the Brisbane River to its source.
	Tas.	Reformation of the Council.—First land sales.—Reward offered for the capture of natives.
	W.A.	Exploration by Captain Stirling.—Examination of Swan River.
1829	N.S.W. / S.A.	Sturt explores the Murray.
	W.A.	Founding of the Swan River settlement, Captain Stirling in command.
1830	N.S.W.	Sturt's overland journey to the south.—Rising of convicts near Bathurst.—The Bushrangers Act passed through all its stages in one day.
	Vic.	Explorations by Sturt.
	S.A.	Sturt discovers Lake Alexandrina.
	Q'ld.	Logan murdered by convicts.—Captain Clunie succeeds to the administration of the settlement.
	Tas.	Commission to inquire into condition of natives.—George Robinson undertakes to secure the submission of surviving blacks.—The Black Line.
	W.A.	Constitution of first Executive Council.
1831	N.S.W.	Governor Darling superseded by Sir Richard Bourke.—Lord Ripon's Land Regulations.—Sir Thomas Mitchell's explorations to the north of Liverpool Plains.—Launch of first colonial-built steamer.
	S.A.	Wakefield's first colonisation committee formed.—Captain Collet Barker killed by blacks at St. Vincent's Gulf.
	Tas.	Minimum price of land fixed at 5s. per acre by Lord Ripon's regulations.
	W.A.	Route from Perth to King George's Sound discovered by Bannister.—Lord Ripon's land regulations.
1832	W.A.	Captain Irwin undertakes the administration of the settlement. First sitting of Legislative Council.
1833	W.A.	Captain Richard Daniell succeeds Captain Irwin.
1834	N.S.W.	Trouble at Norfolk Island.
	Vic.	Settlement of the brothers Henty at Portland Bay.

1834	S.A.	South Australian Association founded.—The South Australian Act passed.
	W.A.	The Battle of "Pinjarrah."—Sir James Stirling appointed Governor, with full rank.—First shipment of wool to England.
1835	N.S.W.	Mitchell, on his second expedition, establishes the depôt of Fort Bourke on the Darling.
	Vic.	Expeditions of Batman and Fawkner to Port Phillip.
	Q'ld.	Captain Fyans succeeds Captain Clunie.—First ship enters Moreton Bay.
	Tas.	Native settlement formed at Flinders' Island.
	W.A.	The Western Australian Association formed in London.—Memorial against Lord Ripon's regulations addressed to the British Government.
1836	N.S.W.	Mitchell explores the South.—Squatting formally recognised.
	Vic.	Captain Hobson surveys and names Hobson's Bay.—Proclamation of Port Phillip District as open for settlement.—Captain W. Lonsdale first Resident Magistrate.—Sir Thomas Mitchell discovers "Australia Felix."
	S.A.	Founding of South Australia, with Captain Hindmarsh as first Governor.
	Q'ld.	Visit of Backhouse and Walker.
	Tas.	Governor Arthur recalled.
1837	N.S.W.	Governor Bourke resigns.—Select Committee on Transportation appointed in London.
	Vic.	Sites of Melbourne and Williamstown laid out by Governor Bourke.—First sale of land.
	S.A.	First newspaper published in the colony.—Eyre drives a mob of cattle from New South Wales to Adelaide.—Survey of site of Adelaide by Colonel Light.
	Q'ld.	Major Cotton supersedes Captain Fyans.
	Tas.	The Governorship assumed by Sir John Franklin.
	W.A.	Explorations by Grey and Lushington in the north-west.—Murders by natives.
1838	N.S.W.	Discontinuance of the assignment system.—Arrival of Governor Gipps.—Speculative mania sets in.
	Vic.	First census of the settlement (population, 3,511).
	S.A.	Governor Hindmarsh, recalled, is succeeded by Colonel Gawler.—Cattle brought overland from New South Wales, along the Murray route, by Hawdon and Bonney.—Eyre journeys from Port Phillip to Adelaide, discovers Lake Hindmarsh.
	Q'ld.	Abolition of assignment system.—Explorations of the Petries.
	W.A.	Discovery of Fitzroy and Adelaide Rivers.
1839	N.S.W.	Execution of seven stockmen for participation in a massacre of blacks.—Count Strzelecki finds traces of gold near Hartley.
	Vic.	Appointment of Superintendent La Trobe.—First wool ship leaves for England.
	Q'ld.	Lieutenant Gravatt succeeds Major Cotton, and a little later gives place to Lieutenant German.
	W.A.	Governor Stirling succeeded by John Hutt.—Grey's second exploring expedition in the north.
1840	N.S.W.	Abolition of transportation to New South Wales.—Important Land Regulations (proceeds of land sales to be regarded as a Trust for the benefit of the colony which produces them, and to be expended in the maintenance of its public works, and the encouragement of immigration).

1840	Vic.	First Land Regulations; nullified at Port Phillip by Gipps.—The northern boundary of the Port Phillip District fixed at the Murrumbidgee.—Exploration of Gippsland by Angus McMillan.—Port Phillip petitions for separation.
	S.A.	Eyre starts on his overland journey from Adelaide to King George's Sound.—Wreck of the "Maria," and murder of the survivors by the blacks.
	Q'ld.	Suspension of transportation.—Break-up of the penal settlement at Moreton Bay.—Murder of Surveyor Stapleton and his assistants by aborigines.
	Tas.	Assignment ceases.
1840-51	N.S.W.	Depression of varying intensity.
1841	N.S.W.	Rev. W. B. Clarke finds grains of alluvial gold near Bathurst.
	Vic.	Second Census, population 11,738.
	S.A.	Gawler recalled in disgrace and succeeded by Captain George Grey.—Galena discovered in the Mount Lofty Ranges.—Hostilities with natives on the Murray.
	Q'ld.	Explorations by the Russells.—Mission station established by Rev. Mr. Handt.
	Tas.	Renewal of Transportation.
	W.A.	Eyre completes his journey overland from Adelaide to King George's Sound.
1842	N.S.W.	First Representative Constitution.—Crown Land Sales Act (Imperial).—Disaffection among the natives.
	Vic.	Representation granted, to the extent of six members.—Incorporation of Melbourne.
	S.A.	Discovery of Kapunda Copper Mines.—The South Australian Act.
	Q'ld.	Gipps visits Brisbane, and orders that the width of streets be reduced in subsequent surveys.—Proclamation of free settlement at Moreton Bay.—First open sale of land.—Appointment of a Police Magistrate.
1843	N.S.W.	Financial crisis marked by the failure of the Bank of Australia.
	S.A.	Collapse of the Adelaide City Council.—Frome explores Lake Torrens district.
	Q'ld.	Moreton Bay granted Legislative Representation.
	W.A.	Arrival of the "Success" with 134 immigrants.
	Tas.	Governor Franklin recalled, and succeeded by Sir John-Eardley Wilmot.
1844	Vic.	Great flood on the Yarra.—John Dunmore Lang's resolution in favour of separation.
	S.A.	Sturt's last expeditions inland.
	Q'ld.	Leichhardt's expedition from Darling Downs to Port Essington.—Murder of Gilbert by Aborigines.
	Tas.	Explorations of Kentish in the north-west.
1845	N.S.W.	Mitchell's explorations on the Barcoo.
	S.A.	Grey transferred to New Zealand, the government assumed by Colonel Frederic Holt Robe.—Discovery of the Burra Copper Mines.
	Q'ld.	Explorations of Mitchell and Kennedy.
	Tas.	Price's Norfolk Island Pandemonium broken up.—Resignation of the "Patriotic Six."
1846	N.S.W.	Governor Gipps is succeeded by Sir Charles Augustus Fitzroy.—Gladstone proposes to revive transportation to New South Wales.
	Vic.	Third Census, population 32,879.

1846	S.A.	Proclamation of North Australia.—State grants made to certain religious bodies.—Expedition and death of Horrocks.
	Q'ld.	The founding of "Gladstone," an "exile" settlement at Port Curtis.—Explorations by Leichhardt.—Moreton Bay declared a port of entry.—Publication of "Moreton Bay Courier," first Queensland newspaper.
	Tas.	Governor Wilmot recalled by Gladstone.
	W.A.	Reports on immigration despatched to the British Government.—Lieut.-Col. Andrew Clarke assumes office as Governor.—Explorations by the brothers Gregory.—Discovery of coal on the Irwin River.
1847	N.S.W.	Crown Land Leases Act.—Lady Fitzroy killed in a carriage accident.
	Q'ld.	The s.s. "Sovereign" wrecked on Moreton Island.—Explorations by Burnett and Kennedy.
	S.A.	Explorations of Baron Von Mueller.
	Tas.	Sir William Denison assumes office as Governor.—Reinstatement of the "Patriotic Six."—Removal of the surviving blacks, 44 in number, from Flinders Island to Oyster Cove.
	W.A.	Death of Governor Clarke, whose place is taken by Lieut.-Col. Irwin.
		Crown Land Leases Act.—Earl Grey suggests the formation of an Assembly, in which all the Australian colonies should be represented.—Destructive floods on the Swan and Avon Rivers.
1848	N.S.W.	Attempts to revive transportation and assignment.—The University of Sydney founded by Act of Parliament.
	Vic.	Earl Grey returned as the Melbourne member of the Legislative Council.
	S.A.	Governor Robe makes a grant of land as site for an Anglican Cathedral.—Recall of Robe, whose place is taken by Sir Henry Fox Young.
1848	Q'ld.	Last journey of Ludwig Leichhardt.—Kennedy speared by the blacks.—Chinese imported as shepherds.—The Fortitude incident.
	Tas.	Unavailing protests against the landing of convicts from the "Ratcliffe."
	W.A.	Captain Charles Fitzgerald, R.N., assumes office as Governor.—Governor Fitzgerald wounded by the blacks.—Copper and lead discovered in the Champion Bay district.—Explorations by J. S. Roe.-Brown coal discovered on the Fitzgerald River.
1849	N.S.W.	The "Hashemy" incident.—Great exodus of population to gold fields of California.
	Vic.	Public indignation at the arrival of the "Randolphe" with convicts.
	S.A.	Revocation of the North Australian proclamation.
	Q'ld.	Convicts per "Hashemy" assigned to squatters on the Darling Downs.
	Tas.	Convicts to the number of 1,860 landed in accordance with Earl Grey's probation scheme.
	W.A.	Commencement of transportation to Western Australia.
	......	A suggestion for the formation of a General Assembly of Australia made in the report of a Privy Council Committee on Trade and Plantations.
1850	N.S.W.	Final abolition of transportation.—Passing of the Australian Government Act.—New South Wales loses her southern province by separation.—First sod of the first Australian railway turned at Sydney.

1850	Vic.	The Constitution Act.—The Murray fixed upon as the northern boundary of Victoria.
	S.A.	South Australia obtains representative government.
	Tas.	First discovery of coal in the colony.—Tasmania obtains representative government.
	W.A.	Arrival of the "Scindian" with detachment of convicts.—Lieutenant Helpman finds pearls in Shark Bay.
	......	Four of the five Australian colonies obtain representative government (Queensland still a dependency of New South Wales).
1851	N.S.W.	Hargraves discovers payable gold near Bathurst.
	Vic.	Black Thursday (6th February).—Proclamation of Victoria as a separate colony.—Gold discoveries.—Fourth Census, population 77,345.
	S.A.	Depression; withdrawal of specie from the colony.—Abolition of State aid to religion.—The Bullion Act passed.—Revival of the Adelaide Corporation.—Abolition of nominee Council, and appointment of Legislature of one Chamber.
	Q'ld.	First direct shipment of wool to England.—Agitation for separation from New South Wales.
	Tas.	Efflux of population to the gold-fields of "the other side."
	......	Transfer of the Customs establishments to the Colonial Governments.
1852	N.S.W.	The town of Gundagai swept away by a flood; 77 lives lost.
	Vic.	Convicts Prevention Act passed.—An extra regiment brought from England to keep order.
	S.A.	Return of prosperity.—A steamer ascends the Murray to the junction of the Darling.
	Q'ld.	Withdrawal of a large proportion of the population towards the gold-fields of New South Wales and Victoria.—Hovenden Hely's expedition in search of Leichhardt.
	Tas.	First Elective Council meets and passes a resolution against transportation.—Gold discovered at Fingal and Tower Hill Creek.
	......	Arrival of the "Chusan," first P. and O. steamer.
	......	Transfer of the Australian gold revenue to the colonial exchequer.
1853	N.S.W.	University of Sydney opened.
	Vic.	Discontent on the gold-fields.
	Q'ld.	Moreton Bay declared a residency, with Captain Wickham as first Government Resident.
	Tas.	Abolition of transportation.—Tasmania adopted as name of the Island.
	......	Establishment of colonial mints.
1854	N.S.W.	War scare and volunteer movement.
	Vic.	Governor La Trobe retires and is succeeded by Sir Charles Hotham.—The Eureka Stockade rebellion.
	S.A.	Departure of Sir Henry Young.—Organisation of military forces.
	Tas.	Departure of Governor Denison.
	......	Creation of a separate Colonial Office.
1855	N.S.W.	Opening of the first Australian railway.—Governor Fitzroy is succeeded by Sir William Denison.—Norfolk Island cleared for the Pitcairn Islanders.—New scheme for the government of the gold-fields.—Introduction of responsible government.
	Vic.	Reforms on the goldfields.—Introduction of responsible government.—Death of Sir Charles Hotham.
	S.A.	Sir Richard Graves Macdonnell assumes office as Governor.—Introduction of responsible government.

1855	Q'ld.	Gregory's search for Leichhardt.—First navigation of the Fitzroy River.
	Tas.	Sir Henry Edward Fox Young succeeds to the Governorship.—The Hampton Case.—£25,000 contributed to a fund in aid of English sufferers by the Crimean War.—Introduction of responsible government.
	W.A.	Governor Fitzgerald succeeded by Arthur Edward Kennedy.—Discovery of high-grade copper at the Bowes River.
	......	New South Wales, Victoria, South Australia, and Tasmania are granted responsible government.
1856	Vic.	Sir Henry Barkly assumes office as Governor.
	Q'ld.	Grounding of the "Phœbe Dunbar" on Stradbroke Island.—Murders by the blacks.
	W.A.	A. C. Gregory's expedition in search of Leichhardt.—Perth constituted a city.—A Select Committee appointed in New South Wales to consider the best means of legislation on matters of common interest.
1857	N.S.W.	Serious floods.—Wrecks of the "Duncan Dunbar" (119 lives lost), and the "Catherine Adamson" (21 lives lost) at Sydney Heads.
	Vic.	Death, by carriage accident, of Lady Barkly. — Abolition of property qualification for members of the Assembly.—Universal manhood suffrage established.—Sixth Census, population 410,766.
	S.A.	Babbage and Warburton explore northwards.
	Q'ld.	Establishment of Supreme Court sittings.—Garbutt tells his tale of Leichhardt's detention in the interior.—A Select Committee appointed in Victoria to consider best means of legislation on matters of common Australian interest.—
	......	Wentworth's draft Bill with proposal for a General Association of the Australian Colonies.
1858	N.S.W.	Establishment of manhood suffrage and vote by ballot.—Telegraphic communication established between Sydney and Melbourne.
	Vic.	Trial of rebel leaders.—The number of members of the Assembly raised to 78.
	S.A.	Torrens' Real Property Act passed.—Series of exploring expeditions begun by Stuart.
	Q'ld.	Brisbane declared a municipality.—Discovery of gold.—The Canoona Rush.—Exploration by Landsborough and Dalrymple.
	Tas.	Establishment of a State system of Public Instruction.
	W.A.	F. T. Gregory explores the Gascoyne and Shark Bay districts.
1858-61	S.A.	Series of exploring expeditions by John McDouall Stuart.
1859	N.S.W.	The Northern Province separated.
	Q'ld.	Proclamation of Queensland as a separate Colony, with responsible government.—Sir George Bowen appointed Governor.
	Tas.	State aid to religion abolished.—First submarine cable laid from Circular Head to Cape Otway.
1860	N.S.W.	Disastrous floods at Shoalhaven and Araluen.—Discovery of Kiandra gold-field.—Heavy losses of cattle from "Cumberland Disease."
	Vic.	Burke and Wills start on their journey of exploration.
	S.A.	The Wallaroo and Moonta copper discoveries.
	Q'ld.	Bowen founded.—Withdrawal of State aid to religion.

1861	N.S.W.	Governor Denison succeeded by Sir John Young.—Anti-Chinese riots at Lambing Flat.—John Robertson's Land Acts.—Constitutional Crisis.—Regulation and restriction of Chinese immigration.
	Vic.	Seventh Census, population 540,322.
	S.A.	Mr. Justice Boothby claims to be the only legally appointed Judge of the Supreme Court.—McKinlay's expedition in search of Burke and Wills.
	Q'ld.	Burke and Wills perish in the Great Stony Desert; dispatch of expeditions to search for their remains.—Laws made for the transfer of real estate, and for municipal government.—First census taken.—First despatch of a telegraphic message in the colony.—First State trial (Regina v. Pugh) results in a verdict for the defendant establishing the right of free discussion.—A military station established on Albany Island.
	Tas.	Governor Sir Henry Young succeeded by Colonel Thomas Gore-Browne.
	W.A.	Explorations of F. Gregory in the North-west.—Pearling grounds discovered.
	......	Conference at Melbourne to secure uniformity in collection and compilation of the Annual Statistics of the Australian Colonies.
1862	N.S.W.	Daring raid on the Lachlan gold escort (£14,000 carried off).—Abolition of State aid to religion.
	Vic.	Charles Gavan Duffy's Land Act.—Intercolonial Conference at Melbourne.
	S.A.	Departure of Sir Richard Macdonnell.—Stuart crosses the continent from south to north.—Sir Dominick Daly assumes office as Governor.
	Q'ld.	McKinlay's explorations.—Severe floods on the Fitzroy River.
	W.A.	Governor Kennedy succeeded by John S. Hampton.—Formation of the first Legislative Council.—Destructive floods in various parts of the colony.
1863	N.S.W.	The outlaw Gilbert and his confederates rob a jeweller's shop in Bathurst, and hold up the town of Canowindra for three days.—Initiation of the Riverina district dispute.
	Vic.	Retirement of Governor Barkly, who is succeeded by Sir Charles Darling.
	S.A.	South Australia takes over the Northern Territory.
	Q'ld.	Expedition of the brothers Jardine in the Gulf Country.—Extension of the north-west boundary.—Queensland Bank Act passed.
	W.A.	First settlement of north-west district.
	......	Intercolonial Conference held at Melbourne.
1864	N.S.W.	Frequent outrages by bushrangers.
	Q'ld.	First railway begun in the colony.—First sugar manufactured from Queensland cane.
	W.A.	Murder of Messrs. Panton, Harding, and Goldwyer, by aborigines.
1864–5	Tas.	First successful shipment of salmon ova from England.
1865	Q'ld.	First railway opened.—Financial depression.
	Tas.	Act passed to facilitate release and transfer of real estate.
	W.A.	Petition to the Legislative Council urging the introduction of a measure to establish representative government.
1866	N.S.W.	Passage of the Public Schools' Act of (Sir) Henry Parkes.

1866	Vic.	Political deadlock.—Governor Darling recalled and replaced by the Right Hon. F. H. T. Manners-Sutton (afterwards Viscount Canterbury).
	S.A.	Introduction of camels for purposes of exploration, etc.
	Q'ld.	Financial crisis.—Hume's search for Leichhardt.
1867	N.S.W.	Departure of Sir John Young.
	Vic.	Import duty imposed on a number of articles for the purpose of affording protection to home industries.
	S.A.	The Governor and Executive Council investigate charges against Mr. Justice Boothby and remove him from the Bench.—Visit of the Duke of Edinburgh.
	Q'ld.	Rich gold discoveries at Gympie.
	W.A.	Loss of the schooner "Emma," 42 lives lost.
1868	N.S.W.	Lord Belmore takes office as Governor.—Attempt to assassinate the Duke of Edinburgh at Clontarf.—Treason Felony Act passed.
	Vic.	Visit of the Duke of Edinburgh.
	S.A.	Death of Sir Dominick Daly.
	Q'ld.	Departure of Governor Bowen.—Visit of the Duke of Edinburgh.—Act passed to regulate Island Labour traffic.—Colonel S. W. Blackall succeeds to the Government.
	Tas.	The Duke of Edinburgh turns the first sod of the first Tasmanian railway.—Governor Gore-Browne's term of office expires.
	W.A.	Departure of Governor Hampton.—Transportation ceases.
1869	N.S.W.	Select Committee appointed to inquire into existence of alleged conspiracy for treason and murder.
	Vic.	Reduction of the property qualification of members and electors of the Legislative Council.
	Q'ld.	Brisbane Grammar School established.
	S.A.	Sir James Fergusson assumes office as Governor.
	Tas.	Governor Gore-Browne departs and is succeeded by Mr. Charles du Cane.—State aid to religion finally abolished.
	W.A.	Forrest's Expedition in search of Leichhardt.
1870	N.S.W.	Intercolonial Exhibition held at Sydney to celebrate the 100th anniversary of Cook's landing.
	S.A.	The trans-continental telegraph started.
	Tas.	Amendment of the Constitution.
	W.A.	Grant of representative government to Western Australia.—The brothers Forrest journey from Perth to Adelaide *via* Eucla.
	......	Intercolonial Congress held at Melbourne.
1871	Vic.	Increase of import duties.—Eighth Census, population 731,528.
	S.A.	Death of Lady Edith Fergusson.
	Q'ld.	Death of Governor Blackall.—The Marquis of Normanby assumes office as Governor.
	......	The Queensland National Bank founded.
	Tas.	Discovery of Mount Bischoff tin-mines, and other valuable mineral discoveries.
	W.A.	Further explorations to the east by A. Forrest.
1872	N.S.W.	Lord Belmore succeeded by Sir Hercules Robinson.—International Exhibition at Sydney.—Death of Wentworth.
	S.A.	Submarine cable laid from Singapore to Port Darwin.—Completion of trans-continental telegraph line.—Strangway's Act passed.
	Q'ld.	Discovery of tin at Stanthorpe, copper at Mt. Perry, opal in the Warrego district, and coal at Wide Bay.—Discovery of the Palmer gold-field.

1872	**Tas.**	**Launceston and Western Railway transferred to the Government.—Completion of direct telegraphic communication with England.**
	W.A.	**Land Act passed to encourage small settlers and immigrants.—Floods and storms in Victoria district.—Cyclone demolishes Roeburne.**
1873	**N.S.W.**	**Intercolonial Conference at Sydney.**
	Vic.	**Departure of Viscount Canterbury.—Sir George Bowen assumes office as Governor.—Education Act passed.**
	Q'ld.	**Rush to goldfields at Cooktown.—Captain Moresby takes formal possession of New Guinea on behalf of the British Government.**
	S.A.	**Governor Sir James Fergusson succeeded by Mr. (afterwards Sir) Anthony Musgrave.—Attack by natives on Barrow's Creek Station, Trans-continental telegraph line.**
	W.A.	**Colonel Warburton crosses from the trans-continental telegraph line to the head of the De Grey River.—Gosse attempts the overland journey from Alice Springs to Perth.**
	......	**Australian Customs Duties Act passed.**
1874	**N.S.W.**	**Triennial Parliaments Act passed.**
	S.A.	**The Boucaut Policy first advocated.**
	Q'ld.	**Dalrymple extends his researches on the north-eastern seaboard.—Departure of the Marquis of Normanby.**
	Tas.	**Departure of Governor Du Cane.**
	W.A.	**Explorations of E. Giles.—Departure of Governor Weld.—John and Alexander Forrest cross the colony from west to east.**
1875	**S.A.**	**Wreck of the "Gothenburg," involving the death of Judge Wearing and other well-known Adelaide citizens.—Death of Sir Richard Hanson.—Education Act passed.—Explorations by Giles, Gosse, and Warburton.**
	Q'ld.	**Mr. (afterwards Sir) W. W. Cairns succeeds the Marquis of Normanby in the Government.—The Port Albany Settlement transferred to Thursday Island.**
	Tas.	**Mr. Frederick A. Weld assumes the Government.**
	W.A.	**Arrival of Sir William Cleaver Francis Robinson to assume office as Governor.—Giles' third expedition confirms the views of previous explorers as to the desert nature of a great portion of the interior.**
		Intercolonial conference at Hobart to secure uniformity of statistical collection and compilation.
1876	**N.S.W.**	**Completion of telegraphic cable between Sydney and Wellington.**
	Vic.	**Number of members of the Legislative Assembly increased to eighty-six.**
	Tas.	**Railway opened from Hobart to Launceston.—Death of Truganini, the last Tasmanian black.**
	W.A.	**Giles crosses the colony from east to west.—Violent gale at Exmouth Gulf; a number of pearling vessels wrecked, and 69 persons drowned.**
1877	**Vic.**	**Deadlock on the question of payment of members.**
	S.A.	**Governor Musgrave succeeded by Sir W. W. Cairns.—Inauguration of the Senate of the University of Adelaide.—Resignation of Governor Cairns after two months of government.—Sir W. F. D. Jervois appointed Governor.—Completion of the telegraph line from Adelaide to Perth.**
	Q'ld.	**Sir Arthur Kennedy appointed Governor.**
	Tas.	**Further discoveries of gold.**
	W.A.	**Governor Sir William Robinson succeeded by Sir Harry St. George Ord.**

1878	N.S.W.	Unveiling of Woolner's Statue of Captain Cook in Sydney.
	Vic.	"Black Wednesday"; wholesale dismissal of civil servants.—Recall of Sir George Bowen.
	S.A.	New Crown Lands Act.—Founding of the University of Adelaide.—Rifle Companies Act passed.—First sod of the Trans-continental Railway turned by Sir William Jervois.
	Q'ld.	Restriction of Chinese immigration.
	W.A.	Agitation for self-government.
1879	N.S.W.	Sir Hercules Robinson succeeded in the Government by Lord Loftus.—Electoral Act, 1879, passed.—International Exhibition held at the Garden Palace, Sydney.
	Vic.	The Marquis of Normanby assumes office as Governor.—Capture of the "Kelly Gang" of bushrangers.
	W.A.	Alexander Forrest crosses from the De Grey River to Daly Waters Station on Overland Telegraph Line.
1880	N.S.W.	Public Instruction Act abolishes State aid to denominational education.
	Vic.	An International Exhibition held in Melbourne.—Inauguration of mail contract service between Victoria and England.
	Tas.	Governor Weld succeeded by Sir J. H. Lefroy.
	W.A.	Departure of Sir Harry Ord.—Sir William Robinson enters upon his second term of office as Governor.
	......	Federal Conference at Melbourne and Sydney.
1881	N.S.W.	Further restriction of Chinese immigration.
	Vic.	Further reduction of property qualification of members and electors of the Legislative Council, and increase in number of members.—Ninth Census, population 862,346.
	Tas.	Governor Lefroy succeeded by Sir George Cumine Strahan.
	W.A.	Cyclone at Roebourne, several pearling vessels wrecked, number of lives lost.
	......	Prince Albert Victor and Prince George of Wales visit Australia.
	......	First simultaneous census of the Australasian colonies.
1882	N.S.W.	Destruction by fire of the Garden Palace.—Death of the poet Henry Kendall.
	S.A.	Departure of Sir William Jervois.
1882–3	Q'ld.	Favenc examines coast rivers of the Gulf, and crosses to Overland Telegraph Line.
1883	N.S.W.	Discovery of silver at Broken Hill.
	Vic.	Completion of railway between Sydney and Melbourne.
	S.A.	Sir William Robinson appointed Governor.
	Q'ld.	Annexation of New Guinea (repudiated by British Government).—Departure of Governor Kennedy, whose place is taken by Sir Anthony Musgrave.
	Tas.	Period of rash mining speculations.
	W.A.	Sir Frederick Napier Broome appointed Governor.—John Forrest explores in the Kimberley district.—Hardman discovers auriferous deposits.
	......	Federal Conference held at Sydney.
1884	N.S.W.	Land Act passed, involving restriction of sales by auction, &c.
	Vic.	Sir Henry Loch succeeds Lord Normanby in the Government.—Appointment of the Public Service Board.
	W.A.	Explorations by Harry Stockdale.
	......	A Federation Bill passed in Victoria.—A similar Bill rejected in New South Wales.
1885	N.S.W.	Military contingent sent to take part in the Soudan Campaign.—Opening of the Broken Hill silver mines.—Governor Loftus succeeded by the Right Hon. Baron Carrington.
	Q'ld.	Agitation for a division of the colony.

1885	Tas.	Mount Zeehan silver-lead mines discovered.
	W.A.	New Land Act passed.—Discovery of gold in Kimberley district.
	......	Formation of the Federal Council of Australia.
1886	N.S.W.	Industrial depression.
	Q'ld.	Discovery of Mount Morgan gold-mine.
	Tas.	Gold and copper discovered at Mount Lyell.—Retirement of Sir George Strahan.—Extension of the franchise.
	W.A.	Agitation for self-government.—Proclamation of Kimberley gold-field.
	.....	The Federal Council meets at Hobart.
1887	N.S.W.	The Bulli mining disaster, 83 lives lost.
	S.A.	The English Government claims £15,516 as interest on an old loan.—Adelaide Jubilee International Exhibition.
	Tas.	Sir R. G. C. Hamilton assumes office as Governor.
	W.A.	Severe hurricane at Ninety-mile Beach, pearling fleet destroyed, 200 lives lost.—Gold discovered at Yilgarn.
	......	Australasian Conference in London.—Australasian Naval Defence Force Act passed.
1888	N.S.W.	Much damage done by bush fires.—Centennial celebrations.—Drastic legislation against Chinese immigration (imposition of a poll tax of £100).—Strike of colliers at Newcastle.—Inauguration of weekly mail service to England.
	Vic.	International Exhibition at Melbourne.—Number of members increased in both Houses.
	Q'ld.	Death of Sir Anthony Musgrave.—Sir Henry Wylie-Norman assumes office as Governor.—Railway communication opened between Brisbane and Sydney.—Floods at Rockhampton.
	W.A.	Explorations of Ernest Favenc.—Discovery of tin at Greenbushes.
	......	Centenary of first settlement in Australia.—Conference of Australian Ministers at Sydney to consider the question of Chinese immigration.—Imperial Defence Act passed.
1889	N.S.W.	Destructive floods.
	Vic.	Sir Henry Loch succeeded by Lord Hopetoun.
	Q'ld.	Arrival of Governor Norman.
	S.A.	Governor Sir W. C. F. Robinson succeeded by the Earl of Kintore.
	W.A.	Tietkins explores country round L. Amadeus.—New Constitution framed.—Opening of the eastern railway.—Discovery of the Pilbarra gold-field.—Departure of Governor Browne.—Opening of cable from Banjoewangie to Broome.
	......	Report of Imperial Commission on Australian Land Defences.
1890	N.S.W.	Payment of Members of Parliament.—Strike at Broken Hill.—Maritime and other strikes.—Severe bush fires.—Departure of Lord Carrington.
	Vic.	Local Government Bill passed.
	S.A.	Land Act passed, fixing the minimum price of country land at 5s. per acre.
	Q'ld.	Wreck of the "Quetta" (146 lives lost).—Extensive floods, and terrible hurricanes.—Industrial crisis.
	Tas.	Establishment of the University of Tasmania.
	W.A.	Granting of responsible government.—Sir William Robinson enters on his third term of office.
	......	Federal Conference held at Melbourne.
1891	N.S.W.	Lord Jersey assumes office as Governor.—Thirty-five Labour Members returned to the Legislative Assembly.—Arrival of Australasian Auxiliary Squadron.
	W.A.	First Parliament under Responsible Government.—Discovery of Murchison gold-field.

1891	......	Federal Convention called in Sydney.—The Colonial Premiers meet at the New South Wales Colonial Secretary's office.—Australasian Colonies join the Postal Union.
1892	N.S.W.	Strike at Broken Hill.—Temporary run on the Government Savings Bank.
	Vic.	Suspension of the Railway Commissioners.
	Q'ld.	Constitution Act passed, whereby Queensland is divided into two provinces.—Pacific Labourers Extension Act passed.
	Tas.	Departure of Sir Robert Hamilton.
	W.A.	Discovery of Bayley's Reward at Coolgardie.
1893	N.S.W.	Sir Robert Duff succeeds Lord Jersey.—The "Royal Tar" sails with the first New Australian colonists.
	Vic.	Land Act passed providing for village settlements, homestead associations, and labour colonies.—Financial panic in Melbourne.
	Q'ld.	Terrific storms and floods.—First departures for New Australia.
	Tas.	Viscount Gormanston takes office as Governor.
	W.A.	Opening of telegraphic line to Wyndham, 2,125 miles from Perth.—Discovery of Kalgoorlie gold-field.
	......	The Corowa Conference.—Banking crisis in Eastern States.
1894	N.S.W.	Further Land legislation.—Shearers' Strike.
	S.A.	Adult Suffrage Bill receives Royal Assent.
	Q'ld.	Disturbances in the Legislative Assembly over the Peace Preservation Bill.—Payment of Members Bill rejected.
	W.A.	Telegraphic communication opened between Southern Cross, Coolgardie, and Kalgoorlie.—Discovery of Kanowna gold-field.
	......	Serious industrial troubles.
1895	N.S.W.	Death of Sir Robert Duff.—Viscount Hampden takes office as Governor.—Crown Lands Act of 1895 passed.
	Vic.	Departure of Earl of Hopetoun, who is succeeded by Lord Brassey
	S.A.	The Earl of Kintore is succeeded as Governor by Sir Thomas Fowell Buxton.
	Q'ld.	Departure of Sir Henry Norman.—Disastrous floods.
	......	Conference of Premiers at Hobart.
1896	N.S.W.	Death of Sir Henry Parkes.
	S.A.	Establishment of the State Bank.—Floods and storms.—Franchise exercised by women in South Australia.—Departure of the Calvert expedition.
	Q'ld.	Lord Lamington assumes office as Governor.—Sir Henry Norman appointed Agent-General for Queensland.—Gales and floods.—The ferry-boat "Pearl" capsizes at Brisbane (28 lives lost)
	W.A.	Explorations of Wells and Carnegie.—Opening of railway to Coolgardie and Kalgoorlie.—Hübbe journeys from Oodnadatta (S.A.) to Coolgardie.
	......	The People's Federal Convention held at Bathurst.
1897	Vic.	Floods and storms in Gippsland.—Destructive fire in Melbourne.
	S.A.	Earthquake and hurricane in Northern Territory; destruction of the town of Palmerston.—Floods and storms at Adelaide.—Death of Sir Thomas Elder.
1897–98	......	The Federal Convention holds sessions at Adelaide, Sydney, and Melbourne.
1898	Vic.	Destructive forest fires in Gippsland.
	S.A.	Resignation of Sir Thomas Fowell Buxton.
	W.A.	Serious disturbances on the gold-fields.
	......	The Federal Bill accepted by Tasmania, Victoria, and South Australia, but rejected by N. S. Wales.
1899	N.S.W.	Governor Hampden succeeded by Earl Beauchamp.

1899	S A.	Lord Tennyson assumes the Governorship of South Australia.
	Q ld.	Destruction of pearling fleets at Thursday Island by cyclonic storms (200 lives lost).
	W.A.	Opening of Coolgardie Exhibition.—Wreck of "City of York" and "Carlisle Castle," 34 lives lost.
	......	Conference of Premiers at Melbourne.—The Referendum; the Bill is accepted by N. S. Wales, Tasmania, Queensland, Victoria, and S. Australia.
1900	N.S.W.	Departure of Lord Beauchamp.—Old Age Pensions Act passed.
	W.A.	Agitation for separation by gold-fields district.—Strike of drivers and firemen on railways.—Departure of Governor Smith.
	......	The Australian Colonies send military contingents to assist the British forces against the Boer Republics.—The Federal Bill receives the Royal Assent (9th July).—The Honorable Edmund Barton, first Federal Prime Minister.
1901	N.S.W.	Readjustment of industrial conditions in many quarters.—Industrial Arbitration Act passed.
	Vic.	Opening of the Federal Parliament at Melbourne.—Expulsion from the State Assembly of Mr. Findley, member for Melbourne, for alleged disloyalty.—Departure of Lord Brassey.—Swearing in of Governor Sir G. S. Clarke.
	W.A.	Brockman's expedition discovers valuable pastoral country in the north.
	......	Proclamation of the Australian Commonwealth, Lord Hopetoun first Governor-General.—The Federal Parliament opened by the Heir-Apparent to the British Crown, the Duke of Cornwall and York, who visits each State of the Commonwealth.—Contingents sent to S. Africa and to China.
1902	N.S.W.	Arrival of Sir Harry Holdsworth Rawson, K.C.B.—Disastrous explosion at Mount Kembla Colliery, Illawarra District; 95 miners lost their lives.—Jubilee of Sydney University.—Woman's Suffrage Act passed.
	Vic.	Agitation for Reform.—Mr. Irvine becomes Premier.
	Q'ld.	Arrival of Sir Herbert Charles Chermside, the new Governor.—Inland mail service interrupted by drought.
	S.A.	Reduction of members of Assembly from 64 to 42 and of Council from 24 to 18. Ministers reduced from 6 to 4.
	W.A.	Opening of pumping station at Northam in connection with Coolgardie water supply scheme.—Departure of Governor Sir Arthur Lawley.
	Tas.	Conference of State Statisticians, Attorneys-General, and Ministers for Agriculture.—Strong protest against Federal action with reference to letters addressed to "Tattersall."
1903	N.S.W.	Conference of State Premiers and Attorneys-General.—Referendum on question of reduction of number of members of the Legislative Assembly.—Vote in favour of reduction to 90.
	Vic.	Strike of Victorian Railway Employees.—Parliamentary Reform.
	Q'ld.	Cyclone at Townsville.—Resignation of Philp Ministry.
	S.A.	Gold discoveries at Arltunga.—Arrival of Governor Sir E. Le Hunte.
	W.A.	Opening of pumping stations in connection with goldfields water supply at Coolgardie and Kalgoorlie; scheme originated with Sir John Forrest.
	......	Federal High Court constituted.—Federal Electoral Act passed enfranchising women.—Election of Second Parliament.—Lord Northcote appointed Governor-General.
1904	N.S.W.	Meeting of Parliament.—Membership reduced to 90.

CHRONOLOGICAL TABLE FOR NEW ZEALAND.

1642	Discovery of New Zealand by Tasman.
1769	Cook arrives at Poverty Bay.
1770	De Surville kidnaps a "rangatira" (Maori chieftain.)
1772	Marion du Fresne killed and eaten by the Maoris.
1773	Furneaux enters Queen Charlotte Sound.
1790	Chatham Islands discovered by Lieutenant Broughton.
1793	Doubtless Bay visited by Lieutenant-Governor King, of Norfolk Island; a rangatira and a tohunga (Maori priest) kidnapped.
1795	The "Endeavour" sunk in Dusky Sound.
1800	Discovery of Antipodes Island.
1806	Discovery of the Auckland Isles.—The "Venus," with a crew of runaway convicts, visits the East Coast.
1807	Defeat of Hongi and the Nga-Puhi tribe at Kaipara.—Crew of a vessel eaten on the East Coast.
1809	The Boyd massacre.
1810	Discovery of Campbell Island.
1814	Rev. S. Marsden founds a mission station in New Zealand.—First introduction of horses, cattle, sheep, and poultry.—Appointment of Kendall as Resident Magistrate
1815	Attempted capture of the "Trial" and the "Brothers" at Kennedy Bay.
1818	Expedition of Hongi and Te Morenga to East Cape.
1819-20	Raid on Taranaki and Port Nicholson by Patone, Nene, and Te Rauparaha.
1820	Hongi's trip to England.—Coromandel visited by H.M. Store-ship "Coromandel."—Auckland Harbour entered by the "Prince Regent."
1821	Fall of Mauinaina Pa (Auckland Isthmus) and Te Totara Pa (Thames) to Hongi.
1822	Hongi takes Matakitaki Pa (Waikato).—Baron de Thierry attempts to buy land at Hokianga.
1823	Act passed to extend the jurisdiction of the New South Wales Courts to British subjects in New Zealand.—Capture of Mokoia Pa (Rotorua Lake) by Hongi.
1824	Pomare takes Te Whetumatarau Pa, near East Cape.
1825	Formation of Lord Durham's (unsuccessful) New Zealand Association.—Hongi defeats Ngati-Whatua at Te Ikaaranganui (Kaipara).
1825	Brief settlement at Hauraki Gulf.
1827	Destruction of the Whangaroa mission station by Hongi's forces.
1828	Death of Hongi at Whangaroa from wounds received at Hokianga.
1829	Capture of brig "Hawes" by Maoris at Whakatane.
1830	Battle of Taumata-Wiwi (near Cambridge).—Fall of Kaiapohia Pa (Canterbury).—Battle of Kororareka between two Nga-Puhi tribes.—Massacre at Kaiapoi and death of Tama-i-hara-nui at the hands of Te Rauparaha's adherents.

1831	Thirteen chiefs appeal for protection to the English Government.—Waikato captures Pukerangiora Pa (Waitara).
1832	Repulse of Waikato at Nga-motu Pa.
1833	Appointment of James Busby as Resident Magistrate at the Bay of Islands.
1834	Battle of Haowhenua and Pakakutu near Otaki.—Wreck of the "Harriet" at Cape Egmont.—Shelling of Waimate Pa near Opunake by H M.S. "Alligator." Thierry announces himself the Sovereign Chief of New Zealand and defender of its liberties.
1835	Formation of the second New Zealand Association.—Formation of a confederation called "The United Tribes of New Zealand."—Ngati-Awa tribes take possession of Chatham Islands.
1836	Waikato captures Maketu Pa (Bay of Plenty).
1837	Lord Durham and Edward Gibbon Wakefield attempt to revive the New Zealand Association.
1838	The settlers at Kororareka form a vigilance committee.—Arrival at Hokianga of Bishop Pompallier (R.C.).—Discovery of Pelorus Sound by H.M.S. "Pelorus."
1839	French whaler "Jean Bart" captured by Maoris at Chatham Islands.—Founding of the New Zealand Company, and despatch of its first colonising expeditions.—New Zealand incorporated with New South Wales, and Captain Hobson appointed first Lieutenant-Governor.—Battle of Kuititanga (Otaki).
1840	First appearance of a steamer in New Zealand waters.—Arrivals of immigrants at Port Nicholson.—Arrival of Captain Hobson, and the signing of the Treaty of Waitangi.—The Queen's sovereignty proclaimed over all New Zealand.—Auckland founded.—The Nantes-Bordelaise Company send settlers to Akaroa.
1841	Auckland proclaimed the seat of government.—Issue of Charter of Incorporation to the New Zealand Company.—New Zealand proclaimed independent of New South Wales.
1842	Settlement founded at Nelson.—Arrival of Bishop Selwyn.—Death of Governor Hobson.
1843	The Wairau massacre.—Captain Fitzroy takes office as Governor.
1844–5	Governor Fitzroy's mistaken land policy.
1844	Hone Heke hews down the flagstaff at the Bay of Islands.
1845	Destruction of Kororareka by Heke.—Arrival of reinforcements of troops from Sydney and Hobart.—Unsuccessful attack on a pa at Ohaeawae.—Recall of Governor Fitzroy and appointment of Captain George Grey.
1846	Capture of Ruapekapeka pa (Bay of Islands) and conclusion of the war with Heke.—Outbreak of hostilities in the Hutt Valley, near Wellington.—Seizure of Te Rauparaha at Porirua.—New Zealand Government Act passed (dividing the colony into two provinces, and granting representative institutions).—Te Heu Heu overwhelmed and buried by a land-slip at Taupo.
1847	Minor outbreak at Wanganui.—Arrival of the New Zealand Fencibles.
1848	Sir George Grey sworn in as Governor-in-Chief over the islands of New Zealand and Governor of the provinces of New Ulster and New Munster.—Founding of Otago.—Severe earthquake at Wellington.
1849	Incorporation of the Canterbury Association.
1850	Surrender of the New Zealand Company's Charter.—Founding of Canterbury.
1852	Discovery of gold at Coromandel.
1852–3	Third Constitution (division of the colony into six provinces).
1853	Boundaries of the provinces proclaimed.—Departure of Sir George Grey.
1854	Lieutenant-Colonel Wynyard assumes administration of the Government.

1855	Severe earthquakes on both sides of Cook Strait.—Arrival of Governor T. Gore Browne.
1856	Formation of a Maori league against land-selling.—Te Whero Whero proposed as king.—First Ministry under Responsible Government, Mr. Sewell, Colonial Secretary.
1857	First payable gold-field opened at Collingwood, Province of Nelson.
1858	New Provinces Act passed.—Te Whero Whero (Potatau I.) proclaimed King of the Maoris.
1859	Te Teira offers land at Waitara for sale to the Government.
1860	Hostilities begun against Wiremu Kingi te Rangitake.—Capture of Waitara Pa.—Engagements at Waireka and Puketakauere.—Defeat of Kingi's Waikato allies at Mahoetahi.—Capture of Matarikoriko Pa.—Death of the Maori King and succession of his son Matutaera (Tawhaiao).
1861	Repulse of Maoris by Imperial troops at Huirangi redoubt.—Truce agreed upon.—Gold discoveries at Tuapeka River, Clutha, &c.—Recall of Governor Browne.—Sir George Grey enters upon his second term of office as Governor.
1862	First Native Lands Act passed.—Wreck of the "White Swan" on east coast, loss of many valuable public records.
1863	Wreck of H.M.S. "Orpheus" on Manukau Bar (181 lives lost).—The Imperial Government explicitly relinquishes control over the administration of native affairs.—Assault on a military escort at Tataraimaka.—Defeat of Maoris at Katikara.—Commencement of Waikato war; action at Koheroa (Auckland district).—Capture of Rangiriri Pa.—Railway opened from Christchurch to Ferrymead Junction.—New Zealand Settlements Act passed.—Occupation of Ngaruawahia.
1864	Engagement with the Maoris at Mangapiko River.—Defeat of Maoris at Rangiaohia.—Capture of the Orakau Pa.—Engagement near Maketu (Bay of Plenty).—Defeat of the Rawhiti tribes by the Arawa friendlies.—Cameron's repulse at the Gate Pa.—Repulse of the Hauhaus at Sentry Hill (Taranaki).—Battle of Moutoa (Wanganui) and defeat of Hauhaus by friendlies.—Defeat of Maoris at Te Ranga.—Discovery of gold on the west coast of Middle Island.—Escape of Maori prisoners from Kawau.—Wellington chosen as the seat of Government.—Grey confiscates native lands in Waikato.
1865	Submission of Maori Chief Wiremu Tamihana te Waharoa.—Removal of the seat of Government to Wellington.—Murder of Volkner by Hauhaus under Kereopa.—Murder of Fulloon and others by Hauhaus at Whakatane.—Capture by Grey of Wereroa Pa, near Wanganui.—Fraser and Te Mokena capture Kairomiromi Pa (Waiapu).—Proclamation of Peace.—Murder of a friendly messenger by Hauhaus at Kakaramea.—Defeat of rebel natives at Wairoa.
1866	Defeat of Maoris at Okotuku Pa, west coast of North Island.—Chute captures Putahi Pa and Otapawa Pa.—Escape of prisoners from the hulk at Wellington.—Submission of Te Heu Heu and Herekiekie, of Taupo.—Maori prisoners sent to Chatham Islands.—Laying of the Cook Strait submarine cable.—Engagement of Pungarehu.—Natives defeated at Omaranui and Petane (Hawke's Bay).
1867	Admission of Maori members (4) to House of Representatives.
1868	Arrival of Governor Sir George F. Bowen.—Escape of Te Kooti from the Chatham Islands.—Maoris attack the redoubt at Turuturu Mokai. Engagements at Ngatu-o-te-manu.—Departure from New Zealand of Bishop Selwyn.—Colonial forces repulsed with heavy loss at Moturoa. Massacre of 32 Europeans at Poverty Bay.—Engagements between Te Kooti and the friendlies at Patutahi (Poverty Bay district).

1869	Defeat and dispersal of Te Kooti's force at Ngatapa Pa (Poverty Bay).—Murder of Rev. John Whitely and others at White Cliffs.—Defeat of Titokowaru at Otauto.—Outrages by Te Kooti, who captures Mohaka Pa.—First visit to Wellington of the Duke of Edinburgh.—Defeat of Te Kooti at Ahikereru Pa and Oamaru Teangi Pa.—Surrender of Tairua with 122 men, women, and children of the Pakakohe tribe, near Wanganui.—Sentences for treason passed against Maori prisoners.—Storming of Pourere Pa by Lieut.-Colonel McDonnell.
1870	Friendlies under Topia and Keepa pursue Te Kooti (Wanganui River).—Capture of Te Kooti's Pa at Tapapa.—Departure of the last detachment of Imperial troops.—Crushing defeat of Te Kooti at Maraetahi.—Second visit of the Duke of Edinburgh to Wellington.—Act passed to establish the University of New Zealand.—Land Transfer Act passed.
1871	Death of Tamati Waka Nene.—Capture of Kereopa.
1872	Execution of Kereopa at Napier.—First appointment of Rangatiras (2) to the Legislative Council.—Public Trust Office Act passed.—Te Kooti retires to the King country.
1873	Governor Sir George Bowen succeeded by Sir James Fergusson.
1874	Abolition of incarceration for debt.—Departure of Sir James Fergusson; the Governorship assumed by the Marquis of Normanby.
1875	Abolition of Provinces Act passed.—Sir George Grey elected to the Assembly as member for Auckland.
1876	Submarine cable completed between New Zealand and New South Wales.
1877	Education Act passed providing for the free and compulsory education of children.
1878	Sir George Grey's first land tax passed.
1879	Departure of the Marquis of Normanby.—Land dispute with Te Whiti.—Sir Hercules Robinson assumes office as Governor.—Arrest and imprisonment of 180 natives, who had been, by Te Whiti's orders, ploughing lands occupied by Europeans.—Triennial Parliaments Act passed.—Act passed to confer the suffrage on every resident adult male.
1880	Governor Sir Hercules Robinson succeeded by Sir A. H. Gordon.
1881	S.S. "Tararua" wrecked (130 lives lost).—Severe earthquakes in Wellington.—Arrest of Te Whiti and Tohu.
1882	Departure of Sir A. H. Gordon.—Assumption of the Government by Sir J. Prendergast.
1883	Arrival of Governor Sir W. F. D. Jervois.—Proclamation of amnesty to Maori political offenders.—Liberation of Te Whiti and Tohu.
1885	Opening of New Zealand Industrial Exhibition at Wellington.
1886	Volcanic eruptions at Tarawera (101 lives lost).—Destruction of famous Pink and White Terraces.
1887	Kermadec Islands annexed to New Zealand.—Australasian Naval Defence Act passed.
1888	Proclamation of protectorate over Cook Islands.
1889	The Earl of Onslow succeeds Sir W. F. D. Jervois in the Government.—Opening of South Seas exhibition, Dunedin.
1890	First election of the House of Representatives under manhood suffrage and on the one man one vote principle.
1891	Labour laws: Employers Liability Act, 1882 Amendment Act; Truck Act.—Factories Act (repealed 1894).—Land and Income Tax Assessment Act passed for purposes of taxation.
1892	The Earl of Onslow succeeded in the Government by the Earl of Glasgow.—Labour laws: Contractors and Workmen's Lien Act.—Passing of the first Land and Income Tax Act, on basis of Assessment Act of previous year.—Land Act, 1892 (lease in perpetuity without revaluation system introduced; occupation with right of purchase; optional method of selection; small farms associations).

1893	Death of Hon. John Ballance.—Bank Note Issue Act passed.—The Electoral Act, 1893, passed conferring the franchise on women.—Alcoholic Liquors Sale Control Act passed; all new licenses to be granted subject to will of electors; also abolition or reduction of licenses.—Labour laws: Workmen's Wages Act.—Native Land Purchase and Acquisition Act.
1894	Labour laws: Conspiracy Law Amendment; Act to encourage the formation of industrial unions and associations, etc.—Factories Act.—Act for limiting hours of business in shops.—Advances to Settlers Act.—Land for Settlement Act (1894) and Lands Improvement and Native Lands Acquisition Act.—Wreck of the s.s. "Wairarapa" at Great Barrier Island (135 lives lost).
1895	Labour laws: Act to regulate the attachment of wages.—Servants Registry Office Act.—Family Homes Protection Act.
1896	Brunner Mine explosion (67 deaths).—Land for Settlements Act amended.—Alteration of franchise by abolition of non-residential or property qualification.
1897	The Earl of Glasgow succeeded in the Government by the Earl of Ranfurly.—Wreck of the "Tasmania" (10 lives lost).—The Hon. R. J. Seddon called to the Privy Council.
1898	Death of Sir George Grey.—Act to provide old-age pensions passed.—Death of Bishop Selwyn.
1899	Military assistance rendered to the Empire in the Boer war.
1900	Further military assistance to the Empire.—Immigration Restriction Act came into operation.—Maori Councils Act passed.
1901	Universal penny postage adopted by New Zealand.—Visit of the Duke of Cornwall and York.—Annexation of Cook Islands.—Departure of the sixth and seventh contingents.—Visit of the Federation Commission to Australia.—Death of Sir John Mackenzie.—Extension of boundaries of colony to include Cook and other Pacific Islands.
1902	Eighth, ninth, and tenth contingents despatched to South Africa.—Mr. Seddon proceeds to South Africa and thence to London.—Wreck of the "Ventnor" near Hokianga.—Wreck of the "Elingamite" at the Three Kings.
1903	Celebration of Hon. R. J. Seddon's tenth year of office as Premier.

THE COMMONWEALTH.

THE question of the federation of the various provinces of Australia was not overlooked by the framers of the first free Australian Constitution, who proposed the establishment of a General Assembly "to make laws in relation to those intercolonial questions that have arisen, or may hereafter arise," and who, indeed, sketched out a tolerably comprehensive federation scheme. Unfortunately, however, that proposition was included with another for the creation of a colonial hereditary nobility, and in the storm of popular opposition and ridicule with which the latter idea was greeted, the former sank out of sight. Again, in 1853, the Committees appointed in New South Wales and Victoria to draw up the Constitutions of their respective colonies, urged the necessity for the creation of a General Assembly; but the Home Government indefinitely postponed the question by declaring that "the present is not a proper opportunity for such enactment." From time to time, since Responsible Government was established, the evil of want of union among the Australian colonies has been forcibly shown, and the idea of federation has gradually become more and more popular. Some years ago (1883) the movement took such shape that, as the result of an Intercolonial Conference, the matter came before the Imperial Parliament and a measure was passed permitting the formation of a Federal Council to which any colony that felt inclined to join could send delegates. The first meeting of the Federal Council was held at Hobart in January, 1886. The colonies represented were Victoria, Queensland, Tasmania, Western Australia, and Fiji. New South Wales, South Australia, and New Zealand declined to join. South Australia sent representatives to a subsequent meeting, but withdrew shortly afterwards. The Council held eight meetings, at which many matters of intercolonial interest were discussed, the last having been held in Melbourne, early in 1899. One meeting every two years was necessary to keep the Council in existence. Being, from its inherent constitution, a purely deliberative body, having no executive functions whatever, the Federal Council possessed no control of funds or other means to put its legislation into force, and those zealous in the cause of federation had to look elsewhere for the full realisation of their wishes. The Council naturally ceased to exist at the inception of the Commonwealth.

An important step towards the federation of the Australasian colonies was taken early in 1890, when a Conference, consisting of representatives from each of the seven colonies of Australasia, was held in the Parliament House, Melbourne. The Conference met on the 6th February, thirteen members being present, comprising two representatives from each of the colonies, except Western Australia which sent only one. Mr. Duncan Gillies, Premier of Victoria, was elected President. Seven meetings were held, the question of federation being discussed at considerable length; and in the end the Conference adopted an address to the Queen, expressing their loyalty and attachment, and submitting certain resolutions which affirmed the desirability of an early union, under the Crown of the Australian colonies on principles just to all, suggested that the remoter Australasian colonies should be entitled to admission upon terms to be afterwards agreed upon, and recommended that steps should be taken for the appointment of delegates to a National Australasian Convention, to consider and report upon an adequate scheme for a Federal Constitution.

In accordance with the terms of that resolution, delegates were appointed by the Australasian Parliaments, and on the 2nd March, 1891, the National Australasian Convention commenced its sittings in the Legislative Assembly Chambers, Sydney, having been convened at the instance of Mr. James Munro, the Premier of Victoria. There were forty-five members of the Convention altogether, New South Wales, Victoria, Queensland, Tasmania, and Western Australia (which had only recently been placed in possession of the privilege of Responsible Government) each sending seven delegates, and New Zealand three. Sir Henry Parkes, then Premier of the mother colony, was unanimously elected President of the Convention; Mr. F. W. Webb, Clerk of the Legislative Assembly of New South Wales, was appointed Secretary; Sir Samuel Griffith, Premier of Queensland, was elected Vice-President; and Mr. (later Sir) J. P. Abbott, Speaker of the New South Wales Legislative Assembly, was elected Chairman of Committees.

A series of resolutions was moved by the President, Sir Henry Parkes, setting forth certain principles necessary to establish and secure an enduring foundation for the structure of a Federal Government, and approving of the framing of a Federal Constitution; and after discussion and amendment, the resolutions were finally adopted, affirming the following principles:—

1. The powers and rights of existing colonies to remain intact, except as regards such powers as it may be necessary to hand over to the Federal Government.

2. No alteration to be made in State boundaries without the consent of the Legislatures of such States, as well as of the Federal Parliament.

3. Trade between the federated colonies to be absolutely free.

4. Power to impose Customs and Excise Duties to rest with the Federal Government and Parliament.
5. Military and Naval Defence Forces to be under one command.
6. The Federal Constitution to make provision to enable each State to make amendments in its Constitution if necessary for the purposes of Federation.

Further resolutions approved of the framing of a Federal Constitution which should establish a Senate and a House of Representatives—the latter to possess the sole power of originating money Bills; also a Federal Supreme Court of Appeal, and an Executive consisting of a Governor-General, with such persons as might be appointed his advisers. On the 31st March, Sir Samuel Griffith, as Chairman of the Committee on Constitutional Machinery, brought up a draft Constitution Bill, which was fully and carefully considered by the Convention in Committee of the Whole, and adopted on the 9th April, when the Convention was formally dissolved.

The Bill of 1891 aroused no popular enthusiasm, and parliamentary sanction to its provisions was not sought in any of the colonies; thus federation fell into the background of politics.

At this juncture a section of the public began to exhibit an active interest in the cause which seemed in danger of being temporarily lost through the neglect of politicians. Public Associations showed sympathy with the movement, and Federation Leagues were organised to discuss the Bill and to urge the importance of federal union upon the people. A conference of delegates from Federation Leagues and similar Associations in New South Wales and Victoria was called at Corowa in 1893. The most important suggestion made at this Conference was that the Constitution should be framed by a Convention to be directly elected by the people of each colony for that purpose. This new proposal attracted the favourable attention of Mr. G. H. Reid, then Premier of New South Wales, who perceived that a greater measure of success could be secured by enlisting the active sympathy and aid of the electors, and who brought the principle to the test in 1895. In January of that year he invited the Premiers of the other colonies to meet in conference for the purpose of devising a definite and concerted scheme of action. At this Conference, which was held at Hobart, all the Australasian colonies except New Zealand were represented. It was decided to ask the Parliament of each colony to pass a Bill enabling the electors qualified to vote for members of the Lower House to choose ten persons to represent the colony on a Federal Convention. The work of the Convention, it was determined, should be the framing of a Federal Constitution, to be submitted, in the first instance, to the local Parliaments for suggested amendments, and, after final adoption by the Convention, to the electors of the various colonies for their approval by means of the referendum.

In 1896 a People's Federal Convention, an unofficial gathering of delegates from various Australian organisations, met at Bathurst to discuss the Commonwealth Bill in detail, and by its numbers and enthusiasm gave valuable evidence of the increasing popularity of the movement.

In accordance with the resolutions of the Convention of 1895, Enabling Acts were passed during the following year by New South Wales, Victoria, South Australia, Tasmania, and Western Australia; and were brought into operation by proclamation on the 4th January, 1897. Meanwhile Queensland held aloof from the movement, after several attempts to agree on the question of the representation of the Colony. The Convention met in Adelaide, Mr. C. C. Kingston, Premier of South Australia, being elected President; and Sir Richard Baker, President of the Legislative Council of South Australia, Chairman of Committees; while Mr. Edmund Barton, Q.C., one of the representatives of the mother colony, and a gentleman who had taken a deep interest in the movement, acted as leader of the Convention. The final meeting of the session was held on the 23rd April, when a draft Constitution was adopted for the consideration of the various Parliaments, and at a formal meeting on the 5th May, the Convention adjourned until the 2nd September. On that date the delegates re-assembled in Sydney, and debated the Bill in the light of suggestions made by the Legislatures of the federating colonies. In the course of the proceedings, it was announced that Queensland desired to come within the proposed union; and, in view of this development, and in order to give further opportunity for the consideration of the Bill, the Convention again adjourned. The third and final session was opened in Melbourne on the 20th January, 1898, the Colony of Queensland being still unrepresented; and, after further consideration, the Draft Bill was finally adopted by the Convention on the 16th March for submission to the people.

In its main provisions the Bill of 1898 followed generally that of 1891, yet with some very important alterations. It proposed to establish, under the Crown, a federal union of the Australasian colonies, to be designated the Commonwealth of Australia. A Federal Executive Council was created, to be presided over by a Governor-General appointed by the Queen. The Legislature was to consist of two Houses—a Senate, in which each colony joining the Federation at its inception was conceded the equal representation of six members; and a House of Representatives, to consist of, as nearly as possible, twice the number of Senators, to which the provinces were to send members in proportion to population, with a minimum number of five representatives for each of the original federating states. The principle of payment of members was adopted for the Senate as well as for the House of Representatives, the honorarium being fixed at £400 per annum. The nominative principle for the Upper House was rejected, both Houses being elective, on a suffrage similar to that existing in each colony for the popular Chamber at the foundation of the Commonwealth. At the same time, it was left to the Federal Parliament to establish a federal franchise, which, however, could only operate in the direction of the extension, not the restriction, of any of the existing privileges of the individual colonies; so that in those States where the franchise has been granted to women their right to vote cannot be withdrawn by the central authority so long as adult suffrage prevails. While the House of Representatives was to be elected for a period of three years, Senators were to be appointed for twice that term, provision being made for the retirement of half their number every third year. The capital of the Commonwealth was to be established in federal territory.

Warmly received in Victoria, South Australia, and Tasmania, the Bill was viewed somewhat coldly by a section of the people of New South Wales, and this feeling rapidly developed into one of active hostility, the main points of objection being the financial provisions, equal representation in the Senate, and the difficulty which the larger colonies must experience in securing an amendment of the Constitution in the event of a conflict with the smaller States. So far as the other colonies were concerned, it was evident that the Bill was safe, and public attention throughout Australasia was riveted on New South Wales, where a fierce political contest was raging, which it was recognised would decide the fate of the measure for the time being. The fears expressed by its advocates were not so much in regard to securing a majority in favour of the Bill, as to whether the statutory number of 80,000 votes necessary for its acceptance would be reached. These fears proved to be well founded; for on the 3rd June, 1898, the result of the referendum in New South Wales showed 71,595 votes in favour of the Bill, and 66,228 against it, and it was accordingly lost. In Victoria, Tasmania, and South Australia, on the other hand, the Bill was accepted by triumphant majorities. Western Australia did not put it to the vote; indeed, it was useless to do so, as the Enabling Act of that colony only provided for joining a Federation of which New South Wales should form a part.

The existence of such a strong opposition to the Bill in the mother colony convinced even its most zealous advocates that some changes would have to be made in the Constitution before it would be accepted by the people; consequently, although the general election in New South Wales, held six or seven weeks later, was fought on the Federal issue, yet the opposing parties seemed to occupy somewhat the same ground, and the question narrowed itself down to one as to which should be entrusted with the negotiations to be conducted on behalf of the colony with the view to securing a modification of the objectionable features of the Bill. The new Parliament decided to adopt the procedure of sending the Premier, Mr. Reid, into conference, armed with a series of resolutions affirming its desire to bring about the completion of federal union, but asking the other colonies to agree to the reconsideration of the provisions which were most generally objected to in New South Wales. As they left the Assembly, these resolutions submitted—first, that, with equal representation in the Senate, the three-fifths majority at the joint sitting of the two Houses should give way to a simple majority, or the joint sitting be replaced by a provision for a national referendum; second, that the clause making it incumbent upon the Federal Government to raise, in order to provide for the needs of the States, £3 for every £1 derived from Customs and Excise Duties for its own purposes, and thus ensuring a very high tariff, should be eliminated from the Bill; third, that the site of the Federal Capital should be fixed within the boundaries of New South Wales; fourth, that better provision should be made against the alteration of the boundaries of a State without its own consent; fifth, that the use of inland rivers for the purposes of water conservation and irrigation should be more clearly safeguarded; sixth, that all money Bills should be dealt with in the same manner as Taxation and Appropriation Bills; and seventh, that appeals from the Supreme Courts of the States should uniformly be taken, either to the Privy Council or to the Federal High Court, and not indiscriminately to either; while the House also invited further inquiry into the financial provisions of the Bill, although avowing its willingness to accept these provisions if in other respects the Bill were amended. These were all the resolutions submitted by the Government to the House, but the Assembly appended others in respect to the alteration of the Constitution and the number of Senators, submitting, on the first of these points, that an alteration of the Constitution should take effect, if approved by both Houses and a national referendum; that a proposed alteration should be submitted to the national referendum, if affirmed in two succeeding sessions by an absolute majority in one House, and rejected by the other; and that no proposed alteration, transferring to the Commonwealth any powers retained by a State at the establishment of the federation, should take effect in that State, unless approved by a majority of electors voting therein; and, on the second point, that the number of Senators should be increased from six to not less than eight for each State.

The Legislative Council adopted the resolutions with some important amendments, discarding the suggestion in the first resolution for a national referendum; submitting that the seat of the Federal Government should be established at Sydney; more clearly preserving the rights of the people of the colony to the use of the waters of its inland rivers for purposes of water conservation and irrigation; carrying all appeals from the Supreme Courts of the States to the Privy Council; and declining to affirm its preparedness to accept the financial scheme embodied in the Bill. Further, the House suggested that the plan of submitting proposed alterations of the Constitution to the people by means of the referendum should be altered, and that no rights or powers retained by a State should be afterwards transferred to the Commonwealth without the consent of both Houses of Parliament of that State. The New South Wales Premier decided to submit the resolutions of both Houses to the other Premiers in conference, attaching, however, greater importance to those of the Assembly, as embodying the views of a House which had just returned from the country. This conference was held in Melbourne at the end of January, 1899, Queensland being represented; and an agreement was arrived at, whereby it was decided that, in the event of a disagreement between the two Houses of Parliament, the decision of an absolute majority of the members of the two Houses should be final; that the provision for the retention by the Commonwealth of only one-fourth of the Customs and Excise revenue might be altered or repealed at the end of ten years, another clause being added, permitting the Parliament to grant financial assistance to a State; that no alterations in the boundaries of a State should be made without the approval of the people as well as of the Parliament of that State; and that the seat of Government should be in New South Wales, at such place, at least 100 miles from Sydney, as might be determined by the Federal Parliament, and within an area of 100 square miles of territory, to be acquired by the Commonwealth, it being provided that the Parliament should sit at Melbourne until it met at the seat of Government. A special session of the New South Wales Parliament was convened to deal with this agreement, and the Legislative Assembly passed an Enabling Bill, referring the amended Constitution to the electors. The Council, however, amended the Bill demanding—first, the postponement of the referendum for a period of three months; second, making it necessary for the minimum vote cast in favour of the Bill to be one-fourth of the total number of electors on the roll; third, deferring the entrance of New South Wales into the Federation until Queensland should come in. These amendments were not accepted by the Assembly, and a conference between representatives of the two Houses was arranged; but this proved abortive, and twelve new members were appointed to the Upper House in order to secure the passage of the Bill. This course had the effect desired by the Government; for the Council passed the Bill on the 19th April, an amendment postponing the referendum for eight weeks being accepted by the Assembly. The Bill received its final assent on the 22nd April, and the 20th June following was appointed as the date of the referendum. The poll resulted in a majority of 24,679 in favour of the Bill, the votes recorded for and against being 107,420 and 82,741 respectively. South Australia on the 29th April had re-affirmed its acceptance of the Bill by a majority of 48,937 votes, in Victoria it was again passed with a majority of 142,848 on the 27th July, while on the same date the Bill passed in Tasmania with a margin in its favour of 12,646 votes. Queensland adopted the measure on the 2nd September by a majority of 6,216. Western Australia still hung back, but at a referendum taken on the 31st July, 1900, the Bill was accepted with the decisive majority of 25,109 votes.

Though the Bill was favourably received by the Imperial Government, certain amendments, the most important of which referred to the appeal to the Privy Council, were proposed by Mr. Chamberlain, the Secretary of State for the Colonies. At a Premier's Conference, held in Sydney at the end of January, it was decided to send delegates to England from each of the federating colonies, who were to give their joint support to the Bill, but were not to consent to any amendment of its provisions. The six delegates arrived in England in March, 1900, and a series of conferences took place amongst themselves, and also with officers representing the Imperial Government. The most serious ground of contention was Clause 74, which prohibited appeals to Her Majesty in Council in matters involving the interpretation of the Constitution of the Commonwealth or of a State unless the public interests of other parts of Her Majesty's dominions were concerned. On all other questions the right of appeal from Supreme Courts of the States, as well as from the Federal High Court, was left untouched. Mr. Chamberlain proposed that, notwithstanding anything in the Constitution, the prerogative of Her Majesty of granting special leave to appeal might be exercised with respect to any judgment or order of the High Court of the Commonwealth or of the Supreme Court of any State. In other words, the Secretary of State insisted that Clause 74 should be amended so as to maintain the royal prerogative as to appeals on constitutional questions as well as other matters, while at the same time he promised a re-constituted Court of Appeal for the Empire in which the Australian Colonies would find representation. The delegates opposed most strongly the submission of constitutional disputes to the decision of the Privy Council under any pretext. A compromise, supported by four of the six delegates, was therefore agreed upon, by which the consent of the Executive Government or Governments was made a necessary condition precedent to an appeal from the High Court to the Privy Council on constitutional questions. The new arrangement, however, evoked such hostile criticism in the colonies that the Premiers cabled a rejection of it. A fresh compromise was thereupon arrived at, by which it was determined that the right of appeal to the Privy Council, where a constitutional point purely Australian in character was involved, might be granted at the pleasure of the High Court. By this settlement the finality of the decisions of the High Court upon matters of constitutional interpretation is preserved. The arrangement proved satisfactory to both sides, and the amendment was accepted by the legislatures of the federating colonies. Thenceforward no further objection was made to the passing of the measure, and it received the royal assent on the 9th July.

Lord Hopetoun, who had formerly occupied the position of Governor of Victoria, was appointed first Governor-General of the Commonwealth of Australia, and arrived in Sydney on the 15th December. Meanwhile, by royal proclamation, the first day of January, 1901, was fixed on as the date of inauguration of the new Commonwealth. The first Federal Ministry was formed under the leadership of Mr. (now Sir) E. Barton, and was composed of the following members:—

Mr. (now Sir) E. Barton (N.S.W.), Prime Minister and Minister of State for External Affairs; Sir William Lyne (N.S.W.), Minister of State for

Home Affairs; Sir George Turner (Vic.), Treasurer; Mr. Alfred Deakin (Vic.), Attorney-General and Minister for Justice; Mr. C. C. Kingston (S.A.), Minister for Trade and Customs; Sir J. R. Dickson (Q.), Minister for Defence; Sir John Forrest (W.A.), Postmaster-General. Mr. R. E. O'Connor (N.S.W.), and Mr. (now Sir) N. E. Lewis (Tas.) were also appointed as Ministers without portfolio, the former occupying the position of Vice-President of the Executive Council. A few days later Sir James Dickson died after a short illness, and the portfolio of Minister of Defence was assigned to Sir John Forrest, while Mr. J. G. Drake, who held office as Postmaster-General of Queensland, was appointed to a similar position in the Federal Executive. Mr. Lewis only held office in the Commonwealth Cabinet until the Federal elections had taken place, when he resigned, and was succeeded by Sir Philip O. Fysh. The Ministry as above constituted was sworn in on the 1st January, 1901, the ceremony taking place in a specially-erected pavilion in the Centennial Park, Sydney. The festivities in connection with this epoch-making event in Australian history lasted for several days, additional interest being lent to the proceedings by the presence of detachments of troops from Great Britain, India, and the various provinces of Australasia. The death of Queen Victoria, which took place on the 22nd January, 1901, possesses a melancholy interest for these States from the fact that one of the last great public acts of the deceased sovereign was the signing of the proclamation establishing the Commonwealth. Under the Constitution, the control of Customs and Excise in the various States passed over to the Federal authority with the inauguration of the Commonwealth, and attention was at once devoted to placing matters in connection with these services in working order. The taking over of the postal administrations of the States was not finally dealt with till the 1st March, and the same date saw the transfer of the Defence Departments. These were the only divisions of State administration over which the Commonwealth Government thought necessary to assume control, though the Constitution rendered it permissible to take over lighthouses, lightships, beacons, buoys, and quarantine, by the simple act of proclaiming the dates, and without further legislation.

As it was necessary for the Federal elections to take place early in 1901, much detail work was cast upon the Ministry in the shape of arranging for the various preliminaries in connection with recording the votes in the six States. In the first Parliament each State returned six members to the Senate, while section 26 of the Constitution provided for the number of representatives in the Lower House as follows:—New South Wales, 26; Victoria, 23; Queensland, 9; South Australia, 7; Western Australia, 5; Tasmania, 5. Parliament may increase or diminish the number of members, provided that it does not alter the proportion of members to Senators, and does not bring the number of members returned from an original State below five. The chief interest in the elections settled round the question of the fiscal policy of the new

Commonwealth. When the Constitution Act was under consideration, the problem arose of ensuring a sufficient Customs Revenue to enable each State to receive back from the Federal Treasurer an amount equal to what its own receipts would have been, less the net expenditure of the Commonwealth. This necessity was met by the "Braddon Clause," as section 87 was called, providing that during a period of ten years after the establishment of the Commonwealth, and thereafter until further legislative action is taken by Parliament, not more than one-fourth of the net revenue of the Commonwealth from Customs and Excise shall be applied annually towards Commonwealth Expenditure. The balance of three-fourths is to be returned to the States, or applied towards the payment of interest on the debts of the several States taken over by the Commonwealth. Under these circumstances it was recognised that it would be necessary to raise a revenue, certainly over £6,000,000 and more probably approximating £8,500,000, so that the States should be recouped in the manner indicated. It was, therefore, apparent that the elections could not be contested on a clear-cut Freetrade-Protection issue, and the parties divided on the question as to whether the tariff should be revenue-producing alone, or of a more or less protective character. The Prime Minister, in his official declaration of ministerial policy, announced himself in favour of a tariff that would yield revenue without destroying industries, or a policy of "moderate protection." The fiscal issue was made most prominent in New South Wales and Victoria, although in the other States more or less powerful organisations ranged themselves on either side. Representatives of labour, for the most part, took up an independent position.

The elections were conducted as provided by the different State laws. Each State voted as one constituency for the Senate, and in Tasmania and South Australia the same procedure was adopted in voting for the House of Representatives. The elections took place on the 29th and 30th March, each of the opposing parties claiming the victory when the final results were published. From the declared policy of the candidates it appeared probable that the protectionists would have a majority in the Lower House, while the "revenue-tariffists" had a stronger hand in the Senate. The attitude of the Labour Party, which had secured 23 seats in the two Houses, was now of prime importance, but a semi-official statement from one of their number made it clear that the party intended to "retain the balance of power and use their strength only to defeat a government which refused to obey the will of the people." In addition to completing arrangements for the mechanical working of both Houses, preliminary action with regard to the framing of a tariff had to be initiated in the interval between the elections and the meeting of Parliament. The Prime Minister was also called upon to deal with questions affecting the condition of affairs in the New Hebrides, and the ownership of Kerguelen Island, and the policy pursued in these matters showed that the Commonwealth was prepared to take cognisance of subjects that lay outside the dominion of Australia. This development met with some adverse criticism, but, generally speaking, the introduction into Australian politics of a more-extended range of interests and a broader aspect of national life was hailed with satisfaction.

The ceremony of opening the first session of the first Federal Parliament of the Commonwealth took place on the 9th May, 1901, in the Exhibition Building at Melbourne, which had been specially decorated for the occasion. Under commission from His Majesty King Edward VII., His Royal Highness the Duke of Cornwall and York formally opened the Parliament and in his speech from the throne, reference was made to His Majesty's deep interest in the consummation of Australian union, and eloquent testimony was given to the loyalty and devotion of the Colonies to the Empire. On the same day the Senate elected Sir Richard Chaffey Baker, of South Australia, as its first President, while the House of Representatives elected Mr. Frederick William Holder, also of South Australia, as Speaker. The Governor-General delivered his speech to members of both Houses on the following day, in which an outline was given of the policy of the Commonwealth. In addition to proposals necessary for adapting the recently transferred Customs and Excise, Posts and Telegraphs, and Defence Departments to the new conditions, measures covering a wide range of subjects were promised. Bills establishing a High Court of Australia, a Commission for the execution and maintenance of the provisions of the Constitution relating to Trade and Commerce, and for regulating the Public Service of the Federation were included in the first part of the Government programme, and the selection of the site for a Federal capital was looked upon as a matter of comparative urgency. As regards the fiscal policy, it was stated that "The fiscal proposals of any Government must be largely dependent on the financial exigencies of the States. The adoption of the existing tariff of any one of these States is impracticable, and would be unfair. To secure a reasonably sufficient return of surplus revenue to each State, so as fully to observe the intention of the Constitution, while avoiding unnecessary destruction of sources of employment, is a work which prohibits a rigid adherence to fiscal theories. Revenue must, of course, be the first consideration, but existing tariffs have in all States given rise to industries, many of which are so substantial that my advisers consider that any policy tending to destroy them is inadmissible. A tariff which gives fair consideration to these factors must necessarily operate protectively as well as for production of revenue."

Bills were also promised dealing with the restriction of immigration of Asiatics, and the diminution and gradual abolition of the introduction of labour from the South Sea Islands, while measures were stated to be in preparation providing for conciliation and arbitration in cases of industrial disputes extending beyond the limits of any one State, for the uniform administration of the law relating to patents and inventions, and for a uniform franchise in all federal elections. Amongst other legislation foreshadowed, but not designed for immediate consideration, were Bills dealing with Old Age Pensions, Banking Laws, Federal Elections, Navigation, Shipping, Quarantine, and the management of State Debts. Reference was also made, and attention promised to the question of the relations of the Commonwealth with the islands of the Pacific, the construction of railways, connecting the eastern states with Western Australia, and also the Northern Territory of South Australia, while with regard to the latter its transference to the Commonwealth was also projected. Mention was also made of such matters as the strengthening of Commonwealth defences, the assimilation of postal and telegraph rates, and the adoption of universal penny postage. After the formal opening of Parliament, both Houses adjourned until the 21st May, when the real work of the session began. Early in the debate on the Address in Reply the Labour Party raised the question of a "White Australia" by moving amendments to the effect that black labour on the sugar plantations of Queensland and northern New South Wales should cease at once, but on the assurance being given that the Ministry had the matter under consideration the amendments were negatived. The address was finally adopted in the Senate on the 31st May, and in the House of Representatives on June 5th, and the way was then clear for practical legislation.

The first measure introduced into the House of Representatives was the Acts of Parliament Interpretation Bill on the 10th May, while in the Senate leave to introduce the Service and Execution of Process Bill was moved for on the opening day. On June 5th notification was given of several bills dealing with such subjects as Pacific Island Labourers, Judiciary, High Court of Procedure, Federal Elections, Federal Franchise, Conciliation and Arbitration, Immigration Restriction, Public Service, Interstate Commission, Acquisition of Property for Public Purposes, Defence, and Customs. On the same date the Postmaster-General introduced the Post and Telegraphs Bill in the Senate.

Early in the session the Senate gave token of its intention to maintain strictly the privileges granted to it by the Constitution. Exception was taken to the first Supply Bill sent from the House of Representatives because the accounts of proposed expenditure had not been incorporated in the measure, but submitted in the form of a schedule. The Bill was returned to the Lower House, which consented to amend it in accordance with the wishes of the Senate. In the House of Representatives deliberations were commenced on the Public Service Bill, and although the Lower House had passed the measure on to the Senate by the end of July it was not till near the close of the session that it finally became law. The second reading of the Customs Bill, a purely machinery measure, passed the Lower House early in July, but the Defence Bill, which proposed to introduce compulsory military service, was shelved. Another measure which met with little success was the Property Acquisition Bill, the various schemes devised for payment for property acquired from individuals or States evoking much opposition from the State Governments, while the Government did not persevere with the bill to institute the Interstate Commission. During Jul and August, in addition to Supply Bills, the Acts Interpretation Actyand an Audit Act received royal assent, while the State Laws and Records Recognition Bill had been practically finally dealt with, and the Postal Bill (assented to on the 20th November) was also in a fair way towards completion, a novel clause being inserted in the latter measure at the instigation of the Labour Party providing for the employment of white labour only in the carriage of mails. While awaiting the completion of these and of other measures preparatory to the introduction of the tariff, some important legislation was introduced in the shape of the Immigration Restriction Bill and the Pacific Islands Labourers Bill.

Under the Constitution, a period of two years was allowed before the imposition of uniform duties became compulsory, but the feeling, both in Parliament and amongst the people of the various States, was in favour of its early introduction in order to secure adequate adjustment of commercial relations. Before the tariff proposals proper could be tabled, however, various machinery measures, such as the Customs Bill, already mentioned, the Excise Bill, and the Beer Excise and Distillery Bills had to be dealt with. Attention was again devoted to the Immigration Restriction Bill, and the Pacific Islands Labourers Bill. After a long debate the first of these measures was passed, but not quite in the form desired by the labour organisation. The Pacific Island Labourers Bill provides for a gradual lessening of the number of Kanakas employed in the northern plantations up till 1904, and none were to enter Australia after the 31st March in that year, while no agreement was to be made, or remain in force, after the same date in 1906. As it stood, the measure met with strenuous opposition in Queensland, where it was maintained that the sugar industry would be extinguished if the Bill became law. Despite the efforts made, both in Parliament and outside, the Bill passed both Houses practically unamended, and received the royal assent at the end of the year.

While the above-mentioned Bills were before the House, in some form or another, the Treasurer delivered his budget speech, and the tariff was laid on the table by the Minister for Trade and Customs on the 8th October. Reference was made by the Treasurer to the financial considerations involved in constructing the proposals. The Cabinet had decided that £21,000,000 represented the value of goods available for taxation in a normal year, and on this amount duties had been framed to produce £2 7s. 6d. per head of revenue. In a normal year the yield from the Customs was estimated at £7,388,056, which with £1,554,345 from Excise, brought the total to £8,942,401. It was proposed to raise a loan of £1,000,000, and a sinking fund for redemption of loans was to be provided, such fund to be invested in Commonwealth Stock. The Minister of Trade and Customs, upon whom devolved the duty of tabling the tariff, did so with the declaration that interstate freetrade had arrived. After stating that the tariff was neither freetrade nor protectionist in character, the Minister proceeded to detail the methods under which it had been drawn up. From the total annual value of imports into the Commonwealth, calculated at £63,000,000, various deductions were to be made. The establishment of interstate freetrade took away £29,000,000 from this sum, and it was estimated that the total taxable balance left amounted to £21,000,000. Of this amount the value of narcotics and stimulants was £1,910,000, and the duties proposed on these articles, together with £1,131,000 from excise would yield £4,100,000. From fixed and composite duties averaging 30·94 per cent. £2,020,471 would be raised on £6,530,000 worth of goods, and ad valorem duties ranging from 10 per cent. to 25 per cent. would yield £2,362,211 on £12,583,740 worth of goods, or an average of 18·7 per cent. The excise on sugar was to be charged from the 1st July, 1902, and would cease in 1907, when, according to the terms of the Kanaka Bill, sugar would be produced by white labour. In the course of his speech the Minister indicated that the Government intended to adopt a reasonable system of bonuses to encourage the establishment or extension of industries which were not yet established, or to which protection could not be immediately extended.

It was to be expected that a tariff constructed under such difficulties as beset the framers would not meet with unqualified approval, and immediate signs were not wanting that extensive amendments would be proposed. On the 15th October the Right Hon. G. H. Reid, the leader of the Opposition, moved a vote of censure to the effect that the financial and tariff proposals of the Government did not meet with the approval of the House. After a protracted debate the motion was put to the vote on the 1st November, and resulted in a victory for the Government by a majority of 14, every member of the House being represented.

When finally dealt with in Committee the tariff had undergone extensive alteration. Amongst the more important changes was the abolition of composite duties, a novel form of impost in most of the States, and in many instances the rates were lessened. The duties on tea and kerosene were abandoned, and the placing of these items on the free list deprived the Treasurer of some £500,000 of his anticipated revenue. The abolition of these duties was viewed with dismay by the Treasurers of the smaller States, and Queensland, South Australia, and Tasmania were united in their protest. Assurance was, however, given by the Government that if it were found necessary fresh duties would be imposed at a ater date. The tariff finally emerged from the House of Representatives during the second week in April, and the necessary machinery measures were thereupon pushed through. Under the Constitution the Senate has no power to alter the tariff, but it may uggest alterations and refuse o pass the duties until such suggestions have been acceded ;

The transfer of British New Guinea to the Commonwealth, effected towards the close of 1901, is interesting, as the territory possesses great, though almost undeveloped, resources, while in connection with Commonwealth defences, the position may prove of strategic importance.

One of the disabilities under which the Commonwealth laboured during the first months of its existence was the absence of a Federal Judicature to deal with cases arising out of the administration of the Federal laws. In some instances, of course, the State Courts were appealed to, but there was some doubt as to whether the Commonwealth itself could be sued under the existing legislation. To obviate in some measure this inconvenience, the State Laws and Records Recognition Act and the Service and Execution of Process Act were introduced at the beginning of the session, and the Punishment of Offences Act was also passed to provide that offenders against the Commonwealth might be dealt with by State laws. It was recognised, however, that a Judiciary Bill and High Court of Procedure Bill were still urgently needed. The second reading of the former was moved on the 18th March. This Bill provided for a High Court, with one Chief Justice and four other justices; the principal seat of the Court to be at the Federal capital. Power was given to appoint a judge of the Supreme Court of any State as a judge of the High Court sitting in Chambers, in order to enable the initiatory steps to actual hearing to be proceeded with prior to the visit of a High Court judge. The measure also allotted certain Federal jurisdiction to State Courts, and permitted the transfer in certain instances of cases from the State Courts to the High Court. Subsequently the Bill was shelved by the Government until a more favourable opportunity presented itself for its discussion.

During 1901 efforts were made, both in Parliament and by public men outside, to have a site fixed on for the Federal Capital. Several localities were suggested and discussed, and the Government of New South Wales obtained reports as to their suitableness, but it was not till 1902 that any definite move was made by the Federal Parliament. In February certain members of the Senate made a tour of inspection to several of the suggested sites, while members of the House of Representatives were given a similar opportunity in May. Both excursions were of necessity somewhat hurried, but they at least served the useful purpose of giving members some knowledge as to the localities suggested. The sites visited included Albury, Tumut, Dalgety, Wagga, Yass, Goulburn, Orange, Cooma, Bombala, and Armidale.

Towards the close of 1901 a commencement was made with the laying of a Pacific Cable, the Australian terminal of which is at Southport, in Queensland. From this point the line runs to Norfolk Island, thence to New Zealand, to Fiji, to Fanning Island, and to Vancouver. The cable was completed and opened for business in November, 1902.

During the adjournment at the end of 1901 the Premier received a request from the Imperial Authorities for 1,000 troops for service in South Africa. This contingent was made up of 348 men each from

Victoria and New South Wales, 116 each from Queensland and South Australia, and 116 from Tasmania and Western Australia combined, the united forces being known, at a later date, as the Australian Commonwealth Horse. When the House met after vacation, the Premier took occasion to refer to the charges made against the people and army of the Empire, and moved resolutions expressive of the determination of the Commonwealth to give all the assistance in its power to His Majesty's Government with a view to a speedy termination of the war. On the 20th January the Government sent another contingent of 1,000 men, and in March a request was received for 2,000 additional troops, and these were also despatched.

At one time it seemed as though the new legislation of the Commonwealth would involve the Federal Government in international complications. By the operation of the Customs Act it was provided that deep sea vessels should pay duty on all stores consumed by passengers and crew during the period between their first touching at an Australian port until they finally left the coast. When a mail steamer arrived at a Western Australian port, therefore, a Customs official boarded the vessel, superintended the removal of sufficient stores to last till the next port of call, and sealed up the storeroom. If on arrival at the next port these seals were found to have been broken, prosecution followed. The first case occurred in connection with an English mailboat, and the Full Court of Victoria decided in favour of the Commonwealth. The owners of the vessel pleaded that, as they were on the high seas between the ports, the Commonwealth had no jurisdiction. When the law was enforced with reference to the German vessels, the matter was taken up warmly by the authorities in Germany, and representations were made to the British Government on the matter. An amicable settlement was, however, arrived at, both English and foreign steamship companies agreeing to the payment of the duties until the matter had been decided by the Privy Council. Judgment was given by the Privy Council in favour of the Commonwealth towards the close of 1903.

Universal regret was expressed throughout the Commonwealth when it became known in May, 1902, that the Earl of Hopetoun had resigned his office as Governor-General. Lord Tennyson, Governor of South Australia, was appointed to the position in November; but, in accordance with his wishes, held office only until January, 1904, when he was succeeded by Lord Northcote.

In June an Imperial Conference was held in London, the Hon. E. Barton being delegated to represent the Commonwealth of Australia. The subjects for discussion suggested by the Commonwealth included (1) Army and Navy supply contracts; (2) Ocean cables and purchase thereof; (3) Imperial Court of Appeal; (4) Mutual protection of patents; (5) Loss of most favoured nation treatment if preference given to British manufacturers; (6) Imperial stamp charges for colonial bonds. The decisions of the Conference were to be brought before Parliament on its re-assembling.

In August the Tariff Bill was again under consideration by the Senate. After some three or four months spent in revising the Bill as passed by the House of Representatives, the Senate sent down requests for 103 amendments to be made. Of these 51 were acceded to by the Lower Chamber and the remaining 52 were rejected. The Senate pressed for consideration of its requests, and the Lower House proving obdurate, it was feared that a deadlock would ensue. The conciliatory attitude of both Houses after maturer consideration happily averted this crisis, the Lower Chamber agreeing to a number of the Senate's proposals, while the two Houses compromised as to the main points at issue. The Bill finally became law on the 10th September, a little over eleven months after its introduction.

The important matter of re-arranging the electorates of the Commonwealth was dealt with at the close of the session, and a Commissioner for each State was appointed. The duty of the Commissioner was to divide his State into electorates embracing, as far as possible, equal numbers of electors, deviations from equality on account of special circumstances detailed in the Federal Elections Act being permitted within certain specified limits. The total number of members to which a state is entitled is determined by section 24 of the Constitution Act, which provides that the population of the Commonwealth shall be determined according to the latest statistics, and a quota thereof ascertained by dividing that population by twice the number of the Senate (72). The number of representatives to which a State is entitled being determined by dividing the population by the ascertained quota, any remainder on such division greater than one-half of the quota is taken as entitling a State to one more member. In reckoning the number of people, aborigines are to be excluded as well as all persons of any race disqualified from voting at elections for the more numerous House of Parliament.

This last provision is an extremely important one. It will be found on reference to the Acts governing the exercise of the franchise that several states have an alien exclusion provision; thus Section 6 of the Queensland Act of 1885 provides that "No aboriginal native of Australia, India, China, or of the South Sea Islands shall be entitled to be entered on the roll except in respect of freehold qualification."

The question arises whether it can be said that all persons of any race are disqualified from voting in view of the exception in regard to a freehold qualification. The matter was submitted to the Attorney-General of the Commonwealth, who decided that the provision of the Queensland Act does disqualify all persons of the races named within the meaning of Section 25 of the Constitution, and persons of those races cannot therefore be reckoned for electoral purposes as people of the Commonwealth. This decision affects Queensland, South Australia, and Western Australia only, as the laws in force in New South Wales, Victoria, and Tasmania do not exclude "all persons of any specified race."

The persons disqualified under the various State Acts are the aboriginal natives of India, China, and the South Sea Islands by

Queensland; the aboriginal natives of Asia and Africa, and persons of half-blood, by Western Australia; and the immigrants under the "Indian Immigration Act, 1882," in the Northern Territory of South Australia.

In establishing a quota it will be necessary, therefore, to exclude from consideration the aliens disqualified by state electoral laws, and, making this exclusion, the population of the Commonwealth on the 30th June, 1902, was 3,827,859 persons, distributed as follows:—

State.	Population, 30th June, 1902, exclusive of Aborigines.	Aliens, Disqualified by State Electoral Acts.	Population, excluding Aborigines and Aliens.	Number of Representatives.
New South Wales	1,391,822	......	1,391,822	26·2
Victoria	1,206,478	......	1,206,478	22·7
Queensland	509,585	18,038	491,547	9·2
South Australia	363,686	2,862	360,824	6·8
Western Australia	208,325	3,709	204,616	3·9
Tasmania	172,572	......	172,572	3·2
Total	3,852,468	24,609	3,827,859	72·0

A quota was therefore 53,165, and the number of members which the various states were entitled to return at the last election was therefore—

New South Wales	26	Western Australia	5
Victoria	23	Tasmania	5
Queensland	9		
South Australia	7		75

Later returns than those available when the above table was compiled give the number of aliens in South Australia as 2,805, and in Western Australia, 3,668. If the number of aliens in Western Australia shown to be disqualified by the State Electoral Acts be compared with the number of persons set down in a later chapter as natives of Asia and Africa, it will be found that the former is apparently below the truth. This is due to the fact that the census returns do not enable a distinction to be made between aboriginal natives and persons born of white parents, and the number for Western Australia will lie somewhere between 3,668 and 5,066, shown on page 189. What the true figure is it is now impossible to say. The minimum number, therefore, in the absence of absolute evidence to the contrary, must be taken in forming an estimate of the Commonwealth population for electoral purposes. The present representation of the different States in the House of Representatives was determined on the population of the Commonwealth on the 30th June, 1902. If the population of twelve months later had been taken, the existing representation would have remained unaltered.

Towards the close of 1902, a difficulty arose in connection with granting permission to enter the Commonwealth to six operatives who had been brought out from England under contract to labour in a hat factory at Sydney. The Immigration Restriction Act expressly forbids the introduction of immigrants under contract to perform manual labour in the Commonwealth, unless it can be shown that such persons possess special qualifications required in the Commonwealth. As soon as a declaration was made to the effect that the men were specially skilled, they were permitted to land. The incident aroused a good deal of angry comment at the time, but it is clear that the Federal authorities simply complied with the law in detaining the operatives on board ship until the necessary declaration was forthcoming.

In view of the senatorial elections to be held at the close of 1903, and consequent on the extension of the Commonwealth franchise to all adults, the work of re-adjustment of the various Federal electorates was vigorously pushed forward. When the returns were published early in 1903, it was found that there were marked discrepancies in some districts between the number of electors shown and the persons of voting age as recorded at the census. Special efforts were therefore made to ensure the enrolment of all persons qualified to vote, and the rolls, as finally compiled, accounted for all but a very small proportion of those entitled to the suffrage.

The first session of the first Federal Parliament concluded its labours on the 10th October, 1902, after a period of activity lasting seventeen months. The second session opened on the 26th May, 1903. Attention was at once devoted to the passage of a Judiciary Bill and a Sugar Bonus Bill. The need for the former measure had already been made apparent, for early in April a decision given by the Chief Justice of Victoria impugned the validity of the Customs Act, while just previously the Supreme Court of New South Wales had denied the power of the Commonwealth to tax State Government imports. "The Constitution," as has been pointed out, "is in effect a deed of national partnership between the States, and until a Federal Court is established there exists no authority competent to settle its true meaning where differences take place as to its interpretation." The Government showed its earnestness in the matter by introducing the Judiciary Bill on the 26th May, while the first reading of the High Court Procedure Bill took place on the 9th June.

The question of the division of cost of the excise rebate of £2 per ton granted to Australian sugar planters who employ white labour occupied the attention of the Cabinet in the early months of 1903. It was anticipated when the Bill was passed that a fair division of the rebate would fall to the share of each State but the system broke down owing to the large importation of foreign sugar into Victoria and South Australia, which consequently consumed little white-grown Australian sugar, and it was found that Queensland and New South Wales, the sugar producing States, had to bear the brunt of the payment. Both of these

States urged the necessity for treating the payment as a bonus, and charging it to all the States in proportion to population. This course eventually was adopted, and the Sugar Rebate Abolition Bill was presented and read the first time on the 10th June, and the Sugar Bonus Bill was also introduced on the same date.

On the 12th June the Report of the Select Committee on Commonwealth Coinage, which was ordered to be printed on the 4th April, 1902, was presented to Parliament, and a motion for its adoption was proposed. The Committee recommended that the Commonwealth should have its own silver coinage with the profits arising therefrom, and in addition proposed the introduction of a decimal system. Under this system the sovereign, half-sovereign, florin, shilling, and sixpence were to be retained, but provision was made for four new coins—a mixed coin equal to a tenth of a florin (2·4d), and three bronze coins, equal respectively to 0·96d, 0·48d, and 0·24d. The question of reform in the coinage has not evoked widespread interest, but the useful labours of the Committee will sooner or later be recognised.

Royal assent to the Sugar Bounty Bill and the Sugar Rebate Abolition Bill was reported on the 31st July, and on the 26th August following the Judiciary Bill became law. In consequence of the retirement of Mr. Kingston from the portfolio of Trade and Customs on the 24th July some rearrangement of the Cabinet became necessary. Sir William Lyne took over the administration of the Customs Department on the 11th August, and Sir John Forrest assumed the direction of the Department of Home Affairs on the same date. On the 10th August the Hon. J. G. Drake accepted the portfolio of Minister of Defence, and the portfolio of Postmaster-General was filled by the appointment of the Hon. Sir P. O. Fysh. On the 18th August Mr. G. H. Reid, leader of the Opposition, resigned his seat in the House of Representatives as a protest against the action of the Government in connection with the re-arrangement of the Federal electorates. Early in the following month Mr Reid was re-elected, a remarkable feature of the election contest being that out of a total of 13,000 electors on the rolls in the East Sydney division, only about 2,000 took the trouble to record their votes.

On the 24th September it was announced in the House of Representatives that the Premier, Sir Edmund Barton, had tendered his resignation, and that the Governor-General had called upon Mr. Deakin to undertake the task of re-arranging the Ministry. The new administration comprised the following members :—Minister for External Affairs, Hon. Alfred Deakin ; Attorney-General, Hon. James George Drake ; Minister for Home Affairs, Right Hon. Sir John Forrest, P.C., G.C.M.G. ; Treasurer, Right Hon. Sir George Turner, P.C., K.C.M.G. ; Minister of Trade and Customs, Hon. Sir William John Lyne, K.C.M.G. ; Minister of Defence, Hon. Austin Chapman ; Postmaster-General, Hon. Sir Philip Oakley Fysh, K.C.M.G. ; Vice-President of Executive Council, Hon. Thomas Playford. On the same day it was announced that Sir S. W. Griffith had accepted the position of Chief Justice of the Federal High Court, while Sir Edmund Barton and Mr. R. E. O'Connor had agreed to accept positions on the High Court Bench. The first sitting of the newly-constituted Court was held in Melbourne on the 7th October.

It was hoped that the question of selecting a site for the Federal capital would have been disposed of during the session of 1903, but this matter will now have to be dealt with by the parliament of 1904. The House of Representatives favoured Tumut as the site, while the Senate selected Bombala, a bill introduced by the Government to deal with the matter being allowed to lapse.

Prior to the formal prorogation on the 22nd October, assent was given to several important legislative enactments. The Defence Bill provides for a uniform system of defence for the Commonwealth, which it is hoped will increase the efficiency of the forces, while avoiding unnecessary expense; and the Patents Bill enables inventors to secure protection for their inventions throughout the Commonwealth with the minimum of expense and trouble. Under the provisions of the "Naturalisation Act of 1903," which was assented to on the 13th October, the right of issuing certificates of naturalisation is exclusively vested in the government of the Commonwealth, and after the commencement of this Act no certificate of naturalisation or letters of naturalisation issued under any state Act shall have any effect.

Parliament was dissolved on the 24th November, and the elections of members of the House of Representatives and of Senators to replace those who retired in accordance with the terms of the Constitution Act, took place on the 16th December. The following table shows the number of electors on the roll, together with the number and proportion of those who recorded their votes at the election of Senators in each state. The figures have been obtained from preliminary returns, the complete official records not being available at the time of publication of this volume.

State.	Electors on the Rolls.	Effective Voters.	Proportion of Effective Voters to Total Electors.
			per cent.
New South Wales	679,791	313,239	46·1
Victoria	603,000	306,617	50·8
Queensland	227,186	120,401	53·0
South Australia	165,742	53,580	32·3
Western Australia	116,195	31,149	26·8
Tasmania	81,880	35,546	43·4
Commonwealth	1,873,794	860,532	45·9

As the table shows, the proportion of effective voters represented only 45·9 per cent. of the total voters enrolled, the percentages ranging from 26·8 in Western Australia to 50·8 in Victoria. The figures point to a remarkable degree of apathy on the part of a large proportion of the population with respect to the exercise of the franchise, and it would appear as if the value placed on the privilege of voting varied in the different states. It is not possible, however, to draw any hard and fast inference from the above figures, as the proportions are liable to be affected by various causes, such as weather conditions, accessibility of polling places, and other local influences.

CONSTITUTION OF THE COMMONWEALTH.

WHEREAS the people of New South Wales, Victoria, South Australia, Queensland, and Tasmania humbly relying on the blessing of Almighty God, have agreed to unite in one indissoluble Federal Commonwealth under the Crown of the United Kingdom of Great Britain and Ireland, and under the Constitution hereby established:

And whereas it is expedient to provide for the admission into the Commonwealth of other Australasian Colonies and possessions of the Queen:

Be it therefore enacted by the Queen's Most Excellent Majesty, by and with the advice and consent of the Lords Spiritual and Temporal, and Commons, in this present Parliament assembled, and by the authority of the same, as follows:—

1. This Act may be cited as "The Commonwealth of Australia Constitution Act."

2. The provisions of this Act referring to the Queen shall extend to Her Majesty's heirs and successors in the sovereignty of the United Kingdom.

3. It shall be lawful for the Queen, with the advice of the Privy Council, to declare by Proclamation that, on and after a day therein appointed, not being later than one year after the passing of this Act, the people of New South Wales, Victoria, South Australia, Queensland, and Tasmania, and also, if Her Majesty is satisfied that the people of Western Australia have agreed thereto, of Western Australia, shall be united in a Federal Commonwealth under the name of "The Commonwealth of Australia." But the Queen may, at any time after the Proclamation, appoint a Governor-General for the Commonwealth.

4. The Commonwealth shall be established, and the Constitution of the Commonwealth shall take effect on and after the day so appointed. But the Parliaments of the several Colonies may at any time after the passing of this Act make any such laws, to come into operation on the day so appointed, as they might have made if the Constitution had taken effect at the passing of this Act.

5. This Act, and all laws made by the Parliament of the Commonwealth under the Constitution, shall be binding on the Courts, Judges, and people of every State, and of every part of the Commonwealth, notwithstanding anything in the laws of any State; and the laws of the Commonwealth shall be in force on all British ships, the Queen's ships of war excepted, whose first port of clearance and whose port of destination are in the Commonwealth.

6. "The Commonwealth" shall mean the Commonwealth of Australia as established under this Act.

"The States" shall mean such of the Colonies of New South Wales New Zealand, Queensland, Tasmania, Victoria, Western Australia, and South Australia, including the Northern Territory of South Australia, as for the time being are parts of the Commonwealth, and such Colonies or Territories as may be admitted into or established by the Commonwealth as States; and each of such parts of the Commonwealth shall be called a "State."

"Original States" shall mean such States as are parts of the Commonwealth at its establishment.

7. The Federal Council of Australasia Act, 1885, is hereby repealed, but so as not to affect any laws passed by the Federal Council of Australasia and in force at the establishment of the Commonwealth.

Any such law may be repealed as to any State by The Parliament of the Commonwealth, or as to any colony not being a State by The Parliament thereof.

8. After the passing of this Act the Colonial Boundaries Act, 1895, shall not apply to any colony which becomes a State of the Commonwealth; but the Commonwealth shall be taken to be a self-governing colony for the purposes of that Act.

9. The Constitution of the Commonwealth shall be as follows:—

CHAPTER I.

THE PARLIAMENT.

Part I.—General.

1. The legislative power of the Commonwealth shall be vested in a Federal Parliament, which shall consist of the Queen, a Senate, and a House of Representatives, and which is hereinafter called "The Parliament," or "The Parliament of the Commonwealth."

2. A Governor-General appointed by the Queen shall be Her Majesty's representative in the Commonwealth, and shall have and may exercise in the Commonwealth during the Queen's pleasure, but subject to this Constitution, such powers and functions of the Queen as Her Majesty may be pleased to assign to him.

3. There shall be payable to the Queen out of the Consolidated Revenue Fund of the Commonwealth, for the salary of the Governor-General, an annual sum which, until the Parliament otherwise provides, shall be ten thousand pounds.

The salary of a Governor-General shall not be altered during his continuance in office.

4. The provisions of this Constitution relating to the Governor-General extend and apply to the Governor-General for the time being, or such person as the Queen may appoint to administer the Government of the Commonwealth; but no such person shall be entitled to receive any salary from the Commonwealth in respect of any other office during his administration of the Government of the Commonwealth.

5. The Governor-General may appoint such times for holding the sessions of the Parliament as he thinks fit, and may also from time to

time, by Proclamation or otherwise, prorogue The Parliament, and may in like manner dissolve the House of Representatives.

After any general election The Parliament shall be summoned to meet not later than thirty days after the day appointed for the return of the writs.

The Parliament shall be summoned to meet not later than six months after the establishment of the Commonwealth.

6. There shall be a session of The Parliament once at least in every year, so that twelve months shall not intervene between the last sitting of The Parliament in one session and its first sitting in the next session.

Part II.—The Senate.

7. The Senate shall be composed of senators for each State, directly chosen by the people of the State, voting, until The Parliament otherwise provides, as one electorate.

But until The Parliament of the Commonwealth otherwise provides, the Parliament of the State of Queensland, if that State be an Original State, may make laws dividing the State into divisions and determining the number of senators to be chosen for each division, and in the absence of such provisions the State shall be one electorate.

Until The Parliament otherwise provides, there shall be six senators for each Original State. The Parliament may make laws increasing or diminishing the number of senators for each State, but so that equal representation of the several Original States shall be maintained and that no Original State shall have less than six senators.

The senators shall be chosen for a term of six years, and the names of the senators chosen for each State shall be certified by the Governor to the Governor-General.

8. The qualification of electors of senators shall be in each State that which is prescribed by this Constitution, or by the Parliament, as the qualification for electors of members of the House of Representatives, but in the choosing of senators each elector shall vote only once.

9. The Parliament of the Commonwealth may make laws prescribing the method of choosing senators, but so that the method shall be uniform for all the States. Subject to any such law, the Parliament of each State may make laws prescribing the method of choosing the senators for that State.

The Parliament of a State may make laws for determining the times and places of election of senators for the State.

10. Until The Parliament otherwise provides, but subject to this Constitution, the laws in force in each State, for the time being, relating to elections for the more numerous House of the Parliament of the State shall, as nearly as practicable, apply to elections of senators for the State.

11. The Senate may proceed to the despatch of business, notwithstanding the failure of any State to provide for its representation in the Senate.

12. The Governor of any State may cause writs to be issued for elections of senators for the State. In case of the dissolution of the Senate the writs shall be issued within ten days from the proclamation of such dissolution.

13. As soon as may be after the Senate first meets, and after each first meeting of the Senate following a dissolution thereof, the Senate shall divide the senators chosen for each State into two classes, as nearly equal in number as practicable; and the places of the senators of the first class shall become vacant at the expiration of the third year, and the places of those of the second class at the expiration of the sixth year from the beginning of their term of service; and afterwards the places of senators shall become vacant at the expiration of six years from the beginning of their term of service

The election to fill vacant places shall be made in the year at the expiration of which the places are to become vacant.

For the purposes of this section the term of service of a senator shall be taken to begin on the first day of January following the day of his election, except in the cases of the first election and of th election next after any dissolution of the Senate, when it shall be taken to begin on the first day of January preceding the day of his election.

14. Whenever the number of senators for a State is increased or diminished, The Parliament of the Commonwealth may make such provision for the vacating of the places of senators for the State as it deems necessary to maintain regularity in the rotation.

15. If the place of a senator becomes vacant before the expiration of his term of service The Houses of Parliament of the State for which he was chosen shall, sitting and voting together, choose a person to hold the place until the expiration of the term, or until the election of a successor as hereinafter provided, whichever first happens. But if the Houses of Parliament of the State are not in session at the time when the vacancy is notified, the Governor of the State, with the advice of the Executive Council thereof, may appoint a person to hold the place until the expiration of fourteen days after the beginning of the next session of The Parliament of the State, or until the election of a successor, whichever first happens.

At the next general election of members of the House of Representatives, or at the next election of senators for the State, whichever first happens, a successor shall, if the term has not then expired, be chosen to hold the place from the date of his election until the expiration of the term.

The name of any senator so chosen or appointed shall be certified by the Governor of the State to the Governor-General.

16. The qualifications of a senator shall be the same as those of a member of the House of Representatives.

17. The Senate shall, before proceeding to the despatch of any other business, choose a senator to be the President of the Senate; and as

often as the office of President becomes vacant the Senate shall again choose a senator to be the President.

The President shall cease to hold his office if he ceases to be a senator. He may be removed from office by a vote of the Senate, or he may resign his office or his seat by writing addressed to the Governor-General.

18. Before or during any absence of the President, the Senate may choose a senator to perform his duties in his absence.

19. A senator may, by writing, addressed to the President, or to the Governor-General if there is no President, or if the President is absent from the Commonwealth, resign his place, which thereupon shall become vacant.

20. The place of a senator shall become vacant if for two consecutive months of any session of The Parliament he, without the permission of the Senate, fails to attend the Senate.

21. Whenever a vacancy happens in the Senate, the President, or if there is no President, or if the President is absent from the Commonwealth, the Governor-General shall notify the same to the Governor of the State in the representation of which the vacancy has happened.

22. Until The Parliament otherwise provides, the presence of at least one-third of the whole number of the senators shall be necessary to constitute a meeting of the Senate for the exercise of its powers.

23. Questions arising in the Senate shall be determined by a majority of votes, and each senator shall have one vote. The President shall in all cases be entitled to a vote; and when the votes are equal the question shall pass in the negative.

Part III.—The House of Representatives.

24. The House of Representatives shall be composed of members directly chosen by the people of the Commonwealth, and the number of such members shall be, as nearly as practicable, twice the number of the senators.

The number of members chosen in the several States shall be in proportion to the respective numbers of their people, and shall, until The Parliament otherwise provides, be determined, whenever necessary, in the following manner:—

I. A quota shall be ascertained by dividing the number of the people of the Commonwealth as shown by the latest statistics of the Commonwealth, by twice the number of the senators.

II. The number of members to be chosen in each State shall be determined by dividing the number of the people of the State, as shown by the latest statistics of the Commonwealth, by the quota; and if on such division there is a remainder greater than one-half of the quota, one more member shall be chosen in the State.

But notwithstanding anything in this section, five members at least shall be chosen in each Original State.

25. For the purposes of the last section, if by the law of any State all persons of any race are disqualified from voting at elections for the more numerous House of the Parliament of the State, then, in reckoning the number of the people of the State or of the Commonwealth, persons of that race resident in that State shall not be counted.

26. Notwithstanding anything in section 24, the number of members to be chosen in each State at the first election shall be as follows:—

New South Wales...	Twenty-three.	South Australia ...	Six.
Victoria	Twenty.	Tasmania	Five.
Queensland ...	Eight.		

Provided that if Western Australia is an Original State, the numbers shall be as follows:—

New South Wales...	Twenty-six.	South Australia ...	Seven.
Victoria	Twenty-three.	Western Australia...	Five.
Queensland ...	Nine.	Tasmania	Five.

27. Subject to this Constitution, The Parliament may make laws for increasing or diminishing the number of the members of the House of Representatives.

28. Every House of Representatives shall continue for three years from the first meeting of the House, and no longer, but may be sooner dissolved by the Governor-General.

29. Until the Parliament of The Commonwealth otherwise provides, the Parliament of any State may make laws for determining the divisions in each State for which members of the House of Representatives may be chosen, and the number of members to be chosen for each division. A division shall not be formed out of parts of different States.

In the absence of other provision, each State shall be one electorate.

30. Until The Parliament otherwise provides, the qualification of electors of members of the House of Representatives shall be in each State that which is prescribed by the law of the State as the qualification of electors of the more numerous House of the Parliament of the State; but in the choosing of members each elector shall vote only once.

31. Until The Parliament otherwise provides, but subject to this Constitution, the laws in force in each State for the time being relating to elections for the more numerous House of The Parliament of the State shall, as nearly as practicable, apply to elections in the State of members of the House of Representatives.

32. The Governor-General in Council may cause writs to be issued for general elections of members of the House of Representatives.

After the first general election, the writs shall be issued within ten days from the expiry of a House of Representatives, or from the proclamation of a dissolution thereof.

33. Whenever a vacancy happens in the House of Representatives, the Speaker shall issue his writ for the election of a new member, or if there is no Speaker, or if he is absent from the Commonwealth, the Governor-General in Council may issue the writ.

34. Until The Parliament otherwise provides, the qualifications of a member of the House of Representatives shall be as follows :—

I. He must be of the full age of twenty-one years, and must be an elector entitled to vote at the election of members of the House of Representatives, or a person qualified to become such elector, and must have been for three years at the least a resident within the limits of the Commonwealth as existing at the time when he is chosen :

II. He must be a subject of the Queen, either natural-born or for at least five years naturalised under a law of the United Kingdom, or of a Colony which has become or becomes a State, or of the Commonwealth, or of a State.

35. The House of Representatives shall, before proceeding to the despatch of any other business, choose a member to be the Speaker of the House, and as often as the office of Speaker becomes vacant the House shall again choose a member to be the Speaker.

The Speaker shall cease to hold his office if he ceases to be a member. He may be removed from office by a vote of the House, or he may resign his office or his seat by writing addressed to the Governor-General.

36. Before or during any absence of the Speaker, the House of Representatives may choose a member to perform his duties in his absence.

37. A member may by writing addressed to the Speaker, or to the Governor-General if there is no Speaker or if the Speaker is absent from the Commonwealth, resign his place, which thereupon shall become vacant.

38. The place of a member shall become vacant if for two consecutive months of any session of The Parliament he, without the permission of the House, fails to attend the House.

39. Until the Parliament otherwise provides, the presence of at least one-third of the whole number of the members of the House of Representatives shall be necessary to constitute a meeting of the House for the exercise of its powers.

40. Questions arising in the House of Representatives shall be determined by a majority of votes other than that of the Speaker. The Speaker shall not vote unless the numbers are equal, when he shall have a casting vote.

Part IV.—Both Houses of the Parliament.

41. No adult person who has or acquires a right to vote at elections for the more numerous House of the Parliament of a State, shall, while the right continues, be prevented by any law of the Commonwealth from voting at elections for either House of The Parliament of the Commonwealth.

42. Every senator and every member of the House of Representatives shall before taking his seat make and subscribe before the Governor-General, or some person authorised by him, an oath or affirmation of allegiance in the form set forth in the Schedule to this Constitution.

43 A member of either House of The Parliament shall be incapable of being chosen or of sitting as a member of the other House.

44. Any person who—

I. Is under any acknowledgment of allegiance, obedience, or adherence to a foreign power, or is a subject or a citizen or entitled to the rights or privileges of a subject or a citizen of a foreign power: or

II. Is attainted of treason, or has been convicted and is under sentence, or subject to be sentenced, for any offence punishable under the law of the Commonwealth or of a State by imprisonment for one year or longer: or

III. Is an undischarged bankrupt or insolvent: or

IV. Holds any office of profit under the Crown, or any pension payable during the pleasure of the Crown out of any of the revenues of the Commonwealth: or

V. Has any direct or indirect pecuniary interest in any agreement with the public service of the Commonwealth, otherwise than as a member and in common with the other members of an incorporated company consisting of more than twenty-five persons:

shall be incapable of being chosen or of sitting as a senator or as a member of the House of Representatives.

But subsection IV does not apply to the office of any of the Queen's Ministers of State for the Commonwealth, or of any of the Queen's Ministers for a State, or to the receipt of pay, half-pay, or a pension by any person as an officer or member of the Queen's navy or army, or to the receipt of pay as an officer or member of the naval or military forces of the Commonwealth by any person whose services are not wholly employed by the Commonwealth.

45. If a senator or member of the House of Representatives—

I. Becomes subject to any of the disabilities mentioned in the last preceding section: or

II. Takes the benefit, whether by assignment, composition, or otherwise, of any law relating to bankrupt or insolvent debtors: or

III. Directly or indirectly takes or agrees to take any fee or honorarium for services rendered to the Commonwealth, or for services rendered in The Parliament to any person or State:

his place shall thereupon become vacant.

46. Until The Parliament otherwise provides, any person declared by this Constitution to be incapable of sitting as a senator or as a member of the House of Representatives shall, for every day on which he so sits, be liable to pay the sum of one hundred pounds to any person who sues for it in any court of competent jurisdiction.

47. Until The Parliament otherwise provides, any question respecting the qualification of a senator or of a member of the House of Representatives, or respecting a vacancy in either House of the Parliament, and any question of a disputed election to either House, shall be determined by the House in which the question arises.

48. Until The Parliament otherwise provides, each senator and each member of the House of Representatives shall receive an allowance of Four Hundred Pounds a year, to be reckoned from the day on which he takes his seat.

49. The powers, privileges, and immunities of the Senate and of the House of Representatives, and of the members and the committees of each House shall be such as are declared by The Parliament, and until declared shall be those of the Commons House of Parliament of the United Kingdom, and of its members and committees, at the establishment of the Commonwealth.

50. Each House of The Parliament may make rules and orders with respect to—

i. The mode in which its powers, privileges, and immunities may be exercised and upheld :

ii. The order and conduct of its business and proceedings either separately or jointly with the other House.

Part V.—Powers of The Parliament.

51. The Parliament shall, subject to this Constitution, have power to make laws for the peace, order, and good government of the Commonwealth, with respect to :—

i. Trade and commerce with other countries, and among the States:

ii. Taxation ; but so as not to discriminate between States or parts of States :

iii. Bounties on the production or export of goods, but so that such bounties shall be uniform throughout the Commonwealth :

iv. Borrowing money on the public credit of the Commonwealth :

v. Postal, telegraphic, telephonic, and other like services :

vi. The naval and military defence of the Commonwealth and of the several States, and the control of the forces to execute and maintain the laws of the Commonwealth :

vii. Light-houses, light-ships, beacons, and buoys :

viii. Astronomical and meteorological observations :

ix. Quarantine :

x. Fisheries in Australian waters beyond territorial limits :

xi. Census and statistics :

xii. Currency, coinage, and legal tender :

xiii. Banking other than State banking ; also State banking extending beyond the limits of the State concerned, the incorporation of banks, and the issue of paper money :

xiv. Insurance, other than State Insurance ; also State Insurance extending beyond the limits of the State concerned :

xv. Weights and measures :

xvi. Bills of exchange and promissory notes :

xvii. Bankruptcy and insolvency :

xviii. Copyrights, patents of inventions and designs, and trade-marks :

xix. Naturalization and aliens:

xx. Foreign corporations, and trading or financial corporations formed within the limits of the Commonwealth:

xxi. Marriage:

xxii. Divorce and matrimonial causes; and in relation thereto, parental rights, and the custody and guardianship of infants:

xxiii. Invalid and old-age pensions:

xxiv. The service and execution throughout the Commonwealth of the civil and criminal process and the judgments of the courts of the States:

xxv. The recognition throughout the Commonwealth of the laws, the public acts and records, and the judicial proceedings of the States:

xxvi. The people of any race, other than the aboriginal race in any State, for whom it is deemed necessary to make special laws:

xxvii. Immigration and emigration:

xxviii. The influx of criminals:

xxix. External affairs:

xxx. The relations of the Commonwealth with the islands of the Pacific:

xxxi. The acquisition of property on just terms from any State or person for any purpose in respect of which The Parliament has power to make laws:

xxxii. The control of railways with respect to transport for the naval and military purposes of the Commonwealth:

xxxiii. The acquisition, with the consent of a State, of any railways of the State on terms arranged between the Commonwealth and the State:

xxxiv. Railway construction and extension in any State with the consent of that State:

xxxv. Conciliation and arbitration for the prevention and settlement of industrial disputes extending beyond the limits of any one State:

xxxvi. Matters in respect of which this Constitution makes provision until The Parliament otherwise provides:

xxxvii. Matters referred to the Parliament of the Commonwealth by the Parliament or Parliaments of any State or States, but so that the law shall extend only to States by whose Parliament the matter is referred, or which afterwards adopt the law:

xxxviii. The exercise within the Commonwealth, at the request or with the concurrence of the Parliaments of all the States directly concerned, of any power which can at the establishment of this Constitution be exercised only by the Parliament of the United Kingdom or by the Federal Council of Australasia:

XXXIX. Matters incidental to the execution of any power vested by this Constitution in the Parliament or in either House thereof, or in the Government of the Commonwealth, or in the Federal Judicature, or in any department or officer of the Commonwealth.

52. The Parliament shall, subject to this Constitution, have exclusive power to make laws for the peace, order, and good government of the Commonwealth with respect to—

I. The seat of Government of the Commonwealth, and all places acquired by the Commonwealth for public purposes:

II. Matters relating to any department of the public service the control of which is by this Constitution transferred to the Executive Government of the Commonwealth:

III. Other matters declared by this Constitution to be within the exclusive power of The Parliament.

53. Proposed laws appropriating revenue or moneys, or imposing taxation, shall not originate in the Senate. But a proposed law shall not be taken to appropriate revenue or moneys, or to impose taxation, by reason only of its containing provisions for the imposition or appropriation of fines or other pecuniary penalties, or for the demand or payment or appropriation of fees for licenses, or fees for services under the proposed law.

The Senate may not amend proposed laws imposing taxation, or proposed laws appropriating revenue or moneys for the ordinary annual services of the Government.

The Senate may not amend any proposed law so as to increase any proposed charge or burden on the people.

The Senate may at any stage return to the House of Representatives any proposed law which the Senate may not amend, requesting, by message, the omission or amendment of any items or provisions therein. And the House of Representatives may if it thinks fit make any of such omissions or amendments, with or without modifications.

Except as provided in this section, the Senate shall have equal power with the House of Representatives in respect of all proposed laws.

54. The proposed law which appropriates revenue or moneys for the ordinary annual services of the Government shall deal only with such appropriations.

55. Laws imposing taxation shall deal only with the imposition of taxation, and any provision therein dealing with any other matter shall be of no effect.

Laws imposing taxation, except laws imposing duties of customs or of excise, shall deal with one subject of taxation only; but laws imposing duties of customs shall deal with duties of customs only, and laws imposing duties of excise shall deal with duties of excise only.

56. A vote, resolution, or proposed law for the appropriation of revenue or moneys shall not be passed unless the purpose of the

appropriation has in the same session been recommended by message of the Governor-General to the House in which the proposal originated.

57. If the House of Representatives passes any proposed law and the Senate rejects or fails to pass it, or passes it with amendments to which the House of Representatives will not agree, and if after an interval of three months the House of Representatives, in the same or the next session, again passes the proposed law with or without any amendments which have been made, suggested, or agreed to by the Senate, and the Senate rejects or fails to pass it, or passes it with amendments to which the House of Representatives will not agree, the Governor-General may dissolve the Senate and the House of Representatives simultaneously. But such dissolution shall not take place within six months before the date of the expiry of the House of Representatives by effluxion of time.

If after such dissolution the House of Representatives again passes the proposed law with or without any amendments which have been made, suggested, or agreed to by the Senate, and the Senate rejects or fails to pass it, or passes it with amendments to which the House of Representatives will not agree, the Governor-General may convene a joint sitting of the members of the Senate and of the House of Representatives.

The members present at the joint sitting may deliberate and shall vote together upon the proposed law as last proposed by the House of Representatives, and upon amendments, if any, which have been made therein by one House and not agreed to by the other, and any such amendments which are affirmed by an absolute majority of the total number of the members of the Senate and House of Representatives shall be taken to have been carried, and if the proposed law, with the amendments, if any, so carried is affirmed by an absolute majority of the total number of the members of the Senate and the House of Representatives it shall be taken to have been duly passed by both Houses of The Parliament, and shall be presented to the Governor-General for the Queen's assent.

58. When a proposed law passed by both Houses of The Parliament is presented to the Governor-General for the Queen's assent, he shall declare, according to his discretion, but subject to this Constitution, that he assents in the Queen's name, or that he withholds assent, or that he reserves the law for the Queen's pleasure.

The Governor-General may return to the House in which it originated any proposed law so presented to him, may transmit therewith any amendments which he may recommend, and the Houses may deal with the recommendations.

59. The Queen may disallow any law within one year from the Governor-General's assent, and such disallowance on being made known by the Governor-General, by speech or message to each of the Houses of the Parliament, or by Proclamation, shall annul the law from the day when the disallowance is so made known.

60. A proposed law reserved for the Queen's pleasure shall not have any force unless and until within two years from the day on which it was presented to the Governor-General for the Queen's assent the Governor-General makes known, by speech or message to each of the Houses of The Parliament, or by Proclamation, that it has received the Queen's assent.

CHAPTER II.

THE EXECUTIVE GOVERNMENT.

61. The Executive power of the Commonwealth is vested in the Queen, and is exercisable by the Governor-General as the Queen's representative, and extends to the execution and maintenance of this Constitution, and of the laws of the Commonwealth.

62. There shall be a Federal Executive Council to advise the Governor-General in the government of the Commonwealth, and the members of the Council shall be chosen and summoned by the Governor-General and sworn as Executive Councillors, and shall hold office during his pleasure.

63. The provisions of this Constitution referring to the Governor-General in Council shall be construed as referring to the Governor-General acting with the advice of the Federal Executive Council.

64. The Governor-General may appoint officers to administer such Departments of State of the Commonwealth as the Governor-General in Council may establish.

Such officers shall hold office during the pleasure of the Governor-General. They shall be members of the Federal Executive Council, and shall be the Queen's Ministers of State for the Commonwealth.

After the first general election no Minister of State shall hold office for a longer period than three months unless he is or becomes a senator or a member of the House of Representatives.

65. Until The Parliament otherwise provides, the Ministers of State shall not exceed seven in number, and shall hold such offices as The Parliament prescribes, or, in the absence of provision, as the Governor-General directs.

66. There shall be payable to the Queen, out of the Consolidated Revenue Fund of the Commonwealth, for the salaries of Ministers of State, an annual sum which, until The Parliament otherwise provides, shall not exceed twelve thousand pounds a year.

67. Until The Parliament otherwise provides, the appointment and removal of all other officers of the Executive Government of the Commonwealth shall be vested in the Governor-General in Council, unless the appointment is delegated by the Governor-General in Council or by law of the Commonwealth to some other authority.

68. The command in chief of the naval and military forces of the Commonwealth is vested in the Governor-General as the Queen's representative.

69. On a date or dates to be proclaimed by the Governor-General after the establishment of the Commonwealth, the following Departments of the public service in each State shall become transferred to the Commonwealth:—

Posts, telegraphs, and telephones:
Naval and military defence:
Light-houses, light-ships, beacons, and buoys:
Quarantine.

But the Departments of customs and of excise in each State shall become transferred to the Commonwealth on its establishment.

70. In respect of matters which, under this Constitution, pass to the Executive Government of the Commonwealth, all powers and functions which at the establishment of the Commonwealth are vested in the Governor of a colony, or in the Governor of a colony with the advice of his Executive Council, or in any authority of a colony, shall vest in the Governor-General, or in the Governor-General in Council, or in the authority exercising similar powers under the Commonwealth, as the case requires.

CHAPTER III.

THE JUDICATURE.

71. The judicial power of the Commonwealth shall be vested in a Federal Supreme Court, to be called the High Court of Australia, and in such other federal courts as The Parliament creates, and in such other courts as it invests with federal jurisdiction. The High Court shall consist of a Chief Justice, and so many other Justices, not less than two, as The Parliament prescribes.

72. The Justices of the High Court and of the other courts created by The Parliament

I. Shall be appointed by the Governor-General in Council:
II. Shall not be removed except by the Governor-General in Council, on an Address from both Houses of The Parliament in the same session praying for such removal on the ground of proved misbehaviour or incapacity:
III. Shall receive such remuneration as The Parliament may fix; but the remuneration shall not be diminished during their continuance in office.

73. The High Court shall have jurisdiction, with such exceptions and subject to such regulations as The Parliament prescribes, to hear and determine appeals from all judgments, decrees, orders, and sentences:

I. Of any Justice or Justices exercising the original jurisdiction of the High Court:
II. Of any other federal court, or court exercising federal jurisdiction; or of the Supreme Court of any State, or of any other court of any State from which at the establishment of the Commonwealth an appeal lies to the Queen in Council:

III. Of the Inter-State Commission, but as to questions of law only:

and the judgment of the High Court in all such cases shall be final and conclusive.

But no exception or regulation prescribed by The Parliament shall prevent the High Court from hearing and determining any appeal from the Supreme Court of a State in any matter in which at the establishment of the Commonwealth an appeal lies from such Supreme Court to the Queen in Council.

Until The Parliament otherwise provides, the conditions of and restrictions on appeals to the Queen in Council from the Supreme Courts of the several States shall be applicable to appeals from them to the High Court.

74. No appeal shall be permitted to the Queen in Council from a decision of the High Court upon any question, howsoever arising, as to the limits inter se of the Constitutional powers of the Commonwealth and those of any State or States, or as to the limits inter se of the Constitutional powers of any two or more States, unless the High Court shall certify that the question is one which ought to be determined by Her Majesty in Council.

The High Court may so certify if satisfied that for any special reason the certificate should be granted, and thereupon an appeal shall lie to Her Majesty in Council on the question without further leave.

Except as provided in this section, this Constitution shall not impair any right which the Queen may be pleased to exercise, by virtue of Her Royal Prerogative, to grant special leave of appeal from the High Court to Her Majesty in Council. The Parliament may make laws limiting the matters in which such leave may be asked, but proposed laws containing any such limitation shall be reserved by the Governor-General for Her Majesty's pleasure.

75. In all matters—

I. Arising under any treaty:
II. Affecting consuls or other representatives of other countries:
III. In which the Commonwealth, or a person suing or being sued on behalf of the Commonwealth, is a party:
IV. Between States, or between residents of different States, or between a State and a resident of another State:
V. In which a writ of mandamus or prohibition or an injunction is sought against an officer of the Commonwealth:

the High Court shall have original jurisdiction.

76. The Parliament may make laws conferring original jurisdiction on the High Court in any matter—

I. Arising under this Constitution, or involving its interpretation:
II. Arising under any laws made by The Parliament:
III. Of admiralty and maritime jurisdiction:
IV. Relating to the same subject-matter claimed under the laws of different States.

77. With respect to any of the matters mentioned in the last two sections, The Parliament may make laws—

i. Defining the jurisdiction of any federal court other than the High Court:

ii. Defining the extent to which the jurisdiction of any federal court shall be exclusive of that which belongs to or is vested in the courts of the States:

iii. Investing any court of a State with federal jurisdiction.

78. The Parliament may make laws conferring rights to proceed against the Commonwealth or a State in respect of matters within the limits of the judicial power.

79. The federal jurisdiction of any court may be exercised by such number of judges as The Parliament prescribes.

80. The trial on indictment of any offence against any law of the Commonwealth shall be by jury, and every such trial shall be held in the State where the offence was committed, and if the offence was not committed within any State the trial shall be held at such place or places as The Parliament prescribes.

CHAPTER IV.

FINANCE AND TRADE.

81. All revenues or moneys raised or received by the Executive Government of the Commonwealth shall form one Consolidated Revenue Fund, to be appropriated for the purposes of the Commonwealth in the manner and subject to the charges and liabilities imposed by this Constitution.

82. The costs, charges, and expenses incident to the collection, management, and receipt of the Consolidated Revenue Fund shall form the first charge thereon; and the revenue of the Commonwealth shall in the first instance be applied to the payment of the expenditure of the Commonwealth.

83. No money shall be drawn from the Treasury of the Commonwealth except under appropriation made by law.

But until the expiration of one month after the first meeting of The Parliament, the Governor-General in Council may draw from the Treasury and expend such moneys as may be necessary for the maintenance of any department transferred to the Commonwealth and for the holding of the first elections for The Parliament.

84. When any department of the public service of a State becomes transferred to the Commonwealth, all officers of the department shall become subject to the control of the Executive Government of the Commonwealth.

Any such officer who is not retained in the service of the Commonwealth shall, unless he is appointed to some other office of equal emolument in the public service of the State, be entitled to receive from the State any pension, gratuity, or other compensation payable under the law of the State on the abolition of his office.

Any such officer who is retained in the service of the Commonwealth shall preserve all his existing and accruing rights, and shall be entitled to retire from office at the time, and on the pension or retiring allowance, which would be permitted by the law of the State if his services with the Commonwealth were a continuation of his service with the State. Such pension or retiring allowance shall be paid to him by the Commonwealth; but the State shall pay to the Commonwealth a part thereof, to be calculated on the proportion which his term of service with the State bears to his whole term of service, and for the purpose of the calculation his salary shall be taken to be that paid to him by the State at the time of the transfer.

Any officer who is, at the establishment of the Commonwealth, in the public service of a State, and who is, by consent of the Governor of the State with the advice of the Executive Council thereof, transferred to the public service of the Commonwealth, shall have the same rights as if he had been an officer of a department transferred to the Commonwealth and were retained in the service of the Commonwealth.

85. When any department of the public service of a State is transferred to the Commonwealth—

i. All property of the State, of any kind, used exclusively in connection with the department, shall become vested in the Commonwealth; but, in the case of the departments controlling customs and excise and bounties, for such time only as the Governor-General in Council may declare to be necessary.

ii. The Commonwealth may acquire any property of the State, of any kind, used, but not exclusively used, in connection with the department; the value thereof shall, if no agreement can be made, be ascertained in, as nearly as may be, the manner in which the value of land, or of an interest in land, taken by the State for public purposes, is ascertained under the law of the State in force at the establishment of the Commonwealth.

iii. The Commonwealth shall compensate the State for the value of any property passing to the Commonwealth under this section; if no agreement can be made as to the mode of compensation, it shall be determined under laws to be made by The Parliament.

iv. The Commonwealth shall, at the date of the transfer, assume the current obligations of the State in respect of the department transferred.

86. On the establishment of the Commonwealth, the collection and control of duties of customs and of excise, and the control of the payment of bounties, shall pass to the Executive Government of the Commonwealth.

87. During a period of ten years after the establishment of the Commonwealth, and thereafter until the Parliament otherwise provides, of the net revenue of the Commonwealth from duties of customs and of excise, not more than one-fourth shall be applied annually by the Commonwealth towards its expenditure.

The balance shall in accordance with this Constitution, be paid to the several States, or applied towards the payment of interest on debts of the several States taken over by the Commonwealth.

88. Uniform duties of customs shall be imposed within two years after the establishment of the Commonwealth.

89. Until the imposition of uniform duties of customs—

I. The Commonwealth shall credit to each State the revenues collected therein by the Commonwealth.

II. The Commonwealth shall debit to each State—

(*a*) the expenditure therein of the Commonwealth incurred solely for the maintenanee or continuance, as at the time of transfer, of any department transferred from the State to the Commonwealth.

(*b*) The proportion of the State, according to the number of its people, in the other expenditure of the Commonwealth.

III. The Commonwealth shall pay to each State month by month the balance (if any) in favour of the State.

90. On the imposition of uniform duties of customs the power of the Parliament to impose duties of customs and of excise, and to grant bounties on the production or export of goods, shall become exclusive.

On the imposition of uniform duties of customs all laws of the several States imposing duties of customs or of excise, or offering bounties on the production or export of goods, shall cease to have effect; but any grant of or agreement for any such bounty lawfully made by or under the authority of the Government of any State shall be taken to be good if made before the thirtieth day of June, one thousand eight hundred and ninety-eight, and not otherwise.

91. Nothing in this Constitution prohibits a State from granting any aid to or bounty on mining for gold, silver, or other metals, nor from granting, with the consent of both Houses of the Parliament of the Commonwealth expressed by resolution, any aid to or bounty on the production or export of goods.

92. On the imposition of uniform duties of customs, trade, commerce, and intercourse among the States, whether by means of internal carriage or ocean navigation, shall be absolutely free.

But notwithstanding anything in this Constitution, goods imported before the imposition of uniform duties of customs into any State, or into any Colony which, whilst the goods remain therein, becomes a State, shall, on thence passing into another State within two years after the imposition of such duties, be liable to any duty chargeable on the importation of such goods into the Commonwealth, less any duty paid in respect of the goods on their importation.

93. During the first five years after the imposition of uniform duties of customs, and thereafter until The Parliament otherwise provides :—

I. The duties of customs chargeable on goods imported into a State and afterwards passing into another State for consumption, and the duties of excise paid on goods produced or manufactured in a State and afterwards passing into another State for consumption, shall be taken to have been collected not in the former but in the latter State :

II. Subject to the last subsection, the Commonwealth shall credit revenue, debit expenditure, and pay balances to the several States as prescribed for the period preceding the imposition of uniform duties of customs.

94. After five years from the imposition of uniform duties of customs, The Parliament may provide, on such basis as it deems fair, for the monthly payment to the several States of all surplus revenue of the Commonwealth.

95. Notwithstanding anything in this Constitution, the Parliament of the State of Western Australia, if that State be an Original State, may, during the first five years after the imposition of uniform duties of customs, impose duties of customs on goods passing into that State, and not originally imported from beyond the limits of the Commonwealth ; and such duties shall be collected by the Commonwealth.

But any duty so imposed on any goods shall not exceed during the first of such years the duty chargeable on the goods under the law of Western Australia in force at the imposition of uniform duties, and shall not exceed during the second, third, fourth, and fifth of such years respectively, four-fifths, three-fifths, two-fifths, and one-fifth of such latter duty, and all duties imposed under this section shall cease at the expiration of the fifth year after the imposition of uniform duties.

If at any time during the five years the duty on any goods under this section is higher than the duty imposed by the Commonwealth on the importation of the like goods, then such higher duty shall be collected on the goods when imported into Western Australia from beyond the limits of the Commonwealth.

96. During a period of ten years after the establishment of the Commonwealth and thereafter until The Parliament otherwise provides, The Parliament may grant financial assistance to any State on such terms and conditions as The Parliament thinks fit.

97. Until the Parliament otherwise provides, the laws in force in any colony which has become or becomes a State with respect to the receipt of revenue and the expenditure of money on account of the Government of the colony, and the review and audit of such receipt and expenditure, shall apply to the receipt of revenue and the expenditure

of money on account of the Commonwealth in the State in the same manner as if the Commonwealth, or the Government, or an officer of the Commonwealth, were mentioned whenever the colony, or the Government, or an officer of the colony is mentioned.

98. The power of The Parliament to make laws with respect to trade and commerce extends to navigation and shipping, and to railways the property of any State.

99. The Commonwealth shall not, by any law or regulation of trade, commerce, or revenue, give preference to one State or any part thereof over another State or any part thereof.

100. The Commonwealth shall not, by any law or regulation of trade or commerce, abridge the right of a State or of the residents therein to the reasonable use of the waters of rivers for conservation or irrigation.

101. There shall be an Inter-State Commission, with such powers of adjudication and administration as The Parliament deems necessary for the execution and maintenance, within the Commonwealth, of the provisions of this Constitution relating to trade and commerce, and of all laws made thereunder.

102. The Parliament may by any law with respect to trade or commerce forbid, as to railways, any preference or discrimination by any State, or by any authority constituted under a State, if such preference or discrimination is undue and unreasonable, or unjust to any State: due regard being had to the financial responsibilities incurred by any State in connection with the construction and maintenance of its railways. But no preference or discrimination shall, within the meaning of this section, be taken to be undue and unreasonable, or unjust to any State, unless so adjudged by the Inter-State Commission.

103. The members of the Inter-State Commission—

I. Shall be appointed by the Governor-General in Council:

II. Shall hold office for seven years, but may be removed within that time by the Governor-General in Council, on an address from both Houses of the Parliament in the same Session praying for such removal on the ground of proved misbehaviour or incapacity:

III. Shall receive such remuneration as The Parliament may fix; but such remuneration shall not be diminished during their continuance in office.

104. Nothing in this Constitution shall render unlawful any rate for the carriage of goods upon a railway, the property of a State, if the rate is deemed by the Inter-State Commission to be necessary for the development of the territory of the State, and if the rate applies equally to goods within the State and to goods passing into the State from other States.

105. The Parliament may take over from the States their public debts as existing at the establishment of the Commonwealth, or a proportion thereof, according to the respective numbers of their people as

shown by the latest statistics of the Commonwealth, and may convert, renew, or consolidate such debts, or any part thereof; and the States shall indemnify the Commonwealth in respect of the debts taken over, and thereafter the interest payable in respect of the debts shall be deducted and retained from the portions of the surplus revenue of the Commonwealth payable to the several States, or if such surplus is insufficient, or if there is no surplus, then the deficiency or the whole amount shall be paid by the several States.

CHAPTER V.

THE STATES.

106. The Constitution of each State of the Commonwealth shall, subject to this Constitution, continue as at the establishment of the Commonwealth, or as at the admission or establishment of the State, as the case may be, until altered in accordance with the Constitution of the State.

107. Every power of the Parliament of a colony which has become or becomes a State, shall, unless it is by this Constitution exclusively vested in The Parliament of the Commonwealth or withdrawn from the Parliament of the State, continue as at the establishment of the Commonwealth, or as at the admission or establishment of the State, as the case may be.

108. Every law in force in a colony which has become or becomes a State, and relating to any matter within the powers of The Parliament of the Commonwealth, shall, subject to this Constitution, continue in force in the State; and until provision is made in that behalf by The Parliament of the Commonwealth, the Parliament of the State shall have such powers of alteration and of repeal in respect of any such law as the Parliament of the colony had until the colony became a State.

109. When a law of a State is inconsistent with a law of the Commonwealth, the latter shall prevail, and the former shall, to the extent of the inconsistency, be invalid.

110. The provisions of this Constitution relating to the Governor of a State extend and apply to the Governor for the time being of the State, or other chief executive officer or administrator of the government of the State.

111. The Parliament of a State may surrender any part of the State to the Commonwealth: and upon such surrender, and the acceptance thereof by the Commonwealth, such part of the State shall become subject to the exclusive jurisdiction of the Commonwealth.

112. After uniform duties of customs have been imposed, a State may levy on imports or exports, or on goods passing into or out of the State, such charges as may be necessary for executing the inspection laws of the State; but the net produce of all charges so levied shall be for the use of the Commonwealth; and any such inspection laws may be annulled by The Parliament of the Commonwealth.

113. All fermented, distilled, or other intoxicating liquids passing into any State or remaining therein for use, consumption, sale, or storage shall be subject to the laws of the State as if such liquids had been produced in the State.

114. A State shall not, without the consent of The Parliament of the Commonwealth, raise or maintain any naval or military force, or impose any tax on property of any kind belonging to the Commonwealth; nor shall the Commonwealth impose any tax on property of any kind belonging to a State.

115. A State shall not coin money, nor make anything but gold and silver coin a legal tender in payment of debts.

116. The Commonwealth shall not make any law for establishing any religion, or for imposing any religious observance, or for prohibiting the free exercise of any religion, and no religious test shall be required as a qualification for any office or public trust under the Commonwealth.

117. A subject of the Queen, resident in any State, shall not be subject in any other State to any disability or discrimination which would not be equally applicable to him if he were a subject of the Queen resident in such other State.

118. Full faith and credit shall be given, throughout the Commonwealth, to the laws, the public acts and records, and the judicial proceedings, of every State.

119. The Commonwealth shall protect every State against invasion and, on the application of the Executive Government of the State, against domestic violence.

120. Every State shall make provision for the detention in its prisons of persons accused or convicted of offences against the laws of the Commonwealth, and for the punishment of persons convicted of such offences, and the Parliament of the Commonwealth may make laws to give effect to this provision.

CHAPTER VI.

NEW STATES.

121. The Parliament may admit to the Commonwealth or establish new States, and may upon such admission or establishment make or impose such terms and conditions, including the extent of representation in either House of The Parliament, as it thinks fit.

122. The Parliament may make laws for the Government of any territory surrendered by any State to and accepted by the Commonwealth, or of any territory placed by the Queen under the authority of and accepted by the Commonwealth, or otherwise acquired by the Commonwealth, and may allow the representation of such territory in either House of the Parliament to the extent and on the terms which it thinks fit.

123. The Parliament of the Commonwealth may, with the consent of the Parliament of a State and the approval of the majority of the

electors of the State voting upon the question, increase, diminish, or otherwise alter the limits of the State, upon such terms and conditions as may be agreed on, and may, with the like consent, make provision respecting the effect and operation of any increase or diminution or alteration of territory in relation to any State affected.

124. A new State may be formed by separation of territory from a State, but only with the consent of the Parliament thereof, and a new State may be formed by the union of two or more States or parts of States, but only with the consent of the Parliaments of the States affected.

CHAPTER VII.

MISCELLANEOUS.

125. The seat of Government of the Commonwealth shall be determined by The Parliament and shall be within territory which shall have been granted to or acquired by the Commonwealth and shall be vested in and belong to the Commonwealth, and if New South Wales be an Original State shall be in that State, and be distant not less than one hundred miles from Sydney.

Such territory shall contain an area of not less than one hundred square miles, and such portion thereof as shall consist of Crown lands shall be granted to the Commonwealth without any payment therefor.

The Parliament shall sit at Melbourne until it meet at the seat of Government.

126. The Queen may authorise the Governor-General to appoint any person or any persons jointly or severally to be his deputy or deputies within any part of the Commonwealth, and in that capacity to exercise during the pleasure of the Governor-General such powers and functions of the Governor-General as he thinks fit to assign to such deputy or deputies, subject to any limitations expressed or directions given by the Queen, but the appointment of such deputy or deputies shall not affect the exercise by the Governor-General himself of any power or function.

127. In reckoning the numbers of the people of the Commonwealth or of a State or other part of the Commonwealth, aboriginal natives shall not be counted.

CHAPTER VIII.

ALTERATION OF THE CONSTITUTION.

128. This Constitution shall not be altered except in the following manner:

The proposed law for the alteration thereof must be passed by an absolute majority of each House of The Parliament, and not less than two nor more than six months after its passage through both Houses the proposed law shall be submitted in each State to the electors qualified to vote for the election of members of the House of Representatives.

But if either House passes any such proposed law by an absolute majority and the other House rejects or fails to pass it or passes it with any amendment to which the first-mentioned House will not agree, and if after an interval of three months the first-mentioned House in the same or the next session again passes the proposed law by an absolute majority with or without any amendment which has been made or agreed to by the other House, and such other House rejects or fails to pass it, or passes it with any amendment to which the first-mentioned House will not agree, the Governor-General may submit the proposed law as last proposed by the first-mentioned House, and either with or without any amendments subsequently agreed to by both Houses to the electors in each State qualified to vote for the election of the House of Representatives.

When a proposed law is submitted to the electors, the vote shall be taken in such manner as The Parliament prescribes. But until the qualification of electors of members of the House of Representatives becomes uniform throughout the Commonwealth only one-half the electors voting for and against the proposed law shall be counted in any State in which adult suffrage prevails.

And if in a majority of the States a majority of the electors voting approve the proposed law, and if a majority of all the electors voting also approve the proposed law, it shall be presented to the Governor-General for the Queen's assent.

No alteration diminishing the proportionate representation of any State in either House of The Parliament, or the minimum number of representatives of a State in the House of Representatives, or increasing diminishing, or otherwise altering the limits of the State, or in any manner affecting the provisions of the Constitution in relation thereto, shall become law unless the majority of the electors voting in that State approve the proposed law.

SCHEDULE.

OATH.

I, A.B., do swear that I will be faithful and bear true allegiance to Her Majesty Queen Victoria, Her heirs and successors, according to law. So HELP ME GOD!

AFFIRMATION.

I, A.B., do solemnly and sincerely affirm and declare that I will be faithful and bear true allegiance to Her Majesty Queen Victoria, Her heirs and successors, according to law.

(NOTE.—*The name of the King or Queen of the United Kingdom of Great Britain and Ireland for the time being is to be substituted from time to time.*)

CONSTITUTIONS OF THE STATES OF THE COMMONWEALTH AND OF NEW ZEALAND.

NEW SOUTH WALES.

THE present form of government in New South Wales was inaugurated forty-eight years ago, the "Act to confer a Constitution on New South Wales, and to grant a Civil List to Her Majesty," having received the Royal assent on the 16th July, 1855. This important statute was proclaimed in Sydney on the 24th November of the same year, and at once came into operation, sweeping away entirely the former system, and constituting an elective representative Chamber —thus, by the granting of equal privileges, making the colonists of New South Wales the equals of their countrymen in other parts of the Empire. The ties which bound the state to the mother country were in no way loosened, for the Constitution Act simply conceded to the people of New South Wales the rights which prevailed in the United Kingdom, namely, of taxing themselves, and of being governed by Ministers responsible to a Parliament elected by popular vote. The authority vested in the Sovereign remains the same as before, though the mode of its exercise is widely different. Prior to Responsible Government, the Sovereign exercised, through the Governor, almost despotic power, this official uniting in himself the executive and legislative functions. Personal liberty and independence were, therefore, to no small degree in his control; but with the establishment of Responsible Government this state of things ceased, and the greatest measure of individual liberty is now found compatible with the full protection of public rights. The readiness with which the people of the state adapted themselves to the forms and practice of their new government was not a little remarkable, and fully justified their assumption of its privileges.

All laws are enacted in the name of the King, "by and with the advice of the Legislative Council and Legislative Assembly," the Governor, as the Royal Deputy, immediately giving the assent of the Sovereign to Acts of Parliament, or, if he should think fit, reserving them for the consideration of His Majesty. In order that the Constitution may be clearly understood, it will be well to consider, under distinct heads, the several elements of which the Government and Legislature consist.

The Governor.

Prior to 1879 the Governor of the state was appointed by Letters Patent under the Great Seal; but in that year the practice was discontinued on the advice of Sir Alfred Stephen, given during the tenure of office of Sir Hercules Robinson. The change was first carried out in the appointment of Sir Augustus Loftus. The office of Governor is now constituted by permanent Letters Patent, and by a standing Commission, instead of as formerly by letters issued *pro hac vice* only. The Governor receives his appointment at present by Commission under the Royal sign manual and signet, which recites the Letters Patent of the 29th April, 1879, as well as the instructions issued (under sign manual and signet) in further declaration of the King's "will and pleasure." The original Letters Patent, thus recited and enforced, declare that the Governor is directed and empowered "to do and execute all things that belong to his office according to the tenor of the Letters Patent, and of such Commission as may be issued to him under our sign manual and signet, and according to such instructions as may from time to time be given to him under our sign manual and signet, or by our order in our Privy Council, or by us through one of our Principal Secretaries of State, and to such laws as are now or shall hereafter be in force in the colony." In accordance with a custom which has long prevailed, no Governor retains his office for a longer period than six years; and should he die or become incapable of performing his duties during his tenure of office, or be removed before the arrival of his successor, or should he have occasion to leave the state for any considerable period, the government is to be administered (1) by the Lieutenant-Governor; or, if there be no Lieutenant-Governor, (2) by an Administrator to be appointed according to the provisions of the Letters Patent and Instructions. The present Lieutenant-Governor is Sir Frederick Matthew Darley, G.C.M.G., C.J., who was appointed by a Commission, dated the 23rd November, 1891; and in recent years the duties of Administrator have been fulfilled by Sir John Lackey, K.C.M.G., President of the Legislative Council, and since his decease by Judge M. H. Stephen.

The Lieutenant-Governor, or, in his absence, the Administrator, is empowered by his Commission to fill the office of Governor during any temporary absence of the Governor from the state; but the Governor may not be absent from the state, except in accordance with the terms of his instructions. Without the King's special leave he may not leave the state for a period exceeding one month at a time, or exceeding in the aggregate one month for every year of his service, unless on a visit to the Governor of a neighbouring state; but, on the other hand, he may leave the state for any period not exceeding one month without its being reckoned as a departure, if he shall have previously informed the Executive Council in writing of his intention, and appointed a deputy to act for him till his return. This deputy must, in the first instance, be the Lieutenant-Governor; but if, from any cause, the services of the Lieutenant-Governor should not be available, the Governor may appoint whomsoever he pleases as his deputy.

The Governor's functions, according to the Letters Patent, Commission, and Instructions, may be recapitulated as follow :—

The Governor is the custodian of the Great Seal, under which all Crown grants, etc., must pass.

The Governor has the appointment of his own Council—the Executive. He is also to summon that Council, and is ordinarily its President; but in his absence some other member may be nominated to preside. It is usual, however, to appoint some member of the Ministry permanent Vice-President, who presides in the absence of the Governor.

The Governor is the fountain of honour within the state, since to him belongs the power to appoint, in the King's name, all Judges, Justices of the Peace, Commissioners, and other "necessary officers and Ministers"; and, by virtue of his powers as Viceroy, he may remove from the exercise of his office any official so appointed.

The Governor is also the depositary of the prerogative of mercy within the state, having it in his power to pardon, either absolutely or conditionally, any offender convicted in New South Wales. He can also remit fines, penalties, and forfeitures due to the Crown, but he cannot pardon or remit on the condition of the offender voluntarily leaving the state, unless the offence has been a political one only. In all capital cases until recently the final responsibility of deciding whether or not the death penalty should be carried out rested solely with the Governor, but, by a new arrangement which has been agreed to by all the Australasian colonies, such final power is now exercised by the Governor "with the advice of the Executive Council." This places the procedure of these colonies, in regard to capital cases, on similar lines to the system that has for some time past been in force in Canada. Its adoption was suggested and strongly urged by Lord Onslow, the former Governor of New Zealand; and Lord Knutsford, the Secretary of State for the Colonies in the second Salisbury Administration, ascertained the views of the various Australasian colonies upon the subject. It being found that they all accepted the proposal as an improvement upon the practice then existing, a circular despatch was sent to each colony with instructions for its adoption. The new system was first brought into operation in New South Wales towards the end of October, 1892.

The Governor is also vested with the authority of the Crown, enabling him to nominate the members of the Upper House of the Legislature, and to summon, prorogue to a future day, or dissolve "any legislative body" existing in the state. His instructions, however, provide that in the exercise of the above powers he is to act by the advice of the Executive Council in all cases except those whose nature is such that in his opinion the public service "would sustain material prejudice were he to follow such advice," or in matters too trivial to submit to the Council, or "too urgent to admit of their advice being given"; but in all such urgent cases he must communicate to the Council as soon as practicable the measures taken by him, and his reasons for acting. It is expressly provided, however, that the Governor may, if he think fit, disregard the advice of the Executive and act in direct opposition to the declared will of his advisers, but in such cases he is required to make a full report of the whole circumstances for the information of the Secretary of State for the Colonies.

The Governor acts as Viceroy as regards giving the Royal assent to or vetoing Bills passed by the Legislature, or reserving them for the special consideration of the Sovereign. The instructions deal at large with this matter, but it is usual in practice to be guided to a large extent by the advice of the law officers of the Crown. There are eight different classes of Bills, however, to which the Governor is bound to refuse the Royal assent. They are:—

(1.) Divorce Bills (that is, private bills divorcing particular persons).

(2.) Bills making any kind of grant, gratuity, or donation to the Governor.

(3.) Bills affecting the currency.

(4.) Bills imposing differential duties, which are not in accordance with the Australian Colonies Duties Act, 1873.

(5.) Bills apparently contrary to Imperial treaty obligations.

(6.) Bills interfering with the discipline or control of His Majesty's land or sea forces employed in the state.

(7.) Bills of great importance, or extraordinary in their nature, whereby the Royal prerogative, or the rights and property of His Majesty's subjects residing beyond the state, or the trade and shipping of the United Kingdom and its dependencies, may be prejudiced.

(8.) Bills containing provisions to which the Royal assent has already been refused, or which have been once disallowed, unless they contain a clause suspending their operation until the King's pleasure has been signified, or unless the Governor is satisfied that there is urgent necessity for bringing any such Bill into immediate operation, in which case he is empowered to assent to the Bill on behalf of the King, if it is not repugnant to the law of England, or inconsistent with Imperial treaty obligations; and in every such case he is required to transmit the Bill to His Majesty, together with his reasons for assenting to it.

The following Acts of Parliament regulate the action of the Governor in assenting to Bills on behalf of the King, or reserving them for the consideration of the Sovereign:—5 and 6 Vic., cap. 76, secs. 31–32; 7 and 8 Vic., cap. 74, sec. 7; and 13 and 14 Vic., cap. 59, secs. 13, 32, and 33. The effect of these enactments is to deprive any reserved Bill of all force and legality until the King's assent thereto has been formally communicated to the Governor; and power is given to His Majesty to veto any Bill to which the Governor has assented on his behalf within two years after the receipt of such Bill by the Secretary of State for the Colonies, in which case the Bill is to be declared null and void by message of the Governor, and proclamation. Reserved Bills are to be laid before His Majesty in Council, and the King may allow them or not within a period of two years from the day on which they were reserved by the Governor. The King's assent to reserved Bills may be transmitted by telegram.

By Act 7 Vic., No. 16, all Acts of Parliament which become law are required to be registered by the Registrar-General within ten days of their so becoming law.

The Governor of New South Wales is also Governor of Norfolk Island, under an order dated October 18, 1900, and it is incumbent on him to visit the possession once at least during his term of office.

The above is a summary of the powers and duties of the Governor, as defined by his instructions and the Letters Patent; but additional duties have been imposed upon him by the Constitution and Electoral Acts. In accordance with these enactments he must summon the Legislative Assembly; appoint the President of the Legislative Council; prorogue or dissolve Parliament; appoint his ministers *proprio motu;* also appoint, with the advice of the Executive, all public officers whose appointment is not vested in heads of departments; issue all warrants for the payment of money; issue the writs for general elections, and, in the absence of the Speaker, issue writs to fill vacancies occurring in the Assembly.

In summoning, proroguing, or dissolving Parliament, the Governor usually acts according to the advice tendered him by the Cabinet; but he is in no way bound to do so, and, as a matter of fact, he has sometimes declined to be guided by his Ministers. This, however, has never happened except in respect to granting a dissolution. As to summoning or proroguing, a difference of opinion is hardly likely to arise. The relations established between the Ministry and the representatives of the people are in accordance with the time-honoured precedents prevailing in Great Britain, which may be thus defined. The Cabinet must be chosen from—"(1) Members of the Legislature; (2) holding the same political views, and chosen from the party possessing a majority in the House of Commons; (3) carrying out a concerted policy; (4) under a common responsibility, to be signified by a collective resignation in the event of Parliamentary censure; and (5) acknowledging a common subordination to one Chief Minister."

The Imperial rule as to the circumstances under which a Government is bound to resign is as follows:—Censure, involving loss of office, rests entirely with the Lower House, or popular branch of the Legislature; hence, directly a Ministry fails to command a majority of the House of Commons, it must give place to another. Want of confidence in a Cabinet may be shown in three ways: first, by a direct vote of censure, or a specific declaration of want of confidence; second, by a vote disapproving of some act of the Government; or, third, by the rejection of some important measure introduced by the Ministry. In any of these cases Ministers must either resign, or appeal to the country if they can get the Sovereign to sanction a new election.

These rules have been virtually adopted in New South Wales, and the undoubted right of the Governor, as the depositary of the Royal prerogative, to refuse to grant a dissolution, if he think fit, has been more than once exercised. In March, 1877, Sir Hercules Robinson refused to grant a dissolution to Sir John Robertson, and in September of the same year he also declined to enable Sir Henry Parkes to go to the country. The reason alleged in each case was that the Assembly refused to make provision for the expenditure of the year. It will thus be seen that a grave responsibility is thrown upon the Governor in the exercise of the unquestioned right of granting or refusing a dissolution of Parliament, and in the cases mentioned it can hardly be doubted that Sir Hercules Robinson acted within his powers. The Viceroy is the conservator of the rights and interests of the whole population, and it must be evident that grave evils would ensue were a dissolution to take place before supplies had been granted.

The exercise of the prerogative of mercy is such an important function of the Governor, and he is so liable on some occasions to have strong pressure brought to bear upon him in connection with it, that it will be well to quote at length the instructions received a few years ago upon this point. The mode of procedure in capital cases has already been referred to, and in other cases the Governor is instructed not to pardon or reprieve any offender without receiving the advice of one, at least, of his Ministers; and in any case in which such pardon or reprieve might directly affect the interests of the Empire, or of any country or place beyond the jurisdiction of the Government of the state, the Governor must, before deciding as to either pardon or reprieve, take those interests specially into his own personal consideration in conjunction with such advice as aforesaid. In another part of his instructions the Governor is permitted to act in opposition to the advice of the Executive Council "if he see sufficient cause," but he is to report any such matter to the Sovereign without delay.

The Executive.

The Executive Council is now composed of seven salaried Ministers, namely: the Premier and Chief Secretary, the Colonial Treasurer and Minister for Railways, the Attorney-General and Minister of Justice, the Secretary for Lands, the Secretary for Public Works, the Minister of Public Instruction and Minister for Labour and Industry, the Secretary for Mines and Agriculture, with a Vice-President, and three members without portfolio. These form the Cabinet, and, of course, are responsible to Parliament. The Ministry, as the advisers of the Governor, must also retain his confidence; but, practically, this is seldom likely to be withdrawn, so long as they command a working majority in the Assembly. The Governor may dissolve

Parliament although the Ministry have not sustained a defeat, and in this case the continued existence of any Government would depend directly on the vote of the constituencies, but such a contingency can happen but seldom.

Apart from the Vice-President of the Executive Council, who holds no portfolio, it is rare for more than one Minister to be selected from the Upper House, and it will thus be seen that the principle of the responsibility of members of the Government to Parliament is fully carried out. For every act of the Governor as Viceroy some Minister is responsible to Parliament; and even in matters of Imperial interest, where the final onus rests upon the Governor, he himself is responsible to the Imperial Government, whose members are under the control of the House of Commons, so that no loophole is left for the exercise of any arbitrary act. The Crown, except in two instances (appeals to the Privy Council, and the bestowal of titles), acts towards the Executive through its representative, the Governor; and so long ago as the inception of Responsible Government, Earl Grey declared, in an official despatch, that he should make "a judicious use of the influence, rather than of the authority, of his office," which wise maxim has usually been followed. But in extreme cases, such as when his sanction is requested to any illegal proceeding, the Governor is bound, without question, to keep the law, though he may thereby be brought into hostile relations with the Cabinet. Sir Michael Hicks-Beach, in a communication to the Governor-General of Canada in 1879, clearly laid down the doctrine that the Governor of any British Colony "has an unquestionable constitutional right to dismiss his Ministers, if from any cause he feels it incumbent on him to do so." This does not militate against the doctrine of responsibility; for if the Ministry appointed by the Governor do not possess the confidence of Parliament, they cannot hold office, and the Governor will be forced to give way, or else persevere till he can select a Ministry whom the Assembly will accept. The final control will thus be, as in every other case, with the representatives of the people. In matters of routine the Governor will necessarily act on the advice of his Ministers, and in most cases relating to the internal economy of the departments, he will even adopt the individual recommendations of the Ministers by whom they are severally controlled.

As regards matters of purely Imperial interest, the Governor is responsible to the British authorities for their due conservation. If in consequence of his action in any such matter, he is involved in a dispute with his Ministers, he is bound to refer them to the Sovereign, should his action have been endorsed by the Colonial Office. If his conduct were not approved of in England he would most likely be recalled. It follows from this, that in no case can the Governor be held to be responsible directly to Parliament for his conduct. His Ministers are responsible, but personally he has only to render an account to the Crown itself—that is, to the Imperial Parliament.

The Executive Council cannot discharge any function unless duly summoned by the Governor, and unless at least two members, in addition to the Governor or presiding member, be present to form a quorum. Formal minutes are, of course, kept of all proceedings.

Since the introduction of Responsible Government there have been thirty Ministries; but as four of these became merged into those next succeeding without the resignation of their members, the actual number of cabinets holding power may properly be said to have been twenty-six, whose average tenure of office, excluding the Ministry at present in power, has been about one year and six and a half months. Ten Governments were displaced by votes of censure, expressed or implied; three resigned in consequence of defeat on important measures of policy; two retired on being saved from defeat only by the Speaker's casting-vote, and three others through a motion for the adjournment of the House being carried against them; four, as previously stated, were merged into the succeeding Ministries; five resigned without a direct vote being carried against them, but in consequence of not possessing a working majority; one Government fell to pieces through internal disagreements; and one resigned in consequence of the Governor declining to appoint to the Legislative Council a certain number of its nominees.

The Parliament.

It seems a singular omission in the Constitution Act that no definition is given of the relative powers of the Legislative Council and Legislative Assembly. Such is the fact, but little inconvenience has arisen thereby, since by common consent it has been agreed that the precedents regulating the proceedings and relations, *inter se*, of the two Houses of the Imperial Parliament shall be followed, so far as applicable, in New South Wales. The Constitution Act provides that all money Bills shall be introduced in the Lower House only. The important rule of the House of Commons, affirmed two hundred years ago and constantly enforced ever since, that "all aids and supplies, and aids to His Majesty in Parliament, are the sole gift of the Commons, and it is the undoubted right of the Commons to direct, limit, and appoint in such Bills the ends, purposes, considerations, conditions, limitations, and qualifications of such grants, which ought not to be changed or altered by the House of Lords," is also held to be in force as regards the Parliament of this state, and has generally been recognised and acted upon.

The two Houses, however, do not possess the most important of the privileges of the Imperial Parliament, namely, the right of punishing for contempt, although the Legislative Assembly has, on one occasion, punished one of its members, by expelling him for conduct, beyond its precincts, assumed to be dishonourable. As regards disorderly conduct within the walls of the Chamber, it has been held by the Supreme Court, and affirmed by the Privy Council, that the Assembly only possesses the power of suspending a member for disorderly conduct for the period of the sitting at which he displays such conduct. A member may also be removed from the House by order of the Speaker if he persists in obstruction or contemns the Standing Orders; but fortunately this course has seldom been rendered necessary.

Witnesses may be summoned to give evidence before either House, or before committees of the Council or Assembly, the necessary powers for compelling their attendance having been conferred by an Act passed in 1881. Any person disobeying a summons may be arrested on a Judge's warrant; and the maximum penalty for refusing to give evidence is imprisonment for one calendar month.

The number of members of the Legislative Council is not limited by the Constitution Act, although the minimum number is fixed at twenty-one. It will be seen that this gives power to a Governor to quash any possible obstruction on the part of the Council to the will of the Government and the Lower House by "swamping" the Council. Such a proceeding, however, can hardly be held to be allowable, except under extreme circumstances. As a matter of fact, an attempt to "swamp" the Council was made during one of the premierships of Sir Charles Cowper, but public opinion condemned the course most strongly, although the somewhat peculiar circumstances of the case were thought at the time to justify the Governor's action. The authorities in England severely rebuked the Governor (Sir John Young) for the course he had taken, and since then "swamping" the Council has never been seriously entertained, nor is there much chance that it will ever again be attempted. The principle in fact has been affirmed, on the basis of an understanding entered into between Sir John Young and the leading statesmen of the day (on both sides of the House), that the members of the Legislative Council should be limited to a convenient number, and that no nominations should ever be made merely for the purpose of strengthening the party which happens to be in power. A deadlock between the two Houses is provided against by the universal feeling that the Assembly represents the will of the people, and in such case the Council would certainly have to give way to the deliberate will of the people's representatives. The Council is intended as a check to hasty legislation; and it doubtless acts as a useful "brake" to violent party feeling.

The Legislative Council.

As before stated, the members of the Upper House are nominated by the Governor, the minimum number composing the House being fixed at twenty-one. No limit to the number is fixed by the Constitution Act, but, in accordance with the arrangement already described, the number of members is practically kept down by the exclusion of all purely political appointments. As the number of members of the Assembly has increased to 125, the number of members composing the Council in October, 1903 (fifty-eight), cannot be considered an unfair proportion, as the ratio of increase has not been much greater than in the case of the Lower House. Every member of the Council must be of full age, and either a natural-born or a duly naturalised subject. Four-fifths of the members must be persons not holding any paid office under the Crown, but this is not held to include officers "in His Majesty's sea and land forces on full or half pay, or retired officers on pensions." Though the appointment is for life, a member may resign his seat, and he also forfeits it by absence from the House for two consecutive sessions without leave, by becoming naturalised in a foreign State, by becoming bankrupt, by becoming a public contractor or a defaulter, and by being attainted of treason or being convicted of felony or any infamous crime. The Governor appoints, and, if necessary, removes the President, who may speak in debate, but can only give a casting-vote. An attendance of one-third of the members on the roll was formerly necessary to con stitute a quorum, but an Act has been carried reducing the proportion to one-fourth. The Council must hold a sitting at least once in every year, and no greater interval than twelve months must elapse between session and session. The proceedings are regulated by standing orders, which are, in the main, similar to those of the Assembly, the latter being framed on the model of the rules obtaining in the House of Commons. No member may sit or vote till he has taken the oath of allegiance, or the affirmation prescribed in lieu of that oath.

The Legislative Assembly.

In the Session of 1892–3, an Act was passed, entitled the Parliamentary Electorates and Elections Act of 1893, by which the course of procedure in regard to elections for the Legislative Assembly of New South Wales was almost entirely changed. The enactments under which such elections had been conducted up to that time—the Electoral Act of 1880, and the Wentworth Subdivision Act—were repealed upon the passing of the Act of 1893, with the exception of certain provisions which have since been abrogated by proclamation. During the year 1896 several important alterations were made in the 1893 Act in the direction of the extension of the franchise, and of the removal of restrictions placed upon electors changing their residence from one district to another. In 1902 the franchise was extended to women. The main principles of the new electoral system may be thus summarised:—

The number of members of the Legislative Assembly, which had grown by virtue of the Expansion Clauses of the Act of 1880 from 108 to 147, was reduced to 125, and the number of electorates, now denominated Electoral Districts, was increased from seventy-four to 125. Under the new system, therefore, there are exactly as many members as electorates, or, in other words, there are single electorates. This, of course, involved a complete re-distribution of the electorates, and special machinery had to be created in order that this might be done. In accordance with the Act three Commissioners were appointed, to whom was entrusted the duty of dividing the state into 125 districts, each containing as nearly as might be the same number of electors. In order to ascertain the quota of electors to be apportioned to each electorate, the number of resident electors on the roll for 1892–3, which happened to be 282,851, was divided by 125, and the quotient, 2,263, was fixed as the standard number of electors entitled to one representative. In mapping out the new Electoral Districts, the Commissioners were required to form them so as to include the standard number of electors as nearly as possible; at the same time, in order to avoid inconvenient divisions, a margin of 200 voters either above or below the standard number was allowed, which margin it was permitted, in exceptional cases, to increase to 600 either way, on satisfactory reason for taking that action being furnished by the Commissioners. No adjustment of electorates has taken place since the first made under the Act of 1893; but the Act contemplates re-adjustments shortly after the taking of a census, and also, if necessary, every four or five years. The last census was taken in 1901. As a result of the referendum on the question of reduction of members, taken in December, 1903, when the voting favoured a reduction from 125 to 90 members, a redistribution of electoral divisions will shortly be carried out.

The qualification for an elector is that he must be a natural-born subject who has resided in New South Wales for a continuous period of one year, or a naturalised subject who has resided in the state continuously for one year after naturalisation. It was provided in the principal Act that in either case he must have resided three months continuously in the electoral district for which he claimed to vote; but by the amending Act 60 Vic. No. 25 the period of residence was reduced to one month in the case of a person already on the rolls, and who had but removed from one district to another. Every such person, being of the full age of 21 years, and not otherwise disqualified, is entitled to have his name on the electoral roll, and to have an elector's right issued to him. The disqualifications, under the Constitution Act, apply to persons attainted or convicted of treason, felony, or other infamous offence in any part of His Majesty's dominions, unless they have received a free or conditional pardon, or have undergone the sentence passed on them for such offence; and, under subsequent enactments, to persons in the Naval and Military Service on full pay (except the militia and volunteers), and to persons of unsound mind, or in receipt of public charity. All other disqualifications have now been removed. The Woman's Franchise Act, passed in 1902, entitles all females of the age of 21 years and upwards to vote, but this right is not to be exercised until the first general election thereafter.

Power was given to the Governor under the Act of 1893 to subdivide each electoral district into divisions, and to appoint to each district an Electoral Registrar, with Deputy Registrars for the several divisions. It is one of the duties of these Registrars and Deputy Registrars to issue certificates known as electors' rights to those entitled to them. These electors' rights are printed in red ink upon paper specially prepared to prevent fraudulent imitations, with butts, like cheques, in accordance with the forms shown in Schedule A of the principal and amending Acts. They are bound in books, and numbered consecutively in black figures. Every person who has established his qualification to vote, and who has been placed on the electoral roll, is entitled to receive an elector's right upon signing his name in a book kept for that purpose, as well as on the butt and the face of the right itself. Under the principal Act an elector who removed from one district to another within three months of an election was practically disfranchised; but, as stated above, this period has now been reduced to one month, and until the elector is qualified to vote in the district to which he has removed he may use his right in his old district. Provision is also made for the issue of a substituted right in the event of a right being lost or defaced. Every elector's right remains in force until cancelled in the prescribed manner. It is provided by the amending legislation of 1896 that an elector who has changed his abode from one district to another may obtain a right for his new district after he has resided one month therein, and may have his name inscribed on the Additional Roll on a declaration by the Registrar of his original district stating that he was enrolled there. When the Registrar of any district grants an application for an elector's right other than in lieu of one held for another district, he inscribes the name of the elector in a Provisional List, copies of which, during the first week of each month, are exhibited at every post-office and police-office within the district, so that objection to any name may be taken and heard at the Revision Court of the district, to be presided over by a Stipendiary or Police Magistrate, specially appointed as a Revising Magistrate. All names passed at the monthly Revision Court are then inscribed on the Additional Roll.

During the first week in August of each year, the Registrar must make out a general list of all persons on the electoral roll for his district, as well as of those to whom electors' rights have been issued since the last roll was printed; and copies of all such lists are exhibited for public inspection at every post-office in the electoral district. Any person objecting to any name upon the list must give to the Registrar, in writing, his reasons for such objection, and the Registrar must notify the same to the person to whom objection is taken. Every Registrar is supplied quarterly, by the District Registrar of Births, Deaths, and Marriages, with a list of all males above the age of 21 years whose deaths have been registered within the quarter in that particular district. As no provision is made for the exchange of these lists of deceased persons between different districts, it is possible for the names of electors who died outside their own districts to remain on the roll, and it is known that this often happens, unless sufficient proof of death is furnished by objectors. The Comptroller-General of Prisons and the Inspector-General of Police must forward quarterly to the Minister charged with the administration of the Act a list of all males above the age of 20 years in any gaol, lock-up, or other place of detention; and the Minister must send to the Registrar of each district such particulars as may be necessary for the purification of the electoral roll for such district. The Registrar must then write on a copy of the electoral roll, against the name of every person on the lists supplied to him as above, the words "dead" or "in custody, disqualified," or simply "in custody" where the particulars supplied do not appear to be such as to disqualify the person. Under the principal Act a Revision Court was held in October each year; but under the amending Act a monthly Revision Court is now held, at which objections may be heard, and claims for insertion on the lists considered; and from the lists, when duly corrected and certified to by the magistrate presiding at the Court, the electoral roll is printed. In the year 1900 and every third year thereafter the General List is to be made up from the butts of the electors' rights issued to persons "then" entitled to vote. A new issue of electors rights was made at the beginning of 1901, and these remain in force until duly cancelled.

Writs for the election of members of the Assembly are issued by the Governor in the case of a general election, and by the Speaker, or, in his absence or if there should be no Speaker, by the Governor, in the case of a bye-election. The writs for a general election are required to be issued within four clear days from the proclamation dissolving Parliament, and are made returnable not later than thirty-five days from the date of issue. Parliament must meet not later than seven days from the return of the writs. The polling day for a general election is fixed as the eighteenth day from the date of the issue of the writs.

A person, to be qualified as a candidate, must be the holder of an elector's right. Each candidate must be nominated by at least six electors for the district. The nomination must be made in writing, signed by the nominators, and endorsed by the candidate, consenting to the nomination. No elector can have more than one vote in the state, or, in other words, the "one man one vote" principle is enforced. No elector can nominate more than one candidate. No deposit from a candidate is required. Proper provision is made for the appointment of Returning Officers, substitutes, deputies, poll-clerks, and scrutineers, much as in the Act of 1880. Under the principal Act the poll was open from 8 a.m. to 6 p.m. in the months from October to March inclusive, and from 8 a.m. to 5 p.m. from April to September inclusive; but under the Parliamentary Elections (Polling) Act (No. 20 of 1898) the poll remains open from 8 a.m. to 6 p.m., irrespective of the season of the year when the election is held. Every person claiming to vote must exhibit his elector's right, satisfy the Returning Officer that he is the person on the roll who should possess that right, and demand a ballot-paper. He is then furnished with a ballot-paper, containing the names of the candidates; and his elector's right, as well as the butt, is punctured to denote that he has voted at that election. The elector has then to retire to some unoccupied compartment of the polling-booth. there to strike out the names of all the candidates on the paper except the one for whom he votes, and the ballot-paper, folded so that the names are not visible, but that the puncture can be seen by the Returning Officer or his deputy, is placed by him in the ballot-box.

No provision is made whereby an elector can record his vote if away from his own electorate, except where outside polling places have been appointed, under the provisions of the Act, before the issue of the writs. At the close of the poll the votes are counted, and the result declared by a notice signed by the Returning Officer, and posted in some conspicuous position in the principal polling place, and published in some newspaper circulating in the district.

Very stringent clauses against bribery, treating, or intimidation are included in the Act. It is even forbidden to make a wager on the result of an election under a penalty of from £5 to £50. There are also sections providing for the appointment of a Committee of Elections and Qualifications, with powers similar to those conferred by the Act of 1880.

The disqualifications for membership of the Legislative Assembly, provided by the Constitution Act, still remain in force. They are as follow:—

1. He must not be a member of the Legislative Council.
2. He must not hold any office of profit under the Crown, either for a term of years or during pleasure.
3. He must not be in any way interested in any contract for the public service.

By the Constitution Act Amendment Act of 1884, the disqualification of persons holding offices of profit was declared not to apply to the Colonial Secretary or any other member of the Ministry. The third disqualification also does not apply to any contract made by a company consisting of more than twenty persons. If any disqualified person be elected, the election is voided by the House, and should such person presume to sit or vote he is liable to a fine of £500.

By an Act assented to on the 21st September, 1889, members of the Assembly are allowed the sum of £300 per annum to reimburse them for expenses incurred in the discharge of their duties. Members of both Houses are allowed free passes on the railways and tramways of the State.

Before taking his seat each member must take the oath of allegiance in the prescribed form, or make an affirmation in lieu of it. A member may resign his seat at any time, and he is held to have vacated it under any of the following conditions:—Absence during a whole session without leave, naturalisation in a foreign country, bankruptcy, being a defaulter, or convicted of treason, felony, or other infamous crime; becoming pecuniarily interested in any contract for the public service excepting as member of a Company exceeding twenty in number, acceptance of an office of profit under the Crown, becoming a member of either House of Parliament of the Australian Commonwealth.

The Act 37 Vic. No. 7 provides that no Assembly can prolong its existence beyond the term of three years. One session, at least, must be held every year, and twelve months must not elapse between any two sessions. On meeting after a general election, the first business is to elect a Speaker, who has only a casting vote.

The first Parliament elected under the Constitution Act met on the 22nd May, 1856, just six months after the proclamation of the

Constitution. The duration of Parliament, unless it should be previously prorogued, was originally fixed at five years; but in 1874 an Act was passed establishing triennial Parliaments, which has ever since remained law. Since the inauguration of Responsible Government there have been nineteen appeals to the people, so that it will be seen the duration of each Assembly has not averaged even the shorter period of life to which its existence is now limited. The subjoined table gives the duration of each Parliament elected under Constitutional Government:—

Parliament.	Opened.	Dissolved.	Duration. Yr.	mth.	dy.	No. of Sessions.
First	22 May, 1856	19 Dec., 1857	1	6	27	2
Second	23 March, 1858	11 April, 1859	1	0	19	2
Third	30 Aug., 1859	10 Nov., 1860	1	2	11	2
Fourth	10 Jan., 1861	10 Nov., 1864	3	10	0	5
Fifth	24 Jan., 1865	15 Nov., 1869	4	9	22	6
Sixth	27 Jan., 1870	3 Feb., 1872	2	0	7	3
Seventh	30 April, 1872	28 Nov., 1874	2	6	29	4
Eighth	27 Jan., 1875	12 Oct., 1877	2	8	15	3
Ninth	27 Nov., 1877	9 Nov., 1880	2	11	13	3
Tenth	15 Dec., 1880	23 Nov., 1882	1	11	8	3
Eleventh	3 Jan., 1883	7 Oct., 1885	2	9	4	6
Twelfth	17 Nov., 1885	26 Jan., 1887	1	2	9	2
Thirteenth	8 March, 1887	19 Jan., 1889	1	10	11	3
Fourteenth	27 Feb., 1889	6 June, 1891	2	3	10	4
Fifteenth	14 July, 1891	25 June, 1894	2	11	12	4
Sixteenth	7 Aug., 1894	5 July, 1895	0	10	29	1
Seventeenth	13 Aug., 1895	8 July, 1898	2	10	26	4
Eighteenth	16 Aug., 1898	11 June, 1901	2	9	26	5
Nineteenth	23 July, 1901	...	...			...
	Average		2	4	7	3 to 4

The system of one man one vote came into operation on the dissolution of the fifteenth Parliament. At the first election under the new system in 1894, a total poll of 204,246 votes was recorded. The electors on the rolls numbered 298,817, and those qualified to vote in districts that were contested, 254,105. The poll, therefore, represented 80·38 per cent. of effective voters—by far the best percentage of votes recorded at a general election in New South Wales. The second election under the new Act gave a poll of 153,034 votes out of a total enrolment of 238,233 electors in contested constituencies, the proportion of votes cast being 64·24 per cent. At the election held in July, 1901, 195,359 votes were recorded, the electors enrolled numbering altogether 346,184, and those qualified in contested electorates only, 270,861, so that the percentage of votes recorded was 72·13.

The number of males of full age compared with the total population is very large, the proportion at the last Census being 28 per cent. According to the official lists the number of persons enrolled at the general election in 1901 amounted to 25·4 per cent., or over one-fourth of the total population. The average number of electors on the roll per member was 2,769, and the estimated population to each member was 10,977.

The subjoined table gives the result of the four general elections which have taken place since the principle of one man one vote became law :—

Parliament.	Voters on Roll.	Number of Electors to a Member.	Total Members returned.	Members unopposed.	Contested Electorates.				
					Electors on Roll.	Votes recorded.	Percentage of Votes recorded.	Informal Votes.	Percentage of Informal Votes.
Sixteenth	298,817	2,296	125	1	254,105	204,246	80·38	3,310	1·62
Seventeenth ...	267,458	2,139	125	8	238,233	153,034	64·24	1,354	0·88
Eighteenth ...	324,338	2,595	125	3	294,481	178,717	60·69	1,638	0·92
Nineteenth ...	346,184	2,769	125	13	270,861	195,359	72·13	1,534	0·79

At the referendum for reduction of members on the 16th December, 1903, the votes for 90 members numbered 206,273, for 125, 63,171, and for 100 the votes were 13,316.

VICTORIA.

UP to the 1st July, 1851, Victoria formed a part of New South Wales, being included with the parent settlement under the name of Port Phillip District. The separation was effected in pursuance of an Act of the Imperial Parliament, dated 5th August, 1850, entitled "An Act for the better government of Her Majesty's Australian Colonies." This measure provided that "the territories now comprised within the said district of Port Phillip, including the town of Melbourne, and bounded on the north and north-east by a straight line drawn from Cape Howe to the nearest course of the River Murray, and thence by the course of that river to the eastern boundary of the colony of South Australia, shall be separated from the colony of New South Wales, and shall cease to return members to the Legislative Council of such colony, and shall be created into and thenceforth form a separate colony, to be known and designated as the Colony of Victoria."

It was also enacted that there should be a separate Legislative Council for Victoria, one third of the number of members to be appointed by Her Majesty and the remainder to be elected by the inhabitants of the colony. Authority was given to the Governor and Legislative Council of New South Wales to determine by Act of Parliament the number of members of which the Legislative Council of Victoria was to consist, and to make provision for dividing the new colony into electoral districts, for appointing the number of members for each district, and generally for carrying on the necessary elections.

The measure provided also that electors should be possessed of freehold estate of the clear value of £100, or be occupiers or three-years leaseholders of the clear annual value of £10 a year.

On the issuing of writs for the first election of members of the Legislative Council of Victoria, the colony was to be accounted as legally established, and the powers of the Governor and Council of New South Wales over the territories comprised in Victoria thereupon ceased.

In accordance with the provisions of the Imperial Act the Governor and Legislative Council of New South Wales passed the Victoria Electoral Act of 1851, which provided that the Legislative Council of Victoria should consist of thirty members, ten to be appointed and twenty elected. The new colony was also divided into sixteen electoral districts.

On the 1st July, 1851, Sir Charles Fitzroy, the Governor-General of Australia, issued the writs for the election of members, and declared the district of Port Phillip to be separated from New South Wales, and established as an independent colony to be known and designated as the colony of Victoria. The constitution thus established continued until the 23rd November, 1855.

At the close of 1852 the Secretary of State for the Colonies forwarded a despatch to Lieutenant-Governor La Trobe, in which the Legislative Council of the colony was invited to consider the question of forming a second Legislative Chamber. This suggestion was shortly afterwards acted upon, and on the 24th March, 1854, a Bill "to establish a constitution in and for the Colony of Victoria" was passed and submitted to the Lieutenant-Governor, who at once forwarded it to the Secretary of State. On the 16th July, 1855, the Imperial Parliament passed an Act "to enable Her Majesty to assent to a Bill as amended of the Legislature of Victoria to establish a constitution in and for the Colony of Victoria." The Bill itself appeared as the first schedule to the Imperial Act, and was assented to on the 21st July, 1855. This course of procedure was rendered necessary owing to the fact that the Legislative Council of Victoria had exceeded its powers in passing the Bill before submitting it to the Imperial Government. It was, however, explained by the Secretary of State that the Parliament did not consider it necessary to supersede the Bill by direct legislation, as it was thought that the colonial legislature should be trusted for all the details of local representation and internal administration.

The new "Constitution Act" was formally proclaimed on the 23rd November, 1855, and the first meeting of the new Parliament was held on the 21st November, 1856.

Under the terms of the Act the elective and nominee Council was abolished, and an elective Council and Assembly were established, "with power to make laws in and for Victoria in all cases whatsoever." Subject to certain limitations, the Parliament may alter, repeal, or vary the Constitution." This power, which was conferred by Section 60, has been extensively availed of. Thus, under the Act as originally passed, the Legislative Council consisted of thirty members, elected for ten years, representing six districts. At present, the Council consists of thirty-five members, elected for six years, of these thirty-four are representatives of, and elected by, the electors of the seventeen provinces, and one member is representative of, and elected by, the public officers and railway officers. The Legislative Assembly, as first constituted, consisted of sixty members, representing thirty-seven districts; at present there are sixty-eight members, of whom sixty-five are representative of, and elected by, the electors of the sixty-five electoral districts, one member representative of, and elected by, the public officers, and two members representative of, and elected by, the railway officers. The property qualification for members and electors of the Upper House has been considerably reduced, while at present no property qualification is required in the case of members and electors for the Legislative Assembly. Amongst other important changes which might be mentioned was the abolition in 1865 of pensions, or retiring allowances, to persons who, on political grounds, retired or were released from certain responsible offices.

The powers and duties of the Governor are very similar in all the states, and the subject is referred to at some length in the previous sub-chapter, dealing with the constitution of New South Wales.

The Governor is, *ex officio*, President of the Executive Council, the other members, consisting of not more than ten Ministers, holding paid offices. There are two legislative chambers—a Legislative Council, consisting of forty-eight members, returned for fourteen provinces; and a Legislative Assembly, composed of ninety-five members, returned from eighty-four districts. Councillors are elected for a term of six years, while members of the Lower House occupy their seats for a period of three years. The qualification for members of the Upper House is the possession of freehold rateable property of an annual rateable value of £100, and a minimum age limit of 30 years. Electors for this Chamber must possess freehold property rated in some municipal district at not less than £10 per annum, or be lessees, assignees, or occupying tenants of property of an annual rateable value of not less than £15. Resident graduates of Universities within the British dominions, legal and medical practitioners, clergymen, certificated schoolmasters, matriculated students of Melbourne University, and naval and military officers are also entitled to vote for the Legislative Council. All voters not being natural born subjects of His Majesty must have resided in Victoria for twelve months previous to 1st January, or 1st July, in any year, and must have taken out letters of naturalisation at least three years previously. Every elector must be a male of the full age of 21 years.

For the Legislative Assembly, the qualifications required of members are that they have reached the age of 21 years, and are natural-born subjects of the King, or, in case of aliens, have been naturalised for five years; but judges of Victorian courts, ministers of religion, and persons who have been attainted of treason, or convicted of any felony or infamous crime, are not eligible. Persons holding offices of profit, uncertificated bankrupts or insolvents, and members of either House of the Federal Legislature are also ineligible. There is no property qualification required, either for members or electors. Manhood suffrage is the basis on which electors vote, and they must be natural-born subjects, or naturalised for one year prior to the 1st January, or 1st July, in any year, possessing an elector's right, and untainted by crime, or be enrolled on the roll of ratepaying electors, or hold a voter's certificate under the provisions of section 23 of Act No. 1601. The Plural Voting Abolition Act of 1899 provides, however, that it shall not be lawful for any one person to vote more than once at the same election, nor to vote in more than one district.

Women are not eligible as members or electors of either House of Parliament.

Members of the Legislative Council receive no remuneration for their services, while in the Lower Chamber the members receive "reimbursement of expenses" at the rate of £300 per annum.

Ratepayers in the municipal districts have their names placed on the roll without any action on their own part; but non-ratepayers and freeholders residing in another electorate and not enrolled as ratepayers, must take out "electors' rights." To qualify for an elector's right a person must have resided in Victoria for twelve months, and in a division of his district for at least one month prior to application. The non-residential qualification for a right consists in possessing property of the clear value of £50, or an annual value of £5, in an electoral district. As before stated, no person is permitted to exercise more than one vote at the same election.

Since the inauguration of responsible government in Victoria, there have been eighteen complete Parliaments, the first of which was opened on the 21st November, 1856, and dissolved on the 9th August, 1859, and the eighteenth opened on the 13th November, 1900, and dissolved on the 16th September, 1902. The present Parliament began its sessions on the 14th October, 1902. The table below shows the date of opening and dissolution of each Parliament up till the present time:—

Parliament.	Opened.	Dissolved.	Duration.			Number of Sessions.
			yr.	mth.	dy.	
First	21 Nov., 1856	9 Aug., 1859	2	8	19	3
Second	13 Oct., 1859	11 July, 1861	1	9	0	2
Third	30 Aug., 1861	25 Aug., 1864	2	11	27	3
Fourth	28 Nov., 1864	11 Dec., 1865	1	0	14	1
Fifth	12 Feb., 1866	30 Dec., 1867	1	10	17	6
Sixth	13 Mar., 1868	25 Jan., 1871	2	10	14	4
Seventh	25 April, 1871	9 Mar., 1874	2	10	15	3
Eighth	19 May, 1874	25 April, 1877	2	11	8	3
Ninth	22 May, 1877	9 Feb., 1880	2	8	19	3
Tenth	11 May, 1880	29 June, 1880	0	1	20	1
Eleventh	22 July, 1880	3 Feb., 1883	2	6	13	3
Twelfth	27 Feb., 1883	19 Feb., 1886	2	11	24	4
Thirteenth	16 Mar., 1886	11 Mar., 1889	2	11	27	3
Fourteenth	9 April, 1889	5 April, 1892	2	11	27	3
Fifteenth	11 May, 1892	4 Sept., 1894	2	3	25	3
Sixteenth	4 Oct., 1894	28 Sept., 1897	2	11	26	4
Seventeenth	25 Oct., 1897	18 Oct., 1900	2	11	25	4
Eighteenth	13 Nov., 1900	16 Sept., 1902	1	10	4	3
Nineteenth	14 Oct., 1902	....	...	...	...	......
		Average	2	5	1	3 to 4

The following table gives particulars of the voting at the last six general elections :—

Year.	Legislative Council.				Legislative Assembly.			
	Electors on Roll.	Electors in Contested Districts.	Voters in Contested Districts.	Percentage	Electors on Roll.	Electors in Contested Districts.	Voters in Contested Districts.	Percentage.
1889	151,803	31,134	14,726	47·29	243,730	220,973	147,129	66·58
1892	163,286	25,300	10,536	41·64	278,812	243,585	158,611	65·12
1894	145,629	*	*	*	234,552	196,482	139,501	70·99
1897	133,575	*	*	*	254,155	224,987	158,225	70·33
1900	129,363	15,551	6,388	41·08	280,600	203,200	128,980	63·47
1902	134,087	*	*	*	290,241	216,063	141,471	65·47

* No contest.

Queensland.

Queensland was formerly included in New South Wales, but was separated from the mother colony by Her Majesty's Letters Patent, dated the 6th June, 1859. The Letters Patent provided that a form of government should be established in Queensland, based on similar lines to that existing in New South Wales, and ordered the constitution of a Legislative Council and Legislative Assembly "to make laws for the peace, welfare, and good government of the colony in all cases whatsoever."

On the 10th December, 1859, Sir George Bowen, the first Governor, landed, assumed the government, and formally proclaimed the establishment of the colony.

The administration is carried on by the Governor with the advice of an Executive Council, consisting of eight salaried members and one member without portfolio. The Premier is usually, but not invariably, the Vice-President of the Executive.

The Orders in Council provided that the Legislative Council should be summoned and appointed by the Governor. As first constituted it consisted of such persons as the Governor nominated, who were to be not fewer than five, and to hold their seats for five years. All subsequent appointments were to be for life. Members of the Council were to be of the full age of 21 years, and natural-born or naturalised subjects of Her Majesty.

It was also provided that four-fifths of the members nominated should be persons not holding any office or emolument under the Crown, except officers of Her Majesty's sea and land forces, on full or half pay, or retired officers on pension. One-third of the members of the Legislative Council, exclusive of the President, are required to form a quorum. The Governor was also authorized by the Orders in Council to summon a Legislative Assembly, to fix the number of members of which it was to be composed, and to divide the colony into electoral districts. It was also provided that every Legislative Assembly so elected should continue for five years, subject to prorogation or dissolution by the Governor before the expiration of such period. The qualifications of persons who could be elected to the Assembly and of those eligible to vote at elections of members were ordered to be arranged in accordance with the qualifications then in force in New South Wales.

As thus constituted, the Parliament was to have power to make laws for the peace, welfare, and good government of the colony; also to make laws altering or repealing any of the provisions of the Orders in Council, except such as related to the giving and withholding of Royal assent to Bills, the reservation of Bills for Her Majesty's pleasure, the instructions to Governors for their guidance in such matters, and the disallowance of Bills by Her Majesty. The Orders in Council also provided that in the event of any Bill being passed making the Legislative Council elective wholly or in part, it should be reserved for Her Majesty's pleasure, and a copy of the Bill should be laid before both Houses of the Imperial Parliament for at least thirty days before Her Majesty's pleasure should be signified. It was further provided that no alteration in the constitution of the colony could be made unless the second and third readings of the Bill containing such alterations should have been passed with the concurrence of two-thirds of the members for the time being of the Legislative Council and Legislative Assembly, and that such Bill be reserved for the signification of Her Majesty's pleasure thereon; also that all Bills for appropriating any part of the public revenue, or for imposing any new rate, tax, or impost, subject to certain limitations, should originate in the Legislative Assembly; the limitation referred to being that it should not be lawful for the Legislative Assembly to pass any such Bill that had not first been recommended to them by a message from the Governor, sent during the session in which such Bill should be passed. The power of the Legislative Council to alter Money Bills is doubtful, and although it has done so, objection to the course has always been taken by the Queensland Legislative Assembly.

In 1867 the Queensland Parliament passed an Act which consolidated the law relating to the Constitution and embodied the Orders in Council with the exception of two sections, namely, that relating to the giving or withholding of Her Majesty's assent to Bills, and the one referring to the power of altering the Constitution.

This Act is now the Constitution Act of Queensland, the amendments introduced later being of a comparatively unimportant character.

At present the Legislative Council consists of thirty-nine members nominated by the Governor in Council, and contingent on the observation of certain rules of the Chamber, such as attendance at each session, &c.; these members hold their seats for life. The Legislative Councillors receive no remuneration for their services, but are allowed a free railway pass from the date of being sworn in. The qualification has already been stated.

The number of members to be elected to the Legislative Assembly has been altered by various Acts of Parliament. At present there are seventy-two members, representing sixty-one electorates, eleven returning two members each, while the remainder are single electorates. Members of the Assembly receive a remuneration of £300 per annum each, with free railway pass and allowances for travelling expenses. To be qualified for membership of the Legislative Assembly a person must be absolutely free, and qualified and registered as a voter in and for any electoral district. The disqualifications preventing election to the Assembly are:—being a minister of religion; being at the time a member of the Legislative Council; holding any office of profit under the Crown except as member of the Ministry, and excepting also such officers, not more than two, whom the Governor may declare capable of being elected; being in receipt of a pension from the Crown (officers of Her Majesty's army and navy excepted). Every male of the full age of 21 years, who is a natural born or naturalised subject of His Majesty, or legally made a denizen of Queensland, is entitled to have his name entered on the electoral roll, subject to the following qualifications:—(*a*) Six months residence in an electoral district; (*b*) Freehold estate of the clear value of £100; (*c*) Household occupation for six months of clear annual value of £10; (*d*) Leasehold estate. Natives of China, South Sea Islands and India, and Australian aborigines are entitled to vote under freehold qualifications. The persons disqualified comprise members of the military and police forces, police magistrates and clerks of petty sessions, insane, and persons tainted with crime.

Since the introduction of responsible government in Queensland there have been thirteen complete Parliaments. The first Parliament was opened on the 29th May, 1860, and dissolved on the 20th May, 1863. The fourteenth Parliament was opened on the 8th July, 1902. At the last general election for the Legislative Assembly in March, 1902, the total number of electors on the roll was 108,548. The number of electors recording votes was returned at 80,076, and the percentage of voters to the total enrolment in contested districts was 78·9.

South Australia.

The Constitution of the state of South Australia is based upon the Imperial Statute 13 and 14 Vic. c. 59. Under section 32 of that Act the Governor and Legislative Council established thereby were empowered to alter, from time to time, the provisions and laws in force under the said Act for the time being, and to constitute separate Legislative Chambers, in place of the said Legislative Council. The present form of Constitution was embodied in "An Act to establish a Constitution for South Australia, and to grant a civil list to Her Majesty," passed by the old Legislative Council in 1855, and reserved for the signification of Her Majesty's pleasure in January, 1856.

By proclamation dated October 24th, 1856, Her Majesty's assent to the Constitution Act, No. 2 of 1855–6, was made known in the colony. This statute provided for two Houses of Parliament—a Legislative Council and a Legislative Assembly. The Legislative Council, which consisted of eighteen members, was elected by the whole province, voting as a single electorate. Each member was elected for twelve years, but it was provided that at the expiration of each period of four years the first six members on the roll, their places in the first instance having been determined by ballot, should retire, and an election take place to supply the vacancies. The names of the members who were elected to fill their places were inscribed at the bottom of the list, and at the end of a further term of four years six others retired, and the same order was observed in placing the newly-elected members. In this way frequent changes were made in the personnel of the Council, in addition to those which occurred by death, resignation, or other causes, such as bankruptcy, etc. By an amendment in the Constitution it is provided that at the end of three years from the 3rd May, 1902, three members from the central and two members from each of the other electoral districts retire, and new members will be elected to fill their seats. A similar number will thereafter retire every three years, but it is provided that no member is necessarily to retire until he has sat for six years, except those elected to fill vacancies, who retire at the time when their predecessors would have retired. The qualification of a member for the Council consists in being of the full age of 30 years, a natural-born or naturalised subject of His Majesty, or legally made a denizen of the province, and a resident therein of the full period of three years. For an elector the age was fixed at 21 years, with a property qualification of a freehold estate of the value of £50; or a leasehold of £20 annual value, with three years to run; or occupation of a dwelling-house of £25 annual value, and being registered on the electoral roll of the province for six months prior to the election. The same qualification with regard to citizenship was demanded of both members and electors. By Act No. 236 of 1881 the number of members of the Council was increased to twenty-four, and the province divided into four electoral districts, each returning six members, but from the end of March, 1902, the membership was reduced to eighteen.

As originally constituted, the House of Assembly consisted of thirty-six members elected for three years. By an amendment of the Constitution Act the number was increased to fifty-four, but in accordance with the scheme of Parliamentary economy the House was reduced to forty-two members after the end of March, 1902. The qualification of a member was that he should be entitled to be registered as a voter in and for an electoral district within the province, and that he should have resided in the province for the full period of five years. All that was required of an elector was that he should be 21 years of age, a natural-born or naturalised subject of Her Majesty, and registered on the electoral roll of any electoral district for six months previous to the election.

By the Constitution Amendment Act of 1894 the franchise was extended to women.

The disqualifications for both Houses comprise persons attainted of treason or convicted of felony who have not been pardoned, or who have not served their sentence, persons brought into the Northern Territory under the Northern Territory Indian Immigration Act of 1882, and persons residing in the Northern Territory who are not natural-born or naturalised subjects of His Majesty, of European nationality or citizens of the United States, naturalised as subjects of His Majesty, and insane persons.

The powers of both Houses of Parliament, with one important exception, are similar. The first clause of the Constitution Act requires that all Bills for appropriating any part of the revenue of the province, or for imposing, altering, or repealing any rate, tax, duty, or impost, shall originate in the House of Assembly. By an agreement between the two Houses, the Council may suggest amendments, and if acceptable the Assembly may embody them in a "money" Bill, but the Council has no power to force their acceptance on the Assembly.

The duration of Parliament is for three years, but the Governor, on the advice of his Ministers, or "*ex mero motu*," may dissolve it at any time. Members of both Houses receive £200 per annum each, and a free pass over Government railways. As originally constituted, the Ministry was formed by five members of the Legislature—the Chief Secretary, the Attorney-General, the Treasurer, the Commissioner of Crown Lands, and the Commissioner of Public Works. Later on a sixth Minister was added to the number. Five of these were members of the House of Assembly and one of the Legislative Council. Under the terms of the Constitution Amendment Act of 1901 the number of responsible Ministers has been reduced to four since the 31st March, 1902. The Ministers are removable by adverse vote of the Legislative Assembly, or if the contingency arose to require the exercise of the prerogative they may be dismissed by the Governor. The Ministry formulates the policy to be submitted to the Legislature, and advises the Governor as to his course of procedure. It also forms the Executive Council, over which the Governor "*ex officio*" is President, while the Lieutenant-Governor also occupies a seat.

Since the inauguration of responsible Government there have been sixteen complete Parliaments. The first Parliament was opened on the 22nd April, 1857, and dissolved on the 1st March, 1860, while the seventeenth was opened on the 3rd July, 1902. The number of electors on the roll of the Legislative Council at the last general election in May, 1903, was 51,909, and of these, 37,918, or 73 per cent., recorded their votes. At the general election for the House of Assembly there were 77,147 males and 72,030 females on the rolls, or a total of 149,177, and of these, 53,471 males and 36,545 females recorded votes, the percentage of males voting being 69·3, and of females, 50·7.

Western Australia.

The Bill enabling Her Majesty "to grant a Constitution to Western Australia," received the Royal assent on the 15th August, 1890. When the measure was first discussed in the Imperial Parliament strong opposition was aroused, chiefly owing to a misunderstanding of questions relating to the Crown lands. It was argued that to hand over the control of such a vast territory to the 45,000 inhabitants thinly scattered over it was a piece of political folly. But, through the exertions of the colonial delegates then in England, aided by the influence of Sir William Robinson, and supported by the assistance of the Agents-General of the other Australasian provinces, the final obstacles were swept away. In all essential points, the Constitution of Western Australia is similar to those of the other states of Australia.

The executive power is vested in the Governor, who is appointed by the Crown, and who acts under the advice of a Cabinet.

The legislative authority is vested in a Parliament, composed of two Houses—a Legislative Council and a Legislative Assembly.

After the establishment of responsible government, the members of the Upper House were, in the first instance, nominated by the Governor, but it was provided that, in the event of the population of the province reaching 60,000, the Chamber should be elective. This limit was reached in 1893, and the constitution was shortly afterwards amended so as to give effect to the proviso mentioned. There are at present thirty members of the Legislative Council, each of the ten electorates returning three members. The qualification for membership is as follows:—being (1) a man of 30 years of age and free from legal incapacity; (2) a resident in Western Australia for at least two years; (3) a natural-born subject of His Majesty, or naturalised for five years and resident in Western Australia during that period. The disqualifications are:—being (1) a member of the Legislative Assembly; (2) a Judge of the Supreme Court; (3) Sheriff of Western Australia; (4) a clergyman or minister of religion; (5) an undischarged bankrupt; (6) attainted of treason or convicted of felony in any part of the King's dominions; (7) directly or indirectly concerned in any contracts for the public service, except as member of an incorporated trading society; (8) holding an office of profit under the Crown other than that of Minister, President of the Council, or officer of His Majesty's sea or land forces on full, half, or retired pay.

Members of the Legislative Council are paid at the rate of £200 per annum, and are provided with free railway passes. At the expiration of two years from the date of election, and every two years thereafter, the senior member for the time being for each province retires. Seniority is determined (1) by date of election; (2) if two or more members are elected on the same day, then the senior is the one who polled the smaller number of votes; (3) if the election be uncontested, or in case of an equality of votes, then the seniority is determined by the alphabetical precedence of surnames, and, if necessary, of Christian names.

The electoral qualification for the Upper House is as follows:—Being (1) at least 21 years of age, and not subject to legal incapacity; (2) a natural-born or naturalised subject of His Majesty resident in the state for twelve months, or a denizen of Western Australia; (3) either (a) have possessed for at least one year before being registered in his electoral province a freehold estate of the clear value of £100 above all charges or encumbrances; or (b) have been a householder for the last preceding twelve months of a dwelling of the clear annual value of £25; or (c) be a holder of a leasehold of the clear annual value of £25, the lease having eighteen months to run; or (d) have been a holder of a leasehold for the last preceding eighteen months of the annual value of £25; or (e) be a holder of a lease or license from the Crown at an annual rental of at least £10; or (f) have his name on the electoral list of a municipality or Roads Board in respect of property in the province of the annual ratable value of £25. Foreigners or persons who are not naturalised subjects of His Majesty, insane persons, and those who are in receipt of charitable aid, or any person attainted or convicted of treason, felony, or any infamous offence in His Majesty's dominions who has not served the sentence for the same, or received a pardon for the offence, are disqualified as electors.

For the Legislative Assembly in Western Australia there are fifty electorates, each returning a single member. The tenure of seat is three years, and members are paid at the rate of £200 per annum, with a free railway pass over all Government lines, and by courtesy the same privilege is extended to them on private lines. The qualification for membership is as follows:—being (a) a man of 21 years of age and free from legal incapacity; (b) a natural-born subject of the King, or naturalised for five years, and resident in Western Australia for two years; (c) resident in Western Australia for at least twelve months. A person is disqualified if (a) a member of the Legislative Council; (b) a Judge of the Supreme Court; (c) Sheriff of Western Australia; (d) clergyman or minister of religion; (e) an undischarged bankrupt or debtor whose affairs are in course of liquidation or arrangement; (f) under attainder of treason or conviction of felony in any part of the King's dominions; (g) directly or indirectly concerned in contracts for the public service except as member of an incorporated trading society. Paid officers under the Crown, except officers of His Majesty's sea and land forces on full, half, or retired pay, or political officers, are also ineligible.

The electoral qualification for the Legislative Assembly is as follows:—electors must be 21 years of age, natural-born or naturalised subjects of the King, and must have resided in the state for six months and been six months on the roll. They must also be resident in the district or hold freehold estate there of the clear value of £50, or be householders occupying a dwelling of the annual value of £10, or holders of an annual lease of the value of £10, or holders of a lease or license or Crown lands of an annual rental of £5, or have their names on the electoral list of a municipality or Roads Board in respect of property within the district. Electors for both Houses may be of either sex. Aboriginals, natives of Asia and Africa, and persons of half-blood, are not entitled to vote except in respect of freehold qualifications.

Since the establishment of responsible Government in Western Australia there have been three complete Parliaments. The first Parliament was opened on the 30th December, 1890, and dissolved on the 1st June, 1894. The third Parliament was opened on the 17th August, 1897, and was dissolved on the 15th March, 1901. The present Parliament commenced its sittings on the 28th June, 1901. At the beginning of 1902 the number of electors on the roll for the Legislative Council was 23,608, and for the Assembly 89,442. The electors on the rolls in contested districts at the general election for the Legislative Assembly in 1901 numbered 83,114, and of these, 33,479, or 40·3 per cent., recorded their votes.

Tasmania.

The Constitution of Tasmania is embodied in Act 18 Vic. No. 17, known as the "Constitutional Act," and in the amending acts subsequently introduced, viz, 23 Vic. No. 23, 34 Vic. No. 42, 48 Vic. No. 54, 49 Vic. No. 8, 54 Vic. No. 58, 60 Vic. No. 1, 60 Vic. No. 54, 62 Vic. No. 67, 64 Vic. No. 5, and 1 Edward VII Nos. 57, 58. A form of government is provided for, consisting of a Governor, appointed by the Crown, and a Legislative Council and House of Assembly, elected by the people. These constitute the "Parliament of Tasmania." Amongst the most important of the powers of the Governor are the appointment, according to law, of the members of the Executive, Ministers of the state, judges, commissioners, and other necessary officers. The Governor also possesses the prerogative of mercy, in the exercise of which he is guided by the advice of the Executive. He may dissolve the House of Assembly at any time ; but he cannot adopt this procedure with the Legislative Council, the members of which are appointed for six years. The Governor, in the exercise of his powers, is generally supposed to consult the Executive Council ; but in some cases he may act on his own authority, should he consider that circumstances demand such procedure. In all such cases, however, he is required to report immediately to the Imperial authorities, setting out the reasons for his action. The Governor is not permitted to leave the state for more than one month at a time without first obtaining His Majesty's sanction.

The Legislative Council consists of eighteen members, appointed for a term of six years. Members must be natural-born or naturalised subjects of His Majesty, not holding offices of profit under the Crown, and not less than 30 years of age. There are fifteen electorates, each returning a single member, with the exception of Hobart, which returns three, and Launceston two.

Electors for the Legislative Council must be natural-born or naturalised male subjects of His Majesty, 21 years of age, resident in Tasmania for twelve months, and possessing freehold of the annual value of £10, or leasehold of the annual value of £30, within the electoral district, or be graduates of any university in the British dominions, or associates of arts of Tasmania, or legal practitioners in the Supreme Court of Tasmania, or legally-qualified medical practitioners, or officiating ministers of religion, or officers or retired officers of His Majesty's land and sea forces not on actual service, or retired officers of the Volunteer Force of Tasmania.

The Legislative Council may, within constitutional limits, originate legislation in respect of any matter, with the exception of bills for appropriating revenue or imposing taxation. The Constitution, however, really leaves to either branch of the Legislature the task of determining the form and extent of its rights and privileges.

Members of the Legislative Council, and also of the House of Assembly, receive an honorarium of £100 each per annum.

The House of Assembly consists of thirty-five members, elected for three years. Members must be 21 years of age and natural-born or naturalised subjects of His Majesty. The following list of disqualifications applies to both Houses as regards right of election or membership:—(*a*) accepting office of profit under the Crown; (*b*) being a contractor for the Government, except as member of a company of more than six persons; (*c*) declaring allegiance to any foreign power; (*d*) holding the office of Judge of the Supreme Court; (*e*) being insane, attainted or convicted of treason, felony, or any infamous offence. The electoral qualification for the House of Assembly is as follows:—Every man of the age of 21 years, who is a natural-born or naturalized subject of His Majesty, and has resided in Tasmania for a period of twelve months, is entitled to have his name placed on the electoral roll, and to vote at an election of a Member of the House of Assembly for the district in which he resides.

An Act to confer the franchise on women has been reserved for the Royal assent.

Since the inauguration of responsible Government, there have been thirteen complete Parliaments in Tasmania. The first Parliament was opened on the 2nd December, 1856, and dissolved on the 8th May, 1861. The fourth session of the thirteenth Parliament terminated on the 20th December, 1902. On the 31st March, 1902, the number of electors on the roll for the Legislative Council was 10,502. In contested electorates the number was 7,613, and of these, 4,919, or 64·6 per cent., recorded votes. On the 2nd April, 1903, there were 43,999 electors on the roll of the Legislative Assembly. At the election in contested districts the number of ballot-papers was 24,111. The votes recorded numbered 23,766, or 59·9 per cent. of the enrolment, and there were 345 informal ballot-papers.

New Zealand.

The Act of the Imperial Legislature granting representative institutions to New Zealand was assented to in 1852. Under this Act the constitution of a General Assembly for the whole colony was provided for, to consist of a Legislative Council, the members of which were to be nominated by the Governor and a House of Representatives on an elective basis. By the Act of 1852 the colony was divided into six provinces, each presided over by an elective Superintendent, and with a separate Provincial Council, empowered to legislate except on certain specified subjects. These Provincial Councils, the number of which was afterwards increased to nine, remained as integral parts of the Constitution until 1876, when they were abolished by the General Assembly that body having the power of amending the Constitution Act. The powers previously exercised by Superintendents and provincial officers were delegated to local boards called County Councils, or vested in the Governor.

The Governor is appointed by the Crown, but his salary and allowances are paid by the colony, the present salary being £5,000 per annum with allowances amounting to £2,000. Executive administration is vested in the Governor, and is conducted according to the principles of responsible government. The Governor can appoint or dismiss his Ministers, but his Ministers must possess the confidence of the majority in the House of Representatives. He can assent to bills or withhold assent therefrom, or reserve them for the signification of His Majesty's pleasure. He can summon, prorogue, and dissolve the colonial Parliament. He can send drafts of bills to either House for consideration, and can return bills to either House for specific amendment after they have been passed by both Houses, and before they are assented to or reserved by him. The Commission from the King delegates to the Governor certain powers of the royal prerogative, and provides for the constitution of an Executive Council to advise him in matters of importance, such Executive Council consisting of responsible Ministers for the time being. The number of members constituting the Legislative Council cannot be less than ten, but otherwise is practically unlimited. At present the number is forty-six. Councillors are remunerated for their services at the rate of £150 per annum, payable monthly, and actual travelling expenses to and from Wellington are also allowed. A deduction of £1 5s. per sitting day is made in case of absence, except through illness or other unavoidable cause, exceeding five sitting days in any one session. To be qualified as a member of the Council a person must be of the full age of 21 years, and a British subject either by birth or by Act of the Imperial Parliament or the Parliament of New Zealand. All contractors to the public service to an amount of over £50, and civil servants of the colony are ineligible. Prior to 1891, Councillors held their appointments for life, but on the 17th

September of that year an Act was passed making seven years the period of tenure of a seat, though members may be re-appointed. Two members of the Council are aboriginal native chiefs.

The House of Representatives consists of eighty members, of whom four are representatives of native constituencies. All the electoral districts for European representation, which number sixty-eight, return one member each, with the exception of the cities of Auckland, Wellington, Christchurch, and Dunedin, each of which returns three members. Representatives are remunerated for their services at the rate of £240 per annum, but £2 per day for every sitting day exceeding five is deducted on account of absence during the session not due to illness or other unavoidable cause. To be qualified for membership of the House of Representatives a person must be of the male sex, duly registered on the electoral roll, and free from the disabilities mentioned in Section 8 of the Electoral Act of 1893. All contractors to the public service of New Zealand to whom any public money above the sum of £50 is payable, directly or indirectly, in any one financial year, as well as civil servants of the colony, are incapable of being elected, or of sitting and voting as members.

Every man or woman of the full age of 21 years, who is either a natural-born or naturalised British subject, and resident in the colony one year, and three months in one electoral district, is qualified to be registered as an elector and vote at elections of members for the House of Representatives. In the Maori districts, adult Maoris are entitled to vote without registration. Under the provisions of the Electoral Act of 1893, the franchise is extended to women of both races in accordance with the qualifications specified above, but women may not be elected as members of the House of Representatives. No person may be represented on more than one electoral roll. The Act also provides that the name of every qualified elector who fails to record his vote shall be removed from the roll after the election. Since the passing of the Constitution Act conferring representative institutions upon the colony of New Zealand there have been fourteen complete Parliaments. The first Parliament was opened on the 27th May, 1854, and dissolved on the 15th September, 1855, and the fourteenth opened on the 22nd June, 1900, and dissolved on the 4th October, 1902.

At the general election for the first Parliament, which took place in 1853, the population of the colony numbered 30,000, and the electors on the roll 5,934. At the last general election for the House of Representatives, in November, 1902, the electors on the roll numbered 415,789 of whom 185,944 were females. The male and female electors numbered respectively 229,845 and 185,944, and the male voters numbered 175,320, or 76·3 per cent. of the enrolment, while 138,565, or 74·5 per cent. of the females recorded their votes.

POPULATION.

ON the 26th January, 1788, Captain Phillip arrived in Sydney Harbour, bringing with him an establishment of about 1,030 people all told. Settlement soon spread from the parent colony, first to Tasmania in 1803, and afterwards to other parts of the continent and to New Zealand. At the census of 1901 the population of Australasia, exclusive of aborigines and Maoris, was 4,545,967, distributed as follows:—

State.	Males.	Females.	Total.
New South Wales	710,005	644,841	1,354,846
Victoria	603,720	597,350	1,201,070
Queensland	277,003	221,126	498,129
South Australia	184,422	178,182	362,604
Western Australia	112,875	71,249	184,124
Tasmania	89,624	82,851	172,475
Commonwealth	1,977,649	1,795,599	3,773,248
New Zealand	405,992	366,727	772,719
Australasia	2,383,641	2,162,326	4,545,967

The figures are inclusive of half-caste aborigines living in a civilised condition, and if there be added an estimated population of 148,000 Australian aborigines in an uncivilised state and of 43,000 Maoris in New Zealand, the total population of Australasia at the date of the census would be about 4,737,000.

The growth of the population of Australasia from the date of the first settlement is shown in the following table. An official enumeration of the people was made in most of the years quoted:—

Year.	Commonwealth.		New Zealand.		Australasia.	
	Population.	Annual Increase per cent.	Population.	Annual Increase per cent.	Population.	Annual Increase per cent.
1788	1,030	......	....	......	1,030	......
1801	6,508	15·25	....	......	6,508	15·25
1811	11,525	5·88	....	......	11,525	5·88
1821	35,610	11·94	....	......	35,610	11·94
1831	79,306	8·34	....	......	79,306	8·34
1841	206,095	10·02	5,000	......	211,095	10·28
1851	403,889	6·96	26,707	18·24	430,596	7·39
1861	1,153,973	11·07	99,021	14·00	1,252,994	11·27
1871	1,668,377	3·75	256,393	9·98	1,924,770	4·39
1881	2,252,617	3·05	489,933	6·69	2,742,550	3·60
1891	3,183,237	3·52	626,658	2·49	3,809,895	3·34
1901	3,773,248	1·71	772,719	2·12	4,545,967	1·78

The high rate prior to 1831 arose from the small numbers on which the increase was calculated; while between 1831 and 1841, it was due to the policy of state-aided immigration which was then in vogue. The discovery of gold, which proved a strong incentive towards emigration to Australia, accounted for the high rate during the period from 1851 to 1861. The rate of increase since 1861 has shown a regular decline during each decennial period, and from 1891 to 1901 the annual increase was only 1·78 per cent., which is but slightly in excess of the natural increase due to the excess of births over deaths.

The chief factor determining the increase of population in Australia prior to 1860 was immigration, and until recent years the states of Queensland and Western Australia gained more largely from this source than from births; but taking the whole period of forty-two years from 1861 to 1902 embraced in the following table, the two elements of increase compare as follows:—

Arrivals from abroad in excess of departures...........	779,345
Births in excess of deaths	1,965,093

The population of each state (exclusive of aborigines of full blood and nomadic half-castes) at the last five census periods, and at the 30th June, 1903, is shown below:—

State.	1861.	1871.	1881.	1891.	1901.	30th June, 1903.
New South Wales...	350,860	503,981	751,468	1,132,234	1,354,846	1,415,760
Victoria	540,322	731,528	862,346	1,140,405	1,201,070	1,208,070
Queensland	30,059	120,104	213,525	393,718	498,129	512,760
South Australia ...	126,830	185,626	279,865	320,431	362,604	365,020
Western Australia..	15,691	25,353	29,708	49,782	184,124	221,990
Tasmania	90,211	101,785	115,705	146,667	172,475	176,960
Commonwealth	1,153,973	1,668,377	2,252,617	3,183,237	3,773,248	3,900,560
New Zealand........	99,021	256,393	489,933	626,658	772,719	818,830
Australasia ...	1,252,994	1,924,770	2,742,550	3,809,895	4,545,967	4,719,390

In order to show the great differences in the growth of the population of the individual states during the last ten years, the appended table has been prepared, giving the population at the end of each year since 1893, and at the middle of 1903. In this table aborigines are included:—

Year.	New South Wales.	Victoria.	Queensland.	South Australia.	Western Australia.	Tasmania.	New Zealand.	Australasia.
1893	1,214,550	1,176,450	417,970	343,050	65,060	150,530	672,260	4,039,870
1894	1,239,250	1,182,630	428,540	347,220	82,070	152,600	686,130	4,118,440
1895	1,262,270	1,186,300	441,110	350,810	101,240	154,930	698,710	4,195,370
1896	1,278,970	1,180,710	450,300	351,600	137,950	159,280	714,160	4,272,970
1897	1,301,730	1,183,090	460,430	352,370	161,920	163,870	729,060	4,357,520
1898	1,323,130	1,188,370	471,510	355,210	168,130	168,320	743,460	4,418,130
1899	1,344,030	1,189,670	482,400	359,290	171,030	172,220	756,500	4,475,190
1900	1,364,590	1,197,390	498,250	361,350	190,150	172,980	770,630	4,545,390
1901	1,379,530	1,211,150	511,080	365,180	194,110	174,380	787,660	4,623,090
1902	1,407,710	1,211,720	515,990	366,110	213,330	177,460	807,930	4,700,250
1903—June 30	1,420,050	1,208,350	517,900	365,020	221,990	176,960	818,830	4,729,100

The average annual rates of increase in the various states during each period of ten years from the beginning of 1861 to the end of 1900, and for the years 1901-2 were as follow:—

State.	Average Annual Rate of Increase.				
	1861-70.	1871-80.	1881-90.	1891-1900.	1901-2.
	per cent.	per cent.	per cent.	per cent.	per cent.
New South Wales	3·65	4·14	4·14	1·98	1·56
Victoria	3·05	1·71	2·80	0·55	0·59
Queensland	15·21	6·95	5·68	2·40	1·76
South Australia	4·00	3·83	1·79	1·24	0·66
Western Australia	5·12	1·47	4·78	14·56	8·82
Tasmania	1·39	1·31	2·39	1·76	1·29
Commonwealth	3·76	3·13	3·47	1·80	1·55
New Zealand	12·04	6·92	2·59	2·10	2·39
Australasia	4·51	3·70	3·33	1·85	1·69

The total populations, at the end of each of the last ten years, of the six states which form the Australian Commonwealth are given below:—

Year	Population	Year	Population
1893	3,367,610	1898	3,669,670
1894	3,432,310	1899	3,718,690
1895	3,496,660	1900	3,774,710
1896	3,558,810	1901	3,835,430
1897	3,623,460	1902	3,892,320

The following table gives the total increase in each state during the forty-two years, 1861–1902, distinguishing the natural increase arising from the excess of births over deaths from the increase due to the excess of arrivals over departures:—

State.	Excess of—		Total Increase.
	Births over Deaths.	Immigration over Emigration.	
New South Wales	723,845	335,329	1,059,174
Victoria	659,366	14,507	673,873
Queensland	225,690	262,244	487,934
South Australia	228,026	13,972	241,998
Western Australia	37,499	160,604	198,103
Tasmania	90,667	(−) 982	89,685
Commonwealth	1,965,093	785,674	2,750,767
New Zealand	427,829	300,390	728,219
Australasia	2,392,922	1,086,064	3,478,986

(—) Excess of Emigration over Immigration.

The information conveyed by the above figures is important, as illustrating, not only the movement of population, but also the effect upon immigration, of local influences, such as the attraction of liberal land laws, the fertility of the soil, the permanence of employment, and the policy of assisted immigration. But a bare statement of the gross increase to each state from immigration is apt to be misleading, since the original density of population must be deemed a factor affecting the current of immigration. The following figures show the density of population per square mile in each state at the time of taking the census on the last five occasions and also at the close of 1902:—

State.	1861.	1871.	1881.	1891.	1901.	31st Dec., 1902.
New South Wales	1·13	1·62	2·42	3·65	4·36	4·53
Victoria	6·15	8·32	9·81	12·98	13·66	13·78
Queensland	0·04	0·18	0·32	0·59	0·75	0·77
South Australia	0·14	0·20	0·31	0·35	0·40	0·40
Western Australia	0·02	0·03	0·03	0·05	0·19	0·22
Tasmania	3·44	3·88	4·41	5·59	6·57	6·75
Commonwealth	0·39	0·56	0·76	1·07	1·27	1·31
New Zealand	0·95	2·45	4·69	6·00	7·39	7·73
Australasia	0·41	0·63	0·89	1·24	1·48	1·52

At the close of the year 1902 the population of Australasia, including the native races, only reached a density of 1·59 persons per square mile—a rate which is far below that of any other civilised country; and excluding Australian aborigines and Maoris, the density was only 1·52 per square mile. But a comparison of the density of population in Australasia with that in older countries of the world is of little practical use, beyond affording some indication of the future of these states when their population shall have reached the proportions to be found in the old world. The latest authoritative statements give the density of the populations of the great divisions of the world as follows:—

Continent.	Area in square Miles.	Population.	Persons per square Mile.
Europe	3,742,000	372,925,000	99·66
Asia	17,101,000	830,558,000	48·57
Africa	11,510,000	170,050,000	14·77
America	14,805,000	132,718,000	8·96
Australasia and Pacific Islands	3,457,000	5,907,000	1·71
Polar Regions	1,732,000	82,000	0·05
The World	52,347,000	1,512,240,000	28·89

From the earliest years of settlement there was a steady if not powerful stream of immigration into these states; but in 1851, memorable for the finding of gold, the current was swollen by thousands of men in the prime of life who were attracted to the shores of Australia by the hope of speedily acquiring wealth. By far the greater number of these new arrivals settled in Victoria, which had just been separated from New South Wales, and for some years afterwards Victoria had an unprecedented addition to its population. The vast changes which took place will be evident when it is stated that in 1850, just prior to the gold rush, the population of the northern and southern portions of New South Wales was:—

Port Phillip (afterwards Victoria)	76,162
Remaining portion of the Colony	189,341

While five years afterwards the population of each was :—

Victoria	364,324
New South Wales	277,579

Victoria enjoyed the advantage in population and increased its lead yearly until 1871, when its inhabitants exceeded in number those of New South Wales by no less than 229,654. But from that time almost every year showed a nearer approach in the numbers of the inhabitants of the two States, until at the census of 1891 Victoria had a lead of only 8,171, while at the end of that year New South Wales had the greater population by about 5,800. At the 30th June, 1903, the parent state had increased its lead to 211,700. In considering the question of increase of population, attention should be paid to the density as well as to the actual number of the population; in regard to the case in point, the density of Victoria is 13·72 per square mile, and in New South Wales only 4·53.

New Zealand and Queensland, and Western Australia also in recent years, owe much of their remarkable progress to the discovery of gold. In New Zealand the gold fever broke out in 1861, when the population numbered only 99,021, and the period of its activity extended over many years. At the end of 1902 the population had reached 807,930 souls, exclusive of Maoris, or more than eight times that of 1861. In Queensland the attractive force of the goldfields was exerted at a later date, and was a powerful factor in stimulating the growth of population in that state; while the development of Western Australia during the past twelve years has been wholly due to the gold deposits discovered there, the population increasing from the small number of 46,290 at the end of 1890 to 215,140 at the close of 1902. The great rush of a few years ago has moderated considerably, but the net increase by excess of immigration over emigration during 1902 amounted, nevertheless, to 16,858; and in view of the vast mineral possibilities of the state it will not be surprising if fresh discoveries should at any time be made, and immigration on an extensive scale again set in.

Much of the increase of population, especially in New South Wales, Victoria, Queensland, and New Zealand, was due to the state policy of assisted immigration. The following table shows the number of all immigrants introduced into Australasia either wholly or partly at the expense of the State, up to the end of 1902:—

State.	Prior to 1881.	1881 to 1902.	Total.
New South Wales	177,234	34,738	211,972
Victoria	140,102	....	140,102
Queensland	52,399	116,804	169,203
South Australia	88,050	7,298	95,348
Western Australia	889	* 6,243	7,132
Tasmania	18,965	2,734	21,699
Commonwealth	477,639	167,817	645,456
New Zealand	*100,920	14,658	*115,578
Australasia	578,559	182,475	761,034

* Exclusive of a number prior to 1870, of which no record can be found.

Queensland and Western Australia are the only States that at present assist immigrants; New South Wales ceased to do so in 1888, Victoria practically ceased assisted immigration in 1873, South Australia in 1886, Tasmania and New Zealand in 1891.

The following table shows the increase of population by excess of immigration over emigration for the five decennial periods ended 1900, and for the years 1901–2:—

State.	1851–60.	1861–70.	1871–80.	1881–90.	1891–1900.	1901–2.
New South Wales	123,097	45,539	109,341	164,205	16,167	12*
Victoria	398,753	38,935	12,672*	112,097	108,795*	15,060*
Queensland	†	68,191	73,849	101,525	17,247	1,428
South Australia	33,024	17,949	34,569	17,004*	16,623*	4,919*
Western Australia	7,187	5,891	638*	10,170	118,592	26,573
Tasmania	6,767	3,228*	1,427*	5,572	73*	1,823*
Commonwealth	568,828	173,277	203,022	376,565	26,515	6,187
New Zealand	44,742	118,637	132,976	9,453	27,211	12,113
Australasia	613,570	291,914	335,998	386,018	53,726	18,300

* Denotes excess of emigrants. † Included in New South Wales figures.

It will be seen that Australasia has gained but little by excess of immigration over emigration during the past twelve years. For the period 1881–90 the gain from this source was 386,018; but in the ensuing period it fell to 53,726, and in three of the states there was an actual loss by emigration. Of all the states, Western Australia alone seems to attract intending emigrants from other countries, and but for excess of arrivals shown by that state during 1901 and 1902, the Commonwealth would have suffered a considerable net loss by emigration as in the two preceding years.

If the results for the last twelve years be compared, it will be seen that there was an exodus both from Victoria and South Australia, the former losing 123,855 persons, and the latter 21,542, by excess of emigration, while Tasmania also lost 2,279 persons from the same source. The gain in the other States of the Commonwealth was very limited, with the exception of Western Australia, where there was a net increase of 146,991 persons; the remaining states showed an increase of only 33,783 persons. The following table shows the increase of population by excess of arrivals over departures in each state for the twenty-two years ending 1902:—

Year.	New South Wales.	Victoria.	Queensland.	South Australia.	Western Australia.	Tasmania.	Commonwealth.	New Zealand.	Australasia.
1881	16,673	4,976	*4,009	12,055	401	1,166	31,262	1,970	33,232
1882	16,034	6,563	17,043	*3,679	94	587	36,642	2,375	39,017
1883	27,278	6,597	34,371	4,266	436	689	73,637	8,657	82,294
1884	23,944	8,525	18,620	275	871	816	53,051	7,724	60,775
1885	24,829	9,027	7,056	*9,280	1,628	*388	32,872	2,757	35,629
1886	18,073	15,436	7,695	*8,819	3,738	*302	35,821	*199	35,622
1887	7,202	15,445	11,527	*3,008	2,049	1,797	35,012	211	35,223
1888	6,633	25,757	5,651	*8,325	*1,196	*383	28,137	*10,548	17,589
1889	8,241	9,794	4,340	*2,346	578	1,172	21,779	*700	21,079
1890	15,298	9,977	*769	1,857	1,571	418	28,352	*2,794	25,558
1891	17,158	5,256	*2,375	*1,878	6,073	3,303	27,537	*3,745	23,792
1892	3,969	*11,490	*727	2,981	4,473	*3,846	*4,640	4,953	313
1893	*1,560	*12,484	231	3,041	5,223	*2,995	*8,544	10,410	1,866
1894	919	*12,648	1,891	*2,288	15,968	*844	2,998	2,260	5,258
1895	*840	*14,400	2,848	*3,014	18,401	*649	2,346	897	3,243
1896	*3,967	*22,054	818	*5,175	35,948	1,648	7,218	3,270	10,488
1897	*173	*13,804	1,240	*4,748	22,592	1,853	6,960	2,758	9,718
1898	1,789	*11,197	3,390	*1,398	3,958	2,229	*1,229	2,689	1,460
1899	390	*8,130	3,135	*864	50	1,430	*3,989	1,885	*2,104
1900	*1,518	*7,844	6,796	*3,280	5,906	*2,202	*2,142	1,834	*308
1901	*6,914	*1,344	4,534	*1,216	10,761	*1,725	4,096	4,123	8,219
1902	6,902	*13,716	*3,106	*3,703	15,812	*98	2,091	7,990	10,081

* Denotes excess of departures.

The great bulk of the movement of population within recent years, shown above, is only inter-state; and it is evident that immigrants are not attracted to these shores from abroad, the long sea voyage and cost of passage probably being the chief deterring reasons.

Centralisation of Population.

One of the most notable problems in the progress of modern civilisation is the tendency of the population, everywhere exhibited in the chief countries of the world, to accumulate in great cities. Not only is this apparent in England, France, and other countries where the development of manufactures has brought about an entire change in the employments of the people, and has necessarily caused the aggregation of workers in towns, but it is seen also in the United States, the most favoured country for the agricultural labourer.

The progress of the chief cities of Australasia has been remarkable, and has no parallel among the cities of the old world. Even in America the rise of the great cities has been accompanied by a corresponding increase in the rural population, but in Australia, perhaps for the first time in history, was presented the spectacle of magnificent cities growing with marvellous rapidity, and embracing within their limits one-third of the population of the states of which they are the seat of government. The abnormal aggregation of the population into their capital cities is a most unfortunate element in the progress of these states, and as regards some of them is becoming more marked each year.

One satisfactory feature in connection with the growth of population in the chief cities of Australia is that, until very recently, such increase did not take place through absorption of the rural population. In all new countries the tendency has been for immigrants to settle in or near the principal towns which mostly lie near the seaboard, and the fact that these states possess no good navigable waterways leading from the interior tends still further to the aggregation of population in the cities.

The population of the chief cities of Australasia and the estimated numbers of their inhabitants at the various census periods, and at the close of 1902, are shown in the following table, which illustrates the remarkable progress referred to:—

City.	1841.	1851.	1861.	1871.	1881.	1891.	1901.	1902.
Sydney	29,973	53,924	95,789	137,776	224,939	383,283	487,900	508,510
Melbourne	4,479	23,143	139,916	206,780	282,947	490,896	494,129	502,610
Brisbane	*829	2,543	6,051	15,029	31,109	93,657	119,428	122,815
Adelaide	†6,480	‡14,577	18,303	42,744	103,864	133,252	162,261	165,723
Perth	....	....	....	5,244	5,822	8,447	36,274	42,474
Hobart	....	....	19,449	19,092	21,118	33,450	34,626	34,809
Wellington	....	....	....	7,908	20,563	33,224	49,344	52,590

* In 1846. † In 1840. ‡ In 1850.

The aggregation of population is most marked in the cases of Adelaide and Melbourne, while Sydney is also conspicuous. The other cities are not so remarkable, the proportion of the people resident in Wellington especially being very small. The proportion of population in each capital compared with that of the whole state at the last four census periods, and on the 31st December 1902, is shown below.

City.	1871.	1881.	1891.	1901.	1902.
	per cent.	per cent.	per cent.	per cent.	per cent.
Sydney	27·34	29·93	33·86	35·90	36·13
Melbourne	28·27	32·81	43·05	41·13	41·69
Brisbane	12·51	14·57	23·79	23·73	23·85
Adelaide	23·03	37·11	41·59	44·75	45·31
Perth	20·68	19·60	16·97	19·70	19·74
Hobart	18·76	18·25	22·81	20·08	19·66
Wellington	3·08	4·20	5·30	6·39	6·51

Although Wellington is the capital of New Zealand, it is exceeded in population by Auckland and Christchurch, and probably by Dunedin.

Still, even in the largest of these cities—Auckland,—the population is not more than 8·70 per cent., and in the four together is only 29·25 per cent. of that of the whole colony.

The following is a list of the cities and most important towns of Australasia, with their populations at the latest available dates. In the case of the capital cities, the populations are as at the 31st December, 1902; the dates to which the other figures refer are as follow:—New South Wales, 2nd February, 1902; Victoria, Western Australia, and New Zealand, 31st March, 1901; Queensland and Tasmania, 31st December, 1902; while the figures for South Australia show the mean populations for 1902. In all but the most important towns, where the suburbs are included, the populations quoted are those of the boroughs or municipal districts:—

City or Town.	Population.	City or Town.	Population.
New South Wales—		South Australia—	
Sydney	508,510	Adelaide	165,723
Newcastle	58,010	Port Adelaide	20,458
Broken Hill	26,970	Port Pirie	8,481
Parramatta	12,560	Mount Gambier	3,225
Goulburn	10,500		
Maitland	10,100	Western Australia—	
Bathurst	9,340	Perth	42,474
Orange	6,510	Fremantle	20,448
Albury	6,310	Kalgoorlie	6,652
Tamworth	5,980	Boulder	4,601
Lithgow	5,720	Coolgardie	4,249
Grafton	5,340	Albany	3,594
Wagga Wagga	4,890		
Victoria—		Tasmania—	
Melbourne	502,610	Hobart	34,809
Ballarat	43,823	Launceston	21,466
Bendigo	30,774	Queenstown	5,203
Geelong	18,289	Zeehan	5,162
Eaglehawk	8,367	Beaconsfield	2,658
Warrnambool	6,404		
Stawell	5,318	New Zealand—	
Castlemaine	5,703	Auckland	67,226
Maryborough	5,622	Christchurch	57,041
Queensland—		Dunedin	52,390
Brisbane	122,815	Wellington	52,590
Rockhampton	18,376	Napier	8,774
Townsville	12,075	Wanganui	7,329
Gympie	13,100	Nelson	7,010
Maryborough	10,159	Palmerston North	6,534
Toowoomba	10,550	Timaru	6,424
Ipswich	8,637	Invercargill	6,215
Mount Morgan	6,800	Oamaru	4,836
Charters Towers	5,000	New Plymouth	4,405
Bundaberg	5,000	Thames	4,009

The above statement shows clearly where the people have settled, for, excluding the capitals, there are only five cities in the whole of Australasia with a population of over 40,000, viz., Newcastle, 58,010; Auckland, 67,226; Dunedin, 52,390; Ballarat, 43,823; Christchurch, 57,041; and of these five, three are in New Zealand.

Ages of the People.

The ages of the people, as ascertained at the census of 1901, were as shown by the following statement, in which the population has been arranged in five-year groups. There is the same tendency in Australia as in other countries for the people to state their ages at the nearest decennial or quinquennial period, hence it is necessary to adjust the census figures before they can be stated under individual ages. The grouping in five-year periods, as indicated below, although not entirely satisfactory, is sufficiently accurate for practical purposes. The following table shows the ages of males, exclusive of aborigines:—

Males.

Age Group.	New South Wales.	Victoria.	Queensland.	South Australia.	Western Australia.	Tasmania.	Commonwealth.	New Zealand.
Under 5	80,308	66,792	31,307	20,260	10,441	10,702	219,810	44,324
5 and under 10 ..	84,189	72,045	31,908	22,756	8,891	11,160	230,949	43,314
10 ,, 15 ..	81,582	67,374	29,005	22,193	7,505	10,649	218,308	43,100
15 ,, 20 ..	70,423	58,882	23,684	20,007	7,088	9,388	189,472	42,456
20 ,, 21 ..	12,754	10,429	4,830	3,618	1,957	1,764	35,352	8,559
21 ,, 25 ..	49,694	40,150	19,760	13,023	9,884	6,497	139,008	32,637
25 ,, 30 ..	56,273	45,458	23,634	13,771	15,822	7,276	162,234	35,307
30 ,, 35 ..	52,596	46,028	22,639	12,945	14,845	6,422	156,075	29,694
35 ,, 40 ..	52,335	46,715	22,088	12,013	12,441	6,262	151,849	24,301
40 ,, 45 ..	44,930	37,111	18,419	11,371	8,722	5,278	125,826	21,589
45 ,, 50 ..	33,338	24,126	13,046	9,083	5,220	3,760	88,523	19,134
50 ,, 55 ..	25,615	18,387	10,187	6,767	3,453	2,797	67,156	15,413
55 ,, 60 ..	19,634	15,337	7,081	5,336	2,311	1,996	52,595	13,711
60 ,, 65 ..	16,788	14,972	6,788	3,992	1,767	1,729	45,976	12,803
65 ,, 70 ..	13,005	16,077	4,131	2,872	1,101	1,292	38,478	10,150
70 ,, 75 ..	7,772	11,777	2,230	2,282	692	1,123	25,876	5,348
75 ,, 80 ..	3,578	5,732	959	1,290	290	756	12,605	2,285
80 ,, 85 ..	1,888	2,452	453	646	140	459	6,033	1,050
85 and over	800	775	143	247	36	199	2,200	375
Unspecified (children)	277	502	5	....	8	....	792	24
Unspecified (adults)	2,286	2,049	3,043	....	261	120	7,759	408
Aboriginal half-castes (unspecified)	....	...	773	....	....	....	773	....
Total	710,005	603,720	277,008	184,422	112,875	89,624	1,977,649	405,992

In the next table similar information is given regarding females.

Females.

Age Group.	New South Wales.	Victoria.	Queensland.	South Australia.	Western Australia.	Tasmania.	Commonwealth.	New Zealand.
Under 5	78,553	65,163	30,687	19,317	10,234	10,163	214,617	42,482
5 and under 10 ..	81,946	70,483	30,947	22,612	8,356	10,864	225,708	42,422
10 „ 15 ..	80,097	66,628	28,557	21,599	7,320	10,487	214,688	42,125
15 „ 20 ..	70,736	59,712	22,792	20,162	5,849	9,063	188,314	42,358
20 „ 21 ..	13,457	11,629	4,368	3,727	1,278	1,836	36,295	8,583
21 „ 25 ..	51,361	45,989	16,818	13,813	6,001	6,313	140,295	33,377
25 „ 30 ..	56,043	52,822	18,284	14,253	8,677	6,561	156,640	33,233
30 „ 35 ..	46,697	48,150	15,958	12,308	7,298	5,576	136,047	27,272
35 „ 40 ..	41,593	43,388	13,705	11,213	5,322	5,217	120,438	21,217
40 „ 45 ..	33,436	33,546	10,710	9,596	3,391	4,467	95,146	17,347
45 „ 50 ..	24,001	21,804	7,402	7,277	2,151	3,094	65,729	13,997
50 „ 55 ..	19,327	17,589	6,042	5,573	1,678	2,379	52,588	11,991
55 „ 60 ..	15,376	15,156	4,918	4,545	1,177	1,885	43,057	9,963
60 „ 65 ..	12,192	14,288	3,957	4,026	908	1,725	37,096	8,017
65 „ 70 ..	9,237	13,842	2,400	3,051	570	1,321	30,421	6,028
70 „ 75 ..	5,202	8,359	1,382	2,280	279	910	18,412	3,236
75 „ 80 ..	2,844	4,231	705	1,262	183	514	9,689	1,679
80 „ 85 ..	1,574	2,065	343	698	56	802	5,038	852
85 and over	678	750	127	310	25	147	2,037	340
Unspecified (children)	44	376	11	....	15	....	446	15
Unspecified(adults)	447	1,380	253	....	31	27	2,138	193
Aboriginal half-castes (unspecified)	....	....	760	....	....	....	760	....
Total	644,841	597,350	221,126	178,182	71,249	82,851	1,795,599	366,727

In the following table will be found the ages of the total population, exclusive of aborigines.

TOTAL POPULATION.

Age Group.	New South Wales.	Victoria.	Queensland.	South Australia.	Western Australia.	Tasmania.	Commonwealth.	New Zealand.
Under 5	158,861	131,955	61,004	40,077	20,675	20,865	434,427	86,806
5 and under 10 ..	166,135	142,528	62,855	45,368	17,747	22,024	456,657	85,736
10 „ 15 ..	161,679	134,002	57,562	43,792	14,825	21,136	432,996	85,225
15 „ 20 ..	141,159	118,594	46,476	40,169	12,937	18,451	377,786	84,814
20 „ 21 ..	26,211	22,058	9,198	7,345	3,235	3,600	71,647	17,142
21 „ 25 ..	101,055	86,139	36,578	26,236	15,885	12,810	279,303	66,014
25 „ 30 ..	112,316	98,280	41,018	28,024	24,499	13,837	318,874	68,540
30 „ 35 ..	99,293	94,778	38,597	25,318	22,143	11,998	292,122	56,966
35 „ 40 ..	93,928	90,103	35,788	23,226	17,763	11,479	272,287	45,518
40 „ 45 ..	78,366	70,657	29,129	20,967	12,113	9,740	220,972	38,936
45 „ 50 ..	57,339	45,930	20,448	16,310	7,371	6,854	154,252	33,131
50 „ 55 ..	44,942	35,926	16,229	12,340	5,131	5,176	119,744	27,404
55 „ 60 ..	35,010	30,493	12,899	9,881	3,488	3,881	95,652	23,674
60 „ 65 ..	28,925	29,260	10,740	8,018	2,675	3,454	83,072	20,820
65 „ 70 ..	22,242	29,919	6,531	5,923	1,671	2,613	68,899	16,188
70 „ 75 ..	12,974	20,136	3,612	4,562	971	2,033	44,288	8,584
75 „ 80 ..	6,422	9,963	1,664	2,552	423	1,270	22,294	3,964
80 „ 85 ..	3,457	4,517	796	1,344	196	761	11,071	1,902
85 and over	1,478	1,525	270	557	61	346	4,237	715
Unspecified (children)	321	878	16	....	23	....	1,238	39
Unspecified(adults)	3,733	3,429	3,296	....	292	147	9,897	601
Aboriginal half-castes (unspecified)	......	......	1,533	....	....	....	1,533	....
Total	1,354,846	1,201,070	498,129	362,604	184,124	172,475	3,773,248	772,719

Of the total population of Australasia, 53·03 per cent were over 21 years of age. The largest proportion of adults is to be found in

Western Australia, where they comprise 62·29 per cent. of the population; and the lowest proportion in Tasmania, where they represent 50·09 per cent. The following table shows the number of persons under 21 years of age, and those 21 and over, with the proportion of adults of each sex to the total population in the several states:—

State.	Under 21 years.			21 years and over.			Proportion per cent. of adults.	
	Males.	Females.	Total.	Males.	Females.	Total.	Males.	Females
New South Wales	329,533	324,833	654,366	380,472	320,008	700,480	58·59	49·62
Victoria	276,024	273,991	550,015	327,696	323,359	651,055	54·28	54·18
Queensland	120,739	117,362	238,101	155,491	103,004	258,495	56·29	46·74
South Australia	88,834	87,917	176,751	95,588	90,265	185,853	51·83	50·66
Western Australia	35,890	33,552	69,442	76,985	37,697	114,682	68·20	52·91
Tasmania	43,663	42,413	86,076	45,961	40,438	86,399	51·28	48·81
Commonwealth	894,683	880,068	1,774,751	1,082,193	914,771	1,996,964	54·74	50·97
New Zealand	181,777	177,985	359,762	224,215	188,742	412,957	55·22	51·47
Australasia	1,076,460	1,058,053	2,134,513	1,306,408	1,103,513	2,409,921	54·82	51·05

These figures show that the proportion of adults differs considerably in the various states. Western Australia has the largest percentage of males, a result due to the large accession of adult immigrants during recent years, and the same cause also slightly affected the proportion of females. The differences, however, will be more readily apprehended by considering the population in the conventional groups of dependent and supporting ages. The figures, therefore, have been arranged so as to show the number of males at the dependent ages from infancy to 15 years; at the supporting ages, from 15 to 65; in the old-age group, from 65 years upwards; and at the military ages, from 20 to 40 years:—

State.	Dependent Ages, up to 15 years.		Supporting Ages, 15 and under 65.		Old Ages, 65 and over.		Military Ages, 20 to 40 years.	
	Number.	Proportion of total male population.	Number.	Proportion of total male population.	Number.	Proportion of total male population.	Number.	Proportion of total male population.
		per cent.		per cent.		per cent.		per cent.
New South Wales	246,079	34·79	434,325	61·39	27,098	3·82	223,652	31·61
Victoria	206,211	34·30	358,145	59·57	36,813	6·13	189,880	31·60
Queensland	92,220	33·76	173,046	63·34	7,916	2·90	92,946	34·02
South Australia	65,209	35·36	111,876	60·66	7,387	3·98	55,370	30·02
Western Australia	26,837	23·83	83,510	74·16	2,259	2·01	54,949	48·68
Tasmania	32,511	36·32	53,164	59·40	3,829	4·28	28,221	31·53
Commonwealth	669,067	33·99	1,214,066	61·68	85,192	4·33	644,518	32·74
New Zealand	130,738	32·24	255,664	63·02	19,218	4·74	130,498	32·18
Australasia	799,805	33·69	1,469,730	61·91	104,410	4·40	775,016	32·65

In Western Australia the males in the supporting ages represent 74·16 per cent. of the male population, while the average for the remaining states is only 60·92 per cent.; the male dependents in Western Australia constitute 23·83 per cent., and those who have reached old age only 2·01 per cent. of the total male population. In the other states the most marked difference is in the old age group, where Victoria shows by far the largest proportion. The proportion of population in the dependent groups ranges from 32·24 per cent. in New Zealand to 36·32 per cent. in Tasmania; the variation is a trifle greater in the supporting ages, the proportion for Tasmania being 59·40 per cent. as against 63·34 per cent. in Queensland. In the old age group there is a comparatively wider margin, the proportions ranging from 2·90 per cent. in Queensland to 6·13 per cent. in Victoria. Western Australia and Queensland show the greatest proportions of males at the military ages, the other states being remarkably even. On the 31st March, 1901, there were 644,500 men in the Commonwealth who could be called upon to perform military service, and 130,500 in New Zealand.

The female population of Australasia may be conveniently grouped in four divisions, namely, dependent ages from infancy to 15 years; reproductive ages, from 15 to 45; mature ages from 45 and under 65; and old ages from 65 years. The numbers of each class in the different states at the time of the census are shown below:—

State.	Dependent Ages, up to 15 years.		Reproductive Ages, 15 and under 45.		Ages of 45 and under 65.		Old Ages, 65 years and over.	
	Number.	Proportion of total female population.	Number.	Proportion of total female population.	Number.	Proportion of total female population.	Number.	Proportion of total female population.
		per cent.		per cent.		per cent.		per cent.
New South Wales	240,596	37·34	313,323	48·63	70,896	11·00	19,535	3·03
Victoria	202,274	33·96	295,236	49·57	68,837	11·56	29,247	4·91
Queensland	90,191	40·98	102,635	46·63	22,319	10·14	4,957	2·25
South Australia	64,028	35·93	85,132	47·78	21,421	12·02	7,601	4·27
Western Australia	26,410	37·09	37,816	53·11	5,914	8·31	1,063	1·49
Tasmania	31,514	38·05	39,083	47·13	9,083	10·97	3,194	3·85
Commonwealth	655,013	36·55	873,175	48·72	198,470	11·07	65,597	3·66
New Zealand	127,029	34·66	183,387	50·03	43,968	12·00	12,135	3·31
Australasia	782,042	36·23	1,056,562	48·94	242,438	11·23	77,732	3·60

The age constitution of the female population shows more general variation in the different states than that of the male population, but

Western Australia does not differ from the other states in any marked degree. In the dependent group there is a considerable margin, for while in Victoria this division comprises but 33·96 per cent. of the total female population, in Queensland it constitutes 40·98 per cent. In the reproductive ages Queensland has the smallest proportionate number, representing 46·63 per cent. of the population, as against 53·11 per cent. in Western Australia. The next age group embraces females aged 45 and under 65, and in Western Australia these comprise 8·31 per cent. only, as against 12·02 per cent. in South Australia. In the old age group Victoria has the largest proportion with 4·91 per cent., while Western Australia only shows 1·49 per cent.

From a consideration of the two preceding tables it will be evident that in Western Australia a fairly large element of the male population consists of married men whose wives and families are living elsewhere, for while the number of males above the dependent age is 85,769, the females of corresponding ages number only 44,793. This is borne out by the information referring to the conjugal condition of the people of Australasia, which appears later on in this chapter

As regards some of the states great changes have taken place in the age constitution of the population during the ten years from 1891 to 1901, and a notable feature is the decline in the proportionate number of dependents under 15 years of age. This decline is general throughout Australasia, and when it is considered that 93 per cent. of the increase of population during the ten years was due to natural increase by excess of births over deaths, the decline in the birth rate is evidenced in a striking manner.

The proportion of the male population in the different groups at each census period was as shown below.

Males.

State.	Under 15 years. Per cent of male population.		15 and under 65. Per cent. of male population.		65 and over. Per cent. of male population.	
	1891.	1901.	1891.	1901.	1891.	1901.
New South Wales	35·85	34·79	61·41	61·39	2·74	3·82
Victoria........................	33·37	34·30	62·68	59·57	3·95	6·13
Queensland	33·15	33·76	65·22	63·34	1·63	2·90
South Australia	38·37	35·36	58·33	60·66	3·30	3·98
Western Australia	28·73	23·83	67·59	74·16	3·68	2·01
Tasmania	37·39	36·32	57·06	59·40	5·55	4·28
Commonwealth	34·82	33·99	61·96	61·68	3·22	4·33
New Zealand	38·01	32·24	59·48	63·02	2·51	4·74
Australasia	35·34	33·69	61·56	61·91	3·10	4·40

There has been a decrease in the proportion of males at dependent ages in all the states with the exception of Victoria and Queensland.

The largest decrease is shown in Western Australia where the proportion has fallen from 28·73 per cent. in 1891 to 23·83 per cent. in 1901. The changes were more general in the supporting ages, for while South Australia, Western Australia, Tasmania, and New Zealand show increases, the proportions in the other states decreased. In 1891 Western Australia had the highest proportionate population at supporting ages with 67·59 per cent., but in 1901 this had been increased to 74·16 per cent., a proportion greatly in advance of that for any other State. In regard to the population which has reached old age, the proportions in most of the states have increased, and Victoria with 6·13 per cent. holds the position occupied in 1891 by Tasmania when 5·55 per cent. of the population of the latter state were aged 65 years and over.

The proportions of female populations in the various groups at the two periods under review were as follow:—

State.	Under 15 years. Per cent of female population.		15 and under 45. Per cent. of female population.		45 and under 65. Per cent. of female population.		65 and over. Per cent. of Female population.	
	1891.	1901.	1891.	1901.	1891.	1901.	1891.	1901.
New South Wales	41·32	37·34	46·42	48·63	9·99	11·00	2·27	3·03
Victoria	36·05	33·96	48·46	49·57	12·58	11·56	2·91	4·91
Queensland	42·61	40·98	46·72	46·63	9·28	10·14	1·39	2·25
South Australia	40·47	35·93	44·78	47·78	11·41	12·02	3·34	4·27
Western Australia	41·89	37·09	46·45	53·11	9·76	8·31	1·90	1·49
Tasmania	40·99	38·05	44·27	47·13	11·22	10·97	3·52	3·85
Commonwealth	39·43	36·55	46·93	48·72	11·07	11·07	2·57	3·66
New Zealand	42·17	34·66	44·74	50·03	11·04	12·00	2·05	3·31
Australasia	39·89	36·23	46·57	48·94	11·06	11·23	2·48	3·60

The proportionate number of female dependents decreased in each of the states during the ten years, and the average for Australasia was only 36·23 per cent. in 1901 compared with 39·89 per cent. in 1891. In Queensland only does the proportion of women at reproductive ages show a decline during the period; the greatest increase is shown in Western Australia, where the proportion is now much higher than in any other state. There were many changes in the proportions of female population in the various states at ages from 45 to 65, but the general average for Australasia is much the same, in fact the figures for the Commonwealth show exactly the same proportion as existed ten years ago. A general increase is noticeable in all the states regarding the number of females aged 65 and over, the only exception being Western Australia.

Conjugal Condition.

At a conference of statisticians held at Sydney, during February, 1900' it was decided to tabulate the conjugal condition of the people, as ascertained by the census of 1901, under the heads of "Never married," "Married,' "Widowed," and "Divorced"; but this decision was not adhered to in South Australia, where the divorced were probably included under the heading of unmarried. For the sake of comparison a similar classification has therefore been made in the tabulation of the other states. The people who returned themselves as "divorced" were very few in number, and it is reasonable to assume that the numbers were wide of the truth, owing to the reluctance on the part of many people whose marriage bonds had been severed to return themselves as "divorced" in the census schedules.

The following table shows the number of males in each state under the headings of "Unmarried," "Married," and "Widowers"; and the proportion of each to the male population. The figures are exclusive of aborigines, and the proportions are calculated only on the number of those persons whose conjugal condition was set down :—

Males.

State.	Unmarried.		Married.		Widowers.		Total.
	Number.	Proportion of Male Population.	Number.	Proportion of Male Population.	Number.	Proportion of Male Population.	
		per cent.		per cent.		per cent.	
New South Wales ...	484,942	68·56	202,922	28·69	19,451	2·75	707,315
Victoria	405,977	67·25	177,629	29·42	20,114	3·33	603,720
Queensland	196,740	71·34	72,213	26·19	6,812	2·47	275,765
South Australia	124,566	67·54	54,754	29·69	5,102	2·77	184,422
Western Australia ...	77,567	68·91	32,063	28·48	2,932	2·61	112,562
Tasmania	60,952	68·24	25,807	28·89	2,560	2·87	89,319
Commonwealth ...	1,350,744	68·46	565,388	28·65	56,971	2·89	1,973,103
New Zealand	275,864	68·10	118,536	29·26	10,666	2·64	405,066
Australasia	1,626,608	68·40	683,924	28·76	67,637	2·84	2,378,169

The figures show that only 28·65 per cent. of the male population of the Commonwealth is married. The rates are fairly uniform throughout Australasia with the single exception of Queensland, where unmarried males form 71·34 per cent. of the male population. The following table shows similar information regarding the female population of Australasia :—

Females.

State.	Unmarried.		Married.		Widows.		Total.
	Number.	Proportion of Female Population.	Number.	Proportion of Female Population.	Number.	Proportion of Female Population.	
		per cent.		per cent.		per cent.	
New South Wales ...	403,034	62·54	206,186	32·00	35,207	5·46	644,427
Victoria	370,809	62·08	183,390	30·70	43,151	7·22	597,350
Queensland	138,568	62·91	71,469	32·45	10,218	4·64	220,255
South Australia	112,122	62·92	55,341	31·06	10,719	6·02	178,182
Western Australia ...	41,046	57·65	27,043	37·98	3,112	4·37	71,201
Tasmania	52,593	63·57	25,460	30·78	4,672	5·65	82,725
Commonwealth ...	1,118,172	62·32	568,889	31·71	107,079	5·97	1,794,140
New Zealand	230,524	62·94	117,839	32·17	17,902	4·89	366,265
Australasia	1,348,696	62·43	686,728	31·79	124,981	5·78	2,160,405

The smallest proportion of unmarried females is in Western Australia, where the number of adult males is relatively large. From the foregoing figures it will be seen that unmarried males are largely in excess of unmarried females in each state. Amongst the widowed, females largely outnumber males, as was to be expected from the higher death-rate and the proportionately larger number of males remarried. The following table shows the excess of unmarried males 21 years of age and upwards, over unmarried females of like ages, and the number of unmarried females to 1,000 unmarried males of these ages. Age 21 is taken as the beginning of the marriageable period, and the figures include the widowed and divorced as well as those who have never been married:—

State.	Excess of Unmarried Males over Unmarried Females.	Number of Unmarried Females to 1,000 Unmarried Males.
New South Wales	58,893	668
Victoria	7,098	952
Queensland	49,898	398
South Australia	5,236	848
Western Australia	33,335	254
Tasmania	4,469	776
Commonwealth	158,929	691
New Zealand	32,705	688
Australasia	191,634	691

The proportion of unmarried females is lowest in Western Australia and Queensland, the two states which have gained most through immigration during the past ten years, and is highest in South Australia, Victoria, and Tasmania, where there has been a loss by excess of emigration. As the population of the two states first mentioned has been largely recruited from the other states, it is evident that the movement of population has been chiefly of unmarried males animated by a desire to better their position.

Birthplaces.

One of the subjects of inquiry at the census of 1901, as at previous enumerations, was the birthplaces of the population. The result of the tabulation shows that while there are differences in the component parts of the population in the several states, these differences are slight, and the great majority of the people in Australasia—to the extent, indeed, of fully 95 per cent.—are of British origin. Probably the population of Australasia is more homogeneous than that of most European countries; for even in Queensland, where people of foreign descent are proportionately more numerous than in any of the other states, they only amount to 8·71 per cent. of the total population. The subjoined table shows in a condensed form the results of the tabulation of the birthplaces of the population of each state, the figures being exclusive of aborigines :—

Birthplaces.	New South Wales.	Victoria.	Queensland.	South Australia	Western Australia	Tasmania	New Zealand.
New South Wales	977,176	22,404	24,868	4,128	14,122	2,075	6,492
Victoria	56,019	875,775	10,272	10,324	39,491	7,949	12,583
Queensland	14,968	3,018	282,861	606	2,595	288	1,271
South Australia	22,059	21,924	2,384	271,671	16,250	887	1,575
Western Australia	887	1,467	199	956	52,368	96	190
Tasmania	7,577	15,368	1,308	819	1,750	136,629	3,720
Australia, State not specified	468	875	19	936	81	14	1,222
Total, Commonwealth	1,079,154	940,826	321,911	289,440	126,962	147,938	27,053
New Zealand	10,589	9,020	1,571	711	2,704	1,193	516,106
Total, Australasia	1,089,743	949,846	323,482	290,151	129,656	149,131	543,159
England	126,117	113,432	} 68,589	37,789	25,380	12,658	111,964
Wales	3,622	3,676		865	909	284	1,765
Scotland	30,717	35,751	19,934	6,965	5,400	2,986	47,858
Ireland	59,945	61,512	37,636	11,248	9,862	3,887	43,524
Total, United Kingdom	220,401	214,371	126,159	56,862	41,551	19,815	205,111
India and Ceylon	2,957	1,939	1,476	710	842	382	1,286
Canada	1,063	995	404	190	267	87	1,439
Other British Possessions	1,933	1,617	857	439	871	168	1,497
Total, British Empire	1,316,097	1,168,768	452,378	348,352	173,187	169,583	752,492
German Empire	8,716	7,608	13,166	6,664	1,527	773	4,217
France and Possessions	2,129	955	370	225	280	56	610
Russia	1,262	954	454	251	400	37	484
Austria	667	404	240	162	418	23	1,874
Switzerland	454	903	441	104	118	19	333
Denmark and Possessions	1,368	1,022	3,161	262	320	155	2,120
Sweden and Norway	3,190	2,207	2,142	931	1,174	219	2,827
Italy	1,577	1,526	847	327	1,354	50	428
Other European Countries and Possessions.	1,910	1,315	682	470	989	129	870
United States of America	3,130	2,135	1,315	523	1,035	234	1,671
Chinese Empire	9,993	6,230	8,472	3,253	1,475	484	2,902
Other Foreign Countries	948	823	11,964	335	1,288	44	246
Total, Foreign Countries.	35,344	25,582	43,254	13,507	10,378	2,223	18,582
Born at Sea	1,967	1,564	634	539	317	182	1,203
Unspecified	1,438	5,156	330	206	242	487	442
Aboriginal half-castes	......	......	1,583	....	....	....	....
Total	1,354,846	1,201,070	498,129	362,604	184,124	172,475	772,719

It will be seen at a glance that natives of the Australasian states formed three-fourths of the population, and that the great majority of the Australasian-born population were natives of the particular state in which they were enumerated, the only exception being in the case of Western Australia. The proportion of the people born in the state in which they were resident at the time of the census, of those born in the other states, and of the total Australasian-born population to the total population of each state, are shown below :—

State.	Percentage of Total Population of—		
	Natives of State of Enumeration.	Natives of other States.	Australasian-born Population.
New South Wales	72·20	8·32	80·52
Victoria	73·23	6·19	79·42
Queensland	57·01	8·19	65·20
South Australia	74·96	5·10	80·06
Western Australia	28·64	41·87	70·51
Tasmania	79·44	7·27	86·71
New Zealand	66·83	3·50	70·33

These figures show that proportionately the largest Australasian-born population is to be found in Tasmania, where nearly 80 out of every 100 of the inhabitants were born in the state, and over 86 per cent. were Australasians. In Queensland, on the contrary, more than one-third of the population were natives of countries outside Australasia, and only 57 per cent. were Queenslanders by birth. The low proportion of native-born in this state is due to the policy of state assisted immigration, which is still in force, the addition to the population from this source during the twenty-one years ended with 1902, amounting to 116,804 souls. The exodus of population from other parts of the Continent to Western Australia is evidenced in a striking manner, as persons born in the other Australasian provinces, comprised 42 per cent. of the total in that state. The following figures set forth still more clearly the extent to which each state is indebted for population to its neighbours :—

State.	Number of Natives of other six States enumerated.	Number of Natives enumerated in other six States.	Net gain from other States.	Net loss to other States.
New South Wales	112,099	74,089	38,010	....
Victoria	73,196	136,638	....	63,442
Queensland	40,602	22,746	17,856	....
South Australia	17,544	65,079	....	47,535
Western Australia	76,912	3,795	73,117	....
Tasmania	12,488	30,537	....	18,049
New Zealand	25,831	25,788	43	....

Next to the Australasian-born population, natives of the United Kingdom were by far the most numerous class in each state. The following table shows the percentages of natives of England and Wales, Scotland, and Ireland to the total population of each state :—

State.	Natives of—			
	England and Wales.	Scotland.	Ireland.	United Kingdom.
New South Wales.....	9·58	2·27	4·43	16·28
Victoria	9·79	2·99	5·14	17·92
Queensland........	13·82	4·02	7·58	25·42
South Australia.........	10·67	1·92	3·10	15·69
Western Australia ...	14·30	2·94	5·36	22·60
Tasmania	7·52	1·74	2·26	11·52
New Zealand	14·73	6·20	5·63	26·56
Australasia	11·18	3·30	5·02	19·50

It was to be expected that the percentage of natives of the United Kingdom would be highest in Queensland which has introduced a large number of assisted immigrants during the last twenty years. Although natives of England and Wales are numerically stronger, if the composition of the population of the United Kingdom be taken into consideration, it will be seen that Scotch and Irish colonists are proportionately much more numerous than those of English birth. A curious feature is the apparent preference on the part of Irishmen for Queensland and Scotsmen for New Zealand.

The number of natives of parts of the British Empire other than the United Kingdom and Australasia enumerated in these states was very small, amounting only to the following percentages of the total population :—In New South Wales, 0·44 per cent. ; in Victoria, 0·38 per cent. ; in Queensland, 0·55 per cent. ; in South Australia, 0·37 per cent. ; in Western Australia, 1·07 per cent. ; in Tasmania, 0·37 per cent. ; and in New Zealand, 0·54 per cent. ; average for Australasia, 0·47 per cent. Natives of Canada and of India and Ceylon make up the majority of this class, which numbered only 21,409 altogether. It is not considered necessary to give a complete tabulation of natives of all foreign countries, and only the more numerous are quoted. Immigrants from Germany formed by far the largest proportion. The Chinese are next in point of numbers, followed by Scandinavians, while natives of the United States, France and Italy are also fairly numerous. Polynesians constitute a considerable section of the community in Queensland, but are almost unknown in some of the other states. The percentages of the total population in each state of natives of Germany, of the Scandinavian Kingdoms (Sweden and Norway and

Denmark), and of the total foreign-born population, are shown in the subjoined table :—

State.	Percentage of—		
	Germans.	Scandinavians.	Total Foreign-born Population.
New South Wales	0·64	0·33	2·61
Victoria	0·64	0·27	2·15
Queensland	2·65	1·07	8·71
South Australia	1·84	0·26	3·73
Western Australia	0·83	0·81	5·65
Tasmania	0·45	0·22	1·29
New Zealand	0·55	0·64	2·41
Australasia	0·94	0·28	3·28

It will be seen that both Germans and Scandinavians are proportionately most numerous in Queensland, where together they amount to 3·72 per cent. of the population. Germans are also very numerous in South Australia, and Scandinavians in Western Australia and New Zealand.

The remainder of the population whose birthplaces were stated, is made up of those born at sea ; the persons whose birthplaces were unspecified numbered 8,301, and have been excluded from consideration in computing the proportions arrived at in these pages. The proportion of the population born at sea to the total population of each state is shown below :—

State.	Persons born at Sea. Per cent.
New South Wales	0·15
Victoria	0·13
Queensland	0·12
South Australia	0·15
Western Australia	0·17
Tasmania	0·11
New Zealand	0·16
Australasia	0·14

From the returns of those states where the people born at sea have been classified into those born of British and of foreign parentage, it appears that the great majority are of British parentage.

Native Races.

At the census of 1901 only 48,248 aborigines were enumerated, of whom 40,880 were full-blooded and 7,368 half-castes. The following table shows the distribution of each class amongst the various states.

State.	Aborigines enumerated at Census of 1901.		
	Full-blooded.	Half-castes.	Total.
New South Wales	3,778	3,656	7,434
Victoria	271	381	652
Queensland	5,137	1,533	6,670
South Australia	26,433	690	27,123
Western Australia	5,261	951	6,212
Tasmania	....	157	157
Total	40,880	7,368	48,248

These figures only represent aborigines enumerated at the census, and except in Victoria, Tasmania, and New South Wales, they must not be taken as indicating the strength of the aboriginal population. At the various mission stations and schools, numbers of the aboriginal population who have abandoned their wild habits are following settled occupations. This is more especially the case with half-castes, many of whom have received a rudimentary education and are in constant employment on farms and stations. In view of their civilised condition, a number of half-castes have been included with the general population of the states as follows:—New South Wales, 3,147; Victoria, 381; Queensland, 1,533; Western Australia, 951; and Tasmania, 157. The native aboriginal race is extinct in Tasmania, and practically so in Victoria where the number recorded was only 271. The aborigines in New South Wales totalled 7,434 at the census of 1901, and as their number was 8,280 ten years previously, they are apparently decreasing at a rate slightly in excess of 1 per cent. yearly. In Queensland, only 6,670 aborigines were enumerated, but their full strength is estimated at 25,000; while in South Australia, although 27,123 were enumerated, the total number cannot be far short of 50,000. The census of Western Australia included only those aboriginals within the bounds of settlement, and as large portions of this, the greatest in area of all the Australian states, are as yet unexplored, it is evident that the number shown, 6,212, gives no idea as to the total aboriginal population. It is estimated that the aborigines in Western Australia are fully 70,000 in number, which would make the total aboriginal population of the continent about 153,000. The difficulty of enumerating the aborigines, even in the civilised area of Australia, will be apparent when their migratory habits are considered; and as by far the greater portion of their number lives outside the bounds of civilisation, in practically unexplored territory, this estimate of their numerical strength is advanced with the utmost diffidence. The Maoris, who are popularly supposed to be the original natives of New Zealand, are quite a different race from the aborigines of Australia. They are gifted with a considerable amount of intelligence, are quick at imitation, and brave even to rashness.

Their numbers, as ascertained at various census periods, were as follow:—

Year.	Males.	Females.	Total.
1881	24,368	19,729	44,097
1886	22,840	19,129	41,969
1891	22,861	19,132	41,993
1896	21,673	18,181	39,854
1901	23,112	20,031	43,143

The figures for 1901 include 31 Morioris, who are supposed to be a branch of the same race as the Maoris. It is thought that both races came from the islands of the Pacific, but the Morioris preceded the Maoris by many years. They held possession until the arrival of the Maoris, whose superior numbers enabled them to overcome the original possessors and drive them from the mainland to the surrounding isles, and it is only in the Chatham Islands that a small remnant of their race is left.

In the totals given for 1896 and 1901 there are included 3,503 and 3,123 half-castes respectively, who were living as members of Maori tribes. It is said that when New Zealand was first colonised, the number of Maoris was fully 120,000; but this, like all other estimates of aboriginal population, is founded on very imperfect information. So far as the above table shows, their number has been almost stationary during the last twenty years; in fact, during the last quinquennial period there was an increase of 3,289 persons.

Alien Races.

The number of coloured aliens enumerated in the Commonwealth at the census of 1901 was 54,441, distributed amongst the various states as follows. The figures in this table are not exact in the case of South Australia and Western Australia. The former state published part of the information only, and there are included among the "others" 266 persons who are probably coloured, but in regard to whom there is no certainty. Western Australia did not publish the information, and with the exception of the Chinese and Japanese, the persons shown in the table may or may not be coloured, since, although the persons enumerated were born in a country such as India, where the aboriginal natives are coloured, it does not necessarily follow that they were also of coloured race, and some of them certainly were persons of European origin. It may be reasonably assumed, however, that the great majority of those shown were coloured.

State.	Chinese (full-blood.)	Japanese.	Hindoos and Cingalese.	Pacific Islanders.	Others.	Total Coloured Aliens.
New South Wales	10,222	161	1,681	467	1,261	13,792
Victoria	6,347	55	789	2	435	7,628
Queensland	8,587	2,269	939	9,327	1,787	22,909
South Australia	3,359	205	439	2	453	4,458
Western Australia	1,521	864	833	31	1,817	5,066
Tasmania	506	...	...	...	82	588
Commonwealth	30,542	3,554	4,681	9,829	5,835	54,441

These figures show that coloured aliens number 14·43 per 1,000 of the population (exclusive of aborigines) in the Commonwealth. The highest proportion is found in Queensland, where large numbers of Pacific Islanders have been imported to work on the sugar plantations. The coloured aliens in that state number 46·13 per 1,000 of the population; in Western Australia, 27·51; in South Australia, 12·29; in New South Wales, 10·18; in Victoria, 6·35; and in Tasmania, 3·41 per 1,000. Amongst the Chinese included in the table there are a certain number who were born outside the Chinese Empire. The figures for New South Wales include 282; Victoria, 187; Queensland, 142; South Australia, 129; Western Australia, 54; and Tasmania, 22.

The further immigration of Pacific Islanders to Australia is now restricted by the Pacific Islands Labourers Bill. This Act is particularly directed against the continued employment of these aliens on the sugar plantations, and under its provisions only a certain limited number will be allowed to enter Australia up to the 31st March, 1904. After that date their further immigration is prohibited, and all agreements for their employment must terminate on the 31st December, 1906, when any Pacific Islander found in Australia will be deported.

The influx of Hindoos and other Eastern races has long caused a feeling of uneasiness amongst the people of Australia, and restrictive legislation was already in force in some of the states prior to federation. One of the first measures passed by the Federal Parliament was the Immigration Restriction Act, which provides for the exclusion of any person who, when asked to do so, fails to write out and sign a passage of fifty words in a European language specified by an officer of the Customs. The Act does not apply, however, to persons in possession of certificates of exemption, to His Majesty's land and sea forces, to the master and crew of any public vessel of any Government, to any person duly accredited by any Government, to a wife accompanying her husband if he is not a prohibited immigrant, to all children under 18 years of age accompanying their father or mother if the latter are not prohibited immigrants, or to any person who satisfies an officer of the Customs that he has been formerly domiciled in the Commonwealth.

The number of Chinese in the various states had increased so rapidly prior to 1880 that it was deemed expedient by the Governments to enact prohibitive laws against the immigration of these aliens, and their migration from one state to another. For several years a poll-tax of £10 was imposed, but this was not considered sufficiently deterrent, and in New South Wales, in accordance with the most recent legislation on the subject, masters of vessels are forbidden under a heavy penalty to bring more than one Chinese to every 300 tons, and a poll-tax of £100 is charged on landing. In Victoria, Queensland, and South Australia no poll-tax is imposed, but masters of vessels may bring only one Chinese to every 500 tons burden. The Western Australian Act was similar to that in the three last-named states until recently, but has now been superseded by the Coloured Immigrants Restriction Act. Tasmania allows one Chinese passenger to every 100 tons, and imposes a poll-tax of £10. In New Zealand an Act similar to the Tasmanian Act was in force until 1896, when the poll-tax was raised to £100, and the number of passengers restricted to one for every 200 tons burden. These stringent regulations have had the effect of greatly restricting the influx of this undesirable class of immigrants, and at the census of 1901 they numbered only 36,022, as against 42,521 ten years previously. The following table shows the number of Chinese in each state at the five last census periods: the figures for 1891 and 1901 including half-castes :—

State.	1861.	1871.	1881.	1891.	1901.
New South Wales	12,988	7,220	10,205	14,156	11,263
Victoria	24,732	17,935	12,128	9,377	6,956
Queensland	538	3,305	11,229	8,574	9,313
South Australia	40	*	4,151	3,997	3,455
Western Australia	......	*	145	917	1,569
Tasmania	......	*	844	1,056	609
Commonwealth	38,298	28,460	38,702	38,077	33,165
New Zealand	......	*	5,004	4,444	2,857
Australasia	......	......	43,706	42,521	36,022

* Information not available.

The decrease in the Chinese population will be more apparent when it is stated that in 1901 they only numbered 7·92 per 1,000 of the population in Australasia as against 11·16 in 1891.

NATURALISATION.

Up to the 30th October, 1903, certificates of naturalisation were granted to aliens in the various states in accordance with enactments which did not differ materially, but with the passing of the

Commonwealth Naturalisation Act this power was taken away from the states, and vested exclusively in the Commonwealth Government. No letters or certificates of naturalisation granted in the states after the coming into operation of the Federal law are to have any effect.

Under the Commonwealth Act, any person who had, before the passing of the Act, obtained a certificate of naturalisation in any state is deemed to be naturalised. Any person resident in the Commonwealth not being a British subject, and not being an aboriginal native of Asia, Africa, or the islands of the Pacific, excepting New Zealand, who intends to settle in the Commonwealth, and who has resided in Australia continuously for two years immediately preceding the application, or who has obtained in the United Kingdom a certificate of naturalisation, may apply to be naturalised.

An applicant under the first heading must produce, in support of his application, his own statutory declaration exhibiting his name, age, birth-place, occupation, residence, the length of his residence in Australia, and stating that he intends to settle in the Commonwealth, as well as a certificate signed by some competent person that the applicant is known to him and is of good repute. An applicant under the second heading must produce, in support of his application, his certificate of naturalisation and his own statutory declaration that he is the person named in the certificate, that he obtained it without fraud, that the signature thereto is genuine, and that he intends to settle in the Commonwealth.

The Governor-General, if satisfied with the evidence adduced, may in his discretion grant or withhold a certificate as he thinks most conducive to the public good, provided that he shall not issue the certificate until the applicant has taken the necessary oath of allegiance.

Any person to whom a certificate of naturalisation is granted shall be entitled to all political and other rights, powers and privileges, and be subject to all the obligations of a natural-born British subject, provided that where, by the provisions of any state Act, a distinction is made between the rights of natural-born British subjects and those naturalised in the state, the rights conferred by the Commonwealth Act shall be only those to which persons naturalised by the state Act are entitled. Under the previously existing Acts in New South Wales, Victoria, South Australia, and Western Australia, aliens may hold and acquire both real and personal property, but may not qualify for any office, nor have any rights or privileges except such as are expressly conferred upon them, while in Queensland and Tasmania they may hold personal property, but lands for twenty-one years only.

Any alien woman who marries a British subject shall be deemed to be thereby naturalised. Any infant, not being a natural-born British subject, whose father has become naturalised, or whose mother is married to a natural-born British subject or to a naturalised person, and who has at any time resided in Australia with such father or mother, shall be deemed to be naturalised.

On the whole, the conditions to be fulfilled under the Commonwealth Act do not differ greatly from those under the old state Acts, but the term of residence necessary is now two years, whereas in New South Wales it was five years, in South Australia six months, and in the other states no specified time. Under the Commonwealth Act Asiatics, Africans, and Pacific Islanders are refused the rights of naturalisation; previously only the Chinese were so treated in New South Wales, Queensland, and Western Australia. In Queensland it was necessary for an Asiatic or African alien to be married and have his wife living in the state, and to have resided in the state for three years. On naturalisation he became entitled to all privileges except that of becoming a member of the Legislature.

In New Zealand, every alien of good repute residing within the colony who desires to become naturalised may present a memorial signed by himself and verified upon oath, stating his name, age, birthplace, residence, occupation, and length of residence in the colony, and his desire to settle therein, together with all other grounds on which he seeks to obtain the rights of naturalisation, and apply for a certificate, which the Governor may grant if he thinks fit. After the letters of naturalisation have been received, and the oath of allegiance taken, the holder becomes entitled to all the privileges which are conferred upon subjects of His Majesty. Naturalised persons may hold and acquire both real and personal property, but may not qualify for any office.

Excluding Queensland, where the information was not ascertained, the number of naturalised foreigners in the Commonwealth at the census of 1901 was 10,910, distributed as follows:—New South Wales, 3,265 males, 354 females; Victoria, 3,304 males, 1,262 females; South Australia, 1,360 males, 545 females; Western Australia, 576 males, 101 females; Tasmania, 119 males, 24 females. In New Zealand the number of naturalised persons was 4,672. It is probable, however, that the above numbers are under-stated. Germans have availed themselves most largely of the privileges of naturalisation, having taken out about one-half of the certificates granted.

The number of persons naturalised in Australasia during 1902 distributed amongst the various states was as follows:—

State.	Germans and other German-speaking nations.	Scandinavians.	Chinese.	Others.	Total.
New South Wales ...	133	110	......	143	386
Victoria	204	19	......	277	500
Queensland	153	110	21	91	375
South Australia	21	14	......	19	54
Western Australia ...	196	121	22	237	576
Tasmania	7	4	14	3	28
Commonwealth...	714	378	57	770	1,919
New Zealand...........	112	107	5	98	322
Australasia	826	485	62	868	2,241

MINERAL RESOURCES.

ALMOST all the principal metals of economic value are found in Australasia, and many are common to several of the States. In dealing with the occurrence and value of mineral deposits, a classification has been made into noble and other metals, carbon minerals, salts, stones and clays, and diamonds and other gem stones.

GOLD.

Gold, the most valuable of noble metals, is found throughout Australasia, and the important position at present occupied by these States is largely due to discoveries of this metal, the development of other industries being, in a country of varied resources, a natural sequence to the acquisition of mineral treasure. Settlement in Australia was still young when many-tongued rumour spoke of the existence of the precious metal, but it was not until the 16th February, 1823, that the Government was officially apprised of a discovery destined to be the precursor of a prosperity seldom surpassed in the history of nations. On the date mentioned Mr. Assistant-Surveyor M'Brien reported that at a spot on the Fish River, about 15 miles east of Bathurst, he had discovered gold. Mention is made in the early records of New South Wales of several other finds, but it remained for Count Strzelecki and the Rev. W. B. Clarke to demonstrate the existence of the precious metal in payable quantities, and to assert their belief in its abundance, an opinion strongly supported in England by several eminent authorities, and substantiated by Hargraves' discovery in the year 1851. The gold-fields of Lewis Ponds and Summer Hill Creek had hardly been opened up when, on the day that witnessed the severance of the Port Phillip district from the mother colony of New South Wales, Mr. J. M. Esmond discovered gold in Victoria. Shortly afterwards a rush set in for Ballarat, and the gold fever took possession of Australia. The following year (1852) saw gold found in South Australia, Tasmania, and New Zealand, though it was not until 1861 that a large population was, by the prospect of rapidly obtaining wealth, attracted to the last-mentioned colony. The rush to Canoona, in what is now Queensland, took place in 1858. The last of the States in which extensive deposits of the precious metal were found was Western Australia, but the mines there are now the richest in Australasia, and have proved an enormous source of wealth to the state.

G

From the date of its first discovery, gold to the value of nearly 476 million pounds sterling has been obtained in Australasia. Towards this total Victoria has contributed 263½ millions, and for many years that state was the largest gold producer of Australasia. In the year 1897, however, for the first time, the production was surpassed by that of Western Australia, and the latter state increased its advantage each year until in 1902 the output was valued at £7,947,662, as against £3,062,028 in Victoria. The yield of gold in Victoria has been well maintained for many years, and each successive year from 1893 to 1899 showed an increase. In the last-mentioned year the production was 854,500 oz., valued at £3,418,000, but during the last three years there has been a decline, and the output in 1902 amounted to only 777,738 oz., or 720,866 oz. fine, valued at £3,062,028. The Bendigo district was again the chief centre of production, with 190,165 oz., followed by Ballarat with 172,599 oz., and Beechworth with 96,518 oz. The richest fields in the state are at Bendigo and Ballarat which, after yielding uninterruptedly for half a century, still give no evidence of depletion. The output of the former field in 1902 was 184,959 oz., and of the latter 62,712 oz. Of the total yield of the state 33,109 oz. were obtained by means of dredging and hydraulic sluicing. There were 11 dredges and 29 sluicing plants in operation at the close of the year, and their value was estimated at £270,000, the number of men employed in connection with them being 956. The total number of men engaged in gold-mining on the 31st December, 1902, was 26,103, of whom 11,963 were alluvial miners, and 14,140 quartz miners. The machinery and plant in use on the same date were valued at £1,958,560.

Queensland promised at one time to overtake Victoria in the annual production of gold, but so far the southern state has maintained its position, although the production of Queensland advanced steadily up to the year 1900. In 1889 the output was valued at £2,586,860, but thenceforward the yield declined, and this amount was not again reached until 1898, when the value was £2,750,349. During the next two years there was again an increase, the value of the gold won in 1900 being £2,871,709, the highest yet recorded. The production in 1901 was 589,382 oz. fine, valued at £2,541,892, while in 1902 it amounted to 640,463 oz. fine, with a value of £2,720,639. The decreased output of the past two years is not due to the waning productiveness of the mines, as the yield of 1902 is the largest obtained from stone raised and reduced in any one year. Although the yield in 1900 was higher, it included a considerable quantity of gold obtained from old tailings, and from creeks which had served as channels for the escape of residue from the mills. Want of water hampered operations in 1902, especially at Mount Morgan; nevertheless, great activity was displayed in gold-mining circles, and, encouraged by the increased dividends paid, many new ventures were launched, while developmental work at established mines was prosecuted with renewed vigour.

Arranged in order of productiveness, the principal goldfields in Queensland in 1902 were Charters Towers, Mount Morgan, and Gympie, while Ravenswood and Croydon also produced a considerable quantity of the precious metal. For many years Charters Towers has been the chief gold-producing centre, and the year 1902 was perhaps the most prosperous experienced on the field since its discovery in 1872. The production in 1902 amounted to 265,244 oz. fine, valued at £1,126,735, or £127,190 more than in the preceding year. There are three great ore shoots on this field, known as The Day Dawn, Brilliant, and Victoria Reefs, and the rich developments in the Queen Cross, one of the mines engaged in working the Victoria reef, was mainly responsible for the increased activity in the mining operations. The dividends paid by this mine during the year amounted to £111,666, and present appearances indicate that the yield of last year will be fully maintained during the present year. Of the mines engaged on the Day Dawn reef, the most important in point of production was the Day Dawn Block and Wyndham, which returned dividends amounting to £49,840 during the year. In consequence of the success attending the operations of the mines on this reef, two new mines were started in 1902 which hope to strike the Day Dawn reef at depths of 2,600 feet and 2,500 feet respectively. The Brilliant Central was the most productivo and profitable mine of the Brilliant group, and paid £68,750 in dividends during 1902. Scarcity of water has hitherto retarded operations at Charters Towers, and in order to secure a constant supply a weir was constructed across the Burdekin River. Shortly after its completion a flood occurred most opportunely in the river, and no less than 400,000,000 gallons of water were impounded. By an arrangement with the Railway Commissioners, who provided a daily supply of 200,000 gallons of water, the Mount Morgan mine was enabled to carry on operations during the dry period of 1902. The yield of this field for the year amounted to 142,826 oz. of fine gold, valued at £606,714, or £8,965 less than in the preceding year. The Mount Morgan mine was responsible for almost the whole of the production, and yielded 145,347 oz. of gold, with a value of £585,007, obtained from 218,214 tons of stone. Up to the 31st May, 1903, no less than 2,624,319 oz. of gold, valued at £10,652,339, had been obtained from this mine. During the year a large body of ore was located at the 750-feet level, a depth much lower than that from which stone has hitherto been raised. The machinery employed at the Mount Morgan mine on the 31st December, 1902, was valued at £517,229, and about 1,700 hands were engaged at the mine and works. The yield of the Gympie mining district, in 1902, surpassed that of any previous year, and amounted to 120,662 oz. fine gold, with a value of £512,562. The chief contributing mines were the No. 2 South Great Eastern, Scottish Gympie, and South Glanmire and Monkland, which produced 44,571 oz., 36,003 oz., and 33,188 oz. of gold, and paid dividends amounting to £98,800, £50,250, and £79,500 respectively.

The deepest mine on the field was the West of Scotland, which is down 3,000 feet, while several others exceed 2,000 feet in depth. This field gives employment to 1,740 quartz miners, and 22 alluvial miners, and the machinery in use is valued at £247,000. The Ravenswood gold-field, which had been comparatively neglected for some years, has again attracted attention owing to rich discoveries made in 1902, and the production last year showed a considerable advance on that of 1901, amounting to 40,969 oz. fine gold, valued at £174,034. The Sunset is the principal mine in the locality, and during the year produced 21,978 oz. of gold, valued at £90,000. There were 849 miners working at the end of 1902, of whom 806 were engaged in gold-mining. The yield of the Croydon field amounted to 28,355 oz. fine gold, valued at £120,451. The number of men employed on the 31st December, 1902, was 500, and the machinery in use was valued at £73,600. The total number of men engaged in gold-mining in Queensland at the end of 1902 was 9,045, of whom 7,129 were quartz-miners and 1,916 alluvial miners, 560 of the latter being Chinese.

In New South Wales the greatest annual production of gold occurred in 1852, soon after the first discovery of the precious metal, when the output was valued at £2,660,946. The only other year which saw a production in excess of two millions sterling was 1862, when the return reached £2,467,780. In 1874 the yield had fallen to 271,166 oz., valued at £1,041,614, and thenceforth the industry declined considerably in importance, reaching its lowest point in 1888, when only 87,541 oz., valued at £317,241, were produced. From that date onward there was a steady improvement, and in 1894 the Government took the step of furnishing large numbers of the unemployed with miners' rights and free railway passes, and sending them to the abandoned alluvial fields as fossickers. This action, with the increased attention paid to quartz-mining, nearly doubled the production, the quantity obtained during the year being set down at 324,787 oz., valued at £1,156,717, being the first time since 1874 that it had exceeded one million sterling; while in 1895 the yield reached 360,165 oz., and the value £1,315,929. During the next three years there was a falling off, but in 1899 the output reached the value of £1,623,320, the highest since 1872. From that year onwards want of water was responsible for a diminished production. The value of the yield in 1902 was £684,970, and the total up to the end of that year £49,844,135. The figures now published referring to the years 1897 to 1901 include gold obtained from native ores only, and differ from those shown in previous editions of this work, which included also gold obtained from imported ores. The yield of gold for 1902 is the lowest since 1893, but this is accounted for by the fact that want of water caused many of the mines to shut down for more than half the year. Of the gold produced in 1902, 25,473 oz., valued at £97,891, were obtained by dredging, the output from this branch of the industry showing an increase of £8,263 on that of the previous year. On the 31st December, 1902, there were 36 dredging plants in commission, valued at £262,700, while 5 others, which had been working unsuccessfully, were in course of removal to more favourable sites. The area held and applied for under lease for gold dredging was 11,719 acres. The principal seats of alluvial mining in the State are the Bathurst, Mudgee, Tumut and Adelong, and Braidwood districts, together with the country watered by the various feeders of the Upper Lachlan; while the principal quartz-veins are situated near Adelong, Armidale, Bathurst, Cobar, Hill End, Orange, Parkes, and Wyalong. Cobar again maintained the position occupied in preceding years as the chief gold-producing centre, the output for 1902 being valued at £90,200. The next in importance was Wyalong, with £77,046; followed by Araluen £53,155, and Adelong £51,700. The mines in this State are not so productive as those of Western Australia or Queensland, the largest yield from any one mine in 1902 being 9,808 oz., valued at £34,142. This was obtained from the Gibraltar mine in the Adelong district, while the Myall United, situated near Peak Hill, produced 7,829 oz., valued at £30,486, and the Lachlan Gold-fields, Limited, 5,542 oz., valued at £22,103. Of the mines recently developed, that at Mount Boppy, near Cobar, is by far the most promising. The lode is 5 feet and upwards in width at a depth of 300 feet, and samples taken from it averaged 79·70 dwt. to the ton. The estimated value of the machinery on the gold-fields, including dredging plant, at the end of 1902 was £992,742. The men engaged in the industry numbered 10,610, of whom 5,176 were quartz miners and 5,434 alluvial miners, the latter including 336 Chinese.

Until a comparatively recent date, Western Australia was considered to be destitute of mineral deposits of any value, but it is now known that a rich belt of mineral country extends from north to south. The first important discovery made in 1882, when gold was found in the Kimberley district, it was not until a few years later that this rich and extensive developed. In 1887 gold was found at Yilgarn, about east of Perth, the find possessing importance as the pre- the discovery of the immense tracts of gold-bearing, the knowledge of the existence of which has drawn population was parts of Australasia and brought the state into the prominent but which it occupies at the present time. General attention was [illegible]cted to these fields by further discoveries at Southern Cross, [illegible] of Yilgarn; and the sensational finds at Coolgardie, which followed in 1892, resulted in a rush to Western Australia which was reminiscent of the experiences of the fifties in the older-settled portions of the continent. Thereafter, before the march of the prospector, the known gold-bearing area was rapidly extended, and in 1894 the country was divided into separate gold-fields, so extensive were the preparations for its exploitation. At the present time, there are nineteen gold-fields in the state, the most important, from the point of production in 1902, being East Coolgardie, Mount Margaret, and North Coolgardie, in the eastern district; and Murchison, in the central district. For the past five years Western Australia has held the premier position among the Australian States in regard to gold production, and the annual output is still increasing. The production during 1901 was 1,879,391 oz., representing 1,703,417 oz. fine, with a value of £7,235,653, and ranked as the highest recorded up that year; but this return was exceeded in 1902 when the production amounted to 2,177,441 oz., or 1,871,037 oz. fine, valued at £7,947,662. Of the total yield, no less than 1,172,405 oz. were obtained from the East Coolgardie field, where some of the richest mines in the world are to be found. Those which contributed chiefly to the large output were the Great Boulder Perseverance, 193,297 oz.; Golden Horseshoe, 192,573 oz.; Great Boulder Proprietary, 166,518 oz.; and the Ivanhoe, 142,298 oz. The Mount Margaret and Murchison gold-fields produced 216,637 oz. and 212,570 oz. respectively, while 187,273 oz. were obtained from North Coolgardie. The dividends returned by some of the gold-mining companies in 1902 were enormous, the total being £1,424,272. Of this amount the Great Boulder Perseverance paid £350,000, the Golden Horseshoe £270,000, and the Great Boulder Proprietary £218,750. The importance of the gold-mining industry to Western Australia may be gauged from the fact that the number of men engaged therein at the end of 1902 was 20,476, comprising 15·67 of the whole male population, while the machinery in use was valued at £4,304,397.

Although gold was discovered in New Zealand at Coromandel during the year 1852 there is no record of the production prior to 1857, when there was an export valued at £40,422. For many years the colony was a large producer of gold, and from 1865 to 1871 the value amounted to over £2,000,000 each year. The production then declined and in 1894 it was only £887,839, but this amount has been considerably increased of late years, and in 1902 the total amounted to 508,045 oz., valued at £1,951,433, the highest recorded since 1873. Up to the 31st December, 1902, gold to the value of £61,111,316 has been raised in the colony. The largest proportion of the yield in 1902 was obtained in the Auckland district; the value of the gold entered for exportation from each district being:—Auckland, £721,977; Otago, £728,124; West Coast, £475,272; Nelson, £23,649; Marlborough, £2,404; and Canterbury, £7. In the early years the gold was obtained from alluvial diggings, but at the present time much is obtained from quartz reefs, which are widely distributed throughout New Zealand. The Auckland district is the principal seat of quartz mining in the colony, and the chief centre of production is at Waihi. The only mine on this field which has reached the productive stage is that of the Waihi Gold-mining Company, from which gold to the value of £520,138 was obtained during 1902. The company paid dividends to the amount of £208,645 during the year, the total paid since the commencement of operations being £1,005,934. From the mines at Karangahake gold valued at £107,362 was won, but the yield from the Thames and Coromandel fields was small. At Thames only tributors and small mining parties are now at work, but at Coromandel renewed interest has been infused into mining operations by the discovery of some rich gold-bearing patches in 1902. From the Reefton district in the Middle Island gold to the value of £188,839 was obtained during 1902. Considerable attention is directed to the recovery of gold by dredging, and at the end of 1902 there were 201 dredges in operation, while there were 37 in course of construction or removal and 52 out of commission. The number of men engaged in gold-mining at the end of 1902 was 11,398, and the machinery in use was valued at £2,082,384.

Although payable gold was found in Tasmania in 1852, it was not until the seventies that the metal was mined for on an extensive scale, the total production to the end of 1870 being less than 4,000 oz. In 1878 the value of gold produced suddenly rose to £100,000, and this total has been gradually increased, until in 1899 it was valued at £327,545, being the highest yet recorded. The production in 1902 amounted to 70,996 oz. fine, valued at £301,573, and showed an increase of £6,397 on the value of the preceding year. Beaconsfield is the principal gold-field in the State. It is situated on the west side of the river Tamar, 26 miles north-west cf Launceston, and formerly produced a large quantity of alluvial gold, while there is also a rich deep lead. The Tasmania mine, on this field, is the largest gold-producer in the state, and up to 30th June, 1903, yielded 569,778 oz., valued at £2,090,938, out of which £772,072 has been paid in dividends. The Lefroy field has been another important centre of gold-production, but although payable gold is still obtained the yield is not nearly so large as in former years. At Mathinna a large quantity of gold has also been obtained. The principal mine on this field is the New Golden Gate, the deepest in the state, its main shaft being 1,500 feet. This mine has yielded 191,357 oz. of gold, valued at about £730,599, and up to 30th June, 1903, had paid £326,400 in dividends. From the Volunteer Consolidated Mine on this field some good stone has been obtained from two lodes struck at a depth of 450 feet. In the Western District a little alluvial gold is obtained, while north of the Pieman River there is a large extent of auriferous country, but owing to the dense vegetation prospecting is difficult. Attempts are being made on the Whyte River to recover gold by the process of dredging, but as the results have not been satisfactory, the dredge is to be transferred to the Pieman River. The men engaged in gold-mining during 1902 numbered 1,038.

Of all the Australian States, South Australia has produced the smallest quantity of gold, the total output from the commencement of mining operations being valued at less than £2,500,000. The highest production was in 1893, when it reached £153,132; but it has gradually declined, and the value has not amounted to £100,000 in any of the last five years. In the state proper the yield is very small, amounting to but 7,245 oz. in 1902, the balance of 20,967 oz. being obtained from the Northern Territory, the total value amounting to £95,129. Some excitement was caused during 1902 by reports of a rich discovery at Arltunga, and visions of easily acquired wealth caused the usual rush of gold seekers. The field, however, proved most disappointing, and although a mild boom in Arltunga shares existed for a few weeks, it did not long survive the discouraging reports received from the scene of operations. Gold undoubtedly exists in considerable quantities, but capital is required for its exploitation. A report by the Government Geologist states that with good management and economic mining and treatment of the ore large and payable returns may be obtained for many years. The mines in the Northern Territory are largely in the hands of Chinese, but a number of properties have been acquired by an English company, which has erected the works necessary for their development. The total number of men engaged in gold-mining in South Australia at the end of 1902 was 2,000. A considerable number of these are Chinese, physically incapable of doing a fair day's work, and dangerous from a sanitary point of view. Possessed of no means whatever, and with no proper tools adapted to the search for the precious metal, they eke out a miserable existence by mining a little alluvial gold.

The following table gives the value of gold raised in each State up to the end of 1902, with the proportion of the total amount:—

State.	Production of Gold.	
	Value.	Proportion raised in each State.
	£	per cent.
New South Wales	49,844,135	10·48
Victoria	263,551,229	55·39
Queensland	55,472,314	11·66
South Australia	2,483,326	0·52
Western Australia	38,097,374	8·01
Tasmania	5,195,161	1·09
Commonwealth	414,643,539	87·15
New Zealand	61,111,316	12·85
Australasia	475,754,855	100·00

It will be readily understood from this and the following table how Victoria, although in area the smallest of the group with the exception of Tasmania, achieved the foremost position amongst the Australasian

States, and retained that place so long as the powerful attraction of gold continued, while the source of Western Australia's progress is also fully disclosed. The following table shows the value of the gold raised in the various States during each year for which records are available, but, for reasons which are explained in the next paragraph, discrepancies exist in the total values shown for several of the States :—

Year.	New South Wales.	Victoria.	Queensland.	South Australia.	Western Australia.	Tasmania.	Commonwealth.	New Zealand.
	£	£	£	£	£	£	£	£
1851	468,336	580,548	......	......	......	......	1,048,884	......
1852	2,660,946	10,953,966	......	......	......	......	13,614,882	......
1853	1,781,172	12,600,084	......	......	......	......	14,381,256	......
1854	773,209	9,568,260	......	......	......	......	10,341,469	......
1855	654,594	11,172,260	......	......	......	......	11,826,854	......
1856	689,174	11,942,940	......	......	......	......	12,632,114	......
1857	674,477	11,046,268	......	......	......	......	11,720,745	40,422
1858	1,104,175	10,112,908	......	......	......	......	11,217,083	52,464
1859	1,259,127	9,122,868	......	730	......	......	10,382,725	28,427
1860	1,465,373	8,626,800	......	......	......	......	10,092,173	17,585
1861	1,806,171	7,869,812	......	......	......	......	9,675,983	751,873
1862	2,467,780	6,633,124	......	12,442	......	......	9,113,346	1,591,389
1863	1,796,170	6,508,420	30,000	880	......	......	8,335,470	2,431,723
1864	1,304,926	6,181,748	......	......	......	......	7,486,674	1,856,837
1865	1,231,243	6,172,752	......	......	......	......	7,403,995	2,226,474
1866	1,116,404	5,913,120	79,148	......	......	4,382	7,113,049	2,844,517
1867	1,053,578	5,732,984	170,090	......	......	2,536	6,959,188	2,698,862
1868	994,665	6,536,800	429,907	2,986	......	514	7,964,822	2,504,326
1869	974,149	5,349,184	451,352	15,593	......	7,475	6,797,753	2,362,995
1870	931,016	4,891,192	351,412	24,217	......	14,218	6,212,055	2,157,585
1871	1,250,485	5,421,908	504,876	6,000	......	16,055	7,199,324	2,787,520
1872	1,644,177	5,180,084	592,998	6,363	......	15,309	7,388,926	1,731,261
1873	1,396,375	4,964,820	555,310	293	......	18,390	6,935,188	1,987,425
1874	1,041,614	4,623,888	561,255	4,175	......	18,491	6,249,423	1,505,331
1875	877,694	4,383,148	596,242	7,034	......	11,982	5,876,100	1,407,770
1876	613,190	3,855,040	660,136	9,888	......	44,923	5,183,177	1,284,328
1877	471,448	3,238,612	838,544	......	......	23,289	4,571,893	1,496,080
1878	430,200	3,101,088	1,085,864	1,225	......	100,000	4,718,377	1,240,079
1879	407,219	3,035,788	1,009,946	90	......	230,895	4,683,938	1,148,108
1880	444,253	3,316,484	934,976	......	......	201,297	4,897,010	1,227,252
1881	573,582	3,435,400	948,318	112,825	......	216,901	5,287,026	1,080,790
1882	526,522	3,594,144	787,125	80,720	......	187,337	5,175,848	1,002,720
1883	458,580	3,240,188	744,731	87,729	......	176,442	4,707,620	993,352
1884	396,059	3,114,472	1,077,314	93,404	......	160,404	4,841,653	921,797
1885	378,665	2,940,872	1,088,294	88,709	......	155,309	4,651,849	948,615
1886	366,294	2,660,784	1,198,493	95,674	1,148	117,250	4,434,643	903,569
1887	394,579	2,471,004	1,490,730	188,302	18,517	158,583	4,671,665	811,100
1888	317,241	2,500,104	1,685,750	66,160	13,273	147,154	4,729,682	801,066
1889	434,784	2,459,356	2,586,860	76,780	58,872	119,703	5,736,355	808,549
1890	460,285	2,354,244	2,137,064	106,105	86,664	87,114	5,231,466	773,438
1891	559,231	2,305,600	2,017,586	125,529	115,182	149,816	5,272,894	1,007,488
1892	575,299	2,617,824	2,154,453	139,370	226,284	174,070	5,887,300	954,744
1893	651,286	2,684,504	2,159,290	153,132	421,385	145,875	6,215,472	913,138
1894	1,156,717	2,694,720	2,378,289	152,092	787,099	225,485	7,394,402	887,839
1895	1,315,929	2,960,344	2,210,887	128,792	879,748	212,329	7,708,029	1,162,164
1896	1,073,360	3,220,348	2,241,347	112,759	1,068,808	237,574	7,954,196	1,041,428
1897	1,104,315	3,251,064	2,553,141	120,044	2,564,977	289,241	9,882,782	980,204
1898	1,201,743	3,349,028	2,750,349	95,143	3,990,698	281,485	11,668,446	1,080,691
1899	1,623,320	3,418,000	2,838,119	79,041	6,246,733	327,545	14,532,758	1,513,173
1900	1,070,920	3,229,628	2,871,709	82,188	6,007,610	316,220	13,578,275	1,439,602
1901	737,164	3,102,758	2,541,892	93,222	7,235,653	295,176	14,005,860	1,753,783
1902	684,970	3,062,028	2,720,639	95,129	7,947,662	301,573	14,812,001	1,961,433

These figures do not in all cases add up to the total value of the production given elsewhere, as the information regarding earlier years is imperfect. The total for Victoria is £297,952 less than the actual value of production, while for Queensland the amount is deficient to the extent of £3,442,948, accounted for by the fact that prior to 1878 the figures only represent the gold sent by escort. There is a deficiency of £68,611 in South Australia which cannot be traced owing to the imperfect nature of the returns available in earlier years. The figures shown for Western Australia are £427,061 less than the total value of gold produced, as prior to 1899 they only show the value of gold exported. There is also a deficiency of £2,869 in the total shown for Tasmania. The information relating to New South Wales for the years 1897 to 1901 inclusive differs from that previously published, which included gold won from other than native ores. The gross production of gold in each State during 1902 and the contents in fine gold are given below:—

State.	Weight of Gold.		Value of Gold.	
	Gross.	Fine Gold.	Total.	Proportion raised in each State.
	oz.	oz.	£	per cent.
New South Wales	190,316	161,256	684,970	4·08
Victoria	777,738	720,866	3,062,028	18·27
Queensland	860,453	640,463	2,720,639	16·23
South Australia	28,212	22,395	95,129	0·57
Western Australia	2,177,441	1,871,037	7,947,662	47·41
Tasmania	....	70,996	301,573	1·80
Commonwealth	....	3,487,013	14,812,001	88·36
New Zealand	508,045	447,529	1,951,433	11·64
Australasia	....	3,934,542	16,763,434	100·00

The number of men engaged in mining for gold is shown in the following table, and it would appear that the average value of gold won by each miner is £207 16s. 1d. per annum. It is probable that the number of gold miners in several of the states is largely overstated, otherwise the industry must be carried on at a great loss; and this will be the more apparent when it is remembered that a fairly large quantity of gold is obtained with other metals, the men employed in the exploitation of which are not classified as gold-miners. Moreover, many of the men employ themselves in mining for only a portion of their time, and devote the remainder to more remunerative pursuits. But when full allowance is made on this score, it will be evident that, in some of the states at least, the search for gold is not a profitable occupation. The small return for South Australia is due to the large number of Chinese engaged in the industry, many of them not possessing proper appliances for working the claims.

State.	Miners Employed.	Average production of Gold.	
		Quantity.	Value.
	No.	oz. fine.	£ s. d.
New South Wales............	10,610	15·19	64 11 2
Victoria	26,103	27·62	117 6 1
Queensland	9,045	70·81	300 15 9
South Australia...............	2,000	11·20	47 11 3
Western Australia	20,476	91·38	388 2 11
Tasmania.........................	1,038	68·40	290 10 8
Commonwealth	69,272	50·34	213 16 6
New Zealand	11,398	39·26	171 4 2
Australasia	80,670	48·77	207 16 1

The most extensive development of quartz-reefing is found in Victoria, some of the mines being of a great depth. At the end of 1902 there were eight mines in the Bendigo district over 3,000 feet deep, and fourteen over 2,500 feet. In the Victoria mine a depth of 3,750 feet had been reached, and in the Lazarus Mine, 3,424 feet. On other fields there were six mines over 1,500 feet deep, the deepest of which were the South Star mine in the Ballarat district, where the shaft is down 2,520 feet, and the North Long Tunnel mine in the Walhalla district where a depth of 2,516 feet has been reached.

A notice of gold-mining would be incomplete without some reference to the remarkably large finds made at various times. Information on this point is meagre and not altogether reliable, as doubtless many nuggets were unearthed of which particulars were never published. Victoria's record is the best, and includes the following nuggets:—

	lb.	oz.	dwt.
"The Welcome Stranger," found 9th February, 1869............	190	0	0
"The Welcome," found 9th June, 1858	184	9	16
Nugget found at Canadian Gully, 31st January, 1853	134	11	0

And others of the following weights:—98 lb. 1 oz. 17 dwt., 93 lb. 1 oz. 11 dwt., 84 lb. 3 oz. 15 dwt., 69 lb. 6 oz., 52 lb. 1 oz., 30 lb. 11 oz. 8 dwt., and 30 lb. 11 oz. 2 dwt.

New South Wales can boast of having produced some splendid specimens. In 1851 a mass of gold was found on the Turon, weighing 106 lb.; another, from Burrandong, near Orange, produced when melted at the Sydney Mint 98 lb 6 oz. 6 dwt. of pure gold; and a third, the "Brenman," was sold in Sydney in 1851 for £1,156. During 1880–82 several nuggets were discovered at Temora, weighing from 59 oz. to 1,393 oz.; and others, of 357 oz., 347 oz. (the "Jubilee"), 200 oz., 47 oz., and 32 oz. respectively, were found during the year 1887 in various parts of the State. Veins of gold of extraordinary richness have been worked in New South Wales. In January, 1873, at Beyers and Holterman's claim, at Hill End, 1·02 cwt. of gold was obtained from 10 tons of quartz, and a mass of ore, weighing 630 lb. and estimated to contain £2,000 worth of gold, was exhibited. The Mint returns for this mine during the year 1873 were 16,279·63 oz., valued at £63,234 12s., obtained from 415 tons of stone. From Krohman's claim, at Hill End, gold to the value of £93,616 11s. 9d. was obtained during the same year. The foregoing figures, however, are insignificant when compared with the enormous yield of the Mount Morgan Mine, in Queensland, which has paid over £5,750,000 in dividends. This mine, which may be designated one of the wonders of the world, is a huge mound of ore, highly ferruginous, the peculiar formation, in the opinion of the Government Geologist of Queensland, being due to the action of thermal springs. To the end of May, 1903, 2,624,319 oz. of gold had been won from 2,005,396 tons of ore, yielding an average of 1 oz. 6 dwt. 4 gr. per ton of ore treated.

For the ten years ended 1902, the world's production of gold is estimated to have been as follows:—

Year.	Value.	Year.	Value.
	£		£
1893	30,731,000	1898	58,137,000
1894	37,345,000	1899	63,057,000
1895	39,191,000	1900	51,578,000
1896	41,009,000	1901	52,738,000
1897	48,088,000	1902	60,197,000

Of the production of £60,197,000 in 1902, Australasia produced 27·85 per cent.

SILVER.

Silver has been discovered in all the states, either alone or in the form of sulphides, antimonial and arsenical ores, chloride, bromide iodide, and chloro-bromide of silver, and argentiferous lead ores, the largest deposits of the metal being found in the last-mentioned form. The leading silver mines are in New South Wales, the returns from the other states being comparatively insignificant. Up to the year 1882 the quantity of silver raised in New South Wales was very small, but in that and the following years extensive discoveries of the metal, associated principally with lead and copper ore, were made in various parts of the State, notably at Boorook, in the New England district, and later on at Sunny Corner, near Bathurst, and at Silverton and Broken Hill on the Barrier Ranges in the Western district. The Sunny Corner Silver mines in 1886 paid handsome dividends, and produced £160,000 worth of silver, but since that period the yield has largely fallen off.

The fields of the Western district of New South Wales have proved to be of immense value. The yield of silver-lead ore in the Broken Hill and Silverton districts during 1902 was valued at £1,052,916; while the machinery employed was valued at £606,484. This is much less than the value set down some years ago, the reduction being chiefly due to the removal of machinery to Port Pirie, in South Australia, where the smelting operations of the Proprietary Company are now wholly carried on. The aggregate output of the mines in the Barrier country to the end of the year named was valued at £30,945,073. This rich silver-field, which was discovered in 1883 by Charles Rasp, a boundary rider on Mount Gipps Run, extends over 2,500 square miles of country, and has developed into one of the principal mining centres of the world. It is situated beyond the river Darling, and close to the boundary between New South Wales and South Australia. In the Barrier Range district the lodes occur in Silurian metamorphic micaceous schists, intruded by granite, porphyry, and diorite, and traversed by numerous quartz reefs, some of which are gold-bearing. The Broken Hill lode is the largest as yet discovered. It varies in width from 10 feet to 200 feet, and may be traced for several miles, the country having been taken up all along the line of the lode, and subdivided into numerous leases, held by mining companies and syndicates.

The Broken Hill Proprietary Company hold the premier position. They have at Port Pirie, in South Australia, a complete smelting plant on the latest and most approved principles. From the commencement of mining operations in 1885 to the end of May, 1903, the company treated 6,544,468 tons of silver and silver-lead ores, producing 119,564,327 oz. of silver and 598,835 tons of lead, valued in the London market at £25,688,000. Dividends and bonuses to the amount of £7,592,000 have been paid, besides the nominal value of shares from the several "Blocks." The sum spent in the erection and construction of plant, from the opening of the property, has been about £1,271,502. The mine wages and salary sheet for the twelve months represented a sum of £622,515, including £155,961 paid to contractors, and £10,933 for quarrying. The net profit for the year was £113,416.

The quantity and value of silver and silver-lead ore exported by New South Wales to the end of 1902 is shown in the following table :—

Year.	Silver.		Silver-Lead.			Total value.
	Quantity.	Value.	Quantity.		Value.	
			Ore.	Metal.		
Up to	oz.	£	tons cwt.	tons cwt.	£	£
1882	765,397	187,429	203 12	....	5,385	192,814
1883	77,066	16,488	105 17	....	1,625	18,113
1884	93,660	19,780	4,668 1	....	123,174	142,954
1885	794,174	159,187	2,095 16	190 8	107,626	266,813
1886	1,015,434	197,544	4,802 2	....	294,485	492,029
1887	177,308	32,458	12,529 3	....	541,952	574,410
1888	375,064	66,668	11,739 7	18,102 5	1,075,737	1,142,405
1889	416,895	72,001	46,965 9	34,579 17	1,899,197	1,971,198
1890	496,552	95,410	89,719 15	41,319 18	2,667,144	2,762,554
1891	729,590	134,850	92,383 11	55,396 3	3,484,739	3,619,589
1892	350,661	56,884	87,504 15	45,850 4	2,420,952	2,477,836
1893	531,972	78,131	155,859 1	58,401 3	2,953,589	3,031,720
1894	846,822	94,150	137,813 8	42,513 2	2,195,339	2,289,489
1895	550,142	81,858	190,192 19	29,687 7	1,560,813	1,642,671
1896	202,789	26,518	267,363 1	19,573 4	1,758,933	1,785,451
1897	150,005	16,711	270,913 14	18,105 7	1,681,528	1,698,239
1898	533,059	59,278	388,460 4	10,108 13	1,644,777	1,704,055
1899	692,036	76,913	424,337 5	20,289 10	1,993,744	2,070,657
1900	774,203	90,243	420,909 11	17,928 6	2,513,874	2,604,117
1901	448,501	50,484	400,156 18	16,921 5	1,803,979	1,854,463
1902	1,067,224	105,360	365,646 1	15,412 18	1,334,819	1,440,179
Total	11,088,554	1,718,345	3,374,369 10	444,379 10	32,063,411	33,781,756

This amount was approximately made up of 154,696,388 oz. of silver, valued at £24,056,883; and of 772,198 tons of lead, valued at £9,724,873. It will be seen that the production of silver in New South Wales rapidly increased until 1891, when it exceeded in value the largest annual production of gold, even in the palmiest days of the diggings. Since that year, however, there has been a decreased output consequent upon the lower grade of the ores now being worked, while the value has been still further reduced by the serious decline in the prices of silver and lead. The price of silver has been declining steadily for some years, and in 1902 it fell below all previous records, while lead also depreciated in value. As many of the lower-grade mines at Broken Hill had only been worked at a profit on account of the high value of the lead contained in the ores, the heavy fall in the price of lead combined with a decline in the value of silver caused all but four of the principal Barrier mines temporarily to suspend the output of ore.

The serious effects of the decline may be judged from a comparison of the employment afforded by the industry during the last three years. The number of miners engaged in silver and lead mines in 1900 was 8,196, and the average value of the metals won amounted to £317 14s. 7d.; in 1901 the number of men employed had fallen to 6,298, and the average value won to £294 9s. 1d.; while in 1902 the men engaged numbered only 5,382, and the average value won £267 11s. 6d.

There are two large smelting works in New South Wales, one of which is situated at Cockle Creek, near Newcastle, and the other at Dapto. These works have proved of great service to the mining communities, both in this and neighbouring States, as large supplies of ore are received for treatment from all parts of Australasia. The quantity of ore, the product of the state, treated during the year, was 53,508 tons, the metal obtained being as follows:—

Gold	21,427 oz.
Silver	1,537,656 oz.
Lead	23,849 tons.
Copper	179 tons.
Spelter	220 tons.

The number of men employed on these works at the end of 1902 was 745.

The only other state where silver has been produced to any extent is Tasmania. The industry has been steadily developed, and the production for the last few years shows a considerable advance on that in former years. The value of the output during each of the last five years was—

1898	£270,893
1899	377,788
1900	252,080
1901	207,228
1902	218,864

In this state, as in New South Wales, the result of the fall in silver and lead values is seen in the diminished value of production, and in this connection it must be remembered that a decline in price not only decreases the value of the output, but checks production inasmuch as operations are restricted to dealing only with higher-grade ores. The principal silver fields are in the West Coast District, where the most important mines are the Zeehan-Montana, British Zeehan, and Mount Zeehan; and in the North-Western District where the Mount Magnet mine is located. The largest output of silver, however, is from the Mount Lyell mine, where the metal is found in conjunction with copper, and the output from this and the mines first mentioned, together with that from the Zeehan Queen and Hercules mines, comprises nearly the whole of the production. The latter mine, situated in the Mount Read district, has abundance of silver ore in sight, while copper is also found.

Silver is found in various districts in Queensland, but generally associated with some other mineral, and the mines where silver predominates are but few. The chief of these is the Silver Spur mine at

Texas, in the Stanthorpe district, on the border of New South Wales, from which 74,820 oz. of silver, valued at £7,482, were obtained during 1902. The year 1901 saw a distinct improvement in the production of silver, and this in the face of a great decline in the prices of silver and lead. This improvement was more than maintained during 1902, and the production for the year was 701,312 oz., valued at £70,145, being the highest total recorded since 1887, when the yield was valued at £80,092. The great advance made in copper-mining during recent years is responsible for the increased silver production, as these minerals are usually found in association. This may be seen from the fact that the Herberton district, which was the chief copper-producing centre in 1902, also contributed the greater portion of the silver produced.

In New Zealand, silver is found in various localities, principally on the Te Aroha, Thames, and Coromandel fields, but the metal is generally obtained in conjunction with gold. The production of the colony during the year 1902 was 674,196 oz., valued at £71,975.

There are no silver-mines in Victoria or Western Australia, the small amount of silver produced in those States being usually found associated with gold. During 1902 the value of the silver produced in Western Australia was only £9,467, and in Victoria £4,900. The production of silver in South Australia is not large, the value in 1902 being £19,740, and it would seem that the argentiferous lead-ore fields of Broken Hill and Silverton, which are almost on the border of the two States, are exclusively confined within the boundaries of New South Wales.

Up to the end of 1902 New South Wales had produced 87·3 per cent. of the total value of silver raised in Australasia; Tasmania came second with 6·7 per cent.; and of the remaining small proportion, Victoria claimed the largest share. The total production of silver in Australasia in 1902, and up to the end of that year, was as follows:—

State.	Value of Silver produced—	
	During 1902.	To end of 1902.
	£	£
New South Wales	1,440,179	33,781,756
Victoria	4,900	861,439
Queensland	70,145	858,187
South Australia	19,740	138,370
Western Australia	9,467	21,072
Tasmania	218,864	2,603,750
Commonwealth	1,763,295	38,264,574
New Zealand	71,975	452,781
Australasia	1,835,270	38,717,355

The world's production of silver during the ten years ended 1902 is estimated to have been as follows:—

Year.	Ounces.	Year.	Ounces.
1893	162,162,000	1898	179,252,000
1894	178,668,000	1899	177,837,000
1895	182,220,000	1900	180,093,000
1896	176,707,000	1901	174,851,000
1897	182,061,000	1902	175,691,000

The output of New South Wales during 1902 therefore represented about 7·5 per cent. of the total production of silver.

Copper.

Copper is known to exist in all the States, and has been mined for extensively in South Australia, Tasmania, New South Wales, and Queensland. The fluctuations in the market value of the metal have always been a check to the progress of the industry, and at various periods in the last two years some of the lower-grade mines have been compelled to suspend operations. South Australia has produced the greatest quantity of copper, but of late years Tasmania has had by far the largest output. In Tasmania deposits were worked on a limited scale for a number of years; but the discovery of a rich belt of copper-bearing country, extending from Mount Lyell past Mount Tyndall, Mount Read, Mount Murchison, and north of the Pieman to the Rocky and Savage Rivers, has completely changed the character of the mining industry in the State, and from a small export of copper ore valued at £1,659 in 1896, the annual production has become the largest in Australasia. The following table, which shows the annual production of copper during the last five years, will give some idea of the development of this branch of the mining industry. The output would appear to have fallen considerably in 1902, but this is due to the fact that in previous years the gold contents of the ore have been included in the values given.

	£
1898	408,796
1899	762,138
1900	970,877
1901	1,010,037
1902	577,533

The chief mines belong to the Mount Lyell Mining and Railway Company which is reported to have spent over £400,000 on railway construction and developmental work at the mines before receiving any return. The company possesses reduction works at Queenstown, from which a railway has been constructed through most difficult country to Teepookana and thence to Strahan. The output from these mines during the year ended 30th June, 1903, averaged 1,000 tons of ore daily, and the contents were 6,141 tons of copper, 604,860 oz. of silver, and 22,278 oz. of gold, the total value thereof being £513,351.

The discovery of copper had a marked effect upon the fortunes of South Australia at a time when the young and struggling colony was surrounded by difficulties. The first important mine, the Kapunda, was opened up in 1842. It is estimated that at one time 2,000 tons were produced annually, but the mine was closed in 1879. In 1845 the celebrated Burra Burra mine was discovered. This mine proved to be very rich, and paid £800,000 in dividends to the original owners. For many years the average yield was from 10,000 to 13,000 tons of ore, yielding from 22 to 23 per cent. of copper. For the period of thirty years during which the mine was worked the output of ore amounted to 234,648 tons, equal to 51,622 tons of copper, valued at £4,749,224. Boring operations were conducted at the mine for the purpose of determining whether payable ore exists at greater depths than those reached by the original workings. One bore was put down to a depth of 1,004 feet, and in the the opinion of the Government Geologist, the result was highly satisfactory, as it proved the continuance downwards of the copper-bearing strata sufficiently to warrant the reopening of a portion of the mine. The Wallaroo and Moonta mines, discovered in 1860 and 1861, proved to be even more valuable than the Burra Burra. The Moonta mine employed at one time upwards of 1,600 hands, and still keeps 1,138 men at work. In 1890 these mines were amalgamated, and the estimated value of the copper produced to the end of 1898 is set down at £9,218,482, out of which about £7,000,000 had been expended in wages. About 1,800 miners are now employed. The total dividends paid by these mines were stated to be upwards of £1,700,000. The production of copper in South Australia during the last few years has again increased, the output in 1901 being valued at £500,077, and in 1902 at £432,525.

The copper-mining industry in New South Wales has been subject to great variations. The production reached its highest point in 1883, when the value was £472,982. From that year, however, there was a general decline, and in 1894 the value was only £63,617. As in the other States, so in New South Wales, the increased prices of later years caused more attention to be directed to the industry, and the production in 1901 had attained a value of £412,292. A heavy fall in prices occurred during that year, however, which, combined with the drought, caused a considerable falling off in production and value. The value of the output in 1902 was only £307,806, a decrease of £104,486 on that of the preceding year. The chief copper-mines are in the western districts, and lack of water led to the closing of several of the most important during portion of the year. At the Great Cobar Mine the company was enabled to carry on operations through the Government arranging to despatch a supply by water train during the dry period. In other districts those mines which were working on low-grade ores were compelled to suspend operations, as at the prevailing prices the ore would not realise a profit on the cost of raising and carriage to the smelting works at Cockle Creek or Dapto. The principal deposits are found in the central part of the state, between the Macquarie, Bogan, and Darling Rivers. Cupriferous strata have also been located in the New England and Southern districts, as well as at Broken Hill, thus showing that the mineral is widely distributed. The largest proportion of the copper produced during 1902 was obtained in the Cobar mining district. The value of the metal raised in the Cobar division of the district amounted to £130,802. It is in this district that the Great Cobar, the largest copper-mine in New South Wales, is situated. The Nymagee division of the Cobar district produced copper to the value of £133,350. In the Burraga division of the Bathurst district one of the leading mines, the Lloyd Copper mine, is situated, and from this mine which was only worked during the first eight months of 1902, owing to the failure of the water supply, 29,440 tons of ore, valued at £66,200, were raised. The lode, which averages 5 feet in width, still maintains its richness, and there are sufficient supplies in sight to last some years. The company employs about 500 men in the mine and works, which are lighted throughout by electricity. The Crowl Creek mine, at Shuttleton, which was opened in 1901 has been further developed with satisfactory results. The total number of men engaged in copper-mining during 1902 was 1,699, a decrease of 1,265 on the numbers of the preceding year.

Copper is found in many parts of Queensland, the principal deposits being in the Herberton and Mount Perry districts. In earlier years the state occupied a prominent position as a producer of copper, but the output in recent years was very small. The year 1901, however, saw a sudden revival in this branch of the mining industry, despite a great fall in prices, and the value of the production rose to £194,227, being the highest value recorded with the exception of 1872, when it reached £196,000. This figure, however, was not maintained in 1902, the production for that year amounting to 3,784 tons, valued at £189,200. A noteworthy feature of the revival was the re-opening of the Mount Perry mine, which afforded employment for over 300 men in 1902, and promises to rank, as in former years, amongst the foremost mines in the State. The Herberton district has for many years been the chief copper-producing centre, the output in 1902 being valued at £122,950. Of the copper-mines in this district, and in the State as a whole, the foremost is Mount Garnet, which produced copper and silver to the value of £164,267 during 1902. The mine is well equipped with machinery, and a railway has been constructed to connect with the Chillagoe line. On the 31st March, 1902, the New Chillagoe Railway and Mines which had been closed since December, 1901, were re-opened, and systematic prospecting is being carried on in the mines with favourable results. One of the chief obstacles to the successful development of copper and silver-mining has been the lack of facilities for transport, but with the increased advantages in this respect which are being afforded year by year, the output of copper and silver may be expected to increase materially.

In Western Australia, copper deposits have been worked for some years. Very rich lodes of the metal have been found in the Mount Malcolm, Northampton, Murchison, West Pilbarra, and Phillips River districts, but operations appear to be carried on systematically only in the first mentioned. The ore raised in this district is treated locally, while in the others it is exported for treatment, and, as the cost of carriage is heavy and the facilities for transport unfavourable, only high-grade ores can be profitably worked. The copper ore raised in the State during 1901 amounted to 10,156 tons, valued at £75,246, but in 1902 only 2,262 tons, with a value of £8,090 were produced. The unfortunate fall in the price of the metal has restricted operations, but as there seems no doubt that eminently payable copper lodes, carrying a little gold, exist in the state, it is surprising that the success of the preceding three years has not further stimulated the progress of the industry. The number of men engaged in copper-mining in 1902 was only 113, as against 321 in the preceding year.

Copper-mining has not attained any great proportions in Victoria, although deposits have been found in several parts of the State, particularly in the Beechworth district, where they have been traced over an area of some 50 square miles. The value of the total production is estimated at £206,395, but there has not been any output during the last few years.

The copper deposits of New Zealand have been worked to a small extent only, and for a number of years have been almost entirely neglected, the output in 1901 being valued at only £105, while in 1902 there was no production.

Copper is sometimes found in the Australasian mines in a virgin state, and beautiful specimens of the pure metal have been exhibited at different times, but it occurs generally in the form of oxidised copper ores, carbonates, sulphates, phosphates, and silicates of copper. The museums of South Australia, Victoria, and New South Wales contain striking samples of azurite and malachite, magnificent blocks of which have been shown from time to time at exhibitions, not only in Australasia, but also in Europe and America. Copper sulphides and arsenides are generally found in deep sinkings, The metal has also been found associated with tin in the form of stannine.

The total value of copper produced in each State during 1902 and up to the end of that year are given below :—

State.	Value of Copper produced.	
	During 1902.	To end of year 1902.
	£	£
New South Wales	307,806	6,164,879
Victoria	....	206,395
Queensland	189,200	2,438,892
South Australia	432,525	23,254,571
Western Australia	8,090	335,062
Tasmania	577,533	4,499,028
Commonwealth	1,515,154	36,898,827
New Zealand	....	18,088
Australasia	1,515,154	36,916,915

In June, 1872, copper realised as much as £112 per ton, whilst in December, 1886, the lowest price on record until that time was touched, and only £44 could be obtained for South Australian copper. At the end of 1887 the price had risen to £70 per ton, and in September, 1888, to £93. In March, 1889, there was a great fall in the price of the metal, and in April of that year the quotation in London was as low as £43 per ton. This was the lowest price reached until June, 1894, when it fell to £41 10s. From that date there was an upward movement, as the following quotations will show. At the close of 1896 the London price of copper stood at £52 10s. per ton; in February, 1897, £54 10s. was reached; and at the 31st December, 1898, £60 was the market value. This price was further increased during 1899, and in September of that year no less than £77 per ton was quoted. The price was well maintained during 1900, and, at the close of the year, stood at £73 per ton; but in 1901 a heavy fall occurred, and the quotations for the last week of the year were as low as £49 15s. per ton. During 1902 prices remained low, but gradually improved towards the end of the year. In the first week of January, 1903, the value was £53 12s. 6d. per ton.

TIN.

Tin was known to exist in Australasia almost from the first years of colonisation, the earliest mention of the metal appearing in a report of a discovery by Surgeon Bass on the north coast of Tasmania. In the form of cassiterite (oxide of tin) it occurs in all the states, but the richest deposits have been found in Tasmania—the Mount Bischoff being the most celebrated tin-mine in Australasia. Expert authorities have also stated that Queensland and the Northern Territory of South Australia possess rich deposits of tin ore.

Tasmania has been the largest producer of tin in Australasia. As in New South Wales, a very large proportion of the metal hitherto produced has been from alluvial deposits, and the want of water has proved a great drawback to the successful development of the industry. There are, however, many promising lodes in the island, and the Waratah, Blue Tier, Ben Lomond, St. Helen's, Derby, and West Coast districts all produce large quantities of the metal. In the district first mentioned is situated the Mount Bischoff mine, worked as an open quarry, which, during the year ended 30th June, 1903, produced 1,276 tons of tin, and paid £54,000 in dividends. In the Blue Tier district, the Australian and Anchor mines are working on good payable stone, and from the latter mine 250 tons of tin, valued at £19,686, were obtained during the year ended 30th June, 1903. Of the mines in the North-Eastern District, the most important are the Briseis, at Derby, and the Pioneer, at Bradshaw's Creek. The former gave employment to 111 men during the year ended 30th June, 1903, and produced 387 tons of tin, while the latter yielded 692 tons of stream tin, and paid dividends amounting to £16,875. Tin-dredging has been carried on in some parts of the island; but, so far, only a moderate measure of success has been achieved. The production of tin during 1902 was valued at £242,990, the value for 1901 being £216,186.

In New South Wales lode tin occurs principally in the granite and stream tin under the basaltic country in the extreme northern portion of the State, at Tenterfield, Emmaville, Tingha, and in other districts of New England. The metal has also been discovered in the Barrier Ranges, at Poolamacca and Euriowie; near Bombala in the Monaro district; at Gundle, near Kempsey; at Jingellic, on the Upper Murray; at Dora Dora, on the Upper Murray; and in the Valley of the Lachlan; but in none of these districts has it been worked to any extent. The mineral was discovered by the Rev. W. B. Clarke so far back as the year 1853, but the opening of the tin-fields of New South Wales only took place in the year 1872. The industry soon attained considerable importance, the value of the output in 1881 amounting to £568,795. In 1889 the total production had fallen to £207,670, and in 1893 to £126,114, while in 1898 the lowest point was reached, when the value was only £45,638. Owing to a recovery in prices there was an increase in value of production during the next two years when the totals were £90,482 and £142,724 respectively, but in 1901 there was a decline to £76,544, and in 1902 to £59,593. The fluctuations in the market price of the metal have always had a discouraging effect on the industry and the heavy fall which occurred during 1901 no doubt tended to diminish the production of that and the following year. In addition to the fall in prices, the industry has had to contend with a long-sustained drought, and as a large proportion of the tin obtained is recovered from alluvial deposits, any scarcity of water diminishes the production by retarding successful washing operations. Lack of sufficient water during the year 1902 was responsible for the closing of the Leviathan mine near Inverell, which was opened in 1901, and gave promise of very favourable results. What appeared to be an extension of the Leviathan lode was discovered at a place about 5 miles distant, where the Dolcoath Syndicate opened a mine, but so far with negative results. Success has attended the attempts to recover tin by dredging, good returns being obtained in 1902 by dredges operating at Cope's Creek in the Tingha district. The total quantity of tin won by dredging in 1902 amounted to 110 tons, valued at £8,300. The number of persons engaged in tin-mining during 1902 was 1,288, of whom 302 were Chinese.

In Queensland, the value of tin produced during 1873 reached £606,184, being next in importance to that of gold, but thenceforward there was a decline, the yield in 1898 falling to £36,502. Since that year, however, there has been a considerable improvement, and some attempt has been made to develop the industry in a manner more worthy of its resources, the returns for 1901 and 1902 being £93,723 and £116,171 respectively. The Herberton district was again the chief centre of production, the output in 1902 being valued at £84,297. The most important mines in this district are situated at Irvinebank, and from one of them, the Vulcan, 5,468 tons of black tin, valued at £181,000, have been obtained since October, 1890. The output of the mine for 1902 was 528 tons, valued at £24,784. In 1901 a rich discovery of tin was made at Smith's Creek, near the Mount Garnet railway, and shafts sunk to a depth of 300 feet have proved the lode to be continuous. The number of persons engaged in tin-mining on the 31st December, 1902, was 1,467.

In Western Australia, tin has been found to exist in large quantities, but the ore is of inferior quality, and, until recent years the industry languished owing to the superior attractions of the goldfields, the average annual production for the three years ending with 1898 being only £3,960. The advance in price gave a stimulus to the industry in the following year, and the output increased considerably, being valued at £25,270. In 1900 the yield amounted to £56,702, but declined during the next year to £40,000, while in 1902 only 620 tons, valued at £39,783, were produced. Of the total output in 1902 the Greenbushes district contributed 403 tons, valued at £24,680, and the Pilbarra field, in the Marble Bar district, 217 tons, valued at £15,103. The full development of the industry in both districts is retarded by the inadequacy of the water supply.

The yield of tin in Victoria is small, no discoveries of any importance having been recorded prior to 1890, but towards the end of that year extensive deposits were reported to exist in the Gippsland district at Omeo and Tarwin. In 1902 the production was only 10 tons, valued at £500, this small return being obtained in connection with gold-dredging.

In South Australia very little tin is produced. During 1902 the production was 126 tons of ore, valued at £6,078, of which the Northern Territory was responsible for 119 tons, valued at £5,985. There is no record of any production of tin in New Zealand.

The tin-mining industry has been subject to frequent fluctuations, especially of late years. The value of the metal in the European market was £159 per ton in 1872, £52 in 1878, £114 in 1880 and 1882, and £72 in 1884. A gradual recovery then took place, until in 1888 the price reached £121. During the ten years from 1888 to 1898 tin was subject to an almost continuous fall in price, realising in 1898 only one-half of that obtained a decade before. The metal, however, made a great advance in price during 1900, London quotations in December being £125 10s. per ton, as compared with £82 in 1898, and £63 in 1897, and although this value was not maintained during 1901, the prices current at the end of the year averaged £109 10s. per ton. In 1902 there was a further improvement, and for the first week of 1903 the quotations were £123 10s. per ton.

The value of the production of tin in Australasia during 1902, and up to the end of that year, was as given below :—

State.	Value of Tin produced.	
	During 1902.	To end of year 1902.
	£	£
New South Wales	59,593	6,661,399
Victoria	500	715,998
Queensland	116,171	4,810,037
South Australia	6,078	38,758
Western Australia	39,783	237,982
Tasmania	242,990	7,519,284
Australasia	465,115	19,983,458

The number of persons engaged in tin-mining in 1902 was as follows :—In New South Wales, 1,288 ; Tasmania, 1,254 ; Queensland, 1,467 ; and Western Australia, 249.

IRON.

Iron is distributed throughout Australasia, but for want of capital in developing the fields this industry has not progressed. In New South Wales extensive deposits of iron ore exist in the Mittagong, Piper's Flat, Goulburn, Queanbeyan, and Port Stephens districts.

At Carcoar and Cadia there are large deposits of rich ore, the quantities in sight being estimated by the Government Geological surveyor at 3,100,000 and 39,000,000 tons respectively. The pig iron produced from the Carcoar ore would be admirably adapted for foundry purposes, and is suitable for use in the basic process of steel manufacture, while the ore at Cadia contains little phosphorus and could be utilised in the manufacture of steel by the cheaper acid processes. Considerable attention has been given to the question of establishing ironworks in this state, capable of supplying the requirements of Australia, and in 1901 the idea assumed a definite shape. Two schemes were advocated—one to smelt ore at Lithgow from the Carcoar and Cadia deposits, and the other to bring ore from the Blythe River, Tasmania, and smelt it in Sydney or elsewhere on the seaboard. Had the Bonus for Manufactures Bill, introduced into the Federal Parliament, been passed in the same form as submitted, there is no doubt that the first of these schemes would have been adopted and the industry established immediately by private enterprise. The amendments made in the Bill, however, provide only for a bonus to works established by a State of the Commonwealth, and in view of the importance of the question, the Federal Government appointed a Royal Commission to inquire into the whole matter, and this Commission by a majority reported in favour of granting a bonus on the manufacture of iron and steel from Australian ores.

The principal works in New South Wales for the manufacture of iron from the ore are situated at Eskbank, near Lithgow, where red siliceous ores, averaging 22 per cent., and brown hematite, yielding 50 per cent., metallic iron, have been successfully treated. Abundance of coal and limestone are found in the neighbourhood. The manufacture of pig-iron, for which the establishment was originally built, has been abandoned for some years, and the work now carried on consists of the re-rolling of old rails, and the manufacture of iron bars, rods, and nails, and of ordinary castings. The quantity manufactured from scrap during 1902 was 6003 tons, valued at £82,273. During the past four years considerable quantities of iron ore have been raised from the deposits situated in the Marulan, Picton, and Carcoar districts and despatched to the smelting-works at Dapto and Cockle Creek, where they have been used as flux, the gold contents of the ore helping to defray the extra cost of railway carriage. The total raised in 1902 was 13,555 tons, valued at £10,690, and up to the end of that year 41,358 tons, valued at £33,588, had been raised. A considerable quantity of iron oxide is also raised each year and used for flux, while there is also a slight export, the amount, in 1902, being 188 tons, valued at £395.

In Tasmania a huge deposit of iron ore has long been known to exist at the Blythe River, near Burnie. During 1901 the deposit was tested by tunnelling and found to maintain its size and quality, and although arrangements for its exploitation are not yet completed, there is little doubt that in the near future it will prove an important addition to the industrial wealth of the State. Up to the present the production of iron ore has not been great, but in 1902 2,386 tons, valued at £1,075 were raised.

In Queensland deposits of iron ore have been found at Stanthorpe, and 430 tons, valued at £215, were raised in 1901, but there has since been no further production.

Magnetite occurs in great abundance in Western Australia, together with hematite, and the ores would prove of enormous value if a sufficiency of cheap labour were available. A considerable quantity of ironstone is raised in the state and used for fluxing purposes, the production in 1901 being 20,569 tons, valued at £13,246. Owing to the closing down of the smelting works at Fremantle the quantity raised in 1902 was only 4,800 tons, valued at £2,040.

In New Zealand 17 tons of hematite, valued at £116, were raised in 1902.

Goethite, limonite, and hematite are found in New South Wales, at the junction of the Hawkesbury sandstone formation and the Wianamatta shale near Nattai, and are enhanced in value by their proximity to coal-beds. Near Lithgow extensive deposits of limonite or clay-band ore are interbedded with coal. Siderite or spathic iron (carbonate of iron) and vivianite (phosphate of iron) are found in New Zealand. The latter also occurs in New South Wales, intermingled with copper and tin ores.

The Government of South Australia has offered a bonus of £2,000 for the first 500 tons of pig-iron produced in that State.

Antimony.

Antimony is widely diffused throughout Australasia, and is sometimes found associated with gold. The low price of the metal during late years has discouraged operations in this branch of the mining industry, and the output in all the States has fallen away considerably. In New South Wales, deposits of antimony occur in various places, chiefly in the Armidale, Bathurst, and Rylstone districts; and at Bowraville on the North Coast. The production, however, is confined to the Hillgrove mines, and in 1902 was valued at only £542, the total production to the end of the year being £194,775.

In Victoria the production up to the end of 1898 was valued at £177,174, but there has been no further output since that year, while in Queensland the production ceased in 1899, when the value raised was only £200. In New Zealand also, the production of antimony has practically ceased, although during 1901 there was an export of 3 tons, valued at £101. Good lodes of stibnite (sulphide of antimony) have been found near Roebourne, in Western Australia; but no attempt has yet been made to work them.

The following table shows the value of antimony produced in Australasia up to the end of 1902:—

State.	Value.
New South Wales	£194,775
Victoria	177,174
Queensland	35,458
Commonwealth	£407,407
New Zealand	52,462
Australasia	£459,869

BISMUTH.

Bismuth is known to exist in all the Australian states, but up to the present time it has been mined for in New South Wales, Queensland, South Australia, and Tasmania only. The demand for the metal is limited, and mining is hardly remunerative at present prices. The output in New South Wales during 1902 was valued at £3,100, and in Queensland £123, while the total production for each state up to the end of the year was £66,285 and £64,535 respectively.

MANGANESE.

Manganese probably exists in all the states, although no deposits have as yet been found in Tasmania. Little, however, has been done to utilise the deposits, the demands of the local markets being extremely limited; but in the event of the extensive iron ores of New South Wales being worked on a large scale, the manganese deposits in that State will become of commercial importance. The ore generally occurs in the form of oxides, manganite, and pyrolusite, and contains a high percentage of sesquioxide of manganese. The production has never attained much importance in any of the States. The value of the output in New South Wales during 1901 was £24, making a total of £1,401 up to the end of that year. There is no record of production in 1902.

In Queensland the output for 1902, valued at £3,000, was obtained solely from the Mount Miller mine, the entire yield being absorbed by the works of the Mount Morgan mines. The total value of the production of this metal in Queensland to the end of 1902 was £24,980.

In New Zealand the value during 1900 was £588, and the total raised to the end of that year £60,232, but there has since been no further production. In South Australia there was an export during 1902 of 18 tons, valued at £62.

PLATINUM.

Platinum and the allied compound metal iridosmine have been found in New South Wales, but so far in inconsiderable quantities, the latter occurring commonly with gold or tin in alluvial drifts. At present mining operations are confined to the deposits in the Fifield district, which, however, give evidence of depletion. A lease of 130 acres has been taken up at Macauley's Lead, about 20 miles from Woodburn, while the old claims at Little Darling Springs and Mulga Springs, in the Broken Hill district, are again to be thoroughly prospected. The value of the production during 1902 was £750, and the total to the end of that year, £13,961. Platinum and iridosmine have also been found in New Zealand.

Tellurium.

The noble metal tellurium has been found in New Zealand, associated with gold and silver (petzite) and with silver only (hessite). It has also been discovered in New South Wales at Bingara and other parts of the northern districts, as well as at Tarana, on the Western Line, though at present only in such minute quantities as would not repay the cost of working; while at Captain's Flat it has been found in association with bismuth.

At many of the mines at Kalgoorlie, Western Australia, large quantities of ores of telluride of gold have been discovered in the lode formations.

Lead.

Lead is found in each of the Australasian States, but is worked only when associated with silver. In Western Australia the metal occurs in the form of sulphides and carbonates of great richness, but the quantity of silver mixed with it is small, and the production of late years has been very limited. In 1902 it amounted to 36 tons, valued at £277.

In Queensland the lead raised during 1902 amounted to 267 tons, valued at £2,706, and from South Australia lead to the value of £22,303 was exported during the year. As will be gathered from the remarks made in a previous portion of this chapter, the association of lead with silver has proved a source of much wealth to the silver mines in New South Wales—those at Broken Hill particularly—several of these mines being only enabled to continue operations owing to the high price of the lead contained in the ore.

Other Metals.

Mercury, in the form of sulphides or cinnabar, is found in New South Wales, Queensland, and New Zealand. In New South Wales cinnabar has been discovered on the Cudgegong River, near Rylstone, and it also occurs at Bingara, Solferino, Yulgilbar, and Cooma. In the latter place the assays of ore yielded 22 per cent. of mercury. Very large and rich deposits have been found on Noggriga Creek, near Yulgilbar.

A series of experiments conducted with small parcels of the ore gave satisfactory results, and 1 ton of ore yielded 2 per cent. of mercury. A furnace, capable of treating between 40 and 50 tons per week, is being erected, and some 400 tons of ore have been raised and are awaiting treatment

Titanium, of the varieties known as octahedrite and brookite, is found in alluvial deposits in New South Wales, in conjunction with diamonds.

Wolfram (tungstate of iron and manganese) occurs in most of the States, notably in New South Wales, Tasmania, Queensland, and

New Zealand. For some years there has been a small output in Queensland, and a rise in the price of the mineral so stimulated the industry that in 1899 the production reached £10,060. As the demand is limited, the increased price soon led to overproduction and a consequent fall in prices, and at present they are not sufficiently remunerative to encourage search for this mineral. The value of the production in 1902 was only £1,167. There was a little wolfram exported from South Australia during 1901, the quantity being 5 tons, valued at £175. In 1900 Tasmania produced a small quantity of the metal, valued at £2,058. Scheelite, another variety of tungsten, is found in Queensland and New Zealand, a little mining being carried on in the latter colony, where 39 tons, valued at £1,200, were raised in 1902. Molybdenum, in the form of molybdenite (sulphide of molybdenum), is found in New South Wales, Victoria, and Queensland, but only in the last-mentioned State was there any production during 1902, the value being £5,502.

Zinc ores, in the several varieties of carbonates, silicates, oxide, sulphide, and sulphate of zinc, have been found in several of the Australasian States, but have attracted little attention, except in New South Wales, where the metal is usually found associated with silver, lead, and copper; and various experiments are being made for the purpose of ascertaining whether it can be profitably extracted. For some years attention has been directed by the Broken Hill Companies to the production of a high grade zinc concentrate from the sulphide ores, and a fair measure of success has attended their efforts. The Sulphide Corporation has a magnetic separating plant in operation at Cockle Creek, and is producing high-grade zinc concentrates from the old dump of middlings, while the Australian Metal Company has found the magnetic separator, invented by their engineer, to work so satisfactorily that they have arranged to have a number of the machines in operation during 1903. The Broken Hill Proprietary are reported to hold possession of a process which will revolutionise the treatment of zinc-containing ores. The experiments made so far have proved satisfactory, but it remains to be seen whether the process can be worked successfully on a commercial scale. The value of zinc produced and exported reached a total of £49,207 in 1899, and £44,187 in 1900; but in 1901 there was a decline to £4,057. The value in 1902 was £10,625, and up to the end of that year £171,748. It is estimated that Europe alone requires 160,000 tons of spelter annually for the manufacture of roofing iron, and the heavy imports of the article into the Australian States show that there is a wide field here for the development of the industry.

Nickel, so abundant in the island of New Caledonia, has up to the present been found only in Queensland and Tasmania; but few attempts have been made to prospect systematically for this valuable mineral. In 1894 Tasmania produced 136 tons of nickel ore, valued at £544; but none has been raised since that date.

Cobalt occurs in New South Wales and Victoria, and efforts have been made in the former State to treat the ore, the metal having a high commercial value; but the market is small, and no attempt has yet been made to produce it on any large scale. The manganese ores of the Bathurst district of New South Wales often contain a small percentage of cobalt—sufficient, indeed, to warrant further attempts towards its extraction. The only deposits being worked at the present time are at Port Macquarie, where very promising ore has been opened up. During 1902, 34 tons, valued at £304, were exported.

Chrome iron or chrome ore has been found in New Zealand and Tasmania. In New South Wales chromium is found in the northern portion of the State in the Clarence and Tamworth districts, and also near Gundagai, usually in association with serpentine. Mining operations in New South Wales have been confined to the deposits at Gobarralong, near Gundagai, as it is uncertain whether those at Bowling Alley Point could be profitably worked. The accessible deposits at these mines are now almost worked out, and the production has consequently slackened. In 1899 the export was valued at £17,416, but in 1902 it had declined to £1,740. In New Zealand chrome ore to the value of £37,367 was extracted between 1858 and 1866, but there was no further production until the year 1900, when the value amounted to only £110. In 1902 there was also a small output, amounting to 175 tons, valued at £525.

Sulphur exists in large quantities in the volcanic regions of New Zealand, where it will doubtless some day become an important article of commerce. The output in 1900 was 1,692 tons, valued at £4,824, but in 1902 only 100 tons, valued at £475, were raised. It is also said to occur in small quantities at Mount Wingen, in the Upper Hunter district of New South Wales; at Tarcutta, near Wagga Wagga; and at Louisa Creek, near Mudgee.

Arsenic, in its well-known and beautiful forms, orpiment and realgar, is found in New South Wales and Victoria. It usually occurs in association with other minerals, in veins.

Coal.

Australasia has been bountifully supplied by Nature with mineral fuel. Five distinct varieties of black coal, of well characterised types, may be distinguished, and these, with the two extremes of brown coal or lignite, and anthracite, form a perfectly continuous series. For statistical purposes, however, they are all included under the generic name of "coal," and therefore these minerals will be considered here only under the three main heads—lignite, coal, and anthracite.

Brown coal or lignite occurs principally in New Zealand and Victoria. Attempts have frequently been made to employ the mineral for ordinary [illegible]oses, but its inferior quality has prevented its general use. In

Victoria there is usually a small annual output, the quantity raised in 1901 amounting to 150 tons, but there was no production in 1902. The fields of lignite in New Zealand are roughly estimated to contain about 500 million tons; the quantity raised annually is increasing, and in 1902 it amounted to 65,239 tons.

Black coal forms one of the principal mineral resources of New South Wales; and in the other states and New Zealand the rich deposits of this valuable substance are rapidly being developed. That they form an important source of commercial prosperity cannot be doubted, as the known areas of the coal-fields of this class in New South Wales have been roughly estimated to contain about 79,198 million tons, and in New Zealand 500 million tons. New Zealand also possesses a superior quality of bituminous coal, which is found on the west coast of the Middle Island. An estimate of the probable contents of these coal-fields is given as 200 million tons. Coal of a very fair description was discovered in the basin of the Irwin River, in Western Australia, as far back as the year 1846. It has been ascertained from recent explorations that the area of carboniferous formation in that state extends from the Irwin northwards to the Gascoyne River, about 300 miles distant, and probably all the way to the Kimberley district. The most important discovery of coal in the state so far is that made in the bed of the Collie River, near Bunbury, to the south of Perth. The coal has been tested and found to be of good quality; and there are grounds for supposing that there are 250 million tons on this field. Mr. Jack, formerly Government Geologist of Queensland, gave it as his opinion that the extent of the coal-fields of that state is practically unlimited, and that the carboniferous formations extend to a considerable distance under the Great Western Plains. It is roughly estimated that the coal measures at present practically explored extend over an area of about 24,000 square miles. In Tasmania and Victoria large deposits of coal have also been found; and in all the states the industry is being prosecuted with vigour.

Coal was first discovered in New South Wales in the year 1797, near Mount Keira, by a man named Clark, the supercargo of a vessel called the Sydney Cove which had been wrecked in Bass Straits. Later in the same year Lieutenant Shortland discovered the river Hunter, with the coal-beds situated at its mouth. Little or no use, however, was made of the discovery, and in 1826 the Australian Agricultural Company obtained a grant of 1,000,000 acres of land, together with the sole right, conferred upon them by charter, of working the coal-seams that were known to exist in the Hunter River district. Although the company held this valuable privilege for twenty years, very little enterprise was exhibited by them in the direction of winning coal, and it was not until the year 1847, when their monopoly ceased and public competition stepped in, that the coal-mining industry began to show signs of progress and prosperity. From the 40,732 tons extracted in 1847, the quantity raised had in 1901 expanded to the large figure of 5,968,426 tons, valued at £2,178,929, both the output and value in the latter year being the highest recorded to that date. The production in 1902 was 5,942,011 tons, valued at £2,206,598, and the total quantity of coal extracted from the New South Wales mines, from the date of their opening up to the end of that year, amounted to 103,387,070 tons, valued at £41,701,442.

The coal-fields of New South Wales are classed in three districts—the Northern, Southern, and Western districts, but it is thought that coal deposits extend over nearly the whole length of the sea-coast. The first of these comprises chiefly the mines of the Hunter River district; the second includes the Illawarra district and, generally, the coastal regions to the south of Sydney, together with Berrima, on the table-land; and the third consists of the mountainous regions on the Great Western Railway, and extends as far as Dubbo. The total area of the carboniferous strata of New South Wales is estimated at 23,950 square miles. The seams vary in thickness. One of the richest has been found at Greta, in the Hunter River district; it contains an average thickness of 41 feet of clean coal, and the quantity underlying each acre of ground has been computed to be 63,700 tons.

It has long been known that a seam of coal existed under Sydney Harbour, and in 1899 a syndicate was formed to determine at what depth the deposit was situated. After boring operations had been carried on to a depth of 2,917 feet, a seam of coal 10 feet 3 inches—supposed to be identical with that at Bulli—was struck, and the syndicate now known as the Sydney Harbour Collieries (Limited) acquired mining rights extending over 10,167 acres. Some difficulty occurred in the selection of a site, but it was at length determined to sink the mine at Balmain, and a small seam of coal was found at a depth of 2,880 feet, while two other seams were struck at depths of 2,933 feet and 2,950 feet. It is fully expected that these seams will be found to unite at a distance of about 300 yards from the shaft, and should this prove to be the case, the effect on the industrial progress of Sydney will be of the utmost importance. At present the output from the mine is limited, but the coal is of good quality, and its capabilities for steaming purposes have been very favourably spoken of.

The number of coal-mines under inspection in New South Wales at the end of the year 1902 was 97 as compared with 96 in the previous year. They gave employment to 12,815 persons, of whom 10,050 were employed under ground, and 2,765 above ground. The average quantity of coal extracted per miner was 591 tons, as against an average of 619 tons in the previous year, and 612 tons in 1900. For the ten years ended 1902, the average quantity of coal extracted per miner was 546 tons, which, at the mean price of coal at the pit's mouth, was equivalent to £172 10s. 7d. Taking all persons employed at the mines, both above and under ground, the average for the ten years would be 440 tons, equivalent to £138 15s. 8d. per man. This production is certainly large, and compares favourably with the results exhibited by the principal coal-raising countries of the world, as will be evident from the following figures, giving the averages for the leading countries, based on the number of persons employed :—

Country.	Quantity of coal raised per miner.	Value at the pit's mouth per ton.	Total value of coal raised per miner.
	tons.	s. d.	£ s. d.
New South Wales	440	6 4	138 15 8
Great Britain	272	10 1	137 2 8
United States	536	5 6	147 8 0
Germany	317	7 3	114 18 3
France	203	11 9	119 15 3
Belgium	174	13 5	116 12 6
Austria	605	6 3	189 1 3

A large proportion of the coal raised is consumed in the state, and out of a total production of 5,942,011 tons in 1902, 2,680,552 tons—or 45·11 per cent.—were used locally. The exports to Australasian ports amounted to 1,678,725 tons, or 28·25 per cent., and to ports outside Australasia 1,582,734 tons, or 26·64 per cent. The quantity required for home consumption increases every year, and the annual consumption per head of population has risen from 16 cwt. in 1877 to 38 cwt. in 1902. The increased steam power employed in the manufacturing industries and on the railways accounts for a great deal of the advance in consumption, while the quantities of coal used in smelting works and gas works also account for a large proportion, but it must be borne in mind that the figures include the bunker coal used in the ocean-going steamers, and this amounted in 1902 to about 430,000 tons.

The progress of the export trade of New South Wales, from 1881 to 1902, is shown in the following table:—

Exported to—	Quantity.			Value.		
	1881.	1891.	1902.	1881.	1891.	1902.
	tons.	tons.	tons.	£	£	£
Australasian states	521,025	1,342,055	1,678,725	200,829	664,847	815,859
New Zealand	136,110	168,921	250,879	54,743	90,662	111,043
India, Ceylon, and China	136,511	188,000	99,402	59,944	105,208	48,203
Mauritius	6,249	19,760	10,120	2,414	10,818	5,242
Pacific Islands	19,526	141,055	324,748	8,011	75,808	163,513
United States	150,002	365,623	185,093	63,172	200,851	100,734
South America	8,017	221,700	489,200	3,243	123,136	265,501
Other countries	52,404	67,254	223,297	20,174	35,310	115,285
Total	1,029,844	2,514,368	3,261,459	417,530	1,306,630	1,625,380

None of the other states is in a position to export coal, but New Zealand is slowly working up an export trade, the progress of which since 1881 is shown below.

Exported to—	Quantity.			Value.		
	1881.	1891.	1902.	1881.	1891.	1902.
	tons.	tons.	tons.	£	£	£
Australasian States	6,049	14,277	9,060	5,022	8,488	10,605
United Kingdom	......	68,871	82,399	......	76,027	76,698
Fiji and Norfolk Island ...	21	3,282	9,476	25	2,469	7,621
Pacific Islands, etc.	551	5,234	87,742	563	4,189	59,823
Total.....................	6,621	91,664	188,677	5,610	91,173	154,747

The exports to the United Kingdom from New Zealand, as well as from New South Wales, consisted entirely of bunker coal for the steamers. The production of the former colony in 1902 was 1,362,702 tons, valued at £741,759. A large proportion is raised from the mines in the Westport district of the Middle Island, which showed an output of 528,462 tons in 1902. The Otago and Greymouth districts produced respectively 308,310 and 216,594 tons.

There is a steady increase in the quantity of coal raised in the colony, and a corresponding decrease in the importation. In 1902 there were 180 coal-mines in operation in New Zealand, giving employment to 2,885 men, the average value of the output per man being £257 2s. 2d.

As showing the various kinds of coal found in New Zealand the following figures relating to the production in 1902 will be of interest:—

Bituminous coal	845,046	tons.
Pitch coal	25,245	,,
Brown coal......................................	427,172	,,
Lignite	65,239	,,
Total	1,362,702	,,

Coal-mining is an established industry in Queensland, and is progressing satisfactorily. The production increased steadily up to the year 1901, when it amounted to 539,472 tons, valued at £189,877, but in 1902 there was a decline to 501,531 tons, valued at £172,286. The collieries now in operation are situated in the Ipswich and Wide Bay districts, on the Darling Downs, and at Clermont; but deposits of coal are known to exist in the neighbourhood of Rockhampton and Gladstone, and also at various localities in Central Queensland. Operations are being conducted at the places mentioned with the view of testing and developing the seams, and the foundation of an export trade will depend on the success of the results obtained in the coastal area. Of the total production of 501,531 tons during 1902, 390,603 tons were obtained in the Ipswich district, 105,181 tons at Wide Bay, and 5,747 tons in the Clermont district. There were 1,336 men engaged in the industry in 1902.

In Tasmania coal of good quality has been found in the Lower Measures of the Permo-Carboniferous rocks, principally in the basins of the Mersey and the Don in the north, and at Adventure Bay and Port Cygnet in the south, as well as in the Upper Measures of the Triassic or Jurassic rocks, which are extensively developed in the eastern and north-eastern parts of the state. The production of coal in the state during 1902 amounted to 48,863 tons, valued at £41,533, the output for the preceding year being 43,010 tons, valued at £21,711. The two largest collieries are the Mount Nicholas and the Cornwall, which give employment to 127 men. The work at the latter mine was greatly interfered with by a strike which occurred during the year and forced the owners to abandon their contract to supply coal to the Melbourne Harbour Trust.

Tasmania still relies largely on New South Wales for its supply of coal for local requirements. Since 1896 the export from New South Wales to the island has increased from 57,000 tons to 100,000 tons. During 1902 there were 164 men engaged in coal-mining in the State, and the average output per man amounted to 296·73 tons, valued at £253 5s.

The output of coal in Victoria is steadily increasing, and, although operations were greatly interfered with by the unfortunate strike in 1902, the output during the year was 225,164 tons, valued at £155,850, an increase of 15,835 tons on the production in 1901. In 1891 the coal produced amounted to 22,834 tons, but notwithstanding the great increase in production since that year Victoria is still a large consumer of New South Wales coal, its import in 1902 amounting to 871,066 tons. The principal collieries in the state are the Outtrim Howitt, Jumbunna, and the Coal Creek Proprietary, the output from these during 1902 being 114, 685, 67,876, and 39,256 tons respectively. Boring operations are in progress, but the only seam struck during 1902 was at Boyle's Creek, near Leongatha, with a proved thickness of about 2 feet.

In South Australia, coal-beds were discovered at Leigh's Creek, north of Port Augusta, but the results of a trial on the Government railways proved the coal to be unsuitable for use. There was no output during 1902. The export of coal from New South Wales to South Australia during 1902 was 467,476 tons.

The only coal-field in Western Australia is situated at Collie, and the output in 1902 reached 140,884 tons, valued at £86,188, an increase of about 23,000 tons on the total of the preceding year. This production could be increased considerably were there sufficient demand, but at present the coal is not extensively used except on the railways.

The quantity of coal extracted annually in Australasia now exceeds 8,221,000 tons, valued at about £3,400,000. The production of each state during the year 1902 was as follows:—

State.	Quantity.	Value.	
		Total.	Proportion raised in each State.
	tons.	£	per cent.
New South Wales	5,942,011	2,206,598	64·82
Victoria	225,164	155,850	4·58
Queensland	501,531	172,286	5·06
Western Australia	140,884	86,188	2·53
Tasmania	48,863	41,533	1·22
Commonwealth	6,858,453	2,662,455	78·21
New Zealand	1,362,702	741,759	21·79
Australasia	8,221,155	3,404,214	100·00

The total quantity and value of the coal produced in Australasia up to the end of 1902 are shown below. A small quantity has been raised in South Australia, but is not yet of sufficient importance to warrant inclusion in the table:—

State.	Quantity.	Value.
New South Wales	103,387,070 tons	£41,701,442
Victoria	2,173,057 ,,	1,198,208
Queensland	7,197,054 ,,	2,994,275
Western Australia	434,974 ,,	237,160
Tasmania	849,127 ,,	486,998
Commonwealth	114,041,282 ,,	£46,618,083
New Zealand	17,143,210 ,,	£9,106,326
Australasia	131,184,492 ,,	£55,724,409

During the year 1902 this industry gave direct employment in and about the mines to the following numbers of persons in the several states:—

	No.
New South Wales	12,815
Victoria	1,303
Queensland	1,336
South Australia	50
Western Australia	368
Tasmania	164
New Zealand	2,885

A large proportion of the coal-mining industry of New South Wales is carried on in the Lower Hunter district, which includes the mines in the locality of Newcastle. The following table shows the birthplaces of the miners in this district at the census of 1901, from which it will be seen that out of a total of 8,556 persons, only 3,878, or about 45 per cent. were natives of New South Wales:—

Birthplace.	No.
New South Wales	3,878
Other Australian States and New Zealand	525
England and Wales	2,833
Scotland	972
Ireland	173
Other British Possessions	15
Germany	45
France	4
Russia	8
Scandinavia	30
Italy	7
Other European Countries	11
United States	29
Other Countries	26
Total	8,556

The average price of coal per ton varies considerably in the states. In New South Wales, from the date of the commencement of mining to the end of the year 1902, the average price obtained has been 8s. 1d., but the mean of the last ten years has not been more than 6s. 4d. In 1902 the average price per ton of coal at the pit's mouth was as follows:—

	s.	d.
New South Wales	7	5
Victoria	13	10
Queensland	6	11
Western Australia	12	3
Tasmania	17	0
Commonwealth	7	9
New Zealand	10	11
Australasia	8	3

The question of cost of raising coal is of considerable importance in connection with the export trade. In New South Wales, miners in the Northern District were paid at the rate of 4s. 2d. per ton for screened coal, while in the Southern District the rate was 2s. 6d. In New Zealand it is computed that to deliver coal at the pit's mouth costs in labour 6s. per ton. The returns of the United States show that of the 20,172,779 tons of coal mined by manual labour, 87,841 tons were paid for by daily wages, varying from 9s. 5d. to 11s. 4d.; 600,060 tons were paid for by weight after screening at 3s. 9½d., and the balance at an average price of 2s. 3½d per ton. In 29 mines machinery was exclusively used for winning the coal and 280 machines were thus employed, while 184 machines were in use at 34 mines, in addition to manual labour. The machine-mined coal was paid for at the rate of 1s. 8¼d. per ton. In France surface workers are paid at the rate of 2s. 10½d., underground hands at 4s. 2½d., and those employed both within and without the mines at 3s. 9d. per day.

Anthracite is found in several of the Australian states, but systematic attempts to develop the deposits have as yet been restricted to Queensland. While not possessing the combustible properties or commercial value of coal, anthracite has proved a fairly efficient substitute in countries where coal is not available. The deposits in Queensland exist in the localities of the Dawson and Mackenzie Rivers, and bores have been sunk with a view of determining the best position for shafts. Two bulk samples obtained from the outcrop on the Dawson River have been tested with satisfactory results.

The following table shows the annual coal production of the principal countries of the world. The figures refer to the year 1902, except those for United States and Canada, which refer to the year 1901 :—

Country.*	Tons of 2,240 lb.
United Kingdom	227,095,000
United States	261,874,000
Germany	105,709,000
Austria	10,867,000
France	29,099,000
Belgium	22,403,000
Canada	6,186,000
Australasia	8,221,000

* Including lignite.

Kerosene shale (torbanite) is found in several parts of New South Wales. It is a species of cannel-coal, somewhat similar to the boghead mineral of Scotland, but yielding a much larger percentage of volatile hydro-carbon than the Scottish product. The richest quality yields about 100 to 130 gallons of crude oil per ton, or 17,000 to 18,000 cubic feet of gas, with an illuminating power of 35 to 40 sperm candles when gas only is extracted from the shale. The New South Wales Shale and Oil Company, at Hartley Vale, and the Australian Kerosene Oil and Mineral Company, at Joadja Creek and Katoomba, not only raise kerosene shale for export, but also manufacture from it petroleum oil and other products. From the year 1865, when the mines were first opened, to the end of 1902, the quantity of kerosene shale raised has amounted to 1,136,348 tons, worth £2,030,340. The average price realised during that period has been £1 15s. 9d. per ton. The prices ruling in 1902, when 62,880 tons were extracted, averaged 19s. per ton, representing a total value of £59,716 for the production of that year.

Extensive formations of oil shale have been found in New Zealand, in Otago, and at Orepuki, in Southland, where a mine has been opened and extensive works erected to treat the mineral for the extraction of oils, paraffin wax, ammonia, &c. The quantity of shale raised in 1901 was 12,048 tons, valued at £6,024, but during 1902 the production was only 2,338 tons, valued at £1,169. Crude petroleum has been obtained in several districts in New Zealand, and boring is in progress with a view to testing the oil-bearing strata.

The annual import of kerosene oil into Australasia, based on the returns of the last three years, is shown below :—

State.	Quantity.		Value.
New South Wales	4,240,966	gallons	£142,793
Victoria	4,667,841	,,	140,290
Queensland	1,878,894	,,	79,809
South Australia	1,178,747	,,	35,821
Western Australia	1,410,246	,,	46,506
Tasmania	362,192	,,	14,589
Commonwealth	13,738,886	,,	459,808
New Zealand	2,897,065	,,	110,949
Australasia	16,635,951	,,	570,757

Other Carbon Minerals.

Of all the mineral forms of carbon the diamond is the purest; but as it is usual to class this precious substance under the head of gems that custom will be followed in the present instance.

Graphite, or plumbago, which stands second to the diamond in point of purity, has been discovered in New Zealand, in the form of detached boulders of pure mineral. It also occurs in impure masses where it comes into contact with the coal measures. This mineral, up to the present time, has not been found in any of the other states except New South Wales, where in 1889 a lode 6 feet wide, but of inferior quality, was discovered near Undercliff, in the New England district; and in Western Australia, where, however, owing principally to difficulties of transit, very little of it has been worked.

Ozokerite, or mineral wax, is reported to have been found at Coolah, in New South Wales.

Elaterite, mineral caoutchouc, or elastic bitumen, is said to have been discovered in New South Wales and South Australia. In the last-named state a substance very similar to elaterite has been discovered in the Coorong Lagoons, and has received the name of coorongite. Up to the present time neither the extent of these finds nor their commercial value has been ascertained.

Bitumen is known to exist in Victoria, and is reported to have been found near the township of Coonabarabran, in New South Wales.

Kauri gum, a resinous substance somewhat resembling amber in appearance, and like that product an exudation from trees, is found only in the Auckland province of New Zealand, and is included under the head of minerals, although more logically entitled to be considered as a vegetable product. The best is that dug out of the ground;

but considerable quantities of inferior grades are taken from the forks of standing trees. In New Zealand an extensive and lucrative commerce is carried on in kauri gum. It is computed that the total value of this product obtained from 1853 to the end of 1902 was £11,226,168. In the year 1902 the quantity obtained represented a value of £450,223, and gave employment to about 7,000 persons, both European and Maori. Kauri gum is included in the figures in this chapter giving the total mineral production.

Salts.

Common rock salt has been found in rock crevices in several parts of New South Wales, but it is not known to exist in deposits large enough to be of commercial importance. Large quantities of salt are obtained from the salt lakes in South Australia by means of evaporation. The principal source of supply is Lake Fowler, and in summer the entire area is covered with a deposit of salt. In 1902 there were 300 persons engaged collecting and refining salt, and the quantity produced during the year amounted to 41,500 tons, valued at £45,650.

Natron is said to occur in the neighbourhood of the Namoi River, in New South Wales. It appears as a deposit from the mud-wells of that region. Epsomite, or epsom salt (sulphate of magnesia), is seen as an efflorescence in caves and overhanging rocks of the Hawkesbury sandstone formation, and is also found in various other parts of New South Wales.

Large deposits of alum occur close to the village of Bulladelah, 30 miles from Port Stephens, New South Wales. Up to the end of the year 1902, 19,386 tons of alunite had been raised in the locality, most of the product having been sent to England for treatment. During 1902 the Bulladelah mine yielded 3,644 tons of stone, valued at £10,932.

Stones and Clays.

Marble is found in many parts of New South Wales, South Australia, New Zealand, and Tasmania. In New South Wales marble quarries have been opened in several districts, and some very fine specimens of the stone have been obtained.

The Hawkesbury sandstone formation, which underlies the city of Sydney, provides an inexhaustible supply of stone admirably adapted for building purposes, and capable of lending itself to fine architectural effects.

Lithographic stone has been found in New Zealand, where another beautiful species of limestone known as Oamaru stone is also procured. This stone has a fine, smooth grain, and is of a beautiful creamy tint. It is in great demand for public buildings, not only in the colony where it is found, but in the great cities of continental Australia, which import quantities of the stone for the embellishment of public edifices.

Limestone is mined for in New South Wales, and is now being largely used in the manufacture of hydraulic cement, as well as for fluxing purposes in smelting works. At Portland, near Wallerawang, extensive works for manufacturing cement have been erected, and works are also in operation at Granville, near Sydney. In other parts of the state limestone is also raised, the total production in 1902 being 20,054 tons, valued at £16,018. Of this quantity 17,352 tons were used in smelting works. In Western Australia a considerable quantity of limestone is raised for fluxing purposes, the production in 1902 being 5,080 tons, valued at £1,340. The establishment of the cyanide process for the recovery of gold, in which lime is freely used, has led to the opening up of limestone mines in various parts of Queensland, and the production in 1902 amounted to 4,743 tons, valued at £3,672, the total production up to the end of that year being 14,921 tons, valued at £12,435.

Gypsum is found crystallised in clay-beds in New South Wales, and in isolated crystals in the Salt Lakes of South Australia, where a small proportion of sulphate of lime is present in the water. It is also found in portions of Victoria, the production in that state for 1902 being 3,227 tons, valued at £3,630. This mineral is of commercial value for the manufacture of cement and plaster of Paris, and also as a fertiliser. A considerable quantity has been raised in South Australia for the latter purpose. Gypsum is also found in the form of an insoluble salt in New South Wales, Victoria, and New Zealand.

Apatite, another mineral of considerable commercial importance, and very valuable as a manure, occurs in several districts of New South Wales, principally on the Lachlan River, at the head of the Abercrombie, and in the Clarence River district.

Quartz is of common occurrence in all parts of Australasia. Rock crystal, white, tinted, and smoky quartz are frequently met with, as well as varieties of crystalline quartz, such as amethyst, jasper, and agate, which possess some commercial value.

Tripoli, or rotten stone, an infusorial earth, consisting of hydrous silica, which has some value for commercial purposes, has been found in New South Wales, Victoria, and New Zealand. Meerschaum is reported to have been discovered near Tamworth and in the Richmond River district, in New South Wales.

Mica is also found in granitic country, and has been discovered in the New England and Barrier districts of New South Wales. In Western Australia very good mica has been found at Bindoon, and also on the Blackwood River, near Cape Leeuwin. Several attempts at mining were made, but they proved unsuccessful, and have been abandoned. Deposits have also been found near Herberton, in Northern Queensland. In the Northern Territory of South Australia mica has been obtained on a small scale. In 1895 the production was valued at £2,638, and in 1896 at £732; but of late years there has been no production.

Kaolin, fire-clays, and brick-clays are common to all the states. Except in the vicinity of cities and townships, however, little use has been made of the abundant deposits of clay. Kaolin, or porcelain clay, although capable of application to commercial purposes, has not as yet been utilised to any extent, though found in several places in New South Wales and in Western Australia.

Asbestos has been found in New South Wales in the Gundagai, Bathurst, and Broken Hill districts—in the last-mentioned district in considerable quantities. Several specimens of very fair quality have also been met with in Western Australia; and the Government of the state offered a bonus not exceeding £500 for the export of 50 tons of asbestos, of a value of not less than £10 per ton. In Tasmania asbestos is known to exist in considerable quantities in the vicinity of Beaconsfield.

In New Zealand fairly extensive deposits of phosphates have been discovered, and with large supplies of this valuable fertiliser near at hand the necessity for importing phosphatic manures should shortly cease to exist.

Gems and Gemstones.

Many descriptions of gems and gemstones have been discovered in various parts of the Australasian states, but systematic search has been made principally for the diamond and the noble opal.

Diamonds are found in New South Wales, Victoria, Queensland, and South Australia, but only in the first-named state have any attempts been made to work the diamond drifts. The existence of diamonds and other gem-stones in the territory of New South Wales had been known for years before an attempt was made to work the deposits in 1872. In the course of the following year several deposits of adamantiferous wash were discovered at Bingara, in the New England district, and in later years at Boggy Camp, Copeton. The output has never been very considerable, the largest value realised in any year being £15,375. In 1899 the value amounted to £10,350; the output declined in the next two years, but increased to £11,326 in 1902. The total value of the diamonds produced up to the end of 1902 was £76,617; but this amount is believed to be considerably understated.

The finest opal known is obtained in the Upper Cretaceous formation at White Cliffs, near Wilcannia, New South Wales. During the year 1895 good stone was found at a depth of 50 feet, and as the lower levels are reached the patches of opal appear to improve in quality and to become more regular and frequent. On block 7 a patch of stone was found which realised over £3,000. It is difficult to state with exactitude the value of the production, but it is believed that stone to the value of £716,600 has been sold up to the end of 1902. In 1901 a Special Commission was appointed to inquire into matters connected with the opal industry at White Cliffs, and their investigations tended to show that the annual value of production for some years had amounted to £100,000. Despite the fact that operations were hampered in 1902 by lack of water, the production for the year was valued at £140,000. The number of men engaged in the opal mining industry was 1,100.

In Queensland opal is found in rocks of the desert sandstone formation, sometimes on the surface, but generally at a depth of about 14 feet. The chief fields are at Cunnamulla, Paroo, and Opalton, in the far western and north-western parts of the State, but the scanty water supply has been a great barrier to the progress of the industry. During 1902 the production was valued at £7,000, and the total up to the end of that year, at £138,845

Other gem-stones, including the sapphire, emerald, oriental emerald, ruby, opal, amethyst, garnet, chrysolite, topaz, cairngorm, onyx, zircon, etc., have been found in the gold and tin-bearing drifts and river gravels in numerous localities throughout the states. The Emerald Proprietary Company, in the Emmaville district, near Glen Innes, New South Wales, have sunk two shafts, 100 feet and 50 feet respectively; and 25,000 carats have been won in a rough state. Their value when cut and finished, if of the best quality, is about £2 per carat. Owing to the difficulties of extraction, and the low price of the gems in the London market, the mines were closed for three years. In 1897 they were again opened up, and, although worked for some time during 1898, they are now closed, the company having obtained a suspension of the labour conditions. No gems were produced during the year.

The sapphire is found in all the states, and considerable attention has lately been directed to the sapphire fields of Anakie, in Queensland. The fields are extensive, but the gems are of a peculiar colour, quite distinct from those of any other country, a characteristic that prejudicially affects their value. The value of the gems produced in 1901 was £6,000, but owing to the low prices and the lack of sufficient water supply on the field, the returns fell away to £5,000 in 1902. The oriental topaz has been found in New South Wales. Oriental amethysts also have been found in that State; and the ruby has been found in Queensland, as well as in New South Wales.

According to an authority on the subject of gemstones, rubies, oriental amethysts, emeralds, and topaz have been chiefly obtained from alluvial deposits, but have rarely been met with in a matrix from which it would pay to extract them.

Turquoises have been found near Wangaratta, in Victoria.

Chrysoberyls have been found in New South Wales; spinel rubies, in New South Wales and Victoria; white topaz, in all the states; and yellow topaz, in Tasmania. Chalcedony, carnelian, onyx, and cat's-eye are found in New South Wales; and it is probable that they are also to be met with in the other states, particularly in Queensland. Zircon, tourmaline, garnet, and other gemstones of little commercial value are found throughout Australasia.

In South Australia some very fine specimens of garnet were found, causing some excitement at the time, as the gems were mistaken for rubies. The stones were submitted to the examination of experts, whose reports disclosed the true nature of the gems, and dispelled the hopes of those who had invested in the supposed ruby-mines of that state.

Production of Minerals.

The foregoing pages show that Australasia possesses invaluable mineral resources, and although enormous quantities of minerals of all kinds have been won since their first discovery, yet the deposits, with the exception perhaps of gold, silver, and coal have only reached the first period of their exploitation. The development of the deposits of various other minerals has not reached a sufficiently advanced stage to enable an exact opinion to be expressed regarding their commercial value, though it is confidently held by mining experts that this must be enormous. The mineral production of the various states in 1902 will be found below:—

State.	Total Value.	Proportion in each State.	Average value per head.
	£	per cent.	£ s. d.
New South Wales	5,078,029	20·35	3 12 11
Victoria	3,288,908	13·18	2 14 6
Queensland	3,310,600	13·27	6 9 2
South Australia	576,374	2·31	1 11 7
Western Australia	8,094,617	32·44	39 9 8
Tasmania	1,383,568	5·54	7 17 6
Commonwealth	21,732,096	87·09	5 12 7
New Zealand	3,221,622	12·91	4 0 9
Australasia	24,953,718	100·00	5 7 2

The total value of the minerals raised in Australasia during 1902 was £24,953,718, being £18,289 below the value for 1901, which is the highest recorded in any one year. The great advance of gold-mining in Western Australia and the increased activity displayed in coal-mining in New South Wales have been the chief contributing factors in maintaining the high figures of the past few years. Gold has always constituted the largest proportion of the value raised, but the search for this mineral has led to the expansion of other branches of the mining industry which are commanding more attention each year. At the present time the number of persons in Australasia who gain their livelihood by mining is nearly 123,000. The total employment in each branch of mining during 1902 was :—

State.	Number of Persons engaged in Mining for--						Total.
	Gold.	Silver and Lead.	Copper.	Tin.	* Coal, Coke, and Shale.	Other Minerals & Precious Stones.	
New South Wales	10,610	5,382	1,699	1,288	13,114	1,602	33,695
Victoria	26,103	......	......	......	1,303	73	27,479
Queensland	9,045	100	666	1,467	1,336	328	12,942
South Australia......	2,000	150	4,100	......	50	750	7,050
Western Australia....	20,476	2	113	249	368	2	21,210
Tasmania	1,038	.....	*3,780	1,254	164	......	6,236
Commonwealth ..	69,272	5,634	10,358	4,258	16,335	2,755	108,612
New Zealand	*11,398	......	......	......	2,885	......	14,283
Australasia	80,670	5,634	10,358	4,258	19,220	2,755	122,895

* Includes silver miners.

The greatest number of persons engaged in mining is in New South Wales, where, owing to the large employment afforded by the coal-mines, the total is 33,695 ; the greatest number of gold-miners is in Victoria. The total number of persons in the Commonwealth engaged in mining pursuits is 108,612, and in view of the known resources which await development, this number is likely to be still further increased.

The following table shows the value of the mineral production of each state during the five years 1871, 1881, 1891, 1901 and 1902, as well as the value per inhabitant for the whole of Australasia :—

State.		1871.	1881.	1891.	1901.	1902.
		£	£	£	£	£
New South Wales.........		1,650,000	2,121,000	6,396,000	5,854,150	5,078,029
Victoria		5,400,000	3,467,000	2,339,000	3,312,162	3,288,908
Queensland		806,000	3,165,000	2,300,000	3,114,702	3,310,600
South Australia............		725,000	421,000	366,000	613,930	576,374
Western Australia		5,000	11,000	130,000	7,445,772	8,094,617
Tasmania		25,000	604,000	516,000	1,675,290	1,383,568
Commonwealth......		8,611,000	9,789,000	12,047,000	22,016,006	21,732,096
New Zealand..............		3,100,000	1,528,000	1,841,000	2,956,001	3,221,622
Australasia	Total	11,711,000	11,317,000	13,888,000	24,972,007	24,953,718
	Per head ..	£ s. d. 6 1 0	£ s. d. 4 1 6	£ s. d. 3 12 3	£ s. d. 5 9 0	£ s. d. 5 7 2

The foregoing table shows that the mineral production of 1902 was over eleven millions more than that of 1891. There were increases in all the states with the exception of New South Wales, in which state a decrease of slightly over £1,318,000 has to be recorded, owing to the fall in the value of silver and lead. The most notable increases were in Western Australia and Tasmania; the production of the former state exceeded that of 1891 by nearly £7,965,000, mainly on account of the great increase in the gold yield, which advanced in value from £115,182 to £7,947,662 during the period under review. The large expansion in the Tasmanian production was due to the output of the Mount Lyell Copper-mines. In the other states, the increases were also substantial, and New Zealand had an increase of £1,380,000.

Comparing the value of the mineral production in 1902 with the population, the largest amount is shown by Western Australia, with £39 9s. 8d. per inhabitant; Tasmania ranks second, with £7 17s. 6d. per inhabitant; Queensland third, with £6 9s. 2d.; New Zealand fourth, with £4 0s. 9d.; New South Wales fifth, with £3 12s. 11d. Victoria follows with an average of £2 14s. 6d. per head, and in South Australia the production per inhabitant was only £1 11s. 7d. The average per inhabitant for Australasia was £5 7s. 2d., and the average for the states constituting the Commonwealth was £5 12s. 7d. per head.

The following table shows the value of production in each of the states during 1902, distinguishing the principal minerals. With regard to some of the states the data are defective in respect to "other minerals," but not to such an extent as to seriously affect the gross total. The column "other minerals" includes kerosene shale in New South Wales and kauri gum in New Zealand, but does not include salt in South Australia :—

State.	Gold.	Silver and Silver-lead.	Copper.	Tin.	Coal.	Other Minerals.	Total.
	£	£	£	£	£	£	£
New South Wales	684,970	1,440,179	307,806	59,593	2,206,598	378,883	5,078,029
Victoria	3,062,028	4,900	......	500	155,850	65,630	3,288,908
Queensland	2,720,639	70,145	189,200	116,171	172,286	42,159	3,310,600
South Australia	95,129	19,740	432,525	6,078	......	22,902	576,374
Western Australia....	7,947,662	9,467	8,090	39,783	86,188	3,427	8,094,617
Tasmania	301,573	218,864	577,533	242,990	41,533	1,075	1,383,568
Commonwealth ..	14,812,001	1,763,295	1,515,154	465,115	2,662,455	514,076	21,732,096
New Zealand	1,951,433	71,975	......	......	741,759	*456,455	3,221,622
Australasia	16,763,434	1,835,270	1,515,154	465,115	3,404,214	970,531	24,953,718

* Inclusive of kauri gum of the value of £450,223.

The total mineral production to the end of 1902 is shown in the following table, in which the column "other minerals" again includes kerosene shale and kauri gum :—

State.	Gold.	Silver and Silver-lead.	Copper.	Tin.	Coal.	Other Minerals.	Total.
	£	£	£	£	£	£	£
New South Wales ..	49,844,135	33,781,756	6,164,879	6,661,399	41,701,442	4,678,830	142,832,441
Victoria	263,551,229	861,439	206,395	715,998	1,198,208	411,661	266,944,930
Queensland	55,472,314	858,187	2,438,892	4,810,037	2,994,275	362,569	66,936,274
South Australia	2,483,326	138,370	23,254,571	38,758	......	532,444	26,447,469
Western Australia ..	38,097,374	21,072	335,062	237,982	237,160	417,809	39,346,459
Tasmania	5,195,161	2,603,750	4,499,028	7,519,284	486,998	338,007	20,642,228
Commonwealth ..	414,643,539	38,264,574	36,898,827	19,983,458	46,618,083	6,741,320	563,149,801
New Zealand	61,111,316	452,781	18,088	......	9,106,326	*11,487,002	82,175,513
Australasia	475,754,855	38,717,355	36,916,915	19,983,458	55,724,409	18,228,322	645,325,314

* Inclusive of kauri gum of the value of £11,226,168.

Coal was the only mineral raised in New South Wales prior to 1852, and its production up to that date was valued at £279,923. Deducting that amount from the total value of Australasian minerals raised up to the end of 1902, the remainder, £645,045,391, represents the value of mineral production from 1852, equal to an average of £12,647,949 per annum for the fifty-one years.

AGRICULTURE.

TAKEN as a whole, Australasia may be said to be just emerging from the first phase of agricultural settlement; indeed, several states have not yet wholly passed from the pastoral stage. Nevertheless the value of agricultural produce, estimated at farm prices, is considerable, and amounts to over 50 per cent. of the value of the pastoral and dairy produce. The average production from agriculture in each state for the last five years is shown below. While the returns in 1902 from several of the states were lower than usual, owing to adverse seasons, New Zealand had a remarkably favourable year, the wheat harvest in that colony being nearly 7,500,000 bushels as compared with 4,100,000 bushels in New South Wales and Victoria combined. In 1900, however, these two states produced 34,000,000 bushels as compared with 6,500,000 bushels in New Zealand, while present conditions are so favourable that in all probability the combined yield of the two states will amount to 54,000,000 bushels.

State.	Average value of Crops for last five years.	Average Value of Produce per acre for last five years.	Proportion of Total Value.
	£	£ s. d.	per cent.
New South Wales	5,563,000	2 7 11	19·30
Victoria	7,216,000	2 5 11	25·03
Queensland	1,876,000	4 13 9	6·51
South Australia	3,287,000	1 9 1	11·40
Western Australia	759,000	3 15 6	2·63
Tasmania	1,506,000	6 7 1	5·23
Commonwealth	20,207,000	2 7 3	70·10
New Zealand	8,619,000	5 1 8	29·90
Australasia	28,826,000	2 16 3	100·00

From this estimate it would seem that the value of crops per acre cultivated is much larger in Queensland and Tasmania than in the other states of the Commonwealth, a fact which is due to the proportionately large area under sugar-cane in the former state, while in Tasmania the area devoted to fruit and hops, and the larger returns of cereals, account for the high average per acre which that province shows; in Western Australia, where the greater part of the produce consumed is imported, prices are higher than in the eastern states, and the small area devoted to the plough returns on an average a better price per acre than in the states where agriculture has received greater attention. In point of gross value, Victoria occupies the first position among the members of the Commonwealth group, the produce of that province having a value slightly in excess of one-fourth of that of all Australasia. The high position occupied by Victoria is in great measure due to the large return from wheat, potatoes, and from gardens and orchards. New Zealand also produces over one-fourth of the total, and New South Wales over one-sixth. The average value of the principal crops, and the percentage of each to the total production for the quinquennial period, 1899 to 1903, are given in the following statement:—

Name of Crop.	Value.	Proportion to Total.
	£	per cent.
Wheat	6,619,000	23·0
Maize	1,371,000	4·8
Barley	428,000	1·5
Oats	2,700,000	9·4
Hay	6,522,000	22·6
Grass seed	260,000	0·9
Potatoes	2,104,000	7·3
Grapes	915,000	3·2
Hops	56,000	0·2
Tobacco	14,000	0·0
Sugar-cane	636,000	2·2
Orchards and Gardens	2,247,000	7·8
Green forage	1,051,000	3·6
Other crops (other grain, root, &c.)	3,903,000	13·5
Total	28,826,000	100·0

The principal crop is wheat, which returned 23 per cent. of the total value, hay coming next with 22·6 per cent. "Other" crops returned the large sum of £3,903,000—13·5 per cent.—to which, New Zealand alone contributed £3,020,000, the high value of the production in that province being due to the fact that there is an area of considerably over half a million acres devoted to the cultivation of turnips and other root crops, which are grown mostly as food for sheep.

The average value of agricultural produce per head of population in each of the Australasian provinces during the last five years is represented by the following figures. It will be seen that New Zealand shows the highest value, followed in order by South Australia, Tasmania, Victoria, Western Australia, and New South Wales. Queensland occupies the lowest position with a value of less than half that of South

Australia. Comparisons of this kind are however somewhat misleading, as the main consideration is the extent of employment afforded by the industry and the return to the persons engaged therein.

State.	Average value per head.		
	£	s.	d.
New South Wales	4	1	[illegible]
Victoria	6	[illegible]	
Queensland	3	1	
South Australia	9		1
Western Australia	4		
Tasmania	8	1	
Commonwealth	5	7	1
New Zealand	11	3	0
Australasia	6	6	9

Below will be found the value of the agricultural production of the Commonwealth and New Zealand in the years 1871, 1881, and 1891. Comparing these figures with those given above, it will be seen that while the total production of Australasia now averages nearly £9,000,000 more than in 1881, the average value per head has declined over 12 per cent., and that, as compared with 1891, the value per head shows an increase of 12s. 3d. As subsequent tables will show, a decrease in prices, and not want of productiveness, was responsible for the decline in value since 1881. The fall in prices, especially of wheat, was very rapid down to 1895; for the next three years there was a very material increase; in 1899 they fell again to the 1895 level, but in 1901 there was a more or less general increase; while towards the close of 1902, when the effects of the adverse season were acutely felt, prices rose to double those of the previous year.

State.	1871.	1881.	1891.
	£	£	£
New South Wales	2,220,000	3,830,000	3,584,500
Victoria	3,300,000	5,894,000	7,009,100
Queensland	650,000	1,283,000	1,414,000
South Australia	1,789,000	3,283,000	3,045,000
Western Australia	258,000	248,000	380,900
Tasmania	724,000	981,000	1,046,500
Commonwealth	8,941,000	15,519,000	16,480,000
New Zealand	1,955,000	4,650,000	5,518,000
Australasia — Total	10,896,000	20,169,000	21,998,000
	£ s. d.	£ s. d.	£ s. d.
Australasia — Per head	5 12 8	7 5 3	5 14 6

Compared with the principal countries of the world, Australasia does not take a high position in regard to the gross value of the produce of its tillage, but in value per inhabitant it compares fairly well; indeed, some of the provinces, such as South Australia, New Zealand, and Tasmania, show averages which surpass those of the leading agricultural countries. This may be partly seen from the following table, which gives approximately for 1891–95 the value of agricultural production in the principal countries of the world, with the average amount per head of population :—

Countries.	Value in millions.	Per head.	Countries.	Value in millions.	Per head.
	£	£		£	£
United Kingdom	126	3·2	Holland	18	4·0
France	284	7·3	Belgium	29	4·6
Germany	262	5·1	Switzerland	9	3·0
Russia	370	3·5	United States	487	7·7
Austria	210	5·7	Canada	33	6·9
Italy	141	4·6	Cape Colony	2	1·3
Spain	94	5·5	Argentina	24	6·0
Portugal	18	4·0	Uruguay	2	2·7
Sweden	20	4·9			
Norway	3	1·7			
Denmark	19	8·6	Australasia (average for years 1897–1902)	29	6·5

Area under Cultivation.

The following figures, giving the total extent of land in cultivation in each of the Commonwealth states and New Zealand at different periods since the year 1871, will serve to illustrate the progress which agriculture has made. In this table, and in the others which follow, the years 1871, 1881, 1891, and 1902 embrace the period from the 1st April in each of those years to the 31st March in the following year :—

State.	1871.	1881.	1891.	1901.	1902.
	acres.	acres.	acres.	acres.	acres.
New South Wales	390,099	578,243	846,383	2,276,628	2,245,839
Victoria	851,354	1,435,446	2,116,654	2,965,681	3,246,568
Queensland	59,969	117,664	242,629	483,460	275,383
South Australia	837,730	2,156,407	1,927,689	2,236,552	2,224,593
Western Australia	51,724	53,353	64,209	216,824	228,118
Tasmania	155,046	148,494	168,121	232,550	246,923
Commonwealth	2,345,922	4,489,607	5,365,685	8,411,695	8,467,424
New Zealand	337,282	1,070,906	1,424,777	1,545,683	1,603,602
Australasia	2,683,204	5,560,513	6,790,462	9,957,378	10,071,026

In addition to the 1,603,602 acres under crop in New Zealand as shown above, there were in 1902, 69,342 acres of grass land cut for hay, and 61,444 acres of clover and grass were cultivated for seed. If these areas be taken into consideration, the total acreage in cultivation in New Zealand will be 1,734,388. In 1861, the cultivated area in Australasia was 1,337,548 acres, so that the extent of land under crop is now over seven times as large as it was in that year. If, however, the land artificially grassed be included, the total will come to 23,289,517 acres, or nearly eighteen times the area in cultivation in 1861. A comparison of the acreage under crop on the basis of population, may perhaps best serve to give an idea of the progress of agriculture, and this is shown in the table given below. South Australia still holds, as it has done for many years, the first position, followed at a long interval by Victoria and New Zealand.

State.	1861.	1871.	1881.	1891.	1901.	1902.
	acres.	acres.	acres.	acres.	acres.	acres.
New South Wales	0·7	0·8	0·8	0·7	1·7	1·6
Victoria	0·8	1·1	1·7	1·8	2·6	2·7
Queensland	0·1	0·5	0·5	0·6	1·0	0.5
South Australia	3·2	4·5	7·5	5·9	6·2	6·1
Western Australia	1·6	2·0	1·8	1·2	1·2	1·6
Tasmania	1·8	1·5	1·2	1·1	1·3	1·4
Commonwealth	1·1	1·4	2·0	1·6	2·2	2·2
New Zealand	0·7	1·3	2·1	2·2	2·1	2·0
Australasia	1·1	1·4	2·0	1·7	2·2	2·2

For the whole of Australasia the decennial increase of agriculture as compared with population is shown in the following table:—

Increase of—	1861-71.	1871-81.	1881-91.	1891-1901
	per cent.	per cent.	per cent.	per cent.
Acreage under crop	100·6	107·2	22·1	47·6
Population	55·6	43·2	38·1	21·3

Although during the period of forty-one years the population of Australasia was nearly quadrupled, the area of land devoted to agriculture increased almost eightfold, and the rate of agricultural progress was more than twice that of the population. The chief progress was made during the twenty years from 1861 to 1881, and the ten years from 1891 to 1901. During the period intervening from 1881 to 1891 the population increased nearly twice as rapidly as the agricultural industry.

The progress in the seventies is what naturally might be expected, as the gold fever had altogether subsided about the end of the first period, and a large portion of the population was seeking employment of a more settled nature than was afforded by the gold-fields. It was not to be anticipated that the same rate of progress could be maintained, and the comparative decline in the eighties may be accounted for by the fact that most of the best land had been taken up. The earnest attempts of the state to assist the agriculturist in obtaining land on easy terms, however, together with the satisfactory advance in the price of wheat during the three years 1896–98, enabled the industry to show a substantial rate of progress during the ten years prior to 1902, when, although the area under crop was greater than in the previous year, the return was small.

In the following table will be found the proportion of land under crop to the total area of each state, and the same with regard to Australasia as a whole. In instituting comparisons between the several states, however, it must be borne in mind that circumstances other than the mere area in cultivation require to be taken into consideration. It would not be fair, for instance, to compare Tasmania, which has 6·57 persons per square mile, with Western Australia, which has only 0·19 inhabitant to the square mile. The table has a value chiefly because it shows how each province has progressed in cultivation of the soil during the periods quoted :—

State.	1861.	1871.	1881.	1891.	1901.	1902.
	per cent.	per cent.	per cent.	per cent.	per cent.	per cent.
New South Wales	0·15	0·20	0·29	0·44	1·44	1·13
Victoria	0·73	1·51	2·55	3·76	5·27	5·77
Queensland	0·001	0·01	0·03	0·06	0·11	0·06
South Australia	0·07	0·15	0·37	0·33	0·39	0·38
Western Australia	0·006	0·008	0·009	0·01	0·03	0·04
Tasmania	0·97	0·92	0·88	0·99	1·39	1·47
Commonwealth	0·07	0·12	0·24	0·28	0·44	0·45
New Zealand	0·10	0·50	1·60	2·13	2·40	2·40
Australasia	0·07	0·14	0·28	0·34	0·51	0·51

The subjoined table shows the proportion of cultivated area devoted to the principal crops in each province, during the year 1902. It will be seen that wheat forms the greatest percentage of the total tillage in Australasia as a whole, and in New South Wales, Victoria, South Australia, and Western Australia. Maize and sugar-cane are the principal crops in Queensland, and oats in New Zealand. In Tasmania only 16·6 per cent. of the land cultivated was under wheat, the area cut for hay forming 26·7 per cent. of the total acreage. "Other crops" also show a considerable increase in the Queensland returns—the figures being 26·6 as against 15·3 in the previous year. The advance is chiefly due to the extensive planting of quick-growing green crops in favoured places for stock-feed during the dry season.

Crop.	New South Wales.	Victoria.	Queensland.	South Australia.	Western Australia.	Tasmania.	Commonwealth.	New Zealand.	Australasia.
	per cent.	per cent.	per cent.	per cent.	per cent.	per cent.	per cent.	per cent.	per cent.
Wheat	57·0	61·4	0·7	78·5	40·3	16·6	60·9	12·1	53·1
Maize	9·0	0·3	32·6	....	0·1	....	3·6	0·8	3·1
Barley	0·2	1·2	0·2	1·0	1·7	3·4	0·9	1·7	1·0
Oats	1·9	13·4	0·0	2·3	4·5	22·3	7·0	30·2	10·7
Potatoes	0·9	1·5	1·0	0·3	0·9	14·0	1·4	2·0	1·5
Hay	21·9	17·9	7·3	14·6	45·3	26·7	18·8	4·3	16·5
Vines	0·4	0·9	0·6	1·0	1·5	....	0·7	....	0·6
Sugar-cane ..	0·9	....	31·0	....	....	....	1·2	....	1·1
Other crops..	7·3	3·4	26·6	2·3	5·2	17·0	5·5	48·9	12·4
Total	100·0	100·0	100·0	100·0	100·0	100·0	100·0	100·0	100·0

The position in which each of the principal agricultural products stood in relation to the total area under crop in Australasia, at various periods since the year 1861, may be ascertained from the following table. The figures should, however, be taken in conjunction with those giving the actual areas cultivated, for a decline in the proportion of land under any particular crop does not necessarily mean a falling-off in the area devoted to that product; on the contrary, in few instances has there been any actual retrogression. It is satisfactory to observe that there is a greater proportionate increase in the cultivation of the more valuable crops, and that, despite checks from causes due to unfavourable seasons, the area devoted to vines, sugar-cane, and "other crops" formed 14·1 per cent. of the whole in 1902, as compared with 8·6 per cent. in 1861:—

Product.	1861.	1871.	1881.	1891.	1901.	1902.
	per cent.	per cent.	per cent.	per cent.	per cent.	per cent.
Wheat	53·6	51·4	60·7	55·0	52·7	53·1
Oats	10·6	13·5	7·9	8·4	8·7	10·7
Maize	4·6	5·3	3·0	4·3	3·3	3·1
Barley	2·2	2·3	1·9	1·4	1·0	1·0
Potatoes..............	4·2	3·0	1·8	2·0	1·4	1·5
Hay	16·2	11·9	15·1	16·0	17·6	16·5
Vines	0·5	0·7	0·3	0·7	0·6	0·6
Sugar-cane............	......	0·5	0·7	1·1	1·3	1·1
Other crops	8·1	11·4	8·6	11·1	13·4	12·4
Total	100·0	100·0	100·0	100·0	100·0	100·0

WHEAT.

With the exception of Queensland and Western Australia, all the states during 1901 produced sufficient wheat for their own requirements.

and in good seasons there is a large and steadily increasing balance available for export, which finds a ready market in Great Britain, where Australian wheat is well and favourably known. For the season 1902–3, although a larger area was sown than at any previous period, the long continued dry weather caused a decline in production, the returns for Victoria and New South Wales averaging only 1·3 and 1·2 bushels per acre respectively. Taking Australasia as a whole, there was a net export of breadstuffs, during 1902, equivalent to 11,678,845 bushels of grain, valued at £2,628,000.

The subjoined table shows the progress of wheat-growing during the period of the last forty-two years:—

State.	1861.	1871.	1881.	1891.	1901.	1902.
	acres.	acres.	acres.	acres.	acres.	acres.
New South Wales	123,468	154,030	221,888	356,666	1,392,070	1,279,760
Victoria	196,922	334,609	926,729	1,332,683	1,754,417	1,994,271
Queensland	392	3,024	10,958	19,306	87,232	1,880
South Australia ...	310,636	692,508	1,768,781	1,552,423	1,743,452	1,746,842
Western Australia	13,584	25,697	21,951	26,866	93,707	92,065
Tasmania	58,823	63,332	51,757	47,584	44,084	40,898
Commonwealth	703,825	1,273,200	3,002,064	3,335,528	5,114,962	5,155,716
New Zealand	29,531	108,720	365,715	402,273	163,462	194,355
Australasia ...	733,356	1,381,920	3,367,779	3,737,801	5,278,424	5,350,071

It will be seen that, during the twenty years extending from 1861 to 1881, all the states, with the exception of Tasmania, made considerable additions to the area under wheat, the increase for the whole of Australasia being 2,634,423 acres, or an advance of 359 per cent. From 1881 to 1902 the extension of this form of cultivation has not been so general, most of the increase in area having taken place during the last few seasons, in consequence of the rise in the prices of wheat which was taken advantage of by the agriculturists of all the states, excepting South Australia and Tasmania. In these two states there were decreases in acreage, although the falling-off was partly due to the unfavourable seasons. In Australasia, as a whole, the increase in area since 1881 amounts to 1,982,292 acres—but while New South Wales shows an extension of cultivation during the period amounting to 1,057,872 acres, and Victoria an increase of 1,067,542 acres, the total increase was considerably reduced by the falling off mentioned above. At present more than one-half of the land in cultivation is devoted to wheat-growing, and in an ordinary season the produce of 750,000 acres is available for export to Europe.

The production of wheat at intervals since 1871 was as follows:—

State.	1871.	1881.	1891.	1901.	1902.
	bushels.	bushels.	bushels.	bushels.	bushels.
New South Wales	2,229,642	3,405,966	3,963,668	14,808,705	1,585,097
Victoria	4,500,795	8,714,377	13,629,370	12,127,382	2,569,364
Queensland	36,288	39,612	392,309	1,692,222	6,165
South Australia	3,967,079	8,087,032	6,436,488	8,012,762	6,354,912
Western Australia	345,368	153,657	288,810	933,101	970,571
Tasmania	847,962	977,365	930,841	963,662	876,971
Commonwealth......	11,927,134	21,378,009	25,641,486	38,537,834	12,363,080
New Zealand	2,448,203	8,297,890	10,257,738	4,046,589	7,457,915
Australasia	14,375,337	29,675,899	35,899,224	42,584,423	19,820,995

The adverse weather conditions which prevailed over the greater part of Australasia caused the wheat crop of 1901 to fall far below expectations, and it is estimated that the harvest was affected to the extent of over seventeen million bushels, while in 1902 the expected crop fell off by at least forty million bushels. In New Zealand the harvest was an exceptionally good one, the yield being at the rate of over 38 bushels per acre, an increase of nearly 14 bushels on the average of the previous year.

The greatest increase in production between 1881 and 1901 is shown by New South Wales, which in 1901 produced nearly eleven million bushels more than in 1891, and from the following statement, which gives the proportion of the total crop produced by each state in 1881, 1891, and 1901, the progress made by New South Wales will be evident, for whereas in 1881 and 1891 it only produced 11 per cent. of the total crop, in 1901 it produced nearly 35 per cent. Victoria and New Zealand show the largest declines during the period, the proportions falling from 38 per cent. and 28·6 per cent. in 1891 to 28·5 per cent. and 9·5 per cent. respectively in 1901:—

State.	1881.	1891.	1901.
	per cent.	per cent.	per cent.
New South Wales	11·5	11·0	34·8
Victoria	29·4	38·0	28·5
Queensland	0·1	1·1	3·9
South Australia	27·2	17·9	18·8
Western Australia	0·5	0·8	2·2
Tasmania.........................	3·3	2·6	2·3
New Zealand	28·0	28·6	9·5
Australasia..............	100·0	100·0	100·0

From a preceding table it will, however, be seen that in 1902 New Zealand produced nearly 40 per cent. of the total wheat crop in Australasia, and New Zealand and South Australia together, about 70 per cent.

As producers of wheat, these states are of little account when viewed in comparison with the great wheat-producing countries of the world, Australasian grown wheat last year forming less than 0·7 per cent. of the world's wheat crop. According to the estimate published by Beerbohm, the world's production of wheat in 1902 was 375,000,000 quarters, of which Australasia produced only 2,500,000 quarters. The figures for each country are appended :—

Country.	In Quarters of 480 lb.	Country.	In Quarters of 480 lb.
Europe—	000's omitted.	Africa—	000's omitted.
Russia	61,000	Algeria	3,500
France	42,000	Egypt	1,500
Hungary	22,800	Tunis	1,000
Germany	17,900	Cape Colony	500
Italy	16,000		
Spain	13,500	Total	6,500
United Kingdom	7,250		
Austria	6,200		
Roumania	9,900	America—	
Bulgaria	5,000		
Turkey	5,000	United States	85,000
Belgium	1,750	Argentine Republic	13,500
Servia	1,500	Canada	12,000
Portugal	750	Mexico	1,550
Sweden and Norway	500	Chili	1,500
Holland	750	Uruguay	1,000
Switzerland	500		
Denmark	400	Total	114,550
Greece	750		
Total	213,450	Australasia—	2,500
Asia—		Grand Total	375,000
India	28,000		
Asia Minor	5,000		
Syria	2,500		
Persia	2,500		
Total	38,000		

The yield of wheat per acre during the season 1902–3 ranged from 1·2 bushels in New South Wales to 38 bushels in New Zealand, and, with the exception of New Zealand, Tasmania, and Western Australia, was far below the average for the last ten years. The average yields per acre for each state for 1902 and during the ten years 1893–1902 are shown below :—

State.	Average Yield per acre.	
	1902.	1893–1902.
	bushels.	bushels.
New South Wales	1·20	8·8
Victoria	1·29	6·7
Queensland	3·28	15·9
South Australia	3·64	4·6
Western Australia	10·54	10·5
Tasmania	21·44	19·7
Commonwealth	2·40	6·7
New Zealand	38·37	27·2
Australasia	3·70	7·7

A yield of 7·7 bushels per acre is a very small one when compared with the following results obtained in some of the principal wheat-growing countries of the world. The averages shown are mostly based on the yields during the last ten years :—

Country.	Average Yield per acre.	Country.	Average Yield per acre.
	bushels.		bushels.
United Kingdom	32·9	India	10·5
Germany	25·6	Russia	7·6
France	18·5	Argentine Republic	11·3
Hungary	15·5	Canada (Ontario and Manitoba)	18·2
United States	13·3		

A bare statement of averages, however, is somewhat misleading. In South Australia, for example, it is found that owing to favourable conditions of culture a yield of 7 bushels is financially as satisfactory a crop as one of 15 bushels in New South Wales or of 20 bushels in New Zealand. In these states the yield could be greatly increased if cultivation of a more scientific character were adopted. Progress in this direction is being made yearly, however; but not to the extent which should prevail, although the tendency in former years simply to put the seed in the ground and await results has been outgrown, and better cultivation and the use of artificial fertilizers are becoming more general.

The average value of the wheat crop for the last five years and the value of the return per acre in each state and in New Zealand are shown below:—

State.	Value of Production.	Value per Acre.
New South Wales	£1,664,000	£1 3 11
Victoria	1,920,000	0 19 0
Queensland	137,000	2 11 3
South Australia	1,352,000	0 15 0
Western Australia	191,000	2 5 6
Tasmania	202,000	3 10 6
Commonwealth	£5,466,000	£1 0 3
New Zealand	1,153,000	4 13 6
Australasia	£6,619,000	£1 3 5

The very high value returned in New Zealand is due to the heavy yield of grain, the area under cultivation being comparatively small and specially selected; the values in Tasmania and Queensland also appear high for similar reasons; while in Western Australia the value of production was increased by the high prices obtained for wheat during portions of the years.

A detailed table of the value of the yield per acre during each of the last thirteen years is shown below for the three principal wheat-growing states—New South Wales, Victoria, and South Australia. The values are estimated on the basis of the market rates ruling in February and March of each year. It will be seen that a considerable decline took place between 1891 and 1895, due for the most part to the fall in prices rather than to any decrease of production. The effect of the rise in prices is seen in the more satisfactory results in New South Wales during the seasons ending March, 1896, 1897, and 1898; for Victoria and South Australia the drought is largely responsible for the low values in those years, also for the very low values shown in 1902–3 for Victoria and New South Wales:—

Year ending March.	Average Yield per acre.			Value of Average Yield per acre.		
	New South Wales.	Victoria.	South Australia.	New South Wales.	Victoria.	South Australia.
	bushels.	bushels.	bushels.	£ s. d.	£ s. d.	£ s. d.
1891	10·9	11·1	5·6	2 0 10	1 19 9	0 19 7
1892	11·1	10·3	4·3	2 2 6	2 2 3	0 17 11
1893	15·1	11·0	6·1	2 5 2	1 14 0	0 19 3
1894	11·0	10·4	7·9	1 10 1	1 0 1	0 18 4
1895	10·9	8·3	4·9	1 4 6	0 13 6	0 8 0
1896	8·7	4·0	4·2	1 17 0	0 17 9	0 19 10
1897	10·2	4·5	1·7	2 3 5	1 3 8	0 8 7
1898	10·6	6·4	2·6	2 4 2	1 6 2	0 11 3
1899	7·0	9·1	4·9	0 19 0	0 19 9	0 13 7
1900	9·5	7·0	4·6	1 5 0	0 18 9	0 12 4
1901	10·6	8·9	5·9	1 6 9	1 1 0	0 16 2
1902	10·6	6·9	4·6	1 16 3	1 3 7	0 17 3
1903	1·2	1·3	3·6	0 7 11	0 7 10	1 1 7
*1904	19·2	12·6	7·6	......	......	......

* Estimated.

The rates just given, as well as elsewhere in this chapter, represent farm prices, and not values at the place of consumption.

The average consumption of wheat per head of population in each of the six states and in New Zealand for the last decade was as stated below. The large proportion of adult male population in Western Australia accounts for the high figures for that province :—

	Bushels.
New South Wales	5·9
Victoria	5·2
Queensland	5·6
South Australia	6·3
Western Australia	8·6
Tasmania	7·2
New Zealand	7·7

For the whole of Australasia, the average consumption was 6·2 bushels per head, which is larger than the quantity consumed in any other part of the world for which records are available, with the exception of France and Canada.

The following table shows the net imports or exports of wheat and flour of each of the states during the year 1902, 1 ton of flour being taken as equal to 50 bushels of grain. The exporting states were New South Wales, Victoria, and South Australia. Between 1896 and 1902, New South Wales has almost been able to supply the wheat required for the food of its inhabitants, and in 1901 exported over 7,700,000 bushels. In the early part of 1902, heavy exports were also made, but towards the close of the year, when the harvest prospects were discouraging, shipments ceased and extensive imports were arranged for. The year, nevertheless, showed an excess of exports amounting to 2,774,782 bushels. During the last few years Tasmania as a rule produced enough wheat for home consumption, and in 1901 had a small surplus available for export :—

State.	Net Imports. Bushels.	Net Exports. Bushels.
New South Wales	....	2,774,782
Victoria	....	5,233,255
Queensland	1,957,187	....
South Australia	....	6,541,495
Western Australia	804,348	....
Tasmania	51,732	....
Commonwealth	....	11,736,265
New Zealand	57,420	....
Australasia	....	11,678,845

The records for the six states which form the Commonwealth show that since 1879 there were only four years during which they were forced to import wheat from places outside their boundaries. These years were 1886, 1889, 1896, and 1897. In the first-named year the wheat crop was a partial failure in Victoria and South Australia, and almost a complete failure in New South Wales and Queensland. In 1889 there was a general failure in New South Wales and Victoria. In 1896 the crop failed in Victoria, and in the following year, that state for the first time in twenty-two years was compelled to import wheat, the net import, however, being only 61,160 bushels. The following statement gives the figures for the Commonwealth for the twenty years since 1882:—

Year.	Wheat Crop.	Net Export of Breadstuffs.	Year.	Wheat Crop.	Net Export of Breadstuffs.
	bushels.	bushels.		bushels.	bushels.
1882	21,378,009	5,751,130	1893	32,759,693	8,829,941
1883	21,492,505	4,742,290	1894	36,929,947	11,916,782
1884	35,714,456	17,130,843	1895	30,855,812	6,774,377
1885	30,559,060	11,583,644	1896	19,557,726	(—) 4,347,168
1886	20,165,988	(—) 603,532	1897	20,880,479	(—) 3,641,306
1887	28,899,220	4,265,924	1898	28,241,409	1,341,596
1888	35,930,697	10,643,673	1899	41,417,853	11,581,198
1889	19,757,509	(—) 2,107,136	1900	48,353,402	13,965,610
1890	34,039,289	8,836,170	1901	38,537,834	24,770,592
1891	27,118,259	10,646,298	1902	12,363,080	11,736,265
1892	25,675,265	4,126,538			

(—) denotes excess of imports.

In ordinary seasons Australasia ranks about sixth amongst the exporting countries; still, its contribution to the world's markets does not form more than one-thirtieth of the demand, and it cannot, therefore, be said to form a factor of any consequence in the trade.

The United Kingdom is the largest importer of wheat, and the British demand largely influences the price throughout the world. The average London prices per quarter of 8 bushels during the last decennial period were as follow:—

Year.	Price per quarter.	Year.	Price per quarter.
	s. d.		s. d.
1893	26 4	1898	34 0
1894	22 10	1899	25 8
1895	23 1	1900	26 11
1896	26 2	1901	26 8
1897	30 2	1902	28 1

During 1902, Great Britain imported 5,396,000 tons of wheat and flour, the countries of origin being as follows :—

	tons.	per cent.
United States	3,248,000	60·19
Argentine Republic..................	227,000	4·21
Russia and Austria..................	379,000	7·03
Other Foreign Countries	270,000	5·00
Total from Foreign Countries ...	4,124,000	76·43
India	442,000	8·19
Canada	611,000	11·32
Australasia	219,000	4·06
Total from British Possessions ...	1,272,000	23·57
Total	5,396,000	100·00

OATS.

The cultivation of oats, which come next to wheat in importance as a grain crop, is increasing in Australasia, as the following figures show:—

State.	1871.	1881.	1891.	1901.	1902.
	acres.	acres.	acres.	acres.	acres.
New South Wales...... .	13,795	16,348	12,958	32,245	42,992
Victoria	175,944	146,995	190,157	329,150	433,489
Queensland	131	88	715	1,535	78
South Australia	3,586	3,023	12,637	34,660	50,296
Western Australia	1,474	827	1,301	9,641	10,180
Tasmania	29,631	27,535	28,360	54,089	55,058
Commonwealth......	224,561	194,816	246,128	461,320	592,093
New Zealand............	139,185	243,387	323,508	405,924	483,659
Australasia...........	363,746	438,203	569,636	867,244	1,075,752

During 1900 there was a considerable increase in cultivation of oats, owing to the demand for this cereal created by the South African war. The colony of New Zealand furnishes two-thirds of the production. In New South Wales the cultivation has been comparatively neglected; in Victoria and Tasmania, however, it is next to wheat in importance; whilst in Queensland and Western Australia the climate is ill-adapted to the cultivation of oats, and the yield is small and counts for very little in the total production of the grain. In 1902 the yield of oats in all the Commonwealth states was small. The output of New Zealand, however, increased by over 6,700,000 bushels, the increase being nearly equal to the whole yield of the Commonwealth.

The total yield in each state for the period covered by the preceding table was as follows :—

State.	1871.	1881.	1891.	1901	1902.
	bushels.	bushels.	bushels.	bushels.	bushels.
New South Wales ...	280,887	356,566	276,259	687,179	351,758
Victoria	3,299,889	3,612,111	4,412,730	6,724,900	4,402,982
Queensland	......	1,121	16,669	42,208	520
South Australia	38,894	32,219	80,876	469,254	620,823
Western Australia...	28,330	8,270	18,539	158,638	161,714
Tasmania	593,477	783,129	873,173	1,702,659	1,752,745
Commonwealth ...	4,241,477	4,793,416	5,678,246	9,784,838	7,290,542
New Zealand	3,726,810	6,924,848	11,009,020	15,045,233	21,766,708
Australasia	7,968,287	11,718,264	16,687,266	24,830,071	29,057,250

The average yields per acre in each state in 1902, and during the ten years 1893–1902 are shown below :—

State.	Average yield per acre.	
	1902.	1893–1902.
	bushels.	bushels.
New South Wales	8·2	17·9
Victoria	10·2	18·4
Queensland	6·7	18·8
South Australia	12·3	10·4
Western Australia	15·9	16·3
Tasmania	31·8	29·4
Commonwealth	12·2	18·8
New Zealand	45·0	36·6
Australasia	27·0	27·4

In all the provinces which grow oats to any extent, with the exception of New Zealand, Tasmania, and South Australia, the yield last year was considerably below the decennial average. New Zealand had the very high average of 45 bushels per acre, which compares very favourably with the averages which prevailed during 1894–99 in the following principal oat-growing countries of the world :—

Country.	Average yield per acre.	Country.	Average yield per acre.
	bushels.		bushels.
United Kingdom ...	40·0	United States	23·7
Germany	35·6	France	26·0
Canada	31·1	Austria.............	22·7
Hungary..............	27·4	Russia, in Europe.	15·5

The average value of the oats crop and the return per acre, in each of the Commonwealth states and New Zealand, for the last five seasons, will be found below :—

State.	Value.	Value per acre.
New South Wales	£63,000	£2 0 8
Victoria	690,000	2 1 5
Queensland	2,000	3 6 11
South Australia	46,000	1 8 9
Western Australia	16,000	2 13 4
Tasmania	180,000	3 9 3
Commonwealth.	£997,000	£2 3 11
New Zealand................	1,703,000	3 19 0
Australasia.............	£2,700,000	£3 1 1

The high values per acre shown by New Zealand and Tasmania were caused by an increase in the local quotations, consequent on the demands from the drought-stricken states. Large quantities of oats and oaten hay were also exported during 1902 to South Africa by the two provinces mentioned.

The net import or export of oats by each of the states is given in the following table. New Zealand was the only province which exported this cereal to any considerable extent in 1902, although Tasmania and Victoria also exported fairly large quantities. Owing to the late war in South Africa, a large demand for oats as horse-feed was created, and for the year ended 31st March, 1903, no less than 3,988,000 bushels of oats, valued at £511,558, were exported to that country by New Zealand alone. The total export of oats from New Zealand amounted to £666,644, of which a quantity valued at over £60,000 was sent to New South Wales. Tasmania also took advantage of the shortage on the mainland, and exported oats to the value of £139,265, of which an amount of £109,695 was consigned to New South Wales.

State.	Net Imports.		Net Exports.	
New South Wales............	1,577,236	bushels.	....	bushels.
Victoria	....	,,	1,643,130	,,
Queensland.....................	301,747	,,	....	,,
South Australia...............	....	,,	134,277	
Western Australia	638,912	,,	....	,,
Tasmania..........	....	,,	972,839	
Commonwealth ...	....	,,	232,351	
New Zealand..................	....	,,	5,182,240	,,
Australasia.........	....	,,	5,414,591	,,

According to a carefully-compiled estimate of the average production in the principal countries growing oats throughout the world, issued by the Board of Agriculture of the United Kingdom, the yield of this grain in 1902 was as follows:—

	Quarters.
Europe	250,953,112
North America	109,000,449
Africa	514,125
Australasia	3,632,156
Total	364,099,842

To this may probably be added 5,250,000 quarters raised in Asia and South America, making the total output about 370,000,000 quarters.

MAIZE.

Maize is, next to sugar-cane, the principal crop grown in Queensland, and is one of the most important products of New South Wales. In the other states the climate is not suited to its growth, and the cultivation of the cereal extends to only about 23,000 acres. The following figures show that fair progress has been made since 1861 in the area devoted to this crop:—

State.	1871.	1881.	1891.	1901.	1902.
	acres.	acres.	acres.	acres.	acres.
New South Wales	119,956	117,478	174,577	167,733	202,437
Victoria	1,709	1,783	8,230	10,020	10,906
Queensland	20,329	46,480	101,598	116,983	89,923
Other States.........	113	36	23	530	186
Commonwealth	142,107	165,777	284,428	295,266	303,452
New Zealand	....	3,177	5,447	12,503	12,038
Australasia ...	142,107	168,954	289,875	307,769	315,490

The production in the same years was as follows:—

State.	1871.	1881.	1891.	1901.	1902.
	bushels.	bushels.	bushels.	bushels.	bushels.
New South Wales	4,015,973	4,330,956	5,721,706	3,844,993	3,049,269
Victoria	39,833	81,007	461,447	615,472	750,524
Queensland	508,090	1,313,655	3,077,915	2,569,118	1,033,329
Other States	2,600	648	483	5,611	2,498
Commonwealth	4,556,896	5,726,266	9,261,551	7,035,194	4,835,620
New Zealand	....	127,257	238,746	571,834	607,609
Australasia ...	4,556,806	5,853,523	9,500,297	7,607,028	5,443,229

It will be seen from the tables given above that although there has been an increase in acreage amounting to over 25,000 acres since

1891, the production declined by about 1,894,000 bushels in 1901, and by about 4,000,000 bushels in 1902, the falling off being accounted for by the unfavourable seasons.

The following table shows the average yield of each state and of Australasia for 1902, and for the ten years ended 1902:—

State.	Average yield per acre.	
	1902.	1893-1902.
	bushels.	bushels.
New South Wales	15·1	27·6
Victoria	68·8	55·4
Queensland	11·5	21·5
Western Australia	13·4	16·6
Commonwealth	15·9	26·3
New Zealand	50·4	42·1
Australasia	17·2	26·9

The averages for Victoria and New Zealand are of little value, as the area under maize in those provinces is small and very favourably situated; while Western Australia, during the period, has never had more than 250 acres under this crop—the average yield for ten years being less than 17 bushels per acre under cultivation, producing 12,498 bushels.

The average value of the crop for the last five seasons, and the average return per acre, will be found below:—

State.	Average value of crop.	Average value per acre.		
	£	£	s.	d.
New South Wales	838,000	4	5	1
Victoria	101,000	9	16	1
Queensland	340,000	3	1	10
Other States	400	3	14	9
Commonwealth	1,279,400	4	0	8
New Zealand	90,000	5	19	11
Australasia	1,369,400	4	2	5

The net import or export of maize by each state during 1902 was as follows:—

State.	Net Imports. bushels.	Net Exports. bushels.
New South Wales	1,218,668	....
Victoria	....	445,293
Queensland	1,100,955	....
South Australia	3,878	....
Western Australia	6,034	....
Commonwealth	1,884,242	....
New Zealand	....	225,829
Australasia	1,658,413	....

Of the maize imported by New South Wales and Queensland, over 1,500,000 bushels, valued at £246,000, was shipped by the Argentine Republic.

It is rather curious that the only states which import maize to any extent are New South Wales and Queensland, where it is principally grown. In Australasia, this grain does not enter into consumption as an article of food, as it does in other countries, and particularly in America, which produces and consumes more than 80 per cent. of the whole maize crop of the world. The following statement shows the world's production of maize during the past two years :—

	1901.	1902.
	Quarters, 000's omitted.	Quarters, 000's omitted.
North America	160,000	310,000
South East Europe	40,000	24,000
Argentine	9,500	10,000
Australasia	950	700
Africa and elsewhere	50,550	47,300
Total	261,000	392,000

In 1901, owing to the low yields in the United States, the world's production of maize was the smallest in recent records. This shortage was responsible for a marked decrease during 1902 in the American exports of bacon and hams, the exports to Great Britain alone showing a decline of 150,000,000 lb. on the figures of the previous year.

Barley.

Of the cereal productions of Australasia, barley is grown on the smallest acreage. The area under this crop at different periods was as follows :—

State.	1871.	1881.	1891.	1901.	1902.
	acres.	acres.	acres.	acres.	acres.
New South Wales	3,461	6,427	4,459	6,023	4,557
Victoria	16,772	48,652	45,021	32,423	37,716
Queensland	971	256	739	11,775	430
South Australia	17,225	11,953	11,461	15,517	21,493
Western Australia	5,083	3,679	3,738	2,719	3,874
Tasmania	4,275	4,597	2,650	6,104	8,281
Commonwealth	47,787	75,564	68,068	74,561	76,351
New Zealand	13,305	29,808	24,268	26,514	27,921
Australasia	61,092	105,372	92,336	101,075	104,272

For the same years the production was as stated below :—

State.	1871.	1881.	1891.	1901.	1902.
	bushels.	bushels.	bushels.	bushels.	bushels.
New South Wales........	55,284	135,218	98,446	106,361	18,233
Victoria	335,506	927,566	830,741	693,851	561,144
Queensland.................	11,836	3,207	21,302	277,037	3,595
South Australia...........	164,161	137,165	167,183	243,362	317,155
Western Australia	5,083	36,790	48,594	35,841	45,778
Tasmania	76,812	102,475	71,686	167,485	201,133
Commonwealth	648,682	1,342,421	1,172,952	1,523,937	1,147,038
New Zealand	287,646	664,093	688,683	855,993	1,136,232
Australasia..............	936,328	2,006,514	1,861,635	2,379,930	2,283,270

The average yield of barley per acre in each state for 1902, and for the ten years ended 1902, is given in the following table :—

State.	Average Yield per Acre.	
	1902.	1893–1902.
	bushels.	bushels.
New South Wales	4·0	15·3
Victoria	15·0	17·2
Queensland	8·4	19·0
South Australia	14·8	13·3
Western Australia	11·8	11·9
Tasmania	24·3	23·7
Commonwealth	15·0	16·7
New Zealand	40·7	30·2
Australasia	21·9	20·4

As in the case of the other three cereals which have just been dealt with, New Zealand had a far larger yield of barley per acre than any of the Commonwealth states, and compares favourably with the following countries, which averaged during 1894–99—United Kingdom, 32·7 bushels per acre; Germany, 30·3; United States, 21·8; and France, 20·3 bushels per acre. Barley is not cultivated in these states to the extent it deserves, and to the total world's production of 1,050,100,000 bushels in 1902 Australasia contributed only a little over 2,000,000 bushels. In fruitful seasons Australasia produces sufficient barley, exclusive of that required for malt, for home requirements, and a small surplus for export; but if the combined trade in barley and malt be considered, all the provinces, with the exception of Tasmania and New Zealand, were dependent in 1902 upon external sources. The trade in barley and malt for the Commonwealth and New Zealand in 1902 was as follows:—

State.	Barley.		Malt.	
	Net Imports.	Net Exports.	Net Imports.	Net Exports.
	bushels.	bushels.	bushels.	bushels.
New South Wales	214,141	....	356,639	....
Victoria	661,122	....	....	305,390
Queensland	....	82,184	111,277	....
South Australia	....	8,240	....	10,097
Western Australia	61,780	....	149,665	....
Tasmania	....	25,375	....	4,457
Commonwealth	821,244	....	297,637	....
New Zealand	....	151,314	828	....
Australasia	669,930	....	298,465	....

The average value of the barley crop and the return of this cereal per acre during the past five seasons will be found below:—

State.	Average value of barley crop.	Average value per acre.
	£	£ s. d.
New South Wales	11,000	1 14 9
Victoria	161,000	3 2 9
Queensland	20,000	3 6 9
South Australia	38,000	2 4 8
Western Australia	7,000	2 6 9
Tasmania	24,000	3 15 0
Commonwealth	261,000	2 18 0
New Zealand	167,000	4 7 11
Australasia	428,000	3 6 10

Owing to the rapid progress of the brewing industry in Australia, increased attention is now being given to the cultivation of barley for malting purposes. Several of the larger malting companies are offering special inducements to farmers to cultivate the crop, and it is expected that the area devoted to it will show a considerable increase in the near future.

POTATOES.

The cultivation of the potato is not confined to any particular state. Victoria, New Zealand, and Tasmania have the largest areas under this crop, but New Zealand shows the greatest production. The largest area under potatoes was recorded in 1899, when no less than 176,381 acres were cultivated. Of this area New South Wales, Victoria, and New Zealand supplied 127,421 acres as against 96,409 acres in 1900. The decrease is accounted for chiefly by the two states last mentioned, where this crop was abandoned to a certain extent in favour of oats for which a large demand was created by the South African war The following table shows the acreage under potatoes in each state :—

State.	1871.	1881.	1891.	1901.	1902.
	acres.	acres.	acres.	acres.	acres.
New South Wales	14,770	15,943	22,560	26,158	19,444
Victoria	39,064	39,129	57,334	40,058	49,706
Queensland..................	3,121	5,086	9,173	13,338	2,899
South Australia	3,156	6,136	6,892	6,248	7,763
Western Australia	494	278	532	1,829	2,069
Tasmania	8,154	9,670	16,393	25,444	34,625
Commonwealth...	68,759	76,242	112,884	113,075	116,506
New Zealand...............	11,933	22,540	27,266	31,259	31,408
Australasia	80,692	98,782	140,150	144,334	147,914

As in the case of the area the production was highest in 1899, when it amounted to 629,275 tons. Of this New South Wales, Victoria, and New Zealand contributed 476,842 tons, as against 392,758 tons in 1902. The production for each state was as follows :—

State.	1871.	1881.	1891.	1901.	1902.
	tons.	tons.	tons.	tons.	tons.
New South Wales	44,758	44,323	62,283	39,146	30,732
Victoria	125,841	134,290	109,786	125,474	168,759
Queensland	6,585	11,984	25,018	39,530	3,257
South Australia	10,989	18,154	27,824	15,059	28,312
Western Australia	1,457	556	1,596	5,665	6,200
Tasmania	22,608	33,565	63,100	114,704	163,518
Commonwealth...	212,238	242,872	289,607	339,578	400,778
New Zealand...............	42,130	121,890	162,046	206,815	193,267
Australasia	254,368	364,762	451,653	546,393	594,045

The average production of potatoes per acre is next given, for 1902, and for the ten years ended 1902. New Zealand, it will be seen, shows a considerably larger return than any of the other provinces :—

State.	Average Yield per Acre.	
	1902.	1893-1902.
	tons.	tons.
New South Wales	1·6	2·3
Victoria	3·4	3·1
Queensland	1·1	2·1
South Australia	3·6	2·6
Western Australia	3·0	3·1
Tasmania	4·7	3·9
Commonwealth	3·4	3·0
New Zealand	6·1	5·9
Australasia	4·0	3·6

Only three of the states are in a position to export potatoes in any quantity—Tasmania, Victoria, and New Zealand. The surplus in Victoria, though at one time considerable, has now very much decreased. The following were the imports or exports of potatoes by each state and New Zealand in 1902 :—

State.	Net Imports.	Net Exports.
	tons.	tons.
New South Wales	50,284	......
Victoria	......	22,053
Queensland	27,759	......
South Australia	1,974	
Western Australia	12,116	......
Tasmania	......	67,944
Commonwealth	2,136	......
New Zealand	......	17,679
Australasia	......	15,543

The average value of the potato crop and the return per acre for the past five years will be found below :—

State.	Value of crop.	Average value per acre.
	£	£ s. d.
New South Wales	230,000	8 6 4
Victoria	606,000	13 4 10
Queensland	82,000	9 12 11
South Australia	76,000	10 12 11
Western Australia	34,000	16 13 2
Tasmania	440,000	16 17 2
Commonwealth	1,468,000	12 12 4
New Zealand	636,000	19 0 10
Australasia	2,104,000	14 0 6

These values are remarkably high, but the ruling prices in 1901 and 1902 were far in excess of those realised for some considerable time.

Hay.

Considerable quantities of wheat, oats, barley, and lucerne are grown for the purpose of being converted into hay, but the area cut varies, of course, according to the season. The area cut for hay has largely increased since 1881, as will be seen from the table appended :—

State.	1871.	1881.	1891.	1901.	1902.
	acres.	acres.	acres.	acres.	acres.
New South Wales	51,805	146,610	163,863	442,163	491,918
Victoria	103,206	212,150	369,498	659,239	580,884
Queensland	3,828	16,926	30,655	63,055	20,068
South Australia	97,812	333,467	304,171	369,796	325,789
Western Australia	*14,342	24,445	28,534	92,964	104,505
Tasmania	31,578	34,790	45,445	61,495	66,038
Commonwealth	302,571	768,388	942,166	1,688,712	1,589,202
New Zealand	30,717	68,423	46,652	236,465	258,479
Australasia	333,288	836,811	988,818	1,925,177	1,847,681

* In 1869.

In New Zealand, for all the years prior to 1901, the areas shown only include the extent of sown grasses cut for hay. It is not possible to quote for the earlier years the area under wheat, oats, &c., cut for this purpose. Similarly, the production shown below only includes the quantity of grass cut :—

State.	1871.	1881.	1891.	1901.	1902.
	tons.	tons.	tons.	tons.	tons.
New South Wales.........	77,460	198,532	209,417	472,621	243,379
Victoria	144,637	238,793	505,246	884,369	601,272
Queensland	6,278	19,640	58,842	122,039	23,181
South Australia............	98,266	240,827	193,317	346,467	308,825
Western Australia	14,288	24,445	28,534	91,517	91,593
Tasmania	30,891	44,957	66,996	109,383	89,210
Commonwealth...	371,820	767,194	1,062,352	2,026,396	1,357,460
New Zealand..............	35,674	89,081	67,361	94,476	104,016
Australasia.........	407,494	856,275	1,129,713	2,120,872	1,461,476

The average yield of hay per acre will be found in the next table, the periods covered being the year 1902 and the ten years which closed with 1902 :—

State.	Average yield per acre.	
	1902.	1893–1902.
	tons.	tons.
New South Wales	0·5	0·9
Victoria	1·0	1·2
Queensland	1·1	1·9
South Australia	0·9	0·8
Western Australia	0·9	0·9
Tasmania	1·4	1·4
Commonwealth	0·8	1·0
New Zealand	1·5	1·8
Australasia	0·9	1·1

The greater portion of the hay is produced from wheat, although in New South Wales, Victoria, Queensland, and New Zealand there are large areas under oaten and lucerne hay, which are in great demand and readily sell at remunerative prices; in fact, so profitable is the return from oaten hay, that in New South Wales and Queensland the cultivation of oats for threshing is practically neglected for the sake of hay. For the most part, hay is grown in each province in quantities sufficient for its own requirements, New South Wales, Queensland, and Western Australia ordinarily being the only states which import to any extent.

The net import or export of hay and chaff by each state and New Zealand during the year 1902 was as follows:—

State.	Net Imports. tons.	Net Exports. tons.
New South Wales	293,810	....
Victoria	....	264,221
Queensland	48,870	....
South Australia	....	98,279
Western Australia	932	....
Tasmania	....	30,626
Commonwealth	....	49,514
New Zealand	....	1,636
Australasia	....	51,150

The value of the return from hay in 1902–3 was higher than that of any other crop; the value in each state and the return per acre will be found below:—

State.	Total Value of Hay Crop. £	Average Value per Acre. £	s.	d.
New South Wales	1,303,000	2	12	10
Victoria	3,070,000	5	5	8
Queensland	125,000	6	4	0
South Australia	1,535,000	4	14	2
Western Australia	554,000	5	5	6
Tasmania	451,000	6	16	4
Commonwealth	7,038,000	4	8	7
New Zealand	1,195,000	4	12	5
Australasia	8,233,000	4	9	1

The above averages, with the exception of New South Wales, are higher than those realised for some years past, the increase being accounted for by the enhanced prices realised for all descriptions of fodder owing to the unfavourable season experienced over a great part of Australasia. In 1902 Victoria and South Australia found profitable markets in New South Wales and Queensland for their hay and chaff. It will be seen that the net imports into New South Wales were 293,810 tons, and into Queensland 48,870 tons. Of the New South Wales supplies 160,000 tons, or more than one-half, came from Victoria, while nearly 90,000 tons came from South Australia. With the improved conditions now prevailing, New South Wales should be in a position to supply her own requirements, and the other states will, therefore, have to secure a market elsewhere for the disposal of their surplus products.

Green Forage and Sown Grasses.

The cultivation of maize, sorghum, barley, oats, and other cereals or green food in addition to lucerne and grass is confined chiefly to the districts where dairy farming is carried on. The following table shows the area under such green food in 1891, 1901, and 1902, and it will be seen that there have been large developments in most of the states especially in New South Wales.

The return from the cultivation of green forage in all the states during the season 1901-1902 is estimated at £1,003,000, or nearly £3 an acre.

State.	Green Food.			Sown Grasses.		
	1891.	1901.	1902.	1891.	1901.	1902.
	acres.	acres.	acres.	acres.	acres.	acres.
New South Wales..	32,138	110,215	109,146	333,238	467,339	477,629
Victoria...	9,202	32,795	30,720	174,982	162,954	565,635
Queensland	10,727	39,793	51,279	20,921	34,679	24,286
South Australia ...	6,416	13,695	14,937	17,519	23,510	23,636
Western Australia	238	1,024	*1,000	......	11,132	*12,000
Tasmania	1,101	4,082	3,355	208,596	314,422	319,090
Commonwealth	59,822	201,604	210,437	755,256	1,014,536	1,422,276
New Zealand	118,484	199,508	205,357	7,357,229	11,620,178	11,808,215
Australasia ...	178,306	401,112	415,794	8,112,485	12,634,714	13,230,491

* Estimated.

In Victoria, Tasmania, and New Zealand various areas of sown grasses are cut for seed, chiefly rye grass and cocksfoot, the total quantity of grass seed produced in 1902 being 8,778 tons, valued at £202,964. The production in Victoria was 141 tons; in Tasmania, 536 tons; and in New Zealand, 8,101 tons. The acreage on which this grass seed was produced is included in the total given above for sown grasses, and amounted to 1,568 acres in Victoria, 3,879 acres in Tasmania and 55,765 acres in New Zealand. The prosperity of New Zealand is largely due to its rich meadow lands, which have been created by human industry and were not the free gift of nature. Last year nearly 12,000,000 acres were under artificial grasses in the colony, or about ten times the area devoted to the crop in the Commonwealth. The productiveness of these pastures is very great.

In the Victorian returns "sown grasses" show an increase of over 400,000 acres on the figures of the previous year. This is accounted for by the fact that the total includes for the first time bush land on cultivated holdings on which imported grass, clover, &c., has spread without cultivation, also burnt off scrub land on which grass has been sown without ploughing.

THE VINE.

The history of the vine in Australia dates from the year 1828, when cuttings from the celebrated vineyards of France, Spain, and the Rhine Valley were planted in the Hunter River District of New South Wales, forming the nursery for the principal vineyards of that state. Years afterwards the vine was planted in the Murray River District and other parts of New South Wales, and was afterwards introduced into Victoria and South Australia, and is now cultivated in all the provinces of the Australian continent. In South Australia a large number of Germans are employed in the industry of wine-making.

The climate and soil of Australia are peculiarly adapted to the successful cultivation of the vine, and with an increasing local demand, and the opening up of a market in England, where Australian wines have obtained due appreciation, the future expansion of wine-growing appears fairly assured. The fact that the vineyards in these States have suffered comparatively little from the ravages of phylloxera, which have had such a disastrous effect on immense areas of the European vineyards, is an additional reason why the vine-growers of Australia should look forward to largely-increased operations for their industry.

The progress of vine cultivation since the year 1861 is illustrated by the table subjoined. The areas given include the vines producing table-fruit, as well as those cultivated for wine-making, also the young vines not yet in bearing :—

State.	1871.	1881.	1891.	1901.	1902.
	acres.	acres.	acres.	acres.	acres.
New South Wales	4,152	4,027	8,281	8,606	8,790
Victoria	5,523	4,928	24,483	28,592	28,374
Queensland	568	1,212	1,988	1,990	1,559
South Australia............	5,455	4,202	12,314	20,960	21,692
Western Australia	692	527	1,604	3,724	3,425
Australia	16,290	14,891	48,079	62,772	63,840
New Zealand...............	....	....	....	543	705
Australasia...........	....	....	....	64,315	64,545

At present the area devoted to vines is much larger in Victoria and South Australia than in the other states; in the former state 3,891 and in the latter 9,378 acres have been added to the vineyard area since 1891. This is not great progress compared with Algeria, for example, which has already 375,136 acres under vines, although systematic planting dates only from 1849, or the Argentine with 112,467 acres; nevertheless it is a hopeful sign in Australia, where patient waiting for the harvest to be gathered years hence is not a characteristic of the agriculturist. The progress of New South Wales has been very slight, the area under vines in 1902 being only 509 acres more than in 1891. The introduction of phylloxera into the county of Cumberland somewhat retarded this industry as most of the table grapes are grown there, but recently the Government has propagated a large number of phylloxera-resistant stocks, which are being disposed of to vignerons at cost price, and better progress may be expected in the near future. Vine-growing has never been carried on to any extent in Tasmania or New Zealand, although there are numerous places in the latter colony suited for growing vines for the manufacture of both wine and raisins. The area under vines in New Zealand in 1901 was returned at 543 acres, and in 1902 at 705 acres.

The following tables show the progress made in wine-growing during the last thirty-two years :—

State.	1871.	1881.	1891.	1901.	1902.
	gallons.	gallons.	gallons.	gallons.	gallons.
New South Wales.........	413,321	513,688	913,107	868,479	806,140
Victoria	713,589	539,191	1,554,130	1,981,475	1,547,188
Queensland..................	....	72,121	168,526	148,835	100,852
South Australia............	852,315	313,060	801,835	2,077,923	2,145,525
Western Australia	....	99,600	166,664	119,500	185,735
Australia	1,979,225	1,537,660	3,604,262	5,196,212	4,785,440

The production of table-grapes during the same period is shown below :—

State.	1871.	1881.	1891.	1901.	1902.
	tons.	tons.	tons.	tons.	tons.
New South Wales.........	508	1,103	3,694	3,475	3,561
Victoria	1,545	740	2,791	5,110	4,327
Queensland..................	....	255	1,169	1,814	400
South Australia............	1,692	1,498	4,590	12,608	11,797
Western Australia	....	....	....	400	*400
Australia...	3,745	3,596	12,244	23,407	20,485

* Estimated.

Among other produce of the vineyards may be mentioned 6,800 gallons of brandy in New South Wales, while Victoria and South

Australia produced respectively 39,256 cwt. and 16,448 cwt. of raisins and currants, the latter being an advance of nearly 6,000 cwt. on the output of the previous year. Victoria produces much more brandy than any of the other states, but it is not wholly made from grapes, and the figures cannot be ascertained.

It is impossible to tabulate the average wine-yield of all the states, as in many instances the acreage under cultivation for wine-making purposes cannot be separated from young unproductive vineyards or areas cultivated for table varieties of the grape only. Making due allowance for this fact, it would appear that the average production for the season 1901–1902, which was a very unfavourable one, was about 177 gallons in New South Wales, 88 gallons in Queensland, 72 gallons in Western Australia, and 77 gallons in Victoria. Taking an average year, the production for Australia may be set down at 190 gallons.

Compared with the wine production of other countries, that of Australia is certainly trifling. In 1898, the latest year for which information is available, the world's production was estimated at 2,716,000,000 gallons, to which Australia only contributed 4,000,000 gallons; while in 1901 the production of Australia was returned at 5,000,000 gallons.

The following table illustrates the progress made in the export of Australian wine to countries outside of Australasia since 1881. It will be noticed that in 1901, the trade with foreign countries had grown to seventeen times the value in 1881, while the number of gallons exported had also increased very largely. The 1901 figures are exclusive of Queensland, 39 gallons, valued at £19; and Western Australia, 173 gallons, valued at £116:—

State.	1881.		1891.		1901.	
	Quantity.	Value.	Quantity.	Value.	Quantity.	Value.
	gallons.	£	gallons.	£	gallons.	£
New South Wales..	13,271	3,520	12,368	2,904	8,242	1,923
Victoria	5,588	2,341	142,294	26,152	340,353	43,327
South Australia	1,751	580	227,681	39,054	485,671	67,136
Australia ...	20,610	6,441	382,343	68,110	834,266	112,386

In 1902 the export of Australian wine to countries outside of Australasia had increased to 1,011,487 gallons, valued at £122,362.

Including the inter-state as well as the foreign trade, the exports of each state during the same years are shown below. The figures for 1901 are exclusive of Queensland, 39 gallons, valued at £19;

Western Australia, 185 gallons, valued at £122; and Tasmania, 24 gallons, valued at £27.

State.	1881.		1891.		901.	
	Quantity.	Value.	Quantity.	Value.	Quantity.	Value.
	gallons.	£	gallons.	£	gallons.	£
New South Wales..	22,377	7,233	54,143	11,644	39,651	12,256
Victoria	12,544	5,388	160,982	32,516	364,413	50,950
South Australia......	54,001	12,637	285,107	58,282	593,357	91,548
Australia ...	88,922	25,258	500,232	102,442	997,421	154,754

In 1902 the inter-state and foreign exports had increased to 1,338,419 gallons, valued at £205,655.

The total value of the grape crop and the average return per acre in the Australian states, for the year 1902, will be found below:—

State.	Total value of crop.	Average value per acre—	
		Of Total Area under Vines.	Of Productive Vines.
	£	£ s. d.	£ s. d.
New South Wales	102,278	11 12 8	13 4 3
Victoria	320,376	11 5 10	12 11 0
Queensland	18,618	11 18 10	14 6 0
South Australia	260,846	12 0 6	14 1 8
Western Australia............	41,593	11 15 9	14 12 6
Commonwealth	743,711	11 15 8	13 5 11
New Zealand	8,570	12 3 1	....
Australasia	752,281	11 12 7	13 5 11

The average value per acre of productive vines cannot be shown for New Zealand, as the area is not distinguished.

The Government of Victoria made provision for assisting the wine industry in that state by establishing wineries. Under safeguarding regulations it undertook to advance up to £3,000 to each company on its formation, and a sum of £8,600 was advanced to companies at Rutherglen, Stawell, Mooroopna, and Yarrawonga.

The removal of the border duties has had a remarkably invigorating effect upon the South Australian inter-state wine trade. During the five years which preceded federation, South Australian inter-state exports averaged only 48,000 gallons; while last year the total reached 160,000 gallons. The progress of the trade with New South Wales is especially noticeable, the increase during the period mentioned being over 61,000 gallons. Victorian growers have also taken advantage of the removal of the border duties, and during the last three years the inter-state trade has increased from 5,000 to 55,000 gallons. Vignerons in the county of Cumberland in New South Wales, who depend upon table grapes for their chief returns, have suffered severely in recent years owing to New Zealand closing her markets to their grapes, through fear of introducing phylloxera, and the loss of this market has probably depreciated the value of table grapes in Cumberland and Camden at least 30 per cent.

Sugar-cane.

The growth of the cane and the manufacture of sugar are important industries in Queensland and New South Wales; but whilst in the former state the industry if not increasing has so far maintained its position, in the latter the area under crop has declined by nearly one-third since 1896. The area under cane in each state in the various years shown was as follows:—

Year.	Queensland.	New South Wales.
	acres.	acres.
1865	94	22
1872	9,581	4,394
1882	28,026	12,167
1892	50,948	22,262
1897	83,093	32,927
1902	112,031	20,809
1903	85,338	20,301

The conditions of cultivation in the two states are not precisely the same. In New South Wales, taking one year with another the area under cane is usually twice as great as the area from which cane is cut, but in Queensland the proportion of productive area is very much larger. This will be seen from the following statement:—

Year ended 31st March.	Total Area.		Area from which Cane was cut.		Yield of Cane per acre.	
	Queensland.	New South Wales.	Queensland.	New South Wales.	Queensland.	New South Wales.
	acres.	acres.	acres.	acres.	tons.	tons.
1899	111,012	24,759	82,391	14,578	18·7	19·8
1900	110,657	22,517	79,435	9,435	14·8	18·1
1901	108,535	22,114	72,651	10,472	11·7	19·0
1902	112,031	20,809	78,160	8,790	15·1	21·4
1903	85,338	20,301	59,102	8,899	10·8	20·9

For the five years the average for Queensland was 14·5 tons per acre, as against 19·7 tons in New South Wales. This does not by any means prove the superiority of the land in New South Wales for cane-growing, for if the whole area under cane be taken into account very different results are arrived at. The following figures cover five years:—

Yield of cane from total area under crop—

Queensland	10·2 tons per acre.
New South Wales	9·3 „ „

In New South Wales cane is cut every second year, but in the

Northern state a crop is obtained from the greater part of the cane area yearly, and this is the explanation of the difference in the yields and the large area in New South Wales apparently unproductive.

The quantity of sugar obtained from the cane-fields has varied during the last ten years between 77,752 and 192,844 tons per annum, the average being 118,518 tons, of which 94,497 tons were produced by Queensland, and 24,021 tons by New South Wales. The yield of sugar per ton of cane varies, of course, with the density of the juice. In an ordinary season it may be set down at 9·75 per cent. Hitherto little attention has been given in Queensland to the question of irrigating sugar-cane plantations, but last year 7,500 acres were irrigated, being an increase of 3,000 acres on the figures for the previous year.

The greater part of the field-work on the plantations in Queensland has hitherto been performed by coloured labour, chiefly South Sea Islanders. In New South Wales the work was formerly done entirely by white labour, but latterly there has been a considerable proportion of coloured persons, chiefly Hindoos, employed on the cane-fields. In Queensland during 1901 the number of coloured labourers was about 8,850, and as the area cut was 78,160 acres, the employment of coloured labour was in the proportion of one man to every 8·8 acres. In New South Wales the coloured labourers numbered about 1,010, and the area cut being 8,790 acres, the proportion was one man to every 8·7 acres. From this statement it would appear that there is little difference between the states in regard to the employment of coloured labour compared with the area cropped. There is, however, a further difference between the states. In Queensland the law restricts the employment of Kanakas to the field-work of a cane plantation; in New South Wales no similar restriction exists, and coloured labour is employed in several occupations reserved for white labour in Queensland. This, of course, refers to the conditions obtaining anterior to recent federal legislation.

In 1901 the Federal Parliament passed an Act which greatly affects the sugar industry, especially in Queensland. Under the provisions of this measure, which is entitled the Pacific Island Labourers Bill, a limited number of Pacific Islanders are allowed to enter Australia up to the 31st day of March, 1904, but on and after that date their coming is prohibited. All agreements for their employment terminate on the 31st December, 1906, and after that date any Pacific Islander found in Australia will be deported. On the 1st December, 1903, there were 8,454 islanders in Queensland; 874 were returned to their homes in 1901, 1,775 in 1902, and 932 during the first eleven months of 1903.

The duty on imported cane sugar is £6 per ton, while the excise duty is fixed at £3 per ton, but a bounty of 4s. per ton of cane (equal to £2 per ton of sugar) is allowed on Australian sugar grown by white labour, the bounty being paid to the grower. The employment of white against black labour is thus protected to the extent of £2 per ton of sugar, or equal to about 4s. 5d. per ton of cane.

In New South Wales last year 85 per cent. of the sugar was white grown and 15 per cent. black, while in Queensland the figures were reversed, 86 per cent. being black and 14 per cent. white grown. Of the total production, 98,170 tons, Queensland raised 76,626 as against 21,544 in New South Wales.

The cost of growing cane may be set down at from 2s. 11d. to 3s. 5d. per ton of cane, according as black or white labour is employed, the lower figures representing the cost of black labour.

In New South Wales the cost of harvesting the cane is somewhat as follows, the average being for areas on which white labour is employed:—

	s.	d.
Cutting	3	3
Carting to riverside	1	0
Transfer to Mills	0	9
Sundry Expenses	0	3
	5	3
Average price paid for standing cane	11	3
Total, per ton	16	6

In Queensland the plantations are more favourably situated in regard to the mills, and the cost delivered to the mill is about 12s. 2d. per ton. This represents 4s. 4d. per ton of cane, and at the rate of 9 tons of cane per ton of sugar the comparison is 39s. per ton in favour of Queensland. From Dr. Maxwell's report to the Federal Premier it would appear that the wages of coloured labourers working in the fields, after making all necessary allowances, may be set down at 2s. 4½d. per day.

The following table shows the quantities of sugar locally produced together with the net import or export during 1902. Queensland was the only province which was able to meet its own requirements, and spare a quantity of sugar for export. The net export from that state amounted to 71,173 tons, valued at £932,610 almost the whole of which was consigned to the other Commonwealth states.

State.	Locally Produced.	Net Import.	Total Locally Produced or Imported.
	tons.	tons.	tons.
New South Wales	21,544	50,746	72,290
Victoria	....	58,227	58,227
Queensland	76,626	*71,173	5,453
South Australia	....	19,260	19,260
Western Australia	....	9,123	9,123
Tasmania	....	7,270	7,270
Commonwealth	98,170	73,453	171,623
New Zealand	....	34,886	34,886
Australasia	98,170	108,339	206,509

* Net Export.

The quantity shown above does not represent the consumption of sugar during the year, as the surplus available from previous years and the amount carried over at the end of the year have to be considered. The trade returns present certain anomalies in the light of the information given in the succeeding table, and the figures are therefore advanced only for what they are worth.

A fairly correct estimate of the consumption of sugar in the states of the Commonwealth may be gathered from the statement below, which shows the quantities on which import duty and excise were paid after allowing for inter-state adjustments:—

State.	Quantity of sugar on which import duty was paid.	Quantity on which excise was paid.	Apparent consumption.	Consumption per head of population.
	tons.	tons.	tons.	lb.
New South Wales	11,662	55,911	67,573	107·5
Victoria	47,851	3,722	51,573	95·8
Queensland	1,077	20,561	21,638	94·1
South Australia	16,014	446	16,460	100·8
Western Australia	7,389	2,431	9,820	102·2
Tasmania	4,346	4,622	8,968	113·4
Commonwealth	88,339	87,693	176,032	101·5

In New Zealand the net import of sugar in 1902 was 34,886 tons, or 96·7 lb. per head of population.

In the chapter on "Food Supply" the average consumption of sugar in the Commonwealth is given at 105·7 lb. per head for the last ten years, and on this basis the annual consumption would appear to be 183,400 tons, which is slightly more than shown in the table.

In 1898, Queensland produced 163,734 tons of sugar, which is the highest output recorded for that state; 1,542,090 tons of cane were crushed, yielding sugar at the rate of 1·99 tons per acre. In 1902, owing to the dry season, only 641,927 tons were crushed, but the juice attained a high degree of density, and 76,626 tons of sugar were produced, only 8·38 tons of cane being required to make a ton of sugar. It is estimated that the decrease of 538,000 tons of cane on the return of the previous year represented a loss of £486,500, of which the growers' share, with cane at 10s. per ton, would be £269,000. Of the 641,126 tons of cane produced in Queensland in 1902, 10·9 per cent. was produced in the Southern or Bundaberg District, 33·5 per cent. in the Central or Mackay, and 55·6 per cent. in the Northern or Cairns District.

It may be estimated that the Commonwealth consumes annually about 179,000 tons of sugar. In average years the production is about 142,400 tons, leaving to be imported or for further production 36,600 tons. The year 1902 was, therefore, below the required average to the extent of about 81,000 tons.

The country of origin of 93,302 tons of the sugar which were imported into Australia from abroad during 1902 can be ascertained, and was as shown below. The unspecified balance consisted partly of small quantities imported from other countries, but mostly of re-exports, the original port of shipment of which could not be traced from one state to another. The quantity shown as imported from Europe was probably beet sugar :—

Country of Origin.	Quantity Imported.
Mauritius	20,924 tons
Fiji	25 ,,
Java	61,738 ,,
Hongkong	7,923 ,,
Europe	500 ,,
China	2,163 ,,
United States	16 ,,
India	13 ,,
Total	93,302 ,,

The re-export of foreign sugar from Australia amounted to 3,086 tons, while 296 tons of Australian sugar were exported outside the Commonwealth.

With the abolition of inter-state duties and the imposition of a uniform federal tariff, Queensland and New South Wales have been placed in a better position as regards competition with the foreign-grown imported article. Consideration will have to be given to the question of establishing an export trade, as in a good season these states can produce sugar more than sufficient for the needs of the Commonwealth.

Prior to last year, the area of cane cut as food for stock had no bearing on the question of sugar production, but in 1902 the adverse season caused such a demand for fodder that over 15,000 acres were cut for this purpose.

The total value of the cane crop in the sugar-growing states of Australia for the year 1902 was :—

State.	Value of Cane grown.
New South Wales	£135,421
Queensland	320,963
Total	£456,384

These amounts are, however, exclusive of rebate on white-grown sugar amounting to £36,731 in the case of New South Wales, and £24,536 in the case of Queensland. The value of the sugar manufactured during the year was about £1,000,000 sterling. In 1902, however, the returns were considerably below the average for the last five years, when the cane crop was equal to £636,000 and the sugar manufactured £1,510,000 per annum.

Sugar-beet.

The question of cultivating beet-root for the production of sugar has attracted attention in these states, principally in Victoria, where experiments were made in this direction over thirty years ago. The results obtained were not considered satisfactory enough to induce growers to cultivate this particular crop, and it was not until the year 1896 that a systematic attempt was made to establish the industry.

On the 6th March, 1896, the Victorian Parliament passed an Act empowering the Government to assist in the establishment of the sugar-beet industry by granting loans to duly registered public companies which might be formed for the purpose of erecting mills and equipping them with the necessary machinery and plant for the extraction of sugar from the roots. The company applying for aid had to satisfy the Treasurer of the state of certain conditions, and if he were of opinion that these conditions were likely to be fulfilled, and it was shown that the company had a paid-up capital of not less than £20,000, he was authorised to advance a sum not exceeding twice the amount raised by the shareholders.

As a result of these concessions a company was formed in Victoria, and erected a factory at Maffra, with a capacity of 420 tons per day. The first campaign in 1898 created disappointment, though the factory had at its disposal 9,109 tons of roots, grown on 1,287 acres. In the second year, the supply of beets had fallen to 6,271 tons from over 1,500 acres under crop. The industry had the misfortune to start with two very bad seasons, the average yield of beet being only 7·08 and 4·15 tons per acre. The low yield in these years was, however, due not only to unfavourable seasons but to want of experience on the part of the growers. The cultivation was further persevered with until May, 1900, when the factory was closed down. The percentage of sugar produced during the three seasons was as follows:—

1897–98	14·0 per cent.
1898–99	11·8 „
1899–1900	14·6 „

while the sugar produced had a standard of purity of 80 per cent., 78 per cent., and 85 per cent. respectively, these figures comparing favourably with the United States yields, which vary from 12·9 in the case of the Oxnard Company, Grand Island, Nebraska, to 15 per cent. at the works of the Western Company, Watsonville, California, where over 30,000,000 lb. of sugar are produced annually.

The Government expenditure on plant and machinery at Maffra amounted to £60,000, and altogether upwards of £100,000 of public money has been laid out in connection with the venture. Although the industry so far has been a failure, it is well known that there are large areas of Victorian soil suitable for the cultivation of beet, but before the factory can be re-started vigorous efforts will have to be put forward in the direction of securing a good and plentiful crop each year.

In New South Wales, although, as already stated, portions of the soil, particularly in the New England district, have been demonstrated to be admirably adapted to the cultivation of beet of excellent saccharine properties, no systematic effort has yet been made towards the establishment of the sugar-beet industry on a commercial basis.

It must not, however, be forgotten that the abolition of the border duties and the stoppage of any system of state bounties in aid of such an enterprise will compel the beet sugar to compete on level terms with the cane-grown sugars of Queensland and New South Wales, the supply of which already, in favourable years, more than meets local demands.

Tobacco.

The cultivation of the tobacco-plant has received attention in the three eastern states. The following table shows the area and production of tobacco at various periods :—

Year.	New South Wales.		Victoria.		Queensland.		Australia.	
	Area.	Production.	Area.	Production.	Area.	Production.	Area.	Production.
	acres.	cwt.	acres.	cwt.	acres.	cwt.	acres.	cwt.
1861	224	2,647	220	2,552	..	....	444	5,199
1871	567	4,475	299	2,307	44	....	910	6,782
1881	1,625	18,311	1,461	12,876	68	521	3,154	31,708
1888	4,833	55,478	1,685	18,355	123	1,418	6,641	70,251
1891	886	9,314	545	2,579	790	7,704	2,221	19,597
1892	848	8,344	477	658	318	3,808	1,643	12,810
1893	854	10,858	1,057	8,952	475	4,577	2,386	24,387
1894	716	8,132	1,412	7,155	915	9,571	3,043	24,858
1895	1,231	10,548	2,029	15,223	1,061	7,511	4,321	33,282
1896	2,744	27,468	1,264	7,890	994	8,629	5,002	43,987
1897	2,181	19,718	522	3,419	755	5,703	3,458	28,840
1898	1,405	12,706	78	190	617	3,276	2,100	16,172
1899	546	6,641	155	1,365	745	6,551	1,446	14,557
1900	199	1,905	109	311	665	4,082	973	6,248
1901	182	1,971	103	345	768	5,848	1,053	8,164
1902	317	2,604	171	781	722	1,818	1,210	5,203

Owing to over-production and the want of a foreign market, the area devoted to tobacco-culture greatly declined from 1888 to 1892, after which it showed signs of development until 1896, but since then consistently declined until 1901, when the acreage showed a slight increase over that of the previous season. The Australasian tobacco-leaf has not yet been prepared in such a way as to find acceptance abroad, and until such is accomplished it will be useless to expect the cultivation of the plant to become a settled industry. The soil and climate of Australia appear to be suitable for the growth of the plant, but sufficient care and skill have not been expended upon the preparation of the leaf. The quantity of 70,251 cwt. of leaf produced in 1888 was so greatly in excess of local requirements that very low prices only could be obtained, and a large portion of the crop was left upon the growers' hands. The result was that many farmers abandoned the cultivation of tobacco, so that the area under this crop during 1889 was only 3,239 acres in New South Wales, and 955 acres in Victoria, producing respectively 27,724 cwt. and 4,123 cwt. of leaf—less than half the crop of the previous year. In 1891 the area showed a further decline in the case of New South Wales and Victoria. In the mother state this decline continued until 1894; but in Victoria and Queensland the smallest area devoted to the crop was during the season 1892. The year 1895 saw a great increase in the cultivation of tobacco in all three states, and in New South Wales in 1896 there was again a large extension of the area under the plant, although in Victoria and Queensland the advance made in 1895 was not maintained. Since that year the area under cultivation and the production have both steadily declined in each state until, in 1900, the total production was only 6,248 cwt., the lowest since 1861. The production in 1901 was very small, being only about 8,000 cwt. In 1898 the crop in Victoria was almost a complete failure.

The average production per acre of tobacco in 1902, and during the ten years ended 1901, were as shown below:—

State.	Average Production per Acre.	
	1902.	1892-1901.
	cwt.	cwt.
New South Wales	8·2	9·9
Victoria	4·6	6·6
Queensland	2·5	7·5
Australia	4·3	8·2

The Agricultural Department of Queensland is endeavouring to assist the tobacco-growers by the importation of American seed of first quality, suited to the Queensland climate, and, following the example set by Victoria and New South Wales, the services of an American expert have been secured. At Texas, Queensland, leaf of fine quality has been raised, which realises a high price in the Sydney markets. In 1902, however, owing to the dry weather, only 70 tons were produced as against 275 in ordinary seasons. The price obtained for the leaf ranges from 6d. to 9d. per lb. New Zealand, also, has commenced the cultivation of tobacco, but so far it is only in the nature of an experiment; and a small area has been planted in the Northern Territory of South Australia. In 1897 the Victorian Government decided to grant a bonus of 3d. per lb. on all tobacco-leaf of approved quality grown in the state, and cured and shipped under the supervision of the tobacco expert. The bonus was only payable to the actual grower of the leaf, and 3 tons were assigned as the maximum quantity for which payment was to be made to any one grower or association. The bonuses have now lapsed, but during 1902 samples of tobacco were exported to England from Victoria, and the price obtained—5½d. per lb., was fair, considering that leaf, from new sources, is treated with caution by buyers, who hesitate to alter the flavour of their well known brands by using an unknown product. The flavour of the leaf was reported to be good, but the packing was inferior. This will, however, doubtless be remedied by experience.

The following table shows the imports of tobacco, cigars, and cigarettes for home consumption during 1902; the amounts for this year however are below the normal consumption owing to the excessive imports during 1901 in anticipation of the Federal Tariff.

State	Quantity. lb.
New South Wales	2,134,450
Victoria	1,644,590
Queensland	727,820
South Australia	494,076
Western Australia	975,005
Tasmania	240,917
Commonwealth	6,216,858
New Zealand	1,971,120
Australasia	8,187,978

The proportion of waste in the manufacture of tobacco is about one-third, so that the quantity of leaf represented above may be set down as 12,282,000 lb. Applying the decennial average of 8·2 cwt. per acre, it would appear that the produce of 13,370 acres is required annually to supply the demand for tobacco in Australasia. The total value of the tobacco crop for 1902 in Australia was only £14,000, returning an average value of £11 11s. 5d. per acre. In the United States, last year, 1,030,734 acres were under tobacco, producing 821,823,963 lb., valued at £11,927,000, or £11 11s. 3d. per acre.

Gardens and Orchards.

The cultivation of fruit in Australasia does not attract anything like the attention it deserves, although the soil and climate of large areas in all the provinces are well adapted to fruit-growing. Still, some progress has been made, especially in recent years. In 1902 the proportion of the total cultivation allotted to fruit was 2·0 per cent., while in 1881 the proportion was 1·5 per cent. The area per 1,000 persons, in 1902, was 43·8 acres; in 1891, 36 acres; and in 1881, 29·4 acres. Grapes, oranges, apples, pears, and peaches are the principal fruits grown; but with an unlimited area suitable for fruit-cultivation, and with climatic conditions so varied, ranging from comparative cold in New Zealand and on the high lands of New South Wales and Victoria to tropical heat in Queensland, a large variety of fruits could be cultivated. The industry, however, languishes partly on account of the lack of skill and care on the part of the grower—good fruits commanding high prices, while those placed within the reach of the multitude are generally of lower quality—and partly owing to the lack of means of rapid transit to market at reasonable rates. The inferior quality of much of the fruit produced was due to the ravages of fruit pests. The pests were almost wholly imported from Europe and America on fruit and cuttings, and as the orchards of Australia were threatened, and the fruit industry likely to be seriously interfered with, Acts have been passed in all the states prohibiting the importation of diseased fruit. The result of this legislation has been wholly beneficial, and if supplemented by legislation aimed at eradicating diseases existing in the orchards themselves, the future of the fruit industry would be assured.

Fruit-drying is a growing industry, and promises before long to attain considerable dimensions. At Mildura, on the left bank of the Murray, in Victoria, between 9,000 and 10,000 acres are under intense culture, the crops raised including currants, sultanas, peaches, and citrus fruits. The rainfall is only about 9 inches per annum, but a plentiful supply of water is obtained by pumping from the Murray, and the channels command an irrigable area of about 35,000 acres. Last year the returns from the sale of fruits amounted to about £110,000.

At Renmark, in South Australia, somewhat similar work is being carried on. Some 3,000 acres are under irrigation, and maintain a population of nearly 1,000 persons. The value of the fruits and olive oil sold last year amounted to over £30,000. As an evidence of the value of irrigation, it may be noted that an adjoining station, with much land as productive as that at Renmark, consisting of 250,000 acres, only carried 5,000 sheep last year.

The area under orchards and gardens in 1881, 1891, and 1902 was as follows:—

State.	1881.		1891.		1902.	
	Acres.	Percentage to total area under Crops.	Acres.	Percentage to total area under Crops.	Acres.	Percentage to total area under Crops.
New South Wales	24,565	4·3	40,116	4·7	55,847	2·5
Victoria	20,630	1·4	37,435	1·8	58,415	1·8
Queensland	3,262	2·8	9,758	4·0	13,023	4·6
South Australia	9,864	0·4	14,422	0·7	26,865	1·2
Western Australia	....	...	....	...	6,765	3·0
Tasmania	6,717	4·5	10,696	6·4	14,568	5·6
Commonwealth	65,038	1·5	112,427	2·1	175,483	2·1
New Zealand	16,360	1·5	29,235	2·0	30,056	1·9
Australasia	81,398	1·5	141,662	2·1	205,539	2·0

With the extension of artificial irrigation, and the increased facilities for export afforded by the adoption of cool chambers for the preservation of fruit during long voyages, the orchardists of Australasia are now enabled to compete with foreign states in the fruit supply for the English market, which averages about £11,000,000 in value annually. The Tasmanian fruit trade with England has passed the experimental stage, and every season large steamers visit Hobart to receive fruit for the home market. During the year 1902, Tasmania exported £163,000 worth of apples to Great Britain; but, as that country imports annually some £2,000,000 worth of such fruit, there is ample scope for increasing the exports from Australia.

The following table shows the import and export trade of each state in green fruit and pulp for 1902, from which it will be seen that Tasmania is, as yet, the only state whose export largely exceeds its import, although in both Queensland and South Australia the exports of domestic produce are now well above the imports:—

State.	Imports.	Exports of Domestic Produce.
	£	£
New South Wales	335,321	97,475
Victoria	81,932	81,348
Queensland	78,655	120,252
South Australia	29,066	37,315
Western Australia	31,106	20
Tasmania	25,544	300,899
Commonwealth	581,624	637,309
New Zealand	88,728	3,107
Australasia	670,352	640,416

The average value of the produce of gardens and orchards, and the average return per acre, during the past five years were as given below:—

State.	Average Value of Crop.	Average Value per Acre.		
	£	£	s.	d.
New South Wales	457,000	10	3	0
Victoria	696,000	12	4	2
Queensland	179,000	13	3	3
South Australia	358,000	14	10	0
Western Australia	81,000	12	10	0
Tasmania	177,000	13	12	3
Commonwealth	1,948,000	12	19	0
New Zealand	299,000	11	1	6
Australasia	2,247,000	12	1	1

. The average returns per acre have but little value for purposes of comparison, as much depends on the proportion of the areas under certain kinds of fruit and under vegetable gardens, which tends to increase or decrease, as the case may be, the general average of a state. It will be seen that Victoria shows the largest return from this class of cultivation, the total value of the produce being £696,000, equal to an average of £12 4s. 2d. an acre. In this state there are great facilities for disposing of the crop, while the bonuses offered by the Government caused increased attention to be devoted to the fruit industry. Under the planting bonus of £3 an acre offered for trees planted after the 8th May, 1890, over 8,000 acres were cropped during the period of eleven years up till 1901. A sum of £25,000 was set apart for payment of these allowances, but the amount has now been expended and the payment of further bonuses is dependent upon the will of the Federal Parliament. The export trade also greatly benefited by the system of bonuses. Prior to 1896 the amount was 2s. per case, but since that date, up to 1901, when the bonuses ceased, it was at the rate of 1s. per case. Last season over 12,000 cwt. of apples and pears were exported, several of the shipments realising very high prices in the English market. In New South Wales the smallness of the average is explained by the fact that in a great number of instances, owing to lack of facilities for disposing of the fruit crops, the produce of the orchards did not reach the markets, and in some cases was not even gathered. In Tasmania, English fruits, such as apples and pears, are principally grown, and the gross returns from these are smaller than the returns obtained from the cultivation of sub-tropical fruits such as the orange and lemon, which tend to increase the average returns in some of the other provinces. In South Australia, the large area cultivated as market gardens, which return a greater value per acre than orchards, accounts for the high value of production shown, while in Queensland over 6,000 acres are under bananas and pineapples, from which excellent returns are received.

Minor Crops.

Besides the crops already specifically noticed, there are small areas on which are grown a variety of products, chiefly rye, onions, beans, peas, turnips, rape, mangold wurzel, and hops; but they are not sufficiently important to warrant special mention, except turnips and rape in New Zealand, where no less an area than 523,000 acres was planted with these crops. The area under minor crops in each province in 1902 was as follows :—

State.	Acres.
New South Wales	13,148
Victoria	22,087
Queensland	18,414
South Australia	8,916
Western Australia	5,049
Tasmania	24,200
Commonwealth	91,814
New Zealand	618,103
Australasia	709,917

In 1902 there were 396 acres under coffee in Queensland, of which 314 acres were in bearing, which produced on an average 360 lb. per acre. There were also 296 acres under arrowroot, with an average production of 5·9 tons per acre, and 38 acres under rice, which returned a yield of 1,093 bushels, or an average of 29 bushels to the acre. Small quantities of cotton, also, are grown in Queensland; and it has been found that heavy crops of cotton can be raised in many parts of New South Wales. In 1897 the South Australian Government granted a lease of Bathurst Island, comprising an area of 500,000 acres, to a syndicate, which proposed to plant india-rubber trees on a large scale.

In British New Guinea, coffee-planting has been initiated with good prospects of success, and on one of the estates some 20,000 plants are already in full bearing.

Dissemination of Agricultural Knowledge.

Although considerable progress has of late years been made in some directions, yet it must be admitted generally that agriculture in Australasia has only now passed the tentative stage. The typical Australian agriculturist, relying largely on a bountiful Nature, does not exercise upon his crops anything approaching the same patience, care, and labour that are bestowed by the European cultivator, nor as a rule does he avail himself of the benefits of scientific farming and improved implements to the extent that prevails in America and Europe. Improvements are, however, already noticeable in this respect, and the efforts made by the Governments of the various States for the promotion of scientific farming are beginning to bear good fruit. In most of the provinces, agricultural colleges and model farms have been established, and travelling lecturers are sent to agricultural centres. At present New South Wales possesses the Hawkesbury Agricultural College and Experimental Farm, and the experimental farms at Wagga, Wollongbar, Grafton, Bathurst, Coolabah, Cowra, Glen Innes, the Pera Bore, and Moree. Victoria has the two agricultural colleges of Dookie and Longerenong, with experimental farms attached to them, and another farm at Framlingham, together with a viticultural college at Rutherglen. South Australia has an agricultural college and experimental farm at Roseworthy. The Queensland Government established an agricultural college and farm at Gatton in 1896. By a change in the distribution of the money voted for state scholarships, four bursaries have been allotted, entitling the holders to free board and instruction for a period of three years as resident students of the college. State farms have also been established at Westbrook, Hermitage, Biggenden, and Gindie. New Zealand possesses an agricultural college and an experimental farm at Lincoln, in Canterbury.

In New South Wales experimental cultivation by means of irrigation with artesian and catchment water has been successfully conducted at some of the tanks and bores owned by the state, notably at the Pera and Moree

Bores. In South Australia a central agricultural bureau in Adelaide, with about one hundred branch bureaus in the country, assists the farmers by disseminating valuable information, publishing papers, introducing new economic plants, and improving the breed of dairy cattle. A state school has been established in Adelaide for the purpose of affording instruction to "secondary agricultural pupils." The fees paid by the scholars, who must be over 13 years of age and have passed the compulsory examination, are at the same rate as those paid in the ordinary state schools. In Tasmania, the Council of Agriculture gives valuable advice to farmers concerning improved methods of agriculture, extermination of insect pests, etc.; while Western Australia possesses seventeen agricultural halls subsidised by the Government, where the latest literature of interest to farmers may be examined, and where lectures are delivered on agricultural subjects.

In Victoria, South Australia, and New Zealand, the Governments have established export depôts, where consignments of meat, butter, and other produce are inspected by Government experts, and graded and branded according to their quality. By this means little but produce of prime quality is exported, and the Colonies are gaining a high name in Great Britain for the excellence of the goods despatched.

State Advances to Farmers.

The oldest system by which advances of money are made to farmers is probably that which was established, as early as 1770, by the German "Landschaften Bank"; and the principle, assuming different forms according to the circumstances of the countries into which it was introduced, was gradually extended to the other great countries of Europe, with the exception of the United Kingdom, where an unwieldy system of land transfer, and the growing accumulation of large estates, form obstacles in the way of its successful application. Since 1849, mainly by the efforts of Raiffeisen, the German Land Credit Banks have taken the form of purely co-operative institutions, and in this respect they have been followed by Sweden, the Baltic provinces of Russia, and Poland, as well as, to some extent, by Austria-Hungary; but in most of the European countries the institutions may be classed as partly state and partly co-operative. In France alone is the system exclusively administered by the state; and it is the French *Credit Foncier* which has been adopted in Australasia wherever the idea of rendering financial aid to agriculturists has been carried into effect, namely, in the states of New South Wales, Victoria, South Australia, Western Australia, Queensland, and New Zealand; while in Tasmania the system has received consideration.

It was not till very recently that New South Wales adopted the principle of advances to settlers. Act No. 1, of 1899, was passed to assist settlers who were in necessitous circumstances, or who were financially embarrassed owing to the droughts. Under this Act a Board was appointed to consider applications for relief, and determine whether such relief should be granted. No advance to any settler was to exceed £200, to be repaid in ten years at 4 per cent. per annum. An Amending Act (No. 1 of 1902) was passed, giving to the Board power to advance up to £500, and providing that the advances with interest thereon should be repaid within thirty-one years. Up to 31st December, 1902, 7,632 applications had been received for advances, the amount applied for being £994,276. Of these applications, 7,363 have been dealt with by the Board, and 2,929 have been refused. The number of applications approved is 4,434, representing advances to the amount of £371,127. Repayments of principal amount to £61,344, in addition to which £15,457 has been received in interest. The Government has in contemplation the introduction of a scheme somewhat on the lines followed in Victoria, in which the system will be carried on in connection with the Savings Bank.

In Victoria, a section of the Savings Banks Act of 1890 empowered the Commissioners to entertain applications for loans, and to lend sums of money on security by way of mortgage of any lands and hereditaments held in fee-simple free of all prior charges, quit-rents excepted, at such rate of interest as might, from time to time, be fixed by them. The conditions were not very liberal, but they endured for a number of years. Five per cent. was the rate of interest charged, and 2 per cent. was payable annually in redemption of the principal. Opportunity was taken in the Act for the amalgamation of the Savings Banks, assented to on the 24th December, 1896, to definitely grant advances to farmers under the land-credit system. Under the new Act the Commissioners of Savings Banks are empowered to assist farmers, graziers, market-gardeners, or persons employed in agricultural, horticultural, viticultural, or pastoral pursuits, by making advances, either by instalments or otherwise, upon the security of any agricultural, horticultural, viticultural, or pastoral land held by them, either in fee simple, or under a lease from the Crown in which the rent reserved is taken in part payment of the purchase money of the land demised by such lease. The Commissioners have the option of making such advances either in cash or in mortgage bonds; and it is provided that all advances, together with interest at the rate of 4½ per cent. per annum, are to be repaid in sixty-three half-yearly instalments, or such smaller number as may be agreed upon by the Commissioners and the borrower. From the commencement of the Act to the 30th June, 1902, advances to the amount of £1,364,510 had been made. The total number of loans in existence on that date was 2,625, representing the sum of £1,145,961, averaging £437 each. The actual advances made during the financial year 1901–2 amounted to £201,405, of which £179,992 was advanced to pay liabilities, £6,148 to pay Crown rents, and £15,265 to improve resources of land, and to carry on. To enable them to make the necessary advances the Commissioners had sold Treasury bonds and debentures to the nominal value of £1,383,600, of which £184,750 have been redeemed, leaving a balance of £1,198,850.

In Queensland the Agricultural Bank Act, assented to on the 31st December, 1901, empowered the Government to establish a bank for the purpose of promoting the occupation, cultivation, and improvement of the agricultural lands of the state. The amount to be raised must not exceed £250,000, and may be advanced to farmers and settlers in sums not greater than £800. Applications for advances not exceeding £200 are to be given priority over those of a greater amount, and no advance must exceed 13s. in the £ of the fair estimated value of the improvements to be made. Interest at the rate of 5 per cent. per annum is to be paid on advances for a period of five years, and thereafter the advances must be repaid within twenty years by half-yearly instalments of £4 0s. 3d. for every £100 advanced. During the year 267 applications were received for advances, amounting in the aggregate to £38,050, of which 188 were approved for £23,486. Eleven applicants declined the partial advances offered, leaving 177 actually made, amounting to £22,613. Interest in arrear, on which a penalty has been incurred, amounted to £52. The average of advances approved was £127 15s. 1d. It has been pointed out by the authorities charged with the administration of the act that it would be desirable to extend the scope of the measure in the direction of allowing advances for such purposes as purchasing seed wheat, dairy stock, etc.

The South Australian Parliament, on the 20th December of that year, passed the State Advance Act of 1895, providing for the establishment of a State Bank for the purpose of making advances to farmers and producers, to local authorities, and in aid of industries, on proper security, consisting either of lands held in fee-simple or under Crown lease; the funds for this purpose to be raised by the issue of mortgage bonds guaranteed by the state. The rate of interest was to be a matter of arrangement between the bank and the borrower, the maximum being 5 per cent. per annum. To the 31st March, 1903, the South Australian State Bank, thus established, had advanced £794,008, and received repayments to the amount of £232,262. On that date there were arrears of interest to the amount of £1,734 outstanding. In order to enable these advances to be made, mortgage bonds had been sold to the amount of £773,740, of which £230,740 had been repurchased, leaving the amount current at £543,000. The advances made during the last financial year amounted to £81,281.

In Western Australia the Agricultural Bank Act of 1894 authorised the establishment of a bank for the purpose of assisting persons in the occupation, cultivation, and improvement of agricultural lands. Under the provisions of the Act the manager of the bank is empowered to make advances to farmers and other cultivators of the soil on the security of their holdings in fee-simple, or under special occupation lease, or under conditional purchase from the Crown, or under the Homestead Farms Act of 1893. The advances are granted either for the purpose of making improvements on unimproved holdings, or of making additional improvements on holdings already improved, and, under the original Act, could not exceed in amount one-half of the fair estimated value of the improvements proposed to be made. The maximum rate of interest chargeable was fixed at 6 per cent. per annum payable half-yearly, and it was provided that the largest sum to be advanced to any one person was to be £400. Repayment is made in half-yearly instalments of one-fiftieth of the principal sum, to commence on the 1st January or the 1st July next following the expiration of five years from the date of the advance, until the whole amount is repaid with interest. Arrangements can, however, be made for the repayment of advances at shorter intervals, and in larger instalments. For the purposes of the Act, improvements were defined as clearing, cultivating, and ringbarking; but by an Amending Act passed in 1896 the term was extended so as to include fencing, drainage works, wells of fresh water, reservoirs, buildings, or any other works enhancing the value of the holding. The same Act raised the largest sum which can be advanced to £800, reduced the maximum rate of interest to 5 per cent., made provision for the acceptance of pastoral leases as security, and allowed advances to be made up to three-fourths of the estimated value of the proposed improvements. A further Amending Act, passed in 1902, empowers the manager to advance up to two-thirds the value of improved agricultural, and one-half the value of improved horticultural, properties, the maximum grant to any one person being raised to £1,000. At least one-third of any sum borrowed under this Act must be expended in further improvements; the balance may be applied to the liquidation of liabilities, or to the purchase of stock, plant, or other farm requisites. Where portion of an advance is made to pay off liabilities, the repayment of so much of the advance begins after the expiration of one year from the date of the advance. The capital allotted to the bank is £300,000, and to the 30th June, 1903, loans to the value of £201,200 had been approved; while repayments to the value of £13,630 had been made. During the financial year 1902–3, loans were advanced to 335 applicants, the total granted being £44,975. The transactions of the bank for the same period resulted in a net profit of £617.

In New Zealand the Government Advances to Settlers Act of 1894 provided for the establishment of an Advances to Settlers Office, empowered to lend money on first mortgages of land occupied for farming, dairying, or market-gardening purposes, urban and suburban lands used for residential or manufacturing purposes being expressly excluded from the scope of the Act. At that time one class of loans only was contemplated, viz., loans on mortgage security, which were repayable by seventy-three half-yearly instalments, subject, however, to redemption at any time; but by an Amending Act passed in 1896 authority was given for the granting of fixed loans for any term not exceeding ten years. These loans are chiefly granted on freehold lands, and are repayable without sinking fund at the end of the period for which they are made. The amount advanced on fixed loan is not to exceed one-half the estimated value of the security; while under the instalment system the Board of Control has power to grant loans up to 60 per cent. of the realisable value of freehold securities, and up to 50 per cent. of the lessee's interest in leasehold securities. In both cases interest is fixed at the rate of 5 per cent. per annum, and the amount advanced cannot be less than £25 nor more than £3,000—the maximum under the 1894 Act having been £2,500. Instalment loans are repayable in 36½ years, in half-yearly payments, at the rate of 5 per cent. for interest and 1 per cent. in redemption of the principal sum. The first meeting of the General Board for the purpose of considering applications for loans was held on 23rd February, 1895; and up to 31st March, 1903, the Board had authorised 12,922 advances, amounting to £4,316,940. The total amount applied for in the 12,922 applications granted in full, or in part, was £4,903,515. 1,629 applicants declined the partial grants offered to them, amounting to £735,280; so that the net advances authorised at 31st March, 1903, numbered 11,293, and amounted to £3,581,660. The security for the advances authorised was valued at £7,849,728. The number of applications received up to 31st March, 1903, was 16,643, and the amount applied for, £5,927,495.

Water Conservation.

The necessity of providing water for stock in the dry portions of the interior of the Australian continent induced the Governments of the States to devote certain funds to the purpose of sinking for water, and bringing to the surface such supplies as might be obtained from the underground sources which geologists stated to exist in the tertiary drifts and the cretaceous beds which extend under an immense portion of the area of Central Australia, from the western districts of New South Wales to a yet unknown limit into Western Australia.

In New South Wales the question of the existence of underground water had long been a subject of earnest discussion, but doubts were set at rest in 1879 by the discovery on the Kallara run, at a depth of 140 feet, of an artesian supply of water, which, when tapped, rose 26 feet above the surface. The Government then undertook the work of searching for water, and since the year 1884 the sinking of artesian wells has proceeded in a scientific and systematic manner, under the direction of specially-trained officers. Private enterprise, which had shown the way, has also followed up its first successes.

Up to 1902 the Government of New South Wales had undertaken the sinking of 110 wells; of these, 103 have been completed, and 7 are in progress. Of the total number of wells, 74 are flowing, 23 are sub-artesian, yielding pumping supplies, and 13 have been failures; these wells represent 149,858 feet of boring, while with the uncompleted wells the total depth bored has been 191,677 feet. From the completed wells about 60,000,000 gallons of water flow every day to the surface. The deepest bore completed is that at the Dolgelly, on the road from Moree to Boggabilla, where boring has been carried to a depth of 4,086 feet; this well yields a supply of approximately 745,200 gallons per diem. The largest flow obtained in the State is from the Oreel No. 2 Bore, in the Narrabri district; the depth of this well is 3,116 feet, and the estimated flow about 3,500,000 gallons per diem. The bore at Walgett, with a depth of 2,036 feet, has a daily flow of some 3,000,000 gallons. Another important bore is that at Pera, 8 miles from Bourke, on the Wanaaring road, where at a depth of 1,154 feet a flow of 350,000 gallons per diem is obtained. At this bore the most extensive system of irrigation by artesian water as yet undertaken in the State is being carried out. An area of 57 acres has been set apart for experimental cultivation by the Government, and certain fruits and other products indigenous to the temperate and torrid zones are being grown with success. Equally good results have been obtained at Native Dog, Barringun, Enngonia, and Belalie bores, on the road from Bourke to Barringun. Lucerne, maize, wheat tobacco, millet, planter's friend, sugar-cane, date palms, pineapples, bananas, and many other fruits and vegetables of tropical and sub-tropical character have been found to thrive there exceedingly well.

On the road from Wanaaring to Milparinka, once a waterless track, successful boring operations have been carried on. Seven bores have been completed. Four of these give a pumping supply, and three are flowing, yielding an aggregate supply of 3,150,000 gallons daily. Boring operations have been extended farther to the north-west, and two bores have been sunk at Paldrumata and Oarnoo, on the Tibooburra to Yalpunga road. These two bores are sub-artesian, and yield pumping supplies at depths of 80 and 1,357 feet respectively. A remarkable flow has also been obtained at the Moree bore, amounting to 1,108,000 gallons daily. This bore has been carried to a depth of 2,792 feet, through formations of the same age as the Ipswich coal measures (*Trias Jura*), thus demonstrating the fact that water can be obtained in other than the lower cretaceous formation. An experimental farm has been established at this site, where sub-tropical fruits and plants are grown.

Much has been done in the way of artesian boring by private enterprise. As far as can be ascertained, 166 private bores have been undertaken in New South Wales, of which 16 were failures, 2 were abandoned, and 4 are in progress. Amongst the most important are two wells on Lissington Holding, one with a flow of 4,000,000 gallons and the other with 3,000,000 gallons per day; one at Cuttabulla (Lila Springs), with a daily flow of 4,000,000 gallons; one at Toulby with 3,500,000 gallons per day; and one at Goondabluie with 3,000,000 gallons per day. From the private wells approximately 82,000,000 gallons are discharged daily.

A better idea of the value of artesian wells to the community will be obtained when it is known that the aggregate daily flow of underground water in New South Wales is now approximately 117,000,000 gallons, and that, in addition, large supplies can be pumped from sub-artesian wells. The average depth of the 103 wells completed by the Government is 1,454 feet 1 inch, with a range from 165 to 4,086 feet, while the temperature of the water varies from 80 to 139 degrees Fah. The total cost of the wells (including actual boring, casing, carriage, and incidental expenses) was £288,234, or an average of £2,620 6s. 2d. per bore, or £1 18s. 6d. per foot.

In Queensland up to the 30th June, 1903, there were 960 completed bores, of which 70 were Government, 32 Local Government, and 858 private bores.

Of the Government bores, 25 were artesian, 18 sub-artesian, and 27 were abandoned as failures. The daily flow of water from the successful bores amounted to 10,827,300 gallons. The Local Government bores included 11 artesian and 19 sub-artesian, while 2 were abandoned From the successful bores a daily flow of 6,346,300 gallons is obtained. Of the private bores, 540 were artesian, 174 were sub-artesian, and 135 were failures or uncertain. It is estimated that the daily flow of water from private bores amounts to no less than 368,331,200 gallons The large proportion of abandoned Government bores is due to the fact that many of them were sunk for experimental purposes in order to ascertain the prospects of obtaining artesian water. Others were put down by the old methods of boring, by which depths over 1,000 feet could not be penetrated in the swelling clays of Queensland. The total expenditure by the Government up to the 30th June, 1903, amounted to £368,629 on water conservation, of which £124,039 was expended on artesian bores. The deepest Government bore is at Winton, and reaches 4,010 feet, while the most copious supply, namely, 3,000,000 gallons per day, is obtained at the Charleville bore. The deepest private bore, and also the deepest bore in the State, is the Whitewood on the Bimerah run, and reaches 5,045 feet. The largest supplies are obtained from the Longlands bore, which yields 6,000,000 gallons daily; Corio-Cunnamulla East, 4,500,000; Burrambilla and Gooia, Cunnamulla West, 4,000,000; Boatman, 3,500,000; and Savannah Downs yielding 3,400,000 gallons daily. The total depth bored in search of artesian water up to 30th June, 1903, was 1,171,461 feet, the average depth per bore being 1,220 feet. At Helidon water of so low a temperature as 60 degrees Fah. was flowing; while at Elderslie No. 2 the water had a temperature of 202 degrees. Large areas are served by the water from the bores for irrigation purposes; in 1902 there were 14,344 acres under irrigation as compared with 6,526 acres in 1901. In addition several stations, which made no returns, also used the water for purposes of irrigation. Some of the bore waters contain soda in various forms, and these it is impossible to use, except for a limited period, and in small quantities.

At the end of 1902 the Water Conservation Department of South Australia had completed 104 bores, of which, however, only fifty-six were successful. These are spread over widely-distant parts of the territory, successful bores existing at Nullarbor Plains, on the boundary of Western Australia; at Oodnadatta, the present terminus of the Northern Railway system; and at Tintinara, in the south-eastern extremity of the State. The bore at Tintinara has proved that the marine tertiary area is water-bearing. The south-western portion of the great artesian basin lies under the north-east corner of South Australia proper, and a portion of it is under the south-eastern corner of the Northern Territory. This portion of the basin covers an area of 120,000 square miles, and towards its southern and western fringe occur the well-known mound springs, naturally indicating the existence of artesian water. Of the Government borings in this basin, there are seven flowing artesian wells under 1,000 feet in depth, seven from 1,000 to 3,000 feet, one between 3,000 and 4,000 feet, and three from 4,000 to 5,000 feet. It will therefore be seen that the South Australian Government has had considerable difficulties to overcome in prosecuting the work of opening up these sources of national wealth. The sea basin, which at one time existed within what is now South Australia, was of great depth, and many of the bores pierced through a thickness of strata varying from three-quarters of a mile to nearly a mile before striking the artesian water. The daily flow from the bores ranges from 100,000 to 1,500,000 gallons. The quality of the water varies considerably. Most of the bores furnish excellent drinking water, but towards the fringe of the basin, where there is little or no circulation, the supply is too salt for domestic use, and is only fit for cattle. The average increase in the temperature of the water has been found to be 1 degree Fah. to every 27 feet in depth. From certain of the deep borings, the water flows over the surface at a temperature of about 200 degrees Fah. Some very successful bores have also been put down on pastoral holdings. In some other parts of South Australia there are comparatively small local artesian basins from which good supplies have been obtained. Four successful bores have been put down in these districts by the Government, and the artesian areas have also been tapped by private persons. The depth of the private bores, however, is seldom over 200 feet. In parts of the state, where flowing supplies are not obtainable, the Government has for many years carried on boring operations, and in a fair number of cases sub-artesian water has been struck.

The results from Government bores up to 31st December, 1902, are as follows:—

Flowing artesian wells	22
Sub-artesian wells of good water	34
Salt, or otherwise unsuccessful bores	48
Total	104

In addition to these, four deep borings are in progress. The total expenditure by the Government on boring has been £233,186, of which £20,595 was expended during the year 1902.

The Government of Western Australia, following the example set by those of the eastern states has sunk 25 bores in various parts of the state, and 14 bores have been sunk by private owners. Of the Government bores, 19 have been successful, and yield a daily supply of 7,131,500 gallons, and 6 were failures. All the private bores yield supplies of water with the exception of two—the daily flow being 2,414,000 gallons. The deepest flowing bore is at Carnarvon, and reached a depth of 3,011 feet; while the largest supply is obtained from the municipal bore at Guildford, and amounts to 1,120,000 gallons daily. Up to the 31st December, 1902, the Government had expended £40,835 on artesian boring, while £9,819 had been spent by private owners.

In Victoria the attempts to obtain water by means of artesian boring have not been successful. Up to the 30th June, 1903, 46 bores had been sunk, 16 of which were driven to bed-rock, but none yielded artesian supplies. The expenditure on these bores amounted to £68,864, and the cost of water conservation, including Government expenditure on Melbourne Water Supply, was £8,684,922.

Employment in Agricultural Pursuits.

The following table shows the number of persons engaged in agricultural pursuits in Australasia during the years 1891 and 1901. The figures relate to the direct producers who were employed on holdings at the end of March in each year, and are exclusive of persons engaged in the manufacture of raw materials, as well as of casual hands who may have been employed at other periods of the year than that stated.

State.	1891.			1901.		
	Males.	Females.	Total.	Males.	Females.	Total.
New South Wales	67,576	7,022	74,598	75,884	1,735	77,619
Victoria	79,090	6,028	85,118	78,539	17,381	95,920
Queensland	33,891	6,089	39,980	38,260	2,081	40,341
South Australia	27,961	886	28,847	33,039	1,147	34,186
Western Australia	4,378	164	4,542	8,322	285	8,607
Tasmania	14,584	1,447	16,031	17,348	2,074	19,422
Commonwealth	227,480	21,636	249,116	251,392	24,703	276,095
New Zealand	56,671	2,387	59,058	65,723	2,089	67,812
Australasia	284,151	24,023	308,174	317,115	26,792	343,907

A classification of the returns for 1901 according as the persons employed in agricultural pursuits were engaged therein as proprietors and managers, relatives assisting, or servants, is given below for all the states except Queensland, where the information has not been published.

State.	Proprietors and Managers.			Relatives assisting.			Servants.		
	Males.	Females.	Total.	Males.	Females.	Total.	Males.	Females.	Total.
New South Wales..	32,466	1,607	34,073	10,271	111	10,382	33,147	17	33,164
Victoria	33,383	3,031	36,411	17,609	13,625	31,234	27,547	725	28,272
South Australia....	13,796	691	14,487	4,108	240	4,348	15,135	216	15,351
Western Australia	3,747	131	3,878	1,426	139	1,565	3,149	15	3,164
Tasmania	7,028	371	7,399	3,373	1,205	4,578	6,947	498	7,445
New Zealand	29,340	1,091	30,431	12,301	841	13,142	24,082	157	24,239

With regard to Victoria it appears that females engaged in domestic duties, who also gave some assistance in farming, were classified as relatives assisting in agricultural pursuits, whereas, in other states, these were included in the category of dependents performing domestic duties.

In proportion to population the persons engaged in agricultural pursuits numbered 8·9 per cent. in 1891, compared with 7·6 in 1901. The decrease in the latter year is accounted for partly by the rapid extension of the dairying industry which has absorbed many of those formerly engaged in agriculture, and partly by the increased cultivation of wheat, which does not require such a large proportion of labour as other miscellaneous crops.

RELIGION.

THE progress of all matters relating to denominational Religion since the early years of Australasian settlement has been steady and remarkable. For the first fifteen years after the foundation of the colony of New South Wales, only a single denomination was recognised by Government or possessed either minister or organisation—the Established Church of England. In those days the whole of Australasia was ecclesiastically within the diocese of the Bishop of Calcutta, of which it formed an Archdeaconry; this continued until 1836, when the bishopric of Australia was constituted, and the Rev. William Grant Broughton, D.D. (formerly Archdeacon), was consecrated the first Bishop. In 1841 the bishopric of New Zealand was established, and in 1842 that of Tasmania. Considerable changes took place in 1847, when the dioceses of Melbourne, Adelaide (including South Australia and Western Australia), and Newcastle (including the northern portion of what is now New South Wales, and the whole of Queensland) were established, and the Bishop of Australia was styled Bishop of Sydney and Metropolitan of Australia and Tasmania. In 1857 the diocese of Perth was formed out of that of Adelaide, and in 1859 the diocese of Brisbane out of that of Newcastle; in 1863 the bishopric of Goulburn was separated from Sydney; in 1867 the bishopric of Grafton and Armidale was formed out of part of the diocese of Newcastle; in 1869 Bathurst was separated from Sydney; in 1875 Victoria was divided into the two dioceses of Melbourne and Ballarat; in 1878 the bishopric of Northern Queensland was established, with Townsville as seat of its Bishop; in 1884 the diocese of Riverina was formed out of parts of the dioceses of Bathurst and Goulburn; in 1892 parts of the bishoprics of Brisbane and Northern Queensland were formed into the new diocese of Rockhampton; in 1898 the bishopric of British New Guinea was established, and in 1900 the new diocese of Carpentaria was formed in Northern Queensland. While the six dioceses of New South Wales were united under a provincial constitution, with the Bishop of Sydney as Metropolitan, no such union existed in Victoria or Queensland, and the decision of the Lambeth Conference of 1897, granting the title of

Archbishop to Colonial Metropolitans applied, therefore, only to Sydney, whose Bishop thereby became Archbishop of Sydney.

Each state preserves its autonomy in church matters, but the Archbishop of Sydney is nominal head or Primate within the boundaries of Australia and Tasmania. In 1872 the ties between the churches in the various states under the jurisdiction of the Primacy were strengthened by the adoption of one common constitution. A general synod of representatives of each of these states meets in Sydney every five years to discuss Church affairs in general. New Zealand is excluded from this amalgamation, and possesses a Primacy of its own. As already stated, a Bishop of New Zealand was appointed in 1841. After various changes the constitution of the Church in New Zealand was finally settled in 1874, when the whole colony was divided into the six dioceses of Auckland, Waiapu (Napier), Wellington, Nelson, Christchurch, and Dunedin. After the departure of Bishop Selwyn, who has been the only Bishop of New Zealand, the Primacy was transferred to the see of Christchurch, where it remained until 1895. In that year the Bishop of Auckland was elected Primate of New Zealand. The missionary Bishop of Melanesia, whose headquarters are at Norfolk Island, is under the jurisdiction of the New Zealand primacy. At present, therefore, there are twenty-three bishops in the States, including the Bishop of Melanesia, but excluding assistant bishops. The synodical system of Church Government, by means of a legislative body, consisting of the clergy and representatives of the laity, prevails throughout Australasia, both in the individual states and as a group.

The Church of England has a larger number of adherents than any other church as well in each state as in the Commonwealth; its position is strongest in Tasmania and New South Wales, where its doctrines are professed by nearly half of the population; in Western Australia also it is a very powerful body, numbering 42 per cent. of the people of the state. The Church is proportionately weakest in South Australia with adherents numbering 30 per cent. of the total population. The adherents of the Church of England in Australia numbered 644,490 in 1871, 867,791 in 1881, 1,234,121 in 1891, and 1,497,579 in 1901, an increase of 853,089 in thirty years; in New Zealand the increase has been from 107,241 in 1871 to 314,024 in 1901, or 206,783 in thirty years.

In 1803 a grudging recognition was extended to Roman Catholics, one of whose chaplains was for some time placed on the Government establishment; but it was not until 1820 that any regular provision was made for the due representation of the clergy of this body. Until 1834 the Roman Catholics of Australia and Tasmania were under the jurisdiction of the Bishop of Mauritius (the Rev. Dr. Ullathorne being Vicar-General from 1830 to 1834), but in that year Sydney was constituted a see, and the Rev. John Bede Polding, D.D., was consecrated Bishop, with jurisdiction over the whole of the Continent and

Tasmania. In 1842 Hobart was established as a separate diocese, and Sydney became an archiepiscopal see. The diocese of Adelaide dates from 1843, that of Perth from 1845, and those of Melbourne, Maitland, Bathurst, and Wellington from 1848. During this year a diocese was established in the Northern Territory of South Australia, which since 1888 has been designated the diocese of Port Victoria and Palmerston. The bishopric of Brisbane was founded in 1859, and that of Goulburn in 1864. In 1867 the Abbey-nullius of New Norcia (Western Australia) was established. The dioceses of Armidale and Auckland date from 1869, and those of Ballarat and Sandhurst from 1874. In 1876 Melbourne became an archdiocese, and Cooktown was formed into a Vicariate-Apostolic. Other changes took place in Queensland in 1882, when the diocese of Rockhampton was founded, and in 1884, when the Vicariate-Apostolic of British New Guinea (with residence at Thursday Island) was established. In 1885 the Archbishop of Sydney was created a cardinal, and placed at the head of the Roman Catholic Church throughout Australasia. Following upon this appointment great alterations took place in the arrangement of dioceses in 1887, when the new dioceses of Lismore, Wilcannia, Sale, Port Augusta, and Christchurch, and the Vicariates-Apostolic of Kimberley and Queensland (the latter with jurisdiction over all the aborigines of the State) were established, and Adelaide, Brisbane, and Wellington became archdioceses. In 1888 Hobart was also made an archiepiscopal see; and a new see was established in 1898 at Geraldton, in Western Australia. At the present time there are six archbishops, sixteen bishops, three vicars-apostolic, and one abbot-nullius, or in all twenty-six heads of the Church with episcopal jurisdiction, irrespective of the Vicariate-Apostolic of British New Guinea and of several auxiliary and coadjutor-bishops.

The Roman Catholic Church occupies the second place in importance among the Churches of Australasia, and in each State, except South Australia, where the Methodist church is numerically stronger, and in New Zealand where its adherents are less numerous than the Presbyterians. In 1871, the Roman Catholics returned at the census of the Commonwealth States numbered 408,279, in 1881, 539,558, in 1891, 713,846, and in 1901, 855,799; this shows an increase of 447,520, in thirty years. In New Zealand the increase was from 35,608 to 109,822 in the same period, that is to say, of 74,214. Compared with the total population the Roman Catholic adherents were 23·1 per cent. in 1871 compared with 21·6 per cent. in 1901, thus showing a slight decrease.

Amongst the earliest free colonists who settled in the Hawkesbury district of New South Wales was a small party of Presbyterians, and one of the first places of worship erected in the state was put up in 1810 at Portland Head by their voluntary exertions. Services were conducted there for years before any ordained minister of the denomination reached New South Wales; indeed, it was not until 1823 that the Rev. Dr. Lang and the Rev. Archibald Macarthur, the first Presbyterian ministers in Australasia, arrived in Sydney and Hobart respectively. The Presbyterian Churches of New South Wales, Victoria, Queensland, South Australia, Western Australia, and Tasmania, are united in a Federal Assembly which meets every year in rotation in the capital cities of the states mentioned. On the 24th July, 1901, representatives of the churches within the various states met at Sydney, when the union of the Presbyterian churches of the States of Australia was accomplished, and the first General Assembly met in pursuance of the scheme of union agreed upon by the Federal Assembly. The United Church is known as "The Presbyterian Church of Australia." New Zealand is not included in this federation, and the Presbyterian Church in that colony is divided into the Presbyterian Church of New Zealand and the Presbyterian Church of Otago and Southland. Besides the churches mentioned, there are several small bodies of Presbyterians unconnected with the larger churches, such as the Presbyterian Church of Eastern Australia in New South Wales, and the Free Church in Victoria. The church in each state, however, acts independently as regards local ecclesiastical administration, and preserves its autonomy in respect of funds and property.

The Presbyterian Church is strongest in New Zealand where its adherents number 176,503, equal to 23·4 per cent. of the population; in Victoria the Presbyterians form 16·2 per cent., and in Queensland 11·7 per cent. of the total population; in none of the other states does the proportion reach 10 per cent. Since 1871 the Presbyterian population of the Commonwealth has increased from 199,195 to 426,105, or by 226,910. In New Zealand the increase has amounted to 112,879.

The first Wesleyan minister came to New South Wales in 1815, but it was not until 1821 that a Wesleyan place of worship was erected in Sydney, and it was even later before the denomination was allowed to share in the Government provision for religion. The first Wesleyan Church in Hobart was established in 1820. From 1815 to 1855 the Wesleyan Church in the colonies was regarded as a mission of the British Wesleyan Church, and from 1855 to 1873 it was affiliated to the British Wesleyan Conference; but in the latter year it was constituted into a separate and independent Conference as the Australasian Wesleyan Methodist Church. At the conference of 1890, held in Sydney, the church districts in Queensland were formed into a separate body, and in 1898, the union of the Methodist churches took place in accordance with resolutions approved by the Wesleyan Conference and Primitive Methodist District Assembly. The union of the Methodist churches of South Australia took place in January, 1900. Western Australia formed a district of the South Australian Conference until March, 1899, when it was constituted a separate conference, its first meeting being held at Perth in March, 1900. At present the Church is divided into six Conferences, viz., New South Wales, Victoria and Tasmania, Queensland, South Australia, Western Australia, and New Zealand. These Conferences meet annually, while a General Conference is held at triennial periods within the boundaries of each annual Conference in the order decided upon. On the 1st January, 1902, the Wesleyan Methodist, Primitive Methodist, and United Methodist Free Churches, entered into organic union, under the name of "The Methodist Church of Australasia." The members of the various Methodist churches in Australia now number 504,139, an increase of 323,556 on the total for 1871, which was returned at 180,583. During the twenty years from 1871 to 1901, the number of adherents in New Zealand increased from 22,004 to 83,789. The denomination at present is proportionately strongest in South Australia, where it forms 25·5 per cent. of the total population, and in Victoria where the proportion amounts to 15·2 per cent. In 1871 the Methodists formed 10·5 per cent of the total population, and the percentage has steadily grown from census to census. In 1881 the proportion was 10·9 per cent., in 1891 11·4, and in 1901 it reached 13·2 per cent.

A Congregational minister arrived in Sydney as early as 1798; and in Hobart the Congregational Church was established in 1830. At present there exists a separate Congregational Union in each of the Australasian provinces. Federal meetings have been held, and a Congregational Union of Australasia has been established. The first meeting of this body was held at Wellington, New Zealand, in 1892. It is intended to hold similar gatherings from time to time in the capital cities of the various states. In 1901 the Congregationalists in Australia numbered 73,561 as against 41,595 in 1871. The membership of this body has, however, remained almost stationary since 1891, when the adherents in Australia numbered 72,738. In New Zealand there were 3,941 Congregationalists in 1871, 6,685 in 1891, and 6,844 at the census of 1901.

The Baptist Church in Australasia dates from a much later period, the establishment of the first four Baptist Churches being as follows:— Sydney, 1834; Launceston, 1839; Adelaide, 1840; and Melbourne, 1841. Churches were established in Auckland in 1852, in Brisbane in 1855, and in Perth in 1895. The adherents of this church in 1871 numbered 33,632, and in 1901 92,670, the increase in Australia for the thirty years being 59,038. In New Zealand the numbers for 1871 and 1901 were 4,732 and 16,035 respectively. The denomination is proportionately strongest in South Australia where it forms 6·2 per cent. of the total population.

The Jewish community in the Commonwealth had a membership in 1901 of 15,239 as compared with 13,805 in 1891, 8,815 in 1881, and 7,059 in 1871. In New Zealand this body numbered 1,262 in 1871, 1,536 in 1881, 1,463 in 1891, and 1,612 in 1901.

Leaving out of consideration some churches with but a small number of adherents, the Salvation Army may be said to be the youngest of the denominations in Australasia. It commenced operations in South Australia towards the close of the year 1880, and in 1882 officers were despatched from Adelaide to Victoria, New South Wales, and Tasmania, for the purpose of organising corps in those states. New Zealand was invaded in 1883, Queensland in 1886, and Western Australia in 1891. The headquarters of the Army are in Melbourne, and its head in Australasia ranks as a Commissioner. He is directly responsible to General Booth, and controls the officers commanding in each of the states, who bear the rank of colonel or brigadier. Each state is divided into districts, which are placed in the charge of superior officers; and each of these districts is subdivided into local corps under subaltern officers, assisted by secretaries, etc. These subaltern officers are responsible to the officers commanding their division, and the latter to the colonel or brigadier in charge of the Army of the whole state. In 1891 there were 33,428 members of the Salvation Army in Australia, and at the census of 1901 the total was returned at 31,100, so that there has been a falling off in membership to the extent of 2,328. For New Zealand the numbers in 1891 and 1901 were respectively 9,383 and 7,999, showing a decrease of 1,384 adherents.

In the eyes of the state all religions are equal in Australasia, and state aid to the denominations has now been abolished in all the provinces of the group. South Australia, in 1851, was the first state to withdraw such aid, after it had been in force only three years; and Queensland, in 1860, shortly after the assembling of the first Parliament, abolished the system inherited from the mother colony, and limited future payments to the clergy then actually in receipt of state aid. New South Wales passed a similar Act in 1862, and the expenditure on this account, which in that year was over £32,000, had fallen in 1903 to £3,036. The total amount paid by the state up to the 30th June, 1903, amounted to £572,236. The other states of the group subsequently abolished state aid, Victoria withdrawing its denominational grants as late as 1875. In Western Australia the system lasted until 1895, when it was abolished from that year; and, in lieu of the annual grants, two sums of £17,715 each were distributed amongst the religious bodies affected, namely, the Anglicans, Roman Catholics, Wesleyans, and Presbyterians, on the 1st October, 1895, and 1st July, 1896.

The only denominations which ever received state aid were the Church of England, Roman Catholics, Presbyterians, and Wesleyans; other denominations to which it was tendered refusing to accept it. The greater portion of the inhabitants belonged to these four persuasions, and the enormous increase of population during the last forty-five years has not in any considerable degree altered this condition of things, though in some states different bodies of Christians have represented a larger proportion of the people than in others.

The following table shows the proportions held by the principal denominations to the total population of each state at the enumerations of 1871, 1881, 1891, and 1901:—

	State.	Church of England.	Roman Catholics.	Presbyterians.	Wesleyan and other Methodists.	Congregationalists.	Baptists.	Jew, Hebrew.	All Others.
		₩ cent.	₩ cent.	₩ cent.	₩ cent.	₩ cent.	₩ cent.	₩ cent.	₩ cent.
1871	New South Wales	45·5	29·3	9·7	7·9	1·8	0·8	0·5	4·5
	Victoria	34·4	23·3	15·5	12·3	2·5	2·2	0·5	9·3
	Queensland	36·5	26·5	12·8	6·0	2·2	2·4	0·2	13·4
	South Australia ...	27·1	15·2	6·4	18·9	3·5	5·0	0·3	23·6
	Western Australia	59·0	28·7	2·1	5·6	3·6	0·2	0·2	0·6
	Tasmania	53·5	22·3	9·1	7·2	4·0	0·9	0·2	2·8
	New Zealand	41·8	13·9	24·8	8·6	1·5	1·9	0·5	7·0
	Australasia	39·1	23·1	13·6	10·5	2·4	2·0	0·4	8·9
1881	New South Wales	45·6	27·6	9·6	8·6	1·9	1·0	0·4	5·3
	Victoria	34·7	23·6	15·4	12·6	2·3	2·4	0·5	8·5
	Queensland	34·6	25·5	10·6	6·7	2·2	2·6	0·2	17·6
	South Australia ...	27·1	15·2	6·4	18·9	3·5	5·0	0·3	23·6
	Western Australia	54·7	28·3	3·4	7·0	4·3	...	...	2·3
	Tasmania	51·7	19·9	7·9	9·5	3·5	1·6	...	5·9
	New Zealand	41·5	14·1	23·1	9·4	1·4	2·3	0·3	7·9
	Australasia	39·1	22·2	13·4	10·9	2·2	2·2	0·4	9·6
1891	New South Wales	44·8	25·5	9·7	9·8	2·1	1·2	0·5	6·4
	Victoria........	35·2	21·8	14·7	13·0	1·9	2·5	0·6	10·3
	Queensland	36·2	23·6	11·6	7·8	2·2	2·6	0·2	15·8
	South Australia ..	27·9	14·7	5·7	19·0	3·7	5·5	0·3	23·2
	Western Australia	49·7	25·3	4·0	9·2	3·2	0·6	0·3	7·7
	Tasmania	49·9	17·6	6·6	11·7	3·1	2·2	...	8·9
	New Zealand	40·0	13·9	22·6	9·9	1·1	2·4	0·2	9·9
	Australasia	39·1	21·1	13·0	11·4	2·1	2·3	0·4	10·6
1901	New South Wales	46·6	26·0	9·9	10·3	1·9	1·2	0·5	3·6
	Victoria	35·8	22·3	16·2	15·2	1·5	2·8	0·[illegible]	5·7
	Queensland	37·5	24·5	11·7	9·5	·7	2·6		12·3
	South Australia ...	30·3	14·8	5·2	25·5	·8	6·2		14·0
	Western Australia	42·0	23·3	8·2	13·6	·5	1·7		8·0
	Tasmania	49·6	17·9	6·8	14·8	·3	2·8	..	4·8
	New Zealand	41·7	14·6	23·4	11·1	·9	2·1	0·2	6·0
	Australasia	40·5	21·6	13·5	13·2	1·8	2·4	0·4	6·6

From the foregoing table it will be seen that while there were fluctuations in individual states, the relative strength of the principal denominations in the whole of Australasia showed but little alteration during the thirty years from 1871 to 1901. The Church of England at the census of 1871 embraced 39·1 per cent. of the population, and at that of 1901 40·5 per cent. The Roman Catholic Church receded from 23·1 per cent. in 1871 to 22·2 per cent. in 1881, and to 21·1 per cent. in 1891 while there was a slight increase to 21·6 per cent. in

1901. The Presbyterian Church receded from 13·6 per cent. in 1871 to 13·4 per cent. in 1881 and 13·0 in 1891, rising again in 1901 to 13·5 per cent. The various Methodist bodies, which have been classed together, increased from 10·5 per cent. in 1871 to 10·9 per cent. in 1881, 11·4 per cent. in 1891, and 13·2 per cent. in 1901. Congregationalists remained almost stationary during the first three enumerations, but in 1901 the proportion receded to 1·8 per cent of the total. The percentage of Baptists at the enumeration of 1871 was 2 per cent., rising gradually to 2·4 per cent, at the census of 1901. At each of the four census periods the proportion of Jews remained the same, namely, 0·4 per cent. The column headed "All others" shows a decrease from 8·9 per cent. to 6·6 per cent. during the period. This column contains all the minor denominations, of which none are at all numerous except Lutherans in Queensland and South Australia; those whose denomination could hardly be classed as a religion; and all those who, from conscientious scruples, took advantage of the clauses of the Census Acts by which the filling in of the column "Religious Denomination" was left optional.

The Denominations in 1901.

The numbers of adherents of the various denominations in each state of the Australian Commonwealth at the census of 1901 were as follows:—

Denominations.	New South Wales.	Victoria.	Queensland.	South Australia.	West'n Australia.	Tasmania.	Australian Commonwealth.
Church of England	623,131	423,914	184,078	106,987	75,654	83,815	1,497,579
Roman Catholic	347,286	263,708	120,405	52,193	41,893	30,314	855,799
Presbyterian	132,617	191,459	57,442	18,357	14,707	11,523	426,105
Methodist	137,638	180,263	46,574	90,125	24,540	24,999	504,139
Baptist	16,618	33,730	12,717	21,764	3,125	4,716	92,670
Congregational	24,834	17,141	8,300	18,338	4,404	5,544	73,561
Lutheran	7,387	13,984	25,470	26,140	1,708	387	75,021
Salvation Army	9,585	8,829	5,512	4,030	1,690	1,454	31,100
Unitarian	770	788	212	621	150	88	2,629
Other Christian	18,635	27,429	6,896	10,612	3,626	4,770	66,968
Jew, Hebrew	6,447	5,907	733	786	1,259	107	15,239
Mahometan	1,072	467	*......	449	1,191	27	3,206
Buddhist, Confucian	5,471	4,806	1,750	3,190	835	353	16,405
Hindoo, Brahmin	468	195	122	24	37	......	846
Other Non-Christian	1,024	1,029	16,489	160	120	72	18,894
Freethinker, Agnostic, &c.	3,434	2,368	2,228	590	1,431	351	10,402
Indefinite	130	204	......	......	145	......	479
Others	23,299	24,899	7,668	13,238	7,614	3,955	80,673
Total	1,354,846	1,201,070	496,596	362,604	184,124	172,475	3,771,715

* Included with other Non-Christian.

The last heading, "Others," includes persons of no professed religious persuasion, those who objected to state their religious belief, and those whose religion was not ascertained. The large number of non-Christians in Queensland is accounted for by the presence in that state of numbers of Asiatics and other coloured aliens.

The numbers in New Zealand and in the whole of Australasia were as shown below :—

Denominations.	New Zealand.	Australasia.
Church of England	314,024	1,811,603
Roman Catholic	109,822	965,621
Presbyterian	176,503	602,608
Methodist	83,789	587,928
Baptist	16,035	108,705
Congregationalist	6,844	80,405
Lutheran	4,833	79,854
Salvation Army	7,999	39,099
Unitarian	468	3,097
Other Christian	18,827	85,795
Jew, Hebrew	1,612	16,851
Mahometan	41	3,247
Buddhist, Confucian	2,432	18,837
Hindoo, Brahmin	2	848
Other Non-Christian	1,041	19,935
Freethinker, Agnostic, &c.	3,495	13,897
Indefinite	377	856
Others	24,575	105,248
Total	772,719	4,544,434

The approximate strength of the various denominations in the Commonwealth and in Australasia at the end of 1902 was as follows :—

Denominations.	Commonwealth State.	Australia.
Church of England	1,543,035	1.871,085
Roman Catholic	881,749	997,324
Presbyterian	439,030	622,388
Methodist	519,429	607,228
Baptist	95,477	112,270
Congregationalist	75,789	83,043
Lutheran	77,294	82,475
Salvation Army	32,042	40,382
Unitarian	2,708	3,198
Other Christian	68,997	88,709
Jew, Hebrew	15,700	17,403
Mahometan	3,303	3,353
Buddhist, Confucian	16,902	19,454
Hindoo, Brahmin	871	875
Other Non-Christian	19,466	20,688
Freethinker, Agnostic	10,355	13,991
Indefinite	493	884
Others	83,440	109,260
Total	3,886,080	4,694,010

PRIVATE PROPERTY AND INCOMES.

THE first century of Australasian history closed on the 26th January, 1888, and though it is impossible to trace step by step the progress made during that period, as the data for the purpose are for the most part wanting, sufficient material is available from which a comparative statement of the wealth of the states at different periods may be deduced. In the following figures the private property of the people has alone been considered, the value of the unsold lands of the state, as well as the value of public works, having been omitted. The table shows the value of private property for the whole of Australasia, and the increase thereof at intervals of twenty-five years from the date when this territory was first colonised:—

Year.	Value of Private Property.
1788	Country first colonised.
1813	£1,000,000
1838	26,000,000
1863	181,000,000
1888	1,015,000,000
1901	1,083,838,000

Though Australasia has but the population of a province of some of the great European powers, in the wealth and earnings of its people it stands before most of the secondary states, and as regards wealth and income per head of population it compares very favourably with any country.

The plan adopted in valuing the elements of private wealth is given in detail in previous issues of this work, and has not been greatly varied on this occasion. Land, houses, and other improvements thereon, represent more than two-thirds of the private wealth. There are now ample data for assessing the value of these, for besides the municipal returns which are available for each state, there are complete land-tax returns for New South Wales, New Zealand, and South Australia. From the information thus to hand, there has been no difficulty in arriving at the value of land separately from its improvements. Estimates of the value of property of all kinds were made with great care for the year 1901; these have since been reviewed, and as there does not appear to have been any change of sufficient consequence to warrant an alteration of the estimates arrived at in the census year, the figures have, therefore, been reproduced in this chapter. For all Australasia, the value of land in private hands is £411,747,000, out of a total wealth of £1,083,838,000; this represents a proportion of 38 per cent., varying in each state, as follows:—

State.	Value of Land.	Proportion of Value of all Property.
New South Wales	£142,617,000	39·74 per cent.
Victoria	112,396,000	40·30 ,,
Queensland	35,887,000	31·80 ,,
South Australia	34,080,000	41·73 ,,
Western Australia	8,813,000	21·78 ,,
Tasmania	16,488,000	45·86 ,,
Commonwealth	350,281,000	38·54 ,,
New Zealand	61,466,000	35·11 ,,
Australasia	411,747,000	37·99 ,,

The value of land and improvements together amounts to £738,910,000, or 68·18 per cent. of the total value of property. The following is a statement of the values for each state:—

State.	Value of Land and Improvements.	Proportion of Value of all Property.
New South Wales	£263,052,000	73·29 per cent.
Victoria	204,294,000	73·25 ,,
Queensland	63,796,000	56·53 ,,
South Australia	56,060,000	68·65 ,,
Western Australia	14,360,000	35·49 ,,
Tasmania	26,243,000	72·99 ,,
Commonwealth	627,805,000	69·08 ,,
New Zealand	111,105,000	63·46 ,,
Australasia	738,910,000	68·18 ,,

The improvements on the lands of the Commonwealth and New Zealand are valued at £327,163,000, which sum represents 79·46 per cent. of the value of land, ranging between 84·45 per cent. in New South Wales and 59·16 per cent. in Tasmania.

Distributing the total value of private property into the ten subdivisions usually adopted in the classification of the elements of private wealth, the following results are arrived at:—

Classification.	Commonwealth States.	New Zealand.	Total.
	£	£	£
Land	350,281,000	61,466,000	411,747,000
Houses and permanent improvements	277,524,000	49,639,000	327,163,000
Live stock	85,048,000	27,184,000	112,232,000
Furniture and household goods and effects	29,746,000	5,254,000	35,000,000
Personal effects	12,066,000	2,318,000	14,384,000
Machinery and implements of trade, excluding mining machinery	29,852,000	6,121,000	35,973,000
Shipping	5,874,000	1,777,000	7,651,000
Mining properties and plant	32,299,000	2,950,000	35,249,000
Merchandise and produce on hand	59,711,000	14,021,000	73,732,000
Coin and bullion	26,361.000	4,346,000	30,707,000
Total	908,762,000	175,076,000	1,083,838,000

The foregoing gives an average of £240 per inhabitant for Australasia, and £243 for the Commonwealth, which figures show a considerable reduction on those of 1890, when the average was not less than £309 per inhabitant. The results fall somewhat short of the truth, inasmuch as they do not take into account property rights, the value of which is not represented by land, buildings, machinery, etc. The case of gas companies may be cited as an example. The total value of the shares of and interests in these companies throughout Australasia is approximately £6,900,000, but in the statement of values of properties given above, the actual property of gas companies appears as value of land, machinery, plant, etc., £4,350,000, no note being taken of value of goodwill and other items which form an appreciable proportion of the value of these works. The actual selling value of the gas undertakings of Australasia is therefore £2,550,000 in excess of the value of their tangible assets, and there are many other cases where a like anomaly exists. For New South Wales it is found that the sum of £18,000,000 might be added to the valuation on this score, and probably a like amount for Victoria, but the data even for these states are imperfect, and it has not been considered desirable to take into consideration an item about which there is any uncertainty.

The distribution of the property amongst the various states is as follows :—

State.	Value of Property.	
	Total.	Per Inhabitant.
	£	£
New South Wales	358,934,000	265
Victoria	278,887,000	234
Queensland	112,860,000	230
South Australia	81,664,000	227
Western Australia	40,462,000	230
Tasmania	35,955,000	208
Commonwealth	908,762,000	243
New Zealand	175,076,000	229
Australasia	1,083,838,000	240

These figures must be taken with some qualification. The foregoing table shows the state wherein the property lies, but gives no indication as to the place of residence of the owners. As is well known, residents in Great Britain have very large interests in Australia and New Zealand, and persons residing in one state have large holdings in other states : thus residents of Victoria and South Australia have large investments in New South Wales, Queensland, and Western Australia, while residents of Victoria and New South Wales are largely interested in Queensland properties. If it were possible to locate the actual ownership of property throughout Australasia it would probably be found that the actual distribution is very different from the apparent distribution as shown above.

The figures available to illustrate the amount of property possessed by persons not living within the state in which their property is situated are by no means complete; indeed details of any kind are obtainable only for New South Wales, Victoria, and New Zealand.

An analysis of the information gathered by the Stamps Office in Sydney for the purpose of assessing the values of the estates of deceased persons shows that the ownership of the £32,638,705 on which stamp duty was paid during the last seven years was as follows:—

	Total. £	Proportion per cent.
New South Wales	26,319,141	80·6
Europe, including Great Britain	3,093,692	9·5
Victoria	2,076,792	6·4
Other States of Australia and New Zealand	993,925	3·0
Elsewhere	155,155	0·5
	£32,638,705	100·0

It may, therefore, be assumed that 20 per cent. of the property in New South Wales is owned by persons who live outside its boundaries, about 10 per cent. being held in Great Britain and 6½ per cent. in Victoria.

In regard to Victoria, there is no direct evidence of ownership available, but the place of residence of the persons who pay income tax affords indirect evidence of great value. During the last five years the incomes of persons paying taxation in respect of incomes derived from property in Victoria were £21,364,000, and of this amount £3,932,500 was enjoyed by persons who resided out of Victoria, This gives about 18½ per cent. as the apparent proportion of absentee incomes. The actual proportion, however, is not so great, as incomes of residents of Victoria below £200 a year do not pay tax, while all absentee incomes are liable; making due allowance on this score it will be found that in all probability 16 per cent. of property in Victoria is owned by absentees.

So far as New Zealand is concerned, there is both direct and indirect evidence. In the year 1888 the value of property assessed for property tax was £135,881,176, and of this sum £24,313,706, or 18 per cent., was returned as belonging to persons not residing in the colony. Since then the proportion of property held by absentees has greatly declined; there has of late years been no great import of capital into the colony, while during some years there have been considerable withdrawals. On the other hand, the total value of property has largely increased, so that at the present time the proportion of New Zealand property held by absentees is only about 9 per cent.

The proportion for Queensland and Western Australia is probably greater than in the other states; for South Australia and Tasmania it is probably less. Adopting a reasonable estimate for these states, it may be said that, apart from Government stock held in London, the value of property in Australia belonging to non-residents of the states in which such property is situated, is not less than £152,000,000, and in New Zealand £15,350,000. In the case of Australia, a considerable portion of this property is held by persons residing in other states than those where the property is situated, and, if allowance be made on this account, it will be found that the value of property belonging to other than Australian residents is approximately £110,000,000. The question of the indebtedness of the Australasian states is referred to at length in another part of this chapter, and for further information the reader is referred to page 314.

DISTRIBUTION OF PROPERTY.

It is a somewhat prevalent practice amongst statisticians to make the valuations for probate purposes the basis of their estimates of the wealth of a country, but no reliance whatever can be placed upon the returns of values of estates assumed for probate purposes, for such returns at best only profess to give the apparent amount of property left by deceased persons, without any allowance for debts. There is, however, some show of reason for using the valuation of estates for stamp-duty purposes. These valuations are far below the values for probate purposes, for while during the twelve years ended with 1902 the probate returns in New South Wales give a total of £66,708,000, the sworn valuation of the very same estates for stamp duty was £52,187,000, or a little more than 78 per cent., and there can hardly be any doubt that all the other states would show similar discrepancies. Much greater reliance could be placed upon estimates depending upon the amount of stamp duty paid, if the ages of the persons dying were taken into consideration; but information on this point is not procurable, except at excessive trouble, and the idea of using the valuations for stamp duty for estimating the amount of wealth in the country cannot, therefore, be resorted to.

The probate returns, however, are not without considerable statistical value, as will presently appear, and the returns for the seven years ended with 1902 are, therefore, given below:—

State.	Number of Estates.	Total Value of Estates.	Average Value of Estate left by each Deceased Person leaving Property.	Corrected values to allow for overstatement of Probate Returns.
		£	£	£
New South Wales	17,325	41,180,987	2,378	1,855
Victoria	21,664	37,508,811	1,731	1,350
Queensland	4,176	10,971,064	2,627	2,049
South Australia	6,008	11,400,680	1,898	1,480
*Western Australia	1,342	2,137,181	1,592	1,242
Tasmania	1,349	2,188,948	1,623	1,266
Commonwealth	51,864	105,387,671	2,032	1,585
New Zealand	7,399	12,762,606	1,725	1,345
Australasia	59,263	118,150,277	1,994	1,555

* Five years only.

On the preceding page it is pointed out that the probate returns in New South Wales over-state the actual value of property by some 20 per cent.: assuming that there is an equal over-statement in all the states, the figures shown in the last column of the foregoing table would represent the true average values of the estates of persons having property in each state.

By comparing the number of persons who leave property at death with the number of persons dying some idea is obtained of the proportion of the whole population possessing estates sufficiently valuable to become the objects of specific bequest. This has been done for each year since 1880, and the following table shows the number of persons per hundred dying who were possessed of property, while the figures may also be taken as the proportion of the whole population owning property to the value of at least £100:—

State.	Proportion of Estates per 100 deaths of total population.				
	1880-84.	1885-89.	1890-94.	1895-1900.	1901-2.
	per cent.	per cent.	per cent.	per cent.	per cent.
New South Wales	11·0	11·6	13·2	15·15	16·65
Victoria	12·7	13·1	17·3	21·63	24·18*
Queensland	6·6	8·8	10·2	10·17	10·08
South Australia	12·3	15·3	17·4	19·95	21·96
Western Australia	10·8	10·7	12·0	11·56	†
Tasmania	9·6	11·5	11·9	10·72	12·62*
Commonwealth	11·1	12·0	14·1	17·23	*
New Zealand	......	......	9·4	15·97	19·09
Australasia	......	....	14·0	16·75	.. ...

* 1901 only. † No later information.

These figures show a distribution of property not to be paralleled in any other part of the world; and in a country where so much is said about the poor growing poorer and the rich richer, it is pleasing to find that in the whole population one in six is the possessor of property, and that the ratio of distribution has been increasing with fair regularity in every province of the group. Victoria has the widest diffusion of wealth of the individual states; South Australia comes next to Victoria; then come New Zealand, New South Wales, Tasmania, Western Australia; and lastly, Queensland. Too much stress, however, may be laid on the apparently wider distribution of wealth in one state than in another, for it is obvious that a province with a stationary or decreasing population will naturally come out of a comparison of this kind more favourably than another with a rapidly-increasing population.

To show the wide distribution of property in these states, the following statement is even more useful than the figures just given. The comparison is made as for every hundred deaths of adult males, and for the same number of deaths of adult males and females. This latter method is undoubtedly the proper basis of comparison, as large numbers of females are possessors of a substantial amount of property :—

State.	Proportion of Estates per 100 deaths of adult males.					Proportion of Estates per 100 deaths of adult males and females.				
	1880-1884.	1885-1889.	1890-1894.	1895-1900.	1901-1902.	1880-1884.	1885-1889.	1890-1894.	1895-1900.	1901-1902.
	per cent.	per cent.	per cent.	per cent.	per cent.	per cent.	per cent.	per cent.	per cent.	per cent.
New South Wales	34·6	37·5	41·2	43·4	45·8	22·3	23·8	25·8	26·8	27·8
Victoria	38·8	39·7	49·8	58·8	63·0*	23·4	24·2	30·2	34·3	36·6*
Queensland	18·3	23·1	28·6	26·2	23·9	18·8	16·9	20·2	18·2	16·4
South Australia	50·0	53·5	59·4	62·7	65·9	29·1	30·9	32·3	34·2	36·1
Western Australia	29·5	29·3	31·2	27·0	..†	19·8	19·6	21·1	20·4	..†
Tasmania	26·0	31·6	33·2	29·5	36·5*	15·8	19·4	20·1	17·2	19·3*
Commonwealth	34·6	37·0	42·1	46 6	..	22·0	23·4	26·1	28·5	..
New Zealand	..	..	27·3	42·1	48·1	..	..	16·7	25·5	28·4*
Australasia	..	..	41·6	46·0	..	..	..	25·8	28·1	..

* 1901 only. † No later information.

There is the same weakness in these figures as in those representing the values. Taking the last ten years it has been ascertained that in New South Wales nearly six in each hundred estates, for which probate or letters of administration are granted, prove to be without assets; it is possible a like condition obtains in other states, and the proportion of persons having property is therefore somewhat overstated.

Taking the returns of estates subject to stamp duties as the basis of comparison, and making allowance for those escaping duty, such as the circumstances seem to warrant, the following table gives for each State the number of adults with property to the value of at least £100 :—

State.	Number of Estates exceeding £100 in value.
New South Wales	188,800
Victoria	226,200
Queensland	41,200
South Australia	63,800
Western Australia	24,600
Tasmania	16,400
Commonwealth	561,000
New Zealand	114,400
Australasia	675,400

The figures for some of the states may appear to be extraordinarily large, but they find strong support in the banking returns, especially those of the Savings Banks, given elsewhere in this chapter. There is a general assumption in dealing with this branch of statistics that few women possess property, and in dealing with property and incomes the position of women is often lost sight of. Full information regarding women's property is obtainable for New South Wales, and the following comparisons are interesting; the figures refer to the seven years 1896 to 1902, but they differ somewhat in regard to the percentages from those in the preceding pages, which include all properties over £100 in value :—

	Males.	Females.
Number of persons dying who had property in excess of £200	12,043	4,311
Number residing in the State of New South Wales	11,244	4,120
Number residing elsewhere	799	191
Value of property devised	£28,458,600	£4,180,105
Average value of estates...............	£2,363	£970
Proportion of total adult population with estates over £200 in value	31 per cent.	17½ per cent.

Importation of Capital.

Australasia ranks among the debtor nations. In June, 1903, its people owed to persons outside its boundaries, or, more correctly speaking, there was invested in it by non-residents, and owing by its various Governments, a sum approximating to £408,078,000, or £87 per inhabitant. Of this large sum, £156,875,000 represents the private investments, and £251,203,000 the outstanding liabilities of the states and local governing bodies. More important in some respects than the corpus of the debt are the annual payments made in respect thereof. These can be stated with some exactitude. The yearly interest paid on account of state debts to other than Australasian creditors amounts to £8,297,000, and on account of local government debts, £562,000, while the income from private investments may be stated at £8,350,000, and the absentee incomes and return on shares held in London, £400,000. These various sums make up a total of £17,609,000, which is the tribute paid yearly by Australasia to London.

It has been stated above that the gross amount of investments by non-residents is £408,078,000. This sum may be divided into what was received prior to 1871, and what was received subsequent to that date, for 1871 may be conveniently taken as the opening year of latter-day Australasian finance. At the opening of 1871 these states stood indebted to Great Britain as follows :—

	Commonwealth States.	New Zealand.	Total.
	£	£	£
On account of State and Municipalities	26,520,000	7,842,000	34,362,000
Private investments.......................	33,090,000	5,504,000	38,594,000
Total	59,610,000	13,346,000	72,956,000

From 1871 to 1902 the increase of indebtedness was :—

	Commonwealth States.	New Zealand.	Total.
	£	£	£
On account of State and Municipalities	166,464,000	50,377,000	216,841,000
Private investments	114,282,000	3,999,000	118,281,000
Total..............................	280,746,000	54,376,000	335,122,000

The figures just given are irrespective of the money brought by persons taking up their abode in Australasia; the amount of such money is very considerable, as will presently appear.

The interests of the various states are so intertwined that there is not a little difficulty in accurately determining the amount of capital imported on private account, in which each stands indebted to Great Britain. In former editions of this work such a distribution was made, but the changes that have taken place since 1893, in which year the bank crisis occurred, have been so many and so extensive, that a separation of the respective interests of the various States is well-nigh impossible.

In considering the question of the annual payment made by Australasia to Great Britain—which is its sole creditor—it is important to have distinctly in view the fact that part of this income is payable irrespective of production, and part only arises when there has been antecedent production. In the first of these categories is the charge on state and municipal borrowings to the amount already stated (£8,859,000), and from two-fifths to a half of the income from private investments, or, in round figures, £3,500,000—the two taken together making a sum of £12,359,000, or £2 12s. 8d. per inhabitant, which must be exported entirely irrespective of the condition of productive industry. It may here be remarked that there is another source of drainage from these states to be considered in estimating the tributary stream flowing from Australasia to England—that is, the income of absentee colonists, which for 1902 probably reached £400,000, a figure very greatly below that of previous years. The total payments to outside creditors or investors during 1902 may be summarised as follow :—

	£
Payments on account of state or municipal borrowings, and on account of private investments on which interest must be paid irrespective of the condition of production	12,359,000
Return dependent on antecedent production	4,850,000
Absentee incomes	400,000
Total..	£17,609,000

Of the sum just given, £14,866,000 is paid by the states of the Commonwealth, and £2,743,000 by New Zealand.

From these figures it will be gathered that for these states to pay their way there ought to be an excess of exports over imports equal to the interest on loans outstanding and the earnings of investments —that is to say, if no capital were introduced and none withdrawn. But equilibrium in this respect is not to be looked for. Even now there is a stream of capital coming here in excess of what is withdrawn; and in the worst years several thousand persons arrive in Australasia with the intention of settling, a large proportion of whom bring with them some little capital with which to begin their career in their new home. In the foregoing pages the expression "capital introduced" must be taken in a qualified sense. Under the condition of equilibrium between the introduction and withdrawal of capital, as already demonstrated, Australasia would show an excess of exports representing the interest on state and other public loans and the tribute due to private investors. This export for 1902 was about £17,609,000, and it is therefore plain that Australasia might increase its indebtedness to the extent of over seventeen and a half millions in any one year and at the same time show an equality between its imports and exports. With this explanation in mind it will not be difficult to understand how, in spite of the fact that during the last thirty-two years the indebtedness of Australasia was increased by £335,117,000, the balance of trade during the same period was against the country to the extent of £10,908,000. Such is the operation of interest as affecting a debtor country. In further explanation of this view of the matter the following figures are given; they refer to the borrowings of the Governments and local bodies during the thirty-two years 1871–1902:—

State.	Borrowings of State and Local Government Bodies.	Interest on State and Local Government Loans.	Net Amount of Money introduced.
	£	£	£
New South Wales	53,261,000	42,836,000	10,425,000
Victoria	40,117,000	43,930,000	(—) 3,813,000
Queensland	31,425,000	25,308,000	6,117,000
South Australia	20,150,000	19,127,000	1,023,000
Western Australia	14,353,000	2,914,000	11,439,000
Tasmania	7,158,000	5,909,000	1,249,000
Commonwealth	166,464,000	140,024,000	26,440,000
New Zealand	50,377,000	49,994,000	383,000
Australasia	216,841,000	190,018,000	26,823,000

It will be seen that out of loans aggregating £216,841,000 a sum of only £26,823,000 reached Australasia, the balance of £190,018,000 being retained in London to meet interest charges, as a set-off against a similar sum which otherwise it would have been necessary to remit from Australasia. The figures in regard to private borrowings are still more striking:—

Private borrowings in excess of withdrawals	£118,281,000
Capital introduced by persons taking up their abode in Australasia	27,141,000
Total inflow of capital	£145,422,000
Earnings of investments of non-residents and incomes of absentees in excess of income derived by residents in Australasia from investments abroad	183,152,000
Excess of outflow over inflow	£37,730,000

Leaving out of consideration the capital introduced by immigrants, it will be seen that since 1871 the return to investors, together with absentee incomes, has exceeded by nearly sixty-five millions the amount invested in Australasia, although of the principal sum, £118,281,000 still remains due. It may be difficult to conceive how such a result has been possible, but the difficulty will be lessened when it is remembered that at the beginning of the period embraced in the tables the Australasian states were already paying an annual tribute to private investors of £3,517,000, and, therefore, on account of debts incurred and investments made prior to 1871 something like 112 millions might have been paid away during the last thirty-two years without any reduction in the principal owing.

Movement of Capital.

The movement of capital towards Australasia up to the end of 1870 presented no features of unusual importance, for the total sum received, though large, representing as it did rather more than £38 per inhabitant, was not larger than might reasonably have been expected to be introduced into a country so rapidly adding to its population and so fertile in resources. During this period the investments on private account and by the various Governments were almost equal in amount, but in the thirty years that followed, the borrowing operations of the Governments far outstripped private investments. The following table shows the borrowings of the state and on private account up to the end of 1870, and in five-year periods subsequent to that date:—

Period.	Money raised by Government or Local Bodies.	Private Investments, excluding Immigrants' Capital.	Total.
	£	£	£
Prior to 1871	34,362,000	38,594,000	72,956,000
1871–75	20,999,000	*2,392,000	18,607,000
1876–80	32,804,000	11,407,000	44,211,000
1881–85	46,944,000	37,186,000	84,130,000
1886–90	53,374,000	49,077,000	102,451,000
1891–95	28,653,000	*1,322,000	27,331,000
1896–1900	21,982,000	18,400,000	40,382,000
1901–1902	12,085,000	5,925,000	18,010,000
Total	251,203,000	156,875,000	408,078,000

* Excess of withdrawals over investments.

In the foregoing table the importation of capital by immigrants has been neglected; if this be taken into consideration, the figures given in the next table show the full amount for the period subsequent to 1870:—

Period.	Total Capital Introduced.
1871–75	£23,010,000
1876–80	48,959,000
1881–85	90,504,000
1886–90	107,088,000
1891–95	30,705,000
1896–1900	42,847,000
1901–1902	19,150,000
Total	£362,263,000

The total indebtedness of Australasia to British investors is set down in the foregoing pages at £408,078,000, and the annual return therefrom, excluding absentee incomes, £17,209,000. The capital sum represents a weight of £86 18s. 9d. per inhabitant, and the annual return £3 13s. 4d. The apparent interest earned is, therefore, slightly above 4 per cent., a rate which must be considered very favourable, seeing that £251,203,000, or three-fifths of the total, comprises Government and Municipal securities. The indebtedness of the states of the Commonwealth to British creditors amounts to £340,356,000, or £87 11s. 8d. per inhabitant, of which £192,984,000 is due by the central and local governing bodies, and £147,372,000 represents private investments. The indebtedness of New Zealand is £67,722,000, or £83 16s. 5d. per inhabitant, of which £58,219,000 is owing by the central and local governing bodies, and £9,503,000 represents private investments.

From the table given above showing the total amount of money including that brought to the country by immigrants introduced during each quinquennial period since 1870, it will be seen that the net introduction of capital during the first period was £23,010,000, and of this New Zealand received £10,707,000, or nearly one-half, principally the proceeds of Governmental borrowings, the withdrawals of private capital being nearly as large as the amount introduced. Queensland and New South Wales had, during the period, an accession of capital to the extent of £4,329,000 and £4,321,000 respectively; in the one case the sum obtained by the state was £2,389,000, and by the public, £1,940,000, while in the other case the sum introduced by the state was £2,861,000, and by private persons something less than £1,460,000. The net sum introduced into Victoria was £2,982,000, the state having imported £3,352,000, while the export of private capital was some £370,000. Tasmania received in all £1,210,000, of which £220,000 was introduced by the state, and nearly one million by private persons, which must be reckoned a very considerable sum in view of the smallness of the population of the island. Nearly the whole sum introduced into Western Australia (£400,000) was by the

Government. South Australia, even so far back as 1871–75, was in a very different position to the other states in regard to private investments. During the five years the state introduced £1,722,000, but £2,661,000 was withdrawn by lenders or sent out of the state for investment. Speaking generally, the period 1871 to 1875 was marked by large public borrowing, with a very moderate influx of private capital. During this interval the importation by the various Governments amounted to £2 per inhabitant yearly, the private investments being not more than 4s. per inhabitant.

The period from 1876 to 1880 showed a net importation of capital to the amount of £48,959,000, or more than twice the sum received during the preceding five years. Of the sum named, New Zealand received £15,396,000, or slightly less than one-third, although its population was only one-eighth of the whole of Australasia. The larger portion of the money brought to New Zealand was in the shape of Government loans, which amounted to £10,884,000, the net sum received on account of private investment being £4,512,000. New South Wales stood next as regards the amount of capital received, but the borrowing by the state and local bodies only amounted to £5,458,000, or half the sum raised by New Zealand, while the private investments amounted to about £8,168,000, of which nearly two millions were received with immigrants taking up their permanent abode in the state. The total capital imported into New South Wales during the five years was £13,626,000. Queensland received £8,028,000 during the period—an enormous sum, considering that the population was not more than 150,000. The money imported by the Government was £4,980,000, and that invested by private persons, £3,048,000. The Victorian Government imported £5,229,000, while the sum sent to the state by private investors, over and above the amount withdrawn, was £1,949,000. The South Australian Government borrowed largely during the five years, the sum raised being £5,217,000, but, as in the previous period, the sum withdrawn by investors or sent to other states for investment exceeded the capital introduced by £1,644,000. Both Tasmania and Western Australia received less capital from abroad from 1876 to 1880 than in the previous five years, the amounts being £954,000 and £204,000 respectively. The Government borrowings were £671,000 in the one case and £365,000 in the other; but in Tasmania there was an investment of £283,000 by private persons, and a withdrawal of £161,000 in the case of Western Australia. Taking Australasia as a whole, the public borrowings during 1876–80 were large, amounting to £32,804,000, or a yearly sum of about £2 12s. per inhabitant. The import of private money continued on a more extended scale, the sum received in excess of withdrawals being £16,155,000, but nearly five millions of this sum were brought in by immigrants.

The facility with which New Zealand had been able to obtain money on loan during the five years 1876–80 was an object lesson not lost on the Australian states, for during the five years from 1881 to 1885 the sum of £46,944,000 was raised by the various Governments and local bodies; while private investors, banks, and financial institutions poured in money at an almost equal rate, the net sum received on private account being, in round figures, £43,560,000. These sums represent yearly amounts of £3 2s. 4d. and £2 18s. 1d., or together over £6 per inhabitant —a rate of increase in indebtedness quite unparalleled in any country except in the next succeeding five years of Australasian history. Of the large sum of £90,504,000 received by these states, the share of New South Wales was £30,473,000. In the light of this statement it is easy to understand how, during this same period, though one of drought and restricted production, the industrial life of the state was marked by increasing wages, shorter hours, and full employment. The importation by the state amounted to £16,066,000, and by private investors to £14,407,000, but of the sum last quoted £2,719,000 represented the money brought by immigrants and entailed no burthen on the state for future interest to be exported. This period was, so far as New South Wales is concerned, the one marked by the most lavish borrowing by the state, though it yields to the subsequent quinquennium in regard to the importation of private capital. Queensland was next to New South Wales in receipt of most money during the period under review, the Government of that state having obtained £7,094,000, while private investments amounted to £12,505,000—enormous sums for a population of a quarter of a million. Included in the private investments, however, is the sum of £1,927,000 introduced by immigrants taking up their abode permanently in the state. The imports of capital into New Zealand during the quinquennium were still very heavy, amounting to £7,442,000 by the Government, and £10,475,000 on private account, or £17,917,000 in all. Of the private importation, £587,000 accompanied the owners who settled in the colony. The capital received by Victoria, which in the two preceding periods amounted to very moderate sums, now rose to £13,002,000, viz., £8,519,000 on account of the Government, and £4,483,000 by private investors. The South Australian Government in 1881–85 was still a large borrower, £5,895,000 being raised and expended during that time, while, contrary to the experiences of previous periods, there was an importation on private account of £1,000,000. Tasmania, also, considerably increased its borrowings, the state raising £1,465,000 in the five years, while £425,000 was sent for investment or was received with the owners. The borrowing of the Western Australian Government for 1881–85 amounted to £463,000, but not more than £265,000 was received for private investment, or in all £728,000.

The next period, 1886–90, was marked by very extraordinary features. The average population of Australasia was 3,540,000, yet during the short space of five years the various states governing these people raised and expended £53,374,000, while an additional sum of £53,714,000 was received for investment on private account, or was introduced into the country by persons who made it their abode. But even more astonishment will be evinced on considering the detailed figures for each state. Of the large total received by the various states, considerably more than one-half—£54,690,000—was obtained by Victoria, and, as the population during the five years under review was 1,070,000, the inflow of capital amounted to over £51 per inhabitant. The state and local bodies borrowed and disbursed £16,987,000, which was the largest expenditure from the proceeds of loans that any state contrived to crowd into the short space of five years. The private capital introduced was £35,792,000, and the sum brought by persons taking up their abode in the country was £1,911,000. These figures afford a sufficient clue to the astounding impetus which trade received during these years, and the corresponding rise in land values. New South Wales, though not the recipient of so much money as its southern neighbour, nevertheless contrived to obtain £28,145,000—a far larger sum than could be conveniently absorbed in five years, especially as in the like preceding period £30,000,000 was absorbed. The capital introduced represented £11,571,000 of Government borrowings, £15,187,000 of private investments, and £1,387,000 brought by persons making New South Wales their home. The Queensland Government was also a large borrower, its loan expenditure during the five years, 1886–90, being not less than £9,581,000. The private capital introduced, however, fell off largely. The sum received, allowing for withdrawals to the amount of £3,360,000, was £1,574,000. The flow of private money to New Zealand practically ceased during the period now under consideration, amounting only to £632,000, as compared with £10,475,000 in the preceding five years; but Government borrowings still continued, and a sum of £6,560,000 was raised and expended. South Australia occupied an exceptional position, for though the Government introduced some £5,693,000, there was a large withdrawal of private capital, or, as it may be, an export of capital for investment in other states, so that the net import on public and private account amounted to £1,345,000. Tasmania, with its population of 150,000, was well in the struggle for British investments, the State importation being £2,557,000, and the investment by private persons, £570,000; of this last sum £85,000 was introduced by persons taking up their abode in the state. It was about this period, too, that Western Australia began to attract attention as a field for investment, for over and above the sum of £425,000 introduced by the Government, about £1,009,000 was invested by private persons, perhaps one-fifth of the amount being accompanied by the investors themselves.

The recitation of borrowing just given brings the financial history of the Australias down to the close of 1890. Two years more of credit and investment remain to be traced, after which came the collapse of credit, and the events of May, 1893, still fresh in the public memory. That two years elapsed after the close of 1890 before Australasian public credit in London finally collapsed is true only of Victoria, and in a modified sense of New South Wales, Western Australia, and Tasmania. These states continued to be the recipients of British money, but private investments were—excepting in the case of Victoria—on a minor scale. Victoria received fresh capital to the extent of £8,834,000, of which amount only £464,000 was brought in by immigrants. New South Wales received from private investments over £3,000,000, but the withdrawals were also extensive, so that the net amount of capital invested was only £1,711,000. Western Australia received £952,000, of which £408,000 was accompanied by the owners. Tasmania received £792,000, and of this about £271,000 was introduced by permanent residents. Withdrawals of private capital were already in progress before the close of 1890, and were continued from South Australia, but to a less extent than in the preceding period. New Zealand ceased to receive any private money, while Queensland, for the first time in its history, showed a net withdrawal of capital, the amount of which during the two years was £2,011,000, but as the state had introduced £1,917,000, there was an actual withdrawal of £3,928,000. During the two years 1891 and 1892 the total capital imported into Australasia was £25,083,000, and of this £18,786,000 was introduced by the various Governments and local bodies.

During the three years which followed there was a withdrawal of private capital from Australasia to the extent of £7,619,000, so that in spite of the importation during the years 1891 and 1892, the quinquennium showed a net withdrawal of £1,322,000. There was during the period a movement of £20,088,000 apparently introduced, and £21,410,000 withdrawn; but this movement was mainly between the states themselves, and not between Australasia and Great Britain. Looking at the figures in detail, it would seem that there was an importation in excess of withdrawals of £14,686,000 into Victoria, and £2,382,000 into Western Australia. So far as Victoria is concerned, this introduction of money was not by way of investment; it was merely the recall by the large financial institutions of their capital from other states. This withdrawal affected New South Wales and Queensland most largely; £10,162,000 was withdrawn from the latter province during the five years, and it is a great tribute to its resources and stability that this withdrawal should have been effected with so little disturbance to its financial position. New South Wales lost £4,481,000, part of which represents deposits gathered in London and withdrawn during the panic, and part transference of capital by branch institutions to the head offices in Melbourne. From New Zealand £2,143,000 was withdrawn, and from South Australia £1,698,000. The withdrawal in nearly all cases was a silent one; and it was only when a financial institution absolutely failed and the courts were invoked to consent to the removal of assets that the community at large realised the process that had been going on.

Taking the whole period of five years the net amount introduced was £30,705,000, the various governments obtaining £28,653,300 from abroad, while private investors withdrew £1,322,000, but as immigration did not entirely cease it is estimated that £3,374,000 was introduced during the period by persons who took up their permanent abode in the country. The respective shares of the state Governments in the money obtained in London on loan was as follows :—

New South Wales	£11,655,000
Victoria	5,430,000
Queensland	2,996,000
South Australia	638,000
Western Australia	2,291,000
Tasmania	1,835,000
Commonwealth	24,845,000
New Zealand	3,808,000
Australasia	£28,653,000

The withdrawal from Australia practically ceased in 1895, but during the next five years the movement of capital between the States and Europe was much involved, and cannot be traced very definitely. In 1896 and 1897 there was a considerable amount of money introduced into Western Australia, where the gold-fields claimed much attention from British mining speculators. In the same years, about £4,000,000 of private capital was brought to New South Wales ; a large part of this, however, was money that had been withdrawn during the period following the bank crisis. In 1898 and the two following years, considerable sums were also brought to New South Wales, so that in the five years ending with 1900 the State received altogether some £10,000,000 of private capital. During these five years the imports and exports of Victoria were practically equal in amount, and as the payments on behalf of the Government in London exceeded its borrowings by £7,350,000, and as there were also large payments on private account, this equality could only have been brought about by private borrowing. Careful estimates place the money so introduced at about £10,600,000. This money, however, may not have been required for investment in Victoria, as Melbourne is the headquarters of many important financial institutions, whose interests extend over the whole of Australia. A certain amount was also sent to Tasmania for investment during these five years ; on the other hand the process of withdrawing capital from Queensland was continued, and it is probable that an average of £1,500,000 a year left that state. During the five years, 1896-1900, the various state Governments increased their indebtedness to outside creditors by £14,735,000, more than half of which (£7,600,000) was obtained by Western Australia. New South Wales obtained £2,650,000 ; Queensland, £2,900,000 ; South Australia, £985,000 ; and Victoria, £600,000. The New Zealand Government also borrowed freely, and increased its indebtedness to the London market, including small sums borrowed by local bodies, by £7,187,000. Owing to its exceptionally prosperous condition, the colony was able to repay £4,450,000 to its private creditors. It has been claimed in some quarters that this withdrawal of capital from New Zealand was the voluntary act of investors dissatisfied with the trend of New Zealand legislation. Be that as it may, the fact remains that at the present time the indebtedness of New Zealand to various non-resident creditors is less than £10,000,000 sterling, and during the whole period over which the process of withdrawal has extended, the industries of the colony have undergone rapid expansion.

Taking Australia and New Zealand together, during the five years 1896–1900 the introduction of money on government account amounted to £21,982,000; besides this £18,400,000 was invested by persons living outside Australia in excess of money withdrawn, while the introduction of capital by immigrants amounted to £2,465,000.

During the two years, 1901–1902, the governments of the Australian States obtained £7,695,000 from the London market, New South Wales, Western Australia and Queensland being the chief borrowers. In these two years also considerable sums were sent to the country for investment, the introduction of capital in excess of withdrawals amounting approximately to £7,570,000, while the money brought by immigrants during the same period was estimated to have been £1,140,000. The New Zealand Government continued its borrowing policy and £4,390,000 was obtained by it in London. The repayment of British money on private investment continued, and it is estimated that £1,645,000 was withdrawn from the colony during the two years on this account. Taking Australia and New Zealand together, during the years 1901–1902 the sum of £19,150,000 was invested either with the Government or in private enterprise, in excess of the loans repaid and capital withdrawn.

In speaking of the British capital invested in Australasia no mention has been made of the amount lost by the owners in unprofitable speculations, of which there have been not a few. From the nature of the case the sum total of these losses cannot be stated with any degree of accuracy; but there is no reason to suppose that the proportion is greater than would have occurred in like investments if made in the British Isles.

Income.

The incomes received by the people of Australasia can be determined with considerable accuracy, as the information available for such an estimate is fairly extensive. For New South Wales, Victoria, South Australia, and New Zealand there are income-tax figures, in Queensland and Tasmania particulars of collections under dividend and income-tax acts, and for several of the states very full returns relating to land-values. Besides these direct sources of information there are official estimates of incomes for New South Wales and New Zealand. Excluding the revenues of the various state governments, the yearly income derived from Australasia amounts to £224,101,000, and of this sum local residents draw £206,492,000, and British investors and absentees

£17,609,000, and of this last-mentioned sum £8,859,000 represents income derived from Government or municipal stocks, and £8,750,000 the amount from private sources. Of the total income (£224,101,000) the states of the Commonwealth claim £184,674,000, and New Zealand £39,427,000, the incomes of non-residents in each case being £14,866,000 and £2,743,000.

Leaving out of consideration the income drawn by debenture-holders in England, it would appear that the income derived from private sources for each of the states was :—

State.	Total.	Per Inhabitant.
New South Wales	£63,927,000	£45·9
Victoria	52,819,000	43·7
Queensland	22,940,000	44·8
South Australia	14,724,000	40·3
Western Australia	15,864,000	77·4
Tasmania	7,834,000	44·6
Commonwealth	£178,108,000	£46·2
New Zealand	37,134,000	46·5
Australasia	£215,242,000	46·2

The amount of income derived from private sources (that is to say, all incomes except payments made by the various governments and local bodies to their debenture-holders), is thus £215,242,000, and of this amount £8,750,000, or slightly over 4 per cent., is drawn by non-residents.

Dividing the incomes into two categories, viz., those below and those above £200 a year, very interesting results are obtained; the figures do not include the sum of £8,859,000 paid to non-resident debenture-holders and holders of local government stock :—

State.	Number of persons with incomes of £200 and over.	Total Incomes £200 and over.	Total Incomes under £200.
	No.	£	£
New South Wales	29,700	19,539,000	44,388,000
Victoria	24,557	15,852,000	36,967,000
Queensland	8,100	5,613,000	17,327,000
South Australia	13,610	4,319,000	10,405,000
Western Australia	5,000	3,630,000	12,234,000
Tasmania	3,780	2,120,000	5,714,000
Commonwealth	84,747	51,073,000	127,035,000
New Zealand	14,470	8,318,000	28,816,000
Australasia	99,217	59,391,000	155,851,000

The incomes of the various states depend in a very large measure upon the number of adult male workers in those States, and the variations in the rates per inhabitant disclosed by the foregoing table, are largely due to the different proportions which these workers form of the general population. Amongst the Australian States Victoria and Western Australia stand at the extremes, the former with 307 adult males per thousand of the population, and the latter with 477 per thousand, and it is, therefore, easy to understand how, in such circumstances, the revenue per head of population in Western Australia so greatly exceeds that of Victoria.

In the edition of this work, published in 1900, attention was directed to the smallness of the aggregate incomes in Victoria subject to taxation —that is, incomes in excess of £200. In the year then reviewed the total of such incomes was £10,080,000, and the opinion was hazarded that the amount was greatly under-stated. Confirmation of this opinion was given by the increase, in the year immediately following, of the amount of taxable incomes, and in the present calculation the Victorian incomes over £200 have been set down at £15,852,000, which is an increase of over 57·2 per cent.

The incomes drawn from investments by persons non-resident amount to £8,350,000, and about £400,000 is spent by Australians resident in Europe. Of the first-mentioned amount, £2,850,000 is drawn from New South Wales, or nearly 4½ per cent. of the total incomes of the state apart from payments to debenture-holders; £1,800,000 is drawn from Victoria, or 3½ per cent.; £1,800,000 from Queensland, or nearly 8 per cent.; and £450,000 or less than 1¼ per cent. from New Zealand. As pointed out elsewhere in this volume the people of New Zealand are rapidly paying off their private indebtedness to the British moneylender, and as the process of repayment has been accompanied by an increase in the private wealth of the colony and in the output of its industries, it must be accepted as a satisfactory evidence of progress. In the case of some of the states the absentee income derived from them, is largely counterbalanced by incomes derived from other states. This is especially true of South Australia and Victoria. The absentee incomes of the first-named are equalled, if not exceeded, by the revenue which its residents derive from investments in Western Australia, New South Wales, and Queensland; while as regards Victoria there is evidence that New South Wales makes to the southern state an annual payment of from £480,000 to £600,000, according to the character of the season, while Queensland and Western Australia also make large payments, so that the excess of absentee incomes over the earnings of Victorian capital abroad is not very great.

The detailed figures of the incomes of the people, read with those in regard to property and production, admit of several very interesting comparisons as to the relation of one to the other. The following table shows the percentage which the incomes drawn in each state bear to the value of private wealth, the incomes being distinguished into total incomes and those over £200 a year:—

State.	Percentage which Total Incomes bear to value of private property.	Percentage which Incomes over £200 bear to private property.
New South Wales	17·8	5·4
Victoria	19·0	5·4
Queensland	20·3	4·1
South Australia	18·0	5·3
Western Australia	39·2	9·0
Tasmania	21·8	5·9
Commonwealth	19·5	5·4
New Zealand	21·2	4·8
Total	19·8	5·3

Taking Australia as a whole, the assessment placed upon private property appears to be about five times the annual income; Western Australia being the only state which departs in any marked degree from this proportion. In that state the assessment is only two and a half times, and this low ratio is accounted for by the circumstance that a large proportion of the private property of the state is represented by gold-mines, and the value of a gold-mine is rarely large compared with the payments made for wages and other services connected with its working.

As the fair distribution of the income of a country is of more importance to the population at large than the aggregate amount of all incomes, it is interesting to know what proportion of the population enjoys large incomes, and if the incomes of the great mass of the population are affected by the accumulation of large incomes in few hands. In the present condition of statistics no great amount of light can be thrown upon the question, although some interesting facts may be gleaned from the particulars already given. The unit for the most useful comparison in regard to incomes is the bread-winner; but as there are both male and female bread-winners it is necessary to take into account the less commercial and productive value of women's work compared with men's. Taking the productive employments of New South Wales and Victoria as a basis, it is found that the earnings of thirty-six men equal those of one hundred women, and if this wage efficiency holds good throughout Australia the work of the 1,560,784 male and 422,123 female bread-winners at the census of 1901 would be equivalent to that of 1,712,748 male bread-winners alone; and comparisons of earnings should therefore be made on the basis of this last number and not on the total 1,982,907 of male and female bread-winners taken together. There is, however, another consideration. Australia has not yet developed a class of independent women workers.

It is true there are considerable numbers of women who are the main bread-winners of their families, but as a rule the earnings of the woman go to supplement the earnings of the head of the family, usually the house-father, and there are some cogent reasons why the comparison of earnings and population should be made on the basis of the number of families to be supported, and this, for practical purposes, may be taken as indicated by the number of male bread-winners, and on such basis the following table has been compiled :—

State.	Average income Male Bread-winners whose income is less than £200 a year.	Average income Male Bread-winners whose income exceeds £200 a year.	Proportion of Male Bread-winners whose income exceeds £200 a year.
	£	£	
New South Wales	103	658	6·6 per cent.
Victoria	103	645	6·1 "
Queensland	103	569	4·5 "
South Australia	97	317	11·3 "
Western Australia	137	725	5·9 "
Tasmania	104	561	6·6 "
Commonwealth	105	530	7·2 "
New Zealand	107	575	5·3 "

This statement forms a corrective to the table on page 322 giving the average income per inhabitant. In that table South Australia and Victoria show the smallest incomes of any of the states, viz., £40·3 and £43·7 respectively, as compared with an average of £45·9 for New South Wales and £44·8 for Queensland; it would now appear that compared with the male bread-winners the average income below £200 a year is equal in Victoria to what it is in Queensland and in New South Wales, viz., £103, while in South Australia it is £97. As regards incomes over £200, the return for Victoria (£645) is largely in excess of the average for the Commonwealth; but for South Australia the average (£317) is much below that of the other states, although there is compensation in the fact that such incomes are widely distributed; thus in South Australia 11·3 per cent of all incomes exceed £200 as compared with 4·5 in Queensland, 5·9 in Western Australia, and 6·6 in New South Wales and Tasmania, and the comparison would be still more favourable if the absentee incomes drawn by Victoria and South Australia from the other states could have been brought into consideration.

As the income of every country depends largely upon its production, a comparison of incomes and production is interesting. No general law can be laid down as to the relation between the two, but it will be found that the more various and developed the industries the greater will be the income which results from production.

The following is the ratio of the incomes obtained in each state to the value of production in that state, as set out on page 913.

It will be seen that in each case the incomes exceed the production ; in Western Australia, however, the excess is very little above 2 per cent., whereas in the case of Victoria the excess is nearly 78 per cent. The low percentage of income given off by production in the case of Western Australia is explained by the fact that of the total production of £12,544,000, the value of gold won exceeds £7,000,000, and the income given off, so to speak, by this production is far less than the value of the production itself, for the winning of gold not only is a costly process, but when the precious metal is obtained, the cost of carriage and handling and other expenses form but a trifling percentage of its value.

State.	Percentage which Total Incomes bear to value of production.	Percentage which Incomes over £200 bear to production.
New South Wales	166·7	49·6
Victoria	177·8	46·8
Queensland	141·0	31·8
South Australia	158·8	47·8
Western Australia	102·2	19·2
Tasmania	144·7	32·9
New Zealand	128·0	26·6

RAILWAYS.

TO the proper development of a country like Australasia, ill-supplied with navigable rivers, railway construction is absolutely essential. This has been recognised from an early period, and for the last forty years the Governments of the principal states have been fully alive to the importance of carrying on the work. For a long time, however, they were hampered in their efforts by the difficulty of borrowing money in London at a reasonable rate of interest; but since the year 1871 considerable progress has been made in the work of construction; indeed, by far the greater portion of the public debt of Australasia has been contracted for railway purposes. As the area of the six states and New Zealand almost equals that of Europe or the United States of America, while the population numbers a little over four and a half millions, it is almost needless to say that many of the lines run through districts very sparsely peopled. This is particularly the case in the states of Queensland, South Australia, and Western Australia, where there are vast tracts of territory in which little in the nature of permanent settlement has yet been accomplished, and in none of the states can it be said that the railway lines traverse thickly-settled areas. Indeed, if a fault may be found with the state policy pursued in the past, it is that in some cases expensive lines have been laid down in empty country the requirements of which could have been effectually met for many years to come by light and cheap lines, and that in consequence the railway administrators find themselves heavily burdened with a number of unprofitable lines. A few of these have been closed, and the remainder are worked at a loss. Notwithstanding these drawbacks, however, the railways of the Commonwealth of Australia collectively yield a net return equal to 2·51 per cent., and those of Australasia 2·61 per cent. on the cost of construction.

History of Railway Construction.

An agitation for the introduction of the railway into the colony of New South Wales was afoot as early as 1846, and in August of that year it was decided at a public meeting held in Sydney to survey a line to connect the capital with Goulburn. But no decided step was taken towards construction until September, 1848, when the Sydney Railroad and Tramway Company was formed for the purpose of laying down a line between Sydney and Parramatta and Liverpool, to be after wards extended to Bathurst and to Goulburn. The first sod was turned by the Hon. Mrs. Keith Stewart, daughter of Sir Charles Fitzroy, the

Governor of the colony, on the 3rd July, 1850. Although started during a period of trade depression, when there was an abundant supply of labour, the scheme was only well under weigh when the discovery of gold caused a stampede from the city, and the company was left without workmen to carry on the undertaking. Undeterred, however, by the difficulties into which the changing conditions of the country had plunged the Sydney Railroad and Tramway Company, private enterprise in 1853 essayed the further task of constructing a line between Newcastle and Maitland; but this project proved no more successful than the other, and in the following year the Government was forced to step in and carry out the schemes for which the two companies had been promoted. From that time the work of construction was vigorously pressed forward, and on the 26th September, 1855, the line from Sydney to Parramatta, 14 miles in length, was opened to traffic; and on the 11th April, 1857, Newcastle was connected with East Maitland. The extension to Goulburn of the Sydney line was completed on the 27th May, 1869.

While the Sydney Railroad and Tramway Company was endeavouring to surmount the obstacles that had arisen in its path, the work of railway construction was begun in the neighbouring state of Victoria, no fewer than three private companies being promoted in 1853 for that purpose. Material assistance in the shape of land grants and guarantee of interest was afforded by the Government; and on the 13th September, 1854, the first completed railway in Australasia, a line extending from Flinders-street, Melbourne, to Port Melbourne, was opened to traffic. It had been begun nearly three years after the line to connect Sydney with Parramatta, but was only 2½ miles long. No further mileage was brought into operation until May 13, 1857, when the Melbourne and Hobson's Bay Railway Company, which had constructed the first line, effected communication with St. Kilda; and on the 17th June of the same year a line from Williamstown to Geelong, 39 miles in length, which had been built by another company, was declared open. Meanwhile the Government of the state had not remained inactive. In addition to assisting private enterprise with liberal concessions, it had taken over in 1855 an unfinished line started by the third of the companies referred to, and was carrying on the work of construction on its own account. By the year 1863 it had acquired all the lines in the state with the exception of those owned by the Melbourne and Hobson's Bay Company, which were not purchased until the year 1878.

Although a line from Goolwa to Port Elliot, 6 miles in length, over which the locomotive now passes, was opened on the 18th May, 1854, it was at that time merely a horse tramway; and the first railway in South Australia was a line connecting the city with Port Adelaide, 7½ miles long, which was thrown open to traffic on the 21st April, 1856. The following year saw a railway constructed as far north as Gawler; while on the 1st October, 1889, a line from Palmerston to Pine Creek, in the Northern Territory, which had been built by the South Australian Government, was opened, the length being 145½ miles.

The northern state of Queensland had enjoyed the privilege of self-government for several years when, early in 1864, a line to connect Ipswich with Grandchester was commenced, and on the 31st July of the same year it was opened.

Although the Tasmanian Parliament granted a sum of £5,000 in 1863 for the survey of a line to connect Hobart with Launceston, the first railway in the island was one between Launceston and Deloraine, 45 miles in length, which was opened on the 10th February, 1871, having been commenced three years before. It was built by a private company, to whose capital, however, the Government had subscribed eight-ninths of the total amount of £450,000, on condition that the interest should be a first charge on the net receipts, and on the 3rd August, 1872, the line passed entirely into the ownership of the state. Communication between Hobart and Launceston was effected in 1876 by the completion of a line, connecting the southern city with Evandale Junction, which was constructed by an English company. The last of the states comprised in the Commonwealth to introduce the railway was Western Australia, where a line from the port of Geraldton to Northampton was begun during 1874 and opened in 1878. The commencement of railway construction in New Zealand was due to an agitation on the part of the settlers of Canterbury, who were desirous of facilitating communication between the city of Christchurch and the port of Lyttleton. The first portion of the line, as far as Ferrymead Junction, was brought into use on the 1st December, 1863.

The progress of railway construction, except, perhaps, in the state of Victoria, was anything but rapid during the earlier years. This was in a great measure owing to the sparseness of the population and the natural fear that the return would not justify the expenditure which would have to be incurred in making lengthy extensions of the lines. It was also due, as previously pointed out, to the low estimation in which Australasian securities were held in London, and the consequent high rate of interest at which money for railway construction had to be borrowed. Since the year 1871, however, all the states and New Zealand have made satisfactory progress. In the following table will be found the length of line opened during each year, and the total mileage at the close of the working year:—

Year.	Miles opened.					
	Total.			During each year.		
	Commonwealth.	New Zealand.	Australasia.	Commonwealth.	New Zealand	Australasia.
1854	2½	....	2½	2½	....	2½
1855	16½	....	16½	14	....	14
1856	32½	....	32½	16	....	16
1857	117	....	117	84½	....	84½
1858	132	....	132	15	....	15
1859	171	....	171	39	....	39
1860	215	....	215	44	....	44

Year.	Miles opened.					
	Total.			During each year.		
	Common-wealth.	New Zealand.	Australasia.	Common-wealth.	New Zealand.	Australasia
1861	243	....	243	28	....	28
1862	373	....	373	130	....	130
1863	395	5	400	22	5	27
1864	469	5	474	74	....	74
1865	490	5	495	21	.. ..	21
1866	519	5	524	29	....	29
1867	711	7	718	192	2	194
1868	782	7	789	71	....	71
1869	911	7	918	129	....	129
1870	994	46	1,040	83	39	122
1871	1,030	105	1,135	36	59	95
1872	1,168	105	1,273	138	....	138
1873	1,353	145	1.498	185	40	225
1874	1,491	209	1,700	138	64	202
1875	1,602	542	2,144	111	333	444
1876	1,961	718	2,679	359	176	535
1877	2,493	954	3,447	532	236	768
1878	2,906	1,070	3,976	413	116	529
1879	3,222	1,171	4,393	316	101	417
1880	3,675	1,258	4,933	453	87	540
1881	4,192	1.334	5,526	517	76	593
1882	4,704	1,465	6.169	512	131	643
1883	5,107	1,480	6,587	403	15	418
1884	5,855	1,570	7,425	748	90	838
1885	6,227	1,654	7,881	372	84	456
1886	6,859	1,810	8,669	632	156	788
1887	7,657	1,841	9,498	798	31	829
1888	8,365	1,865	10,230	708	24	732
1889	9,162	1,912	11,074	797	47	844
1890	9,757	1,956	11,713	595	44	639
1891	10,163	2,011	12,174	406	55	461
1892	10,394	2,011	12,405	231	....	231
1893	10,688	2,108	12,796	294	97	391
1894	10,974	2,168	13,142	286	60	346
1895	11,600	2,190	13,790	626	22	648
1896	11,641	2,190	13,831	41	....	41
1897	11,970	2,185	14,155	329	(—) 5	324
1898	12,170	2,222	14,392	200	37	237
1899	12,702	2,257	14,959	532	35	567
1900	12,995	2,271	15,266	293	14	307
1901	13,497	2,300	15,797	502	29	531
1902	13,821	2,323	16,144	324	23	347
1903	13,730	2,404	16,134	(-) 91	81	(—) 10

It will be seen from the foregoing table that the lines opened in the Commonwealth and Australasia averaged 30 miles in length during each year from 1854 to 1861; from 1862 to 1871 the annual average was 82 miles in the Commonwealth and 89 in Australasia; from 1872 to 1881, 312 miles in the Commonwealth and 439 in Australasia; from 1882 to 1891, 597 miles in the Commonwealth and 665 in Australasia; and from 1892 to 1903, 333 miles in the Commonwealth and 372 in Australasia. It is now the established policy of each state to keep the railways under state control, and only in exceptional circumstances is that policy departed from. Excluding coal, timber, and other lines which are not open to general traffic, there are within the Commonwealth only 640¼ miles of private lines, equal to but 4·66 per cent. of the total mileage open; and in Australasia only 728¼ miles, or 4·51 per cent. of the total mileage open. In Victoria the railways are entirely in the hands of the Government; while in Western Australia there are 277 miles of private lines, or 15·44 per cent. of the total mileage of the state; in New South Wales, 81¼ miles; in Tasmania, 160 miles, and in South Australia, 20 miles. A departure from the ordinary policy of the state has also been made in Queensland, where the construction of the railway from Mareeba to Chillagoe, a distance of 102 miles, has been carried out by private persons. The private lines of New Zealand have a total length of 88 miles. Except in the case of Western Australia, none of these private railways are trunk lines, the most important of them being primarily intended to facilitate the development of important mines, and not for general traffic.

The divergence of the policy of Western Australia from that pursued by the other states was caused by the inability of the Government to construct lines when railway extension was urgently required in the interests of settlement. Private enterprise was therefore encouraged by liberal grants of land to undertake the work of construction; but the changing conditions of the state have modified its policy, and on the 1st January, 1897, the Government acquired the Great Southern Railway, 243 miles in length, one of the two trunk lines in private hands. This railway, which was owned by the West Australian Land Company, Limited, was built on the land-grant system, the state concession being 12,000 acres for every mile of line laid down, of which the original concessionaire retained 2,000 acres. The total price paid by the Government for the railway, with all the interests of the company and of the original concessionaire, was £1,100,000, of which £800,000 is set down as the capital sum on which the railway authorities are expected to provide interest, exclusive of the amount invested in rolling stock. The other trunk line is the Midland Railway, 277 miles in length, owned by the Midland Railway Company of Western Australia, Limited. In this case the land granted by the state was also 12,000 acres per mile of line. In 1891 the Government granted some slight assistance to the company, and in the following year guaranteed £500,000 of 4 per cent. debentures, the security being a first charge upon the railway and its equipment, and 2,400,000 acres selected land. At three months' notice, the state may foreclose should the company be indebted to it to the amount of £20,000.

The following statement shows the gauge and length of the private railways of Australasia, excluding coal, timber, and other lines which are not open to general traffic :—

Line	Gauge.		Length.
New South Wales—	ft.	in.	miles.
Deniliquin-Moama	5	3	45
Cockburn-Broken Hill	3	6	35½
Warwick Farm	4	8½	¾
Queensland—			
Mareeba to Chillagoe	3	6	102
South Australia—			
Glenelg Railway Co.'s lines :			
Holdfast Bay	5	3	7
Victoria Square	5	3	7
Sidings, loops, &c.	5	3	6
Western Australia—			
Midland : Midland Junction-Walkaway Junction	3	6	277
Tasmania—			
Emu Bay-Waratah-Guildford Junction-Zeehan	3	6	98
Lyell-Strahan	3	6	22
Gormanston to Kelly's Basin	3	6	33
Dundas-Zeehan	3	6	7
New Zealand—			
Wellington-Manawatu	3	6	84
Kaitangata-Stirling	3	6	4

A proviso has been inserted in the charters of the companies owning the private lines in New South Wales, whereby after a certain date the Government can, if so disposed, acquire the lines at a valuation. Similar conditions are found in most of the charters granted by the other states permitting the construction of private lines.

In the construction of railways during the last working year the state of Western Australia displayed most activity, 156 miles of new line having been opened for traffic during the year. It will be observed, on reference to the following table, that notwithstanding the opening of new lines, the total mileage is less than that shown in the previous year. The decrease is due to the closing in 1902 of several lines which were unable to pay working expenses.

The following table shows the extent of railway mileage in each state since 1861 :—

State.	1861	1866	1871	1876	1881	1886	1891-2	1901-2	1902-3
New South Wales..	73	148	358	554	1,040	1,941	2,266	3,107	3,220
Victoria	114	270	276	718	1,247	1,754	2,908	3,302	3,383
Queensland........	*	50	218	298	800	1,433	2,320	2,903	2,813
South Australia....	56	56	133	308	845	1,226	1,823	1,901	1,901
Western Australia..	*	*	*	38	92	202	657	1,990	1,793
Tasmania	*	*	45	45	168	303	425	618	620
Commonwealth	243	519	1,030	1,961	4,192	6,859	10,394	13,821	13,730
New Zealand	*	5	105	718	1,334	1,810	2,011	2,323	2,404
Australasia....	243	524	1,135	2,679	5,526	8,669	12,405	16,144	16,134

* Railways not in existence.

In 1883 a junction was effected between the New South Wales and Victorian lines at the river Murray ; three years later direct communication was established between Victoria and South Australia ; and in 1888 the last mile of line connecting Sydney with the northern state of Queensland was completed, thus placing the four capitals, Brisbane, Sydney, Melbourne, and Adelaide, in direct communication with each other. A few years ago proposals were made to the Government of Western Australia to construct a railway upon the land-grant system, connecting the eastern districts of the state with South Australia. It was proposed to extend the lines to Eucla, close to the South Australian border, and when that state had extended its railways to the same point, Perth would be connected with all the capitals of the Australian states. In June, 1897, the South Australian Railways Commissioner, in a report to the Commissioner of Public Works, estimated the cost of construction and equipment of a line to the Western Australian border, a distance of 553 miles, at £1,903,000. When the railways of the two states shall have been connected, as they will possibly be at no far distant date, the European mails will, in all likelihood, be landed at Fremantle, and sent overland to all parts of the continent.

The following table shows the length of Government railways in course of construction and authorised on the 30th June, 1903 :—

	Miles.
New South Wales	312
Victoria	127
Queensland	216
South Australia	3
Western Australia	48
Commonwealth	706
New Zealand	194
Australasia...	900

Notwithstanding the energetic expansion of the railway systems throughout Australasia since 1871, there is still room for considerable extension. In the state of South Australia construction is entirely confined to the south-eastern corner and to the extension of the Northern Line, which has its present terminus at Oodnadatta, 686 miles from Adelaide. It is proposed eventually to extend this line as far north as Pine Creek, the southern terminus of the Port Darwin line. In the course of the year 1896 offers were made on behalf of various syndicates for the construction of the transcontinental railway, with the acquisition of the section from Palmerston to Pine Creek; but the Government was not prepared to recommend to Parliament the acceptance of any offer based on the land grant or guarantee system. When this railway is completed, direct overland communication will be established between the northern and southern portions of the continent. The length of the gap between the terminus at Oodnadatta and that at Pine Creek is 1,140 miles on the telegraph route.

In New South Wales the railway extensions will be chiefly confined to perfecting the various systems already constructed. At the present time several lines of what is termed the "pioneer" class are in course of construction in level pastoral country. These are of a light and cheap kind, on which the produce of the settlers may be conveyed to the trunk lines at a reasonable speed and at a cheaper rate than carriage by road. In Queensland, with its vast expanse of partly-settled territory and extensive seaboard, the railways are being constructed in separate systems. The lines commence from each of the principal ports and run inland, but there is no doubt that not many years will elapse before these systems will become branches of a main trunk-line which, in all likelihood, will be the Brisbane-Charleville line extended as far as Normanton at the Gulf of Carpentaria. In this state a system has been introduced by which railways are constructed under a guarantee given by the local authority on behalf of the ratepayers of the district. Details of this system are given on a subsequent page. In Victoria, Tasmania, and New Zealand the railways are well developed compared with size of territory, and any future extensions will hardly be on so large a scale as in the other states. Western Australia has accomplished much useful work in the direction of extending the lines to the gold-fields, and also to the south-western portion of the state.

Control of State Railways.

The states of Victoria, South Australia, New South Wales, Queensland and Western Australia have found it expedient to place the management and maintenance of railways under the control of commissioners. Victoria, in 1883, was the first state to adopt this system; four years later South Australia made the change, while New South Wales and Queensland followed in 1888, and Western Australia in 1902. Each of these states (with the exception of Western Australia, where there is only one commissioner) appointed three officials as commissioners, and conferred upon them large executive powers, amounting to almost independent control, the object aimed at being to obtain economical management of the lines free from political interference. Subsequently Queensland, Victoria, and South Australia reduced the number of commissioners to one; but in New South Wales, where the administration has been most successful, no changes in the system have been made. On the 1st June, 1903, the control of the railways in Victoria was again vested in three commissioners. The control of the New Zealand railways was also handed over to a body of three commissioners in 1887; but at the beginning of 1895 the Government resumed charge of the lines, a general manager being appointed, responsible to a Minister for Railways.

In New South Wales and Victoria all proposals for new lines are submitted to committees selected from Members of the Houses of Parliament. These committees take evidence regarding the suitability of the route suggested, the probable cost of construction, the financial prospects of the line, and the grades to be adopted; and thereupon advise Parliament to adopt or reject the schemes proposed. This supervision of railway development may be said to have been attended with success, although lines that are not likely to be commercially successful have been recommended by the committee and sanctioned by Parliament.

Diversity of Gauge.

Unfortunately for interstate communication, railway construction in Australia has proceeded without uniformity of gauge, and the accomplishment of this work, which it is everywhere admitted must be secured, becomes more formidable to contemplate as the years roll on. In 1846 Mr. Gladstone advised that the 4-ft. 8½-in. gauge should be adopted for any lines constructed in New South Wales; and two years later this gauge was adopted as the standard by the Royal Commission appointed for the purpose of determining a uniform gauge for England and Scotland. In 1850, however, the Sydney Railroad and Tramway Company decided to adopt the 5-ft. 3-in. gauge, and in 1852 an Act was passed which provided that all railways in the state should be laid down to that gauge. But in 1853 the company mentioned, having changed their engineer, altered their views on the gauge question, and applied to have the 4-ft. 8½-in. gauge substituted for the 5-ft. 3-in., succeeding in repealing the Act and in passing another which made the narrower gauge imperative. This step was taken without the concurrence of the other states, and feeling ran very high in Victoria in consequence, as two of the railway companies in that state had already given large orders for rolling-stock on the 5-ft. 3-in. gauge. Until the lines of the two states met on the boundary no discomfort was, of course, experienced; but since then the break of gauge, with the consequent change of trains, has been a source of irritation and inconvenience. The South Australian

Government adopted at the outset the 5-ft. 3-in. gauge of Victoria; but finding that the construction of lines of this class involved a heavier expense than they were prepared to face, the more recent lines were built on a gauge of 3 ft. 6 in. In that state there are 507 miles laid to the 5-ft. 3-in. gauge, and 1,229¼ to that of 3-ft. 6-in., which is also the gauge of the 145½ miles of railway in the Northern Territory. The line joining Adelaide with the Victorian border, as well as several of the other trunk-lines, has been constructed on the wide gauge, so that the line from Melbourne to Adelaide is uniform. The private line which prolongs the South Australian system into New South Wales as far as Broken Hill is on the 3-ft. 6-in. gauge. All the Queensland lines are built on the gauge of 3 ft. 6 in., so that transhipment is necessary on the boundary between that state and New South Wales. Tasmania, Western Australia, and New Zealand have adopted the 3-ft. 6-in. gauge. The first line laid down in Tasmania was on the 5-ft. 3-in. gauge, but it was soon altered to 3 ft. 6 in. On the west coast of that island an experiment is being made in the construction of a 2-ft. gauge line, at one-fourth the cost of a line laid down to the Tasmanian standard gauge. The advisableness of constructing lines of this class is also being considered in Victoria. The total length of line in Australasia laid down to a gauge of 5 ft. 3 in. is 3,890½ miles; there are 3,138½ miles on the 4-ft. 8½-in. gauge, and 8,354½ miles on the 3-ft. 6-in. gauge.

As far back as May, 1889, Mr. Eddy urged the Government of New South Wales to take action with the object of securing a uniform gauge for the states, and frequently since that date the Railway Commissioners have directed attention to the urgency of dealing with this important question before the states incur greater expenditure in railway construction. They have suggested that the settlement of the difficult question of the adoption of a standard gauge should be approached from the standpoint of which of the two gauges, 4 ft. 8½ in. and 5 ft. 3 in., can be adopted at the least cost and with the smallest amount of inconvenience to the country; and that the whole of the railways of New South Wales and Victoria, with that part of the South Australian lines laid to the 5-ft. 3-in. gauge, as well as the line to Cockburn, and all the lines in Queensland south of Brisbane leading to New South Wales, shall be altered to the standard, the cost of altering the railways and the rolling stock necessary to work them to be a national charge.

Comparison of Railway Facilities.

The population and area of territory per mile of line open vary considerably in the different states and New Zealand. In comparison with population, Western Australia, Queensland, and South Australia—the most extensive states—have the greatest mileage; but in proportion to the area of territory, Victoria, Tasmania, and New Zealand take the lead. The annexed table shows the relation of the railway mileage to population and to the area of each state and New Zealand for the year 1902–3 :—

State.	Per Mile of Line Open.	
	Population.	Area.
	No.	sq. miles.
New South Wales	437	97
Victoria	356	26
Queensland	183	237
South Australia*	192	475
Western Australia	142	644
Tasmania	283	42
Commonwealth	289	222
New Zealand	336	43
Australasia	296	194

* Including Northern Territory.

In the following table are given the average population and area of territory per mile of line open in the principal countries of the world. Of course a comparison can only be made fairly between Australasia and other young countries in process of development :—

Countries.	Length of Railway.	Per Mile of Line Open.	
		Population.	Area.
	miles.	No.	sq. miles.
United Kingdom	22,078	1,900	5·5
France	23,910	1,639	8·6
Germany	30,974	1,820	6·7
Austria-Hungary	22,691	2,001	10·4
Belgium	2,843	2,354	4·0
Netherlands	1,730	3,042	7·3
Switzerland	2,490	1,331	6·4
Sweden	7,023	737	24·5
Norway	1,308	1,712	94·9
Russia (exclusive of Finland)	29,646	3,497	65·8
Spain	8,315	2,239	23·4
Italy	9,852	3,296	11·2
India (inclusive of Native States)	25,373	11,601	69·6
Canada	18,868	285	161·6
Cape Colony	2,994	812	73·9
Argentine Republic	10,300	465	110·2
Brazil	8,718	1,644	25·0
Chili	2,880	1,092	97·2
United States of America	198,787	384	17·9
Commonwealth of Australia	13,730	289	222
Australasia	16,134	296	194

Cost of Construction.

At the close of the year 1902–1903, the cost of construction and equipment of the state railways completed and open to traffic in the Commonwealth was, in round figures, £129,490,000, or 58·7 per cent. of the public debts of the states comprised in the Federation, after deducting sinking funds. The construction and equipment of the railways of Australasia cost £148,572,700, or 54·1 per cent. of the public debt of Australasia, after deducting sinking funds. To what extent the states have contributed to this expenditure will be apparent from the subjoined table, showing the total cost and the average per mile :—

State.	Year.	Length of line open.	Gauge.	Total cost of Construction and Equipment.	Average cost per mile.
		miles.	ft. in.	£	£
New South Wales	1903	3,138½	4 8½	41,654,977	13,272
Victoria	,,	3,383⅓	5 3	40,974,493	12,110
Queensland	,,	2,711	3 6	20,302,177	7,488
South Australia	,,	1,736¼	5 3 / 3 6	13,400,796	7,718
Northern Territory	,,	145⅓	3 6	1,175,056	8,080
Western Australia	,,	1,516	3 6	8,141,782	5,370
Tasmania	1902	461¾	3 6	3,840,747	8,302
Commonwealth	......	13,092⅓	......	129,490,028	9,890
New Zealand	1903	2,291	3 6	19,081,735	8,329
Australasia	......	15,383⅓	......	148,571,763	9,658

It will be seen that the lines which have been constructed most cheaply are those of Western Australia, where the average cost per mile has only been £5,370, as compared with an average of £9,890 for the Commonwealth and £9,658 for the whole of Australasia. In that state there have been few engineering difficulties to contend with, and the lines laid down have been of a light kind. In New South Wales, the average cost, given as £13,272, has been somewhat reduced lately, in consequence of the construction of light "Pioneer" lines, built at an expenditure of £2,019 per mile. The Minister for Public Works has constructed 12, and is constructing 5 new lines by day labour, as the Railway Construction Department has had a somewhat unfortunate experience in regard to claims for extras to contracts, and expensive litigation in resisting such claims. In Victoria the average cost has been reduced from £13,153 to £12,110 since 1891. At that date it was decided to apply the "butty-gang" system to the construction of railways in the state, and to build all new country lines as cheaply as possible, and this principle has been strictly adhered to. Fairly substantial permanent-way has been laid down, with reduced ballast; unless absolutely necessary, fencing and gatehouses have been dispensed with; and only a skeleton equipment for stations and water supplies has been provided. As settlement progresses and traffic is developed, it is intended to raise these lines to the requisite standard of efficiency.

It would hardly be fair to institute a comparison between the cost of construction per mile in Australasia and in the densely-populated countries of Europe, for while in Europe the resumption of valuable ground is perhaps the heaviest expense in connection with the building of railways, in the states and New Zealand this item of expenditure is not of leading importance. The cost per mile in certain sparsely-settled countries is as follows:—

Canada	£12,067
Cape Colony	10,363
United States	12,810
Argentina	10,213
Mexico	9,417
Chili	10,103
Brazil	14,355

while for the Commonwealth of Australia it is £9,890, and for New Zealand £8,329.

Revenue and Working Expenses.

The avowed object of state railway construction in Australasia has been to promote settlement, apart from considerations of the profitable working of the lines; but at the same time the principle has been kept in view that in the main the railways should be self-supporting, and some of the states have, with more or less success, handed them over to Commissioners to be worked according to commercial principles, free from political interference. With the exception of South Australia, so far as the Palmerston-Pine Creek line in the Northern Territory is concerned, in all the states the revenue derived from the railway traffic exceeds the working expenses. During 1898-9 the states of New South Wales and Western Australia derived a profit from the working of the lines; and for the year ended 30th June, 1900, the states of South Australia proper and Western Australia were similarly favoured. During 1900–1, the lines of New South Wales and Western Australia, and for the years ended 30th June, 1902 and 1903, those of Western Australia, not only paid working expenses and interest but left a slight margin of profit. Even in New South Wales, where the Commissioners have achieved most commendable results during the term of their administration, there is a fairly large deficiency for the year ended 30th June, 1903, when it is borne in mind that the average price received for the loans of the state is but £96·37 per £100 of stock, and the interest payable is calculated accordingly. The net sum available to meet interest charges during the last two working years will be found in the following table, showing the earnings and working expenses:—

State.	Working year, 1901–1902.			Working year, 1902–1903.		
	Gross Earnings.	Working Expenses.	Net Earnings.	Gross Earnings.	Working Expenses.	Net Earnings.
	£	£	£	£	£	£
New South Wales......	3,668,686	2,267,369	1,401,317	3,314,893	2,266,299	1,048,594
Victoria	3,367,843	2,166,118	1,201,725	3,046,858	2,032,087	1,014,771
Queensland	1,382,179	992,751	389,428	1,234,230	863,382	370,848
South Australia	1,085,175	689,517	395,658	1,076,612	624,511	452,101
Northern Territory	12,522	34,649	(—) 22,127	11,298	12,812	(—) 1,514
Western Australia	1,521,429	1,256,370	265,059	1,553,485	1,247,873	305,612
Tasmania*	205,791	173,400	32,391	233,210	173,292	59,918
Commonwealth ..	11,243,625	7,580,174	3,663,451	10,470,586	7,220,256	3,250,330
New Zealand†	1,874,586	1,252,237	622,349	1,974,088	1,343,415	630,673
Australasia	13,118,211	8,832,411	4,285,800	12,444,674	8,563,671	3,880,953

* Years ended 31st December, 1901 and 1902. † Years ended 31st March, 1902 and 1903

(—) Denotes deficiency in amount available to meet working expenses.

The proportion of gross earnings absorbed by working expenses during each of the last five years will be found below :—

State.	Percentage of Gross Earnings absorbed by Working Expenses.				
	1898–9.	1899–1900.	1900–01.	1901–02.	1902–3.
New South Wales	53·75	55·93	57·17	61·80	68·37
Victoria	62·55	62·89	62·17	64·31	66·69
Queensland	57·14	64·78	80·34	71·82	69·95
South Australia	58·33	56·37	58·95	63·54	58·01
Northern Territory	117·73	164·47	182·59	276·70	113·40
Western Australia	70·91	68·40	77·19	82·58	80·33
Tasmania*	79·23	79·10	79·07	84·26	74·31
Commonwealth	59·71	61·46	64·66	67·41	68·96
New Zealand†	63·26	64·80	65·30	66·80	68·05
Australasia	60·18	61·94	64·75	67·33	68·73

* Years ended 31st December, 1898–1902. † Years ended 31st March, 1899–1903.

It will be seen from this table that the percentage of working expenses for the states comprised in the Commonwealth has increased from 59·71 to 68·96 in the course of the five years; the increase for Australasia as a whole being from 60·18 to 68·73. In each state of the Commonwealth and New Zealand, with the exception of South Australia, Northern Territory and Tasmania, the working expenses have increased during the quinquennial period. In New South Wales, the increase was 14·62 per cent.; in Victoria, 4·14 per cent.; in Queensland, 12·81 per cent.; in Western Australia, 9·42 per cent.; and in New Zealand, 4·79 per cent. While the reduction in South Australia proper was 0·32 per cent.; in the Northern Territory, 4·33 per cent.; and in Tasmania, 4·92 per cent. At the present time the proportion of gross earnings absorbed by working expenses is smallest in South Australia proper, and, setting aside the Northern Territory railway, highest in Western Australia.

The following statement gives an analysis of the working expenses for the year 1903 for all the states except Tasmania, where the figures refer to the year 1902, distinguishing the expenditure on maintenance, locomotive power, repairs and renewals, traffic expenses, and general charges. The distribution under the various heads is that made by the railway authorities, and, so far as can be seen, like charges have been grouped together in every case. For New South Wales and Victoria the table shows an item "Pensions and Gratuities"; in the other states expenditure under this heading is included with general charges. The item of "Compensation" can be given for all the states with the exception of Queensland, Tasmania, and New Zealand, where it is not separately shown. The important distinction of repairs to carriages and waggons and of maintenance of locomotive power is unfortunately not observed by Western Australia and Tasmania, the manner in which such repairs are carried out precluding the possibility of an exact distribution of the outlay. It is not proposed to enter into a comparison of the various branches of expenditure, since the differences disclosed by the table arise not from exigencies of working, but from the needs of the treasurers of the states, and the freedom of control, or otherwise, allowed to the managers. In a subsequent part of this chapter which deals with the railway systems of the states individually, an analysis is given of the working expenses for ten years.

Expenditure on—	New South Wales.	Victoria.	Queensland.	South Australia (Proper).	Northern Territory.	Western Australia.	Tasmania.	New Zealand.
Maintenance—								
Total.................£	486.596	523,253	292,952	139,297	6,981	265,548	58,612	460,398
Per train mile ......d.	10·11	12·33	14·21	8·87	55·07	13·82	15·6	20·30
Per mile open ......£	160·4	158·4	106·5	80·0	48·00	185·2	125·2	203·55
Locomotive Power—								
Total.................£	925,584	611,319	270,162	205,343	2,479	642,808	63,791	378,575
Per train mile ......d.	19·23	14·96	13·10	16·89	19·56	33·46	16·9	16·69
Per mile open ....£	306·1	192·3	97·2	153·0	17·05	448·3	136·3	167·36
Carriage and Waggon Repairs—								
Total.................£	164,245	133,614	73,513	51,874	972	Included under		105,976
Per train mile ......d.	3·41	3·12	3·57	3·30	7·67	Locomotive		4·67
Per mile open........£	54·1	40·1	26·5	30·0	6·68	Power.		46·85
Traffic Expenses—								
Total.................£	605,210	582,167	207,303	151,738	1,935	312,364	42,416	360,061
Per train mile ......d.	12·58	13·58	10·06	9·66	15·26	16·26	11·2	15·88
Per mile open... ....£	199·5	174.6	74·6	87·0	13·81	217·7	90·6	159·17
Compensation—								
Total.................£	7,070	10,729	....	1,663	4	4,808	....	....
Per train mile ......d.	0·15	0·25	....	0·10	0·03	0·25	....	....
Per mile open........£	2·4	3·2	....	1·0	0·03	3·4	....	....
Pensions and Gratuities—								
Total.................£	8,126	93,507	....	....	....	....	....	....
Per train mile ......d.	0·17	2·18	....	....	....	....	....	....
Per mile open........£	2·7	28·0	....	....	....	....	....	....
General Charges—								
Total.................£	69,468	42,498	19,452	14,596	441	22,845	8,473	38,405
Per train mile ......d.	1·45	0·99	0·94	0·93	3·48	1·16	2·3	1·69
Per mile open........£	22·8	12·7	7·0	9.0	3·03	15·6	13·1	16·97
Total Expenses—								
Total.................£	2,266,299	2,032,087	863,382	624,511	12,812	1,247,873	173,292	1,343,415
Per train mile ......d.	47·10	47·41	41·88	39·75	101·07	64·95	46·0	59·23
Per mile open........£	747·0	609·3	310·8	360·0	88·10	870·2	370·2	593·90

Interest returned on Capital

In establishing the financial results of the working of the lines, it is the practice of the railway authorities to compare the net returns with the nominal rate of interest payable on the railway loans outstanding, ignoring the fact that many loans were floated below par and that the nominal is not the actual rate of interest. A true comparison, of course, is afforded by taking the rate of interest payable on the actual sum obtained by the state for its outstanding loans. On this basis the only state which shows out advantageously during the year ended 30th June, 1903, was Western Australia, where the lines returned a profit of 0·27 per cent. after defraying interest charges on the capital cost. In New South Wales the receipts were adversely affected by the unfavourable season, and the interest returned only reached 2·52 per cent., while the actual rate payable on outstanding loans was 3·67 per cent., so that there was a deficiency of 1·15 per cent. on the year's transactions. Victoria also experienced the effects of the adverse season, the net receipts being only 2·47 per cent. on the capital cost, while the actual rate of interest on outstanding loans was 3·86 per cent., there being thus a shortage of 1·39 per cent. on the year's working. The receipts of the Queensland lines also suffered, the return being at the rate of 1·48 per cent. on the capital cost, while the interest charge on the loans of the state was equal to 3·92 per cent., the loss on the year's business being therefore 2·44 per cent. In South Australia proper, the net return for the year was equal to 3·08 per cent. on capital cost, and according to the method of comparison above adopted, this represents a loss of 0·66 per cent. for the year. As explained in subsequent pages, the lines in the Northern Territory are handicapped to such an extent that they do not pay even working expenses, the loss on capital cost being at the rate of 0·13 per cent., and this figure added to 4·37, the actual rate of interest payable on outstanding loans gives a deficiency of 4·50 per cent. on the year's transactions. The Tasmanian railway revenue showed a return equal to 1·56 per cent. on the capital cost, an improvement on the figures of previous years, but as the actual rate of interest on loans outstanding was 3·76 per cent., there was a deficiency equal to 2·20 per cent. For New Zealand lines the net revenue for the year was 3·31 per cent. on capital cost. No data exist on which a comparison can be made with actual rate of interest on outstanding loans, but the interest paid on the loans without taking into consideration the price received for the stock was 3·71 per cent., and on this basis the year shows a loss of 0·40 per cent.

The rate of return on capital represents the interest on the gross cost of the lines. In some cases the nominal amount of outstanding debentures is less than the actual expenditure on construction and equipment, owing to the fact that some loans have been redeemed; but as the redemption has been effected by means of fresh loans charged to general services, or by payments from the general revenue, and not out of railway earnings, no allowance on this account can reasonably be claimed.

The table given below shows the rate of interest returned on the capital expenditure for each of the last five years, with the sum by which such return falls short of the actual rate of interest payable on cost of construction. In the case of New Zealand, only the nominal loss is shown; the actual loss was somewhat higher :—

State.	1898-9.	1899-1900.	1900-01.	1901-2.	1902-3.
	Per cent.	Per cent.	Per cent.	Per cent.	Per cent.
INTEREST RETURNED ON CAPITAL EXPENDITURE.					
New South Wales	3·83	3·62	3·93	3·45	2·52
Victoria	2·75	2·83	3·14	2·96	2·47
Queensland	3·15	2·67	1·31	1·93	1·48
South Australia	3·42	3·91	3·86	2·98	3·08
Northern Territory	(—)0·22	(—)0·82	(—)0·98	(—)1·99	(—)0·13
Western Australia	4·55	5·81	4·35	3·54	3·75
Tasmania*	1·03	1·12	1·16	0·85	1·56
Commonwealth	3·31	3·25	3·14	2·88	2·51
New Zealand	3·29	3·42	3·48	3·43	3·31
Australasia	3·31	3·27	3·18	2·95	2·61
NET LOSS ON WORKING LINES.					
New South Wales	†0·08	0·14	†0·19	0·23	1·15
Victoria	1·08	1·06	0·62	0·76	1·39
Queensland	0·85	1·35	2·67	2·01	2·44
South Australia	0·53	†0·02	0·01	0·83	0·66
Northern Territory	4·17	4·86	5·03	6·36	4·50
Western Australia	†1·01	†2·29	†0·83	†0·07	†0·27
Tasmania*	2·79	2·69	2·62	2·91	2·20
Commonwealth	0·53	0·59	0·65	0·86	1·26
New Zealand	0·52	0·37	0·30	0·33	0·40
Australasia	0·52	0·55	0·60	0·80	1·14

* Years 1898 to 1902. † Net profit.

In 1881 the New South Wales railways yielded 5·31 per cent.—a higher rate of interest on the capital cost than was ever reached before or since. In the same year the Victorian lines yielded a return of 4·04 per cent., which is the highest on record in that state, with the exception of 4·18 in the year 1886. The decline in the net profits was largely due to the extension of the lines in sparsely-populated districts; but with the adoption of a more prudent policy in the matter of construction, rendered necessary by the severe financial pressure to which the states were subjected, and with more careful management, the returns, as will be evident from the foregoing table, are again showing improvement.

Earnings and Expenses per Mile.

The gross earnings, expenditure, and net earnings per average mile worked during the last two years were as follow :—

State.	Gross Earnings.		Expenditure.		Net Earnings.	
	1901–02.	1902–3.	1901–02.	1902–3.	1901–02.	1902–3.
	£	£	£	£	£	£
New South Wales..	1,259	1,093	778	747	481	346
Victoria	1,031	913	663	609	368	304
Queensland	493	444	354	311	139	133
South Australia ...	625	620	397	360	228	260
Northern Territory	86	78	238	88	(—)152	(—) 10
Western Australia.	1,122	1,083	927	870	195	213
Tasmania*	448	498	377	370	71	128
Commonwealth	887	811	598	559	289	252
New Zealand	842	873	562	594	280	279
Australasia...	880	815	592	561	288	254

* 1901 and 1902.

For the states comprised in the Commonwealth the gross earnings per average mile worked during 1902–3 were £76 less than in the the previous year, and the working expenses were less by £39, leaving the net earnings at £252 in 1902–3, as compared with £289 in 1901–2. For the whole of Australasia the gross earnings per average mile worked during 1902–3 were £65 less than in the previous year, and the working expenses were reduced by £31, leaving the net earnings at £254 in 1902–3 as against £288 in 1901–2. On the next page will be found a table giving the returns per train mile. The states of New South Wales, Victoria, Queensland, and South Australia proper, show a reduction in the train mileage during 1902–3, in comparison with that of the previous year :—

State.	Gross Earnings.		Working Expenses.		Net Earnings.	
	1901–02.	1902–3.	1901–02.	1902–3.	1901–02.	1902–3.
	d.	d.	d.	d.	d.	d.
New South Wales	75·58	68·89	46·71	47·10	28·87	21·79
Victoria	71·63	71·09	46·06	47·41	25·57	23·68
Queensland	58·54	59·87	42·05	41·88	16·49	17·99
South Australia	62·06	68·53	39·44	39·75	22·62	28·78
Northern Territory	99·26	89·13	274·67	101·07	(–)175·41	(–)11·94
Western Australia	81·00	80·85	66·89	64·95	14·11	15·90
Tasmania*	55·14	61·99	46·46	46·06	8·68	15·93
Commonwealth	70·59	69·62	47·59	48·01	23·00	21·61
New Zealand	88·80	87·02	59·32	59·23	29·48	27·79
Australasia	72.72	71·90	48·96	49·48	23·76	22·42

* 1900 and 1901.

Financial Results of Foreign Railways.

The interest on capital cost, the proportion of working expenses to the gross revenue, and the return per train mile for the railways of some of the principal countries of the world are given below. The figures for the countries other than Australasia refer to the years 1902 or 1901, but in some cases there is no later information than for the year 1899.

Country.	Capital Cost.			Working Expenses: Proportion to Gross Revenue.	Per Train Mile.		
	Total.	Per Mile Open.	Return Per Cent.		Gross Revenue.	Working Expenses.	Net Revenue.
	£	£	p. cent.	per cent.	d.	d.	d.
United Kingdom	1,216,861,421	54,932	3·42	62·0	65·7	40·7	25·0
France	657,680,000	27,697	4 21	54·3	67·1	36·5	30·6
Germany	620,152,000	20,885	6·05	61·4	77·3	46·3	31·0
Belgium	78,544,948	27,725	4 08	66·2	55·3	37·6	17·7
United States	2,393,966,000	12,810	5·99	64·6	83 0	53·5	29·5
Canada	225,822,484	12,067	2·39	68·5	74·0	50·7	23·3
Cape Colony	22,125,085	10,363	4·41	74·6	89 0	66·4	22·6
Commonwealth of Australia	129,490,028	9,890	2·51	69·0	69·6	48·0	21·6
Australasia	148,571,763	9,658	2·61	68·7	71·9	49·5	22·4

The figures given above for Cape Colony are for state lines only.

Coaching and Goods Traffic.

The following table shows the number of passengers carried on the lines of the various states during the years 1881, 1891–2, 1901–2, and 1902–3. The number of journeys on the Victorian lines during the year ended 30th June, 1902, approximates to those of 1888–9, 1889–90, and 1890–91, and though, in common with the rest of the states, a great reduction occurred in 1893–94, the traffic, since the latter year, has manifested an upward movement. All the states have experienced the effects of the diminished spending power of the people, following on the financial crisis, but in every case a recovery has taken place. The number of passenger journeys in Tasmania in 1902 shows a small increase compared with the returns for 1891:—

State.	Passengers carried.			
	1881.	1891–2.	1901–2.	1902–3.
New South Wales	6,907,312	19,918,916	30,885,214	32,384,138
Victoria	18,964,214	55,148,122	57,465,077	54,798,073
Queensland*	247,284	2,370,219	4,636,174	4,048,161
South Australia	3,032,714	5,744,487	9,497,222	9,061,488
Northern Territory	....	4,541	3,755	3,631
Western Australia	67,144	456,631	8,158,299	9,106,396
Tasmania	102,495	704,531	777,445	761,345
Commonwealth	29,321,163	84,347,447	111,423,186	110,163,232
New Zealand	2,911,477	3,555,764	7,356,136	7,575,390
Australasia	32,232,640	87,903,211	118,779,322	117,738,622

* Exclusive of journeys of season ticket-holders.

The amount of goods tonnage is shown in the subjoined table. In the period from 1881 to 1891 there was an increase of about 102 per cent., varying from 44 per cent. in New Zealand to 747 per cent. in Tasmania. During the decennial period 1891–2 to 1901–2, the increase in tonnage has varied from 4 per cent. in South Australia to 1,401 per cent. in Western Australia, with an average increase of nearly 63 per cent. for the Commonwealth, and 64 per cent. for the whole of Australasia.

State.	1881.	1891-2.	1901-2.	1902-3.
	tons.	tons.	tons.	tons.
New South Wales	2,033,850	4,296,713	6,467,552	6,596,241
Victoria	1,366,603	2,720,886	3,433,627	3,093,997
Queensland	161,006	768,527	1,725,520	1,566,960
South Australia	646,625	1,337,859	1,392,257	1,349,617
Northern Territory	....	2,633	2,436	2,455
Western Australia	27,816	135,890	2,040,092	1,968,331
Tasmania	21,043	178,224	314,628	407,505
Commonwealth	4,256,945	9,440,732	15,376,112	14,985,106
New Zealand	1,437,714	2,066,791	3,529,177	3,730,394
Australasia	5,694,659	11,507,523	18,905,289	18,715,500

The percentage of receipts from coaching traffic to the total receipts is somewhat less in the states of the Commonwealth and New Zealand than in the United Kingdom, where for the year 1902 the coaching receipts formed 46·43 per cent. of the total obtained from goods and passenger traffic. The figures for each state are given below :—

State.	Coaching Traffic. per cent.	Goods Traffic. per cent.
New South Wales	42·41	57·59
Victoria	52·25	47·75
Queensland	37·88	62·12
South Australia	32·71	67·29
Northern Territory	29·38	70·62
Western Australia	30·77	69·23
Tasmania	46·06	53·94
Commonwealth	42·25	57·75
New Zealand	37·48	62·52
Australasia	41·51	58·49

Average Weight of Train Load.

The useful comparisons that may be made between the railway systems of the various states are very limited, and greater uniformity in the presentation of the railway reports is extremely desirable in view of the provisions of the Commonwealth Act for the possible control of the railway systems by the central government. An example of want of uniformity in an important particular is the absence of information which would enable the average train load to be ascertained. This information can only be given for two states—South Australia and New South Wales—and for the latter state, complete returns are available for three years only. The figures for South Australia show a considerable variation in the average weight during the last eight years; but, for the years 1899, 1900, and 1901, the average is uniformly high when compared with that for each of the preceding three years. In 1902 a considerable fall occurred, consequent on a falling off in tonnage carried without a commensurate reduction in mileage; a slight improvement, however, was manifested during 1903. The figures quoted do not include the business of the Northern Territory:—

Year.	Goods mileage.	Ton mileage.	Average weight of train.
			tons.
1896	2,089,911	134,846,696	64·52
1897	2,265,277	159,454,588	70·34
1898	2,273,537	157,143,651	69·11
1899	2,426,477	191,041,569	78·73
1900	2,569,958	197,079,956	76·68
1901	2,686,789	202,649,157	75·42
1902	2,468,326	170,523,167	69·08
1903	2,311,250	165,357,307	71·54

The average tonnage for goods trains is, therefore, 72·2 tons, which is 5·3 tons higher than in New South Wales, the only other system with which a comparison can be made. The New South Wales figures, with the exception of those for the years 1900, 1901, 1902, and 1903, are unsatisfactory, inasmuch as the goods mileage relates to the year ended 30th June, while the ton mileage is for the year ending 31st December following. There are no returns for 1899:—

Year.	Goods mileage.	Ton mileage.	Average weight of train.
			tons.
1896	4,001,164	255,621,932	63·9
1897	4,244,385	273,400,624	64·4
1898	4,260,368	314,996,969	73·9
1900	4,610,343	320,364,852	69·5
1901	5,836,587	404,740,360	69·4
1902	6,586,032	436,814,308	66·3
1903	6,405,756	399,578,918	62·4

The average for the period was 66·9 tons. The figures for New South Wales and for South Australia compare very favourably with the returns of the British railways, but are very far behind those of some of the great American lines, as the following figures show :—

BRITISH RAILWAYS, 1900.

Company.	Goods mileage.	Ton mileage.	Average weight of train.
			tons.
Lond. North-Western	22,668,940	1,311,000,000	57
Midland	27,270,791	1,377,000,000	50
Great Western	23,096,578	1,056,000,000	46
North-Eastern	17,565,768	1,055,000,000	60
Great Northern...............	12,027,759	534,000,000	44½
Lancashire and Yorkshire	6,681,695	450,000,000	67
Great Eastern	8,564,851	322,000,000	37½
Great Central..................	8,328,551	360,000,000	43
Total	126,204,933	6,465,000,000	51

The New York Central appears to great advantage compared with the British lines; the average weight of train for the years quoted was :—

	tons.		tons.
1894	249	1897	270
1895	252	1898	299
1896	268	1899	322

ROLLING STOCK.

The following table gives the different classes of rolling stock in the possession of the several Australasian Governments at the end of the year 1902–3, and, considerable as are the numbers in each class, they could with advantage be largely increased in most of the states :—

State.	Engines.	Coaching Stock.	Goods Stock.
New South Wales	559	1,115	11,443
Victoria	547	1,482	9,872
Queensland	342	446	7,183
South Australia...............	346	435	6,021
Northern Territory	6	7	134
Western Australia...........	316	264	5,991
Tasmania........................	75	172	1,274
Commonwealth ...	2,191	3,921	41,918
New Zealand	372	751	12,992
Australasia	2,563	4,672	54,910

RAILWAY ACCIDENTS.

The persons meeting with accidents on railway lines may be grouped in three classes—passengers, servants of the railways, and trespassers ;

and the accidents themselves might be classified into those arising from causes beyond the control of the person injured, and those due to misconduct or want of caution. The following table shows the number of persons killed and injured on the Government railways during 1902–1903 in those states for which returns are available :—

State.	Passengers.		Railway Employés.		Trespassers, &c.		Total.	
	Killed.	Injured.	Killed.	Injured.	Killed.	Injured.	Killed.	Injured.
New South Wales	2	37	14	737	26	34	42	808
Victoria	2	177	10	317	28	80	40	574
South Australia	1	8	2	23	5	4	8	35
Northern Territory	...	......	...	......	...	......	...	......

The railways of Australasia have been as free from accidents of a serious character as the lines of most other countries. In order to obtain a common basis of comparison it is usual to find the proportion which the number of persons killed or injured bears to the total passengers carried. There is, however, no necessary connection between the two, for it is obvious that accidents may occur on lines chiefly devoted to goods traffic, and a more reasonable basis would be the accidents to passengers only compared with the number of passengers carried. The data from which such a comparison could be made are wanting for some countries. As far as the figures can be given they are shown in the following table, which exhibits the number of passengers killed and injured per million carried. The figures are calculated over a period of ten years and brought down to the latest available dates :—

Country.	Number of Passengers.		Average per million passengers carried.	
	Killed.	Injured.	Killed.	Injured.
Germany	609	2,484	0·1	0·4
Austria-Hungary	200	1,896	0·1	1·3
Belgium	142	1,929	0·1	1·8
Sweden	24	43	0·2	0·3
France	793	3,696	0·2	1·5
Norway	8	16	0·1	0·2
Holland	28	133	0·1	0·5
Switzerland	177	709	0·4	1·5
Russia	576	2,315	0·9	3·7
United Kingdom	137	5,707	0·01	0·56
Spain	155	924	0·5	3·3
Canada	118	934	0·7	5·4
New South Wales	57	461	0·23	1·85
Victoria	29	1,490	0·06	3·17
South Australia	11	28	0·16	0·41

New South Wales.

The progress of railway construction during the twenty years which followed the opening of the first line was very slow, for in 1875 the length of line in operation had only reached 435 miles. From 1876 to 1889, greater activity prevailed, no less than 1,748 miles being constructed during the period, but this rate of increase was not continued, and only 14 miles were opened during the next three years. Subsequently there was renewed activity, and the length of line opened to 30th June, 1903, was 3,138½ miles, the amount expended thereon for construction and equipment being £41,654,977, or at the rate of £13,272 per mile.

The railways of the state are divided into three branches, each representing a system of its own. The southern system, which is the most important, serving as it does the richest and most thickly-populated districts, and placing Sydney, Melbourne, and Adelaide in direct communication, has several offshoots. From Culcairn, there are two branch lines, one connecting with Corowa on the Murray River, and the other with Germanton; from The Rock a line extends to Lockhart; from Junee a branch extends as far as the town of Hay in one direction, and Finley in another, and places the important district of Riverina in direct communication with Sydney. From Cootamundra a southerly branch carries the line to Tumut, and another in a north-westerly direction to Temora; the latter will shortly be extended to Wyalong. From Murrumburrah a branch has been constructed to Blayney, on the western line, thus connecting the southern and western systems of the state. From Koorawatha a branch has been laid down to connect Grenfell with the railway system. Nearer the metropolis, the important town of Goulburn is connected with Cooma, bringing the rich pastoral district of Monaro into direct communication with Sydney. From Goulburn, a branch line has also been opened to Crookwell. Another line that forms part of the southern system has been constructed to Nowra, connecting the metropolis with the coastal district of Illawarra, which is rich alike in coal and in the produce of agriculture. The western system of railways extends from Sydney over the Blue Mountains, and has its terminus at Bourke, a distance of 503 miles from the metropolis. Leaving the mountains, the western line, after throwing out a branch from Wallerawang to Mudgee, enters the Bathurst Plains, and connects with the metropolis the rich agricultural lands of the Bathurst, Orange, and Wellington districts. Beyond Dubbo it enters the pastoral country. At Blayney, as before stated, the western line is connected with the southern system by a branch line to Murrumburrah; at Orange a branch connects that town with Forbes on the Lachlan River, and from Parkes, one of the stations on this branch line, an extension to Condobolin on the Lachlan River has been constructed. Further west, at Dubbo, a branch line extends to Coonamble, and from the main line at Nevertire, a short line extends to the town of Warren, and at Nyngan a branch line connects the important mining district of Cobar with Sydney. From Byrock a line branches off to Brewarrina. The western system also includes a short line from Blacktown to Richmond on the Hawkesbury River. The northern system originally commenced at Newcastle, but a connecting line has been constructed, making Sydney the head of the whole of the railway systems of the state. This connecting line permits of direct communication between Adelaide, Melbourne, Sydney, and Brisbane, a distance from end to end of 1,808 miles, or altogether between the terminus of Oodnadatta, in South Australia, and Cunnamulla, in Queensland, there is one continuous line of railway, 3,100 miles in length. The northern system comprises a branch from Werris Creek, *via* Narrabri and Moree, to Inverell, thus placing the Namoi and Gwydir districts in direct communication with the ports of Newcastle and Sydney. There is also under construction a line from Narrabri to Walgett, with a branch to Collarendabri. A portion of the North Coast railway has also been constructed from Murwillumbah, on the Tweed River, to Lismore on the Richmond River, and an extension through Casino to Grafton is now in course of construction. A short line branches off the main northern line at Hornsby, and connects with the north shore of Port Jackson at Milson's Point.

Up to October, 1888, the control of the railways was vested in the Minister for Works, the direct management being undertaken by an officer under the title of Commissioner. It was, however, recognised that political influence entered unduly into the management of this large public asset, and, as a consequence, the "Government Railways Act of 1888" was passed, with the object of removing the control and management of the railways from the political arena, and vesting them in three railway Commissioners, who were required to prepare for presentation to Parliament an annual report of their proceedings, and an account of all moneys received and expended during the preceding year. While the avowed object of state railway construction has been to promote settlement, apart from consideration of the profitable working of the lines, the principle has nevertheless been kept in view that in the main the railways should be self-supporting. It will be seen, from subsequent pages, that, despite the fact that the Commissioners are hampered by a large number of unprofitable lines, they have succeeded in placing the railways of the state in a satisfactory financial position.

Revenue and Working Expenses.

The net sum available to meet interest charges during the last decennial period is set forth in the following table, and the returns show that the Commissioners have achieved most important results during their term of administration. A reference to the table on page 357 will show that on two occasions during the last decennial period the railways returned a small profit after meeting the charges for working expenses and interest on capital, while, with the exception of the last year, there has been a considerable reduction in the percentage of average loss during the ten years. Owing to the adverse season, the year 1903 has been financially the worst in the history of the railways of the state.

Year.	Gross Earnings.	Working Expenses.	Net Earnings.	Proportion of Working Expenses to Gross Earnings.
	£	£	£	per cent.
1894	2,813,541	1,591,842	1,221,699	56·58
1895	2,878,204	1,567,589	1,310,615	54·46
1896	2,820,417	1,551,888	1,268,529	55·02
1897	3,014,742	1,601,218	1,413,524	53·11
1898	3,026,748	1,614,605	1,412,143	53·34
1899	3,145,273	1,690,442	1,454,831	53·75
1900	3,163,572	1,769,520	1,394,052	55·93
1901	3,573,779	2,043,201	1,530,578	57·17
1902	3,668,686	2,267,369	1,401,317	61·80
1903	3,314,893	2,266,299	1,048,594	68·37

In the foregoing table will be found ample evidence of the economical working of the state railways under their present management, for, despite the exceedingly unfavourable conditions, the net earnings for the financial year ended 30th June, 1903, were 31·63 per cent. of the total earnings, as against 33·31 per cent. when the Commissioners took office. The financial depression of 1893, which brought about a great change in the character of the coaching traffic, and the continued unfavourable character of the seasons, adversely affected the earnings of several years; the fall in earnings, however, was met by a reduction in working expenses, so that the satisfactory results of the railway management were not greatly affected. The year 1900 compares somewhat unfavourably with the three years immediately preceding. This is due to the fact that, notwithstanding a much larger tonnage carried, the merchandise and live stock traffic showed a decrease in freight earned, clearly indicating that the traffic from these sources had been carried at less profitable rates than hitherto. The traffic in wool and hay also showed a large falling off, but there was no further diminution in the net earnings for the year 1901, the total, £1,530,578, being the largest for the period shown in the table. The revenue exceeded that of the previous year by £410,207, towards which all classes of traffic contributed. The increased traffic, the greater cost of coal and materials, and the more liberal advances granted to the wages staff, were responsible for the rise of £273,681 in the working expenses. For the year ended 30th June, 1902, however, a considerable falling off in the net earnings occurred. The rise from 57·17 to 61·80 in the percentage of working expenses to gross earnings was due to the increased volume of traffic carried at exceptionally low rates, largely contributed to by the concessions made in the carriage of starving stock and fodder. The increased cost of fuel, the additional repairs to the rolling stock and permanent way, the necessity for hauling water for locomotive and other purposes, and the increments granted to the staff, also contributed to the reduction in net earnings. As previously pointed out, the year ended June, 1903, was the most disastrous in the history of the railways of New South Wales. Owing to the long-continued dry weather, water had to be despatched by train to several remote parts of the state, and large quantities for locomotive uses had also to be transported for long distances. The latter, of course, was carried free, while merely a nominal rate was charged for the former, the working expenses being thereby heavily burdened, with practically no corresponding gain to revenue. During the year live stock was carried at greatly reduced rates from the drought-stricken areas to places where feed was obtainable, while fodder for starving animals was carried at an extremely low charge. Exclusive of terminal charges, the average rate on all fodder carried fell to 0·04d., and on all live stock to 1·23d. per ton per mile, without taking into consideration the amount of empty, and consequently unprofitable, running involved.

The cost of working has steadily increased over the last three years of the decade, and this has in great measure been brought about by the increased cost of fuel, the heavier expenditure on stores, and the large outlay on wages. Much of the additional charge under the last-mentioned heading has been necessitated by the adoption of eight hours instead of nine hours per day for the running staff. Renewals and replacement of old stock also added a heavy burden to the total expenditure. For the last quinquennial period the average charge for maintenance amounted to £421,758, as against £313,806 for the preceding five years, the capital account having been debited only with expenditure on new lines and the outlay necessary to meet the heavy growth of passenger and goods traffic.

For 1903–4 the prospect is very encouraging. The copious rainfall over the whole of New South Wales has resulted in a prolific growth of herbage for stock, while from present appearances the wheat harvest will be the best experienced in the history of the state.

The proportion of working expenses to earnings is less in New South Wales than in any other part of Australia, as the following figures, which are the average of the five years 1899–1903, will show:—

	Per cent.
New South Wales	59·51
Victoria	63·72
Queensland	68·63
South Australia	60·32
Western Australia	76·54
Tasmania	79·06
New Zealand	65·81

An analysis is given hereunder of the working expenses of the New South Wales railways for the ten years, 1894-1903; in this statement the total expenses as well as the expenses per train mile and per mile of line in operation, are given. It will be seen that there has been a general reduction in the expenditure per train mile, and this reduction is visible in all the details included in the total, with the exception of the expenditure upon locomotive power, which has slightly increased during the ten years. In regard to the working expenses generally, it may be said that the condition of affairs revealed by the table is satisfactory. When the Commissioners took over the management of the railways in 1888, large renewals of rolling stock were needed, while additional expenditure had to be incurred on permanent way and buildings. The result of this will be seen in the high outlay per train mile and per mile open in the earlier years of the decade. By the year 1896, the lines were in thorough working order, and have been so maintained since that date. The rolling stock has been very greatly improved; the tractive power of the engines has been increased, and types of locomotives adapted to the special and general needs of the traffic introduced.

Year ended 30th June.	Maintenance of Way, Works, and Buildings.	Locomotive Power.	Carriage and Waggon Repairs and Renewals.	Traffic Expenses.	Compensation.	Pensions and Gratuities.	General Charges.	Total.
	£	£	£	£	£	£	£	£
1894	418,989	507,649	127,221	458,011	5,186	10,744	64,042	1,591,842
1895	399,679	494,657	130,776	441,798	33,232	8,446	59,001	1,567,589
1896	350,964	533,255	150,073	437,591	15,248	3,878	60,879	1,551,888
1897	358,057	574,255	152,886	444,857	2,894	5,203	63,067	1,601,218
1898	353,969	597,455	139,161	455,545	3,296	4,504	60,675	1,614,605
1899	370,197	635,145	141,942	471,532	5,451	2,652	63,523	1,690,442
1900	406,044	648,767	159,630	478,818	4,164	4,250	67,847	1,769,520
1901	484,750	761,625	174,478	537,227	11,111	4,764	69,246	2,043,201
1902	521,983	875,582	184,232	588,988	20,234	6,296	70,104	2,267,369
1903	486,596	925,584	164,245	605,210	7,070	8,126	69,468	2,266,299
				Per Train Mile.				
	d.	d.	d.	d.	d.	d.	d.	d.
1894	14·03	16·99	4·26	15·33	·18	·36	2·14	53·29
1895	12·63	15·63	4·13	13·96	1·05	·27	1·87	49·54
1896	10·91	16·58	4·67	13·60	·47	·12	1·89	48·24
1897	10·57	16·95	4·51	13·13	·09	·15	1·86	47·26
1898	10·18	17·19	4·00	13·11	·10	13	1·75	46·46
1899	10·09	17·32	3·87	12·85	·14	·07	1·73	46·07
1900	10·96	17·51	4·31	12·92	·11	·11	1·83	47·75
1901	10·81	16·98	3·89	11·98	·25	·10	1·55	45·56
1902	10·75	18·04	3·79	12·13	·42	·13	1·45	46·71
1903	10·11	19·23	3·41	12·58	·15	·17	1·45	47.10
				Per Mile Open.				
	£	£	£	£	£	£	£	£
1894	172·6	209·1	52·4	188·7	2·1	4·4	26·4	655·7
1895	158·9	196·6	52·0	175·6	13·2	3·4	23·4	623·1
1896	138·6	210·6	59·3	172·9	6·0	1·5	24·1	613·0
1897	139·0	223·0	59·4	172·7	1·1	2·0	24·5	621·7
1898	133·1	224·7	52·3	171·3	1·3	1·7	22·8	607·2
1899	136·9	234·9	52·5	174·4	2·0	1·0	23·5	625·2
1900	147·9	236·4	58·1	174·5	1·5	1·7	24·7	644·8
1901	174·5	274·2	62·8	193·2	4·1	1·7	25·0	785·5
1902	179·2	300·6	63·2	202·2	6·9	2·2	24·1	778·4
1903	160·4	305·1	54·1	199·5	2·4	2·7	22·8	747·0

Interest returned on Capital.

In establishing the financial results of the working of the lines it is the practice of railway authorities to compare the net returns with the nominal rate of interest payable on the railway loans or on the public debt of the state. As previously pointed out, an accurate comparison can only be made by taking the average rate of interest payable on the actual sum obtained by the state for its outstanding loans. On this basis, the lines of the state have met the interest on construction and equipment during five years only, viz., 1881, 1882, 1883, 1899, and 1901. In 1901 the lines yielded a net sum of £74,000 after paying working expenses, interest, and all charges, but the year 1902 showed a loss of £91,000, while during the year ended 30th June, 1903, the loss was £480,000. The following table shows the average loss for each year during the period 1894–1903 :—

Year.	Interest returned on Capital.	Actual Rate of Interest payable on Outstanding Loans.	Average Loss.
	per cent.	per cent.	per cent.
1894	3·46	3·89	0·43
1895	3·58	3·94	0·36
1896	3·44	3·86	0·42
1897	3·78	3·81	0·03
1898	3·74	3·78	0·04
1899	3·83	3·75	*0·08
1900	3·62	3·76	0·14
1901	3·93	3·74	*0·19
1902	3·45	3·68	0·23
1903	2·52	3·67	1·15

* Average gain.

The fluctuation of the profits is partly owing to the extension of the lines in sparsely-populated districts ; but as a result of more economical working the returns show an improvement during the period, with the exception of 1903, the position of that year being due to the special circumstances dealt with in preceding pages. Regard must be paid to the fact, moreover, that there are twenty-four branch lines on which over thirteen millions sterling have been expended which do not pay their way, the loss on these lines being about £280,000 per annum.

Earnings and Expenses per Mile.

Two important facts which demonstrate the financial position of the railways and the character of the management are the earnings per train mile and per average mile open. Although the returns now being realised cannot be compared with those of 1875, when the net earnings per train mile fell little short of 52d., and per mile open of £775, the earnings, with the exception of those for the years 1902 and 1903, are in every way encouraging. The falling off in 1902 was largely due to the increased volume of traffic carried at exceptionally low rates, the average revenue derived from all descriptions of merchandise and live stock traffic, exclusive of terminal charges, having decreased from 1·13d. to 1·07d. per ton per mile. Under the control of the Commissioners the net return per train mile during that year was increased from 27·4d. to 28·9d., or 5·5 per cent.; while per mile of line open for traffic the advance has been from £374 to £481, or 28·6 per cent. During the year ended 30th June, 1903, the adverse circumstances already alluded to brought about a considerable reduction, and the net earnings per train mile fell to 21·79d., and per mile open for traffic to £346. The gross earnings, expenditure, and net earnings per train mile for the past ten years are shown in the following table:—

Year.	Gross Earnings per train mile.	Expenditure per train mile.	Net Earnings per train mile.
	d.	d.	d.
1894	94·18	53·29	40·89
1895	90·96	49·54	41·42
1896	87·68	48·24	39·44
1897	88·99	47·26	41·73
1898	87·10	46·46	40·64
1899	85·72	46·07	39·65
1900	85·36	47·75	37·61
1901	79·69	45·56	34·13
1902	75·58	46·71	28·87
1903	68·89	47·10	21·79

The gross earnings, expenditure, and net earnings per average mile open for the past ten years, were as follow:—

Year.	Gross Earnings per average mile open.	Expenditure per average mile open.	Net Earnings per average mile open.
	£	£	£
1894	1,159	656	503
1895	1,144	623	521
1896	1,114	613	501
1897	1,171	622	549
1898	1,138	607	531
1899	1,163	625	538
1900	1,153	645	508
1901	1,286	735	551
1902	1,259	778	481
1903	1,093	747	346

In many cases the railways of the state pass through heavy and mountainous country, involving steep gradients. For the more expeditious and economical working of the traffic, important deviations have been and are being carried out to secure better grades and to ease the curves. While much has been done in this direction, much remains to be accomplished, as many of the lines have been constructed with an unusual proportion of steep gradients, of which the worst are on the trunk lines, and are so situated that the whole of the traffic must pass over them. In the southern system, the line at Cooma reaches an altitude of 2,659 feet above the sea level; in the western, at the Clarence station, Blue Mountains, a height of 3,658 feet is attained; while on the northern line the highest point, 4,471 feet, is reached at Ben Lomond. In no other state of the Commonwealth or New Zealand do the lines attain such an altitude. In Queensland, the maximum height is 3,008 feet; in Victoria, 2,452 feet; in South Australia, 2,024 feet; in Western Australia, 1,522 feet; and in New Zealand, 1,252 feet. Where heavy gradients prevail, the working expenditure must necessarily be heavier than in the states where the surface configuration is more level.

Coaching and Goods Traffic.

The following table shows the number of passengers carried on the lines of the state during the year 1881, and for the last ten years, together with the receipts from the traffic, and the average receipts per journey:—

Year.	Passengers carried.	Receipts from Coaching Traffic.	Average Receipts per journey.
	No.	£	d.
1881	6,907,312	488,675	16·97
1894	19,265,732	1,047,029	13·04
1895	19,725,418	1,022,901	12·45
1896	21,005,048	1,043,922	11·93
1897	22,672,924	1,098,696	11·63
1898	23,233,206	1,126,257	11·63
1899	24,726,067	1,158,198	11·22
1900	26,486,873	1,227,355	11·12
1901	29,261,324	1,370,530	11·23
1902	30,885,214	1,403,744	10·91
1903	32,384,138	1,405,888	10·42

It will be seen that the years 1896 to 1903 show far larger numbers of passenger journeys than preceding years, but less satisfactory results in the way of average receipts per journey. This does not so much arise from curtailment of long-distance travelling as from the change of a large body of travellers from first to second class—a result due to diminished means, and doubtless to some extent to the more comfortable carriages now provided for second-class passengers. A return to prosperous times should show an increase in first-class travellers, but it frequently happens that the removal of the original impelling cause is not followed by a return to previous habits, so that the railways may not altogether recover the revenue lost by the change on the part of the travelling public.

The amount of goods tonnage for the year 1881, and from 1894 to 1903 is shown in the following table:—

Year.	Tonnage of Goods and Live Stock.	Earnings.
	tons.	£
1881	2,033,850	955,551
1894	3,493,919	1,766,512
1895	4,075,093	1,855,303
1896	3,953,575	1,776,495
1897	4,567,041	1,916,046
1898	4,630,564	1,900,491
1899	5,248,320	1,987,075
1900	5,531,511	1,936,217
1901	6,398,227	2,203,249
1902	6,467,552	2,264,942
1903	6,536,241	1,909,005

The subdivision of the tonnage of goods and live stock for the year ended 30th June, 1903, into a general classification is set forth in the subjoined statement. Particulars of the tonnage are given under nine broad classes, while the table also shows the average distance goods of each class were carried, and the average earnings per ton per mile. The last figure, however, does not include the terminal charges, which would probably increase the revenue per ton per mile by about 0·20d., from 0·98d. to 1·18d. The "miscellaneous" traffic comprises timber, bark, agricultural and vegetable seeds, in 5-ton lots; firewood, in 5 ton lots; bricks, drain pipes, and various other goods. "A" and "B" classes consist of lime, fruit, vegetables, hides, tobacco leaf, lead and silver ore, caustic soda and potash, cement, copper ingots, fat and tallow, mining machinery, ore tailings, leather, agricultural implements in 5 ton lots; and various other goods.

Description of Traffic.	Tons carried.	Average number of miles each ton of traffic is carried.	Earnings per ton per mile.
		miles.	d.
Coal, coke, and shale	3,890,932	18·91	0·56
Firewood......	196,895	27·08	0·75
Grain, flour, &c.	83,105	177·47	0·31
Hay, straw, and chaff	257,910	275·24	0·04
Miscellaneous..................	785,778	66·30	0·62
Wool	76,179	259·64	1·94
Live stock	282,058	243·76	1·23
"A" and "B" classes......	517,339	119·81	0·98
All other goods	213,998	151·09	3·75
	6,304,194	63·38	0·98
Terminal charges	......	......	0·20
Total	6,304,194	63·38	1·18

The charge for carrying goods one mile along the lines of the state in 1872 was 3·6d. per ton, while after an interval of thirty-one years, it has fallen to 1·18d. The decrease, however, is to some extent more apparent than real, inasmuch as it represents a more extensive development of the mineral traffic than of the carriage of general merchandise; but, when due allowance has been made on this score, it will be found that the benefit to the general producer and consumer has been very substantial, and it may safely be taken as indicating generally the lessened cost of carriage to persons forwarding goods by rail.

VICTORIA.

Railway operations in Victoria began with the opening of the line from Flinders-street, Melbourne, to Port Melbourne. In the early years the lines constructed were chiefly in the vicinity of the metropolis, and up to the year 1865, that is in ten years, only 274 miles were laid down; during the next decennial period a further length of 312 miles was constructed. As in the case of other states, more energy was manifested during the decade ended 1885, when no less than 1,092 miles were constructed; during the next ten years the rate of progress was maintained, and a further length of 1,444 miles was opened. The length of line open for traffic on 30th June, 1903, was 3,383½ miles, upon which the sum of £40,974,493 has been expended for construction and equipment, or an average of £12,110 per mile.

The railways of the state are grouped under seven systems—the Northern, North-Eastern, Eastern, South-Eastern, North-Western, South-Western, and Suburban lines. The Northern system extends from Melbourne to Echuca; the North-Eastern stretches from Kensington to Wodonga, and is the main line connecting Melbourne with Sydney; the Eastern connects Prince's Bridge, Melbourne, with Bairnsdale; the South-Eastern runs from Lyndhurst to Port Albert; the North-Western, joining Laverton with Serviceton, is the main line connecting Melbourne with Adelaide; the South-Western runs from Breakwater to Port Fairy; and the suburban system makes provision for the requirements of the population within a distance of about 20 miles from the metropolis. Included in the seven systems are no less than ninety main, branch, and connecting lines. With the exception of the eastern and extreme north-western portions of the state, where settlement is sparse, the railway facilities provided are in advance of those of any other state, in so far as the length of the line open for traffic is concerned.

Victoria, in 1883, was the first state of the group to adopt the system of placing the management and maintenance of the railways under the control of three Commissioners. From the 1st February, 1884, to the end of 1891 the construction as well as the working of the lines was vested in this body; but on the 1st January, 1892, the duty of construction was transferred to the Board of Land and Works under the provisions of the "Railways Act, 1891." During 1896 the number of commissioners was reduced to one; but under the Victorian Railway Commissioners Act, 1903, the control of the lines of the state was placed in the hands of three commissioners from the 1st June, 1903.

Revenue and Working Expenses.

The net earnings, that is the sum available to meet interest charges during the last decennial period, are shown in the following table:—

Year.	Gross Earnings.	Working Expenses.	Net Earnings.	Proportion of Working Expenses to Gross Earnings.
	£	£	£	per cent.
1894	2,726,159	1,651,186	1,074,973	60·57
1895	2,581,591	1,547,698	1,033,893	59·95
1896	2,401,392	1,551,433	849,959	64·61
1897	2,615,935	1,568,365	1,047,570	59·95
1898	2,608,896	1,649,793	959,103	63·24
1899	2,873,729	1,797,725	1,076,004	62·55
1900	3,025,162	1,902,540	1,122,622	62·89
1901	3,337,797	2,075,239	1,262,558	62·17
1902	3,367,843	2,166,118	1,201,725	64·31
1903	3,046,858	2,032,087	1,014,771	66·69

It will be observed that while the gross earnings for the closing year of the decade are larger than those of the opening year, the net earnings for 1903 show a considerable falling off from those of the year 1894, while the proportion of working expenses to gross earnings was also much larger during the former year. The decrease in the gross revenue in comparison with that earned during the previous twelve months, is largely, if not entirely, attributable to the almost total failure of the harvest, the collateral loss in the passenger traffic, and the partial cessation of transport facilities owing to a strike of a section of the railway service. The intervening years show similar fluctuations to those of the other states comprised within the Commonwealth, due to a variety of causes, among the principal of which are—the financial crisis, the drought that has uniformly affected the whole of Australasia for some years past, and the fact that Victoria adopted the construction of a number of branch "cockspur" lines, which had to be worked at absolute loss. In many instances the lines did not even pay working expenses, apart from interest. Continued losses resulted in the closing to traffic of some of these lines during 1896 and subsequent years, and the Report for the year ended 30th June, 1902, shows that the average loss per annum on non-paying lines is £294,697. Notwithstanding the fall in 1902, the net revenue shows a gradual tendency to improvement during the previous six years, the fall in 1898 in comparison with the previous year being due to the fact that in 1897 the receipts were swollen by the exceptional traffic occasioned by the Jubilee celebrations. In 1898 additional expenditure, arising from increases of pay to the lower-grade employees, and from improvements and renewals of permanent-way works and rolling stock caused a large inflation in working expenses. The proportion of working expenses to gross earnings shows a decided improvement with the exception of 1902 and 1903; and consequent on extensive renewals of way, repairs and renewals of stock, the payment of increments to employees, the heavy compensation for settlement of claims for personal injury, the extra price paid for coal under new contracts, and the inclusion of a sum of £78,913 expended on "belated repairs," this figure now stands somewhat higher than it did at the commencement of the decennial period.

The necessity for reducing expenditure has received serious considera tion, and, as a consequence, a considerable reduction in train mileage has taken place. The operation of the principle of percentage deductions in respect of salaries and wages has resulted in a considerable saving, while the limitation of a large proportion of the staff to an average of five days' work per week, has enabled a saving in wages for the year to be effected to the extent of £73,000. In addition, economy was practised in various matters of detail, and; generally speaking, only such works were undertaken as were regarded essential in the interests of safety and efficiency.

Great care seems to have been taken to keep down the working expenses during the first four years of the decade shown in the following analysis of the working expenditure of Victorian railways, and a reduction of over £200,000 per annum was made in spite of an addition of 200 miles to the length of line in operation. After 1896, concessions in regard to salary or wages were made to the staff, amounting to £35,000 in 1897, and £66,312 in the following year. In 1899 and 1900 additional concessions were made, involving an annual expenditure of £41,000.

The following analysis, which is on the same basis as that already given for New South Wales, gives the details of the expenditure during the ten years. It will be observed that there is an item of £93,507 per annum for pensions and gratuities. The charges for this service for New South Wales amount to £8,126, and in none of the other railway systems is there any like expenditure.

Year ended 30th June.	Maintenance of Way, Works, and Buildings.	Locomotive Power.	Carriage and Waggon Repairs and Renewals.	Traffic Expenses.	Compensation.	Pensions and Gratuities.	General Charges.	Total.
	£	£	£	£	£	£	£	£
1894	320,981	528,309	104,050	562,226	4,316	93,620	37,684	1,651,186
1895	331,198	478,439	89,129	514,131	6,806	84,509	43,486	1,547.698
1896	365,848	450,489	97,353	486,433	7,321	94,695	49,294	1,551,433
1897	381,293	451,548	101,946	497,080	4,689	88,958	47,901	1,568,365
1898	408,837	459,992	111,113	526.958	7,892	83,720	51,281	1,649,793
1899	480,792	502,763	130,659	546,754	3,611	81,284	51,862	1,797,725
1900	498,459	537,340	142,639	564.908	6,862	95,289	57,093	1,902,540
1901	518,488	646,192	147,153	609,000	7,945	90,443	56,018	2,075,239
1902	501,938	710,105	145,359	640,442	31,145	93,744	43,385	2,166,118
1903	523,253	641,819	133,614	582,167	10,729	93,507	42,498	2,032,087

Year ended 30th June.	Maintenance of Way, Works, and Buildings.	Loco-motive Power.	Carriage and Waggon Repairs and Renewals.	Traffic Expenses.	Compen-sation.	Pensions and Gratuities.	General Charges.	Total.
				PER TRAIN MILE.				
	d.	d.	d.	d.	d.	d.	d.	d.
1894	7·59	12·50	2·46	13·30	·10	2·21	·89	39·05
1895	8·31	12·00	2·24	12·90	·17	2·11	1·09	38·82
1896	9·77	12·03	2·60	12·99	·19	2·53	1·32	41·43
1897	9·92	11·74	2·65	12·93	·12	2·18	1·25	40·79
1898	10·62	11·95	2·89	13·69	·20	2·17	1·33	42·85
1899	11·88	12·42	3·23	13·51	·09	2·01	1·28	44·42
1900	11·84	12·76	3·39	13·41	·16	2·26	1·35	45·17
1901	11·25	14·02	3·19	13·21	·17	1·96	1·21	45·01
1902	10·68	15·10	3·09	13·62	·66	1·99	·92	46·06
1903	12·33	14·96	3·12	13·58	·25	2·18	·99	47·41
				PER MILE OPEN.				
	£	£	£	£	£	£	£	£
1894	107·7	177·2	34·9	188·6	1·5	31·1	12·6	553·6
1895	107·4	155·1	28·9	166·8	2·2	27·5	14·1	502·0
1896	117·2	144·3	31·2	155·9	2·4	30·3	15·8	497·1
1897	122·0	144·4	32·6	159·0	1·5	26·9	15·3	501·7
1898	130·9	147·2	35·6	168·7	2·5	26·8	16·4	528·1
1899	154·0	161·0	41·9	175·1	1·2	26·0	16·6	575·8
1900	156·5	168·7	44·8	177·3	2·1	29·9	17·9	597·2
1901	160·6	200·2	45·6	188·6	2·2	28·0	17·4	642·6
1902	153·8	217·5	44·5	196·2	9·5	28·7	13·3	663·5
1903	158·4	192·3	40·1	174·6	3·2	28·0	12·7	609·3

Interest returned on Capital.

Continuing the basis adopted in the case of New South Wales of taking into consideration the absolute interest paid on the loans of the state and comparing this with the net earnings, the following table furnishes a review for the past ten years, and shows the average loss for each year of the period :—

Year.	Interest returned on Capital.	Actual Rate of Interest payable on Outstanding Loans.	Average Loss.
	per cent.	per cent.	per cent.
1894	2·88	4·04	1·16
1895	2·73	3·96	1·23
1896	2·24	3·98	1·74
1897	2·74	3·96	1·22
1898	2·49	3·93	1·44
1899	2·75	3·83	1·08
1900	2·83	3·89	1·06
1901	3·14	3·76	0·62
1902	2·96	3·72	0·76
1903	2·47	3·86	1·39

The earnings of the Victorian lines are largely reduced by the necessity of working of the lines upon which there is an annual loss of £294,697. The fluctuations in net profits are due to the opening of new lines in sparsely-settled districts and the effect of the drought upon the traffic. A gradual improvement is, however, manifest in the returns of the seven years prior to 1903, and the large shortage in the concluding year is due to the reasons already adverted to.

Earnings and Expenses per Mile.

While the present returns bear no comparison with those of 1872, when the net earnings per train mile were 73·29d. and per mile open £1,342, they are also below those secured during 1894, owing to the special circumstances already dealt with. The gross earnings, expenditure, and net earnings per train mile for the past ten years are set forth in the following table:—

Year.	Gross Earnings per train mile.	Expenditure per train mile.	Net Earnings per train mile.
	d.	d.	d.
1894	64·49	39·05	25·44
1895	64·76	38·82	25·94
1896	64·11	41·43	22·68
1897	68·03	40·79	27·24
1898	67·77	42·85	24·92
1899	71·00	44·42	26·58
1900	71·83	45·17	26·66
1901	72·39	45·01	27·38
1902	71·63	46·06	25·57
1903	71·09	47·41	23·68

The gross earnings, expenditure, and net earnings per average mile open for the past ten years were as follow:—

Year.	Gross Earnings per average mile open.	Expenditure per average mile open.	Net Earnings per average mile open.
	£	£	£
1894	914	553	361
1895	837	502	335
1896	769	497	272
1897	837	501	336
1898	835	528	307
1899	920	576	344
1900	949	597	352
1901	1,034	642	392
1902	1,031	663	368
1903	913	609	304

The tables indicate that while the gross earnings gradually improved up to 1902, the peculiar conditions of 1903 resulted in a considerable reduction on those of the previous two years. It is evident that the strictest economy will be necessary in the matter of expenditure, for the improvement in the revenue has so far been almost wholly neutralised by an increase in the working expenses.

Coaching and Goods Traffic.

The following table shows the number of passengers carried on the lines of the state during the year 1881, and for each of the last ten years, with the receipts from coaching traffic and the average receipts per journey :—

Year.	Passengers carried.	Receipts from Coaching Traffic.	Average Receipts per journey.
	No.	£	d.
1881	18,964,214	770,617	9·75
1894	40,880,378	1,359,675	7·98
1895	40,210,733	1,259,609	7·51
1896	40,993,798	1,264,219	7·40
1897	42,263,638	1,328,687	7·55
1898	43,090,749	1,325,062	7·38
1899	45,805,043	1,372,000	7·19
1900	49,332,899	1,469,910	7·15
1901	54,704,062	1,625,903	7·13
1902	57,465,077	1,648,381	6·89
1903	54,798,073	1,592,088	6·96

The number of passengers carried on the railways of Victoria reached its maximum in 1890, when no less than 58,951,796 persons made use of the lines. The reaction following on the banking crises of 1893 considerably affected the traffic, and in 1895 the number of passengers was reduced to 40,210,733; a gradual improvement, however, has since been manifest in the returns. Victoria occupies the leading position among the states as regards the number of passengers carried, the latest figures being as follow :—New South Wales, 32,384,138; Victoria, 54,798,073; Queensland, 4,048,161; South Australia, including the Northern Territory, 9,065,119; Western Australia, 9,106,396; Tasmania, 761,345; and New Zealand, 7,575,390. The superiority of the Victorian figures results from the large number of passengers carried on the suburban railways, the Melbourne system effectively serving the population within a distance of 20 miles from the centre, and carrying upwards of 88 per cent. of the total passengers. The magnitude of the suburban traffic is evidenced by the fact that the average receipts per journey during the last year are shown to be 6·96d., as against 10·42d. in New South Wales; 27·72d. in Queensland; 9·12d. in South Australia, including Northern Territory; 11·52d. in Western Australia; 31·25d. in Tasmania; and 18·26d. in New Zealand.

The amount of goods and live stock tonnage in 1881, and for each of the ten years from 1894 to 1903, with the earnings therefrom, is shown in the following table :—

Year.	Tonnage of Goods and Live Stock.	Earnings.
	Tons.	£
1881	1,366,603	894,592
1894	2,455,811	1,366,484
1895	2,435,857	1,321,982
1896	2,163,722	1,137,173
1897	2,383,445	1,287,248
1898	2,408,665	1,283,834
1899	2,779,748	1,501,729
1900	2,998,303	1,555,252
1901	3,381,860	1,711,894
1902	3,433,627	1,719,462
1903	3,093,997	1,454,770

The table indicates a gradual increase in the tonnage carried and earnings therefrom during the seven years preceding 1903. The figures for 1902 must be considered highly satisfactory, especially when it is remembered that the harvest conditions generally were not so good as in the preceding year. The considerable falling off in 1903 was due, as already pointed out, to the total failure of the harvest. Particulars of the subdivision of the tonnage of goods and live stock into a general classification are not available, and no information is furnished that will admit of a comparison being made in order to determine how far the cost of carriage per mile has been reduced during the period under review.

Queensland.

The progress of railway construction in Queensland for the first ten years after the opening of the Ipswich to Grandchester line was somewhat slow, only 268 miles having been constructed. In the decade ending in 1885, more energy was displayed, and a further length of 1,167¼ miles was constructed, while during the quinquennial periods ending in 1890 and 1895, extensions of 712 and 250 miles were opened. The length of line open on 30th June, 1903, was 2,710¾ miles, and the amount expended thereon for construction and equipment was £20,302,177, or at the rate of £7,480 per mile. During the year ended 30th June, 1903, the length of line open for traffic was increased by the opening of the extensions of the Kilkivan Branch and Mackay railways, but the total length was again reduced to 2,710¾ miles by the c osing of the Bowen and Cooktown lines.

The railways of the state may be grouped into three divisions, comprising six systems. The southern division extends from Brisbane to Wallangarra in a southerly direction, to Cunnamulla in a westerly direction, and to Gladstone northerly along the coast, and has fifteen branch lines connected with it. The central division extends from Archer Park to Longreach, and has five branch lines connected with it. The northern division comprises the line from Mackay to Eton, Mirani and Pinnacle; the line from Townsville to Winton, with a branch to Ravenswood; the line from Cairns to Mareeba; and the line from Normanton to Croydon.

For many years the construction, maintenance, and control of the railways were carried out by a branch of the Public Works Office, and subsequently by a separate Ministerial Department with a Secretary responsible to Parliament and administering the details of the office in a manner similar to any other Crown Minister. The "Railways Act of 1888," however, while leaving the Minister in charge of the Department, vested the construction, management, and control of all Government railways in three Commissioners, of whom one was to be Chief Commissioner. The number was subsequently reduced to two, and later a single commissioner was appointed holding the authority formerly vested in the three. In undertaking railway construction the state is guided by other considerations than those which would direct the action of private investors, and is content, for a time at least, to recoup the expenditure in an indirect form. The disastrous result of the continued drought has operated against successful management during recent years, and in consequence of the fact that the rate of interest returned on capital expenditure during the past three years does not compare favourably with the previous years, a policy of stringent economy is to be pursued in the management of the railways, and the rates and fares have been increased with the object of reducing the deficit.

Revenue and Working Expenses.

The net sum available to meet interest charges during the last decennial period is shown in the following table:—

Year.	Gross Earnings.	Working Expenses.	Net Earnings.	Proportion of Working Expenses to Gross Earnings.
	£	£	£	per cent.
1894	955,747	598,403	357,344	62·61
1895	1,025,512	581,973	443,539	56·75
1896	1,085,494	644,362	441,132	59·36
1897	1,179,273	684,146	495,127	58·01
1898	1,215,811	686,066	529,745	56·43
1899	1,373,475	784,811	588,664	57·14
1900	1,464,399	948,691	515,708	64·78
1901	1,316,936	1,057,981	258,955	80·34
1902	1,382,179	992,751	389,428	71·82
1903	1,234,230	863,382	370,848	69·95

With the exception of the last three years the foregoing table shows a gradual tendency towards an increase in revenue, but there have been considerable fluctuations in the proportion of working expenses to gross earnings. The net earnings for the year ended 30th June, 1900, were 35·22 per cent. of the total earnings, as against 36·33 per cent. when the railways were placed under their present control. It will be observed that the result secured for that year is considerably lower than those of the preceding two years, and is due to the fact that the railways were compelled to carry very large numbers of starving stock and large quantities of fodder at unremunerative rates. There were also heavy disbursements to replace and increase the stock of locomotives, and to carry out works which, though improving the equipment of the railways and ensuring safe running, have not been of a reproductive character, while during the year substantial increases in pay were conceded to all classes of railway employees. There was consequently a large increase in expenditure which was not accompanied by a corresponding improvement in the earnings. For the year ended 30th June, 1901, the revenue from passenger traffic showed a substantial increase; the decrease in earnings shown in the preceding table was entirely due to the loss of live stock by drought and consequent stoppage of station improvements, and to the necessity of carrying starving stock and fodder at merely nominal rates. The net earnings for the year were thus reduced to 19·66 per cent. of the total earnings. A slight improvement was manifested in the year ended 30th June, 1902, the percentage gained being 28·18 of the total earnings, the increase in rates and fares being responsible for the advance. Working expenses were curtailed by a reduction in the train mileage, and by the exercise of stringent economy in administration, and with the return of favourable seasons it was hoped that more satisfactory results would be secured. The adversity of the season during the year ended the 30th June, 1903, however, was responsible for a heavy decline. Less wool and live stock were carried, while the traffic in produce from the agricultural districts decreased by as much as 43 per cent.

An analysis of the working expenses of the Queensland railways for the ten years, 1894–1903, is given below. Taking the first year with the last it will be seen that there has been a substantial increase in the total cost, as well as in the rate per train mile and per mile of line open. In 1899 the expenditure per train mile had been reduced to 32·35d., as compared with 40·82d. in 1893 and 42·05d. in 1902. There can be no doubt that the expenditure for 1899 had been reduced below the point of safety and some services had been starved, and this necessitated in the following years an abnormal expenditure on improvements of the locomotive, carriage and waggon stock, and in bringing the equipment generally up to a better standard to ensure the safe working of the lines. In 1901 there was a considerable outlay on relaying and other heavy works; similar expenditure, or, at least, expenditure on so large a scale, will not, of course, be needed for some little time.

Year ended 30th June.	Maintenance of Way, Works, and Buildings.	Locomotive Power.	Carriage and Waggon Repairs and Renewals.	Traffic Expenses.	General Charges.	Total.
	£	£	£	£	£	£
1894	251,946	139,231	31,201	150,045	25,980	598,403
1895	233,772	141,568	33,702	144,483	28,448	581,973
1896	248,468	172,373	34,936	161,656	26,929	644,362
1897	271,602	184,817	37,714	164,097	25,916	684,146
1898	261,706	186,226	38,719	172,503	26,912	686,066
1899	289,005	225,033	45,462	196,680	28,631	784,811
1900	335,777	302,752	56,256	221,640	32,266	948,691
1901	401,013	322,879	68,088	229,902	36,099	1,057,981
1902	355,793	317,831	71,915	226,745	20,467	992,751
1903	292,952	270,162	73,513	207,303	19,452	863,382

PER TRAIN MILE.

	d.	d.	d.	d.	d.	d.
894	16·89	9·33	2·10	10·06	1·74	40·12
1895	14·32	8·67	2·07	8·85	1·74	35·65
1896	12·57	8·72	1·77	8·18	1·36	32·60
1897	13·20	8·98	1·83	7·97	1·26	33·24
1898	12·54	8·92	1·86	8·27	1·29	32·88
1899	11·91	9·28	1·87	8·11	1·18	32·35
1900	12·54	11·31	2·10	8·28	1·20	35·43
1901	16·63	13·39	2·82	9·53	1·50	43·87
1902	15·07	13·46	3·05	9·60	0·87	42·05
1903	14·21	13·10	3·57	10·06	0·94	41·88

PER MILE OPEN.

	£	£	£	£	£	£
1894	106·0	58·6	13·1	63·1	10·9	251·7
1895	98·3	59·5	14·2	60·7	11·9	244·6
1896	104·3	72·3	14·7	67·8	11·3	270·4
1897	111·9	76·2	15·5	67·6	10·7	281·9
1898	101·2	72·0	15·0	66·7	10·4	265·3
1899	106·5	82·9	16·8	72·5	10·6	289·3
1900	120·1	108·3	20·1	79·3	11·5	339·3
1901	143·1	115·3	24·3	82·1	12·9	377·7
1902	127·0	113·5	25·7	81·0	7·3	354·5
1903	105·5	97·2	26·5	74·6	7·0	310·8

Interest returned on Capital.

The financial results of the working of the lines are exhibited in the following table which covers a period of ten years :—

Year.	Interest returned on Capital.	Actual Rate of Interest payable on Outstanding Loans.	Average Loss.
	per cent.	per cent.	per cent.
1894	2·18	4·17	1·99
1895	2·68	4·16	1·48
1896	2·63	4·09	1·46
1897	2·87	4·04	1·17
1898	2·92	4·04	1·12
1899	3·15	4·00	0·85
1900	2·67	4·02	1·35
1901	1·31	3·98	2·67
1902	1·93	3·94	2·01
1903	1·48	3·92	2·44

A fair proportion of the railway construction of recent years has been in country of a purely pastoral character, and it is manifest that a sufficient traffic to prove remunerative cannot be looked for immediately from localities possessed of only a scattered and limited population ; but it is confidently expected that these lines will ultimately pay interest on cost of construction. Unfortunately, Queensland, in common with the other provinces, is burdened with lines of railway not warranted by existing or prospective traffic, and these will always be a handicap to successful management.

Earnings and Expenses per Mile.

While the results now secured cannot be compared with those of 1880, when the net earnings per train mile were a little over 43d., and per mile open £222, a satisfactory state of affairs is disclosed by a review of the figures for earnings shown in the subjoined tables. It will be seen that the net earnings per train mile, as well as the net return for each mile of line open, have, except in the last four years, been fairly well sustained. The fall in 1900, 1901, 1902, and 1903, as compared with the previous three years, is due to the fact that the continuance of the drought and the consequent loss in sheep and cattle have operated against the revenue from the carriage of wool and live stock, while the increased traffic which was obtained consisted largely of the removal of starving stock from and the carriage of fodder to drought-stricken districts, a class of traffic which had to be undertaken at unremunerative rates. The gross earnings, expenditure, and net earnings per train mile for the past ten years are shown in the following table:—

Year.	Gross Earnings per train mile.	Expenditure per train mile.	Net Earnings per train mile.
	d.	d.	d.
1894	64·18	40·12	24·06
1895	62·82	35·65	27·17
1896	54·91	32·60	22·31
1897	57·30	33·24	24·06
1898	58·27	32·88	25·39
1899	56·62	32·35	24·27
1900	54·69	35·43	19·26
1901	54·61	43·87	10·74
1902	58·54	42·05	16·49
1903	59·87	41·88	17·99

The gross earnings, expenditure, and net earnings per average mile open for the past ten years were as follow:—

Year.	Gross Earnings per average mile open.	Expenditure per average mile open.	Net Earnings per average mile open.
	£	£	£
1894	402	251	151
1895	431	244	187
1896	455	270	185
1897	486	281	205
1898	470	265	205
1899	506	289	217
1900	523	339	184
1901	470	377	93
1902	493	354	139
1903	444	311	133

Coaching and Goods Traffic.

The number of passengers carried on the lines of the state during the year 1881, and for the last ten years, together with the receipts fro mthe traffic, and the average receipts per journey, are set forth in the following table :—

Year.	Passengers carried.	Receipts from Coaching traffic.	Average Receipts per Journey.
	No.	£	d.
1881	247,284	113,490	110·14
1894	2,024,450	307,430	36·44
1895	2,054,416	308,025	35·98
1896	2,274,219	324,790	34·27
1897	2,633,556	359,811	32·79
1898	2,742,108	391,270	34·24
1899	3,716,425	447,123	28·87
1900	4,395,841	505,536	27·60
1901	4,760,559	536,462	27·05
1902	4,636,174	513,257	26·59
1903	4,048,161	467,594	27·72

It will be seen that the years 1899, 1900, 1901, 1902, and 1903 show a far larger number of passenger journeys than preceding years; this was largely due to an extraordinary expansion in the suburban traffic. The falling off in 1903 as compared with the three preceding years occurred almost wholly on the lines of the Southern Division. During the period the average receipts per journey show a decline, which may be expected to continue as the suburban traffic expands, so that in a few years the receipts per person carried will approximate closely to the average for the rest of Australia, viz., one shilling per journey.

The amount of goods tonnage for a similar period is shown in the following table :—

Year.	Tonnage of Goods.	Earnings.
1881	161,008	£235,100
1894	785,475	648,317
1895	900,591	717,487
1896	1,026,889	760,704
1897	1,243,603	819,462
1898	1,323,782	824,541
1899	1,684,858	926,352
1900	1,688,635	958,863
1901	1,530,440	780,474
1902	1,725,520	868,922
1903	1,566,960	766,636

In the foregoing statement the tonnage of live stock is not included, the information not being available, but the earnings shown include the revenue derived from this class of traffic. The general traffic is divided into eight classes, particulars of which, for the year ended 30th June, 1903, together with the receipts for each class, are shown in the subjoined table. No information is available as to the average number of miles each ton of traffic is carried, or the earnings per ton per mile.

Description of Traffic.	Tons carried.		Receipts from traffic.
General merchandise	241,938	...	£353,877
Agricultural produce	229,217	...	94,239
Wool	18,490	...	57,021
Coal........................	372,947	...	56,700
Minerals other than coal...	313,473	...	34,815
Timber	390,895	...	83,606
Live stock	......	...	86,378
Total	1,566,960	...	£766,636

Guaranteed Railways.

Up to the 30th June, 1903, four railways, having a total length of 36 miles 55 chains, were constructed under "The Railways Guarantee Act of 1895." In accordance with this Act the local authority, representing the ratepayers of a district, agrees to pay up to one-half of the deficiency in working expenses with interest at the rate of 4 per cent. on the capital cost during the first fourteen years after opening, the sum to be raised by means of a rate not exceeding 3d. in the £ of value of ratable lands. Should the operations of any year provide a surplus, half of this is retained by the Government and the other half paid to the local authority for distribution among the ratepayers in return for the payments made on account of the deficiency in previous years. When the line has been payable for three years, the Government may cancel the agreement. The results of the working of three out of the four railways do not afford much encouragement to apply the provisions of the Act to other lines which may be projected in the future. The Pialba branch, on which the expenditure to 30th June, 1903, was £46,085, showed, without taking into consideration the interest on capital cost, a net revenue for the year 1899 of £715; in 1900, £966; in 1901, £994; in 1902, £1,139; while in 1903, there was a loss of £219. Leaving out of consideration the interest on a capital cost of £11,385, the Allora branch shows a net revenue of £262 in 1899; £120 in 1900; and £105 in 1902; while in the year 1901, there was a loss of £182, and in the year just closed a further loss of £187. A capital expenditure of £47,632 has been incurred in connection with the Enoggera branch, and leaving out of consideration the interest charge thereon, there was a net revenue of £159 in 1899, and £67 in 1900, while the loss in 1901 was £440; in 1902, £235; and in 1903, £737. The Mount Morgan branch, which up to the 30th June, 1902, had involved a capital expenditure of £84,407, has given satisfactory results. The net revenue, leaving out of consideration the interest on capital cost, was £7,127 in 1899; £9,084 in 1900; £6,297 in 1901; £4,872 in 1902; and £4,147 in 1903.

South Australia.

While the beginning of railway construction in South Australia dates as far back as 1854, very little progress was made in the subsequent twenty years, and in 1874 the total length of line in operation was only 234 miles; in 1880 this had increased to 627 miles; in 1890 to 1,610 miles; and in 1895 to 1,722 miles. The length of line in operation on the 30th June, 1903, was 1,736¼ miles, and the amount expended thereon for construction and equipment, £13,400,796, or at the rate of £7,718 per mile.

The railways of South Australia proper are divided for the purposes of management into five systems. The Midland system, constructed on the 5ft. 3in. gauge, has a length of 236¾ miles, and extends from Adelaide to Terowie in a northerly direction, and to Morgan, on the Murray River, in a north-easterly direction. The Northern system has a total length of 1,008¼ miles, 1,003 of which are 3 ft. 6 in. gauge, and 5¼ miles 5 ft. 3 in. gauge. This system includes that portion of the transcontinental line which extends to Oodnadatta, a distance of 550 miles from Adelaide; the line to Cockburn, which provides for the requirements of the Broken Hill district of New South Wales; and branches to Port Augusta, Port Pirie, Wallaroo, and Port Wakefield. The Southern system comprises a length of 265¼ miles on a gauge of 5 ft. 3 in., and includes the main line connecting Adelaide with Melbourne, and branches—Wolseley to Naracoorte and from Naracoorte to Kingston, Mount Gambier, and Beechport. The line from Port Broughton to Barunga has a length of 10 miles.

During 1887 the control of the railways was entrusted to three commissioners; in 1895, however, the number was reduced to one, who is responsible to Parliament.

Revenue and Working Expenses.

The net sum available to meet interest charges is set forth in the following table:—

Year.	Gross Earnings.	Working Expenses.	Net Earnings.	Proportion of Working Expenses to Gross Earnings.
	£	£	£	£
1894	999,707	569,592	430,115	56·98
1895	960,155	568,973	391,182	59·26
1896	986,500	583,022	403,478	59·10
1897	1,025,035	614,254	410,781	59·92
1898	984,228	603,474	380,754	61·31
1899	1,058,397	617,380	441,017	58·33
1900	1,166,987	657,841	509,146	56·37
1901	1,236,616	729,039	507,577	58·95
1902	1,085,175	689,517	395,658	63·54
1903	1,076,612	624,511	452,101	58·01

The foregoing table shows that the gross earnings in 1901 were the largest during the decade, while the proportion of working expenses to gross earnings was lowest in 1900, the net earnings in the latter year being the highest for the period. The failure of the harvest and the succession of adverse seasons which South Australia laboured under during part of the decennial period are the causes of the falling off in the revenue for several years. No other railway system in Australia depends so much upon the carriage of agricultural produce for its traffic, and years of shrinkage in the railway revenue are coincident with years of harvest failure. The increase in working expenses during the years 1899 and 1900 was due to the renewal of rolling stock, the relaying of portion of the permanent way, and other outlay expended from the improved revenue. The further increase during 1901 is explained by the rise in the price of coal and materials; by the increased train mileage; and by the fact that opportunity was taken of a fairly good year's revenue to debit working expenses with an unusual outlay under the head of "replacements." The operations of the year ended 30th June, 1902, show a considerable reduction in the gross earnings, which is attributable to the shrinkage in the Barrier traffic caused by the fall in the price of lead reducing the output of the mines. Moreover, consequent on the decrease in mining profits, the department was compelled to carry ore and concentrates at much lower rates, so that there was a diminished receipt from every ton of a smaller volume of traffic, and an increase in the proportion of working expenses to gross earnings. While the gross earnings for the year ended 30th June, 1903, exhibit a slight shortage in comparison with those of the previous year, a large reduction is manifest in the working expenses. This has been secured by restricting expenditure in every branch, and the postponement of repairs and renewals, which it would have been the truest economy to effect. The results secured may be looked upon as fairly satisfactory, when it is considered that the management is burdened with some very unproductive lines, notably that from Hergott Springs to Oodnadatta, which barely pays working expenses, and entails an annual payment of about £44,000 in interest.

The working expenditure of the South Australian lines, an analysis of which is given below, does not show very much variation from year to year. The average reached its lowest point in the year 1900 with 37·78d. per train mile; since then there has been a rise of about 2d. per train mile, which the railway managers attribute to the increased price of coal and materials, to larger expenditure on repairs and rolling stock, and to increases in the wages of the employees.

Year ended 30th June.	Maintenance of Way, Works, and Buildings.	Locomotive Power.	Carriage and Waggon Repairs and Renewals.	Traffic Expenses.	Compensation.	General Charges.	Total.
	£	£	£	£	£	£	£
1894	141,625	225,871	37,292	147,755	166	16,883	569,592
1895	138,983	214,271	51,956	147,173	73	16,517	568,973
1896	137,855	221,706	62,882	146,127	162	14,290	583,022
1897	159,798	244,235	50,546	144,935	718	14,027	614,254
1898	152,091	234,233	52,323	150,033	836	13,968	603,474
1899	160,514	236,604	58,754	146,962	645	13,901	617,380
1900	163,851	255,582	62,832	160,641	687	14,298	[illegible]
1901	185,292	298,913	68,654	164,589	1,568	15,029	[illegible]
1902	166,691	278,830	64,733	162,626	1,394	15,234	689,517
1903	139,297	265,346	51,874	151,738	1,668	14,596	6[illegible]

Year ended 30th June.	Maintenance of Way, Works, and Buildings.	Locomotive Power.	Carriage and Waggon Repairs and Renewals.	Traffic Expenses.	Compensation.	General Charges.	Total.
Per Train Mile.							
	d.	d.	d.	d.	d.	d.	d.
1894	9·80	15·61	2·58	10·22	0·01	1·17	39·39
1895	9·83	15·15	3·67	10·41	0·01	1·17	40·24
1896	9·58	15·42	4·37	10·16	0·01	0·99	40·53
1897	10·44	15·94	3·30	9·47	0·05	0·92	40·12
1898	9·82	15·14	3·38	9·69	0·05	0·90	38·98
1899	9·88	14·56	3·62	9·05	0·04	0·85	38·00
1900	9·41	14·67	3·61	9·23	0·04	0·82	37·78
1901	10·12	16·06	3·75	8·99	0·09	0·82	39·83
1902	9·53	15·96	3·70	9·30	0·08	0·87	39·44
1903	8·87	16·89	3·30	9·66	0·10	0·93	39·75
Per Mile Open.							
	£	£	£	£	£	£	£
1894	85·1	135·7	22·4	88·8	....	10·1	342·1
1895	80·7	124·4	30·2	85·5	....	9·6	330·4
1896	80·1	128·7	36·5	84·9	....	8·3	338·5
1897	92·8	141·8	29·3	84·1	0·4	8·1	356·5
1898	88·2	135·9	30·4	87·0	0·5	8·1	350·1
1899	93·1	137·3	34·1	85·3	0·4	8·0	358·2
1900	94·7	147·7	36·3	92·8	0·4	8·2	380·1
1901	106·7	169·3	39·5	94·8	0·9	8·7	419·9
1902	96·0	160·6	37·3	93·6	0·8	8·8	397·1
1903	80·0	153·0	30·0	87·0	1·0	9·0	360·0

Interest returned on Capital.

The following table exhibits the financial results of the working of the lines during the last ten years :—

Year.	Interest returned on Capital.	Actual rate of Interest payable on Outstanding Loans.	Average Loss.
	per cent.	per cent.	per cent.
1894	3·54	4·27	0·73
1895	3·12	4·22	1·10
1896	3·21	4·12	0·91
1897	3·26	4·05	0·79
1898	2·98	4·03	1·05
1899	3·42	3·95	0·53
1900	3·91	3·89	0·02*
1901	3·86	3·87	0·01
1902	2·98	3·81	0·83
1903	3·08	3·74	0·66

* Represents profit.

The interest returned on capital during 1900 was the highest secured since 1892, when the railways returned 4·78 per cent. on capital expenditure, and exceeded by a slight amount the interest rate on the debt of the province. South Australia possesses one advantage not shared by any other province, namely, a large and steady long-distance traffic from a neighbouring state. The Broken Hill traffic is a very important factor in the railway revenue, as the greater portion of the line connecting the mines with the seaports runs through South Australian territory. The extent of the Broken Hill traffic will be found mentioned on page 380.

Earnings and Expenses per Mile.

The net earnings now secured are very much below those of 1891 when the return per train mile was 38·64d., and per mile open £370; a gradual improvement is, however, noticeable up to 1900, the fall in 1901 and 1902 being due to the reasons already adverted to on a previous page. The figures for 1903 again show an upward tendency. The gross earnings, expenditure, and net earnings per train mile for the past ten years are shown in the following table:—

Year.	Gross Earnings per train mile.	Expenditure per train mile.	Net Earnings per train mile.
	d.	d.	d.
1894	69·14	39·39	29·75
1895	67·90	40·24	27·66
1896	68·57	40·53	28·04
1897	66·95	40·12	26·83
1898	63·57	38·98	24·59
1899	65·14	38·00	27·14
1900	67·02	37·78	29·24
1901	67·56	39·83	27·73
1902	62·06	39·44	22·62
1903	68·53	39·75	28·78

The gross earnings, expenditure, and net earnings per average mile open for the past ten years are set forth in the following table:—

Year.	Gross Earnings per average mile open.	Expenditure per average mile open.	Net Earnings per average mile open.
	£	£	£
1894	601	342	259
1895	558	330	228
1896	573	338	235
1897	595	356	239
1898	571	350	221
1899	614	358	256
1900	674	380	294
1901	712	419	293
1902	625	397	228
1903	620	360	260

The results for the year 1900 may be viewed as satisfactory, taking into consideration the fact that the number of train miles run during that year was higher than in any previous year during the period. It will be seen that there was a substantial fall in the net earnings per train mile for the year ended 30th June, 1902, due to the reasons already referred to. The present earnings per train mile, and the return per mile of line open are above the average of the Commonwealth as a whole.

Coaching and Goods Traffic.

The following table shows the number of passengers carried on the lines of the state during the year 1881, and for each of the last ten years, together with the receipts from the traffic, and the average receipts per journey:—

Year.	Passengers carried.	Receipts from Coaching Traffic.	Average Receipts per Journey.
	No.	£	d.
1881	3,032,714	151,867	12·01
1894	5,260,079	274,243	12·51
1895	5,224,854	263,448	12·09
1896	5,435,956	288,594	12·73
1897	5,789,297	297,026	12·31
1898	6,050,189	291,411	11·56
1899	6,171,081	297,207	11·56
1900	7,416,506	337,723	10·93
1901	8,863,632	359,172	9·74
1902	9,643,058	369,677	9·34
1903	9,061,488	342,037	9·05

The table indicates an improvement in the number of passengers carried; the falling off during the last year in comparison with 1902 being due to the less prosperous season; the average receipts per journey have, however, gradually declined.

The amount of goods tonnage for the same period is shown in the following table:—

Year.	Tonnage of Goods and Live Stock.	Earnings.
	No.	£
1881	646,625	222,184
1894	1,014,010	694,724
1895	1,000,408	666,600
1896	1,056,963	670,961
1897	1,146,293	700,629
1898	1,189,095	664,348
1899	1,403,727	731,156
1900	1,485,976	798,231
1901	1,628,444	843,019
1902	1,392,257	681,045
1903	1,349,617	703,522

Fluctuation in the tonnage of goods carried is presented by the figures in the foregoing table, and the considerable decrease manifested in the past two years, in comparison with 1901, is due to the continuous fall in the metal market not only reducing the output, but leading to a general slackness of business on the Barrier, while, in addition, ore and concentrates were carried at lower rates. The volume of traffic secured by South Australia from the Barrier District of New South Wales amounted to 491,711 tons out of the total of 1,349,617 tons, and the receipts from all traffic passing through Cockburn to £339,341 out of a revenue of £1,076,612.

The following table shows a classification of the goods carried during 1903, and the amount received for carriage. It would have been interesting to exhibit also the charge for haulage of each description of goods during the last ten years, but no information is available which will enable such particulars to be compiled. There has been a general reduction in freight charges, and the average charge per ton per mile for all goods has fallen from 1·05d. in 1897 to 1·03d. in 1903:—

Description of Traffic.	Tons Carried.	Receipts from Traffic.
		£
Minerals	546,701	226,728
Grain	101,602	29,578
Wool	14,798	19,690
Goods other than above	647,066	355,166
Live stock	39,450	72,360

Northern Territory.

Railway construction in the Northern Territory has been confined to the line from Palmerston to Pine Creek, opened on the 1st October, 1889, and the returns for the past eight years show that the traffic does not even pay working expenses.

Revenue and Working Expenses.

The gross earnings, expenditure, and net earnings, with the proportion of working expenses to gross earnings of the line are set forth in the following table, which covers a period of ten years:—

Year.	Gross Earnings.	Working Expenses.	Net Earnings.	Proportion of Working Expenses to Gross Earnings.
	£	£	£	per cent.
1894	16,193	11,403	4,790	70·42
1895	14,722	11,477	3,245	77·96
1896	15,105	15,289	(—) 184	101·22
1897	17,908	18,966	(—) 1,058	105·91
1898	14,124	20,268	(—) 6,144	143·50
1899	14,758	17,375	(—) 2,617	117·73
1900	14,799	24,340	(—) 9,541	164·47
1901	13,845	25,280	(—)11,435	182·59
1902	12,522	34,649	(—)22,127	276·70
1903	11,298	12,812	(—) 1,514	113·40

(—) Denotes loss.

The experience of the past eight years offers no encouragement to any further extension of railways in the Northern Territory. The actual results of working have not been quite so unfavourable as would appear from the foregoing table, as each of the two years 1900 and 1901 was charged with the payment of an instalment of £10,000, and 1902 with the final instalment of £21,931, towards the reconstruction of the jetty which was destroyed by a hurricane in 1896.

The expenditure on working for 1903 may be divided as follows :—

	£
Maintenance of Permanent Way Buildings, &c.	6,981
Locomotive Power	2,479
Carriage and Waggon Repairs	972
Traffic Expenses	1,935
General Charges	445
Total	12,812

These figures are equivalent to 101·07d. per train mile, and £88·10 per mile of line open for traffic.

Interest returned on Capital.

The following table shows the average loss for each year during the last ten years, after the interest on cost of construction has been deducted from the net earnings :—

Year.	Interest returned on Capital.	Actual Rate of Interest payable on Outstanding Loans.	Average Loss.
	per cent.	per cent.	per cent.
1894	0·42	4·08	3·66
1895	0·28	4·22	3·94
1896	(—) 0·02	4·12	4·14
1897	(—) 0·09	4·05	4·14
1898	(—) 0·53	4·03	4·56
1899	(—) 0·22	3·95	4·17
1900	(—) 0·82	4·04	4·86
1901	(—) 0·98	4·05	5·03
1902	(—) 1·99	4·37	6·36
1903	(—) 0·13	4·37	4·50

(—) Denotes loss.

From the outset there was very little prospect that the traffic on this line would meet the interest on the cost of construction and equipment; and although for the first five years there was a margin after paying working expenses, the results of the past eight years show that even working expenses have not been met. The deficiency is in part due to the heavy expenditure necessitated by the ravages of the teredo in the sub-structure of the jetty at Palmerston, and the large outlay to repair damages caused by the cyclone which struck Port Darwin in the early part of 1897. Fluctuations in the volume of traffic are also partly responsible for the deficiency.

Earnings and Expenses per Mile.

The gross earnings, expenditure, and net earnings per train mile for a period of ten years are shown in the following table :—

Year.	Gross Earnings per Train Mile.	Expenditure per Train Mile.	Net Earnings per Train Mile.
	d.	d.	d.
1894	125·14	88·12	37·02
1895	115·10	89·73	25·37
1896	114·28	115·67	(—) 1·39
1897	137·28	145·38	(—) 8·10
1898	112·97	162·12	(—) 49·15
1899	115·53	136·02	(—) 20·49
1900	114·53	188·37	(—) 73·84
1901	109·75	200·39	(—) 90·64
1902	99·26	274·65	(—) 175·39
1903	89·13	101·07	(—) 11·94

(—) Denotes loss.

The gross earnings, expenditure, and net earnings per average mile open for the last decennial period were as follow :—

Year.	Gross Earnings per average mile open.	Expenditure per average mile open.	Net Earnings per average mile open.
	£	£	£
1894	111	78	33
1895	101	79	22
1896	104	105	(—) 1
1897	123	130	(—) 7
1898	97	139	(—) 42
1899	102	119	(—) 17
1900	102	167	(—) 65
1901	95	174	(—) 79
1902	86	238	(—) 152
1903	78	88	(—) 10

(—) Denotes loss.

The gross earnings show little variation from year to year, but the expenditure was increased through the series of accidents at the terminal port, to which reference has already been made.

Coaching and Goods Traffic.

The following table shows the number of passengers carried on the Palmerston to Pine Creek Line since its opening, together with the receipts from the traffic and the average receipts per journey :—

Year.	Passengers carried.	Receipts from Coaching Traffic.	Average Receipts per journey.
	No.	£	d.
1890 (nine months)	4,567	4,330	227·54
1891	4,515	4,693	249·45
1892	4,541	4,159	219·80
1893	6,169	4,007	155·89
1894	4,076	3,820	224·91
1895	2,950	3,755	305·48
1896	2,901	3,772	312·04
1897	3,080	4,055	315·97
1898	3,126	3,556	273·01
1899	3,191	3,173	238·64
1900	3,374	3,556	260·48
1901	4,097	3,415	200·05
1902	3,755	3,032	193·80
1903	3,631	2,913	192·53

The table shows an increase in the number of passengers carried during 1893; but the promise of the year was not sustained, and the traffic fell away by more than one-half during 1895, 1896, and 1897, although the earnings did not decline in anything like the same proportion. Since the year last mentioned there has been a steady, though small, increase in the number of passengers; but without a corresponding addition to the revenue. The receipts per journey indicate that a large proportion of the traffic is of a long-distance character.

The amount of goods tonnage for a similar period is shown in the following table :—

Year.	Tonnage of Goods and Live Stock.	Earnings.
	Tons.	£
1890 (nine months)	2,114	7,499
1891	2,426	9,035
1892	2,633	9,267
1893	2,328	9,470
1894	2,524	10,260
1895	2,053	8,643
1896	2,493	9,149
1897	3,150	11,222
1898	2,678	8,570
1899	3,187	10,091
1900	3,009	9,626
1901	2,981	8,892
1902	2,436	7,996
1903	2,455	7,000

The average receipts per ton per mile during the year 1903 were 7·39d., as against 8·43d. in 1896.

Western Australia.

The first railway constructed in Western Australia was that from Geraldton to Northampton, a length of 34 miles 17 chains, opened for traffic on the 26th July, 1879. Between that date and the close of 1885, a further length of 91 miles 55 chains was constructed. To the end of 1890, only 200½ miles were constructed, and on the 30th June, 1895, there were 573 miles open for traffic. Railway construction received a considerable impetus subsequent to 1895, and on the 30th June, 1903, there were 1,516 miles open for traffic, at a cost of £8,141,782 for construction and equipment, or at the rate of £5,370 per mile.

The state railways of Western Australia are comprised in five systems. The Eastern system has a length of 196 miles, and includes the line from Fremantle to Northam, with branches to Newcastle, Beverley, Greenhills, Perth Racecourse, and Owen's Anchorage, the Mahogany Creek deviation, and Goomalling; the Eastern Gold Fields system extends eastward from Northam, and includes the Kanowna, Menzies, Leonora, and Boulder branches, the total length being 491 miles; the South-western system comprises the line from East Perth to Bunbury, with branches to Colliefields, Bridgetown, Busselton, and Canning and Bunbury Racecourses, and has a length of 234 miles; the Northern system includes the line from Geraldton to Cue and Nannine, with branches to Walkaway, Mullewa, and Northampton, the total length being 352 miles; and the Great Southern system, from Beverley to Albany, is 243 miles in length.

The control of the state railways was formerly vested in the Commissioner for Railways as member of the Government, the active management being undertaken by an officer with the title of General Manager, but on the 1st July, 1902, the administration was placed in the hands of an independent Commissioner.

Revenue and Working Expenses.

The net sum available to meet interest charges during the last ten years is shown in the following table:—

Year.	Gross Earnings.	Working Expenses.	Net Earnings.	Proportion of Working Expenses to Gross Earnings.
	£	£	£	per cent.
1894	140,564	103,973	36,591	73·96
1895	296,000	182,046	113,954	61·50
1896	529,616	263,704	265,912	49·79
1897	915,483	577,655	337,828	63·09
1898	1,019,677	786,318	233,359	77·11
1899	1,004,620	712,329	292,291	70·91
1900	1,259,512	861,470	398,042	68·40
1901	1,353,704	1,044,920	308,784	77·19
1902	1,521,429	1,256,370	265,059	82·58
1903	1,553,485	1,247,873	305,612	80·33

From the foregoing statement it will be seen that the gross earnings have increased from £140,564 in 1894 to £1,553,485 in 1903. The rush to the gold-fields of Western Australia has brought an enormous amount of traffic to the railways of that state, and the lines stand in a position which it is impossible for those of any other province to attain, except under similar circumstances. The proportion of working expenses to gross earnings during the ten years has increased from 73·96 per cent. to 80·33 per cent., the intervening years showing considerable irregularity. The rates for the carriage of merchandise are so low that the revenue derived from the traffic is hardly sufficient to pay for working it, and with a view to economy during 1899 the train service was considerably curtailed, and trains previously confined to passenger traffic were converted into mixed trains, conveying both passengers and goods, the result being a substantial reduction in working expenses proportionately to the gross earnings.

The relation of working expenses to gross earnings for 1903 showed a percentage of 80·33, as compared with 82·58, 77·19, and 68·40 in the preceding three years. The comparatively large increase during the period is attributable to several causes. There was a substantial addition to the tonnage of coal, timber, and goods hauled at low rates, but no profit was returned therefrom, the receipts only about equalling the working expenses in connection therewith. A heavy expenditure was incurred on locomotive repairs, and among other contributing causes were the rise in price of coal and stores, and increased rates of wages.

Western Australian lines show much greater variation from year to year than the lines of any other state. During the ten years 1894–1903, the lowest expenditure was in 1894 with 38·92d. per train mile, which rose to 66·89d. in 1902, but dropped to 64·95d. in 1903. The conditions, however, in the earlier years of the decade, when only 321 miles of line were open for traffic, and the train miles run amounted only to 641,080, were entirely different from those of 1903 with 1,516 miles open for traffic and an aggregate train mileage of 4,611,315. In 1899 there was a reduction in the total working expenses, brought about mainly by the curtailment of the mileage; this was accomplished by reducing the number of passenger trains and adopting a system of mixed trains. In the year 1900 there was a large increase in the number of locomotives, and in the repairs to carriages, waggons, &c. This increase, so far as can be seen, was attributable, partly to the natural development of the traffic, but chiefly to the inadequate workshop accommodation and to the fact that the water supply for railways was both inferior and expensive. The year 1901 showed a great advance in the cost of the railways, the expenditure per train mile rising from 49·04d. to 60·78d., every branch participating in the increase. It was in this year that the fifty-four hours per week system was introduced, involving the employment of an increased wages staff, and in addition thereto there was a general increase in the rates of wages. The conditions of working at Fremantle locomotive shops entailed a large outlay, and, in addition, there was an increased expenditure on locomotives due to the compulsory use of bad water, and the overwork of rolling stock owing to a shortage of hauling power and waggons. During the year named the railways were undoubtedly worked at a very great disadvantage.

The increased expenditure per train mile in 1901 was continued during 1902, when it rose from 60·78d. to 66·89d., in consequence of the expanded outlay in all branches of the service. There was a specially heavy expenditure in the locomotive branch, amounting to £173,297. In 1903, however, the average per train mile fell to 64·95d.

Year.	Maintenance of Way, Works, and Buildings.	Locomotive Power, Carriage and Waggon Repairs.	Traffic Expenses.	Compensation.	General Charges.	Total.
	£	£	£	£	£	£
1894	20,493	47,129	31,250	......	5,101	103,973
1895	36,202	86,453	50,725	......	8,666	182,046
1896	56,036	101,692	94,388	......	11,588	263,704
1897	97,184	221,884	225,615	11,651	21,321	577,655
1898	176,741	315,066	266,167	9,803	18,541	786,318
1899	165,277	297,500	227,225	3,568	18,759	712,329
1900	183,096	406,565	252,750	4,455	14,604	861,470
1901	221,451	497,188	296,045	6,926	23,310	1,044,920
1902	246,931	670,485	306,408	7,246	25,300	1,256,370
1903	265,548	642,808	312,364	4,808	22,345	1,247,873
PER TRAIN MILE.						
	d.	d.	d.	d.	d.	d.
1894	7·67	17·64	11·70	......	1·91	38·92
1895	8·71	20·80	12·21	......	2·08	43·80
1896	8·72	15·83	14·69	......	1·81	41·05
1897	9·19	20·99	21·34	1·10	2·02	54·64
1898	11·74	20·92	17·68	0·65	1·23	52·22
1899	12·18	21·92	16·74	0·26	1·38	52·48
1900	10·42	23·15	14·39	0·25	0·83	49·04
1901	12·88	28·92	17·22	0·40	1·36	60·78
1902	13·15	35·70	16·31	0·38	1·35	66·89
1903	13·82	33·46	16·26	0·25	1·16	64·95
PER MILE OPEN.						
	£	£	£	£	£	£
1894	63·8	146·8	97·4	......	15·9	323·9
1895	65·8	157·2	92·2	......	15·8	331·0
1896	96·6	175·3	162·7	......	20·0	454·6
1897	117·1	267·3	271·8	14·0	25·7	695·9
1898	181·5	323·5	273·3	10·0	19·0	807·3
1899	130·1	234·3	178·9	2·8	14·8	560·9
1900	135·1	300·0	186·5	3·3	10·8	635·7
1901	163·4	366·9	218·5	5·1	17·2	771·1
1902	182·1	494·5	225·9	5·3	18·7	926·5
1903	185·2	448·3	217·7	3·4	15·6	870·2

Interest returned on Capital.

The following is a statement of the average interest earned by the railways on the money invested in them, and affords a comparison with the interest paid on the public debt of the state :—

Year.	Interest returned on Capital.	Actual Rate of Interest payable on Outstanding Loans.	Average gain.
	per cent.	per cent.	per cent.
1894	3·12	4·09	*0·97
1895	5·45	4·57	0·88
1896	11·48	3·84	7·64
1897	9·05	3·61	5·44
1898	4·62	3·59	1·03
1899	4·55	3·54	1·01
1900	5·81	3·52	2·29
1901	4·35	3·52	0·83
1902	3·54	3·47	0·07
1903	3·75	3·48	0·27

* Average loss.

The railways of Western Australia have not only met working expenses during the past nine years, but have left a margin after making provision for the payment of interest on capital expenditure. In the construction of these railways, few engineering difficulties were met with, and the lines, which are of a light character, were constructed at a cheaper rate than those of any other state. This fact, together with the enormous increase in coaching and goods traffic, due to the development of the gold-fields, has been instrumental in securing such a favourable return.

Earnings and Expenses per Mile.

The gross earnings, expenditure, and net earnings per train mile for the last ten years are shown in the following table :—

Year.	Gross Earnings per train mile.	Expenditure per train mile.	Net Earnings per train mile.
	d.	d.	d.
1894	52·59	38·92	13·67
1895	71·22	43·80	27·42
1896	82·44	41·05	41·39
1897	86·59	54·64	31·95
1898	67·72	52·22	15·50
1899	74·01	52·48	21·53
1900	71·70	49·04	22·66
1901	78·74	60·78	17·96
1902	81·00	66·89	14·11
1903	80·85	64·95	15·90

The gross earnings, expenditure, and net earnings per average mile open for the past ten years were as follow:—

Year.	Gross Earnings per average mile open.	Expenditure per average mile open.	Net Earnings per average mile open.
	£	£	£
1894	438	324	114
1895	538	331	207
1896	913	454	459
1897	1,103	696	407
1898	1,047	807	240
1899	791	561	230
1900	930	636	294
1901	999	771	228
1902	1,122	927	195
1903	1,083	870	213

While the gross earnings per train mile have increased from 52·59d. in 1894 to 80·85d. in 1903, the net earnings also show a slight improvement during the period, having risen from 13·67d. in the former year to 15·90d. in the latter. The causes that have led up to this have already been indicated. It will be observed that the expenses per train mile for 1902 are the highest for the period. From 1898 to 1900 a reduction was secured by the adoption of mixed trains. The volume of coaching and goods traffic carried during 1898 was larger than in previous years, but the net earnings per average mile open show a marked reduction. The increased traffic, of course, necessitated extra expenditure; and being accompanied by a reduction in rates, had the temporary effect of reducing the net earnings. It is estimated that the adoption of the new rates, as compared with the old, involved a loss during 1898 of at least £232,000 in the working of the Northam, Southern Cross, Coolgardie, and Kalgoorlie railways, but the wisdom of the railway policy of the country was justified by the results of the following two years. The abnormal rise in the expenditure for 1901 has already been explained.

Coaching and Goods Traffic.

The following table shows the number of passengers carried on the lines of the state during the year 1887, the earliest for which particulars are available, and for the last ten years, together with the receipts from the traffic, and the average receipts per journey :—

Year.	Passengers carried.	Receipts from Coaching Traffic.	Average Receipts per Journey.
	No.	£	d.
1887	173,656	19,032	26·29
1894	617,080	64,409	25·05
1895	1,022,248	122,051	28·65
1896	1,679,816	188,765	26·97
1897	3,607,486	410,750	27·33
1898	5,669,444	458,402	19·41
1899	5,872,200	364,687	14·90
1900	6,225,068	402,500	15·52
1901	6,823,453	407,319	14·33
1902	8,158,299	430,093	12·65
1903	9,106,396	437,232	11·52

The statement shows a large increase in the number of passengers carried each year; the gradual reduction in the average receipts per journey indicates the expansion of the suburban and local traffic.

The amount of goods tonnage for a similar period is shown in the following table :—

Year.	Tonnage of Goods.	Earnings.
1887	52,151	£20,380
1894	204,686	76,155
1895	255,839	173,949
1896	435,855	340,850
1897	858,748	494,733
1898	1,203,911	561,275
1899	1,132,246	639,933
1900	1,384,040	857,012
1901	1,719,720	946,385
1902	2,040,092	970,684
1903	1,968,331	983,877

It will be seen that the increase in the goods traffic has been considerable since 1897, while the tonnage in 1902 was nearly two and a half times that of 1897. Owing to reduction in the charges for carriage, the earnings have not shown so considerable an expansion.

TASMANIA.

The progress of railway construction in Tasmania has been somewhat slow, for owing to the fact that the island is small and possesses numerous harbours, the railways have had to face severe competition with sea-borne traffic. As stated earlier in the chapter, the line from Launceston to

Deloraine, 45 miles in length, was opened on 10th February, 1871, and though an agitation long existed for the construction of a railway between the principal centres, Hobart and Launceston, it was not till the 1st November, 1876, that it was opened for traffic. No further extension was carried out until 1884, when an increase of 48 miles was made, and up to 1890 the total mileage opened was only 398, of which 48, opened in 1884, were constructed by a private company. The length of state railways opened to 31st December, 1902, was 461¾ miles, at a cost of £3,840,747 for construction and equipment, or at the rate of £8,302 per mile.

The lines of state railway in operation in Tasmania are the Western, from Launceston to Burnie, with branch to Chudleigh; the Main line from Hobart to Launceston, with branches from Launceston to Scottsdale, Parattah to Oatlands, Conara Junction to St. Mary's, Bridgewater to Glenora, and Brighton Junction to Apsley; the Sorell line, from Bellerive to Sorell; and the West Coast line, from Strahan Wharf to Maestris.

The control of the railways is vested in the Department of Lands and Works, the active management being undertaken by an officer with the title of General Manager.

Revenue and Working Expenses.

The net sum available to meet interest charges in connection with the railways of the state for each of the years during the last decennial period was as follows:—

Year.	Gross Earnings.	Working Expenses.	Net Earnings.	Proportion of Working Expenses to Gross Earnings.
	£	£	£	£
1893	152,083	136,468	15,615	89·73
1894	144,488	122,850	21,638	85·02
1895	149,642	120,351	29,291	80·42
1896	162,932	122,171	40,761	74·98
1897	166,834	128,544	38,290	77·04
1898	178,180	141,179	37,001	79·23
1899	193,158	152,798	40,360	79·10
1900	202,959	160,487	42,472	79·07
1901	205,791	173,400	32,391	84·26
1902	233,210	173,292	59,918	74·31

The cost of working the Tasmanian railways is comparatively high, and, as in New Zealand, the lines have to face severe competition with sea-borne traffic while there are no large inland centres that could support railways. There is a marked decrease year by year in the Australian traffic *viâ* Launceston, which is attributed to the great improvement in the direct steamer service between Melbourne and Hobart

The following analysis of the working expenses of Tasmanian railways for the ten years 1893–1902 does not call for special comment. There has, of late years, been a slight upward tendency in the cost of train mileage, partly due to the increased price of coal. In the years 1895, 1896 and 1897 it is evident that necessary expenditure on rolling stock was not carried out, thus throwing the burthen of repairs on to later years—this was especially the case in regard to locomotive repairs. In 1901 there were extensive renewals of locomotive boilers, but a portion of the expenditure in connection therewith might have been saved by earlier attention :—

Year ended 31st December.	Maintenance of Way, Works, and Buildings.	Locomotive Power, Carriage and Waggon Repairs and Renewals.	Traffic Expenses.	General Charges.	Total.
	£	£	£	£	£
1893	50,191	48,623	31,152	6,502	136,468
1894	44,762	42,483	29,507	6,098	122,850
1895	46,548	38,381	29,424	5,998	120,351
1896	46,813	38,326	30,909	6,123	122,171
1897	48,561	40,683	32,989	6,311	128,544
1898	54,927	45,180	33,765	7,307	141,179
1899	56,238	51,662	37,370	7,528	152,798
1900	58,862	53,865	39,300	8,460	160,487
1901	59,897	63,580	41,138	8,785	173,400
1902	58,612	63,791	42,416	8,473	173,292
Per Train Mile.					
	d.	d.	d.	d.	d.
1893	15·1	14·6	9·3	1·9	40·9
1894	14·2	13·5	9·3	1·9	38·9
1895	15·4	12·6	9·7	2·0	39·7
1896	15·2	12·4	10·0	2·0	39·6
1897	15·2	12·8	10·3	2·0	40·3
1898	17·3	14·2	10·7	2·3	44·5
1899	16·7	15·4	11·1	2·2	45·4
1900	17·3	15·8	11·6	2·5	47·2
1901	16·1	17·0	11·0	2·3	46·4
1902	15·6	16·9	11·2	2·3	46·0
Per Mile Open.					
	£	£	£	£	£
1893	117·5	113·8	72·9	15·2	319·4
1894	104·8	99·4	69·0	14·3	287·5
1895	109·0	89·8	68·8	14·0	281·6
1896	109·6	89·7	72·3	14·3	285·9
1897	112·4	94·1	76·3	14·5	297·3
1898	123·3	101·5	75·8	16·4	317·0
1899	126·3	116·0	83·9	16·9	343·1
1900	132·1	120·9	88·2	19·0	360·2
1901	130·3	138·4	89·5	19·1	377·3
1902	125·2	136·3	90·6	18·1	370·2

Interest returned on Capital.

The following table shows the average loss on the working of the Tasmanian railways for each year during the last ten years :—

Year.	Interest returned on Capital.	Actual rate of Interest payable on Outstanding Loans.	Average Loss.
	per cent.	per cent.	per cent.
1893	0·44	4·11	3·67
1894	0·61	3·96	3·35
1895	0·83	3·88	3·05
1896	1·16	3·87	2·71
1897	1·09	3·85	2·76
1898	1·03	3·82	2·79
1899	1·12	3·81	2·69
1900	1·16	3·78	2·62
1901	0·85	3·76	2·91
1902	1·56	3·76	2·20

The foregoing table shows that there was a slight improvement in the condition of the railway revenue during the five years preceding 1901. During 1901 the interest returned on capital expenditure fell to nearly that of the year 1895. Among the causes leading to this was the reduction in passenger fares, in the case of single fares by 45 per cent., and return fares by 27½ per cent. These large reductions did not result in the fulfilment of anticipations, and on the 1st December, 1901, a revised scale was adopted, which is still 20 per cent. below that in force in 1900. The competition of the Emu Bay Company and the low prices ruling for lead and silver have brought about a decrease in revenue on the Government West Coast line. Working expenses have absorbed 84·26 per cent. of total revenue, and the large increase over the previous five years is due to increased mileage, more extensive renewals of locomotive boilers paid for out of working expenses, and the increased price of coal. The competition already referred to, together with the heavy initial cost of the railways themselves, especially of the main line connecting Hobart with Launceston, for which the price paid by the Government on its resumption was at the rate of £9,069 per mile, as against an average of £8,304 per mile for the lines of the state generally, render it extremely difficult, even with the most careful management, to effect any considerable diminution in the average loss. Even in the case of the Western line from Launceston to Burnie, which passes through the finest agricultural land in the state, the return, after paying working expenses for the year ended 31st December, 1902, was only 2·69 per cent. on the cost of construction and equipment. The returns for the year ended 31st December, 1902, however, show a considerable improvement on those of the previous year, the gross and net earnings being the highest for the decennial period.

Earnings and Expenses per Mile.

The following tables indicate the gross earnings, expenditure, and net earnings per train mile and per average mile of line open. It will be observed that the net earnings per train mile reached 15d. in 1902, a point beyond which it does not seem likely there will be much expansion. The considerable reduction in net earnings during 1901, in comparison with the previous five years, is due to the shrinkage of revenue consequent on the reduction of fares, and the contraction in revenue from goods traffic already referred to. This compares very unfavourably with the results for other parts of Australia.

Year.	Gross Earnings per train mile.	Expenditure per train mile.	Net Earnings. per train mile.
	d.	d.	d.
1893	45·63	40·94	4·69
1894	45·83	38·96	6·87
1895	49·36	39·69	9·67
1896	52·85	39·63	13·22
1897	52·34	40·33	12·01
1898	56·17	44·50	11·67
1899	57·50	45·49	12·01
1900	59·70	47·20	12·50
1901	55·14	46·46	8·68
1902	61·99	46·06	15·93

The earnings and expenditure per average mile open were as shown in the following statement:—

Year.	Gross Earnings per average mile open.	Expenditure per average mile open.	Net Earnings per average mile open.
	£	£	£
1892	424	387	37
1893	356	319	37
1894	338	287	51
1895	350	281	69
1896	381	286	95
1897	386	297	89
1898	400	317	83
1899	434	343	91
1900	456	360	96
1901	448	377	71
1902	498	370	128

The peculiar position of Tasmania has already been referred to. The portions of the lines at first constructed were within the more densely populated districts, and the later extensions were projected into the more thinly-peopled areas, which were without sufficient production to afford a payable traffic. In comparison with the other states the proportion of expenses to gross earnings is extremely high, and while for the five years ended 1900 an improvement was shown, the increase in 1901 and 1902 indicates that it is not possible under present conditions to reduce expenditure.

Coaching and Goods Traffic.

Particulars in respect of the number of passengers carried on the state lines of Tasmania during the year 1881, and for the last ten years, together with receipts from the traffic and the average receipts per journey, are set forth in the following table:—

Year.	Passengers carried.	Receipts from Coaching Traffic.	Average Receipts per Journey.
	No.	£	d.
1881	102,495	10,396	24·34
1893	546,671	64,428	28·28
1894	514,461	58,070	27·09
1895	526,814	57,947	26·39
1896	542,825	59,771	26·43
1897	603,530	62,447	24·88
1898	617,643	68,317	26·54
1899	640,587	73,147	27·40
1900	683,015	76,184	26·77
1901	777,445	78,328	24·18
1902	761,345	99,115	31·25

During the year 1892 there was a comparatively large number of passengers carried. This was due to the resumption of the main line connecting Hobart with Launceston, the returns for the years in question being swollen by the traffic over the increased length of line. The traffic, however, was not sustained, for in the subsequent year a large diminution in the number of persons making use of the lines was recorded. There has since been a revival, and there are good grounds for supposing that this improvement will be continued. The average receipts per journey do not vary to any considerable extent, the amount of suburban traffic properly so-called being very small. The fall in 1901 is largely due to the considerable reduction in fares already alluded to. A reaction, however, set in during 1902, and the average receipts per journey for that year are the highest during the decennial period.

The amount of goods tonnage for a similar period is shown in the following table :—

Year.	Tonnage of Goods and Live Stock.	Earnings.
		£
1881	21,043	8,332
1893	164,962	73,490
1894	174,457	73,639
1895	204,480	78,797
1896	229,707	85,780
1897	229,620	86,941
1898	235,096	93,620
1899	312,446	107,661
1900	308,453	111,904
1901	314,628	108,698
1902	407,505	134,096

No information is available showing the subdivision of the tonnage of goods and live stock for the year into a general classification. The average distance each ton of goods was carried was 35·30 miles, and the average receipts per ton per mile 1·82d.

New Zealand.

The continuance of the native war in New Zealand, militated against the rapid extension of the railways, and at the close of the war in 1870 there were only 46 miles in operation. In 1875 the length of line opened for traffic had increased to 542 miles; in 1885, to 1,613 miles; in 1890, to 1,842 miles; and in 1895 to 2,014 miles. The length of line opened to 31st March, 1903, was 2,291 miles, at a cost of £19,081,735 for construction and equipment, or at the rate of £8,329 per mile.

The railway system of the colony is divided into ten sections. The Kawakawa and Whangarei sections, in the extreme north of the North Island, are short lines to coal-fields, and the Kaihu section was built for the purpose of tapping large timber areas inland. The Auckland section forms the northern portion of the North Island main trunk railway, which, when complete, will terminate at Wellington, on the shores of Cook's Strait. The Wellington-Napier-New Plymouth section comprises the group of lines which serve the southern portion of North Island. In the northern portion of Middle Island, the Westland, Westport, Nelson, and Picton sections form only the first link in the chain of through communication. On the East Coast of Middle Island, the actual working portion of the main trunk line is to be found. The present terminus is at Culverden, from whence extension will be made northward. This is known as the Hurunui-Bluff section, and includes the service to Christchurch, Dunedin, Invercargill, and the Bluff.

During the year ended March, 1901, the whole of the Midland railways were formally taken possession of by the Government and incorporated with the Westland section of the Government railways. They had previously been worked by the Government as a trust. The total length of these lines was about 83 miles.

The management of the railways of New Zealand was placed in the hands of three Commissioners in 1887, but early in 1895 the Government resumed charge of the lines, the active control being vested in an officer with the title of General Manager, who is responsible to the Minister for Railways.

Revenue and Working Expenses.

The net sum available to meet interest charges during each year of he last decennial period is set forth in the following table:—

Year.	Gross Earnings.	Working Expenses.	Net Earnings.	Proportion of Working Expenses to Gross Earnings.
	£	£	£	£
1894	1,172,793	735,360	437,433	62·70
1895	1,150,851	732,161	418,690	63·62
1896	1,183,041	751,368	431,673	63·51
1897	1,286,158	789,054	497,104	61·35
1898	1,376,008	857,191	518,817	62·30
1899	1,469,665	929,738	539,927	63·26
1900	1,623,891	1,052,358	571,533	64·80
1901	1,727,236	1,127,848	599,388	65·30
1902	1,874,586	1,252,237	622,349	66·80
1903	1,974,038	1,343,415	630,623	68·05

The foregoing table shows that the serious fluctuations which at times characterise the returns of the states on the mainland of Australia are absent from those of New Zealand, the configuration of the islands and their higher latitude rendering them to a very great extent immune from the periodical droughts to which the Australian states are so subject. The proportion of working expenses to gross earnings does not vary to any considerable extent, and the rise during the past four years is attributed to the payment of an increased rate of wages to employees, replacing old engines with new, extensive repairs due to the increased age of the stock, and the relaying of a portion of the permanent way with heavier rails. The traffic has, in many places, practically outgrown the carrying capacity of the lines, which were originally intended as the pioneers of settlement, and were not built to cope with a business such as exists in many parts of the colony. The management urges the employment of the heaviest type of locomotive as a matter of the utmost importance in the interests of economy, together with the running of trains at frequent intervals and higher speeds. There are, however, considerable portions of main line still laid with light rails, and until such time as these can be replaced with rails of a heavier type, and the bridges strengthened to carry the heavier class of engine, it is impossible to obtain the best results of working.

The analysis of the working expenses of the New Zealand railways for the ten years, 1894-1903, which is here presented, shows that there has been a regular increase since 1895, in which year the expenditure amounted to £732,161, equal to 54·54d. per train mile compared with 59·23d. per train mile in 1903.

In 1902 the Minister for Railways drew attention to the increasing age of the lines, the necessity for employing heavier rolling stock, and the accelerated speed which render the efficient maintenance of the track an imperative necessity; if the Minister's ideas are fully carried out an increased expenditure may be looked for. The advance in the cost of working from £372 to £594 per mile of line open is of no significance, such expenditure being due merely to the continued growth of the traffic.

Year ended 31st March.	Maintenance of Way, Works, and Buildings.	Locomotive Power.	Carriage and Waggon Repairs and Renewals.	Traffic Expenses.	General Charges.	Total.
	£	£	£	£	£	£
1894	268,451	177,833	56,470	201,166	31,440	735,360
1895	272,718	175,758	50,949	201,641	31,095	732,161
1896	282,593	185,669	54,692	207,253	21,161	751,368
1897	301,981	190,543	65,825	213,914	16,791	789,054
1898	327,987	209,289	65,344	232,646	21,925	857,191
1899	357,189	231,532	73,680	244,932	22,405	929,738
1900	394,619	295,542	76,555	262,552	23,090	1,052,358
1901	426,405	293,383	91,532	296,159	20,369	1,127,848
1902	436,847	351,172	99,522	333,211	31,485	1,252,237
1903	460,398	378,575	105,976	360,061	38,405	1,343,415
Per Train Mile.						
	d.	d.	d.	d.	d.	d.
1894	20·70	13·71	4·35	15·51	2·42	56·69
1895	20·32	13·09	3·79	15·02	2·32	54·54
1896	20·51	13·47	3·97	15·04	1·54	54·53
1897	21·26	13·41	4·64	15·06	1·18	55·55
1898	21·47	13·70	4·27	15·23	1·44	56·11
1899	21·60	14·00	4·46	14·81	1·35	56·22
1900	22·61	16·93	4·39	15·05	1·33	60·31
1901	22·15	15·24	4·75	15·38	1·06	58·58
1902	20·69	16·64	4·71	15·79	1·49	59·32
1903	20·30	16·69	4·67	15·88	1·69	59·23
Per Mile Open.						
	£	£	£	£	£	£
1894	140·35	92·96	29·52	105·15	16·43	384·41
1895	138·57	89·31	25·89	102·45	15·80	372·02
1896	141·45	92·93	27·37	103·74	10·59	376·08
1897	149·77	94·50	32·65	106·09	8·33	391·34
1898	160·53	102·43	31·98	113·86	10·73	419·53
1899	172·92	112·09	35·67	118·56	10·85	450·09
1900	187·99	140·80	36·47	125·08	11·00	501·34
1901	196·14	134·95	42·11	136·23	9·37	518·80
1902	196·17	157·69	44·69	149·63	14·14	562·32
1903	203·55	167·36	46·85	159·17	16·97	593·90

Interest Returned on Capital.

The basis employed in the case of the states comprised within the Commonwealth for ascertaining the net interest payable on the railway debts cannot be adopted for New Zealand, the necessary data not being available. The nominal loss is, therefore, shown in the following statement, the actual loss being somewhat higher:—

Year.	Interest Returned on Capital.	Average rate of Interest payable on Outstanding Loans.	Average Loss.
	per cent.	per cent.	per cent.
1894	2·88	4·59	1·71
1895	2·73	4·00	1·27
1896	2·80	3·94	1·14
1897	3·19	3·92	0·73
1898	3·24	3·89	0·65
1899	3·29	3·81	0·52
1900	3·42	3·79	0·37
1901	3·48	3·78	0·30
1902	3·43	3·76	0·33
1903	3·31	3·71	0·40

The foregoing table indicates that the railways are approaching the stage of being self-supporting, the interest returned on capital cost for the past nine years showing an improvement each year.

Earnings and Expenses per Mile.

The gross earnings, expenditure, and net earnings per train mile for the past ten years are shown in the following table:—

Year.	Gross Earnings per train mile.	Expenditure per train mile.	Net Earnings per train mile.
	d.	d.	d.
1894	90·25	56·69	33·56
1895	85·75	54·54	31·21
1896	85·75	54·53	31·22
1897	90·50	55·55	34·95
1898	90·00	56·11	33·89
1899	89·00	56·22	32·78
1900	93·00	60·31	32·69
1901	89·75	58·58	31·17
1902	88·80	59·32	29·48
1903	87·02	59·23	27·79

The gross earnings per train mile have varied very little during the ten years, the lowest point touched being 85¾d., and the highest, 93d., while the expenditure has varied even less. The expenditure during 1900 was higher than in any other year during the decennial period. The gross earnings per train mile for the past three years were less than those of 1900, and the net earnings show a slight but gradual reduction during the past six years. The results, however, compare very favourably with the other states, and are only exceeded by those of New South Wales, with the exception of the year just closed, when New Zealand showed a slightly higher net return.

The gross earnings, expenditure, and net earnings per average mile open for the past ten years are as follow :—

Year.	Gross Earnings per average mile open.	Expenditure per average mile open.	Net Earnings per average mile open.
	£	£	£
1894	613	384	229
1895	585	372	213
1896	592	376	216
1897	638	391	247
1898	673	419	254
1899	712	450	262
1900	774	501	273
1901	794	519	275
1902	842	562	280
1903	873	594	279

The foregoing table indicates that the gross earnings have increased from £613 per average mile open to £873, and the net earnings from £229 to £279, the return for 1902 being the highest secured during the decennial period, and that for 1903 being only £1 less—evidence of the fact that the extensions in recent years have been judicious, and that the volume of traffic has been maintained.

Coaching and Goods Traffic.

The following table shows the number of passengers carried on the lines of the colony during the year ended 31st March, 1882, and for the last ten years, together with the traffic, and the average receipts per journey :—

Year.	Passengers carried.	Receipts from Coaching traffic.	Average Receipts per Journey.
	No.	£	d.
1882	2,911,477	329,492	27·16
1894	3,972,701	378,480	22·89
1895	3,905,578	360,243	22·14
1896	4,162,426	359,822	20·74
1897	4,439,387	378,684	20·47
1898	4,672,264	399,262	20·51
1899	4,955,553	438,367	21·23
1900	5,468,284	474,793	20·83
1901	6,243,593	503,051	19·34
1902	7,356,136	575,697	18·78
1903	7,575,390	576,529	18·26

It will be observed that there was a falling off during the decennial period in the average receipts per journey. The continued increase in the number of passengers carried is, however, very marked, the advance for the closing year of the period being upwards of 219,000, while the receipts from the traffic rose by £832. Taking the returns for the year ended 31st March, 1884, as a basis, it has been found that those for 1903 show an increase of only 37 per cent. in the number of passengers who travelled first-class, while the increase in those who travelled second-class was not less than 113 per cent. While the marked prosperity of the past four years has induced more passengers to travel first-class, it is none the less evident that the tendency is towards one class of carriage, as already exists in the case of tramways.

The amount of goods tonnage for a similar period is shown in the following table :—

Year.	Tonnage of Goods exclusive of Live Stock.	Earnings.
		£
1882	1,437,714	491,057
1894	2,060,645	686,469
1895	2,048,391	683,726
1896	2,087,798	698,115
1897	2,368,927	774,163
1898	2,518,367	837,590
1899	2,624,059	882,077
1900	3,127,874	985,723
1901	3,339,687	1,051,695
1902	3,529,177	1,110,575
1903	3,730,394	1,189,101

The large increase in the tonnage of goods carried during 1900 over preceding years was caused by the bountiful harvest in the Middle Island, which was carried at freight rates averaging 20 per cent. below those ruling in the previous year. The further increase of 211,813 tons for 1901 was contributed to by all descriptions of goods, with the exception of wool, the grain traffic alone being 84 per cent. higher than in 1899. The returns for 1902 show an advance of 189,490 tons over the traffic in 1901. Increases occur under all the various headings, the largest being in grain and timber, the traffic in each class, with the exception of wool, being the largest on record.

The subdivision of the tonnage of goods and live stock for the year ended 31st March, 1903, is shown in the following table. Particulars of the goods traffic are set forth in seven classes, but the average distance for which goods of each class were carried cannot be given, and there are no data available showing the average earnings per ton per mile.

Description of Traffic.	Tons carried.	Number carried.
Lime and Chaff	121,092	....
Wool	116,309	....
Firewood	100,498	....
Timber	436,008	....
Grain	718,376	....
Merchandise	633,685	....
Minerals	1,604,426	....
Cattle	....	102,461
Sheep	....	3,821,333
Pigs	....	61,844

TRAMWAYS.

In all the Australasian states tramways are in operation, but it is chiefly in Sydney and Melbourne, the inhabitants of which numbered at the latest date 508,510 and 502,610 respectively, that the density of settlement has necessitated the general adoption of this mode of transit.

In New South Wales the three systems of electric, cable, and steam traction are in vogue. Within the metropolitan area, however, the electric is being substituted for steam power. The length of line under electric traction on the 30th June, 1903, was 67 miles 69 chains, comprising 11 miles 68 chains at North Sydney; 4 miles 18 chains, Ocean-street, Woollahra, to South Head; 3 miles 36 chains, George-street–Harris-street tramway; 4 miles 11 chains, Glebe Junction to Newtown, Marrickville, and Dulwich Hill; 2 miles 73 chains, Forest Lodge Junction to Leichhardt; 2 miles 57½ chains, Newtown to St. Peters and Cook's River; 1 mile 63 chains, Railway to Bridge-street; 5 miles 55 chains, Waverley and Bondi; 2 miles 28 chains, Railway to Glebe and Forest Lodge; 3 miles 34 chains, Forest Lodge to Balmain; 1 mile 26 chains, Redfern to Moore Park; 3 miles 20 chains, Pitt and Castlereagh streets to Fort Macquarie; 55 chains, George-street to Miller's Point; 5 miles 33 chains, Randwick and Coogee; 1 mile 18 chains, Waverley to Randwick; 69 chains, Crown-street to Cleveland-street; 2 miles 12 chains, Drummoyne; 6 miles 66 chains, Railway Station junction to Botany; 1 mile 45 chains, Zetland; 1 mile 34 chains, Mitchell-road; and 48 chains, Bridge and Phillip streets to Circular Quay. The only line worked by cable traction is that from King-street, Sydney, to Ocean-street, in the suburb of Woollahra, a distance of 2 miles 32 chains. On the remaining lines steam motors are still used. The length of Government tram lines open to 30th June, 1903, was 124½ miles, which had cost for construction and equipment £3,371,587. The receipts for the year were £752,034, and the working expenses £654,165, leaving a profit of £97,869, or 2·90 per cent. on the invested capital. The number of passengers carried during 1903 was 130,405,402.

In Victoria the cable system is in operation in the metropolitan area, the lines having been constructed by a municipal trust at a cost of £1,705,794. The tramways are leased to a company, and the receipts for the year ended 30th June, 1903, were £488,540. The number of passengers carried during the year was 47,564,942. The miles of track operated on were 43½ cable and 4½ horse lines, or 48 miles of double track. Besides the lines of the Tramway Trust, there are additional suburban systems worked by limited liability companies, as follows:—Horse, 8½ miles; electric, 4 miles; and cable, 2¼ miles.

In Queensland there is a system of electric trams controlled by a private company. The only information available shows that the capital of the company is £750,000 fully paid up, and that there are also debentures to the amount of £400,000. Particulars as to receipts and disbursements are not available, but the report presented to the shareholders in London during May, 1902, showed a net profit of £42,815 for the period from 20th November, 1900, to 31st December, 1901. The length of the tramways is 25 miles, or 43 miles of single line. The company owned seventy-nine electric cars, and during the year 1901, 16,183,801 passengers were carried.

In South Australia there are no Government tramways, but horse trams are run in the principal streets of Adelaide by private companies. No particulars have been collected respecting the length of the lines, nor of the returns therefrom. A proposal is under consideration for the substitution of electric traction on these lines.

The Western Australian Government owns a line of horse tramway on a 2-foot gauge between Roeburne and Cossack, a length of 8½ miles, constructed at a cost of £24,022. For the year ended 30th June, 1903, the gross earnings were £2,211, and the working expenses £2,161, leaving the gain on working expenses at £50.

In Tasmania there is an electric tramway from Hobart railway station, about 9 miles in length, owned by a private company. The cost of construction and equipment was £90,000; and the company possesses 20 cars. For the year ended 31st December, 1902, the receipts amounted to £17,802, and the working expenses, to £12,900. The passengers carried during the twelve months numbered 1,848,104. There is also a steam system at Zeehan, 2 miles in length, constructed at a cost of £5,388. No information is available as to the receipts, but the working expenses for the year ended 31st December, 1901, were £1,848. The number of passengers carried during the twelve months ended 31st December, 1902, was 7,302.

There are also tramways in existence in New Zealand under municipal and private management, but no particulars in regard to them are at present available.

PASTORAL RESOURCES AND DAIRY INDUSTRY.

NOTWITHSTANDING the fact that the soil, climate, and indigenous herbage of Australasia are admirably adapted to the sustenance of animal life, no attempt was made to test the capabilities of the land as a feeding-ground for flocks and herds on a large scale until the example of Captain Macarthur had demonstrated beyond doubt that Nature favoured the production in Australasia of a quality of wool which was unsurpassed by that grown in any part of the world. Then the settlers began to understand and utilise the natural resources of the country; and as the indomitable spirit of exploration gradually opened up the apparently boundless plains of the interior, pastoralists extended their domain, and sheep and cattle in increasing numbers spread over the face of eastern Australia. Now the expansion of the pastoral industry is gradually converting the central and western portions of the continent into holdings devoted to the production of the greatest element of the wealth of Australasia.

The beginnings of pastoral enterprise in Australia were very humble. The live stock of the community which accompanied Captain Phillip comprised only 1 bull, 4 cows, 1 calf, 1 stallion, 3 mares, 3 foals, 29 sheep, 12 pigs, and a few goats; and although the whole of the present flocks and herds of Australasia have not sprung from these animals alone, yet the figures show the small scale on which the business of stock-raising was first attempted. No systematic record of the arrival of stock seems to have been kept in the early days of settlement; but it would appear that during the period between Governor Phillip's landing and the year 1800 there were some slight importations, chiefly of sheep from India. In 1800 the stock in Australasia comprised 6,124 sheep, 1,044 cattle, 203 horses, and 4,017 swine; while at the end of the year 1901, there were no less than 92,358,824 sheep, 9,827,433 cattle, 1,905,172 horses, and 1,171,381 swine.

The following figures give the number of stock in Australasia at various dates up to 1851:—

Year.	Sheep.	Cattle.	Horses.	Swine.
1792	105	23	11	43
1800	6,124	1,044	203	4,017
1810	33,818	11,276	1,114	8,992
1821	290,158	102,939	4,564	33,906
1842	6,312,004	1,014,833	70,615	66,086
1851	17,326,021	1,921,963	166,421	121,035

The increase in the number of each kind of live stock since the year 1861 is illustrated in the following table :—

Year.	Sheep.	Cattle.	Horses.	Swine.
1861	23,741,706	4,039,839	459,970	362,417
1871	49,773,584	4,713,820	782,558	737,477
1881	78,063,426	8,709,628	1,249,765	903,271
1891	124,547,937	11,861,330	1,785,835	1,154,553
1901	92,358,824	9,827,433	1,905,172	1,171,381
1902	74,348,003	8,472,880	1,821,431	1,002,057

The average number of sheep, cattle, horses, and swine per head of the population of Australasia at the same periods was as follows :—

Year.	Sheep.	Cattle.	Horses.	Swine.
1861	18·8	3·2	0·4	0·3
1871	25·3	2·4	0·4	0·4
1881	27·7	3·1	0·4	0·3
1891	31·8	3·0	0·5	0·3
1901	20·2	2·1	0·4	0·3
1902	15·8	1·8	0·4	0·2

It will be seen that in 1861 there were 18·8 sheep for every person in Australasia, and that this number had increased to 31·8 in 1891. In consequence of the continued dry seasons, and the demands made upon the flocks for the export trade, the average for the last five years has fallen to 20·9 per inhabitant. The average number of cattle depastured during the last five years per inhabitant was 2·3, as against 3·2 forty-two years ago. The breeding of horses and swine has about kept pace with the population.

Sheep.

The suitableness for pastoral pursuits of the land discovered in the early days was undoubtedly the means of inducing the infant colony of New South Wales to take its first step on the path of commercial progress, and, looking backward, it is not a little surprising to find how steadily some of the settlers, in the face of the almost insurmountable difficulty of transport which existed a century ago, availed themselves of the opportunities at their disposal. The importation of valuable specimens of sheep from England or the Cape of Good Hope prior to the introduction of steam was at all times attended with great risk, and it frequently happened that many of these costly animals died during the tedious voyage. These enterprises were, however, on the whole successful, and thus the flocks and herds of the colonists surely, if at first slowly, increased and multiplied.

By the year 1795, Captain Macarthur, one of the first promoters of sheep-breeding in New South Wales, had accumulated a flock of 1,000 sheep, which were held in great estimation, and gradually increased in value until, as recorded by an entry in his journal ten years later, the market price of a fat wether had risen to £5. Not satisfied with the natural increase of his flocks, Macarthur sought to improve the quality of his fleeces, by which means he could see opening before him the promise of great wealth and the prospect of establishing important commercial relations with Great Britain. With these ends in view, he procured from the Cape of Good Hope, at great cost and trouble, a number of superior rams and ewes. A happy circumstance favoured his enterprise; for he had the good fortune to secure three rams and five ewes of very fine Spanish breed, which had been presented by the King of Spain to the Dutch Government. These animals, out of a total of twenty-nine purchased at the Cape, arrived in Sydney in 1797, and were disposed of to various breeders. With the exception of Macarthur, however, those who had secured sheep of the superior breed made no attempt to follow up this advantage, being probably amply satisfied with the larger gains from the sale of an increased number of animals. Macarthur, on the other hand, thought little of present profits, and still less of breeding entirely for human consumption. He attentively watched the results of crossing his imported rams with the old stock, and by systematically selecting the finer ewes which were the offspring, for further mingling with the sires, he gradually improved the strain, and in a few years obtained fleeces of very fine texture which met with the ready appreciation of English manufacturers. It has been asserted that Macarthur was not the first to introduce merino sheep into Australia; but whether this be so or not, there is no doubt that to him is due the credit of having been the first to prove that the production of fine wool could be made a profitable industry in New South Wales.

Prior to the present century the production of the finest wool had been confined chiefly to Spain, and woollen manufactures were necessarily carried on in England upon a somewhat limited scale, which was not likely to improve in face of certain restrictions which the operatives endeavoured to place upon their employers. These men, in support of their contention that the woollen trade could not be expanded on account of the limited supply of raw material, argued that fine wool was obtainable only in Spain; and it was at this favourable period that Macarthur arrived in England with specimens of the wool obtained from his finest sheep, conclusively proving the capabilities of Australia as a wool-producing country. In this way he opened up with English manufacturers a small trade which, as Australasian wool rose in public estimation, gradually increased until it reached its present enormous dimensions. During his visit to England, Macarthur purchased an additional stock of ten rams and ewes of the noted Spanish breed, nearly equal in quality to those which in 1797 he had procured from the Cape of Good Hope. That these animals were the finest obtainable in Europe may be gathered from the fact they also had formed portion of a present from the King of Spain to George III. After his return to New South Wales, Macarthur patiently continued for many years the process of selection, with such success that in 1858, when his flock was finally dispersed, it was estimated that his superior ewes numbered fully 1,000. Victoria secured a considerable portion of his flock, and the process of breeding proceeded simultaneously in that and other adjacent states.

Although the increase in the numbers of the finer sheep was satisfactory, yet the importation of superior stock was not discontinued, and the stock of the states was augmented in 1823 and 1825 by the further introduction of Spanish sheep. Sheep-breeding was about this period commenced in the Mudgee district of New South Wales; the climate of that region had a more favourable effect upon the quality of the fleeces than that of any other part of the state, and it was thence that the finest merinos were for a long time procured. As was to be expected, the climate has in some respects changed the character of the Spanish fleece. The wool has become softer and more elastic, and while it has diminished in density it has increased in length, and the weight of the fleece has considerably increased. Thus, on the whole, the quality of the wool has improved under the beneficial influence of the climate, and if no further enhancement of its intrinsic value can be reasonably hoped for, there is at least every reason to believe that Australasian wool will maintain its present high standard of excellence.

The following table shows the number of sheep in each state at intervals of ten years since 1871:—

State.	Number of Sheep.				
	1871.	1881.	1891.	1901.	1902.
New South Wales	16,278,697	36,591,946	61,831,416	41,857,099	26,649,424
Victoria	10,002,381	10,267,265	12,928,148	10,841,790	*10,841,790
Queensland	7,403,334	8,292,883	20,289,633	10,030,971	7,213,985
South Australia	4,412,055	6,810,856	7,745,541	5,060,540	4,922,662
Western Australia	670,999	1,267,912	1,962,212	2,542,844	2,697,897
Tasmania	1,305,489	1,847,479	1,662,801	1,792,481	1,679,518
Commonwealth	40,072,955	65,078,341	106,419,751	72,125,725	54,005,276
New Zealand	9,700,629	12,985,085	18,128,186	20,233,099	20,342,727
Australasia	49,773,584	78,063,426	124,547,937	92,358,824	74,348,003

* 1901 figures: no later information available.

In all the states the number of sheep depastured had prior to 1902 largely increased during the period shown above with the exception of Tasmania. In that state, however, more attention is directed towards the breeding of stud sheep than to raising immense flocks, and the stud farms of the island have gained considerable distinction, and are annually drawn upon to improve the breed of sheep in the other states.

In South Australia the area adapted to sheep is limited, and no great expansion in sheep-farming can be looked for. As regards Victoria, the important strides made in agriculture and kindred pursuits afford sufficient explanation of the diminished attention paid to sheep farming. The statement given below shows, for 1901, the proportion of sheep in each state to the total flocks of Australasia, the Victorian figures for 1902 being not available. New South Wales, with 45·32 per cent. of the total flock, comes first, and New Zealand, with 21·91 per cent., second, while Victoria, with 11·74 per cent., and Queensland, with 10·86 per cent., are next in order. The other three states together possess only a little over 10 per cent. of the whole.

State.	1901. per cent.
New South Wales	45·32
Victoria	11·74
Queensland	10·86
South Australia	5·48
Western Australia	2·75
Tasmania	1·94
New Zealand	21·91
Australasia	100·00

In order to show the increase or decrease in sheep during the last eighteen years, the following table has been prepared, giving the numbers in the various states at the end of each year since 1885. It will be seen that returns were not collected in some years in Victoria, South Australia, and New Zealand, and that the figures for those states are therefore incomplete :—

Year.	New South Wales.	Victoria.	Queensland.	South Australia.	Western Australia.	Tasmania.	New Zealand.
1885	37,820,906	10,681,837	8,994,322	*	1,702,719	1,648,027	16,564,595
1886	39,169,304	10,700,403	9,690,445	*	1,809,071	1,609,046	*
1887	46,965,152	10,623,985	12,926,158	*	1,909,940	1,547,242	*
1888	46,503,460	10,818,575	13,444,005	*	2,112,392	1,430,065	15,468,860
1889	50,106,768	10,882,231	14,470,095	6,432,401	2,366,681	1,551,429	15,503,263
1890	55,986,431	12,692,843	18,007,234	7,050,544	2,524,913	1,619,256	18,128,186
1891	61,831,416	12,928,148	20,289,633	7,745,541	1,962,212	1,604,218	18,570,752
1892	58,080,114	12,965,306	21,708,310	7,209,500	1,685,500	1,623,338	19,380,369
1893	56,980,688	13,098,725	18,697,015	7,325,003	2,200,642	1,535,047	20,230,829
1894	56,977,270	13,180,943	19,587,091	*	2,132,311	1,727,200	19,826,604
1895	47,617,687	*	19,856,959	*	2,295,832	1,523,846	19,138,493
1896	48,318,790	*	19,593,696	6,402,593	2,248,976	1,650,567	19,687,954
1897	43,952,897	*	17,797,883	5,092,078	2,210,742	1,578,611	19,673,725
1898	41,241,004	*	17,552,608	5,076,696	2,251,548	1,493,638	19,348,506
1899	36,213 514	*	15,226,479	5,721,493	2,282,306	1,672,068	19,347,346
1900	40,020,506	*	10,339,185	5,283,247	2,431,861	1,683,956	19,355,195
1901	41,857,099	10,841,790	10,030,971	5,060,540	2,542,344	1,792,481	20,233,099
1902	26,649,424	*	7,213,985	4,922,662	2,697,397	1,679,518	20,342,727

* Returns not collected.

The number of sheep depastured in the Commonwealth increased with great regularity each year until 1891, when it reached 106,400,000;

since that year there has been an almost continuous succession of unfavourable seasons in New South Wales and Queensland, the two states chiefly interested in pastoral pursuits, with the result that the number of sheep depastured in these states has decreased by over 47,000,000 during the last ten years. In Queensland the number fell from 15,226,000 in 1899, to 10,339,000 in 1900, a decrease of 4,887,000 in one year, and at the present time the number is only just over 7,200,000. In New South Wales the returns place the number of sheep depastured in December, 1902, at 26,649,424, which is lower than in any year since 1884. The other states did not suffer to the same extent from adverse seasons, although the number of sheep in both Victoria and South Australia has decreased considerably since 1891. In Western Australia and Tasmania there were increases in the numbers, and in New Zealand, although the figures have been practically stationary for some years past, they show an advance on the number in 1891.

During the last ten years there has been a tendency towards dividing the sheep into smaller flocks. This is especially noticeable in New South Wales and Queensland. In the former state there are now 18,074 sheep-owners as compared with 14,033 in 1893, while the average size of the flocks in 1901 was about 2,390, as against 4,050 in the former year.

In Queensland, at the present time, there are 2,052 sheep-owners as compared with 1,440 in 1893, the average size of the flocks in 1901 being 4,970 as compared with 12,984 in 1893.

Adverse seasons during the period had, of course, the effect of considerably diminishing the number of sheep in each state, but, when full allowance has been made on this score, it will be found that the size of the flock has greatly decreased.

In New Zealand there are at the present time 18,803 flock-owners, as compared with 14,779 ten years ago; while 15,119 persons possess flocks of 1,000 sheep and under, as against 11,868 in 1893. There are now only 131 flocks of 20,000 and upwards, as compared with 178 ten years ago.

Of the 571,217 stud sheep in New Zealand, the proportions of the various breeds are as follows:—

	Per cent.
Lincoln	29·58
English Leicester	13·92
Romney	18·59
Merino	12·75
Border	11·65
Shropshire	6·43
South Devon	1·84
Other	5·24
Total	100·00

Out of a total of 19,771,510 flock sheep there were 87·03 per cent. cross breds and other long wools, while 12·97 per cent. were merinos.

The total number of sheep (including lambs) slaughtered in the various states from which the information is available during the seven years ended 1902 is shown below. For South Australia and New Zealand no slaughtering returns are available, while the figures for Tasmania refer to the numbers killed in Hobart and Launceston only.

Year.	New South Wales.	Victoria.	Queensland.	Western Australia.	Tasmania (Hobart and Launceston).
1896	6,196,749	2,559,088	1,726,125	420,952	102,266
1897	5,790,103	2,434,519	1,902,735	505,091	107,223
1898	5,665,763	2,352,694	1,262,313	433,867	104,303
1899	4,795,259	2,557,858	1,497,546	......	93,913
1900	4,359,513	2,371,415	860,648	445,046	91,829
1901	4,519,133	2,469,797	554,705	428,234	101,627
1902	4,635,850	2,827,938	715,443	482,907	114,900

The value of the sheep depastured in Australasia, on the basis of the average prices ruling in 1902, was £39,630,000, thus distributed among the various states:—

	£
New South Wales	13,324,000
*Victoria	4,791,000
Queensland	3,607,000
South Australia	1,707,000
Western Australia	1,484,000
Tasmania	994,000
Commonwealth	25,907,000
New Zealand	13,723,000
Australasia	£39,630,000

* Victorian sheep estimated at 1,716,000 less than in 1901.

CATTLE.

Except in Queensland, cattle-breeding in the Australasian States is secondary to that of sheep. Indeed, in New South Wales in 1902 the number of the herds was even less than in 1861, the decrease amounting to 530,697. The lowest point was reached by that state in 1885, when the herds only numbered 1,317,315, the result partly of continuous bad seasons, but principally of the more profitable character of sheep-farming, which had induced graziers on many runs to substitute sheep for cattle. From that period up till 1894, when the herds numbered 2,465,411, there was a gradual improvement, which seemed to indicate a disposition on the part of pastoralists in some parts of the state to devote more attention to cattle-breeding. The serious droughts which have been experienced, however, have militated against the expansion of the cattle industry, and the numbers again fell away until the year 1899, but increased slightly during the next two years, when the adversity of the season was responsible for a shrinkage of over 300,000. The progress of Victoria in the breeding of cattle was steady until 1894, but since that year the numbers have decreased. In Queensland the number reached 7,012,997 in 1894, but owing to the combined effects of drought and tick fever, the herds have since diminished greatly, and in 1902 there were but 2,543,471. New Zealand, after having neglected the cattle industry for a long time, has during recent years largely increased its herds, the increase being the result of the special attention bestowed upon the dairy industry.

The following table shows the number of cattle in each state at ten-year intervals since 1861:—

State.	Number of Cattle.					
	1861.	1871.	1881.	1891.	1901.	1902.
New South Wales	2,271,923	2,014,888	2,597,348	2,046,347	2,047,454	1,741,226
Victoria	628,092	799,509	1,286,677	1,812,104	1,602,384	*1,602,384
Queensland	560,196	1,168,235	3,618,513	6,192,759	3,772,707	2,543,471
South Australia	265,434	143,463	314,918	676,933	479,863	519,163
Western Australia	33,795	49,593	63,009	133,690	394,580	437,588
Tasmania	87,114	101,540	130,526	167,666	168,661	178,385
Commonwealth	3,846,554	4,277,228	8,010,991	11,029,499	8,465,649	7,022,217
New Zealand	193,285	436,592	698,637	831,831	1,361,784	1,460,663
Australasia	4,039,839	4,713,820	8,709,628	11,861,330	9,827,433	8,482,880

*Latest returns available.

The statement below shows the proportion of cattle in each state to the total herds in Australasia, at the end of 1901, the Victorian figures for 1902 not being available:—

State.	Per cent.
New South Wales	20·83
Victoria	16·31
Queensland	38·39
South Australia	4·88
Western Australia	4·01
Tasmania	1·72
New Zealand	13·86
Australasia	100·00

In spite of the vast losses in recent years, Queensland has still the largest number of cattle, but the extent of its losses will be realised when it is remembered that out of a total of 11,049,065 in 1899, nearly 46 per cent. were in Queensland, while in 1901, out of a total of 9,827,433 only 38 per cent. were in that state.

A clearer idea of the changes which late years have brought about in the cattle industry is afforded by the next table, showing the number in the various states at the close of each year since 1885. As will be seen, returns were not collected in three of the states—Victoria, South Australia, and New Zealand—for several of the years under review :—

Year.	New South Wales.	Victoria.	Queensland.	South Australia.	Western Australia.	Tasmania.	New Zealand.
1885	1,317,315	1,290,790	4,162,653	*	70,408	138,642	853,358
1886	1,367,844	1,303,265	4,071,563	*	88,254	148,665	*
1887	1,575,487	1,333,873	4,473,716	*	93,544	147,092	*
1888	1,622,907	1,370,660	4,654,932	*	95,822	142,019	853,358
1889	1,741,592	1,394,209	4,872,416	531,296	119,571	150,004	895,461
1890	2,091,229	1,782,881	5,558,264	574,032	130,970	162,440	831,831
1891	2,128,838	1,812,104	6,192,759	676,933	133,600	167,788	*
1892	2,221,459	1,824,704	6,591,416	631,522	162,886	170,085	851,801
1893	2,269,852	1,817,291	6,693,200	675,284	173,747	169,141	885,306
1894	2,465,411	1,833,900	7,012,997	*	187,214	177,038	964,034
1895	2,150,057	*	6,822,401	*	200,091	162,801	1,047,90[illegible]
1896	2,226,163	*	6,507,377	638,591	199,793	157,736	1,138,572
1897	2,085,096	*	6,089,013	540,149	244,971	157,486	1,209,165
1898	2,029,516	*	5,571,292	613,894	269,947	149,754	1,203,024
1899	1,967,081	*	5,053,836	526,524	297,081	160,204	1,210,439
1900	1,983,116	*	4,078,191	472,428	338,665	165,516	1,256,680
1901	2,047,454	1,602,384	3,772,707	479,863	394,580	168,661	1,361,784
1902	1,741,226	*	2,543,471	519,163	437,568	178,885	1,460,663

* Returns not collected.

The number of cattle (including calves) slaughtered during each of the seven years ended 1902 is shown in the following table for all the states except South Australia and New Zealand, which do not furnish returns. The Tasmanian figures represent the numbers killed in Hobart and Launceston only :—

Year.	New South Wales.	Victoria.	Queensland.	Western Australia.	Tasmania. (Hobart and Launceston).
1896	351,246	245,477	474,946	30,664	9,393
1897	365,898	240,958	498,583	41,665	10,615
1898	364,042	244,319	572,735	33,203	10,029
1899	383,948	249,177	640,898	38,577	10,276
1900	399,992	248,797	503,223	40,950	9,114
1901	335,823	251,477	377,433	39,424	8,365
1902	288,131	233,206	344,731	43,914	9,793

The value of the cattle in Australasia, on the basis of the average prices ruling in 1901, was £49,934,000, thus divided amongst the various states :—

	£
New South Wales	10,421,000
Victoria	10,262,000
Queensland	11,726,000
South Australia	3,031,000
Western Australia	2,762,000
Tasmania	1,137,000
Commonwealth	39,339,000
New Zealand	10,595,000
Australasia	£49,934,000

Since 1901 the number of cattle in the Commonwealth has diminished considerably, but on the other hand prices have advanced. There is much uncertainty as to the true values at the time of writing, and for this reason it has been thought desirable to allow the figures for 1901 to stand, as they represent average values under normal conditions.

Horses.

Australasia is eminently fitted for the breeding of most descriptions of horses, and attention has long been directed to this industry. At an early period the stock of colonial-bred horses was enriched by the importation of some excellent thoroughbred Arabians from India, and to this cause the high name which was acquired by the horses of Australia was largely due. The abundance of good pasture everywhere obtainable also contributed to this result. The native kangaroo-grass, especially when in seed, is full of saccharine matter, and young stock thrive excellently upon it. This plenitude of natural provender permitted a large increase in the stock of the settlers, which would have been of great advantage had it not been that the general cheapness of the animals led to a neglect of the canons of breeding. In consequence of the discovery of gold, horses became very high priced. Under ordinary conditions this circumstance would have been favourable to breeding, and such was actually the case in Victoria. In New South Wales, however, it was far otherwise. The best of its stock, including a large proportion of the most valuable breeding mares, was taken by Victoria, with the result that for twenty years after the gold rush the horses of the mother state greatly deteriorated. One class of stock only escaped—the thoroughbred racer, which was probably improved both by the importation of fresh stock from England, and by the judicious selection of mares.

The states are specially adapted to the breeding of saddle and light-harness horses, and it is doubtful whether these particular breeds of Australasian horses are anywhere surpassed. The bush horse is hardy and swift, and capable of making very long and rapid journeys when fed only on the ordinary herbage of the country; and in times of drought, when the grass and water have become scanty, these animals often perform astonishing feats of endurance. Generally speaking, the breed is improving, owing to the introduction of superior stud horses and the breeding from good mares. Where there has been a deterioration in the stock, it has been due to breeding from weedy mares for racing purposes and to the effects of drought.

The following table shows the number of horses in each state at ten-year intervals since 1861. In 1902, New South Wales possessed the largest number of horses, followed by Queensland and Victoria :—

State.	Number of Horses.					
	1861.	1871.	1881.	1891.	1901.	1902.
New South Wales	233,220	304,100	398,577	459,755	486,716	450,125
Victoria	84,057	181,643	278,195	440,696	392,237	*392,237
Queensland	28,983	91,910	194,217	399,364	462,119	399,122
South Australia	52,597	78,125	159,678	202,906	178,199	179,413
Western Australia ..	10,720	22,698	31,755	40,812	73,830	80,114
Tasmania	22,118	23,054	25,607	31,262	32,399	33,465
Commonwealth...	431,695	701,530	1,088,029	1,574,795	1,625,500	1,534,476
New Zealand............	28,275	81,028	161,736	211,040	279,672	286,955
Australasia	459,970	782,558	1,249,765	1,785,835	1,905,172	1,821,431

* Latest figures available.

There is at present a considerable demand in India for Australian horses, especially for those of a superior class, and although the speculation of shipping horses to that country is attended with some risk, owing to the dangers of the voyage, there is reason to believe that in the near future the trade will assume considerable dimensions, as Australia is the natural market from which supplies may be derived. The number and value of the horses exported to India during 1902 from each state and New Zealand was as follows :—

State.	Number.	Value.
New South Wales	858	£15,764
Victoria	1,828	35,975
Queensland	2,928	27,848
Western Australia	24	300
New Zealand..........................	147	1,085
Australasia	5,785	£80,972

The export from Australasia to India in 1901 consisted of 5,672 horses, valued at £80,313.

The war in South Africa created a demand for Australian horses as army remounts during the last few years, and in 1901 no less than 24,995 horses, valued at £320,152, were exported from Australasia to South African ports. In 1902 there was a considerable falling off, the horses exported only numbering 11,491, valued at £159,040.

The number from each state exported to South Africa during 1901 and 1902 was as follows:—

State.	1901.		1902.	
	Number.	Value.	Number.	Value.
		£		£
New South Wales ...	6,300	81,204	2,918	38,116
Victoria	6,857	129,642	2,977	56,747
Queensland	11,069	96,841	4,105	36,178
South Australia	15	355	455	5,821
Western Australia ...	472	7,080	5	265
Tasmania	280	5,000	....	....
Commonwealth ...	24,993	320,122	10,460	137,127
New Zealand.......... ...	2	30	1,031	21,913
Australasia	24,995	320,152	11,491	159,040

The following table shows the proportion of horses in each state to the total number in Australasia, at the end of 1901:—

State.	Per cent.
New South Wales	25·55
Victoria......................	20·59
Queensland	24·26
South Australia	9·35
Western Australia	3·87
Tasmania	1·70
New Zealand	14·68
Australasia	100·00

The value of horses in 1901, in the various states, is estimated as follows:—

New South Wales	£3,901,000
Victoria	4,707,000
Queensland	2,311,000
South Australia	1,247,000
Western Australia	923,000
Tasmania	356,000
Commonwealth	£13,445,000
New Zealand	3,636,000
Australasia	£17,081,000

ANGORA GOATS.

The breeding of the Angora goat, with a view to the production of mohair, has recently attracted attention in Queensland and New South Wales, and considerable numbers of pure-bred animals have been imported from the United States. It is found that the Angora thrives admirably in the warm dry climate existing in a great portion of the states mentioned, and, with the steady demand for mohair, it is confidently expected that the export of the product will in time form an important element in the trade of the Commonwealth.

STOCK-CARRYING CAPACITY OF AUSTRALASIA.

None of the states is stocked to its full capacity; indeed, in the large territory of Western Australia and in the Northern Territory of South Australia the process has only begun. A clear idea of the comparative extent to which each state is stocked cannot be given unless the different kinds of animals are reduced to a common value. Assuming, therefore, that one head of large stock is equivalent to ten sheep, and expressing cattle and horses in terms of sheep, it will be found that the number of acres to a sheep in each state is as follows:—

State.	No. of acres per sheep.
New South Wales	4·09
Victoria	1·93
Queensland	11·86
South Australia	48·57
Western Australia	79·31
Tasmania	4·54
New Zealand	1·77
Australasia	11·22

The most closely-stocked of the Commonwealth states is Victoria, with 1·93 acres per sheep, but this is by no means the limit to the carrying-capacity of that state; on the contrary, there is still a considerable tract to be brought under the sway of the pastoralist. The figures for this state, however, refer to the year 1901, there being no later information available, and it is probable that the area is slightly understated, as no estimate can be made of Victorian losses of cattle and horses. New Zealand is stocked to a slightly heavier extent, but neither that colony nor New South Wales, which averages 4 acres per sheep, can be said to have reached its full carrying-capacity. If the 1901 average of New South Wales, viz., 3 acres to a sheep, be taken as the possible limit to which Australasia may be stocked, there is room in these states for nearly 450 million sheep, or 45 million cattle more than were then depastured. That Australasia could carry 1 sheep to 3 acres, however, is an improbable supposition; in almost every state the best land is under occupation, and the demands of the farmer must diminish the area at present at the disposal of the grazier. This will more especially prove true of Victoria, New Zealand, and Tasmania. On the other hand, by resisting the temptation to overstock inferior country, and by increasing the natural carrying-capacity by water conservation and irrigation and by the artificial cultivation of grasses, the states in which agriculture has made most progress will be able to carry stock in even larger numbers than they have hitherto attempted. Taking all circumstances into consideration, it may be fairly estimated that under the present system the states are capable of maintaining, in ordinary seasons, stock equivalent to 390,000,000 sheep—that is, about 180,000,000 sheep, or their equivalent in cattle, more than depastured in 1901.

The evil effects of the adverse seasons experienced in the Commonwealth during recent years have caused renewed attention to be devoted to the questions of water conservation and irrigation. Movements are on foot at the present time in New South Wales for the utilisation of the natural reservoirs such as that at the head of the Murrumbidgee and other suitable places where, at a comparatively small cost, supplies of water could be conserved to feed the rivers in time of drought. It is not alone the actual loss of stock that makes a drought so disastrous, but the fact that, even with the return of good seasons, a considerable period elapses before the country regains its full carrying-capacity. That much can be done in the direction of providing fodder during the dry season was shown in isolated instances during 1902. At Forbes, in New South Wales, 22 acres of irrigated lucerne maintained nearly 1,600 sheep in good condition for a period of four months prior to the breaking up of the drought. At Rodney, in Victoria, the farmers who utilised the waters of the Goulburn for irrigation purposes were able to send fat stock to the Melbourne and Bendigo markets, in addition to supplying the squatters of Riverina with lucerne and other fodder for their starving stock. With proper provision for water conservation, it may be safely said that the Commonwealth was not overstocked in 1896, when there were over 90,000,000 sheep and 11,000,000 head of cattle, whereas in 1902 there were but 54,000,000 sheep and 7,000,000 cattle.

It is a difficult task satisfactorily to estimate the losses occasioned by adverse seasons, but a careful computation shows that during the last six years the Commonwealth has carried on an average over 19,000,000 sheep and 2,300,000 head of cattle less than in 1896. The lesson of the past season has been taken to heart in those parts of the continent liable to drought conditions, and it is safe to say that no disaster such as that of 1902 is likely again to occur.

The wonderful recuperative powers of the states were amply evidenced in 1903 by the bountiful harvest and prolific growth of herbage over the major portion of the districts which were most keenly affected by the adversity of the season in the year before. The lambing returns have been excellent, while the weight and quality of the fleece have surpassed expectations. There is every hope, therefore, that ere long Australia will resume its position as the foremost pastoral country of the world.

The expenditure on water conservation of a moiety of the sum represented by the losses of the season of 1901-2 would go far towards solving the problem of how to utilise to their best advantage the fertile but comparatively rainless districts of the interior. Outside of a system of water conservation the only other alternative appears to be the construction of light lines of railway in the pastoral districts to enable the stock to be moved quickly from place to place in periods of drought, but these would not be of much avail in some seasons.

The number of stock in Australasia, expressed in terms of sheep, the number of acres per sheep, and the number of sheep per head of population, at various dates since 1861, were as given below :—

Year.	Sheep.	Cattle, in terms of Sheep.	Horses, in terms of Sheep.	Total.	Acres per Sheep.	Sheep per head of Population.
1861	23,741,706	40,398,390	4,599,700	68,739,796	28·7	54
1871	49,773,584	47,138,200	7,825,580	104,737,364	18·8	53
1881	78,063,426	87,096,280	12,497,650	177,657,356	11·1	63
1891	124,547,937	118,613,300	17,858,350	261,019,587	7·5	67
1901	92,358,824	98,274,330	19,051,720	209,684,874	9·4	46
1902	74,348,003	84,728,800	18,214,310	177,291,113	11·1	39

Value of Pastoral Property and Production.

The total value of pastoral property in Australasia—that is, of improvements, plant, and stock—was estimated a few years ago at £242,000,000. This estimate does not include land, but merely the stock, other than swine, depastured, and the improvements effected in the grazing area. It is difficult if not impossible to assign an exact value to the lands devoted to pastoral purposes, for though much purchased land is used for depasturing stock, the larger area comprises lands leased from the state, so that a statement which omitted to take into account the value of the state lands would be misleading.

The annual return from pastoral pursuits in 1902 was £28,688,673, the share of each state in the total production being as follows :—

New South Wales	£10,731,132
Victoria	4,347,964
Queensland	3,187,236
South Australia	1,900,313
Western Australia	1,035,871
Tasmania	610,619
Commonwealth	21,813,135
New Zealand	6,875,538
Australasia	£28,688,673

The products of dairy cattle and swine are not included in the foregoing statement, the figures being given in another place. It should be understood that the values quoted are those at the place of production. The value of the return from each class of stock may be approximately reckoned as follows :—

Sheep	£20,337,329
Cattle	5,237,668
Horses	3,113,676
Total	£28,688,673

Wool.

As might be supposed, the greater part of the value of production from sheep is due to wool. Thus, out of the £20,337,329 shown above, £15,982,000 is the value of wool, viz. :—£15,746,000 for wool exported, and £236,000 for wool used locally. The value of the wool exported, according to the Customs returns, was £16,116,119—that is to say, £370,119 more than the figures shown above. The excess represents the charges for freight, handling, etc., between the sheep-walks and the port of shipment.

The price of wool, which in 1899 was much higher than for many years previously, declined almost as suddenly as it had advanced, and as the production for 1901 did not show much increase, except in New Zealand, the total value compares unfavourably with preceding years, and fell short of that of 1899 by £6,165,000. In 1902 wool again rose considerably in value, and though the production was less than in 1901, the increased price added over £1,700,000 to the figures of the previous wool year ended 30th June.

The following figures show the chief sources of origin of the wool sold in London during the years 1900-1-2.

Year.	Total Sales.	Australasian.	Cape.	Argentine.
	bales.	per cent.	per cent.	per cent.
1900	2,064,000	70·55	6·78	22.67
1901	2,494,000	69·97	8·70	21·33
1902	2,445,000	69·49	9.57	20·94

Nearly all the wool produced in Australasia is exported, the home consumption being small, amounting to only 1·76 lb. greasy, per head of population; while in Europe and America the quantity of wool available for consumption by the industry amounts to about 5 lb. per head. During the last two quinquennial periods the consumption of wool in Europe and America has averaged as follows :—

1891-94	5·12 lb.	per head of population
1895-99	5·19 lb.	,, ,,

The quantity, in the grease, of wool produced by each state at decennial periods since 1871 was as follows :—

State.	1871.	1881.	1891.	1901.	1902.
	lb.	lb.	lb.	lb.	lb.
New South Wales...	74,401,300	161,022,900	321,416,000	301,942,000	221,565,900
Victoria	63,641,100	67,794,300	69,205,600	74,879,300	65,490,400
Queensland	36,553,200	34,275,300	83,118,100	70,141,800	41,659,100
South Australia......	28,242,100	46,013,900	50,151,500	39,951,700	36,862,600
Western Australia..	1,888,000	4,654,600	9,501,700	14,049,000	13,377,700
Tasmania	6,687,800	10,525,100	10,102,900	8,939,000	8,304,400
Commonwealth	211,413,500	324,286,100	543,495,800	509,902,800	387,260,100
New Zealand.........	46,192,300	69,055,600	117,733,500	164,011,500	167,448,100
Australasia......	257,605,800	393,341,700	661,229,300	673,914,300	554,708,200

The great fall in production is seen from the above table, which shows that the only states where an increase has taken place since 1891 are Western Australia and New Zealand, all the others showing a large decline. The increase in New Zealand has taken place in spite of the heavy demands upon the resources of the colony for the supply of sheep to meet the requirements of the London market in frozen mutton.

The weight of wool per sheep has been increasing regularly in each of the states, as will be seen from the following table, which shows the weight of clip per sheep at each decennial interval since 1861. It is manifest that the Victorian figures are unreliable, because there is no reason to suppose that there was a decline in the weight of the fleece in 1891; on the contrary, it is known to have been steadily improving. The Western Australian and Tasmanian results also show irregularities, and are omitted from the table. The values for New South Wales and Queensland best represent the increase in the weight of the fleece on the mainland, and the New Zealand figures are also believed to be correct. In South Australia the weight of wool per sheep has been consistently higher than in the other states, but the results are derived from the official statistics, and it would appear that the number of sheep in that state has been under-estimated.

State.	1861.	1871.	1881.	1891.	1901.
	lb.	lb.	lb.	lb.	lb.
New South Wales..................	3·28	4·57	4·47	5·74	7·2
Victoria	4·52	6·17	6·87	5·68	6·9
Queensland	3·40	4·73	4·50	4·73	7·1
South Australia.....................	4·69	6·41	6·93	6·85	7·9
New Zealand.......................	3·48	4·76	5·32	6·42	8·1

The values of the excess of exports over imports in each state for the period 1871–1902 were as follows. A careful examination of the figures proves rather conclusively that less care than might have been expected has been taken in stating the values, except in New South Wales and New Zealand, but they are obtained from the official records, and are given for what they are worth :—

State.	Excess of Exports over Imports.				
	1871.	1881.	1891.	1901.	1902.
	£	£	£	£	£
New South Wales ...	4,705,820	7,173,166	10,927,487	9,050,884	7,316,148
Victoria	4,483,461	2,562,769	3,792,938	2,510,219	2,331,657
Queensland	1,158,833	1,331,869	3,453,548	2,130,778	1,305,871
South Australia	1,113,825	1,573,313	1,540,079	1,021,283	1,092,482
Western Australia ..	122,637	256,690	329,365	378,135	458,078
Tasmania	298,160	498,400	418,460	279,022	262,243
Commonwealth ..	11,882,736	13,396,207	20,461,877	15,370,321	12,766,479
New Zealand	1,606,144	2,914,046	4,129,686	3,669,642	3,349,640
Australasia	13,488,880	16,310,253	24,591,563	19,039,963	16,116,119

Western Australia was the only state to show an increase in the value during the year over that obtained in 1891.

The Customs figures are not necessarily a reliable guide as to the value of the wool clip in any particular year, since the returns show the exports up to the 31st December only, whereas the wool year does not close until six months later. Consequently, if the clip be late, as was the case last season, a large proportion of the quantity exported appears in the Customs returns for the following year. The figures for 1902 are therefore considerably less than they would have been under ordinary conditions.

According to the London returns, the imports of Australasian wool into Europe and America during the 1902 wool season comprised 1,699,000 bales, which at an average of £11 16s. 7d. per bale represents a total value of £20,097,754. For the previous season the imports were 1,745,000 bales, averaging £10 10s., equivalent to a total value of £18,322,500, so that notwithstanding the smaller import in 1902 the returns for that year exceeded the total for 1901 by £1,775,000.

Wool realised a high price in Australia at the sales closing in June, 1903, the average per bale being £11 18s. 4d., as against £9 6s. 4d. for the preceding year. In a comparison between London and Australian prices it may be taken that freight and other charges add from 15s. to £1 per bale to the Australian rates, while the former returns include also New Zealand wool, which is not so valuable as that grown in Australia. The shipments of wool from Australasia during the twelve months ending June, 1903, show a decrease of 250,000 bales on the totals for the preceding year. The quantity shipped by the Commonwealth fell off by 284,000 bales, but the exports from New Zealand increased by about 30,000 bales, while there was also a slight expansion in the Tasmanian trade. From present indications the current season will be a phenomenal one as far as concerns the yield of wool per sheep. Copious rains have fallen throughout almost the whole of the Commonwealth, the lambing has been excellent, and the growth of wool extraordinary. It seems not unlikely that on many large runs the flocks will yield an average of from 9 to 10 lbs. of wool per head, which at present prices is equivalent to a return of about 7s. per head of sheep shorn. It is probable that the growth of wool has never been exceeded, and notwithstanding the greatly reduced numbers of the sheep, indications are so favourable that the net return of wool will approximate very closely to the returns for last year, while the quality of the wool will be vastly superior. The continental demand for last season's clip was very keen, and of the 739,338 bales sold in Australian markets no less than 56 per cent. was taken by continental buyers, while 26 per cent. was secured by Great Britain, 4 per cent. by America, and the remaining 14 per cent. by local manufacturers and Japanese and Eastern buyers. Of the 1,971,000 bales of Australasian and South African wool consumed in England, the Continent, and America during 1902, the respective proportions taken by each were 42.5 per cent., 54 per cent., and 3.5 per cent.

The price per lb. obtained for wool in grease in London at the end of each year from 1890 was as follows:—

Year.	New South Wales. (Average Merino).	Victoria. (Good Average Merino.)	New Zealand. (Average Cross-bred.)
	d.	d.	d.
1890	8½	10	10
1891	7½	9	9½
1892	7	8½	9½
1893	7	8½	9½
1894	6	7¾	8½
1895	7¼	9½	9½
1896	7	9	8½
1897	7¼	9	8¼
1898	7¾	9½	7
1899	13	15½	10½
1900	7	9	7½
1901	7¾	10	5¼
1902	10½	12	7½

Taking the last sixteen years, the highest prices were realised for New South Wales and Victorian wools during 1899, namely, 13d. per lb. and 15½d. per lb. respectively. The maximum price for New Zealand wool, 11½d. per lb., was obtained in 1889. The lowest prices—6d. for New South Wales, and 7½d. for Victoria—were experienced in 1895, while owing to the heavy fall in the value of cross-breds, New Zealand wool realised as little as 4¾d. per lb. during 1901. The average prices realised during the whole period were 9d. per lb. for New South Wales average merino, 11d. for good average Victorian merino, and 7½d. for average New Zealand cross-bred. From these figures it will be seen that Victorian wool averages about 2d. per lb. higher than New South Wales wool. The figures must be taken with some qualification. Much of the New South Wales wool, the product of the Riverina districts, is exported *via* Melbourne and sold as Port Phillip wool, and brings a price considerably in excess of the average given in the table for the State of which it is the produce. The quantity of wool sold at the local sales in the Australasian States is increasing. Particulars of these sales will be found in the chapter on "Commerce."

The Frozen-Meat Trade.

In view of the large increase in the live stock of Australasia during favourable seasons, the question of the disposal of the surplus cast has become a matter of serious consequence. In New South Wales especially, and in the Riverina district in particular, it was found necessary to have recourse to the old method of boiling down, which a fortunate rise in the price of tallow made it possible to carry on with a margin of profit. The price of tallow during the last few years has however been low, and offered little inducement to pastoralists, while the loss of stock will prevent the trade being of much importance to Australia for some considerable time.

In New Zealand a much better solution of the question of disposal of the surplus cast was found, and a trade in frozen mutton with the United Kingdom has been established on a thoroughly payable basis—an example which some of the other states are endeavouring to follow, although considerably handicapped by the want of cross-bred sheep and the prejudice of the English consumer against merino mutton.

The first successful attempt at shipping frozen mutton to England was made by New Zealand in 1882, and since then the trade has attained great proportions, to the immediate benefit of the colonial producer as well as the English consumer. In 1882 the exports amounted to 1,700,000 lb., at that time regarded as a considerable quantity, but in 1902 the total was no less 226,000,000 lb., and there is every prospect of a further increase in 1903. The value of the trade in frozen and preserved meat has risen from £1,281,000 in 1895 to £2,686,000 in 1902, or by £1,405,000. The bulk of the trade was carried on with

Great Britain, the exports thereto in 1902 being valued at £2,457,000, but a market is opening up in South Africa, to which New Zealand consigned frozen and preserved meat to the value of £140,000 in 1902. The trade initiated by the New Zealand Land Company has been extended by the formation of numerous joint stock companies, which now own twenty-one meat-freezing works in the two islands, having an aggregate capacity for freezing about 4,000,000 sheep per year. The sheep are generally killed in the country, and transported by rail to the freezing works. Several fleets of steamers are engaged in the trade, and the freight rates charged enable the companies to realise satisfactory profits. The growth of the frozen and preserved meat industries of New Zealand since 1881 is shown in the following table. The shipments are almost exclusively made to the United Kingdom :—

Year.	Frozen or Chilled Meat.						Preserved Meat.	
	Beef.	Mutton.	Lamb.	Mutton and Lamb.	Total Weight.	Total Value.	Weight.	Value.
	cwt.	carcases.	carcases.	cwt.	cwt.	£	lb.	£
1881	....	......	......	......	......	......	1,074,640	22,391
1882	....	......	......	......	15,244	19,339	2,913,904	54,397
1883	937	......	......	86,995	87,932	118,261	3,868,480	72,778
1884	1,644	......	......	252,422	254,066	345,081	3,103,744	59,224
1885	9,170	......	......	286,961	296,131	373,326	4,047,904	81,401
1886	9,391	......	......	336,405	345,796	426,556	2,592,464	47,426
1887	6,630	656,823	110,816	421,405	428,035	454,942	4,706,016	79,246
1888	44,613	885,843	94,681	507,306	551,919	629,110	4,912,544	86,128
1889	68,298	990,486	118,794	588,524	656,822	783,374	5,325,152	106,772
1890	98,234	1,330,176	279,741	798,625	896,859	1,084,992	6,702,752	136,182
1891	103,007	1.447.583	338,344	889,012	992,019	1,185,122	5,447,904	111,133
1892	55,020	1,316,758	290,996	806,304	861,324	1,021,838	3,039,712	69,420
1893	11,059	1,355,247	475,365	888,455	899,514	1,078,427	2,656,416	46,601
1894	912	1,633,213	459,048	1,001,342	1,002,254	1,102,770	3,368,736	57,325
1895	12,090	1,632,590	735,254	1,078,640	1,090,730	1,214,778	4,124,400	66,137
1896	25,905	1,505,969	792,037	1,065,292	1,091,197	1,239,969	5,006,848	75,661
1897	50,044	1,653,170	1,038,316	1,291,582	1,341,626	1,512,286	5,046,216	78,235
1898	95,218	1,719,282	1,168,888	1,338,175	1,433,393	1,596,543	6,245,792	97,197
1899	172,345	2,102,583	1,272,525	1,557,439	1,729,784	1,905,164	5,382,272	90,919
1900	312,291	1,585,238	1,351,145	1,354,730	1,667,021	1,952,610	4,973,024	94,524
1901	221,211	1,806,671	1,513,017	1,499,124	1,720,335	2,116,360	3,048,896	87,688
1902	286,699	2,058,622	1,852,050	1,708,738	1,995,437	2,561,327	6,087,096	124,633

Amongst the states of the Commonwealth the export of meat has reached the largest dimensions in Queensland, although of course it consists chiefly of beef, the trade in mutton being proportionately very small. Of the total exports of frozen and preserved meat, amounting to £1,465,203 in 1902, South Africa took £771,333 worth, or more than one half, while of the remainder, £275,229 worth went to the United Kingdom. Three years previously Queensland exported over £750,000 worth of frozen beef to England. Existing contracts with South Africa and Manilla will keep the meat works in operation for some considerable time, and with the return of good seasons it is hoped that much of the British trade will be recovered. So far as they can be given, the figures showing the growth of the Queensland frozen-meat trade, as well as the exports of preserved meat, will be found below:—

Year.	Frozen or Chilled Meat.				Preserved Meat.	
	Beef.	Mutton.	Total Weight.	Total Value.	Weight.	Value.
	cwt.	cwt.	cwt.	£	lb.	£
1881	......	......	....	....	2,276,409	39,956
1882	......	......	....	....	5,689,189	112,343
1883	......	......	1,951	2,151	6,729,721	151,001
1884	......	......	8,082	11,240	2,298,696	57,101
1885	......	......	3,926	5,003	8,306,432	171,432
1886	......	......	9,289	12,103	130,658	1,586
1887	.....	......	....	....	5,272,170	99,653
1888	.....	......	....	....	3,964,419	77,887
1889	8,745	15,542	24,287	62,240	853,621	16,743
1890	30,253	23,799	54,052	75,908	2,769,881	44,040
1891	52,609	53,698	106,307	161,345	3,333,317	59,032
1892	123,196	51,595	174,791	276,113	6,035,035	96,828
1893	204,349	21,898	226,247	377,039	8,001,788	143,146
1894	301,837	32,187	334,024	498,652	15,544,826	250,646
1895	461,733	28,221	489,954	580,489	25,941,400	393,492
1896	434,683	31,874	466,557	501,498	21,583,658	330,728
1897	529,162	31,162	560,324	659,260	15,699,098	241,189
1898	511,629	10,935	522,564	672,970	13,188,836	217,684
1899	651,029	32,529	683,558	833,733	25,148,815	383,899
1900	689,423	16,239	705,662	976,878	25,250,226	427,062
1901	675,221	19,208	694,429	1,016,038	13,310,615	221,709
1902	770,423	39,844	810,267	1,207,345	12,838,507	257,858

Next to New Zealand, the largest exporter of frozen mutton is New South Wales. During the last few years greater efforts have been made in this State to expand the trade, and the exports show a considerable increase, although a temporary check was experienced during the last four years in consequence of the unfavourable seasons. But New South Wales has laboured under the disadvantage of possessing few cross-bred sheep for export, and the food qualities of the merino are scarcely appreciated in the English market, where New Zealand mutton is favourably known, and brings on an average 1¼d. per lb. more than Australian. A great expanse of New South Wales, however, is suited to the breeding of large-carcase sheep, and the pastoralists have become alive to the importance of securing a share of the meat trade of the United Kingdom. Attention is being directed to the introduction of British rams, and a large increase in the cross-bred flocks has already taken place. The following table shows the growth of the frozen-meat trade of New South Wales; the exports of preserved meat consist almost wholly of tinned mutton :—

Year.	Frozen or Chilled Meat.				Preserved Meat.	
	Beef.	Mutton.	Total Weight.	Total Value.	Weight.	Value.
	quarters.	carcases.	cwt.	£	lb.	£
1881	......	....	9,980	8,554	....	*176,721
1882	......	....	13,782	22,910	....	*143,601
1883	......	....	34,911	43,100	....	*221,912
1884	......	....	13,309	12,321	....	*161,477
1885	......	....	6,271	6,064	....	*166,561
1886	......	....	4,852	4,671	....	*77,756
1887	......	....	21,831	19,310	9,761,154	150,714
1888	......	....	52,262	44,537	4,528,269	69,481
1889	......	....	37,868	33,426	2,877,303	52,321
1890	......	....	72,304	71,534	4,655,523	74,329
1891	......	....	105,013	101,828	6,581,713	87,632
1892	......	....	223,074	169,425	8,620,747	105,922
1893	4,773	364,958	220,584	141,640	13,092,942	164,592
1894	9,538	533,995	339,404	193,760	16,382,597	206,054
1895	88,719	1,021,006	607,818	380,107	22,384,285	302,828
1896	16,286	1,372,373	642,188	343,397	16,351,936	218,292
1897	28,529	1,065,990	503,925	275,118	10,903,611	147,165
1898	39,593	1,095,568	539,495	330,325	13,930,801	227,288
1899	32,855	956,222	459,553	331,904	11,453,332	185,804
1900	86,948	951,891	540,426	541,395	11,966,326	221,604
1901	72,662	963,614	510,148	578,923	12,398,011	260,455
1902	12,130	510,466	221,126	263,170	10,884,786	242,915

* Including Extract of Meat.

The total capacity of the boiling-down works in New South Wales is stated at 683,900 head of cattle or 16,965,000 sheep; of chilling works, 488,500 head of cattle or 5,422,800 sheep; of freezing works, 76,500 head of cattle or 3,150,000 sheep; and of meat-preserving works, 183,000 head of cattle or 5,445,000 sheep.

The only other state in which the meat-export trade has reached dimensions of any importance is Victoria, although its exports fall far below those of the states already dealt with. A statement of the Victorian trade from 1881 to 1902 will be found below:—

Year.	Frozen or Chilled Meat.				Preserved Meat.	
	Beef.	Mutton.	Total Weight.	Total Value.	Weight.	Value.
	cwt.	cwt.	cwt.	£	lb	£
1881	......	......	....	....	4,026,072	102,306
1882	......	......	18,522	18,969	1,274,066	30,705
1883	......	......	9,944	12,220	3,225,657	76,015
1884	......	......	41,373	53,196	2,667,866	63,707
1885	......	......	39,107	61,617	1,486,849	38,244
1886	......	......	39,384	70,319	616,652	17,868
1887	......	......	15,245	27,270	629,054	14,291
1888	......	......	....	....	714,856	16,115
1889	......	......	....	....	805,580	16,156
1890	......	......	....	....	893,114	20,197
1891	......	......	....	....	1,052,887	19,230
1892	......	......	....	....	1,982,151	51,624
1893	......	......	1,307	1,838	777,953	14,349
1894	53	27,182	27,235	25,370	2,267,791	40,082
1895	268	24,563	24,831	31,673	2,917,730	43,408
1896	127	23,634	23,761	25,827	4,335,511	71,576
1897	62	21,416	21,478	20,248	5,498,315	84,914
1898	233	7,556	7,789	9,101	2,852,191	38,516
1899	1,458	74,960	76,418	86,087	4,760,047	50,174
1900	2,814	79,507	82,321	112,040	4,776,979	67,265
1901	3,931	85,053	88,984	131,529	3,856,381	63,284
1902	5,210	118,700	123,910	195,674	2,216,862	47,959

There are at present depastured in Australasia 74,348,003 sheep and 8,472,880 cattle, of which 20,342,727 sheep and 1,460,663 cattle are in New Zealand. In that colony the industry of sheep and cattle raising has now reached such a stage that practically the whole of the stock available for market is used up every year either locally or for export, and as a consequence the numbers of both kinds of stock are stationary, and have been so for some years past. In the states of the Commonwealth a different state of things prevails. In New South Wales there is usually a large surplus of sheep beyond the state's requirements; while the cast of cattle is below the local demand, and is supplemented by the importation of stock from Queensland, the net import from that State for the past four years being 306,766 head. The other four States have each a deficiency of cattle and sheep.

It is estimated that in an average year the "cast" of cattle is 10·25 per cent.—that is to say, that percentage of all the cattle depastured would be of marketable age, could they be made fit for slaughtering. Assuming this is as the basis of calculation it is estimated that in the Commonwealth there are annually 250,000 head of cattle in excess of those required for food and independent of those preserved or frozen.

The year 1902 was a disastrous one to sheep and cattle breeders in the Commonwealth, and especially to those of Queensland and New South Wales, but owing to the copious rains which have fallen the prospects for the 1903 season are remarkably bright. Fodder is abundant, and the lambing returns are very satisfactory, nevertheless it will be some time before there is any great quantity of meat available for export. This is unfortunate in view of the export trade which has been so patiently built up; but as it is now an established fact that Australian meat is greatly appreciated in England, and can be exported largely at remunerative prices, there are strong elements of hope for future progress when better seasons are experienced.

During the years 1894 and 1895 several attempts, more or less successful, were made to place live cattle and sheep in the English market. A great difficulty in the way of establishing such a trade was the wildness of the cattle, the mortality in some of the shipments being sufficiently high to provoke strong criticism in England as to the cruelty to which the cattle were subjected by being shipped on such a long voyage. It is to be feared, however, that these expressions of opinion were prompted, not altogether by the alleged sufferings of the cattle, but to a large extent by the interests of the English producer and the American exporter. At the same time, it is clear that a permanent and profitable trade cannot be established until the cattle have been handled sufficiently to bring them into a tractable condition, for the present system of depasturing followed in Australia renders the stock too wild to endure a long stay on shipboard. In view of the vast population of the United States, any increase in the export of live cattle from that country cannot be anticipated. The trade of the Argentine Republic with Great Britain in chilled and frozen beef has increased during the last three years from £200,000 to £1,700,000. The increase is partly due to the stoppage of the export of live cattle owing to disease, and partly to the falling off in Australian exports, and at the present time about one-fourth of the British imports of chilled and frozen beef comes from the Argentine. With the revocation of the order restricting the importation of live cattle both from the Argentine and Uruguay, it is expected that the primest beeves will be shipped from these countries alive. As far as concerns Great Britain it may be noted here that the 1902 returns show a decrease in cattle and sheep as compared with 1892. With the growth of population and general advance in the standard of living among the middle and lower classes, the home supplies of meat become yearly more inadequate to meet demands, and there is consequently an annual increase in the imports from abroad. The comparative figures for population and live stock in the United Kingdom during the years 1892 and 1902 are as follows:—

	Population.	Cattle.	Sheep.
1892	38,110,250	11,519,400	33,642,800
1902	41,869,120	11,376,970	30,056,600

Dairy-farming.

Dairy-farming has of late years made fair progress in Australasia, especially in New South Wales, Victoria, New Zealand, and, more recently, in Queensland. The introduction of the factory system at convenient centres and the use of the cream-separator have done much to cause the extension of the industry. The number of dairy cows at the end of 1902, and the estimated quantity of milk produced in each state during that year, were as follow:—

State.	No. of Dairy Cows.	Quantity of Milk produced (estimated).
New South Wales	351,287	114,742,000 gallons
Victoria	456,000*	149,145,000 ,,
Queensland	108,800*	25,483,000 ,,
South Australia	75,638	23,084,000 ,,
Western Australia	24,324	5,624,000 ,,
Tasmania	33,316	10,590,000 ,,
Commonwealth	1,049,365	328,668,000 ,,
New Zealand	428,773	155,250,000 ,,
Australasia	1,478,138	483,918,000 ,,

* Estimated; actual figures not available.

The estimated value of the milk and its products, butter and cheese, and of the return obtained from swine, together with the total value of dairy produce for each state in 1902, will be found below:—

State.	Value of Milk, Butter, and Cheese.	Value of Return from Swine.	Total Value of Dairy and Swine Produce.
	£	£	£
New South Wales	2,275,000	372,000	2,647,000
Victoria	2,910,000	490,000	3,400,000
Queensland	772,000	170,000	942,000
South Australia	447,000	148,000	595,000
Western Australia	128,000	113,000	241,000
Tasmania	446,000	97,000	543,000
Commonwealth	6,978,000	1,390,000	8,368,000
New Zealand	2,608,000	371,000	2,979,000
Australasia	9,586,000	1,761,000	11,347,000

The value of production shown in the foregoing table for 1902 is, notwithstanding the drought, greater than in the previous year, for, though the quantity of milk products was less in most of the states, the prices obtained by the farmers were considerably higher than those realised in 1901.

The production of butter and cheese in each state during 1902 is estimated to have been as follows :—

State.	Butter.	Cheese.
New South Wales	29,950,977 lb.	4,148,038 lb.
Victoria	39,227,754 ,,	3,849,561 ,,
Queensland	4,851,362 ,,	952,013 ,,
South Australia	4,521,246 ,,	705,969 ,,
Western Australia	359,670 ,,	....
Tasmania	700,402 ,,	327,934 ,,
Commonwealth	79,611,411 ,,	9,983,515 ,,
New Zealand	43,530,000 ,,	11,500,000 ,,
Australasia	123,141,414 ,,	21,483,515 ,,

The states having a surplus of butter and cheese available for exportation during 1902 are shown in the following table :—

State.	Butter.	Cheese.
Victoria	14,194,875 lb.	493,727 lb.
New Zealand	28,444,304 ,,	8,368,080 ,,
Tasmania	....	124,086 ,,
Total	42,639,179 ,,	8,985,893 ,,

New South Wales was formerly both an importer and an exporter of butter, for only during the spring and early summer months was the production larger than the local requirements, while during the remainder of the year butter had to be imported to meet the local demand. In favourable seasons this state now exports butter to the United Kingdom on a fair scale ; but a large quantity of New Zealand butter is still sent to the New South Wales markets on account of the more satisfactory price realised there. There is also an importation from South Australia and Victoria for the supply of the districts adjacent to those states. Queensland has lately become an exporter of butter, 1897 being the first year when the export exceeded the import. The net export in that year was 179,490 lb., which in 1901 had increased to 2,044,073 lb. Owing to an unfavourable season in 1902, however, the imports exceeded the exports by 2,718,434 lb.

The net imports of butter and cheese during 1902 are shown below:—

State.	Butter.	Cheese.
New South Wales	1,779,613 lb.	873,627 lb.
Queensland	2,718,434 ,,	708,295 ,,
South Australia	881,499 ,,	166,522 ,,
Western Australia	5,727,011 ,,	1,153,665 ,,
Tasmania	553,172 ,,	
Total	11,659,729 ,,	2,902,109 ,,

From the foregoing figures it will be seen that those states which produce a surplus of butter and cheese have, after providing for the deficiency of the other states, a balance available for exportation to outside countries, this balance in 1902 amounting to 30,979,450 lb. of butter and 6,083,784 lb. of cheese. An export trade in butter and cheese has long been maintained by New Zealand, while in recent years Victorian, New South Wales, and South Australian butters and, more recently still, Queensland butters have been sent to the London market, and their very favourable reception has given a fresh stimulus to the dairying industry in those states. The unfavourable season in 1902, however, caused a falling off of 50 per cent. in Queensland's butter production. Recently a fair number of co-operative factories has been established, and with a continuance of favourable climatic conditions there is a bright prospect before the industry. It is hoped that before long facilities will be available for shipping the product direct from Brisbane to London, thus avoiding the double handling of the butter, much of which is at present shipped *via* Sydney. The rapidity with which this trade is growing may be gauged from the following table, which shows the quantity of butter exported to the United Kingdom during the fourteen years ended 1902:—

Year.	Exporting State.				
	New South Wales.	Victoria.	Queensland.	South Australia.	New Zealand.
	lb.	lb.	lb.	lb.	lb.
1889	284,251	505,478	....	....	2,363,088
1890	589,160	1,286,583	....	10,850	2,976,848
1891	391,180	3,778,775	....	23,864	3,246,768
1892	1,532,782	6,446,900	....	....	4,648,980
1893	2,846,989	13,141,423	1,064	357,087	5,864,656
1894	4,333,927	22,139,521	....	1,233,539	6,590,640
1895	1,852,360	21,127,025	31,420	1,017,629	6,181,728
1896	1,741,272	16,452,649	....	242,872	6,730,304
1897	5,431,109	15,450,857	407,199	16,240	8,943,088
1898	5,309,811	13,548,293	628,296	389,836	9,051,168
1899	7,006,701	26,045,210	741,308	894,992	13,608,224
1900	8,477,617	26,185,679	872,244	707,448	18,577,552
1901	5,985,784	17,180,468	208,740	162,456	19,141,136
1902	121,672	1,424,460	....	....	19,063,184

Tasmania also sent about 20,000 lb. of butter to the United Kingdom in 1902, but the effects of the unfavourable seasons in the past two years on the general totals for the Commonwealth will be apparent from the above table.

In average years the price obtained for Australian butter in London is higher than the rates ruling in the local market; and as there can hardly be a limit placed to the capacity of Australasia to produce butter and cheese, it is probable that these higher prices will have the effect of greatly stimulating the dairy industry throughout all these states. In connection with this subject, it may be mentioned that the value of the butter, cheese, and eggs imported into the United Kingdom during 1902 was £20,526,690, £6,412,002, and £6,308,985 respectively. The supply is chiefly drawn from the Continent of Europe and from America, and of the total amounts mentioned, the only imports from Australasia were butter to the value of £1,183,966, and cheese to the value of £131,054, practically the whole of the cheese, and £781,872 worth of butter from New Zealand being included in the Australasian figures.

It may not be out of place to remark that in one or two of the states the export of butter has helped to maintain prices in the local markets, and tended to restrict home consumption. If a season of great prosperity visits Australia there will be a very large increase in the local demand, with a consequent limitation in the supply available for export, so that it may be concluded that under any circumstances the prospects of the industry are encouraging. Even under existing circumstances local consumption shows a considerable increase. For example, in Victoria, the consumption in 1899 was 33,006,718 lb., in 1900, 35,968,878 lb., and in 1901, 39,208,646 lb., being a gradual increase in the local demand at the rate of about 3,000,000 lb. per annum.

It is interesting to note that the imports of dairy produce and margarine into the United Kingdom during 1902 reached a total value of £31,350,000, the highest yet recorded. The following figures furnished by the Board of Agriculture, London, show the percentages of imports of butter contributed by the various countries from which supplies were drawn during the last five years. It will be seen that Denmark maintains the leading position, while Russia occupies second place, having more than doubled its contribution during the five years, and that Australasia in 1902 only furnished 6 per cent. of the total, of which New Zealand's share was nearly 4 per cent:—

Year.	Denmark	Russia.	France.	Holland.	Sweden.	Canada.	New Zealand.	Australia	Other Countries
	per cent.	per cent.	per cent.	per cent.	per cent.	per cent.	per cent.	per cent.	per cent.
1898	45·65	5·62	12·99	8·39	9·19	4·89	2·18	6·21	5·88
1899	42·19	4·10	10·44	8·40	7·25	7·33	3·29	7·79	9·16
1900	43·99	6·21	9·53	8·37	5·80	4·09	4·85	10·45	6·71
1901	43·13	10·22	8·42	8·07	4·87	5·82	4·52	6·70	8·25
1902	42·85	12·32	10·42	9·90	4·82	7·19	3·98	2·02	6·50

During the last decade the average yearly increase in the quantity of butter imported into the United Kingdom was about 8,500 tons. The increase is partly accounted for by the rapid growth of the population generally, but more by reason of the fact that the enlarging population of the towns is drawing more and more new milk from the churn and leaving less for butter and cheese making. Moreover, the number of cows per head of the population is decreasing rapidly, and at the present time there are 11 cows less per 1,000 inhabitants than was the case ten years ago.

SWINE.

The breeding of swine is usually carried on in conjunction with dairy-farming, and the following table shows the number of swine in each state at ten-year intervals since 1871 :—

State.	Number of Swine.				
	1871.	1881.	1891.	1901.	1902.
New South Wales ...	213,193	213,916	253,189	265,730	192,097
Victoria	177,447	239,926	286,780	350,370	350,370*
Queensland	32,707	56,438	122,672	121,641	77,202
South Australia..	95,542	120,718	83,797	89,875	83,791
Western Australia.....	14,265	22,530	25,930	61,025	52,765
Tasmania................	52,863	49,660	73,520	58,716	52,093
Commonwealth ..	586,017	703,188	845,888	947,357	808,317
New Zealand........ ...	151,460	200,083	308,812	224,024	193,740
Australasia.........	737,477	903,271	1,154,700	1,171,381	1,002,057

* Year 1901, no later information.

The production of swine should be a large factor in dairy-farming, but the increase in the number of pigs has not been so large as might have been expected. In Queensland, Tasmania, South Australia, and New Zealand the number of swine is actually less now than in 1891. Victoria possessed the largest stock in 1901, with 29·9 per cent. of the total number in Australasia ; then came New South Wales and New Zealand with 22·7 per cent. and 19·1 per cent. respectively ; Queensland had 10·4 per cent. of the total ; South Australia, 7·7 per cent. ; Western Australia, 5·2 per cent. ; and Tasmania, 5·0 per cent.

The products of the swine—bacon, ham, lard, and salt pork—are now exported by all the states with the exception of New South Wales and Western Australia, as is shown by the following table, which shows the excess of exports in the year 1902 :—

State.	Bacon and Ham.	Salt and Frozen Pork.	Lard.	Net Value exported.
	£	£	£	£
New South Wales...........	*63,216	5,356	*11,555	*69,415
Victoria	131,903	514	9,836	142,253
Queensland	16,706	3,667	1,803	22,176
South Australia	27,990	.....	*13,453	14,537
Western Australia...........	*134,430	*1,312	*1,985	*137,727
Tasmania	2,247	....	*1,380	867
Commonwealth.........	*18,800	8,225	*16,734	*27,309
New Zealand	18,450	9,858	2,470	30,778
Australasia	*350	18,083	*14,264	3,469

* Excess of imports.

Poultry and Minor Industries.

An estimate is given below of the value of the production of poultry and eggs, together with that arising from bee-farming, in each state during the year 1902 :—

State	Poultry and Eggs.	Honey and Beeswax.
New South Wales	£732,000	£24,000
Victoria	716,000	15,000
Queensland	305,000	5,000
South Australia	343,000	10,000
Western Australia	178,000	3,000
Tasmania	105,000	4,000
Commonwealth	£2,379,000	£61,000
New Zealand	471,000	16,000
Australasia	£2,850,000	£77,000

The most remarkable feature is the trade in eggs between South Australia as supplier and New South Wales, Victoria, and Western Australia as buyers. The returns for 1902 show that during that year South Australia exported eggs to the value of £105,463 to these States, viz., £4,585 to Victoria, £27,168 to New South Wales, and £73,710 to Western Australia. The bulk of the trade with New South Wales is transacted with the Barrier district, which is commercially a dependency of South Australia.

During the last few years an important trade has sprung up in the export of frozen poultry, and frozen rabbits and hares. In 1902, 98,462 fowls, 21,699 ducks, geese, and turkeys, 113,125 pairs of rabbits, and 61,448 hares were exported from New South Wales through the Government Depôt. The total value of frozen poultry, game, and rabbits exported during 1902 amounted to £43,181, of which about £24,000 worth was sent to South Africa.

In Victoria the export of rabbits and hares has reached much larger dimensions, over 3,250,000 pairs, valued at £160,000, being sent away in 1902. In addition to this there was an export of over £30,000 worth of frozen poultry and game. In this state, as in New South Wales, a large number of persons find remunerative employment in trapping hares and rabbits.

At the Government Depôt in New Zealand during 1902, 75,000 head of poultry were dressed and exported, the bulk of which was consigned to South African markets.

The exports of poultry and game from South Australia in 1902 amounted to about £20,000.

Pastoral and Dairy Production.

The total value of pastoral and dairy production, including that from poultry and bee farming, during the year 1902, in each state and in the whole of Australasia, together with the value per inhabitant, were as shown in the following table:—

State.	Total Value of Pastoral and Dairy Production.	Value per Inhabitant.
	£	£ s. d.
New South Wales	14,134,000	10 1 0
Victoria	8,479,000	7 0 6
Queensland	4,439,000	8 12 6
South Australia	2,848,000	7 14 0
Western Australia	1,458,000	6 14 0
Tasmania	1,263,000	7 3 0
Commonwealth	32,621,000	8 8 0
New Zealand	10,342,000	12 16 0
Australasia	42,963,000	9 3 0

The following table gives similar information for the last four census periods. It will be seen that the only states which show increases since 1891 are Western Australia, Tasmania, and New Zealand:—

State.	1871.	1881.	1891.	1901.
	£	£	£	£
New South Wales	8,709,000	13,151,000	17,460,000	15,598,000
Victoria	7,260,000	7,499,000	9,321,000	9,242,000
Queensland	1,959,000	4,186,000	7,561,400	6,670,000
South Australia	1,800,000	3,178,000	3,148,525	2,936,000
Western Australia	274,000	431,000	647,350	1,344,000
Tasmania	734,000	1,093,000	1,117,550	1,100,000
Commonwealth	20,736,000	29,538,000	39,255,825	36,890,000
New Zealand	3,210,000	7,096,000	9,153,225	9,970,000
Australasia — Total	23,946,000	36,634,000	48,409,050	46,860,000
	£ s. d.	£ s. d.	£ s. d.	£ s. d.
Australasia — Per head	12 7 7	13 3 11	12 12 0	10 4 6

On reference to the above table, it will be seen that although the total production has been nearly doubled since 1871 the value per head has decreased considerably. In 1901 the value of pastoral and dairy production was £1,549,000 less than in 1891; but to a great extent this was due to diminished production caused by a succession of dry seasons—the cast of both sheep and cattle being much reduced as compared with 1891. On the other hand, the production of butter was larger, and also the export of meat, as will be seen below:—

Produce.		1891.	1901.
Wool, as in grease	Lb.	661,229,000	673,914,000
Cast of sheep	No.	17,000,000	10,345,000
Cast of cattle	No.	1,216,000	1,014,000
Butter produced	Lb.	70,628,000	131,398,606
Meat export.....................	Cwt.	1,454,000	3,322,939

The movement in prices will be seen from the following tabulation, which is based chiefly on an analysis of the New South Wales trade. The prices of 1902 are represented by 1,000:—

Year.	Price Levels of—				
	Wool.	Butter.	Cattle.	Tallow.	Hides.
1891	836	838	464	715	802
1892	821	844	457	730	685
1893	735	781	377	809	607
1894	680	647	289	751	560
1895	757	562	285	695	728
1896	809	790	474	626	611
1897	780	783	371	590	804
1898	829	832	490	669	855
1899	1,171	863	455	801	969
1900	951	830	564	869	1,025
1901	863	858	724	836	1,134
1902	1,000	1,000	1,000	1,000	1,000

The price of wool, which advanced suddenly in 1899, declined again during 1900 and 1901, but there was an advance in 1902, which partly compensated for the small clip.

Employment in Pastoral and Dairying Pursuits.

The following tables show the total number of persons engaged in pastoral and dairying pursuits in Australasia for the years 1891 and 1901. In each case the figures include only the direct producers who were working on holdings in March of the respective years, and do not take into account persons employed in butter factories, or casual hands engaged at other periods of the year:—

PASTORAL.

	1891.		1901.	
	Males.	Females.	Males.	Females.
New South Wales	26,176	334	31,312	595
Victoria	5,660	1,881	11,650	1,692
Queensland	12,530	198	16,714	180
South Australia	3,582	317	4,112	81
Western Australia	1,530	98	1,633	52
Tasmania	1,859	142	957	26
New Zealand	6,486	90	12,014	156
Total	57,823	3,060	78,392	2,782
Total—Males and Females :	60,883		81,174.	

DAIRYING.

	Males.	Females.	Males.	Females.
New South Wales	4,996	4,758	15,850	2,285
Victoria	4,850	2,933	11,701	5,877
Queensland	1,121	455	3,170	826
South Australia	419	1,014	839	2,029
Western Australia	175	72	350	144
Tasmania	181	265	561	337
New Zealand	2,793	180	7,586	1,654
Total	14,535	9,677	40,057	13,152
Total—Males and Females :	24,212		53,209.	

From the above table it will be seen that there has been an increase equal to 58 per cent. in the number of persons engaged in pastoral and dairying pursuits during the last ten years. This is chiefly owing to the rapid expansion of the dairying industry, especially in the three larger provinces, where the increase in this branch was more than double that of the first year of the period. Comparing the number of persons employed with the total stock expressed in terms of sheep, it will be found that the proportion in 1901 was 1 person to every 1,552 sheep, as against 1 to every 3,070 sheep in 1891. The decreased proportion in 1901 is of course partly attributable to the loss in stock from unfavourable seasons, but it arises chiefly from the greater amount of employment in the dairying industry, as well as from the tendency previously mentioned to divide the sheep into smaller flocks.

DEFENCE.

THE colonists of Australasia have always manifested an objection to the maintenance of a large standing army, and shown a disposition to rely mainly upon the patriotism and valour of the citizens for their own defence. As the Commonwealth, however, possesses a more or less complete system of fortifications armed with expensive ordnance, which requires a more regular and constant attendance than could well be bestowed by those who devote only a portion of their time to military affairs, it is necessary that there should be in each of the states a small permanent military force, consisting for the most part of artillery and submarine miners, whose chief duty is to man the fortifications and keep the valuable armaments therein in a state of efficiency, to be ready for any emergency. At the same time, it is expected that they will prove the nucleus for an effective defence force if ever hostilities should unfortunately occur. The responsibility for the defence of Australia now lies with the Federal Government, and, since it assumed control many improvements in organization have been effected, while the expenditure has been considerably reduced.

The greater portion of the Australian forces consists of volunteers enrolled under a system of partial payment, which affords a defence force without the disadvantages and expense of a standing army. The men receive payment according to the number of parades and night drills they attend, as compensation for wages lost while absent from their employment for the purpose of receiving military instruction. For privates the pay is eight shillings per day. The remuneration has hitherto varied in the different states, but under the new scheme introduced by Sir John Forrest an uniform rate is to be adopted in each state with the exception of Tasmania. Very little encouragement is extended by the Commonwealth to those who are purely volunteers, as the system has been tried in the various states and found unsatisfactory, and in New Zealand alone is the volunteer system the mainstay of defence.

The following table shows the strength of the military forces maintained in each state as at 30th June, 1903. The total number of men of military ages (from 20 to 40 years) in Australasia was ascertained at the Census of 1901 to be 775,000, and compared with this figure the forces of the states appear extremely small.

State.	Paid.	Militia or Partially Paid.	Volunteers.	Total Forces.
[Headquarters Staff	25	......	......	25]
New South Wales............	485	4,932	2,740	8,157
Victoria	366	3,272	2,432	6,070
Queensland	210	2,431	248	2,889
South Australia...............	51	1,857	......	1,908
Western Australia	51	6	1,390	1,447
Tasmania	40	3	1,807	1,850
Commonwealth	1,228	12,501	8,617	22,346
New Zealand	400	......	14,086	14,486
Australasia..	1,628	12,501	22,703	36,832

The relative strength of the various arms in the Commonwealth states may be summarised as follows:—

Staff, administrative and educational	283
Artillery—	
Field	987
Garrison	2,199
Engineers	625
Mounted troops..	4,419
Infantry	12,962
Army Service Corps	210
Army Medical Corps	512
Veterinary department	7
Ordnance department	102
Pay department	40
Total..........................	22,346

In addition to the above there are small bodies of reserves in New South Wales and Victoria, and rifle clubs are enrolled in all the states except Tasmania. These men are all trained to the use of the rifle, and have a slight knowledge of drill, and would be available in time of war to complete the establishment of the regular forces. The following table shows the strength of reservists, members of rifle clubs, and school cadets in the various states, on the 30th June, 1903:—

State.	Reservists and Members of Rifle Clubs.	Cadets.
New South Wales	4,043	89
Victoria	20,504	4,150
Queensland	3,274	964
South Australia	3,497	....
Western Australia	....	....
Tasmania	....	172
Commonwealth	31,318	5,375
New Zealand	2,455	2,429
Australasia	33,773	7,804

In addition to the military forces enumerated, there are in each state, with the exception of Tasmania and Western Australia, small corps of Naval Volunteer Artillery, or partially-paid forces of a similar character, capable of being employed either as light artillery land forces or on board the local war vessels. The strength of these marine forces on the 30th June, 1903, was as follows:—

State.	Paid.	Partially Paid.	Unpaid.	Total.
New South Wales	3	377	1	381
Victoria	105	115	....	220
Queensland	41	454	206	701
South Australia	20	133	8	161
Commonwealth	169	1,079	215	1,463

On their present footing the combined forces of the Commonwealth states are nearly 24,000 strong, as will be seen above, and of these about 20,000 could be mobilised in a very short time in any one of the states of Queensland, New South Wales, Victoria, or South Australia. Most of the states have also cadet companies, consisting of youths attending school, who are taught the use of arms so as to fit them, on reaching manhood, for taking a patriotic share in the defence of their country.

The outbreak of hostilities with the Boers in October, 1899, served to demonstrate the strength of the loyalty of these states to the mother country. From all parts of Australasia members of the various defence forces, as well as civilians, volunteered for service with the Imperial troops in South Africa. The total number of men despatched in the various contingents was 22,928. The table below shows the number of men and horses sent from each state:—

State.	Officers.	Non-commissioned Officers and Men.	Horses.
New South Wales	327	6,000	5,877
Victoria	183	3,393	3,878
Queensland	143	2,756	3,085
South Australia	78	1,450	1,524
Western Australia	63	1,160	1,044
Tasmania	35	827	725
Commonwealth	829	15,586	16,133
New Zealand	342	6,171	6,662
Australasia	1,171	21,757	22,795

In addition to the above, several special service officers were, at the request of the colonial Governments, attached to the British troops for the purpose of gaining experience, and 14 nurses were despatched from New South Wales.

The states again offered to assist Great Britain on the outbreak of hostilities in China. The Imperial Authorities accepted the offer, and contingents of naval volunteers were despatched from New South Wales and Victoria numbering 260 and 200 men respectively, while South Australia equipped and sent the gunboat Protector.

Naval Defence.

The boundaries of the Australian Naval Station have been defined as follow:—From 95° E. long. by the parallel of 10° S. lat. to 130° E. long.; thence north to 2° N. lat., and along that parallel to 136° E. long.; thence north to 12° N. lat., and along that parallel to 160° W. long.; thence south to the Equator, and east to 149° 30′ W. long.;

bounded on the south by the Antarctic Circle; and including the numerous groups of islands situated within the limits specified.

The defence of Australasia and its trade is entrusted to ships of the Imperial navy, under an agreement entered into between the British Government and the Governments of the Commonwealth and New Zealand. The agreement provides that the naval force on the Australian Station shall consist of not less than—

1 Armoured cruiser, first-class;

2 Second-class cruisers;

4 Third-class cruisers;

4 Sloops;

and of a Royal Naval Reserve of 25 officers and 700 seamen and stokers.

This force is under the control and orders of the Naval Commander-in-Chief on the Australian Station. One of the ships is to be kept in reserve, and three are to be partly manned and used as drill ships for training the Royal Naval Reserve, the remainder being kept in commission and fully manned. The three drill ships and one other vessel are to be manned by Australians and New Zealanders as far as procurable, paid at special rates, and enrolled in proportion to the relative population of the Commonwealth and New Zealand, but the vessels are to be officered by officers of the Royal Navy and of the Royal Naval Reserve. In order to insure the inclusion of Australian-born officers in the Royal Navy, 8 nominations for cadetships are to be given annually in the Commonwealth and 2 in New Zealand. In consideration of the services rendered, the Commonwealth is to pay five-twelfths and New Zealand one-twelfth of the total annual cost of maintenance, provided that the total amount to be paid in one year shall not exceed £200,000 and £40,000 respectively. In reckoning the total annual cost, a sum equal to 5 per cent. on the prime cost of the ships composing the naval force is to be included. The agreement covers a period of ten years, and only terminates if notice to that effect shall have been given two years previously, viz., at the end of the eighth year, or at the end of any subsequent year, and then two years from such date. In time of peace one drill ship and one other cruiser are to be stationed in the waters of New Zealand as their headquarters, but they may be temporarily removed if any emergency arises to justify such a course. The base of the naval force is to be the ports of Australia and New Zealand, and their sphere of operations the waters of the Australia, China, and East Indies Stations where the Admiralty believe they can most effectively act against hostile vessels which threaten the trade or interests of Australia and New Zealand. No change in this arrangement can be made without the consent of the Governments of the Commonwealth and New Zealand, and nothing in the agreement shall be taken to mean that the naval force named therein shall be the only force used in Australasian waters should the necessity arise for a larger force.

The agreement was embodied in the Naval Agreement Bill and passed by the Commonwealth Parliament, being assented to on the 28th August, 1903. It has also been passed by the New Zealand Parliament. Prior to this agreement the defence of the Australasian coast was entrusted to the British ships on the Australian Station and the Australasian Auxiliary Squadron, and these vessels are still on duty.

The vessels of the Imperial fleet which are still on service are detailed below. The Penguin and Dart are engaged in surveying service.

Name.	Class.	Displacement.	Indicated horse-power.	Draught of water extreme.	Length.	Beam.	Armament. Guns.	Speed.	Coal endurance. Coal that can be carried in bunkers.	Coal endurance. Distance that can be steamed at 10 knots' speed.
		tons.		ft. in.	ft. in.	ft. in.		knots.	tons.	knots.
Royal Arthur (flagship)	Twin-screw cruiser, 1st class, protected.	7,700	10,000	24 10	360 0	60 8	One 9·2-in. B.L., 12 6-in. B.L.Q.F., 12 6-Pr., 5 3-Pr., 7 Nordenfeldt.	19·75	1,250	10,000
Phœbe ..	Twin-screw cruiser, 3rd class.	2,575	7,500	15 6	265 0	41 0	Eight 4·7 Q.F., 8 3-in. Pr. Q.F., 4 M., 1 L.	19·2	300	4,800
Archer ..	Twin-screw cruiser, 3rd class.	1,770	3,500	15 7	225 0	36 0	Six 6-in. 5-ton B.L. V.C.P. 8 3-Pr., 2 Nordenfeldt.	16·5	325	7,000
Pylades..	Screw cruiser, 3rd class.	1,420	1,510	16 11	200 0	38 0	Eleven 5-in. 38-cwt. B.L. R., 8 M., 1 L.	12·6	425	6,600
Sparrow	Screw gun-boat, 1st class.	805	1,200	13 3	165 0	30 0	Six 4-in. 26-cwt. B.L.R., 2 Q.F. Hotchkiss, 2 M.	13·7	105	..
Lizard	Screw gun-boat, 1st class	715	1,000	12 6	165 0	29 0	Six 4-in. 25-cwt. B.L. 4 M.	12·6	105	..
Torch ..	Screw sloop..	960	1,100	14 6	180 0	32 6	Six 4-in. Q.F., 2 3-Pr. Q.F. Hotchkiss, 2 0·45-in. Maxim.	13·25	130	2,000
Penguin.	Screw sloop..	1,130	700	14 0	180 0	38 0	Two 64-pr. M., 1 L., 2 M.	10·1	200	..
Dart	Screw yacht..	470	250	12 11	133 0	25 2	2 L., 2 M.	7·5	64	..

Q.F., Quick-firing guns; M., Machine guns; L., Light guns under 15 cwt.; B.L.R., Breech-loading rifled guns; V.C.P., Vavasseur Centre Pivot.

The Royal Arthur has no armour, but carries a protective deck of steel, varying in thickness from 1 to 5 inches. Her 6-inch guns are also enclosed in casemates of steel 6 inches thick. Sydney is the headquarters of the fleet, and ranks as a first-class naval station, extensive repairing yards and store-houses having been provided for the accommodation of ships of war.

The ships which formed the Australian Auxiliary Squadron are still in Australian waters, and the fleet consists of five fast cruisers and two torpedo gunboats of the Archer (improved type) and Rattlesnake classes of the British Navy. The squadron is commanded by the Admiral on the Australian Station, whose headquarters are in Sydney, where a residence is provided for him by the state of New South Wales. The squadron, which arrived in Port Jackson on the 5th September, 1891, consists of the following vessels :—

Name.	Displacement.	Indicated horse-power.	Draught of water extreme.	Length.	Beam.	Armament.		Speed.	Coal endurance.	
						Guns.	Torpedo tubes.		Coal that can be carried in bunkers.	Distance that can be steamed at 10 knots' speed.
	tons.		ft. in.	ft. in.	ft. in.			knots.	tons.	knots.
*Katoomba ..	2,575	7,500	17 6	265 0	41 0	Eight 4·7 Q.F. guns, eight 3-pr. Q.F. guns, one 7-pr. M.L.R. gun (boat and field), four 4·45-in. 5-barrel Nordenfeldt.	4	19·2	300	6,000
Ringarooma ..	2,575	7,500	17 6	265 0	41 0		4	19·2	300	6,000
Mildura	2,575	7,500	16 6	265 0	41 0		4	19·2	300	6,000
Wallaroo	2,575	7,500	17 3	265 0	41 0		4	19·2	300	6,000
Tauranga	2,575	7,500	17 6	265 0	41 0		4	16·5	300	6,000
Boomerang ..	785	3,500	10 8	230 0	27 0	Two 4·7 in. Q.F. guns, four 3-pr. Q.F. guns.	3	19·0	160	2,500
Karrakatta ..	785	3,500	10 9	230 0	27 0		3	19·0	160	2,500

* Guard ship of reserve. Q.F.—Quick-firing guns. M.L.R.—Muzzle-loading rifled guns.

The Boomerang and Karrakatta are classed as torpedo gun-boats; all the other vessels are third-class screw cruisers. The hull of each vessel is of steel. The deck armour over machinery space is 2-in. and 1-in., and the conning-towers are protected by 3-inch armour, except in the case of the torpedo gun-boats, the towers of which have 1-in. armour. Each of the cruisers carries four, and each of the torpedo gun-boats three torpedo tubes. In the event of any of the squadron being lost, the vessel is to be replaced by the British Government.

The Commonwealth possesses a number of vessels which are available for harbour defence in Victoria, Queensland, and South Australia. The names and classes of the vessels in Victoria are :—

Name.	Class.	Displacement.	Armament.
		tons.	
Cerberus	Armoured turret ship (twin screw).	3,480	Four 10-in. 18-ton M.L.R., six 6-pdr. Q.F., four 1-in. Nordenfeldt—4 barrels.
Countess of Hopetoun.	First-class steel torpedo boat.	120	Three 14-in. Mark IX R.G.F. torpedoes, and two 2-barrel Nordenfeldt 1-in. M. guns.
Childers	do do ..	63	Two 14-in. Fiume torpedoes, and two 1-pdr. Hotchkiss Q.F. guns.
Nepean	Second-class steel torpedo boat.	12	Two 14-in. Mark IV Fiume torpedoes.
Lonsdale	do do ..	12	do do do
Gordon	Wooden torpedo boat ..	12	Two 14-in. Mark IV Fiume torpedoes, three 2-barrel 1-in. Nordenfeldt guns.

The turret ship Cerberus is in good condition, and it is proposed to re-arm her with modern B.L. guns, in which case the vessel will be an efficient harbour defence.

There are two vessels available for harbour defence in Queensland, and particulars of their armament are shown below :—

Name.	Class.	Displacement.	Armament.
		Tons.	
Gayundah........	Steel gunboat (twin screw)	360	One 8-in. B.L., one 6-in. B.L. Armstrong, two 3-pdr. 1½-in. Nordenfeldt, one 1-in. four-barrelled Nordenfeldt, one Maxim.
Paluma	do ..	360	One 6-in. B.L. ; two 5-in. B.L. ; two 1½-in. Q F. Nordenfeldts ; one 1-in. four-barrelled Nordenfeldt ; one 0·45-in five-barrelled Nordenfeldt.

In South Australia one twin-screw steel cruiser, the Protector, of 920 tons, is available. The armament of the Protector consists of one 8-in. 12-ton B.L., five 6-in. 4-ton B.L., and four 3-pdr. Q.F. This vessel has lately seen service in the war with China, and was reported by the Commander-in-Chief of that station to be "an efficient and well-kept man-of-war, reflecting credit on captain, officers, and men." There are also some large arms available in South Australia, comprising two 6-in. 5-ton B.L. guns, intended for use in an auxiliary gun-vessel, and five Gatling machine guns for boat or land service, while in Tasmania there is one torpedo boat with dropping gear for Whitehead torpedoes. New Zealand possesses three Thorneycroft torpedo boats and two steam launches fitted for torpedo work.

Cost of Defence.

The following table shows the expenditure by the Commonwealth Government on naval and military defence for the year ended 30th June, 1903 :—

State.	Amount.	Per head.
	£	s. d.
New South Wales	274,928	3 11
Victoria..................................	265,722	4 5
Queensland	110,640	4 4
South Australia	56,062	3 1
Western Australia	33,661	3 1
Tasmania	26,075	2 11
Commonwealth	£767,088	4 0

In all the states, with the exception of Western Australia, a certain amount of money has been spent out of loans for purposes of defence. The amounts thus spent during 1902–3 were as follow :—

	£
Queensland	12,931
South Australia..	3,393
Tasmania	346
Commonwealth	16,670
New Zealand	37,004
Australasia	£53,674

The total loan expenditure in each state for defence purposes to the end of the financial year 1902–3 was as follows:—

State.	Amount.	Per head.		
	£	£.	s.	d.
New South Wales	*1,421,976	1	0	3
Victoria	149,324	0	2	4
Queensland	377,097	0	14	8
South Australia	292,683	0	16	0
Tasmania	128,180	0	14	7
Commonwealth	2,369,260	0	12	3
New Zealand	733,839	0	18	2
Australasia	£3,103,099	0	13	3

* Inclusive of £812,485 for naval station, Port Jackson.

This does not represent the whole cost of the fortifications, as large sums have from time to time been expended from the general revenues of the states in the construction of works of defence; the amount of such payments, however, it is now impossible to determine.

In 1890 a military commission was appointed by the Imperial and the different Australian Governments to take evidence and report on the question of fortifying King George's Sound, Hobart, Thursday Island, and Port Darwin, at the joint expense of the states. The commission visited the points mentioned during 1891, and as a result of the evidence taken fortifications were erected at King George's Sound and Thursday Island, and it is probable that similar works will eventually be erected at Hobart and Port Darwin.

SOCIAL CONDITION.

THE high rates of wages which have generally prevailed in Australasia and the cheapness of food have permitted the enjoyment of a great degree of comfort, if not of luxury, by a class which elsewhere knows little of the one and nothing of the other; and even in times of trade depression and reduced wages it may safely be said that the position of the wage-earner in Australia is equal to that occupied by his compeers in any other part of the world. Although a high standard of living is not conducive to thrift, saving has gone on with marked rapidity, notwithstanding the industrial disturbances resulting from the great strikes and the bank crisis of 1893. Some idea of the rate and extent of this accumulation of wealth may be obtained from the tables showing the growth of deposits with banks. The banking returns, however, afford in themselves but an incomplete view of the picture; it should also be regarded from the standpoint of the expenditure of the people. Both of these subjects are dealt with in their proper places in this volume, and these evidences of the social condition of the people need not, therefore, be further considered here.

Newspapers and Letters.

Few things show more plainly the social superiority of a civilized people than a heavy correspondence and a large distribution of newspapers. In these respects all the provinces of Australasia have for many years been remarkable. In proportion to population it is doubtful whether any country in the world can boast of a larger number or a better class of newspapers than they publish. Great advances were made in this respect between 1871 and 1891, but the rate of progress, both in number and in excellence of production, has been even more rapid since the year last named. There are no means of correctly estimating the number of newspapers actually printed and distributed in the states, because the Post-office carries but a small proportion of the circulation. For purposes of comparison with other countries, however, it may be stated that during the year 1902 no less than 122,297,000 newspapers passed through the Post-offices of the various states, giving the large proportion of 26 per head of population. In the same year the number of letters and post-cards carried was

301,563,000, being over 64 for every person in Australasia. An examination of the statistics of other countries shows that these States stand third among the countries of the world in the transmission of correspondence, being only exceeded by the United Kingdom and the United States of America per head of population. The following table shows the increase which has taken place in the quantity of postal matter carried, together with the proportion of letters and newspapers carried per head of population at the last six census periods and in 1902:—

Year.	Letters and Post Cards.	Newspapers.	Letters per head.	Newspapers per head.
1851	2,165,000	2,150,000	4·7	4·7
1861	14,061,000	10,941,400	11·3	8·8
1871	30,435,300	17,252,700	15·7	8·9
1881	80,791,700	43,802,000	29·1	15·8
1891	183,694,900	95,879,760	47·9	25·0
1901	273,582,000	121,000,000	59·7	26·4
1902	301,563,000	122,297,000	64·2	26·1

There are 989 newspapers published in Australasia; 306 in New South Wales, of which 92 are published in Sydney and suburbs; 324 in Victoria, of which 130 are published in Melbourne and suburbs; 118 in Queensland; 46 in South Australia; 22 in Western Australia; 16 in Tasmania; and 157 in New Zealand.

Parks, Museums, and Art Galleries.

All the Australasian capitals are liberally supplied with parks and recreation-grounds. In Sydney and suburbs there are parks, squares, and public gardens comprising an area of 4,335 acres, including 530 acres which form the Centennial Park. Then there is the picturesque National Park, of 36,810 acres, situated about 16 miles from the centre of the metropolis; and, in addition to this, an area of 35,300 acres, in the valley of the Hawkesbury, and distant about 12 miles from the railway terminus on the northern shore of Sydney Harbour, has been reserved for public recreation under the name of Ku-ring-gai Chase. Thus Sydney has two extensive and picturesque domains for the enjoyment of the people at almost equal distances north and south from the city, and both accessible by railway. Melbourne has about 5,400 acres of recreation-grounds, of which about 1,750 acres are within the city boundaries, 2,850 acres in the suburban municipalities, and 800 acres outside those municipalities. Adelaide is surrounded by a broad belt of park lands, and also contains a number of squares within the city boundaries, covering altogether an area of 2,300 acres. Brisbane, Hobart, Perth, and the chief cities of New Zealand are also well provided for in this respect, and in all the provincial towns large areas have been dedicated as public parks. There are fine Botanic Gardens in Sydney, Melbourne, Brisbane, Adelaide, Perth, and Hobart, which are included in the areas above referred to. Each of these gardens has a special attraction of its own. They are all well kept, and reflect great credit upon the communities to which they belong.

The various capitals of the states, and also some of the prominent inland towns, are provided with museums for the purposes of instruction as well as recreation; and in Sydney, Melbourne, Brisbane, Adelaide, Perth, and Hobart there are art galleries containing excellent collections of paintings and statuary. All these institutions are open to the public free of charge.

Public Charities.

One of the most satisfactory features of the social condition of the Australian communities is the wide distribution of wealth, and the consequently small proportion of people who are brought within the reach of want. In the United Kingdom, the richest country of Europe, only nine out of every hundred of the population possess property of the value of £100, while in Australasia the number is about fifteen, and the violent contrast between the rich and the poor which blots the civilisation of the old world is not observable in these young states. It is, unfortunately, only too plain that a certain amount of poverty does exist; but there is a complete absence of an hereditary pauper class, and no one is born into the hopeless conditions which characterise the lives of so many millions in Europe, and from which there is absolutely no possibility of escape. No poor-rate is levied in Australasia, the assistance granted by the state to able-bodied men who find themselves out of employment in times of depression, taking the form of payment, in money or in rations, for work done by them.

The chief efforts of the authorities, as regards charity, are directed towards the rescue of the young from criminal companionship and temptation to crime, the support of the aged and infirm, the care of the imbecile or insane, and the subsidising of private institutions for the cure of the sick and injured and the amelioration of want. Even where the state grants aid for philanthropic purposes, the management of the institutions supervising the expenditure is in private hands, and in addition to state-aided institutions there are numerous charities wholly maintained by private subscriptions, whose efforts for the relief of those whom penury, sickness, or misfortune has afflicted are beyond all praise.

The rescue of the young from crime is attempted in two ways—first, by means of Orphanages and Industrial Schools, where children who have been abandoned by their natural guardians, or who are likely, from the poverty or incapacity of their parents, to be so neglected as to render them liable to lapse into crime, are taken care of, educated, and afterwards apprenticed to some useful calling; and second, by sequestering in Reformatories children who have already committed crime, or whose parents or guardians find themselves unable to control them; but the accommodation in the latter class is very limited, and might well be extended.

Although more than a century has elapsed since settlement commenced in Australasia, its resources are by no means developed, and very many men are at work far away from the home comforts of everyday life, and from home attendance in case of sickness or injury. Owing to the peculiar nature of the occupations in which a great part of the adult male population is employed, accidents are very common, the annual death-rate being about 7 per 10,000 living, and the majority of the cases treated, especially in the districts outside the metropolitan area are injuries arising out of accidents to men following hazardous pursuits. Hospitals are therefore absolutely essential under the conditions of life in the rural districts of the states, and they are accordingly found in every important country town. Below will be found the number of hospitals in each state, with the number of indoor patients treated during the year mentioned, and the total expenditure for the same year. Unfortunately, the South Australian and Western Australian returns are defective, as will be seen by the note appended to the table :—

State.	Year.	Hospitals.	Indoor patients treated.	Expenditure.
		No.	No.	£
New South Wales ...	1901	118	33,012	176,118
Victoria	1901-02	53	26,526	157,918
Queensland............	1901	68	19,194	120,781
South Australia	1901	8	3,354*	20,104*
Western Australia...	1901	24	5,390	16,969†
Tasmania	1901	13	3,606	22,754
Commonwealth	......	284	91,082	514,644
New Zealand	1901-02	45	14,233	123,366
Australasia ...	......	329	105,315	638,010

* Adelaide Hospital only. † Perth and Fremantle Hospitals.

All the states possess institutions for the care of the insane, which are under Government control. The treatment meted out to the inmates is that dictated by the greatest humanity, and the hospitals are fitted with all the conveniences and appliances which modern science points out as most calculated to mitigate or remove the affliction from which these unfortunate people suffer. The following table shows the number of insane patients under treatment, the total expenditure on hospitals for the insane during the year, and the average expenditure per inmate under treatment. The question of insanity is treated farther on in this chapter :—

State.	Insane Patients under treatment.	Total Expenditure.	Average Expenditure per Inmate under treatment.
	No.	£	£ s. d.
New South Wales	5,335	123,531	23 3 1
Victoria	5,168	122,611	23 14 6
Queensland	2,054	44,009	21 8 5
South Australia	1,192	27,669	23 4 3
Western Australia	418	8,167	19 10 9
Tasmania	470	14,890	31 13 7
Commonwealth	14,637	340,877	23 5 9
New Zealand	3,271	58,532	17 17 10
Australasia	17,908	399,409	22 4 1

The amounts expended on Destitute Asylums and Benevolent Societies cannot be separated from other items of expenditure in some of the states. As far as they can be ascertained they are given in the following table, together with the number of adult inmates of the various asylums for the year 1901 :—

State.	Inmates.	Expenditure.
	No.	£
New South Wales	4,959	139,942
Victoria	3,072	84,949
Queensland	2,314	38,376
South Australia	713	18,306
Western Australia	1,115	18,350
Tasmania	860	6,673
Commonwealth	13,033	306,596
New Zealand	1,813	49,914
Australasia	14,846	356,510

In addition to the above, a liberal amount of out-door relief is given in all the Australasian provinces, and destitute children are taken care of, either by being supported in the Government institutions or by being boarded out to persons deemed able to take care of them properly.

The expenditure by the Governments of the six states of the Commonwealth on hospitals, benevolent asylums, orphanages, and poor relief generally, amounted in 1902 to £1,346,927, the total for New Zealand for the same year being £188,044. This sum does not include payments to old-age pensioners, but as want of means is a necessary qualification for a pension, it is very doubtful whether this service does not come under the general description of poor relief. Including payments for old-age pensions, the total expenditure of the various states reaches £2,075,561, and of New Zealand £395,512, the distribution among the states being as follows. The figures refer to expenditure from revenue only, the outlay from loans being separately shown in a subsequent table :—

State.	Hospitals, Asylums, and Poor Relief.	Old-Age Pensions.	Total.
	£	£	£
New South Wales	449,268	436,202	885,470
Victoria	351,919	292,432	644,351
Queensland	229,203	....	229,203
South Australia	122,458	....	122,458
Western Australia	142,288	....	142,288
Tasmania	51,791	....	51,791
Commonwealth	1,346,927	728,634	2,075,561
New Zealand	188,044	207,468	395,512
Australasia	1,534,971	936,102	2,471,073

Comparing these amounts with the population of the various states the following results are obtained :—

State.	Expenditure per head in 1902.		
	Hospitals, Asylums, and Poor Relief.	Old-Age Pensions.	Total.
	£ s. d.	£ s. d.	£ s. d.
New South Wales	0 6 5	0 6 3	0 12 8
Victoria	0 5 10	0 4 10	0 10 8
Queensland	0 9 11	....	0 9 11
South Australia	0 6 8	....	0 6 8
Western Australia	0 13 10	....	0 13 10
Tasmania	0 5 11	....	0 5 11
Commonwealth	0 7 0	0 3 9	0 10 9
New Zealand	0 4 9	0 5 2	0 9 11
Australasia	0 6 7	0 4 0	0 10 7

It will be seen that the expenditure was proportionately highest in Western Australia, with 13s. 10d. per inhabitant, followed by New South Wales, with 12s. 8d., and Victoria, with 10s. 8d., whilst Tasmania showed the lowest average, with 5s. 11d. per inhabitant. For the Commonwealth the average was 10s. 9d. per head, and for Australasia, 10s. 7d.

In addition to the amounts shown in the preceding table there is a fairly considerable expenditure from loans in some of the states on hospitals and charitable institutions. The total loan expenditure under this heading is given below :—

State.	Expenditure from Loans on Hospitals and Charities.
	£
New South Wales	55,033
Victoria	65,050
Queensland	9,007
Tasmania	11,366
Commonwealth	140,456
New Zealand	18,733
Australasia	159,189

Including expenditure from revenue and from loans the total outlay by the Commonwealth for the year 1902, on all forms of charitable relief, amounted to £2,216,000, or at the rate of 11s. 6d. per head of population, and for Australasia, £2,630,000, equal to 11s. 4d. per inhabitant.

It was anticipated by the introducers of the old age pension system that there would be a reduction in the expenditure on poor relief, especially on asylums. The expectation was without reasonable foundation, as the classes of people affected by the two systems of relief are essentially distinct, and little or no reduction in the expenditure on poor relief can be traced to the establishment of the pension system. The following is a statement of the expenditure in 1896 ; the total for 1902 has been given on a previous page. It will be seen that on the whole there has been a large increase in expenditure during the period, the rate per inhabitant—excluding old-age pensions—being 6s. 7d. in 1902, as compared with 6s. per head in 1896.

State.	Expenditure in 1896 on Hospitals, Asylums, and Poor Relief.	
	Total.	Per Inhabitant
	£	£ s. d.
New South Wales	410,800	0 6 6
Victoria	266,300	0 4 6
Queensland	158,900	0 7 2
South Australia	94,600	0 5 4
Western Australia	110,100	0 18 5
Tasmania	42,100	0 5 4
Commonwealth	1,082,800	0 6 2
New Zealand	179,400	0 5 1
Australasia	1,262,200	0 6 0

As far as can be judged from the imperfect returns, adding together the amount received from the Government and the amount of private subscriptions, the expenditure in the whole of the Australasian states in connection with all forms of relief and in aid of hospitals and other charitable institutions excluding old age pensions is certainly not less than £1,823,000 per annum. This sum, though not excessive in proportion to the population, may yet appear large in view of the general wealth of the states, which should preclude the necessity of so many seeking assistance; and there is the risk that the charitable institutions may encourage the growth of the pauper element, for while free quarters and free food are so accessible, those who are disinclined to work are tempted to live at the public expense. It should be stated, however, that of the total number of persons who seek hospital relief, less than one-half are natives of the states, the remainder being mostly natives of the United Kingdom, with a few who were born in a European country or in China. This, however, cannot be taken as evidence of the superiority of the Australian born. The inmates of the institutions referred to are in almost all cases aged persons, and probably not more than half the number of aged persons are Australian born.

Old-Age Pensions.

The question of granting pensions to aged persons has been of late years much discussed throughout Australia and New Zealand, and at the present time the old age pension system is in operation in New South Wales, Victoria, and New Zealand. The last-named province was the first to legislate in regard to the matter, and pensions were payable from 1st April, 1898.

Every person in New Zealand, of the full age of sixty-five years, or upwards, is eligible for a pension, provided he has resided continuously in the colony for twenty-five years, certain concessions in regard to residence being made in favour of seamen and others. To be entitled to a pension, a person must not possess an income in excess of £52 a year, nor property exceeding £270 in value. There are also other qualifications, principally affecting good citizenship. The full pension is £18 a year, payable in monthly instalments. For each £1 of income above £34 a year, and for each £15 of property above £50, £1 per annum is deducted from the amount of the pension. In March, 1903, there were 32,800 persons in New Zealand whose ages exceeded sixty-five years, and of these 12,481 had already been granted pensions. The average pension paid was £16 19s., and the sum payable in respect of all pensions, excluding management, was £211,594. The proportion of the population who claim old-age pensions varies according to the locality. This variation is due partly to the differences in the proportion of the persons above the pension age, and partly to the fact that in districts where mining is the chief industry, few persons are able to earn their living after they reach sixty-five years. The proportion of pensioners to the population over sixty-five years of age is about 35 per cent., and the proportion of pensioners to those qualified, both by age and residence, is about 45 per cent.

The old-age pension scheme sanctioned by the Parliament of New South Wales specifies a pension of £26 a year, diminished by £1 for every £1 of income above £26 a year, and by £1 for every £15 of property that the pensioner possesses. Where a husband and wife are each entitled to a pension, the amount is fixed at £19 10s. a year each, unless they are living apart under a decree of the Court or a deed of separation, when the full sum of £26 will be allowed. Persons under 65 years of age but over 60 years are entitled to pensions if they are incapacitated by sickness or injury from earning their livelihood, but debility due merely to age is not considered as an incapacitating sickness.

The pension system came into force on the 1st August, 1901, and at the close of the first pension year there were 22,252 pensions current, representing an annual payment of £531,823 or £23 18s. per pension. On the 31st December, 1903, there were 22,884 pensions current, representing an annual payment of £547,019, and an average pension of £23 18s. per annum, being the same as in August, 1902. It will be seen that the number of pensioners has remained practically at the same figure, notwithstanding the increase in the total persons of pension-age. This is owing to the strict supervision which the Central Board is now able to exercise in the granting of pensions. During 1903, 1,446 pensioners died, and 308 pensions were cancelled or withdrawn.

The pension system of Victoria differs very materially from that in operation in New South Wales and New Zealand. The average weekly income of a claimant in Victoria during the six months immediately preceding the grant of a pension must not have amounted to 8s. per week (in New South Wales the sum allowed is £1 per week); he must also have made reasonable efforts to provide for himself, and this is not necessary either in New South Wales or New Zealand, where the pension is granted in consideration of old age, and a citizen may enjoy his pension on attaining the age of 65, whether he is able to work or not; indeed, the law allows him to supplement his income to the extent of 10s. per week, in the case of New South Wales, and 13s. in that of New Zealand; the total income enjoyed by the pensioner may, therefore, in these two states, amount to 20s. per week. In Victoria, under the original Act of 1901, the amount of pension was determined by the Commissioners appointed to adjudicate on the matter, and 8s. was the maximum allowed; but the Commissioners had power to determine what sum less than 8s. might be reasonable and sufficient to meet the wants of the claimant. Under the Amending Act of 1903, however, the control and management of "this charitable grant," as the Premier styled it, was taken out of the hands of the Commissioners and vested in the Treasurer, the object being to secure greater uniformity of administration. The rate of pension and date of commencement of the claim is fixed by the Treasurer and specified in the pensioner's pass-book

Moreover, when a claimant, although he has attained the statutory age of 65 years appears to be physically capable of earning or partly earning his living, a pension may be refused or fixed at a lower sum than 8s. As noted before, the total income of a pensioner in New South Wales may reach 20s., that is 10s. over and above a full pension; but in Victoria, the limit of a pensioner's income from all sources is 8s., although, subject to certain conditions, he was allowed, under the original Act, to earn a sum which, with his pension, would amount to 10s. in all. The power to increase the pension was, however, taken away by the Amending Act. The statutory maximum of pension is diminished by 6d. per week for every £10 of savings accumulated by the claimant, or by the value of the board and lodging which he may receive; the value of such board and lodging, however, may be taken at any sum not exceeding 5s. per week. Proceedings to obtain an old-age pension are usually in open court, but the Commissioners dealing with the claim may dispense with the personal attendance of the claimant where the latter is physically unfit, or where the claim is one that obviously should be granted. The Commissioners may not now determine the rate of pension and the manner of payment, but must forward particulars of each case to the Registrar, and no pass-book may be issued to any claimant except by authority of the Treasurer. Relatives —if the father, mother, brother, sister, or child of the claimant—are required to assist in the maintenance of the pensioner, where their means are sufficient to allow them to do so, and they may be brought before the Commissioners' Court to prove their inability to contribute to the maintenance of the pensioner to whom they are said to be related. An important section in the 1903 Act is that providing for the gradual reduction of the total sum paid in old-age pensions to £150,000 a year. The Bill does not, however, propose to affect existing pensioners' rights. The average rate of pension, when the maximum was 10s., came to 7s. 5½d. The present average is 6s. 8d., or a difference of 9½d. The expenditure on old-age pensions in Victoria for the financial year ending June, 1902, was £292,342, and for the year 1903, £215,754, or about £76,000 less. At the end of 1901 the number of old-age pensioners was 16,233. In November, 1903, the total had fallen to 12,067.

It will be seen that, whereas in New South Wales and New Zealand the old-age pension is a gift by the state to citizens who have contributed by taxation, and who, as the preamble to the New South Wales Act declares, have during the prime of life helped to bear the public burthens of the state by the payment of taxes, and by opening up its resources by their labour and skill, in Victoria the pension partakes more of the nature of a charitable dole. It is easy to understand, therefore, how it is that in New South Wales there are 22,884 persons who are in receipt of pensions, and in New Zealand 12,481, while in Victoria the number is only 12,067, although the persons of 65 years and upwards in Victoria number 67,200, compared with 49,000 in New South Wales and 33,500 in New Zealand.

The estimated number of persons of 65 years and upwards in Australasia was, at the beginning of 1904, 189,700, of whom 156,200 resided in the Commonwealth and 33,500 in New Zealand. These figures are deduced from the census returns and are probably in excess of the truth, as a large number of persons, in anticipation of the establishment of a general system of old-age pensions, described themselves as over 65 years of age, though in reality they had not reached that age. However, accepting the figures as they stand, the following are the numbers in the various states of the Commonwealth :—

New South Wales	49,000
Victoria	67,200
Queensland	13,300
South Australia	15,200
Western Australia	4,200
Tasmania	7,300
	156,200

Proposals have been made from time to time for the Commonwealth Government to institute a system of old-age pensions applicable to persons resident in any of the states, an objection to the present state system being that residence of twenty years in the case of Victoria and of twenty-five years in the case of New South Wales is a condition precedent to the granting of a pension. There are a large number of persons who have been twenty-five years in Australia but whose time has been spent in two or more states and who, therefore, would not under any state system likely to be put into operation be entitled to a state pension. These persons would be eligible under a federal system to receive pensions in virtue of their residence in Australia.

The proportion of the 156,200 persons of 65 years and upwards now in the Commonwealth, who were born or have resided for twenty-five years in Australia, is probably about 87 per cent., and the proportion qualified to receive a pension about 42 per cent., so that if a federal pension scheme had been in operation on 1st January, 1904, there would have been 65,600 pensioners over 65 years of age. The cost of this scheme, according to the New South Wales rates, would be £1,568,000 per annum, and according to the New Zealand rates, £1,112,000. The New South Wales system, as before stated, provides for pensions to persons between the ages of 60 and 65 years, incapacitated, by reason of physical infirmity from earning their livelihood. If provision were to be made by the Commonwealth for such persons according to the New South Wales scale, the cost of the pension system would be about £1,735,000. The pension payments will not tend to increase very rapidly, as the experience of both New South Wales and New Zealand shows that the pension was not larger in 1904 than in the first year after the system was established.

CRIME.

In all the states proceedings against a person accused of an offence may be initiated either by the arrest of the culprit or by summoning him to appear before a magistrate. Serious offences, of course, are rarely dealt with by process of summons; but, on the other hand, it is not uncommon for a person to be apprehended on a very trivial charge, and this circumstance should not be forgotten in dealing with arrests by the police, which are unusually numerous in some of the states. Unfortunately, it is not easy to say how far the police of one state are disposed to treat offenders with such consideration as to proceed against them by summons, and how far those of another state are content to adopt similar action; for in most of the provinces the records do not draw a distinction between the two classes of cases; and in the table given on page 459, showing the number of persons charged before magistrates in each state during the year 1901, offenders who were summoned to appear are included with those arrested, except in the case of Victoria, whose criminal statistics seem to deal only with arrests. It is likewise difficult to make a true comparison between the various states in the matter of the prevalence of crime, for there are a number of circumstances which must considerably affect the criminal returns and modify their meaning. The first of these, of course, is the question of the strength of the police force and its ability to cope with lawlessness, which must be decided chiefly by the proportion of undetected crime which takes place in the states. The policy adopted by the chief of police in regard to trivial breaches of the public peace and other minor offences against good order must also be taken into consideration; and then there are considerable differences between the criminal codes of the states, and in the number of local enactments, breaches of which form a large proportion of the minor offences taken before the Courts. Also, when the returns of the lower Courts are laid aside and the convictions in superior Courts taken up, the comparison is affected by the jurisdiction of the magistrates who committed the prisoners. In New South Wales, for example, the jurisdiction of the lower Courts is limited to imprisonment for six months, except in regard to cases brought under one or two Acts of Parliament, such as the Chinese Restriction Act, prosecutions under which are very few; while in Victoria a large number of persons are every year sentenced in Magistrates' Courts to imprisonment for terms ranging from six months to three years. It is apparent, therefore, that in any comparison drawn between the number of convictions in the superior Courts of New South Wales and of Victoria, the former state must appear to great disadvantage.

An investigation into the differences between the law of New South Wales and of Victoria in respect to the jurisdiction of magistrates discloses some important results. Under the Victorian Crimes Act of 1890, 54 Victoriæ No. 1,079, it is provided by section 67 that Justices may try persons under sixteen years of age for the offence of simple larceny or for any offence punishable as simple larceny no matter what the value of the property in question may be, and persons over sixteen years of age where the property said to have been stolen is not of greater value than £2; and it is further provided by the same section that if upon the hearing of such a charge the Justices shall be of opinion that there are circumstances in the case which render it inexpedient to inflict any punishment, they shall have power to dismiss the charge without proceeding to a conviction. This provision, it is needless to say, is likely to reduce materially the number of convictions for larceny in Victoria. In New South Wales, on the other hand, the law does not give Justices any such power. In every case where the offence is proved they must convict the accused person, although in the case of offenders under the age of sixteen years they may discharge the convicted person on his making restitution, or in other cases deal with him under the First Offenders' Act and suspend the sentence; but in all such cases the conviction is placed on record and is accounted for in the criminal statistics of the state. Section 69 of the same Victorian Act gives Justices power to deal with any case of simple larceny, or of larceny as a clerk or servant, or of stealing from the person, when the accused pleads guilty, the punishment being imprisonment for any term not exceeding twelve months; while in New South Wales the law does not give Justices the power to deal with such cases when the property alleged to have been stolen exceeds the value of £20. This section must therefore tend materially to reduce the number of cases committed for trial in Victoria for the offences mentioned, although in all such cases the Justices may commit the accused person if they think fit to do so. Furthermore, it is provided by section 370 of the Crimes Act of 1890 that suspected persons who have been convicted of capital or transportable felony elsewhere and are found in Victoria may be arrested and sentenced to imprisonment for three years in the case of a male, and for one year in the case of a female. Such a protective provision is in force in some of the other provinces as well as in Victoria, and its absence in New South Wales has made that state the chosen refuge of many of the criminals of the other states; for there they may lay their plots in peace and enjoy immunity from arrest until the police discover some proof of their complicity in fresh crime or can charge them with being in possession of property which may reasonably be regarded as having been stolen. It is not, however, only in respect to serious offences that the law of Victoria differs from that of New South Wales, for under the Victorian Police Offences Act of 1890 drunkenness in itself is no crime, and must be allied with disorderly conduct before the person may be punished. These statements all go to show in what important respects the criminal statistics of the states must differ from each other, and how great care must be taken in making comparisons.

The number of persons arrested during the year 1901, together with the proportion per 10,000 of the population for four of the

Commonwealth states, is given below. The returns from the other states do not show apprehensions separately.

State.	No. of Arrests.	Per 10,000 of Population.
New South Wales	28,112	205
Victoria	29,039	241
Queensland	18,373	364
Tasmania	1,896	109

Taking into consideration only the more serious crimes, such as offences against the person and against property, including forgery, the rates for New South Wales, Victoria, and Tasmania, were respectively 39, 28, and 28 per 10,000 of the population.

During the year 1901, so far as can be gathered, 164,524 persons were charged before magistrates in Australasia, 129,044 being summarily convicted and 31,862 discharged, while 3,618 were committed. The returns of each of the Commonwealth states and New Zealand will be found below. It should be explained that in the case of New Zealand and Western Australia each charge is counted as a separate person—a proceeding which, of course, tells against those provinces; while in Victoria the returns only deal with arrested persons, no record being published of the summons cases dealt with in that state :—

State.	Persons charged.	Summarily dealt with.		Committed.
		Discharged.	Convicted.	
New South Wales	58,681	8,457	48,962	1,262
Victoria	29,039	8,801	19,614	624
Queensland	23,920	3,573	19,844	503
South Australia	6,227	1,015	5,000	212
Western Australia	15,333	4,263	10,829	241
Tasmania	5,499	963	4,469	67
Commonwealth	138,699	27,072	108,718	2,909
New Zealand	25,825	4,790	20,326	709
Australasia	164,524	31,862	129,044	3,618

Taking the whole of Australasia, rather more than thirty-five persons out of every thousand were charged before magistrates during the year 1901—a figure which compares favourably with the rates for previous years. Only three states—Western Australia, Queensland, and New South Wales—exceed the average amount of disorder and crime as disclosed by the police court returns. The very large proportion of adult males to the population of the first-named state, and its present industrial conditions, place it, of course, in quite an exceptional position; while in Queensland and New South Wales there are greater floating populations, from the ranks of which a large percentage of offenders is drawn, than in the other states which have better records.

The province with the least disorder and crime is South Australia, where the persons answering to charges in the lower Courts only form 17·15 per thousand of the population. Next come Victoria with 24·14 per thousand; Tasmania, with 31·68; and New Zealand, with 33·14; while, as before stated, Western Australia, Queensland, and New South Wales have the highest proportions, namely, 71·27, 47·42, and 42·77 per thousand respectively. In the case of Western Australia, the returns leave little doubt that there has been a large influx of criminals from the eastern states, because the rate is over 50 per cent. higher than that of Queensland, the next state. The rate is, however, unduly increased by including the charges brought against the aborigines, and also from the fact that as stated before, each offence is counted as a separate person; but in the absence of any exact statistical information, there is no option but to use the figures presented. In New South Wales and Victoria, about every ninety persons charged are accused of 100 offences, and assuming the same ratio to hold in Western Australia, it is estimated that if these two mentioned factors were excluded, the rate in Western Australia would be about 64 per 1,000. The New Zealand rate is also affected by the last-mentioned circumstance. The following table shows the proportion of persons charged before magistrates in each state during the year; also the percentages of the persons discharged, convicted, and committed of the whole number charged:—

State.	Persons charged per 1,000 of Population.	Percentages of total persons charged.			
		Discharged.	Convicted.	Summarily dealt with.	Committed.
New South Wales	42·77	14·41	83·44	97·85	2·15
Victoria	24·14	30·31	67·54	97·85	2·15
Queensland	47·42	14·94	82·96	97·90	2·10
South Australia	17·15	16·30	80·30	96·60	3·40
Western Australia	71·27	27·80	70·63	98·43	1·57
Tasmania	31·68	17·51	81·27	98·78	1·22
Commonwealth	35·69	19·52	78·38	97·90	2·10
New Zealand	33·14	18·55	78·71	97·26	2·74
Australasia	35·05	19·37	78·43	97·80	2·20

It will be seen from the above table that out of every hundred persons charged before magistrates in Australasia in 1901, 97·80 were summarily dealt with, 19·37 being discharged and 78·43 convicted, while only 2·20 were committed to higher courts. The state with the highest percentage of cases summarily disposed of and the smallest proportion of committals was Tasmania; while Victoria, although the magistrates there have a much wider jurisdiction, showed an equal proportion of cases summarily dealt with to New South Wales. This was without doubt due to the fact that, as already pointed out, summons cases, which usually cover minor offences, are not included in the criminal statistics of the first-mentioned state. As a matter of fact, the Victorian returns should show a very high percentage of cases summarily disposed of; for an inspection of the statistics discloses the fact that, owing to this wider jurisdiction, the magistracy of the state, in 1901, sentenced 15 persons to two years' imprisonment, 67 to periods between one year and two years, and 421 to terms of six months and under one year. Many of these persons, had they been tried in New South Wales, would have been convicted in higher courts. Another important point to be noted is that Victoria and Western Australia have by far the largest proportion of discharges, and if the theory be dismissed as untenable that the police in those states are more prone to charge persons on insufficient grounds than in the other states, it must be concluded that the magistrates of Victoria and Western Australia deal more leniently with accused persons than is the case elsewhere; indeed, so far as Victoria is concerned, it has already been shown that the Crimes Act of 1890 provides for the discharge without conviction of persons found guilty of certain offences. The lowest proportion of discharges is to be found in New South Wales and Queensland, which also have the highest percentage of summary convictions; and the figures testify to the stringency with which the criminal laws are administered in those states.

Of the 164,524 persons brought before magistrates during the year 1901, only 26,842 were charged with offences which can fairly be classed as criminal, the overwhelming majority being accused of drunkenness and other offences against good order, and of breaches of Acts of Parliament, which have a tendency to multiply to a great extent. For present purposes the accused persons may be divided as in the table given below, offences against the person and against property being regarded as serious crime. Of course, amongst the other offenders are to be found a few charged with grave misdemeanours, but against these may be put trifling assaults, which are included with crimes against the person :—

State.	All Offenders.	Serious Offenders.			Minor Offenders.
		Against the Person.	Against Property.	Total.	
New South Wales	58,681	4,032	5,575	9,607	49,074
Victoria	29,039	993	2,409	3,402	25,637
Queensland	23,920	1,846	2,547	4,393	19,527
South Australia	6,227	434	712	1,146	5,081
Western Australia	15,333	1,040	1,615	2,655	12,678
Tasmania	5,499	341	664	1,005	4,494
Commonwealth	138,699	8,686	13,522	22,208	116,491
New Zealand	25,825	1,586	3,048	4,634	21,191
Australasia	164,524	10,272	16,570	26,842	137,682

This examination into the nature of the offences explains in some measure the comparatively unfavourable position of New South Wales as shown by the previous tables; for of the 58,681 accused persons in that state, the minor offenders numbered 49,074, or 83·6 per cent. No doubt the large number of trivial cases in New South Wales is accounted for by the greater strictness of police administration. Victoria shows 88·3 per cent. of minor offenders, but in consequence of a difference in the tabulation of the returns its position is not nearly so favourable as it appears to be on the surface. In New South Wales, and, it is to be presumed, in most of the other states, a person accused of two or more offences is entered as charged with the most serious in the eyes of the law; while in Victoria he is entered as charged with the first offence committed, any others, however serious, arising out of his capture, being left out of consideration. For example, if a person is arrested for drunkenness, and he assaults his captors while on the way to the station, he is entered in the returns of New South Wales, as they are here presented, as charged with an offence against the person, and thereby helps to swell the amount of serious crime; but in Victoria he is entered as charged with drunkenness and disorderly conduct, and the charge of assault, on which he may be convicted and sentenced to a term of imprisonment, is not disclosed. This fact must therefore be taken into account in comparing the proportions of the various classes of offenders per thousand of population, which are appended :—

State.	Per 1,000 of Population.				
	All Offenders.	Serious Offenders.			Minor Offenders.
		Against the Person.	Against Property.	Total.	
New South Wales	42·77	2·94	4·06	7·00	35·77
Victoria	24·14	0·83	2·C0	2·83	21·31
Queensland	47·42	3·66	5·05	8·71	38·71
South Australia	17·15	1·20	1·96	3·16	13·99
Western Australia	71·27	4·83	7·51	12·34	58·93
Tasmania	31·68	1·97	3·82	5·79	25·89
Commonwealth	35·69	2·23	3·48	5·71	29·98
New Zealand	33·14	2·04	3·91	5·95	27·19
Australasia	35·05	2·19	3·53	5·72	29·33

It will be seen that, relatively to population, the state with the largest number of serious offenders was Western Australia, which had a proportion of 12·34 per thousand. Queensland followed with a proportion of 8·71, while New South Wales and Tasmania occupied third and fourth positions with 7·00 and 5·79 per thousand respectively. The rate of New Zealand was 5·95 per thousand, while that of South Australia is set down at 3·16, and Victoria closes the list with 2·83. It would be interesting to compare the crime of the principal states on the basis of the number of males of such ages as contribute to the ranks of offenders; but the records unfortunately do not give sufficient data to enable such a comparison to be made. In explanation of the position of Western Australia, it is well known to the police of Victoria and New South Wales—and, indeed, the fact is proved by the records of the prisoners received into Fremantle gaol—that a large number of criminals have left those states for the west during the last few years.

About two-fifths of the minor offenders of Australasia are charged with drunkenness. From the table given below it will be seen that in all the states 64,036 cases of drunkenness were heard during the year 1901, convictions being recorded in 56,883 cases, or 88·83 per cent. of the total number. The state with the highest number of cases relatively to population was Queensland, the rate of which was 19·02 per thousand persons, followed by Western Australia with 15·56, New South Wales with 15·39, and Victoria with 14·43, while Tasmania was last with a rate of only 4·28 per thousand. The figures for Victoria, however, only refer to apprehensions, information respecting persons summoned to answer a charge of drunkenness not being available, while, as already pointed out, drunkenness in itself is not a crime in that state, but must be aggravated by disorderly conduct. In the case of Western Australia, it must be remembered that the proportion of adult male population is very high. From the figures showing the number of convictions, it will be seen that the magistrates of Victoria take a somewhat lenient view of this offence, and only record convictions in about 62 per cent. of the cases, while in the other states the percentage ranges from 94·9 to 99·8:—

State.	Charges of Drunkenness.	Convictions.		Per 1,000 Persons.	
		Total.	Percentage of Charges.	Charges.	Convictions.
New South Wales	21,123	21,005	99·44	15·39	15·31
Victoria	17,360	10,846	62·48	14·43	9·02
Queensland	9,791	9,773	99·82	19·02	18·99
South Australia	2,049	2,011	98·14	5·64	5·54
Western Australia	3,348	3,237	96·68	15·56	15·05
Tasmania	743	705	94·88	4·28	4·06
Commonwealth	54,414	47,577	87·43	14·00	12·24
New Zealand	9,622	9,306	96·72	12·35	11·94
Australasia	64,036	56,883	88·83	13·64	12·12

A return showing only the number of cases of drunkenness is not, however, a safe index of the abuse of alcoholic liquors, for a great deal depends on the state of the law and the manner in which it is administered, and it is evident that the maintenance of the law intended to preserve public decency will always be less strict in sparsely-settled country districts than in larger centres of population where the police are comparatively more numerous, if not in proportion to the population, at least in proportion to the area they have under their supervision; and further, will vary according to the diverse nature of the duties performed by the police. The quantity of intoxicants consumed per head is another index of the habits of communities living under like conditions; but comparisons so based should not be pushed to extremes, for, as has often been pointed out, the larger part of the alcohol which enters into consumption is that consumed by the population who are not drunkards. The average quantity of intoxicants used in each state during the three years ended 1902, is given below, wines and beer being reduced to their equivalent of proof spirit. The consumption of the various kinds of intoxicants will be found in the chapter on "Food Supply and Cost of Living":—

State.	Proof Gallons of Alcohol per head population.
New South Wales	2·44
Victoria	2·74
Queensland	2·57
South Australia	1·95
Western Australia	5·13
Tasmania	1·75
Commonwealth	2·61
New Zealand	2·00
Australasia	2·50

The strength of the police force in each of the states and New Zealand at the end of 1901 is given below. These figures show the importance which must be attached to police administration when studying the question of drunkenness.

State.	Police.			Inhabitants to each Police Officer.	Area to each Constable in Country Districts.
	Metropolitan.	Country.	Total.		
	No.	No.	No.	No.	Sq. miles.
New South Wales	909	1,263	2,172	635	246
Victoria	806	709	1,515	798	124
Queensland	217	640	857	596	1,044
South Australia	171	200	371	983	4,517
Western Australia	155	357	512	381	2,734
Tasmania	60	195	255	683	134
Commonwealth	2,318	3,364	5,682	675	883
New Zealand	105	521	626	1,258	200
Australasia	2,423	3,885	6,308	732	792

A comparison of the cost of the police forces of the various states will be found below. The greater number of mounted troopers in those states where very large and thinly-populated districts have to be controlled, tends to make the average cost somewhat higher than in the other provinces :—

State.	Total Cost of Police Force.	Average Cost per Constable.	Average Cost per Inhabitant.
	£	£ s. d.	£ s. d.
New South Wales	400,947	184 12 0	0 5 10
Victoria	271,561	179 5 0	0 4 6
Queensland	170,873	199 7 8	0 6 8
South Australia	84,874	228 15 5	0 4 8
Western Australia	123,724	241 12 11	0 12 8
Tasmania	37,806	148 5 2	0 4 4
Commonwealth	1,089,785	191 15 11	0 5 8
New Zealand	120,629	192 14 0	0 4 0
Australasia	1,210,414	191 17 8	0 5 2

The record of cases heard before a Court of Magistrates cannot be regarded as altogether a trustworthy indication of the social progress of Australasia, because, as has been pointed out, it includes many kinds of offences which cannot fairly be classed as criminal, and the number of these has a tendency to increase with the increase of local enactments. The committals for trial, taken in conjunction with the convictions for crime in the Superior Courts may be regarded as much more conclusive on the question of the progress of society or the reverse. In some respects even this evidence is misleading, for, as already shown, in the less populous provinces there are no Courts intermediary between the Magistrates' and the Supreme Courts, so that many offences which in New South Wales, for example, are tried by a jury, are in some of the other provinces dealt with by magistrates; and even in Victoria, where there are Courts of General Sessions, magistrates have a much wider jurisdiction than in New South Wales. But for the purpose of showing the decrease of serious crime in Australasia as a whole, the proportion of committals and of convictions in Superior Courts may fairly be taken; and this information is given below. It will be seen that during the forty-one years, from 1861 to 1901, the rate of committals per thousand of population has dropped from 2·2 to 0·8, and of convictions from 1·3 to 0·4 :—

Year.	Per 1,000 of Population.	
	Committals.	Convictions in Superior Courts.
1861	2·2	1·3
1871	1·4	0·8
1881	1·2	0·7
1891	1·1	0·6
1901	0·8	0·4

In noting these facts and comparing the results with those obtained in Great Britain during the same period, it must not be forgotten that some of the provinces of Australasia have been compelled gradually to reform a portion of their original population, and that in the case of states such as Victoria and Queensland, not originally peopled in any degree by convicts, the attractions of the gold-fields have drawn within their borders a population by no means free from criminal instincts and antecedents. Viewed in this light, the steady progress made cannot but be regarded as exceedingly satisfactory, and the expectation may not unreasonably be entertained that the same improvement will be continued until the ratio of crime to population will compare favourably with that of any part of the world.

Below will be found the number of convictions in the Superior Courts of each state, at decennial periods from 1861 to 1901 :—

State.	1861.	1871.	1881.	1891.	1901.
New South Wales	437	628	1,066	964	730
Victoria	846	511	332	729	393
Queensland	24	91	92	232	285
South Australia	62	91	213	90	134
Western Australia	35	65	61	44	162
Tasmania	127	74	51	63	39
Commonwealth	1,531	1,460	1,815	2,122	1,743
New Zealand	100	162	270	276	328
Australasia	1,631	1,622	2,085	2,398	2,071

The following table gives a classification of the offences for which the accused persons were convicted during 1901 ; also the rate of convictions and of committals per 1,000 of population. It will be seen that the rate of convictions in the Superior Courts of Victoria is 0·33 per thousand ; but if the persons who received sentences of over six months' imprisonment at the hands of magistrates were taken into account, the proportion would be as high as that of most of the other states. Tasmania and South Australia for the period in question show a smaller proportion of convictions in Superior Courts than Victoria; but in those two provinces, as already pointed out, no intermediate Courts exist:—

State.	Convictions in Superior Courts.					Committals per 1,000 of Population.
	Classification of Offences.			All Convictions.	Per 1,000 of Population.	
	Against the Person.	Against Property.	Other.			
New South Wales	179	513	38	730	0·53	0·92
Victoria	106	273	14	393	0·33	0·52
Queensland	70	195	20	285	0·57	1·00
South Australia	21	110	3	134	0·37	0·58
Western Australia	49	103	10	162	0·75	1·12
Tasmania	11	16	12	39	0·22	0·39
Commonwealth	436	1,210	97	1,743	0·45	0·75
New Zealand	91	213	24	328	0·43	0·91
Australasia	527	1,423	121	2,071	0·44	0·77

There is no doubt that New South Wales would appear to much greater advantage in a comparison of crime statistics if there existed in that state any law preventing the entrance of criminals, such as is rigidly enforced in most of the other provinces. That there is ground for this assertion is shown by the fact that whereas in New South Wales offenders born in the state only formed 42 per cent. of the total apprehensions in 1901, in Victoria 47 per cent. of arrested persons were of local birth; while at the census of 1901 the element of the population of local birth was fairly equal, being 72·1 per cent. for New South Wales and 72·9 for Victoria. In July, 1903, a bill was introduced into the New South Wales Parliament to prevent the influx of habitual criminals into the state, and will probably be passed into law during the session of 1904.

The punishment of death is very seldom resorted to except in cases of murder, though formerly such was not the case. Thus the number of executions steadily declined from 151 during the decade 1841–50 to 66 during the ten years 1881–90. In South Australia the extreme penalty has been most sparingly inflicted, there having been only 11 executions in the thirty years which closed with 1901. The following table shows the number of executions in each province during each decade of the 50 years ended 1890, also those which took place in 1891–95 and 1896–1900. Queensland was incorporated with

New South Wales until the end of 1859, though Victoria became a separate colony in 1851. It will be noticed that the returns are defective so far as Western Australia is concerned:—

State.	1841-1850.	1851-1860.	1861-1870.	1871-1880.	1881-1890.	1891-1895.	1896-1900.	1901.
New South Wales	68	38	34	27	23	15	7	3
Queensland			14	18	15	16	1	5
Victoria		47	41	19	13	12	4	......
South Australia	......	7	12	6	2	2	1	......
Western Australia	......	......	......	......	......	6	10	......
Tasmania	83	32	15	3	5	1	...	......
New Zealand	......	......	......	12	8	1	5	1
Total	151	124	116	85	66	53	28	9

The returns relating to the prisons of the states are in some cases very incomplete. The prisoners in confinement at any specified time may be divided into those who have been tried and sentenced, those who are awaiting their trial, and debtors. The returns of five of the states allow of this distinction being made. The number and classification of prisoners in confinement on the 31st December, 1901, were as follow:—

State.	Tried and Sentenced.	Awaiting Trial.	Debtors.	Total.
New South Wales	1,696	116	2	1,814
Victoria	1,082	68	....	1,150
Queensland	624	32	1	657
South Australia	231*	7	....	238
Western Australia	451	32	....	483
New Zealand	661	52	....	713
Total	4,745	307	3	5,055

* Including debtors.

The returns of Tasmania do not enable the distinction made in the above table to be drawn, but there were 117 prisoners in Tasmanian gaols at the end of 1901; so that the total number of persons in confinement in the gaols of Australasia, at the close of 1901, may be stated as 5,172, equal to 1·15 in every thousand of the population.

Law and Crime.

The cost of the administration of justice, the police, and the penal services of the Commonwealth during the last five years was at the rate of £1,826,388 per annum or 9s. 9d. per inhabitant. This large sum is made up of £569,494 for the administration of justice, £226,070 for

prisons, and £1,030,824 for police. For each of these five years the expenditure was :—

Year.	Justice.	Prisons.	Police.
	£	£	£
1898	542,948	224,933	960,149
1899	558,617	231,943	1,007,642
1900	567,074	220,901	1,028,210
1901	587,447	226,615	1,068,232
1902	591,391	225,960	1,089,785

The expenditure varies greatly in the different states, the range per inhabitant being from 6s. 10d. in Tasmania to 22s. 1d. in Western Australia. The distribution of the expenditure for 1902 amongst the six States was :—

State.	Justice.	Prisons.	Police.	Total.
	£	£	£	£
New South Wales	234,428	101,370	400,947	736,745
Victoria	179,136	51,948	271,561	502,645
Queensland	76,046	26,322	170,873	273,241
South Australia	29,512	15,772	84,874	130,158
Western Australia	53,667	24,869	123,724	202,260
Tasmania	18,592	5,679	37,806	62,077
Total	591,381	225,960	1,089,785	1,907,126

The expenditure per inhabitant in each state, and in the Commonwealth, for the year 1902 was as follows :—

State.	Justice.			Prisons.			Police.			Total.		
	£	s.	d.	£	s.	d.	£	s.	d.	£	s.	d.
New South Wales	0	3	4	0	1	6	0	5	9	0	10	7
Victoria	0	3	0	0	0	10	0	4	6	0	8	4
Queensland	0	3	0	0	1	0	0	6	8	0	10	8
South Australia	0	1	7	0	0	10	0	4	8	0	7	1
Western Australia	0	5	6	0	2	7	0	12	8	1	0	9
Tasmania	0	2	1	0	0	8	0	4	4	0	7	1
Total	0	3	1	0	1	2	0	5	8	0	9	11

It will be seen that, in proportion to population, the total cost, as well as the expenditure per head on each service, was much higher in Western Australia than in any of the other states. This of course is only to be expected, if regard be paid to the peculiar industrial conditions of that state, and also to the fact that the provision for efficient police protection must necessarily entail a heavy expenditure in a large and sparsely-peopled country.

SUICIDES.

The total number of persons who committed suicide in Australasia during 1902 was 531—462 males and 69 females—corresponding to a rate of 1·13 per 10,000 living. The table below shows the number of deaths and the rates in each state, in five-year periods since 1870. It is believed that the actual number of suicides is even larger than is shown in the tables, especially during recent years; for there is a growing disposition on the part of coroners' juries to attribute to accident what is really the result of an impulse of self-destruction.

TOTAL NUMBER of Deaths.

State.	1871-75.	1876-80.	1881-85.	1886-90.	1891-95.	1896-1900	1901-2.
New South Wales	212	297	368	578	713	874	270
Victoria	446	505	463	638	630	565	255
Queensland	72	141	179	292	349	400	195
South Australia ..	79	93	146	134	156	192	78
Western Australia	3*	7	23	22	73	157	89
Tasmania............	28	37	27	43	63	63	18
New Zealand	89*	195	261	267	339	340	159
Australasia...	......	1,275	1,467	1,974	2,323	2,591	1,064

DEATH RATE per 10,000 living.

State.	1871-75.	1876-80.	1881-85.	1886-90.	1891-95.	1896-1900	1901-2.
New South Wales	·78	·90	·87	1·12	1·19	1·33	0·98
Victoria	1·17	1·23	1·02	1·21	1·08	0·95	1·06
Queensland...	1·00	1·38	1·33	1·62	1·69	1·71	1·92
South Australia ...	·81	·77	·99	·87	·92	1·07	1·07
Western Australia	·29*	·50	1·46	1·05	2·25	1·99	2·27
Tasmania............	·54	·68	·44	·63	·85	0·79	0·52
New Zealand	·72*	·91	·99	·89	1·03	0·92	1·01
Australasia...	......	1·02	·98	1·12	1·16	1·18	1·15

* Four years—1872-75.

Speaking generally, the experience of Australasia agrees with that of other countries, namely, that the tendency to self-destruction is increasing. From the table above it is seen that the rate slowly but steadily advanced from 1870 up till the end of 1900, but the results for the last two years show a slight falling off. Tasmania has always had the lowest rate, while in New Zealand the rate is slightly above that in England, where it is 0·92 per 10,000 living. Up to 1893, the three first named states in the table exhibited the highest rates, Queensland coming first; but since that year Western Australia has shown the largest proportional number of victims by suicide, due, no doubt, to the relatively large number of males in the state, since males are three or four times as prone to take their own lives as females.

The means of committing suicide most favoured in all the states, are poisoning, drowning, shooting, which is more common now than formerly, and hanging amongst males, and poisoning and drowning amongst females.

ILLEGITIMACY.

Illegitimate births are rather numerous in these states, the total number in the whole of Australasia during 1902 being 6,901, equal to 5·59 per cent. of the total births. A comparison of the results for the last two years shows that in 1902 the rates decreased in New South Wales, Victoria, and New Zealand, while the other states showed increases, the most remarkable being in the case of Tasmania, where the proportion advanced from 3·91 to 6·12 per 100 births. The following table shows the number of illegitimate births which have occurred in each state and New Zealand in quinquennial periods since 1875, and the proportion per cent. of total births :—

State.	1876–80.	1881–85.	1886–90.	1891–95.	1896–1900.	1901.	1902.
TOTAL NUMBER of Illegitimate Births.							
New South Wales	5,401	6,949	9,394	11,875	12,622	2,712	2,497
Victoria	5,646	6,491	8,425	9,858	8,625	1,729	1,677
Queensland	1,447	1,990	3,117	3,516	4,213	848	859
South Australia	...	1,222	1,331	1,577	1,767	361	389
Western Australia	...	...	...	†402	1,133	222	247
Tasmania	...	*762	911	1,136	1,322	193	311
New Zealand	2,027	2,831	3,011	3,443	4,196	937	921
Australasia	...	20,245	26,189	31,807	33,878	7,002	6,901
PROPORTION per cent. of Total Births.							
New South Wales	4·22	4·36	4·90	6·01	6·88	7·16	6·59
Victoria	4·27	4·63	4·89	5·45	5·57	5·57	5·55
Queensland	3·85	4·06	4·44	4·83	5·92	5·93	6·04
South Australia	...	2·16	2·50	2·98	3·76	3·96	4·35
Western Australia	...	...	...	†4·75	5·06	3·88	3·96
Tasmania	...	*4·35	3·84	4·58	5·65	3·91	6·11
New Zealand	2·30	2·93	3·20	3·77	4·43	4·57	4·46
Australasia	...	3·90	4·35	5·06	5·67	5·67	5·59

* Four years—1882-85. † Four years—1892-95.

It is seen that New South Wales has always been in the unenviable position of exhibiting the highest proportion of illegitimate births, although up to 1890 it was closely followed by Victoria. Since 1890, however, the rate in New South Wales has increased very rapidly, as also in Queensland. Tasmania showed the second highest proportion in 1902 with 6·11 per cent., a remarkable increase on the figure for the previous year, which stood at 3·91. In all the states illegitimacy is on the increase; and whereas less than twenty years ago each province had a lower rate than prevailed in England, they all, with the exception of South Australia, have now a higher rate.

The increase, however, is more apparent than real, since the general decline in the birth-rate affects the proportion of illegitimates. A proper comparison would be obtained by relating the number of illegitimate births to the number of unmarried women of child-bearing ages during the period. If this were done it would be found that illegitimacy is not increasing in Australia.

The following table shows the proportion of illegitimate births in the United Kingdom, and in the chief countries of Europe, based on the experience of the latest five years available, the figures referring, in most cases, to the period 1895-9. In a majority of the European countries illegitimacy appears to be on the increase.

Country.	Illegitimate Births per cent.	Country.	Illegitimate Births per cent.
England and Wales	4·15	Hungary	9·01
Scotland	6·97	France	8·26
Ireland	2·65	Belgium	8·51
Germany	9·21	Netherlands	2·71
Prussia	7·84	Sweden	10·80
Bavaria	14·00	Norway	7·35
Saxony	12·90	Italy	6·34
Austria	14·55		

Divorce.

The question of divorce is one of much interest to Australasia, as some of the states, especially New South Wales and Victoria, now offer great facilities for the dissolution of the marriage bond. The general opinion was that such facilities were calculated to increase divorce to an extent that would prove hurtful to public morals; and so far as the experience of New South Wales was concerned, for the first few years after the passing of the Act multiplying the grounds on which divorce could be granted, the fear did not seem to be altogether groundless; for in 1893 the number of decrees *nisi* granted rose to 305, from 102 in 1892, and in 1901 was still as high as 252. When, however, it is remembered that advantage would be taken of the change in law to dissolve marriages the bonds of which would have been broken long before under other circumstances, it is evident that there was little ground for the fear that this somewhat alarming increase would continue, and it was, therefore, not surprising to find a decline to 245 in 1902. In Victoria, where a very similar law came into operation in 1890, the number of divorces increased considerably, immediately after the passing of the Act, although not to the alarming extent experienced in New South Wales.

In New South Wales, under the Matrimonial Causes Act of 1873, the chief grounds on which divorce was granted were adultery after marriage on the part of the wife, and adultery with cruelty on the part of the husband. Under the Act of 1892 and the Amending Act passed in 1893 petitions for divorce can be granted for the following causes, in addition to those already mentioned:—*Husband v. Wife.*—Desertion for not less than three years; habitual drunkenness and neglect of domestic duties for a similar period; refusing to obey an order for restitution of conjugal rights; being imprisoned under sentence for three years or upwards; attempt to murder or inflict grievous bodily harm, or repeated assault on the husband within a year preceding the date of the filing of the petition. *Wife v. Husband.*—Adultery, provided that at the time of the institution of the suit the husband is domiciled in the state; desertion for not less than three years; habitual drunkenness with cruelty or neglect to support for a similar period; refusing to obey an order for restitution of conjugal rights; being imprisoned for three years or upwards, or having within five years undergone various sentences amounting in all to not less than three years; attempt to murder or assault with intent to inflict grievous bodily harm, or repeated assault within one year previously. Relief can only be sought on these grounds should the petitioner have been domiciled in the state for three years or upwards at the time of instituting the suit, and not have resorted to the state for the purpose of having the marriage dissolved. In Queensland, South Australia, Western Australia, Tasmania, and New Zealand, divorces are granted principally for adultery on the part of the wife, and adultery coupled with desertion for over two years on the part of the husband.

In the subjoined table will be found the actual number of divorces and judicial separations granted during each of the years 1895–1901. It will be seen that, taking the states as a whole, with the exception of that for 1898, the rate for 1900 is the lowest shown in the table:—

State.	1895.		1896.		1897.		1898.		1899.		1900.		1901.	
	Divorces.	Judicial Separations.	Divorces.	Judicial Separations.	Divorces.	Judicial Separations.	Divorces.	Judicial Separations.	Divorces.	Judicial Separations.	Divorces.	Judicial Separations.	Divorces.	Judicial Separations.
New South Wales	301	11	234	8	246	13	247	17	232	17	219	14	252	20
Victoria	85	..	106	2	117	..	87	..	105	2	93	..	83	..
Queensland	4	..	3	2	10	1	7	..	10	1	12	1	14	..
South Australia	5	..	6	1	3	..	7	1	11	..	7	1	6	..
Western Australia	2	..	1	..	4	..	3	..	8	..	16	..	12	1
Tasmania	4	1	3	..	5	..	4	..	4	..	4	..	11	..
New Zealand	18	5	36	2	33	1	32	2	46	16	85	3	103	1
Australasia	419	17	389	15	418	15	387	20	411	36	436	19	481	22
Totals	436		404		433		407		447		455		503	
Divorces and separations per 10,000 marriages	169·9		144·2		150·6		137·7		142·3		138·0		148·6	

The following table shows the number of decrees of dissolution of marriage and judicial separation granted in each state, in quinquennial periods since 1871, so far as it is possible to procure the information. Divorce was legalised in New South Wales in 1873, and the figures of that state for 1871–75 only cover the two years 1874 and 1875.

State.	1871-75.		1876-80.		1881-85.		1886-90.		1891-95.		1896-1901.	
	Divorces.	Judicial Separations.	Divorces.	Judicial Separations.	Divorces.	Judicial Separations.	Divorces.	Judicial Separations.	Divorces.	Judicial Separations.	Divorces.	Judicial Separations.
New South Wales	21	...	87	...	116	6	212	12	1087	55	1430	89
Victoria	33	6	41	2	74	8	124	9	441	10	591	4
Queensland	4	1	14	...	5	2	26	3	26	3	56	5
South Australia	22	3	35	2	31	10	23	2	30	2	40	3
Western Australia	...	...	1	1	5	...	8	...	9	...	39	1
Tasmania	9	...	9	...	9	...	15	2	21	2	31	...
New Zealand	*...	*...	*...	*...	*...	*..	110	5	101	14	335	25
Australasia	89	10	187	5	240	26	518	33	1715	86	2522	127

* Information not available.

Taking the figures given in the foregoing table, and comparing them with the number of marriages celebrated during the same periods, the rates of divorce for the individual states, per 10,000 marriages, will be found below. It will be seen that the rate for New South Wales is higher than that of any country of the world except the United States and Switzerland :—

State.	1871-75.	1876-80.	1881-85.	1886-90.	1891-95.	1896-1901.
New South Wales	†23·5	33·6	32·5	54·8	272·3	271·2
Victoria	16·0	16·9	24·4	31·1	119·6	124·8
Queensland	8·0	18·7	6·0	19·0	21·4	32·4
South Australia	33·5	34·6	33·1	24·3	29·9	32·5
Western Australia	...	20·5	44·8	53·5	38·6	41·3
Tasmania	27·4	22·0	18·0	35·4	50·8	44·7
New Zealand	*...	*...	*...	63·5	56·9	111·5

* Information not available. † 1874 and 1875 only.

From the appended statement, which sets forth the latest divorce rates of the countries for which accurate statistics are obtainable, such rates being calculated on an experience of ten years wherever possible, it will be seen that there is a larger proportion of marriages dissolved in Australasia than in any other part of the British Empire, but that the rate for these provinces as a whole is largely exceeded by a number of foreign countries. Of countries where divorce laws are in force, no reliable statistics are available for Denmark, Hungary, Russia, and Spain. In Italy and Portugal divorce is not recognised by law :—

Country.	Divorces per 10,000 Marriages.	Country.	Divorces per 10,000 Marriages.
Canadian Dominion ...	4	Cape Colony	98
United Kingdom	11	Netherlands	103
Norway	16	Germany	165
Austria Proper	43	France	180
Greece	50	Roumania	204
Belgium	81	Switzerland	432
Sweden	87	United States	612

In the United States of America no general system of registration of births, deaths, and marriages is in force. For the purpose of comparison, the marriage-rate of that country has been assumed to be 6·50 per 1,000 of mean population, and on that basis the 20,660 divorces granted annually during ten years would give an average of not less than 612 per 10,000 marriages.

In the Dominion of Canada divorce was, under the Union Act, assigned to the Federal Parliament; but those provinces which had established divorce courts before the accomplishment of federation were permitted to retain the jurisdiction which they already exercised. In the remaining provinces no divorce courts have been established since the constitution of the Dominion, and divorce can only be obtained by legislation, the matter being dealt with in each case as an ordinary private Act of Parliament, with this difference, however, that the Senate requires the production of such evidence in support of the application for relief as would be deemed sufficient in a court of law.

Insanity.

The number of insane persons in Australasia, under official cognizance in the various Government hospitals for the treatment of the insane, at the end of 1901 was 15,266, equal to 3·30 per 1,000 of the population, or corresponding to one insane person in about every 303. This rate is below that prevailing in England, where one person in every 298 is officially known to be insane.

An inspection of the table given below of the insane persons, both male and female, in each state and New Zealand on 31st December, 1901, and the rate per 1,000 inhabitants of each sex, will disclose the fact that the rate of insanity varies greatly in the different provinces, and that the rate for males is everywhere higher than that for females.

State.	Number of Insane.			Per 1,000 of Population.		
	Males.	Females.	Total Persons.	Males.	Females.	Total Persons.
New South Wales	2,684	1,804	4,488	3·71	2·74	3·25
Victoria	2,309	2,195	4,504	3·80	3·65	3·73
Queensland	1,091	656	1,747	3·84	2·90	3·42
South Australia	576	412	988	3·11	2·30	2·71
Western Australia	238	102	340	2·00	1·34	1·74
Tasmania	234	192	426	2·59	2·29	2·45
Commonwealth	7,132	5,361	12,493	3·55	2·94	3·26
New Zealand	1,654	1,119	2,773	3·99	3·00	3·52
Australasia	8,786	6,480	15,266	3·63	2·95	3·30

Victoria has the highest general rate, with 3·73 per 1,000, New Zealand coming next with 3·52, closely followed by Queensland with 3·42. Next comes New South Wales with 3·25; South Australia with 2·71; Tasmania with 2·45; while Western Australia shows the lowest proportion with 1·74 per 1,000. New Zealand shows the highest rate for males with 3·99 per thousand, followed by Queensland with 3·84; and Victoria with 3·65 per thousand has the largest proportion of females.

There is one remarkable difference between the Australasian states and Great Britain, namely, that in England the greater proportion of insanity is found amongst women, whereas in Australasia it is found amongst men.

In England the rate per 1,000 males in 1901 was 3·16, and per 1,000 females 3·54. In Australasia the greatest disproportion was in New Zealand, where the male and female rates were respectively 3·99 and 3·00 per 1,000. The smallest difference between the sexes is found in those states where the male population follow in greater proportion what may be termed the more settled pursuits. In Victoria the excess of the male over the female rate was only 0·15 and in Tasmania 0·30.

There seems to be little doubt that insanity is slowly but steadily increasing in the states, as it is in the United Kingdom and other countries. In England the rate has risen from 2·75 per 1,000 of population in 1879 to 3·36 in 1901, and in Scotland a similar rise has taken place from 2·75 per 1,000 in 1884 to 3·49 in 1901. In Ireland the rate has risen from 2·50 per 1,000 of the population in 1880 to 4·87 per 1,000 in 1901. The greater part of this increase is no doubt rightly attributed to an improvement in the administration of the Commissioners in Lunacy, by which a more accurate knowledge of the number of cases existent in the country has been gained; but the steady growth of the rate in recent years, when statistical information has been brought to a high pitch of perfection, plainly points to the fact that the advance of civilisation, with the increasing strain to which the struggle for existence is subjecting body and mind, has one of its results in the growth of insanity. In all the states of Australasia, with the sole exception of Tasmania, there is seen the same state of affairs as the insanity returns of Great Britain disclose, although the conditions of life press much more lightly on the individual here.

The experience of the various states is fairly represented in the following table, which shows the average number of insane in each state per 1,000 of population, arranged in three five-years periods:—

State.	1887–91. Rate per 1,000 of Population.	1892–96. Rate per 1,000 of Population.	1897–1901. Rate per 1,000 of Population.
New South Wales	2·75	2·89	3·14
Victoria	3·34	3·47	3·69
Queensland	2·66	3·12	3·39
South Australia	2·50	2·59	2·71
Western Australia	3·02	1·68	1·47
Tasmania	2·48	2·37	2·32
Commonwealth	2·92	3·03	3·19
New Zealand	2·85	3·05	3·41
Australasia	2·90	3·04	3·23

The only states where the rate is diminishing are Western Australia and Tasmania. In Western Australia the hospital accommodation is limited, and thereby many insane, especially males, doubtless escape notice.

It has been said that the trade depression experienced a few years ago throughout Australasia, was the cause of an increase in insanity; and at first sight it looks as if this were so, because since 1892 there has been a steady increase in the proportion of the population detained in asylums. But looking at the rates of admissions this view does not seem to be altogether borne out. Probably one effect of depressed times is to send to the asylums a number of harmless but demented persons who, under other circumstances, would be supported by their relatives. In England and Wales it is found that the increase in insanity has taken place amongst those who are termed the "pauper" class—that is, those whose relatives are not in a position to support them after they lose their reason. On the other hand, the admissions in prosperous times are kept up by insanity either directly or indirectly induced by the indulgence which commonly follows high wages and large gains.

The following table shows the average annual number of admissions and readmissions into the asylums in each state, and the rate per 1,000 of population, during each of the two quinquennial periods 1892–96 and 1897–1901:—

State.	1892–96.		1897–1901.	
	Average Number of Admissions per annum.	Rate per 1,000 of Population.	Average Number of Admissions per annum.	Rate per 1,000 of Population.
New South Wales	704	0·57	785	0·58
Victoria	685	0·58	752	0·63
Queensland	256	0·60	318	0·66
South Australia	218	0·63	217	0·61
Western Australia	49	0·55	115	0·64
Tasmania	61	0·40	70	0·40
Commonwealth	1,973	0·57	2,257	0·60
New Zealand	464	0·75	573	0·76
Australasia	2,437	0·59	2,830	0·63

The table shows that the rate of admissions has advanced slightly during the decade, and that while there has been a decrease for the last five years in South Australia, the other states, with the exception of Tasmania, where the rate remained stationary, show increases, the proportion in Western Australia rising from 0·55 per 1,000 in 1892-6 to 0·64 in 1897–1901.

The next table shows the total number of patients who were discharged from the asylums during the ten years 1892–1901, either on account of recovery, permanent or temporary, or on account of death, and the proportion borne by each to the total number who were under treatment during the period.

State.	Total under Treatment.	Discharged—recovered or relieved.		Died.	
		Number.	Per cent. of total under treatment.	Number.	Per cent. of total under treatment.
New South Wales	10,580	3,655	34·55	2,402	22·70
Victoria	11,050	3,184	28·81	3,285	29·72
Queensland	4,062	1,310	32·25	971	23·90
South Australia	2,989	1,199	40·11	743	24·86
Western Australia	923	392	42·47	173	18·74
Tasmania	1,014	282	27·81	280	27·61
Commonwealth	30,618	10,022	32·73	7,854	25·65
New Zealand	7,036	3,125	44·41	1,338	19·01
Australasia	37,654	13,147	34·92	9,192	24·41

It is seen that, of the total number under treatment, 34·92 per cent were discharged either partially or wholly recovered, and that 24·41 per cent. died. New Zealand shows the highest proportion of recoveries, and Victoria the lowest, while Western Australia has the lowest death-rate, and Victoria the highest. The position of Victoria as regards results in treatment of the insane is therefore the worst in Australasia, and this unsatisfactory state of affairs has aroused anxious attention in the southern State. At present the asylums are overcrowded, while the system of classification leaves much to be desired. A serious drawback to efficient administration also lies in the fact that while the inspector and official visitors may make suggestions they have no power to give administrative effect to their recommendations. Speaking generally, it is estimated that of the persons who are discharged from the asylums in Australasia, some 28 per cent. suffer a relapse and are readmitted; and it may be said that out of every 1,000 persons who are admitted for the first time, 420 will recover, and the sufferings of the remaining 580 will only be terminated by death.

Very little information is available as to the exciting or predisposing causes of insanity in the different states, New South Wales being the only one concerning which there is complete information. But that state may be taken as typical of the whole, as the customs and conditions of living do not vary greatly in any of them, and the statement below enables a comparison to be made with the principal assigned causes of insanity in England and Wales. The following figures represent the proportion of each assigned cause to the total known causes for a period of five years:—

Cause.	Males.		Females.	
	New South Wales.	England and Wales.	New South Wales.	England and Wales.
	per cent.	per cent.	per cent.	per cent.
Domestic trouble, Adverse circumstances, Mental anxiety	9·4	8·8	12·0	9·8
Intemperance in drink	15·6	19·3	3·9	7·8
Hereditary influence, ascertained; Congenital defect, ascertained	17·8	20·8	19·5	23 0
Pregnancy, Lactation, Parturition, and Puerperal state, Uterine and Ovarian disorders, Puberty, Change of life	......	......	14·6	11·9
Previous attacks	15·6	13·6	19·3	18·4
Accident, including Sunstroke	5·5	4·8	0·8	0·6
Old Age	7·4	5·7	6·4	6·5
Other Causes ascertained	28·7	27·0	23·5	22·0

Intemperance in drink is popularly supposed to be the most fruitful cause of insanity in Australasia, but as will be seen from the above table hereditary influence is the chief factor both here and in England.

figures moreover prove that insanity arising from intemperance is nearly so common in these states as in the old country. Amongst ales, the chief causes of insanity in the states are hereditary influence 1 pregnancy, etc. It is believed that hereditary influence and congenital defect are responsible in New South Wales for a much larger percentage of cases than the number shown in the table, and that of the unknown causes the great majority should be ascribed to hereditary influences. The small proportion of cases set down to these two causes is simply due to the difficulty of obtaining knowledge of the family history of a large number of those who enter the asylums.

HABITATIONS.

The latest information available concerning the habitations of the people, is that obtained at the census of 1901, when inquiry was made on the householders' schedules respecting the dwellings of the population. The information sought was in respect to whether a building was occupied, unoccupied, or in course of construction; the material of which it was built, and the number of rooms which it contained. The tabulation was not made with the same degree of completeness in all the states; but so far as comparative figures can be given they are shown below:—

Class of Dwelling.	New South Wales.	Victoria	Queensland.	South Australia.	Western Australia.	Tasmania.	New Zealand.
Inhabited	252,502	241,410	96,737	69,856	48,506	34,165	158,898
Uninhabited	14,831	11,629	1,670	5,640	2,263	2,187	10,830
Being built	1,438	617	*	358	201	118	865
Total	268,771	253,656	100,407	75,854	50,970	36,470	170,593

* Information not ascertained.

The materials of which the dwellings in each state were constructed are shown in the following table, so far as the particulars are available. In New South Wales, South Australia, Tasmania, Western Australia, and New Zealand the information is shown for all dwellings; in Victoria and Queensland for inhabited dwellings only. Dwellings made of canvas are most numerous in Western Australia, Queensland, and New South Wales. The large numbers of men living in tents engaged in mining in Western Australia, and in mining and on railway extensions in the two last mentioned states, will sufficiently account for the totals shown in this class.

Material.	New South Wales.	Victoria.	Queensland.	South Australia.	Western Australia.	Tasmania.	New Zealand.
Stone	10,798	8,469	300	45,186	3,981	8,059	7,517
Brick	92,879	63,627	2,248	13,479	8,872		....
Concrete, Pisé	1,525	1,525	83	2,664	1,164	......	....
Iron, metal	5,880	1,337	6,215	2,787	5,589		
Wood	140,482		77,419	9,471	12,296	23,653	153,945
Lath and Plaster		157,112	....	....	....		
Mud, bark	4,952	2,896	1,604	....	495	1,304	1,688
Canvas (including tents)	8,874	3,423	9,609	1,564	18,628	869	5,116
Others and unspecified	3,886	3,021	1,309	758	495	2,585	2,327
Total	268,771	241,410	98,737	75,854	50,970	36,470	170,598

The number of rooms is given below for all houses, whether occupied or unoccupied, in the case of New South Wales, South Australia, Tasmania, and Western Australia; for the other states the figures refer to inhabited dwellings only :—

Dwellings, with—	New South Wales.	Victoria.	Queensland.	South Australia.	Western Australia.	Tasmania.	New Zealand.
One room	7,915	6,841	3,606	2,902	14,485	717	8,147
Two rooms	16,275	11,470	5,782	5,776	7,808	3,529	10,462
Three and four rooms	79,366	80,076	25,108	31,180	17,278	13,028	45,499
Five and six rooms	98,641	84,914	31,924	24,061	7,319	8,193	52,585
Seven to ten rooms	43,844	43,242	16,158		2,886	4,158	
Eleven to fifteen rooms	6,928	5,615	2,104	11,086	647		36,542
Sixteen to twenty rooms	1,612	1,157	548		226	1,968	
More than twenty rooms	1,205	909	529		209		
Number of rooms unspecified	5,889	3,763	423	849	612	2,632	547
Tents, etc.	7,096	3,423	12,555	....	....	2,245	5,116
Total	268,771	241,410	98,737	75,854	50,970	36,470	158,898

In the case of those states where no information is given in the table respecting tents, etc., the returns are incorporated in the first two lines of the table. From the foregoing figures it will be seen that in Australasia there are over 5 persons to every occupied house.

SHIPPING.

THE earliest date for which there is reliable information in regard to the shipping of the states now constituting the Commonwealth of Australia, and also of the colony of New Zealand is the year 1822. Since that time the expansion of the trade has been marvellous, and although population has increased at a high rate, yet the growth of shipping has been even more rapid. In the table given below the increase in the number and tonnage of vessels may be traced. The shipping of New Zealand is treated separately, and all tonnage of this colony, of course, is shown, but it is necessary to point out that the figures for the Commonwealth of Australia include the interstate traffic, and are, therefore, of little value in a comparison between the shipping trade of Australia and that of other countries, as the vessels plying between the various states represent merely coasting trade when the Commonwealth is considered as a whole. This distinction is to be kept in view throughout this chapter, as well as in the later one dealing with commerce:—

Year.	Commonwealth of Australia. Entered and Cleared.		Year.	New Zealand. Entered and Cleared.	
	Vessels.	Tonnage.		Vessels.	Tonnage.
1822	268	147,869	1822	....	....
1841	2,576	552,347	1841	....	....
1851	4,780	975,959	1851	560	112,149
1861	9,174	2,425,148	1861	1,142	403,336
1871	11,836	3,689,643	1871	1,438	540,261
1881	14,408	8,109,924	1881	1,527	833,621
1891	16,987	16,235,213	1891	1,481	1,244,322
1901	18,638	26,197,436	1901	1,379	2,139,180
1902	17,878	26,791,360	1902	1,249	2,137,949

In the year 1822 all the settlements on the mainland were comprised in the designation of New South Wales, and as late as 1859 Queensland formed part of that state. Thus an exact distribution of shipping amongst the states comprising the Commonwealth of Australia can be made only for the period subsequent to the year last named. Such a division of the total tonnage entered and cleared is shown in the following table for the five census years commencing with 1861, and for the year 1902.

State.	Total Tonnage Entered and Cleared.					
	1861.	1871.	1881.	1891.	1901.	1902.
Commonwealth of Australia—						
New South Wales	745,696	1,500,479	2,786,500	5,694,236	8,521,234	8,728,144
Victoria	1,090,002	1,355,025	2,412,534	4,715,100	6,715,491	6,739,040
Queensland	44,045	93,236	882,491	997,118	1,685,820	2,067,611
South Australia	199,331	387,026	1,359,591	2,738,539	4,127,903	4,131,276
Western Australia	115,256	137,717	285,046	1,045,555	3,714,263	3,358,074
Tasmania	230,218	216,160	383,762	1,044,606	1,432,725	1,767,215
Total	2,425,148	3,689,643	8,109,924	16,285,213	26,197,436	26,791,360
Colony of New Zealand	403,336	540,261	833,021	1,244,322	2,139,180	2,137,940

The tonnage of 1891 exceeded that of any preceding year. This result was not altogether due to the actual requirements of the trade of that year, as, in consequence of the maritime strike, a large quantity of goods remained unshipped at the close of 1890, and helped to swell the returns for the succeeding twelve months. It was not until 1895 that the tonnage of 1891 was again reached; but since 1895 there has been a great expansion of shipping, and 1902 showed not only the largest total tonnage recorded but, with the exception of Western Australia, the greatest for each individual state.

For New Zealand the total tonnage of 1902 is slightly below that of the preceding year; but in explanation of this fact it may be pointed out that there was a phenomenal export of certain articles of domestic production from the colony in 1901. The shipments of oats during that year totalled 10,515,000 bushels, as against 5,186,000 in 1902. Of wheat there were 2,301,000 bushels shipped, as against 195,000 in 1902, while the sawn timber exports of 1901 reached nearly 72 million feet, as against 49 million in the following year.

Below will be found the proportion of the tonnage of each state to the total shipping of the Commonwealth of Australia in each of the years quoted above:—

State.	Percentage of Total of Commonwealth.					
	1861.	1871.	1881.	1891.	1901.	1902.
Commonwealth of Australia—						
New South Wales	30·8	40·7	34·4	35·1	32·5	32·6
Victoria	44·9	36·7	29·7	29·0	25·6	25·2
Queensland	1·8	2·5	10·9	6·2	6·4	7·7
South Australia	8·2	10·5	16·8	16·9	15·8	15·4
Western Australia	4·8	3·7	3·5	6·4	14·2	12·5
Tasmania	9·5	5·9	4·7	6·4	5·5	6·6
Total	100·0	100·0	100·0	100·0	100·0	100·0

It cannot be claimed that these figures have much meaning, and they would not have been repeated in this work, except for the purpose of showing how easy it is to make fallacious comparisons from reasonably correct data. Queensland appears almost last amongst the states in point of tonnage, yet, unquestionably, that state ranks third as regards the importance of its trade. The explanation of the discrepancy between the real and apparent trade lies in the fact which will hereafter be reverted to, that the same vessels are again and again included as distinct tonnage in the returns of the southern states. For example, a mail-steamer which calls at Fremantle, in Western Australia, continues its voyage to Sydney by way of Adelaide and Melbourne, sometimes calling at Hobart, and figures as a separate vessel at each port. The Canadian mail-steamers and the vessels of the Nippon Yusen Kaisha, or Imperial Japanese Mail Line, are also counted twice in the New South Wales and Queensland returns, but on account of the less number of trips, and the small tonnage of the vessels, the figures for each of these states are not so much inflated as is the case with those of other Commonwealth states. It is apparent therefore that the returns are only of value as indicating the comparative progress of the trade of each separate state, and not the progress of one state as compared with another.

Interstate Shipping.

The total shipping of the Commonwealth of Australia, dealt with in the preceding section, included the trade between the various states, which represents 56·77 per cent. of the total for Australia. In the following table will be found the number and tonnage of vessels entered at the ports of each state from the other states. As a rule, the expansion of the trade of a state with its neighbours has kept pace with the growth of its commerce with outside countries. It should be remembered that the trade between New Zealand and Australia has been eliminated from the tables showing interstate shipping.

State.	Entered from other States of the Commonwealth.					
	1891.		1901.		1902.	
	Vessels.	Tonnage.	Vessels.	Tonnage.	Vessels.	Tonnage.
Commonwealth of Australia—						
New South Wales	2,111	1,687,300	2,303	2,094,297	2,074	2,280,536
Victoria	1,954	1,461,974	1,745	1,992,118	1,696	2,045,643
Queensland	376	267,753	430	545,469	504	672,556
South Australia	761	683,095	719	1,135,714	709	1,161,641
Western Australia	149	237,708	446	973,474	368	784,547
Tasmania	680	371,205	713	485,023	837	581,242
Total	6,031	4,709,035	6,356	7,226,095	6,188	7,526,165

The peculiar feature of the foregoing table is the large increase in the tonnage of Western Australia and South Australia, due in both cases to the influx of population and expansion of trade resultant on the great gold discoveries in the former state.

State.	Cleared for other States of the Commonwealth.					
	1891.		1901.		1902.	
	Vessels.	Tonnage.	Vessels.	Tonnage.	Vessels.	Tonnage.
Commonwealth of Australia—						
New South Wales	1,861	1,385,357	1,995	1,907,226	1,719	1,971,572
Victoria	2,166	1,761,027	1,794	2,072,747	1,852	2,279,698
Queensland	389	302,723	395	440,659	490	585,215
South Australia	865	854,236	826	1,377,399	830	1,415,499
Western Australia	158	269,256	456	977,846	388	902,496
Tasmania	679	352,406	694	433,735	809	528,524
Total	6,118	4,925,005	6,160	7,209,612	6,088	7,683,004

A comparison of the figures given above with those in the preceding table shows that in the case of Victoria, South Australia and Western Australia the tonnage cleared is largely in excess of that entered. This partly arises from the necessity of many vessels clearing at the southern and Western Australian ports in ballast and proceeding for outward cargo to New South Wales ports, principally Newcastle, where on their outward voyage such vessels are, of course, reckoned amongst the external shipping.

The combined tonnage of inter-state shipping entered and cleared with the percentage for each state to the total inter-state shipping of the Commonwealth, will be found below :—

State.	Entered from and Cleared for other States.					
	Total Tonnage.			Percentage of each State to Total.		
	1891.	1901.	1902.	1891.	1901.	1902.
Commonwealth of Australia—						
New South Wales	3,072,657	4,001,523	4,252,108	31·9	27·7	28·0
Victoria	3,223,001	4,064,865	4,325,341	33·5	28·2	28·4
Queensland	570,476	986,128	1,257,771	5·9	6·8	8·3
South Australia	1,537,331	2,513,113	2,577,140	15·9	17·4	16·9
Western Australia	506,964	1,951,320	1,687,043	5·3	13·5	11·1
Tasmania	723,611	918,758	1,109,766	7·5	6·4	7·3
Total	9,634,040	14,435,707	15,209,169	100·0	100·0	100·0

External Shipping.

It has been explained that in any comparison between the shipping of the Commonwealth of Australia and that of other countries the interstate trade would have to be excluded; but even then the tonnage would be too high, because of the inclusion of mail-steamers and other vessels on the same voyage in the returns of several of the states. However, it is scarcely possible to amend the returns so as to secure the rejection of the tonnage which is reckoned more than once; and in considering the following statement, showing the shipping trade of the Commonwealth with countries beyond Australia, this point should be borne in mind :—

Division.	1891.		1901.		1902.	
	Vessels.	Tonnage.	Vessels.	Tonnage.	Vessels.	Tonnage.
United Kingdom—						
Entered	868	1,699,958	716	2,066,167	735	2,232,861
Cleared	588	1,217,582	784	2,144,587	667	1,967,529
Total	1,456	2,917,540	1,500	4,210,754	1,402	4,200,390
British Possessions—						
Entered	894	790,608	1,403	1,971,931	1,244	1,782,896
Cleared	942	903,972	1,349	2,081,623	1,201	1,996,403
Total	1,836	1,694,580	2,752	4,053,554	2,445	3,779,299
Foreign Countries—						
Entered	681	880,814	906	1,774,013	842	1,839,877
Cleared	865	1,108,239	964	1,723,408	913	1,762,625
Total	1,546	1,989,053	1,870	3,497,421	1,755	3,602,502
All External Trade—						
Entered	2,443	3,371,380	3,025	5,812,111	2,821	5,855,634
Cleared	2,395	3,229,793	3,097	5,949,618	2,781	5,726,557
Total	4,838	6,601,173	6,122	11,761,729	5,602	11,582,191

The external shipping of the Commonwealth of Australia during 1902 was fully 75 per cent. more than the tonnage entered and cleared in 1891, when trade was inflated by the shipment of goods left over from the previous year on account of the maritime strike. A distribution of the traffic amongst the leading divisions of the British Empire and the principal foreign countries with which the states of the Commonwealth have commercial relations will be found below :—

Country.	Entered from and cleared for Countries beyond the Commonwealth.					
	1891.		1901.		1902.	
	Vessels.	Tonnage.	Vessels.	Tonnage.	Vessels.	Tonnage.
British Empire—						
United Kingdom	1,456	2,917,540	1,500	4,210,754	1,402	4,200,390
New Zealand	1,007	749,886	999	1,345,471	943	1,366,783
India and Ceylon	134	276,030	142	330,714	137	374,593
Hong Kong	227	324,820	241	380,174	210	332,889
Canada	27	29,952	61	118,523	90	175,766
Cape Colony	63	55,611	430	681,869	354	593,500
Natal	35	12,950	423	794,583	277	547,980
Fiji	107	105,033	60	58,799	68	71,924
Straits Settlements	61	75,269	90	129,112	144	218,599
Other British Possessions	175	65,029	306	214,309	222	97,265
Total, British	3,292	4,612,120	4,252	8,264,308	3,847	7,979,689
Foreign Countries—						
France	101	255,351	117	304,026	127	322,460
Germany	208	393,001	274	909,798	304	1,141,890
Netherlands	13	15,731	7	14,748	3	5,215
Belgium	27	41,907	14	29,716	10	20,111
United States	418	519,252	385	758,281	359	742,726
China	34	33,135	11	23,797	19	28,436
Japan	7	13,677	80	192,674	100	247,165
New Caledonia	154	155,226	125	179,486	126	205,525
Java	37	58,379	88	183,349	58	101,149
Philippine Islands	29	36,305	52	87,809	39	77,490
Hawaiian Islands	1	430	107	106,205	69	67,451
Peru	16	21,520	39	48,554	34	41,929
Chili	131	146,448	218	324,892	196	292,908
Other Foreign Countries	370	298,691	353	334,086	311	308,047
Total, Foreign	1,546	1,989,053	1,870	3,497,421	1,755	3,602,502
All External Tonnage	4,838	6,601,173	6,122	11,761,729	5,602	11,582,191

It will be seen from the above figures that out of a total external tonnage, amounting to 11,582,191 tons in 1902, vessels from the United Kingdom aggregated 4,200,390 tons, or 36·2 per cent. of the whole. New Zealand furnished the next largest tonnage, with 1,366,783 tons, or 11·8 per cent., followed by Germany, with 1,141,890 tons, equal to 9·8 per cent., and the United States, with 742,726 tons, or 6·4 per cent. of the total. During the eleven years, 1891-1902, the tonnage of the United Kingdom increased by 1,282,850 tons, or 44 per cent., while British tonnage as a whole increased by 3,367,569 tons, or 73 per cent., the German by 748,889 tons, or 191 per cent., and the United States tonnage by 223,474 tons, or 43 per cent.

The enormous increase in the German tonnage is due to the large volume of business captured by the heavily subsidised vessels of the various German lines.

As the following table shows, the largest share of the external tonnage of Australia falls to New South Wales, which takes more than one-third of the total; Victoria comes next with a little over one-fifth, followed by Western Australia with about one-seventh. The figures in the chapter on Commerce, however, give a better idea of the relative importance of the states in external trade, as the tonnage of the mail steamers entered and cleared at Fremantle and Port Adelaide is out of all proportion to the goods landed and shipped there:—

State.	External Tonnage Entered and Cleared.						Percentage of each State to Total of Commonwealth.		
	1891.		1901.		1902.				
	Vessels	Tonnage.	Vessels	Tonnage.	Vessels	Tonnage.	1891.	1901.	1902.
Commonwealth of Australia—									
New South Wales	2,149	2,621,579	2,529	4,519,711	2,373	4,476,036	39·7	38·4	38·6
Victoria	971	1,492,108	1,226	2,650,626	1,016	2,418,699	22·6	22·5	20·9
Queensland	406	426,642	534	699,692	555	809,840	6·5	6·0	7·0
South Australia	803	1,201,258	721	1,614,790	624	1,554,136	18·2	13·7	13·4
Western Australia	291	538,591	883	1,762,943	772	1,671,081	8·1	15·0	14·4
Tasmania	219	320,995	229	513,967	262	657,449	4·9	4·4	5·7
Total	4,838	6,601,173	6,122	11,761,729	5,602	11,582,191	100·0	100·0	100·0

A comparison between the shipping of the principal countries of the world and the external tonnage of the Commonwealth of Australia is appended:—

Country.	Tonnage Entered and Cleared.		Country.	Tonnage Entered and Cleared.	
	Total.	Average per head.		Total.	Average per head.
United Kingdom.....	99,872,719	2·4	Spain	28,892,629	1·6
Russia in Europe.....	17,465,000	0·1	Italy	42,320,578	1·2
Norway	6,097,260	2·7	United States	49,680,318	0·6
Sweden...	16,566,699	3·2	Argentine Republic	13,364,884	2·9
Denmark	11,527,399	4·6	Canada	14,543,062	2·7
Germany	29,493,043	0·5	Cape Colony	9,979,133	4·1
Netherlands...........	18,656,021	3·5	New Zealand.........	2,137,949	2·6
Belgium	18,628,728	2·7	Commonwealth of Australia	11,582,191	3·0
France	38,171,406	1·0			

On the basis of population, therefore, the shipping of the states of the Commonwealth exceeds that of the United Kingdom and the great countries of the United States of America, France, Germany, Italy, Russia, and Spain.

Tonnage in Ballast.

A peculiar feature of the shipping trade is the small though varying proportion of tonnage in ballast arriving from and departing for places beyond Australia. Thus in the year 1881 this description of tonnage amounted to 5·2 per cent., and in 1891 to 4·1 per cent., of the total external shipping; while in 1902, at 9·6 per cent., the proportion was comparatively high. The increase during recent years is chiefly due to the larger number of vessels which come to New South Wales in quest of freights, the proportion of shipping in ballast for that state being over 12 per cent. of the total external tonnage. The figures for Tasmania were abnormally high in 1902, the tonnage in ballast being as high as 14·4 per cent. of the total external tonnage. Of the 94,697 tons entered and cleared this state, 18,358 tons represented sailing vessels entered in ballast from France, and 11,990 tons sailing vessels in ballast from the United Kingdom. Amongst the clearances there were no less than 19,275 tons representing sailing vessels cleared in ballast for America. The total external tonnage entered and cleared the Commonwealth in ballast during the years 1891, 1901, and 1902 was as follows:—

State.	External Tonnage Entered and Cleared in Ballast.			Percentage of Tonnage in Ballast to Total External Tonnage.		
	1891.	1901.	1902.	1891.	190	1902.
Commonwealth of Australia—						
New South Wales	100,167	579,904	554,759	3·8	12·8	12·4
Victoria	47,721	194,442	87,496	3·2	7·3	3·6
Queensland	36,700	24,869	21,901	8·6	3·6	2·7
South Australia	52,515	102,899	197,257	4·4	6·4	12·7
Western Australia	14,104	210,581	160,975	2·6	11·9	9·6
Tasmania	16,357	2,355	94,697	1·6	0·5	14·4
Total	267,564	1,115,050	1,117,085	4·1	9·5	9·6

The reason why so small a proportion of Australian shipping clears in ballast is principally to be found in the great and varied resources of the country; for when the staple produce—wool—is not available, cargoes of wheat, coal, silver, copper, live-stock, frozen meat, butter, fruit, tallow, leather, skins and hides, and other commodities may generally be obtained. Besides, owing to the great distance of the ports of the Commonwealth from the commercial centres of the old world, vessels are not usually sent out without at least some prospect of securing a return cargo. As a rule, it does not pay to send vessels to Australasia seeking freights, as is commonly done with regard to European and American ports. It is strong testimony, therefore, of the value of the trade of New South Wales to shipowners to find entered at the ports of that state direct from outside countries the comparatively large quantity of 442,380 tons of shipping in ballast, the following being the chief countries represented:—Cape Colony, New Zealand, Natal, Philippine Islands, Mauritius, Fiji, Java, Japan.

The tonnage in ballast which entered and cleared at New Zealand ports and the percentage of such to the total tonnage of that colony may be seen in the following table.

Year.	Tonnage in ballast.	Percentage to total tonnage.
1881	76,247	9·0
1891	103,754	8·3
1901	191,266	8·9
1902	215,486	10·1

The proportion of tonnage in ballast to the total shipping of some of the principal countries of the world is subjoined:—

Country.	Percentage of Shipping in Ballast.	Country.	Percentage of Shipping in Ballast.
United Kingdom	17·2	France	17·9
Russia in Europe	33·3	Spain	28·7
Norway	26·1	United States	17·9
Sweden	45·1	New Zealand	8·9
Germany	19·9	Commonwealth of Australia	9·6
Netherlands	26·1		
Belgium	23·0		

Nationality of all Vessels.

The shipping trade of the Commonwealth of Australia and of the colony of New Zealand is almost entirely in British hands, as will be seen from the subjoined tables, which deal with the total tonnage, both inter-state and external. Although direct communication with continental Europe has been established within recent years, and several lines of magnificent steamers, subsidised by foreign Governments, have entered into the trade between Australia and foreign ports, yet the proportion of shipping belonging to Great Britain and her dependencies has only fallen from 86·8 to 84·7 per cent. during the period extending from 1891 to 1902. The chief increases during the period have been amongst vessels trading from Germany and Japan, the proportion of the former rising from 5·2 per cent. to 7·7 per cent., and of the latter from 0·2 per cent. to 1·2 per cent:—

Nationality.	Total Shipping Entered and Cleared the Commonwealth.						Percentage of each Nationality.		
	1891.		1901.		1902.				
	Vessels.	Tonnage.	Vessels.	Tonnage.	Vessels.	Tonnage.	1891.	1901.	1902.
British	15,472	14,087,469	16,544	22,358,652	15,889	22,680,040	86·8	85·3	84·7
French	247	591,524	305	654,475	324	683,317	3·6	2·5	2·6
German	526	843,652	662	1,771,945	659	2,062,267	5·2	6·8	7·7
Scandinavian	319	292,071	408	350,040	340	302,281	1·8	1·3	1·1
Italian	11	9,736	98	118,881	112	141,409	0·1	0 5	0·5
Japanese	17	34,907	120	285,370	119	312,880	0·2	1·1	1·2
American	307	296,096	401	520,705	292	409,815	1·8	2·0	1·5
Other nationalities.	88	79,758	110	137,368	143	199,351	0·5	0·5	0 7
Tota	16,987	16,235,213	18,638	26,197,436	17,878	26,791,360	100·0	100·0	100·0

The returns published by the various states are not in such a form as to admit of the separation of the purely local tonnage from the other shipping of the Empire, and vessels owned in the Commonwealth are classed in the above table as "British." The number and tonnage of the steam and sailing vessels registered in each of the states of the Commonwealth and New Zealand may be found on a succeeding page. Few of the large vessels employed in the inter-state trade have been built in Australia.

The nationality of vessels trading with New Zealand may be seen in the following table :—

Nationality.	Entered and Cleared New Zealand.						Percentage of each Nationality.		
	1891.		1901.		1902.				
	Vessels.	Tonnage.	Vessels.	Tonnage.	Vessels.	Tonnage.	1891.	1901.	1902.
British	1,359	1,120,435	1,234	1,831,590	1,104	1,810,510	90·0	85·6	84·7
French	4	1,862	1	1,562	2	728	0·2	0·1	0·1
German	16	12,876	2	1,684	10	14,727	1·0	0·1	0·7
Scandinavian	17	12,906	39	26,541	37	22,271	1·0	1·2	1·0
American	81	91,887	80	263,134	76	274,424	7·4	12·3	12·8
Other nationalities	4	4,856	23	14,669	20	15,239	0·4	0·7	0·7
Total	1,481	1,244,322	1,379	2,139,180	1,249	2,137,949	100·0	100·0	100·0

The following table shows the relative increase during the last ten years in British, foreign, and colonial trade with New Zealand, and the figures possess a certain amount of interest in view of the laws recently passed in that colony granting preferential trade in certain commodities to Great Britain :—

Year.	Shipping Entered and Cleared New Zealand.								
	British.			Colonial.			Foreign.		
	Vessels.	Tonnage.	Crews.	Vessels.	Tonnage.	Crews.	Vessels.	Tonnage.	Crews.
1893	352	607,453	15,128	805	542,558	23,410	95	108,059	3,845
1902	324	943,554	16,854	780	866,956	30,476	145	327,439	12,228

These figures apply to external trade only ; but in addition thereto, as might be expected in a country with such an extensive seaboard as New Zealand, there is a very large coastal trade, amounting in 1902 to 8,249,623 tons entered, and 8,309,635 cleared.

Steam and Sailing Vessels.

The tendency to substitute steamers for sailing vessels, which is general throughout the world, is very marked in the Australian trade. Unfortunately the subdivision of the total tonnage into steam and sailing was not obtainable for the whole of the Commonwealth States until last year. It is not possible, therefore, to show the total increase of steam tonnage, but appended will be found the figures of the external trade of the various states so far as they can be given :—

State.	Steam Tonnage entered and cleared.			Percentage of Steam to Total Tonnage.		
	1891.	1901.	1902.	1891.	1901.	1902.
Commonwealth of Australia—						
New South Wales	1,582,308	3,258,228	3,395,190	60·3	72·1	75·9
Victoria	1,044,467	2,194,863	2,127,470	70·0	82·8	88·1
Queensland	......	......	762,696	......	......	94·2
South Australia	......	......	1,319,146	......	......	84·9
Western Australia	483,460	1,460,619	1,403,121	89·8	82·9	84·0
Tasmania	287,188	488,379	568,162	89·5	95·0	86·4
Colony of New Zealand	822,086	1,860,622	1,900,813	66·1	87·0	88·9

The substitution of steam for sailing vessels in the shipping trade of some of the principal countries of the world may be gathered from the following table. The figures refer to the year 1900, the latest for which information is obtainable for the places specified :—

Country.	Percentage of Steam to Total Tonnage.		
	1881.	1891.	1901.
United Kingdom	67·7	84·2	92·4
Russia in Europe	74·3	91·0	95·9
Norway	31·1	55·7	70·4
Sweden	46·8	72·1	84·5
Denmark	61·9	81·7	86·6
Germany	70·8	87·2	90·9
Netherlands	74·4	92·5	97·2
Belgium	81·3	94·0	96·1
France	69·5	87·0	94·7
Portugal	82·1	93·6	97·7
Spain	....	94·0	97·6
Italy	72·8	88·3	96·9
United States	55·5	72·3	87·9
Argentine Republic	70·4	86·7	90·7
Canada	....	66·2	82·3
Cape Colony	62·5	79·8	90·4
Natal	....	91·3	93·3
New Zealand	....	66·1	88·9 } 1902
Commonwealth of Australia	68·6	81·8	82·7 } 1902

A comprehensive view of the changes which have taken place since the year 1881 in the class of vessel engaged in the inter-state and the external shipping trade of the Commonwealth is afforded by the following figures :—

Year.	Vessels.	Tonnage.	Crews.	Average Tonnage per vessel	Average Tonnage per hand.
		INTER-STATE SHIPPING.			
1881	10,484	4,941,294	251,189	471	20
1891	12,149	9,634,040	386,798	793	25
1901	12,516	14,435,707	475,457	1,153	30
1902	12,276	15,209,169	490,498	1,239	31
		EXTERNAL SHIPPING.			
1881	3,924	3,168,630	120,193	808	26
1891	4,838	6,601,173	244,171	1,364	27
1901	6,122	11,761,729	350,266	1,921	34
1902	5,602	11,582,191	362,817	2,068	32
		ALL COMMONWEALTH SHIPPING.			
1881	14,408	8,109,924	371,382	563	22
1891	16,987	16,235,213	630,969	956	26
1901	18,638	26,197,436	825,723	1,406	32
1902	17,878	26,791,360	853,315	1,499	31

As the table shows, the total number of vessels engaged in the shipping trade of the Commonwealth of Australia during 1902 was 891 more than the figure for 1891, and the returns of tonnage show an increase of over 10½ millions. The average tonnage of shipping is 1,499, as compared with 956 in 1891, and 563 in 1881. The explanation of this increase of course lies in the fact that a superior type of vessel is now engaged in the shipping trade, and the enterprise of the great British and foreign trading companies will doubtless have the effect of raising still higher the average for succeeding years. Several of the vessels belonging to the fleet of the North German Lloyd are over 10,000 tons, the largest exceeding 13,000 tons. The Peninsular and Oriental Company possesses a magnificent fleet, the steamers ranging in size from 6,600 tons to 10,500 tons. The average tonnage of the steamers of the Orient Pacific Royal Mail Line is over 7,200 tons, of the Messageries Maritimes 6,500 tons, and of the White Star Line, the vessels of which were built principally as cargo carriers, 12,000 tons. Considerable impetus has been given to the foreign shipping trade with Australia through the subsidising of the lines by several of the foreign governments. The North German Lloyd, for example, receives an annual subsidy from the German Government of £115,000, equal to 6s. 8d. per mile. To protect the interests of the German agriculturists it is stipulated in the agreement that the vessels shall not carry on their homeward journey frozen meat, dairy produce, or cereals in the nature of those grown in Germany. The Japanese Government subsidises its steamers trading to Australia to the extent of £50,000 per annum, and the Messageries Maritimes receives a subsidy of 8s. 4d. per mile. The British lines—the Peninsular and Oriental and the Orient Pacific—each receive £85,000 per annum for carrying the mails to and from Australia.

It is somewhat remarkable to find that the vessels engaged in the inter-state trade have more than kept pace in increase of tonnage with those trading between the Commonwealth and other countries. Of course, the increase in the average tonnage of inter-state vessels is represented as greater than it actually has been, because the mail-steamers on their way to Sydney are cleared at Fremantle, Adelaide, and Melbourne for the states further east; but when allowance has been made on this score, the improvement in the class of vessel trading in local waters will be found most noteworthy. It is well known, however, that the steamers running on the Australian coast favourably compare with those engaged in the coasting trade of any of the great maritime countries of the world. Several of the vessels are over 7,000 tons burthen, and are provided with twin screws and fitted with the most modern appliances and conveniences for the transport of passengers and cargo.

The trade of the Commonwealth with New Zealand appears as external shipping in all returns given in this chapter, and has, therefore not been distinguished separately, but in the following table will be found figures showing the total shipping of that colony with all countries:—

Year.	Vessels.	Tonnage.	Crews.	Average Tonnage per Vessel.	Average Tonnage per hand.
1881	1,527	833,621	30,409	546	27
1891	1,481	1,244,322	43,969	840	28
1901	1,379	2,139,180	59,752	1,551	36
1902	1,249	2,137,949	59,558	1,712	36

The improvement in the class of vessel engaged in the trade will be apparent from the fact that although the number of vessels has decreased by 232 since 1891, the total tonnage has increased by about 894,000 tons, while the average per vessel is more than double that of 1891.

Relative Importance of Ports.

The relative importance of the various ports of the Commonwealth of Australia and New Zealand may be ascertained by an inspection of the table given hereunder. Melbourne takes first place in the amount of tonnage; but the figures are inflated by the counting of the great ocean steamers as twice entering and twice clearing at Port Phillip. This remark applies equally to Port Adelaide and Albany, and in the last two years to Fremantle. If allowance be made on this score, it will be found that Sydney has a larger quantity of shipping than any other Australasian port, and that it is followed by Melbourne, Newcastle, and Port Adelaide. The figures for the years 1881 and 1891 given for Queensland ports, other than Brisbane, include coastal trade, and the quantity of tonnage shown for these years is, therefore, somewhat in excess of the truth. As this table is only intended to show the relative importance of ports, the inter-state shipping of the Commonwealth has not been excluded, but no account has been taken of the purely coastal trade within each state:—

Port.	Total Tonnage entered and cleared.			
	1881.	1891.	1901.	1902.
COMMONWEALTH OF AUSTRALIA.				
New South Wales—				
Sydney	1,610,692	3,469,862	5,413,677	5,939,374
Newcastle	1,127,238	1,844,842	2,609,861	2,388,738
Wollongong	14,642	101,888	300,699	271,684
Victoria—				
Melbourne	2,144,949	4,362,138	6,366,103	6,244,033
Geelong	93,347	190,932	259,573	372,273
Queensland—				
Brisbane	406,032	855,993	1,207,295	1,540,492
Townsville	205,886	544,470	95,101	113,844
Rockhampton	207,706	471,837	36,653	54,187
Cooktown	217,144	469,577	31,670	27,220
Cairns	56,447	326,898	4,084	2,488
Mackay	104,174	330,119	4,473	3,375
South Australia—				
Port Adelaide	1,078,920	1,990,938	3,296,108	3,424,017
Port Pirie	33,325	321,781	376,856	242,605
Port Darwin	90,100	170,642	163,705	171,924
Western Australia—				
Fremantle	42,618	63,068	1,864,195	2,095,371
Albany	219,902	931,502	1,667,707	1,068,472
Bunbury	7,905	1,189	8,942	103,147
Tasmania—				
Hobart	204,007	646,683	870,733	1,070,171
Launceston	138,657	293,537	199,444	237,368
Devonport	....	8,121	124,964	173,141
NEW ZEALAND.				
Wellington	119,243	293,451	591,154	666,707
Auckland	238,886	345,183	736,005	779,295
Bluff Harbour	91,592	196,540	303,496	289,370
Lyttelton	167,151	161,387	208,476	144,255
Dunedin	114,637	97,409	112,718	112,773

A better idea of the relative importance of the principal ports of the states is obtainable from the trade figures, which are given below for the year 1902 :—

Port.	Total Trade.	Average per ton of Shipping.	Port.	Total Trade.	Average per ton of Shipping.
New South Wales—	£	£ s. d.	Western Australia—	£	£ s. d.
Sydney	38,828,608	6 10 9	Fremantle	12,026,760	5 14 10
Newcastle	3,021,957	1 5 4	Albany	1,495,126	1 8 0
Victoria—			Tasmania—		
Melbourne	31,451,877	5 0 9	Hobart	1,926,136	1 16 0
Queensland—			Launceston	1,785,923	7 10 6
Brisbane	6,889,198	4 9 5	New Zealand—		
South Australia—			Wellington	5,692,039	8 10 9
Port Adelaide	8,725,941	2 11 0	Auckland	5,178,476	6 12 11

The comparative importance of the ports of the Commonwealth of Australia and New Zealand may be seen by viewing them in connection with the shipping and trade of the chief ports of the United Kingdom, the 1902 figures for which are appended. It will be seen that in aggregate tonnage Melbourne is exceeded only by London, Liverpool, Cardiff, and Newcastle. Sydney comes next on the list, exceeding all other British ports. In value of trade Sydney is exceeded only by London, Liverpool, and Hull. If the Commonwealth of Australia be regarded as one country, however, the comparison is somewhat misleading, as the inter-state trade has been included in the returns :—

Port.	Total Shipping.	Total Trade.	Port.	Total Shipping.	Total Trade.
England and Wales—	tons.	£	Scotland—	tons.	£
London	17,564,108	261,179,647	Glasgow	4,144,217	33,284,117
Liverpool	13,157,714	236,049,898	Leith	1,880,271	17,189,216
Cardiff	12,556,644	14,463,230	Kirkcaldy	2,361,313	1,749,361
Newcastle and N.&S.Shields	8,369,347	17,280,969	Grangemouth.	1,485,658	5,312,242
Hull	4,480,538	51,799,849	Ireland—		
Southampton	3,224,491	32,146,816	Belfast	628,937	8,343,842
Sunderland	1,839,530	2,076,977	Dublin	373,674	2,920,118
Grimsby	1,797,531	18,726,506	Cork	167,992	1,132,123
Dover	1,967,892	13,299,269	Australia—		
Newport	2,464,543	3,787,022	Sydney	5,939,374	38,828,608
Harwich	1,432,968	24,677,991	Melbourne	6,244,033	31,451,877
Bristol	1,237,082	14,067,437	Brisbane	1,540,492	6,889,198
Newhaven	704,679	13,293,981	Adelaide	3,424,017	8,725,941
Swansea	2,400,153	10,002,292	Fremantle	2,095,371	12,026,760
Manchester	1,580,802	25,305,857	Hobart	1,070,171	1,926,136
Middlesbrough	1,733,286	6,016,517	New Zealand—		
			Wellington	666,707	5,692,039
			Auckland	779,295	5,178,476

The yearly movement of tonnage at Melbourne and Sydney far exceeds that of the ports of any other British possession, Hong Kong and Singapore excepted. Two other exceptions might be mentioned—

Gibraltar and Malta; but as these are chiefly ports of call, and the trade is very limited compared with the tonnage, they can scarcely be placed in the same category.

Registration of Vessels.

The number and tonnage of steam and sailing vessels on the registers of each of the six states of the Commonwealth and the colony of New Zealand at the end of 1902 are given below :—

State.	Steam.		Sailing.		Total.	
	Vessels.	Net Tonnage.	Vessels.	Net Tonnage.	Vessels.	Net Tonnage.
Commonwealth of Australia—						
New South Wales	516	71,953	523	57,772	1,039	129,725
Victoria	153	72,805	223	37,545	376	110,350
Queensland	101	15,001	168	10,243	269	25,244
South Australia	110	33,330	221	19,775	331	53,105
Western Australia	30	5,708	197	6,811	227	12,519
Tasmania	55	9,246	151	8,979	206	18,225
Total—Australia ...	965	208,043	1,483	141,125	2,448	349,168
Colony of New Zealand ...	224	62,027	325	42,806	549	104,833

For comparative purposes a statement is subjoined, showing the merchant navies of some of the principal maritime countries of the world. In considering the figures, allowance must be made for the fact that the minimum tonnage of vessels included in the registrations is not the same in every instance. Thus for Norway it is 4 tons ; Sweden, 20 tons ; Denmark, 4 tons ; France, 2 tons ; Italy, 2 tons ; Germany, 17½ tons ; and the United States, 5 tons.

Country.	Steam.		Sailing.		Total.	
	Vessels.	Net Tonnage.	Vessels.	Net Tonnage.	Vessels.	Net Tonnage.
United Kingdom	9,484	7,617,793	10,572	1,990,626	20,056	9,608,419
New Zealand	224	62,027	325	42,806	549	104,833
Canada	2,289	310,253	4,547	342,360	6,836	652,613
Australia	965	208,043	1,483	141,125	2,448	349,168
Russia and Finland	1,333	417,922	4,704	556,614	6,037	974,536
Norway	1,223	531,142	5,445	935,947	6,668	1,467,089
Sweden	943	341,622	2,100	298,589	3,103	640,211
Denmark	536	259,360	3,305	157,188	3,841	416,548
German Empire	1,463	1,506,059	2,496	586,974	3,959	2,093,033
Austria	134	219,446	25	13,483	159	232,929
Hungary	53	62,235	19	9,166	72	71,401
Netherlands	235	306,694	417	75,408	652	382,102
Belgium	66	109,336	6	1,121	72	110,457
France	1,299	546,541	14,393	564,447	15,692	1,110,988
Spain	502	679,392	549	95,187	1,051	774,579
Italy	471	424,711	5,337	575,207	5,808	999,918
United States	7,414	2,920,953	16,643	2,603,265	24,057	5,524,218

Wages of Seamen.

In calculating the average wages paid to seamen, regard must be had to the fact that shipping companies, in some instances, take into consideration personal qualifications and length of service of employees, when fixing rates. The following table shows the average wages, per calendar month, in 1903, paid to white crews of British ocean-going steamers trading with the Commonwealth, and also the rates for white crews of steamers engaged in the inter-state trade. The rates were obtained from the ships' articles deposited with the state shipping officers :—

Capacity	Average monthly wages. White crews.		Capacity.	Average monthly wages. White crews.	
	Ocean-going steamers.	Inter-State steamers.		Ocean-going steamers.	Inter-State steamers.
Navigation—	£ s.	£ s.	Cooking and Providoring—	£ s.	£ s.
1st Mate	15 0	15 0	Purser	£10 to £25	10 0
2nd „	10 0	12 0	Chief Cook	11 0	12 0
3rd „	8 0	10 0	2nd „	6 0	7 0
Boatswain	6 10	7 10	Baker	6 0	8 0
Carpenter	7 10	8 10	Butcher	6 0	5 0
A.B. Seaman	4 0	6 10	Pantryman	4 0	5 10
Ordinary Seaman	2 5	3 0	Attendance—		
Winchman	7 0	9 10	Head Steward	10 0	12 0
Engineer's Department—			2nd „	7 0	7 0
1st Engineer	25 0	£22 to £25	Stewardess	2 10	2 10
2nd „	15 0	£17 to £18	General Servant	3 0	4 0
3rd „	12 10	£14 to £15			
4th „	10 0	12 0			
5th „	8 0	10 0			
6th „	8 0	10 0			
Fireman	4 0	8 10			
Greaser	4 10	8 10			
Trimmer	3 10	6 10			

The crews of some of the British steamers trading to the Commonwealth are composed partly of coloured seamen, chiefly Lascars and

Chinese. In the following table will be found the average rates of wages paid to the various employees in this class:—

Capacity.	Ocean-going steamers. Average monthly wages.		Capacity.	Ocean-going steamers. Average monthly wages.	
	Lascars.	Chinese.		Lascars.	Chinese.
Navigation—	£ s. d.	£ s. d.	Cooking and Providoring—	£ s. d.	£ s. d.
1st Serang (Boatswain) ..	2 8 8	2 8 0	Bhandary (Cook)	1 6 8	1 8 0
1st Tindel (Boatswain's Mate)	1 17 4	....	Baker	2 0 0	....
2nd " " ..	1 14 8	....	Cassub (Storekeeper)	1 10 0	1 18 4
3rd " " ..	1 12 0	....	Butcher	2 6 8	....
Seacauz (Helmsman)	1 17 4	....	Pantryman	1 5 0	....
Carpenter..............	2 17 6	....	Scullion	0 17 4	....
Winchman	1 9 4	1 18 4	Knifeman	0 17 4	....
Oilman	1 18 4	....	Iceman.................	0 18 8	....
Lascars (not otherwise described)	1 4 0	....	Paniwalla (Water Turn-cock)................	1 10 0	....
Engineers Department—			Attendance—		
Fireman	1 2 8	1 10 8	Waiter	1 6 8	1 18 4
Trimmer	0 16 0	1 6 8	Topass (Sweeper)	0 16 0	....
			Cabin Boy	0 16 0	1 8 9

EDUCATION.

IT would have been strange if communities so prosperous as the Australasian States had neglected to provide for the education of the children. This duty, so vitally affecting the welfare of the people, has been recognised as one of the most important which the State could be called upon to discharge. In every province of the group, ample provision has been made for public instruction—such provision, indeed, in some cases, extending far beyond what has been done in most of the countries of the old world. In addition to a system of primary education, in all the states there are grammar and high schools, by means of which those who have the desire may qualify for the higher studies of the University. So bountiful is the provision made by the state that in most cases the cost of education is merely nominal, and the poverty of the parents ceases to be an excuse for the ignorance of the children. It is true that in the very early days of colonisation but little attention was paid to education; but so soon as the sharp struggle for bare existence was over, attempts were made to provide means of instruction for the rising generation, and the foundations were laid of an educational system that is in the highest degree creditable to these young communities. The religious bodies were naturally the first to build schools and provide teachers; but there was always a large proportion of persons who objected to denominationalism, principally those who belonged to denominations which were not subsidised by the state; hence there arose a national or non-sectarian system, which has in the course of time almost monopolised the educational field.

In all the Australasian provinces the state system of education is secular. Compulsory clauses find a place in the Acts of the various states; but the enforcement of these is not everywhere equally strict. In Victoria, for example, compulsory attendance at school has been rigorously insisted upon, while in Queensland the principle of compulsion has been allowed to remain almost in abeyance, and in the other states it has been enforced with varying degrees of strictness. In Victoria, Queensland, New Zealand, Western Australia, and South Australia the primary education provided by the State is entirely free of charge to the parents; in New South Wales and Tasmania small fees are charged, but these are not enforced where the parents can reasonably plead poverty.

The statutory school-age in each state is as follows :—

New South Wales	over 6	and under	14	years.
Victoria	,, 6	,,	13	,,
Queensland	,, 6	,,	12	,,
South Australia	,, 7	,,	13	,,
Western Australia	,, 6	,,	14	,,
Tasmania	,, 7	,,	13	,,
New Zealand............................	,, 7	,,	13	,,

Exemption certificates are granted to pupils below the maximum school age, provided they can pass an examination of a prescribed standard.

In New South Wales, for many years, a dual system of education was in existence. The four State-aided denominations—the Church of England, Roman Catholic, Presbyterian, and Wesleyan bodies—had schools supported by annual votes from Parliament, administered under the control of the head of each denomination for the time being. There were also National schools, likewise supported by the State, but under the control of a Board appointed by the Government. This plan was found to be costly and wasteful in the extreme, for in many country towns there were in existence several small and inefficient competing schools where the total number of children was not more than sufficient for one well-conducted establishment. So strongly was this evil felt that changes in the law were made from time to time, until at length the denominational system was abolished altogether, and one general and comprehensive plan of public instruction adopted in its place. This reform was not accomplished without much agitation, extending over a considerable period. A league was formed with the object of securing the establishment of secular, compulsory, and free education, and in 1880, under the auspices of Sir Henry Parkes, the measure establishing the present system became law. Education in the public schools is now non-sectarian, though facilities are afforded to clergymen to give religious instruction within specified school-hours to children whose parents belong to their denomination and desire that this instruction shall be given. It is compulsory, and free to all who cannot afford to pay, while a merely nominal fee is charged to those who are in a position to contribute towards the cost of the teaching of their children. For secondary education there are a number of superior and high schools entirely supported by the state, besides numerous colleges, grammar schools, and denominational schools which obtain no assistance from the Government, excepting the Sydney Grammar School, which receives a statutory endowment of £1,500. Scholarships and bursaries have been founded in connection with many of these schools. The University of Sydney, which is liberally endowed by private individuals as well as by the state, grants degrees which rank with those of Oxford and Cambridge. Educational affairs in the state are under the direction of a Minister for Public Instruction. In 1902 two Commissioners were appointed by the Government to visit Europe and America and report upon the best educational methods pursued in those countries. Special attention was devoted by this Commission to the question of technical education.

In Victoria, under an Act passed in 1872, a system of free, compulsory, and secular primary education is in force, under a Minister of Public Instruction, who is responsible to Parliament. The compulsory clause is very strictly enforced, especially in the large towns, and education is entirely free as regards the ordinary subjects of primary instruction, while the teachers are allowed to impart instruction in additional subjects, for which a small fee is payable. The teaching of religion is strictly forbidden during school-hours, and at no time must a state teacher give religious instruction. At the close of 1901 an important Amending Bill was passed. The main provisions of this measure were designed to strengthen the compulsory clauses of the Act, and to raise the age at which children can be excused from attendance at school to 14 years. No certificates of exemption can be granted to a child below 12 years of age. A Director of Education has been appointed who will, subject, of course, to the Minister, administer all laws relating to education. Secondary education is almost entirely in the hands of private or denominational establishments. The higher education is supplied by the University, with its affiliated colleges.

The Education Department in Queensland is administered by the Secretary for Public Instruction. The Act now in force was passed in 1875, and is of a tolerably liberal character, primary education being secular and free. An Amendment Act came into operation in 1898, extending the range of subjects taught in State schools and reducing the number taught in the Provisional schools. In July, 1900, seven attendance officers were appointed, and steps taken to put in operation the provisions of the Act of 1875 regarding regular attendance at school. These officers did excellent service during the year, but, with a view to economy, they were retired in 1902, and their duties relegated to the police. The public schools are divided into two classes, termed State and Provisional schools. A State school must have an average daily attendance of not less than thirty children, and the local district must contribute one-fifth of the cost of establishing, maintaining, repairing, and making additions to the building. In 1899, Provisional schools which had previously received a subsidy not exceeding £50 for any single school, and not more than half the cost of new buildings and furniture, were placed on the same footing with regard to Government grants as the State schools. Secondary education is provided by grammar schools, which are liberally assisted by the State. The State has no University of its own, but sends a fair number of students to the Universities of Sydney and Melbourne. The system of extension lectures in connection with the University of Sydney has been extended to Queensland; and the Government has given consideration to the question of the establishment of a University in Brisbane.

The South Australian system of primary education, which was introduced in its present form in 1878, is very similar to the systems already described. Public instruction in the state is presided over by a responsible Minister, with an Inspector-General and other officials. It is compulsory, secular, and free. Until the end of 1891 a small weekly fee was payable by all parents able to do so; but at the beginning of 1892 primary instruction was made free until the scholar reached the age of 13 years or had been educated to the compulsory standard, and in 1898 the remaining fees were abolished by the Minister for Education. Children who have attained a certain standard of education are exempt from compulsory attendance. Religious instruction is not allowed except out of ordinary school-hours. There are two secondary schools in connection with the Department—the Advanced School for Girls at Adelaide, where pupils are prepared for the University Public Examinations, and the Agricultural School, where boys are prepared for entrance to the School of Mines and Agricultural College. In addition there are numerous high-class private and denominational establishments; and the University of Adelaide, though small, is efficient.

Under the Elementary Education Act of 1871, primary education in Western Australia is imparted in Government schools, which are entirely supported by the state. An Amendment Act passed in 1893 placed educational affairs in the state under the control of a responsible Minister, and afforded facilities for special religious teaching, half-an-hour per day being allotted to clergymen for the instruction of children of the same denomination. Another Amendment Act which came into force in 1894 abolished payment by results, and gave powers for the enforcement of compulsory attendance. Until 1895, private schools were also assisted from the public purse, on condition of submitting to Government inspection in secular subjects; but towards the end of that year an Act was passed abolishing the system of annual grants to denominational schools, and providing that during the year 1896 the state should hand over, as compensation for the abolition of these subsidies, the sum of £15,000, to be divided between the schools in like proportions to those which governed the distribution of the annual vote in 1895. Under the regulations of 1895, children were entitled to free education on account of inability to pay the fees, of living more than 1 mile from school, of having made 400 half-day attendances in the previous year, or of other reasons approved by the Minister, but the Education Act which came into operation in 1899 gave free education to all children of compulsory school age. There is a high school at Perth, which is subsidised by the state; and further encouragement is given to secondary instruction by the institution of scholarships which are open to competition.

In Tasmania the Treasurer holds the portfolio of Education, and has especial charge of matters relating to primary instruction. The permanent head of the department is styled Director of Education. There are public schools in every country town throughout the state, and several in Hobart and Launceston. The principle of compulsion is in force in these two towns, the school age being from 7 to 13 years; and special religious instruction is given by the Church of England clergy out of school-hours. Secondary education was at one time encouraged by exhibitions, but none have been granted since 1893. The University of Tasmania was established in 1890, and at first was merely an examining body, but in the beginning of the year 1893 a building was acquired and teaching provided for the purpose of enabling students to graduate in Arts, Science, and Laws. The first degree, one of B.A., was taken in 1894. The Government grants the institution an annual subsidy, the amount voted by Parliament in 1902 being £4,000.

Education at the public schools of New Zealand is free (except that at such as are also district high schools fees are charged for instruction in the higher branches) and purely secular. The attendance of all children between the ages of 6 and 13 years is compulsory, except in cases where special exemptions have been granted. There is a separate Department of Education, presided over by one of the responsible Ministers of the Crown, as in the other provinces of Australasia. The whole colony has been divided into school districts, each presided over by a local Board, and a capitation grant of £3 15s. per head is paid by the State for every child in average attendance, and, in addition, 1s. 6d. per child in support of scholarships, with other grants for school-buildings, training of teachers, etc. In districts where there are few or no Europeans, native schools are maintained for the Maori children. High schools, colleges, and grammar schools provide the means for acquiring secondary education; and the University of New Zealand, like those of the Commonwealth states, is empowered to confer the same degrees as the Universities of Oxford and Cambridge, except as regards Divinity. It is, however, only an examining body, the undergraduates keeping their terms at the affiliated colleges—the University of Otago, the Canterbury College, the Auckland University College, and the Victoria College at Wellington.

Interest in educational matters has undoubtedly undergone a marked revival in the course of the last few years throughout the whole of Australasia. In New South Wales it has been considered that the prevailing system of state education is capable of expansion and modernisation, and a commission was appointed in 1902 to inquire into and report upon the methods employed in the chief continental countries and in America and Great Britain. This Commission presented its report in 1903, and several drastic changes in present methods were advocated. In Victoria the system has been to a large extent remodelled; Queensland and Western Australia have recently revised their standards; South Australia has introduced some valuable improvements, and reform is foreshadowed in New Zealand.

As regards actual school work, Kindergarten methods are more freely employed in the early stages, while throughout greater efforts are being made to avoid the purely abstract and to correlate with the concrete. More attention is being devoted to the cultivation of the powers of observation by the introduction of courses of lessons in nature study in which the pupils are encouraged to observe and where possible handle the objects under discussion. The importance of developing the physical as well as the mental powers of the scholar is also receiving increased recognition in various directions.

State Schools.

Exclusive of the native schools established by the New Zealand Government for the instruction of the Maori children, there were 8,930 public schools in Australasia at the close of the year 1902. The number in operation in each of the states, as well as in New Zealand, will be seen on reference to the table given below. As a rule, secondary education is provided by private institutions, and the figures quoted may be taken as representing primary schools; but in New South Wales there are four high schools, which it is customary to include with the others. The secondary schools in New Zealand are excluded from the returns:—

State.	State Schools.	Teachers employed, exclusive of Sewing Mistresses.		
		Males.	Females.	Total.
New South Wales	2,846	2,988	2,333	5,321
Victoria	2,070	1,917	2,739	4,656
Queensland	991	1,144	1,247	2,391
South Australia	716	411	930	1,341
Western Australia	250	261	356	617
Tasmania	349	232	446	678
Commonwealth	7,222	6,953	8,051	15,004
New Zealand	1,708	1,415	2,289	3,704
Australasia	8,930	8,368	10,340	18,708

In all the states, with the exception of Victoria, there has been a steady increase in the number of State schools during the past few years. In Victoria the reverse has been the case, for since 1891 the number in operation has decreased from 2,233 to 2,070. This is the result of a scheme of retrenchment, initiated at that time, by which there has been an amalgamation of schools in large centres of population; and in other districts schools have been closed and the pupils conveyed to other institutions at the cost of the state. Under the first part of this scheme no fewer than 84 schools have been converted into adjuncts to others in the neighbourhood. At these adjuncts—which are not included in the number of schools set down in the table—instruction is now imparted only to young children, in junior classes. The system of conveyance, brought into operation under the second part of the scheme, has been the means of closing 270 schools, an allowance being made by the state to parents to defray the cost of conveyance of their children to schools further removed from their place of abode. Notwithstanding the reduction in the number of schools during the past five years, consequent on the above retrenchment policy, the increased proportion of average attendance shows that educational facilities are well distributed.

The 991 schools in Queensland include 449 State schools, 77 special provisional schools, 462 ordinary provisional schools, and 3 schools at benevolent establishments. In compliance with a resolution of the Legislative Assembly, the provisional schools, which had previously been receiving a subsidy not exceeding £50, and not more than half the cost of new buildings and furniture, were placed on the same footing as State schools in regard to subsidy. By this step the state assumed the responsibility for four-fifths of the cost of building and equipment without limitation as to the amount. For Western Australia, the returns for years prior to 1896 included State-aided denominational schools. From these establishments the Government subsidy was withdrawn at the end of 1895, and thenceforth they are not included in the returns of the Education Department. The private schools are, however, examined by the Departmental inspectors in order to ascertain that sufficient instruction is given in arithmetic, writing, reading, spelling, and geography, while the various registers are supplied to the principals free of cost. This should be borne in mind when comparing the figures with those given for previous years, otherwise the extension of public instruction in that state would seem to be incommensurate with the growth of population. As a matter of fact, the progress has been rapid, and 8 new state schools were opened in 1902.

As shown in the previous table, the total number of teachers employed in the 8,930 state schools was 18,708—8,368 males and 10,340 females—exclusive of sewing-mistresses, of whom there were 80 in New South Wales, 410 in Victoria, 10 in South Australia, 60 in Western Australia, and 176 in New Zealand. New South Wales is the only state where employment is afforded to a greater number of male teachers in comparison with females; in all the other provinces there is a large preponderance of female instructors. In most of the states provision is made for the training of teachers. In New South Wales, the Fort-street Training School for male students had 35 students in training in 1902, 16 of whom held full-scholarships, 9 held half-scholarships, and 10 were non-scholarship students; while at the Hurlstone Training School for female students there were 41 students in residence, 16 of whom held full-scholarships, 9 half, and 16 non-scholarships. At the Fort Street Training College, residence and board and lodging are not provided, but full-scholarship students receive an allowance of £72 per annum, and half-scholarship £36, while no allowance is granted to non-scholarship students. The Hurlstone College is a residential institution, and scholarship students receive free board and lodging with an allowance of £1 per month, half-scholarship students pay £15 a year and receive an allowance of 10s. per month, and non-scholarship students pay £30 per annum. The Victorian Training College, which was closed for some time in accordance with the policy of retrenchment, was re-opened in 1900. On the 1st January, 1902, there were 50 students holding scholarships, while 20 others paid fees for the training received. There were 38 students in the training college in South Australia. A scheme for the more efficient training of pupil-teachers has been arranged, under which, for the first two years of their course, these young people will not be required to teach, but will receive instruction at the Pupil Teachers' School. For the third and fourth years they will engage in practical teaching, and may then be entered as students at Adelaide University for a period of two years. In addition to the 79 pupil teachers of the first and second grade who attended daily at the institution, 53 others received tuition on Saturday mornings, and 7 were taught by correspondence, while 14 boys were also in attendance who had gained exhibitions entitling them to free tuition for three years, in accordance with the Education Regulations of 1900. In 1902 a Training College was opened in Western Australia. The building is situated at Claremont, about half-way between Perth and Fremantle, and is open for both day and resident students of both sexes. There is accommodation for 60 students and the first session opened with a total of 41, of whom 30 were females. In New Zealand, teachers are trained at normal schools in Christchurch and Dunedin and at the Napier Training School. An interesting experiment in connection with the training of teachers was the holding of a Summer School in Victoria at the close of 1901. About 600 teachers applied for permission to attend, and of these 120 were selected. Lectures on such subjects as Principles of Education, Kindergarten, etc., were given by experts, and the experiment proved so successful that it is intended to make the institution an annual one, and the idea has been taken up with enthusiasm in some of the other states.

Within recent years it has come to be more or less clearly recognised that the pupil teacher system, as prevailing in these states, is not conducive to the acquirement of a satisfactory degree of professional ability, while the Training Colleges are hampered in their operations from the fact that they are dependent on the pupil teachers for their main supply of students. Instead of allowing these young people to teach with varying degrees of success for a certain period and then admitting them to a Training College, it is proposed to give a course of training antecedent to appointment in the schools. It will be seen from a preceding page that this idea has received practical application in the state of South Australia.

Enrolment at State Schools.

The average enrolment of pupils at the State schools of Australasia for the year 1902 and the proportion such figures bear to the total population is given in the following table :—

State.	Average Enrolment.	Percentage of Population.
New South Wales	212,848	15·12
Victoria	195,425	16·21
Queensland	89,531	17·39
South Australia	57,973	15·85
Western Australia	22,605	10·51
Tasmania	19,553	11·04
Commonwealth	597,935	14·89
New Zealand	133,952	16·58
Australasia	731,887	15·59

It will be seen that the largest percentage of the population enrolled at state schools was to be found in Queensland, and the lowest in Western Australia. Such a comparison, however, is of very little value, because the proportion which the children of school age bear to the total population varies considerably in the different states, being as low as 14 per cent. in Western Australia, up to 17 per cent. in Queensland and South Australia, and 19 per cent. in New South Wales. In Western Australia, which is still at its pioneer stage, there must of necessity be a much smaller percentage of dependent children than in the more widely settled states.

More important, perhaps, than the number of children enrolled is the average attendance. This, for scholars at the state schools during the year 1902, was 569,054, representing about 64 per school and 30 per teacher, and 12·12 per cent. of the population of Australasia. The figures for the individual states will be found appended :—

State.	Scholars in average attendance.			
	Total.	Per School.	Per Teacher.	Percentage of population.
New South Wales	155,916	55	29	11·08
Victoria	150,939	73	32	12·52
Queensland	72,809	73	30	14·14
South Australia	42,690	60	32	11·67
Western Australia	18,448	74	30	8·57
Tasmania	14,541	42	22	8·21
Commonwealth	455,343	63	30	11·72
New Zealand	113,711	67	31	14·07
Australasia	569,054	64	30	12·12

It will be seen from the above table that the highest percentage was shown by Queensland with 14·14 per 100 of the population, closely followed by New Zealand with 14·07 per cent. The percentage of the population of New Zealand—14·07—shown as in average attendance at the state schools, it must be remarked, is rather higher than it should be, on account of a number of Maori children attending the ordinary schools in districts where there are none established for the "natives," while the basis on which the proportion has been calculated is the population exclusive of aborigines. The "Native" schools in New Zealand, of which the number was 107, had a teaching-staff of 180, exclusive of 11 sewing-mistresses, in 1902, with an enrolment of 3,742 and an average attendance of 3,005 scholars, and the expenditure on the schools during the year amounted to £27,076. Of the 3,742 children enrolled at these schools, 3,043 were Maoris, or between Maori and half-caste, 336 were half-castes, and 363 were Europeans, or between half-caste and European.

Cost of Primary Education.

The official reports of the various states show that during the year 1902 the cost of administration and maintenance of the State schools of Australasia was £2,497,012, while the revenue from fees, rents, sales of books, etc., amounted to £126,296, leaving a net cost to the state of £2,370,716, excluding a sum of £288,165 expended on school premises. Assistance to private schools where primary or secondary education is given is not included in these figures. The expenditure for each of the states will be found below. In the case of New Zealand, the amounts given in the table represent the disbursements of the Education Boards, and not the actual capitation grant received from the Government during 1902, as the former figures more accurately represent the cost of the state schools for the twelve months. From the total cost to the state in that colony, the receipts from the Education Reserves, £43,047, have not been deducted, as the capitation grant is now reduced by an amount equivalent to the rents derived from these reserves, so that practically they are paid into the Consolidated Revenue. The figures do not give the whole expense to the state, as most of the principal teachers enjoy residences for which no rent charge is made. In the case of New South Wales, the annual value of these residences is about £38,000 :—

State.	Expended on Administration and Maintenance.	Receipts from Fees, Rents, &c.	Net Cost to State, excluding Premises.	Expended on School Premises.
	£	£	£	£
New South Wales	738,090	85,230	652,860	76,794
Victoria*	689,299	7,947	681,352	81,946
Queensland	261,317	....	261,317	9,443
South Australia	162,713	11,250	151,463	18,591
Western Australia	92,654	1,589	91,065	31,833
Tasmania	58,318	12,232	46,086	7,795
Commonwealth	2,002,391	118,248	1,884,143	226,402
New Zealand	494,621	8,048	486,573	61,763
Australasia	2,497,012	126,296	2,370,716	288,165

* Year ending 30th June, 1902.

In the states of Victoria, Queensland, South Australia, Western Australia, and in the colony of New Zealand, primary education is free; in the other states a small fee is charged, but, as will be seen from the table, the revenue derived from this source is very small in Tasmania. In New South Wales the fee charged is 3d. per week for each child, the sum payable by one family being limited to one shilling; and the receipts amount to a considerable sum annually, totalling £85,230 in 1902. Free education is, of course, given to those children whose parents cannot afford to pay for them, and the number of children so treated during last year was 28,701—equal to 11·8 per cent. of the gross enrolment of distinct pupils; the average for the last five years being 12·6. In Tasmania, at the beginning of 1901, new regulations came into force, under which school fees, which had till then constituted part of teachers' incomes, are paid into the Treasury, the teachers receiving, by way of compensation, an addition to their salaries to an extent and for a period exactly defined. Free education is granted in cases of necessity, and for this purpose free public schools were established in Hobart and Launceston; but as it was considered that this system affixed a brand of pauperism to the children making use of them, they have now been abolished, and the pupils find free education at the ordinary schools. In 1899 an Education Act was passed in Western Australia, which had for its chief object the granting of free education to all children of compulsory school age. The work of compulsion was also systematised, and the returns for 1902 show the highest percentage of attendance for any year since 1872.

Although primary instruction is free in Victoria, Queensland, South Australia, Western Australia, and New Zealand, yet Queensland is the only state where no fees were received in 1902; but, as pointed out on a previous page, the state receives contributions from local districts towards the construction of school buildings, the amount of such contributions in 1902 being £1,329. In Victoria fees are charged for instruction in extra subjects, such as book-keeping, shorthand, algebra, Euclid, French, Latin, Science, &c., but the instruction is given by visiting teachers as well as the regular staff teachers outside of statutory school hours. During last year extra subjects were taught in 131 schools, and the fees collected represent £2,859. This amount has not been included in the receipts which totalled £7,947 and were made up of fines, rents, and the amount realised by the sale of publications; and although not directly applied by the state towards the reduction of departmental expenditure, have been so treated here. In South Australia the receipts during 1902 included £4,215 from sale of books and school materials, £5,426 from rent of dedicated land, and sundry receipts amounting to £1,609.

It will be seen from the previous table that, excluding the expenditure on school premises, the net cost of public instruction in Australasia in 1902 was £2,370,716. This is equivalent to £4 3s. 3d. for each child in average attendance during the year; while, if the expenditure on buildings is taken into account, the amount reaches £4 13s. 5d. per child. The figures for each of the six states and for the colony of New Zealand are presented below:—

State.	Net Cost to State, per scholar in average attendance.	
	Excluding School Premises.	Including School Premises.
	£ s. d.	£ s. d.
New South Wales	4 3 9	4 13 7
Victoria	4 10 3	5 1 2
Queensland	3 11 9	3 14 5
South Australia	3 10 11	3 19 8
Western Australia	4 18 9	6 13 3
Tasmania	3 3 5	3 14 1
Commonwealth	4 2 9	4 12 8
New Zealand	4 5 7	4 16 5
Australasia	4 3 3	4 13 5

Expenditure on education in a large State like Western Australia, with a sparse but rapidly-expanding population, must of necessity be proportionately higher than in the older settled Eastern States. For the provisional schools, the cost per scholar in average attendance during 1902 was as high as £7 1s. 11d, while for the special schools in the North-west the expenditure was no less than £8 6s. 6d. per head of the average attendance. The figures for administration are also swollen by reason of the fact that private schools are inspected by the Departmental officers, and also receive various registers free of cost. The increased figures for total expenditure in Victoria during the year were caused by the large outlay on buildings, which amounted to £81,946, or more than twice as much as in the preceding year, and considerably over six times higher than that shown under this heading for 1897-8. Twenty-eight new school buildings and four detached residences were erected, the new infant schools in particular being built on the latest and most approved lines. Under the heading administration there was an increase of £15,700 in teachers' salaries, while the expenditure was further augmented by extension of the manual training and Kindergarten work. All the states show increases in expenditure on administration and maintenance per child in average attendance as compared with the figures for 1897–98. In New Zealand increases to teachers' salaries were responsible for the high average compared with previous years. The expenditure under this heading amounted to £419,000 in 1902, as against £382,000 for the preceding year. For New South Wales the increase amounted to 10s. 8d. per scholar; for Victoria, to 8s. 2d.; for Queensland, to 4s. 11d.; for South Australia, to 9s. 10d.; for Western Australia, to 5s. 5d.; for Tasmania, to 7s. 10d.; and for New Zealand, to 8s. 11d.

Encouragement of Secondary Education.

Before passing to the consideration of private schools, reference may be made to the encouragement of secondary education by the State, apart from grants to the Universities. In New South Wales there are numerous private colleges of a high class, and there are four State High Schools—two for boys and two for girls—where higher education may be obtained at a moderate cost; as well as 121 Superior Schools, in the higher classes of which pupils are prepared for the public examinations. In 1902 the expenditure on the High Schools amounted to £6,593. A scheme of scholarships for the Sydney Grammar School, for High and Superior Schools, and for the University, is in existence. In 1902, 105 candidates were successful at these examinations. Fifty secured scholarships and 38 bursaries for High and Superior Schools; 7, bursaries at the Sydney Grammar School; and 10, University bursaries.

In Victoria, as previously pointed out, extra subjects are taught for a small fee at 131 of the public schools. For the encouragement of secondary education, 200 scholarships were granted from 1886 to 1890, but in 1891 the number was reduced to 100, and in 1892 to 75. Consequent on the retrenchment policy already alluded to, these scholarships were abolished in 1893, but the principals of private colleges offered a large number of exhibitions to children attending State schools. The Department, however, decided to introduce paid scholarships similar to those withdrawn in 1893; and under the new scheme, 60 exhibitions of the annual value of £10 are awarded, the first examination for which was held in December, 1900. In 1902 there were 60 scholarships allotted, while 110 scholarships were awarded in 1902 to State school pupils by principals of the various secondary schools. The Department annually bestows a number of exhibitions to the University on pupils who have gained scholarships at secondary schools. At the examinations for these exhibitions, held in January, 1902, 10 candidates were successful. There are at present 80 exhibitions.

Steps have recently been taken in Queensland to add to the curriculum of the State schools, in order that they may be brought more into line with the superior public schools of New South Wales. Secondary education, however, has long been provided for by the liberal endowment of the private grammar schools, and by a system of scholarships for these schools, which at present number ten. Each school is subsidised to the extent of £1,000 annually; and the total amount of endowments and grants by the State to these institutions to the end of 1902 was £281,937. At the annual examinations for scholarships, 157 boys and 68 girls competed, and scholarships were gained by 27 boys and 9 girls, while 6 boys and 2 girls were awarded bursaries. Three pupils of secondary schools also qualified for exhibitions to Universities. In the last quarter of 1902 there were altogether 114 State scholars in attendance at the various grammar schools. Of the 75 exhibitions granted since the year 1878, when they were first instituted, 56 have been gained by students who had previously won scholarships from State schools.

In South Australia the Advanced School for Girls was attended by 115 pupils in 1901. The fees amounted to £1,043, and the expenditure to £1,287, so that there was a loss on the year's transactions of £244, against which must be set the fact that 45 bursary-holders were taught free. There are twelve bursaries for this school annually awarded to State school pupils. Six University scholarships of the value of £35 each are annually awarded to day students on the recommendation of the University Council, and 18 other scholarships of £10 each are awarded to evening students. There are also available 24 exhibitions and 24 bursaries for boys and girls, and 20 junior scholarships are also offered annually to pupils attending schools under the Minister. In Western Australia there is a high school for boys at Perth, which in 1901 received Government aid to the extent of £1,083. In 1901 the number of pupils on the roll, including boarders, was 96, and the average daily attendance was 93. Two State scholarships for this school, valued at £75 each and tenable for three years, are awarded annually. The Government also offers annually ten bursaries of the value of £10 to children attending the elementary schools of the state—five to boys, and five to girls. In Tasmania a system of exhibitions was at one time in force, but none have been granted since 1893. New Zealand has 25 incorporated or endowed secondary schools, with a regular teaching staff of 155, and a visiting staff of 59. At the end of 1902 there were 3,072 pupils on the rolls, and the average attendance for the year was 2,836. The receipts for 1902 amounted to £73,229, including £25,926 derived from interest on investments and rents of reserves, and £36,773 from fees. These schools, it should be noted, are not supported directly by the state. Some have endowments of land, and others receive aid from the rents derived from the Education Reserves administered by the School Commissioners.

PRIVATE SCHOOLS.

At the end of 1902 there were 2,718 private schools in Australasia, with a total teaching staff estimated at 9,163. The total number of pupils on the rolls was 163,469, and the average attendance, 128,743. Below will be found the figures for the individual states and for New Zealand. At the end of 1895, the Government subsidy was withdrawn from the assisted schools in Western Australia, and, thenceforward, information respecting these institutions is incorporated in the returns for private schools :—

State.	Schools.	Teachers.	Enrolment.		Average Attendance.
			Total.	Percentage of Population.	
New South Wales...	868	3,339	58,939	4·19	47,195
Victoria...............	872	2,616	47,030	3·90	33,624
Queensland	180	692	15,051	2·92	12,867
South Australia ...	224	678	10,602	2·90	9,393
Western Australia	80	294	6,260	2·91	4,922
Tasmania	197	690	9,963	5·63	7,200
Commonwealth	2,421	8,309	147,845	3·80	115,201
New Zealand	297	854	15,624	1·93	13,542
Australasia ...	2,718	9,163	163,469	3·48	128,743

In New South Wales during the ten years 1893–1902 the number of private schools reached its highest point in 1899, when there were no less than 1,053 schools, with 47,560 scholars in average attendance. Since that year, however, the numbers steadily declined, until in 1902 the returns showed 868 schools, with an average attendance of 47,195. The decrease is partly attributable to the extension of the public school system. Of the private schools in the state, 342 are Roman Catholic, as compared with 67 connected with the other Churches, while 459 are undenominational; but of the scholars enrolled, 40,868, or over 69 per cent., are in attendance at Roman Catholic schools, while 4,263 attend Church of England schools; 1,372, schools belonging to other denominations; and 12,436, the undenominational schools. Since 1893 the pupils of the Roman Catholic schools have increased by 31 per cent., which is about 1 per cent. higher than the general rate of increase. Many of the private schools are institutions of a high class. Only one—the Sydney Grammar School—is assisted by the State, which provides a statutory endowment of £1,500 per annum. In 1902 the staff of this school consisted of 26 teachers; the total enrolment was 626; the average enrolment, 534; and the average daily attendance, 514. The receipts for the year totalled £10,654, of which £9,015 represented fees; while the expenditure was £10,251.

From returns furnished by the principals of private schools in Victoria, it appears that the total number of institutions has increased from 867 in 1894 to 872 at the end of 1902, while the gross enrolment increased from 44,038 to 47,030 during the same period. In this state the principals of a number of the private colleges have granted scholarships at their institutions to state school pupils since the Government retrenched in this respect, 110 scholarships being granted in 1902. These colleges are not subsidised by the state.

Of the 180 private schools in Queensland, the principal are the ten grammar schools, which are situated at Brisbane, Ipswich, Maryborough, Rockhampton, Townsville, and Toowoomba. In each of the first four towns there are two schools—one for girls and one for boys. In 1902 the teaching staff of the grammar schools consisted of 56 permanent and 22 visiting teachers; the aggregate number of pupils on the rolls was 1,017; and the average daily attendance, 861. As previously mentioned, each of the ten schools receives an annual grant of £1,000 from the state. During 1902 the total receipts amounted to £27,971, and the expenditure, including salaries, to £28,251.

There is no special information available with respect to the private schools in South Australia. Of the 80 private schools open in Western Australia at the end of 1902, 43 were Roman Catholic institutions, with an enrolment of 4,921 pupils, or 78·6 per cent. of the total. The principal private institution is the Perth High School for Boys, which, in 1902, received Government aid to the extent of £1,000. The school is under the supervision of a Board of Governors. In 1902 the teaching staff numbered 5; the total number of pupils enrolled was 96, of whom 26 were boarders; and the average daily attendance was 93.

Included with the 215 private schools in Tasmania are 19 grammar schools and colleges, 6 of which are undenominational in character, 7 are connected with the Church of England, 3 with the Roman Catholic Church, 1 with the Wesleyan Church, 1 with the Presbyterian Church, and 1 with the Society of Friends. There were 119 permanent teachers at these institutions in 1900, and accommodation was provided for 2,819 students. The average attendance during the year was 2,191, of whom 467 were of the age of 15 years and upwards. As in New South Wales, the majority of the pupils at private institutions in New Zealand are enrolled at the Roman Catholic Schools. At the end of 1902 the number of schools belonging to this denomination was 139, at which 10,802 scholars were enrolled, with an average daily attendance of 9,303.

Diffusion of Education.

It will be seen that the Governments of the various states have done much for the instruction of the children, and throughout Australia and New Zealand attendance at school of children of certain ages is compulsory. Unfortunately, in spite of the law and in spite of the educational facilities afforded by the states, large numbers of children are growing up in total ignorance, and a large number with very little instruction. It must not be supposed that the officials of the public departments controlling instruction are to blame for this lamentable state of affairs; on the contrary, they have made, and continue to make, protests against the continuance of the evil, but the rescuing of children from the neglect of parents, and the effects of their own depraved inclinations, does not seem to appeal very strongly to the legislatures of these States.

As regards New South Wales the census returns for 1901 showed that there were 17,464 children of school age, that is 6 and under 14 years, who were not receiving instruction either at school or at home. If allowance be made for those who possessed certificates showing that they had been educated up to the requirements of the Education Act, and who numbered approximately 5 per cent. of the number quoted, there still remain about 16,600 children presumably growing up in blank ignorance. In addition to these a large proportion of the scholars enrolled at State schools fail to attend the requisite 70 days in each half-year. With respect to private schools the State has no means of ascertaining whether the teachers are competent to impart instruction, while nothing can be said regarding regularity of attendance at these institutions as the principals are not compelled to produce returns. Legislation to cope with the truancy evil is in contemplation by the State. At present the parents of children attending public schools are liable to prosecution if their children do not attend the number of days prescribed by the Act. Private schools are not interfered with, while there is no adequate provision made for tracing and dealing with children who are not enrolled at any school.

In Victoria, the census returns for 1901 showed that the total number of children of school age, that is 6 to 13 years, was 197,704, and of these the number receiving instruction either at school or at home was 184,200, so that apparently there were 13,504 children growing up in ignorance. Deducting a small percentage on account of those who while not at school were yet in possession of certificates of exemption there will be left upwards of 12,000 uneducated.

In Queensland there were at the census of 1901, 75,179 children of school age, that is over 6 and under 12 years of age, and of these 71,830 were receiving instruction at school or being taught at home, so that there were 3,349 uneducated. Of these it appears that in the majority of instances the degree of education was not stated on the schedule, but there is every probability that the greater number were uninstructed. With respect to the 3,100 children who were presumably taught at home, there is of course no guarantee that the instruction received was up to standard requirements.

In South Australia the children of school age, that is 7 to 13 years, numbered 62,720 at the census of 1901. Of these the total number under instruction at school or at home was returned as 54,471, leaving 8,249 not attending school, and presumably growing up in ignorance. In Western Australia the children of school age, that is 6 and under 14 years, numbered 26,335 at the census of 1901. The total under instruction was returned as 24,333, and the remaining 2,002 were therefore uneducated.

The Tasmanian census returns for 1901 showed a total of 26,122 children of the school ages 7 to 13 years, of whom 23,676 received instruction at school or at home, the remaining 2,446 apparently being illiterate. The New Zealand census returns for 1901 record a total of 170,961 children between 5 and 15, of whom 157,803 were receiving education, leaving the apparently illiterate as 13,158.

In addition to the numbers recorded as not receiving instruction in the various States there is also to be reckoned the percentage of children who while attending school do not comply with the standard requirements respecting the yearly attendances. To what extent irregularity prevails in regard to private schools there is no means of ascertaining, the returns from the public schools, however, indicate a greater or less degree of laxity in this respect.

UNIVERSITY EDUCATION.

The advance of education is hardly more clearly indicated by the institution and success of Colleges and Universities than is the progress of wealth or the attainment of leisure. In Australia the earliest attempts to provide for what may be termed the luxuries of education were made in New South Wales in 1852, and in Victoria in 1855, when the Universities of Sydney and Melbourne respectively were established. No other province of Australasia was at that time sufficiently advanced in wealth and population to follow the example thus set; but New Zealand in 1870, South Australia in 1874, and Tasmania in 1890, each founded a University. The Universities are in part supported by grants from the public funds, and in part by private endowments and the fees paid by students.

The income received by the Sydney, Melbourne, Adelaide, and Tasmanian Universities in 1902 was as follows :—

University.	Government Endowment.	Lecture Fees.	Other Sources.	Total.
	£	£	£	£
Sydney	12,317	11,950	15,387	39,654
Melbourne	14,625	9,352	5,747	29,724
Adelaide	6,572	8,747	5,113	20,432
Tasmania	4,000	1,007	987	5,994

In addition to the above annual endowment, the Adelaide University has received a perpetual endowment of 50,000 acres of land from the Government of South Australia. The University of New Zealand has a statutory grant of £3,000 a year from Government, and an additional income of about £2,500 from degree and examination fees. Of the affiliated colleges, Auckland University College is in receipt of a statutory grant of £4,000 a year from Government. The University of Otago derives a sum of about £5,500 annually from rents of reserves.

The number of students attending lectures in 1902 is shown below. In New Zealand the students keep their terms principally at the University of Otago, the Canterbury College, the Victoria College, and the Auckland University College.

University.	Students attending Lectures.		
	Matriculated.	Not Matriculated.	Total.
Sydney	667	63	730
Melbourne	485	30	515
Adelaide	311	287	598
New Zealand	588	276	864
Tasmania	54	4	58
Total	2,105	660	2,765

Attached to the University of Sydney there are three denominational colleges for male students, and a fourth, undenominational in character, for female students. In Melbourne there are three affiliated denominational colleges, one of which contains a hall for the accommodation of female students. In Adelaide and Hobart there are no affiliated colleges attached to the University; and in New Zealand the University itself is an examining and not a teaching body, the students keeping their terms at three undenominational colleges at Dunedin, Christchurch, and Auckland, besides several smaller institutions which have supplied a few graduates.

The Australasian Universities are empowered to grant the same degrees as the British Universities, with the exception of degrees in Divinity. In all the Universities women have now been admitted to the corporate privileges extended to male students; and at the Sydney, Melbourne, and Adelaide Universities this includes qualifying for degrees in medicine.

The number of degrees conferred by the five Universities, including those bestowed on graduates admitted *ad eundem gradum*, is as follows:—

Sydney	2,107
Melbourne	3,442
Adelaide	513
New Zealand	1,012
Tasmania	157

TECHNICAL EDUCATION.

Technical instruction is given in nearly all the capital cities of Australasia, as well as in many other parts of the country, and there is every probability that instruction in such matters will before long be still further extended. The State expenditure on this important branch of education in five of the Commonwealth provinces and in New Zealand will be found below; information for South Australia is not available:—

	£
New South Wales	33,408
Victoria	22,958
Queensland	19,653
Western Australia	4,319
Tasmania	1,338
New Zealand	15,459

In New South Wales, during the year 1878, a sum of £2,000 was granted by Parliament towards the organisation of a Technical College, and for five years the work of the institution was carried on in connection with the Sydney School of Arts. In 1883, however, a Board was appointed by the Government to take over its management, and the Technical College thenceforth became a State institution. Towards the end of 1889 the Board was dissolved, and the institution came under the direct control of the Minister of Public Instruction. The College, which, with the Technological Museum, is housed in a fine building at Ultimo, Sydney, is open to both male and female students. Branch technical schools have been established in the suburbs of Sydney and in many of the country districts, and technical instruction is also given in some of the public schools. In 1902 there were 428 technical classes in operation, of which 185 were held in Sydney and suburbs, 212 in the country districts, and 31 in connection with the public schools. The enrolment at these classes was 13,680, namely, 7,954 in Sydney and suburbs, 4,156 in the country districts, and 1,570 at the public schools. The number of individual students under instruction during the year was 10,405, and the average weekly attendance 8,842. In 1896 a Technical College was opened at Newcastle, and a new College at Bathurst in June, 1898. In 1902 a Technical School was built at Lithgow, and Mechanical Engineering Shops were provided at Newcastle. During the year the expenditure by the Government on technical education amounted to £33,408, exclusive of expenditure on the Technical Museum and branches. Fees to the amount of £7,278 were received from the students.

Technical education in Victoria has extended rapidly, but while the Government of New South Wales has wholly borne the cost of this branch of instruction, that of Victoria has received great assistance from private munificence, the Hon. F. Ormond, M.L.C., having given £15,500 to assist in the establishment of a Working Men's College. In 1902 there were 18 Schools of Mines and Technical Schools receiving aid from the State. The total State expenditure during the year was £22,958, and the fees received from students amounted to £10,232. The question of more closely relating the work of the schools to the industrial conditions of the districts wherein they are situated is under consideration, and it is intended to withdraw the subsidy from those schools which fail to attract a sufficient number of students, or which do not supply a real need in local industrial requirements.

Technical education has well advanced in South Australia. The School of Design in Adelaide during 1902 had 575 students on the roll, and there were branch schools at Port Adelaide and Gawler with an enrolment of 22 and 18 students respectively. The School of Mines and Industries, founded in 1889, received Government aid in 1901 to the extent of £3,250, while the receipts from fees and sale of materials to students amounted to £2,532. Manual instruction is imparted in the public schools, and special instruction in agriculture is also given at various country centres. At the Adelaide Agricultural School 117 pupils were enrolled during the year, and there was an average attendance of 77·3.

In Queensland technical education has received some attention, and a Board of Technical Instruction was appointed in 1902, its functions being to report concerning existing colleges and advise with respect to the establishment of new institutions. The Board will also conduct examinations, and report generally with reference to matters concerning technical education. The sum of £10,650 was voted by Parliament for "Grants in aid of Technical Education," for the financial year 1902-3, subject to the condition that the aid should not exceed 15s. for every £1 raised locally. There were 23 technical schools distributed in various centres in 1902, and the number of individual students was given as 5,084. The receipts of the various colleges amounted in 1902 to £20,271, and the expenditure to £19,653.

In Tasmania the foundations of new Technical Schools were laid in 1889 in Hobart, and there is a branch school in Launceston. The schools are under the direction of local Boards of Advice, the members of which act directly under the Minister in charge of education. The average attendance of students in 1901, including those in the two Schools of Mines, was 689. The total receipts for the year came to £3,235.

In Western Australia a Technical School was opened in Perth during 1900. The total number of students enrolled in 1902 was 145, of whom 122 were males, and 23 females. The receipts during the year were £414, chiefly from fees, and the expenditure amounted to £4,319. There are also classes for manual training at Perth, Boulder, Coolgardie, and Northam, and a cookery class at Perth. In the former branch 789 boys attended during the year, and 146 girls were entered in the cookery class.

In New Zealand the Manual and Technical Instruction Acts of 1900 and 1902 provide for instruction in manual and technical subjects in accordance with specified regulations, and the recognised classes are entitled to receive capitation allowances in addition to grants in aid of buildings, furniture, and apparatus. The subjects taught in the school classes include woodwork, cottage gardening, swimming and life-saving, ambulance work, dressmaking, laundry work, and cookery. In 1902 there were fifteen technical or art schools, with 360 classes attended by 4,500 students. There is a school of engineering and technical science at the Canterbury College, which was attended by 92 students in 1902. The Canterbury Agricultural College has an endowment of 60,000 acres of land, and possesses complete and up-to-date plant and buildings. Thirty students attended at the institution in 1902. Several schools of mines are located in the chief mining centres, and at the Otago University there is a chair of mining and metallurgy endowed by the Government, with a yearly grant of £500. The number of mining students in 1902 was 300, of whom 60 attended the course of instruction at Otago University.

General Education.

Striking evidence of the rapid progress made by these states in regard to education is afforded by a comparison of the educational status of the people as disclosed by the five census enumerations of 1861, 1871, 1881, 1891, and 1901. In those years the numbers who could read and write, read only, and who were unable to read were as follow, children under five being considered unable to read, no matter how returned at the census :—

Degree of Education.	New South Wales.	Victoria.	Queensland.	South Australia.	Western Australia.	Tasmania.	Commonwealth.	New Zealand.	Australasia.
1861.									
Read and write..	188,543	327,800	17,181	72,207	8,446	48,281	662,458	67,998	730,456
Read only	46,024	56,945	3,714	18,629	1,559	18,137	140,008	8,922	148,930
Cannot read	116,293	155,577	9,164	35,994	5,585	28,559	351,172	22,101	373,273
1871.									
Read and write..	296,741	478,572	74,940	115,246	18,703	55,939	1,040.141	177,419	1,217,560
Read only	56,391	70,999	12,080	21,123	2,614	13,945	177,152	19,240	196,392
Cannot read	150,849	181,957	33,084	49,257	4,036	29,444	443,627	59,734	508,361
1881.									
Read and write..	507,067	651,567	136,718	200,057	19,697	74,967	1,590,073	346,228	1,936,301
Read only	49,372	49,535	13,681	15,267	2,429	9,605	139,839	27,323	167,162
Cannot read	195,029	161,244	63,176	64,541	7,582	31,133	522,705	116,382	639,087
1891.									
Read and write..	835,570	908,767	276,381	236,514	34,254	103,138	2,394,624	484,198	2,878,822
Read only	43,536	32,817	14,618	9,571	2,061	6,287	108,890	24,902	133,792
Cannot read	244,848	198,821	102,719	74,346	18,467	37,242	671,443	117,558	789,001
1901.									
Read and write..	1,071,939	999,620	375,874	290,748	150,194	133,579	3,021,454	638,889	3,660,343
Read only	29,725	21,402	11,387	8,222	2,982	3,825	77,543	14,752	92,295
Cannot read	253,182	180,048	109,835	63,634	30,948	35,071	672,718	119,078	791,796

The figures in the preceding table refer to the total population, and the number of illiterates is therefore swollen by the inclusion of children under school-going age. If the population over 5 years of age be considered in comparison with the total population, the results for the whole of Australasia will be as follow :—

Degree of Education.	Whole Population.				
	1861.	1871.	1881.	1891.	1901.
Read and write	730,456	1,217,560	1,936,301	2,878,822	3,660,343
Read only	148,930	196,392	167,162	133,792	92,295
Cannot read	373,273	508,361	639,087	789,001	791,796
Total..................	1 252,659	1,922,313	2,742,550	3,801,615	4,544,434

Degree of Education.	Population over 5 years of age.				
	1861.	1871.	1881.	1891.	1901.
Bead and write	730,339	1,180,145	1,936,111	2,878,813	3,660,343
Read only	143,908	190,545	161,295	128,445	92,295
Cannot read	168,929	235,236	243,583	262,515	270,552
Total.	1,043,176	1,605,976	2,340,989	3,269,773	4,023,190

The following table affords a comparison of the number of each class in every 10,000 of the population for the same periods:—

Degree of Education.	Whole Population.					Population over 5 years of age.				
	1861.	1871.	1881.	1891.	1901.	1861.	1871.	1881.	1891.	1901.
Read and write	5,831	6,334	7,060	7,578	8,054	7,001	7,038	8,270	8,804	9,099
Read only	1,189	1,022	610	352	204	1,380	1,186	689	393	229
Cannot read	2,980	2,644	2,330	2,075	1,742	1,619	1,776	1,041	808	672
Total	10,000	10,000	10,000	10,000	10,000	10,000	10,000	10,000	10,000	10,000

It will be seen, therefore, that while in 1861 there were only 7,001 persons who could read and write out of every 10,000 people over 5 years of age, the number in 1901 had increased to 9,099, while those who were totally illiterate had in the same period decreased from 1,619 to 672.

Looking at the matter still more closely with reference to age, it will be seen that the improvement in education is most marked in the case of the rising generation. The following table shows the degree of education of all children between the ages of 5 and 15 years in 1861, 1871, 1881, 1891, and 1901, numerically and per 10,000:—

Degree of Education.	Total between 5 and 15 years.					Per 10,000 children.				
	1861.	1871.	1881.	1891.	1901.	1861.	1871.	1881.	1891.	1901.
Read and write	114,353	288,154	482,719	674,012	850,188	4,637	5,911	7,058	7,565	8,009
Read only	68,038	102,316	86,574	69,640	52,428	2,759	2,099	1,266	782	494
Cannot read ..	64,237	96,986	114,654	147,280	158,984	2,604	1,990	1,676	1,653	1,49
Total ..	246,628	487,456	683,947	890,932	1,061,600	10,000	10,000	10,000	10,000	10,00

The proportion of those able to read and write has, therefore, grown from 4,637 to 8,009 in every 10,000 children during the forty years which the table covers, while the number of those able to read only in 1901 was one-sixth of what it was in 1861, and the wholly illiterate had decreased by nearly one-half during the period.

The Marriage Register affords further proof of the advance of education, and it has the further advantage of giving annual data, while the census figures are only available for decennial periods,

The numbers of those who signed the Marriage Register by marks were as appended. Where a blank is shown the information is not available.

State.	1861.			1871.			1881.			1891.			1902.		
	Marriages.	Marks.		Marriages.	Marks.		Marriages.	Marks.		Marriages.	Marks.		Marriages.	Marks.	
		M.	F.		M.	F.		M.	F.		M.	F.		M.	F.
New South Wales.	3,222	596	989	3,953	573	768	6,284	347	525	8,457	278	248	10,486	135	120
Victoria	4,434	..	..	4,698	342	650	5,896	171	245	8,780	110	133	8,477	57	46
Queensland	320	..	..	970	..	..	1,708	84	169	2,905	88	109	3,243	50	75
South Australia ..	1,158	..	..	1,250	..	..	2,308	100	159	2,315	40	49	2,383	33	21
Western Australia.	149	..	..	159	..	..	197	..	..	418	..	..	2,024	12	16
Tasmania	717	..	..	598	..	..	856	..	..	988	..	..	1,313	52	30
Commonwealth	10,000	..	..	11,628	..	..	17,244	..	..	23,858	..	..	27,926	339	308
New Zealand	878	..	..	1,864	..	..	3,279	105	190	3,805	53	64	6,394	16	28
Australasia	10,878	..	..	13,487	..	..	20,523	..	..	27,663	..	..	34,320	355	336

The percentages for those states for which the necessary information is available are worked out in the following table :—

Year.	Males.	Females.	Total.
1861	18·50	30·69	24·60
1871	10·58	16·40	13·49
1881	4·14	6·61	5·38
1891	2·12	2·27	2·20
1902	1·03	0·98	1·01

The percentage in 1902 was, therefore, less than a twenty-fourth of that in 1861, and there is every reason to expect that in the course of another few years it will be still further diminished.

Public Libraries.

In all the states public libraries have been established. The Public Libraries in Melbourne and Sydney are splendid institutions, the former comparing favourably with many of the libraries in European capitals. The following table shows the number of libraries which furnished returns, and the number of books belonging to them, for the latest year for which information is available :—

	No. of Libraries.	No. of Books.
New South Wales	340	520,000
Victoria	389	1,198,085
Queensland	157	187,805
South Australia	166	266,157
Western Australia	155	86,000
Tasmania	44	90,493
New Zealand	369	516,300
Australasia	1,620	2,864,840

FOOD SUPPLY AND COST OF LIVING.

CONSIDERING the comparatively high rate of wages which prevails, food of all kinds is fairly cheap in Australasia, and articles of diet which in other countries are almost within the category of luxuries are largely used even by the poorer classes. The average annual consumption per inhabitant of the principal articles of common diet, based on the experience of the last ten years, is given below :—

Article.	New South Wales.	Victoria.	Queensland.	South Australia.	Western Australia.	Tasmania.	Common-wealth.	New Zealand.	Australasia.
Grain—	lb.	lb.	lb.	lb.	lb.	lb.	lb.	lb.	lb.
Wheat	360·2	330·8	344·0	389·0	474·1	418·1	357·2	400·1	364·4
Rice	9·4	7·3	17·7	9·3	18·2	5·9	9·9	8·8	9·8
Oatmeal	6·1	6·9	4·3	5·5	10·2	15·6	6·6	9·3	7·1
Potatoes	181·4	239·3	157·0	126·1	187·7	624·7	212·3	522·5	264·4
Sugar	109·0	95·0	128·9	102·1	110·1	96·1	105·7	96·7	104·2
Tea	7·7	6·8	7·3	8·3	9·9	6·2	7·4	6·4	7·2
Coffee	0·5	0·7	0·5	0·7	0·8	0·4	0·6	0·4	0·6
Cheese	3·6	3·2	4·2	2·7	6·0	1·6	3·5	4·4	3·7
Butter	20·6	13·7	13·3	12·9	28·5	17·4	16·7	17·8	16·9
Salt	42·1	15·4	63·7	17·0	19·2	19·7	31·7	34·4	32·1
Meat—									
Beef	159·7	117·3	280·0	127·0	141·8	117·8	155·5	90·0	144·4
Mutton	120·4	71·8	90·0	75·0	133·9	84·9	94·1	110·0	96·8
Pork and Bacon	12·2	12·2	13·3	11·4	31·4	14·0	13·0	12·5	12·9

It will be seen that the consumption of wheat in the Commonwealth is 357 lb., ranging from 331 lb. in Victoria to 474 lb. in Western Australia, the average consumption for Australasia being 364 lb. per head. There is in all the states a tendency towards reducing the consumption of bread-stuffs, the place of bread being taken by potatoes and other vegetables. In Western Australia and in Tasmania the large influx of miners some years ago materially increased the consumption of breadstuffs, as shown by the high figures in the above table, but of late years the tendency in these, as in the other states, is towards a smaller consumption. The consumption of rice remains about the same from year to year, the average being 9·8 lb., varying from 5·9 lb. in Tasmania to 18·2 lb. in Western Australia. The use of tea is universal in Australia, but there has been a perceptible decline in the quantity used during the last fifteen years. The consumption is largest in Western Australia, with 9·9 lb. per head, while South Australia comes next with 8·3 lb. per head. Sugar also enters largely into consumption, the average in the two principal states being 109 lb. per head in New South Wales and 95 lb. in Victoria. The figure for Queensland is based on the returns of production and export; the consumption for 1902 appears to have been only 94·1 lb. per head. Coffee is not a universal beverage in Australasia, the consumption being only one-twelfth that of tea. It is used most largely in Western Australia, where the annual demand amounts to 12·8 oz. per head; but, like tea, the consumption of this beverage is not now so great as formerly.

In some of the states the consumption of potatoes per head of population may be less than is shown in the table. It is probable that the high average consumption of 624·7 lb. in Tasmania and 522·5 lb. in New Zealand is caused by the failure of the New South Wales and other continental markets to absorb the production of potatoes in excess of local requirements in those states, with the result that a quantity has to be given to live stock and poultry. Under these circumstances, it is impossible to determine with exactitude the quantity entering into the food consumption of the population.

The consumption of meat has been ascertained with exactness for five of the states, but these may be taken as fairly representing the whole group. The average quantity of beef annually consumed in the Commonwealth amounts to 155·5 lb. per head; of mutton, to 94·1 lb.; and of pork, 13·0 lb.; in all, 262·6 lb. It would thus appear that each inhabitant requires daily nearly three-quarters of a pound of meat, and that during the year two sheep are killed for each member of the community, and one bullock to every five persons. It is obvious, therefore, that much meat must be wasted. The consumption in New Zealand cannot be accurately determined, but it is probable that about 212·5 lb. of meat is the average annual consumption per inhabitant, of which beef comprises 90·0 lb.; mutton, 110·0 lb.; and pork, 12·5 lb.

The quantity of meat used by the Australasian people, as shown by the above figures, is the most remarkable feature of their diet. The consumption per inhabitant in Germany is 64 lb., while in Australia it is nearly four times that quantity. In the United States, a meat exporting country, the consumption is abont three-fifths of that of Australasia. The following table shows the meat consumption per head for the principal countries of the world:—

ountry.	Per Inhabitant.	Country.	Per Inhabitant.
	lb.		lb.
Great Britain	109	Holland	57
France	77	Sweden	62
Germany	64	Norway	78
Russia	51	Denmark	64
Austria	61	Switzerland	62
Italy	26	United States	150
Spain	71	Canada	90
Belgium	65	Australasia	254

Judged by the standard of the food consumed, the lot of the population of Australasia appears to be far more tolerable than that of the people of most other countries. This will be seen most clearly from the following table, the particulars given in which, with the exception of the figures referring to Australasia, have been taken from Mulhall's *Dictionary of Statistics*:—

Country.	Lb. per Inhabitant.						Tea and Coffee—Oz.
	Grain.	Meat.	Sugar.	Butter and Cheese.	Potatoes.	Salt.	
United Kingdom	378	109	75	19	380	40	91
France	540	77	20	8	570	20	66
Germany	550	64	18	8	1,020	17	78
Russia	635	51	11	5	180	19	6
Austria	460	61	18	7	560	14	28
Italy	400	26	8	4	50	18	20
Spain	480	71	6	3	20	17	6
Portugal	500	49	12	3	40	17	18
Sweden	560	62	22	11	500	28	112
Norway	440	78	13	14	500	40	144
Denmark	560	64	22	22	410	25	140
Holland	560	57	35	15	820	20	240
Belgium	590	65	27	15	1,050	...	142
Switzerland	440	62	26	11	140	...	110
Roumania	400	82	4	9	80	...	8
Servia	400	84	4	9	80	...	8
United States	370	150	53	20	170	39	162
Canada	400	90	45	22	600	40	72
Australasia	381	254	104	21	264	32	125

Taking the articles in the foregoing list, with the exception of tea and coffee, and reducing them to a common basis of comparison, it will be found that the amount of thermo-dynamic power capable of being generated by the food consumed in Australasia is only exceeded by that eaten in Germany, Holland, and Belgium. For the purpose of comparison the figures of Dr. Edward Smith, F.R.S., in his well known work on *Foods*, have been used, and the heat developed has been reduced to the equivalent weight lifted 1 foot high. In estimating the thermo-dynamic effect of food, grain has been reduced to its equivalent in flour, and regard has been paid to the probable nature of the meat consumed. The figures for potatoes are given as they appear in the *Dictionary of Statistics;* but it is a probable supposition that but a small proportion of the quantity over 400 lb. set down for any country is required for human consumption, and the figures relating to some of the countries—notably the three just mentioned—are therefore excessive. The substances specified above are largely supplemented by other foods, both in America and in Europe, but not more so than in these states, and the figures in the table may be taken as affording an accurate view of the comparative quantity and food value of the articles of consumption in the countries mentioned. To make such a comparison perfectly just, however, the average amount of work which each individual in the community is called upon to perform should be taken into consideration. In Australasia the proportion of women and children engaged in laborious occupations is far smaller than in Europe and America, and the hours of labour of all persons are also less, so that the amount of food-energy required is reduced in proportion. In his *Dictionary of Statistics*, under the heading of "Diet," Mulhall gives a measure of the aggregate amount of work performed by persons doing physical and mental labour, and it would appear that when burnt in the body the food of an average man should be equal to at least 3,300 foot tons of work daily; of a woman, 2,200; and of a child, 1,100 foot tons. For Australasia the average of all persons would be about 2,000 foot tons, whereas from the table just given it would appear that the amount of work to which the daily food consumed by each individual in Australasia is equivalent is not less than 4,146 foot tons.

It must be admitted, however, that the method of comparison adopted in the preceding paragraph is not entirely satisfactory, as the functions of various kinds of food have not been considered. Experiments and observations made in Europe show that a standard may be set up by which the amount of nutrients required to maintain different classes of people may be measured. Professor Voit, of Munich, has ascertained that to sustain a labouring man engaged in moderately hard muscular work there are required 118 grams of protein and quantities of carbo-hydrates and fats sufficient with the protein to yield 3,050 calories of energy. There are 454 grams in a pound avoirdupois, and the calorie is the amount of heat that would raise the temperature of 4 lb. of water 1° Fahrenheit. Applying the ascertained values of the various foods, the consumption of which has just been given, it will be found that the daily consumption per inhabitant is equivalent to 105 grams of protein and 3,195 calories, or about the quantity Professor Voit declares to be sufficient for a labouring man. If allowance be made for the fact that only 29 per cent. of the population are adult males, 24 per cent. women, and 47 per cent. children, the quantity of food consumed in Australasia would appear to be far in excess of the actual requirements of the population, and though the excess may be looked upon as so much waste, it is none the less evidence of the condition of a people whose circumstances permit them to indulge in it.

The consumption of many other articles of common use can be ascertained with some exactness, and this is given for the seventeen specified in the following list. In all cases where the commodities are wholly imported the actual quantities entering into consumption can be given; where there is a local manufacture it has been necessary in some instances to make an estimate, but as the data for such are ample the figures given may be taken as fairly reliable.

The principal feature of the table is the high consumption of Western Australia of most of the articles comprised in the list. Amongst the most notable of these are tinned fish, 8·83 lb. per inhabitant, compared with the Commonwealth average of 4·38 lb.; preserved milk 27·82 lb., compared with 3·68 lb.; onions 27·96 lb., compared with 16·82 lb.; candles 10·43 lb., compared with 4·7 lb.; kerosene oil 7·4 gallons, compared with 3·51 gallons; and soap 18·38 lb., compared with 14·24 lb.

The annual consumption per inhabitant based on the experience of the last four years was :—

Article.	New South Wales.	Victoria.	Queensland.	South Australia.	Western Australia.	Tasmania.	Commonwealth.	New Zealand.	Australasia.
	lb.	lb.	lb.	lb.	lb.	lb.	lb.	lb.	lb.
Cocoa and chocolate ...	0·83	0·78	0·41	1·08	0·93	0·72	0·78	0·69	0·77
Currants and raisins ...	4·09	4·30	4·16	5·10	5·51	4·16	4·34	6·57	4·72
Dates ...	1·41	1·42	0·80	0·68	1·06	0·37	1·20	0·60	1·10
Fish (tinned) ...	5·01	3·40	4·22	3·62	8·83	3·50	4·38	3·77	4·28
Honey ...	1·72	0·73	1·36	2·10	1·27	0·55	1·32	0·60	1·20
Maizena (cornflour) ...	2·39	1·58	0·74	1·23	1·88	0·55	1·70	1·58	1·68
Milk (condensed) ...	3·52	1·50	2·86	1·39	27·82	1·39	3·68	1·87	3·37
Mustard ...	0·27	0·20	0·24	0·26	0·37	0·19	0·24	0·28	0·25
Onions ...	12·79	22·71	17·17	9·50	27·96	10·23	16·82	...	...
Pepper ...	0·21	0·36	0·26	0·39	0·29	0·26	0·29	0·30	0·29
Sago ...	0·29	0·30	0·85	0·29	0·21	0·56	0·38	0·61	0·42
Tapioca ...	1·63	1·73	1·24	1·48	1·71	1·04	1·58	1·98	1·64
Blue (washing) ...	0·38	0·30	0·25	0·27	0·36	0·31	0·32	0·24	0·31
Candles ...	4·43	4·51	3·76	4·00	10·43	6·29	4·70	6·38	4·99
Soap ...	15·10	12·39	15·52	12·00	18·38	16·78	14·24	13·92	14·18
Starch ...	4·01	4·70	3·15	2·18	2·24	2·33	3·78	2·50	3·56
	galls.	galls.	galls.	galls.	galls.	galls.	galls.	galls.	galls.
Kerosene oil ...	3·04	3·58	3·77	3·45	7·40	2·01	3·51	3·27	3·47

The following table gives the annual consumption of tobacco in Australasia and the principal countries of the world. The use of tobacco is more prevalent in Western Australia and Queensland than in any of the other states, but not to the extent which the figures of consumption would indicate, as both Western Australia and Queensland have a larger proportion of adult males amongst their population than the other states, and the proportionate number of smokers is larger, though the actual consumption per smoker may not be so. Compared with other parts of the world, the average consumption of Australasia will not appear excessive :—

Country.	lb.	Country.	lb.
Australasia	2·52	Austria-Hungary	3·77
New South Wales	2·70	Italy	1·34
Victoria	2·22	Spain	1·70
Queensland	2·97	Holland	6·92
South Australia	2·00	Belgium	3·15
Western Australia	4·81	Switzerland	3·24
Tasmania	2·05	Sweden	1·87
New Zealand	2·30	Denmark	3·70
United Kingdom	1·41	Turkey	4·37
France	2·05	United States	4·40
Germany	3·00	Canada	2·11
Russia	1·23	Brazil	4·37

Taking Australia as a whole, the consumption of tobacco per inhabitant is slightly less than it was ten years ago; but there has been a considerable change in the consumption in some of the states. In Queensland there has been a fall in amount consumed per inhabitant of nearly half a pound, in New South Wales one-fifth, in Tasmania one-seventh, in South Australia one-eighth, and in Victoria one-twelfth of a pound. In Western Australia there has been an increase of nearly three-fourths of a pound, and in New Zealand of one-eighth of a pound. In regard to the description of tobacco used, the chief point noticeable is the large increase in the consumption of cigarettes. In 1890 about 88·4 per cent. of the total consumption was of ordinary tobacco; in 1902 the proportion had fallen to 84·1 per cent.; of cigars, the consumption in 1890 was about 8·5 per cent., compared with 5 per cent. at present, and of cigarettes 3·1 per cent. in 1890, compared with 10·9 per cent. for the year 1902.

All the states except Tasmania manufacture tobacco, and the following figures show the average consumption of the locally-made and of the imported article during the last three years. The imported tobacco is inclusive of tobacco made in other Commonwealth states :—

State.	Consumption of locally-made—			Consumption of imported—		
	Tobacco.	Cigars.	Cigarettes.	Tobacco.	Cigars.	Cigarettes.
	lb.	lb.	lb.	lb.	lb.	lb.
New South Wales	2,512,134	45,892	476,400	787,471	186,948	58,119
Victoria	1,867,313	94,318	200,515	736,087	121,424	51,128
Queensland	617,668	1,246	20,189	792,968	68,299	80,469
South Australia	324,500	35,468	34,843	238,107	29,521	29,388
Western Australia	103,565	13,719	7,208	625,597	62,142	71,904
Tasmania	*	*	*	355,562	19,663	18,054
New Zealand	47,120	2,084	240	1,647,174	83,468	169,998

* Information not available.

Australasia as a whole compares very favourably with most European countries in the average quantity of intoxicants consumed, as the following statement shows. The figures, which are reduced to gallons of proof spirit from data given in Mulhall's *Dictionary of Statistics*, would appear even more favourable to Australasia were the fact of the large preponderance of males over females in these states made a feature of the comparison :—

Country.	Proof gallons.	Country.	Proof gallons.
United Kingdom	3·57	Portugal	3·00
France	5·10	Holland	4·00
Germany	3·08	Belgium	4·00
Russia	2·02	Denmark	5·00
Austria	2·80	Scandinavia	4·36
Italy	3·40	United States	2·65
Spain	2·85	Australasia	2·50

The following table shows the average consumption for all the states during the last three years :—

State.	Spirits.		Wine.		Beer, &c.		Equivalent in Alcohol (proof) per Inhabitant
	Total.	Per Inhabitant.	Total.	Per Inhabitant.	Total.	Per Inhabitant.	
	galls.	galls.	galls.	galls.	galls.	galls.	galls.
New South Wales	1,203,353	0·88	905,798	0·66	14,777,499	10·75	2·44
Victoria	953,534	0·79	1,469,004	1·22	15,260,957	12·70	2·74
Queensland	516,254	1·03	189,862	0·38	5,584,377	11·14	2·57
South Australia	172,732	0·48	466,599	1·29	3,261,121	8·99	1·95
Western Australia	293,151	1·55	164,699	0·87	4,891,940	25·83	5·13
Tasmania	88,551	0·51	28,378	0·16	1,596,315	9·18	1·75
Commonwealth	3,227,575	0·85	3,224,340	0·85	45,372,209	11·93	2·61
New Zealand	582,675	0·75	122,077	0·16	7,230,358	9·27	2·00
Australasia	3,810,250	0·83	3,346,417	0·73	52,602,567	11·48	2·50

The largest consumption of spirits per inhabitant is in Western Australia, Queensland being second. Wine is used most freely in South Australia and Victoria, and beer in Western Australia. The average consumption of alcohol in the Commonwealth for the last three years amounted to 2·61 gallons of proof spirit per inhabitant, ranging from 5·13 gallons in Western Australia to 1·75 gallons in Tasmania. There was a great diminution in the quantity of alcohol consumed in Australasia in the year immediately following the bank crisis, and in 1895 the consumption fell to 2·1 gallons, as compared with 2·94 gallons in 1891. From 1895 there was a gradual increase, and the consumption for the last seven years has ranged between 2·4 and 2·5 gallons.

During the last ten years there has been a considerable change as regards some of the states in the character of the beverages consumed. This change is most noticeable in the consumption of beer in Victoria and Western Australia. In the first-named state during the year 1892 there was a consumption of 16,817,930 gallons of malt liquors; this is equal to 14·47 gallons per head; in 1902 the total consumption had fallen to 15,519,211 gallons, equal to 12·86 gallons per head. In Western Australia the experience was of the opposite character, as the accompanying table shows:—

State.	Consumption of Malt Liquors in 1892.		Consumption of Malt Liquors in 1902.	
	Total.	Per Inhabitant.	Total.	Per Inhabitant.
	galls.	galls.	galls.	galls.
New South Wales	12,869,059	10·91	14,564,552	10·45
Victoria	16,817,930	14·47	15,519,211	12·86
Queensland	3,939,618	9·47	5,482,246	10·69
South Australia	3,762,818	11·36	3,231,355	8·85
Western Australia	635,921	11·36	5,354,877	26·12
Tasmania	1,486,621	9·72	1,699,945	9·68
Commonwealth	39,531,967	11·98	45,852,186	11·88
New Zealand	5,013,781	7·81	7,380,883	9·25
Australasia	44,545,748	11·30	53,233,069	11·42

The consumption per inhabitant of malt liquors for the Commonwealth showed a slight decrease during the ten years, but there was an increase in New Zealand. The consumption of spirits has declined in all the states of the Commonwealth, but in New Zealand there has been an increase in the volume per inhabitant. For the Commonwealth the decline during the ten years is strikingly evidenced by the fact that the total consumption of spirits in 1892 exceeded that of 1902 by

145,478 gallons. The following is a statement of the consumption in 1892 and 1902 respectively :—

State.	Consumption of Spirits in 1892.		Consumption of Spirits in 1902.	
	Total.	Per Inhabitant.	Total.	Per Inhabitant.
	galls.	galls.	galls.	galls.
New South Wales	1,184,042	1·00	1,260,438	0·90
Victoria	1,164,750	1·00	708,341	0·59
Queensland	446,146	1·07	492,272	0·96
South Australia	204,907	0·62	181,037	0·50
Western Australia	86,865	1·55	314,114	1·58
Tasmania	104,759	0·69	89,789	0·51
Commonwealth	3,191,469	0·97	3,045,991	0·79
New Zealand	454,036	0·71	602,021	0·75
Australasia	3,645,505	0·92	3,648,012	0·78

The consumption of wine can be determined only approximately. Wine is an article of local production not subject to excise duty, and it is quite possible some wine may be consumed without its production being noted. The following statement gives the probable consumption for the periods named :—

State.	Consumption of Wine in 1892.		Consumption of Wine in 1902.	
	Total.	Per Inhabitant.	Total.	Per Inhabitant.
	galls.	galls.	galls.	galls.
New South Wales	1,021,144	0·86	1,019,460	0·73
Victoria	1,414,965	1·22	2,249,909	*1·85
Queensland	231,025	0·56	202,114	0·39
South Australia	486,229	1·47	554,517	1·52
Western Australia	124,618	2·23	159,141	0·78
Tasmania	31,155	0·20	36,503	0·21
Commonwealth	3,309,136	1·00	4,221,644	1·09
New Zealand	111,707	0·17	126,450	0·16
Australasia	3,420,843	0·87	4,348,094	0·93

* Consumption in 1901 was 1·29 gallons.

Several descriptions of Australian wines have a natural strength of 30 per cent. of proof spirit, while from analyses which have been made it would appear that the strength of these wines offered for sale varies from 24 to 37 per cent. of spirit. Imported beers range from 13·88 per cent. to 15·42 per cent. in the case of English, and from 9·58 per cent. to 11·76 per cent. of proof spirit in Lager, while the local manufacture varied according to the make from 6·1 to 13·8, the average being 9·97 per cent. Four of the states manufacture spirits, and five make wine, while beer is brewed in all of them. The average consumption of locally-manufactured spirits, wine, and beer for the last three years has been estimated, and will be found in the following statement:—

State.	Spirits.		Wine.		Beer, &c.	
	Total.	Per Inhabitant.	Total.	Per Inhabitant.	Total.	Per Inhabitant.
	galls.	galls.	galls.	galls.	galls.	galls.
New South Wales	47,844	0·03	789,486	0·57	13,278,116	9·67
Victoria	170,928	0·14	1,419,575	1·18	14,674,543	12·22
Queensland	72,780	0·14	132,536	0·26	5,047,158	10·04
South Australia	29,545	0·08	459,014	1·26	3,108,858	0·86
Western Australia	....	...	107,379	0·57	4,337,080	22·90
Tasmania	....	...	....	...	1,523,822	8·76
Commonwealth	321,097	0·08	2,907,992	0·76	41,969,577	11·04
New Zealand	....	...	....	...	7,041,813	9·03
Australasia	321,097	0·07	2,907,992	0·63	49,011,390	10·69

If the figures in this table be subtracted from those in the table on page 531 the consumption of imported goods will be found.

Expenditure on Living.

In previous issues of this volume statements appeared showing the annual expenditure of the people of New South Wales and of the other states of the Commonwealth on food, clothing, house rent, and other services usually grouped together under the term "cost of living." The necessity for some such table arose from the circumstance that the states lived under separate tariffs, which in various ways influenced the prices of commodities. But with the uniform system of Customs that prevails throughout Australia, the conditions governing the cost of commodities are, so far as they are affected by the operation of tariff charges, made practically the same.

The explanation of the differences that exist in the total expenditure of the peoples of the various states will be found rather in difference of consumption than of prices, and the extent of this difference in consumption will be seen from a scrutiny of the tables relating to the annual consumption of thirty-four articles of common use given in the earlier part of this chapter.

The cost of providing food, and beverages other than intoxicants, consumed in Australia during the year 1902 may be set down at £64,057,000. This sum represents the price to the consumer, and covers all charges except that of cooking and preparing the food for the table. The expenditure on wines, spirits, and beer amounted to £15,058,000, so that the total expenditure for all food and beverages was £79,115,000, equal to £20 10s. per inhabitant, or 1s. 1·3d. daily. Excluding intoxicants, the yearly expenditure per inhabitant was £16 12s., and the average per day, 10·9d. Compared with the cost of food supply in other countries, this may appear considerable, but the year 1902 was an abnormal one, while allowance must also be made for the profusion with which flesh meat is consumed and wasted in Australia.

Of the total cost of food and beverages, viz., £79,115,000, the expenditure on fresh meat is the largest item, being 23·92 per cent. of the whole; bread is 9·48 per cent.; milk, butter, and cheese, 14·89 per cent.; vegetables and fruits, 11·92 per cent.; sugar, 5·16 per cent.; tea, coffee, cocoa, 2·87 per cent.; and wines, beers, and other spirituous liquors, 19·03 per cent. The following is the approximate retail cost of the chief articles that enter into daily consumption :—

	£
Bread	7,498,000
Fresh meat	18,927,000
Vegetables and fruits	9,428,000
Milk, butter, cheese, etc.	11,777,000
Other farm produce	1,742,000
Sugar	4,085,000
Tea, coffee, etc.	2,271,000
Other foods	6,803,000
Non-alcoholic beverages	1,526,000
Total expenditure on food	£64,057,000
Wines, beer, and spirituous liquors	15,058,000
Total expenditure on food and beverages...	£79,115,000

The total expenditure on food just given works out at an average of £16 12s. per inhabitant, which is considerably higher than in ordinary years, but the high prices of meat, butter, etc., are accountable for the increase. The amount is probably higher than in any other country, but the mere statement of expenditure affords but a partial view of the question, as the earnings of the people must be taken into consideration, otherwise the comparison is of little value. If this be done it will be found that few countries approach Australia in the small proportion of income absorbed in providing food for their people, for although in 1902 the ratio amounted to 44·5 per cent. of the total earnings, it must be borne in mind that the prices of foods of all kinds were abnormally high in that year; in an ordinary year the proportion would be about 37 per cent. The following table taken from Mulhall's *Dictionary of Statistics*, shows that while the actual cost of food and drink is £20 10s. in Australia, as against £14 4s. 9d. in Great Britain, the earnings required to pay for that food are not larger proportionately than in the countries which show most favourably in the table. The number of working days in the year is assumed to be 300, allowing for thirteen days' sickness and fifty-two Sundays. It should, however, be borne in mind that comparisons of this kind are more or less fanciful. The economic condition of a people is more readily and conclusively ascertained by reference to the actual quantities of foods of various kinds entering into consumption, than by the nominal value of such foods and the proportion of the average income spent in their attainment :—

Country.	Average annual cost of food and beverage.	Ratio of cost of food to earnings.	Days' earnings equal to annual cost of food.
	£ s. d.	per cent.	days.
United Kingdom ...	14 4 9	42·2	127
France	12 4 5	44·0	142
Germany	10 18 5	49·1	148
Russia	5 19 7	52·0	156
Austria	7 17 4	50·8	152
Italy	6 4 10	51·2	153
Spain	8 9 0	51·2	154
Portugal	7 3 0	59·1	177
Sweden	9 18 11	45·2	136
Norway	9 15 0	47·6	143
Denmark	11 14 0	36·0	108
Holland	10 8 0	46·0	138
Belgium	12 3 1	43·4	130
Switzerland	8 11 7	45·2	135
United States	9 17 7	25·3	76
Canada	8 9 0	32·5	97
Australia	20 10 0	44·5	133

The expenditure of Australia coming under the designation "cost of living" amounted in 1902 to £43 13s. 2d., made up of the following items. The expenditure of New Zealand is not included.

Division of Expenditure.	Total Expenditure.	Per Inhabitant.
	£	£ s. d.
Food and non-alcoholic beverages	64,057,000	16 12 0
Fermented and spirituous liquors	15,058,000	3 18 0
Tobacco	3,554,000	0 18 5
Clothing and drapery	20,667,000	5 7 1
Furniture	1,856,000	0 9 8
Rent or value of buildings used as dwellings	19,057,000	4 18 9
Locomotion	6,642,000	1 14 5
Fuel and light	5,281,000	1 7 4
Personal attendance, service, and lodging	6,944,000	1 16 0
Medical attendance, medicine, and nursing	4,579,000	1 3 8
Religion, charities, education (not including state expenditure)	2,830,000	0 14 8
Art and amusement	4,380,000	1 2 8
Books, newspapers, etc.	1,831,000	0 9 6
Postage and telegrams, not incidental to earning the incomes	1,079,000	0 5 7
Direct taxes not falling on trade	1,810,000	0 9 5
Household expenses not included elsewhere	5,314,000	1 7 7
Miscellaneous expenses	3,557,000	0 18 5
Total	£168,496,000	43 13 2

According to Mulhall, the expenditure per inhabitant in the leading countries of Europe and in America is as follows :—

Country.	Expenditure per Inhabitant.			Country.	Expenditure per Inhabitant.		
	£	s.	d.		£	s.	d.
United Kingdom	29	14	9	Norway	19	0	0
France	23	19	4	Denmark	28	11	5
Germany	20	3	4	Holland	20	17	4
Russia	10	1	11	Belgium	25	8	2
Austria	14	4	9	Switzerland	18	0	0
Italy	11	11	0	United States	32	16	2
Spain	15	12	6	Canada	23	6	2
Portugal	11	5	6				
Sweden	20	8	4	Australia	43	13	2

The expenditure of Australia as compared with population is, according to this table, largely in excess of that of other countries, but as expenditure depends upon income, a table such as the above has little meaning unless regard be paid to the amount of income available for expenditure and the purchasing power of money. This latter question is too involved to be dealt with, so far as European and American countries are concerned, within the limits at disposal in this volume. It may, however, be mentioned that so far as the primary food requirements are concerned the purchasing power of money is greater in Australia than in any of the countries mentioned in the foregoing list: house rents, however, are higher, as well as the price of most descriptions of wearing apparel. The question of cost of living is further dealt with in another place.

Prices of Commodities.

The area of Australia is so extensive, and the population, except on the sea-board, so scattered, that the determination with any exactness of the average prices of the various commodities consumed is almost a matter of impossibility. No attempt has therefore been made to ascertain the average for the whole continent, and in the following pages the prices refer to the Sydney markets alone. There is a further reason. Until the discovery of gold there were virtually only two important markets in all Australia—Sydney and Hobart—and of these Sydney was much the more considerable. Any comparisons of the prices of commodities extending back beyond 1852 must be based mainly upon the experience of Sydney, although from 1840 onwards there is sufficient information in the chapter on the Industrial Progress of Australia in this volume to enable Sydney prices to be adjusted for Melbourne, Hobart, Adelaide, and the other chief centres of population. For the earlier years the authority of contemporary newspapers has been followed where the official records are obscure or silent, but since 1836 these records have been available, and have for the most part been followed.

The accompanying table exhibits the average prices of eight commodities during each year since 1820 :—

Year.	Bread per 2-lb. loaf.	Fresh Beef per lb.	Butter per lb.	Cheese per lb.	Sugar per lb.	Tea per lb.	Potatoes per cwt.	Maize per bushel.
	d.	d.	s. d.	s. d.	d.	s. d.	s. d.	s. d.
1820	5	5½	2 9	1 1	......	......	7 3	5 6
1821	6	5½	2 8	1 2	......	......	7 3	5 0
1822	5	5½	2 6	1 3	......	......	5 9	4 9
1823	3½	5½	2 2	1 2	......	......	6 1	2 6
1824	5	5½	3 0	1 4	......	......	6 10	4 10
1825	4½	6	2 2	1 5	......	......	8 4	5 6
1826	5½	5½	2 4	0 10	......	......	9 0	4 0
1827	4½	6¼	2 3	1 1	......	......	8 0	5 0
1828	6	5	2 6	1 4	......	......	18 6	9 0
1829	7	6	1 10	1 1	......	......	12 6	7 9
1830	4½	3½	1 0	0 11	3½	2 6	8 0	3 10
1831	4	4½	1 8	0 6	3½	2 6	5 0	3 8
1832	5	5	2 3	0 7	3½	2 6	5 0	4 7
1833	4	3½	1 5	0 6	3½	2 6	10 0	2 11
1834	5	4	1 6	0 6	3½	2 6	14 0	4 4
1835	4	3½	1 10	0 5	3½	2 6	10 0	4 6
1836	5½	3	1 9	0 8½	3½	2 6	7 0	6 9
1837	3	4½	1 9	0 7½	3½	2 6	10 0	4 2
1838	5	5¾	1 6	0 8½	3½	1 5	6 0	3 7
1839	11½	4¾	2 6	1 1	3½	1 6	10 0	9 0
1840	7½	6¾	2 0	1 0	3½	2 6	10 0	5 3
1841	4¼	6¾	2 6	0 10	3½	3 3	10 0	2 10
1842	5	4½	2 6	1 1½	3¼	2 0	7 0	4 9
1843	3½	2¾	1 9	0 9	3	2 6	5 0	2 9
1844	2½	2¼	1 5	0 4½	2½	1 6	4 0	1 5
1845	2½	2¼	1 6	0 6	3	1 6	4 6	2 11
1846	3½	2½	1 8	0 6	4	2 3	3 0	4 1
1847	3½	2½	1 2	0 7	4	2 4	5 10	2 1
1848	3½	2½	1 1	0 8	3¾	2 0	4 4	1 8
1849	2½	2¼	1 2	0 6¼	3¾	1 9	3 0	3 9
1850	4½	2¼	1 3	0 7	3½	1 10	4 0	4 1
1851	5	2¾	1 3	0 7	3½	1 4	6 0	3 7
1852	4½	3	1 3	0 7	3½	1 4	6 0	3 11
1853	6½	3½	1 5¼	0 7¼	3½	1 4	13 0	9 3
1854	7½	4½	2 3	0 9	5	2 6	18 6	10 0
1855	9	6	2 4	1 3	7	2 5	21 4	8 7
1856	7½	3½	1 11	1 2	5½	2 2½	10 0	3 8
1857	5	3½	2 0	1 0	7½	2 6	14 6	8 2
1858	6	4	2 0	1 0	7	2 6	15 6	6 5
1859	6	4	1 10	1 0	5	2 6	8 0	3 5

Year.	Bread per 2-lb. loaf.	Fresh Beef per lb.	Butter per lb.		Cheese per lb.		Sugar per lb.	Tea per lb.		Potatoes per cwt.		Maize per bushel.	
	d.	d.	s.	d.	s.	d.	d.	s.	d.	s.	d.	s.	d.
1860	6½	4	1	6	1	10	5½	2	3	7	6	2	10
1861	6½	3	1	8	0	9	5½	2	4	7	3	5	1
1862	4½	4½	2	3	0	9	4½	2	0	8	0	5	0
1863	4	4¼	1	6	0	10	4½	2	0	7	0	3	10
1864	5½	4	1	6	0	8	4½	2	0	5	0	3	11
1865	7½	3	1	9	0	9	4½	2	0	8	0	3	7
1866	6½	3	1	3	1	0	4	2	6	6	0	4	1
1867	3½	2½	1	6	0	7½	4	2	0	7	0	2	5
1868	4	3½	1	3	0	9	4	2	0	9	0	2	11
1869	3½	2	1	6	0	6	4	2	0	4	0	3	8
1870	3½	3½	1	3	0	6	4	2	0	5	0	3	4
1871	3½	2½	1	3	0	7½	4	2	3	4	0	3	0
1872	3½	2½	1	0	0	9	4	1	9	5	0	2	2
1873	4	2½	1	3	0	5	4	1	9	3	6	3	1
1874	3½	4	1	7	0	6	4	1	9	4	9	4	6
1875	3	3½	1	3	0	9	4½	1	9	5	6	4	3
1876	3½	5½	1	3	0	7	4	1	9	4	9	3	1
1877	4	4½	1	6	0	6	4	2	0	4	9	3	4
1878	4	4	1	3	0	6	4	1	9	5	10	4	0
1879	3½	4	0	10½	0	6	3½	1	6	6	0	3	1
1880	3	3½	0	10	0	7	4	2	0	4	3	2	6
1881	3½	3½	0	10½	0	6½	3½	2	0	4	0	3	7
1882	4	4½	1	3	0	8	4	2	0	5	6	5	4
1883	3½	4	1	4	0	10	4	2	0	6	0	4	0
1884	3	4½	1	3	0	9	3½	1	6	6	6	5	0
1885	3	4½	1	9	1	0	3	1	9	5	6	3	11
1886	3½	4½	1	9	1	1	3½	1	9	6	3	3	9
1887	3½	4	1	4	0	10½	3½	1	9	5	0	3	11
1888	3	4	1	7	0	8½	3½	1	6	6	0	3	4
1889	3½	3	1	4	0	9	3¼	1	6	9	0	3	7
1890	3½	4	1	0	0	8	3½	1	6	6	0	3	10
1891	3½	4	1	1	0	9	3¼	2	0	5	0	2	11
1892	3½	4	1	3	0	8	3	1	6	5	6	3	4
1893	3¼	4	1	1½	0	8	2½	1	6	6	4	4	0
1894	2¾	3	1	0	0	8	2½	1	6	4	6	2	6
1895	2¾	3	1	0	0	8	2½	1	6	4	3	2	9
1896	3	3	1	0	0	8	2½	1	6	5	6	2	7
1897	3	2½	1	0	0	8	2½	1	6	5	3	2	3
1898	2½	2½	1	0	0	8	2	1	6	9	0	2	9
1899	3	3½	1	0	0	8	2¼	1	6	9	4	3	4
1900	3	3½	0	11	0	7½	2¼	1	4	6	9	3	0
1901	3	5	1	0	0	8	2¼	1	3	7	6	3	6
1902	3¼	6	1	2	0	10	2½	1	3	7	6	5	10

The most noteworthy feature of the history of prices in Australia—the great range of some of the commodities during the year—is not disclosed by the foregoing table. This variation is most noticeable during the early years, and amongst articles of local production, and was the result of the almost complete isolation of the country from the markets of the world. Prior to the discovery of gold, communication by letter with the outside world was at best uncertain, and as late as 1878 the regular mails were made up but once a month. The establishment of telegraphic communication, amongst other results, has had a marked effect on prices, so that except in rare instances, and for goods produced in excess of the demand, the production of Australia no longer determines the prices of goods required for the local markets. Exception must, of course, be made for perishable produce, which is still liable to a great range in price during the course of a single year, as will be shown by some examples hereafter given.

Potatoes have varied in price from year to year. The lowest average for a whole twelvemonth was 3s. 6d. per cwt. in 1873, and the highest was 21s. 5d. in 1855, shortly after the discovery of gold; and it may not be without interest to note that from 1853 to 1855 the price of potatoes was extraordinarily high. Commencing with the year first named, the averages were 13s., 18s. 6d., 21s. 4d., 10s., 14s. 6d., and 15s. 6d. per cwt. With regard to the variation ir a single year, the following examples may be cited:—In 1820, from 4s. 6d. to 10s. per cwt.; in 1825, from 4s. to 12s.; in 1829, from 9s. to 26s.; in 1834, from 9s. to 19s.; in 1839, from 7s. to 25s.; in 1854, from 11s. to 24s.; in 1856, from 3s. to 11s.; and in 1888, from 2s. to 24s.

The price of maize has not been subject to very great fluctuation, since, being little used except for horse-feed, this grain is capable of being replaced by other products; nevertheless the prices have ranged from 1s. 5d. in 1844 to 10s. in 1854.

In the list given on pages 538 and 539 are included quotations for bread at per 2-lb. loaf. In most years the price varied somewhat regularly with that of wheat. There are, however, exceptions to this rule, chiefly in the years during which wheat brought an unusually high figure, when the price of bread was generally less than might have been expected. The lowest price at which bread has been retailed was 2½d. in 1849, and the highest was 14d. the 2-lb. loaf, which figure was paid for a short time in 1839.

In addition to the eight commodities which are given on pages 538 and 539, the following list of the average retail prices of articles largely used may not be without interest. The information begins with 1836, beyond which year it is difficult to determine the exact average.

Year.	Bacon per lb.	Eggs per doz.	Rice per lb.	Oat-meal per lb.	Coffee per lb.	Salt per lb.	Beer (Col.) per gal.	Soap per lb.	Starch per lb.	Tobacco per lb. (Col.)	Tobacco per lb. (Imp.)
	s. d.	s. d.	d.	d.	s. d.	d.	s. d.	d.	s. d.	s. d.	s. d.
1836	...	2 2	9	...	...	...	...	4½	...	...	3 3
1837	...	2 6	...	...	1 6	1	1 0	...	...	...	4 0
1838	...	4 0	3	...	...	...	...	...	...	...	...
1839	...	3 0	3	...	1 6	...	...	4½	...	...	3 3
1840	0 10	2 9	2½	...	1 4	...	...	4½	...	...	3 3
1841	0 11	2 3	2½	...	1 4	...	...	4½	...	...	3 3
1842	0 10½	1 11	2	...	1 4	1	1 9	4½	...	...	3 6
1843	0 10	2 0	1½	...	0 10	0½	2 3	...	...	1 4	3 6
1844	0 5½	0 11	1¾	...	0 8½	1¼	1 3	3¾	...	1 6	3 6
1845	0 6½	1 1	3	...	0 7½	1½	1 1	3½	...	1 6	4 6
1846	0 9½	1 3	1½	...	0 10	1½	2 0	5	...	1 9	4 6
1847	0 6½	1 1	3¾	6	1 1	1½	3 4	5	1 0	1 9	4 4
1848	0 9	1 3	3½	6	1 1	1½	3 3	5	1 0	1 9	4 4
1849	0 8½	1 1	3¾	5¾	1 0	1½	2 8	5¼	1 1	2 0	4 7
1850	0 8½	1 4	4	6	1 2	1¾	2 9	5½	1 0	2 7	4 10
1851	0 9½	1 8	4	6	1 3	1½	2 6	5¼	1 0	3 8	7 9
1852	1 1	1 6	4	6	1 3	1½	2 6	6	1 0	4 0	6 0
1853	1 2½	2 3	4¼	6	1 3	1½	2 4½	6	1 0	4 0	7 6
1854	1 4½	2 9	5	7½	1 6	2½	3 6	8	1 6	4 0	5 6
1855	0 11½	2 8	6	9	1 8	4	4 7	8	1 6	3 0	5 0
1856	0 10	2 2	5¼	7	1 7¼	3	3 6	7¼	1 1¼	2 6½	5 3
1857	0 9½	1 11	5	7	1 8	2¾	4 0	7	1 0	2 7	5 0
1858	0 7½	2 3	6	7	1 8	4½	4 3	7	1 5	2 6	5 0
1859	0 8½	1 10	4¼	7	1 8	2½	4 0	6½	1 0	2 6	5 0
1860	1 0	1 3	5	6	1 6	2½	3 6	7	1 0	2 3	5 0
1861	0 10	1 6	4	6	1 6	2½	3 6	6	0 10½	2 0	5 6
1862	0 10	1 5	3	5	1 5	1½	2 0	4½	0 8	4 6	6 0
1863	0 10½	1 7	3	4	1 4	1½	1 6	4	0 7	3 0	7 6
1864	0 10	1 6	3	4	1 4	1½	2 0	4	0 8	1 6	5 6
1865	0 9¾	1 6	3	4	1 4	1½	2 0	4	0 8	2 6	5 6
1866	1 0	1 6	4	4	1 4	1½	2 0	4½	0 7	2 6	5 0
1867	0 10	1 7	3½	4	1 4	1	1 6	4	0 7	1 9	4 6
1868	0 9½	1 2	4	4	1 4	1½	2 0	4	0 7	1 9	5 0
1869	0 10	1 3	3	4	1 0	1	1 4	4	0 8	1 0	3 6
1870	0 10½	1 4	3	4	1 2	1	1 4	4	0 7	1 3	3 6
1871	0 9½	1 4	2½	2½	1 0	0½	2 3	3	0 4½	1 0	3 0
1872	0 9	1 1	3	3	1 1	0¾	1 4	3	0 5	1 4	3 6
1873	0 9	1 4	2½	2¾	1 2	0½	2 3	3	0 5	2 0	3 6
1874	0 8¾	1 6	3	3¾	1 4	0½	2 0	2¾	0 6	1 9	3 3

Year.	Bacon per lb.	Eggs per doz.	Rice per lb.	Oat-meal per lb.	Coffee per lb.	Salt per lb.	Beer (Col.) per gal.	Soap per lb.	Starch per lb.	Tobacco per lb. (Col.)	Tobacco per lb. (imp.)
	s. d.	s. d.	d.	d.	s. d.	d.	s. d.	d.	s. d.	s. d.	s. d.
1875	0 9½	1 6	3	3	1 2	1½	3 0	3	0 5	2 0	3 9
1876	0 9	1 0	3	3	1 2	1	2 0	2¾	0 5	1 9	3 0
1877	0 8½	1 6	3	3¼	1 3	1	2 0	2¾	0 5	2 0	3 9
1878	0 9	1 3	3	3	1 3	0½	2 0	2	0 5	1 6	3 9
1879	0 8	1 7	2½	2¼	1 0	0½	2 0	2	0 5	1 6	3 0
1880	0 7½	1 4	3	3	1 5	0¾	2 0	3	0 5½	2 0	4 0
1881	0 7½	1 0	3	3	1 5	0¾	2 0	3	0 5½	2 0	4 0
1882	1 0	2 0	3¼	4	1 5	1	2 0	2½	0 6	3 0	5 0
1883	1 0	1 11	3	4	1 9	1	2 0	3	0 7	3 0	6 0
1884	0 11½	1 11	2½	3	1 4	1	2 0	3	0 6	3 0	5 0
1885	0 10½	1 10	3	3	1 5	0¾	2 0	3	0 6½	3 0	6 0
1886	0 10½	1 8	3¼	2¾	1 6	1	2 0	4	0 6½	4 0	5 6
1887	0 10	1 7	3	2¾	1 6	1	2 0	3½	0 6½	4 0	5 6
1888	0 10½	1 7	3	2½	1 6	1	2 0	3¼	0 6	4 0	5 6
1889	0 11	1 8	3	3¼	1 6	1	2 0	3½	0 6	4 0	5 6
1890	1 0½	1 6	4	3	2 0	1	2 0	3½	0 5	4 0	6 0
1891	0 10	1 6	3	2½	2 0	1	2 0	3½	0 5	4 0	6 0
1892	0 9	1 6	3	2½	1 10	0¾	2 0	3	0 4½	4 0	6 0
1893	0 11	1 6	3	2¼	1 10	0¾	2 0	3	0 4½	4 0	6 0
1894	0 7	1 3	3	2¼	1 10	0¾	2 0	3	0 4½	4 0	6 0
1895	0 7½	1 0	2½	2	1 9	0¾	2 0	2	0 4	4 0	6 0
1896	0 7½	1 0	2	2	1 9	0½	2 0	2	0 4	4 0	6 0
1897	0 8	1 0	2½	2½	1 9	0¾	2 0	2½	0 4	4 0	6 0
1898	0 8½	1 0	2	2½	1 9	0¾	2 0	2½	0 4	4 0	6 0
1899	0 8	0 11	2	2¼	1 10	1	2 0	2½	0 3¾	4 0	6 0
1900	0 7½	0 11	2¼	2¼	1 6	0½	2 0	3	0 3½	4 0	6 0
1901	0 8½	1 3	2¼	2¼	1 6	0½	2 0	3	0 4	4 0	6 0
1902	0 10	1 6	2½	2¼	1 6	0½	2 0	3	0 4	4 0	6 0

In the quotation of prices in the foregoing tables the figures given are those charged in the retail shops. It is quite possible that produce of all kinds may have been bought at cheaper rates than those stated, but higher rates were also paid, and the figures will be found to represent the fair average rates, having regard to the class of goods consumed. It is of importance to take into consideration the quality of the produce consumed, for very considerable changes in the direction of improvement have taken place in this respect. Thus, the ordinary sugar now used, and obtainable for about 2d. per lb., is a good white sugar, whereas some years ago only a common quality of moist sugar was found on the tables of the people. A very material improvement has been effected in the quality of flour, a large proportion of the present consumption being roller-made. Salt-butter still forms the bulk of the supply, but it is usually of recent make; while formerly the butter was imported from Great Britain, and was several months old before reaching the dining-table. The candles now used are made of stearine, but the time is not remote when only the common tallow candle was in general use; and so with many other articles of ordinary consumption. The retail prices are those actually paid from day to day, irrespective of the nominal wholesale rates of the commodities in the metropolitan markets.

Price-levels of Articles of Common Use.

A consideration of retail prices would not be complete without a statement of the price-level in different years. This can be given for foods; but at present the data are hardly sufficient to establish an exact series of price-levels, taking into consideration all the elements of ordinary expenditure. The information in regard to foods is given below, the assumption being made that the quantities entering into consumption were the same formerly as at the present day. This assumption, however, is in some respects erroneous; but there appear to be no other means within reach to effect a just comparison. Sugar, tea, coffee, butter, cheese, and potatoes are now more largely used than (say) prior to 1870; but bread, or other forms in which flour is used, and meat, are not consumed so largely. However, when full allowance is made on this score, the following table will still be found to approximate closely to the truth. The price-level is calculated on the prices ruling for beef, mutton, bread, sugar, rice, potatoes, tea, beer, and tobacco :—

Period.	Price-level of principal Articles of Consumption.	
	1821-37 prices =1,000.	1901-02 prices =1,000.
1821 to 1825	1,000	1,223
1826 „ 1830	1,000	1,223
1831 „ 1835	802	980
1836 „ 1840	930	1,137
1841 „ 1845	676	826
1846 „ 1850	669	818
1851 „ 1855	1,038	1,269
1856 „ 1860	1,153	1,410
1861 „ 1865	959	1,173
1866 „ 1870	753	921
1871 „ 1875	709	867
1876 „ 1880	759	928
1881 „ 1885	756	924
1886 „ 1890	730	892
1891 „ 1895	670	819
1896 „ 1900	646	790
1901 „ 1902	818	1,000

During the past forty years prices of food stuffs have changed very slightly, such changes as there have been tending in the direction of a reduction. The average of 1896–1900 was less than in any previous period, but in 1901–2 there was a considerable increase, and prices ruled higher than in any period since 1861–65. Little practical good can be gained by comparing the prices of one period with those of another, unless regard is also paid to the earnings of labour, and as means of comparison are afforded in the chapter of this work dealing with wages, it will be unnecessary to pursue the subject further in this chapter.

Price-levels of Imports and Exports.

The following tables have been compiled with the object of showing to what extent Australia has been affected by the variation in the prices of commodities imported and exported during the past forty-one years. The figures refer to New South Wales alone, but they may be accepted as also indicating in a fairly accurate degree the position in which the other states of Australasia stand in regard to this matter. The total value of the exports of each of the states is greatly affected by the prices obtained for certain leading lines of raw produce, of which wool, wheat and flour, tallow, silver and silver lead, hides, leather, tin, copper, coal, fruit, butter, sugar, meat and timber are the most important. The value of these articles represents a total of about seventeen and a half millions or ninety per cent. of the total export of domestic produce.

In the subjoined table the price-level of domestic exports is given for the forty-one years beginning with 1860. In order to ascertain the price-level, all the principal articles of domestic produce exported have been taken, the prices of 1902 have been applied to the quantities of each of the other years, and the result has been compared with the actual total of such year: the level of the year being found by dividing the actual sum obtained into the amount which would have been obtained had the prices of 1902 prevailed. The average for 1902 is assumed to be 1,000, the price-levels or index numbers of the other years being as shown in the table. In order to further facilitate comparison, the average of the five years 1870–74 has been assumed to be 1,000, and the prices of other years have been adjusted to that basis. The average of these years has been taken because the question is frequently raised as to the comparative prices of commodities before and after the demonetisation of silver by Germany in 1873. In compiling the price-level for exports, only articles of insignificant value have been omitted from consideration, and in no year does the value of articles excluded form more than 15 per cent. of the total exports, while in some years the proportion falls as low as 5 per cent., the average of all years being about 10 per cent. It is considered that this system enables a more reliable estimate of the relative prices to be obtained than that of selecting the prices of certain articles without giving due weight to the quantities of such articles exported.

These figures show that there has been a great fall in the prices of Australian produce exported since 1860, or still greater since 1864, viz., from the index number 1,316 to 700, or nearly 47 per cent. Marked fluctuations, ranging to about 10 per cent., occurred between 1860 and 1866, when the index number was about the same as in the first-named year. From 1866 to 1870 there was a drop from 1,249 to 879, or about 30 per cent. A rise followed in 1871 to 1,075, or about 22 per cent., after which for four years prices continued fairly steady, until there was a further decline to 887 in 1878. In 1879 the level rose to 921 and for the next four years prices continued without much change, but from 1884 to 1885 there was a fall from 919 to 806. This was succeeded by a fairly even range until 1889, when the level stood at 785. From 1889 there was a steep decline to 532 in 1894, a fall of 32 per cent. for the five years, but in 1895 and 1896 prices recovered a little, and the level rose to 573—an advance of 7·7 per cent. In 1897 there was again a slight fall from 573 to 557, equivalent to 2·8 per cent., but in 1898 the level rose to 590, and in 1899 to 736, a rise of 32 per cent. for the two years. The sharp rise in 1899 was entirely due to the improved price obtained for wool, and the fluctuation in the last three years has been mainly caused by the varying price of that commodity.

Year.	Price-level of Exports.		Year.	Price-level of Exports.	
	1902 prices = 1,000.	Average of 1870-74 prices = 1,000.		1902 prices = 1,000.	Average of 1870-74 prices = 1,000.
1860	1,782	1,247	1882	1,324	926
1861	1,780	1,244	1883	1,324	926
1862	1,874	1,310	1884	1,311	919
1863	1,702	1,191	1885	1,152	806
1864	1,883	1,316	1886	1,108	775
1865	1,723	1,203	1887	1,138	797
1866	1,784	1,249	1888	1,104	773
1867	1,650	1,154	1889	1,121	785
1868	1,651	1,155	1890	1,083	758
1869	1,505	1,053	1891	985	689
1870	1,257	879	1892	933	652
1871	1,537	1,075	1893	843	590
1872	1,401	979	1894	760	532
1873	1,485	1,037	1895	779	546
1874	1,471	1,028	1896	820	573
1875	1,465	1,027	1897	796	557
1876	1,389	972	1898	842	590
1877	1,274	891	1899	1,052	736
1878	1,268	887	1900	975	682
1879	1,315	921	1901	942	659
1880	1,292	903	1902	1,000	700
1881	1,282	897			

It will be seen that the purchasing power of money has steadily increased since 1864 and that 20s. in 1902 would purchase the same articles of domestic export which in 1864 would have cost 37s. 7d., prices having fallen 46·8 per cent. during the period of thirty-eight years. The greatest decline has taken place in the three staple exports of wool, silver, and coal, many of the minor articles having maintained or increased their price during the last fifteen years.

It must not be supposed that Australia has been a loser by the fall in the prices of its exports to the extent which the price-level shows, because the power of the exports to purchase imports must also be taken into consideration. It will, therefore, be necessary to consider also the price-level of imports. As there exist no reliable data on which price-levels for imports can be based prior to 1870, the table commences with that year :—

Year.	Price-level of Imports.		Year.	Price-level of Imports.	
	1902 prices = 1,000.	Average of 1870–74 prices = 1,000.		1902 prices = 1,000.	Average of 1870–74 prices = 1,000.
1870	1,271	966	1887	1,031	783
1871	1,277	970	1888	1,026	779
1872	1,335	1,014	1889	1,069	812
1873	1,357	1,030	1890	1,058	804
1874	1,343	1,020	1891	1,011	767
1875	1,265	962	1892	969	736
1876	1,243	944	1893	932	708
1877	1,195	908	1894	885	673
1878	1,186	900	1895	877	666
1879	1,136	862	1896	912	693
1880	1,143	868	1897	921	700
1881	1,131	859	1898	932	708
1882	1,125	855	1899	927	704
1883	1,144	869	1900	989	752
1884	1,134	862	1901	972	738
1885	1,041	790	1902	1,000	760
1886	1,022	776			

It may be said generally that the fall in prices was somewhat in favour of the exports up to the year 1889. Since then the exports have fallen away on the average values at a much more rapid rate than the imports. A clearer view of the operation of the fall in prices will be obtained from the table which is given below, showing the price-levels of imports of merchandise for home consumption and exports of domestic produce, for periods of five years to the end of 1899, and for the three years ended with 1902, with the relative fall per cent. :—

Period.	Imports.		Exports.	
	Average of five years, 1870-4, prices = 1,000.	Decline in prices in five years, per cent.	Average of five years, 1870-4, prices = 1,000.	Decline in prices in five years, per cent.
1870-74	1,000	....	1,000	....
1875-79	915	8·5	940	6·0
1880-84	863	5·9	914	2·9
1885-89	788	8·5	787	13·8
1890-94	737	6·5	645	18·0
1895-99	694	5·8	600	7·0
1900-02	750	8·1 (rise)	680	13·3 (rise)

It will be seen that, assuming the index number of the five years 1870-74 to be 1,000, the fall in the succeeding five years was 8·5 per cent. for the imports, as compared with 6 per cent. for the exports. The average value of the imports for the five years ending with 1884 was 5·9 per cent. less than in the preceding quinquennial period, whereas the difference in the value of the exports was 2·9 per cent. During the next five years the average value of the imports declined 8·5 per cent., while the fall in the value of the exports was no less than 13·8 per cent., so that the index number for 1885-89 for both imports and exports was practically the same figure. As already mentioned, the fall for the period 1890-94 was much more heavy in regard to the exports than the imports, amounting to 18 as compared with 6·5 per cent.; but during the period 1895-99 the fall in the exports was not much greater than that in the imports, 7·0 per cent. compared with 5·8 per cent. In the last three years the exports have risen by 13·3 per cent., and the imports by 8·1 per cent., so that the last two periods were the most favourable, as far as prices go, that have been experienced in Australia for many years.

The Australian states and New Zealand are chiefly affected by the fall in prices because they are debtor countries. In the chapter on "Private Finance" will be found certain calculations showing that the annual charge payable by the states and municipalities on their indebtedness to British creditors is £12,359,000, while the earnings of investments made in Australasia by private persons, or drawn by absentees, amount to £5,250,000 per annum. As the whole of the interest on Government and municipal loans has to be paid by exports, irrespective of the fall in prices, and as a large portion also of the interest payable to private investors is in the same category, the fall is a matter of very serious importance to these states. Fortunately the increase of production, as compared with the population, has been large enough in normal seasons to counteract the fall in prices, and if the change in regard to the price of Australian produce which began in 1895 be continued, the condition of these states will be in every respect more hopeful.

LAND AND SETTLEMENT.

IN each of the Commonwealth States and New Zealand a different system has been adopted to secure the settlement of an industrial population upon the Crown lands, the conditions upon which land may be acquired being of a more or less liberal nature according to the circumstances in which the province has found itself placed. The legislation of Victoria, Queensland, and Tasmania, which at one time formed part of New South Wales, bears a strong resemblance to that of the mother state, practically the same form of conditional occupation with deferred payments being in existence in all four states. In the other provinces, however, the influence of New South Wales was not so directly felt, and new experiments were made. South Australia, for instance, was originally settled upon the Wakefield system—alike remarkable for its originality and its failure. In Western Australia and New Zealand, under pressure of a different set of circumstances, settlement was effected by legislation of a novel character. An attempt is made here to give a description of the Land Laws of Australasia, although the radical changes which are constantly being made render the task of giving a serviceable account of the various systems a somewhat difficult one. During the past ten years, numerous Acts affecting State lands have been placed on the statute book, so that it is impossible to say how long the information given in this chapter can be taken as representing the latest phases of land legislation in Australasia.

New South Wales.

With the progress and development of the state, the Land Laws of New South Wales have naturally undergone considerable alteration. In the earliest period alienation was effected by grants, orders, and dedications, the power of disposal resting solely with the Governor. In August, 1831, the principle of sale by auction was introduced, the minimum price for country lands being fixed at 5s. per acre. This was raised to 12s. in 1839, and to 20s. in 1843, power being given in the latter year to select, at the upset price, country portions for which a bid was not forthcoming at auction, or upon which the deposit paid at the time of sale had been forfeited. This was the first appearance of the principle of selection in the laws of the state, but it was limited to lands which had been surveyed for sale by auction.

The discovery of gold in 1851, and the consequent rush of population to Australia, greatly altered the conditions of colonisation. As the interest in gold-digging declined, so did the desire for settlement on the land increase, and the question had to be dealt with in an entirely new spirit, to meet the wants of the class of immigrants desirous of being placed upon the soil. The agitation which thus sprang up resulted in the passing of the Crown Lands Act of 1861, under the leadership of Sir John Robertson. This measure was designed to secure the establishment of an agricultural population side by side with the pastoral tenants. With this object in view an entirely new principle was introduced—that of free selection in limited areas before survey, coupled with conditions of residence and improvement—and country lands were sold at 20s. per acre, payable by annual instalments carrying interest.

The occupation of waste lands for pastoral purposes was at first allowed under a system of yearly licenses. Any person could apply for such a license, the extent of the run which it was desired to occupy being limited only by the boundaries of the surrounding stations. The fee was fixed at £10 per annum for a section of 25 square miles, with £2 10s. for every additional 5 square miles. This system of yearly licenses was succeeded by one under which the squatter was given fixity of tenure, the fee payable being calculated upon the stock-carrying capacity instead of upon the area of the run. Still another system was inaugurated by the Occupation Act of 1861, the period of tenure being limited to five years in all but first-class settled districts, and the whole of the pastoral leases left open to the operations of the free selectors. But such evils were found to result from this system that in 1884, in 1889, in 1895, in 1901, so far as the western division is concerned, and again in 1903, so far as the eastern and central divisions are concerned, Parliament was led to adopt amendments which are now in force, and which, while maintaining the principle of selection before survey, aim at giving fixity of tenure to the pastoral lessee and obtaining a larger rental from the public lands, while at the same time securing land to *bonâ-fide* settlers on terms and conditions within the reach of all.

For the purposes of land administration, the state is split up into three divisions, each of which is subdivided into land districts. In the eastern and central divisions one or more of these land districts form a local division, the administration of which is entrusted to a Local Land Board, comprising a chairman and not more than two assessors, the control of the western division being vested in the Western Land Board. The decisions of these Local Land Boards may be appealed against to the Land Appeal Court. This Court is composed of a President and two members appointed by the Executive, and its decisions in matters of administration have the force of judgments of the Supreme Court; but whenever questions of law become involved, a case may be submitted to the Supreme Court, upon the written request of the parties interested, or by the Land Appeal Court of its own initiative. The judgment given in this appeal is final.

Under the Acts at present in force, land may be acquired by the following methods:—(1) By conditional and additional conditional purchase with residence; (2) by conditional purchase without residence; (3) by classified conditional purchase; (4) by the preferent right of purchase attached to conditional leases; (5) by improvement purchases on goldfields; (6) by auction sales; (7) by after auction sales; (8) by special sales without competition; and (9) by homestead selection.

The maximum area which may be conditionally purchased differs in the eastern and central divisions. In the western division land can only be occupied under lease, or alienated by auction.

Eastern Division.

The conditions for the purchase and occupation of Crown lands are more restricted in the eastern division than in the central and western divisions. Nevertheless, any person above the age of 16 years may, upon any Crown lands not specially exempted, select an area of 40 to 640 acres, together with a lease of contiguous land not exceeding thrice the area of the conditional purchase. The combined area of purchase and lease must not, however, exceed 1,280 acres. The price demanded is £1 per acre, of which 2s. must be deposited when application is made, and the balance, together with interest at the rate of 2½ per cent., paid by instalments of 5 per cent. of the value of the land, as determined, per annum. Payment of instalments commences at the end of the third year, and after the expiry of the period of enforced residence the balance may be paid in one sum at any time. The selector must reside on his selection for a period of ten years, and within three years erect a substantial fence around the land; in some cases, however, other permanent improvements are allowed in lieu of fencing. He is restricted to one selection during his lifetime; but after the expiry of the residential period he may purchase additional areas, whether contiguous or not, to his original purchase up to the maximum area, but all available land adjoining the original or prior additional purchases or leases of the same series must first be exhausted, and the land applied for as such additional purchase must, in the opinion of the land board, be within a reasonable working distance of the original purchase by virtue of which the application is made, or he may purchase his conditional leasehold. In such a case, however, he must extend his period of residence, and enclose his additional purchase. Married women judicially separated may select in their own right; and minors taking up lands adjoining the selection of their parents may fulfil the condition of residence under the paternal roof until the age of 21 in the case of males and 24 in that of females.

A conditional leasehold, in conjunction with a selection, may be held for twenty-eight years, but on application the period may be extended to forty years, and all leases granted subsequent to the 1st January, 1904, are for a period of forty years. The rental is fixed by the Land Board. The leasehold must be enclosed within three years; one fence, however, may enclose both the conditional purchase and the lease. A lease may at any time be converted into a purchase. The term of residence on the conditional purchase and leasehold must aggregate ten years from the date of application.

When land is conditionally purchased without residence, the maximum area is limited to 320 acres, and no conditional lease is granted. The selection must be enclosed within twelve months after survey, and within five years additional improvements must be made to the value of £1 per acre. The price demanded is £2 per acre, and the deposit and instalments payable are twice as high as those required in the case of an ordinary conditional purchase. No person under 21 years of age may select land on non-residential conditions; and anyone who takes advantage of the provisions permitting the acquirement of a conditional purchase without residence is not allowed to make any other conditional purchase.

Special areas may be thrown open to selection under special conditions. The price is not less than £1 10s. per acre, and the maximum area which may be taken up is 320 acres. Non-resident selectors are charged double the rates payable by those who reside on the land.

At the close of 1899 an Act was passed introducing a new feature in the form of classified conditional purchases. Under this system land set apart for conditional purchase or conditional lease becomes available for conditional purchase at prices specified at the time of notification, whether above or below £1 per acre. The area which may be selected in the Eastern Division is restricted to 640 acres. The conditions as to residence and improvements are similar to those in the case of an ordinary conditional purchase.

The capital value of conditional purchases and conditional leases applied for prior to the 30th December, 1899, and held *bonâ fide* for the applicant's sole use and benefit may be the subject of reappraisement up to an area, sufficient, in the opinion of the Local Land Board, to enable him to maintain a home thereon, provided the application therefor was lodged prior to the 30th December, 1901.

Central Division.

In the central division land may be conditionally purchased on terms as to residence, fencing, improvements, price, and mode of payment similar to those which govern selection in the eastern division. The maximum area which may be selected is 2,560 acres, and a conditional lease in the proportion granted in the eastern division may be secured, but the aggregate area of both selection and lease must not exceed 2,560 acres. The area which may be purchased without residence, and the conditions in regard thereto, are the same as in the eastern division. Within special areas the maximum extent of a selection has been fixed at 640 acres.

The system of classified conditional purchases applies to this Division and the area that may be selected, and the conditions of residence and improvements imposed are similar to those in respect of ordinary conditional purchases.

Western Division.

The western division embraces an area of 79,970,000 acres, watered entirely by the Darling River and its tributaries. This part of the state is essentially devoted to pastoral pursuits.

The administration of the western division by the "Western Lands Act of 1901" is vested in a Board of three Commissioners, entitled "The Western Land Board of New South Wales," and all Local Land Boards constituted prior to the 1st January, 1902, cease to have jurisdiction within the area. The Commissioners, sitting in open Court, are empowered to exercise all the powers conferred upon Local Land Boards by the Crown Lands Acts, and for all purposes of the Crown Lands Acts shall be a Local Land Board in all cases, as well as in any cases that may be or are required to be referred to any Local Land Board under the provisions of any Act, now or hereafter in force.

Subject to existing rights and the extension of tenure referred to in a subsequent paragraph, all forms of alienation, other than by auction, and leases, prescribed by the Crown Lands Acts, ceased to operate within the Western Land Division from the 1st January, 1902.

Before any Crown lands in the western division, not held under lease, shall become available for lease, the Commissioners must recommend the areas and boundaries of the land to be offered for lease and the rent to be charged therefor, and, should there be any improvements on the land, determine the amount to be paid for them. The Minister may, by giving thirty days' notice in the *Government Gazette*, declare such lands open for lease, and applications therefor must be made to the Commissioners on a prescribed form, accompanied by a deposit at the rate of 20 per cent. on the amount of the first year's rent, as notified in the *Government Gazette*, and the Commissioners may recommend a lease to such applicant as they shall consider most entitled to it. Upon the issue of a lease the notification thereof is published in the *Government Gazette*, and within one month therefrom the successful applicant must pay the balance of the first year's rent and execute the lease within the time and manner prescribed.

The registered holder of a pastoral, homestead, improvement, scrub, or inferior lease or occupation license of land in the western division, or in the event of any such holding being mortgaged, then any owner of the equity of redemption in the same, could apply before the 30th June, 1902, to bring his lease or license under the provisions of the "Western Lands Act of 1901." In cases where no application was made to bring the lease or license under the provisions of the Act, such lease or license is to be dealt with as if the Act had not been passed, and the Commissioners as constituted are to be deemed the Local Land Board to deal with such cases.

All leases issued or brought under the provisions of the "Western Lands Act of 1901" expire on the 30th June, 1943, except in cases where a withdrawal is made for the purpose of sale by auction or to provide small holdings, when the Governor shall, after report by the

Commissioners, add to the remainder of the lease such term as may be considered reasonable as compensation, but in no case shall it exceed six years.

The rent on all leases current after the commencement of the Act is determined by the Commissioners for the unexpired portion of such leases. No rent or license fee is to be less than 2s. 6d. per square mile or part thereof, and in no case shall the rent or license fee be fixed at a higher rate than 7d. per sheep on the carrying capacity determined by the Commissioners. In the case of new leases, the rents are determined for periods not exceeding ten years, and in the case of leases extended under the provisions of the Act for periods ending 30th June, 1930, and 30th June, 1943. The rent fixed in the case of existing leases, and for the first term in the case of new leases, cannot on reappraisement be either increased or decreased more than 25 per cent. on the first reappraisement, and the provision applies at each subsequent reappraisement to the rent last determined.

Homestead Selection.

Among the special features of the Act of 1895 was the introduction of the principle of classification and measurement of lands prior to selection. Under this system suitable land is set apart and rendered available for the purposes of the selector. The appropriation of areas for homestead selection is another prominent feature of the Act. The tenure of such a selection is freehold, subject to perpetual residence and perpetual rent, and the construction of a dwelling-house at a cost of not less than £20. Six months' rent and part of the survey fee must be lodged when application is made. Until the grant issues, the rent is fixed at 1¼ per cent. on the capital value of the land; but from and after the expiration of the first six years of the selection, the annual rent is 2½ per cent. of the capital value of the land; and the selection is subject to reappraisement every ten years. Provided an application was made before the 31st December, 1900, the capital value of homestead selections applied for, on or before 29th December, 1899, could be reappraised. In cases where the application for the homestead selection is of a subsequent date, reappraisement may be made before the selection is confirmed, or within twelve months after, but not later. Tenant-right in improvements is secured, and the holding may be so protected that it cannot by any legal procedure, or under any circumstances, be wrested from the selector. This form of alienation ceased to operate within the Western Land Division from the 1st January, 1902, existing rights being preserved.

Settlement Leases.

Another departure under the Act referred to is the provision for settlement leases for agricultural and grazing purposes. Under this form of tenancy, lands gazetted in any division as available for settlement lease are obtainable on application, accompanied by a deposit consisting of six months' rent and survey fee. Of agricultural land the maximum area which may thus be taken up is 1,280 acres, and of grazing land, 10,240 acres. The lease is issued for a period of twenty-eight years, but on application may be extended to forty years. All leases granted subsequent to the 1st January, 1904, are for a period of forty years, and the conditions attached to them are that the lessees shall reside on the land throughout the term, and fence it in during the first five years. Provided an application was made before the 31st December, 1900, the capital value of settlement leases applied for on or before the 29th December, 1899, could be reappraised. In cases where the application for the settlement lease is of a subsequent date, reappraisement may be made before the lease is confirmed, or within twelve months after, but not later. Tenant-right in improvements is secured to the outgoing lessee, who may, during the last year of the term, convert a portion not exceeding 1,280 acres into a homestead selection. This form of lease ceased to operate within the Western Land Division from the 1st January, 1902, existing rights being preserved.

Scrub and Inferior Lands.

The principle of improvement leases secures, in the Eastern and Central Divisions, the utilisation of scrub or inferior lands that would otherwise remain unoccupied, the form of lease having ceased to operate in the Western Division since the 1st January, 1902, subject to existing rights being preserved and the extension of tenure referred to later on. The term for which such a lease is issued is twenty-eight years, except in those cases in the western division brought under the provisions of the "Western Lands Act of 1901," when the lease expires on the 30th June, 1943, and the rent is determined according to the circumstances of each case, the object being to secure the profitable occupation of otherwise valueless lands. The maximum area obtainable is 20,480 acres. The outgoing lessee has tenant-right in improvements, and may, during the last year of the term of his lease, convert into a homestead selection 640 acres on which his dwelling-house is erected.

Pastoral and other Leases.

Under the Act of 1884 pastoral leases were surrendered to the Crown, and divided into two equal parts. One of these parts was returned to the lessee under an indefeasible lease for a fixed term of years; the other half, called the resumed area, might be held under an annual occupation license, but was always open to selection—by conditional purchase in the eastern and central divisions, and by homestead lease in the western division. Under the Act of 1895, the tenure of pastoral leases in the western division was fixed at twenty-eight years, but if the leases are brought under the "Western Land Act of 1901," they expire on the 30th June, 1943. In the central division a pastoral lease extends to ten years. In certain cases a further extension ranging up to five years has been secured by virtue of improvements effected; beyond this, however, the Crown has power to further extend the term of the lease for the remainder of a pastoral holding where a portion of such holding has been resumed for the purpose of settlement. Tenant-right in improvements made with the consent of the Crown is secured to the outgoing lessee. If in the western division he may, during the last year of his lease, convert into a homestead selection 640 acres on which his dwelling-house is erected. When application is made for an occupation license for the expired leasehold area, a license-fee, equal in amount to the sum formerly payable as rent, must be lodged as a deposit. This form of lease ceased to operate in the Western Land Division since the 1st January, 1902, subject to existing rights being preserved and the extension of tenure referred to.

In addition to pastoral leases, special leases on favourable terms are granted of scrub lands, snow lands—that is, lands covered with snow during a part of the year,—and inferior lands. Annual leases for pastoral purposes, and residential leases on gold and mineral fields, are also granted; and special leases are allowed in certain cases. Within the Western Land Division all forms of lease prescribed by the Crown Lands Act ceased to operate on the 1st January, 1902, subject to existing rights and the extension of tenure provided in respect of pastoral, homestead and improvement leases, and occupation licenses. Within that division all new leases are to be submitted to competition and expire on 30th June, 1943.

Auction Sales.

Auction sales to the extent of not more than 200,000 acres in any one year are permitted. The upset price is fixed by the Minister for Lands. For town lands it must not be less than £8 per acre; for suburban lands, £2 10s.; and for country lands, £1 5s. Special terms can be made for the purchase of land on gold-fields, and for reclaimed lands.

Labour Settlements.

In the middle of 1893 an Act was passed to establish and regulate labour settlements on Crown lands, following the example set by New Zealand, and imitated by several other states. Under this Act the Minister may set apart certain areas for the purpose of establishing labour settlements. A settlement is placed under the control of a Board, which enrols such persons as it may think fit to become members of the settlement; makes regulations concerning the work to be done; apportions the work among the members; and equitably distributes wages, profits, and emoluments after providing for the cost of the maintenance of the members. Any trade or industry may be established by the Board, and the profits apportioned among the enrolled members. A Board is constituted as a corporate body, with perpetual succession and a common seal; and the land is leased to the Board as such, in trust for the members of the settlement, for a period of twenty-eight years, with right of renewal for a like term.

When a Board has enrolled such a number of persons as the Minister for Lands may approve, it may apply for monetary assistance on behalf of the members of the settlement. The Minister has power to grant an amount not exceeding £25 for each enrolled member who is the head of a family dependent upon him; £20 for each married person without a family; and £15 for each unmarried person. On the expiration of four years from the commencement of the lease, and at the end of each year following, 8 per cent. of the total sum paid to the Board becomes a charge on its revenues, until the total amount advanced, with interest at the rate of 4 per cent. per annum, has been repaid.

Victoria.

During the earlier period of the colonisation of Victoria, then known as the District of Port Phillip, in New South Wales, the alienation of Crown lands was regulated by the Orders in Council of the mother state, to which reference has already been made. In the year 1840, however, the upset price of country lands, which in New South Wales was limited to 12s. per acre, was specially raised to 20s. in the District of Port Phillip. The Orders in Council continued in force until 1860, when the system of free selection of surveyed country lands was inaugurated, the uniform upset price being fixed at £1 per acre. No condition was required to be fulfilled by the selector other than that of making a cash payment for the whole of his purchase—or for one-half only, the other half being occupied at a yearly rental of 1s. per acre, with right of purchase at the original price. In 1862 a new Act was passed. Large agricultural areas were proclaimed, within which land could be selected at a uniform price of £1 per acre. Modifications were introduced in the mode of payment; the maximum area which could be selected by one person was limited to 640 acres; and it was stipulated that certain improvements should be effected or part of the land placed in cultivation. This Act was amended in 1865, when the principle was introduced of leasing Crown lands within agricultural areas, with right of purchase after the fulfilment of certain conditions as to residence and improvements; and a new provision was added to meet the demand for land adjacent to gold-fields.

The legislation in force was, however, superseded by the Land Act of 1869 and the Pastoral Act of the same year. Until that time the free selection system in the state had been limited to certain lands proclaimed within agricultural areas, and to allotments previously surveyed, thus avoiding the conflict which was then beginning to take place in New South Wales between the selector and the pastoralist. Under pressure of a sudden increase in the demand for land, arising from the enormous immigration into Victoria which had followed the discovery of gold, and the necessity for the people finding other means of employment, and other and more permanent sources of income, the Victorian

Legislature adopted the system in vogue in the neighbouring state, with modifications to suit the local conditions. The Act of 1869, which was amended in 1878, was further amended in 1884, the main tendency of the latter amendment being towards the restriction of the further alienation of the public estate by limiting the area which might be sold by auction, and substituting for the existing method of selecting agricultural land a system of leasing in certain defined areas, and at the same time conserving to the lessee the privilege of acquiring from his leasehold the fee-simple of 320 acres under the system of deferred payments. A portion of the public domain, known as the "Mallee Scrub," comprising some 11½ million acres wholly or partly covered with various species of stunted trees, was separately dealt with by the Mallee Pastoral Leases Act of 1883. The land legislation of 1869, and the special enactment just referred to, were again modified by the Acts of 1890, 1891, 1893, 1896, 1898, and 1900, the whole being consolidated as the "Land Act, 1901," which came into force on the 31st December, 1901.

The Land Act of 1869 is inoperative as to future selections, but concessions as to payments of arrears of rent, the option of converting their present leases into perpetual leases, and of surrendering part of and obtaining new leases on better terms for the balance of their holdings, have been granted to selectors thereunder by the most recent legislation.

For the purposes of land administration, the state is divided into districts which are merely arbitrary divisions, and in each district there are land offices under the management of land officers. As occasion requires, the land officers hold board meetings to deal with applications for, and any matter pertaining to, Crown lands.

Unalienated Crown lands are divided into the following classes:—Good agricultural or grazing land; agricultural and grazing lands; grazing lands; inferior grazing lands; pastoral lands (large areas); swamp or reclaimed lands; lands which may be sold by auction (not including swamp or reclaimed lands); auriferous lands; State forest reserves; timber reserves; and water reserves. Provision is made for a reclassification of lands within the first, second, third, and fourth classes, where it is recognised that an inequality exists, and for this purpose Land Classification Boards are constituted, each Board to consist of three members who will be officers of the Lands Department or other competent persons. Land may be acquired in the following manner:—(1) By the lessee of pastoral lands, by selection of a homestead up to 640 acres of land not superior to third-class land out of his leasehold at 10s. per acre; (2) by the lessee of a "grazing area" who is entitled to select thereout an agricultural allotment, obtaining a perpetual lease of the allotment in lieu of a license; (3) by licensee or lessee of an agricultural allotment on the surrender of his license or lease, obtaining in its stead a perpetual lease; (4) by the holder of a mallee allotment, eligible to select an agricultural allotment thereout, obtaining a perpetual lease instead of a license; (5) by perpetual leases of any

Crown lands available as agricultural or grazing allotments, or mallee lands available as agricultural allotments, or swamp, or reclaimed lands; (6) by purchase at auction of town or country lands within specified areas; (7) by purchase at auction of detached portions of Crown lands of an area not exceeding 50 acres; (8) by the holder of a residential agricultural allotment under license within mallee territory; (9) by farm allotment under conditional purchase lease, within areas required for the purpose of closer settlement.

Pastoral Lands.

Pastoral leases are granted to the person first lodging an application after public notice has been given that the land is available, and expire on the 29th December, 1909. The maximum area is 40,000 acres, and the minimum 1,920 acres. Should more than one application be lodged, the right to a lease is sold by public auction, after at least one month's notice has been given in the *Government Gazette*, and the highest bidder by way of premium is, on payment of same, entitled to the lease. The annual rent reserved on every lease of pastoral lands is computed at 1s. per head of sheep, and 5s. per head of cattle, the number of such sheep or cattle to be determined by the grazing capacity of the area, and the rent must be paid in advance every six months. The lessee cannot assign, sublet, or subdivide without the consent of the Board in writing; he must destroy all vermin and noxious growths, and keep in good condition all improvements on the land; and he must not destroy growing timber, except for fencing purposes or for building on the land, without the Board's consent. The Crown has the right to resume any portion of the area required for any railway or public purposes, and may issue licenses to enter on the land to obtain timber, stone, earth, etc. The right is reserved to other pastoral lessees to pass over the area, and the Governor may at any time by proclamation grant to the public the use of any track leading to a public road or track. The lessee is also required to erect swing gates where there is a fence across any track required by any other pastoral lessee or the public. Upon compliance with all conditions the lessee may select 200 acres of first-class, or 320 acres of second-class, or 640 acres of third-class land, or 960 acres of fourth-class land, as a homestead. Upon the expiration of a lease the lessee is entitled to payment from an incoming tenant for all fences, wells, reservoirs, tanks, and dams—but such payment shall be determined in the manner provided by the Lands Compensation Acts—and all other improvements revert to the Crown.

Agricultural and Grazing Lands.—Grazing Areas.

Agricultural and grazing lands are leased in "grazing areas" of first, second, third, or fourth-class land, to any person of the age of 18 years and upwards, for any term of years expiring not later than 29th December, 1920. No such lease can be granted for more than 200 acres of first-class, or 640 acres of second-class, or 1,280 acres of third-class land, or

1,920 acres of fourth-class land; but the lease may comprise two or more "grazing areas," provided the total acreage does not exceed the maximum limit of any class. The rent is fixed at 3d. per acre for first-class, 2d. per acre for second-class, and 1d. per acre for third-class lands, and ½d. per acre for fourth-class lands; but an additional rent of 4 per cent. per annum on the capital value of any substantial and permanent improvements on the "grazing area" at the date of the commencement of the lease is imposed. On the expiration of the lease the incoming tenant is required to pay to the late lessee the value of all improvements, effected during the currency of the lease, calculated to increase its capacity for carrying sheep or cattle; but the sum to be paid in respect of such improvements must not be more than 10s. per acre of the "grazing area" if first-class, or 7s. 6d. per acre if second-class, or 5s. per acre if third-class land, or 2s. 6d. per acre if fourth-class land. All other improvements revert absolutely to the Crown, unless specially provided for in the lease of the "grazing area." The rent is payable half-yearly in advance, and the lessee cannot assign, sublet, or subdivide, without the consent of the Board; he must destroy all vermin and noxious growths and keep in good condition all improvements on the land. The lessee cannot ring or destroy, or, except for the purpose of fencing, or building, or domestic use on the land, cut down any timber thereon, without the consent of the Board, and he must enclose the land with a fence and keep it in good repair. The Crown may resume possession at any time of any of the land which may be required for public or mining purposes, or for removal of material or timber, or for industrial purposes, on payment of reasonable compensation. Every other lessee of a "grazing area" and his agents and servants have the right of ingress, egress, and regress to and from his "grazing area" through, from, and to any public road or track. The lessee, after the issue of the lease, may, if the "grazing area" consist of first-class land, select not more than 200 acres thereout as an "agricultural allotment"; if of second-class land, an "agricultural allotment of" of 320 acres; and if of third-class land a "grazing allotment" of 640 acres. A lessee of a "grazing area" in respect of which no rent is due, and who has reasonably and sufficiently fulfilled the conditions and covenants of his lease, may surrender any part of his "grazing area" in order that a new "grazing area" lease of such surrendered part may be granted to his wife or any eligible child, without public competition.

Agricultural Allotments.

Residence licenses are issued to any person of the age of 18 years and upwards, who has not made a selection under the Land Acts, or who is not in respect of the license applied for or any part thereof an agent, servant, or a trustee for any other person, or who has not at any time entered into an agreement to permit any other person to acquire by purchase or otherwise the applicant's interest therein, to occupy an "agricultural allotment" not exceeding in the aggregate 200 acres of first-class or 320 acres of second-class land. The period of license is six years, and the fee for occupation is 1s. per annum in the case of first-class land, or 9d. per annum in the case of second-class land for each and every one acre or part thereof, payable half-yearly in advance. The licensee cannot assign, transfer, or sublet; he must enclose the land with a fence and keep it in repair; and he must effect substantial and permanent improvements to the value of 20s. per acre, or fractional part of an acre, where the land is first-class, and 15s. an acre, or fractional part of an acre, where the land is second-class, during the currency of the license. The licensee must enter into occupation within twelve months from the issue of the license, and occupy the agricultural allotment for not less than five years during its currency. If a licensee satisfactorily prove that the home of his family is situate upon the land held by him under residential license, the Board may consent, for a specified period, to substituted occupation by the wife or any stated child over the age of 18 years; or, if he has no wife or child, by the father or mother of the licensee, provided he or she is dependent on him for support. A licensee may, in each and every year of the term of residence on residential license, apply to the land officer of the district to register a written notice of intention to absent himself from the agricultural allotment for a period or periods not exceeding on the whole three months, and any absence between the registered dates is not deemed a breach of the condition of occupation. If the conditions be complied with, the licensee is entitled at any time within twelve months after six years from the commencement of the license to obtain a Crown grant upon payment of the difference between the amount of rent actually paid and the entire sum payable for the purchase of the land, or obtain a lease for a term of fourteen years. The Crown may resume any portion of the land during the currency of the license that may be required for public or mining purposes, subject to the repayment of moneys paid by the licensee to the Crown or expended by him on the land resumed.

Non-residential licenses for a period of six years are issued to persons similarly qualified on identical conditions, with the exception that the improvements to be effected are 6s. 8d. per acre, or fractional part of an acre each year of the license on first-class land, and 5s. per acre, or fractional part of an acre for each of the first three years of the license in respect of second-class lands.

The licensee or lessee of an agricultural allotment may surrender his license or lease, and in its stead obtain a perpetual lease. The rent chargeable therefor to 29th December, 1909, is based upon the unimproved value of the land, which is assumed at £1 per acre if first-class and 15s. per acre if second-class land; thereafter the rent is fixed by the Board at the end of every successive ten years. The holder of an agricultural allotment who desires to establish and cultivate a vineyard, hop-garden, or orchard may, during the term of his license or lease, upon payment of the difference between the amount of rent actually paid and the entire purchase-money payable in respect of any part, not more than 20 acres, of his allotment, obtain a Crown grant of such part subject to such covenants, conditions, exceptions, and reservations as the Governor may direct.

Grazing Allotments.

Licenses, either residential or non-residential, are issued to persons, qualified in a similar manner to those entitled to hold agricultural allotments, to occupy an allotment of third-class land not exceeding 640 acres, or 960 acres of fourth-class land. The period of license is six years, and the rent payable 6d. per acre for third-class land, and 3d. per acre for fourth-class land, half-yearly in advance. In the case of a residential license, the licensee must enter into occupation within twelve months from the issue of the license, and occupy the grazing allotment for not less than five years during the currency of the license. If a licensee satisfactorily prove that the home of his family is situate upon the land held by him under residential license, the Board may consent, for a specified period, to substituted occupation by the wife or any stated child over the age of 18 years; or, if he has no wife or child, by the father or mother of the licensee, provided he or she is dependent on him for support. A licensee may, in each and every year of the term of residence on residential license, apply to the land officer of the district to register a written notice of intention to absent himself from the grazing allotment for a period or periods not exceeding on the whole three months, and any absence between the registered dates is not deemed a breach of the condition of occupation. Substantial and permanent improvements must be effected to the value of 10s. per acre, or fractional part of an acre, on third-class lands, or 5s. an acre on fourth-class lands in respect of residential licenses, and 3s. 4d. each year of the first three years for each acre, or fractional part of an acre, in the case of non-residential licenses of third-class lands, or 1s. 8d. in the case of fourth-class lands. The licensee cannot assign, transfer, or sublet; he is required to keep the land free from vermin, and must enclose the land and keep the fence in repair. The Crown may resume any portion of the land during the currency of the license that may be required for public or mining purposes, subject to the repayment of moneys paid by the licensee to the Crown or expended by him on the land resumed. If the conditions be complied with, the licensee is entitled, at any time within twelve months after six years from the commencement of the license, to obtain a Crown grant upon payment of the difference between the amount of rent actually paid and the entire sum payable for the purchase of the land, or obtain a lease for a term of fourteen years, at a yearly rent of 6d. for each acre of third-class land, or 3d. per acre for fourth-class lands. The holder of a grazing allotment, who desires to establish and cultivate a vineyard, hop-garden, or orchard, may, during the term of his license or lease, upon payment of the difference between the amount of rent actually paid and the entire purchase-money payable in respect of any part, not exceeding 20 acres, of his allotment, obtain a Crown grant of such part, subject to such covenants, conditions, exceptions, and reservations as the Governor may direct. Any person who is entitled to select a grazing allotment may apply for a perpetual lease of the allotment in lieu of the license.

Perpetual Leases.

Perpetual leases may be granted over any Crown lands available as agricultural or grazing allotments; over mallee lands available as agricultural allotments; and over swamp or reclaimed lands. They may also be granted to holders of grazing areas who are entitled to select thereout an agricultural or grazing allotment; to holders of mallee allotments or parts thereof eligible to select an agricultural allotment; to holders of permits or leases to occupy allotments on swamp lands; and to village settlers on other than swamp lands who may desire to surrender the same and obtain perpetual leases in lieu thereof. No person is allowed to hold by transfer or otherwise more than 600 acres of first-class, or 960 acres of second-class, or 1,920 acres of third-class land, or 2,880 acres of fourth-class land, outside the mallee country. The rent on every perpetual lease, outside mallee and swamp or reclaimed lands, to 29th December, 1909, is 1¼ per cent. on the unimproved value of the land, which is deemed to be £1 per acre for first-class, 15s. per acre for second-class, 10s. per acre for third-class land, and 5s. per acre for fourth-class land. For every successive period of ten years the value, exclusive of all improvements made by the lessee, will be such amount as may be fixed by the Board, and the annual rent will be 1¼ per cent. of such value. The rent must be paid yearly in advance. The lessee must destroy all vermin within two years, and keep the land free from vermin and noxious growths; he must enclose the land within six years, or sooner if called upon under the Fences Act, 1890; he must reside for six months on the land, or within 5 miles thereof during the first year, and eight months during each of the four following years. In the event of the cultivation by the lessee of one-fourth of the area during the first two years, and one-half before the end of the fourth year, the residence covenant ceases to operate. Improvements must be effected to the value of 10s. per acre on first-class, 7s. 6d. per acre on second-class, and 5s. per acre on third-class land, or 2s. 6d. per acre on fourth-class land, before the end of the third year, and further improvements to a like value before the end of the sixth year of the lease. The lessee may not transfer, assign, mortgage, sublet, or part with the whole or any portion of the area within six years; and any portion required for railways, roads, mining, or other public purposes may be resumed on payment for non-removable improvements thereon or cost of removable improvements. A perpetual lessee whose rent is not in arrear may surrender his lease within six months after 29th December, 1909, or within six months after any successive period of ten years, with a view of obtaining an agricultural or grazing allotment license, either residential or non-residential. The improvements made will be credited to the licensee, and should there be a mortgage on the perpetual lease, the licensee may, after the issue of the license, give to the mortgagee a license lien on his improvements to the full amount due on the mortgage at the time of surrender.

Lands within Auriferous Areas.

Licenses to reside on or cultivate lands comprised within an auriferous area may be granted for a period not exceeding one year, and for areas not exceeding 20 acres, at an annual license fee of 1s. per acre. No person can hold more than one license. The license is subject to the following conditions:—Right to use surface of land only; licensee not to assign or sublet without permission of the Minister; licensee either to reside on or fence the land within four months from date of license and cultivate one-fifth of area, allowance being made for any portion occupied by buildings; miners to have free access to any part of the land without making compensation to the licensee for surface or other drainage; and notices to be posted on the land by the licensee indicating that it is auriferous.

Grazing licenses, renewable annually at the option of the licensee, are issued for a period expiring not later than 29th December, 1905, for areas not exceeding 1,000 acres, at a rent to be fixed by appraisement. The licensee may, with the consent of the Minister of Mines, enclose the whole or any specified part of the holding with a fence, which may be removed by him upon or at any time before the expiration of his license; but such fence must be removed, without compensation, by the licensee when so ordered by the Board. Free access to such area must be allowed at all times to miners and other persons specially licensed to enter thereon; the ringbarking of the timber on the land by the licensee is strictly forbidden; and the licensee is subject to a penalty, not exceeding £20, if he fails to place upon the outside of the corner posts of the fence, if any, enclosing the lands such distinguishing marks as may be prescribed.

Auction Lands.

Lands comprised within certain areas notified in a schedule attached to the Act of 1891, and lands within proclaimed towns or townships, or within any city, town, or borough proclaimed before the passing of the Lands Act of 1884, may be sold at auction, the upset price for town lands being determined in the proclamation for sale, and that for country lands, £1 per acre. The maximum area that may be sold in any one year is 100,000 acres. Of the price, 12½ per cent. must be paid in cash, and the balance in forty half-yearly instalments, carrying interest at 4 per cent. per annum. Where, in the opinion of the Board, it is undesirable that the residue of the price of any land should be paid for by instalments extending over twenty years, such residue may be made payable in any number of half-yearly instalments less than forty.

Stringent provisions are enacted prohibiting agreements preventing fair competition at auction sales. Isolated portions of Crown lands not exceeding 50 acres and not adjoining other Crown lands, or any portion of Crown lands not exceeding 3 acres required for a site for a church or for any charitable purpose, may be sold at auction.

Swamp Lands.

The swamp or reclaimed lands comprise the areas known as Condah, Koo-wee-rup, Moe, Panyzabyr, Mokoan, Black Swamp, Borodomanin, and Brankeet, Greta, Kelfeera, and Pieracle Swamps, and any swamp or reclaimed lands that may be proclaimed as such in the *Government Gazette.* The lands are divided into allotments of an area not exceeding 160 acres, and may be leased for twenty-one years, or be leased under perpetual lease at a rental of 4 per cent. on the value of the land, or be leased under conditional purchase lease, or be disposed of by sale at public auction, subject to general conditions of sale. Every lease for twenty-one years, every perpetual lease, every conditional purchase lease, and every contract of sale for an allotment of swamp or reclaimed lands contains the condition that the lessee or purchaser shall make substantial improvements on the land to the extent of 10s. per acre in each of the first three years and keep open all canals and drains. The condition of residence is not obligatory in all cases. For determining the rent on the upset price the Board will fix the value of each allotment. Village settlers on swamp or reclaimed lands may surrender their permits or leases, and acquire in place thereof perpetual leases or conditional purchase leases. In the event of a perpetual lease being granted, the annual rent thereon till 29th December, 1909, will be 4 per cent. on the price of the land as fixed in the surrendered permit or lease, the improvements at time of surrender to be credited towards compliance with conditions of new lease. In the event of a conditional purchase lease being granted, the price to be paid will be that fixed in the surrendered permit or lease, carrying interest at 4½ per cent. per annum.

Lands enhanced in Value.

Where Crown lands are enhanced in value by the proximity of a railway, or of waterworks for irrigation purposes, etc., the Governor is empowered to increase the minimum sum per acre for which such lands may be sold, as well as the minimum amount of rent or license fee, by not less than one-eighth nor more than double the sum. But where lands have been sold, leased, or licensed at an enhanced price, and the works by reason of which the extra payment has been demanded have not been constructed within ten years from the date of the Order in Council fixing the enhanced price, the additional sum paid must be returned.

Forest Lands.

Land situated within the State forests, and timber and water reserves, cannot be alienated, except as hereinafter provided; and the administration of the Forest Domain of the Crown is placed in the hands of local Forest Boards, which are empowered to receive fees for licenses to cut or remove timber. Where any person has made his home, or the home of his family, for a period of five years on forest lands, whether permanently reserved or not, and has effected thereon improvements of the value of not less than £2 per acre, he may apply to purchase an area not exceeding 10 acres at a price to be determined by appraisement; and if there be no mining or other valid objection a Crown grant may issue.

Mallee Lands.

The territory known generally as the "Mallee" is situated in the north-western district of the state, and comprises an area of about 10,000,000 acres. The mallee land bordering on the plain country is mostly of a light chocolate and sandy loam character, and in its natural state is covered with mallee scrub, interspersed with plains lightly timbered with box, oak, and pines. The scrub can be cleared at a moderate expenditure, and the land is well adapted for wheat-growing. The smaller areas are known as "mallee allotments," and the larger areas, extending further north and where the soil is more sandy in character, as "mallee blocks." The "blocks" are practically in their natural state, are many square miles in extent, and are used for pastoral purposes only.

Mallee Blocks.

The "mallee blocks" are of various sizes. One portion of a block may be held for five years under an occupation license, and the other under lease for a period expiring not later than the 1st December, 1903. The lease is granted for a period of twenty years. For the first five years the rent payable is at the rate of 2d. per head of sheep and 1s. per head of cattle depastured on the land; for the second five years twice this amount; and for the remainder of the term at an additional increase equal to one-half the amount payable during the second period of five years; but in no case may the yearly rent be less than 2s. 6d. for each square mile or part of a square mile of land. Leases issued after the 20th February, 1896, have the rent fixed by the Board. The lessee cannot assign, subdivide, or cultivate any part without the consent of the Board of Land and Works; he must destroy the vermin upon the land, and fulfil certain other conditions. The Government retain the right of resuming the land after giving due notice, compensation for improvements effected being given on assessment. Licenses may be granted to enter on the block to obtain timber, stone, earth, etc., and other lessees may cross the area to get to any public road or track.

Mallee Allotments.

The mallee allotments are situated on the southern and eastern fringe of the mallee territory, and have a maximum area of 20,000 acres, and are leased for terms expiring not later than 30th November, 1903.

No assignment of the lease of a mallee allotment by operation of law can take effect without the consent of the Board, and the lessee without such consent cannot execute any mortgage or lien thereon. The lessee is required, within six months of the granting of the lease, to take up his residence on the land or within 5 miles thereof, and to remain there for at least six months in the first year, and nine months during each of the next four years; or, instead, to cultivate at least one-fourth of the allotment within two years, and at least one-half before the end of the fourth year. In the event of the insolvency or death of the lessee, residence is not obligatory on the assignee, executor, or administrator. Without the consent of the Board, the lessee cannot clear or cultivate any part of his allotment, and not more than five crops in succession may be raised, after which for one year the land must be allowed to lie fallow. A uniform rental of 1d. per acre per annum is now charged in all cases where the Board's consent has been obtained to clear and cultivate.

It is provided that the lessee may select out of his mallee allotment an agricultural allotment not exceeding 640 acres, either under license or perpetual lease. When this is done the remainder of the mallee allotment may be resumed, compensation being awarded for improvements only. Should the lessee have actually resided on the land and destroyed the vermin thereon, the period of six years for which the agricultural allotment license is issued may be so shortened as not to exceed the length of such residence, conditionally on the payment of the license fees.

Agricultural Allotments under License or Perpetual Lease.

Any person of the age of 18 years or upwards may select 640 acres of first-class, or 1,000 acres of second-class land, or 1,280 acres of third-class land, or 1,600 acres of fourth-class land, out of any area made available as an agricultural allotment under residential or non-residential license or perpetual lease. A similar concession is made to any holder of a mallee allotment who may make application at any time before the 30th November, 1903, to select out of his mallee allotment a similar area in like manner. The period of residence attached to residential licenses is five years. When the area is first-class land, the purchase money in full for a residential license is £1 per acre, and the license is for a term of six years, at a yearly rent of 1s. per acre; the improvements at the expiration of the license must be of the value of £1 per acre. If all the conditions be complied with, the licensee is entitled, at the expiration of the license, to a lease for fourteen years at the same rent, or to a Crown grant at any time, on paying the difference between the amount paid and £1 per acre. If the applicant prefer, he may obtain a license at a reduced rental of 6d. per acre per annum for the term of six years, with a lease for thirty-four years at 6d. per acre yearly. When the area is second-class land, the purchase money in full is 10s. per acre, and the license is for a term of six years at a yearly rent of

6d. per acre, and the lease for fourteen years at the same rent, or a license may be issued, with conditions varied in these respects, that the rent shall be 3d. per acre yearly for six years, with a subsequent lease for thirty-four years at the same rent. The improvements at the end of the six years must be of the value of 10s. per acre. A non-residential license on first-class land is granted for a term of six years at 1s. per acre per annum, and the lease for a period of fourteen years at the same rent. Improvements to the value of 6s. 8d. per acre must be made in each of the six years. The period of non-residential license on second-class land is six years, at an annual rent of 6d. per acre, and the lease is for fourteen years at the same rent. Improvements to the value of 3s. 4d. an acre must be made during each of the first three years. Except for the purpose of building, fencing, or other improvements, the licensee may not cut or remove any live pine, box, or red gum, on the land.

Perpetual leases of mallee country are issued, in areas not exceeding 1,920 acres, at a yearly rental not to exceed 2d. per acre to 31st December, 1903, and thereafter as the Board may determine. The rent must be paid yearly in advance, and the lessee must destroy any vermin on the land, and within two years have made a complete clearance of such pests, while during the remainder of his lease he must see that the land is kept free from them. Within six months, the lessee must reside on or within 5 miles of the land, and do so for a period of eight months in each of the second, third, fourth, and fifth years. In the event of the lessee cultivating one-fourth of the area within two years, and at least one-half within four years, the residence condition ceases to operate.

Vermin Districts.

Under the Land Act of 1890, districts which are proclaimed as vermin-infested are, for the purpose of securing the extinction of these animal pests, administered by local committees appointed by the owners, lessees, and occupiers of the lands. In order to secure the erection of vermin-proof wire-fencing, a fencing rate may be levied, and the Minister has power to deduct 5 per cent. of the amount levied in vermin districts for the purpose of erecting a vermin-proof fence between the mallee country and the mallee border.

Wattle Cultivation.

During 1890 legislation was enacted having for its object the granting of leases of any unoccupied Crown lands for the cultivation of wattle-trees, for any term not exceeding twenty-one years, at a rent of 2d. per acre per annum for the first seven years, 4d. per acre for the second seven years, and 6d. per acre for the remainder of the term. A lease is not granted for more than 1,000 acres; and the rent is payable half-yearly in advance. The lessee covenants not to assign, sublet, or divide the lease without the consent of the Board of Land and Works; to keep all improvements in repair during each of the first six years following the year after the granting of the lease; to sow or plant wattle-trees or any other approved tannin-producing trees or plants on at least one-fifth of the land leased, and within six years to occupy the whole area in a similar manner. He must within two years enclose a third, within three years two-thirds, and within four years the whole of the land leased; and he is required to keep the fence in good repair, and to destroy all vermin which may be upon the land. The lessee may select out of his lease an agricultural or grazing allotment under license or perpetual lease.

Village Settlements.

Under the Settlement on Lands Act of 1893 there may be set apart and appropriated for the purposes of village communities any lands not alienated from the Crown, provided they are not auriferous or permanently reserved for any purpose. Such lands are surveyed into allotments of 1 to 20 acres each, according to the quality of the soil and the situation. Subject to certain restrictions, any person of the age of 18 years may obtain a permit to occupy a village community allotment for a period not exceeding three years. The rent is merely nominal, but conditions are laid down with the object of ensuring *bona-fide* occupancy. On the expiration of the permit a lease may be obtained, provided the conditions of the permissive occupancy have been fulfilled. The lease is granted for a period of twenty years. The lessee must pay in advance, every half-year, rent equal to one-fortieth of what is regarded as the price of the allotment, which is to be not less than £1 per acre. Within two years from the date of the lease he must have brought into cultivation not less than one-tenth, and within four years, one-fifth of the land; and within six years, have effected substantial improvements of a permanent character to the value of £1 for every acre leased. He must also keep all improvements in good repair; and he cannot assign, transfer, or sublet the land, or borrow money on the security of his lease without the consent of the Board of Land and Works. He must reside personally on the land, and use it for agriculture, gardening, grazing, or other like purpose. Any person in occupation of an allotment under permit or lease may surrender the same, and acquire the land under a perpetual lease, or a conditional purchase lease. In the event of the land being granted under perpetual lease, the rental thereon to 29th December, 1909, will be 250 per cent. on the price set out in the original permit or lease; should the land be granted as a conditional purchase lease, the price to be paid is that fixed in the surrendered permit or lease carrying interest at 4½ per cent. per annum.

Homestead Associations.

Areas of similar lands to the foregoing may also be set apart and appropriated for occupation by members of associations or societies; but no proclamation can remain in force for a longer period than three years in the case of a society, nor for more than six months in the case of an association, after the survey and subdivision of the block; and land in any block not occupied or leased at the expiration of these periods becomes unoccupied Crown land again. No block of land set apart for the purposes of associations or societies can exceed in area 2,000 acres. A block is subdivided into lots of not more than 50 acres each, and the number of persons to be located in each block must not be less than one for every 50 acres of its total area. A permissive occupancy of a section may be granted to any member of an association or a society for a period of three years. The rent is a nominal one, and after proof of fulfilment of conditions a lease may be obtained by the member, provided he is of the age of 18 years. The lessee covenants to pay the annual rent and the cost of survey; to repay all moneys advanced by the Board; to bring into cultivation within two years not less than one-tenth, and within four years not less than one-fifth of the land; and within six years to effect substantial improvements of a permanent character to the value of £1 for every acre leased. He must also keep the improvements in good repair; and he cannot assign, transfer, or sublet the land, or borrow money upon it without the consent of the Board of Land and Works. He must personally reside on his section or its appurtenant township allotment, and use the land for agriculture, gardening, grazing, dairying, or other like purpose. Adjoining to or within every block of land appropriated in this manner, an area of not more than 100 acres may be set apart for the purposes of a township, and the Board of Land and Works may subdivide it into allotments not exceeding 1 acre, in order to provide a township allotment for each homestead selection. Power is reserved to alienate the fee-simple of those allotments not required for the purpose; and every settler may, within one year from the commencement of his permit or lease, obtain a lease of such an allotment, with the right to a Crown grant in fee on making the payment prescribed.

Labour Colonies.

Areas of similar land, not exceeding 1,500 acres in extent, may also be set apart for the purpose of labour colonies, to be vested in five trustees, appointed by the Governor. For the purpose of aiding the trustees, provision is made whereby persons subscribing to the funds of such a colony may annually elect a committee of management, consisting of four members. The joint body (trustees and committee) is empowered, on a day to be determined in each case by the Minister, to admit to such a colony any person who shall be entitled to such benefits as the rules of the colony may prescribe. The trustees and committee of each colony must establish and conduct the same; and they have all the powers and authority necessary to enable them to improve the position of the colony and make it self-supporting. They may establish and maintain any industry they please, and dispose of the proceeds thereof. A subsidy of £2 for every £1 received by the trustees and committee from public and private subscriptions is payable by the Government. The moneys received are to be disbursed in the payment of allowances for work to persons employed in the colony; in the construction and maintenance of necessary buildings; and in purchasing provisions, clothing, building materials, stock, seed, and agricultural implements.

Besides the foregoing provisions, there are numerous others, dealing with minor interests, which in a general statement of this kind it is not necessary to recapitulate.

Acquisition of Land for Closer Settlement.

The acquisition of private lands for the purpose of closer settlement is an entirely new feature in Victorian land legislation. The Board of Lands and Works may, subject to the approval of Parliament, purchase for the Crown, blocks of good agricultural private land in any farming district. The portion of the acquired land to be disposed of is to be subdivided into farm allotments of a value not exceeding £1,000 each, which are to be available under conditional purchase lease. Any person of the age of 21 years, who is not already the holder of land of the value of £1,000, or who would not thereby become the holder of land exceeding such value, may be granted a farm under conditional purchase lease. The price of the land to be disposed of is to be so fixed as to cover the cost of original purchase, cost of survey and subdivision, the value of lands absorbed by roads and reserves, and the cost of clearing, draining, fencing, or other improvements which the Board may effect prior to the disposal of the land as farm allotments. The purchase money, with interest at 4½ per cent. per annum, must be paid by sixty-three or a less number of half-yearly instalments. The conditional purchase lease may be for such a term of years (not exceeding thirty-one and a-half) as may be agreed upon between the lessee and the Board. The lease is subject to the following conditions:—Improvements to be effected to the value of 10s. an acre, or if the Board so determines, to the value of 10 per cent. of the purchase money, before the end of the third year of the lease, and to the value of a further 10s. an acre, or if the Board so determines, to the value of a further 10 per cent. of the purchase money before the end of the sixth year of the lease; personal residence by the lessee, or by his wife, or any child not less than 18 years of age, on the allotment for eight months during each year of the first six years; lessee not to transfer, assign, mortgage or sublet within the first six years; and such other conditions and covenants relating to mining, cultivation, vermin destruction, and other matters as may be prescribed by regulation. Upon or at any time after the expiration of the first six years of the lease, provided all conditions have been complied with, the lessee may, on payment of the balance of the principal, acquire the fee-simple of his farm allotment.

QUEENSLAND.

The land legislation of New South Wales in force on the date when the Moreton Bay District was formed into the colony of Queensland, gave place soon after that event to a new system of settlement, better adapted to the requirements of the newly constituted province. Following to a certain extent the lines adopted by their neighbours, the Queensland legislators introduced into their regulations the principle of free selection before survey, and of sales under the deferred payment system. Having to dispose of a vast territory which, not being endowed with so temperate a climate, had not the same attractions as the southern provinces, it was considered necessary to exercise greater liberality in offering the land than was shown to settlers in the other states. Large areas and small prices were therefore features of Queensland land sales. Most liberal, also, were the provisions to facilitate the exploration and occupation for pastoral purposes of the vast interior country, and the Pastoral Act of 1869 led to the occupation by an energetic race of pioneers of nearly the whole of the waste lands of the province. The rapid development of the resources of the state, and the consequent increase of population, necessitated later on a revision of the conditions under which land might be alienated or occupied; but although the tendency has been to curtail the privileges of the pastoralists, the alienation of the public estate by selection—conditional and unconditional—has been placed under enactments of a still more liberal character than those which existed in the earlier days. Under pressure of the new social movement, Queensland has followed in the wake of New Zealand and South Australia, and has granted to the working classes great facilities for acquiring possession of the soil. The regulations at present in force are based upon the legislation enacted under the Crown Lands Act of 1884, and its subsequent amendments in 1886, 1889, 1891, 1893, 1897, 1900, and 1902.

Land may be acquired in the following manner:—(1) By conditional selection: agricultural homesteads from 160 to 640 acres, at prices ranging from not less than 20s. for 160 acres to less than 15s. per acre for 640 acres, and agricultural selections up to 1,280 acres, at a price determined by the proclamation rendering the land available for settlement—residence in both cases to be personal or by agent; (2) by unconditional selection, at prices one-third greater than those payable in respect of agricultural selections, the area being limited to 1,280 acres; (3) by grazing-farm selection up to 20,000 acres, the period of lease ranging from fourteen to twenty-eight years at a varying rental, ½d. per acre being the minimum; (4) by scrub selection of areas not exceeding 10,000 acres for a term of thirty years, at rentals ranging from a peppercorn to 1d. per acre; and (5) by purchase at auction, of town lands at an upset price of £8 per acre, suburban lands at £2 per acre, and country lands at £1 per acre for land classed as agricultural, and 10s. per acre for any other.

The state is, so far as is necessary, divided into Land Agents' Districts, in each of which there are a Public Lands Office and a Government Land Agent with whom applications for farms must be lodged. Applications must be made in the prescribed form, and be signed by the applicant, but they may be lodged in the Lands Office by a duly authorised attorney. There is connected with the Survey Department, in Brisbane, an office for the exhibition and sale of maps, and there full information respecting lands available for selection throughout the state can be obtained on personal application. Plans can also be obtained at the District Offices.

The conditions under which country lands may be acquired for settlement by persons of either sex over 16 years of age—married women excepted, unless they are judicially separated or possess separate estate, or living apart from their husbands, provided the husbands have never acquired a homestead of the character sought—are substantially as stated below.

Grazing Farms.

Areas of land already surveyed are available for selection as grazing farms over a great extent of territory within accessible distance of the seaboard. Intending settlers can obtain up to 20,000 acres on lease, for a term of fourteen, twenty-one, or twenty-eight years, at an annual rent varying according to the quality of the land, ½d. an acre being the minimum. This rent is subject to reassessment by the Land Court after the first seven years, and subsequently at intervals of seven years, but it cannot be decreased at any reassessment, nor can it be increased by more than one-half of the rent for the period immediately preceding. The applicant must first obtain an occupation license, which is not transferable, and which may be exchanged for a lease for the balance of the term of fourteen, twenty-one, or twenty-eight years as soon as the farm is enclosed with a substantial fence, which must be done within three years, or such extended time, not exceeding two years, as the Land Court may allow. The lease may be transferred or mortgaged after the expiration of five years from the commencement of the lease, and the farm may be subdivided, or, with the consent of the Land Court, sublet. The land must be continuously occupied by the lessee or his agent for the whole term of the lease, and cannot be made freehold. The Commissioner may issue a license to a group of two or more selectors, enabling any one of the selectors to perform the condition of occupation in respect of any of the selections as well as on his own behalf, but the number of selectors personally residing is not at any time to be less than half the whole number interested. One-fifth of the cost of survey, ranging from about £30 for a farm of 2,560 acres to about £65 for 20,000 acres—subject to increase or decrease according to locality—must be paid with a year's rent when application is made for the farm, and the balance in equal instalments without interest.

Grazing Homesteads.

Lands available as grazing farms are also open for selection as grazing homesteads at the same rental and for the same term of lease. An application to select as a grazing homestead takes precedence of a simultaneous application to select the same land as a grazing farm. The conditions and other provisions mentioned in respect of grazing farms are applicable also to grazing homesteads, with the exception that during the first five years of the term of a grazing homestead the condition of occupation must be performed by the continuous personal residence of the selector on the land.

Agricultural Farms.

The more accessible lands near lines of railway, centres of population, and navigable waters, are set apart for agricultural farm selection in areas up to 1,280 acres. The period of license is five years, during which the selector must fence in the land, or expend an equivalent sum in effecting other substantial improvements. As soon as the improvement condition has been complied with, a lease is issued for a term of twenty years from the date of the license, with right of purchase at any time after continuous occupation of the lease for a period of five years. The annual rent is one-fortieth of the purchasing price specified in the proclamation declaring the land open, and varies according to the quality and situation of the land, its natural supply of water, etc. The selector must occupy the land continuously, either in person or by an agent —who must be a person qualified to select a similar selection—for the whole term of the lease; but if the selector is the holder of two or more agricultural selections each of which is at a distance not exceeding fifteen miles from the others, the residence of the selector or his agent on one of the selections is sufficient. The cost of survey, ranging from about £10 to £12 for a farm of 160 acres to £20 to £40 for a farm of 1,280 acres, must be borne by the selector.

Agricultural Homesteads.

When land is taken up as an agricultural homestead, the area is restricted to 160 acres, 320 acres, or 640 acres, according as the price specified in the proclamation is determined at not less than 20s., less than 20s. but not less than 15s., or less than 15s. per acre respectively. The selection must be enclosed within a period of five years, or permanent improvements effected at an expenditure dependent on the capital value of the land. The applicant is entitled to a lease for a period of ten years, at a rental of 3d. per acre; but he may acquire the fee-simple of the land on the terms prescribed in the proclamation, after the expiration of five years from the commencement of the lease.

Two or more selectors of agricultural homesteads may associate for mutual assistance under license from the Land Board. A selector may perform conditions of residence for himself and any other member of the association, provided that at least one-half of the whole number of selectors interested are in actual occupation; and any sum expended on permanent improvements on any one homestead in excess of the required amount may be credited to any other farm or farms in the group. In other respects the conditions are similar to those governing agricultural homesteads.

Village Settlements.

With regard to village settlement, special provision is made by law for the settlement of little communities, so that settlers may live together in townships for mutual convenience, on allotments not exceeding 1 acre in extent, and with farms of 80 acres in close proximity to their residences. The freehold of these farms may be secured generally on the same terms as those upon which agricultural farms not exceeding 160 acres in area may be acquired, with the additional privileges that residence on an allotment in the township is held to be equivalent to residence on the farm, and one-fifth of the required improvements may be made on the allotment.

Unconditional Selection.

Areas of land are also available for unconditional selection at prices one-third greater than those payable in respect of agricultural selections. The term of lease is twenty years, and the annual rent one-twentieth of the purchasing price, which may not be less than 13s. 4d. per acre. At any time during the currency of the lease the freehold may be acquired. As the term implies, no other conditions than the payment of the purchase money are attached to this mode of selection—the maximum area allowed to be selected being 1,280 acres. The proportion of cost of survey, on the same scale as for agricultural selection, must be deposited with the first instalment of purchase money at the time of application, the balance to be paid in equal annual instalments.

Scrub Selections.

Lands which are entirely or extensively overgrown with scrub are available for selection in four classes, determined by the extent of scrub. The area selected must not exceed 10,000 acres, and the term of lease is thirty years, the rent ranging from a peppercorn per acre in the first five years, ½d. an acre for the next succeeding ten years, and 1d. per acre for the remaining fifteen years in respect of lands in the first class, to a peppercorn for the first twenty years, and 1d. per acre for the remaining ten years in relation to those of the fourth class. During the period of lease under which the selector pays a peppercorn rent the whole of the scrub must be cleared—a proportionate area in each year—and the land enclosed. Compensation is paid in respect of clearing on any land resumed, but upon determination of the lease the clearing improvements revert to the Crown.

Auction Lands.

The alienation in fee of allotments in towns is restricted to areas ranging from 1 rood to 1 acre, at an upset price of £8 per acre; while in respect of suburban lands, areas of 1 to 5 acres may be acquired within 1 mile of town lands, and the limit is extended to 10 acres in regard to lands situated over 1 mile from such town lands, the upset price being £2 per acre. In respect of country lands, the maximum area that may be sold in any one year is limited to 150,000 acres in lots not exceeding 320 acres, and the upset price is fixed at £1 per acre for land classed as agricultural, and not less than 10s. per acre for any other. A deposit of 20 per cent. is to be paid at time of sale, and the balance, with deed, assurance, and survey fees, within one month thereof.

Pastoral Leases.

Under the provisions of the Land Act, 1902, the lessee of any holding held at the passing of the Act, may make application prior to the 1st January, 1904, for the classification of the same by the Land Court. The leases of classified holdings which may be granted are: 1. For a term consisting of the unexpired part of the term of the surrendered pastoral lease and ten years more; provided that no such lease shall be for a longer term than twenty years, or in the case of a holding the lease whereof was extended under previous enactments, twenty-four years. 2. For a term consisting of the unexpired part of the term of the surrendered pastoral lease and twenty years more: provided that no such lease shall be for a longer term than thirty years, or, in the case of a holding the lease whereof was extended under previous enactments, thirty-four years. 3. For a term consisting of the unexpired part of the term of the surrendered pastoral lease and thirty years more; provided that no such lease shall be for a longer term than forty years, or in the case of a holding the lease whereof was extended under previous enactments forty two-years. 4. For the term of forty two years.

The rent payable is determined by the Land Court.

Co-operative Settlement.

The Co-operative Communities Land Settlement Act of 1893 provides for the setting apart of a portion of Crown lands for the purposes of a group or association of persons for co-operative land settlement, and the condition annexed thereto is that the group shall consist of not less than thirty persons, each of whom is eligible to apply for and hold land under the provisions of the Crown Lands Act of 1884. It is requisite that the group shall be recognised by the Minister, and the rules of the community must be deposited with him. None but natural born or naturalised subjects are eligible to become members of a group, and no person may be a member of more than one community. It is open to a group to register itself under the Friendly Societies Act of 1876, and in such case certain provisions at law dealing with the internal government of the community become inoperative.

The area available for a co-operative community is set apart by proclamation, and cannot exceed in area more than 160 acres for each member. The proclamation specifies and defines the name of the group; the persons included therein; the boundaries and a description of the area; the improvements to be made; the period for which the area is set apart (not exceeding twelve nor less than six years); and the rent payable for the land. A sum equal to at least 2s. 6d. per acre must be expended during each of four equal portions of the lease, and failing that, resumption of the land and consequent dissolution of the group ensue.

No member of a co-operative community possesses an individual interest or property in the improvements effected on the land, the same being vested in the Minister; but on the expiry of the lease, with the conditions satisfactorily performed, the members, on payment of the proclaimed price (if any) and deed and assurance fees, are entitled to a deed of grant in fee-simple of so much land as was specified in the proclamation, the division of the area being left to the members themselves. In certain cases the acquisition of freehold may be prohibited by the rules of the group, and provision is made for dissolution when the membership falls below a certain number.

Labour Colonies.

Provision is also made for the proclamation of Labour Colonies. The area granted to a colony, which must not exceed 10,000 acres in extent, is vested in five trustees, who are empowered to establish and manage any trade or industry. A subsidy not exceeding £1,000, either conditionally or otherwise, may be granted to a labour colony from Parliamentary appropriations for such purposes.

South Australia.

The settlement of the state of South Australia was the outcome of an attempt to put into actual practice one of those remarkable theories which logically seem founded upon apparently solid ground, but which are apt to weaken and give way when subjected to the pressure of hard practical facts. The policy by which a wealthy colony was to be created in a few years on the edge of a supposed desert continent, was based upon principles enunciated by Edward Gibbon Wakefield, in a pamphlet published in England about the year 1836. The main idea of his scheme of colonisation was the sale of land in the new possession at a high price, and the application of the amount thus realised to the introduction of immigrants, whom the landowners would at once employ to reclaim the virgin forest, and create wealth and abundance where desolation existed. But although Wakefield had fairly calculated upon the results which would follow the action of man if left to himself, the part which Nature might be expected to play was not taken into consideration, and the scheme quickly proved an empty failure and a distressful speculation for the many whom its apparent feasibility had deluded into investing their means in the lands of the new colony. Had not the discovery of great mineral resources occurred at an opportune time, the exodus into the eastern colonies of the immigrants imported or attracted to South Australia would have emptied the province of its population, and considerably retarded the progress of a territory not inferior in natural resources to other portions of the Australian continent.

Steps were soon taken to modify the Wakefield system, but it was only in 1872 that an Act was passed more in conformity with the legislation of the neighbouring states, and giving to the poorer classes of the population a chance to settle upon the lands of the Crown under fair conditions. The Lands Act of 1872, adapted as it was to the needs of the time, gave way to other measures, and the regulations now in force are those of the Crown Lands Act of 1888, as amended in 1889, 1890, 1893, 1894, 1895, 1896, 1897, 1898, and 1899.

General Provisions.

The law as it now stands gives power to the Government to alienate Crown lands in the following manner:—(1) By auction, town lands, Crown lands within hundreds, and special blocks may be alienated, but no sales of country lands may be made at a price of less than 5s. per acre; a deposit of 20 per cent. is required at time of sale, the residue to be paid within one month therefrom; (2) by lease with right of purchase, the period of lease being twenty-one years, with option of renewal for a further period of twenty-one years, and right of purchase exercisable at any time after the expiration of the first six years of the term, at a price of not less than 5s. per acre. The grant in fee-simple of any land cannot be construed to convey any property in any mineral or mineral oil in or upon the land, the same being reserved by the Crown, although authority may be given to persons at any time to search for and remove any of the minerals reserved.

Leases with Right of Purchase.

No lands may be leased unless they have been surveyed; and the area that a lessee may at any one time hold with a right of purchase is restricted to 1,000 acres. No lease with right of purchase, or perpetual lease, can be granted of lands of such value that the purchase money will exceed £5,000 unimproved value. The Land Boards are entrusted with the duty of classifying lands, and of fixing the area of blocks, the price and annual rent at which each block may be taken up on lease with right of purchase, and the annual rent at which such block may be taken up on perpetual lease. Applications must be made in writing to the Commissioner, and must cover a deposit equal to 20 per cent. of the first year's rent of the block which it is desired to take up. All applications are dealt with by the Land Board, which has power to subdivide or to alter the boundaries of blocks, and to decide what pric or annual rent shall be payable. A lessee must execute his lease and pay the balance of the first year's assessment and prescribed fees within twenty-eight days after the acceptance of his application has been notified and the lease has issued, otherwise he forfeits the deposit paid and all rights to a lease of the land.

Leases with right of purchase are granted for a term of twenty-one years, with the right of renewal for a similar term. Purchase may be made at any time after the first six years. The price must not be less than 5s. an acre.

The rent chargeable on a perpetual lease for the first fourteen years is fixed by the Land Board and notified in the *Government Gazette*, and for every subsequent period of fourteen years a revaluation is made. Every lease contains a reservation to the Crown of all minerals, timber, and mineral oils in or upon the land. The lessee undertakes to fulfil the following conditions :—(1) To pay rent annually; (2) to pay all taxes and other impositions; (3) to fence in the land within the first five years, and thereafter to keep the fences in repair; (4) to commence forthwith to destroy and to keep the land free from vermin; (5) to keep in good order and repair all improvements which are the property of the Crown; (6) to keep insured to their full value all buildings which are the property of the Crown; and (7) to give access to the land to persons holding mining licenses or mineral leases.

A pastoral lessee may surrender his lease for a perpetual lease where the unimproved value of the land comprised therein, together with that of all other lands held by him, does not exceed £5,000, or where, in the opinion of the Commissioner, the land is suitable only for pastoral purposes, and the carrying capacity thereof unimproved, and of all other lands held by the lessee under any tenure does not exceed 5,000 sheep. The annual rent of the perpetual lease in such case is to be determined by the Surveyor-General, subject to the approval of the Commissioner, according to the actual value, irrespective of the amount of the right of purchase granted in respect thereof.

Sale of Lands.

All Crown lands within hundreds which have been offered for lease and not taken up, may be offered for sale at auction for cash within two years of the date on which they were first offered for lease. Other lands may be sold at auction for cash, and not upon credit or by private contract, the Commissioners fixing the upset price of both town and country lots offered; but no country lands may be sold for less than 5s. per acre.

Pastoral Leases.

The administration of the law in respect of pastoral lands is controlled by a Pastoral Board consisting of three members, including the Surveyor-General. Legislation passed in 1899 provides that in future pastoral leases the classification hitherto existing is abolished, and the term of such leases is to be forty-two years, subject to a revaluation of the rent for the second twenty-one years, the rent to be determined by the carrying capacity of the land for the depasturing of stock, the value of the land for agricultural and other purposes, and the proximity and facilities of approach to railway stations, ports, rivers, and markets. Pastoral leases current at the time of the passage of the legislation referred to are divided into three classes. Class A includes all pastoral lands within district A, the boundaries of which are set out in the

Schedule to the Pastoral Act of 1893; Class B includes similar land in district B; and Class C includes all pastoral lands to the south of the 26th parallel of south latitude, and not included in Classes A and B. Leases in Classes A and B have a currency of twenty-one years, and in Class C of twenty-one years, with a right of renewal for a similar term at a revaluation.

No mining by the lessee is allowed, but he may use the surface of the land for any purpose, whether pastoral or not. Improvements are valued solely in connection with their worth to the incoming lessee, and may in no case exceed in value such as are necessary for the working of a run of 5,000 sheep in Class A, of 10,000 sheep in Class B, or of 30,000 sheep in Class C, or a proportionate number of cattle, five sheep being taken as the equivalent of one head of cattle. Revaluations may be made during the currency of a lease if, by the construction of Government works in the neighbourhood, such as railways and waterworks, the land should have received an enhanced value. Leases are granted to discoverers of pastoral lands, or to any person for inferior lands, for forty-two years—the first five years at a peppercorn rental; the next five years at 1s. per annum per square mile; and the remainder of the term at 2s. 6d. per annum per square mile. For all other leases the minimum rent is fixed at 2s. 6d. per annum per square mile, together with 2d. for each sheep depastured in Classes A and B, and 1d. for each sheep in Class C. Provision is made for the resumption of leases and the granting of compensation. All disputed cases are decided according to the terms of the Arbitration Act, 1891.

A pastoral lessee may surrender his lease for a perpetual lease where the unimproved value of the land comprised therein, together with that of all other lands held by him, does not exceed £5,000, or where, in the opinion of the Commissioner, the land is suitable only for pastoral purposes, and the carrying capacity thereof unimproved and of all other lands held by the lessee under any tenure does not exceed 5,000 sheep.

In cases where the area held by an outgoing lessee is reduced by subdivision below a certain minimum, the improvements are to be valued for the protection of such lessee as if the area were of the minimum carrying capacity, and any difference between their value and that paid by the incoming lessee is to be borne by the Commissioner. The Commissioner is not bound to recover improvement moneys or to protect improvements, and any moneys paid to an incoming lessee for depreciation of improvements are to be laid out in their repair; but a lessee may be released from the liability to repair improvements provided others in lieu thereof are made to the satisfaction of the Commissioner.

The lessee covenants to stock the land, before the end of the third year, with sheep, in the proportion of at least five head, or with cattle, in the proportion of at least one head, for every square mile leased: and before the end of the seventh year to increase the stock to at least twenty sheep or four head of cattle per square mile, and to maintain the numbers at that rate. In addition, pastoral leases granted subsequent to 28th January, 1899, contain a covenant binding the lessee to expend in improvements such sum, not to exceed 10s. per mile per annum as shall be recommended by the Pastoral Board, and approved by the Commissioner, the covenant to cease so soon as an expenditure of at least £3 per mile in improvements has been made on the land.

In cases where the Commissioner is satisfied that the country is waterless or infested with vermin, the covenant relating to stocking the land may be qualified, provided that a sum equal to £5 per square mile of the leased land has been expended in the destruction of vermin or in the construction of water improvements. Where artesian water yielding not less than 5,000 gallons per diem is discovered, the lessee is entitled to a remission of five years' future rent in respect of an area of 100 square miles surrounding such well, but this concession cannot be claimed on account of more than four wells on any one run.

Forfeiture of a lease does not take effect until after three months' notice has been given to the lessee, who may thereupon apply for relief to the Tenants' Relief Board, which consists of a Judge of the Supreme Court assisted by two assessors. After consideration of all matters affecting the question, the Board may determine as they think fit.

Working-men's Leases.

A new feature has been introduced into the land legislation of the state, in response to the claims of the working classes. It is enacted that certain lands of the province may be surveyed into blocks exceeding 20 acres in area, so long as the unimproved value does not exceed £100, and leased under the conditions affecting leases granted with the right of purchase and perpetual leases. No one except a person who gains his livelihood by his own labour, and who has attained the age of 18 years, is entitled to a working-man's lease. Either husband or wife may hold a working-man's block, but not both at the same time. The rent is payable annually in advance. The lessee is bound to reside on the land for at least nine months in every year, but residence by his wife or any member of his family is held as a fulfilment of the residential condition. Working men's leases situated within a radius of 10 miles from the Post Office, Adelaide, cannot be taken up with the right of purchase.

Exchange of Lands.

Crown lands may be exchanged for any other lands, notwithstanding the existence of any lease that may have been issued in connection with the former. The Crown lands proposed to be given in exchange may be granted in fee simple or under perpetual lease.

Village Settlements.

Twenty or more persons of the age of eighteen and upwards may form an association for the purpose of founding a village settlement. The memorandum, on approval of the Commissioner, is deemed to be registered, and the association becomes a corporate body, with the right to sue and to be sued. The proclamation sets forth the name, situation, and boundaries of the village; the names of the villagers and of the trustees of the association; the maximum area to be allotted to each villager; and the nature and aggregate value of the improvements to be made on the land, and the period within which they are to be effected. Within two months of the publication of the proclamation constituting a village, the Commissioner is to issue to the association a perpetual lease thereof. The conditions attached are that, after the first six months from the date of issue of the lease, at least one-half of the villagers shall reside upon and utilise the land in the manner prescribed; that during each of the first ten years the sum of 2s. per acre at least shall be expended in improvements, which are to be kept in good repair; and that the lands are not to be sub-let. The Commissioner may make advances to registered associations, to the extent of £100 for each villager, for the purchase of tools or to effect improvements, such advances to be repaid in ten equal yearly instalments, with interest at the rate of 5 per cent. per annum. Power is vested in the Commissioner to expel from an association any villager who has become liable to expulsion under the rules; to control and direct the expenditure of any money advanced; to call upon a trustee to resign where the welfare of the association calls for such action; and to require an association to increase the number of villagers so that it may not be less than the number who signed the rules when first registered—the total to be not more than 500.

Registration of Homesteads.

The Homestead Act of 1895 has for its object a simple method of securely settling homesteads for the benefit of settlers and their families. It is essential that applicants for the registration of their homesteads should be residing, and have resided for at least one year prior to making the application, on the land to be registered. Homesteads with improvements thereon of the value of more than £1,000, or in respect of which the applicant is not either the owner of an unencumbered estate in fee-simple or the holder of a perpetual lease from the Crown, are not eligible for registration. The effect of registration is to settle the homestead for the benefit of the settler and family until the period of distribution, either under his will, or when his children have all attained the age of 21 years. No alienation or attempted alienation by the settler or his family has any force or effect other than as provided for, and their interest continues unaffected to the value of £1,000 only. Provision is made for the leasing of the homestead, but for no period longer than three years. Registration may be rescinded should the settler become bankrupt or make an assignment for the benefit of his creditors within twelve months from the date of registration; and a similar course may be adopted in the event of his death within a like period and should it be shown that the estate is insufficient for the payment of his debts and liabilities without recourse to the homestead. The Act applies to land brought under the provisions of the Real Property Act of 1886, as well as to land not subject to that Act.

Closer Settlement.

With a view to the encouragement of closer settlement in the public interest by facilitating the acquisition by the Crown of large estates for subdivision and letting for agricultural purposes at reasonable rents, power is given to the Commissioner to acquire such. The price to be paid for lands compulsorily taken is not to exceed the unimproved value of the land, together with the value of the improvements thereon, with an additional 10 per cent. for compulsory resumption.

Mining Areas.

Provision is made for the issue of business and occupation licenses. Business claims cannot be more than ¼ acre in townships nor more than 1 acre on other lands, and they must not be situated within 5 miles of any Government township, except they come within a gold-field. The cost of a business license is 10s. for six months or £1 for a year. Occupation licenses of blocks not exceeding ½ acre are granted for a period of fourteen years, at an annual rental of 2s. or less.

The Northern Territory.

The Northern Territory of South Australia includes the whole of the lands situated to the north of the 26th degree of south latitude, bounded by Queensland on the east, Western Australia on the west, and the Ocean on the north. This portion of the Continent is under the administration of a Resident, appointed by the Government of South Australia; and the alienation and occupation of lands within the Territory are conducted under regulations enacted by the South Australian Legislature, in accordance with the Northern Territory Crown Lands Consolidation Act of 1882.

It is provided that lands may be purchased for cash, without conditions, in blocks not exceeding 1,280 acres, for 12s. 6d. per acre. They may also be bought under the deferred payment system to the same maximum area, and at the same price, payable in ten years, together with an annual rent of 6d. per acre.

Leases for pastoral occupation may be issued for a term not exceeding twenty-five years, for blocks up to 400 square miles, the annual rental for the first seven years being 6d. per square mile, while 2s. 6d. per square mile is charged during the remainder of the term.

In order to encourage the cultivation of tropical produce, such as rice, sugar, coffee, tea, indigo, cotton, tobacco, etc., special provisions have been enacted. Blocks of 320 acres to 1,280 acres may be let for such purposes at the rate of 6d. per acre per annum. If, on the expiration of five years, the lessee can prove that he had cultivated one-fifth of his area by the end of the second year, and one-half by the end of the fifth year, he is relieved from all further payment of rent, and the amount already so paid is credited to him towards the purchase of the land in fee.

Western Australia.

The first regulations referring to land settlement in Western Australia were issued by the Colonial Office in 1829' at the time when Captain James Stirling was appointed Civil Superintendent of the Swan River settlement. The first special grants were made in favour of Captain Stirling himself for an area of 100,000 acres near Geographe Bay; and of Mr. Thomas Peel, for 250,000 acres on the southern bank of the Swan River and across the Channing to Cockburn Bay—Mr. Peel covenanting to introduce at his own cost 400 immigrants into the state by a certain date. Persons proceeding to the settlement at their own cost, in parties in which the numbers were in the proportion of five females to every six male settlers, received grants in proportion to the amount of capital introduced, at the rate of 40 acres for every sum of £3. Capitalists were granted land at the rate of 200 acres for every labouring settler introduced at their expense, but these grants were subject to cancellation if the land was not brought into cultivation or reclaimed within twenty-one years. These regulations were amended by others of a similar nature, issued on the 20th July, 1830. In 1832, however, the mode of disposing of Crown lands by sale came into force, the regulations issued in that year assimilating the system of settlement to that in force in the colonies of New South Wales and Van Diemen's Land. Other alterations were made from time to time, until in October, 1898, an Act amending and consolidating the laws relating to the sale, occupation, and management of Crown lands received assent.

For the purposes of administration, the state is divided into six divisions, namely, the South-west division, the Western division, the North-west division, the Kimberley division, the Eucla division, and the Eastern division. Land may be acquired in the following manner:—(1) By auction of town and suburban lands in all divisions, at an upset price to be determined by the Governor; (2) by conditional purchase—(*a*) by deferred payments with residence within agricultural areas in all divisions; (*b*) by deferred payments with residence on any land other than agricultural in the south-west division; (*c*) by deferred payments with residence on any land within 40 miles of a railway within the eastern and Eucla divisions, at a price of not less than 10s. per acre, payable in twenty yearly instalments, and in areas not exceeding 1,000 acres nor less than 100 acres; (*d*) by deferred payments without residence within an agricultural area, also over any other land within the south-west division, or within 40 miles of a railway within the eastern and Eucla divisions, which may from time to time be declared open to selection; (*e*) by direct payment without residence within agricultural areas of not less than 100 acres nor more than 1,000 acres, at a price of not less than 10s. per acre, 10 per cent. of which is to be paid on application and the balance within twelve months of date of the commencement of the license, by four equal quarterly instalments; (*f*) by direct payment without residence, for gardens, in all divisions, of areas of not less than 5 nor more than 50 acres, at not less than 20s. per acre; (*g*) of poison lands; (*h*) working-men's blocks; (*i*) free homestead farms; (*j*) of grazing lands, second and third class lands.

Auction Lands.

Town and suburban lands in all divisions may be sold by public auction, at an upset price to be determined by the Governor-in-Council. Any person may apply to the Commissioner to put up for sale by auction any town or suburban lands already surveyed, on depositing 10 per cent. of the upset price, which is returned if such person does not become the purchaser. Should the purchaser not be the applicant, he must pay 10 per cent. on the fall of the hammer, the balance of the purchase money, in the case of town lots, by two equal instalments at the end of three and six months; in the case of suburban lots, by four equal quarterly instalments, subject to alteration by regulation, the Crown grant and registration fees being payable with the last instalment. All suburban land is sold subject to the condition that each lot shall, within two years from the date of sale, be enclosed with a fence of a prescribed description.

Conditional Purchase.

In all the divisions, agricultural areas of not less than 2,000 acres are set apart by the Governor-in-Council. The maximum quantity of land which may be held by any one person is 1,000 acres, and the minimum 100 acres. The price is fixed at 10s. an acre, payable in twenty yearly instalments of 6d. an acre, or sooner, in the occupier's option. Upon the approval of an application, a lease is granted for twenty years. Within six months the lessee must take up his residence on some portion of the land; and make it his usual home without any other habitual residence, during, at least, six months in each year for the first five years. The lessee must within two years from the date of the commencement of his lease fence at least one-tenth of the area, and within five years enclose the whole of the land, and must within ten years, expend upon the land, upon prescribed improvements, in addition to the exterior fencing, an amount equal to the full purchase money. After the lease has expired, provided that the fence is in good order, and the improvements have been maintained, and the full purchase money has been paid, a Crown grant is given.

Land may be purchased outside agricultural areas in the south-west division, also within 40 miles of a railway within the eastern and Eucla divisions, by free selection, on deferred payments with residence, and otherwise subject to all the conditions required within agricultural areas as already stated.

Under the fourth mode of purchase, the applicant is subject to all the conditions, except that of residence, imposed under the first mode, but he has to expend twice the amount on improvements in lieu of residence.

By the fifth mode, land of a minimum extent of 100 acres and a maximum of 1,000 acres, within an agricultural area, and not more than 5,000 acres outside an agricultural area, may be applied for at a price (not less than 10s. per acre) fixed by the Governor-in-Council. Within three years the land must be enclosed, and within seven years a sum equal to 5s. per acre must be spent on improvements, in addition to the exterior fencing.

For garden purposes, small areas of not less than 5 acres nor more than 50 acres (except in special cases) may be purchased within all divisions at 20s. per acre on condition that within three years the land shall be fenced in, and one-tenth of the area planted with vines or fruit-trees or vegetables.

Lands infested with poisonous indigenous plants, so that sheep or cattle cannot be depastured thereon, are available for conditional purchase, in areas of not more than 10,000 acres nor less than 3,000 acres, at a price not less than 1s. per acre, payable half-yearly, at the rate of one-thirtieth of the total purchase money per annum. Upon approval of the application, a lease for thirty years is granted, subject to the conditions that the lessee shall, within two years, fence one-tenth, and within five years enclose the whole area, with a fence of the prescribed description, and, during the term of his lease, eradicate the whole of the poisonous indigenous plants. At the expiration of the lease, or at any time during the currency of the same, provided all the conditions have been complied with, the fencing properly maintained, and the full balance of the purchase money and fees paid, and provided that the land has been rendered safe for depasturing cattle and sheep at all seasons, and has continued so for a term of two years, a Crown grant of the land issues. A pastoral lessee has the first right to select land within his lease under these terms.

Every person who does not own land within the state in freehold, or under special occupation, or conditional purchase, or a homestead farm, who is the head of a family, or a male who has attained the age of 18 years, is entitled to obtain a lease of lands set apart for working-men's blocks. The maximum area that may be selected by one person is, if within a gold-field, ½ an acre, or 5 acres elsewhere. The price of the land is not less than £1 per acre, payable half-yearly, at the rate of one-tenth of the total purchase money per annum. The application is to be accompanied by a deposit of half a year's rent, and, on approval, a lease for ten years issues. Within three months from the date of the lease, the lessee must take personal possession and reside upon it during at least nine months in each of the first five years of the lease ; possession and residence may, however, be performed by the lessee's wife or a member of his family. Within three years the land must be fenced, and within five years an amount equal to double the full purchase money, in addition to his house and exterior fencing, must be expended on the land in prescribed improvements. At the expiration of the lease, or at any time after five years from commencement of lease, provided all the conditions have been complied with, and the fencing and improvements maintained, and the full purchase money and fees paid, a Crown grant issues.

Any person who does not already own more than 100 acres of land within the state, in freehold or conditional purchase, and being the head of a family, or a male who has attained the age of 18 years, may apply for a free homestead farm of not more than 160 acres, from lands declared open for such selection within the south-west division, and within 40 miles of a railway in the eastern or Eucla division, not being within a gold-field. The application is to be accompanied by a statutory declaration and a fee of £1, and, upon approval, an occupation certificate authorising the applicant to enter upon and take possession of the land for the term of seven years is issued. Within six months from the date of the occupation certificate, the selector must take personal possession of the land, and reside upon it for at least six months in each year for the first five years of the term. Within two years from the date of the certificate, a habitable house must be erected of not less than £30 in value, or the selector must expend £30 in clearing, or clearing and cropping, or prepare and plant 2 acres of orchard and vineyard. Within five years, one-fourth of the land must be fenced and one-eighth cleared and cropped. Within seven years, the whole must be enclosed, and at least one-fourth cleared and cropped. At the expiration of seven years, provided the conditions have been complied with, a Crown grant issues on payment of the usual fees.

Leases for thirty years of second and third class lands are granted, called grazing leases, but which are really another form of conditional purchase. The maximum area allowed to be taken up is 3,000 acres of second-class, and 5,000 acres of third-class, land, and the minimum in both cases is 1,000 acres; and if one person selects two leases in different classes, the total quantity must not exceed 4,000 acres. The price of second class land is not less than 6s. 3d. per acre, and of third class land 3s. 9d. per acre, payable half-yearly at the rate of 2½d. and 1½d. per acre respectively. The lessee is required to pay one-half the cost of survey in ten half-yearly instalments. Within six months from the date of the commencement of the lease, the lessee must take possession of the land and reside upon it during at least six months of the first year, and nine months in each year of the next four years. Residence may, however, be complied with by the lessee's agent or servant. Within two years from the date of the commencement of the lease, the lessee is required to fence at least one-tenth of the area contained therein, and within five years to fence the whole of the land, and within fifteen years to expend upon the land in prescribed improvements an amount equal to the full purchase money in addition to the exterior fencing.

Pastoral Lands.

Pastoral lands are granted on lease, which gives no right to the soil or to the timber, except for fencing and other improvements on the land leased, and the lands may be reserved, sold, or otherwise disposed of by the Crown during the term. The following are the terms of pastoral leases in the several divisions; all leases expire on the 31st December, 1928, and the rental named is for every 1,000 acres:—South-west division.—In blocks of not less than 3,000 acres, at 20s. per annum for each 1,000 acres or part of 1,000 acres; if, however, the land is in that part of the division situated eastward of a line from the mouth of the Fitzgerald River in the direction of Mount Stirling, the rental is 10s. per annum for each 1,000 acres or part thereof. Western and north-west division.—In blocks of not less than 20,000 acres, at 10s. per annum for each 1,000 acres or part thereof. Eucla division.—In blocks of not less than 20,000 acres, at 5s. per annum for each 1,000 acres or part thereof. Eastern division.—In blocks of not less than 20,000 acres, at the following rental:—For each 1,000 acres or part thereof, 2s. 6d. for each of the first seven years, and 5s. for each of the remaining years of the lease. Kimberley division.—In blocks of not less than 50,000 acres when on a frontage, nor less than 20,000 acres when no part of the boundary is on a frontage, at a rental of 10s. per annum for each 1,000 acres or part thereof. Any lessee in the Kimberley Division, or in that part of the south-west division situated to the eastward of a line from the mouth of the Fitzgerald River in the direction of Mount Stirling may obtain a reduction of one-half the rent due for the remaining years of his lease, who at any time during its term shall have in his possession within the division ten head of sheep or one head of large stock for each 1,000 acres leased. Except in the south-western division, a penalty of double rental for the remaining portion of the lease is imposed should the lessee within seven years have failed to comply with the stocking clause.

Any Crown land within a gold-field or mining district, not required to be reserved for any public purpose, may be leased for pastoral purposes in blocks of not less than 2,000 acres at a rental of 10s. per 1,000 acres. In the event of the land, or any portion of it, being taken for an agricultural area, the lessee is only entitled to three months notice.

Miner's Homestead Leases.

Any miner resident on a gold-field, being not less than 18 years of age, may apply for a miner's homestead lease of any Crown lands within the limits of a gold-field set apart for the purpose. The area which may be taken up is as follows:—Within 2 miles of the nearest boundary of any town site or suburban area, 20 acres; and beyond 2 miles from such boundary, 500 acres; and the aggregate area applied for by any one person within the same gold-field shall in no case exceed 500 acres. Upon the approval and notification of the lease in the *Government Gazette*, the applicant is entitled to enter upon and occupy the land; but if at the expiration of six months he has not used or occupied the land, either by himself residing upon it, or by enclosing one-tenth part of it with a substantial fence, or by substantial improvements upon the land, or by carrying on some manufacture upon or in connection with the land, he is deemed to have abandoned it. The lessee is required, within three years from the date of survey of the land, to fence the whole of it with a substantial fence, not being a bush fence, sufficient to resist the trespass of great stock; and within five years from the said date to expend upon the land in prescribed improvements an amount equal to 10s. per acre. If the area does not exceed 20 acres, the annual rent is at the rate of 2s. for every acre or part of an acre; if the area exceeds 20 acres, the annual rent is at the rate of 6d. per acre or part of an acre, payable during the first twenty years of the lease, and thereafter an annual rent of 1s. The minimum annual rent for the first twenty years to be reserved by any lease shall not be less than 10s.

TASMANIA.

In the earlier period of the occupation of Tasmania, from 1804 to 1825, the island was administered as a part of New South Wales, and its settlement was subject to the regulations affecting the disposal of the Crown domain in that colony. After its constitution under a separate administration, the regulations issued from the Colonial Office for the settlement of the Crown lands in the mother colony were made applicable also to Tasmania. New measures were introduced after self-government had been granted to the province, but they became so complicated and cumbersome that in 1890 the necessity was felt of passing an Act consolidating into one comprehensive and general measure the twelve Acts then in force. Amendments of the 1890 Act have, however, been made in 1895 and 1900.

The business of the Lands and Survey Departments is now transacted by virtue of the Crown Lands Act of 1890, and its amendments in 1895 and 1900, under which, for the convenience of survey operations, the island is divided into fifteen districts. Lands of the Crown are divided into two classes—town lands and rural lands, the latter being further subdivided into first-class agricultural lands and second-class lands. Lands which are known to be auriferous, or to contain other minerals, and such lands as may be necessary for the preservation and growth of timbers, are dealt with under separate sections; and the Governor-in-Council is empowered to reserve such lands as he may think fit for a variety of public purposes.

Land may be acquired in the following manner:—(1) By selection of rural lands in areas of not less than 15 nor more than 320 acres, at an upset price of £1 per acre, with one-third added for credit; (2) by selection of rural lands of not less than 15 nor more than 50 acres, at an upset price of £1 per acre, with one-third added for credit; (3) by selection of lands within mining areas—if situated within 1 mile of a town reserve, of an area of not less than 1 nor more than 10 acres; and if at a greater distance than 1 mile, of not less than 10 nor more than 100 acres—the upset price of first-class lands being not less than £1 per acre, payable in fourteen years, and that for second-class lands not less than 10s. per acre, payable in ten years; (4) by auction—(*a*) of town lands at the upset price notified in the *Gazette*, (*b*) of second-class lands at an upset price of 10s. per acre in lots of not less than 30 nor more than 230 acres, (*c*) of second-class rural lands at an upset price of not less than 10s. per acre (maximum area 320 acres), (*d*) of third-class rural land at an upset price of not less than 5s. per acre, in lots of not less than 60 acres nor more than 320 acres; (5) as settlement areas by any persons, styled "the purchasing body," in areas not exceeding 1,000 acres.

In the rural division any person of the age of 18 years may select by private contract at the price and upon the terms set forth hereunder:—

One lot of rural lands not exceeding 320 acres nor less than 15 acres.

	£	s.	d.
100 acres at 20s.	100	0	0
Add ⅓ for credit	33	6	8
	133	6	8

Payable as follows:—

	£	s.	d.	£	s.	d.
Cash at time of purchase	3	6	8			
First year	5	0	0			
Second year	5	0	0			
Third year	10	0	0			
And for every one of the eleven successive years to the fourteenth year inclusive at the rate of £10 per annum	110	0	0			
				133	6	8

The same proportions are allowed for any greater or smaller area than 100 acres; but credit is not given for any sum less than £15. Additional selections may be taken up, provided the total area held by one selector does not exceed 320 acres. Selection by agent is not allowed.

Sales of Land on Credit.

Any person of the full age of 18 years, who has not purchased under the Crown Lands Acts, may select and purchase one lot of rural land of not more than 50 acres nor less than 15 acres; and on payment of a registration fee of £1 an authority is issued to the selector to enter upon and take possession of the land, which must be done in person within six months from the date of issue of certificate. The purchase money, which is calculated on the upset price of £1 per acre, together with the survey fee, and with one-third of the whole added for credit, is payable in fifteen annual instalments, the first of which is due in the fourth year of occupation. A condition of purchase is that the selector shall expend a sum equal to £1 per acre in effecting substantial improvements (other than buildings) on the land, or reside habitually thereon for the full term of eighteen years, before a grant deed is issued. Where a purchaser is unable to pay the instalments as they become due, they may be deferred for any period up to five years on payment of interest at the rate of 5 per cent., if all other conditions have been fulfilled; and the selector may take possession of his land as soon as his application has been approved by the Commissioner and the survey fee paid.

The conditions in connection with the credit system are as follow:—The purchaser must commence to make improvements on the expiration of one year from the date of contract, and during eight consecutive years must expend not less than 2s. 6d. per acre per annum, under penalty of forfeiture. Any surplus over 2s. 6d. per acre spent in any year may be set against a deficiency in another year, so that £1 per acre shall be spent in the course of the eight years. In the event of improvements to the full amount being made before the expiration of the eight years, the purchaser may pay off any balance due, discount being allowed. Payment of instalments may in certain cases be postponed, but under such circumstances interest must be paid at the rate of 5 per cent. per annum. In certain cases the time for making the improvements may be extended for two years. Should an instalment not be paid within sixty days after becoming due, the land may be put up to auction, the defaulter having the privilege of redeeming his land up to the time of sale by payment of the amount due, with interest and costs. If land sold at auction by reason of default should realise more than the upset price, the excess is handed to the defaulter. Land purchased on credit is not alienable until paid for, but transfers are allowed. For five years after alienation land is liable to be resumed for mining purposes, compensation being paid to the occupier. All grant-deeds contain a reservation by the Crown of the right to mine for minerals.

Second-class lands may be sold by auction at the upset price of 10s. per acre in lots of 30 to 320 acres, the latter being the maximum quantity which any one purchaser can hold under the Act on credit. One-half of the purchase money is to be expended in making roads. Improvements, other than buildings, to the value of 5s. per acre are to be effected by the purchaser, beginning at the expiration of one year from the date of contract, and to be continued for the next five years at the rate of 1s. per acre per annum, the deed of grant issuing only when the amount of 5s. per acre has been expended. Non-fulfilment of the conditions entails forfeiture. Where the purchaser has fulfilled the conditions, but is unable to complete the purchase of the whole, a grant may issue for so much as has been paid for upon the cost of survey being defrayed. On approval of the application by the Commissioner, and payment of the survey fee, the selector may at once enter into possession.

Third-class lands may be sold by auction at an upset price of not less than 5s. per acre, and in lots of not less than 60 acres nor more than 320 acres. Within one year from the sale of the land, the purchaser must begin to effect substantial improvements other than buildings on the land, and continue in each year during the five consecutive years thereafter to effect such substantial improvements to the value of 1s. for every acre of land so purchased.

Rural lands not alienated and not exempt from sale may be sold by auction. Town lands are sold only in this way. Ten shillings per acre is the lowest upset price, and agricultural lots must not exceed 320 acres. Lands unsold by auction may be disposed of by contract. No private lands may be sold by private contract within 5 miles of Hobart or Launceston.

Mining Areas.

Mining areas may be proclaimed, within which land may be selected or sold by auction, in lots varying with the situation—from 1 to 10 acres if within a mile from a town, and up to 100 acres if at a greater distance. In such cases residence for three years is required, and in default the land is forfeited to the Crown. Occupation licenses are granted to holders of miners' rights or residence licenses for cultivation or pasture within areas withdrawn from the operation of the Crown Lands Act, in lots of not more than 20 acres, for a period of two years at 5s. per acre, on terms prescribed by regulation, and an area not exceeding ¼ of an acre may be sold by auction, the person in occupation having a preferential right of private purchase at the upset price fixed by the Land Commissioner. A deposit of one-sixth of the purchase money must be made on the approval of the sale, the balance to be paid in eleven equal monthly instalments.

Land selected or bought within a mining area is open to any person in search of gold or other mineral, after notice has been given to the owner or occupier, to whom compensation must be made for damage done. Persons who occupy land in a mining town, under a business license, and who have made improvements to the value of £50, may purchase one quarter of an acre at not less than £10 nor more than £50, exclusive of the value of improvements and cost of survey and deed fee.

Residence licenses may be issued to mining associations for a period of 21 years at 10s. for each year of the term. The same party may hold two licenses if the areas are 5 miles apart.

Grazing Leases.

Grazing leases of unoccupied country may be offered at auction, but such runs are liable at any time to be sold or licensed, or occupied for other than pastoral purposes. The rent is fixed by the Commissioner, and the run is put up to auction, the highest bidder receiving a lease for fourteen years. The lessee may cultivate such portion of the land as is necessary for the use of his family and establishment, but not for sale or barter of produce. Should any portion of the run be sold or otherwise disposed of, a corresponding reduction may be made in the rent, which is payable half-yearly in advance. A lease is determinable should the rent not be paid within one month of becoming due. In the event of the land being required for sale or any public purpose, six months' notice must be given to the lessee, who receives compensation for permanent improvements. Leases for not more than fourteen years may be granted for various public purposes, such as the erection of wharfs, docks, etc. Portions of a Crown reserve may also be leased for thirty years for manufacturing purposes.

New Zealand.

The first settlements in New Zealand were founded upon land obtained from the various native tribes, and the task of distinguishing between the few *bona-fide* and the numerous bogus claims to the possession of land thus acquired was the first difficulty which confronted Captain Hobson when, in 1840, he assumed the government of the colony. Trading in land with the natives had, from 1815 to 1840, attained such proportions that the claims to be adjudicated upon covered 45,000,000 acres—the New Zealand Company, of which Mr. Edward Gibbon Wakefield, of South Australian fame, was the managing director, claiming an estate of no less than 20,000,000 acres in area. In the year 1840, the Legislature of New South Wales passed a Bill empowering the Governor of that state to appoint a Commissioner to examine and report upon all claims to grants of land in New Zealand—all titles, except those allowed by Her Majesty, being declared null and void. This Bill, before receiving the Royal assent, was superseded by an Act of the local Council, passed in 1841, under which the remaining claims were settled, and new regulations were adopted for the future disposal of the Crown lands. When, later on, the colony became divided into independent provinces, each district had its own regulations, but in 1858 an Act was passed by the General Assembly embodying all the regulations under which land could be alienated or demised in the various provinces of the colony. This Act was repealed in 1876, and the enactments of 1885, 1887, and 1888 which followed have been superseded by the Lands Act of 1892 and its Amending Acts of 1893, 1895, 1896, 1897, and 1899, under which the Crown lands are now administered. For convenience the colony is divided into ten land districts, each being under the direction of a local Commissioner and a Land Board.

Classification of Lands.

Crown lands are divided into three classes:—1. Town and village lands, the upset prices of which are respectively not less than £20 and £3 per acre: such lands are sold by auction. 2. Suburban lands, being lands in the vicinity of any town lands, the upset price of which may not be less than £2 per acre; these lands are also sold by auction. 3. Rural lands, being lands not reserved for towns and villages, classified into first and second class lands, which may be disposed of at not less than £1 per acre for first-class, and 5s. an acre for second-class lands; such lands may be either sold by auction after survey, if of special value, as those covered with valuable timber, etc., or be declared open for application as hereafter described. Pastoral lands are included within the term "rural lands," and are disposed of by lease. No person can select more than 640 acres of first-class or 2,000 acres of second-class land, inclusive of any land already held; but this proviso does not apply to pastoral land.

Mode of Alienation.

Crown lands may be acquired as follows:—(1) At auction, after survey, in which case one-fifth of the price must be paid down at the time of sale, and the balance, with the Crown grant fee, within thirty days; and (2) by application, after the lands have been notified as open to selection, in which case the applicant must fill up a form and make the declaration and deposit required by the particular system under which he wishes to select. All applications, whether for surveyed or unsurveyed lands, are deemed to be simultaneous if made on the same day, and, if there be more than one applicant for the same land, the right of selection is determined by ballot.

The Optional System of Selection.

After lands have been notified as open under the optional system, they may be obtained on any of the three following tenures:—(*a*) Freehold, (*b*) occupation with the right of purchase, (*c*) lease in perpetuity.

(*a*) Freehold.

If the land is surveyed, one-fifth of the price is payable at the time of application, and the balance within thirty days; or if the land is unsurveyed, the survey fee, which goes towards the purchase of the land, is deposited when the application is agreed to, and the balance within thirty days of notice that survey is completed. Freehold-tenure lands must be improved within seven years to an amount of £1 an acre for first-class lands, and 10s. an acre for second-class land. A certificate of occupation issues to the purchaser on the final payment being made, and is exchanged for a Crown grant so soon as the Board is satisfied that the improvements have been completed.

(*b*) Occupation with Right of Purchase.

After notification, lands may be selected for occupation, with right of purchase, under a license for twenty-five years. At any time subsequent to the first ten years, and after having resided on the land and made the improvements hereafter described, the licensee can, on payment of the upset price, acquire the freehold. If not purchased after the first ten and before the expiry of the twenty-five years of the term, the license may be exchanged for a lease in perpetuity. The rent is 5 per cent. on the cash price of the land. A half-year's rent must be deposited with the application, if for surveyed land, and this sum represents the six months' rent due in advance on the 1st day of January or July following the selection. If the land is unsurveyed, the cost of survey is to be deposited, and is credited to the selector as so much rent paid in advance, counted from the 1st day of January or July following thirty days' notice of the completion of survey.

Residence must commence on bush or swamp lands within four years, and be continuous for six years, and in open or partly open land it must begin within one year from the date of selection, and be continuous for a period of seven years. The land must be improved to an amount equal to 10 per cent. of its value within one year from the date of the license or lease; within two years must be improved to the amount of another 10 per cent.; and within six years to the value of another 10 cent., making 30 per cent. in all within the six years. In addition, the land must be further improved to an amount of £1 an acre for first-class land, and on second-class land to an amount equal to the net price of the land, but not more than 10s. per acre. Two or more persons may make a joint application to hold as tenants in common under this tenure. Land held on deferred payment may be mortgaged under the Government Advances to Settlers Act of 1894.

(c) Leases in Perpetuity.

Lands notified under the optional system may be selected on a lease for 999 years (or in perpetuity), subject to the undernoted conditions of residence and improvements. The rental is 4 per cent. on the cash price of the land. In the case of surveyed lands, the application must be accompanied by half a year's rent, which represents that due on the 1st day of January or July following the date of selection. In the case of unsurveyed lands, the cost of survey must be deposited, and is credited to the selector as so much rent paid in advance, dating from the 1st day of January or July after thirty days' notice of completion of survey. Two or more persons may make a joint application to hold as tenants in common under this tenure. The residence must be continuous for a term of ten years, and the conditions of improvements are similar to those imposed in connection with occupation with the right of purchase.

Residence and Improvement Conditions.

Residence is compulsory (with a few exceptions mentioned in the Act). The Board has power to dispense with residence in certain cases, such as where the selector resides on adjacent lands, or is a youth or an unmarried woman living with his or her parents. The term "residence" includes the erection of a habitable house to be approved of by the Board.

Improvements comprise the reclamation of swamps, the clearing of bush, cultivation, the planting of trees, the making of hedges, the cultivation of gardens, fencing, draining, the making of roads, wells, water-tanks, water-races, sheep-dips, embankments or protective works, or the effecting of any improvement in the character or fertility of the soil, or the erection of any building, etc.; and cultivation includes the clearing of land for cropping, or clearing and ploughing for laying down artificial grasses, etc.

Special Settlement Associations.

Under the existing regulations, any group of persons numbering not less than twelve may apply for a block of land of not less than 1,000 acres nor more than 11,000 acres in extent; but the number of members must be such that there shall be one for every 200 acres in the block, and no one may hold more than 320 acres, except of swamp lands, of which the area may be 500 acres. The price of lands within a special settlement is fixed by special valuation, but it cannot be less than 10s. an acre. The rental may not be less than 4 per cent. on the capital value of the land; the tenure is lease in perpetuity. Residence, occupation, and improvements are generally the same as required in connection with selections under the optional system of selection, and applications have to be made in the manner prescribed by the regulations.

Improved Farm Settlements.

Special regulations are in force for this class of settlement, and those who form settlements are selected from the applicants by the Commissioner, preference being given to married men. The area of the farms may vary from 10 to 200 acres, according to locality, and no settler can select more than one farm. The land is leased for 999 years at a rental of 4 per cent. on the unimproved capital value, to which is added the amount advanced by Government for clearing, grassing, etc. Residence for the first ten years is compulsory, and the improvements to be effected are similar to those on leases in perpetuity.

Village Settlements.

Village settlements are disposed of under regulations made from time to time by the Governor, but the main features are as follow:— Such settlements may be divided into—(1) Village allotments not exceeding 1 acre each, which are disposed of either at auction or upon application as already described, with option of tenure, the cash price being not less than £3 per allotment; and (2) homestead allotments not exceeding 100 acres each, which are leased in perpetuity at a 4-per-cent. rental on a capital value of not less than 10s. per acre. Where a village-settlement selector has taken up less than the maximum area prescribed, he may obtain an additional area in certain cases without competition on the same tenure and terms as the original holding. Residence, improvements, and applications are the same as already described. The leases are exempt from liability to be seized or sold for debt or bankruptcy. The Governor is empowered in certain cases to advance small sums for the purpose of enabling selectors to profitably occupy their allotments.

Grazing Areas.

Small grazing runs are divided into two classes: first-class, in which they cannot exceed 5,000 acres; and second-class, in which they cannot exceed 20,000 acres in area. These runs are leased for terms of twenty-one years, with right of renewal for a like term, at a rent of $2\frac{1}{2}$ per cent. on the capital value of the land, but such capital value cannot be less than 5s. per acre. The runs are declared open for selection, and applications and declarations on the forms provided have to be filled in and left at the Lands Office, together with a deposit of six months' rent, representing that due on the 1st day of March or September following selection. A selector may not hold more than one small grazing run, nor may he hold any freehold or leasehold land of any kind whatsoever over 1,000 acres, exclusive of the area for which he applies under this system. The lease entitles the holder to the grazing rights and to the cultivation of any part of the run, and to the reservation of 150 acres around his homestead through which no road may be taken; but the runs are subject to the mining laws. Residence is compulsory on bush or swamp land within three years, and on open land within one year; and it must be continuous to the end of the term, though this latter condition may in certain cases be relaxed. Improvements are necessary as follow:—Within the first year, to the amount of one year's rent; within the second year, to the amount of another year's rent; and within the next four years, to the value of two years' rent;—making a sum equal to four years' rental to be spent on the run in six years. In addition to this, a first-class run must be improved to an amount of 10s. an acre, and a second-class run to an amount of 5s., if the land be under bush. After three years' compliance with these conditions, the run may be divided among the members of the selector's family who are of the age of 17 years and upwards, and new leases may be issued to them on the terms and subject to the conditions of residence and improvements contained in the original lease.

Pastoral Leases.

Purely pastoral country is let by auction for a term not exceeding twenty-one years; but, except in extraordinary circumstances, no run can be of a carrying capacity greater than 20,000 sheep or 4,000 cattle. Runs are classified from time to time into those which are suitable for carrying more than 5,000 sheep (let as above), and into pastoral-agricultural country, which may either be let as pastoral runs, generally for short terms, or be cut up for settlement in some form. Leases of pastoral-agricultural lands may be resumed without compensation at any time after twelve months' notice has been given. No one can hold more than one run unless it possesses a smaller carrying capacity than 10,000 sheep or 2,000 cattle, in which case the lessee may hold additional country up to that limit. Runs are offered at auction from time to time, and half a year's rent must be paid down at the time of sale, representing that due in advance on the 1st March or September following; and the purchaser has to make the declaration required by the Act. All leases begin on the 1st March; they entitle the holder to the grazing rights, but not to the soil, timber, or minerals. A lease terminates over any part of the run which may be leased for another purpose, purchased, or reserved. The tenant must prevent the burning of timber or bush, and the growth of gorse, broom or sweet-briar, and destroy the rabbits on his run. With the consent of the Land Board, the interest in a run may be transferred or mortgaged, but power of sale under a mortgage must be exercised within two years. In case it is determined again to lease any run, it must be offered at auction twelve months before expiry of the term, and if, on leasing, it is purchased by some person other than the previous lessee, valuation for improvements, to be made by an appraiser, must be paid by the incoming tenant, to an amount not greater than three times the annual rent, except in the case of a rabbit-proof fence, which is valued separately. Runs may also be divided with the approval of the Land Board. Where a lessee seeks relief, and the application is favourably reported on by the Board, the whole or part of one year's rent payable or paid may be remitted or refunded, or the lease may be extended, or a new lease or license issued in lieu thereof. The Minister may also postpone payment of rent or sheep rate where a tenant has applied or signified his intention of applying for relief.

Acquisition of Land for Settlement.

The administration of the law in respect of the acquisition of land for settlement is vested in a Board styled the Board of Land Purchase Commissioners, and consisting of the Surveyor-General, the Commissioner of Taxes, and the Commissioner of Crown Lands for any district in which it is proposed to acquire land, the Land Purchase Inspector, and a member of the Land Board of the district. The duties devolving upon the Board are to ascertain the value of any lands proposed to be acquired, and to report to the Minister as to their character and suitableness for settlement, and as to the demand for settlement in the locality. Land may be compulsorily taken for the purposes of the Act. The rent of land acquired and disposed of under the Act is at the rate of 5 per cent. on the capital value of the land, and the capital value is to be fixed at a rate sufficient to cover the cost of the original acquisition, together with the cost of survey, subdivision, and making due provision for roads. Where land acquired contains a homestead, a lease in perpetuity of the homestead and land surrounding it, not exceeding 640 acres, may be granted to the person from whom it was acquired, on conditions prescribed, at a yearly rental of 5 per cent. on the capital value of the land, such capital value to be determined in the manner set forth above.

A large area, principally in the North Island, remains in the hands of the native race, and this land may be acquired for settlement after a report upon its character, suitableness for settlement, and value, has been made by a Board specifically appointed for the purpose. On notification, the land becomes Crown land, subject to trust for native owners.

Australasian Settlement.

The particulars given in the foregoing pages will have made the fact abundantly clear that the main object of the land legislation, however variously expressed, has been to secure the settlement of the public estate by an industrious class, who, confining their efforts to areas of moderate extent, would thoroughly develop the resources of the land; but where the character of the country does not favour agricultural occupation or mixed farming, the laws contemplated that the State lands should be leased in blocks of considerable size for pastoral occupation, and it was hoped that by this form of settlement vast tracts which, when first opened up, seemed ill-adapted even for the sustenance of live-stock, might ultimately be made available for industrial settlement. To how small an extent the express determination of the legislators to settle an industrious peasantry on the soil was accomplished will presently be illustrated from the records of several of the provinces; but in regard to pastoral settlement the purpose was fully achieved—large areas, which were pronounced even by experienced explorers to be uninhabitable wilds, have since been occupied by thriving flocks, and every year sees the great Australian desert of the early explorers receding step by step. The following statement shows the area of land alienated by each province, the area leased, and the area neither alienated nor leased at the close of 1902. The term "alienated" is used for the purpose of denoting that the figures include lands granted without purchase. The area so disposed of has not been inconsiderable in several provinces:—

State.	Area.	Area alienated or in process of alienation.	Area leased.	Area neither alienated nor leased.
	acres.	acres.	acres.	acres.
New South Wales	198,848,000	48,507,192	131,099,305	19,241,503
Victoria	56,245,760	24,058,181	17,244,278	14,943,301
Queensland	427,838,080	16,824,355	289,495,477	121,518,248
South Australia	578,361,600	14,207,490	197,570,367	366,583,743
Western Australia	624,588,800	9,856,592	112,086,002	502,646,206
Tasmania	16,778,000	4,955,550	1,518,895	10,303,555
Commonwealth	1,902,660,240	118,409,360	749,014,324	1,035,236,556
New Zealand	66,861,440	24,029,976	16,254,847	26,576,617
Australasia	1,969,521,680	142,439,336	765,269,171	1,061,813,173

The proportions which these figures bear to the total area of each province are shown below :—

State.	Area alienated or in process of alienation.	Area leased.	Area neither alienated nor leased.
	per cent.	per cent.	per cent.
New South Wales	24·39	65·93	9·68
Victoria	42·77	30·67	26·56
Queensland	3·93	67·67	28·40
South Australia	2·46	34·16	63·38
Western Australia	1·58	17·94	80·48
Tasmania	29·54	9·05	61·41
Commonwealth	6·22	39·37	54·41
New Zealand	35·94	24·31	39·75
Australasia	7·23	38·86	53·91

The figures in the foregoing table disclose many grounds for congratulation. Of 1,902 million acres which comprise the area of the Commonwealth, 868 millions, or 45·59 per cent., are under occupation for productive purposes, and of an extent of 1,969 millions, the area of Australasia, no less than 908 millions, or 46·09 per cent., are similarly occupied, and there is every probability that this area will be greatly added to in the near future. New South Wales shows the least area returning no revenue, for out of nearly 200 million acres only 19 million remain unoccupied, and much of this is represented by lands which the State has reserved from occupation, and which are used for travelling stock or for various public purposes, including lands reserved for future settlement along the track of the great trunk line of railways. The State of Tasmania has nearly 62 per cent. of its area unoccupied, the western part of the island being so rugged as to forbid settlement. Settlement in Western Australia is only in its initial stage ; much of the area of the state is practically unknown, and a large part of what is known is thought to be little worth settlement. Much the same thing was confidently predicted of western New South Wales and South Australia, though, as subsequent events proved, the forebodings were untrue. In South Australia, including the Northern Territory, only 36·62 per cent. is in occupation. New Zealand, favoured with a beneficent climate, has nearly half its area not utilised—a circumstance entirely due to the mountainous character of its territory.

The practice of sales by auction without conditions of settlement was a necessary part of the system of land legislation which prevailed in most of the provinces ; but this ready means of raising revenue offered the temptation to the Governments, where land was freely saleable, to obtain revenue in an easy fashion. The result of the system was not long in making itself felt, for pastoralists and others desirous of accumulating large estates were able to take advantage of such sales, and of the ready manner in which transfers of land conditionally purchased could be made, to acquire large holdings, and in this manner the obvious intentions of the Lands Acts were defeated. Notwithstanding failures in this respect, the Acts have otherwise been successful, as will appear from the following table, as well as from other pages in this volume. It is unfortunate that detailed information regarding settlement can only be given for three of the states of the Commonwealth, viz., New South Wales, South Australia, Western Australia, and for New Zealand, and that in respect of Western Australia the information is deficient in regard to the area of the holdings. The figures given for Western Australia in the table refer to the year 1900, for South Australia to the Census year of 1891, for New South Wales to the year 1902, and for New Zealand to the year 1901 :—

Size of Holdings.	New South Wales.		South Australia.		Western Australia.	New Zealand.	
	Number of Holdings.	Area of Holdings.	Number of Holdings.	Area of Holdings.	Number of Holdings.	Number of Holdings.	Area of Holdings.
		acres.		acres.			acres.
1 to 100 acres......	38,801	1,176,995	6,804	183,443	1,926	36,478	959,462
101 to 1,000 acres......	27,351	9,625,563	10,618	4,711,060	3,019	23,755	7,787,050
1,001 to 5,000 acres	4,661	9,871,924	2,394	4,623,937	607	2,854	5,849,516
5,001 to 20,000 acres......	964	9,467,685	481	4,737,253	111	627	5,811,728
20,001 acres and upwards..	350	17,502,308	58	1,974,995	36	268	15,150,133
Total............	72,127	47,144,475	20,355	16,230,688	5,699	63,982	35,507,889

It will be seen that in the case of South Australia and New Zealand the area included in the foregoing table is greater than the area alienated as shown on page 598; the figures for these states must therefore include some Crown lands held under lease.

Out of the 47,144,475 acres set down to New South Wales in the foregoing, 43,178,955 acres are in the actual occupation of the owners, and 3,965,520 acres are held under rent. In New Zealand the proportion was not stated at the last Census. In South Australia only 5,510,289 acres are occupied by the owners, while 10,720,399 acres, or 66 per cent., are rented. The most remarkable feature of the table is that in New South Wales about one half the alienated land is owned by 738 persons or institutions, in South Australia by 1,283, and in New Zealand by less than 500.

INDUSTRIAL PROGRESS.

The Period Preceding the Gold Discoveries.

THE discovery of gold in 1851 divides the industrial history of Australia into two periods, the main characteristics of which are absolutely dissimilar. Prior to the discoveries of the precious metal, Australia appeared to be destined for a purely pastoral country. Its distance from the world's markets, and the fewness of its population, militated against any decided progress in agriculture; but the people were encouraged to devote their attention to a fuller development of the pastoral industry by the circumstance that a local market was not necessary. Moreover, the products of both sheep and cattle were so valuable that the heavy cost of carriage to England could be borne, and an ample margin still left to compete successfully with Russia, Germany, Spain, Portugal, and America, the great wool-growing countries of that epoch. This one-sided development of the country's resources was manifestly dangerous to industrial stability, as a succession of droughty seasons might have had the effect of disturbing the business of the whole country; and this, indeed, was what from time to time actually happened.

Other industries would doubtless have followed in the wake of the great pastoral industry as time went on, and there were not wanting signs that, with an assured market, attention would be given to agriculture, and the manufacture of certain articles of local consumption.

The development of the industries of Australia along their natural lines must undoubtedly have been attended with ultimate success, but the colonists were not content to grow prosperous in such a humdrum way, and early in the forties there was intense speculation in land allotments in towns. Large and small country areas also were disposed of, and redisposed of, at prices far beyond what was warranted by any return that could be obtained from their immediate or prospective use, and many persons grew rich by the tossing backwards and forwards of title deeds. The business of land jobbing was, moreover, encouraged by the action of the local Government which from time to time disposed of considerable areas of land, and frequently altered its policy in regard to the public estate.

Land speculation, carried to excess, has tended on more than one occasion in Australia to a commercial crisis, and the disasters of 1842 and 1843 were undoubtedly attributable to this cause. They were accelerated, however, by the unwise action of the Government in regard to its financial operations. Having sold much land, the Government was possessed of considerable funds, which were placed with the banks, at one time fully £350,000 being deposited, and the highest rates of interest exacted therefor. The banks accepting these deposits were obliged, on their part, to reissue equivalent sums in discounts, in order to pay the interest demanded of them. They, therefore, readily entered into the spirit of the times, and their willingness to lend stimulated amazingly the dealings in land purchase. It thus happened that business was transacted in a vicious circle. The Government, by selling land, thereby accumulated an amount of money, which was deposited with the banks, the money so deposited being loaned by the latter to their customers for the purpose of buying more land from the Government, the latter depositing the sums paid to them, which again were loaned for the purpose of land buying; and by this means the business of speculation was kept alive so long as the Government maintained its balance with the banks. The immigration policy of the Government, however, made large calls upon it, and the Treasury found itself compelled to withdraw its deposits upon very short notice. To meet this sudden call, the banks were compelled, to the utmost inconvenience of their customers, immediately to restrict their discounts and curtail advances, and it was this sudden contraction of credit that gave the initial downward impulse to the money market. The issue could hardly have been otherwise than as happened, and a financial crisis immediately resulted. The year 1842 was one of acute financial distress. In Sydney, property of all kinds became unsaleable, and many business houses, including some of the principal ones, became insolvent. For nearly two years the failures were at the rate of from fifty to sixty a month. A similar condition of affairs prevailed in Melbourne, and the distress was also keenly felt in Adelaide and Tasmania. The local prices of all descriptions of produce were ruinously low, and were still further depressed by reason of the large number of bankruptcies involving forced sales of real property, stock, wool, furniture, ships—indeed, of everything which promised a return, however small. Historians of that period relate cases of enforced sales at which sheep brought very small prices—as little as 6d. being obtained for them; while cattle occasionally realised only 7s. 6d., and valuable horses only £3 each. Boiling down, meat canning, and other devices were resorted to in order to revive the commerce of the country from the stagnation and lethargy into which it had fallen; yet, notwithstanding all expedients, the outlook steadily became more gloomy, prices continued seriously to decline, and speculation was at a standstill. South Australia was the first to emerge from the all-pervading depression. In 1844, copper arrived in Adelaide from the Kapunda Mine, and in 1845 the famous Burra Burra Mine was discovered. Other finds came in quick succession. Population was speedily attracted, and as the mines yielded beyond all expectation a season of prosperity at once ensued. The discovery of copper in South Australia proved to be of advantage to the rest of Australia. Labourers and others were attracted to Adelaide from the neighbouring provinces, though not in such large numbers as would have relieved the labour markets. The men employed in the copper mines were able to earn 7s. per day, which at the time was considered a very high wage. Skilled mechanics were not so well remunerated; plasterers were paid from 4s. to 7s., very few getting the higher wage; painters' wages ranged from 4s. to 5s. 6d.; blacksmiths' from 4s. to 5s.; wheelwrights' 5s. to 5s. 6d. Carpenters' wages ranged from 5s. 6d. to 6s. 6d. per day—the highest rates paid to mechanics; bricklayers and masons earned from 5s. 6d. to 6s. per day. Farming hands were paid 10s. to 12s. per week with rations and sleeping accommodation, and were in much request. Domestic servants were in demand at wages varying from £14 to £22 per annum with board and lodging, and the supply was insufficient. The wages quoted were greatly in excess of those obtained prior to the discovery of copper and about 20 per cent. higher than for similar employment in New South Wales.

The average wages paid in New South Wales prior to 1851 were as indicated in the accompanying statement. Inferior workers, of whom there was naturally a considerable proportion, considering the origin of a large part of the population, did not receive within 20 per cent. of the rates quoted:—

Trade or Calling.	1843.	1844.	1845.	1846.	1847.	1848.	1849.	1850.
Males, per day, without board and lodging.								
	s. d.	s. d.	s. d.	s. d.	s. d.	s. d.	s. d.	s. d.
Carpenters	5 0	4 0	4 0	5 2	5 6	5 3	4 9	4 6
Smiths	5 0	4 0	4 3	5 2	5 6	5 3	4 9	4 6
Masons	5 0	4 0	4 0	5 2	5 6	5 3	4 9	4 6
Bricklayers	5 0	4 0	4 0	5 2	5 6	5 3	4 9	4 6
Wheelwrights	4 0	3 6	3 3	4 8	5 0	5 3	4 9	4 6
Males, per annum, with board and lodging.								
	£	£	£	£	£	£	£	£
Farm labourers	15	15	18	20	23	21	18	18
Shepherds	14	14	17	20	23	21	18	18
Females, per annum, with board and lodging.								
	£	£	£	£	£	£	£	£
Cooks	15	15	18	20	22	21	17	17
Housemaids	15	15	15	17	17	17	14	13
Laundresses	12	12	15	17	19	18	15	15
Nursemaids	10	10	12	15	16	14	9	9
General servants	12	12	16	16	18	16	12	14
Farm-house servants	10	10	12	16	17	16	12	11
Dairy-women	10	10	12	16	17	16	12	11

These rates show a great reduction on those obtaining in 1841, in which year mechanics' wages stood at 7s. 6d. to 8s. per day, and those of farm servants at £25 a year. In the Port Phillip district wages were generally higher than in Sydney, as also were those of Tasmania. A schedule of the latter is given below. The fall in wages was in a measure compensated for by a lowering of the price of provisions. During this period the average price of beef in the Australian cities ranged from 2¼d. to 6¾d. per lb., and of mutton from 2d. to 3d. per lb. The price of flour ranged from 14s. to 24s. per 100 lb. These prices were very greatly below those paid prior to the crisis. Bread, for example, in 1839 sold at 11½d. the 2 lb. loaf; in 1843 the price was 3½d., and thereafter it did not rise higher than 5d. until after the gold discoveries. House rents, however, continued high.

Throughout the period the demand for pastoral and agricultural labour was always fairly keen, and the stream of bounty-paid immigrants was maintained in spite of the fall in wages and the restriction in employment. The immigrants, however, were mainly of the agricultural class—shepherds, gardeners, and useful mechanics for country employment,—who were readily absorbed by the community. The condition of the mechanics who clung to the towns was one of great distress. Inferior men could not earn more than 2s. 6d. per day, and at no time was the average for good men more than 5s., while even at those rates employment was at times difficult to obtain.

In Tasmania wages were maintained at a higher level than in New South Wales, and in the undermentioned trades the ruling rates per day were :—

Year.	Bricklayers.	Carpenters.	Masons.	Quarrymen.
	s. d.	s. d.	s. d.	s. d.
1839	7 6	7 6	7 6	5 6
1840	7 6	7 6	7 6	5 6
1841	6 6	6 6	7 0	5 1
1842	7 0	7 0	8 0	5 6
1843	7 0	7 0	7 0	5 0
1844	5 0	5 0	4 6	3 0
1845	6 0	6 0	5 0	4 0
1846	5 6	5 6	5 6	3 0
1847	4 11	4 10	4 10	3 0
1848	4 10	4 8	4 10	3 2
1849	6 0	6 0	6 0	3 6
1850	5 6	5 6	5 6	3 4

The financial crisis of 1842 did not affect Tasmania in the same degree as it did New South Wales, since in the island colony there had been less land jobbing and riotous speculation. The fall in wages in 1844 was accompanied, and, in a measure, brought about, by a fall in the cost of living. It is difficult to determine the retail prices of the various commodities in common use, and to account for the causes of the great variation apparent from year to year. The price of flour, for example, seemed to have a very ill-defined relation to the price of wheat. In 1839, wheat was sold throughout the year at 26s. per bushel, and flour at 24s. per cwt.; in 1840 the prices were: Wheat 9s. per bushel, and flour 30s. per. cwt.; and in 1841, wheat 7s. per bushel, and flour 21s. per cwt. The price of tea was 1s. 6d. per lb. in 1839, and 2s. 6d. and 3s. 3d. in the two following years, and similarly with regard to other articles.

The following were the market prices of six of the leading commodities :—

Year.	Fresh Meat.	Sugar.	Tea.		Rice.	Wheat.		Potatoes.	
	per lb.	per lb.	per lb.		per lb.	per bshl.		per cwt.	
	d.	d.	s.	d.	d.	s.	d.	s.	d.
1838	5¾	3½	1	5	3	8	9	6	0
1839	4¾	3½	1	6	3	26	0	10	0
1840	6¾	3½	2	6	2½	9	0	10	0
1841	6¾	3½	3	3	2½	7	0	10	0
1842	4½	3¼	2	0	2	6	6	7	0
1843	2¾	3	2	6	1½	3	6	5	0
1844	2¼	2½	1	6	1¾	3	3	4	0
1845	2¼	3	1	6	3	3	3	4	6
1846	2½	4	2	3	1½	5	0	3	0
1847	2½	4	2	4	3¾	4	10	5	10
1848	2½	3¾	2	0	3½	3	6	4	4
1849	2¼	3¾	1	9	3¾	4	1	3	0
1850	2¼	3½	1	10	4	4	9	4	0

About the year 1849, the labour market in Sydney was relieved in some measure by the emigration to California which commenced immediately on the announcement of the discovery of gold in that country. But as an amount of ready cash was needed before a person could emigrate, the most distressful part of the local population was little affected by the Californian mines, and it is difficult to imagine what would have happened had not the discovery of gold, in 1851, occurred so opportunely. In an instant the face of everything was changed, as if by the wand of a magician, although the full influence of the discoveries was not felt until the following year.

During the period anterior to the gold discoveries agriculture was entirely subsidiary to sheep and cattle raising, being confined to supplying the wants of the handful of persons scattered round the coastal fringe who then comprised the population of these States. The country was, therefore, dependent upon outside sources for the supply of the greater part of the food stuffs required for ordinary consumption. Signs were not wanting, however, of an early extension of the cultivation of wheat, particularly in South Australia. The plains around Adelaide yielded magnificent crops of the cereal, and when a method of harvesting was discovered which enabled the farmers to gather the crops, in spite of the looseness of the grain in the ear and the extreme brittleness of the straw, the future of the industry at once became more hopeful.

Naturally the manufacturing industries did not make much progress. Manufacturing for export was out of the question, handicapped as the infant settlements were by distance from the centres of civilisation. What industries there were had been called into being by the isolation of the country. The largest number of establishments of any kind were flour mills, of which there were in 1848 about 223; of these 87 were worked by steam, 53 by water, 42 by wind, and 38 by horse-power. The next in importance were establishments for the treatment of leather; then came breweries and distilleries, soap and candle works, iron foundries, brick-works and potteries, and ship and boat building, in the order named. As late as 1848 the industrial establishments of Australia were as comprised in the following list, and the employment afforded did not in all probability exceed 1,800 hands:—

Distilleries	2	Blacking manufactories	2
Rectifying and compounding	2	Meat preserving and salting works	5
Breweries	51	Potteries	9
Sugar refineries	2	Glass works	1
Soap and candle works	30	Copper smelting works	1
Tobacco and snuff factories	5	Iron and brass foundries, &c.	27
Woollen mills	8	Gas works	1
Hat manufactories	4	Ship and boat building, repairing	12
Rope works	7	Flour mills	223
Tanneries	62	Oatmeal, groat mills	1
Salt works	5		
Starch manufactories	2		

Of the 479 establishments, 272 were in New South Wales, 41 in the Port Phillip district, 99 in Tasmania, and 67 in South Australia. There were possibly a few others in Western Australia, information in regard to which has not been recorded.

Whale-fishing, although now almost unknown in Australian waters, at one time held a very important place amongst the industries of the country. From 1791 onwards there are records of the take of vessels engaged in the industry. In the twenties there were whaling stations belonging to Sydney merchants in various parts of the southern seas, and whale-fishing was afterwards carried on from a Tasmanian base at Frederick Henry Bay and from Portland Bay, Victoria. The colonists of Western Australia had also engaged in the whale fishery, which appears to have been continued by them until the whales had practically disappeared from local waters. The practice of Australian whalers of killing the calves, in order to secure the capture of the mothers, did great damage to the fishery by wastefully thinning out the product, and in 1843 the animal was remarked as becoming somewhat shy and scarce in southern seas. By the year 1847, the industry was declining in southern waters generally, and Australian shipping was engaging more exclusively in the carrying trade, and in time the whaling industry was prosecuted mainly by American vessels. The value of the total quantity of whale oil exported from New South Wales has been estimated at about £3,000,000, and from Tasmania at about £1,200,000.

The principal exports during the year preceding the gold discoveries were wool, tallow, oil, skins, bark, and salt beef. Wool has been one of the staple products of the country from the earliest days of the century, although in some years the product of the fisheries was equally important. Trade was almost wholly confined to the United Kingdom, and in ten years, 1841-50, the quantity of wool exported to that country was:—

	lb.		lb.
1841	12,959,671	1846	26,056,815
1842	17,433,780	1847	30,034,567
1843	17,589,712	1848	35,774,671
1844	24,150,687	1849	39,018,221
1845	21,865,270	1850	41,426,655

The value of the wool trade for the year 1850 was £1,992,369, and the shares of the present States, according to quantity and value, were:—

	lb.	Value. £
New South Wales	14,270,622	788,051
Victoria	18,091,207	826,190
South Australia	2,841,131	113,259
Western Australia	368,595	16,000
Tasmania	5,855,100	248,869
Total	41,426,655	1,992,369

Sperm oil was principally exported from Sydney and Hobart, the value of the trade in 1850 being £65,499, a slightly larger quantity being despatched from Hobart than from Sydney. The value of tallow exported was £311,900, of which £167,858 was sent from Sydney, and £132,863 from Melbourne. In 1850 South Australia was already a copper producing country of some importance, and its export of metal and ore had reached £275,090. Flour was also becoming an item of export worth considering in South Australia and Tasmania, the former having exported in 1850 wheat and flour to the value of £41,491, and the latter £34,565, besides providing for the local consumption.

In 1850 the export of domestic produce, including products of fisheries, from each division of Australia was:—

	£
New South Wales	1,158,858
Victoria	1,022,064
South Australia	570,816
Western Australia	30,000
Tasmania	558,000

Industrial Period—1851–8.

The Gold Discoveries.

The attention of the people of Australia during the period extending from the year 1851 to 1858 was chiefly directed to gold-seeking. The whole period was one of rapid growth and great change. It is chiefly interesting politically on account of the initiation of responsible government in New South Wales, Victoria, South Australia, and Tasmania, and commercially, because of the construction of the first railroads and the establishment of steam communication with Great Britain.

The discovery of gold not only put an end to the depression of the previous period, but it effected a revolution in all industrial relations. According to contemporary evidence, the supply of labour in many occupations speedily became exhausted, and there were more persons desirous of hiring labourers than there were labourers to be hired. The diggings drained not only Melbourne and Sydney, but Adelaide, Hobart, and every other Australian centre. Most branches of industry and all public works were at a standstill. In New South Wales the sheep and cattle stations were deserted by their hands very shortly after the first great discoveries were made, and for a time it was impossible, in some parts of the colony, to care for the flocks except by the employment of aborigines. In South Australia, during 1852 and 1853, the crops would have remained unharvested if it had not been for the assistance of the blacks, so great was the exodus of farming hands. In Victoria, where the greatest quantity of gold was found, for a brief period no other occupation than gold seeking was thought of, until it was discovered by the reflecting part of the population that trade offered even greater and surer prizes, and there as well as elsewhere every department of industry received a direct stimulus. In Tasmania the people became so infected with the epidemic that there was danger of the island becoming depopulated. The able-bodied men left by every boat, and Bass's Straits became in a brief period a populous waterway from the home of hardship and toil to the visionland of wealth. So great was the exodus that some of the country districts were utterly deserted by the male inhabitants.

The eight or nine years characterised by the rage of the gold fever exercised a very great economic effect on the condition of the working classes ; for had there been no discovery of gold it is not improbable that, with respect to both the standard of living and the remuneration of labour, the conditions existing prior to 1850 would have long remained without any great change for the better. In those days the standard of labour in England was the practical test of the condition of the working classes in Australia, who were thought well off simply because their earnings enabled them to enjoy comforts beyond the reach of their fellows in the Old World. Since the gold era this has been changed, and the standard now made for themselves by Australian workers has no reference to that of any other country. The attractions of the goldfields had also a marked subsequent effect upon industries of an absolutely different character. Many men, of all sorts of trades and professions, who were drawn to these shores by the prospect of acquiring enough of the precious metal to ensure their independence, remained in the country, and pursued less exciting and less precarious callings, while gold-miners themselves in many cases ceased the exploitation of the mineral which was to have made them rich, and turned their attention to the winning of silver, copper, tin, coal, and other minerals.

Another effect of the gold rush must not be lost sight of. Although Australia had ceased to be a place open to the reception of British convicts, yet the old settled parts were permeated with social and economic ideas begotten of the transportation era. The men who had been convicts, or who were born of convict parents, were a considerable element in the population, while the employers had, for the most part, at one period or other of their career, been masters of bond labour. A few years changed all this. It was as if Australia had been newly discovered. Certainly the country was recolonised, and the bond population and their descendants became a small minority of the population which every year made more insignificant, until at the present day it is only in out of the way corners that there is anything to remind the observer that any part of Australia was at one time a penal settlement.

The gold fever brought to Australia not only young, stalwart, enterprising men of great endurance, and capable of adapting themselves to almost any conditions of life, but also multitudes of others whose chief idea was that wealth could be acquired almost without exertion. Unable to endure the hardships of the digger's lot, without trade or profession, and capable of only the lightest manual labour, they mostly drifted back to the chief towns; and there was speedily presented the strange spectacle of thousands of unemployed clamouring for government work, while the more stalwart labourers were earning extraordinary wages in the gold-fields.

At the height of the gold discovery the earnings of miners in some cases were prodigious. The Gold Commissioners of New South Wales estimated the average earnings of diggers to have been about £1 per day; and a comparison of the gold yield with the numbers of licenses issued confirms this calculation. In Victoria the average was probably much higher, and a contemporary calculation fixes the earnings at £42 10s. per month for each miner licensed to dig. Making allowance for illicit digging, there seems ample proof that in the first half of 1852 the average of all miners could hardly have been less than 30s. per day. At one period 50,000 persons held licenses in Victoria and 31,000 in New South Wales; and if allowance be made for the great number of persons who evaded payment of the license fee, the number of gold diggers could scarcely have been less than 100,000 in a total male population in Victoria and New South Wales of 229,562.

The effect of the discoveries on wages was immediate and extraordinary. Governor La Trobe of Victoria, in a despatch, under date 12th January, 1852, remarks on the difference in the wages payable immediately before and after the gold discoveries. The wages of shearers rose from 12s. in 1850 to 20s. in 1851; of reapers, from 10s. to 20s. and 25s. per acre; of common labourers, from 5s. to 15s. and 20s. per day; of coopers, from 5s. to 10s.; of shipwrights, from 6s. to 10s.; of wool-pressers, from 3s. 6d. to 7s. and 8s. per day; sailors, from

£4 to £9 a month (from £50 to £100 being offered for the run to England); stokers, from £12 to £20 a month; men cooks, from 20s. and 25s. to £2 and £3 a week; waiters at hotels, from 20s. to 40s. and 50s. a week; ostlers and stable-men, from 21s. to 50s. a week; men servants in town, from £25 and £30 to £50 and £70 per annum, and none to be had even at these wages; men servants in the country, from £20 and £25 to £35 and £40; salesmen, shopmen, &c., from 25s. and 35s. to 40s. and 70s. a week; porters, from 12s. and 15s. to 25s. and 35s. a week; the increase in the wage of female servants was 25 per cent.; of clerks in banks and mercantile houses, 20 to 50 per cent.; but the figures given by the Governor denoted only the beginning of the advance in wages. Prices rose in response to the altered conditions. From December, 1850, to December, 1851, the prices of provisions, etc., had risen as follows:— Bread, 4 lb. loaf, from 5d. to 1s. 4d. and 1s. 8d.; butter, from 1s. 2d. to 2s. and 2s. 6d.; cheese, from 8d. and 1s. 4d. to 2s. and 3s.; fresh meat doubled; salt meat rose from 1½d. to 2½d.; ham, from 8d. and 1s. to 1s. 6d. and 2s. 6d.; bacon, from 6d. and 8d. to 2s. per lb.; fowls and ducks, from 3s. and 3s. 6d. to 5s. and 6s. a couple; potatoes, from 8s. to 12s. and 15s. a cwt.; tobacco, from 2s. 6d. and 4s. to 7s. and 8s. a lb.; groceries generally, 25 per cent.; vegetables, from 50 to 100 per cent; spirits, wine, beer, etc., from 30 to 50 per cent.; confectionery, 50 per cent.; fruit, 100 per cent. The following are the percentage rates of increase on the prices of some of the supplies furnished under contract for the Government service of Victoria:—Candles, 60 per cent; fresh beef, 33⅓ per cent.; salt pork, 25 per cent.; bread, 50 per cent.; tea, about 21 per cent.; sugar, 10 per cent.; soap, 20 per cent.; milk, 75 per cent.; new horse-shoes, 150 per cent.; cost of removing old ones, 350 per cent.; printing, 100 per cent.; saddlery, 75 per cent.; for boots and shoes no tender could be obtained. "Old furniture," remarks the Governor, "sells at about 75 per cent. advance upon the former price of new. Scarcely any mechanic will work; those few who do, receive an advance on former wages of from 200 to 350 per cent."

The condition of things just described may be looked upon as chaotic, but every month saw the prices of commodities and the remuneration for labour more systematised. As the gold discoveries continued, the wages continued to rise, but there was an essential difference between the conditions of 1851 and 1853. In the former year, men's ideas of the amount of the wages they should receive were, on the one hand, tempered by the remembrance of the wages paid in England and in the colonies before the discovery of gold, and on the other they were excited by the boundless possibilities of easily acquired wealth which loomed before the successful digger, and their demands rose and fell according to the exigencies of the employer. In 1853 the condition of things became more settled. Wages on the average were higher than in previous years, but there was a recognised scale for the payment of the principal classes of labourers and mechanics. In 1853, carpenters, wheelwrights, and bricklayers received, in Melbourne, 15s. per day with board and lodging; masons, without board and lodging, 26s. 9d. per day; bricklayers, 25s. per day; smiths and wheelwrights, 22s. 6d. per day. This would seem to fix the cost of board and lodging at about £3 10s. per week. In the following year the wages of wheelwrights reached 30s. per day; bricklayers, 30s. per day; but the pay of carpenters and other mechanics remained about the same. In the following table the wages given are those ruling in Sydney during the period named. It must be remembered, however, that in some instances the wages quoted were merely nominal, as, owing to the dearth of labour, there was a suspension of many trades which flourished before the gold discoveries, and prices quoted are those paid to the remnant who remained in town :—

Trade or Calling.	1851.	1852.	1853.	1854.	1855.	1856.	1857.	1858.
				Males, per day, without board and lodging.				
	s. d.	s. d.	s. d.	s. s.	s. s.	s. s.	s. s.	s. s.
Bricklayers	6 0	9 0	18 6	25 to 30	18 to 25	16 to 18	12 to 16	10/6 to 11/6
Blacksmiths	6 8		1	20 to 25	14 to 16	8 to 8	10 to 14	10/6
Carpenters	6 5			15 to 20	2 to 15	12 to	0 to 12	10 to 11
Coopers	....	....	....	15 to 20	0 to 2	12 to	2 to 14	......
Cabinetmakers	....	....	....	15 to 20	2 to 5	2 to	2 to 14	......
Farriers	....	....	....	12 to 15	0 to 2	9 to	0 to 12	......
Plumbers and glaziers	....	....	....	16 to 20	2 to 5	12 to 15	2 to 15	......
Joiners	....	....	....	17 to 20	2 to 5	12 to 14	2 to 15	......
Ironfounders	....	....	....	16 to 20	4 to 6	2 to 16	1 to 13	......
Locksmiths	....	....	....	18 to 22	6 to 8	2 to	0 to 13	......
Quarrymen	....	....	....	18 to 21	6 to 8	2/6 to	4 to 16	......
Shoemakers	....	....	....	....	4 to 22	2 to	0 to 12	......
Wheelwrights	6 4	9 0	15 0	18 to 20	4 to 16	2 to	2 to 14	10 to 11
Plasterers	....	....	16 0	25 to 30	4 to 16	3 to	3 to 15	......
Painters	....	....	....	13 to 16/8	3 to	10 to 12	8 to 12	......
Stonemasons	7 8	9 0	16 0	25 to 30	....	12/6 to 15	13 to 15	10/6 to 11
				Females, per annum, with board and lodging.				
	£ £	£ £	£	£	£	£	£	£
Cooks	16 to 25	18 to 25	24	28	28	25	28	26
Housemaids	14 to 18	14 to 18	17	22	22	21	17	23
Laundresses	7 to 12	15 to 18	20	28	28	24	23	26
Nursemaids	9 to 15	16 to 18	17	18	18	18	18	19
General servants	14 to 18	16 to 18	18	28	23	22	23	25
Farm-house servants	13	14	15	25	22	20	19	25
Dairy-women	13	14	15	25	22	20	19	25

In Adelaide, from the time of the discovery of gold, wages were not only daily advancing, but some industries came to a complete standstill. In wheat farming, for example, it was impossible to procure white labour at all, and, as already remarked, settlers were glad to hire the aborigines to gather in their crops, and for this work they were paid at the rate of 10s. an acre. As mentioned elsewhere, Tasmania lost a large portion of its adult population to Victoria, but those who remained behind prospered exceedingly. Everything the island produced found a ready market and at highly remunerative prices.

Prices of articles of ordinary consumption in Victoria have already been alluded to. All over Australia the prices of provisions and of all articles of clothing were, during this golden era, largely increased; indeed, there was hardly a commodity in the market, whether of use or of luxury, the price of which might not be described as "fancy." In 1853 bread sold in Sydney at $3\frac{1}{2}$ to 4d. per lb. and potatoes at 13s. per cwt., but certain lines of provisions were fairly reasonable; for instance, tea was quoted at 1s. 4d. per lb., sugar at $3\frac{1}{2}$d., fresh meat at 3d., butter at 1s. 5d., brandy at 23s. per gallon, and imported beer at 5s. per gallon; flour, however, was quoted at 3d. per lb., the price per ton ranging between £20 and £27. House rents, of course, rose with the influx of population. In Melbourne, the sudden increase of population raised house rents to an unparalleled height, and for a considerable time a large proportion of the community lived in tents. This, of course, gave an extraordinary stimulus to building, and partly from this reason, and partly on account of the mercantile failures consequent on the over-trading of 1853 and 1854, the year 1855 witnessed a heavy fall in rents, so that in that year they did not exceed half the amount paid three years previously.

In Sydney, the number of persons requiring house room was so much in excess of the accommodation available in habitable dwellings that the census of 1856 enumerates no fewer than 709 houses as being in occupation although still in the hands of the builder. As illustrative of the exigencies of the time in this particular, it is interesting to note that out of 39,807 dwellings 1,709 were tents, 31 were drays, and 64 were ships used as residences. Of the total number of habitations in New South Wales, 23,709 were built of wood, and of such inferior materials as bark, slabs, wattle and daub, and the like, and 225 of iron, while more than one-third of the dwellings were roofed with bark and thatch. Owing to the dearth and dearness of skilled labour, a large number of houses were imported in pieces, ready to be put together with little or no carpentering work beyond making the foundations and driving the nails. Some of these were still to be seen in the vicinity of Sydney and other towns until within recent years.

The discovery of gold had an almost immediate effect in establishing Melbourne as the largest city of Australia, and Victoria as the most important state. The total trade of Victoria, New South Wales, and South Australia with places outside their boundaries during the eight years was as given in the following table. The preponderance of Victoria is evident.

Year	New South Wales.		Victoria.		South Australia.		Tasmania.		Western Australia.	
	Imports.	Exports.	Imports.	Exports.	Imports.	Exports.	Imports.	Exports.	Imp.	Exp.
	£	£	£	£	£	£	£	£	£	£
1851	1,563,931	1,796,912	1,056,437	1,422,909	690,777	602,087	641,609	665,790	56,598	26,870
1852	1,900,436	4,604,034	4,069,742	7,451,549	798,811	1,787,741	860,488	1,509,883	97,304	24,181
1853	6,342,397	4,523,346	15,842,637	11,061,544	2,336,290	2,241,814	2,273,397	1,756,316	126,735	31,645
1854	5,981,063	4,050,126	17,659,051	11,775,204	2,147,107	1,322,822	2,604,680	1,433,021	128,260	34,109
1855	4,668,519	2,884,130	12,007,939	13,493,338	1,370,938	988,215	1,559,797	1,428,629	105,320	46,314
1856	5,460,971	3,430,880	14,962,269	15,489,760	1,366,529	1,665,740	1,442,106	1,207,802	122,938	44,740
1857	6,729,408	4,011,952	17,256,209	15,079,512	1,623,022	1,958,572	1,271,087	1,354,655	94,532	59,947
1858	6,059,366	4,186,277	15,108,249	13,989.209	1,769,351	1,512,185	1,328,612	1,151,609	144,932	78,649

The excess of the imports is very marked in the years immediately following the discoveries, and indicates the inflow of capital accompanying the immigrants who poured into the country from Europe and elsewhere. During the eight years included in the foregoing table the excess of arrivals over departures was at least 450,000, probably more; and if each of these immigrants brought with him not more than £25, their capital alone would represent £11,250,000. The imports comprised manufactured goods and articles of luxury, and the exports were almost exclusively gold and wool, and other raw material, the produce of the pastoral industry. As already mentioned, the product of the southern fisheries had greatly fallen off by the beginning of the period, and the export of oil, etc., averaged for five years between £25,000 and £30,000 per annum. In 1858 the exports of the fisheries had fallen to £1,450; in 1859 to £532; and in 1860 to £136. With the last-named year, the industry, around which cluster so many historical associations, and which is so peculiarly reminiscent of the early days of Australian settlement, practically disappears, although a few trifling essays have, from time to time, been made to revive it in southern waters, and small quantities of oil are still exported.

The actual export of gold from Australia cannot now be stated with exactness. The figures given in the following table show the exports in excess of the imports registered in the Customs houses, but doubtless there was a large export of which no account was rendered to the authorities, for, though the influx of population was great, the departures were also numerous, and every ship that left Melbourne carried with it more or less gold in the possession of returning diggers.

Year.	Net Export of Gold from—	
	Victoria.	New South Wales.
	£	£
1851	508,013	468,336
1852	6,912,415	2,660,946
1853	11,090,643	1,781,172
1854	9,214,093	773,209
1855	11,070,270	654,594
1856	11,943,458	689,174
1857	10,987,591	674,477
1858	10,107,836	1,104,175

The figures for Victoria are from the Customs returns, and in the earlier years are probably far below the actual amounts. Competent authorities estimate the yield of 1852 at fifteen millions, or about eight millions in excess of the official returns.

The forego ng table explains the tremendous attraction which the southern colony possessed for the population of the Australasian group. The imports into Victoria during 1854 were no less than £17,659,051; it is therefore easy to understand how it happened that, for a period, the parent colony was quite eclipsed by the growth of its own off-shoot, and that the commerce of the South Pacific gravitated to Melbourne. During a single month as many as 152 ships arrived in Port Phillip, conveying thither 12,000 immigrants.

Agriculture was greatly neglected during the days of the gold fever. In New South Wales about one-third of the area went out of cultivation, the acreage falling from 198,000 acres in 1850 to 131,000 acres in 1852; in Victoria there was a reduction from 52,000 acres to 34,000 n the same period; in Tasmania and South Australia there were also considerable reductions in the area cropped. The check to the industry was, however, only temporary, as the ultimate effect of the gold discoveries upon agriculture was extremely stimulating. In Victoria, especially, there was a great expansion. In 1853 the breadth of land cropped was 34,000 acres; in six years this had been increased to 419,000 acres. In 1857 the cultivated area in Victoria exceeded that of New South Wales by 50,000 acres, a superiority which was afterwards greatly added to and is maintained to this day.

The progress of agriculture in each state may be seen from the ollowing figures:—

AREA UNDER CROP.

Year	New South Wales.	Victoria.	South Australia.	Western Australia.	Tasmania.	Total.
	acres.	acres.	acres.	acres.	acres.	acres.
1850	198,056	52,341	64,728	7,419	168,820	491,364
1854	131,857	54,905	129,692	13,979	127,732	458,165
858	223,295	298,960	264,462	20,904	229,489	1,037,110

The principal crops grown were wheat, oats, potatoes, and hay, chiefly wheaten and oaten; but there were signs of attention being paid, especially in Victoria and Tasmania, to fruit-growing and other forms of culture requiring less land and more labour.

The influence of the gold discoveries on the pastoral industry was twofold—on the one hand retarding its development by depriving it of labour, and on the other, encouraging it by the creation of a demand for carcase meat. Before the discoveries, fat sheep sold in the Melbourne market at 10s. to 12s., in 1852 the price was 30s., and higher prices were subsequently obtained. During the whole period the value of the carcase steadily gained on that of the wool, and it is not surprising, therefore, that the increase of the flocks was arrested. This was especially the case in Victoria, where the number of sheep depastured fell from 6,589,923 in 1851 to 4,577,872 in 1855. In New South Wales the number of sheep fluctuated according to the requirements of the southern districts, but there was no tendency for the flocks to increase. In 1859 the number of sheep depastured fell to 5,162,671, or three millions below the figures of some previous years, a result brought about by the demand for restocking in Victoria, and the opening up of new country in Queensland.

In the first years of the colony's history the coastal belt only was available for settlement, but with the crossing of the Blue Mountains, in 1813, a new horizon stretched before the pastoral imagination, and with each successive discovery by Oxley or Cunningham or Mitchell or Hume, plain was added to plain of pasture, and the paths of the explorers were dotted with chains of squattages. In the earliest years of pastoral settlement it was customary for stock-breeders to drive their herds to the nearest unoccupied good country when they increased beyond the grazing capabilities of their pasturages. In this manner the river-courses in the western districts became stocked, and the country bordering them occupied. The practice came into vogue when cattle were decreasing in value, and when, therefore, it was absolutely necessary to breed them at the least expense. These herds were, however, inferior in strain. They frequently became wild and unmanageable, and it was only with the influx of population during the gold fever days, when high prices were paid for meat, that they acquired any value. The cattle, nevertheless, showed that the interior country was good for stock-grazing, and proved that land which had hitherto been regarded as a desert was very fattening pasture; for they had discovered "salt-bush," a fodder plant which retains its vitality when other kinds of herbage have long withered away. The grazing value of the river country, or Riverina, has never since been challenged.

There were in effect three great waves of pastoral settlement which swept over Australia. The first is that just alluded to, which flowed over the inland plains between the colonies of New South Wales, Victoria, and South Australia. The second rolled farther north, and beyond the occupied country, as far as the central basin of the continent. The third went still northward to the downs of Queensland. The first migration of stock arose from the demands for meat made by the gold-diggers. The success of this pioneer movement inspired the second experiment, which was prompted by the demand for wool. The third essay in pastoral settlement was occasioned by the maintained and increasing value of all squatting property.

The first of these migrations alone concerns the industrial history of the gold period, and began immediately the first fever of discovery had abated, and was the chief factor in producing the agrarian agitation which marked the following decade.

The following is a statement of the values of the chief articles of pastoral produce exported in the years named :—

Year.	Wool.	Tallow and Lard.	Skins and Hides.
	£	£	£
1851	1,979,527	237,402	32,284
1855	3,170,640	152,376	69,602
1859	4,236,693	48,085	271,349

The actual number of stock depastured in Australia was as follows:—

Year.	Sheep.	Horned Cattle.	Horses.	Swine.
1851	17,515,798	1,924,482	167,220	109,911
1852	18,002,140	2,075,256	186,092	132,093
1853	17,191,146	2,141,526	183,360	123,033
1854	17,249,581	2,256,639	208,133	112,062
1855	17,065,979	2,697,390	231,056	131,431
1856	16,193,035	3,054,592	262,448	212,582
1857	17,091,798	3,180,042	289,027	217,352
1858	17,205,653	3,217,600	332,381	196,636
1859	15,443,617	3,275,850	353,388	245,367

Upon the manufacturing industry the first effect of the gold rush was disastrous; but there was an immediate change, especially in Victoria, where the camps of the diggers soon became thriving towns. It was to the population attracted to the country by the gold discoveries that the manufactories owed their subsequent revival and the labour required to operate them. The statistics of these states are not complete enough to enable a statement of the progress of the manufacturing industry to be given; but it is evident, from the rapid increase, after the year 1855, in the number and variety of establishments, that the ultimate effect of the gold discoveries upon the manufacturing industry was extremely stimulating.

Reference has already been made to the opening up of steam communication with England in 1852, during which year the "Chusan," the "Australia," and the "Great Britain"—the last-named the largest ship afloat at that time—visited Australia. In 1856 a steam service, of anything but a satisfactory character, was carried on by the Peninsular and Oriental Company and the Royal Mail Company; but the days of efficient ocean communication were still to come. These early essays, however, had no small effect in encouraging the colonists to agitate for something better, and proposals were made for the establishment of a line of mail-packets *via* Panama, but they did not bear fruit until the year 1866.

The history of railway construction is elsewhere dealt with. It was not until 1846 that the people of Australia began to awaken to the advantages of railroad communication, and not until two years afterwards that a company was formed to construct a railway from Sydney to Parramatta and Liverpool. This line was commenced in 1850 and partly completed in 1855. Meanwhile, the discovery of gold had been made, and attention was directed to railway construction in Melbourne, and in 1854 the first line in Australia was opened for traffic; it ran from Melbourne to Port Melbourne, and was 2½ miles long. For some years railway construction languished, the enthusiasm of its advocates being doubtless considerably damped by the reflection that the short line from Sydney to Parramatta—only 14 miles in length—cost £700,000, or £50,000 a mile. The progress of railway construction is shown by the following figures, which give the length of line open for traffic in the years named :—

Years.	Miles.	Years.	Miles.
1854	2½	1857	117
1855	16½	1858	132
1856	32½	1859	171

With steam communication to other parts of the world, and the introduction into Australia of the railway system, new markets were being created for the trade in coal, although it was not before the subsidence of the gold fever that they began to be availed of. The quantity of coal raised in 1852 was 67,404 tons, and in 1858 over three times as much, viz., 216,397 tons. In 1850 and 1851 the price of coal ranged from 9s. to 10s. per ton; in 1852 it had risen to over 80s. per ton, although it did not remain for an extended period at this high figure. The quantity and value of the production of this mineral during the period under review were as follow :—

Year.	Quantity raised.	Average price per ton.	Approximate total value.
	tons.	s. d.	£
1852	67,404	10 11	36,885
1853	96,809	16 2	78,059
1854	116,642	20 6	119,380
1855	137,076	13 0	89,082
1856	189,960	12 5	117,906
1857	210,434	14 1	148,158
1858	216,397	15 0	162,182

The whole of this coal was mined in New South Wales.

During the whole of this period considerable activity was shown in testing the navigable waters of the Continent, and repeated efforts were made to open up communication by way of the rivers Murray and Darling, which, of course, had a corresponding influence on the great pastoral industry by affording means of cheap transit for the leading staple of the interior. In 1853, W. R. Randall, in his small steamer, the "Mary Anne," was the first to proceed up the Murray, and eventually he reached Maiden's Punt, as the crossing from Echuca to Moama was then named. In the same year Captain Cadell proceeded in a steamer up the Murray to near Albury "with the greatest ease and success." This voyage attracted marked attention, and was the cause of the inauguration of regular steam-service on the river. Captains Cadell, Johnson, and Robertson, and Mr. Randall, subsequently followed up the original essays in the direction of inland river navigation by steaming up the courses of the Murrumbidgee, the Darling, the Barwon, and the Edwards, thus making accessible to population, and opening up to the wool-growing industry, an enormous expanse of territory. In the north, A. C. Gregory (in search of Leichhardt), Dalrymple, and other explorers, were successively unlocking to the squatters, who followed closely in their wake, the broad areas of pasturage, whose almost immediate occupation advanced the northern congeries of squatting localities, known as the Moreton Bay District, in rapid strides to the dignity of the Colony of Queensland. It is noteworthy, and distinctly characteristic of the period, that by the year 1854 the purchase of land for agricultural purposes had almost ceased, territory being taken up instead in large tracts by pastoral lessees for grazing purposes.

The population of Australia in 1850 was 480,120; in 1855 it had risen to 821,452, and in 1860 to 1,141,563. The tendency to crowd into the cities was already visible; in 1861 Melbourne held 139,916 people, and Sydney 95,789, or together 235,705, a total representing one-fifth of the population of the continent.

Industrial Period—1859-62.

The three years, 1860-62, may be regarded as a transition period, during which the country was undergoing the process of recovery from the days of excitement and dreams of chance, when the wealthy speculator of one moment became the beggared adventurer of the next, and the outcast of many years the millionaire of as many months. The community was vaguely restless, as though beginning to realise that the golden era of its recent experience was drifting into a prosaic period of sterner conditions and slower and more arduous growth. There were many, however, still in the daily expectation of hearing of new discoveries as rich as those of the previous decade, and these refused to accept the conditions of settled industry, while the rumour of a new find was sufficient to entice them away from the employment they chanced at the time to be following.

The production of gold in 1859 was nearly ten and a half millions, of which one and a quarter million was from New South Wales, and the balance from Victoria. The following was the yield during tho four years embraced in this period :—

Year.	Victoria.	New South Wales.	Other Districts.	Total.
	£	£	£	£
1859	9,122,868	1,259,127	730	10,382,725
1860	8,626,800	1,465,373	......	10,092,173
1861	7,869,812	1,806,171	......	9,675,983
1862	6,633,124	2,467,780	12,442	9,113,346

It will be seen that, in spite of the improvement in New South Wales the total gold won was steadily declining. The earnings of the working miner were diminishing at even a greatei ratio than the foregoing figures indicate, with the natural and immediate result that there was a return of gold-seekers to their original or other pursuits. Agriculture naturally received more attention, but many successful miners made investments in squattages, and both for farming and grazing there arose a persistent demand for the acquisition of state lands on more equitable terms than had hitherto prevailed in Victoria and New South Wales.

The renewal of attention to agrarian pursuits was general throughout Australia. Victoria and South Australia had about equal areas under tillage, although the value of crop was, perhaps, greatest in the first-named. Victoria had benefited most by the gold discoveries, both directly and indirectly, and was now in all important respects the leading state. It was the chief financial centre, and had the largest population, trade, acreage under tillage, and mining yield, as well as a larger number of sheep, and perhaps sheep of a better class than possessed by any of its neighbours. New South Wales stood first in regard to the possession of cattle and horses; Queensland and South Australia had already large interests in live stock, especially in sheep and cattle; and Tasmania depastured more sheep than it does at the present time, while the number of cattle and horses in the state was considerable. The following were the numbers of stock of each class at the close of the year 1862 :—

State.	Sheep.	Cattle.	Horses.
New South Wales	6,145,651	2,620,383	273,389
Victoria	6,764,851	576,601	86,067
Queensland.....................	4,553,353	637,296	36,532
South Australia..............	3,431,000	258,342	56,251
Western Australia	295,666	36,887	12,099
Tasmania	1,616,225	83,143	20,742
Total...	22,806,746	4,212,652	485,080

The area under crop at the close of the year 1862 was 1,549,255 acres. In South Australia the acreage was 494,511; in Victoria, 465,430; in New South Wales, 302,138; and in Tasmania, 253,050. The beginning of an important industry was made in Queensland, though the area in crop was only 6,067 acres, while in Western Australia the cultivated area was 28,059 acres. The importance already assumed by South Australia is very noticeable, and from this period that state and Victoria continued to make, for twenty years, rapid and almost equal progress, until in 1892 the superiority in agricultural interests fell to Victoria, where it has remained. Although New South Wales had many advantages over the southern states, its agricultural progress was astonishingly slow; in point of fact, its position was little in advance of Tasmania so far as concerned acreage, and probably below it in point of value.

The permanent effect of the gold discoveries on the industries of Australia is best seen in the trade returns, and especially in the figures relating to exports. In 1850 the total value of exports from Australia was £3,584,000; in 1856, when the gold production was at its height, the value was £21,794,000; in 1861 it was £23,166,607; and thereafter the values showed a constant tendency to increase. The phrase that the gold discoveries "precipitated Australia into nationhood" is no poetic exaggeration, but an actual fact.

The progress made in railway construction during this period was far from satisfactory. The Governments of the different states were not wanting in enterprise, but it was difficult to obtain money at a rate of interest sufficiently low to warrant them in borrowing; and even if loans at moderate rates could be raised, the prospect of sufficient traffic being obtained to make the railways pay was not assured. In 1862 the length of line open for traffic was 368 miles, viz., 214 miles in Victoria, 98 miles in New South Wales, and 56 in South Australia.

Allusion has been made to the demand for land which set in after the more easily worked gold deposits had been exhausted and erstwhile gold-seekers were compelled to look round for other means of livelihood. The beginning of the sixties marks the inception of the agrarian legislation and agitation for cheap land that has persisted in every state to the present day. New South Wales led the way by passing a law, under the provisions of which land was obtainable by free selection before survey. Sir John Robertson's Land Act—the measure referred to—came into operation in 1861, and the new principle it initiated had lasting, if not immediately apparent, effect on the condition of the working classes, giving them opportunities for employment not previously open to them. The main principle of the measure, which did so much to assist recovery from the dead level of conditions that prevailed at the time, is embodied in the following clause:—"Any person may, upon any Land Office day, tender to the Land Agent for the district a written application for the conditional purchase of any such lands, not less than 40 acres nor more than 320 acres, at the price of 20s. per acre, and may pay to such Land Agent a deposit of 25 per centum of the purchase money thereof. And, if no other application and deposit for the same land be tendered at the same time, such person shall be declared the conditional purchaser thereof at the price aforesaid."

The free selector of any portion of Crown lands had three years' credit for the payment of the remainder of his purchase-money. Should he, after that time, be unable or disinclined to make payment, liberty was granted him to defer instalments for an indefinite period on paying 5 per cent. interest per annum on the principal amount remaining unpaid. It was also provided that the purchaser of any area of land from 40 to 320 acres should be entitled to three times the extent of his purchase for grazing ground, so long as it should not be claimed by any other free selector. Certain conditions were imposed regarding residence, which came to be more honoured in the breach than in the observance.

No other state dealt so lavishly with its waste lands as did New South Wales. The amendments made by Victoria were more cautious, and it was not until 1869 that the principle of free selection, as in vogue in New South Wales, was adopted. The pressure of population from abroad was not so great in Tasmania, South Australia, and Western Australia as to compel agrarian legislation of a revolutionary character, and in each of these states the amendments in the law, though frequent, were such as to conserve the public estate. In the period under review Queensland was only beginning its career as an independent state, and having a vast territory to dispose of, which did not offer the same attractions as were offered by the southern provinces, its land legislation was marked by extreme liberality to the intending settler.

The period 1859-62 was peculiarly one of transition so far as wages were concerned; there were no recognised trade rates, and even in the same year there were occasional variations, sometimes as many as four in the daily wages of artisans. An example of this may be given for the year 1861. In that year the daily wages of masons working in Melbourne fell from 14s. in April to 13s. in July and 12s. in October, and the wages of bricklayers were, in the same months, 12s., 11s., and 10s. per day. Other trades were somewhat similarly affected. The following were the current wages in the closing months of the years named, in Melbourne and Sydney:—

Trade or Calling.	1860.				1861.				1862.			
	Melbourne		Sydney.		Melbourne		Sydney.		Melbourne		Sydney.	
	s.	d.	s.	d.	s.	d.	s.	d.	s.	d.	s.	d.
Masons	14	0	11	6	12	0	10	0	10	0	10	0
Plasterers	11	0	10	6	10	0	11	0	8	0	10	0
Bricklayers	12	0	10	6	10	0	11	0	8	0	13	0
Carpenters	11	6	10	6	10	0	10	0	8	0	10	0
Blacksmiths	11	0	10	6	10	0	10	0	10	0	10	0
General Labourers	7	6	6	0	6	0	6	0	5	6	6	0
	per week.		per week.		per week.		per week.		per week.		per week.	
General Servants (female)	10	0	8	6	11	0	9	0	12	0	10	0

The wages of female servants were in addition to board and lodging The figures just given mark the transition from the high rates of the gold-discovery period to those payable under modern conditions. There was, naturally, considerable reluctance on the part of wage-earners to accept the new conditions, and there was considerable fluctuation in wages before a distinct understanding was arrived at between employers and employed.

The prices of commodities fell with the decline in wages, although not to so great an extent, but rents were adjusted to the new conditions. It is not easy to give average prices in each part of Australia at this period; for, although price lists are available, it is difficult, if not impossible, to be certain that the goods mentioned therein are identical with those quoted in similar lists for other places. Speaking generally, the prices of agricultural and dairy produce were lower in Melbourne than in Sydney; agricultural produce was also of lower price in Adelaide than in Sydney. Beef and mutton were cheaper in Sydney than elsewhere. Imported goods were, on the whole, of lower price in Melbourne than in the other capital cities—that is to say, in the retail shops,—the wholesale prices being much the same. The following are the average prices of some of the principal articles of consumption in the retail shops of Sydney during the year named :—

Article of Consumption.	1860.	1861.	1862.
	s. d.	s. d.	s. d.
Wheat, per bushel	8 0	6 6	7 0
Bread, 1st quality, per lb.	0 3½	0 4	0 2½
Flour, " per lb.	0 3½	0 3	0 3
Rice, per lb.	0 5	0 4	2d. to 4d.
Oatmeal, per lb.	0 6	0 6	0 5
Tea, per lb.	2 3	2 4	1/6 to 2/6
Coffee, per lb.	1 6	1 6	1/4 to 1/6
Meat, fresh, per lb.	0 4	0 3	0 4
Butter, fresh, per lb.	1 6	1 8	2 3
Cheese, English, per lb.	1 6	1 7	1 6
Potatoes, per cwt.	7 6	7 3	8 0

Industrial Progress—1863–1872.

During this period of Australia's history the industrial and social conditions now obtaining were gradually evolved. The El Dorado dreams of ten years before almost entirely faded from men's minds, and although large discoveries of gold were made both during this period and afterwards, the impulse towards gold-seeking never again became a dominating passion amongst any large class in the community. All the states had, owing to the increased demand for freehold land consequent upon the large influx of population at the time of the gold discoveries, altered their laws with the avowed object of affording men of small means the opportunity of acquiring land on easy terms, and in the ten years following the passing of the Robertson Lands Acts 11,260,547 acres were disposed of by the six Australian states. Victoria sold 3,607,791 acres, New South Wales 3,969,273 acres, South Australia 2,250,552 acres, and Tasmania 542,061 acres.

It is interesting to note that, taking Australia as a whole, about one-eighth of the land sold by the states was placed under cultivation. The proportions, however, were very different in the different states. In Victoria, it was about one-seventh, in South Australia one-fourth, while in New South Wales it was less than one-thirtieth. These proportions give an indication of the lines upon which the states were progressing. Victoria and South Australia were becoming important agricultural communities, Tasmania was developing grazing and agriculture together, while New South Wales, neglecting agriculture, paid more and more attention to sheep-farming. Gold-mining still maintained a position of great importance in Victoria, but even in that state, at the middle of the period, the industry, measured by the value of its production, ranked below both agriculture and stock-rearing. In 1866 Queensland appears for the first time as a gold producer, and small quantities were obtained in South Australia and Tasmania. The value of the gold exported from Australia in 1859 was £10,382,725; in 1866 it had fallen to £7,108,667.

During this period the coal-mining industry of New South Wales was beginning to obtain some importance. In 1858 the quantity of coal raised barely exceeded 100,000 tons; in 1862 it reached about 300,000 tons; and from 1866 to the end of the period the quantity varied from 500,000 to 600,000 tons.

South Australia was helped very much by its copper industry. In the days preceding the gold discoveries the value of copper won did not fall far short of £400,000. The immediate effect of the gold discoveries, as already indicated, was to deprive South Australia of its able-bodied men, especially its miners. By 1854 the value of copper won had fallen below £100,000. With the subsidence of the first excitement of the gold discoveries, labour again returned to the province. In 1856 the output reached £400,000, and remained between that figure and £450,000 up to the year 1861. From 1861 onward the industry received considerable impetus, and the output in 1866 reached the large total of £824,000. Although the following years do not show so valuable a production, the output declining in 1868 to £624,000, the actual quantity of copper won had not diminished, the fall being due to a decline in the price of the metal.

The climatic conditions of the period in some of the states were not such as to encourage the progress of rural occupation. This was especially the case as regards New South Wales. The year 1862 was one of drought and bush fires. The drought persisted till February, 1863, and was succeeded by heavy rains which deluged the eastern portion of the continent. Floods were recorded from Rockhampton the north to Gippsland on the south, and in the Hawkesbury Valley the water rose 27 feet above its normal level. In New South Wales the floods were succeeded by a long spell of dry weather, which lasted into the opening month of 1865. Farmers petitioned the Government to be released from claims for seed-wheat advanced during the previous year; crops in many parts of the interior were totally destroyed by rust and drought, and in the north by continued rain—for floods were again submerging many districts,—and efforts were being made to provide accommodation for the houseless poor. The floods, which covered a period of six months, extending from February to July, caused rivers to overflow their banks, swept bridges away, and destroyed a vast amount of property. The year 1866 was normal as regards the seasons, but unsettled conditions again prevailed in 1867. In this year the floods were attended by loss of life as well as by destruction of property. Lines of railway were closed in consequence of the heavy rains, and public works in some districts were greatly damaged. The distress of the settlers who had been "washed out" called so loudly for relief that public meetings were held for the purpose of raising subscriptions. The Colonial Secretary and others hastened to the inundated districts with succour, and the butchers and bakers of Sydney sent meat and bread to those who had been rendered destitute. Dry weather supervened from October, 1867, to January, 1868, followed by heavy rains which inundated the valleys of the Hawkesbury and the Hunter. The year 1869 began with a severe drought, and the 13th February was proclaimed by the Government a day of humiliation and prayer for rain. The pastoral industry was severely affected, and the whole country suffered. In 1870 floods prevailed throughout the state; traffic was stopped and much property destroyed. A Flood Relief Committee was formed, and, notwithstanding the presence of many unemployed in Sydney, great efforts were made to send succour to the "washed-out" settlers. The month of November in this year was specially fraught with disaster from floods. The calendar was simply a record of inundations which were general throughout the state.

The effect of the vicissitudes of the seasons is seen in the returns of the acreage cropped in the states chiefly affected. In New South Wales, from 1861 to 1864 the increase of cultivation was barely 20,000 acres; there were large increases in the two succeeding years, but the area was not retained in cultivation, and the year 1871 showed less tillage than 1866. From 1861 to 1865 the seasons in Victoria were on the whole adverse to the farmer, but subsequent years up to the end of the period under review were distinctly favourable. Tasmania is not subject to adverse seasons, but from 1861 to 1865 the climatic conditions were such that no progress was made as regards area under crop. In Queensland little progress is observable up to 1865, in which year the area cropped did not exceed 15,000 acres. Contrary to the experience of the eastern states, South Australia enjoyed a succession of fair seasons, interrupted by a few that were exceptionally good, and the area devoted to tillage made regular progress, being checked only in one year (1868) of the period between 1861 and 1871. As will be seen from the table in regard to acreage under crop, the position of South Australia was higher even than that of Victoria. The following is a statement of the area cropped in each state in the years named:—

Year.	New South Wales.	Victoria.	Queensland.	South Australia.	Western Australia.	Tasmania.	Total. Commonwealth States
	acres.	acres.	acres.	acres.	acres.	acres.	acres.
1861	260,798	439,895	4,440	486,667	27,018	163,385	1,382,203
1866	451,225	592,915	24,433	739,714	43,159	167,866	2,019,312
1871	417,801	937,220	59,969	1,044,656	58,324	154,445	2,672,415

The progress of the sheep-breeding industry was continuous up to the year 1868, the seasons which proved so adverse to the farmer being, on the whole, favourable to the grazier; but from 1868 to 1871, which were good farming years, the seasons were against sheep rearing. The most important economic change observable in the period is the reversal of the positions of New South Wales and Victoria. In 1865 the number of sheep depastured in Victoria exceeded that of New South Wales by about three-quarters of a million; in 1871 the superiority was with the last-mentioned state to the extent of six and a quarter millions. The following is a statement of the numbers of sheep and cattle depastured in the years named:—

State.	Sheep.			Cattle.		
	1861.	1866.	1871.	1861.	1866.	1871.
New South Wales....	5,615,054	11,562,155	16,278,697	2,271,923	1,771,809	2,014,888
Victoria	6,239,258	8,833,139	10,002,381	628,092	598,968	799,509
Queensland	4,093,381	7,278,778	7,403,334	560,196	919,414	1,168,235
South Australia	3,038,356	3,911,600	4,412,055	265,434	123,820	143,463
Western Australia ..	279,576	481,040	670,999	33,795	41,323	49,593
Tasmania	1,714,498	1,722,804	1,305,489	87,114	88,370	101,540

In spite of the large fall in the gold returns, the exports of the states increased considerably during the period. There was a steady improvement in the quantity of wool and other pastoral produce exported, and the prices obtained were well sustained. Victoria held the first place in regard to the value of the trade, both of imports and exports, although at the end of the period its advantage over the mother state was very greatly reduced. It was in this period that Victoria adopted the policy of Protection, which it has since strictly adhered to, though that policy was not adopted without a severe legislative struggle. The customs tariff of February, 1867, imposed duties on a number of articles with a view of affording protection to native industries, and four years later (May, 1871) the duties were increased upon many articles with the view of affording further protection.

The position of Melbourne at the end of the period under review was undoubtedly imposing. The population, 206,780, was far greater than that of any other city in Australia, its nearest rival, Sydney, having a population of only 137,776. But Melbourne's superiority was founded on a stronger basis than that of mere population. Early in the sixties the city became the financial centre of Australia. The enormous sums won at the gold-fields were poured into its banks, and filled their coffers to repletion, and fields for investment were eagerly sought after. The Riverina district of New South Wales first attracted attention, and speedily became the property of Melbourne residents, either absolutely or by way of mortgage. From New South Wales their enterprise extended to Queensland and across the sea to New Zealand, until Melbourne was without a rival in the field of Australian finance. The gradual working out of the gold-fields did not alter Melbourne's position. The gains derived from its investments, and the profits flowing to it as the financial centre of the continent, were greater even than those flowing from the gold-fields in the days of their highest production.

The position acquired by Melbourne was not at the expense of Sydney. It is true that the latter was the chief seat of Australian enterprise in the days preceeding the gold discoveries; but it lost nothing by those discoveries, although its position was now second to Melbourne.

The climatic disturbances affecting New South Wales have been alluded to; but it must not be supposed that no progress was achieved during the period. Agriculture, it is true, made only slight advance, and no beginning had yet been made of manufacturing on a large scale, but the great pastoral industry had thriven, in spite of adverse seasons, and Sydney, on its part, had greatly benefited thereby. The stoppage of immigration was severely felt in some of the industries of the state, and immigration lecturers were sent to England to attract attention to the resources of New South Wales. There was, as is frequently the case in Australia, a demand for labourers in some pursuits in excess of the supply, while there was a dearth of employment in other branches of industry. All the trades connected with the pastoral industry were fully employed; those connected with the building industry, depending for their expansion upon an increase of population were in a very different condition, especially in Sydney. In 1866 there was very keen distress amongst mechanics; and the Government of the state established relief works at Haslem's Creek, where considerable numbers of men were employed clearing and forming a large area to serve as a cemetery. Later in the same year rumours of rich gold discoveries in the Weddin Mountains attracted many of the workers away from the city, and so relieved the tension of the labour market. Queensland was troubled about the same time with a large number of persons willing to work, for whom no employment was available; but the Queensland difficulty differed from that of New South Wales, both as to its origin and the class affected. The want of employment arose from a neglect of the ordinary canons of good government. It was the credit of the Government that was impaired, general business remaining unaffected. A brief description of the position of affairs at this period will be found in the historical sketch of Queensland in the early part of the volume for 1901–2. The persons who felt the crisis most acutely were the unskilled labourers discharged from public works by reason of the inability of the Government to pay its way. A return to the principles of sound finance, which of course was not accomplished in a moment, removed the cause of the crisis and with it the labour difficulty.

Wages for like employment were fairly level throughout Australia during the whole period, the tendency being for the rate for skilled tradesmen to fall to 8s. per day, and that for general labourers to 5s. per day. The following tables show the wages in some of the principal mechanical trades, and for day labourers and general servants, paid in 1861 and 1871 in the cities of Melbourne, Sydney, Adelaide, and Hobart. It will be seen that a considerable range is shown for most of the rates paid in Melbourne. There were two reasons for this: First, there was a greater range in the quality of the workmen than in the other cities; and, secondly, the Melbourne artisan resisted the inevitable fall in wages more strenuously than did his fellows in the other cities.

Class of Workers.	1861.				1871.			
	New South Wales.	Victoria.	South Australia.	Tasmania.	New South Wales.	Victoria.	South Australia.	Tasmania.
	s. d.	s. s.	s. d.	s. d.	s. d.	s. s.	s. d.	s. d.
Carpenters	10 0	8 to 10	9 0	7 0	8 6	8 10	8 0	6 6
Blacksmiths ...	10 0	8 to 12	10 0	9 6	8 6	8 10	8 0	6 6
Bricklayers	13 0	8 to 12	10 0	8 6	9 0	8 to 10	8 0	6 0
Masons	10 0	8 to 12	9 0	7 9	8 6	8 to 10	8 0	6 6
Day labourers ...	5 6	5/7	6 0	7 0	5 0	5/-	5 6	4 0

The lower rates shown for 1871 were not accepted without demur, and meetings were held at various places to protest against the reduction in wages; but protests were unavailing when there were large numbers of qualified men unable to obtain employment even at the rates objected to.

The ratio of wages of female servants was well maintained during this period, the slight fall observable in 1866 being more than recovered. Farm labourers and shepherds suffered a slight reduction in wages towards the end of the period, as large numbers who had quitted their employment on the sheep and cattle stations for the gold-fields returned to their former pursuits. The following are the weekly wages, the rates being in addition to board and lodging provided by the employers:—

	1861.		1866.		1871.	
	s.	d.	s.	d.	s.	d.
Farm labourers	13	0	11	6	10	9
Shepherds	13	0	13	0	11	9
Cooks (female)	11	0	10	0	11	6
Housemaids	9	0	9	0	9	0
Laundresses	11	0	10	0	10	9
Nursemaids	8	0	7	0	8	0
General servants (female)	10	0	9	0	9	0
Farm house-servants and dairywomen	8	6	9	0	9	0

The year 1861 is notable in labour matters, as witnessing a crucial stage in the agitation against the admission of the Chinese to Australia—an agitation which for many years has been an important factor in determining the trend of domestic and industrial legislation. The discovery of gold brought to Australian shores great numbers of these aliens. In 1852 they began to arrive, for prior to that year their presence, except at the seaports, was practically unknown. Victoria was the first place of settlement chosen by them. Although their number at the census of 1854 was not greater than 2,000, the local Legislature took alarm, and passed an Act limiting the number of Chinese to be brought into the country to one for every 10 tons of a vessel's cargo. Five other Acts were passed between 1855 and 1864, regulating the influx of these Asiatics. In 1856 the number in Australia was 26,000, and of these 24,000 were in Victoria, the rest being in New South Wales. In 1859 the Chinese inhabitants in New South Wales and Victoria numbered 37,000, or about $4\frac{1}{4}$ per cent. of the population. The Chinese were almost wholly adult males, and if this number be compared with the adult male population of the two states it will be found that the proportion in the year named was not less than $11\frac{1}{2}$ per cent. Victoria had the largest share of these aliens. In 1861 there were about 38,300 Chinese in New South Wales and Victoria, viz., 12,988 in the first-named, and 24,732 in the latter state. Thenceforward the Chinese population of Victoria rapidly declined, and the majority of those leaving crossed the Murray into New South Wales.

The arrival of Chinese was at no time viewed with equanimity by the whites; but with large numbers of disappointed gold-seekers in the country there was a growing feeling of resentment, and in 1861 matters in regard to this class of immigration reached a crisis. The gold-field opened up at Burrangong, in New South Wales, proved extraordinarily rich; a great rush set in to that place, and large crowds of the Chinese flocked to the diggings there. The miners received this influx of Asiatic fossickers with very bad grace, and convened a public meeting for the purpose of deciding whether "Burrangong was a European or a Chinese territory." They likewise addressed a petition to the Assembly, complaining of the swamping of the field by thousands of Chinese. This agitation against the alien miners resulted in continuous riotings. The unfortunate foreigners were ejected from their claims, their tents were burned, and they were generally ill-used. The Government, determined to uphold order at any cost, despatched to the scene of the riots—a place called Lambing Flat—a mixed force of artillerymen, with two 12-lb. field-pieces, some men of the 12th Regiment, and some members of the mounted police force. The Premier, Mr. (afterwards Sir) Charles Cowper, also visited the field and addressed a monster meeting of the miners, sympathising with their grievances, but informing them that no redress could be obtained until riot and confusion had entirely ceased. When the Premier had returned to Sydney the excitement rapidly ceased. A new rush to a locality named Tipperary Gully lured away 6,000 miners from the scene of their former disputes, and the Chinese departed to other fields. Thus ended the first labour conflict between the Europeans and the Chinese, who from that date onward became a growing menace to the character of the settlement of the Australian States.

At the beginning of the period a Select Committee was appointed by the Parliament of New South Wales to inquire into and report upon the state of the manufacturing and agricultural industries. On the 12th December, 1862, this Committee brought up a report which stated that, from the evidence taken, it was shown that manufactures had not increased during twenty years; that many which had flourished in the past were not in existence; and that in consequence thousands of youths were wandering about the streets in a state of vagrancy, instead of learning some useful trade. This statement is, however, too sweeping to be accepted literally, and is not supported by any evidence of value. It may be taken, however, as indicating the popular opinion of the day, and perhaps as a tribute to the superior condition of affairs on the Victorian side of the Murray and in South Australia. The slight progress made in agriculture in New South Wales, and the more rapid development of Victoria and South Australia, have already been noticed. In regard to manufactures, none of the states could claim a strong position. If there were nothing else against the manufacturers, there was the absence of a local demand for the products, without which the maintenance of industries in their early stages is always difficult, and sometimes impossible. Owing to the imperfection of the statistics it is impossible to speak with exactness of the amount of employment afforded by the manufacturing industries of 1861. So far as the records now existing enable an estimate to be made, the persons employed in the year 1862, in what are now classified as manufacturing industries, were:—

New South Wales	12,225
Victoria	6,405
Queensland	4,966
South Australia	5,066
Western Australia	373
Tasmania	3,372

The chief industries in New South Wales were the grinding or dressing of grain, sugar-making, distilling, and boat-building. In

Victoria, flour and grain mills gave employment to 552 persons, no other industries being on a like scale. In 1871 a very considerable change is observable. Victoria is no longer a minor state, and as regards manufactories it is in every important respect superior to New South Wales. It is still difficult to speak with certainty as to the number of persons employed, but the following may be taken as a fair approximation:—

New South Wales	13,583
Victoria	19,569
Queensland	5,518
South Australia	5,629
Western Australia	414
Tasmania...	3,747

In Victoria the largest employment was afforded by breweries, clothing factories, saw-mills and joinery works, boot factories, tanneries, iron foundries and engineering establishments, and potteries and brick-works; but there were many others of growing importance. In New South Wales the industries on the largest scale were tobacco factories, sugar-mills, tanneries, brick-works, saw-mills, iron foundries and engineering establishments, clothing factories, flour-mills, and coach-building establishments. The state of the industries throughout Australia cannot, however, be gauged from a mere statement of hands employed. Most of the industries were on a small scale. In the four less populous states, the average number of hands to each establishment was not more than three or four, and only in the capital cities was there a considerable employment of machinery.

The prices of the principal articles of consumption were greatly reduced in this period as compared with those of previous years following the gold discoveries; rents also showed a great reduction. Taking the seven articles in common use, prices for which have been given for other periods, the following were the averages for Sydney:—

RETAIL PRICES IN SYDNEY.

Year.	Bread per 2 lb. loaf.	Rice per lb.	Beef per lb.	Sugar per lb.	Beer (Col.) per gal.	Butter per lb.	Potatoes per cwt.
	d.	d.	d.	d.	s. d.	s. d.	s. d.
1859	6	4¼	4	5	4 0	1 10	8 0
1860	6½	5	4	5½	3 6	1 6	7 6
1861	6½	4	3	5½	3 6	1 8	7 3
1862	4½	3	4½	4½	2 0	2 3	8 0
1863	4	3	4¼	4½	1 6	1 6	7 0
1864	5½	3	4	4½	2 0	1 6	5 0
1865	7½	3	3	4½	2 0	1 9	8 0
1866	6½	4	3	4	2 0	1 3	6 0
1867	3½	3½	2½	4	1 6	1 6	7 0
1868	4	4	3½	4	2 0	1 3	9 0
1869	3½	3	2	4	1 4	1 6	4 0
1870	3½	3	3½	4	1 4	1 3	5 0
1871	3½	2½	2½	4	2 3	1 3	4 0

The prices stated above are for articles of good quality. Cheaper articles of low quality went into consumption, but not to any very considerable extent. Bread, for example, was retailed in some places at one penny per loaf less than quoted, while low grade sugar was also retailed at about one penny per pound less than shown. The same remarks apply to the following statement of prices for Melbourne during the same period. The figures in most cases are approximate. It is always difficult in dealing with prices to determine if the quality of the articles is the same in each year compared. It must be understood that the prices given have reference to the total quantity entering into consumption. In some years there was an extraordinary range in the figures quoted. Thus, in 1859, potatoes sold at 37s. 4d. per cwt., and in 1860 at 32s. 8d. per cwt. for a short period; but it is probable that very little entered into consumption at these prices, especially as bread was, weight for weight, much cheaper.

RETAIL PRICES IN MELBOURNE.

Year.	Bread per 2 lb. loaf.	Rice per lb.	Beef per lb.	Sugar per lb.	Fresh Butter per lb.	Potatoes per cwt.
	d.	d.	d.	d.	s. d.	s. d.
1859	7	4	7 to 10	4¼	2 10	9 4
1860	6	3½	4½ „ 6	4	2 6	9 4
1861	5	3½	3½ „ 4½	4	1 6	9 4
1862	4	3½	3 „ 6	4¾	2 3	4 8
1863	4	3½	4 „ 7	4¼	2 6	9 4
1864	6	3½	4 „ 6½	4½	1 3	4 8
1865	6	3½	4 „ 9	5½	3 0	4 8
1866	4½	3½	4 „ 9	5½	3 0	4 8
1867	4½	4	2 „ 7	4½	1 8	4 8
1868	5	3½	2 „ 6½	4½	1 7	9 4
1869	4½	3½	3 „ 7	4½	2 2	10 0
1870	3½	3½	3 „ 6	4½	1 9	4 8
1871	3½	3½	4 „ 8	4¼	0 10	8 2

The prices of commodities in the Adelaide market were, on the whole, less than in Melbourne, but wages ruled higher in the latter city, although, as affairs became settled after the gold rushes had subsided, prices tended to become level in the great centres of population. Bread was usually cheaper in Adelaide than elsewhere, and meat cheaper in Sydney, while potatoes and other vegetables, as well as butter and cheese, were, towards the end of the period under review, of less price in Melbourne. Imported goods varied in price with the duties payable; nevertheless importers continued to keep a semblance of equality in quotations in the various cities by adapting the quality of the goods to the prices obtainable.

The following statement refers to Adelaide :—

RETAIL PRICES IN ADELAIDE.

Year.	Bread per 2 lb. loaf.	Rice per lb.	Beef per lb.	Sugar per lb.	Fresh Butter per lb.	Potatoes per cwt.
	d.	d.	d.	d.	s. d.	s. d.
1859	6	3	5½	5	2 1	8 10
1860	5½	3	6	5	1 8	8 9
1861	3½	3	4½	5	0 11	6 0
1862	3½	3	4½	5	1 0	8 0
1863	3½	3	4¾	5	1 0	10 0
1864	5	3	5	5	1 0	7 3
1865	5	3	7½	5	1 8	8 0
1866	4	3	7¼	5	2 1	7 10
1867	3	3	4¾	5	1 1	5 8
1868	4½	3	3½	5	1 3	5 0
1869	3½	3	4	5	1 6	8 3
1870	4	3	5	5	1 0	4 9
1871	3½	3	4	5	0 10	3 10

The monetary position during the period was very peculiar. Up to 1861 interest allowed on deposits for twelve months by the banks was 5 per cent. In the year named the rate was reduced to 4 per cent., and remained unchanged until 1865, when it was increased to 6 per cent. for some and 6½ per cent. for other banks, private companies offering as much as 7 per cent. These high rates continued till August, 1867, when the interest fell to 5 per cent., and during the following year was reduced by successive stages to 3½ per cent. In the succeeding year the rate was increased, first to 4½ per cent. and then to 5 per cent., at which figure it remained until 1871, when there was again a reduction to 4 per cent.

The money market was much disturbed owing to the necessities of some of the state Governments. There was a large amount of New Zealand Government debentures bearing interest at 8 per cent. on sale in Sydney, and the New South Wales Government was so pressed for money that, at one time, it found itself compelled to place its 5 per cent. debentures at £70 per £100 of stock, allowing for redemption in twenty-eight years at par. This was equal to paying nearly 7½ per cent. interest.

The Governments of several of the states favoured the policy of assisted immigration, and during the ten years 1861–1870, 135,702 persons arrived in Australia, wholly or partly at the public expense. Of these, 18,165 came to New South Wales, 46,594 to Victoria, 56,586 to Queensland, 13,730 to South Australia, and 627 to Tasmania. The total accession of population from abroad during the same period was 173,277, viz., 68,191 to Queensland, 45,539 to New South Wales, 38,935 to Victoria, 17,949 to South Australia, and 5,891 to Western Australia; Tasmania, however, lost 3,228 persons by emigration. Though the country badly needed opening up, little progress was made during this period in railway extension, the average length of line opened being rather less than 80 miles a year.

During this period business was very much disturbed in New South Wales owing to the depredations of the bushrangers. From 1860 to 1870 was the great bushranging epoch in the state's history, which memorised such unworthy names as those of Frank Gardiner, the Clarkes, Dunn, Johnnie Gilbert, Ben Hall, Morgan, Power, "Thunderbolt," and O'Malley. The existence of this dangerous bushranging pest was a source of keen embarrassment to the Government, and a standing challenge to every Ministry which accepted office.

Industrial Period—1872–1893.

The twenty-two years from 1872 to 1893 do not call for such lengthened notice as former epochs, inasmuch as the statistics to be found in various parts of this volume give a detailed illustration of the progress made during the period. The preceding period had closed somewhat tamely. Population was not being attracted in any great numbers; the demand for land was not by any means so great as might have been expected from a consideration of the facilities afforded for its purchase, nor was there any extensive cultivation upon the land which was bought. The efforts that were made for the development of the country were not well sustained, except, perhaps, in Victoria, while railway construction was almost suspended. Expenditure by the Government on public works, either from revenue or from the proceeds of loans, was small, while little private capital found its way to the country. In such circumstances the industrial condition could not be said to have been hopeful. Nevertheless, causes were at work which were to affect materially the progress of Australia, especially of the eastern states.

The great discoveries of gold during the early fifties had given strength to the opinion that mining would speedily and permanently oust pastoral pursuits from the first position amongst the industries of the country. This expectation was soon disproved. From 1872 to

1893 the position of Australia as a gold-producing country greatly declined. In Victoria, the chief producer, the yield of the precious metal fell away from over £5,000,000, at the beginning of the period, to a little over £2,300,000 towards its close. In New South Wales the industry, which seemed very promising in 1872, in which year it yielded £1,644,000, fell away to less than one-fifth of that quantity in 1888. Queensland, on the other hand, began to display the richness of its gold mines. In 1872 the mines of that state already showed the respectable yield of £500,000; this was rapidly increased, and in 1878 the value of gold obtained exceeded a million sterling, and ten years later it was two and a half millions. This satisfactory condition of things was due to large discoveries of the precious metal at Rockhampton and Gympie, and subsequently to the wonderful deposits found at Mount Morgan. Tasmania could scarcely be called a gold-producing country at the beginning of this period; but in 1877 the famous quartz reef, afterwards worked by the Tasmanian Gold Mining Company, was discovered, and in 1879 the yield reached a quarter of a million sterling, and, although it fell away in subsequent years, the discovery was most opportune. The gold discoveries in Western Australia do not belong to this period, but the long-accepted dictum that the country was without minerals was fully disproved, and in 1893, the year which closes the epoch under review, the gold won was valued at £421,000.

The chief coal-fields in the vicinity of Newcastle, New South Wales, yielded in 1872 about 1,000,000 tons; this was increased in 1891 to over 4,000,000 tons; and as 370 tons represents the employment of one man in or about the mines, the benefit of the additional output may be estimated. Queensland, Victoria, and Tasmania also began during the period to open up their coal-fields, but the value of the combined output of the three States, in 1893, was under £200,000.

Valuable deposits of other minerals were also worked to a considerable extent. In New South Wales, tin and copper were mined for during the whole period, the greatest value of production being £568,000 for tin in 1881, and £473,000 for copper in 1883. The quantity of these metals obtained was largely influenced by the weather conditions, which in some years were most unfavourable, while the extraordinary fluctuations in the price of the metals in the European markets also adversely affected their production.

Mining for silver became an important industry in New South Wales in 1885, and for the following year the yield of silver and lead, the two metals being found in conjunction, was about half a million sterling; in 1891 the value of the output was £3,600,000, and in 1893 it was still over £3,000,000.

In South Australia, copper-mining was an important industry, and added much to the wealth of the state, although towards the close of the period the output was greatly diminished, chiefly through labour disturbances. Queensland produced large quantities of tin and copper in the earlier years, but towards the end of the period, both metals being affected by a fall in price, the output, especially of copper, was considerably smaller. In Tasmania, there was an opportune discovery of tin at Mount Bischoff in 1871, when the island stood badly in need of an impetus to trade, and this important find marks the beginning of a new era in the mining and industrial history of the state. The discovery of gold in Tasmania has already been alluded to. Valuable lodes of silver-lead and copper were found in the western parts of the island, notably silver-lead at Mount Zeehan in 1885, gold and copper at Mount Lyell in 1886, and silver and lead at Heazlewood in 1887.

Taking Australia as a whole, agriculture made great progress from 1873 onwards. In 1872 the area under crop, exclusive of that devoted to grass, was 2,491,023 acres; in 1880 this had been increased to 4,583,894 acres; in 1890 to 5,430,221 acres. Of the larger states, the least progress was made by New South Wales, if progress be measured by acres under crop. In the ten years, from 1872 to 1882, the breadth of land devoted to the plough was increased by 247,689 acres, as compared with 709,479 acres in Victoria, and 1,267,482 acres in South Australia. The smallness of the population in Western Australia precluded any attempt at cultivation on a large scale, while Tasmania, with its small home market, and entrance barred to the markets across the straits, made very little progress, the area under crop in 1893 being only 179,000 acres, as compared with 156,000 acres twenty years previously. So early as 1852, South Australia had produced sufficient wheat for its own requirements, and was exporting its surplus, part to Great Britain, and part to New South Wales and other states with deficient production, while, so far as foodstuffs were concerned, Victoria also became independent of outside assistance in 1877. The value of the country's production, however, is not to be estimated merely by the acreage under crop. The maize and sugar crops of New South Wales, estimated by their yield, would represent four times their area in wheat land. A more exact idea of the condition of the agricultural industry may be obtained from the figures relating to the value of production. Judged by this standard, the production of Victoria stood easily first during the whole period, while New South Wales and South Australia, with almost equal values, were second and third. In 1871 the return from agriculture in the Commonwealth States was £8,941,000, equivalent to £5 7s. 2d. per inhabitant; in 1881 the value had increased to £15,519,000, or £6 17s. 9d. per inhabitant; while in 1891 the production reached £16,480,000, or £5 3s. 6d. per inhabitant. This satisfactory result was obtained in spite of a fall of about one-third in the prices of agricultural products. Further details in regard to agriculture will be found in the chapter dealing specifically with this question.

When the development of the pastoral industry during this period is considered, it will be readily understood how it happened that certain states, well fitted for agriculture, showed comparatively little progress in the breadth of land brought under tillage. Leaving aside for the present the question of prices, and considering only the volume of production, it will be found that this period was the one, of all others, most favourable to the pastoral industry. Taking Australia as a whole, the following figures, giving the number of cattle and sheep and the weight of the wool-clip at various periods, illustrate the position of the industry :—

Year.	Cattle.	Sheep.	Wool.
	No.	No.	lb.
1871	4,277,228	40,072,955	211,413,500
1881	8,010,991	65,078,341	324,286,100
1891	11,029,499	106,419,751	543,495,800
1893	11,546,833	99,799,759	601,085,000

The favourable position of the pastoral industry was maintained almost throughout the period in spite of a considerable fall in the prices of the staple articles of production. This was especially the case in New South Wales and Queensland. In New South Wales the wool-clip in 1871 weighed about 74,000,000 lb.; in 1892 it was nearly five times that weight. In Queensland the chief interest was cattle-grazing, and the number of cattle increased nearly sixfold in twenty years—that is to say, from 1,168,000 in 1871 to 6,192,000 in 1891. The first check to this prosperous state of affairs was brought about by the fall in prices. High prices for all classes of local produce obtained in 1875; but from that year to 1877 there was a reduction equal to about 14 per cent. Nevertheless, at the reduced prices the industry was highly profitable, especially as the flocks tended to increase largely in numbers. Good prices prevailed until 1884, but there was a further fall of 16 per cent. in the ensuing two years. In 1886 the country began to feel the effects of price reduction, which almost counterbalanced the larger returns due to the increase in the number of stock depastured. From 1886 to 1890 prices continued with little change, but from 1890 to 1894 there was a steady decline, the fall in the four years being equal to 30 per cent. During the nineteen years, 1875 to 1894, the total decline was equivalent to 49 per cent., and affected all descriptions of pastoral products; and as there was no corresponding reduction in the cost of production, and little in the cost of transport, the reduced prices proved a very severe blow to the staple industry of the country.

The various manufacturing industries prospered over the greater portion of this period. The number of hands employed in Victoria in 1873 was 24,495; in 1880 the number had increased to 38,141; in 1885 to 49,297; and in 1889 to 57,432. This was the year of greatest prosperity in Victoria. Thenceforward the manufacturing industry greatly declined, and in 1893 the number of hands employed was 39,473, or no greater than in the year 1883. In New South Wales, also, there was considerable impetus given to the manufacturing industry, which in 1889 gave employment to 45,564 persons; but, influenced by the same causes that affected Victoria, the number of persons employed fell away in 1893 to 38,918.

In the earlier years of the period the expenditure of borrowed money by the states was very moderate; but as money became easier to obtain in the London markets, the various Governments availed themselves of their opportunities to the fullest extent. The public debt of New South Wales in 1871 stood at about 10½ millions; in 1881 it was still below 17 millions; from 1881 to 1891 it rose to 53 millions, showing an increase of 36 millions in ten years. During the greater part of this period New South Wales had an abundantly large land revenue, which was expended for current purposes; this, added to a huge loan expenditure, rarely less than £4,000,000 a year, gave the state a predominating influence in the labour market of the continent.

In Victoria there was much the same condition of affairs, except that the Government had not any considerable revenue from the sale of its public lands. In 1871 the public debt in Victoria stood at 12 millions; in 1881 at 22½ millions, and in 1891 at 43½ millions. In some years, considering the number of the population, the loan expenditure was prodigious, although never on so lavish a scale as in New South Wales. The largest outpouring in any one year from loan funds was in 1890, when £4,134,000 was expended. Queensland also indulged in borrowing on a scale much beyond its requirements. From 1872 to 1882 the expenditure from loan funds was nearly £900,000 a year. From 1882 to 1892 it averaged between one and two millions. In South Australia the state expenditure from loans during the period 1872 to 1892 was scarcely ever less than one million a year, in some years rising to as much as 1¾ million. Western Australia was the only state in which the loan expenditure was kept within reasonable proportions, its total debt in 1891 being only £1,613,000. In Tasmania, from 1880 to 1890, 4½ millions was added to the public debt, expenditure slackening off after 1891.

In the eastern states the year 1892 was the first to show a restricted loan expenditure, the total for the five states, which in 1889 had been over 11 millions, and in 1890 about 10 millions, falling to less than 3 millions—equivalent to a shrinkage of at least 7 millions. This sudden contraction of expenditure had a most serious effect upon the labour market, and at least 40,000 men, accustomed to look to the Government or to contractors working under the Government for their employment, were thrown upon the labour market, which immediately became disorganised. Indeed, so far as New South Wales was concerned, the labour market was disorganised even in 1888, a state of affairs which did not altogether result from the cessation of expenditure on public works. Large numbers of persons had been attracted from the other states by the extravagant expenditure and vigorous immigration policy of preceding years, and on the Government reducing their expenditure from extravagance to moderation, thereby involving a decrease of about three millions sterling, some 15,000 men were left without employment.

To mitigate the distress consequent upon the inability of the community to absorb so much labour thus thrust upon it, the Government started relief works, still further attracting the unemployed to the vicinity of Sydney, and an expenditure of nearly £400,000 was incurred upon useless works before they were abandoned.

As affecting the industrial condition of the country, the importation of private capital for investment, in addition to that brought by persons taking up their abode in the state, was almost as important as the introduction of money by the various state Governments and by the local governing bodies. During the twenty-two years under review, the amount of private capital sent to New South Wales for investment, in excess of what was withdrawn, amounted to some 19 millions, and the money brought by persons coming to the country was over 23 millions. The bulk of the capital sent for investment came within the five years 1886–1890, and with the assistance of what was expended by the state during the same period and the preceding one, helped to bring about the industrial inflation so characteristic of those years. The investments made during 1871–1885 in Victoria by persons outside that state were very moderate in their amounts, and were probably not greater than the investments of Victorians in other states. During the years 1886–1890, entirely different conditions prevailed. In the short period of five years the private capital introduced or withdrawn from investments outside the state exceeded £31,500,000—a prodigious sum when the population of the state is considered; and when it is remembered that during the same five years the borrowings of the state Government and of the local bodies exceeded 17 millions, it is easy to understand the extraordinary inflation which arose, especially in Melbourne and the surrounding district. Every branch of industry was affected by the large amounts of capital available in the Melbourne market, and wages, rent, and the price of land reached very high figures. Speculation was carried on to the point where it became gambling, and all classes of real property assumed fictitious values. As illustrative of this, it may be mentioned that the rental value of Melbourne and suburbs during the boom period was £6,815,315, which became reduced when the boom collapsed in 1893 to £5,847,079. In Sydney the inflation brought rental values of the metropolitan district to £6,067,882, which was reduced by the year 1897 to £5,022,910. All the states except Western Australia and South Australia were the recipients of the attention of the British investor. Queensland received nearly nine millions of private capital in the five years 1881-85, large investments being also made in the immediately preceding quinquennial period. From 1885 onwards, however, there was a tendency in Queensland to withdraw capital. Tasmania received about one million pounds during the five years 1871–1875 for investment on private account, and in the subsequent five-yearly periods the amount invested varied between £400,000 and £500,000. These sums were not larger than the island State could readily absorb. There can be no doubt whatever that during many years Australia received more capital, both public and private, than could be legitimately utilised, and no small portion of it was necessarily devoted to purposes purely speculative. Many persons became suddenly rich by land speculation; on the other hand, as the land which they sold had a productive value far short of the interest represented by the purchase money, many of the purchasers, of whom there were thousands, became embarrassed, and it was some years before they could free themselves from their difficulties. The financial institutions, which had greatly assisted to promote the speculations, became involved also, and by the failure of their customers to redeem mortgages, these institutions, including several of the banks, became the possessors of a large amount of property on which advances had been made beyond all possibility of recovery. There was, however, an evil of greater consequence than the temporary inflation of values. It will be readily conceived that the introduction of capital within the limits of absorption, and the application of it to productive purposes, are conducive to true progress; while, on the contrary, the over-introduction of capital, however applied, means arrest of progress. An example of this may be taken from the history of New South Wales during this period. Of the twenty-two years comprising this industrial period, 1885 and 1886 witnessed the largest introduction of capital, namely, £11,470,000 in the former, and £10,028,000 in the latter year. It is therefore not astonishing to find that the value of domestic produce exported in those two years, when compared with the population, was less than in any other period since the discovery of gold. It must not, however, be supposed that the money introduced by the state or by private persons was to any large extent absolutely wasted. The states carried out many public works of a remunerative character and highly beneficial to the community generally, and the foundations of many important industries were laid by private enterprise during the period. It is true many private investors suffered great loss by the fall in prices which subsequently occurred, but this was a private evil and not a national one. The most detrimental effect produced by the "boom," as it is called, was the withdrawal of large bodies of men from productive pursuits and the derangement in the labour market which immediately ensued. From the point of view of wages and cost of living, the greater part of this period was an extremely prosperous one, improving year by year from 1872 onwards. At no period, except in the five golden years, 1853–7, were wages so high, and at no previous period was the purchasing power of money so great. The tide of improvement reached its highest level just before 1885, and in 1886 the signs of a reaction were visible. This was unfortunately coincident with the fall in prices already spoken of. The profits of capital became reduced and employers immediately attempted to reduce wages. In 1886 and the five years following, many strikes and trade disputes occurred. In New South Wales, in 1886–87, work in some of the southern district collieries was suspended for nearly twelve months by strikes and disputes; in 1888 the coal miners in the northern districts were on strike for several months; and in 1888 and 1889 the completion of various large public works threw out of employment some 12,000 men—no inconsiderable proportion of the unskilled labour of the country. In 1890 the maritime and pastoral industries were disturbed by strikes and disputes, very hurtful to the community in general and the working class in particular; and in 1892 another disastrous strike occurred, causing the silver-mines at Broken Hill to remain idle for nearly three months.

The bulk of the production of Australia is for export, and a very small proportion of the produce of the pastoral industry, with the exception of meat, is consumed in the country. The mineral products are also almost entirely exported, and there is a surplus production of bread stuffs. The prices, therefore, which the Australian producer can obtain for his produce are determined by prices and conditions in Europe or America, over which he can exercise little or no control. As a consequence, with a fall in prices of staple produce, employers almost invariably seek to balance their accounts by a reduction in wages; and under existing conditions it is practically necessary, if production is to continue, that the employees' wages should fall with the prices obtained for the commodity produced. In 1891 and the following years, Australia as a whole was face to face with a falling off in the quantity of production, and a decline in prices. The wage-earners were slow to concede the necessity of wages sharing in the general decline, and this was the root difficulty which caused the labour troubles preceding the crisis of 1893. It has been attempted in some quarters to fix upon the Labourers' Unions the responsibility for the events of that year. When it is remembered that the country was entirely over-capitalised, that land values had risen exorbitantly in the principal cities, and that the banks and financial institutions were largely concerned in maintaining the position of speculators, and were themselves, contrary to the spirit of the law and of their charters, the holders, either as mortgagees in possession or directly, of large squattages and landed properties in the cities and towns, it is easy to conceive that if the working classes had obediently acquiesced in all the demands for a reduction of wages, the crisis would still have happened. In the light of subsequent events, it must be confessed that the crisis was by no means the disaster which has been pictured. On the contrary, as will be seen from other parts of this volume dealing with the progress of production, all the producing interests of the state can look back to this time as a period of general awakening, and general production has made far greater progress since 1893 than ever before, in spite of adverse seasons and persistently low prices.

The flourishing condition of the pastoral industry throughout the greater portion of this period gave a marked impetus to the export trade. In 1872 the total value of the exports of the six states amounted to £32,212,000; this was an extremely large showing for a population of only 1,708,502. In 1875 the value of exports had grown to

£38,704,000, representing £20 11s. 3d. per head of population; in 1880 it reached £42,671,000 or £19 6s. 8d. per head of population; in 1885 it was £44,722,000 or £16 15s. 1d. per head; and in 1891 the total reached the enormous figure of £63,138,800, which is equivalent to £19 14s. per head of the population. These figures of course include re-exports and interstate trade; but when every allowance is made on these accounts it will still be found that the production of Australia, as measured by its exports, compared very favourably with that of any country in the world. The year 1891 represented the summit of Australian trade up to that time. In the following year there was a considerable falling off. This, however, was due more to the decline in prices than to any failure in production. The imports into Australia represent the return for the exports in addition to the proceeds of loans raised by the states and the investments made by foreign capitalists, less the interest and earnings of investments held by persons living outside its boundaries. The value of the imports fluctuates considerably, and in years of heavy borrowing shows very large figures; thus, in 1885 the imports exceeded the exports by £11,179,000, in 1889 by £9,305,000, and similarly in respect to other years.

After a long period of neglect the Governments of the various states began in 1873 to attend to the expansion of their railways. In 1872 the mileage in operation was 1,122; in 1874 it had risen to 1,346, and from this time onwards progress was rapid. Within four years the mileage open for traffic was doubled, and in ten years was quadrupled, the mileage in 1884 amounting to 5,694; and by the end of the period under consideration—that is, the year 1893—the length open for traffic exceeded 10,300 miles.

The expansion of general business during the same period may be gauged with considerable accuracy from the extension of the banking facilities. During the twenty-two years under review, banks were opened in every important centre of Australia, and it is estimated that in 1893 there was one bank or branch in operation for every 3,000 of the population. The deposits in 1872 were 23 millions; in three years they had increased 50 per cent; in seven years they had doubled; and in eleven years the increase was threefold—that is to say, in 1884 the sum on deposit reached £69,936,000. In 1891 the business of the banks reached its highest point, and the amount of money deposited was, in round numbers, 100 millions, equivalent to £31 4s. 2d. per head of population. This enormous sum, however, was not derived wholly from the Australian people, as large amounts were obtained in the United Kingdom and transmitted to Australia for investment. After 1891 the banking business slackened off, and in 1893 the great financial crisis occurred, of which mention has been made so frequently, and was accompanied by a very large withdrawal of deposits, chiefly by persons resident in the United Kingdon. In 1895 the amount on deposit was reduced to 86 millions, which included a considerable sum, estimated at about 54 millions, locked up in reconstructed banks. The crisis of 1893 involved the suspension of thirteen banks, of which six had their head-quarters in Victoria, two in New South Wales, three in Queensland, and two in London. Coincident with the increase in the money placed with the banks of issue was a very large increase in the deposits in the Savings or people's banks. In 1872, the sum on deposit was £3,810,000; in 1880 it had risen to £5,867,000; in 1885 to £10,199,000; and in 1891 to £15,477,000. From this point it leaped to £18,100,000 in 1893, but the increase was not entirely due to working class deposits, as it represented to some extent money withdrawn from the banks of issue at the time of the crisis. At the highest point in the period, namely, the year 1893, the total deposits represented £5 9s. 5d. per inhabitant; and although this figure has since been greatly exceeded, it was considered at the time, and justly so, a tribute to the earning capacity of the Australian working population and an index of its material condition.

During the twenty-two years from 1872 to 1893 the population of Australia was practically doubled. The greater portion of the increase was due to births, the excess of persons arriving over those departing, though important in some of the states, being not very considerable for Australia, taken as a whole. Several of the states, notably New South Wales and Queensland, maintained the policy of assisted immigration during the larger portion of this term, and in New South Wales alone nearly 50,000 persons were introduced in the ten years preceding 1886, and in Queensland the average number per annum brought to the country at the public expense from 1873 to 1892 was 9,746. Various important changes took place in the positions of the states in regard to population. During nearly the whole of this period Victoria had the premier position, but at the close of 1891 New South Wales took the lead and South Australia yielded the third place to Queensland in 1884. Western Australia was still far in the rear. Established before any of the other states except New South Wales and Tasmania, the population of this huge province did not in 1893 amount to more than 65,000—a condition of affairs due almost entirely to its isolation and the absence of mineral discoveries. Western Australia was on the eve of reaping great benefits from its gold discoveries, but the record of these and of the great influx of population which resulted therefrom belongs to the succeeding period.

It is impossible within the limits of this chapter to give a statement of the wages paid in all industries, or even in the leading industries of the various states. The illustrations given are therefore confined to the rates paid in certain well-known trades, and these it is thought will indicate sufficiently well the general condition of wages in the other trades. In considering these examples it should be remembered that wages in Australia do not always indicate the condition of the productive industries of the country; and especially is this the case when, as from 1882 to 1889, the Governments of the states are large borrowers and large employers of labour. Wages, generally speaking, rose rapidly after 1872, and reached a high level in 1874, thenceforward remaining stationary till 1883, when there was a distinct rise, and continuing fairly level at the advanced rates until 1889. From a labour point of view, these seven years may be considered amongst the best Australia has experienced. During this period carpenters received 11s. a day in Sydney, and from 10s. to 12s. in Melbourne; blacksmiths from 10s. to 14s. in Melbourne and 10s. in Sydney; bricklayers, 12s. 6d. in Sydney and from 10s. to 12s. in Melbourne; stonemasons, 11s. 6d. in Sydney and from 10s. to 12s. in Melbourne; plasterers, 12s. in Sydney, and about the same in Melbourne, and 11s. in Adelaide; painters, 11s. in Sydney, 10s. in Melbourne, and 9s. in Adelaide; boilermakers, up to 14s. in Melbourne; and navvies employed on public works, 8s. in New South Wales, 7s. in South Australia, and from 6s. to 7s. in Victoria. In 1890 wages made their first decided move downwards, and, compared with the previous year, there was a fall equivalent, on an average, to 1s. per day. Consequent on the financial crisis of 1893, wages again fell, and continued falling, until, so far as most trades were concerned, they touched their lowest point in 1895, although for some workers—notably navvies and common labourers—the period of acute depression lasted a year or two longer.

The following is a statement of the average daily wage paid in the four leading cities from 1872 to 1879:—

Trade.	Average daily wage paid in—			
	Melbourne.	Sydney.	Adelaide.	Brisbane.
	s. d.	s. d.	s. d.	s. d.
Carpenter	9 9	9 11	8 8	10 3
Bricklayer	10 0	10 10	9 0	10 4
Mason	10 9	10 7	9 2	9 0
Plasterer	10 0	10 11	9 10	10 0
Painter	9 0	9 3	9 0	9 10
Blacksmith	11 2	10 3	8 10	10 3
Boilermaker	11 0	9 6	9 0	10 6
Navvy or common labourer	6 3	7 1	6 9	6 0

Taking the wages as a whole, those paid in Sydney and Brisbane average about the same figure. In the building trades the wages paid in Sydney and Brisbane were superior to those in Melbourne; but in the iron trade, such as blacksmithing, boilermaking, and the like, the wages in Melbourne were higher than in any of the other cities. Throughout the whole of this period the wages paid in South Australia were distinctly lower than in the other states, except navvies' wages, which were very nearly equal to those paid in New South Wales.

From 1880 to 1891 the average wages in Melbourne, Sydney, and Brisbane were fairly uniform, but in Adelaide the ruling rates were some 10 per cent. below those of the neighbouring states. Navvies and others employed on public works in New South Wales received on an average about 8s. per day throughout the whole period of thirteen years extending from 1879 to 1891. Considering the cost of living, this is the highest wage ever paid in Australia for this description of labour. In Victoria and Queensland the rates touched 7s. 6d.; in South Australia, 7s. The following represent the average wages from 1880 to 1891:—

Trade.	Average daily wage paid in—			
	Melbourne.	Sydney.	Adelaide.	Brisbane.
	s. d.	s. d.	s. d.	s. d.
Carpenter	10 7	10 3	8 6	11 0
Bricklayer	10 9	11 4	9 0	11 0
Mason	10 10	10 10	9 2	9 10
Plasterer	10 9	11 3	10 6	10 0
Painter	9 0	9 10	8 10	10 0
Blacksmith	11 8	10 6	9 6	11 0
Boilermaker	11 10	9 10	9 6	11 0
Navvy or common labourer	6 9	8 0	6 6	6 0

From 1892 to 1896, which was a period of great disturbance, wages remained higher in South Australia than in any of the other states, the reduction from the average of the previous years in the case of this state not being very great; whereas in Victoria, in New South Wales, and in Queensland the reduction in some cases was as much as 25 per cent., and work was much more difficult to procure. The iron trades in Victoria, in spite of the general fall, maintained a strong position during this period, but the building trades generally reached a very low level. Carpenters in Melbourne received 7s. 5d., compared with 8s. 11d. in

New South Wales and 8s. 4d. in Queensland. Bricklayers received 7s. 6d. in Victoria, 9s. 8d. in New South Wales, 9s. in South Australia, and 9s. 3d. in Queensland; blacksmiths, however, were paid 10s. in Victoria, 8s. 6d. in New South Wales, and about the same in South Australia and Queensland. Navvies were paid at the rate of 6s. a day in all the states.

Trade	Average daily wage paid in—			
	Melbourne.	Sydney.	Adelaide.	Brisbane.
	s. d.	s. d.	s. d.	s. d.
Carpenter	7 5	8 11	8 6	8 4
Bricklayer	7 6	9 8	9 0	9 3
Mason	8 6	8 11	9 0	11 2
Plasterer	7 8	8 6	8 10	8 10
Painter	6 8	8 0	8 0	7 6
Blacksmith	10 0	8 6	8 6	8 4
Boilermaker	10 6	9 0	10 0	8 4
Navvy, or common labourer	6 0	6 0	6 0	6 0

The approach of the crisis of 1893 was heralded by many signs. Deposits were shifted from bank to bank; there was a run on the Savings Bank at Sydney, an institution guaranteed by the state; mortgagees required additional security from their debtors; bankruptcies became frequent; and some of the banks began to accumulate gold against the evil day. The building societies and financial institutions in receipt of deposits, or so many of them as were on an unsound footing, failed at an early period of the depression; so also did the weaker banks. There was distrust in the minds of the depositors, especially those whose holdings were small; and the banks, even long before the crisis arrived, were subjected to the strain of repaying a large proportion of their deposits as they fell due. The crisis, however, was by no means a sudden crash; even when the failures began to take place they were spread over some considerable period, the time between the failure of the first bank and that of the last being sixteen weeks.

The first noticeable effect of the crisis was a great scarcity of employment. Wages fell precipitously, as also did rents. There was almost a complete cessation of building, and large numbers of houses in the chief cities remained untenanted, the occupants apparently moving to lodgings, or more than one family living in a single house. Credit became greatly restricted, with the result that all descriptions of speculative enterprise came to an end; and by reason of the lowering of wages and decline in profits, the demand for most articles of domestic consumption declined also. This is seen in the fact that in 1894 there was a reduction in the imports into Australia of £4,300,000. The manufacturing industry was the first to feel the effects of the crisis, and there was a reduction in the average number of persons employed in the two leading states which may be set down at not less than 25,000. This reduction, however, was spread over four years. The closing of the factories was not general; the establishments were kept open, but there was a dismissal of workmen and a restriction of output. Lack of employment in the factories had an immediate effect on the coal-mining industry, the output of coal being about one-fourth less in 1893 than in the previous year.

The crisis was felt in the large cities more keenly than in the country districts, and in Melbourne more severely than in any other capital. The change of fortune proved disastrous to many families, previously, to all appearances, in opulent circumstances; but by all classes alike their reverses were borne with the greatest bravery. In its ultimate effects the crisis was by no means evil; on the contrary, its true meaning was not lost upon a business community that required the chastening of adversity to teach it a salutary lesson, and a few years after its first effects had passed away business was on a much sounder footing than had been the case for very many years.

The banks of issue showed large withdrawals of deposits, practically the whole of the money received from the United Kingdom being withdrawn as it became due; so that in 1898 the Australian banks had on deposit £17,175,000 less than in 1891, their highest point before the crisis occurred. There were also large withdrawals of local deposits, but the bulk of these found their way into the Post Office and other Government Savings Banks.

The compensations which followed the crisis were many, and the country would have recovered with surprising quickness from the blow which the credit of the community and of all its financial institutions had received, were it not for the adverse seasons which afflicted the great pastoral industry.

Prior to the crisis the extent of credit given to storekeepers and other tradespeople was on the whole much greater than sound experience warranted, and one of the first results was to put trade on a sound basis, and to abolish most of the abuses of the credit system. Attention was almost immediately attracted to productive pursuits, and the recovery made by the country as a whole, though slow at first, owing to the depression in the pastoral industry, was steady. Renewed attention was given to agriculture, especially in New South Wales, where, in 1901, 1,450,000 acres were devoted to the plough in excess of the area cultivated in 1893. In Victoria there was an increase of 870,000 acres, in Queensland 210,000 acres, and some slight extensions in the other States.

There was also a complete revival in the mining industry. The production of gold in New South Wales was almost doubled, and was largely increased in Victoria, Queensland, and Tasmania. In Western Australia the great gold discoveries which have placed that state at the head of Australian gold-mining, and amongst the leading gold producers of the world, were made subsequent to the crisis. Taking Australia as a whole, the output of gold in 1893 was £6,215,472; in 1902 it reached a total of £14,817,128, notwithstanding the unfavourable conditions affecting production in several states.

It was unfortunate that this time of financial distress should have been succeeded by a period of low prices for articles of local production, and that the great pastoral industry should have suffered from untoward seasons. The sheep depastured in Australia in 1893 numbered 99,800,000; in 1899 the total was reduced to 74,300,000; and in 1902 to 54,000,000; and it is more than probable that when the losses of the disastrous season of 1902–3 come to be counted up, the number will be found to have still further decreased.

During the years 1894 and 1895 prices reached their lowest level, but a slight recovery took place in the following two years, and this was succeeded by still further improvement, so that at the present time the average level is about equal to that of 1891.

In 1894 the total value of the imports into Australia was £41,930,720, equivalent to £12 6s. 8d. per inhabitant. These figures are far below those recorded in previous years. The imports in 1889, for example, were valued at £62,551,992, or at the rate of £20 13s. 7d. per inhabitant. It must be borne in mind, however, that extensive borrowing took place during 1889, and a considerable proportion of the imports was due to loan money brought to the country by the states, and to deposits in the banks, which were subsequently withdrawn during the financial crisis. From 1895 onward a material expansion took place in the trade of the states, and in 1900 the value of the exports was higher than at any previous period, thus showing that the country had completely recovered from the financial paralysis of 1893. It must be conceded that from every point of view sound industrial progress has been made during the last few years, and this is all the more gratifying when consideration has been given to the fact that, in some part or other of the continent, the main industries—those of sheep and cattle raising—were during the greater portion of the period seriously hampered by adverse weather conditions.

The progress of the manufacturing industries is dealt with at some length in another portion of this volume, and need not be further referred to here. It may be stated, however, that the ground lost during the financial crisis has been more than recovered, and the amount of employment afforded is now greater than ever before in the history of these states.

The movement in wages from 1896 to 1901 was distinctly upward. Carpenters, for example, were in 1896 paid 8s. per day in Sydney, while in 1900 their wages were 9s. 6d., in 1901, 10s., and in 1902, 9s. 6d. Though wages in Melbourne at these periods were lower than in Sydney, their upward movement has been even greater, for in 1896 carpenters' wages in Melbourne ranged between 6s. and 7s. per day, the greater number being employed at the lower figures, while in 1900 the accepted rate was 8s. 3d., in 1901, 10s., and in 1902, 9s. As regards other trades connected with building, there has also been a marked improvement, and the rates of 1902 approach very closely those paid in 1891—that is to say, before the changes accompanying the financial crisis began to be felt.

The building trades suffered more heavily than any others during the period of financial disaster, and their recovery was also more protracted. Over-speculation in business was in part responsible for the crisis; and even after its immediate effects had passed from sight, there was still great reluctance to embark capital in this form of investment, although a reasonable return seemed to be fairly assured. Building operations being therefore carried on only in cases of necessity, and when exceptional profits were looked for, the wages of the artisans employed were less affected by the return of better times than might otherwise have been expected. In other branches of industry there was a marked revival, and wages shared in the upward movement.

Federation undoubtedly is a strong force in the direction of increased production and larger employment of capital, and an expansion of industrial activity should follow in its train; but the pastoral industry, which is the key to the industrial condition of Australia, was seriously affected during 1902 by the adverse climatic conditions which prevailed over a great part of the continent. The year 1903 opened under most favourable conditions. Abundant rains have fallen, and a larger area is now under crop than at any previous period, while the harvest promises to be very bountiful, so that the improvement in the industrial conditions manifested since 1896, but interrupted during 1902, may confidently be expected to continue.

Recent Industrial Legislation.

The conditions of labour in Australia and New Zealand have, since the year 1894, been affected by certain new elements which have the promise of very powerfully influencing the industrial position in the near future, and in order to understand rightly the working of these elements it will be necessary to describe in rough outline the factory, shop, conciliation, and arbitration laws of these states.

Although the condition of workers in factories received attention in England as far back as the year 1802, and comprehensive legislation dates from 1844, it was not until 1873 that there was any Australian enactment on the subject. In the year named the Parliament of Victoria passed a statute, which, amongst other provisions, enacted that no woman or girl should work in a factory for more than eight hours a day. New Zealand followed immediately with an Act, which was practically a transcript of the Victorian measure.

The factory system did not, until recent years, play an important part in the industrial life of Australia; but there have been factories in all the principal towns for many years, and it is a world-wide experience that where there are factories working uncontrolled by legislation there will always be more or less disregard of cleanliness and sanitation. This was sufficiently demonstrated by the Victorian Royal Commission of 1882, which followed upon a vivid exposure of the evil conditions of local factories made by the *Age* newspaper. The Commission did most useful work, and from its report came the Factories and Shop Act of 1885. Under that enactment the number of persons technically required to form a legal factory was fixed at six, including apprentices, and provision was made for ensuring cleanliness, air space, sanitation, the requirements of decency, and for safeguarding the health of workers and their safety in life and limb. Inspectors were appointed, and under the operation of the law the old dilapidated workshops disappeared, and the well-built, well-lit and roomy factories, now found everywhere in Melbourne, took their place. The law remained practically unchanged until 1893, when the number of persons constituting a factory was reduced to four. This, however, was only a preliminary step to further and more radical changes. In 1896 the law was further expanded, and the term factory was extended to every place in which furniture was manufactured, to every place in which a Chinese was engaged in laundry work, and to all laundries in which four persons were employed, excepting laundries carried on by charitable institutions. Powers of prosecution were given to inspectors after a factory or work-room was found to be in an insanitary condition. The Chief Inspector of Factories was empowered to condemn any factory or workroom which was, in his opinion, dilapidated, unsafe, or unfit for use. It was also provided that no portion of a factory or workroom could be used as a sleeping-place unless such sleeping-place were separated from the factory by a substantial wooden partition extending from floor to ceiling. No child under 13 years of age was allowed to work in a factory, and no female whosoever and no boy under 16 years of age could be employed in a factory for more than ten hours in a day or after 9 o'clock at night. It had already been provided that such persons could not be employed for more than forty-eight hours a week. In furniture factories and laundries where a Chinese was working, it was provided that no person was to work before 7.30 o'clock in the morning or after 5 o'clock in the evening, or on Saturday after 2 o'clock or on Sunday at any time whatever. All persons in charge of boilers and steam engines were required to hold certificates of competence, and very special and extensive powers were given to the department administering the Act to enforce cleanliness, ventilation, and sanitation. These were the main provisions in regard to the work of the factories, but the Act of 1896 introduced most important provisions regarding wages, which will be referred to later on.

New South Wales was very slow in taking steps for the proper regulation of work in factories. Various bills had been prepared and one had been introduced into the Legislature, but no serious attempt was made to deal with the matter on behalf of the Government, and, apart from the Government, legislation would have been impossible. In the year 1890 the Census and Industrial Returns Act was passed, under which the Government Statistician was empowered to report on the condition of the factories of the state, and pursuant to the authority contained in the Act, the officers of the Statistical Department made an exhaustive examination of factories and workshops in the large centres of population, and a series of reports was drawn up indicating the condition of the workers. The chief abuse found to exist was the almost uniform absence of due provision for sanitation and for the preservation of decency. Though sweating was not found to exist to any large extent, home workers were found to be grossly underpaid, and in many respects a strong case was made out for the necessity of passing a proper Factories Act on the lines of legislation in force in other states. Parliamentary action, however, was not taken until the year 1896, when the Factories and Shops Act was passed on the lines of the Victorian Act of 1885. Good work has been accomplished under the Act, but the powers conferred on the administration are limited compared with those found in the existing Acts of other states.

In South Australia nothing of importance was accomplished in the way of regulating employment in factories until the year 1894. The Act of 1894 did not, however, go far enough to cope successfully with the evils that had arisen, and in 1900 the law was changed, and an Act based on the Victorian model was passed, but going even farther than the original, for a factory was declared to be any workroom where anyone was working in an owner's employ.

In Queensland work in factories remained unregulated until 1896, when tentative legislation on the lines of the New South Wales Act was passed ; this legislation proved insufficient, and gave way in 1900 to a carefully framed and comprehensive Factories and Shops Act as far-reaching in its provisions as that of any other state.

In Tasmania there is as yet no legislation regarding employment in factories, but there is a law for the protection of persons using machinery.

In Western Australia the factory legislation is much like that of the more advanced eastern states, the most recent legislation on the subject having been passed in 1903.

Although New Zealand cannot claim to be the pioneer of Australian legislation in regard to factories, this being an honour which is due to Victoria, it may be claimed on behalf of that colony that Victorian legislation was closely followed from the outset. In 1873 the Victorian Act was adopted by New Zealand under the title of "The Workshops Act." Like its prototype this Act made but a small advance upon the road to factory legislation. In 1890 a Royal Commission was appointed to inquire into the state of labour and industry, and consequent upon the report of this Commission the Government of the day introduced and passed a Factories and Shops Act somewhat on the lines of the Victorian Act of 1885; but the law was almost immediately amended in 1891 and again in 1894, when one of the most radical measures, dealing with employment in factories, was passed. In 1901 an act was passed superseding all previous enactments, and this remains law in the colony to the present time. New Zealand has been divided into factory districts under the charge of a Chief Inspector and 150 local inspectors. As a "factory" or "workroom" includes any place in which two or more persons are engaged in working for hire or reward in any handicraft, there are few operatives who do not come within the scope of the Act. Children under 14 years of age are not allowed to be employed, and the hours of labour, holidays, etc., of women and youths under 16 are strictly regulated. Good ventilation, sanitary accommodation, and general cleanliness of buildings are insisted upon; machinery has to be properly guarded and fire-escapes provided, while dangerous occupations are specially classified. In order to assist the system of free general education which prevails in the colony, young persons are not allowed to work in factories till they have passed the fourth standard of the state schools, or an equivalent examination. To prevent the introduction of the great evil of "sweating," articles made or partly made in private dwellings or unregistered workshops, have to be labelled when offered for sale, in order that goods so manufactured (likely enough in unsanitary premises), may not be placed in the market for competition with work done in properly inspected factories. Any person removing such labels is liable to a heavy fine. The factory inspectors also exercise supervision over the sleeping accommodation provided for shearers in country districts. A female inspector of factories gives her assistance in the duties of the department, travelling from place to place, and particularly inquiring into the working conditions of the operative women and girls. There are other provisions directed towards preventing the employment of children of tender years, and punishing parents who endeavour to evade the Act in regard to their own children. This Factories Act is one of a long series of other acts passed by the New Zealand Parliament and termed the "Labour Laws." The New Zealand Year Book gives a list of thirty-five acts which come under this category.

Besides the regulations governing employment in factories, there is, in the majority of the states, the corollary of this legislation, viz., laws dealing with the hours during which shops may remain open for the sale of goods. As in the matter of factory legislation, so in regard to the compulsory closing of shops the credit of initiation belongs to Victoria. The Act of 1885 to which allusion has already been made, declared that the hours for closing shops in towns generally should be 7 o'clock in the evening on five days a week, and 10 o'clock on Saturday nights, shops dealing with certain classes of food and perishable products being exempted from the operation of the law. In order that there should be an intelligent application of the law, the various municipal councils were authorised to pass by-laws allowing other classes of shops than those enumerated in the Act to remain open after the hours named, and at the same time the councils were empowered, if they thought fit, to close the shops earlier than 7 o'clock. Penalties for breach of the law were also left to the determination of the councils. The beneficent intentions of the framers of the law failed owing to the perfunctory way in which the municipal councils carried out their duties in regard to early closing, and a very unsatisfactory condition of things prevailed until the amending Factories and Shops Act was passed in 1896, to which allusion will be made later on.

Meanwhile New Zealand had taken the matter in hand, and the Shops and Shop Assistants Act of 1894 was passed. The main provisions of this Act, as amended in 1895, 1896, and 1901, are as follows :—

All shops in towns and boroughs are to be closed for one afternoon in each week, but a few shops, such as those of fishmongers, fruiterers, eating-house keepers, are exempted on account of their convenience to the general public, the assistants in such establishments and in the bars of hotels and in country stores must, however, have a half-holiday allowed them in each week. Very small shops carried on by Europeans without paid assistants are also exempt from closing on a general half-holiday, but these shops must be closed on one afternoon in each week. The hours of work for women and young persons are defined. Sitting accommodation must be provided in all shops, and the necessary time for meals shall be given to all workers and sufficient sanitary accomodation provided. The Act goes still further, and enumerates the working hours, holidays, and such like of clerks employed in banks and mercantile and business offices.

The Victorian Act of 1896 passed to remedy the defects found in the Act of 1885 did not go so far as the New Zealand Act—the initiative of closing was left with the shopkeepers, and considerable power still remained in the hands of the municipal councils. The Victorian Act, however, was an early-closing law, which the New Zealand Act was not. In 1900 the Parliament of Victoria passed an Amending Act, restricting the hours of all males employed in shops to fifty-two, carters, porters, and night watchmen alone being excepted. The law does not, however, apply to the whole state.

The Early Closing Act of New South Wales was passed in December, 1899. This Act provides for the compulsory closing of shops at 6 o'clock on four days in the week, 1 p.m. on one day, and 10 p.m. on one day. The Act, however, does not specify when shops may be opened. It applies to the Metropolitan district and Newcastle; country shop districts, which include all municipalities in the state other than Sydney and Newcastle, may be brought under the Act by proclamation, and this has been done.

In the year 1900 early-closing laws were enacted in South Australia and in Queensland; in both cases the Acts were close copies of that of

New South Wales. In 1897, an Early Closing Act was passed in Western Australia; Tasmania, therefore, is the only state in which there is no law regulating shop hours.

The disastrous strikes which have been spoken of as occurring between 1886 and 1895 were symptoms of an industrial unrest spreading over the whole of the Eastern States and New Zealand. The expenditure of public money on a lavish scale had attracted to these states a larger number of unskilled workers than work could be provided for in ordinary seasons, and even many of the skilled trades were largely overmanned. Under the existing conditions of industrial remuneration a fall in wages was inevitable. The trades unions, however, made a brave stand against any reduction in the wages of their own members, and there can be no question but that up to the year 1888, and in some trades for a year or two longer, their efforts were in the main successful. But the number of workers enrolled in the unions was small compared with the total number of persons following gainful pursuits. The trades unions, too, had an advantage from the fact that the trades which they controlled were skilled trades which required long apprenticeship to learn, and which in the case of a strike could not be swamped by unskilled or partially skilled labour. About the year 1888 the trade unions and others who sympathised with the labour movement, and persons desirous of avoiding further labour conflicts, began to consider very earnestly whether some means might not be taken to regulate the relations of employers and the employed, and so avoid the wasting effects which inevitably follow in the train of strikes. Several distinct methods of arriving at the same desirable end presented themselves, namely :—

Conciliation, in which the parties to a dispute were brought together without legal compulsion.

Compulsory arbitration.

The regulation of wages by a board representing the employers and employed, with an impartial chairman ;

and each of these systems has been tried in these states since 1888.

The question of conciliation and voluntary arbitration has been before the Australian public for some considerable time. In 1882 Mr. (now Sir George) Dibbs introduced into Parliament a bill for the establishment of a council composed of members of the New South Wales Employers' Union and the Trades and Labour Council, in which conciliation was provided for on the lines of the Conseils de Prud'hommes existing in France ; but there was so little parliamentary response that the bill was shelved. In 1887 a scheme based upon English precedent was promulgated by a joint committee of the Victorian Trades Hall Council and the Employers' Union for the establishment of a Board of Conciliation. A similar scheme was drawn up by the joint committee of the New South Wales Employers' Union and the Trades and Labour Council, but was rejected. In the building trade of New South Wales there was for some years a representative Board of Conciliation without any provision for arbitration, and this board is reported to have done very excellent work. In 1887 Mr. J. H. Carruthers introduced a Trades Conciliation Bill, in which the machinery provided was purely voluntary. The measure did not, however, get beyond the stages of a bill. Other schemes of conciliation were proposed, notably one drawn up by the Honorable C. J. Langridge, of Victoria. In South Australia a bill to encourage the formation of industrial unions and associations, and to facilitate the settlement of industrial disputes, was introduced into Parliament by the Hon. C. C. Kingston in December, 1890. This measure is the parent of all the conciliation and arbitration laws now in operation in Australia; the bill met with strong opposition, and it was not until late in 1894 that it was finally passed into law, having been twice rejected by the Legislative Council.

Meanwhile the matter of conciliation had been before the New South Wales Parliament. A commission had been appointed to inquire into th question of strikes, and a report was drawn up and a bill based on the recommendations was drafted and introduced by Sir Henry Parkes on the 5th of August, 1891, but the Government resigned before the bill could become law.

About the same time a measure was before the Victorian Parliament; t consisted of twenty-three clauses, and did not go much farther than to permit the establishment of councils of conciliation under license from the Crown, as no award could be taken into, or enforced by, any court of law. This measure became law at the commencement of 1892, and has, therefore, the distinction of being the first legislative enactment of its kind on the statute books of Australia. The Act, however, was not followed by any consequences, good or bad, being entirely ignored by all parties. When Sir George Dibbs succeeded Sir Henry Parkes as Premier of New South Wales he took up the question of trades disputes, and on 31st March, 1892, his Trades Disputes Conciliation and Arbitration Act was assented to. This Act was in force for four years, when it lapsed, very little use being made of it in spite of the strenuous exertions of the officials in charge of its administration.

In New Zealand a Conciliation and Arbitration Bill was introduced in 1892 by the Minister for Labour, the Hon. W. P. Reeves, and was twice rejected by the Legislative Council; it was, however, presented a third time, and became law on the 31st August, 1894. The following is a short epitome of its leading provisions:—

The object of the Act, as declared in the preamble, is to encourage the formation of industrial unions and associations, and to facilitate the settlement of industrial disputes by conciliation and arbitration.

A society of not less than seven persons, associated for the purpose of protecting or furthering the interests of employers or workmen, may be registered as an industrial union by complying with certain provisions of the Act. Full and detailed information as to constitution, rules, names of officers and members, etc., must be sent to the Registrar, who will issue a certificate of registry and incorporation. The effect of registration will be to render the industrial or trade union so registered subject to the jurisdiction of the Board and Court appointed under the Act.

The parties to industrial agreement may be—(1) trade unions, (2) industrial unions, (3) industrial associations, (4) employers. Every industrial agreement shall bo for a specified time not exceeding three years, and is to be filed in the Supreme Court office within thirty days of making. It is binding on both sides, and if any association or person thus bound fails in carrying it out there is a penalty not exceeding the amount fixed by the agreement, or, if no amount is fixed, not exceeding £500.

"Industrial districts" are to be constituted and gazetted, and for every such industrial district a Board of Conciliation and a Clerk of Awards is to be appointed. The Act defines the powers of the Court and Board and the duties of the Clerk, and provides that, when a dispute is referred to Board or Court, no strike or lock-out may take place until the decision is given. A Board of Conciliation is to consist of not more than six or less than four persons, chosen by the industrial unions of employers and of workmen in the respective districts, and a chairman is to be elected outside the members of the Board. Should a Conciliation Board fail to effect settlement, the dispute may be referred to the Court of Arbitration. There is to be one Court of Arbitration for the whole colony, consisting of three members, one appointed on the recommendation of the council of associations of employers, one on the recommendation of the council of associations of workmen, and the third a judge of the Supreme Court; every member to hold office for three years, and to be eligible for re-appointment. If any party to a proceeding before the Court fail to appear without cause the Court may proceed *ex parte*. The award is to be made within one month, and may include costs and expenses; but no costs will be allowed for agents, counsel, or solicitors appearing for any party, and it shall be framed in such manner as to express the decision of the Court whilst avoiding technicalities. The award may be enforced in the same manner as a judgment of the Supreme Court. The amount for which an award may be enforced against an association is limited to £500.

The fourth part of the Act provides that the Railway Commissioners and the Amalgamated Society of Railway Servants may be respectively registered, and may refer any industrial dispute between them to the Court of Arbitration, but Boards of Conciliation are to have no jurisdiction in these cases.

So novel a piece of legislation could not be expected to work quite smoothly in the first instance; Amending Acts elucidating the provisions of the original measure were therefore passed in 1895, 1896, and 1898, and the law was consolidated and further amended by the Acts of 1900 and 1901. The amendments of the original Act extend the scope of the jurisdiction of the tribunals of arbitration, and carry the principle of compulsion further than contemplated by the Act of 1894. Non-unionist workmen are brought within the jurisdiction of the Arbitration Court in certain circumstances, as well as clerical employees. Conciliation Boards are made courts of first instance; awards are made permanent in default of a further dispute, and, subject to certain safeguards, awards may have force throughout New Zealand.

It has been mentioned that Mr. C. C. Kingston, when Premier of South Australia, introduced his bill to facilitate the settlement of industrial disputes in December, 1890. Various causes tended to delay the passing of the measure, so that it was not until December, 1894, that it passed both Houses of Parliament and received the Royal assent. In point of time the South Australian measure was introduced before that of New Zealand, but it became law a few months later. The South Australian Act has not been availed of to any large extent, for, unlike the New Zealand law, it allows only registered bodies to appear before the Arbitration Court, and as the trade unions of the state have not registered under the Act, they have consequently remained outside its jurisdiction. South Australia, however, is a state in which trade disputes have not been by any means very virulent, and it is probable that the failure of industrial bodies to invoke the aid of the Arbitration Court has been due to the mildness of the disease and not to the inefficacy of the remedy.

The movement to provide means of settling disputes was felt also in Queensland, where a bill, on the lines of the Conseils de Prud'-hommes, was introduced by Sir S. W. Griffith. It was not, however, a measure dealing with industrial disputes between employers and bodies of employees.

Western Australia passed an Arbitration Act in 1900. The law, however, was superseded in February, 1902, by one approximating very closely to the latest New Zealand law, and this is now in active operation.

With the example of New Zealand and South Australia before it, the New South Wales Parliament at the instigation of Mr. B. R. Wise, the Attorney-General, undertook the passing of an Arbitration Act. The first bill was introduced in the middle of 1901, but was rejected by the Council. The bill was afterwards re-introduced, and became law on the 10th December, 1901, an amendment by the Council limiting the law until 1908 being assented to by the Assembly. The New South Wales Act in some respects bears a close resemblance to that of New Zealand, but in other ways there are radical differences. The matter of conciliation is laid great stress upon by the framers of the New Zealand law. As it has been seen that conciliation has been of doubtful success in New Zealand, the New South Wales Act does not attempt to introduce the principle. The Act provides for the registration of industrial unions of employers and of employees. Any employer or association of employers employing fifty or more hands may be registered as an industrial union, but employees must first register as trade unions, as only trade unions can become industrial unions under the Act. Any dispute in regard to industrial matters, whether between industrial unions, or between an employer and an industrial union of employees, or between an employer and a trade union, may be referred to the Court of Arbitration. It is provided, however, that no person or body of persons other than an industrial union (or in certain cases the Registrar) may refer such dispute to the Court, so that the Act has had the effect of fostering the organisation both of employers and employees, and the formation and registration of industrial unions. The provision for restricting the right of approaching the Court to industrial unions is a great departure from the New Zealand law, and in conjunction with the clause making the passing of a resolution by the members of a union a condition precedent to the referring of a dispute, was intended to protect the Court from being burdened with trivial cases. Before seeking the intervention of the Court, employers must be registered; but they may be cited before the Court as defendants although unregistered. The Court consists of a Supreme Court Judge appointed by the Governor, and two members elected respectively by the industrial unions of employers and the industrial unions of employees. The prohibition of strikes and lockouts during the reference of any dispute to arbitration is similar to the New Zealand law. The persons who strike or lockout after a dispute has arisen are, in certain circumstances, guilty of a misdemeanour. The Arbitration Court specifically grants the power of fixing the minimum wage, and has also statutory power to give preference to unionists over non-unionists, other things being equal, when men of both classes offer their labour at the same time. The distinctive feature of the New South Wales Act is the provision regarding the common rule. In New Zealand the process of arbitration is for the court to proceed to district after district, citing all the employers in the industry under review before it. Its decisions in a district are confined only to that district. The decisions therefore bind certain specific employers, whereas in New South Wales the decision of the court can be made to apply to all industries of the state, and the court has power to declare that any custom, regulation, agreement, condition, or dealing in relation to any industrial matter shall be a common rule of the industry.

Another important provision not contained in the New Zealand law is that any industrial dispute may be referred to the court by the Registrar, where the parties—or some or one of them—are not industrial unions.

The description of the various Acts in force in reference to conciliation and arbitration must be taken as the merest outline. The student of this important question who is desirous of getting a clear knowledge of the working of the Acts must consult the original authorities on the subject. The descriptions here given are only intended to illustrate a phase of the industrial position which the student of Australian affairs must not lose sight of.

The aim of the Conciliation and Arbitration Acts is primarily the prevention of strikes and lockouts. In Victoria the amelioration of the industrial situation was approached in an entirely different manner. It was thought that as the Factories Act provided for the protection of the worker, so far as sanitation, working hours, and the surroundings of the workshop were concerned, if his remuneration was determined by an agreement between the employer and the employed, the occasion for strikes would be avoided. In the Factories Act of 1896, to which allusion has already been made, a bold attempt was made to deal with the difficult problem of industrial remuneration. In addition to the provisions regarding workshops, the Factories and Shops Act of 1896 enacted that special boards might be appointed to fix wages and piecework rates for persons employed either inside or outside factories in making clothing or wearing apparel, or furniture, or in breadmaking or baking, or in the business of a butcher or a seller of meat, or maker of small goods. The appointment of special boards was also authorised for any process, trade or business usually or frequently carried on in a factory or workroom, provided a resolution has been passed by either House declaring it to be expedient that such a board should be appointed. Special boards, it was provided, might consist of not less than four and not more than ten members with a chairman, the period of office being two years. Half the members were to be elected by the employers as representing their interests, and half by employees. The right of appointment of a chairman of a board rested with the board itself, the chairman not being an elective member, but in the absence of appointment by the board, the Governor-in-Council has power to appoint the chairman. An exception to the principle of election was made in the case of the furniture trade, where the whole of the members of the board were appointed by the Governor, as it was thought undesirable that the election should be made by the trade itself, as the great majority of the workmen in the furniture trade were Chinese. The boards were given power to fix either wage rates or piece work, or both, as well as the hours for which the wage rate was determined and the rate of pay for overtime; to the boards also was given power to determine the proportion of apprentices or improvers to skilled workmen employed in any process, trade or business, as well as the wage to be paid to them. When a board had determined the minimum wage, manufacturers were allowed to fix the piece-work rates, provided that these rates were based on such minimum wage, and as a check on imposition, it was provided that the Chief Inspector of Factories should have the right to challenge any piece-work rate and submit the matter to the board. Provision was also made for the granting of licenses to aged and infirm workers, who were permitted to work at less than the minimum wage fixed by the board. Agreements in contravention of the decision of the board were held to be null and void, and an employee might sue for his wages as determined by the Wages Board, any agreement to the contrary with his employer notwithstanding. It was further enacted that any person employed in a factory should receive at least 2s. 6d. a week, and that no premium or bonus was to be charged directly or indirectly for engaging or employing any female apprentice or improver in making articles of clothing or wearing apparel.

The Act was not a permanent enactment; it was first passed in 1896, re-enacted with some amendments in 1900, and continued until September, 1902, when it lapsed on the dissolution of Parliament. At the time of the expiry of the Act there were thirty eight special boards in existence. When Parliament met after the elections, amongst the first bills introduced was one to revive and continue in force the Factories and Shop Acts and all regulations thereunder, as well as the determinations of the special boards. The lapsed laws, with some modification in regard to special boards, were continued until the 31st October, 1903, and before that date an Act was passed continuing the then existing law until otherwise provided by Parliament. The Act continued the old laws but modified them in certain important particulars, and constituted a court of appeal to hear appeals against determinations of special boards, and for dealing with references in regard thereto by the Minister. The principles of future determination as to wages and rates were laid down as follows :—

(*a*) The board shall ascertain as a question of fact the average prices or rates of payment (whether piece-work prices or rates or wages prices or rates) paid by reputable employers to employees of average capacity;

(*b*) The lowest prices or rates as fixed by any determination shall in no case exceed the average prices or rates as so ascertained;

(*c*) Where the average prices or rates so ascertained are not in the opinion of the special board sufficient to afford a reasonable limit for the determination of the lowest prices or rates which should be paid, they may so report to the Minister, who shall in such case refer the determination for the consideration of the Court, and the Court in that event may fix the lowest prices or rates to be paid without having regard to the provisions of subsection (b);

(*d*) Where it appears to be just and expedient, special wages prices or rates may be fixed for aged, infirm, or slow workers.

The effect of the provisions of the Factories and Shops Act in regard to the industrial conditions of Victoria has been much discussed. For detailed information on the subject the enquirer should consult the Reports of the Chief Inspector of Factories, and the Report of the Royal Commission on the operation of the factories and shops law of Victoria, dated February 19th, 1903. The apparent results so far as concerns the wages of operatives are considerable. Taking the operatives in trades in respect of which determination as to wages were arrived at, there has been a general increase in the pay of male labour, equivalent to 19 per cent., and of female labour to 17 per cent.—in the one case the increase represents about 5s. 9d. per week, and in the other 2s. 3d. If the industries working under special boards in Victoria be compared with like industries in New South Wales, it will be found that the results work out as follows:—

For all workers—Average wages.

	Males. £ s. d.	Females. s. d.
Victoria	1 15 9	15 11
New South Wales	1 14 6	13 0
Difference in favour of Victoria...	1 3	2 11

For workers 19 years and upwards.

	Males. £ s. d.	Females. s. d.
Victoria	2 3 6	19 2
New South Wales	2 0 6	16 10
Difference in favour of Victoria...	3 0	2 4

The averages for New South Wales are those obtaining before the Industrial Arbitration Act came into force, and both for males and females are uniformly below those for Victoria; this was not the case prior to the establishment of the Special Boards, for the average earnings of all male workers in Victoria were only 30s. per week compared with 34s. 6d. in New South Wales, the remuneration of female workers averaging about the same in both states.

It will be understood that the foregoing comparison deals with only a portion of the workers in these states. If all workers be included, the average wage for males in Victoria is £1 14s. 9d., and in New South Wales £1 15s. 11d.; and for females 14s. 2d. in Victoria, and 13s. 3d. in New South Wales.

A comparison of the average wages paid to workers of various ages (*a*) in trades regulated by Special Boards in Victoria, and (*b*) other factory workers, is interesting reading.

Age of Worker.	Trades under Special Boards.		Other Trades.	
	Males.	Females.	Males.	Females.
Years.	£ s. d.	£ s. d.	£ s. d.	£ s. d.
13	0 6 1	0 4 0	0 6 6	0 3 7
14	0 6 6	0 4 4	0 7 6	0 4 3
15	0 7 7	0 5 1	0 8 9	0 4 5
16	0 9 0	0 6 5	0 10 8	0 5 6
17	0 11 8	0 8 4	0 13 0	0 7 1
18	0 14 8	0 11 4	0 16 4	0 8 10
19	0 18 7	0 12 8	0 19 4	0 10 7
20	1 2 11	0 15 4	1 2 8	0 11 10
21 and upwards	2 4 3	0 19 9	2 1 11	0 17 5
All ages...........	1 15 9	0 15 11	1 11 1	0 12 8

It will be seen that the wages determined for male workers by the special boards are uniformly lower for boys and youths than in the non-regulated factories; but for adult workers the wages are higher, and for females the regulated wages are in every case higher. For all male workers the average in regulated trades is £1 15s. 9d., compared with £1 11s. 1d. in other trades, showing a difference of 4s. 8d. per week; this is higher than an inspection of the figures in the foregoing table would lead one to expect, and is due to the fact that in the regulated trades three-fourths of all workers are adults, whereas in other trades the proportion is not more than three-fifths.

The amendments in the minimum wage law of Victoria made by the Act of October, 1903, will probably modify in some degree the tendency of Special Boards to raise wages, but the law even as it now stands embodies so much that is novel and important in industrial legislation that its working is being watched with very keen interest both in Australia and in Europe and America. Nor is the interest lessened by the fact that while in Victoria and South Australia the principle of the legal establishment of the minimum wage is in operation, side by side as it were, in New South Wales, Western Australia, and New Zealand the essentially different system of conciliation and compulsory arbitration is at work to prevent the occurrence of strikes and lockouts, and regulate the earnings of all classes of labour.

The admirable publications of the New Zealand Statistical Department show the wages in various trades at intervals since 1891, and from these the following summary has been deduced, which gives the average weekly earnings of employees in the various factories and works of the colony at the last three census periods:—

Year.	Weekly Earnings.	
	Males.	Females.
	s. d.	s. d.
1891	29 0	13 4
1896	29 9	11 6
1901	31 5	12 5

It will be seen that the average earnings both for males and females is less in New Zealand than in New South Wales and Victoria. In the absence of the ages of the workers in New Zealand, however, it is impossible to go beyond the statement of the average earnings. As the table shows, the average rate for males has increased by 2s. 5d. per week, which is equivalent to 8½ per cent.; the earnings of females, on the other hand, are slightly lower than they were in 1891.

As already explained, the Arbitration Act of New South Wales has not been in force sufficiently long to admit of statistics being obtained as to its probable effect upon wages; but the average weekly rates of pay for males and females engaged in the various manufactories and works of the state in the year immediately preceding the passage of the Act were as shown below:—

Age.	Average Weekly Wage.	
	Males.	Females.
	s. d.	s. d.
13 years	6 9	4 4
14 ,,	7 5	4 1
15 ,,	8 2	4 9
16 ,,	9 10	6 7
17 ,,	12 7	8 2
18 ,,	16 4	10 5
19 ,, and upwards	42 0	17 2
All ages	35 11	13 3

VITAL STATISTICS.

BIRTHS.

THE total number of births in each state, and the rate per thousand of the population during the year 1902 are shown in the following table:—

State.	Births.			Birth-rate.
	Males.	Females.	Total.	
New South Wales	19,322	18,513	37,835	27·15
Victoria	15,583	14,878	30,461	25·23
Queensland	7,279	6,937	14,216	27·73
South Australia	4,587	4,360	8,947	24·49
Western Australia	3,241	2,991	6,232	30·40
Tasmania	2,604	2,481	5,085	28·94
Commonwealth	52,616	50,160	102,776	26·63
New Zealand	10,653	10,002	20,655	25·89
Australasia	63,269	60,162	123,431	26·50

The variation in the birth-rates disclosed in these figures is not very considerable, and may be set down as due for the most part to the larger proportion of married women found in some states than in others. Taking the general average for the last two years (26·72), the birth-rate of Australia will be found lower than that of most European countries, and very much below the former experience of these states, as shown by the following statement, which gives the number of births in each state and in the whole of Australasia, in quinquennial periods from 1861 to 1900, and for the years 1901–2.

State.	1861–65.	1866–70.	1871–75.	1876–80.	1881–85.	1886–90.	1891–95.	1896–1900.	1901–2.
New South Wales	79,958	92,643	106,543	127,572	158,965	188,300	197,566	183,582	75,710
Victoria..........	123,353	131,062	136,368	132,347	140,258	172,307	180,852	155,437	61,469
Queensland	11,761	22,622	29,279	37,535	48,979	70,150	72,863	70,963	28,519
South Australia ..	30,472	35,067	36,398	46,310	56,618	58,200	53,093	47,179	18,058
Western Australia	3,352	3,724	4,033	4,611	5,446	7,696	10,242	22,399	11,950
Tasmania	15,454	14,679	15,313	17,165	21,425	23,710	24,794	23,494	10,015
Commonwealth	264,350	299,787	327,929	365,540	431,691	515,363	539,410	502,964	205,721
New Zealand	26,611	46,770	59,891	88,205	96,482	94,071	91,410	94,685	41,146
Australasia ..	290,961	346,557	387,820	453,745	528,173	609,434	630,820	597,649	246,867

The average birth-rates per thousand of population for each state during the same periods were as follow :—

State.	1861–65.	1866–70.	1871–75.	1876–80.	1881–85.	1886–90.	1891–95.	1896–1900.	1901–2.
New South Wales	42·71	40·70	39·05	38·53	37·65	36·36	32·93	27·98	27·37
Victoria	43·30	39·27	35·69	31·43	30·76	32·72	30·98	26·22	25·50
Queensland	43·07	43·91	40·81	36·72	36·37	38·81	35·15	30·40	28·04
South Australia ..	44·14	40·60	37·24	38·28	38·52	34·48	31·54	26·59	24·79
Western Australia	39·07	33·86	31·30	32·97	34·57	36·88	30·77	28·73	30·45
Tasmania	33·80	29·65	29·72	31·54	35·02	34·59	32·84	28·28	28·67
Commonwealth	42·29	39·46	36·85	35·09	34·92	35 02	32·32	27·62	26·85
New Zealand	38·22	42·28	40·02	41·32	36·50	31·22	27·66	25·74	26·09
Australasia ..	41·92	39·84	37·34	36·38	35·21	34·43	31·55	27·31	26·72

It is a matter of common knowledge that for some years past the birth-rate in Australasia has been declining, and so important is the subject—not only as regards the growth of the population, but also as affecting general progress—that in 1899 the author made a special investigation into the question of childbirth in Australia, but more particularly with reference to New South Wales. The conclusions arrived at with respect to that state, however, may be held to obtain for all the others, seeing that the conditions of living do not differ materially in any of them. During the course of the investigation it was found, first, that for all women the proportion of fecund marriages was decreasing ; second, that amongst fecund women the birth-rate was much reduced as compared with what it was twenty years ago, and third, that Australian-born women did not bear so many children as the European women who had emigrated to these states. A further and more exhaustive investigation made in 1902 amply bears out the first and second conclusions, but the inferior fecundity amongst Australian women is disproved, and more extended observation supports the opposite view. It was also found that the decline had been persistent and regular since 1881, and this restriction of births in a young country like Australia, where immigration is discouraged, is a matter which must have far-reaching results, although its economic effects are only beginning to be seen, and should claim the serious consideration of all thoughtful people. It would have been interesting to have compared the number of births to married women of specified ages at regular intervals from the date when the birth-rate first showed marked decline. Unfortunately, the information is not available for the different states, but the following figures, relating to New South Wales, possess strong interest. These show the number of legitimate births and the birth-rate per cent. among married women of various ages at each of the four decennial periods 1871, 1881, 1891, and 1901.

Age groups of married women.	Legitimate births.				Birth-rate per 100 married women.			
	1871.	1881.	1891.	1901.	1871.	1881.	1891.	1901.
15 and under 20	741	1,099	1,377	1,448	50·10	51·60	47·71	56·28
20 „ 25	4,280	6,853	8,344	7,806	44·15	45·79	41·63	39·70
25 „ 30	5,918	7,558	11,238	9,742	40·75	40·52	35·87	29·87
30 „ 35	4,340	5,946	8,622	7,848	33·67	33·86	29·22	22·68
35 „ 40	3,019	4,410	5,336	5,711	27·04	27·36	23·68	17·25
40 „ 45	1,027	1,645	2,184	2,369	13·41	12·89	11·84	8·81
45 and over	123	200	225	244	·71	·78	·55	·48

The rates in 1871 and 1881 were practically the same, but at all ages there was a large decline between 1881 and 1891, and again between 1891 and 1901. The apparent increase from 1891 to 1901 among women aged 15 and under 20 is due to the increased number of ante-nuptial conceptions in 1901 compared with 1891.

Although like information cannot be given for the other states, the births compared with the total married women of child-bearing ages have been ascertained for some of the states for the periods 1881, 1891, and 1901, and were as follows :—

State.	1881.	1891.	1901.
New South Wales	33·63	28·87	23·53
Victoria	29·84	29·77	22·86
Queensland	31·62	32·77	25·40
New Zealand	31·22	27·57	24·61

Particulars relating to illegitimate births will be found in the chapter headed "Social Condition."

Deaths.

The following table shows the total number of deaths and the rate per thousand of the population during the year 1902 :—

State.	Deaths.			Death-rate.		
	Males.	Females.	Total.	Males.	Females.	Total.
New South Wales	9,535	7,111	16,646	13·04	10·74	11·94
Victoria	9,152	7,025	16,177	15·13	11·66	13·40
Queensland	3,924	2,280	6,204	13·77	10·01	12·10
South Australia	2,389	1,925	4,314	12·88	10·70	11·81
Western Australia	1,832	991	2,823	14·69	12·34	13·77
Tasmania	1,044	870	1,914	11·45	10·30	10·90
Commonwealth	27,876	20,202	48,078	13·78	11·00	12·46
New Zealand	4,890	3,485	8,375	11·64	9·23	10·50
Australasia	32,766	23,687	56,453	13·41	10·70	12·12

The death-rate of Australia is much below that of any of the European states, and is steadily declining. Every year sees an advance in the sanitary condition of the people in the large centres of population, and to this cause may be ascribed the greater part of the improvement in the death-rate shown in the following tables, but there are other causes. The decline in the birth-rate elsewhere alluded to has an immediate effect on the death-rates. In ordinary years about 30 per cent. of the deaths are of children under one year, and the decline in the birth-rate from 35 to 27 per thousand, which has happened during the last twelve years, means a reduction of 1 per thousand in the death-rate.

Comparing the death-rate of males and females separately, Tasmania shows the lowest rates amongst males, and New Zealand amongst females. New Zealand shows the lowest general rate, followed by Tasmania.

The number of deaths in each state and in the whole of Australasia, in quinquennial periods from 1861 to 1900, and during the years 1901–2, is shown in the following table :—

State.	1861–65.	1866–70.	1871–75.	1876–80.	1881–85.	1886–90.	1891–95.	1896–1900.	1901–2.
New South Wales..	36,466	31,561	40,909	53,256	66,103	71,457	76,802	77,783	32,667
Victoria	55,136	49,452	59,759	62,811	66,811	84,648	82,056	81,328	32,081
Queensland	9,312	5,751	12,869	17,284	25,731	28,040	26,581	29,202	12,211
South Australia ..	12,963	10,840	15,475	18,026	21,616	19,361	20,535	21,174	8,379
Western Australia	1,711	1,399	2,068	2,008	2,709	3,332	5,430	11,943	5,342
Tasmania	6,962	6,953	8,060	8,994	9,790	10,389	10,128	10,313	3,728
Commomwealth	122,550	105,956	139,140	162,374	192,760	217,227	221,527	231,743	94,408
New Zealand	13,328	10,001	19,354	25,254	29,074	29,746	33,525	35,151	16,009
Australasia ..	135,878	115,957	158,494	187,628	221,834	246,973	255,052	266,894	110,417

The average death-rates per thousand of the population of each state for the periods shown in the above table are given below, but the statement does not afford a just comparison between them as no account is taken of the ages of the people :—

State.	1861–65.	1866–70.	1871–75.	1876–80.	1881–85.	1886–90.	1891–95.	1896–1900.	1901–2.
New South Wales	16·86	16·05	14·99	16·09	15·66	13·80	12·80	11·85	11·81
Victoria	17·36	16·52	15·64	14·92	14·65	16·07	14·04	13·72	13·31
Queensland	21·06	18·07	17·94	16·90	19·10	15·52	12·82	12·51	12·01
South Australia ..	15·70	15·01	15·83	14·90	14·71	12·55	12·20	11·93	11·50
Western Australia	16·31	15·55	16·08	14·32	17·19	15·97	16·31	15·32	13·61
Tasmania	15·20	14·06	15·64	16·52	16·00	15·16	13·41	12·46	10·67
Commonwealth	16·98	16·01	15·58	15·54	15·36	14·51	13·27	12·73	12·32
New Zealand	14·36	12·05	12·93	11·83	11·00	9·87	10·14	9·56	10·15
Australasia ..	16·75	15·62	15·26	15·04	14·79	13·95	12·76	12·20	11·95

If this table be compared with that showing the birth-rates, it will be observed that the experience of Australasia corresponds with that of other countries, viz., that a low birth-rate and a low death-rate accompany each other, so that although the birth-rate has been declining it has had an effect in reducing the death-rate, as indicated on the preceding page, and the balance in favour of births has not been reduced so much as it might have been. From the next table, which shows the mean natural increase in various foreign countries during the decennial period 1892–1901, and for Australasia during the period 1893–1902, it will be seen that the case of Australasia is much better than that of any of the countries of the United Kingdom or Europe, for notwithstanding that the birth-rate of these countries in some cases is higher, the death-rate is so much higher as to more than outweigh any advantage in that respect.

Country.	Birth-rate.	Death-rate.	Excess of Births per 1,000 Inhabitants.
New South Wales..	29·01	12·04	16·97
Victoria......................	27·07	13·56	13·51
Queensland	30·87	12·45	18·42
South Australia	27·44	11·92	15·52
Western Australia........	29·27	14·95	14·32
Tasmania	32·53	12·17	20·36
Commonwealth	28·62	12·70	15·92
New Zealand...............	26·22	9·84	16·38
Australasia	28·22	12·22	16·00
England and Wales	29·39	17·59	11·80
Scotland	29·91	18·06	11·85
Ireland........................	23·17	18·08	5·09
United Kingdom.....	28·75	17·70	11·05
Denmark.....	30·52	17·29	13·23
Norway	30·13	15·96	14·17
Sweden	26·90	16·22	10·68
Austria........................	37·27	26·36	10·91
Hungary	40·30	29·22	11·08
Switzerland	28·03	18·59	9·44
German Empire............	35·96	21·94	14·02
Prussia........................	36·82	22·08	14·74
The Netherlands	32·20	17·92	14·28
Belgium	28·89	18·70	10·19
France	22·07	21·23	0·84
Italy	34·53	23·77	10·76

In regard to the above table it must be stated that, had the figures of any of the last five years been taken as the basis of comparison, the gain by natural increase in Australasia would have been below that of some European countries, where the decline in the birth-rate, although distinctly evident, has not been so great as in Australasia.

Index of Mortality

So far consideration has only been given to the actual death-rates as they are obtained by taking the proportion which the number of deaths bears to the number of inhabitants. It is well known, however, that the death-rate of a country is affected by more than the salubrity of its climate, the degree of perfection to which the sanitary condition of its cities and towns and villages has been brought, and the nature of the industrial pursuits of its people. It is known that the ages of the people considerably affect the death-rate of a country; that, for instance, one which has a large proportion of young people will, other things being equal, have a lower death-rate than another which has a comparatively large proportion of old persons; and it is this fact that statistical science now seeks to take into account in establishing the rates of mortality of the various countries of the world. In order to have a comparison of the mortality of the principal countries on a uniform basis, the International Statistical Institute, in its 1895 session, held at Berne, decided to recommend the population of Sweden, in five age-groups, as ascertained at the census of 1890, as the standard population, by which the index of mortality should be calculated. Applying the co-efficient of mortality in each age-group in the Commonwealth and New Zealand to the age constitution of the standard population, the "index of mortality," as distinguished from the actual "death-rate," is found as given below for the year 1902. How greatly the ages of the people of a country affect its mortality will be evident from the fact that whereas in 1902 the death-rates in Australasia ranged from 10·50 in New Zealand to 13·77 in Western Australia, a difference of 3·27 per thousand, the range of the indexes of mortality was 4·66 per thousand, namely, from 13·00 in New Zealand to 17·66 in Western Australia.

State.	1902.
New South Wales	15·45
Victoria	15·89
Queensland	15·85
South Australia	15·12
Western Australia	17·66
Tasmania	14·26
Commonwealth	15·68
New Zealand	13·00
Australasia	15·22

Ages at Death.

A detailed statement of the ages at death of the males who died during the year 1902 in the various states is given below. The

figures for South Australia in this and subsequent detailed tables refer to the province proper exclusive of the Northern Territory.

Ages at Death.	New South Wales.	Victoria.	Queensland.	South Australia.	Western Australia.	Tasmania.	Common-wealth.	New Zealand.	Australasia.
Under 1 year........	2,249	1,793	780	465	496	222	6,005	952	6,957
1 and under 2 years..	410	345	119	129	85	28	1,116	155	1,271
2 ,, 3 ,, ..	163	106	42	56	19	13	399	55	454
3 ,, 4 ,, ..	81	67	30	33	21	10	242	47	289
4 ,, 5 ,, ..	52	37	13	16	12	3	133	22	155
5 ,, 10 ,, ..	201	179	74	80	22	18	574	121	695
10 ,, 15 ,, ..	167	146	61	41	14	27	456	76	532
15 ,, 20 ,, ..	241	186	110	58	34	24	653	123	776
20 ,, 25 ,, ..	279	245	223	63	98	34	942	172	1,114
25 ,, 30 ,, ..	298	259	223	76	140	28	1,024	188	1,212
30 ,, 35 ,, ..	348	307	221	77	120	31	1,104	161	1,265
35 ,, 40 ,, ..	416	352	233	78	118	44	1,241	173	1,414
40 ,, 45 ,, ..	415	384	221	93	116	48	1,277	177	1,454
45 ,, 50 ,, ..	461	340	188	96	90	48	1,213	221	1,434
50 ,, 55 ,, ..	422	342	218	97	75	35	1,184	246	1,430
55 ,, 60 ,, ..	462	393	212	123	72	42	1,304	256	1,560
60 ,, 65 ,, ..	508	495	275	127	70	51	1,526	333	1,859
65 ,, 70 ,, ..	721	801	258	130	64	52	2,021	441	2,462
70 ,, 75 ,, ..	655	987	207	167	66	76	2,158	427	2,585
75 years and upwards	972	1,377	216	310	87	214	3,176	544	3,720
Unspecified..........	14	11	15	1	13	1	55	....	55
Total	9,535	9,152	3,924	2,316	1,882	1,044	27,803	4,890	32,693

Similar information respecting the deaths of females in 1902 is given in the following table :—

Ages at Death.	New South Wales.	Victoria.	Queensland.	South Australia.	Western Australia.	Tasmania.	Common-wealth.	New Zealand.	Australasia.
Under 1 year	1,908	1,515	644	372	389	180	5,008	760	5,768
1 and under 2 years..	390	285	102	105	79	22	983	152	1,135
2 ,, 3 ,, ..	134	110	35	36	19	11	345	63	408
3 ,, 4 ,, ..	72	52	33	21	14	5	197	45	242
4 ,, 5 ,, ..	47	51	20	16	9	6	149	39	188
5 ,, 10 ,, ..	181	171	63	56	25	26	522	87	609
10 ,, 15 ,, ..	143	143	59	40	23	25	433	75	508
15 ,, 20 ,, ..	203	167	63	68	22	50	573	134	707
20 ,, 25 ,, ..	273	237	84	72	51	49	766	153	919
25 ,, 30 ,, ..	309	271	111	75	61	33	860	175	1,035
30 ,, 35 ,, ..	277	323	101	74	64	34	873	138	1,011
35 ,, 40 ,, .	314	344	117	68	46	31	920	151	1,071
40 ,, 45 ,, ..	303	332	103	79	29	45	891	121	1,012
45 ,, 50 ,, ..	239	245	85	66	20	20	675	109	784
50 ,, 55 ,, ..	245	220	76	59	18	21	639	155	794
55 ,, 60 ,, ..	260	257	98	61	25	28	729	173	902
60 ,, 65 ,, ..	314	355	105	73	22	38	907	171	1,078
65 ,, 70 ,, ..	384	508	116	115	29	52	1,204	221	1,425
70 ,, 75 ,, ..	370	541	101	137	15	57	1,221	200	1,421
75 and upwards......	748	898	162	327	30	136	2,296	363	2,659
Unspecified	2	5	2	....	1	1	11	....	11
Total........	7,111	7,025	2,280	1,920	991	870	20,197	3,485	23,682

The next table shows the ages of all the persons who died during 1902 :—

Ages at Death.	New South Wales.	Victoria.	Queensland.	South Australia.	Western Australia.	Tasmania.	Common-wealth.	New Zealand.	Australasia.
Under 1 year	4,152	3,308	1,424	837	885	402	11,008	1,712	12,720
1 and under 2 years	800	630	221	234	164	50	2,099	307	2,406
2 ,, 3 ,,	297	216	77	92	38	24	744	118	862
3 ,, 4 ,,	153	119	63	54	35	15	439	92	531
4 ,, 5 ,,	99	88	33	32	21	9	282	61	343
5 ,, 10 ,,	382	350	187	136	47	44	1,096	208	1,304
10 ,, 15 ,,	310	289	120	81	37	52	889	151	1,040
15 ,, 20 ,,	444	353	178	126	56	74	1,226	257	1,483
20 ,, 25 ,,	552	482	307	135	149	83	1,708	325	2,033
25 ,, 30 ,,	607	530	334	151	201	61	1,884	363	2,247
30 ,, 35 ,,	625	630	322	151	184	65	1,977	299	2,276
35 ,, 40 ,,	730	696	350	146	164	75	2,161	324	2,485
40 ,, 45 ,,	718	716	324	172	145	93	2,168	298	2,466
45 ,, 50 ,,	700	585	268	162	110	63	1,888	330	2,218
50 ,, 55 ,,	667	562	289	156	93	56	1,823	401	2,224
55 ,, 60 ,,	722	650	310	184	97	70	2,033	429	2,462
60 ,, 65 ,,	822	850	380	200	92	89	2,433	504	2,937
65 ,, 70 ,,	1,105	1,309	369	245	93	104	3,225	662	3,887
70 ,, 75 ,,	1,025	1,528	308	304	81	133	3,379	627	4,006
75 and upwards	1,720	2,270	378	637	117	350	5,472	907	6,379
Unspecified	16	16	17	1	14	2	66	....	66
Total	16,646	16,177	6,204	4,236	2,823	1,914	48,000	8,375	56,375

The ages of the people were ascertained at the census of March, 1901, and a comparison of the foregoing figures with the numbers living at each age can now be made. Using the same age groups as for the index of mortality given on page 669, the following rates are obtained. For age 0 (under 1 year) the number of births during the year has been used in place of figures deduced from the census results :—

Age Groups.	Deaths in each Age Group per 1,000 living.								
	New South Wales.	Victoria.	Queensland.	South Australia.	Western Australia.	Tasmania.	Common-wealth.	New Zealand.	Australasia.
Under 1 year	109·74	108·60	100·17	94·00	142·01	79·06	107·15	82·89	103·09
1 and under 20	4·06	4·07	3·67	4·68	5·83	3·38	4·10	3·56	4·02
20 ,, 40	5·63	5·92	7·77	5·44	7·49	5·18	6·12	4·99	5·92
40 ,, 59	12·63	13·61	14·63	11·91	14·20	10·78	13·13	11·46	12·84
60 and over	60·03	61·96	58·97	60·19	57·26	63·35	60·56	50·08	58·64

The superiority of Tasmania over the other states of the Commonwealth is very marked, and New Zealand also shows a much lower rate than any of the states excepting Tasmania. For children under 1 year Tasmania shows a far more favourable mortality than any other state, while Western Australia shows an exceptionally high rate. The most favourable rates among old persons occur in New Zealand, Western Australia, and Queensland in that order.

INFANTILE MORTALITY.

The mortality of infants under 1 year of age may be measured accurately by comparing the deaths with the number of births; this is a most sensitive and reliable test of the healthiness and sanitary condition of a country, since at this early age children are most susceptible to the attacks of disease. The following table shows for each state the number of deaths of children under 1 year of age, and the rate per 1,000 births, since 1870, arranged in five-year periods:—

State.	1871-75.	1876-80.	1881-85.	1886-90.	1891-95.	1896-1900.	1901-2.
DEATHS under 1 Year.							
New South Wales	11,036	14,626	19,709	21,586	21,930	20,819	8,081
Victoria	16,981	15,865	17,043	22,582	20,221	17,299	6,500
Queensland	3,596	5,068	6,732	8,339	7,496	7,337	2,882
South Australia	5,758	6,516	7,594	5,593	5,227	5,266	1,746
Western Australia	......	......	......	939	1,332	3,488	1,622
Tasmania	1,560	1,820	2,391	2,437	2,337	2,284	841
Commonwealth	38,931	43,905	53,409	61,476	58,543	56,493	21,672
New Zealand	6,390	8,432	8,733	7,924	8,005	7,578	3,175
Australasia	45,321	52,337	62,142	69,400	66,548	64,071	24,847
RATE per 1,000 Births.							
New South Wales	103·58	114·65	123·98	114·64	111·00	113·40	106·74
Victoria	124·53	119·87	121·51	131·06	111·81	111·29	105·74
Queensland	122·82	135·02	137·45	118·87	102·88	103·39	101·06
South Australia	158·20	140·70	134·13	105·13	98·67	111·97	96·97
Western Australia	......	......	......	109·15	130·05	155·72	135·73
Tasmania	101·87	106·61	108·75	102·78	94·26	97·59	83·97
Commonwealth	119·47	120·55	123·48	117·51	107·96	112·35	105·35
New Zealand	106·69	95·60	90·51	84·23	87·57	80·03	77·16
Australasia	118·09	116·53	118·88	113·71	105·51	107·23	100·65

In spite of all the sanitary improvements that have been effected in recent years, the rate, as judged from the quinquennial period 1896–1900, did not seem to have decreased very appreciably in any of the states except Queensland, South Australia, and New Zealand. But during the last two years there has been a most satisfactory improvement, and the general rate is now only a little over 10 per cent. In Western Australia the mortality among infants increased rapidly from 11 per cent. in 1886–90 to 16 per cent. in 1896–1900, but during 1901–2 it decreased 2 per cent. as compared with the preceding five years. In South Australia the rate appears very high in the earlier years, the reason given being that the deaths of several children 1 year old were wrongly included by the registering officers with those under 1 year.

Causes of Death.

The system of classifying the causes of death adopted in Australasia is that arranged by Dr. William Ogle on the basis of the older system of Dr. William Farr, his predecessor as Superintendent of the Statistical Department of the Registrar-General's Office, England. Under this classification deaths are divided into eight classes, namely, deaths from specific febrile or zymotic diseases, from parasitic diseases, from dietetic diseases, from constitutional diseases, from developmental diseases, from local diseases, from violence, and from ill-defined or unspecified causes. The following were the assigned causes of death of the 56,375 persons who died in Australasia during 1902:—

Classification	New South Wales.	Victoria.	Queensland.	South Australia.	Western Australia.	Tasmania.	New Zealand.	Australasia.
Specific febrile or zymotic diseases—								
Miasmatic diseases	1,043	872	349	452	262	125	488	3,596
Diarrhœal diseases	656	429	312	151	147	25	275	1,995
Malarial diseases	3	1	55	2	26	1	2	90
Zoogenous diseases	4	....	....	....	....	....	....	4
Venereal diseases	55	68	35	10	7	5	15	190
Septic diseases	201	159	48	28	17	19	64	536
Total	1,962	1,524	799	643	459	175	889	6,401
Parasitic diseases	41	42	24	14	4	5	8	138
Dietetic diseases	200	108	130	19	35	7	68	567
Constitutional diseases	2,570	2,833	1,007	710	314	306	1,549	9,290
Developmental diseases	1,761	1,662	413	520	211	349	846	5,762
Local diseases—								
Diseases of nervous system	1,418	1,498	606	413	204	220	858	5,217
Diseases of organs of special sense	14	23	11	5	1	2	8	64
Diseases of circulatory system	1,415	1,726	549	482	234	209	954	5,569
Diseases of respiratory system	2,297	2,114	746	388	304	192	1,058	7,099
Diseases of digestive system	2,158	2,071	825	404	434	153	734	6,779
Diseases of lymphatic system and ductless glands	29	13	5	10	1	8	28	94
Diseases of urinary system	688	729	286	147	82	3	328	2,313
Diseases of organs of generation	59	61	33	9	6	7	27	202
Diseases of parturition	154	131	59	24	1	18	85	472
Diseases of organs of locomotion	34	42	14	19	32	6	30	177
Diseases of integumentary system	43	72	27	13	16	4	11	196
Total	8,309	8,480	3,161	1,914	1,315	872	4,121	28,172
Violence—								
Accident or negligence	1,026	662	481	183	225	76	523	3,176
Homicide	27	27	15	4	9	....	2	84
Suicide	127	133	97	35	49	10	80	531
Execution	1	2	....	....	1	....	....	4
Violent deaths not classified	58	....	....	....	....	....	....	58
Total	1,239	824	593	222	284	86	605	3,853
Ill-defined and not specified causes	564	704	77	194	201	114	348	2,202
Grand Total	16,646	16,177	6,204	4,236	2,823	1,914	8,375	56,375

Comparing the figures of the total deaths in each class and order with the population, the following results are obtained. The figures represent the number of deaths per 100,000 living based on the experience of the five years ended with 1902.

Classification.	Number of deaths per 100,000 living.		
	Males.	Females.	Total population.
Specific, febrile, or zymotic diseases—			
Miasmatic diseases	96·15	92·04	94·21
Diarrhœal diseases	49·57	43·65	46·77
Venereal diseases	5·31	3·25	4·34
Septic diseases	6·02	17·42	11·40
Other specific, febrile, or zymotic diseases	2·87	0·41	1·71
Total	159·92	156·77	158·43
Parasitic diseases	4·16	3·69	3·94
Dietetic diseases	17·71	8·17	13·21
Constitutional diseases	211·94	184·67	199·07
Developmental diseases	130·32	105·99	118·83
Local diseases—			
Diseases of nervous system	125·86	103·26	115·19
Diseases of circulatory system	130·01	99·79	115·75
Diseases of respiratory system	166·06	122·92	145·69
Diseases of digestive system	141·82	134·53	138·38
Diseases of urinary system	60·84	33·02	47·71
Diseases of organs of generation	0·34	7·75	3·84
Diseases of parturition	....	22·94	10·83
Diseases of organs of locomotion	3·61	2·66	3·16
Diseases of integumentary system	3·91	3·16	3·56
Other local diseases	3·22	3·86	3·52
Total	635·67	533·89	587·63
Violence—			
Accident or negligence	106·21	35·13	72·66
Homicide	2·60	1·88	2·26
Suicide	18·21	4·11	11·55
Other deaths from violence	1·18	0·25	0·74
Total	128·20	41·37	87·21
Ill-defined or not specified causes	55·06	48·81	52·11
Grand total	1,342·98	1,083·36	1,220·43

Specific Febrile or Zymotic Diseases.

The deaths from specific febrile or zymotic diseases in 1902 numbered 6,401, representing 13·76 deaths per 10,000 of the population. Under this class are included the highly infectious diseases—measles, scarlet fever, whooping-cough, and diphtheria—which are especially fatal to children; diarrhœal diseases, chiefly fatal to persons at the extremes of life; and typhoid (enteric) fever, the death-rate from which at times is very high.

It would be interesting to compare the fatality of these diseases in the various states in proportion to the number of cases occurring, but unfortunately the necessary information is lacking. In some of the states legal enactments provide for the notification of infectious diseases, but they are not rigidly enforced, and doubtless many cases escape notice.

In New South Wales, since the beginning of 1898, under the provisions of the Public Health Act of 1896, notification of the three diseases scarlet fever, diphtheria, and typhoid has been compulsory, and careful record has been kept of the number of cases and deaths. The following table shows the number of cases notified during the five years 1898 to 1902 in the metropolis, and the fatality per cent. :—

Disease.	Number of cases notified.	Number of Deaths.	Fatality per cent.
Scarlet Fever	5,582	91	1·6
Diphtheria	2,008	212	10·6
Typhoid	4,032	403	10·

The average annual experience of London during the ten years 1891-1900 is also given.

Disease.	Number of cases notified.	Number of Deaths.	Fatality per cent.
Scarlet Fever	21,156	818	3·9
Diphtheria	11,658	2,192	18·8
Typhoid	3,518	616	17·0

Measles.

Measles, which is mainly a children's disease, was the cause in 1902 of the deaths of 550 persons, equal to a rate of 1·18 per 10,000 living. The disease was epidemic in South Australia, and to a lesser extent in New South Wales and New Zealand; in the state first mentioned the deaths numbered 235. The following tables show the number of deaths in each state from this disease, and the death-rate per 10,000 living, in five-year periods since 1870, and for the years 1901–2:—

State.	1871-75.	1876-80.	1881-85.	1886-90.	1891-95.	1896-1900.	1901-2.
Number of Deaths.							
New South Wales	......	311	200	293	885	784	144
Victoria	1,809	271	386	148	696	827	100
Queensland	179	36	102	4	302	261	5
South Australia ...	256	18	240	8	291	63	240
Western Australia	......	1	129	nil	27	41	64
Tasmania............	132	8	66	1	49	59	1
New Zealand	*359	10	246	85	526	294	140
Australasia ...	......	650	1,369	539	2,776	2,209	694
Death-rate per 10,000 living.							
New South Wales	......	0·94	0·47	0·57	1·48	1·12	0·52
Victoria	4·73	0·66	0·81	0·28	1·19	1·39	0·41
Queensland	2·50	0·35	0·76	0·02	1·46	1·12	0·05
South Australia ...	3·64	0·15	1·63	0·05	1·73	0·47	3·34
Western Australia	......	0·07	8·19	0·00	0·81	0·53	1·63
Tasmania............	2·56	0·06	1·08	0·01	0·65	0·71	0·03
New Zealand	*2·90	0·05	0·93	0·28	1·59	0·55	0·89
Australasia ...	......	0·52	0·91	0·30	1·38	1·01	0·75

* Four years, 1872-75.

With regard to the diseases which are almost solely confined to children, the rates would of course be more accurately stated if the deaths were compared with the children living of like ages. However, taking them as they appear, it will be seen that measles has been more prevalent since 1891 than during the preceding fifteen years, and it seems to have been most common in the first three states shown in the table. In 1901–2 the rate increased largely in South Australia, owing to an epidemic, and in Western Australia and New Zealand. Although the disease is in evidence every year, it usually occurs as an epidemic, and, according to the records, the outbreaks occur with more or less regularity and severity about every five years. Measles was epidemic in nearly all the states in 1875 (when the attack was very severe), in 1880, in 1884 (when Western Australia suffered heavily) in 1889, in 1893, in 1898, and in 1899.

SCARLET FEVER.

The deaths resulting from scarlet fever during 1902 numbered 143 or at the rate of 0·31 per 10,000. In the table below are shown the number of deaths and the death rates in each State arranged quinquennially since 1870:—

State.	1871-75.	1876-80.	1881-85.	1886-90.	1891-95.	1896-1900.	1901-2.
NUMBER of Deaths.							
New South Wales	......	1,295	476	404	460	244	77
Victoria	1,455	2,646	282	148	172	230	17
Queensland	77	37	19	73	31	157	7
South Australia	626	520	141	27	56	47	1
Western Australia	......	......	......	*nil.	1	4	3
Tasmania	72	304	49	9	8	38	23
New Zealand	*58	383	312	96	40	18	56
Australasia	......	5,185	1,279	757	768	738	184
DEATH-RATE per 10,000 living.							
New South Wales	......	3·91	1·13	0·78	0·77	0·37	0·28
Victoria	3·81	6·44	0·59	0·28	0·29	0·39	0·07
Queensland	1·07	0·36	0·14	0·40	0·15	0·67	0·07
South Australia	6·40	4·30	0·96	0·17	0·33	0·26	0·01
Western Australia	......	......	......	0·00	0·03	0·05	0·08
Tasmania	1·40	5·59	0·80	0·13	0·11	0·46	0·66
New Zealand	*0·47	1·79	1·18	0·32	0·12	0·05	0·36
Australasia	......	4·20	0·86	0·43	0·38	0·34	0·20

* Four years, 1872-75.

The rate of mortality from scarlet fever for the first ten years shown in the table was much higher than that recorded for measles, but, in spite of the highly infectious nature and difficulty of isolation of the former disease, the death-rate has since been consistently lower than that of the latter. From 1871 to 1880 the rate of mortality from scarlet fever was high, but during the next five years a great decrease was manifested, and later there was a further decline, while during the three quinquennial periods ending 1900 the rate was practically constant, but with a tendency to rise in Victoria, Queensland, and Tasmania. Since 1900, the rate has risen in Tasmania, New Zealand, and Western Australia, and declined in the other states. In 1902 the disease was epidemic in a mild form in Tasmania, New Zealand, and New South Wales. In Victoria the extremely high rate for 1876–80 was caused by a very virulent outbreak of the disease in 1876, and in Tasmania an outbreak in 1877 largely increased the rate;

in fact, during the three years 1875, 1876, and 1877 all the states were more or less affected by an epidemic of scarlet fever. In Queensland the disease has never been very prevalent, and in Western Australia it is virtually unknown.

Whooping-cough.

A curious fact in connection with whooping-cough, the third of the diseases of infancy and childhood, is that the mortality resulting from it is higher in the case of girls than of boys. During 1902 whooping-cough was responsible for 634 deaths (292 males and 342 females), equal to 1·36 deaths per 10,000 of the population, the male rate being 1·20 and the female 1·54. The table below shows the number of deaths and the death rates in each state since 1870:—

State.	1871-75.	1876-80. *	1881-85.	1886-90.	1891-95.	1896-1900.	1901-2.
Number of Deaths.							
New South Wales	......	676	632	979	1,157	947	520
Victoria	1,053	921	701	691	851	498	373
Queensland	117	198	184	306	381	454	105
South Australia	181	211	341	263	279	264	87
Western Australia	......	nil.	19	65	57	80	36
Tasmania	99	84	59	89	79	88	27
New Zealand	*465	589	592	443	752	245	92
Australasia	......	2,679	2,528	2,836	3,556	2,576	1,240
Death-rate per 10,000 living.							
New South Wales	......	2·04	1·50	1·89	1·93	1·44	1·88
Victoria	2·76	2·24	1·47	1·31	1·46	0·84	1·55
Qeensland	1·63	1·94	1·37	1·69	1·84	1·94	1·03
South Australia	1·85	1·74	2·32	1·70	1·66	1·49	1·21
Western Australia	......	0·00	1·21	3·12	1·71	1·03	0·92
Tasmania	1·92	1·54	0·96	1·30	1·05	1·06	0·77
New Zealand	*3·75	2·76	2·24	1·47	2·28	0·67	0·58
Australasia	......	2·15	1·69	1·60	1·78	1·18	1·34

* Four years, 1872-75.

The death-rate from whooping-cough, which has never been remarkably high, declined after the second quinquennium (1876–80), and thenceforward remained fairly constant during the next twenty years. The returns show an especially gratifying decrease, as the disease was mildly epidemic during 1896–1900. During 1901 and 1902, in both of which years whooping-cough was more or less epidemic, the rates increased as compared with the preceding quinquennium in two States and decreased in five. The increase in Victoria was so large that it had the effect of raising the average. Generally speaking, whooping-cough seems to have been most prevalent in New South Wales,

South Australia, and New Zealand; but it is gradually decreasing in these States, and, in fact, throughout Australasia, with the single exception of Queensland, where, until 1900, the tendency was towards an increase. On the whole, the rates up to the year 1895 were very even amongst themselves in all the states. In Western Australia the rate rose regularly to a maximum during 1886–90—a very severe epidemic being experienced in 1886—and then declined.

DIPHTHERIA.

Diphtheria, the last of the febrile diseases mentioned which mainly affect children, caused, in 1902, a total of 298 deaths, equal to a rate of 0·64 per 10,000 persons living. In the following table are shown the number of deaths, and the death rates in each state since 1870:—

State.	1871–75.	1876–80.	1881–85.	1886–90.	1891–95.	1896–1900.	1901–2.
			NUMBER of Deaths.				
New South Wales	......	1,109	1,005	1,325	1,753	584	205
Victoria	1,609	1,431	681	1,885	994	892	251
Queensland	246	170	224	530	551	273	69
South Australia	379	329	387	570	513	153	46
Western Australia	......	11	28	19	38	79	18
Tasmania	124	329	96	182	208	65	19
New Zealand	*535	316	525	542	577	289	98
Australasia	......	3,695	2,946	5,053	4,634	2,335	706
			DEATH-RATE per 10,000 living.				
New South Wales	......	3·35	2·39	2·56	2·92	0·89	0·74
Victoria	4·21	3·48	1·43	3·58	1·70	1·50	1·04
Queensland	3·43	1·66	1·66	2·93	2·66	1·17	0·68
South Australia	3·88	2·72	2·63	3·69	3·05	0·86	0·64
Western Australia	......	0·79	1·78	0·91	1·14	1·01	0·46
Tasmania	2·41	6·05	1·57	2·66	2·76	0·79	0·54
New Zealand	*4·32	1·48	1·99	1·80	1·75	0·79	0·62
Australasia	......	2·96	1·96	2·85	2·32	1·07	0·76

* Four years, 1872–75.

The present rates for diphtheria, as compared with those of twenty or twenty-five years ago, show a decrease. The decline, however, has been by no means regular, owing to the fact that this disease, in common with the others affecting children, sometimes occurs as an epidemic. Thus the increase in the rates during 1886–90 over those prevailing in the previous five years was due to an epidemic in nearly all the provinces in 1890.

The decreased mortality during the last twenty-five years, from the four diseases just mentioned, together with croup, represents a gain of about 9 children to the population in every 10,000 persons living. This improvement is very gratifying, since it may be taken that cases of these diseases, which are particularly liable to be attended with dangerous after-effects in the shape of lung and other local troubles, are not so numerous, and that in consequence the general health of the people is better.

Croup.

Croup, although classed as a disease of the respiratory system, was formerly classified with the zymotic diseases, and is included here on account of its similarity to diphtheria, and the confusion which often arises between them, and of the deaths set down to a combination of both. It is a disease that may be said to affect children only, and in 1902 caused the death of 80, or 0·17 per 10,000 of the population. In the subsequent table are shown the number of deaths and the death-rate in each state since 1870 :—

State.	1871-75.	1876-80.	1881-85.	1886-90.	1891-95.	1896-1900.	1901-2
				Number of Deaths.			
New South Wales	......	968	971	951	683	278	54
Victoria	647	1,250	795	1,209	458	199	48
Queensland	273	324	483	382	239	103	15
South Australia	258	330	443	192	145	45	11
Western Australia	......	24	31	45	64	26	2
Tasmania	80	76	113	112	101	29	4
New Zealand	*281	277	334	340	304	186	43
Australasia	......	3,249	3,170	3,231	1,994	866	177
				Death-rate per 10,000 living.			
New South Wales	......	2·92	2·31	1·84	1·14	0·42	0·20
Victoria	1·69	3·04	1·66	2·30	0·78	0·34	0·20
Queensland	3·81	3·17	3·59	2·11	1·15	0·44	0·15
South Australia	2·64	2·74	3·01	1·24	0·86	0·25	0·15
Western Australia	......	1·72	1·97	2·16	1·92	0·33	0·05
Tasmania	1·55	1·40	1·85	1·63	1·34	0·35	0·11
New Zealand	*2·27	1·30	1·26	1·13	0·92	0·51	0·27
Australasia	......	2·61	2·11	1·83	1·00	0·40	0·19

* Four years, 1872-75.

Generally speaking, deaths from this disease show a steady and consistent fall from the earliest period, although in some of the states, especially Victoria and South Australia, the rates fluctuate slightly. The greatest decline has taken place in New South Wales, Victoria, Queensland, and South Australia, until at the present time croup is about equally prevalent throughout Australasia. The rate is farthest above the mean in New Zealand, and below it in Western Australia. If croup and diphtheria be taken together, as they usually are, the rates generally have declined to the extent of about 4½ per 10,000 during the last twenty-seven years.

Diarrhœal Diseases.

Diarrhœal diseases, comprising cholera, diarrhœa, and dysentery, carry off mostly young children and old persons. In 1902 these diseases were fatal to 1,995 persons, equal to a death-rate of 4·29 per 10,000 living. The number of deaths and the death-rates in each state in quinquennial periods since 1870, are shown below.

State.	1871-75.	1876-80.	1881-85.	1886-90.	1891-95.	1896-1900.	1901-2
Number of Deaths.							
New South Wales	......	3,913	4,775	4,323	3,794	3,622	1,123
Victoria	6,030	5,006	4,886	5,489	3,290	2,679	865
Queensland	1,618	2,469	3,833	2,865	2,125	1,779	687
South Australia	1,628	1,620	2,105	1,388	1,079	1,205	352
Western Australia	......	140	106	251	323	794	252
Tasmania	437	512	474	605	354	309	98
New Zealand	*1,528	2,375	1,879	1,789	1,280	1,363	414
Australasia	......	16,035	18,058	16,710	12,245	11,751	3,791
Death-rate per 10,000 living.							
New South Wales	......	11·82	11·34	8·34	6·32	5·52	4·06
Victoria	15·78	12·18	10·23	10·42	5·63	4·52	3·59
Queensland	22·56	24·15	28·46	15·85	10·25	7·62	6·75
South Australia	16·65	13·39	14·32	8·99	6·41	6·79	4·89
Western Australia	......	10·01	6·73	12·03	9·70	10·18	6·42
Tasmania	8·48	9·41	7·75	8·83	4·69	3·73	2·81
New Zealand	*12·33	11·13	7·11	5·94	3·87	3·71	2·63
Australasia	......	12·86	12·04	9·44	6·02	5·37	4·11

* Four years, 1872-75.

The high death-rates of earlier years are not surprising, and may be ascribed to the hard fare and exposure incidental to the development of the pastoral and mining industries. This will be evident from a comparison of the present rates in Queensland, South Australia, and New South Wales with those of former periods. In all the states there has been a marked improvement during the last twenty-two years, the only exception being Western Australia, where the rough conditions of life prevailing on the gold-fields exert an adverse influence on the rates. In 1901-2, however, the rate in Western Australia was lower than in Queensland. The most noticeable improvement has occurred in

Queensland, where the rate has declined from 24·15 to 6·75. That temperature and climate have an effect on the death-rates from these diseases is proved from the fact that they are much more prevalent and more fatal in summer than in any other season of the year, and that in Tasmania and New Zealand, where the climate is mild and genial, the rates are much lower than in Queensland and Western Australia, where the climate is very warm, and in some parts tropical, while the other states, whose climates are fairly temperate, show rates between the two extremes.

The decline in the number of deaths from diarrhœa may be in part due to the fact that of late years more skilful diagnosis in some cases makes possible the ascription of death to ailments of which diarrhœa may be only a symptom.

Typhoid (Enteric) Fever.

Seeing that typhoid is entirely a filth disease, the poison of which is propagated by sewage, and that it yields readily to sanitary precautions, it is a matter of very great regret that the annual mortality, although steadily declining, should still be so heavy. In 1902 typhoid was responsible for 956 deaths in Australasia, or at the rate of 2·05 per 10,000 living, as against the English rate of 1·73 for 1900. The table below shows the number of deaths from this disease, and the death rate in each state, arranged in five-year periods since 1870 :—

State.	1871-75.	1876-80.	1881-85.	1886-90.	1891-95.	1896-1900.	1901-2.
Number of Deaths.							
New South Wales	......	1,722	2,132	2,307	1,533	1,968	567
Victoria	1,799	2,174	2,364	3,209	1,571	1,722	383
Queensland	424	525	1,303	990	513	747	281
South Australia	372	446	632	566	369	512	161
Western Australia	......	......	......	59	500	1,379	301
Tasmania	156	184	213	401	230	251	49
New Zealand	*632	739	626	674	561	511	148
Australasia	......	5,790	7,270	8,206	5,277	7,090	1,890
Death-rate per 10,000 living.							
New South Wales	......	5·20	5·06	4·46	2·56	3·00	2·05
Victoria	4·71	5·29	5·18	6·09	2·69	2·90	1·59
Queensland	5·91	5·14	9·67	5·48	2·48	2·20	2·76
South Australia	3·80	3·69	4·30	3·67	2·19	2·89	2·24
Western Australia	......	......	......	2·83	15·02	17·69	7·67
Tasmania	3·03	3·38	3·48	5·85	3·05	3·03	1·40
New Zealand	*5·10	3·46	2·37	2·24	1·70	1·39	0·94
Australasia	......	4·69	4·90	4·64	2·64	3·24	2·05

* Four years, 1872-75.

It will be observed that the rates over the whole period covered by the table show a decline. The disease is of an epidemic nature, but still the rates do not fluctuate greatly, and during the last two years the rates in all the states, excluding Western Australia, were fairly uniform, ranging from ·94 in New Zealand to 2·76 in Queensland. An epidemic occurred in the year 1889 in New South Wales, Victoria, Queensland, and Tasmania, and the disease seems to have since been more prevalent in the last-mentioned state than in any other, with the exception of Western Australia. In that state typhoid was almost unknown prior to the gold rush in 1894, when the disease may be said to have commenced. The maximum was soon reached, for in 1895 the death-rate was 35·46 per 10,000. With improved sanitation the rate is steadily declining, and although the table shows an apparent increase in the quinquennial period, 1896–1900, it must be remembered that, as previously stated, the disease was comparatively unknown prior to 1894, and this accounts for the lower rate of the period 1891–1895. The rapid decline of the death-rate may be seen when it is stated that in 1895 it was 35·46 per 10,000, for the period 1896–8 only 25·38, while in 1901–2 it had fallen to 7·67, less than half the rate for the preceding five years.

In England and Wales since the measures which have been taken to improve the drainage and water supply the rate has steadily fallen from 3·74 in 1871–75 to 1·76 in 1896–1900.

Parasitic Diseases.

The deaths from parasitic diseases in Australasia during 1902 numbered 138, equal to a death-rate of 0·29 per 10,000 living. The chief disease of this group is hydatids, which was responsible for 98 deaths, or 0·21 per 10,000 of the population, and was most common in South Australia, where the rate was 0·36.

Dietetic Diseases.

Dietetic diseases in 1902 carried off 567 persons, or at the rate of 1·22 per 10,000 living, the chief contributing causes being privation and intemperance.

Constitutional Diseases.

The next class of diseases is the constitutional, which caused in 1902 9,280 deaths, giving an average of 19·95 per 10,000 living. Of these diseases, phthisis and cancer stand out most prominently, and deserve special consideration.

Phthisis.

Phthisis claims more victims in Australasia than any other disease, but notwithstanding this fact the death-rates are lower than in the other countries of the world. This is all the more gratifying when it is considered that many persons afflicted with the disease, or predisposed to it, are attracted to this country in the hope of obtaining relief, as the Australian climate is undoubtedly favourable to people suffering from pulmonary complaints. It is estimated that of the total persons who die of phthisis in Australasia, 7 per eent. do so after less than five years' residence. In 1902 phthisis caused 4,181 deaths in Australasia, equal to a rate of 8·99 per 10,000 living. The following table shews the number of deaths and the death-rates in each state since 1870, arranged in five-year periods :—

State.	1871-75.	1876-80.	1881-85.	1886-90.	1891-95.	1896-1900.	1901-2.
Number of Deaths.							
New South Wales	2,532	3,363	4,805	5,127	5,198	5,225	2,325
Victoria	4,594	5,397	6,428	7,662	7,751	7,049	2,828
Queensland	784	1,390	2,332	2,412	2,266	2,117	885
South Australia	872	1,244	1,558	1,640	1,667	1,544	504
Western Australia	*89	120	135	194	250	534	297
Tasmania	522	536	658	671	658	578	205
New Zealand	*1,080	1,805	2,418	2,529	2,693	2,886	1,213
Australasia	......	13,795	18,234	20,235	20,483	19,933	8,347
Death-rate per 10,000 living.							
New South Wales	9·28	10·16	11·41	9·90	8·66	7·96	8·41
Victoria	12·02	13·13	14·10	14·55	13·26	11.89	11·73
Queensland	10·93	13·01	17·31	13·35	10·93	9·07	8·70
South Australia	8·92	10·28	10·60	10·63	9·90	8·98	8·26
Western Australia	*8·58	8·58	8·57	9·30	7·51	6·85	7·57
Tasmania	10·13	9·85	10·76	9·79	8·72	6·98	5·87
New Zealand	*8·72	8·46	9·15	8·39	8·15	7·85	7·[illegible]
Australasia	10·09	11·06	12·22	11·43	·24	9·11	9·03

* Four years, 1872-75.

For the first half of the period eovered by the table, phthisis seems to have been on the increase; but since 1885 it has steadily decreased, and the mortality rate is now lower than that of England—where the rate is over 13 per 10,000 living—or of any European country. The decline is general, and is evidence of the more skilful treatment of the disease and the effectiveness of the preventive measures taken against it. Phthisis has always been most prevalent in Victoria, and up to 1900 the rate was fairly uniform throughout the rest of Australasia, the lowest being in Western Australia. During 1901–2, however, the order was changed; the rate increased in New South Wales and Western Australia, and decreased in the other states, so that now Tasmania has the lowest rate. In Queensland the rate is adversely affected by the peculiar liability of the Pacific Island labourers to contract the disease, while the Maori population of New Zealand is also extremely susceptible to its ravages.

CANCER.

Next to phthisis, cancer is the most deadly of the constitutional diseases, and in 1902 was the cause of the death of 3,003 persons, or at the rate of 6·45 per 10,000 living. In the table below are shown the number of deaths and the death-rates in each state since 1870:—

State.	1871–75.	1876–80.	1881–85.	1886–90.	1891–95.	1896–1900.	1901–2.
NUMBER of Deaths.							
New South Wales	772	984	1,146	1,876	2,587	3,548	1,716
Victoria	1,245	1,712	2,065	2,799	3,621	4,086	1,734
Queensland	125	225	336	508	731	1,071	563
South Australia	189	362	475	592	803	968	483
Western Australia	*16	23	52	85	102	248	168
Tasmania	249	255	308	341	371	459	204
New Zealand	*262	526	806	1,270	1,725	2,153	1,051
Australasia	......	4,027	5,188	7,471	9,940	12,583	5,919
DEATH-RATE per 10,000 living.							
New South Wales	2·83	2·82	2·72	3·62	4·31	5·41	6·26
Victoria	3·28	4·16	4·53	5·32	6·19	6·89	7·19
Queensland	1·74	2·20	2·49	2·81	3·53	4·59	5·54
South Australia	2·04	2·91	3·23	3·84	4·77	5·45	6·71
Western Australia	*1·54	1·64	3·30	4·07	3·06	3·18	4·28
Tasmania	4·83	4·69	5·04	4·98	4·91	5·55	5·84
New Zealand	*2·11	2·46	3·95	4·22	5·22	5·85	6·66
Australasia	2·76	3·23	3·46	4·22	4·97	5·73	6·41

* Four years, 1872–75.

It will be observed that with some slight irregularity the death-rate from cancer has steadily risen in Australasia over the whole period covered by the table. For the first half of the period Tasmania had the highest rate, but so rapid has been the progress of the disease that the rates in all the states except Queensland and Western Australia are now higher than that of Tasmania. With the exception of the ten years 1881 to 1890, Western Australia has always shown the lowest rates.

Although part of the increase may arise from the fact that more skilful diagnosis in recent years enables cancer to be ascribed as the cause of death in obscure malignant diseases more often than was formerly the case, yet after making due allowance on this score, the conclusion must inevitably be arrived at that the spread of the disease is a dread reality.

DEVELOPMENTAL DISEASES.

The deaths from developmental diseases in 1902 were 5,762, or 12·38 per 10,000 persons living, and of these deaths, 3,325, or 7·15 per 10,000 living, were ascribed to the vague cause, old age. Premature birth was set down as the cause of death of 1,882 infants, a mortality equal to 15·25 per thousand children born alive, or 1 in every 66.

Local Diseases.

Local diseases in 1902 were the cause of 28,172 deaths, and averaged 60·55 per 10,000 living. This group comprises diseases of the various systems and special organs of the body, the principal being diseases of the nervous system and of the circulatory system, which are further considered below. Under this heading also are classified diseases of the respiratory system, which caused 7,099 deaths, equal to 15·26 per 10,000; of the digestive system, responsible for 6,779 deaths, or 14·57 per 10,000; and of the urinary system, the deaths from which numbered 2,313, equal to a rate of 4·94 per 10,000.

Diseases of the Nervous System.

It has been asserted that coincident with the advance of civilisation there has been an increase in diseases of the nerves and brain, but from the figures in the following table showing for each state the number of deaths, and the death-rates, since 1870, it will be seen that such has not been the case. Moreover, it has been ascertained that deaths from apoplexy and convulsions in proportion to population are now less frequent than formerly. In 1902 the total deaths from diseases of the nerves and brain numbered 5,217, or at the rate of 11·21 per 10,000 living.

State.	1871-75.	1876-80.	1881-85.	1886-90.	1891-95.	1896-1900.	1901-2.
Number of Deaths.							
New South Wales	5,881	6,844	8,522	8,432	8,256	7,938	2,888
Victoria	6,503	7,029	7,414	8,585	7,852	7,382	3,009
Queensland	1,656	2,190	2,684	3,005	2,778	2,790	1,173
South Australia	2,068	2,249	2,645	2,177	2,127	2,086	827
Western Australia	*230	309	296	379	510	802	385
Tasmania	1,133	1,238	1,577	1,388	1,210	1,142	390
New Zealand	*1,850	2,614	3,244	3,320	3,528	3,842	1,678
Australasia	......	22,473	26,382	27,286	26,261	25,982	10,350
Death-rate per 10,000 living.							
New South Wales	21·56	20·67	20·23	16·28	13·76	12·10	10·44
Victoria	17·02	17·10	16·26	16·30	13·43	12·45	12·48
Queensland	23·09	21·42	19·93	16·63	13·40	11·95	11·53
South Australia	21·15	18·59	17·99	14·11	12·64	11·76	11·49
Western Australia	*22·17	22·09	18·79	18·16	15·32	10·29	9·81
Tasmania	21·99	22·75	25·78	20·25	16·03	13·80	11·17
New Zealand	*14·93	12·25	12·27	11·02	10·67	10·45	10·64
Australasia	18·61	18·02	17·59	15·42	13·13	11·87	11·21

* Four years, 1872-75.

A study of the table shows that the death-rate for diseases of the nervous system in Australasia has decreased by considerably more than one-third during the last twenty-five years ended with 1900, representing a gain of nearly 7 persons to the population in every 10,000 living. Among the various states the rates for 1901–2 were fairly even, ranging from 9·81 in Western Australia to 12·48 in Victoria. Until the quinquennial period ending 1900 the rate was consistently lower in New Zealand than in any other state, while from 1875 to 1900 Tasmania always had the highest rate. During 1901–2 Victoria showed the highest rate.

Diseases of the Circulatory System.

Diseases of the heart, which now command more attention than previously on account of their more frequent occurrence, and also on account of the better knowledge of the organ which now exists, were responsible in 1902 for 5,569 deaths, or 11·97 per 10,000 living. The following table shows the number of deaths and the death-rates in each state since 1870 :—

State.	1871-75.	1876-80.	1881-85.	1886-90.	1891-95.	1896-1900.	1901-2.
				Number of Deaths.			
New South Wales	2,197	2,755	3,262	4,289	4,826	5,724	2,946
Victoria	3,138	3,666	4,453	6,198	7,365	8,056	3,466
Queensland	444	586	991	1,406	1,575	2,353	1,092
South Australia	649	934	1,130	1,359	1,605	1,995	956
Western Australia	*102	147	201	239	408	748	418
Tasmania	499	578	700	799	875	1,089	400
New Zealand	*795	1,422	1,762	2,284	2,767	3,824	1,887
Australasia	......	10,088	12,549	16,574	19,421	23,789	11,165
				Death-rate per 10,000 living.			
New South Wales	8·05	8·32	7·74	8·28	8·04	8·72	10·65
Victoria	8·21	8·92	9·77	11·77	12·60	13·59	14·38
Queensland	6·19	5·73	7·36	7·78	7·60	10·08	10·74
South Australia	6·64	7·72	8·03	8·81	9·53	11·24	13·29
Western Australia	*9·83	10·51	12·76	11·45	12·26	9·59	10·65
Tasmania	9·69	10·62	11·44	11·66	11·60	13·16	11·45
New Zealand	*6·42	6·66	6·67	7·58	8·37	10·40	11·97
Australasia	7·53	8·09	8·37	9·36	9·71	10·87	12·09

* Four years, 1872–75.

It will be seen that deaths from the diseases of the organs of circulation have steadily and rapidly increased during the last twenty-five years. It is questionable whether the increase shown is not partly due to more skilful diagnosis, as many deaths formerly attributed to old age are now assigned to some more definite cause. The highest death-rates prevail in Victoria and South Australia, which contain the largest number of persons of middle and old age who are most prone to this order of diseases. The only state to show a decrease is Tasmania, where the rate is usually high.

Deaths in Childbirth.

Included under the heading of local diseases are diseases of parturition, which, together with puerperal fever, a septic disease of the zymotic group, comprise the causes of death of women in childbed. In 1902, deaths from these diseases averaged 1 in every 167 births, which differs slightly from the ratio to confinements, as some births are multiple. The table below gives the number of deaths from these diseases in each state since 1872, and the deaths per 1,000 births, the usual method of stating the rate :—

State.	1873-77.	1878-82.	1883-87.	1888-92.	1893-97.	1898-1902.
Number of Deaths.						
New South Wales	*448	555	838	824	1,336	1,311
Victoria	997	899	895	916	942	925
Queensland	189	244	311	368	317	319
South Australia	208	255	241	217	263	223
Western Australia	32	27	31	25	58	167
Tasmania	123	74	88	88	106	116
New Zealand	367	435	582	464	459	479
Australasia	......	2,489	2,981	2,902	3,482	3,540
Death-rate per 1,000 Births.						
New South Wales	*6·43	3·99	4·79	4·24	6·96	7·07
Victoria	7·42	6·74	5·96	4·96	5·61	6·03
Queensland	5·75	6·07	5·33	5·00	4·43	4·48
South Australia	5·32	5·00	4·22	4·06	5·13	4·90
Western Australia	7·48	5·54	4·86	3·01	4·32	6·06
Tasmania	7·88	3·94	3·85	3·62	4·39	4·81
New Zealand	5·13	4·68	5·99	5·06	4·96	4·36
Australasia	......	5·18	5·27	4·90	5·68	5·84

* 1875-77.

The rate showed a tendency to decline up till 1893, since when it has risen. The statistics presented above, however, are not absolutely to be relied upon, for the reason that medical attendants do not take sufficient care when furnishing the certificate required of them by law to state the real cause of death; for instance, it is believed that the word *puerperal* is omitted in many cases, especially of pyæmia and septicæmia where death occurred in childbirth. It is absurd to suppose, as the rates indicate, that there is a greater degree of risk attached to childbirth in New South Wales than in the other states, the only assurance that can be given being that since 1890 the figures for New South Wales are absolutely correct.

Deaths from Violence.

Deaths by violence in 1902 numbered 3,853, or at the rate of 8·28 per 10,000 living. Of these, more than 82 per cent. were the results of accidents or negligence, and more than 11 per cent. were due to suicide, the latter being more fully dealt with in the chapter "Social Condition."

Accidents.

The total number of persons who died in 1902 from accidents was 3,176, or 6·83 per 10,000 living. The following table shows the number of deaths in each state from this cause, and the death-rates since 1870:—

State.	1871–75.	1876–80.	1881–85.	1886–90.	1891–95.	1896–1900.	1901–2.
Number of Deaths.							
New South Wales	2,982	3,569	4,174	4,542	4,520	4,852	1,993
Victoria	3,908	3,539	3,662	4,612	4,262	4,016	1,434
Queensland	1,134	1,389	1,874	2,639	2,349	2,681	926
South Australia	610	877	919	1,038	912	1,141	377
Western Australia	*106	184	184	277	400	1,000	461
Tasmania	492	497	441	551	500	583	162
New Zealand	*1,259	2,200	2,216	2,369	2,494	2,415	1,017
Australasia	......	12,255	13,470	16,028	15,437	16,688	6,370
Death-rate per 10,000 living.							
New South Wales	10·93	10·78	9·91	8·77	7·53	7·39	7·21
Victoria	10·23	8·61	8·03	8·76	7·29	6·77	5·95
Queensland	15·81	13·59	13·91	14·60	11·33	11·49	9·10
South Australia	6·24	7·25	6·25	6·73	5·42	6·43	5·24
Western Australia	*10·22	13·16	11·68	13·28	12·02	12·83	11·74
Tasmania	9·55	9·13	7·21	8·04	6·62	7·04	4·64
New Zealand	*10·16	10·31	8·38	7·86	7·55	6·57	6·45
Australasia	10·10	9·83	8·98	9·06	7·72	7·63	6·90

* Four years, 1872–75.

The death-rates from accidents have fallen considerably, as the table shows, but they are still by no means low, and only Tasmania and South Australia exhibit so small a rate as that of England and Wales, viz., 5·6 per 10,000 living. Western Australia and Queensland, which have the most scattered populations, show the largest rates, while South Australia, where accidents seem always to have been less frequent than in the other states, shows the lowest rate. The most common accidents appear to be fractures, contusions, and drowning, the last mentioned causing a large number of deaths in Queensland every year, the high rate during 1886–90 in that state being due to the great number of people (340) who were drowned in 1890.

MARRIAGES.

The number of marriages and the marriage-rate per thousand of the population for each state during the year 1902 are shown below :—

State.	Marriages.	Marriage-rate.
New South Wales	10,486	7·52
Victoria	8,477	7·02
Queensland	3,243	6·33
South Australia	2,383	6·52
Western Australia	2,024	9·87
Tasmania	1,313	7·47
Commonwealth	27,926	7·24
New Zealand	6,394	8·01
Australasia	34,320	7·37

During 1902 the marriage-rate of Australasia decreased from 7·39 to 7·37 per thousand, but it was higher than the average for the preceding ten years, and this may be looked upon as a sure sign of returning prosperity.

The number of marriages in each state and in the whole of Australasia, in quinquennial periods from 1861 to 1900, and for the years 1901-2 was as follows :—

State.	1861–1865.	1866–1870.	1871–1875.	1876–1880.	1881–1885.	1886–1890.	1891–1895.	1896–1900.	1901–1902.
New South Wales	16,920	18,271	21,210	25,904	35,787	38,671	39,924	45,909	21,024
Victoria	22,237	22,902	24,368	25,416	33,589	42,832	37,717	39,245	16,883
Queensland	3,689	4,648	6,276	7,466	11,682	15,271	13,526	15,479	6,584
South Australia	6,226	6,435	7,472	10,682	12,379	10,334	10,686	10,942	4,692
Western Australia	705	828	835	978	1,112	1,495	2,832	7,902	3,845
Tasmania	3,340	3,143	3,290	4,087	5,005	4,796	4,524	5,598	2,651
Commonwealth	53,177	56,227	63,451	74,583	99,454	113,399	108,709	125,075	55,679
New Zealand	7,240	9,955	12,060	16,220	18,102	18,097	20,210	26,418	12,489
Australasia	60,417	66,182	75,501	90,753	117,556	131,496	128,919	151,493	68,168

The average marriage-rates for each state during the same periods are given below. The table shows the ratio of marriages to population; to ascertain the ratio of persons married it is necessary to double the figures:—

State.	1861–1865.	1866–1870.	1871–1875.	1876–1880.	1881–1885.	1886–1890.	1891–1895.	1896–1900.	1901–1902.
New South Wales	9·04	8·04	7·77	7·82	8·46	7·47	6·64	7·00	7·60
Victoria	7·81	6·86	6·38	6·03	7·37	8·13	6·48	6·62	7·00
Queensland	13·51	9·02	8·75	7·30	8·64	8·45	6·53	6·68	6·47
South Australia.......	9·02	7·45	7·64	8·83	8·42	6·70	6·29	6·17	6·44
Western Australia....	8·92	7·53	6·48	6·99	7·06	7·16	7·01	10·13	9·80
Tasmania	7·30	6·35	6·39	7·51	8·18	7·00	5·87	6·76	7·59
Commonwealth ..	8·54	7·36	7·12	7·21	8·02	7·66	6·50	6·87	7·27
New Zealand	10·39	9·00	8·05	7·60	6·85	6·00	6·11	7·18	7·92
Australasia	8·73	7·61	7·27	7·28	7·84	7·43	6·44	6·92	7·38

During the five years ended 1895 the marriage-rate fell considerably in Australasia. With the exception of New Zealand it was lower in every state than during the preceding quinquennial period, and lower everywhere than during the five years 1881–85, while during the last five years the rate rose again in every state except South Australia. This is another proof of the truth of the oft-repeated statement that commercial depression always exerts an adverse influence on the marriage-rate. The abnormal rise in the case of Western Australia is what might be expected from the large number of men whom the industrial activity in that state has placed in a position to take upon their shoulders the responsibility of a household.

As marriage is the great institution by which the birth-rate is controlled, and through which the population is regulated, it will not be out of place to consider the fertility of marriages in Australasia. The two chief elements influencing this are the age at marriage of the parents, especially of the mother, and the duration of married life. The mean age at marriage of bridegrooms in Australasia is a little over 29 years, and of brides about 24·5 years, and it is known that these ages have been increasing for some years past. As regards the duration of married life, it is not possible to speak with certainty; all that is known is that the length of lifetime of married persons surpasses that of the unmarried—both male and female. The fertility of marriages is reckoned by the number of children to each marriage; and as the difference between the mean age of mothers and the mean age of brides in Australia is between 5 and 6 years, the average number of children to a marriage has been computed for the following table by dividing the number of legitimate births during each quinquennium by the number of marriages during the preceding five years :—

NUMBER of Children to a Marriage.

State.	1871-75.	1876-80.	1881-85.	1886-90.	1891-95.	1896-1900.	1901-2.
New South Wales	5·59	5·76	5·87	5·01	4·80	4·28	4·07
Victoria	5·77	5·20	5·26	4·88	3·99	3·89	3·82
Queensland	6·12	5·75	6·29	5·76	4·54	4·93	4·[illegible]
South Australia	5·53	6·06	5·19	4·19	4·97	4·25	4·19
Western Australia	4·72	5·32	5·35	6·62	......	......	4·[illegible]
Tasmania	4·68	5·01	5·01	4·56	4·93	4·88	4·72
Commonwealth	5·63	5·53	5·55	4·95	4·48	4·[illegible]	4·11
New Zealand	5·94	7·15	5·77	5·03	4·86	4·48	4·02
Australasia	5·68	5·79	5·59	4·96	4·53	4·29	4·10

Western Australia has been excluded from the table during the period from 1890 to 1900, as the sudden influx of population, consequent on the discovery of the gold-fields, unduly increased the number of births to be divided by the number of marriages of the preceding five years, and would have made the marriages of that state appear more fertile than they really are. Of course, the above means of determining the fecundity of marriages is only to be used in the absence of more direct methods ; still the results cannot be very far from the truth, as is proved by the case of New South Wales, where accurate computations have shown the number of children to be expected from the present marriages to be only 3·64. The table shows that, on the whole, the fertility of marriages has been steadily declining since 1885, which bears out what has been before remarked in dealing with this question.

Particulars relative to divorce in Australasia will be found in the chapter headed "Social Condition."

LOCAL GOVERNMENT.

MUNICIPAL INSTITUTIONS.

ONLY of recent years has the question of Local Government received the attention which its importance demands, the states of the Commonwealth that have adopted general systems being Victoria, Queensland, South Australia, and Tasmania. New Zealand, however, has also for a number of years been divided into districts with local governing powers. It will be noted, from the information given in the following pages, that the Acts controlling Local Government vary considerably, especially as regards the election of representatives and presiding officers, method of valuation, and rating powers; and the particulars available in regard to each state are not sufficiently exhaustive to admit of the making of any effective comparison between the systems of the different provinces.

The first portion of this chapter is devoted to an account of the local bodies operating under the various Municipal Acts, while the particulars relating to Boards and Trusts, for the establishment and control of which special Acts have in most cases been passed, will be found in the second part.

NEW SOUTH WALES.

The first Act providing for the establishment of a Local Council in this state was passed in 1842, when the City of Sydney was incorporated. In 1867, the Municipalities Act became law, but as that Act left it optional for any district to become constituted as a municipality, only a small proportion of the area of the state is incorporated.

Under the provisions of the original Acts, the aldermen were elected by the ratepayers (except in the City of Sydney, where both owners and occupiers voted), and the mayors were chosen by the aldermen. By legislation enacted in 1900 the franchise was extended to tenants and lodgers in the city of Sydney, and a similar extension is proposed in the Bill to amend the Municipalities Act of 1867.

During 1900 the Sydney Corporation Amending Act became law. Under its provisions the city is divided into twelve wards, each returning two aldermen, instead of into eight wards, each represented by three aldermen, as heretofore. The mayor is still to be elected by the aldermen, as the proposal to provide for his election by the citizens was not carried. Other important amendments are those providing (1) for the abolition of auditors elected by citizens, with the substitution of Government inspectors to audit the accounts; and (2) for the resumption of land for the opening or enlarging of streets or public places. The rating powers have not been altered, the general rate remaining at not more than 2s. in the £ of the annual value, but lighting and other special rates may also be imposed, if necessary.

The Municipalities Act of 1867 provided that the general rate should not exceed 1s. in the £ of the annual value, but that special rates could be levied, so long as the general and special rates together did not come to more than 2s. in the £. A further charge, limited to 6d. in the £, could be made for street-watering, and an additional rate for water supply, where necessary, the amount not to exceed 1s. in the £. The amending Bill, introduced in 1901, and again in 1902, proposed to give power to the councils to increase the general rate to as much as 1s. 6d. in the £ of the annual value if necessary, but the special rates were to remain as quoted in the original Act. A most important alteration in the principles of municipal taxation was the authority to be conferred on the municipalities to levy their rates on the unimproved capital value of the land instead of on the annual value of all property, provided that the ratepayers agreed to the alteration by a special vote. The assessment of the unimproved value was not to exceed 2d. in the £ of the assessed capital value. The Bill referred to has not yet been passed into law, and it is now proposed to submit another measure providing for a more comprehensive scheme of local government as soon as a favourable opportunity offers.

The total area incorporated at the close of the municipal year 1902 was only 2,816 square miles, so that it will be seen that a large area still remains under the control of the central government in New South Wales. For this some justification is claimed on account of the largeness of the territory and the sparseness of the population residing in the unincorporated areas; but this is hardly tenable, seeing that both these conditions exist to a greater degree in Queensland, where the whole territory is under local government. The total area still unincorporated in New South Wales amounts to 307,884 square miles.

The total capital value of all property in municipalities is returned as £130,019,800, and the annual value as £8,080,160, so that the annual return from property is about 6·21 per cent.

Taking the municipalities as a whole, the following particulars in regard to the number of municipalities, the area incorporated, and the annual and capital values of property assessed for municipal purposes, will not be without interest. The figures relate to all municipalities, and cover eleven years :—

Year.	No. of Municipalities.	Area Incorporated.	Annual Value.	Capital Value.
		acres.	£	£
1892	168	1,637,046	8,697,503	144,277,400
1893	171	1,660,675	8,929,475	150,938,000
1894	175	1,683,990	8,460,674	151,226,000
1895	182	1,754,941	7,895,645	136,202,100
1896	183	1,767,079	7,603,735	127,499,700
1897	183	1,767,749	7,430,120	122,787,000
1898	184	1,768,500	7,379,350	120,625,600
1899	184	1,768,500	7,412,100	121,213,800
1900	189	1,807,522	7,905,760	124,546,200
1901	191	1,802,532	8,109,200	127,996,900
1902	191	1,802,532	8,080,160	130,019,800

The annual and capital values of Sydney and suburbs since 1892 are shown below :—

Year.	Sydney and Suburbs.		Year.	Sydney and Suburbs.	
	Annual Value.	Capital Value.		Annual Value.	Capital Value.
	£	£		£	£
1892	6,013,697	106,891,100	1898	4,965,400	86,927,600
1893	6,067,882	110,061,000	1899	4,995,200	87,464,000
1894	5,686,197	108,951,000	1900	5,069,630	88,116,600
1895	5,352,920	96,692,200	1901	5,188,700	90,060,600
1896	5,141,990	91,427,100	1902	5,455,270	93,413,300
1897	5,022,910	88,464,400			

A reference to these figures will show the depreciation which has taken place in the value of real estate since 1892, but it is satisfactory to note that a steady increase is shown from 1898 ; while the annual value for 1902 exceeds that of any previous year since 1894, and the capital value is higher than in any year since 1895.

In view of the fact that it is proposed in the new Bill to levy rates on the unimproved values of land, the following statement will be of some value :—

Division.	Estimated Unimproved Value.
City of Sydney	£20,207,800
Suburban Municipalities	19,583,600
Total Metropolitan	£39,791,400
Country Municipalities	13,942,000
Grand Total	£53,733,400

The values of five of the principal towns are given in the subjoined table, and for the purposes of comparison, the corresponding figures for 1892 are shown. With regard to Broken Hill, it should be remembered that the mines were not fully developed in 1892, and although the capital value in 1899 had increased by about £364,000, the values in the years 1894 and 1895 were stated to be £2,952,000, and £2,862,000 respectively, but for 1897 the figures declined to £1,232,600, which was practically the value in 1899. The annual and capital values shown for 1902 exclude the assessments on the output of the silver mines, as the mining companies were successful in the appeals against the rating of their products :—

Town.	1892.		1902.	
	Annual Value.	Capital Value.	Annual Value.	Capital Value.
	£	£	£	£
Bathurst	70,363	905,000	54,885	935,400
Broken Hill	244,776	1,410,000	223,860	1,438,000
Goulburn	89,222	1,330,000	61,475	940,800
Newcastle and suburbs	496,200	6,784,000	397,675	7,235,000
Parramatta	83,440	1,692,000	66,495	1,330,000

The revenues of municipalities are derived chiefly from rates, but under the Act of 1867 the Government allows an endowment for the first fifteen years following incorporation, the scale being £ for £ of general rates received during the first five years, 10s. per £ during the next five years, and 5s. per £ for the remaining period. The Government also contributes grants in aid of roads and other works, and occasionally a special endowment is given. Rates are levied on nine-tenths of the annual value of improved property, and on 5 per cent. of the capital value of unimproved land, except in the City of Sydney, where the maximum percentage on unimproved is 6 per cent. The following table shows the receipts during 1902, the Government endowments and grants being specified. The total shown is exclusive of refunds and cross entries, but it includes proceeds of loans :—

	£
Total receipts—	
Government	84,866
Rates	567,789
Other Revenue	266,957
Total	919,612

	£	s.	d.
Receipts per inhabitant in incorporated area—			
Government	0	1	11
Rates	0	12	8
Other Revenue	0	6	0
Total	1	0	7

The burthen of rates is, therefore, 1s. 4¾d. per £ of annual improved value, and about 2½d. per £ of estimated unimproved capital value.

The total expenditure, exclusive of refunds, &c., for the same period amounted to £892,076, distributed as follows :—

	£
Public works, services, and improvements	501,050
Interest on loans and overdrafts	132,482
Repayments of loans	110,837
Salaries and office expenses	80,546
Payments to sinking funds	16,637
Other expenditure	50,524
	£892,076

The proportion of the expenditure incurred for salaries and office expenses was slightly over 9 per cent., and for interest on loans and overdrafts it was 14·85 per cent., while the average rate of interest payable on the liabilities was 4·49 per cent.

The amount of loans and secured overdrafts outstanding on the 3rd February, 1902, was £2,882,140, of which £1,316,753 was due to investors in London, principally by the city of Sydney, while of the balance, £18,420 was floated in Victoria, and £1,546,967 in New South Wales. The unsecured overdrafts amounted to £68,405, so that the total liability on which interest was payable was £2,950,545. The interest charged ranged from 3½ to 8 per cent. for the secured loans, and from 4 to 8½ per cent. on the unsecured overdrafts. Against the total liability, sinking funds have been established, the total amount at the credit of such funds being £295,415.

VICTORIA.

In Victoria a comprehensive system of local government has been in force for many years. In 1842 the Act of the Legislative Council of New South Wales, which incorporated Sydney, also constituted Melbourne a municipality, and in 1874 the general system was inaugurated. Under this system the state is divided into cities, towns, boroughs, and shires, and the total area under local control is 87,322 square miles, only 562 square miles remaining unincorporated.

The councillors are elected by the ratepayers, and the mayors of cities, towns, and boroughs, or presidents of shire councils, are elected by the councillors. A general rate of not more than 2s. 6d. or less than 6d. in the £ of the annual value may be imposed, but special rates may be levied, provided that general and special rates together do not exceed 2s. 6d. in the £. A further special rate, limited to 6d., may also be charged for works in particular parts of any district.

The number of municipalities with the annual and capital values of property assessed for local purposes for the ten years ending with 1902, were as follows :—

Year.	No. of Municipalities.	Annual Value.	Capital Value.
		£	£
1893	201	13,605,990	197,366,940
1894	203	12,779,600	189,461,350
1895	207	11,676,079	174,984,851
1896	208	10,641,200	167,197,780
1897	208	10,393,000	168,427,700
1898	208	10,345,535	171,253,984
1899	208	10,152,500	168,611,906
1900	208	10,283,500	169,911,900
1901	208	10,537,497	174,141,754
1902	208	10,885,087	185,101,993

The total capital value of property assessed for municipal purposes in 1902 was £185,101,993, while the annual value was £10,885,087, the figures for Melbourne and suburbs being £66,190,119 and £4,365,297 respectively. The values for the metropolitan district since 1893 are given below, and it will be noticed how great has been the decrease during the period under review, though both the annual and capital values for 1902 show a marked improvement, and are higher than in any year since 1895 :—

Year.	Melbourne and Suburbs.		Year.	Melbourne and Suburbs.	
	Annual Value.	Capital Value.		Annual Value.	Capital Value.
	£	£		£	£
1893	6,639,014	88,510,328	1898	3,968,888	60,404,877
1894	5,847,079	78,916,730	1899	3,973,357	60,626,915
1895	4,984,596	66,824,384	1900	4,042,497	60,255,735
1896	4,299,515	60,962,705	1901	4,144,816	61,296,623
1897	4,168,182	60,352,040	1902	4,365,297	66,190,119

The annual and capital values for the five principal provincial municipalities for 1892 and 1902 will be found in the following statement, the annual return from property having been estimated at 7 per cent. :—

City, Town, or Borough.	1892.		1902.	
	Annual Value.	Capital Value.	Annual Value.	Capital Value.
	£	£	£	£
Ballarat	177,972	2,542,457	160,925	2,298,929
Ballarat, East..................	79,360	1,133,714	79,139	1,130,557
Bendigo	167,305	2,390,071	193,311	2,761,585
Geelong	97,303	1,390,043	89,243	1,274,900
Geelong, West	30,230	431,857	26,490	378,375

The revenue of the local governing bodies is chiefly derived from taxation, under the headings of general and special rates (which are levied on the net annual value), licenses, dog fees, market and weighbridge dues, etc. The total amount collected from all sources during the year 1901 was £1,656,917, of which £181,081 was contributed by the Government, either as endowment, special grant, or loan, while the amount of rates received was £736,004, and £169,087 was received from licenses, fees, &c., the total local taxation thus being £905,091. The balance, £570,745, includes sanitary fees amounting to £42,624, £54,117 received as rents of municipal property, £370,574 as loans, £23,201 for contributions to works, and £80,229 from other sources. The receipts per inhabitant in incorporated areas amounted to £1 7s. 8d. The amount received as rates shown above represents a tax of 1s. 4¼d. in the £ of annual value, and 1½d. per £ of the estimated unimproved capital value.

The total expenditure for the year 1901 was £1,581,352, of which £1,093,193 were spent on public works, &c., while the amount paid for interest was £188,405. The payments to sinking funds were £15,675, and the repayments of loans from revenue, £12,070, the principal items in the balance being—salaries, £139,270, representing 12·74 per cent. of the total, and printing, &c., £22,153. The proportion paid as interest on loans and overdrafts was about 17 per cent. of the total, while the average interest paid on loans and overdrafts amounted to about £4 5s. 5d. per cent.

The municipal loans outstanding were £4,253,304, of which £286,327 were borrowed through the Government, and the bank overdrafts amounted to £157,046, giving a total interest-bearing liability of £4,410,350. The total liabilities were £4,637,041, other items being—amount due on contracts, £103,960; temporary advances from Government, £20,901; overdue interest on loans, £9,413; and other, £92,417. The assets totalled £4,149,471, and consisted of—municipal property, £2,768,848; sinking funds, £676,701; unexpended loan funds, £394,136; outstanding rates, £187,205; bank balances and cash in hand, £29,849; contributions due for streets, &c., £24,507; and miscellaneous, £68,225.

QUEENSLAND.

The beginning of local government in Queensland was the proclamation constituting Brisbane a municipality, the date of which was the 6th September, 1859, or about three months prior to the separation of the colony from New South Wales. A general system of government by local authorities was inaugurated in 1878, when the colony was divided into boroughs, shires, and divisions, and in 1902 the Local Authorities Act was passed, which consolidated and amended all measures relating to local government. This Act also provides that the local areas shall be called cities, towns and shires, and the members are called aldermen in cities and towns, and councillors in the shires.

The aldermen and councillors are elected by ratepayers in each area, while mayors of cities and towns and chairmen of shires are chosen by the representatives.

Under the provisions of the original Act, the rates were levied on the annual value, and the maximum general rate was 1s. in the £ for boroughs, shires, and divisions, but the minimum was 6d. per £ for boroughs and shires, and 4d. per £ in divisions. Special rates could also be imposed for sewerage, drainage, lighting, street-watering, sanitary works, loans, or particular works. By an amending Act passed in December, 1890, the rates thenceforward were to be charged on the unimproved capital value of the land, and this system has been continued in the 1902 Act. The maximum general rate now allowed is 3d. in the £ for all areas, while the minimum is ½d. The separate rates may still be charged, and if waterworks have been established a further rate may be imposed for that service.

The total area controlled by local bodies is 668,252 square miles, leaving only 245 square miles unincorporated. The total capital value was estimated at the end of 1902 to be £43,203,000. This represents the value of land without improvements; if improvements had been considered, the capital value would have been approximately £71,725,000, and the annual value £4,554,000.

The unimproved capital value declined steadily from 1893 to 1896, but from 1897 it improved gradually, and in 1901 it was even greater than in the first year of the period. The 1902 figures show a small falling-off, which was only to be expected owing to the bad season. The following statement shows the total unimproved values from 1893 to 1902:—

Year.	Assessed Value of Unimproved Property.	Year.	Assessed Value of Unimproved Property.
	£		£
1893	43,427,923	1898	41,486,971
1894	41,772,975	1899	42,195,693
1895	40,821,733	1900	42,722,090
1896	40,810,384	1901	43,897,000
1897	41,009,739	1902	43,203,000

The capital values of Brisbane and some of the other large boroughs are given below for 1892 and 1902:—

Municipality.	1892.	1902
	Unimproved Capital Value.	Unimproved Capital Value.
	£	£
Brisbane	5,528,798	5,881,846
South Brisbane	2,391,992	1,426,235
Other Brisbane Suburbs	5,695,195	4,390,853
Rockhampton	1,357,514	1,041,338
North Rockhampton	192,724	156,282
Townsville	1,257,820	864,206
Toowoomba	710,815	618,880

North Rockhampton has been included, as it is a suburb of Rockhampton.

The receipts for the year 1902 amounted to £601,806, the chief sources being—Government endowments, grants, and loans, £157,900, and rates, £321,831 (levied, as already stated, on the unimproved capital value), leaving £122,075 derived from other sources. The amount collected for rates represents 1s. 7d. per £ of the annual value and 1¾d. per £ of capital value. The expenditure for the same period was £595,314, the amount spent on public works being £399,262, while repayments of loans and interest amounted to £39,934, salaries and office expenses to £58,618, or 9·85 per cent. of total, and all other disbursements £97,500.

The outstanding loans, including overdue instalments payable to the Government, amounted to £1,118,307, the whole of which, with the exception of the loans of the city of Brisbane (£335,500), and part of the indebtedness of South Brisbane (£105,000), is due to the Government, as no local body, except the two mentioned, is allowed to borrow from outside sources. The amount of other liabilities was £226,747, making a total of £1,345,054 owing by local bodies.

The total assets on the same date were given as £1,686,247, the only item specified being outstanding rates, which amounted to £125,496.

South Australia.

Adelaide, the capital of South Australia, was proclaimed a municipality as far back as 1840, and was thus the first local body established in Australasia. The present general system of corporations and district councils was instituted in 1887.

In all cases the councillors and mayors are elected by the citizens, the representatives not being empowered to choose their presiding officer. The rates are assessed on the annual value, and the general rate must not exceed 1s. in the £; while lighting rates are limited to

4d., and park improvement rates to 3d. Water rates may also be imposed where necessary, and special rates for works in particular portions of municipalities.

The total area incorporated at the close of the last municipal year was 42,493 square miles, leaving 337,577 square miles still under the control of the central government. The unincorporated territory consists chiefly of the unsettled portion of the state, as the populous centres have all been brought under municipal government. The figures in this chapter relating to South Australia are in all cases exclusive of the Northern Territory.

The annual and capital values of all the incorporated districts for the ten years ending with 1901 are as shown in the following table :—

Year.	Annual Value.	Capital Value.
	£	£
1892	2,538,094	41,031,000
1893	2,561,806	41,428,000
1894	2,552,820	41,325,000
1895	2,494,326	40,512,000
1896	2,463,564	40,076,000
1897	2,485,995	40,472,000
1898	2,518,688	41,047,000
1899	2,553,415	41,668,000
1900	2,576,729	42,080,000
1901	2,590,357	42,341,000

The capital value of the incorporated districts in 1901 as shown above was estimated at £42,341,000, and the annual value at £2,590,357. Adelaide, and its suburbs are the largest corporations, and the following were the values of the most important centres for 1901, compared with those for 1892 :—

Corporation.	1892.	1901.
	Annual Value.	Annual Value.
	£	£
Adelaide	392,820	434,538
Port Adelaide	124,791	152,758
Unley	80,894	116,780
Kensington and Norwood	69,459	75,943
Hindmarsh	45,639	56,310
St. Peters	39,836	52,243
Glenelg	37,099	36,939
Thebarton	22,640	30,673
Brighton	11,015	10,725

The total receipts for 1901 were £369,089, the amount contributed by the Government as subsidy and grants being £110,824, while the rates collected were £150,610, leaving £107,655 from other sources. The rates collected which are levied on the annual value equal 1s. 2d.

in the £ of the annual value and 1d. per £ of unimproved capital value. The expenditure was £368,476 the amount spent on works being £210,787, while salaries and office expenses absorbed £29,823, or 8·09 per cent., and miscellaneous services, £127,866.

The loans outstanding at the close of 1902 amounted to only £81,900. These loans, with the exception of £6,000 owing by the corporation of Kensington and Norwood, were floated by the Adelaide City Council. The interest payable ranges from 3 to 6 per cent., the average being 4·41 per cent.

Western Australia.

The great resources of this state have only been made manifest during recent years, and the limited population, compared with the vast area of the province, has prevented any great extension of local government.

The first Municipalities Act was passed in 1871, but only a few districts were incorporated under it. In 1900 the existing Act, which consolidated the previous Acts, became law, and a considerable increase in the area locally controlled has resulted from its provisions. The local bodies are termed Municipalities, Road Boards, and Health Boards; the latter may be established within or outside municipal boundaries.

The Municipal Act provides for the election of both councillors and mayors by the ratepayers. With regard to Road Boards, however, the members are elected by the ratepayers, and the chairmen by the members.

The general rate imposed in municipalities must not exceed 1s. 6d. in the £ of annual value, and a special rate of 3d. in the £ may be levied under the Health Act. In the City of Perth, however, an additional rate is charged for water-supply; this rate must not exceed 1s. in the £ of annual value. In the Road Board districts the general rate is limited to 1s. in the £ of annual value.

The total area of municipalities is only about 112 square miles. The remainder of the state comprises 975,808 square miles, a large proportion of which is still under the central government. The Road Board Districts occupy a considerable area, but as the general government exercises a certain amount of control over the expenditure, these districts cannot be said to be endowed with full local government.

The capital value for the year 1901 was estimated at £8,181,100, and the annual value at £981,700. The particulars for 1891 are not available, but it may be said generally that since 1895, the earliest year for which figures are obtainable, there has been a considerable increase both in the annual and capital values. The following table shows the annual values of some of the most important towns for 1896 and 1901. These values as shown in the official figures range from 10 to 13 per cent. of the capital values, but as this return from property in old settled districts like Perth and Albany seems improbable, and as the assessments are on the annual value, the capital values cannot be said to have been properly ascertained, and, therefore, are not given:—

Municipality.	Annual Value.	
	1896.	1901.
	£	£
Perth	105,409	277,166
Albany	24,320	29,507
Fremantle	74,140	121,819
,, North	11,810	20,363
,, East	*	19,580
Coolgardie	38,732	47,038
Kalgoorlie	22,355	141,710
Boulder	*	82,289

* Not incorporated.

The total receipts for 1901 amounted to £227,128, included in which is the sum of £66,860 given by the Central Government as subsidy and special allowances. The general and special rates received were £78,022, while the remainder, £82,246, represents £11,740 collections from rents, £7,631 from license fees, &c., £51,264 proceeds of loans, and £11,611 from all other sources. The disbursements in the same year came to £214,415, of which the large proportion of £146,369 was spent on works and improvements. The other important items are:—Salaries and office expenses, £14,218, or 6·63 per cent.; and interest on loans and overdrafts, £15,264; leaving £38,564 expended on other services, including £8,530 for payments to sinking funds.

The amount shown for rates represents a tax of 1s. 7d. per £ of annual value, and 3¾d. per £ of estimated unimproved capital value.

The total liabilities at the close of the year were approximately £371,733, the principal item being outstanding loans, which amounted to £352,000. The unsecured overdrafts (including unpaid cheques) amounted to £1,452, the balance, £18,281, being due for amounts owing on contracts, outstanding accounts, &c. Against the loan indebtedness, however, must be placed the accumulated sinking fund, which amounts to £42,311.

The assets on the same date were estimated at £308,046. The largest proportion of this amount is accounted for by the value of landed property, plant, and furniture, which was stated to be £214,984. The outstanding rates amounted to £8,923; while other important items were:—Bank and cash balances, and fixed deposits, £37,260, and sinking fund, £42,311, leaving £4,568 for other assets.

The information given above is incomplete, as some of the municipalities failed to furnish the necessary financial returns required by the Government.

TASMANIA.

In this state, the city of Hobart was incorporated by a special Act in 1852, and in 1858 the Rural Municipalities Act was passed which provided for the establishment of corporations throughout the state. The whole area of the state is not under the provisions of this Act alone, as there are other bodies, notably Town Boards and Road Trusts, which are authorised to control outlying districts.

In the urban municipalities—Hobart and Launceston—the aldermen are elected by the ratepayers, and the mayors by the aldermen. The ratepayers in the rural districts also elect their representatives, who are termed councillors, and the latter have the privilege of choosing their presiding officer, who is called warden.

The general rate in each class of corporation is limited to 1s. 6d. in the £ of the annual value, while special rates may be levied in rural districts, provided that the general and special rates together do not exceed 1s. 6d. in the £. Road rates may also be imposed in addition to municipal rates.

The area of municipal districts may be set down as 10,771 square miles, leaving 15,444 square miles under the control of the other local bodies, or of the central government. The total capital value at the close of 1901 was estimated at £26,664,500, and the annual value at £1,449,255. These figures may be somewhat over-stated, as the same property may be rated by more than one of the local authorities. The values of the two principal municipalities will be found below, and a reference to the corresponding particulars for 1892 will show that Tasmania has not been very much affected by the depreciation of property, which was so severely felt in the mainland States :—

Municipality.	1892.		1901.	
	Annual Value.	Capital Value.	Annual Value.	Capital Value.
	£	£	£	£
Hobart	180,716	3,614,320	173,813	3,476,260
Launceston	140,253	2,805,060	128,434	2,568,680

The total receipts of Municipalities, Town Boards, and Road Trusts for 1901 were £167,077, the proportion contributed by the central government being only £20,194. The bulk of the collections consisted of rates (which are levied on the annual value), the amount of which was £93,836; and the remainder, £53,047, was accounted for by fees, licenses, proceeds of loans, &c. The total expenditure for the same year amounted to £166,343, but no details relating to this sum are available. The collections for rates are equal to 1s. 3½d. in the £ of annual value, and 1¼d. per £ of the estimated unimproved value.

The total loans outstanding at the close of 1901 for the local bodies under review amounted to £590,773, of which a sum of £86,937 is due to the Government, but in the majority of cases sinking funds have been established for the extinction of the debts, the total amount accumulated at the end of 1901 being £62,356.

New Zealand.

In New Zealand an Act was passed in 1852 which divided the colony into six provinces, the local administration being vested in provincial councils. This system continued till 1876, when the provincial system was abolished, and the whole colony, except the area within the forty-one boroughs then existing, was subdivided into counties, each county having full control of its local affairs.

The provisions for election differ in the boroughs and counties. In the former bodies both the councillors and mayors are elected by "burgesses," but in counties, the councillors are elected by the "county electors," and the chairmen by the councillors. The rating powers are also different. In boroughs, the rates are in most cases levied on the annual value, and the general rate is limited to 1s. 3d. in the £. Special rates may also be imposed, but general and special rates together must not exceed 1s. 3d. in the £. In counties, and in a few of the boroughs (the latter having taken advantage of the "Rating on Unimproved Value Act of 1896"), the rates are charged on the capital value, and the general rate must not exceed three farthings in the £ in counties or boroughs where road boards or town districts exist, and six farthings in other local areas. Separate rates may also be levied, provided the general and special rates do not exceed three farthings and six farthings in the £ respectively; and extra rates for special works, for interest and sinking funds on loans, and, where necessary, for hospitals and charitable aid, may be charged.

In addition to the boroughs and counties, road districts and town districts have been proclaimed, and the area locally governed may practically be set down at 104,471 square miles, the total area of the colony.

The capital value for 1902 may be estimated at £154,816,000, and the annual value at £7,158,000. The remarks with regard to the over-statement of the values in Tasmania may also be applied to New Zealand, as the boundaries of the various districts in some cases may overlap.

The distribution of the population of New Zealand differs from that of the Commonwealth. In the Australian States, especially those in the eastern portion of the continent, the great majority of the people are centred in the metropolitan areas, and consequently the capital and annual values are proportionately great in the chief cities. In New

Zealand, however, there are four large centres of population, and the values of the assessed properties are shown below. The figures for 1893 are also shown, and it will be noticed that the values have largely improved, as New Zealand, like Tasmania, did not experience the great depreciation which took place in some of the other states after the Bank reconstructions in 1893 :—

Borough	1893.		1902.	
	Annual Value.	Capital Value.	Annual Value.	Capital Value.
	£	£	£	£
Wellington	322,450	6,141,900	473,599	9,056,600
Auckland	297,728	4,802,000	351,821	5,676,700
Dunedin	251,000	4,482,100	268,965	4,823,400
Christchurch	196,325	2,804,600	246,086	3,364,900

The total receipts for 1902 amounted to £1,866,422, the Government contributions being £417,698, inclusive of loans. The collections from rates (which are levied chiefly on capital values) were £726,009, and from other sources £722,715, represented chiefly by fees for licenses and rents. The expenditure for the same period was £1,826,378, the amount spent on works being £1,093,171; on hospitals and charitable aid, £76,008; on management, £133,797 or 7·33 per cent. of the total; and on other services, £523,402. The payments for interest, contributions to sinking funds, and repayments of loans, are not shown separately in the total expenditure, and the amounts disbursed under these heads are, therefore, not available. The rates collected represent 2s. 0¼d. per £ of annual value, and 1¾d. per £ of estimated unimproved value.

The total loans outstanding at the close of 1902 for the bodies referred to amounted to £4,496,776, and the sinking fund was £379,568, the net indebtedness, therefore, being £4,117,208. The annual charge for interest and sinking fund is approximately £247,793, the rates of interest ranging from 4 to 7 per cent.

Comparison of Cities.

Estimated by the annual value of its ratable property, Sydney is, and has been for many years, the second city of the British Empire; next comes Glasgow, and then Melbourne, as Manchester, exclusive of Salford, is valued at £3,464,400. None of the other Australasian cities ranks high on the list, but the extreme value of property in relation to population in the Australasian population centres as compared with the principal British cities, will be seen from the following table :—

Cities and Towns.	Population.	Annual Value.	
		Total.	Per Inhabitant.
		£	£ s. d.
Australasia—			
Sydney	516,180	5,455,270	10 11 4
Newcastle and suburbs	56,760	397,675	7 0 2
Melbourne	478,904	4,365,297	9 2 4
Ballarat and Ballarat East	43,823	240,064	5 9 7
Brisbane	122,315	1,187,393	9 14 2
Adelaide	165,723	1,167,740	7 0 11
Perth	42,474	409,545	9 12 10
Hobart	34,809	173,813	4 19 10
Wellington	52,590	511,354	9 14 6
United Kingdom—			
London (County)	4,536,541	40,142,274	8 17 0
Glasgow	760,423	5,100,006	6 14 2
Manchester (including Salford)	764,619	4,434,892	5 16 0
Liverpool	710,337	4,114,875	5 15 10
Edinburgh	316,479	2,924,173	9 4 9
Birmingham	522,182	2,759,032	5 5 8
Leeds	437,341	1,804,410	4 2 6
Bristol	334,632	1,610,276	4 16 3
Sheffield	418,765	1,610,931	3 16 11
Bradford	279,809	1,462,746	5 4 7
Newcastle-on-Tyne	214,803	1,299,388	6 1 0
Belfast	349,180	1,204,430	3 9 0
Cardiff	164,420	1,059,751	6 8 11
Nottingham	239,753	1,110,599	4 12 8
Hull	240,739	1,004,702	4 3 6
Dublin	289,108	844,476	2 18 5

The populations of the Australasian cities and towns given in the table are the estimates at the dates of the annual valuations of the incorporated districts and not the present populations.

Boards and Trusts in New South Wales.

In addition to the municipalities, there are bodies known as Boards or Trusts whose function it is to construct and supervise certain works which have been established for the benefit of districts generally comprising one or more of the ordinary municipalities. These bodies are usually composed of members representing respectively the central Government, the municipalities affected, and other persons directly interested in the particular undertakings; and as a rule they raise the funds necessary for carrying out the works they control, by means of rates on the assessed value of the properties benefited, as is the case with municipalities.

In New South Wales there are the Metropolitan Board of Water Supply and Sewerage, having charge of the water supply, which it assumed in 1888, and of the sewerage system, which it has controlled since 1889, and the Hunter River District Board of Water Supply and Sewerage, formed in 1892. The Wollongong Harbour Trust, which was instituted in 1889, was the only one of the kind in the state up to the year 1900—the works connected with shipping, and the improvements to navigation, at Sydney, Newcastle, and other ports, having always been carried out at the expense and under the supervision of the central Government. The Wollongong Trust, however, failed, and its powers have been assumed by the Government. During the year 1900, an Act was passed for the establishment of a Harbour Trust for the port of Sydney, and in the same year the Wharfs Resumption Act became law, which enabled the Government to acquire certain wharf properties in Darling Harbour; these wharfs, and others, originally the property of the Government, are now controlled by the Harbour Trust. The total receipts for the period 11th February, 1901, to 30th June, 1902, amounted to £277,963, and the expenditure, exclusive of interest on capital, to £85,250, leaving £192,713 to meet charges for interest and sinking fund. There is also a Metropolitan Fire Brigades Board, on which the municipalities within the metropolitan area are represented, and towards the annual expenses of which they contribute one-third. The fire insurance companies and the state Government are also represented, and contribute equally with the municipalities in maintaining the Fire Brigades Board. Thirty-eight country boards have also been established under the Fire Brigades Act of 1884, four of which are, however, within the area administered by the Metropolitan Board, and contribute to its funds.

The Country Towns Water Supply and Sewerage Act of New South Wales was passed in 1880. Under the provisions of this measure municipalities outside the area under the control of the Metropolitan and Hunter District Water Supply and Sewerage Boards were entitled to construct, or to have constructed for them by the Government, works for water supply and sewerage, provided the construction of the same were approved by the Governor-in-Council and the municipalities agreed to pay back the original cost of the works with interest at the rate of 4 per cent. per annum. The Government were to pay the certified cost of the works, and the municipalities were to repay the Government by instalments extending over a period of sixty years. Under the operations of this Act twenty-seven water-supply works have been carried out by the Government (exclusive of Richmond, now administered by the Metropolitan Board of Water Supply and Sewerage), and three by municipal councils, while works in forty-five other places were in course of construction on the 31st December, 1902, including additions to twenty-three existing works. The amount advanced by the Government to local bodies under the Act to the end of 1892 was £370,549, and instalments to the amount of £85,886 were then overdue. It was found that the liability of some of the municipal councils was too heavy for their resources, and in 1894 an amending Act was passed distributing the payments over 100 years and reducing the interest to 3½ per cent. On the 31st December, 1902, the total amount expended by Government, inclusive of interest, stood at £847,613, viz. : £572,333 for works completed under Government control; £27,344 for works carried out under the supervision of municipal councils; and £247,936 for works still in course of construction. Of the total amount of £599,677 due on account of completed works to the 31st December, 1902, £19,266 had been repaid, and £81,162 had been remitted by Government, leaving the debt at £499,249, which is repayable by annual instalments of £18,055.

Boards and Trusts in Victoria.

In Victoria the port of Melbourne is under the control of a Harbour Trust, which was established as far back as 1877. A Tramway Trust, representing twelve of the metropolitan municipalities, viz.:—Melbourne, Prahran, Richmond, Fitzroy, Collingwood, South Melbourne, Hawthorn, Kew, St. Kilda, North Melbourne, Brunswick, and Port Melbourne, was formed under the provisions of an Act passed in 1883. This body was entrusted with power to construct tramways through the streets of the municipalities interested, the requisite funds being raised by loans on the security of the tramways and the revenues of the municipal bodies connected with the undertaking. The trustees had the option either of working the tramways themselves or of leasing them to a private company. They adopted the latter alternative, and the tramways are being worked on a thirty-two years' lease, commencing from 1884. In 1891 the Melbourne and Metropolitan Board of Works was established for the purpose of constructing and supervising all works connected with water supply, sewerage, and drainage in Melbourne and suburbs. The Government is not directly represented on this Board, which differs from the Metropolitan Board of Water Supply in Sydney, of which three members are nominated by the state. The reason for this difference is that in New South Wales the Government constructs the works and is responsible for the debt incurred in doing so, while in Victoria the Board carries out the work of construction in addition to the maintenance and management to which the operations of the Sydney Board are confined. Throughout Victoria there are Water Works Trusts and Irrigation and Water Supply Trusts. During 1901-1902 there were seventy-four Water Works Trusts and thirty-two Irrigation and Water Supply Trusts. The Government authorised an advance of £1,240,934 for the former service, and for the latter £1,452,400, and the amounts outstanding in June, 1902, were £754,450 and £415,282 respectively, the large sum of £723,662 having been written off the debt of the Irrigation Trusts. As in New South Wales, the municipal bodies are represented on the Fire Brigade Boards, and bear a proportionate share of the expenses.

The Government of Victoria, prior to the establishment of the Trusts for Water Works, Irrigation, and Water Supply, advanced money from the Public Loans Account to local bodies requiring assistance to construct these works. The amount advanced for the development of the services to June, 1902, including arrears of interest capitalised, was £421,356, which has to be repaid into a sinking fund, or by annual instalments. The amount outstanding on the date mentioned was only £152,759, owing to large sums having been written off during the last two years. The figures just given are exclusive of the advances to the city of Ballarat for the water-supply works, as these are now under a special commission. The outstanding debt of the Ballarat Water Commission on the 30th June, 1902, was £324,197. Under a special Act the Government have power to advance funds to shires for the construction of tramways, and £60,811 had been so advanced up to June, 1902. The Government, under two different Acts, can also make advances to shires for the purchase of rabbit-proof fencing. The amount so advanced to June, 1902, was £192,370, of which £19,801 was outstanding on that date.

BOARDS AND TRUSTS IN OTHER STATES.

In Queensland the water supply service forms part of the local government system; the works are proposed by the municipal bodies, but the Government constructs and supervises them, and when completed hands them over to the local authorities with their attendant liabilities. The latter form a debt to the state which is repaid in instalments. The total cost of construction to 31st December, 1902, was £1,220,307, and the amount due to the Government on the same date was £831,977.

In South Australia there are no Boards or Trusts of any importance beyond the municipal bodies already mentioned; extensive municipal powers exist, however, for raising loans for the construction of local works, and each corporation and District Council is constituted a Board of Health.

In Western Australia there are Road Boards, Local Boards of Health, and a Metropolitan Water Works Board.

In Tasmania seven Marine Boards, forming part of the local government system, have been established in different parts of the state, and there are fifteen Water Trusts in connection with municipal bodies.

In New Zealand there are, in addition to the ordinary forms of municipal government, River and Harbour Boards, which are established throughout the colony. The number of these at the end of 1902 was respectively thirty-one and twenty-eight. There is a Drainage Board at Christchurch, while there are sixteen Land Drainage Boards, and Water Supply Boards at Waimakariri—Ashley and Manukau.

Complete information relating to the Boards and Trusts in each state is not readily obtainable; the following table, however, which has been compiled from the latest available returns, gives important details in connection with some of these bodies :—

Board or Trust.	Receipts.			Expenditure, including Interest.	Outstanding Loans.
	Government.	Other.	Total.		
New South Wales—	£	£	£	£	£
Metropolitan Board of Water Supply and Sewerage	...	361,083	361,083	379,123	7,638,773
*Hunter District Water Supply and Sewerage	...	29,558	29,558	32,109	494,644
Sydney Harbour Trust	...	277,963	277,963	†85,250	...
Victoria—					
Melbourne Harbour Trust	...	155,513	155,513	162,603	2,000,000
Melbourne and Metropolitan Board of Works	...	315,054	315,054	373,571	7,775,917
Melbourne Tramways Trust	...	462,545	462,545	381,977	1,650,000
Fire Brigade Boards	16,427	36,869	53,296	50,905	130,000
Water Works Trusts	...	...	...	...	754,450
Irrigation and Water Supply Trusts	...	...	...	...	415,282
Ballarat Water Commission	...	...	...	...	324,197
Queensland—					
Water Works, Brisbane	...	62,063	62,063	64,087	449,362
,, ,, Country Towns	35,169	64,916	100,085	95,966	382,615
Western Australia—					
Road Boards	36,011	14,873	50,884	56,072	...
Boards of Health in Municipalities	222	27,386	27,608	29,475	...
,, ,, outside Municipalities	1,225	3,874	5,099	4,869	...
Metropolitan Water Works Board	8,144	24,084	32,228	32,032	372,852
Tasmania—					
Marine Boards (including Light-houses)	61,800	44,114	105,914	104,956	144,139
Water Trusts	..	6,795	6,795	6,391	31,900
Road Trusts	7,323	21,564	28,887	26,263	1,200
Town Boards	9,073	19,861	28,934	28,851	49,800
New Zealand—					
River Boards	5,715	13,380	19,095	24,522	43,670
Harbour Boards	8,512	631,880	640,392	650,056	4,123,631
Drainage Boards	1,720	31,196	32,916	24,268	200,050
Water Supply Boards	...	3,260	3,260	2,868	22,218

* Water supply only. † Exclusive of Interest on Capital Debt.

The Melbourne Tramways Trust shows an expenditure on working and interest of £381,977 ; to this should be added £32,314 placed to reserve, £48,000 paid in dividends, and £254 carried forward in excess of the amount brought over from the previous year. A sinking fund has been established for the purpose of liquidating outstanding loans, but information relating thereto is not available.

The amounts shown in the foregoing table under Road Trusts and Town Boards in Tasmania are included in the figures given on page 705.

The outstanding loans for Tasmania are gross, sinking funds amounting to £21,373, £1,273, £467, and £3,492 respectively being established in connection with the debts of Marine Boards, Water Trusts, Road Trusts, and Town Boards. In New Zealand, also, sinking funds amounting to £10,785, £393,904, £37,687, and £1,119, exist in connection with the liabilities of River, Harbour, Drainage, and Water Supply Boards respectively.

The outstanding loans of the Boards and Trusts of New South Wales constitute part of the public debt. This is true also with regard to the amounts for Victoria, except the loans of the Tramway Trust and the Melbourne Harbour Trust, the Fire Brigades Boards, and part of the loans of the Melbourne and Metropolitan Board of Works, which are not guaranteed. The liabilities shown for Queensland and Western Australia, and a small portion of the Tasmanian indebtedness, also form part of the public debt of those states; but the amounts given for New Zealand are not included in the debt of the Central Government. In the foregoing table the advances made by the Governments to the borrowing bodies are included.

Total Revenue of Local Bodies.

The total revenue of all local bodies was as follows, the receipts from the various Governments being distinguished from the ordinary receipts :—

State.	Receipts from Government.	Other Receipts.	Total.
	£	£	£
New South Wales	84,866	1,503,350	1,588,216
Victoria	197,508	2,445,817	2,643,325
Queensland	193,069	570,885	763,954
South Australia	110,824	258,265	369,089
Western Australia	112,462	230,485	342,947
Tasmania	81,994	197,792	279,786
Commonwealth	780,723	5,206,594	5,987,317
New Zealand	433,645	2,128,440	2,562,085
Australasia	1,214,368	7,335,034	8,549,402

Indebtedness of Local Bodies.

The following table shows the total indebtedness of local bodies in each of the states including the liabilities to the Government. It must also be explained that the liabilities of Road Trusts and Town Boards in

Tasmania, and Town Boards and Road Boards in New Zealand, have been included with municipalities :—

State.	Outstanding Loans.		
	Municipalities.	Boards, Trusts, &c.	Total for local purposes.
	£	£	£
New South Wales	2,882,140	8,133,417	11,015,557
Victoria	4,253,304	13,049,846	17,303,150
Queensland	1,118,307	831,977	1,950,284
South Australia	81,900	....	81,900
Western Australia	352,000	372,852	724,852
Tasmania	590,773	176,039	766,812
Commonwealth	9,278,424	22,564,131	31,842,555
New Zealand	4,496,776	4,389,564	8,886,340
Australasia	13,775,200	26,953,695	40,728,895

For the amounts that have just been given the local bodies are responsible directly to their creditors in part, and the general governments hold themselves directly liable for the balance. In the following table is given a division of the indebtedness of local bodies into the sum due to the state and that due to the public. It may be mentioned that the amount owing to the state is included with the general debt of the state; and in order to estimate the total state and municipal indebtedness the figures in the second column only have to be added to the figures given later on under State Finance.

State.	Amount of Corporation Indebtedness included in the Public Debt.	Loans of Local Bodies floated in open market.	Total Indebtedness.
	£	£	£
New South Wales	8,133,417	2,882,140	11,015,557
Victoria	3,862,593	13,440,557	17,303,150
Queensland	1,509,784	440,500	1,950,284
South Australia	....	81.900	81,900
Western Australia	372,852	352,000	724,852
Tasmania	235,276	531,536	766,812
Commonwealth	14,113,922	17,728,633	31,842,555
New Zealand	1,046,645	7,839,695	8,886,340
Australasia	15,160,567	25,568,328	40,728,895

State and Municipal Rates and Land Values.

The extent of the charges on land levied by the various corporations and other local bodies as rates will have been gathered from the foregoing pages; in addition thereto a land tax is levied by the General Government in all the states except Queensland and Western Australia, and the income tax imposed by Victoria, South Australia, and Tasmania, includes income derived from land and its use; in New South Wales, however, incomes derived from the use and occupancy of land are untaxed. The following table shows the collections for rates and the other taxes mentioned, and also the capital values of property and of land and improvements, with the amount per £ on the value of unimproved land and land and improvements which the rates would equal:—

State.	Amount of Rates and Land and Property taxes collected.	Capital Value.		Amount per £ of—	
		Unimproved Land.	Land and Improvements.	Unimproved Land.	Land and Improvements.
	£	£	£	d.	d.
New South Wales	1,260,411	142,617,000	263,052,000	2·12	1·15
Victoria	1,209,400	112,396,000	204,294,000	2·58	1·42
Queensland	443,338	35,887,000	63,796,000	2·96	1·67
South Australia	345,143	34,080,000	56,060,000	2·43	1·48
Western Australia	111,828	8,813,000	14,360,000	3·05	1·87
Tasmania	140,180	16,488,000	26,243,000	2·04	1·28
Commonwealth	3,510,300	350,281,000	627,805,000	2·40	1·34
New Zealand	1,113,307	61,466,000	111,105,000	4·34	2·40
Australasia	4,623,607	411,747,000	738,910,000	2·69	1·50

The amount of rates collected in Western Australia is only approximate, as the returns are incomplete.

ACCUMULATION.

Banking.

THE laws relating to banks and banking at present in force are susceptible of great improvement, and in 1893 the failure of many monetary institutions which posed as banks directed attention to the urgent necessity for entirely revising the conditions under which deposits might be taken from the general public, but so far no new legislation has been enacted. All institutions transacting the business of banking are required by law to furnish, in a specified form, quarterly statements of their assets and liabilities, and from these statements and the periodic balance-sheets the tables in this chapter have been compiled. The returns furnished by the banks, though in compliance with the laws of the states, are by no means satisfactory, being quite unsuited to the modern methods of transacting banking business, and they cannot be accepted without question as indicating the stability or instability of the institutions by which they are issued. As a rule, nothing can be elicited beyond what is shown in the half-yearly or yearly balance-sheets. No uniformity is observed as regards the dates of closing the accounts, and the modes of presentation are equally diverse. Important items which should be specifically stated are included with others of minor import, and, in some cases, current accounts are blended with other accounts instead of being separately shown. The value of the information vouchsafed to the public is illustrated by the fact that it was impossible to obtain from the publications of several institutions suspending payment in 1893 the amount of their liabilities either to the public or the state, and these particulars were never disclosed.

Capital Resources of Banks.

According to the latest information published, the paid-up capital of the twenty-two banks operating in Australasia is £19,344,119, of which £5,318,629, inclusive of £2,000,000 guaranteed to the Bank of New Zealand by the Government of that colony, has a preferential claim on the profits of the companies. Below will be found a statement of the ordinary and preferential capital of each bank at the date shown, with the amount of the reserve fund of the institution. In the case of several companies which were reconstructed, there are reserves which are held in suspense pending realisation of assets, and of these no account has been taken in the table :—

Bank.	Date of Balance-sheet.	Capital paid up.			Reserve Fund.
		Ordinary.	Preferential.	Total.	
		£	£	£	£
Australian Joint Stock Bank (Ld.)	30 June, 1903	1,168,041	....	1,168,041	*272,830
Bank of Adelaide	31 Mar., 1903	400,000	....	400,000	220,000
Bank of Australasia	13 April, 1903	1,600,000	....	1,600,000	1,100,000
Bank of New South Wales	30 Sept., 1903	2,000,000	....	2,000,000	1,330,000
Bank of New Zealand	31 Mar., 1903	429,688	2,000,000	2,429,688	23,474
Bank of North Queensland (Ld.)	30 June, 1903	100,000	....	100,000	16,000
Bank of Victoria (Ld.)	30 June, 1903	1,061,250	416,760	1,478,010	140,000
City Bank of Sydney	30 June, 1903	400,000	....	400,000	†101,500
Colonial Bank of Australasia (Ld.)	30 Sept., 1903	134,559	304,044	438,603	50,000
Commercial Bank of Australia (Ld.)	30 June, 1903	94,882	2,117,290	2,212,172	....
Commercial Banking Co. of Sydney (Ld.)	30 June, 1903	1,000,000	....	1,000,000	1,025,000
Commercial Bank of Tasmania (Ld.)	31 Aug., 1903	141,493	....	141,493	115,000
English, Scottish, and Australian Bank (Ld.)	30 June, 1903	539,437	....	539,437	‡160,710
London Bank of Australia (Ld.)	31 Dec., 1902	743,985	171,930	915,915	....
National Bank of Australasia (Ld.)	30 Sept., 1903	1,192,440	305,780	1,498,220	85,000
National Bank of New Zealand (Ld.)	31 Mar., 1903	250,000	....	250,000	180,000
National Bank of Tasmania (Ld.)	31 May, 1903	152,040	....	152,040	27,500
Queensland National Bank (Ld.)	30 June, 1903	413,146	....	413,146	39,000
Royal Bank of Australia (Ld.)	30 Sept., 1903	150,000	....	150,000	30,000
Royal Bank of Queensland (Ld.)	30 June, 1903	454,529	2,825	457,354	60,000
Union Bank of Australia (Ld.)	28 Feb., 1903	1,500,000	....	1,500,000	1,000,000
Western Australian Bank	23 Sept., 1903	100,000	....	100,000	250,000

* Includes £220,830, Profit and Loss Special Account. † Includes £100,000 at Contingency Account. ‡ Includes Capital Reserve Account.

During the half-year ended 31st December, 1902, a reduction in the capital of the Commercial Bank of Australia, Limited, took place, resulting in the writing off of £5 10s. per share of the ordinary capital.

The preceding table shows the position of the capital account at date of balancing; but a number of the banks had made calls on their shareholders which will increase their paid-up capital. The amount of these calls and the total working capital that will be available when they are met are appended:—

Bank.	Capital paid and being called up.		
	Paid up.	Being called.	Total Working Capital.
	£	£	£
Australian Joint Stock Bank (Limited)	1,168,041	6,474	1,174,515
Bank of Adelaide	400,000	......	400,000
Bank of Australasia	1,600,000	......	1,600,000
Bank of New South Wales	2,000,000	......	2,000,000
Bank of New Zealand	2,429,688	70,312	2,500,000
Bank of North Queensland (Limited)	100,000	......	100,000
Bank of Victoria (Limited)	1,478,010	......	1,478,010
City Bank of Sydney	400,000	......	400,000
Colonial Bank of Australasia (Limited)	438,603	678	439,281
Commercial Bank of Australia (Limited)	2,212,172	3	2,212,175
Commercial Banking Company of Sydney (Limited)	1,000,000	......	1,000,000
Commercial Bank of Tasmania (Limited)	141,498	......	141,498
English, Scottish, and Australian Bank (Limited)	539,437	......	539,437
London Bank of Australia (Limited)	*915,915	750	916,665
National Bank of Australasia (Limited)	1,498,220	......	1,498,220
National Bank of New Zealand (Limited)	250,000	......	250,000
National Bank of Tasmania (Limited)	152,040	......	152,040
Queensland National Bank (Limited)	413,146	2,102	415,248
Royal Bank of Australia (Limited)	150,000	......	150,000
Royal Bank of Queensland (Limited)	457,354	......	457,354
Union Bank of Australia (Limited)	1,500,000	......	1,500,000
Western Australian Bank	100,000	......	100,000

* Includes £8,190 prepaid on account of Reserve Liability.

The paid-up capital of the banking companies now operating in Australasia has increased from £14,724,587 before the crisis to £19,344,119, or by £4,619,532. In 1893, however, there were in existence two banks, with a combined capital of £900,000, which are now defunct; and it should also be mentioned that capital to the amount of £7,314,205 has been written off during the last ten years, including £500,000, the value of shares of the Bank of New Zealand issued to the Crown, and re-purchased, and £1,071,520, being £5 10s. per share of the ordinary capital of the Commercial Bank of Australia, Limited.

Liabilities and Assets of Banks.

The liabilities of the banks enumerated, at the dates which have been previously given, totalled £141,551,199, against which amount assets aggregating £168,167,266 were shown. The following table gives the liabilities of each institution to the public, notes in circulation and deposits being distinguished from other liabilities. In some cases small items which should be classed with "other liabilities" are included with deposits, as they cannot be distinguished in the balance-sheets; and in the case of the Commercial Bank of Australia (Limited), the accounts of the assets trust have been excluded:—

Bank.	Notes in Circulation.	Deposits.	Other Liabilities to Public.	Total Liabilities to Public.
	£	£	£	£
Australian Joint Stock Bank (Limited)	86,495	5,759,216	182,714	6,028,425
Bank of Adelaide	127,702	2,148,960	227,271	2,503,933
Bank of Australasia	567,903	14,758,614	2,381,115	17,707,632
Bank of New South Wales	928,227	20,628,463	3,321,088	24,877,778
Bank of New Zealand	764,906	10,520,936	924,829	12,210,671
Bank of North Queensland (Limited)	....	290,441	48,736	339,177
Bank of Victoria (Limited)	110,458	4,497,192	744,291	5,351,941
City Bank of Sydney	82,444	1,169,555	804	1,252,803
Colonial Bank of Australasia (Limited)	108,013	2,265,758	214,494	2,588,265
Commercial Bank of Australia (Limited)	146,003	3,417,708	494,104	4,057,905
Commercial Banking Company of Sydney (Ld.)	460,174	11,384,272	777,857	12,622,303
Commercial Bank of Tasmania (Limited)	63,612	1,507,442	....	1,571,054
English, Scottish, and Australian Bank (Ld.)	18,961	5,110,953	271,022	5,400,936
London Bank of Australia (Limited)	168,597	4,280,793	584,480	5,033,870
National Bank of Australasia (Limited)	269,029	6,143,575	485,080	6,897,684
National Bank of New Zealand (Limited)	257,104	2,838,524	308,313	3,403,941
National Bank of Tasmania (Limited)	62,363	492,440	32,120	586,923
Queensland National Bank (Limited)	....	6,717,136	332,600	7,049,736
Royal Bank of Australia (Limited)	8,100	705,472	199,147	912,719
Royal Bank of Queensland (Limited)	....	790,402	42,220	832,622
Union Bank of Australia (Limited)	497,589	15,949,227	1,966,092	18,412,908
Western Australian Bank	113,346	1,671,432	123,195	1,907,973

The assets of each bank are shown below:—

Bank.	Coin and Bullion.	Advances.	Other Assets.	Total Assets.
	£	£	£	£
Australian Joint Stock Bank (Limited)	704,797	5,963,843	831,012	7,499,652
Bank of Adelaide	379,659	1,470,339	1,307,675	3,157,673
Bank of Australasia	3,290,633	14,770,153	2,459,200	20,519,986
Bank of New South Wales	4,195,456	18,947,318	5,183,446	28,326,220
Bank of New Zealand	1,947,779	6,365,040	6,546,604	14,859,423
Bank of North Queensland (Limited)	48,655	322,126	85,731	456,512
Bank of Victoria (Limited)	939,295	4,899,626	1,176,924	7,015,845
City Bank of Sydney	269,598	1,204,941	188,820	1,663,359
Colonial Bank of Australasia (Limited)	428,900	2,045,568	617,948	3,092,446
Commercial Bank of Australia (Limited)	1,095,305	3,804,321	1,595,623	6,495,249
Commercial Banking Company of Sydney (Ltd.)	2,592,357	9,185,532	2,940,029	14,717,918
Commercial Bank of Tasmania (Limited)	235,561	1,259,698	344,950	1,840,209
English, Scottish, and Australian Bank (Ltd.)	988,833	3,977,820	1,186,810	6,153,463
London Bank of Australia (Limited)	788,035	3,973,376	1,212,582	5,973,993
National Bank of Australasia (Limited)	1,371,196	5,024,427	2,126,903	8,522,526
National Bank of New Zealand (Limited)	520,092	3,005,773	319,337	3,854,202
National Bank of Tasmania (Limited)	125,051	594,914	54,041	774,006
Queensland National Bank (Limited)	758,605	5,497,846	1,248,431	7,504,882
Royal Bank of Australia (Limited)	122,428	533,451	445,754	1,101,633
Royal Bank of Queensland (Limited)	193,585	1,008,210	156,061	1,357,856
Union Bank of Australia (Limited)	3,586,523	11,798,914	5,607,264	20,992,701
Western Australian Bank	791,623	1,108,883	387,006	2,287,512

RESULTS OF WORKING OF BANKS.

The results of working of each bank for the latest period for which information is available are given below. With the exception of the Bank of Adelaide, the Bank of New Zealand, the English, Scottish, and Australian Bank, the London Bank of Australia, and the National Bank of New Zealand, for which the figures refer to twelve months' operations, the amounts given cover a period of six months. The dates of the balance-sheets are as shown on page 717 :—

Bank.	Class of Shares.	Amount brought forward.	Net Profits less Rebate on Bills current.	Dividend paid. Rate per cent. per annum.	Dividend paid. Amount.	Amount transferred to Reserve Fund, Contingency Accounts, Reduction of Premises Account, &c.	Amount carried forward.
		£	£		£	£	£
Australian Joint Stock Bank (Ltd.)	Ordinary	26,166	4,190	..	....	....	30,256
Bank of Adelaide	,,	17,423	52,317	8	32,000	20,000	17,740
Bank of Australasia	,,	14,648	157,705	12	96,000	60,000	16,353
Bank of New South Wales	,,	16,072	117,370	10	100,000	15,000	18,442
Bank of New Zealand	Preferential Ordinary	....	195,590	.. 5	 21,180	50,000	124,410
Bank of North Queensland (Limited)	Ordinary	182	2,153	2½	1,313	1,000	22
Bank of Victoria (Limited)	Preferential Ordinary	14,360	29,441	5 3½	10,419 18,572	....	14,810
City Bank of Sydney	Ordinary	961	9,351	4	8,000	1,256	1,056
Colonial Bank of Australasia (Ltd.)	Preferential Ordinary	3,327	17,251	5 5	7,601 3,364	5,000	4,613
Commercial Bank of Australia (Ltd.)	Preferential Ordinary	29,730	32,442	3 ..	31,759	....	30,413
Commercial Banking Co. of Sydney (Limited)	Ordinary	26,847	58,768	10	50,000	15,000	20,615
Commercial Bank of Tasmania (Ltd.)	,,	3,623	14,089	10	8,887	5,000	3,825
English, Scottish, and Australian Bank (Limited)	,,	13,186	41,805	4	22,578	22,192	10,221
London Bank of Australia (Limited)	Preferential Ordinary	10,518	13,690	5¼ ..	14,184	....	10,024
National Bank of Australasia (Ltd.)	Preferential Ordinary	16,748	39,464	5 3½	7,644 20,868	14,590	13,110
National Bank of New Zealand (Ltd.)	Ordinary	8,226	54,534	10	25,000	30,000	7,760
National Bank of Tasmania (Limited)	,,	7,636	4,908	5	3,992	5,000	3,552
Queensland National Bank (Limited)	,,	....	12,000	..	3,000	9,000	..
Royal Bank of Australia (Limited)	,,	2,096	6,819	6	4,500	....	4,414
Royal Bank of Queensland (Limited)	Preferential Ordinary	827	9,052	3¼ 3	7,226	2,000	653
Union Bank of Australia (Limited)	Ordinary	20,144	59,649	8	60,000	....	19,793
Western Australian Bank	,,	8,566	20,974	17½	8,750	....	20,790

The total net profit for the Bank of New Zealand was £290,591, and the interest on guaranteed stock amounted to £80,000, leaving £210,591 for distribution. Of this sum £15,001 was written off the various estate and property accounts; £50,000 was paid to the Assets Realisation Board and £21,180 for dividend on ordinary shares at 5 per cent.: leaving a balance of £124,410 which must be paid to the Assets Realisation Board in accordance with the Act of 1895 which governs the operations of the bank. The dividend paid by the Queensland National Bank represents a repayment to the Government of that state in terms of the scheme of arrangement, and the amount transferred to reserve fund, etc., includes £6,000 paid to private depositors' repayment fund. The total net profit was £21,660, of which £9,660 was allotted to the contingency account. The net profit shown for the London Bank of Australia, and the English, Scottish, and Australian Bank (Limited), is exclusive of the interest on Transferable Fixed Deposits, Debenture Stocks, &c.; while the earnings of the Commercial Bank of Australia (Limited), exclude £5,000 transferred to the Special Assets Trust Reserve Account, and £29,331 to the Special Assets Trust Company. The net profit shown for the Union Bank of Australia (Limited) is exclusive of £50,000 applied to the release of a similar sum which stood in the balance-sheet as a contingent reserve against doubtful debts, and £4,000 in aid of the guarantee and provident funds. The dividend tax payable by the two Tasmanian banks, the Royal Bank of Queensland, and the Bank of North Queensland has been included in the amount of dividend shown in the table. The dividend paid by the Commercial Bank of Tasmania (Limited) includes £1,408 bonus to officers. The dividend paid by the National Bank of Australasia (Limited) includes £4,590, note and income tax. The amount shown as carried to reserve by the Bank of Australasia includes £30,000, to write down the Reserve Fund Consols to £85 per cent. In the case of the English, Scottish, and Australian Bank (Limited) the amount of dividend shown includes £1,000 contribution to Officers' Guarantee and Provident Fund, and the amount shown as carried to reserve includes £7,192 for the purchase and cancellation of Deferred Inscribed Deposit Stock, in accordance with the articles of association.

Banking Business of each State.

Of the twenty-two banks operating in Australasia during 1903, thirteen had offices in New South Wales, eleven in Victoria, eleven in Queensland, seven in South Australia, six in Western Australia, four in Tasmania, and five in New Zealand. There were only two banks doing business in all the seven states; one transacted business in six states; one in five states; two in four; two in three; four in two; and ten banks did not extend their business beyond the limits of one state or colony. The majority of the institutions, however, had offices in London.

The liabilities and assets of the twenty-two banks of issue operating in the different states and New Zealand during the June quarter of 1903 are shown in the following tables. The total liabilities of the banks are given as £117,074,762, and the assets as £135,750,795, showing a surplus of assets of £18,676,033. If the returns gave all the facts in relation to the operations of the banks, this surplus should represent the capital or funds provided out of their own resources; but as the capital and reserve funds amount to £25,619,736, it is evident that there is a balance of £6,943,703 to be otherwise accounted for. This sum represents part of the deposits obtained in Australasia and used in the London business of the banks, the British deposits with Australasian banks having decreased to about twelve millions. The following figures will convey some notion of the business transacted within each state. It should be noted that under the heading of deposits bearing interest has been included perpetual inscribed stock of the English, Scottish, and Australian Bank (Limited), to the amount of £2,055,162, namely, £700,830 in New South Wales, £934,069 in Victoria, £324,655 in South Australia, and £95,608 in Queensland:—

State.	Notes in circulation not bearing Interest.	Bills in circulation not bearing Interest.	Deposits.		Balances due to other Banks, &c.	Total Liabilities.
			Not bearing Interest.	Bearing Interest.		
	£	£	£	£	£	£
New South Wales..........	1,408,060	219,335	13,151,618	20,158,075	142,266	35,079,354
Victoria	936,411	118,069	11,602,187	19,117,147	84,941	31,858,755
Queensland	....	104,026	5,048,281	7,597,444	69,982	12,819,733
South Australia	406,618	18,665	2,620,373	3,952,852	47,944	7,071,452
Western Australia..........	891,427	48,047	3,336,261	1,449,578	62,814	5,238,127
Tasmania	170,725	38,496	1,619,467	2,073,953	....	3,902,640
Commonwealth	3,313,241	541,637	37,378,187	54,379,049	407,947	96,020,061
New Zealand	1,501,247	55,482	8,937,545	10,516,880	43,547	21,054,701
Australasia......... ..	4,814,438	597,119	46,315,732	64,895,929	451,494	117,074,762

The preceding table shows that about 95 per cent. of the Australasian liabilities of the banks consisted of deposits, viz., £111,211,661 out of £117,074,762. The returns of the banks in each state, with the exception of Tasmania, distinguish between deposits at call and deposits bearing interest. In Tasmania, although not obliged by law to do so, a similar distinction has been made by three banks out of four, and assuming that in the case of the other bank the proportion of deposits at call to the total deposits is the same, the total deposits at call are as stated in the table, viz., £46,315,732, or 41 per cent. of all deposits.

The assets for the same period are shown below. Certain assets of small amount, consisting chiefly of Government and other securities, have been included under all debts due to the banks. The value of landed property in Victoria is exclusive of the interest of the Commercial Bank of Australia (Limited), in the Special Assets Trust Company

(Limited). Also, under the heading of "Notes and Bills of other banks," &c., are included Queensland Treasury Notes to the amount of £643,299 :—

State.	Coin.	Bullion.	Landed Property.	Notes and Bills discounted, and all other Debts due to the Banks.	Notes and Bills of other Banks, and Balances due from other Banks.	Total Assets.
	£	£	£	£	£	£
New South Wales........	6,696,857	225,793	1,792,960	34,229,389	567,472	43,502,471
Victoria	5,896,723	445,910	2,005,620	29,906,949	517,201	38,770,403
Queensland	1,967,485	222,368	737,947	13,439,426	800,309	17,167,535
South Australia	1,501,546	15,594	431,387	4,428,983	112,747	6,490,257
Western Australia.......	1,706,690	598,160	204,959	3,683,451	264,762	6,458,022
Tasmania	*755,483	....	116,568	2,541,487	238,153	3,651,691
Commonwealth	18,513,784	1,507,825	5,289,441	88,228,685	2,500,644	116,040,379
New Zealand	3,405,535	192,710	415,052	15,609,023	88,096	19,710,416
Australasia..........	21,919,319	1,700,535	5,704,493	103,837,708	2,588,740	135,750,795

* Includes Bullion.

Metallic Reserves of Banks.

The following table shows the metallic reserves held by the banks as against their total Australasian liabilities, and also against their liabilities at call, viz., deposits at call and note circulation. The table, however, cannot be taken as complete, as some banks receiving deposits in England and elsewhere do not include such liabilities in their returns :—

State.	Coin and Bullion.	Total Liabilities.	Liabilities at Call.	Proportion of Coin and Bullion—	
				To Total Liabilities.	To Liabilities at Call.
	£	£	£	per cent.	per cent.
New South Wales........	6,912,650	35,079,354	14,559,678	19·71	47·48
Victoria	6,341,633	31,858,755	12,538,598	19·90	50·57
Queensland	2,189,853	12,819,733	5,048,281	17·08	43·37
South Australia	1,517,140	7,071,452	3,026,991	21·45	50·12
Western Australia	2,304,850	5,288,127	3,727,688	43·59	61·83
Tasmania	755,483	3,902,640	1,790,192	19·36	42·20
Commonwealth	20,021,609	96,020,061	40,691,428	20·85	49·20
New Zealand...............	3,598,245	21,054,701	10,438,792	17·09	34·47
Australasia	23,619,854	117,074,762	51,130,220	20·18	46·19

It will be seen that Queensland apparently holds the weakest position in the proportion of cash reserves to total liabilities, and New Zealand in proportion to liabilities at call. This, however, means very little, seeing that in some of the states many banks profess to hold gold largely in excess of their wishes or requirements.

Expenses of Banking.

The balance-sheets of banks, as presented to the shareholders, do not usually contain details likely to satisfy the inquirer curious to discover the amount of gross profits as compared with the net amount divisible amongst shareholders. Allowing the same proportion of expenses for the banks not disclosing this information as for those concerning which particulars are available, the following results are obtained for the last working year dealt with in the preceding pages:—

Total trading assets	£161,453,400
Capital and reserves	25,684,100
Gross earnings, less reserve for bad and doubtful debts	6,661,600
Gross expenditure, including interest	4,849,500
Net earnings	1,812,100

Compared with the total assets, the net earnings represent 1·08 per cent.; and compared with the banks' own resources, *i.e.*, capital and reserved profits, 7·01 per cent. The gross expenditure above set down may be divided into expenses of management, £2,163,800, and interest, £2,685,700; these together amount to 72·80 per cent. of the gross earnings, the management expenses being 32·48 per cent., and the interest 40·32 per cent. It would appear, therefore, that for every £1 of net earnings, the sum of £1 3s. 11d. is spent in management expenses, and £1 9s. 8d. in interest. The cost of working banking institutions in Australia is undoubtedly very large; but this class of business is everywhere expensive, and an analysis of the balance-sheets of some thirty British banks shows that the expenses of management amount to about 18s. 3d. for every £1 of net earnings.

Compared with their resources, the net earnings of Australasian banks are far less than those of English banks, as will appear from the following statement, which gives the rate per cent. per annum of earnings compared with total resources, including, of course, deposits and issue, as well as shareholders' capital and reserves:—

	£	s.	d.
Bank of England	1	6	3
English Provincial Banks	1	7	2
Irish Banks	1	9	1
London Banks	1	3	10
Scotch Banks	1	5	1
Banks trading in Australasia	1	3	7

The net earning power of Australian banks has much improved during recent years, and is now larger than at any time since the crisis. The year 1892 showed net earnings equal to £1 0s. 4d. per cent. of the banks' resources; this is, however, as will be seen from the statement below, a reduction on the earnings of previous years. From this there was a steady falling off, until in 1897 the net earnings were only 8s. 5d. per cent., which was perhaps as poor a showing as could be found in the history of Australian banking. After 1897 there was a gradual recovery, and the year closing with June, 1903, showed an improvement even on 1892. The net earnings per cent. during the past fifteen years, were:—

	£	s.	d.		£	s.	d.
1889............	1	8	10	1897............	0	8	5
1890............	1	7	10	1898............	0	10	10
1891............	1	6	4	1899............	0	13	10
1892............	1	0	4	1900............	0	16	1
1893............	0	17	7	1901............	1	0	1
1894............	0	12	10	1902............	1	1	7
1895............	0	9	0	1903............	1	3	7
1896............	0	8	8				

The expense of banking in Australasia is largely due to the number of branches open throughout the country; thus in Australasia there are 1,613 banks and branches, or one to every 2,900 persons, while in England the proportion is one bank to 8,000 persons (exclusive of private banks), in Scotland one to every 4,100, and in Ireland one to every 6,700.

Investment Companies.

In addition to the Banks of Issue, there are numerous Savings Banks, and Land, Building, Investment, Trading, and Commercial Companies receiving money on deposit and transacting much of the business usually undertaken only by banks of issue. The land, building, and other trading companies were presumed to be in a flourishing condition even as late as the year 1890. Their dividends to shareholders were very large, and the rates allowed on deposits were considerably in excess of those current in the banks of issue. As might be expected, the high interest offered was too tempting a bait to be resisted by a section of the investing public, and large sums were placed in these institutions with the utmost confidence that they would be available when required. This confidence, unfortunately, proved to be, in many instances, unmerited. The shrinkage of land values, and the depreciation of real estate generally, put an end to all unsound institutions working on speculative lines, as well as to some other companies that were conducted on reasonable principles. The difficulties into which the deposit companies fell may for the most part be attributed to their practice of borrowing money for short periods, and locking it up for long terms. Besides this, however, many so-called building societies indulged in speculative land purchases, and having retailed the land at enhanced prices, with payments over extended periods, proceeded to divide the presumed profits among the shareholders; with a result that might easily have been foreseen, for in many cases the purchasers, after paying a few instalments towards the price, left the allotments on the hands of the companies, whose anticipated profits were therefore purely visionary, and whose dividends were really never earned, but, in many instances, were merely taken from the deposits. Complete returns of these societies are not available, but the amounts held on deposit in some of the states will be found on page 731.

Savings Banks.

The Savings Banks are on a very different footing, being to a greater or less extent under state control and otherwise safeguarded, so that they enjoy public confidence. The institutions classed as Savings Banks may be divided into two kinds—those worked in conjunction with the Post Office, and, consequently, directly administered by the state; and those under trustees or commissioners, who are generally nominated by the government. The declared objects of these banks are to encourage thrift in the working classes, and to provide a safe investment for the funds of charitable institutions, friendly societies, and such like. The institutions, however, have become so popular that all classes of the community are represented amongst their depositors, and the banking crisis of 1893 had the effect of largely increasing their business.

In New South Wales there are both state and trustee institutions for the receipt of savings, the Post Office Savings Bank having been established in 1871, and the Savings Bank of New South Wales as far back as 1832. In both institutions sums of one shilling and any multiple of that amount may be deposited; but, with the exception of the funds of charitable institutions and friendly societies, deposits exceeding £200 do not bear interest on such excess. From October, 1894, to July, 1896, the Post Office Savings Bank allowed interest at the rate of 3 per cent., with an additional 1 per cent. on accounts open for the full calendar year, but this latter privilege has now been withdrawn. During the year ended 31st December, 1902, the Savings Bank of New South Wales allowed 3 per cent. interest on accounts closed during the year, and 3½ per cent. for those remaining open at the end of the year. It is proposed to increase the interest to depositors to 3½ per cent. during 1904, and by the Amendment Act assented to on 5th December, 1903, the limit of deposits by individuals was raised from £200 to £300. A measure providing for the amalgamation of the two institutions has been presented to Parliament on several occasions, but up to the present the Bill has not been passed.

In Victoria both Commissioners' and Post Office Savings Banks, stablished in 1842 and 1865 respectively, were in operation until the 0th September, 1897, when they were amalgamated under the Savings ank Amendment Act of 1896, the Commissioners assuming the control f the new institution. Amounts of one shilling and any multiple hereof are received. The Act referred to further provided for advances o farmers and others, and this portion of the Act was brought into peration without delay. Interest is allowed at the rate of 2½ per cent. n sums not exceeding £100, and 2 per cent. from £100 to £250, the atter being the maximum amount carrying interest.

In Queensland, a Government Savings Bank, not administered in onnection with the Post Office, is in operation, the system dating from 865. The interest allowed during 1895 was 3½ per cent. on all deposits elow £200; but from July, 1896, the rate was reduced to 3 per cent., which is the rate now being paid. In December, 1895, authority was btained for the issue of Savings Bank Stock at 3 per cent. to enable epositors of upwards of £200 to obtain interest on such excess, as it ras found that large sums were entrusted to the Government which ould not earn interest under the old constitution of the Bank.

In South Australia there is, properly speaking, no Government avings Bank; but an institution administered by trustees was estabshed in 1848. The rate of interest paid by the trustees has been the ubject of many changes. Starting at 3 per cent., it fell as low as per cent. in 1853; rose to 6 per cent. in 1858; and declined to 4 per ent. in 1873. Between the year last mentioned and 1892, interest uctuated between 5½ and 4½ per cent.; and in 1893 it was reduced to per cent., at which it remained during the years 1894 and 1895, while in 1896 and 1897 it was still further reduced to 3½ per cent. and per cent. respectively—the latter rate being allowed in 1901-2—he maximum amount bearing interest being £250.

In Western Australia, Post Office banks have been in operation since 864. One shilling and upwards may be received, provided not more han £150 is deposited in any one year, while the maximum amount of eposits must not exceed £600. Interest is allowed at the rate of 3 er cent. provided the amount at credit is not less than £1, and not nore than £300.

In Tasmania, Post Office and trustee banks are working side by side. ums of one shilling and upwards may be deposited, the interest llowed being 3 per cent. both in the Post Office banks and in the rustee institutions. Interest is not allowed on amounts over £150.

In New Zealand, Post Office and trustee institutions are also estabished. The former commenced operations in February, 1867; but ome of the other class of banks are of much older standing, the Auckand Savings Bank, for instance, having been established as far back as 847. Deposits of one shilling and upwards are received. Interest was formerly allowed in both classes of institutions at the rate of 4½ er cent. up to £200, and 4 per cent. from £200 to £500; but in

July, 1893, the rates allowed in the Government Savings Bank we reduced to 4 per cent. and 3½ per cent. respectively, the maximu amount bearing interest remaining at £500. These rates remained i force until the 1st January, 1896, when the interest was reduced to 3 per cent. and 3 per cent. respectively; while from the 1st November, 189 a further reduction was made, the rates ruling from that date being 3 p cent. up to £200, and 2½ per cent. from £200 to £500, no interest bei allowed on sums in excess of £500. The trustee Savings Banks in 18 allowed 4 per cent., but reduced this rate to 3½ per cent. from th beginning of 1896. In 1897 the interest was increased to 4 per cen on amounts under £100; but in 1900 it was again reduced to 3½ pe cent., which is the rate now allowed. A feature of the New Zeala Post Office Savings Bank is that deposits of one shilling may be mad by means of postage stamps affixed to cards specially issued for th purpose. This plan was adopted to encourage thrift among childre It was recognised to be a difficult matter for a child to save its pen until they accumulated to a shilling; but under the present syste whenever a child receives a penny it may purchase a postage stamp an affix it to the card in its possession.

The returns of the Savings Banks show an enormous developme since the year 1861. At that period the number of depositors i Australasia (excluding Tasmania, for which there are no returns) wa 29,062, with the sum of £1,367,396 to their credit, or an average o £47 to each depositor. In 1871 the number of depositors had risen t 115,074, with deposits amounting to £3,675,772; but the averag amount credited to each depositor was only £31 18s. 10d. In the yea 1881 there were 311,124 depositors, with a total of £9,442,979, averagin £30 7s. for each account. In 1891 the number of depositors had increas to 741,627, and the amount of deposits to £18,943,541, the averag being £25 10s. 1d. In 1901–2 the number of depositors had risen t 1,252,219, with deposits amounting to £40,126,061, giving an averag sum of £32 0s. 11d. to each account. In 1902–3 the number o depositors had increased to 1,299,681, with deposits amounting t £41,736,977, or an average sum of £32 2s. 3d. to each account. I will thus be seen that there has been a decline in the amount pe depositor from the period first mentioned; but this is no sign of retro gression, for the large increase in the number of depositors, which mus be taken into consideration, evidences the fact that the less affluen classes of the community are more largely represented in the books o the banks than was formerly the case. In point of fact, the proportio of depositors to the entire population has increased all along. Thus, i 1861 the number of persons who had accounts in the Savings Bank represented only 2·31 per cent. of the entire population of Australasia but in 1871 the percentage had risen to 5·98; in 1881, to 11·33; i 1891, to 19·47; in 1900–1, to 25·52 per cent.; while in 1902–3 th proportion was 27·69 per cent. Dealing with the individual state the Queensland depositors have the largest amount at their credit veraging £47 2s. 8d. per head; Western Australian depositors come next with £40 16s. 3d.; New South Wales depositors occupy the third position with £38 8s. 10d.; while those of Victoria have the smallest sum, their average being only £24 14s. 3d. The subjoined table shows the progress of accumulation in the Savings Banks of each of the states and of New Zealand since 1871:—

Year.	New South Wales.	Victoria.	Queensland.	South Australia	Western Australia	Tasmania.	Commonwealth.	New Zealand.	Australasia.
				NUMBER OF DEPOSITORS.					
1871	24,379	45,819	6,769	14,270	1,062	8,500	100,799	14,275	115,074
1881	72,384	101,829	20,168	37,742	3,219	14,728	250,070	61,054	311,124
1891	158,426	300,731	46,259	78,795	3,564	26,916	614,741	126,886	741,627
1900–1	282,643	393,026	81,025	111,587	39,339	42,509	950,079	228,883	1,178,962
1902–3	323,212	418,511	80,048	120,349	48,015	47,626	1,037,759	261,922	1,299,681
				AMOUNT OF DEPOSITS.					
	£	£	£	£	£	£	£	£	£
1871	945,915	1,117,761	407,134	517,000	15,583	217,413	3,220,806	454,966	3,675,772
1881	2,698,708	2,569,488	944,251	1,288,450	23,344	369,278	7,893,464	1,549,515	9,442,979
1891	5,342,135	5,715,687	1,660,753	2,217,419	46,181	554,417	15,536,592	3,406,949	18,943,541
1900–1	10,901,882	9,662,007	3,896,170	3,782,575	1,618,359	1,009,098	30,869,591	6,665,344	37,534,935
1902–3	12,425,464	10,341,757	3,772,686	4,172,720	1,941,231	1,206,242	33,860,100	7,876,877	41,736,977
				AVERAGE AMOUNT PER DEPOSITOR.					
	£ s. d.	£ s. d	£ s. d.	£ s. d.	£ s. d.	£ s. d.	£ s. d.	£ s. d.	£ s. d.
1871	38 16 0	24 7 11	60 2 11	36 4 7	14 13 6	25 11 7	31 19 0	31 17 5	31 18 10
1881	37 5 8	25 4 7	46 16 5	34 2 9	7 5 0	25 1 6	31 11 4	25 7 7	30 7 0
1891	33 14 5	19 0 1	35 18 0	28 2 10	12 19 2	20 12 0	25 5 6	26 17 0	25 10 1
1901–2	38 11 4	24 11 8	48 1 8	33 18 3	41 2 9	23 14 8	32 9 10	29 2 5	31 16 9
1902–3	38 8 10	24 14 3	47 2 8	34 13 3	40 8 6	25 6 6	32 12 7	30 1 6	32 2 3

The following table shows the average amount per head of population, and the average number of depositors per 100 of population, in each of the states for the year 1902–3:—

State.	Average amount per head of population.	Depositors per 100 of population.
	£ s. d.	
New South Wales	8 15 3	23
Victoria	8 11 7	35
Queensland	7 6 10	15
South Australia	11 9 3	33
Western Australia	8 13 1	21
Tasmania	6 16 3	27
Commonwealth	8 13 5	26
New Zealand	9 13 4	32
Australasia	8 16 10	28

It will be observed that Victoria had the largest number of depositors per 100 of population; while the largest amount per head of population was reached in South Australia.

The following table shows the number of depositors in the savin banks of the principal countries of the world, the total amount standi at their credit, and the average amount per depositor. The figures a compiled from the latest available returns :—

Country.	Depositors.	Amount of Deposits in Savings Bank.	Average Amount per Depositor.
	No.	£	£ s. d.
United Kingdom	10,803,555	192,359,302	17 16 1
Sweden	1,828,362	28,200,319	15 8 6
Norway	695,524	17,888,148	25 14 9
Holland	1,188,821	13,719,166	11 10 10
Austria-Hungary	5,162,594	174,131,742	33 14 7
Belgium	1,757,906	26,224,296	14 18 4
Italy	6,395,956	99,233,856	15 10 4
France	10,922,283	172,225,339	15 15 4
Denmark	1,176,853	36,534,856	31 0 11
Russia	3,935,773	76,425,159	19 8 4
United States	6,666,672	565,880,101	84 17 8
*Canada	211,762	12,024,318	56 15 8
Australasia	1,299,681	41,736,977	32 2 3

* Exclusive of £4,189,483 in special Savings Banks—number of depositors not available.

The figures for the United States are given on the authority of tl official *Statistical Abstract*, and are, to all appearances, correct.

Total Deposits in Banks.

If to the amounts deposited in the savings banks of the states l added the deposits in banks of issue, it will be seen that the total su on deposit in banking institutions is equal to over £32 for each inhabita of Australasia. The largest amount on deposit as compared with pop lation is found in Victoria, with £34 1s. 4d., or £1 13s. 3d. above th average of all the states. The particulars for each state will be foun below :—

State.	Deposits in Banks of Issue (Averages for the second quarter of 1903.)	Deposits in Savings Banks.	Total Deposits.	Amount of Deposits per head of Population.
	£	£	£	£ s. d
New South Wales	33,309,693	12,425,464	45,735,157	32 5 [illegible]
Victoria	30,719,334	10,341,757	41,061,091	34 1 [illegible]
Queensland	12,645,725	3,772,686	16,418,411	31 15 [illegible]
South Australia	6,603,225	4,172,720	10,775,945	29 12 [illegible]
Western Australia	4,785,839	1,941,231	6,727,070	29 19 [illegible]
Tasmania	3,693,420	1,206,242	4,899,662	27 13 [illegible]
Commonwealth	91,757,236	33,860,100	125,617,336	32 3 [illegible]
New Zealand	19,454,425	7,876,877	27,331,302	33 10 [illegible]
Australasia	111,211,661	41,736,977	152,948,638	32 8 [illegible]

As already mentioned, large sums are also deposited with various building and investment societies, but the returns with reference to these are incomplete. The latest available figures show that the amounts so invested were:—In New South Wales, £1,330,463; in Victoria, £471,861; in Tasmania, £139,427; and in New Zealand, £249,530.

In the following table are given the deposits in banks, including savings banks, and, where available, building societies, &c., at five decennial periods, as well as for the year 1902–3:—

State.		1861.	1871.	1881.	1891.	1900–1.	1902–3.
		£	£	£	£	£	£
New South Wales		5,645,106	7,989,801	23,006,720	42,988,550	44,954,947	47,065,620
Victoria		7,575,406	12,476,677	23,721,345	50,183,551	42,006,957	41,532,952
Queensland		334,503	1,647,830	5,633,097	12,154,657	17,099,659	16,418,411
South Australia		875,320	2,038,719	6,231,004	9,992,338	10,052,971	10,775,945
Western Australia		*2,487	*15,583	*23,344	1,365,906	6,020,578	6,727,070
Tasmania		†729,085	875,512	2,969,390	4,220,292	4,327,871	5,089,089
Commonwealth	Total	15,161,909	25,044,122	61,584,[illegible]	120,905,294	124,462,783	127,559,087
	Per head	£13	£15	£27	£35	£33	£33
New Zealand		905,675	3,789,639	10,618,893	17,497,436	23,306,265	27,580,832
Australasia	Total	16,067,584	28,833,761	72,203,798	138,402,730	147,769,048	155,139,919
	Per head	£13	£15	£26	£36	£33	£33

*Savings Banks only. † Banks of Issue only.

From this table it will be seen that the increase of deposits in all classes of banks between 1861 and 1881 was exactly 100 per cent., allowing for the growth of population; while between 1871 and 1891 the deposits per head of population increased by 140 per cent. When compared with the figures for Great Britain, the amount of deposits per head of population in Australasia far exceeds that in the older country. In 1861, indeed, the sum per head in Great Britain was higher than in Australasia, amounting to £15 as against £13 in the colonies, and in 1874 the British average stood at £25 per head; but ten years later, in 1884, it had sunk to £23, and in 1890 to £16; while in 1901 the rate per head had increased to over £24. In the colonies there was no falling-off at any period until 1893—the total deposits per head in 1888 far exceeding the highest level ever reached in Great Britain. In 1893, however, there was a decline of about ten millions in the sum total of Australasian deposits; that is to say, the commercial depression which prevailed more or less throughout Australasia during that year caused the amount just mentioned to be withdrawn from the savings of the people and to be employed in meeting current expenses and in the maintenance of credit. During 1894 and 1895 there was a further falling-off in Victoria and Tasmania; but the other states showed larger deposits in 1895 than in 1893—the Queensland, Western Australia, and New Zealand deposits being even larger than in 1891. In 1902–3 the savings in all the states were greater than in 1895, the net increase in the seven and a half years being nearly twenty-five millions, while, compared with 1891, there was an increase of about sixteen and a half millions. It will thus be seen that the states have entirely recovered from the effects of the financial crisis of 1893.

In some of the states the *Credit Foncier* system has been established in connection with the Savings Banks, and particulars relating to the operations of the system will be found in the chapter dealing with Agriculture.

CURRENCY.

There is no universal currency in Australia except the British sovereign, the silver and bronze current being more properly tokens than coins. The bank notes issued by the banks of issue are not legal tender in any state, and do not circulate beyond the state in which they are issued. In Queensland there is a legal paper currency in the shape of Treasury notes, which have superseded the ordinary bank notes. The total note currency of the Commonwealth comprises £3,313,241 bank notes issued in the various states in the proportions shown on page 722, and £643,299 Treasury notes of Queensland, in all £3,956,540, equal to £1 0s. 3d. per inhabitant. The coin in circulation is a doubtful quantity; if the ratio found for New South Wales, viz., gold, £1 8s. 7d., silver, 5s. 7d., and bronze, 6d., obtains throughout the Commonwealth—the total coin circulation of Australia is gold, £5,477,800, silver, £1,070,000, and bronze, £95,800. These sums, with the note circulation, bring the total currency to £10,600,140, or £2 14s. 11d. per inhabitant. The coin and bullion held in reserve by the banks amount to £20,021,609, so that the total currency of the Commonwealth, both active and reserved, amounts to £30,621,749. Gold coins are legal tender to any amount, silver for an amount not exceeding forty shillings, and bronze for one shilling. The standard weight and fineness of each coin are given below. The least current weight of a sovereign is 122·5 Imperial grains, and of a half-sovereign, 61·125 grains:—

Denomination of Coin.		Standard Weight.	Standard Fineness.
		Imperial grains. Troy.	
Gold	Sovereign	123·27447	Eleven-twelfths fine gold, one-twelfth alloy, or decimal fineness ·91666
	Half-sovereign	61·63723	
Silver	Crown	436·36363	Thirty-seven-fortieths fine silver, three-fortieths alloy, or decimal fineness ·925.
	Double Florin	349·09090	
	Half-crown	218·18181	
	Florin	174·54545	
	Shilling	87·27272	
	Sixpence	43·63636	
	Threepence	21·81818	
		Avoirdupois.	
Bronze	Penny	145·83333	Mixed metal:—Copper, 95 parts; tin, 4 parts; and zinc, 1 part.
	Halfpenny	87·50000	
	Farthing	43·75000	

The only coins struck at the Sydney, Melbourne, and Perth Mints are of gold, though silver and bronze of English coinage are also issued at Sydney and Melbourne. The amounts of silver and bronze issued during

1902 were, at the Sydney Mint, silver, £11,800, and bronze, £3,000; and at the Melbourne Mint, £16,065 and £1,430 respectively. No silver or bronze coin had been issued at the Perth Mint up to the end of 1902. The Sydney Branch of the Royal Mint was opened on the 14th May, 1855, the Melbourne Branch on the 12th June, 1872, and a third branch was established at Perth on the 20th June, 1899. The amount of gold received for coinage up to the end of 1902, at the Sydney Mint, was 27,807,912 oz., valued at £102,914,214; the amount received at the Melbourne Mint to the same date was 25,762,522 oz., valued at £101,742,228; while at the Perth Branch the amount received was 2,877,264 oz, the value being £10,228,251.

The following table shows the quantity of gold received into the three Mints to the end of 1902, the metal received from outside sources being distinguished from that locally produced :—

Where produced.	Gold received for Coinage.		
	Sydney Mint.	Melbourne Mint.	Perth Mint.
	oz.	oz.	oz.
New South Wales	9,765,788	117,279	....
Victoria	1,443,182	18,670,392	19
Queensland	12,934,014	11,956	....
South Australia	86,299	617,674	21
Western Australia	12,709	2,676,045	2,877,034
Tasmania	94,341	975,864	....
New Zealand	3,160,442	2,472,534	....
Other Countries	50,104	209,691	174
Old Coin, etc.	261,033	11,087	16
Total	27,807,912	25,762,522	2,877,264

The total value of gold raised in Australasia to the end of 1902 was £475,759,982, of which amount 45 per cent. passed through the Sydney, Melbourne, and Perth Mints.

The following table shows the amount of gold coin and bullion issued by each Mint to the end of 1902 :—

Mint.	Sovereigns.	Half-sovereigns.	Bullion.	Total Value of Coin and Bullion issued.
	£	£	£	£
Sydney	96,501,500	2,909,500	3,286,031	102,697,031
Melbourne	94,257,340	547,362	6,923,430	101,728,132
Perth	9,755,536	59,688	407,245	10,222,469
Total	200,514,376	3,516,550	10,616,706	214,647.632

The quantity of gold received into the Sydney Mint in 1902 was 796,327 oz., valued at £2,874,297, of which only 167,215 oz., or about 21 per cent., was the produce of New South Wales. Queensland contributed 502,403 oz., or about 63 per cent. of the whole, while of the remainder, 113,254 oz. came from New Zealand, and 9,448 oz. from Tasmania. The amount of gold received into the Melbourne Mint for the same year was 1,142,243 oz., of which 825,335 oz., or 72 per cent., was the produce of Victoria, while 55,387 oz. came from Western Australia, notwithstanding the fact that the Perth Mint was opened on the 30th June, 1899; and 185,848 oz. were the produce of New Zealand. With the exception of 230 oz. the whole of the gold coined at the Perth Mint was the produce of Western Australia.

The gold coins issued from the Sydney Mint in 1902 consisted of 2,813,000 sovereigns and 84,000 half-sovereigns, while the Melbourne Mint issued 4,267,157 sovereigns, and the Perth Mint, 4,289,122 sovereigns during the year.

The value of the gold coinage issued from Sydney, Melbourne, Perth, and London Mints during the year 1902 was as follows:—

	£
Sydney	2,855,000
Melbourne	4,267,157
Perth	4,289,122
London	6,908,000

Besides gold coin, the Sydney Mint during 1902 issued gold bullion to the value of £2,553; the Melbourne Mint to the value of £195,410; and the Perth Mint to the value of £385,988.

The annual report of the Deputy-Master of the Royal Mint for 1902 shows the value of silver coin issued to and withdrawn from, and the value of bronze coin issued to each of the Commonwealth States and New Zealand during the thirty-one years 1872–1902, to have been as follows:—

State.	Silver Coin.			* Bronze Coin issued.
	Issued.	Withdrawn.	Net Issue.	
	£	£	£	£
New South Wales	1,034,700	203,467	831,233	51,350
Victoria	1,036,150	297,829	738,321	44,535
Queensland	267,245	4,750	262,495	3,650
South Australia	290,800	2,176	288,624	14,065
Western Australia	111,950	3,927	108,023	4,915
Tasmania	50,400	23,443	26,957	1,320
Commonwealth	2,791,245	535,592	2,255,653	119,835
New Zealand	287,035	....	287,035	17,285
Australasia	3,078,280	535,592	2,542,688	137,120

* From 1874.

These figures show a net annual average circulation of silver of £82,022 and of bronze of £4,728, but no allowance is made in the figures for coin brought to the states or taken away by passengers.

Complete information regarding worn coin is not available for the Melbourne Mint; the following figures, therefore, refer to Sydney only. From 1873, when the Mint first received worn silver coin, until 1902, the amount of silver withdrawn from circulation was of the nominal value of £212,263. The actual weight after melting was 680,297 oz., and the corresponding weight of new coinage would be 771,862 oz. The loss while the coins were in circulation was therefore 91,565 oz., the average loss being 11·9 per cent. From 1876 to 1902 gold coin of the nominal value of £826,700 was received at the Sydney Mint for recoinage, and was found to have an actual value of £823,933. The loss amounted, therefore, to £2,767, or 0·33 per cent.

As has already been pointed out, standard silver consists of ·925 pure metal and ·075 alloy. A pound troy of standard silver is coined into sixty-six shillings; that is to say, 11·1 ounces of fine metal produce coin to the value of £3 6s. The average price of silver during 1902 was 2s. 0⅛d. per ounce, which for 11·1 ounces gives the sum of £1 2s. 3¾d.; so that, after making due allowance for Mint expenses and loss entailed by abrasion of the coinage, it is evident that the British Government derives a fairly large profit from the silver coin issued to Australasia. This explains why the Governments of New South Wales and Victoria have approached the Imperial authorities for permission to coin silver to the value required for circulation in the States. With the present limited population of Australasia, however, it is doubtful whether the profits would do more than pay for the outlay necessary in connection with the minting.

Life Assurance.

All the states save New South Wales have special laws regulating the business of life assurance. Except that of Queensland, the Life Assurance Acts require yearly statements to be made showing the total business of companies in operation, and also certain particulars regarding the transactions within their own state, and the Western Australian Act also enforces particulars of the business in each of the other states. In New South Wales no special law has been passed, and companies doing this class of business are either registered under the Companies or Friendly Societies Act, or incorporated by special Act. In the other states the Acts regulating the business of life assurance deal chiefly with deposits to be made by companies commencing business, and with returns of business transacted. In no province are the full returns officially published; nevertheless, interesting and valuable reports are prepared and circulated by several of the companies, and all information reasonably to be desired is given in their pages. Other companies pursue a different course, and disclose very few particulars of their business. However, from such sources as are available, the information contained in the following pages has been compiled.

Of the twenty-two companies doing ordinary and industrial business in the states, eight have their head-offices in New South Wales, six in

Victoria, one in South Australia, two in New Zealand, one in the United Kingdom, three in the United States, and one in Canada. Some of the British companies have agencies in the states, principally for the collection of renewal premiums on policies effected in the United Kingdom, but as particulars of the business in the states are not available, these companies have also been excluded. The Mutual Assurance Society of Victoria was amalgamated with the National Mutual Life Association at the beginning of 1897, and consequently the figures in the tables show the transactions of the new company. The particulars in respect of the Victoria Life and General Insurance Company and the Adelaide Life Assurance and Guarantee Company have been omitted in this issue, as the information available in regard to them is incomplete.

The results of the latest published actuarial investigations of the various societies are appended:—

Institution.	Year of Foundation.	Basis of Valuation.	Date of last Valuation.	Net or Present Liability.	Total Assets.
		per cent.		£	£
Australian Mutual Provident Society	1849	3½ (a)	31 Dec., 1902	18,160,160	19,245,287
Mutual Life Association of Australasia ...	1869	4 (q)	31 ,, 1899	1,234,990	1,372,331
City Mutual Life Assurance Society (Ltd.) ..	1879	4 (t)	31 ,, 1900	199,898	211,498
*Citizens' Life Assurance Company (Ltd.) ..	1886	3½ (a)	31 ,, 1902	563,814	632,739
Standard Life Association (Ltd.)	1899	§..(q)	§........	§......	‡19,230
Australian Metropolitan Life Assurance Company (Ltd.)	1895	4 (q)	31 Aug., 1900	*3,347	‡22,976
Australian Alliance Assurance Company	1862	3½ (t)	31 Dec., 1900	253,108	†256,566
National Mutual Life Association of Australasia (Ltd.)	1869	3½ (t)	30 Sept., 1901	3,068,319	3,399,231
Australian Widows' Fund Life Assurance Society (Ltd.)	1871	3½ (q)	31 Oct., 1901	1,418,509	1,527,566
Colonial Mutual Life Assurance Society (Ltd.)	1874	3½, 4 (q)	31 Dec., 1899	2,071,579	2,391,882
Australasian Temperance and General Mutual Life Assurance Society (Ltd.)	1876	3½ (q)	30 Sept., 1900	*233,142	‡280,751
People's Prudential Assurance Company (Ltd.)	1896	3½ (q)	31 Aug., 1901	**3,256	††9,934
Phœnix Mutual Provident Society (Ltd.)	1902	‖	‖	‖	‖
New Zealand Government Life Insurance Department	1870	3½ (t)	31 Dec., 1902	3,214,409	3,882,817
Provident and Industrial Insurance Company of New Zealand	1889	4 (q)	30 June, 1899	7,211	13,376
Liverpool, London, and Globe Insurance Company	1836	3 (q)	31 Dec., 1898	4,891,268	‡‡10,376,224
Independent Order of Foresters	1877	4 (q)	31 ,, 1897	7,159,342	‖
Equitable Life Assurance Society of the United States	1859	3, 3½, 4 (a)	31 ,, 1902	58,437,632	78,855,785
New York Life Insurance Company	1845	3, 4 (a)	31 ,, 1902	55,141,153	66,339,443
Mutual Life Insurance Company of New York	1843	3, 4 (a)	31 ,, 1902	64,536,644	78,528,271

(a) Annual. (t) Triennial. (q) Quinquennial. (d) Decennial.

* Ordinary branch only. † Exclusive of Fire, Marine, and Guarantee branches.

‡ Includes assets of Industrial branch. § The first investigation will be made in June, 1904.

‖ Information not available. ** Includes Industrial branch.

†† Includes Industrial and Medical Benefit branches. ‡‡ Includes Fire branch.

The net or present liability represents the present value of the sums assured in respect of whole life and endowment assurance, reversionary bonuses, endowments, and annuities in force at date of valuation, less the present value of the future pure premiums thereon.

Of the twenty-two companies, twelve are mutual, and the remainder are what is termed in insurance parlance "mixed"—that is, proprietary companies dividing profits with the policy-holders. Six of the institutions also transact industrial business, while one company also undertakes fire, marine, and guarantee risks, and another does guarantee as well as life business. Most of the offices have representatives in all the states. Three institutions have extended their operations to London, and two also to South Africa. The New Zealand Government institution does not transact any business outside that colony.

The following table gives the policies in force and the sums assured in each society at the close of 1902. The item "Sums assured" means the sums payable, exclusive of reversionary bonuses, at death, or on attaining a certain age, or at death before that age:—

Institution.	Policies in force, exclusive of Annuities.	Assurances.			Annual Premium Income.
		Sums Assured, exclusive of Bonuses.	Bonus Additions.	Total.	
	No.	£	£	£	£
Australian Mutual Provident Society	176,012	50,763,589	10,048,346	60,811,935	1,663,382
Mutual Life Association of Australasia	22,638	5,816,259	¶	¶	202,406
City Mutual Life Assurance Society (Ltd.)	10,923	1,389,508	44,711	1,434,219	53,649
Citizens' Life Assurance Company (Ltd.)	33,604	4,608,160	145,318	4,753,478	181,415
Standard Life Association (Ltd.)	1,573	159,327	478	159,805	7,467
‖ Australian Metropolitan Life Assurance Company (Ltd.)	985	77,907	919	78,826	3,639
Australian Alliance Assurance Company	1,054	371,341	33,407	404,748	11,423
National Mutual Life Association of Australasia (Ltd.)	50,082	11,336,347	728,160	12,064,507	371,943
Australian Widows' Fund Life Assurance Society (Ltd.)	23,622	5,025,229	168,406	5,193,635	185,506
Colonial Mutual Life Assurance Society (Ltd.)	33,906	10,420,684	325,430	10,746,114	325,877
‖ Australasian Temperance and General Mutual Life Assurance Society (Ltd.)	10,375	1,512,740	12,433	1,525,173	53,597
People's Prudential Assurance Company (Ltd.)	177	12,400	¶	¶	448
Phœnix Mutual Provident Society (Ltd.)	¶	¶	¶	¶	¶
New Zealand Government Life Insurance Department	42,105	9,896,572	838,088	10,734,660	296,373
Provident and Industrial Insurance Company of New Zealand	¶	¶	¶	¶	¶
‡ Liverpool, London, and Globe Insurance Company	904	373,558	¶	¶	9,961
‡ Independent Order of Foresters	2,167	344,890	¶	¶	6,251
‡ Equitable Life Assurance Society of the United States	13,486	5,205,491	¶	¶	¶
‡ Mutual Life Insurance Company of New York	6,511	2,472,434	¶	¶	199,356
‡ New York Life Insurance Company	4,400	2,017,141	¶	¶	77,649

‡ Australasian business only. ‖ Ordinary branch only. ¶ Not available.

The following table shows the assurances in force at the close of each of the last three years :—

Institution.	Amount Assured, excluding Bonuses and Annuities.		
	1900.	1901.	1902.
	£	£	£
Australian Mutual Provident Society	47,706,765	49,366,565	50,763,589
Mutual Life Association of Australasia	5,179,578	5,501,585	5,816,259
City Mutual Life Assurance Society (Ltd.)	1,274,166	1,385,716	1,389,508
‡Citizens' Life Assurance Company (Ltd.)	3,652,684	4,173,655	4,608,160
‡Standard Life Association (Ltd.)	98,997	§156,817	159,327
‡Australian Metropolitan Life Assurance Company (Ld.)	13,571	75,458	77,907
Australian Alliance Assurance Company	431,892	399,271	371,341
National Mutual Life Association of Australasia (Ltd.)	10,948,504	11,336,347	11,336,347
Australian Widows' Fund Life Assurance Society (Ltd.)	4,742,674	5,025,229	5,025,229
Colonial Mutual Life Assurance Society (Ltd.)	10,418,388	10,420,684	10,420,684
‡Australasian Temperance and General Mutual Life Assurance Society (Ltd.)	1,362,635	1,407,379	1,512,740
People's Prudential Assurance Company (Ltd.)	*	*	12,400
Phœnix Mutual Provident Society (Ltd.)	*	*	*
New Zealand Government Life Insurance Department	9,607,036	9,742,102	9,896,572
Provident and Industrial Insurance Company of New Zealand	*	*	*
Liverpool, London, and Globe Insurance Company	*	*	373,558
Independent Order of Foresters	*	*	344,800
†Equitable Life Assurance Society of the United States	4,284,265	4,729,161	5,305,491
†Mutual Life Insurance Company of New York	1,747,814	1,860,500	2,017,141
†New York Life Insurance Company	2,212,033	2,330,404	2,472,434

* Information not available. † Australasian business only, but inclusive of bonus additions, except for the Mutual Life of New York in 1900 and 1901, and the New York Life Company in 1901, for which the information relating to bonuses is not available. ‡ Ordinary branch only. § June, 1902.

The receipts of the societies are chiefly represented by the collections from premiums on policies and the interest arising from investments of the accumulated funds; while payments on account of claims, surrenders, cash bonuses, and expenses of management chiefly comprise the disbursements. The receipts and disbursements during 1902 of each society having its head office in Australasia were as follow :—

Institution.	Receipts.	Expenditure.	Excess Receipts (Addition to Funds).
	£	£	£
Australian Mutual Provident Society	2,509,729	1,595,130	914,599
Mutual Life Association of Australasia	287,399	182,152	105,247
City Mutual Life Assurance Society (Ltd.)	63,746	59,352	4,394
*Citizens' Life Assurance Company (Ltd.)	197,424	62,271	135,153
‡Standard Life Association (Ltd.)	36,960	30,730	6,180
‡Australian Metropolitan Life Assurance Company (Ld.)	12,698	22,909	†10,211
Australian Alliance Assurance Company	35,965	28,274	7,691
National Mutual Life Association of Australasia (Ltd.)	583,149	387,804	195,345
Australian Widows' Fund Life Assurance Society (Ltd.)	253,661	194,467	59,194
Colonial Mutual Life Assurance Society (Ltd.)	429,263	318,308	110,960
*Australasian Temperance and General Mutual Life Assurance Society (Ltd.)	73,932	43,199	30,733
Victoria Life and General Insurance Company	12,434	41,681	†29,247
People's Prudential Assurance Company (Ltd.)	12,566	13,056	†490
Phœnix Mutual Provident Society (Ltd.)	1,407	1,743	†336
Adelaide Life Assurance and Guarantee Company	66	18,423	†18,357
New Zealand Government Life Insurance Department	451,348	353,946	97,402
Provident and Industrial Insurance Company of New Zealand	12,242	11,239	1,003
Total £	4,973,989	3,364,729	1,609,260

*Ordinary branch only. † Decrease. ‡ Includes Industrial Branch.

The aggregate receipts and disbursements of the seventeen Australasian institutions during 1902 were as follow:—

Receipts.		Expenditure.	
	£		£
Premiums—		Claims	1,919,970
New	374,629	Surrenders	488,074
Renewals	3,055,985	Annuities	68,417
Consideration for Annuities	88,140	Cash Bonuses and Dividends	98,111
Interest	1,443,646	Expenses	688,497
Other Receipts (Rents, etc.)	11,589	Amount written off to Depreciation, Reserves, etc.	101,660
Total £	4,973,989	Total £	3,364,729

The basis of the valuation of the various companies operating in Australia and New Zealand has been shown on a previous page. It will be seen that the assumed rate of interest is either 3½ or 4 per cent., while the actual rate earned on the average amount of funds for last year was 4·45 per cent., so that there is still a good margin above valuation rates. The question of the earnings of investments is one of great concern both to insurers and insured, and the following table covering the last fifteen years, will show the downward tendency of interest during that period:—

Year.	Average rate of interest realised on mean funds. Per cent.
1888	5·91
1889	5·95
1890	5·81
1891	5·96
1892	5·80
1893	5·66
1894	5·44
1895	5·35
1896	5·15
1897	4·77
1898	4·73
1899	4·58
1900	4·47
1901	4·46
1902	4·45

Assets and Liabilities of Assurance Companies.

The societies publish annually a statement of assets and liabilities, with the object of showing the distribution of the accumulated funds and the amount placed to commercial reserve. The return is, however, in no way connected with the valuation balance-sheet prepared at the date of the actuarial investigation. The assets and liabilities for each institution, for the financial year of 1902, were as shown in the subjoined table:—

Institution.	Assets.			Liabilities.		
	Loans on Mortgages and Policies.	Government and Municipal Securities, Freehold Property, Cash on Deposit, etc., etc.	Total.	Assurance Endowment and Annuity Funds.	Paid-up Capital, Reserve Funds, etc., etc.	Total.
	£	£	£	£	£	£
Australian Mutual Provident Society	13,093,917	6,151,370	19,245,287	18,774,641	470,646	19,245,287
Mutual Life Association of Australasia	951,314	698,024	1,649,338	1,638,939	10,399	1,649,338
City Mutual Life Assurance Society (Ltd.)	131,395	108,531	239,926	238,396	1,530	239,926
*Citizens' Life Assurance Company (Ltd.)	272,139	360,600	632,739	626,755	5,984	632,739
§Standard Life Association (Ltd.)	917	25,242	26,159	12,528	13,631	26,159
§Australian Metropolitan Life Assurance Company (Ltd.)	1,820	36,764	38,584	14,788	23,796	38,584
†Australian Alliance Assurance Company	267,315	230,386	497,701	257,469	240,232	497,701
National Mutual Life Association of Australasia (Ltd.)	2,296,172	1,295,819	3,591,991	3,460,471	131,520	3,591,991
Australian Widows' Fund Life Assurance Society (Ltd.)	1,133,049	455,348	1,588,397	1,577,753	10,644	1,588,397
Colonial Mutual Life Assurance Society (Ltd.)	1,387,472	1,328,539	2,716,011	2,620,862	95,140	2,716,011
Australasian Temperance and General Mutual Life Assurance Society (Ltd.)	140,893	185,210	326,103	284,448	41,655	326,103
Victoria Life and General Insurance Company	148,601	167,225	315,826	220,600	95,226	315,826
People's Prudential Assurance Company (Ltd.)	3,885	5,878	9,763	4,831	4,932	9,763
Phœnix Mutual Provident Society (Ltd.)	......	728	728	708	20	728
¶Adelaide Life Assurance and Guarantee Company	5,310	23,160	28,470	10,650	17,820	28,470
New Zealand Government Life Insurance Department	2,416,271	1,057,863	3,474,134	3,382,817	91,317	3,474,134
Provident and Industrial Insurance Company of New Zealand	......	27,759	27,759	6,263	21,496	27,759
Total £	22,250,470	12,158,446	34,408,916	33,132,919	1,275,997	34,408,916

* Ordinary branch only. † Inclusive of Fire, Marine, and Guarantee Branches, which cannot be separated. § Inclusive of the Industrial Branch. ¶ Inclusive of Guarantee Branch.

Loans on mortgages and policies represent about two-thirds of the total assets, and in former years the investment of funds was almost exclusively confined to these securities; but lately the operations in Government stocks, municipal loans, and other securities and shares have greatly increased. The remaining items require no special comment, except loans on personal security, combined with life assurance. Investments of this character are unusual in Australasia, and are decreasing each year, the amount invested aggregating only £47,248. In some of the states the companies are obliged by law to deposit certain sums with the Treasury as a guarantee of good faith, and the amount so lodged is included either under the head of Government securities or of deposits.

Expenses of Management of Assurance Companies.

The ratio of expenses of management to premium income and gross receipts must necessarily vary according to the age of the society and the proportion of new business transacted. The figures are given for what they are worth. That a more exact comparison cannot be made is the fault of certain companies which fail to make a complete disclosure of their affairs, and do not distribute their expenses of management so that the cost of new business may be distinguished from that of old business; the reports of other companies are unequalled in any part of the world:—

Institution.	Expenses of Management.		
	Amount.	Proportion to—	
		Premium Income.	Gross Receipts.
	£	per cent.	per cent.
Australian Mutual Provident Society	220,446	13·16	8·78
Mutual Life Association of Australasia	56,945	26·10	19·81
City Mutual Life Assurance Society (Ltd.)	14,717	28·78	23·69
*Citizens' Life Assurance Company (Ltd.)	27,583	15·76	13·95
‡Standard Life Association (Ltd.)	28,129	77·25	76·11
‡Australian Metropolitan Life Assurance Company (Ltd.)	12,703	109·36	100·94
§Australian Alliance Assurance Company	2,742	10·70	7·62
National Mutual Life Association of Australasia (Ltd.)	100,020	23·52	17·15
Australian Widows' Fund Life Assurance Society (Ltd.)	50,777	27·88	20·02
Colonial Mutual Life Assurance Society (Ltd.)	80,162	24·71	18·66
*Australasian Temperance and General Mutual Life Assurance Society (Ltd.)	18,640	30·10	25·21
Victoria Life and General Insurance Company	1,536	42·13	12·35
People's Prudential Assurance Company (Ltd.)	6,294	51·16	50·09
Phœnix Mutual Provident Society (Ltd.)	1,314	97·26	93·39
Adelaide Life Assurance and Guarantee Company	†......	†......	†......
New Zealand Government Life Insurance Department	59,895	19·71	13·27
Provident Industrial Insurance Company of New Zealand	6,704	56·69	54·76

* Ordinary Branch only. † Included in expenses of Guarantee Branch. ‡ Includes Industrial Branch. § Life branch only.

Assurance in various Countries.

The average amount assured per policy for each state, and for the United Kingdom, Canada, and the United States, is given in the following table. The figures in certain instances are probably somewhat overstated, as all the companies do not show complete returns of the business in each state; but the results may be taken as a fair estimate for each province. The Australasian business of the American institutions excluded from the previous returns, has been included for the purpose of establishing the Australian averages, but the industrial business has been excluded:—

Country.	Average Sum assured per Policy.	Average Premium per £100 of Assurance.		
	£	£	s.	d.
Australasia	257	3	3	8
New South Wales	280	3	2	0
Victoria	233	3	3	10
Queensland	299	2	19	6
South Australia	232	3	5	5
Western Australia	300	2	19	9
Tasmania	254	3	3	2
New Zealand	244	3	0	11
United Kingdom	323			
United States	441			
Canada	330	....		

The average amount of assurance per head of population was, in Australasia, £24; in Canada, £18; in the United Kingdom, £16; and in the United States £20; while the average number of policies per thousand of population was, in Australasia, 92; in Canada, 56; in the United Kingdom, 49; and in the United States, 46.

The average policy is scarcely a fair measure of thrift. In these states mutual assurance is the rule, and members of the various societies have acquired large bonus additions. The average existing policy, including reversionary bonus, of the Australasian companies, on the 31st December, 1902, was £286, as compared with the £257 shown in the comparative table.

It would seem that the practice of assuring life is much more prevalent in Australasia than in any of the other countries instanced; and although the average sum assured by each policy is less, the number of policies is so much greater, as compared with the population, that the amount assured per inhabitant is considerably higher.

INDUSTRIAL ASSURANCE.

In addition to the ordinary life transactions mentioned in the fore going tables, a large industrial business has grown up during the past few years. The policies in this class are usually for small amounts, and the premiums are, in most cases, payable weekly or monthly. The assurances may be effected on the lives of infants and adults, and the introduction of this class of business has proved of great benefit to the industrial population.

As already mentioned there are four of the Australasian companies previously dealt with which combine industrial with ordinary business, while two limit their operations to industrial and medical benefit transactions. The balance-sheets of these companies, however, do not show sufficient information to admit of making a satisfactory comparison of the business transacted, as, in some cases, the two branches are not treated separately. At the close of 1902, the business in force of the six companies showing transactions in the industrial branch, was as follows:—

Company.	Date.	No. of Policies.	Sum Assured.	Annual Premiums
			£	£
Citizens' Life Assurance Company, Ltd.	31 Dec., 1902	196,837	4,197,153	181,172
Australasian Temperance and General Mutual Life Assurance Society, Ltd.	31 Dec., 1902	54,990	1,060,825	61,358
Standard Life Association, Ltd. ...	31 Dec., 1902	21,898	395,123	29,101
Australian Metropolitan Life Assurance Company, Ltd.	31 Dec., 1902	8,656	426,383	12,555
People's Prudential Assurance Company, Ltd.	31 Dec., 1901*	4,055	109,449	5,540
Provident Industrial Insurance Company of New Zealand.	31 Dec., 1902	12,016	305,880	14,410
Total	....	298,452	6,494,813	304,136

* Latest Available.

It will thus be seen that the average amount per policy for these companies was about £21 15s., while the average premium per policy amounted to £1 0s. 5d. per annum, or about 4¾d. per week.

The receipts and disbursements of the companies publishing the information are given below, the dates to which the figures relate being also shown :—

Company.	Date.	Receipts.			Disbursements.		
		Premiums.	Other.	Total.	Claims, Surrenders, and Cash Dividends.	Expenses of Management, Commission on New Business, &c.	Total.
		£.	£.	£.	£.	£.	£.
Citizens' Life Assurance Company, Ltd.	31 Dec., 1902	175,810	12,878	188,088	43,707	108,234	151,941
Australasian Temperance and General Mutual Life Assurance Society, Ltd.	30 Sep., 1903	67,691	1,856	69,547	8,925	46,230	55,155
People's Prudential Assurance Company, Ltd.	31 Aug., 1903	12,313	371	12,684	1,225	*9,966	11,191
Provident and Industrial Insurance Company of New Zealand.	30 June, 1903	13,048	424	13,472	3,988	8,022	12,010
Total	....	268,862	15,529	284,391	57,845	172,452	230,297

* Includes payments to medical practitioners and chemists.

The figures quoted show that about 95 per cent. of the total receipts consists of premiums, the other sources of revenue being interest, rent, fines, &c. With regard to the disbursements it will be noticed that a large amount was paid for expenses of management, commission, etc., the proportions under this head being :—

	Percentage of Total Income.	Percentage of Premium Income.
Citizens' Life Assurance Co., Ltd.	57·4	61·6
Australasian Temperance and General Mutual Life Assurance Society, Ltd....	66·5	68·3
People's Prudential Assurance Co., Ltd.	78·6	80·9
Provident and Industrial Insurance Co. of N.Z.	59·5	61·5

The expenses of all societies transacting this class of business are invariably high, as a large staff of collectors and agents have to be employed, who are required to call at the homes of the assured for payments, but it may be said generally that the above ratios compare not unfavourably with those of old-established societies in the United Kingdom and the United States of America.

A distinctive feature of the liabilities of five of the companies (the Australasian Temperance and General is purely mutual) is the amount of share capital employed, and the profits generally provide for the payment of dividends to shareholders, the policy-holders, as a rule, not being entitled to participate. A complete table of assets and liabilities cannot be given, but the paid-up capital at the latest available date was as follows:—

	£.
Citizens' Life Assurance Company, Ltd.	20,000
Standard Life Association, Ltd	12,500
Australian Metropolitan Life Assurance Co., Ltd.	3,000
People's Prudential Assurance Company, Ltd.	4,721
Provident and Industrial Insurance Co. of N.Z.	19,000

Friendly Societies.

The services which friendly societies directly render to the state in enabling the labouring classes to combine for the making of due provision to meet unforeseen demands in the case of sickness or death, are clearly recognised by the Governments of the various states, and all such societies which are registered according to law are granted certain privileges in consideration of the important part which they play in the social welfare of the community, in relieving the public purse of claims which would otherwise have to be preferred against it, and in maintaining the independence of their members and obviating the necessity of those members accepting aid which would have a tendency to pauperise them. The Acts regulating the operations of friendly societies in the states are all based on English legislation; and, generally speaking, the following privileges, which are granted to members of such societies in the state of New South Wales, may be taken as typical of those enjoyed in Australasia:—

1. A registered Society can legally hold land and other kinds of property in the names of trustees, such property passing from one trustee to another by the mere fact of appointment; and can carry on all legal proceedings in the trustees' names.
2. The Society has a remedy on summary conviction whenever any person—
   - (*a*) Obtains possession of its property by false repre sentation or imposition;
   - (*b*) Having possession of any of its property, withholds or misapplies it;
   - (*c*) Wilfully applies any part of such property to purposes other than those expressed or directed by the rules and authorised by the Act.
3. If an officer of the Society dies or becomes bankrupt or insolvent, or if an execution is issued against him whilst he has money or property of the Society in his possession by virtue of his office, the trustees of the Society are entitled to claim such money or property in preference to any other creditors.
4. The documents of the Society are free from stamp duty.

5. The Society can admit members under twenty-one and take from them binding receipts, which would otherwise be of no effect.

6. If it invests money on mortgage, such mortgages can be discharged by a mere endorsed receipt without reconveyance.

7. Its officers are legally bound to render account and give up all money or property in their possession on demand or notice, and may be compelled to do so.

8. Disputes can be legally settled according to the Society's own rules.

9. Members of registered Friendly Societies have the privilege of legally insuring money, on the deaths of their wives and children, for their funeral expenses, without having an insurable interest in their lives.

10. Members of registered Societies may dispose at death of sums payable by the Society by written nomination without a will; and this nomination may be made by youths of sixteen who cannot make a will till they are twenty-one.

11. Where there is no will and no nomination, the trustees may distribute sums without letters of administration being taken out (a person doing so in any other case would make himself liable for the debts of the deceased).

The Acts contain provisions inserted with the object of securing the solvency of the societies. In most of the states these provisions have been operative; but in others the position of some of the orders is not so satisfactory as it should be.

In the following table will be found the number of societies, the number of lodges or branches of these societies, the aggregate number of members, the total amount of their funds, and the average amount per member in each of the states. The figures are for the latest available periods, the dates being set forth below :—

State.	Date.	Societies.	Lodges or Branches.	Members.	Total Funds.	Average Amount of Funds per member.
		No.	No.	No.	£	£ s. d.
New South Wales	31 Dec., 1901	68	862	88,881	745,405	8 7 9
Victoria..................	31 Dec., 1901	29	1,132	100,783	1,317,811	13 1 6
Queensland	31 Dec., 1902	17	385	31,709	290,919	9 3 6
South Australia	31 Dec., 1899	16	474	48,043	535,198	12 8 8
Western Australia	31 Dec., 1901	*15	146	†9,919	53,142	5 7 2
Tasmania	31 Dec., 1901	18	159	14,716	114,305	7 15 4
Commonwealth	....	163	3,158	289,051	3,056,780	10 11 6
New Zealand	31 Dec., 1901	12	445	41,236	804,753	19 10 4
Australasia		175	3,603	330,287	3,861,533	11 13 10

* Exclusive of 8 specially authorised societies. † Exclusive of honorary members.

It will be seen from the foregoing table that, taking the average amount of funds per member as the basis of comparison, New Zealand occupies first position with the sum of £19 10s. 4d.; Victoria comes next with £13 1s. 6d.; South Australia takes third place with £12 8s. 8d. per member; Queensland comes next with £9 3s. 6d.; and then follow New South Wales and Tasmania in the order named, with £8 7s. 9d. and £7 15s. 4d. respectively; Western Australia having the smallest amount, viz., £5 7s. 2d., to the credit of each individual member.

Money Orders.

The business transacted in the various Postal Departments under the system of money orders has grown to very large dimensions. This increase is due mainly to the greater facilities now afforded for the transmission of money by this method, though it is also to some extent attributable to the more general appreciation of the system by the working classes. The following is a statement of the business transacted during 1902:—

State.	Orders issued.		Orders paid.	
	Number.	Amount.	Number.	Amount.
		£		£
New South Wales	538,796	1,761,149	545,861	1,812,063
Victoria	217,634	706,791	306,510	1,053,313
Queensland	137,168	506,990	105,556	400,042
South Australia	78,041	246,826	82,479	295,372
Western Australia	189,514	768,751	85,700	372,689
Tasmania	121,397	290,113	125,317	228,958
Commonwealth	1,282,550	4,280,620	1,251,423	4,162,437
New Zealand	367,207	1,277,059	286,369	1,118,254
Australasia	1,649,757	5,557,679	1,537,792	5,280,691

The average amount of each money order issued was £3 7s. 5d., and the business done by New South Wales greatly exceeded that of any other state. The average value of money orders issued in the United Kingdom during 1902 was £3 0s. 5d.

POSTAL NOTES.

Besides the money orders mentioned above, a system of postal notes is in force in all the states. The notes are issued for fixed amounts, varying from 1s. to 20s. The number and value of notes issued and paid during 1902 in each of the states were as follows :—

State.	Notes issued.		Notes paid.	
	Number.	Amount.	Number.	Amoun
		£		£
New South Wales......	1,409,180	506,159	1,423,369	514,048
Victoria	1,387,039	528,381	1,432,734	544,979
Queensland	290,663	110,599	259,455	97,045
South Australia	296,997	102,112	293,590	102,651
Western Australia ...	122,877	55,841	112,934	37,529
Tasmania	77,665	24,851	77,445	28,179
Commonwealth...	3,583,821	1,327,853	3,599,527	1,324,431
New Zealand.....	616,264	191,905	610,464	190,375
Australasia.........	4,200,085	1,519,758	4,209,991	1,514,806

These figures show that, for the transmission of small amounts, postal notes are rapidly superseding money orders. While in 1902 the number of money orders issued was less than half that of postal notes, the value of the latter was only slightly over one-fourth of the value of money orders, the average value of postal notes being 7s. 3d. as compared with £3 7s. 5d. for money orders.

BANKRUPTCIES.

The bankruptcy laws of the different states are even more dissimilar than the laws on most other questions of importance; they have also been fluctuating, and the subject of many experiments and amendments. This renders any work of comparison difficult and unsatisfactory. Returns are available for all the states for the year 1902, and are given below. In connection with the table it may be pointed out that the figures are exclusive of 74 liquidations in Queensland, with liabilities stated at £86,999, and assets at £69,876; and also of 183 private arrangements under the Insolvency Act in South Australia, for which the assets and liabilities are not stated. The Victorian figures include

209 Deeds of Arrangement under the Act of 1897, the liabilities of which were £204,956, and the assets £181,139:—

State.	Number of Sequestrations.	As shown in Bankrupts' Schedules.		
		Liabilities.	Assets.	Deficiency.
		£	£	£
New South Wales...	458	281,204	124,427	156,777
Victoria	612	564,758	448,398	116,360
Queensland............	434	88,311	30,321	57,990
South Australia.....	35	40,798	25,138	15,660
Western Australia..	76	51,548	17,247	34,301
Tasmania	60	44,213	29,562	14,651
Commonwealth	1,675	1,070,832	675,093	395,739
New Zealand	205	120,401	61,604	58,797
Australasia......	1,880	1,191,233	736,697	454,536

Little, if any, reliance can be placed upon the statements made by bankrupts as to the position of their affairs, the assets being invariably exaggerated. Taking the figures given above for what they are worth, it would appear that the average amount of liabilities per bankrupt was £634, and of assets, £392, showing a deficiency of £242. In the following table the average figures for the ten years ended 31st December, 1902, are given; the assets, however, have been omitted, since the statements, so far as some of the states are concerned, are palpably worthless. The Victorian figures include the "Deeds of Arrangement" for the years 1898 to 1902, while the South Australian returns are exclusive of private arrangements, which averaged 193 per annum. The Queensland figures are exclusive of liquidations.

State.	Number of Sequestrations.	Liabilities, as shown in Bankrupts' Schedules.
		£
New South Wales	910	791,994
Victoria	748	1,913,261
Queensland	358	107,374
South Australia	55	85,809
Western Australia	70	108,781
Tasmania	100	42,772
Commonwealth	2,241	3,049,991
New Zealand	395	219,707
Australasia	2,636	3,269,698

POSTS AND TELEGRAPHS.

THE first Australasian post-office was established by Governor Macquarie in the year 1810, Mr. Isaac Nichols being appointed Postmaster. The office was in High-street (now known as George-street), Sydney, at the residence of Mr. Nichols, who was, "in consideration of the trouble and expense attendant upon this duty," allowed to charge on delivery to the addressee 8d. for every English or foreign letter of whatever weight, and for every parcel weighing not more than 20 lb., 1s. 6d., and exceeding that weight, 3s. The charge on colonial letters was 4d., irrespective of weight; and soldiers' letters, or those addressed to their wives, were charged 1d. Very little improvement in regard to postal matters took place for some years.

In 1825 an Act was passed by Sir Thomas Brisbane, with the advice of the Council, "to regulate the postage of letters in New South Wales," giving power for the establishment of post-offices, and to fix the rates of postage. It was not, however, until 1828 that the provisions of the Act were put into full force. The rates of postage appear to have depended upon the distance and the difficulty of transmission. The lowest single inland rate was 3d., and the highest 12d., the postage on a letter increasing according to its weight, which was fixed for a single letter at ¼-ounce. Letters between New South Wales and Van Diemen's Land were charged 3d. each (ship rate), and newspapers 1d. Other ship letters were charged 4d. single rate, and 6d. for any weight in excess. The privilege of franking was allowed to the Governor and a number of the chief public officials, and letters to and from convicts passed free under certain regulations.

In 1831 a twopenny post was established in Sydney; and in 1835, under Sir Richard Bourke, the Act of 1825 was repealed and another Act was passed, fixing the charge on a single letter at 4d. for 15 miles, 5d. for 20 miles, 6d. for 30 miles, and so on up to 1s. for 300 miles. In 1837 a post-office was established in Melbourne, and a fortnightly mail was established between that city and Sydney. Stamps were introduced in the same year in the shape of stamped covers or envelopes, which are believed to have been the first postage-stamps ever issued. By 1838 there were 40 post-offices in the state of New South Wales, which at that time, of course, included the territory now known as Victoria and Queensland; and in the Sydney office about 15 persons were employed. The revenue of the Department for the year was

£8,390, and the expenditure £10,347; while payments were made by the New South Wales Government to the post office at Kororareka, in New Zealand, which was not created a separate colony until 1841. In 1847 an overland mail between Sydney and Adelaide was established. Stamps in their present form were issued in 1849, and the postage rates were fixed at 1d. per ½ oz. for town and 2d. for country letters, at which they remain in most of the states to-day.

Regular steam mail communication with Great Britain was first established in 1852. Until that time the Australian colonies had to depend upon the irregular arrival and despatch of sailing vessels for the carriage of mails; but in the year mentioned the steamships Australia, Chusan, and Great Britain were despatched from England, making the voyage in 60 days, and causing a strong desire in the minds of the colonists for a more frequent and steady system of steam communication with the Old World. The outbreak of the Crimean War in 1854 hindered for a while the accomplishment of this object; but in 1856 a line of steamers was again laid on, and the service was carried on by the Peninsular and Oriental Company and the Royal Mail Company for some years, but without giving so much satisfaction to the public as might have been expected.

As far back as 1854 a proposal was made for the establishment of a line of mail packets *via* Panama, and negotiations on the subject were carried on for several years between the British Government and the Governments of New South Wales and New Zealand. The result was that in 1866 the service was started, and continued in operation until the end of 1868, when it was terminated through the failure of the company by which it had been carried out. In the following year New South Wales, in conjunction with New Zealand, inaugurated a mail service *via* San Francisco, which, with a few interruptions and under various conditions, has been continued up to the present time.

The establishment of a mail route *via* America had the effect of stimulating the steamship-owners who were engaged in the service *via* Suez, and from that time there was a marked improvement in the steamers employed, as well as in the punctuality and speed with which the mails were delivered. The Peninsular and Oriental Company have carried mails for the colonies almost from the inception of the ocean steam service, with very few interruptions. Towards the end of 1878 the Orient Company commenced carrying mails between Australia and the United Kingdom, and have continued to do so ever since. In the year 1883 the fine steamers of the Messageries Maritimes of France entered the service, followed in 1887 by the North German Lloyd's, so that there are now sometimes two or even three mails received and despatched every week, and a voyage to Europe, which was formerly a formidable undertaking, involving great loss of time and much discomfort, is regarded as a mere pleasure trip to fill up a holiday.

In the year 1893 another mail service was established, by a line of steamers running from Sydney to Vancouver Island, in British Columbia.

There is also a line of steamers running between Brisbane and London, but the states other than Queensland make little use of these vessels.

Under the provisions of the 51st clause of the Commonwealth of Australia Constitution Act, the control of the Post and Telegraph services became vested in the Commonwealth, and by proclamation these services were taken over on the 1st March, 1901. The systems of administration, and the rates levied in force in each state at the date of union were however continued until the Commonwealth Postal Act was brought into operation on the 1st November, 1902, thus securing uniformity in all the states.

Growth of Postal Business.

The growth of postal business in each of the states during the forty-two years from 1861 to 1902 is shown below. It will be seen that the number of letters for all Australasia in 1861 was less than the present total for any individual state, with the exception of Tasmania. The true total for Australasia is, of course, not to be found by adding the figures of the several states together, as interstate letters are counted both in the state from which they are despatched and in that in which they are received for delivery. A second total is therefore given from which this excess has been excluded :—

State.	Post Offices.		Letters and Post-cards.		Newspapers.		Packets.	
	1861.	1902.	1861.	1902.	1861.	1902.	1861.	1902.
New South Wales....	840	2,216	4,369,463	90,781,395	3,384,245	47,763,360	105,388	16,995,440
Victoria	369	1,649	6,109,929	97,007,069	4,277,179	29,141,619	....	13,509,395
Queensland	24	1,360	515,211	23,537,197	427,489	12,936,847	3,555	7,756,502
South Australia	160	702	1,540,472	20,734,629	1,089,424	10,682,376	....	1,516,611
Western Australia ..	..	197	193,317	18,741,157	137,476	10,511,898	....	5,164,034
Tasmania	100	377	835,873	9,823,246	895,656	6,869,902	....	2,625,795
Commonwealth ..	..	6,441	13,564,265	260,624,713	10,211,469	117,966,002	....	47,567,[illegible]
Commonwealth (excluding Inter-State excess)	..	..	12,844,300	243,674,886	9,603,000	104,780,042	....	43,047,926
New Zealand	..	1,807	1,236,768	59,016,798	1,428,351	18,517,276	....	18,917,994
Australasia........	..	8,248	14,801,033	319,641,511	11,639,820	136,483,278	....	66,485,261
Australasia (excluding intercolonial excess)	..	..	14,061,000	301,563,402	10,941,400	122,296,796	....	61,707,332

A corresponding table to that already given, showing the number of letters, newspapers, and packets per head of population, is appended :—

State.	Letters and Post-cards.		Newspapers.		Packets	
	1861.	1902.	1861.	1902.	1861.	1902.
New South Wales	12	65	10	34	1	12
Victoria	11	80	8	25	......	11
Queensland	17	46	14	25	1	15
South Australia	13	57	9	29	......	4
Western Australia	12	91	9	51	......	25
Tasmania	9	56	10	39	......	15
Commonwealth......	11	68	8	31	......	12
New Zealand	14	74	16	23	......	24
Australasia*	11	65	9	26	......	13

* Interstate excess excluded.

Western Australia takes the lead in the transmission of letters, newspapers, and packets; while Victoria in letters and postcards, Tasmania in newspapers, and New Zealand in packets occupy second place. A comparison of the average number of letters and postcards per head of population in Australasia with similar figures for the principal countries of the world is afforded by the table given below. It will be seen that on a population basis the correspondence of Australasia exceeds that of any of the countries named, with the exception of the United Kingdom :—

Country.	Letters and Post-cards per head.	Country.	Letters and Post-cards per head.
United Kingdom.......	69	France	30
Australasia	65	Norway	27
Argentine Republic ...	59	Hungary	17
Switzerland.........	55	Japan	14
Germany.........	54	Italy	13
Sweden.........	53	Portugal.........	12
Austria	42	Spain.........	7
Denmark	41	Roumania......... ...	6
Canada.........	41	Chili	4
Belgium	36	Greece	3
Netherlands	32	Russia	4

RATES OF POSTAGE.

The inland letter postage is 1d. per ½ oz. on town and 2d. on country letters in all the states of the Commonwealth of Australia, except Victoria and South Australia. In Victoria the rate is 1d. per ½ oz., and in South Australia 2d. per ½ oz. on all letters posted for delivery within the state. In Victoria the minimum charge was altered in 1890 from 2d. per oz. to 1d. per ½ oz.; but the loss at that time was too great, and in 1892 the rate was again raised to 2d. per oz.; in 1901 it was once more reduced to 1d. per ½ oz. In New South Wales the city and suburban rate of 1d. per ½ oz., which is in force in the Metropolitan Suburban District, is also in operation within a 12-mile radius of Newcastle, and a 13-mile radius of nearly sixty of the other principal country towns. The inter-state and intercolonial rate is uniformly 2d. per ½ oz. in Australasia. On the 1st January, 1901, New Zealand adopted a universal penny postage, and the loss attendant thereon for the year may be set down at about £34,000. By arrangement with the Commonwealth, New Zealand letters come to Australia for 1d., but letters to New Zealand are charged 2d. When this matter was settled it was further arranged that New Zealand should reduce its terminal rate on cable messages exchanged with Australia from 1d. to ½d. per word; but, on the other hand, the Commonwealth made a liberal concession by reducing its terminal rate from 1d. per word per state to a uniform 1d. for the whole of Australia.

The diverse rates imposed on the carriage of newspapers in the various states of the Commonwealth, prior to the union, continued after the control became vested in the Federal Government, and up to the 1st November, 1902, when a uniform rate was imposed under the Post and Telegraph Rates Act, 1902. On all newspapers posted for delivery within the Commonwealth by registered newspaper proprietors, or by newsvendors, or returned by an agent or newsvendor to the publishing office, without condition as to the number contained in each addressed wrapper, a charge of 1d. per 20 oz. on the aggregate weight is imposed, and on all other newspapers posted within the Commonwealth for delivery therein, ½d. per 10 oz. or fraction thereof for each newspaper is levied. In New Zealand a charge of ½d. each is levied upon all newspapers, town and inland. The intercolonial postage is 1d. each to all the states except Queensland, to which province the charge is 1d. each if not exceeding 4 oz., and ½d. additional for every succeeding 2 oz.

REGISTERED LETTERS.

The number of registered letters and packets passing through the post-offices of the Australasian states has largely increased of late years. In New South Wales the number of such letters in 1902 was 1,095,095. This number was exceeded during 1901, when the number registered was 1,213,277. Even in 1892, when the total was largely made up of correspondence relating to so-called "consultations," or lottery sweeps connected with horse-racing, which were established in Sydney, and to support which large sums of money were sent to that city from all parts of Australasia, as well as from other countries, the registrations only numbered 1,075,241. Probably not less than 600,000 of the total for New South Wales in 1892 were in connection with these lotteries. The Government of that state dealt with the evil in an amending Postal Bill in 1893, and this illicit branch of the postal traffic was removed to Queensland, where the number of registered letters at once greatly increased, and numbered 541,148 in 1895. But in 1896 the Parliament of Queensland passed an Act making these lotteries illegal, and the evil was transferred to Hobart. The registrations in the northern state in 1902 numbered 357,500. In South Australia 346,902 registered letters were dealt with during the year. In Western Australia 353,522 registered letters and packets were passed through the head office. In Tasmania 235,813 registered letters passed through the post; while in New Zealand the registered articles dealt with numbered 592,258. For Victoria no particulars of registrations are available.

Parcels Posts.

Excepting Western Australia, where there was no inland service, there were inland, intercolonial, and international parcels posts in operation in 1902; but statistics of the services on a uniform basis are not obtainable. During the year 785,528 parcels, weighing 2,755,244 lb., passed through the post-office of New South Wales, the postage collected amounting to £50,100; in Victoria 312,997 parcels, weighing 860,742 lb., yielding a revenue of £15,339, were dealt with; in Queensland the number of parcels which passed through the post-office was 303,427, weighing 1,204,627 lb., and the revenue derived from the service amounted to £17,345; in South Australia 49,505 parcels, weighing 121,613 lb., were forwarded, and the revenue received was £3,080; in Western Australia 39,378 parcels, the declared value of which was £91,301, and which yielded a revenue of £3,374, were dealt with; in Tasmania 47,087 parcels weighing 119,152 lb., with a declared value of £55,390, passed through the post, and yielded a revenue of £2,907; and in New Zealand the parcels dealt with numbered 291,670, weighing 861,069 lb., of which 47,654, weighing 173,230 lb., and valued at £123,912, were received from places outside the colony, and 14,779, weighing 35,853 lb., and valued at £16,313, were despatched from the colony.

Money Orders and Postal Notes.

In all the states there are money order and postal note systems in operation; and in all the states, except Victoria, Queensland, and South Australia, post-office savings banks. In Queensland there is a

Government Savings Bank, but it is not placed under the administration of the Postmaster-General. The Victorian Post Office Savings Bank was amalgamated with the Commissioners' Savings Bank in September, 1897. Particulars of the working of these services will be found in the chapter dealing with "Accumulation."

Postal Facilities.

The following table shows the number of inhabitants and the area in square miles to each post-office for the year 1902. It will be seen that the most sparsely populated states have the greatest number of post-offices in comparison with their population, but in order to judge of the relative extension of postal facilities the area of country to each office must also be taken into account:—

State.	Number of Inhabitants to each Post Office.	Number of Square Miles of Territory to each Office.
New South Wales	629	140
Victoria	732	53
Queensland	394	514
South Australia	516	1,287
Western Australia	1,041	4,954
Tasmania	466	69
Commonwealth	599	462
New Zealand	441	58
Australasia	564	373

Ocean Mail Services.

The Federal Ocean Mail Service, which is carried on by the Orient Pacific and Peninsular and Oriental Steam Navigation Companies, is subsidised by the United Kingdom and all the Australian states. New contracts were entered into on the 1st February, 1898, for a period of seven years. The total amount of the subsidy is £170,000, of which £98,000 is payable by the Imperial authorities and £72,000 by the states in proportion to their population. The sea transit rates collected from other countries and colonies making use of the service are credited to the Imperial and Colonial Governments in proportion to the amount of their contribution towards the subsidy. The following table shows the amount of the subsidy, with exchange, payable by each of the states during 1902, on the basis of the population at the end of the preceding year. In addition to the subsidy, there are other charges in connection with the service, such as transit rates in France and Italy and in Australia. After adding these, and deducting the postages collected in the states, and the proportion of sea transit rates payable by other countries using the service, the net cost charged to New South Wales in 1902 was £3,409, to Queensland £8,837, to Western Australia £3,408, and to Tasmania £3,481, while Victoria reaped a profit of £1,042, and South Australia a profit of £2,219, as shown in the table on the next page.

New Zealand, although not a contracting party, yet avails itself of the Federal Service for the carriage of mail matter, and its net loss during the year amounted to £2,404 :—

		Subsidy, 1902.	Net Cost, 1902.
United Kingdom		£98,000	90,900
Australasia—			
New South Wales	£25,900	......	£3,409
Victoria	23,136	......	......
Queensland	9,413	......	8,837
South Australia	6,908	......	......
Western Australia	3,688	......	3,408
Tasmania	3,481	......	3,481
		£72,526	......
Total		£170,526	......

The mail service has been performed with great regularity and expedition. The average time occupied by the outward and homeward services in 1902 was as follows :—

	Orient Pacific.	P. and O.
London to Sydney	$33\frac{7}{13}$ days.	$32\frac{1}{26}$ days.
Sydney to London	$33\frac{9}{26}$,,	$32\frac{4}{13}$,,

On several occasions the mails from London have been delivered in Sydney in 31 days.

In addition to the Federal Ocean Mail Service *via* Suez, New South Wales and New Zealand until November, 1890, subsidised the Union Steamship Company, in conjunction with the Pacific Steamship Company, for a four-weekly service, *via* San Francisco, to the amount of £37,000, of which New South Wales paid £25,750, and New Zealand £11,250. Under the new contract which was entered into, the amount of the subsidy was largely reduced, the contribution being based on the weight of mail matter carried, and New South Wales made an annual payment of £4,000 to the New Zealand Government, subject to appropriation by Parliament. Various extensions of the contract have been made, and at present the New Zealand Government is working under a temporary agreement with the J. D. Spreckels Company (the Oceanic Steamship Company of San Francisco), until the New Zealand Parliament has had an opportunity of considering the question of the continuance of the service, proposals for which the Government intends to submit at an early date. During the year 1902 the net cost of the service to New Zealand was £14,685 ; no expense being incurred by New South Wales and Victoria. The average time occupied in carrying the mails by the San Francisco route during the same year was as follows :—

London to Sydney	$35\frac{11}{17}$ days.
Sydney to London	$34\frac{11}{15}$,,

During 1893 a calendar monthly service between Sydney and Vancouver was established by the Canadian-Australian Royal Mail Line, the state of New South Wales granting an annual subsidy of £10,000, and the Canadian Dominion one of £25,000. This action was taken more in the interests of trade between the great British colonies in Australasia and America than in those of the postal service. The Government of New Zealand guaranteed a minimum payment of £7,500 annually to this line in consideration of Wellington being made a port of call. But on the expiry of this contract on the 31st March, 1899, a fresh agreement, to hold for four years, was made by the Shipping Company with the Governments of New South Wales and Queensland, by which Brisbane was substituted for Wellington as a port of call, on condition that Queensland paid a subsidy of £7,500. New Zealand, therefore, does not now subscribe to the Vancouver service. During 1902 the net cost of the Vancouver service to New South Wales was £1,952; to Victoria £622; and to Queensland £6,875. The average time occupied by the mails in transit from Sydney to London was $37\frac{8}{19}$ days.

The Queensland line of steamers, sailing from Brisbane, *via* Torres Straits, carries mails for the Queensland Government, payment being made according to weight. This route is from four to ten days longer than those previously mentioned. Queensland, under a former contract, paid the company an annual subsidy of £55,000. This arrangement ceased in January, 1890, and under a new contract the state agreed to pay the company an annual subsidy of £19,800 for a four-weekly, or £32,500 for a fortnightly service. The latter service was commenced on 1st July, 1890, the monthly service having lasted nearly six months; but in November, 1891, the contractors, on account of the heavy losses under the fortnightly system, were allowed to revert to the four-weekly service, the subsidy being reduced to the smaller amount mentioned above, viz., £19,800. When the contract expired, an agreement was arrived at for the institution of a subsidised service for purely commercial purposes. This arrangement lasted but a short time, when the subsidy was abandoned by the shipping company, who preferred to run their steamers without restriction. Payment is now only made in accordance with the weight of the mails carried. The amount of mail matter despatched from the other states by the Torres Straits route is very small.

Besides those mentioned, the other steamship companies trading with the Australasian states carry mails, notably the Messageries Maritimes Company and the North German Lloyd's, sailing from Sydney; and the Shaw, Savill, and Albion Company, and the New Zealand Shipping Company, sailing from Lyttelton, *via* Magellan Straits. The companies are paid by the states in proportion to the weight of mail matter carried, but the Messageries Maritimes Company and the North German Lloyd's are in receipt of large subsidies from the French and German Governments respectively.

The postage to the United Kingdom was reduced in January, 1891, from 6d. per ½ ounce *via* Italy, and 4d. *via* the long sea route, to the uniform rate of 2½d. In 1891 the states were represented at the

Congress of the Universal Postal Union held in Vienna, and on the 4th July a convention was signed on their behalf, by which they joined the Union from the 1st October of that year. From that date the rate of postage to all British colonies and possessions and foreign countries included in the Union was reduced to 2½d.

A common scale of postage on newspapers to the United Kingdom and foreign countries has been adopted by the Australasian states, the rate being 1d. for the first 4 ounces, and ½d. for every additional 2 ounces.

Telegraphs.

The electric telegraph was introduced into these states almost at the time of the earliest railway construction. The first telegraph messages were sent in New South Wales in 1851. In Victoria the telegraph line from Melbourne to Williamstown was opened in 1854. The first line in South Australia, from Adelaide to Port Adelaide, was opened in 1856; and the first Tasmanian line was completed in 1857. In New Zealand the first telegraph office was opened in 1862; and the line from Brisbane to Rockhampton, the first in Queensland, was opened in 1864. Telegraphic communication was established between Sydney, Melbourne, and Adelaide in 1858. The first telegraph in Western Australia was opened in 1869, and communication between that state and all the others of the group was completed in 1877.

All the states show very rapid progress in regard to telegraphic matters during the period from 1871 to 1881. In the case of Queensland this increase was largely a result of the construction of the line to the Gulf of Carpentaria; and in the case of South Australia, to the construction of the lines to Port Darwin and to Eucla, on the boundary of Western Australia. The following table shows the length of telegraphic lines in each state at the last five census periods, and at the end of 1902, so far as the returns are available:—

State.	1861.	1871.	1881.	1891.	1901.	1902.
New South Wales	1,616	*4,674	8,515	11,697	14,272	14,526
Victoria	......	*2,295	3,350	6,840	6,467	6,969
Queensland	169	2,525	6,280	9,996	10,246	10,247
South Australia	597	1,183	4,946	5,640	5,763	5,302
Western Australia	......	*550	1,585	2,921	6,173	6,112
Tasmania	......	*291	928	2,082	2,187	2,187
Commonwealth	......	11,518	25,604	39,176	45,108	45,343
New Zealand	......	2,015	3,824	5,349	7,469	7,749
Australasia	......	13,533	29,428	44,525	52,577	53,092

* In 1873.

The next table gives similar particulars, but the figures represent miles of wire instead of miles of line :—

State.	1861.	1871.	1881.	1891.	1901.	1902.
New South Wales..........	1,981	5,579	14,278	24,780	46,133	58,9[illegible]
Victoria........................	......	3,472	6,626	13,989	13,480	15,611
Queensland	169	2,614	8,585	17,646	20,537	20,695
South Australia	915	1,718	7,228	†12,707	17,853	14,04[illegible]
Western Australia	... ..	*750	1,593	3,546	9,104	9,104
Tasmania	......	241	1,157	3,178	3,565	3,462
Commonwealth........	......	14,374	39,467	75,846	110,672	121,818
New Zealand..................	......	3,287	9,653	13,235	21,705	22,67[illegible]
Australasia	......	17,661	49,120	89,081	132,377	144,49[illegible]

* In 1873. † Including telephone wires.

The number of telegrams passing along the wires of each state and the revenue received by the Telegraph Departments during the year 1902 were as appended. In the total for Australasia a correction has been made for interstate telegrams recorded in both the despatching and the receiving state :—

State.	Number of Telegrams.	Revenue received.
New South Wales	3,423,106	£187,802
Victoria	2,587,121	125,252
Queensland	1,487,957	85,514
South Australia	924,459	84,612
Western Australia	1,215,061	81,824
Tasmania	332,663	16,892
Commonwealth	9,970,367	£581,896
Do (Interstate excess excluded).	8,431,372	....
New Zealand	4,713,354	160,344
Australasia	14,683,721	£742,240
Do (Intercolonial excess excluded).	13,081,373	....

In the whole of Australasia there were on 31st December, 1902, 4,205 telegraph stations, of which 983 were in New South Wales, 880 in Victoria, 475 in Queensland, 287 in South Australia, 167 in Western Australia, 310 in Tasmania, and 1,103 in New Zealand.

In no country in the world has the development of telegraphic communication been so rapid as in Australasia, and in none has it been taken advantage of by the public to anything like the same extent. Taking Australasia as a whole, there are only four countries that possess a greater extent of telegraph lines, and only eight in which a larger number of messages is actually sent. In no other countries, however, except the United Kingdom, and Belgium, does the number of messages bear anything approaching the same ratio to the population. The following table illustrates these remarks:—

Country.	Length of Telegraph Lines.	Messages.	Messages per head of population.
	miles.	No.	No.
United Kingdom	47,786	90,432,041	2·16
France	87,382	50,486,435	1·30
Belgium	3,993	14,322,500	2·14
Netherlands*	3,880	5,693,359	1·08
Germany	81,358	45,146,281	0·80
Denmark	3,762	2,212,433	0·90
Sweden	9,456	2,749,483	0·53
Norway	7,458	2,194,597	0·98
Austria-Hungary	38,662	30,048,910	0·66
Switzerland	4,095	3,914,994	1·18
Italy	27,918	11,175,282	0·34
Spain	20,178	5,131,495	0·27
Portugal	5,180	3,420,453	0·63
Russia	98,570	19,257,456	0·13
Roumania	4,344	2,219,767	0·38
United States†	196,115	69,374,883	0·91
Canada	35,902	5,181,680	0·96
Cape Colony	7,470	4,242,640	1·74
Argentine Republic	28,107	5,296,184	1·15
Japan	6,377	16,713,619	0·38
Commonwealth of Australia	45,343	8,431,372	2·18
Australasia	53,092	13,081,373	2·81

* Government lines only. † Western Union Company only.

From the above table it appears that in Australasia during the year over two and three quarter messages were sent over the telegraph for each inhabitant. In the United Kingdom the number was slightly over two and three-twentieths for each inhabitant; and in the United States of America about one message to every inhabitant. The return for the United States, however, includes only the lines of the Western Union Company, which owns the principal part of the telegraph system of that country. The other countries shown in the table sent messages ranging from two and one-seventh per inhabitant in the case of Belgium, to about one-eighth per inhabitant in the case of Russia.

Telegraph Rates.

The rates for the transmission of telegrams within the Commonwealth were determined by the Post and Telegraph Rates Acts, 1902, and came into force on the 1st November, 1902. For ordinary telegrams, not exceeding sixteen words, including the address and signature, the charges are 6d. in town and suburban districts within prescribed limits or within 15 miles from the sending station, 9d. to other places within the state, and 1s. for inter-state, that is, from any one state to any other, and for each additional word, an extra charge of 1d. in each case is made. On telegrams from and to Tasmania, the cable charges are added to those already specified, and double rates are imposed for the transmission of telegrams on Sunday, Christmas Day, and Good Friday, and for "urgent" telegrams. In New Zealand a charge of 6d. for the first twelve words, including address and signature, and 1d. for each additional word on all inland telegrams is made. Urgent messages are transmitted upon payment of double the ordinary rates.

Cable Services.

Australasia is in telegraphic communication with Europe and the rest of the world by means of five cables three of which are connected with the various Asiatic continental lines, one by America, and one by Durban and along the West Coast of Africa. The first of the three cables by Asia, which were all laid by the Eastern Extension Telegraph Company, Limited, was opened in October, 1872, joining Port Darwin to Banjoewangie, in Java, whence communication is provided with Europe by way of Batavia, Singapore, Madras, and Bombay. In 1879 a duplicate cable was laid down, the states of New South Wales, Victoria, South Australia, Western Australia, and Tasmania agreeing to pay the company a subsidy of £32,400 per annum for a period of 20 years, the amount to be apportioned between the states on the basis of population. At Port Darwin the cables connect with an overland wire, which extends to Adelaide, a distance of 1,971 miles, the construction of which involved an expenditure by the South Australian Government of about half a million sterling. The total length of line between Adelaide and London is 12,570 miles, of which 9,146 miles are submarine cable, and 3,424 miles overland wire. The third cable was laid in 1888 from Broome, in Roebuck Bay, Western Australia, to Banjoewangie. The length of line by this route from Perth to London is 12,296 miles, 10,811 being cable and 1,485 land wire. The eastern states are connected with Broome by a line running from Adelaide, *via* Port Augusta, Eucla, and Albany, to Perth.

The cable joining Tasmania to the continent of Australia was laid in 1869, the length being about 170 miles. It starts from the township of Flinders, near Cape Schanck, in Victoria, and terminates at Low Head, at the mouth of the Tamar, in Tasmania. This line is subsidised to the extent of £4,200 yearly by the states of New South Wales, Victoria, South Australia, Western Australia, and Tasmania, the contributions being based on the population figures.

New Zealand was joined to the continent by a cable laid in 1876, the length being about 1,191 miles. The line has its Australian terminus within sight of the spot where Captain Cook landed on the shores of Botany Bay, and within a stone's throw of the monument of La Perouse. The New Zealand terminus of the cable is at Wakapuaka, near Nelson, on the Middle or South Island, whence another cable, 109 miles in length, is laid to Wanganui, in the North Island, with an alternate line from White's Bay across Cook Strait to Wellington. For the first ten years after its opening, the New Zealand cable was subsidised by the Governments of New South Wales and New Zealand, their annual contributions being £2,500 and £7,500 respectively. Under agreement, dating from the 1st January, 1893, the Company which laid the cable was guaranteed £26,258 per annum in return for the reduction of the cable rates from 8s. 6d. for the first ten words and 10d. for every additional word to 2s. and 3d. respectively, the Company to bear one-fourth of any loss. On the 1st May, 1885, an amended agreement came into operation under which the guarantee was reduced to £20,000, and the Company ceased to share in any loss. This agreement expired on the 30th April, 1900, and the Company in proposing a renewal claimed that the guarantee should be increased to £26,000. This was absolutely declined by New Zealand, and the Company then determined on a uniform word rate of 3d., and abolished the minimum charge of 2s. for the first ten words. This was agreed to, pending the laying of the Pacific Cable.

As a direct result of the completion of the Pacific cable of which the sections, Queensland–Norfolk Island and Norfolk Island–New Zealand, were opened for business on the 23rd April, 1902, the charges for New Zealand–Australian telegrams, except to and from Tasmania, were reduced to one uniform rate of 4½d. per word, and to Tasmania to 5½d.; the additional 1d. to Tasmania is to cover the transmission over the Australia–Tasmania cablo. In addition to the reduction of the rates for telegrams to and from Australia, the opening of the Pacific cable has benefited senders of cable telegrams to places beyond Australia, by bringing about a general reduction of the rates in New Zealand to the more favourable rates obtaining in New South Wales and some of the other Commonwealth states. The rates on ordinary telegrams from New Zealand to Europe were reduced from 1st June, 1902, from 5s. 2d. to 3s. 4d. per word.

A cable connecting New Caledonia with Queensland at Bundaberg was opened in October, 1893. It was constructed by a French company, and is guaranteed by the French Government to the extent of £8,000, and by the states of New South Wales and Queensland to the amount of £2,000 each annually for a period of thirty years, in return for which the Governments of these states are entitled to use the cable for the transmission of official messages up to the amount of the guarantee.

During the year 1890 the states opened negotiations with the Eastern Extension Telegraph Company for a reduction in the cable rates to Europe, which at that time were 9s. 4d. per word for ordinary messages and 2s. 8d. per word for press messages sent from New South Wales; and at a conference of the postal and telegraphic authorities a proposal to reduce the tariff to 4s. per word for ordinary messages and 1s. 10d. per word for press messages was agreed to, the states contributing to the subsidy undertaking to make good half the loss which the company would sustain by this reduction in the schedule of charges, and New South Wales, Victoria, Western Australia, Tasmania, and New Zealand at the same time agreeing to pay to South Australia a proportion of the loss to the revenue of that state which the lower charges would cause in the working of the overland wires. The amended tariff came into force in May, 1891, and the amount to be guaranteed to the company for the portion of the year during which the contract was in existence was £158,491. The sum earned by the company for the same period was £120,141, so that the deficiency on the eight months' business was £38,350, one-half of which was made good by the contributing states according to population. But this sum, combined with the amount of the subsidy, was more than the states were prepared to bear, and on the 1st January, 1893, the rates were fixed at 4s. 11d. per word from Sydney to London for ordinary messages, and 1s. 10d. for press messages. Even at these charges there was a loss to be borne, the total amount payable to the cable company being £21,778 in 1893 (as compared with £27,520 in 1892), and £6,191 in 1894; and to the South Australian Government £7,675 in 1893 (as compared with £10,415 in 1892), £822 in 1894, and £1,125 in 1895. Since the years mentioned the amounts guaranteed—£227,000 to the cable company, and £37,552 to the South Australian Government—have been met by the revenue, and the states have therefore not been called upon to contribute. Queensland later joined the other states in the guarantee.

The agreement between the Australian Governments and the Company expired on the 30th April, 1900. In July, 1899, the Company offered to lay a cable to Australia, *via* the Cape of Good Hope, to reduce the tariff per word from 4s. 11d. to 4s. at once, and later to 2s. 6d. under a sliding scale, if the states would agree to certain conditions. South Australia, Western Australia, and Tasmania accepted the terms offered and now enjoy the reduced rates. The other states refused, but notified the Company that they also would accept if certain alterations were made in the agreement, the alterations being intended to safeguard the Pacific cable, to which these states were definitely committed. On the 16th January, 1901, New South Wales entered into the agreement.

The following table shows the amount paid by each state towards cable subsidies and guarantees during the year 1902. From the 1st May, 1901, the whole of the subsidy in connection with the Tasmanian cable has been paid by Tasmania.

State.	Victoria-Tasmania Subsidy.			Queensland-New Caledonia Guarantee.			Total.		
	£	s.	d.	£	s.	d.	£	s.	d.
New South Wales	....			1,993	2	1	1,993	2	1
Victoria	....			....			....		
Queensland	....			2,000	0	0	2,000	0	0
South Australia	....			....			....		
Western Australia									
Tasmania	6,000	0	0	....			6,000	0	0
Total	6,000	0	0	3,993	2	1	9,993	2	1

The desirableness of constructing a Pacific cable, which shall touch only British territory on its way from Australia to America, was acknowledged by the Governments of most of the Australasian colonies as well as by those of the United Kingdom and Canada, and an informal Conference was held in London in July, 1898, of representatives of Great Britain, Canada, New South Wales, Victoria, Queensland, South Australia, and New Zealand, when it was suggested that Great Britain should pay one-third of the cost of laying such a cable, Canada two-ninths and the Australian colonies the remaining four-ninths. This proposal was eventually adopted, and in July, 1899, a meeting was held in London by the representatives of the countries interested, and it was agreed that the cable should be laid and that the capital necessary to construct and manage it should be raised and controlled by a Board designated the Pacific Cable Board, comprising Sir Spencer Walpole, as president, representing the United Kingdom; Lord Strathcona, Canada; and the Australian Agents-General their respective states. A contract was entered into with the Telegraph Construction and Maintenance Company of Greenwich, and the Australian shore end of the cable was laid at Southport, Queensland, on the 13th March, 1902, and the cable was completed to Vancouver, and opened for traffic on the 3rd November, 1902. The cable comprises four sections, with a branch to New Zealand from Norfolk Island, the length of the sections being: Brisbane to Norfolk Island, 834 nautical miles; Norfolk Island to Fiji, 961 miles; Fiji to Fanning Island, 2,093 miles; and Fanning Island to Vancouver, 3,240 miles, the branch from Norfolk Island to New Zealand measuring 537 miles.

The direct Cape cable, from Durban to Fremantle, which provides an alternative all-British route to that of the Pacific, was completed on the 19th October, 1901.

TELEPHONES.

In connection with the telegraph departments of the various states, telephone exchanges have been established in the capitals and other important centres of population. In order to popularise the use of the instrument, the charges in some of the states have within the last few years been reduced, and the result is seen in a satisfactory extension of this means of communication. Information regarding telephones in the different states during 1901, as far as can be ascertained, will be found in the following table :—

State.	Exchanges.	Telephones.	Length of Telephone Wires.	Revenue.
	No.	No.	miles.	£
New South Wales	51	14,810	.........*	96,278
Victoria	20	6,847	20,894	76,326
Queensland.........	15	3,296	4,912	24,619
South Australia...	11	1,817	4,224	21,925
Western Australia	12	2,941	4,947	29,464
Tasmania............	13	1,437	1,199	8,704
Commonwealth	122	31,148	....	257,316
New Zealand	70	10,633	8,727	62,151
Australasia	192	41,781	....	319,467

* Not ascertained.

In the Australasian states the rates for telephones at places of business range from £5 to £10 for the maximum length of wire—generally one mile, the colonies with a half-mile radius being New Zealand and Queensland—and the charge is higher in the city than in the country. In New South Wales and Victoria the city and suburban rates are £9 per annum, and the country rates £8 in the former state, and £7 in the latter. In South Australia the city rate is higher, being £10 ; but in the suburbs and country the rates range from £6 to £8. Queensland, for a radius of half-a-mile, has a uniform rate of £6, which is also the charge made in Tasmania, for a one mile radius, in Hobart, Launceston, and Zeehan, while for the suburbs and country districts the rate is a matter of arrangement. In New Zealand a distinction is drawn between exchanges continuously open and those not continuously open, the charges being respectively £7 and £5; while in Western Australia, in the towns of Perth, Fremantle, and Guildford, the rate is £7, and £10 where the exchange has less than 100 subscribers. The charges for telephones at private residences are, of course, less than for places of business. In New South Wales, Victoria, and New Zealand, the rate is uniformly £5; and in Queensland, £6. In South Australia the charge is £6 for the city, and from £6 to £8 in the suburbs and country; in Tasmania, it is £4 10s. in Hobart, Launceston, and Zeehan, and a matter of arrangement in the suburbs and country; while in Western Australia, at Perth, Fremantle, and Guildford, the charge is £5, and £6 where the exchange has less than 100 subscribers.

Postal and Telegraphic Finances.

The following table shows the revenue and expenditure of the Postal and Telegraph Departments of the states during 1902:—

State.	Revenue.				Expenditure.
	Posts.	Telegraphs.	Telephones.	Total.	
	£	£	£	£	£
New South Wales	610,434	187,802	96,278	894,514	759,619
Victoria	432,311	125,252	76,326	633,889	550,227
Queensland	204,520	85,514	24,619	314,653	420,904
South Australia	157,474	84,612	21,925	264,011	237,532
Western Australia	121,303	81,824	29,464	232,591	257,283
Tasmania	64,834	16,892	8,704	90,430	101,431
Commonwealth	1,590,876	581,896	257,316	2,430,088	2,326,996
New Zealand	302,604	160,344	62,151	525,099	487,815
Australasia	1,893,480	742,240	319,467	2,955,187	2,814,811

In the expenditure shown in the table, interest on the outlay on post-office buildings and telegraph lines and maintenance of buildings is not taken into account. If allowance be made for these, so far as is possible from the very imperfect returns concerning the expenditure on post-offices in each state, the total expenditure and the deficiency in revenue would be as follow :—

State.	Departmental Expenditure.	Interest and Maintenance of Works and Buildings.	Total charge.	Deficiency in Revenue.
	£	£	£	£
New South Wales	759,619	119,573	879,192	*15,322
Victoria	550,227	89,075	639,302	5,413
Queensland	420,904	67,587	488,491	173,838
South Australia	237,532	59,338	296,870	32,859
Western Australia	257,283	26,783	284,066	51,475
Tasmania	101,431	8,956	110,387	19,957
Commonwealth	2,326,996	371,312	2,698,308	268,220
New Zealand	487,815	75,521	563,336	38,237
Australasia	2,814,811	446,833	3,261,644	306,457

* Excess of Revenue.

With the progress of settlement and the increase of population, the expenditure on the postal and telegraphic services naturally expands year by year, and it is apparent that in order to keep pace with the growing needs of the community the department must be administered on ordinary business principles. Hitherto the application of such principles has not been obvious, and perhaps it has not been possible, but now that the affairs of the six states are centred under one control, much of past extravagant expenditure will be avoided, and there is every prospect of the service becoming self-supporting—that is, returning a revenue sufficient not only to meet current expenditure, but provide a surplus to cover maintenance of works and buildings, together with interest on capital cost.

COMMONWEALTH FINANCE.

The financial obligations of the Commonwealth began with the appointment of the Executive and the proclamation of the Constitution on the 1st January, 1901, at which date also the administration of the Customs passed over to the control of the Commonwealth. Besides the Customs and Excise, the Commonwealth has authority to take over from the states the administration of the following services, viz., posts, telegraphs, and telephones; naval and military defence; lighthouses, lightships, beacons and buoys; astronomical and meteorological observations; quarantine; census and statistics; bankruptcy and insolvency; patents and copyrights; naturalisation and aliens; divorce and matrimonial causes; and immigration and emigration.

In accordance with this power, the Postal Service was transferred to the Commonwealth on the 1st March, 1901, and on the same date the Defence Administration was taken over. None of the other departments has yet been completely transferred.

The expenditure of the Commonwealth is divisible into new expenditure, that is to say, on services called into being after the proclamation of the Federal Union, and other expenditure, or expenditure on services previously existing. The new expenditure is charged to the states proportionately to their population, and the cost of transferred services over and above the revenue derived therefrom being ascertained, the total of the two amounts is deducted from the net revenue from Customs and Excise, and the balance handed back to the states.

Under the provisions of section 87 of the Constitution Act, the Treasurer of the Commonwealth is entitled to retain one-fourth of the net proceeds of Customs and Excise services for the purposes of defraying the expenses of the Commonwealth, the remaining three-fourths, and as much more as the Treasurer does not require, being handed back to the states. It is, therefore, very essential in considering the question of Federal and State Finance to remember that, so far as concerns three-parts of the net revenue derived from customs and excise, such revenue, though appearing in the receipts of the Commonwealth, is not within the disposal of Parliament, but must be returned to the states. A large amount, in a normal year estimated at over seven and three-quarter millions, appears first as a federal receipt and a federal expenditure, and again as received by the states. Therefore in calculating the total sums raised by the Australian Governments, the amount returned to the states by the Federal Treasurer should be deducted from the total receipts. It is necessary, however, that the whole transactions of the

Federal Treasurer should be shown both as to revenue and expenditure; for, unless this is done, a proper understanding of federal and state accounts cannot be obtained.

The financial year of the Commonwealth ends on the 30th June. Since the 1st January, 1901, there have been three periods, the first being the six months, January to June, 1901, the second, the twelve months from 1st July, 1901, to 30th June, 1902, and the third, the twelve months from 1st July, 1902, to 30th June, 1903. The first of these periods was quite abnormal, the transferred departments were not administered by the Commonwealth for the whole period, while in addition there were some exceptional expenses by reason of the federal elections, and the cost of establishing the Commonwealth itself; on the other hand, the federal departments were not organised, and cost less than in an ordinary year.

Operations for Half-year ended 30th June, 1901.

For the half-year ended 30th June, 1901, the following were the income and expenditure of the Treasurer:—

Income.	£	Expenditure.	£
Customs and Excise	4,150,589	New services of Commonwealth	131,255
Posts and Telegraphs	740,665	Customs and Excise collection	121,443
Other	4,502	Posts and Telegraphs	809,840
		Military and Naval	233,515
		Balance carried to following year	5,974
		Returned to States	3,593,729
	£4,895,756		£4,895,756

During this period the state tariffs existing at the establishment of the Commonwealth remained in force, the uniform customs tariff with the abolition of interstate duties not coming into operation until some time later. The collections in each state were:—

State.	Half-year ended 30th June, 1901.				
	Taxation.		Posts and Telegraphs.	Other.	Total.
	Customs.	Excise.			
	£	£	£	£	£
New South Wales	820,012	198,996	276,936	1,019	1,296,963
Victoria	1,123,106	232,993	177,931	2,780	1,536,810
Queensland	643,059	67,771	95,586	301	806,717
South Australia	330,695	21,258	90,702	395	443,050
Western Australia	475,456	15,915	67,736	1	559,108
Tasmania	209,865	11,463	31,774	6	253,108
Total	3,602,193	548,396	740,665	4,502	4,895,756

The expenditure on account of new services distributed on a capitation basis, and the other expenditure chargeable to the states were as follows :—

State.	Expenditure during half-year ended 30 June, 1901.					Balance carried forward to following year.	Total.
	New Expenditure.	Customs and Excise Collections.	Posts and Telegraphs.	Naval and Military.	Total.		
	£	£	£	£	£	£	£
New South Wales	47,606	29,005	262,036	70,743	409,390	Cr. 4,300	413,690
Victoria	41,056	32,645	209,177	77,148	360,026	Dr. 956	359,070
Queensland	17,031	27,944	129,388	49,666	224,029	Dr. 594	223,435
South Australia ..	13,088	11,656	71,030	15,605	111,379	Dr. 567	110,812
Western Australia	6,038	15,338	84,191	8,610	114,177	Cr. 4,070	118,247
Tasmania	6,436	4,855	54,018	11,743	77,052	Dr. 279	76,773
Total	131,255	121,443	809,840	233,515	1,296,053	5,974	1,302,027

The difference between these figures and the amounts set out in the preceding table represents the payments which the states were entitled to receive under the provisions of section 87 of the Constitution Act, and the sums handed back to each were as shown below.

	£
New South Wales	883,273
Victoria	1,177,740
Queensland	583,282
South Australia	332,239
Western Australia	440,860
Tasmania	176,335
Total..........................	£3,593,729

The financial operations of the Commonwealth for its first half-year call for no special comment,—the payments made and the sources of income were in continuation of those of the states; no new sources of revenue were entered on by the Commonwealth, while the amount of new expenditure was comparatively small.

Operations for Year ended 30th June, 1902.

An entirely new set of conditions came into operation on the 9th October, 1901, when the schedule of uniform customs duties was promulgated. Under the new conditions the interstate duties ceased, except, as will be hereafter explained, in the case of Western Australia. The federal customs and excise duties were in force for thirty-eight weeks and the state duties for fourteen weeks, while the Post Office and Defence Services were administered by the Commonwealth for the whole year. The following is a statement of the transactions of the Federal Treasurer for the year:—

Income.	£	Expenditure.	£
Balance brought forward from 30th June, 1901 ...	5,974	New Services of Commonwealth	275,862
Customs and Excise	8,692,750	Customs and Excise collection	260,322
Posts and Telegraphs	2,372,861	Posts and Telegraphs	2,461,916
Customs collected on behalf of Western Australia ...	201,569	Military and Naval	934,646
Other revenue	29,805	Returned to States	7,368,137
		Balance carried forward to 1902–3	2,076
Total...............	£11,302,959	Total	£11,302,959

The amount of revenue collected within each state was as shown in the following table. The Customs and Excise collections of Western Australia include £1,134,045 revenue from the Commonwealth tariff, and £201,569 from interstate duties.

State.	Balance brought forward from previous year.	Collections during year ended 30th June, 1902.				
		Taxation.		Posts and Telegraphs.	Other Revenue.	Total.
		Customs.	Excise.			
	£	£	£	£	£	£
New South Wales...	*Cr.* 4,300	2,324,000	488,732	873,312	8,223	3,698,567
Victoria	*Dr.* 956	1,976,245	400,279	591,470	8,506	2,975,544
Queensland	*Dr.* 594	1,135,562	162,100	312,905	934	1,610,907
South Australia	*Dr.* 567	625,637	73,010	277,811	1,639	977,530
Western Australia...	*Cr.* 4,070	1,273,125	62,489	225,752	172	1,565,608
Tasmania......	*Dr.* 279	335,401	37,739	91,611	10,331	474,803
Total...........	*Cr.* 5,974	7,669,970	1,224,349	2,372,861	29,805	11,302,959

The distribution of the expenditure between the states was as shown in the following table, the new expenditure as it is called being distributed amongst the states according to population, the other expenditure according to the states on behalf of which it was incurred:—

State.	Expenditure during year ended 30th June, 1902.					Balance carried forward to following year.	Total.
	New Expenditure.	Customs and Excise Collections.	Posts and Telegraphs.	Naval and Military.	Total.		
	£	£	£	£	£	£	£
New South Wales	99,252	63,450	840,685	309,147	1,312,584	Cr. 128	1,312,662
Victoria	87,194	63,812	588,888	316,876	1,056,770	Dr. 2200	1,054,570
Queensland	36,464	64,225	419,965	185,958	706,612	Dr. 478	706,134
South Australia	26,320	26,517	246,752	58,670	358,259	Cr. 3403	361,662
Western Australia	14,061	31,991	258,570	34,967	339,589	Cr. 942	340,531
Tasmania	12,571	10,327	107,056	29,028	158,982	Cr. 281	159,263
Total	275,862	260,322	2,461,916	934,646	3,932,746	Cr. 2076	3,934,822

The difference between the collections and disbursements by the Commonwealth on behalf of the states was returned to the latter, and the following sums represent the amount in each case:—

	£
New South Wales	2,385,904
Victoria	1,920,974
Queensland	904,775
South Australia	615,868
Western Australia	1,225,076
Tasmania	315,540
Total	7,368,137

Operations for Year ended 30th June, 1903.

The following statement indicates the transactions of the Federal Treasurer for the year ended 30th June, 1903:—

Income.	£	Expenditure.	£
Balance brought forward from 30th June, 1902	2,076	New services of Commonwealth	316,217
Customs and Excise	9,451,686	Customs and Excise collection	272,286
Posts and Telegraphs	2,404,650	Posts and Telegraphs	2,563,789
Customs collected on behalf of Western Australia	233,467	Military and Naval	745,183
Other revenue	16,075	Other expenditure	4,284
		Returned to States	8,200,457
		Balance carried forward to following year	5,738
Total	£12,107,954	Total	£12,107,954

The revenue collected within each state is set forth in the subjoined table. The Customs and Excise collections of Western Australia include £1,162,530 revenue from the Commonwealth tariff, and £233,467 from interstate duties.

State.	Collections during year ended 30th June, 1903.					Total.
	Balance brought forward from previous year.	Taxation.		Posts and Telegraphs.	Other Revenue.	
		Customs.	Excise.			
	£	£	£	£	£	£
New South Wales	Cr. 128	2,861,710	617,032	906,798	5,460	4,391,128
Victoria	Dr. 2,200	2,096,217	402,797	622,501	5,377	3,124,692
Queensland..	Dr. 478	1,042,341	218,725	300,724	2,105	1,563,417
South Australia...	Cr. 3,403	583,461	106,266	255,480	1,729	950,339
Western Australia	Cr. 942	1,317,785	78,212	225,099	715	1,622,753
Tasmania............	Cr. 281	312,015	48,592	94,048	689	455,625
Total.........	Cr. 2,076	8,213,529	1,471,624	2,404,650	16,075	12,107,954

The distribution of the expenditure between the states, was, as shown in the following table, the new expenditure being distributed amongst the states according to population, the other or transferred expenditure to the states on behalf of which it was incurred :—

State.	Expenditure during year ended 30th June, 1903.						Balance carried forward to following year.	Total.
	New Expenditure.	Customs and Excise Collections.	Posts and Telegraphs.	Naval and Military.	Other.	Total.		
	£	£	£	£	£	£	£	£
New South Wales..	114,367	70,322	890,618	267,006	778	1,343,086	*Dr.* 5,091	1,337,995
Victoria	98,375	64,593	596,810	258,907	..	1,018,685	*Cr.* 557	1,019,242
Queensland	41,605	66,192	437,266	107,758	132	652,953	*Cr.* 5,229	658,182
South Australia ..	29,857	25,799	254,808	53,994	3,017	367,475	*Cr.* 3,935	371,410
Western Australia	17,560	34,740	280,171	32,445	362	365,278	*Cr.* 1,743	367,021
Tasmania	14,458	10,640	104,116	25,073	..	154,282	*Dr.* 635	153,647
Total	316,217	272,286	2,563,789	745,183	4,284	3,901,759	*Cr.* 5,738	3,907,497

The difference between the collections and disbursements by the Commonwealth on behalf of the states was returned to the latter, and the following sums represent the amount in each case :—

	£
New South Wales	3,053,133
Victoria................................	2,105,450
Queensland	905,235
South Australia	578,929
Western Australia	1,255,732
Tasmania	301,978
Tota	8,200,457

Probable Revenue and Expenditure, 1903–4.

Sufficient time has elapsed since the settlement of the tariff to admit of the consumption of goods introduced into the Commonwealth in anticipation of the imposition of new or increased duties, and the passage of the Postal Act having brought about a uniform rate of postage throughout the states, the Federal Treasurer is in a position to forecast the probable revenue and expenditure for the year ending 30th June, 1904, with a reasonable assurance that the forecast will be realised. The following table indicates the revenue estimated to be received during the year :—

State.	Customs and Excise.	Posts and Telegraphs.	Other Revenue.	Total.
	£	£	£	£
New South Wales	3,125,000	925,000	2,296	4,052,296
Victoria	2,400,000	640,000	4,595	3,044,595
Queensland	1,175,000	302,000	782	1,477,782
South Australia	695,000	257,000	507	952,507
Western Australia	1,342,000	229,000	460	1,571,460
Tasmania	370,000	97,000	535	467,535
Total	9,107,000	2,450,000	9,175	11,566,175

The expenditure that will probably be incurred during the same period is as follows :—

State.	New Expenditure.	Customs and Excise Collection.	Posts and Telegraphs.	Naval and Military.	Total.
	£	£	£	£	£
New South Wales	157,912	73,383	984,620	267,530	1,483,445
Victoria	133,533	62,650	645,848	258,530	1,100,561
Queensland	56,848	61,826	461,241	112,226	692,141
South Australia	40,667	28,355	278,039	67,635	414,696
Western Australia	26,040	39,749	329,497	51,852	447,138
Tasmania	19,946	10,248	118,502	33,772	182,468
Total	434,946	276,211	2,817,747	791,545	4,320,449

The probable return to the states, after adding or deducting the balance brought forward from 1902–3, will, therefore, be—

New South Wales	£2,563,760
Victoria	1,944,591
Queensland	790,870
South Australia	541,746
Western Australia	1,126,065
Tasmania	284,432
Total	£7,251,464

The proportions of estimated revenue and expenditure borne by each state, are shown in the following table :—

State.	Estimated Revenue, 1903-4.		Estimated Expenditure, 1903-4.	
	Amount.	Proportion to Total.	Amount.	Proportion to Total.
	£	per cent.	£.	per cent.
New South Wales........ ...	4,052,296	35·04	1,483,445	34·34
Victoria	3,044,595	26·32	1,100,561	25·47
Queensland.........................	1,477,782	12·78	692,141	16·02
South Australia...............	952,507	8·23	414,696	9·60
Western Australia	1,571,460	13·59	447,138	10·35
Tasmania	467,535	4·04	182,468	4·22
Total	11,566,175	100·00	4,320,449	100·00

The proportions of population in each state to the total Commonwealth population, are—New South Wales, 36·30 per cent. ; Victoria, 30·70 ; Queensland, 13·07 ; South Australia, 9·35 ; Western Australia, 5·99 ; and Tasmania, 4·59. It will be seen that Western Australia alone has a revenue in excess of the proportion indicated by its population.

Customs and Excise.

The customs and excise collections during the year ended 30th June, 1901, were under divided control. From the 1st July, 1900, to the 31st December of that year, the collections were made by the state Governments, and for the latter half of the financial year, the administration was carried out by the Commonwealth Government. During the whole period the tariffs existing in the various states at the time of their union remained in force, and afforded no indication of the revenue likely to be received under a uniform tariff. Nor do the collections for the year ended 30th June, 1902, settle satisfactorily this important question. In the first place three months of the twelve were under state tariffs and inter-state duties, and secondly, in some of the states it is believed that there were large importations in anticipation of the federal tariff affecting goods then free or subject to low duties. During the passage of the tariff through Parliament, material alterations were made in the rates proposed, and on that account also the revenue received gives no exact indication of the possibilities of the tariff as a revenue-producing instrument.

The following table shows the Customs and Excise collections for the years ended 30th June, 1901, 1902, and 1903, with the amounts collected in each state, and the average per inhabitant:—

State.	For Year ended 30th June, 1901.				For Year ended 30th June, 1902.		For year ended 30th June, 1903.	
	Collected by State Government.	Collected by Commonwealth Government.	Total Collections.	Average per Inhabitant.	Amount Collected.	Average per Inhabitant.	Amount Collected.	Average per Inhabitant.
	£	£	£	£ s. d.	£	£ s. d.	£	£ s. d.
New South Wales	939,336	1,019,008	1,958,344	1 8 8	2,812,782	2 0 11	3,478,742	2 9 8
Victoria	1,202,999	1,356,099	2,559,098	2 2 9	2,876,524	1 19 4	2,499,014	2 1 6
Queensland	787,695	710,830	1,498,525	3 0 2	1,297,662	2 11 4	1,261,066	2 9 6
South Australia ..	338,228	351,958	690,186	1 18 3	698,647	1 18 4	689,727	1 17 9
Western Australia	500,845	491,371	992,216	5 10 2	1,134,045	5 16 5	1,162,530	5 8 1
Tasmania	253,783	221,328	475,111	2 14 11	373,140	2 2 10	360,607	2 0 9
Total......	4,022,891	4,150,589	8,173,480	2 3 4	8,692,750	2 5 6	9,451,686	2 8 10

Besides the amount set down in the foregoing table as collected in Western Australia during the year ended 30th June, 1902, a sum of £201,569 was received by the Customs Department on interstate goods taxable under the special Western Australian tariff. For the year ended 30th June, 1903, the amount received on interstate goods and on foreign goods taxed at a higher rate under that tariff than under the Federal tariff was £233,467. Under the provisions of the 95th section of the Commonwealth of Australia Constitution Act, Western Australia is empowered for the first five years after the imposition of a uniform tariff to impose duties on goods passing into that state and not originally imported from beyond the limits of the Commonwealth. The duty so imposed on any goods, however, is not to exceed, during the first of such years, that chargeable under the law of Western Australia in force at the imposition of uniform duties, and shall not exceed during the second, third, fourth, and fifth of such years respectively, four-fifths, three-fifths, two-fifths, and one-fifth of such latter duty. This special tariff therefore ceases on the 9th October, 1906. If the collections for the year ended 30th June, 1902, had been included, the total revenue for the Commonwealth would have been £8,894,319, and for Western Australia £1,335,614, equal in the former case to £2 6s. 6d. per inhabitant, and in the latter to £6 17s. 1d. Taking into consideration these collections for the year ended 30th June, 1903, the total revenue for the Commonwealth would have been £9,685,153, and for Western Australia £1,395,997, or in the former case equal to £2 10s., and in the latter £6 9s. 9d. per inhabitant.

In his financial statement made in July, 1903, the Federal Treasurer estimated the revenue that may be expected from duties of customs and excise during the financial year ending 30th June, 1904, at £8,915,000.

Excluding the receipts from the special Western Australian tariff, calculated to yield £192,000, the estimated collections in each state are as follows :—

State.	Estimated Net Revenue from Customs and Excise for year ending 30th June, 1904.
	£
New South Wales	3,125,000
Victoria	2,400,000
Queensland	1,175,000
South Australia	695,000
Western Australia	1,150,000
Tasmania	370,000
Total	8,915,000

Grouping the receipts according to the divisions of the tariff, the estimated return under each head will be—

Estimated Revenue, 1903–4.

Customs—	£
Stimulants	2,077,000
Narcotics	918,000
Sugar	437,000
Agricultural products and groceries	990,500
Apparel and textiles	1,308,500
Metals and machinery	564,250
Oils, paints, and varnishes	116,850
Earthenware, &c.	152,750
Drugs and chemicals	56,100
Wood, wicker, and cane	190,000
Jewellery and fancy goods	168,650
Leather and rubber	165,750

Customs—	£
Paper and stationery	107,200
Vehicles	57,500
Musical instruments	41,950
Miscellaneous receipts, including licenses	130,500
Total customs	7,482,500
Excise	1,556,500
Total collections	9,039,000
Drawbacks and refunds	124,000
Net revenue	8,915,000

The foregoing estimated revenue is equal to £2 5s. 5d. per inhabitant, the rates for each state being :—

	£	s.	d.
New South Wales	2	3	10
Victoria	1	19	10
Queensland	2	5	10
South Australia	1	17	10
Western Australia	4	17	10
Tasmania	2	1	1
Commonwealth	2	5	5

If the yield from its special tariff had been included the rate for Western Australia would be £5 14s. 3d., and for the Commonwealth, £2 6s. 5d. Western Australia stands far above any of the other states in regard to revenue per inhabitant, and in total revenue it exceeds Tasmania and South Australia, and approximates to Queensland. This position it owes to the large consuming power of its population, a population consisting very largely of adult males receiving higher wages than those paid in any other state.

The proportion in which the various states have contributed, and may be expected to contribute to the Commonwealth tariff, is a question of much interest, as under the book-keeping provisions of the Constitution the return made to each state depends upon its contribution to the revenue. The following is a statement of the proportions of customs and excise collected in each state for the nine months of the financial year 1902 during which the uniform tariff was in operation, the proportions for the year ended June, 1903, and the proportions estimated by the Treasurer for the year ending June 1904; in order to throw further light on the question the proportion of population in each state to the total population of the Commonwealth is also given.

State.	Proportion of—			
	Population. 31st December, 1902.	Customs and Excise Revenue raised, 9 months ended 30th June, 1902.	Customs and Excise Revenue raised for year ended 30th June, 1903.	Customs and Excise Revenue estimated for year ending 30th June, 1904
	Per cent.	Per cent.	Per cent.	Per cent.
New South Wales	36·17	35·31	36·81	35·05
Victoria	31·11	25·05	26·44	26·92
Queensland	13·16	14·62	13·33	13·18
South Australia	9·44	7·07	7·30	7·[illegible]
Western Australia...........	5·55	13·18	12·30	12·90
Tasmania.................	4·57	4·17	3·82	4·15

The chief element in determining the amount of revenue to be raised by the Commonwealth was the necessities of the various states, and so long as those necessities exist, a sum approximating to what is now obtained will need to be raised. It can hardly be supposed, however, tha Australia will long continue to raise as large a revenue as £2 5s. 5d. per inhabitant from a customs tariff containing so large a free list, embracing as it does imports amounting to £11,455,000 out of a total import of general merchandise of £38,740,000.

Although indirectly connected with the question of the Commonwealth tariff, the returns obtained in past years from customs and excise by the states under their local tariffs are worth recording. It will be found from a consideration of the subsequent tables that the rate per inhabitant has varied greatly, not only as regards the different states but for the same state in different years. This variation arises from diverse causes. First, the influence of good or bad seasons on the producing power of the people is directly felt in the customs collections, although the rise or fall of the rate per inhabitant is not always a safe indication of such influence. Certain states, notably Queensland and Western Australia, grow insufficient agricultural produce for their own requirements, and in times past a good season—since it enabled those states to depend to a greater extent on their own resources—meant a decrease in the revenue from the importation of agricultural produce. Similar effects have also been felt in regard to revenue derived from live stock and other forms of produce. In addition, it must be remembered that for many years the states have been systematic borrowers from the London market, while they have been the recipients of much money sent for investment by private persons. As loans of all descriptions reach the borrowing country in the form of goods, and a considerable proportion of the importations is the subject of taxation, years of lavish borrowing are naturally years of large revenue collections, and coincident with the cessation of a flow of foreign capital there is a decrease in customs revenue. Furthermore, there have been extensive alterations in the tariffs affecting the revenue during the years which the following table covers. In New South Wales, in 1891 and 1895, and in Western Australia, in 1893 and 1896, radical tariff changes were made, and in other years minor alterations took place in nearly all the other states.

To these changes is chiefly attributable any sharp rise or fall in the rate of revenue per inhabitant. Speaking generally the customs revenue per inhabitant has tended to decline, especially when the tariffs are high, unless adjusted from time to time to meet the decline, for, apart from the specific causes mentioned above, other effective, if less obtrusive, influences are at work. Year by year the industries of the states are being developed, and the local producer is acquiring a firm hold on the domestic markets. Except in drought years little revenue will be received from duties on agricultural produce, as such produce will not be imported from abroad, and many descriptions of manufactured goods have likewise ceased to be introduced, the locally-made article being produced in sufficient quantities to meet the demand. There can be no reasonable doubt that this tendency will be still more marked in the future; and it is, therefore, not surprising that Australasian Treasurers have of late years found it necessary to look to other sources than the customs for the revenue necessary to carry on the business of the country, and under the Commonwealth, with complete interstate freetrade and growing manufactures, this necessity will be greatly accentuated.

The amount of import and excise duties collected in the various states during each of the last thirteen years is set forth in the following table—drawbacks and refunds being deducted from the gross collections of those states for which such information can be obtained :—

State.	1891.	1892.	1893.	1894.	1895.	1896.
	£	£	£	£	£	£
New South Wales	2,417,673	2,865,112	2,328,274	2,265,	2,240,596	1,637,078
Victoria	2,509,551	2,818,218	1,887,474	2,045,	2,021,564	2,050,880
Queensland	1,241,447	1,155,695	1,099,450	1,146	1,295,383	1,330,247
South Australia	647,268	611,723	546,006	539,	551,103	613,199
Western Australia	283,777	271,376	254,995	409,058	614,457	988,829
Tasmania	393,457	336,034	303,682	299,[illegible]	322,755	347,925
Commonwealth	7,448,168	7,558,158	6,418,981	6,706,676	7,045,858	6,967,658

State.	1897.	1898.	1899.	1900.	1901 (Half-year).	1901-2.	1902-3.
	£	£	£	£	£	£	£
New South Wales	1,520,116	1,551,827	1,650,333	1,773,993	1,019,008	2,812,732	3,478,742
Victoria	2,025,836	2,217,541	2,224,811	2,320,555	1,856,099	2,376,524	2,499,014
Queensland	1,244,556	1,418,841	1,568,744	1,565,838	710,830	1,297,662	1,261,066
South Australia	612,382	618,430	641,181	639,005	351,958	698,647	689,727
Western Australia	1,062,026	906,881	859,915	976,411	491,871	1,335,614	1,395,997
Tasmania	370,312	426,799	447,086	489,921	221,323	378,140	360,607
Commonwealth..	6,835,278	7,140,269	7,892,020	7,770,723	4,150,589	8,894,319	9,685,153

The revenue from import and excise duties per head of population probably offers more food for reflection than the figures in the table just given. New South Wales raised the smallest revenue compared with population of any of the states until 1891, a circumstance due to the comparatively low rate of the tariff; in 1892 its collections were about the average for Australasia ; but at the beginning of 1896 a new tariff came into force which was designed to make the ports of the state free to all imports except narcotics and stimulants, and, although this intention was not fully carried out, yet the revenue per head of population was, until the introduction of the Commonwealth tariff, very considerably less than in any of the other states. The variations in the rates from year to year are interesting as illustrating the force of the remarks made a few pages back in introducing the subject of customs duties.

State.	1891.	1892.	1893.	1894.	1895.	1896.	1897.
	£ s. d.	£ s. d.	£ s. d.	£ s. d.	£ s. d.	£ s. d.	£ s. d.
New South Wales............	2 2 4	2 8 8	1 18 8	1 16 11	1 15 10	1 5 9	1 3 7
Victoria	2 3 10	1 19 10	1 12 2	1 14 8	1 14 2	1 14 8	1 14 4
Queensland..................	3 2 7	2 17 2	2 13 2	2 14 2	2 19 7	2 19 8	2 14 8
South Australia...............	2 0 3	1 17 2	1 12 3	1 11 3	1 11 7	1 14 11	1 15 10
Western Australia	4 13 6	4 17 0	4 2 2	5 11 5	6 14 1	8 5 4	7 1 8
Tasmania	2 13 1	2 4 7	2 0 5	1 10 7	2 2 0	2 4 3	2 5 10
Commonwealth	2 6 5	2 6 1	1 18 5	1 19 5	2 0 8	1 19 6	1 18 1

State.	1898.	1899.	1900.	1901 (Half-year).	1901-2.	1902-3.
	£ s. d.	£ s. d.	£ s. d.	£ s. d.	£ s. d.	£ s. d.
New South Wales	1 3 8	1 4 9	1 6 3	0 14 11	2 0 11	2 9 8
Victoria	1 17 6	1 17 6	1 18 11	1 2 8	1 19 4	2 1 6
Queensland	3 0 11	3 5 10	3 3 10	1 8 6	2 11 4	2 9 6
South Australia	1 15 0	1 15 11	1 15 6	0 19 6	1 18 4	1 17 9
Western Australia	5 9 11	5 1 5	5 11 2	2 14 7	6 17 1	6 9 10
Tasmania	2 11 5	2 12 6	2 16 9	1 5 7	2 2 10	2 0 9
Commonwealth	1 19 2	2 0 0	2 1 6	1 2 0	2 6 5	2 10 0

The proportion of the cost of collection of customs and excise duties to the total amount received is less under the Commonwealth than under the separate control of the states. The experience of the five years immediately preceding federation shows that an average of 3·34 per cent. was expended, as against an average of 2·9 per cent. for the two-and-a-half years since the control of the customs and excise was vested in the Commonwealth Government.' The average percentages for each state for the five years previous to federation were as follows:—New South Wales, 3·26; Victoria, 3·07; Queensland, 3·91; South Australia, 4·31; Western Australia, 3·28; and Tasmania, 1·96. For the period subsequent to the consummation of federation, the percentages are, New South Wales, 2·30; Victoria, 2·66; Queensland, 4·90; South Australia, 3·75; Western Australia, 2·57; and Tasmania, 2·77. The proportion of cost to total amount collected has been reduced under Commonwealth control in the states of New South Wales, Victoria, South Australia and Western Australia, and increased in Queensland and Tasmania.

Posts and Telegraphs.

The administration of the Post and Telegraph services was undertaken by the Commonwealth on the 1st March, 1901; the departments consequently were under state direction for a period of eight months in the year ended 30th June, 1901. In discussing the question of the revenue derived from these services, it must be borne in mind that the taking over of the administration by the Commonwealth made no immediate change in the management, which was conducted as if the six states were separate systems. On the coming into operation of the Commonwealth Postal Act on 1st November, 1902, a uniform system was introduced, but the finances of the postal service before that date remained unaffected. In the following table is set out the revenue derived during each of the last three financial years, distinguishing for the earlier year, the amounts received by the state and by the Commonwealth Governments during the period of their control :—

State.	For year ended 30th June, 19			For year ended 30th June, 1902.	For year ended 30th June, 1903.
	Collected by State Government.	Collected by Common-wealth Government.	Total Collections.	Amount Collected.	Amount Collected.
	£	£	£	£	£
New South Wales...	557,006	276,936	833,912	873,312	906,798
Victoria	410,435	177,931	588,366	591,470	622,501
Queensland	213,584	95,586	309,170	312,905	300,724
South Australia......	183,310	90,702	274,012	277,811	255,480
Western Australia	142,391	67,736	210,127	225,752	225,099
Tasmania................	72,551	31,774	104,325	91,611	94,048
Total	1,579,277	740,665	2,319,942	2,372,861	2,404,650

The expenditure during the same periods is shown in the subjoined table :—

State.	For year ended 30th June, 1901.			For year ended 30th June, 1902.	For year ended 30th June, 1903.
	Expenditure by State Government.	Expenditure by Common-wealth Government.	Total Expenditure.	Total Expenditure.	Total Expenditure.
	£	£	£	£	£
New South Wales...	527,254	262,036	789,290	840,685	890,618
Victoria	305,787	209,177	514,964	588,888	596,810
Queensland	246,798	129,388	376,186	419,965	437,266
South Australia ...	152,288	71,030	223,318	246,752	254,808
Western Australia	171,322	84,191	255,513	258,570	280,171
Tasmania	52,812	54,018	106,830	107,056	104,116
Total	1,456,261	809,840	2,266,101	2,461,916	2,563,789

The operations of the past year show an apparent deficiency of £159,139 in the working of the Post and Telegraph Department. The financial position of the postal service, however, cannot be correctly stated unless the interest on the capital cost of the land, buildings, plant and appliances existing at the time of transfer to the Commonwealth, be taken into account. This cost has been variously estimated at from £7,312,000 to £7,514,000, and if an interest payment of £3 6s. per annum be charged to the postal service, the transactions would show a net loss of nearly £404,000. The revenue and expenditure of the Post and Telegraph Department for the year ending 30th June 1904, is estimated by the Treasurer to be, approximately, as follows:—

State.	Revenue.	Expenditure.
New South Wales	£925,000	£984,620
Victoria	640,000	645,848
Queensland	302,000	461,241
South Australia	257,000	278,039
Western Australia	229,000	329,497
Tasmania	97,000	118,502
Total	£2,450,000	£2,817,747

These figures indicate a probable loss of £367,747 on the operations of the year, but included in the proposed expenditure is an amount of £297,744, for the construction of works and buildings. From all the states an increased revenue is expected. A considerable falling off in the receipts from South Australia has occurred during the past two years; this is due to the fact that alterations, by way of reduction in the terminal and other charges in connection with the Eastern Extension Cable Company's business, will not be compensated for by new business. Losses in connection with the Pacific cable have also increased the expenditure of the Department.

Effect of Federation on State Finance.

The question of the effect which the operations of the Commonwealth may have upon the finances of the states is of great moment, and one which will not lessen in importance with the passage of time. That the finances of the states are in a disturbed state is evident from the fact that increased taxation and drastic retrenchment are being carried out, or in contemplation, in several of the states, and some show large deficits on the year's transactions. The existence of financial disturbance immediately following on the loss by the states of the control of their customs revenue is relied upon as proving the allegation so confidently made that this disturbance is due to the action of the Commonwealth Parliament and the Federal Administration. The assumption, more easily made than proved, is one that admits of being tested by the evidence of actual facts.

In dealing with the matter it will be necessary to consider the finances of the states since federation, and for a few years preceding that event. The following is a statement of the net revenue and expenditure of each state upon the services not transferred to the Commonwealth. The period covered is the six years, 1897–1903 :—

State.	1897-8.		1898-9.		1899-1900.	
	Revenue.	Expenditure.	Revenue.	Expenditure.	Revenue.	Expenditure.
	£	£	£	£	£	£
New South Wales	7,652,354	8,808,239	7,208,586	8,569,898	7,436,878	9,057,447
Victoria	4,250,196	6,261,685	4,585,787	6,315,082	4,595,216	6,567,260
Queensland	2,183,676	3,296,141	2,384,940	3,543,201	2,675,751	4,011,211
South Australia	1,768,205	2,479,569	1,844,949	2,505,035	1,935,725	2,659,777
Western Australia	1,516,111	2,906,952	1,414,120	2,255,399	1,733,571	2,316,117
Tasmania*	400,332	702,779	399,882	735,790	408,631	770,613

State.	1900-1.		1901-2.		1902-3.	
	Revenue.	Expenditure.	Revenue.	Expenditure.	Revenue.	Expenditure.
	£	£	£	£	£	£
New South Wales	8,222,587	,990,	8,621,451	11,020,106	8,242,986	11,467,285
Victoria	4,932,081	[illegible],219,682	5,085,359	7,407,781	4,862,601	6,774,084
Queensland	2,511,729	,270,922	2,680,287	3,967,001	2,621,230	3,717,806
South Australia	2,032,153	,801,736	1,853,850	2,823,578	1,952,018	2,641,789
Western Australia	1,875,692	[illegible],806,002	2,129,047	3,151,427	2,374,507	3,521,763
Tasmania*	472,299	812,071	429,787	861,678	469,961	850,684

* Year ended 31st December previous.

The foregoing figures admit of a calculation of the amount of revenue to be obtained from other sources to enable the states to balance their finances, had they not administered the posts and telegraphs, or provided for their own defence during any of these years. The excess of expenditure over revenue for each year was :—

State.	1897-8.	1898-9.	1899-1900.	1900-1.	1901-2.	1902-3.
	£	£	£	£	£	£
New South Wales	1,255,885	1,361,312	1,620,569	1,758,095	2,398,654	3,224,299
Victoria	2,011,489	1,729,295	1,972,044	2,287,740	2,322,422	1,911,483
Queensland	1,112,465	1,158,261	1,335,460	1,759,193	1,336,714	1,096,576
South Australia	711,364	660,086	724,052	769,583	969,728	689,776
Western Australia	1,390,841	841,279	582,546	930,310	1,022,380	1,147,256
Tasmania*	302,447	335,958	361,982	339,772	431,891	380,723

* Year ended 31st December previous.

Taking the averages of the three years preceding federation and comparing them with the results of the year 1902 it will be seen that there was an increase in the expenditure of each state, in no instance warranted by an increase of population. The strong necessity of reducing expenditure was forcibly brought home to the state Treasurers by their inability, in most instances, to balance their accounts. Vigorous curtailment of expenditure ensued, with the result that in 1903 the requirements of Queensland were brought to £151,061 below the average of the three years preceding federation; in Victoria and South Australia the requirements were brought back to a level with the ante-federal period, in Tasmania the Treasurer's requirements were in excess by £47,261 and in Western Australia by £209,034, but in both cases there were causes in operation which made an increase in the expenditure almost inevitable. During the three years preceding federation the sum required by the New South Wales Treasurer to meet the deficiency of revenue, from services not transferred to the Commonwealth, was £1,412,589, in 1903 it was £3,160,866, or an increase of £1,748,277.

Comparing the years 1899 and 1903 the increase for each state has been as follows:—

	£
New South Wales	1,862,987
Victoria	182,188
South Australia	29,690
Western Australia	305,977
Tasmania	44,765

In the case of Queensland there has been a decrease of £61,685.

Western Australia is in a peculiar position, and causes were in operation in the state which make its case quite different from that of the other states.

It is obvious that no action of the Commonwealth could affect in any important degree the services remaining in the hands of the states, and that any increase or decrease in their obligations would arise, if not from causes within the control of the states, at all events from causes beyond the control of the Commonwealth. It must, therefore, be conceded that any confusion apparent in the state finances would have existed even if federation had not taken place. It remains to be seen how far the return made to the states by the Commonwealth differs from what the states provided for themselves before federation became an accomplished fact. The following is a statement of the excess of revenue over expenditure of transferred departments. This excess represents the amount available to meet the deficiency of revenue from the departments not transferred:—

State]	Excess of Revenue over Expenditure, Transferred Services.					
	1897-8.	1898-9.	1899-1900.	1900-1.	1901-2.	1902-3.
	£	£	£	£	£	£
New South Wales	1,261,358	1,371,988	1,508,119	1,692,661	2,473,918	3,160,866
Victoria	1,970,102	2,111,533	2,139,763	2,366,812	2,006,047	2,204,943
Queensland	1,133,189	1,308,177	1,383,249	1,247,275	940,684	951,001
South Australia	594,132	613,679	640,762	661,915	645,894	611,779
Western Australia	888,676	780,782	842,267	848,878	1,235,867	1,274,068
Tasmania*	362,440	414,013	434,498	471,021	331,376	315,235

* Year ended 31st December previous.

The whole of the sum shown as excess on transferred services in 1903 was not returned to the states, as the expenses of the Commonwealth had first to be deducted. After making due allowance for this new expenditure, as shown on page 774, and taking the year 1898–9 as the last of the series for which the states were wholly responsible so far as revenue was concerned, and comparing the excess of revenue therein with that for 1902–3, some interesting results are obtained.

	Excess of 1902-3 over 1898-9.	Deficiency of 1902-3 on 1898-9.
	£	£
New South Wales	1,674,511	......
Victoria	......	4,965
Queensland	......	398,781
South Australia	......	31,757
Western Australia	475,776	......
Tasmania*	......	113,231

* Year ended 31st December, 1902.

To two of the states, therefore, the second complete year of the Commonwealth gave a larger revenue than the last year under state control, while in the case of Queensland, South Australia, and Tasmania the reverse was true. It will be seen from the table on page 785 what efforts had been made to cope with the restriction of income which the re-arrangement of finances under federation would inevitably entail in the majority of the states. Placing side by side the sums representing the movements in revenue and expenditure and the sums charged to each state as its share of the new expenditure under federation, the position of affairs in the Commonwealth will be readily understood.

Taking the states individually it would appear that for New South Wales in 1902–3, as compared with four years previously (1898–9), there were—

	£
Increased revenue from transferred services	1,788,878
Less new expenditure of Commonwealth charged to state	114,367
	1,674,511
Increased state expenditure	1,862,987
Difference	188,476

This statement clearly shows that in New South Wales the new Commonwealth revenue available to the state was £1,674,511, yet this vast addition was insufficient to meet the wants of the State Treasury by £188,476.

In Victoria the conditions were:—

	£
Increased revenue from transferred services	93,410
Less new expenditure of Commonwealth charged to state	98,375
Difference, excess of new expenditure	4,965
Increased state expenditure	182,188
Difference	187,153

The state finances, therefore, were in a worse position to the extent of £187,153 in 1902–3 compared with four years previously, and the increase in the state expenditure was responsible for nearly the whole of this sum (£182,188). It was fully expected that the operation of the Commonwealth would injuriously affect Victorian state finance, since the first result would be a loss of interstate duties to the extent of £350,000; far, however, from injuring the finances of the state, the Commonwealth Treasurer raised from the state £93,410 more than was obtained from customs, and posts and telegraphs in the year immediately before federation, and this notwithstanding the surrender of so large an amount of interstate duties.

The position of Queensland was as follows:—

	£
Decreased revenue from transferred services	357,176
New expenditure of Commonwealth charged to state	41,605
	398,781
Decreased state expenditure	61,685
Difference	337,096

The condition of the state from a revenue point of view has during the four years become worse to the extent of £398,781, but this was reduced to £337,096 by savings in the expenditure. The analysis just given shows that the position is in no way attributable to any action on the part of the state, but was the inevitable result of the establishment of a uniform tariff, as the Queensland tariff prior to federation was considerably above the average of the other states and of the present tariff.

In South Australia the development since 1898–9 has been as follows:—

	£
Decreased revenue from transferred services	1,900
New expenditure of Commonwealth charged to state	29,857
	31,757
Increased state expenditure	29,690
Total	61,447

The state's position is, therefore, worse to the extent of £61,447. The cost of federal services is a charge every state looked forward to paying, and as South Australia has almost as large a revenue from transferred services now as before the uniform tariff was adopted, the financial position of the state has not been affected to any appreciable extent by the establishment of the Commonwealth.

The position of Western Australia differs in one essential respect from that of the other states—duties are still leviable on interstate produce, and will continue leviable until the 8th October, 1906.

Comparing 1898–9 with 1902–3, the following shows the altered conditions.

	£
Increase revenue from transferred services	493,336
Less new expenditure of Commonwealth charged to state	17,560
	475,776
Increasee state expenditure	305,977
Difference..................................	169,799

Compared with four years ago the finances of 1902–3 showed an excess of £169,799 available revenue, above the increased expenditure both of state and Commonwealth, so that it is plain the state finances of Western Australia have not been disturbed by the operation of the uniform tariff.

The financial position of Tasmania has been for several years one of some difficulty. The following figures show the changes that have taken place during the last four years :—

	£
Decreased revenue from transferred services	98,778
New expenditure of the Commonwealth charged to state	14,453
	113,231
Increased state expenditure	44,765
Total	157,996

The state Treasury was, therefore, in a less favourable position on the 31st December, 1902, by £157,996, than four years previously, and of this sum £113,231 was due to the operation of the federal system.

Where the position of the states is now less favourable than in 1898–9, the result may be attributed, first, to increase of expenditure upon the services remaining with the state, and secondly, to the loss of interstate duties. The value of the latter, at the date of the establishment of the Commonwealth, was :—

	£
New South Wales..................................	141,061
Victoria	358,659
Queensland	144,009
South Australia	89,679
Western Australia..................................	256,060
Tasmania..................................	76,829

Western Australia, for the present, retains its interstate duties, while New South Wales receives back more from the new duties than was received from the old duties, including those on interstate goods. In the case of Victoria the return by the Commonwealth was £93,410 in excess of that obtained in 1899, while there was a deficiency in Queensland amounting to £357,176; in South Australia, £1,900; and in Tasmania, £98,778.

As will be seen from the chapter dealing with State Finance, the Treasurers of the states are seeking, by means of retrenchment and increased taxation, to balance their accounts. It is well, perhaps, that this resolution has been taken, for a little consideration will show that it is idle, so far as concerns some of the states, to expect a return from the Commonwealth equal to satisfying their needs on the basis of expenditure indulged in by them during 1902 and 1903. The following would need to be the amount of customs and excise duties to be levied by the Commonwealth to enable each state to receive back sufficient to balance its finances as on the 30th June, 1903. In order to show the measure of responsibility to be attached to the states, a column has been added showing the customs and excise revenue that would have sufficed had their requirements been not greater than in 1899:—

State.	Customs and Excise revenue required, so that the return to each State would be sufficient to balance its expenditure.	
	On the basis of 1899.	On the basis of 1903.
	£	£
New South Wales	5,031,000	10,150,000
Victoria	8,311,000	8,952,000
Queensland	11,418,000	11,120,000
South Australia	9,537,000	11,195,000
Western Australia	7,457,000	8,705,000
Tasmania	10,203,000	12,720,000

It will thus be seen that whereas a tariff from which £8,952,000 is obtainable would, at the present time (1903), satisfy the requirements of the Victorian Treasurer, it would take one yielding £12,720,000 to satisfy Tasmania, the other states occupying positions at various intervals between the extremes. The most remarkable feature of the table is the position of New South Wales. Four years ago there was much talk about the surplus revenue of that state being needed to make up the requirements of the so-called necessitous states. At the present time the revenue necessities of the mother state place a demand on the Commonwealth above that of some of the other states, and very little short of the reqirements of the state standing most in need of revenue.

It will have been observed from a previous table in this chapter, and in the part of this volume dealing with "State Finance," that the requirements of the state Treasurers vary greatly from year to year; it would be hopeless, therefore, for the Commonwealth Treasurer to endeavour to adjust his revenue to the needs of any state; still more hopeless would it be for him to attempt to mould his revenue to suit the variations in the requirements of six states. Hence the obvious policy of fixing a reasonable sum to be raised through the Customs House, and allowing the states to adjust their incomes and expenditures to the revenue thus provided.

STATE FINANCE.

THE functions of government are much alike throughout Australasia, and it is only to be expected, therefore, that similar items of expenditure should be found in the budgets of the various states. The chief point of difference is the extent to which local requirements are provided for out of general revenue. In most of the states provision for local improvements is a matter of which the state has long since divested itself; but in New South Wales and Western Australia the central government still charges itself with the construction of works of a purely local character, especially in the rural districts; hence the appearance, in the statements of public expenditure of those states, of items of large amount which find no parallel in the other states. Also, when comparison is made with outside countries, other points of difference are found. In Australasia, as in other young communities, it has been necessary for the state to initiate works and services which in older countries have come within the province of the local authorities or have been left to be undertaken by private enterprise. Even at the present day it is deemed advisable that the Government should retain the control of services, such as the railways, which in the United Kingdom and some other countries are not regarded as forming part of the functions of the state, and it is on account of the administration of these services that the budgets of the Australasian states reach such comparatively high figures.

The revenues of the Australasian states have been subject to considerable fluctuations, due not so much to changes in the incidence of the revenue, as to variation in the amount of the imports, for it was upon taxation of imports that the states have most largely depended for revenue. The years of highest revenue ought, under normal conditions, to be coincident with the years of greatest prosperity; but some of the states have been able to efface the effect of unfavourable seasons by lavish borrowing, and the inflow of loans, as represented by taxable goods, has, at times, more than counterbalanced the shrinkage in the imports, due to failure in the wool or wheat crops, for which these imports are payment. This effect of the borrowing policy of the various states upon their revenue was not so great in the last decade as in the previous one, but that it was considerable may be gathered from the fact that in the ten years 1894–1903 the various state Governments contrived to borrow and spend £62,000,000, obtained in London. The unsteadiness of the railway revenue, due to variations in the seasons, is another cause of disturbance to Australian finance, and one which will not be obviated until the resources of the states are so developed that wool and wheat will no longer play the important part they do at present in the railway trade of the country. In 1895 large reductions were made in the New South Wales tariff; these account for a reduction in the revenue of the state during that and the three following years, while to other influences must be added the financial crisis of 1893, which had a numbing effect upon trade throughout the states comprised in the Commonwealth. It will be observed from the table that Western Australia and New Zealand are in a different position to the more important mainland states. The financial position of Western Australia is exceptional, being due to the opening up of the goldfields, and the influx of a large amount of capital, and, as the tariff was of a wide range, the importation necessarily involved a large customs revenue, while the trade expansion increased the earnings of the railways. The configuration of the colony of New Zealand renders it to a very great extent immune from the droughts that so much affect the mainland of Australia, and the financial crisis of 1893 had only a comparatively slight influence on its trade; the progress of trade in that colony was, therefore, fairly regular during the years when the finances of the mainland states were most disturbed.

The establishment of the Commonwealth on the 1st January, 1901, necessitated the transfer of the Customs Department to the Federal Government; and, by proclamation, the Postal, Telegraph, and Defence Departments were taken over on the 1st March of the same year. The receipts of the six states are inclusive of the surplus returned by the Commonwealth, but the expenditure excludes all Federal transactions. The finances of the Commonwealth are dealt with on page 769.

The revenue for each state during the past ten years is shown in the following table. For New South Wales and New Zealand the figures shown for the years 1894 and 1895, are those for the twelve months ended on the 31st December of the previous year; while for the remainder of the period the fiscal year ended on the 30th June in the former state, and on the 31st March in New Zealand. The amounts given for Tasmania are for the year ended 31st December prior to the years shown, while for the remaining states the financial year ends on the 30th June:—

Year.	New South Wales.	Victoria.	Queensland.	South Australia, including Northern Territory.	Western Australia.	Tasmania.	Commonwealth.	New Zealand.	Australasia.
	£	£	£	£	£	£	£	£	£
1894	9,499,910	6,716,814	3,343,069	2,591,271	681,946	706,972	23,539,982	4,692,463	28,231,745
1895	9,350,051	6,712,152	3,413,172	2,497,648	1,125,941	696,795	23,795,759	4,447,899	28,243,658
1896	9,091,368	6,458,682	3,641,553	2,585,230	1,858,695	761,971	24,397,529	4,556,015	28,953,544
1897	9,109,253	6,630,217	3,613,150	2,698,759	2,842,751	797,976	25,692,106	4,798,768	30,490,874
1898	9,304,884	6,898,240	3,768,152	2,633,727	2,754,747	845,019	26,204,769	5,079,280	31,283,049
1899	9,573,415	7,378,842	4,174,086	2,781,208	2,478,811	908,228	27,244,585	5,[illegible]	32,5[illegible]
1900	9,973,786	7,450,676	4,588,207	2,853,329	2,875,396	943,970	28,685,314	5,699,618	34,384,932
1901	10,612,422	7,722,397	4,096,290	2,886,854	2,964,121	1,054,980	29,337,064	5,906,916	35,243,980
1902	11,007,356	7,006,378	3,535,662	2,477,432	3,349,460	826,163	28,201,941	6,152,[illegible]	34,[illegible]
1903	11,296,069	6,968,051	3,526,465	2,581,548	3,680,238	724,666	28,687,029	6,447,435	35,134,464

The revenue per inhabitant for each state during the past ten years was as follows :—

Year.	New South Wales.	Victoria.	Queensland.	South Australia, including Northern Territory.	Western Australia.	Tasmania.	Commonwealth.	New Zealand.	Australasia.
	£ s. d.	£ s. d.	£ s. d.	£ s. d.	£ s. d.	£ s. d.	£ s. d.	£ s. d.	£ s. d.
1894	7 17 11	5 14 10	8 0 0	7 9 5	10 9 5	4 12 0	7 0 2	7 1 11	7 0 5
1895	7 12 5	5 14 5	7 19 4	7 1 11	13 14 5	4 9 5	6 19 0	6 11 0	6 17 8
1896	7 4 1	5 10 1	8 5 1	7 5 0	18 7 2	4 15 10	6 19 7	6 11 0	6 18 3
1897	7 2 5	5 13 10	8 0 6	7 10 6	20 12 2	4 17 8	7 4 3	6 15 1	7 2 9
1898	7 2 11	5 18 7	8 3 8	7 5 11	17 0 3	5 0 1	7 4 6	7 0 1	7 3 9
1899	7 4 8	6 7 2	8 17 1	7 9 7	14 14 10	5 4 2	7 8 4	7 2 2	7 7 4
1900	7 8 5	6 8 1	9 10 3	7 13 11	16 16 3	5 5 0	7 14 1	7 11 4	7 13 7
1901	7 15 6	6 9 0	8 4 5	7 19 10	16 9 1	6 2 3	7 15 5	7 13 4	7 15 1
1902	7 19 7	5 15 11	6 12 6	6 15 10	17 4 2	4 15 2	7 7 2	7 16 3	7 8 7
1903	8 0 9	5 15 7	6 17 0	6 18 5	16 17 6	4 3 8	7 7 9	7 19 7	7 9 10

The following statements show that the expenditure of the six Commonwealth states has increased from £24,985,835 in 1894, to £28,973,361 for the year 1902–3, while the amount per inhabitant has decreased from £7 10s. 10d. to £7 9s. 3d. The expenditure of Australasia has increased, during the same period, from £29,440,951 to £35,187,380, while the amount per inhabitant has increased from £7 8s. 7d. to £7 10s. 1d. The expenditure for each state during the past ten years is set forth in the following table :—

Year.	New South Wales.	Victoria.	Queensland.	South Australia, including Northern Territory.	Western Australia.	Tasmania.	Commonwealth.	New Zealand.	Australasia.
	£	£	£	£	£	£	£	£	£
1894	10,082,198	7,310,246	3,351,536	2,749,081	656,357	836,417	24,985,835	4,455,116	29,440,951
1895	9,329,353	6,760,439	3,308,434	2,661,934	936,729	789,806	23,786,695	4,266,712	28,053,407
1896	9,698,891	6,540,182	3,567,947	2,640,688	1,828,863	748,946	25,020,517	4,370,481	29,390,998
1897	9,316,620	6,568,932	3,604,264	2,779,110	2,839,458	750,244	25,858,623	4,509,981	30,368,604
1898	9,299,411	6,928,850	3,747,428	2,750,959	3,256,912	785,026	26,768,586	4,602,372	31,370,958
1899	9,562,739	7,001,663	4,024,170	2,777,614	2,539,358	830,168	26,735,712	4,858,511	31,594,223
1900	10,086,186	7,280,689	4,540,418	2,986,619	2,615,675	871,454	28,331,041	5,140,128	33,471,169
1901	10,729,741	7,683,079	4,624,479	3,007,034	3,051,331	923,731	30,019,395	5,479,703	35,499,098
1902	11,020,105	7,407,781	3,967,001	2,823,578	3,151,427	870,442	29,240,334	5,914,915	35,155,249
1903	11,467,235	6,774,084	3,717,806	2,641,789	3,521,768	850,684	28,973,361	6,214,019	35,187,380

The expenditure per inhabitant in each state for the last ten years is as follows:—

Year.	New South Wales.	Victoria.	Queensland.	South Australia, including Northern Territory.	Western Australia.	Tasmania.	Commonwealth.	New Zealand.	Australasia.
	£ s. d.	£ s. d.	£ s. d.	£ s. d.	£ s. d.	£ s. d.	£ s. d.	£ s. d.	£ s. d.
1894	8 7 7	6 4 11	8 0 4	7 18 6	10 1 9	5 8 10	7 10 10	6 14 9	7 8 7
1895	7 12 1	6 15 3	7 14 5	7 11 3	11 8 3	5 1 4	7 1 3	6 5 8	6 18 11
1896	7 13 8	5 11 5	8 1 9	7 8 1	18 0 4	4 14 2	7 5 9	6 5 8	7 2 9
1897	7 5 9	5 16 10	8 0 1	7 15 0	20 11 8	4 11 10	7 7 11	6 7 0	7 4 9
1898	7 2 10	5 17 2	8 2 9	7 12 5	20 2 3	4 13 0	7 7 10	6 6 11	7 4 3
1899	7 4 6	5 18 4	8 10 8	7 12 2	15 2 1	4 15 2	7 5 10	6 11 4	7 2 3
1900	7 10 1	6 3 1	9 8 3	7 18 5	15 5 10	4 17 0	7 12 5	6 16 6	7 9 8
1901	7 17 3	6 8 4	9 5 8	8 6 5	16 18 9	5 7 0	7 19 1	7 2 3	7 16 3
1902	7 19 9	6 2 7	7 15 5	7 14 10	16 3 5	5 0 3	7 12 7	7 10 2	7 12 0
1903	8 3 2	5 12 4	7 4 5	7 4 5	16 7 5	4 16 10	7 9 3	7 13 10	7 10 1

Below will be found a statement showing the total revenue and expenditure of each state for the financial year 1902–3, with the amounts per head of population. It must be pointed out that from the revenue and expenditure of New South Wales, Victoria, South Australia, Tasmania, and New Zealand, as given in the table, refunds are excluded; while for Queensland and Western Australia there is nothing in the published statements to show whether the amounts are gross or net:—

State.	Year ended—	Total.		Per head of population.	
		Revenue.	Expenditure.	Revenue.	Expenditure.
		£	£	£ s. d.	£ s. d.
New South Wales	30 June, 1903	11,296,069	11,467,235	8 0 9	8 3 2
Victoria	30 June, 1903	6,968,051	6,774,064	5 15 7	5 12 4
Queensland	30 June, 1903	3,526,465	3,717,806	5 17 0	7 4 5
South Australia*	30 June, 1903	2,531,543	2,641,789	6 18 5	7 4 5
Western Australia	30 June, 1903	3,630,238	3,521,763	16 17 6	16 7 5
Tasmania	31 Dec., 1902	734,663	850,684	4 8 8	4 16 10
Commonwealth	....	28,687,029	28,973,361	7 7 9	7 9 3
New Zealand	31 Mar., 1903	6,447,435	6,214,019	7 19 7	7 13 10
Australasia	....	35,134,464	35,187,380	7 9 10	7 10 1

* Including Northern Territory.

As will be seen from the table, the revenue of the states included in the Commonwealth for the financial year 1902–3 was £28,687,029, or £7 7s. 9d. per head of population, and the expenditure £28,973,361, or £7 9s. 3d. per head, showing a total deficiency on the twelve months' transactions of £286,332. The revenue of the whole of Australasia was £35,134,464, or £7 9s. 10d. per head of population, and the expenditure £35,187,380, or £7 10s. 1d. per head, showing a deficiency of £52,916. The only states which had a surplus were Victoria, Western Australia and New Zealand.

Sources of Revenue.

The revenue of the states is mainly derived from taxation and public services. During the year 1902–3 the customs and excise duties, and postal and telegraph revenue of the states forming the Commonwealth were collected by the Federal Government, and the balance, after deducting expenses of the transferred and new services, was returned to the states. These balances amounted to £8,163,781, and other forms of taxation, £3,110,030; while the railways and tramways returned a revenue of £11,276,825, making altogether a sum of £22,550,636 derived from these sources, or 78·61 per cent. of the total receipts. For New Zealand, customs and excise duties yielded £2,426,043 and other taxation, £851,921; railways returned £1,982,551, and posts and telegraphs, £525,099; the receipts from the sources mentioned being £5,785,614, or 89·73 per cent. of the total. It will thus be seen that for the whole of Australasia the collections under the headings mentioned amounted to £28,336,250, or 80·66 per cent. of the gross revenue. A division of the revenue of each state is appended:—

State.	Taxation.		Railways and Tramways	Posts and Telegraphs.	Public Lands.	Surplus Commonwealth Revenue returned to State.	All Other Sources.	Total Revenue.
	Import and Excise Duties.	Other.						
	£	£	£	£	£	£	£	£
New South Wales	....	1,108,781	4,079,788	....	1,805,227	3,058,133	1,249,140	11,296,069
Victoria	....	859,972	3,033,597	....	348,208	2,105,450	620,824	6,968,051
Queensland	....	415,088	1,245,915	....	610,280	905,235	349,347	3,526,465
South Australia..	....	398,941	1,086,758	....	159,850	579,530	306,464	2,581,548
Western Australia	....	221,247	1,598,023	....	273,249	1,255,731	281,988	3,630,238
Tasmania	....	105,401	232,744	....	71,928	264,702	59,888	734,663
Commonwealth	....	3,110,030	11,276,825	....	3,268,742	8,163,781	2,867,651	28,687,029
New Zealand	2,426,043	851,921	1,982,551	525,099	252,278	....	409,543	6,447,435
Australasia	2,426,043	3,961,951	13,259,376	525,099	3,521,020	8,163,781	3,277,194	35,134,464

Below will be found a statement of the revenue in 1902–3 on the basis of population. The average for the states of the Commonwealth was £7 7s. 9d., and for the whole of Australasia £7 9s. 10d. per head, the amounts ranging from £4 3s. 8d. in Tasmania to £16 17s. 6d. in Western Australia. The high revenue in the latter state is attributable partly to the influx of foreign capital for the development of the gold-fields, but chiefly to the large consumption of dutiable goods and the railway revenue yielded by the gold-fields. While oversea goods entering the state are subject to the Federal tariff, importations from the other states are dutiable under the Special Western Australian Tariff, and as a consequence a large importation of capital necessarily means a large customs revenue and increased traffic and earnings for the railways:—

State.	Taxation.		Railways and Tramways.	Posts and Telegraphs.	Public Lands.	Surplus Commonwealth Revenue returned to State.	All Other Sources.	Total Revenue.
	Import and Excise Duties.	Other.						
	£ s. d.	£ s. d.	£ s. d.	£ s. d.	£ s. d.	£ s. d.	£ s. d.	£ s. d.
New South Wales ..	....	0 15 10	2 18 1	....	1 5 8	2 3 5	0 17 9	8 0 9
Victoria	....	0 14 3	2 10 4	....	0 5 9	1 14 11	0 10 4	5 15 7
Queensland	....	0 16 2	2 8 5	....	1 3 8	1 15 2	0 13 7	6 17 0
South Australia....	....	1 1 10	2 19 5	....	0 8 9	1 11 8	0 16 9	6 18 5
Western Australia..	....	1 0 7	7 8 7	....	1 5 5	5 16 9	1 6 2	16 17 6
Tasmania	....	0 12 0	1 6 6	....	0 8 2	1 10 1	0 6 11	4 3 8
Commonwealth ..	....	0 16 0	2 18 1	....	0 16 10	2 2 1	0 14 9	7 7 9
New Zealand	3 0 1	1 1 1	2 9 1	0 13 0	0 6 3	....	0 10 1	7 19 7
Australasia	0 10 4	0 16 11	2 16 6	0 2 3	0 15 0	1 14 10	0 14 0	7 9 10

Dividing the revenue derived from taxation into that payable (*a*) directly and (*b*) indirectly by the people, the former including land and income taxes, stamp duties, &c., and the latter customs and excise, license fees, &c., the appended figures are obtained. The figures for the Commonwealth states include the collections of the Federal Government within each state as shown on page 774. As already stated, the Customs and Excise Duties were collected by the Commonwealth Government during the year ended 30th June, 1903, and from the 9th October, 1901, were not determined by the state, but by the Parliament of the Commonwealth.

State.	Total Taxation, 1902-3.			Per head of population.		
	Direct.	Indirect.	Total.	Direct.	Indirect.	Total.
	£	£	£	£ s. d.	£ s. d.	£ s. d.
New South Wales	986,372	3,601,151	4,587,523	0 14 0	2 11 3	3 5 3
Victoria	844,356	2,514,630	3,358,986	0 14 1	2 1 8	2 15 9
Queensland	363,498	1,313,256	1,676,754	0 14 2	2 11 0	3 5 2
South Australia............	379,361	709,307	1,088,668	1 0 9	1 18 9	2 19 6
Western Australia..	190,059	1,427,185	1,617,244	0 17 8	6 12 8	7 10 4
Tasmania............	91,150	374,858	466,008	0 10 5	2 2 8	2 13 1
Commonwealth	2,854,796	9,940,387	12,795,183	0 14 8	2 11 3	3 5 11
New Zealand	851,921	2,426,043	3,277,964	1 1 1	3 0 1	4 1 2
Australasia	3,706,717	12,366,430	16,073,147	0 15 9	2 12 9	3 8 6

Comparing these figures with the returns for the year 1881, which are given below, it will be found that the general tendency has been to increase both forms of taxation: this is contrary to the general experience, which is that the expenses of government as compared with population, should diminish as population increases.

State.	Total Taxation, 1881.			Per Inhabitant.		
	Direct.	Indirect.	Total.	Direct.	Indirect.	Total.
	£	£	£	£ s. d.	£ s. d.	£ s. d.
New South Wales	192,503	1,578,345	1,770,848	0 5 0	2 1 3	2 6 3
Victoria	347,782	1,635,345	1,983,127	0 8 1	1 18 0	2 6 1
Queensland	49,311	608,443	657,754	0 4 7	2 16 7	3 1 2
South Australia	14,522	569,617	584,139	0 1 1	2 2 7	2 3 8
Western Australia	1,206	114,919	116,125	0 0 10	3 17 10	3 18 8
Tasmania	66,748	283,398	350,146	0 11 5	2 8 6	2 19 11
Commonwealth	672,072	4,790,067	5,462,139	0 5 11	2 1 11	2 7 10
New Zealand	405,802	1,480,507	1,886,309	0 16 6	3 0 1	3 16 7
Australasia	1,077,874	6,270,574	7,348,448	0 7 10	2 5 8	2 13 6

With regard to the proportion of revenue raised at the present time by direct taxation, the states differ considerably. Thus, no less than 12·41 per cent. of the revenue of Tasmania in 1902–3 was derived from that source; while in New Zealand the proportion was 13·21 per cent.; in Queensland, 10·31 per cent.; in Victoria, 12·12 per cent.; in Western Australia, 5·23 per cent.; in South Australia, 14·98 per cent.; and in New South Wales, only 8·73 per cent. The comparison, however, is chiefly interesting as showing the large territorial revenue that New South Wales is fortunate enough to possess.

In all the states probate duties are levied, and except in Western Australia and Queensland, land and income taxes. In Queensland, with few exemptions, all incomes are taxed as well as the dividends of joint-stock companies, and in Western Australia a dividend and companies tax was introduced at the close of the financial year 1898–9. In the edition of this work for 1895–6 the changes in the probate and succession duties, and in the land and income taxes, were traced; the description given below deals only with the duties as they stand at the present time.

Probate and Succession Duties.

New South Wales.—In this state a duty of 1 per cent. was payable to the end of the year 1899 on the value of the real and personal estate of a testator or intestate, and on settlements of property taking effect after death, provided the value of the property was less than £5,000; 2 per cent. was payable on estates of the value of £5,000 and under £12,500; 3 per cent. upon £12,500 and under £25,000; 4 per cent. upon £25,000 and under £50,000; and 5 per cent. upon £50,000 and upwards. Estates not exceeding £200 in gross value were exempt from duty. On the 22nd December, 1899, an amending Act was assented to, under which the following duties on the estates of deceased persons are now payable :—

Exceeding—	Not exceeding—	Rate.	Exceeding—	Not exceeding—	Rate.
£	£	per cent.	£	£	per cent.
....	1,000	Nil.	34,000	36,000	6⅖
1,000	5,000	2	36,000	38,000	6⅗
5,000	6,000	3	38,000	40,000	6⅘
6,000	7,000	3⅕	40,000	44,000	7
7,000	8,000	3⅖	44,000	48,000	7⅕
8,000	9,000	3⅗	48,000	52,000	7⅖
9,000	10,000	3⅘	52,000	56,000	7⅗
10,000	12,000	4	56,000	60,000	7⅘
12,000	14,000	4⅕	60,000	64,000	8
14,000	16,000	4⅖	64,000	68,000	8⅕
16,000	18,000	4⅗	68,000	72,000	8⅖
18,000	20,000	4⅘	72,000	76,000	8⅗
20,000	22,000	5	76,000	80,000	8⅘
22,000	24,000	5⅕	80,000	84,000	9
24,000	26,000	5⅖	84,000	88,000	9⅕
26,000	28,000	5⅗	88,000	92,000	9⅖
28,000	30,000	5⅘	92,000	96,000	9⅗
30,000	32,000	6	96,000	100,000	9⅘
32,000	34,000	6⅕	100,000	....	10

Only one-half of these rates is payable on the net amount received by the widow, children, and grand-children of the testator or intestate, provided the total value of the estate is not more than £50,000 after all debts have been paid.

Victoria.—The succession duties in force in Victoria are the same as those levied in New South Wales under the 1899 Act, with the exception that on estates exceeding £1,000, but not exceeding £5,000, an exemption of £1,000 is allowed in Victoria. The conditions as to half-rates payable by widows, children, and grand-children, on amounts received by them, are the same as in New South Wales.

Queensland.—A succession duty of 2 per cent. is levied in Queensland on property acquired by a person on the death of its former owner when the value of the property is £200 and under £1,000; 3 per cent. is chargeable upon property valued at £1,000 and under £2,500; 4 per cent. upon £2,500 and under £5,000; 6 per cent. upon £5,000 and under £10,000; 8 per cent. upon £10,000 and under £20,000; and 10 per cent. upon £20,000 and upwards. No duty is levied on estates under the net value of £200. When the successor is the wife or husband or lineal issue of the predecessor, one-half of these rates only is charged; and when the successor is a stranger in blood to the predecessor double rates are charged. The following small probate duties are also payable on the net value of the property :—

Value.	Probates.		Letters of Administration.
Under £50	Nil.	....	Nil.
£50 and not exceeding £100.........	10s.	....	£1
Over £100 and not exceeding £200..	£1	....	£2
,, £200 ,, ,, £500...........	£2	....	£4
,, £500	£5	....	£10

Succession duty is chargeable on all property held within the state, although the testator or intestate may have been domiciled elsewhere; but power is taken to compound the duty and to accept one sum in respect of all successions, present and future, where the deceased has been domiciled in the United Kingdom or a British possession, and it has been found difficult to assess the value of the succession. Also, where the British Government or the Government of a British possession exempts from duty property held in Queensland by a person domiciled in the United Kingdom or the British possession referred to, no duty is chargeable by the Queensland Government on property held in the United Kingdom or such British possession by a person domiciled in the state.

South Australia.—Succession duties are imposed on real and personal property derived from the estate of a deceased person; on settlements of property to take effect after the death of the settlor; and on property made over by deed of gift during the lifetime of the donor, and not made before and in consideration of marriage, or in favour of a *bona-fide* purchaser or encumbrancer for valuable consideration. The duty is levied on the net present value, and is fixed at 10 per cent. when the legatee or beneficiary is a stranger in blood to the person from whom the property is received. When the person taking the property is the widow, widower, descendant, or ancestor, it is subject to a duty of 1½ per cent. if the value is £500 and under £700; if £700 and under £1,000, 2 per cent.; £1,000 and under £2,000, 3 per cent.; £2,000 and under £3,000, 3½ per cent.; £3,000 and under £5,000, 4 per cent.; £5,000 and under £7,000, 4½ per cent.; £7,000 and under £10,000, 5 per cent.; £10,000 and under £15,000, 5½ per cent.; £15,000 and under £20,000, 6 per cent.; £20,000 and under £30,000, 6½ per cent.; £30,000 and under £40,000, 7 per cent.; £40,000 and under £60,000, 7½ per cent.; £60,000 and under £80,000, 8 per cent.; £80,000 and under £100,000, 8½ per cent.; £100,000 and under £150,000, 9 per cent.; £150,000 and under £200,000, 9½ per cent.; and £200,000 and upwards, 10 per cent.; one-half of these rates only to be charged when the person taking the property is the child (under 21 years of age) or the widow of the deceased, and the net present value of the whole estate is under £2,000. When the property is taken by a brother or sister, or a descendant of a brother or sister, or a person in any other degree of collateral consanguinity to the deceased person, settlor, or donor, a duty of 1 per cent. is charged if the net present value is under £200; if £200 and under £300, 1½ per cent.; £300 and under £400, 2 per cent.; £400 and under £700, 3 per cent.; £700 and under £1,000, 3½ per cent.; £1,000 and under £2,000, 4 per cent.; £2,000 and under £3,000, 5 per cent.; £3,000 and under £5,000, 6 per cent.; £5,000 and under £10,000, 7 per cent.; £10,000 and under £15,000, 8 per cent.; £15,000 and under £20,000, 9 per cent.; and £20,000 and upwards, 10 per cent.

Western Australia.—Probate duty is payable on the estates of deceased persons, and upon settlements of property to take effect after the death of the donor, with the exception of ante-nuptial settlements, on all post-nuptial settlements made in pursuance of an agreement entered into before marriage, all settlements, on or for the wife, or her issue, or the issue of the settlor, of property which has accrued to the settlor after th marriage in right of his wife; and upon all settlements made in favour of a purchaser or encumbrancer in good faith and for valuable consideration. The duty is imposed on the net value of the estate after all debts have been paid. The lowest sum subject to taxation is £1,500, and this sum is likewise exempted when the net value of the estate is less than £2,500, but when this value is exceeded no exemption is made. The rates of duty are as follow:—

£1,500 and under £2,500 (on excess of £1,500)			1 per cent.
£2,500	,,	£5,000	2 ,,
£5,000	,,	£10,000	3 ,,
£10,000	,,	£20,000	4 ,,
£20,000	,,	£30,000	5 ,,
£30,000	,,	£40,000	6 ,,
£40,000	,,	£60,000	7 ,,
£60,000	,,	£80,000	8 ,,
£80,000	,,	£100,000	9 ,,
Over £100,000			10 ,,

with half these rates when the beneficiaries comprise the parent, issue, husband, wife, or issue of husband or wife of the deceased.

Tasmania.—In this state duties are imposed on probates of wills and letters of administration. The duty is levied on the net value of the personal estate of the testator or intestate. When the amount is under £100 no duty is payable; when it is £100 and not more than £500 the duty is 2 per cent.; and when it is £500 and upwards the duty is 3 per cent. Life policies are exempt from taxation.

New Zealand.—The following duties are imposed in New Zealand on the final balance of the real and personal property left by a testator or intestate; on settlements of property taking effect after the death of the settlor; and on property made over by deed of gift taking effect during the lifetime of the donor, and not being property granted before and in consideration of marriage, or in favour of a *bona-fide* purchaser or encumbrancer in return for valuable consideration:—

Not exceeding £100	Nil.
£100 and not exceeding £1,000—	
On first £100	Nil.
On remainder	$2\frac{1}{2}$ per cent.
Over £1,000 and not exceeding £5,000	$3\frac{1}{2}$,,
Over £5,000 and up to £20,000	7 ,,
On £20,000 and upwards	10 ,,

with 3 per cent. additional in the case of strangers in blood, except adopted children. It is provided that no duty shall be payable on property passing absolutely into the possession of the widow of the deceased, or of the widower of the deceased; and that only half-rates shall be payable on property acquired by the children, step-children, and grand-children of the testator or intestate. It is further provided that in the case of property in which a life estate or interest is acquired by the widow on the death of her husband, or by the widower on the death of his wife, payment of duty shall be made in ordinary course if the property possesses a capital value which would give an annual return of not less than £500 if invested at 6 per cent., and when the property is of lower value the widow or widower shall obtain a refund not exceeding 50 per cent. of the duty.

Land and Income Taxation in New South Wales.

In New South Wales, land tax is levied on the unimproved value; the present rate being 1d. in the £. An exemption of £240 is allowed, and if the unimproved value is in excess of this sum a deduction equal to the exemption is made, but when a person or company holds several blocks of land only one sum of £240 may be deducted from the aggregate unimproved value. Also, when a block of land is mortgaged, the mortgagor is allowed to deduct from the amount of his tax a sum which is equal to the income tax chargeable to the mortgagee on the interest derived from the mortgage of the whole property, including improvements. The exemptions from taxation comprise Crown lands not subject to right of purchase, or held under special or conditional lease, or as homestead selections; other lands vested in His Majesty or his representatives; lands vested in the Railway Commissioners; lands belonging to or vested in local authorities; public roads, reserves, parks, cemeteries, and commons; lands occupied as public pounds, or used exclusively for or in connection with public hospitals, benevolent institutions, and other public charities; churches and chapels, the University and its affiliated colleges, the Sydney Grammar School, and mechanics' institutes and schools of arts; and lands dedicated to and vested in trustees and used for zoological, agricultural, pastoral, or horticultural show purposes, or for other public or scientific purposes. Should the tax remain unpaid for a period of two years after it becomes due the

Commissioners may, after giving another year's notice, let the land for a period not exceeding three years, or, with the permission of a Judge of the Supreme Court, sell so much of it as may be necessary for the payment of the tax, with fines, costs, and expenses added.

A tax is also imposed upon so much of every income as may be in excess of £200, except in so far as it is derived from the ownership or use or cultivation of land upon which land tax is payable; the present rate being 6d. in the £. The exemptions include the revenues of local authorities; the income of life assurance societies and of other societies and companies not carrying on business for purposes of profit or gain, and not being income derived from mortgages; the dividends and profits of the Savings Bank of New South Wales and the Post Office Savings Bank; the funds and income of registered friendly societies and trade unions; the income and revenues of all ecclesiastical, charitable, and educational institutions of a public character; and income accruing to foreign investors from Government stock. The regulations provide that in the case of every company its income shall be taken as the income of the company in New South Wales and from investments within the state. Public companies are not allowed the exemption of £200.

The receipts from the land and income taxes since their imposition were as follows. The amounts are exclusive of refunds rendered necessary through correction of errors by the taxpayer or adjustments by the Department, but include refunds brought about through the income of the year of assessment falling short of the amount of income of the preceding year on which the assessment was made.

Year.	Land Tax.	Income Tax.
	£	£
1896	....	27,658
1897	139,079	295,537
1898	364,131	166,395
1899	253,901	178,032
1900	286,227	183,460
1901	288,369	215,893
1902	301,981	203,625
1903	314,104	214,686

The irregularities noticeable in the first three years are due to the difficulties inseparable from the introduction of a system of direct taxation; the returns for 1899 and subsequent years are under normal conditions.

The value of land assessed for taxation purposes is £124,015,000; but the owners of estates valued at £3,340,000 could not be discovered, while £14,202,000 represents the value of land falling below the minimum taxable value (£240), or untaxable in consequence of mortgage deductions. As an exemption of £240 is allowed for each person, the taxable amount is further reduced by £8,400,000: exemptions in respect of mortgages described in the text still further reduce the taxable balance by £16,800,000, and balances due on land conditionally purchased from the state by £6,633,000, so that the actual taxable value is £74,640,000.

The number of persons owning land in New South Wales is about 110,000, but the deductions allowed by law reduced the actual number of taxpayers to 40,000.

The incomes liable to taxation do not vary greatly either in regard to their number or amount, and during the last four years were as follows :—

Year.	Number of Incomes.	Gross Income.	Net Income.
		£	£
1899	19,775	23,046,181	11,123,343
1900	20,051	25,770,057	12,140,569
1901	19,991	26,293,249	12,065,842
1902	20,299	27,716,525	12,127,129

The difference between the gross and the net income represents the deductions allowed to taxpayers on account of cost of earning their incomes, and certain allowances for life assurance on premium payments up to £50 per annum. A distribution of the incomes subject to taxation according to amounts taxable is given below for the last three years. It should be remembered that these represent only a proportion of the incomes derived from New South Wales, as incomes derived from land, or the use or occupancy of land, are not taxable. The amounts given are the net earnings :—

Grade.	1900.		1901.		1902.	
	Incomes.		Incomes.		Incomes.	
	No.	Net.	No.	Net.	No.	Net.
		£		£		£
£200 and under £250	5,824	1,292,501	5,726	1,277,561	5,496	1,228,625
250 „ 300	3,830	1,035,180	3,923	1,060,673	4,030	1,087,264
300 „ 400	3,946	1,338,668	3,968	1,358,333	4,073	1,386,012
400 „ 500	1,840	814,349	1,836	810,742	1,909	844,482
500 „ 700	1,783	1,035,137	1,839	1,068,134	1,875	1,081,837
700 „ 1,000	1,184	964,218	1,071	879,489	1,171	961,530
1,000 „ 1,200	326	354,290	360	392,947	399	436,012
1,200 „ 2,000	690	1,032,815	671	1,020,669	681	1,032,147
2,000 „ 5,000	434	1,238,487	428	1,252,534	489	1,426,905
5,000 „ 10,000	111	748,346	99	667,483	105	711,508
10,000 „ 20,000	54	709,028	45	617,970	45	621,370
20,000 and upwards ...	29	1,577,550	25	1,659,307	26	1,309,437
Total	20,051	12,140,569	19,991	12,065,842	20,299	12,127,129

Land and Income Taxation in Victoria.

The Land Tax Act in force in Victoria was passed with the object of breaking up large holdings. For this purpose it was declared that all "landed estates" should be subject to taxation; that a "landed estate" should consist of one or more blocks of land not more than 5 miles apart which possessed an aggregate area of upwards of 640 acres and a capital value of more than £2,500; that the value in excess of £2,500 should be taxed at the rate of 1¼ per cent. per annum, but that only one exemption should be allowed to a person or company owning more than one "landed estate"; and that the assessment of the capital value of the "landed estate" should be based upon the average number of sheep which it was estimated to be able to maintain, £4 per acre being fixed as the value of land which could carry 2 sheep or more to that area; £3 per acre if it could carry only 1½ sheep; £2 per acre if it could carry only 1 sheep, and £1 if it could not maintain an average of a single sheep to the acre.

The rate of income tax payable in the state varies according to the source whence the income is derived and the taxable amount of such income. On incomes derived from personal exertion 4d. in the £ is payable up to £500; on every £ in excess of £500 up to £1,000, 5d.; on every £ in excess of £1,000 up to £1,500, 6d.; on every £ in excess of £1,500 up to £2,000, 7d.; and on every £ in excess of £2,000, 8d.; double these rates being payable on incomes the produce of property within the state. All incomes, except those of companies, of and under £125 escape taxation, and where the income exceeds the sum of £125 an exemption of £100 is allowed, but such exemption does not apply to any taxpayer whose income chargeable with tax exceeds £500, or to any company. In the case of a company liable to pay tax, with the exception of those referred to later on, the income chargeable is the profits earned in or derived from Victoria by such company during the year immediately preceding that of assessment. The taxable amount of the income of a company which carries on in Victoria the business of life assurance, is assessed at a sum equal to £30 per cent. of the premiums received by the company during the year immediately preceding that of assessment in respect of insurances or assurances effected in Victoria, and such sum is chargeable with tax as income the produce of property. In respect of companies carrying on fire, fidelity, guarantee, marine assurance or insurance business, the premiums derived from any such business are not included in the premiums received by any such company within the meaning of the previous sentence. The rate of income chargeable in respect of life assurance companies is 12d. in the £ of the taxable amount of income. The income of a taxpayer, from any trade carried on in Victoria, to the extent of £4 per cent. of the surplus of assets employed or used in such trade over and above the liabilities thereof during the year immediately preceding that of assessment, is chargeable with tax as income from property, and beyond such extent with tax as income from personal exertion, the determination of such surplus being left with the Commissioner. Land and buildings used by the owner for residential purposes are regarded as returning an income of 4 per cent. on the capital value. It is provided that shipowners whose principal place of business is outside the state shall pay £5 for every £100 received for the carriage of Victorian passengers, goods, and mails. In the case of sales of property, where the principal is not a resident of Victoria, the taxable amount of his income derived from such sale or disposal of property is assessed at 5 per cent. of the total amount for which the property was sold or otherwise disposed of, unless it should be proved to the satisfaction of the Commissioner that the amount received was less than 5 per cent., when a corresponding reduction will be made. The exemptions include the income of the state, local authorities, savings banks, University of Melbourne and affiliated colleges, Working Men's College, schools of mines, technical schools, religious bodies, registered friendly societies, building societies, and trade unions; of societies and public bodies not carrying on business for purposes of gain to shareholders or members of insurance companies (other than life) taking out an annual license under the Stamps Act; and of mining companies; also such dividends derived from mining companies as may not be in excess of calls paid up during the year; and income derived by foreign investors from the stock of Government or local bodies.

The land tax of Victoria affects an area of 6,777,387 acres of the nominal value of £9,950,429, the actual value being probably twice that amount. Private land having an area of over 16,500,000 acres and land values to the extent of about £100,000,000 therefore escape taxation. The classification of land for taxation purposes has been given in a preceding paragraph, and the following table gives the number of taxpayers of each class, with the area, assessed capital value, and other particulars of taxable land.

Classification of land.	No. of Proprietors.	Area.	Capital Value.	Net taxable value allowing deduction of £2,500 for each proprietor.	Tax payable.
		acres.	£	£	£
I. (2 sheep per acre)............	77	237,620	950,480	757,980	9,474
II. (1½ sheep per acre)	151	498,476	1,480,428	1,102,928	13,786
III. (1 sheep per acre)...	280	1,473,230	2,946,460	2,246,460	28,082
IV. (less than 1 sheep per acre)	348	4,573,061	4,573,061	3,703,061	46,288
Total	856	6,777,387	9,950,429	7,810,429	97,630

The number of payers of income tax in Victoria during 1903, on incomes earned in 1902 was 64,548, comprising 63,978 individuals and 570 companies. Of these 52,533 were from personal exertion only;

5,858 from property only ; and 6,157 combined both classes of income. The total income of taxpayers, who paid tax, was £20,593,386, being £15,609,218 from personal exertion, and £4,984,168 from property. The income on which the tax was assessed after the deduction of the exemption amounted to £14,740,086, and was distributed as follows: In the case of individuals, from personal exertion, £9,511,925, and from property £3,245,568; and in the case of companies £977,193 from personal exertion, and £1,005,400 from property. Taking into consideration 6,157 assessments, which combine income from both personal exertion and property, the taxpayers aggregate 70,705, of whom, 58,690 derived their income from personal exertion, with net incomes valued at £10,489,118, while 12,015 obtained their income from property with a net return of £4,250,968. The following is a statement of the taxpayers and their incomes after deducting the exemption of £100, according to the latest assessment, the tax payable being that for the year 1903 :—

Incomes.	Total Taxpayers.		Taxable Incomes.		
	Personal Exertion.	Property.	From Personal Exertion.	From Property.	Total.
	No.	No.	£	£	£
£200 and under	47,982	8,000	3,617,895	631,978	4,249,873
£201 to £1,200	9,775	3,399	4,059,081	1,559,969	5,619,050
£1,201 to £2,000	527	297	794,448	456,281	1,250,729
£2,001 and upwards	406	319	2,017,694	1,602,740	3,620,434
Total	58,690	12,015	10,489,118	4,250,968	14,740,086

The annual assessments, and the revenue obtained from all sources since the imposition of the income tax, were as follows :—

Year.	Tax Assessed.		Revenue.
	Personal Exertion.	Property.	
	£	£	£
1896	79,928	92,793	169,946
1897	85,977	85,133	168,320
1898	89,140	90,373	178,619
1899	89,444	83,976	172,721
1900	123,457	93,787	215,867
1901	125,824	95,091	218,792
1902	123,333	91,273	213,540

The revenue in arrears is the difference between the total of the second and third columns and the last column.

Income and Dividend Taxes in Queensland.

The Income Tax Act became law in November, 1902, and provided for the imposition from the 1st January, 1902, of a tax on the income of all persons, except males under the age of 21 years and all females whose incomes do not respectively amount to £150. The rates levied are: (1.) If the total income does not amount to £100, a fixed sum of 10s. (2.) If the total income exceeds £100, but does not amount to £150, a fixed sum of £1. (3.) If the total income amounts to £150 and upwards, a fixed sum of £1 on the first £150 and on income over £150, 6d. per £ from personal exertion; and 1s. per £ from produce of property. The incomes, revenues, and funds not liable to taxation are: Governor's salary and incidental expenses; revenues of local bodies; incomes of Mutual Assurance Companies; incomes of societies and institutions not carrying on business for profit or gain; funds of friendly societies and trade-unions; incomes of religious, charitable, and educational institutions; income from dividends which have paid dividend duty; income derived by absentees from debentures, stock, or treasury bills; sums expended on the maintenance of infirm, aged, and indigent relatives up to the amount of £26; premiums on life assurance up to £50; payments for superannuation or into friendly societies up to £50; calls or contributions to companies in liquidation. The Act is limited in its operation to the 31st December, 1904.

The number of taxpayers was 90,419, of whom 15,028 were assessed at over £1; 19,482 at the fixed sum of £1; and 55,899 at 10s. each. The number of taxpayers subject to the tax by way of property was 3,211, with a total income of £563,613, and from personal exertion; 14,187 with an aggregate income of £4,819,837. The total incomes over £150 subject to taxation were £5,383,450, and, allowing for 2,360 appearing under both heads, the number of individual taxpayers was 15,038. The following table shows the grades of assessments, number of taxpayers, and amount of income in relation to those above £150:—

Assessment.	From Property.		From Personal Exertion.	
	Number of Taxpayers.	Amount of Income.	Number of Taxpayers.	Amount of Income.
		£		£
Over £150 up to £210.. ...	1,122	91,279	7,161	1,226,171
,, £210 ,, £310......	808	83,600	3,496	863,980
,, £310 ,, £510......	666	110,869	1,964	748,536
,, £510 ,, £910... ..	395	112,448	930	605,981
,, £910 ,, £2,110...	170	85,362	455	576,189
,, £2,110	50	80,055	181	798,980
	3,211	563,613	14,187	4,819,837

Dividend tax is collected in Queensland on the dividends declared by public companies. The rate is 1s. per £ on dividends declared by all companies having their head office or chief place of business in Queensland, provided that when the operations of such a company extend beyond the state, duty shall only be payable on so much of the dividends as is proportionate to the average capital employed within the state. In the case of companies which have not their head office in Queensland, and which are not companies carrying on insurance business only, the duty is payable on so much of the total dividends as is proportionate to the average amount of capital employed in the state during the year compared with the total average capital of the company; and in the case of insurance companies duty is payable at the rate of 20s. for every £100 or part of £100 of gross premiums received. An exemption is allowed in the case of mining companies, the tax of 1s. per £ being payable only on dividends over and above those applied in repayment of the expenditure actually incurred by the company before the declaration of the first dividend in connection with labour or material employed in developing the mine, and in repayment of three-fourths of the cost of machinery erected for the raising of ores and other materials from the mine.

An additional tax, called the "Totalisator Tax," is imposed at the rate of 2½ per cent. on all moneys received by conductors of authorised totalisators in connection with horse races.

Land and Income Taxation in South Australia.

In South Australia the land tax is calculated on the unimproved value, the rate being ½d. in the £, with an additional tax of ½d. on every £ in excess of £5,000. The amount of tax payable by an absentee, who is defined as a person who has been absent from or resident out of the state for two years, is increased by 20 per cent. The exemptions to the land tax comprise Crown lands which are not subject to any agreement for sale or right of purchase, park lands, public roads, public cemeteries, and other public reserves, and land used solely for religious or charitable purposes, or used by any institute under the provisions of the Institute Act of 1874. It is provided that an assessment shall be made every three years, and that the distribution of the tax shall be made according to the proprietary interest held in the land. It is further provided that if the payment of the tax has been in arrear for a period of two years the Commissioner may, after giving another year's notice of his intention, let the land from year to year, and after deducting from the rents the amount of tax, with costs and expenses, hold the balance for the benefit of the owner; or he may even go so far as to petition the Supreme Court for permission to sell so much of the land as may be necessary for the payment of the tax and costs and expenses.

The income tax varies according to the source whence the income is derived. On incomes derived from personal exertion the rate imposed is 4½d. in the £ up to and including £800, and 7d. for every £ in excess of that sum. On incomes the produce of property the rate imposed is 9d. in the £ up to and including £800, and 13½d. for every £ in excess of that amount. The sum exempted from taxation is £135, but where the net income of a taxpayer from all sources exceeds £400 he is not entitled to any exemption. No exemption is allowed if the taxpayer has been absent from South Australia for twelve consecutive months prior to November, 1902. The exemptions from taxation comprise the incomes of municipal corporations and [illegible] public bodies and societies not carrying

ERRATUM.

On page 808, the first three lines referring to Land and Income Taxation in South Australia should *read*—

> In South Australia the land tax is levied on the unimproved value, and is at the rate of ½d. per £, with an additional tax of ½d. on every £ in excess of £5,000.

The payers of income tax during 1902 numbered 15,226, comprising 16,539 assessments, viz., 13,150 on personal exertion, 2,829 on property, 138 firms, 199 companies, and 223 trustees. The taxable incomes from personal exertion amount to £2,526,682, and from property, £1,265,166 The incomes for the four years, 1899 to 1902, were :—

Year.	Number of Taxable Incomes.	Amount of Assessment.
		£
1899	12,761	3,050,396
1900	8,528	3,384,928
1901	9,632	3,162,423
1902	15,226	3,791,848

These sums do not represent the total income, being exclusive of the exemptions allowed by law to incomes under £135. For the year 1902 the total incomes subject to taxation were :—

15,226 incomes, exclusive of exemption...........	£3,791,848
Exemption of £135 on 11,911 incomes	1,607,985
	£5,399,833

Included in the taxable incomes are those of 721 persons not resident in the state, and 201 companies, both local and with head offices outside the state.

The receipts from income tax during the last ten years are shown in the following table :—

Year.	Income Tax Received.	Year.	Income Tax Received.
	£		£
1893	60,235	1898	82,396
1894	70,853	1899	84,184
1895	55,969	1900	92,281
1896	86,570	1901	85,746
1897	86,476	1902	114,720

Dividend and Companies Tax in Western Australia.

Of all the states, Western Australia was the last to introduce the system of direct taxation ; but, the field of taxation was restricted to the income and dividends of companies. The Act authorising this taxation is known as the Companies Duty Act of 1899. The main object aimed at by Parliament in sanctioning this partial taxation of incomes was to secure to the state some portion of the golden harvest of the mining fields. The Act was regarded as legislation of an experimental character, and as a consequence was limited in its operation to the period of three years ended 31st December, 1902. It is apparent that the fears of the opponents of this method of taxation—that it would scare away capital from the state—have not been realised, for in December, 1902, the Dividend Duties Act was passed into law, imposing a tax of 1s. in the £ on the profits of all companies, exclusive of those engaged in insurance or assurance business. In the case of insurance or assurance companies, other than life assurance companies, which are exempt from the operation of the Act, a tax of 20s. per £100 of gross premiums is imposed.

The net receipts from the tax on companies during the past four years were as follows :—

Year.	Amount of Tax received.
	£
1899...........................	6,117
1900...........................	83,971
1901	81,175
1902...........................	79,221

LAND AND INCOME TAXATION IN TASMANIA.

The land tax payable in Tasmania is at the rate of ½d. in the £ where the assessed value is under £5,000; ⅝d. in the £ where the assessed value is £5,000 and under £15,000; ¾d. in the £ where the value is £15,000 and under £40,000; ⅞d. in the £ where the value is £40,000 and under £80,000; and 1d. in the £ where the value is £80,000 and over, with a deduction of ⅛d. in the £ on account of mortgages. The exemptions comprise land the property of a municipal corporation or other local authority, or of a registered friendly society; the site of a State school under the Education Department; of a public library or museum; of the Tasmanian Museum; of a hospital or benevolent asylum or other building used solely for charitable or religious purposes, or land vested in trust for public purposes; public roads; cemeteries which are not owned by joint-stock or public companies; and public reserves, gardens, and recreation grounds. Crown lands held on lease are also exempted from taxation, but if they have been purchased on credit the occupier is required to pay tax, provided one-half of the price has been paid or has become due. The owner of the land is looked to directly for the amount of the tax, unless he resides out of the state or cannot be found, in which case the occupier becomes responsible, but is allowed to deduct the sum from the amount of his rent. The Commissioner has power to let the land if the tax remains unpaid six months after it has become due, or, with the approval of a Judge of the Supreme Court, to sell it if the tax has remained unpaid for two years; and it is provided that the balance of the proceeds, after the amount of the tax, with costs and expenses, has been deducted, shall be handed over to the owner of the rented property or the original owner of the property which has been sold. As the value of the land rated is declared by law to be the sum which the fee simple would sell for, the tax is not purely a land tax, but a tax on real estate.

The income tax in force in the state provides for the imposition of 1s. in the £ on all income of any company, on the income of any person at the rate of 6d. in the £ of the taxable amount thereof derived from business and 1s. in the £ on that derived from property, and on every dividend not included in either of the foregoing at the rate of 1s. in the £ on such dividend. The chief exemptions are the revenues of municipal corporations and other local authorities, incomes of companies, societies, or public bodies or trusts not carrying on business with a view to a distribution of profits amongst their shareholders or members, the funds and incomes of registered friendly societies and trade unions, income accruing to foreign investors in Tasmanian Government stock, rents from land subject to land tax, income derived from dividends which have already been taxed, income of the Governor of Tasmania, income from all sources that is less than £100 per annum, and incomes of persons who have not been resident in the state for six months. Where any person's income is assessed at

£100 or over and is less than £400 a deduction by way of exemption is allowed as follows :—£100 and under £110, a deduction of £80; £110 and under £120, £70; £120 and under £150, £60; £150 and under £200, £50; £200 and under £250, £40; £250 and under £300, £30; £300 and under £350, £20; £350 and under £400, £10. Where the income is derived partly from business and partly from property the deduction is made upon that from business, and if such income is insufficient to allow the full benefit of the deduction, the balance of the deduction is made from the income from property. No deductions are allowed in respect of the income of a company or on income receivable by a person as a prize in any lottery authorised by law in Tasmania. The taxable amount of the income of companies having their head office in Tasmania is the sum represented by the dividends declared or becoming due to the shareholders. In the case of companies whose head office is outside Tasmania, the income during the year preceding that of assessment is adopted, but in no case is it to be deemed less than £1,000, and the assessment is to be calculated as follows :—In the case of banking companies to be so much of the total dividend declared by the company during the year ended 31st December preceding that of assessment as is proportionate to the average amount of the average quarterly assets and liabilities of the company in Tasmania during the same year compared with the total assets and liabilities of the company for a like period as disclosed by the balance sheet. In the case of fire, accident, fidelity, guarantee or marine assurance or insurance companies, the taxable amount is a sum equal to £50 per cent. of the net premiums received by the company in Tasmania. The taxable amount of life assurance companies is £20 per cent. of the premiums received in Tasmania. In the case of shipping companies the taxable amount is £5 per cent. of the receipts for the carriage of livestock, goods, mails and passengers shipped in Tasmania and carried to any port in or beyond the state. Mercantile and other companies liable to taxation are taxed on £5 per cent. of the turnover of business in Tasmania.

The land tax of Tasmania is levied on a capital value in excess of 20 millions sterling, and yields over £35,000 a year. The estates subject to taxation in 1902 numbered 44,888. The following is the result of seven years' working :—

Year.	Estates subject to Tax.	Capital Value of Land.	Amount of Tax.
	No.	£	£
1896	34,806	19,376,559	37,609
1897	34,980	19,213,591	37,226
1898	34,987	19,261,841	37,577
1899	42,739	20,029,051	38,966
1900	43,132	20,026,162	38,915
1901	44,416	20,259,343	39,337
1902	44,888	20,464,094	35,337

The income tax, or more properly companies dividend tax, was levied on from thirty to forty companies to the 31st December 1902, the major part of the tax being obtained from a few large mining companies. The returns for the last five years were—

Year.	Companies.	No.	Taxable Dividends.	Tax Paid.
			£	£
1898	Mining	7	284,850	14,242
	Other	22	45,746	2,287
	Total	29	330,596	16,529
1899	Mining	16	365,437	18,272
	Other	23	45,732	2,286
	Total	39	411,169	20,558
1900	Mining	13	505,123	25,256
	Other	27	47,983	2,399
	Total	40	553,106	27,655
1901	Mining	9	302,823	15,141
	Other	25	47,934	2,397
	Total	34	350,757	17,538
1902	Mining	12	184,906	9,245
	Other	26	52,937	2,647
	Total	38	237,843	11,892

Land and Income Taxation in New Zealand.

In New Zealand the Land and Income Tax Assessment Act imposes a tax upon incomes and an ordinary tax upon land and mortgages, the amount of which it is provided shall be fixed annually by a Rating Act; and also an additional graduated tax upon the unimproved value of land, the rates of which are fixed by the Assessment Act. The rate of the ordinary tax upon land and mortgages at present stands at 1d. in the £ of capital value. It is provided that the owner of any land shall pay the tax on the actual value of his land, and also on the value of any mortgages which he may hold over other land, less the value of improvements, and of any mortgage which may be owing on his land. If the net value does not then exceed £1,500, an exemption of £500 is allowed, but for every £2 by which the net value exceeds the sum of £1,500 the exemption of £500 is reduced by £1, so that when the value reaches the sum of £2,500 there is no exemption at all. In cases where the income from any land or mortgages, plus income from all other sources, is less than £200 per annum, and the owner is incapacitated by age or infirmity from supplementing such income, a further exemption may be allowed by the Commissioner upon his being satisfied that the payment of the tax would entail hardship on such owner. All mortgages are assessed at their full nominal value, except where it is satisfactorily shown that owing to depreciation of the security or other cause such value has been diminished. In the case of mixed mortgages, that is, mortgages which are secured on both real and personal property, the amount of the mortgage chargeable with land tax is taken to be the assessed value of the land included in the security, the interest derived from the balance of mortgage being liable to income tax.

The graduated land tax is imposed on all land possessing an unimproved value of £5,000 and upwards, an important difference between the two taxes being that the mortgagee escapes the graduated tax, and no deduction is allowed to the mortgagor in consideration of any sum which may be advanced on the property. It is provided that on an unimproved value of £5,000 and under £10,000, ⅛d. per £ shall be payable; on £10,000 and under £15,000, ¼d.; £15,000 and under £20,000, ⅜d.; £20,000 and under £25,000, ½d.; £25,000 and under £30,000, ⅝d.; £30,000 and under £40,000, ¾d.; £40,000 and under £50,000, ⅞d.; £50,000 and under £70,000, 1d.; £70,000 and under £90,000, 1⅛d.; £90,000 and under £110,000, 1¼d.; £110,000 and under £130,000, 1⅜d.; £130,000 and under £150,000, 1½d.; £150,000 and under £170,000, 1⅝d.; £170,000 and under £190,000, 1¾d.; £190,000 and under £210,000, 1⅞d.; and £210,000 and over, 2d. per £.; and it is further provided that an absentee, who is declared to be a person who has been absent from or resident out of the colony for a period of not less than one year next preceding the date of the passing of the annual taxing act, shall pay a graduated tax of 20 per cent. additional to the schedule rates.

It is provided that returns of land and mortgages shall be made biennially. Purchasers of Crown lands on credit are liable to taxation, and the owner of a leasehold interest in land is liable to taxation in respect of the value of such interest. The exemptions comprise Crown lands; lands vested in the Railway Commissioners and in local governing bodies; land used solely in connection with a place of worship or a place of residence for the clergy of any religious body, or in connection with public schools established under the Education Act of 1877, or with any other school not carried on exclusively for gain or profit, but the maximum area of land exempted for the purposes of any school carried on for profit is 15 acres; the site of a university or college, or school incorporated by any Act or Ordinance, or the site of a public library, athenæum, mechanics' institute, or school of mines; a public cemetery or burial-ground; the ground or place of meeting of any agricultural society, provided it be the property of such society; the place of meeting of a friendly society or Masonic lodge, or of a registered building society; land used for the purposes of public charitable institutions constituted under the Hospitals and Charitable Institutions Act, and of other charitable institutions not carried on for gain or profit; public gardens, domains, or recreation or other public reserves not occupied by a tenant, and all public roads and streets; land owned and occupied by Maoris, and not leased to or occupied by any person other than the Maori owner; and any public railway, including the land occupied and used as permanent way and for yards, stations, and sheds, and all buildings used for the purposes of railway traffic only. Further exemptions comprise all land owned and mortgages held by any friendly society within the meaning of the Act; alll and owned and mortgages held by any savings bank constituted under the Savings Bank Act of 1858; all land owned and mortgages held by the Commissioners of Sinking Funds under the Public Debts Sinking Funds Act of 1868, or by the trustees of any local authority whose revenues are exempt from taxation; and all mortgages held by or on behalf of any charitable institution.

Still another exemption is provided for, namely, all land owned and mortgages held by or on behalf of any religious body, the proceeds of which land and mortgages are devoted to the support of aged or infirm ministers, or of widows or orphan children of ministers. It is also declared that native land occupied by any other person than the Maori owner shall be subject to one-half of the ordinary land tax in respect of the Maori landowner's interest therein, while being exempt from the graduated tax, and that all mortgages held by or in trust for Maoris shall be liable to the payment of ordinary land tax. Mortgages held by banking companies are reached by the income tax; and land owned and mortgages held by any registered building society are exempted from taxation, the profits derived by members being subject to income tax. In the event of land being undervalued, the Commissioner may give notice to the owner, within twelve months of the signing of the assessment roll, that he must increase the value of the land to the sum placed upon it by the taxation authorities. If the owner is not willing to increase the value to the sum notified by the Commissioner, he may appeal to the Resident Magistrate to assess the value; but should he neither adopt this course nor consent to the Commissioner's valuation within thirty days, the Commissioner may recommend that the Government shall purchase the land at the returned value plus 10 per cent. On the other hand, if the owner is not satisfied with the value at which the land has been assessed, whether by the Board of Review or not, he may call upon the Commissioner to reduce the valuation to a certain sum or to purchase the land at this price.

The income tax is payable upon income derived from employment and from business, including investments other than those in mortgages of land, upon which ordinary land tax is levied. An exemption of £300 is allowed to every person domiciled in the colony, this concession being withheld from absentees; but no exemption is allowed to a public company. The rate of tax is 6d. in the £ on the first taxable £1,000, and 1s. on every additional £, except in the case of public companies which pay 1s. per £ on the whole sum. The income of public companies is declared to be the amount of dividends earned, sums carried to reserve fund, and any other profits made or income derived by such companies. To this provision exception is made in the case of banking companies, insurance companies, shipping companies, and loan, building, and investment companies. It is provided that every banking company shall be assessed for income tax at the rate of 7s. 6d. per £100 of the average of the total liabilities and assets for the four quarters of the preceding year. The shareholders of loan, building, and investment companies are personally taxed upon the amount of income derived from such societies. The regulations declare that a person or company engaged in business as the owner or charterer of shipping shall be assessed upon the income derived from such business carried on in New Zealand and with places beyond the colony; and that when the head office of a person or company engaged in such business is outside the colony the agent shall be liable to the payment of income tax of 5 per cent. of the receipts from the carriage of passengers, goods, and live stock shipped at New Zealand ports. It is also provided by these regulations that the income of every insurance company shall be taken as the income derived from business carried on in the colony, and from investments within the colony other than those in land and in mortgages of land. The exemptions to the income tax comprise the revenues of any county council, borough council, town board, road board, harbour board, public university, public school, education board, school commissioners, licensing committee, and every other local authority receiving revenue of any kind for the purposes of or in relation to local self-government; the income of friendly societies and building societies, and of all public bodies and societies not carrying on business for purposes of gain to be divided amongst the shareholders or members; and income derived by the owner or occupier from any land on which land tax is payable, and from mortgages of such land. The income of any savings bank constituted under the Savings Bank Act of 1858, and the income of any public charitable institution, are also exempted. Also, when a person occupies for purposes of business or employment land on which he pays land tax, he is allowed to deduct from his income a sum equal to 5 per cent. on the amount on which he is liable to pay land tax. It is imperative that a person who does not reside permanently in the colony, and who offers or exposes goods for sale or disposition by sample or otherwise, shall take out an annual license, the fee for which is fixed by regulation at £50.

There are about 115,000 landowners in New Zealand and of these 18,500 pay tax, the remainder being exempted from one cause or another. The land tax yielded £296,000 for the year ended 31st March, 1903, of which £217,000 came from ordinary land tax and £79,000 from graduated tax, the latter amount including about £1,000, imposed upon persons who have been absent from the colony for not less than one year prior to the passing of the yearly taxing act. The total value of land subject to taxation is about £30,175,000 out of a total unimproved value of £61,460,000. The following is a statement of the tax levied during the past six years :—

Year ended 31st March.	Ordinary Land Tax.	Graduated Land Tax.	Total Amount of Land Tax.
	£	£	£
1898	196,000	73,000	269,000
1899	215,000	83,000	298,000
1900	214,000	80,000	294,000
1901	222,000	72,000	294,000
1902	234,000	79,000	313,000
1903	217,000	79,000	296,000

The income tax returns have shown great expansion during the last three years; indeed, the yield shows substantial increases in almost every year since the first imposition of the tax. The revenue obtained during each of the last ten years was as follows :—

Year ended 31st March.	Income Tax Paid.	Year ended 31st March.	Income Tax Paid.
	£		£
1894	75,238	1899	115,480
1895	89,891	1900	128,721
1896	92,778	1901	173,809
1897	105,504	1902	179,397
1898	115,210	1903	200,684

The number of taxpayers for 1903 was 7,589, including 742 absentees and 599 companies. The total incomes assessed for taxation cannot be stated, but the taxable amount was reduced to £5,051,830 by exemptions. The incomes of companies are assessed at £2,301,823, and of absentees £230,532.

The cost of collection in each of the states imposing either land or income taxes, or both combined, varies considerably. The complex character of the Acts under which the impost is levied necessitates a larger expenditure in some states than in others. In New South Wales, where the machinery for the administration of the land tax is of an elaborate character, taking land and income taxes together, the cost is largely in excess of that of any other state, showing, for the period since the inception of the taxes in 1895–6, an expenditure of 8·64 per cent. of the net receipts. In Victoria, for the ten years ended 30th June, 1903, it was only 3·10 per cent.; In South Australia, for the same period, 5·61 per cent.; in Tasmania, for the same period, 4·69 per cent.; and in New Zealand, for the same period, 3·82 per cent. Queensland has had only one year's experience, and the proportion of cost to net receipts was 3·82 per cent. Covering a period of ten years, the proportion of cost to net receipts, for the whole of Australasia, was 5·16 per cent.

Revenue from Direct Taxation.

The following table shows the amount of revenue received from the various sources of direct taxation during the year 1902–3:—

State.	Stamp Duties: Probate.	Stamp Duties: Other.	Land Tax.	Income Tax.	Dividend Tax.	Total.
	£	£	£	£	£	£
New South Wales	240,445	232,664	314,104	199,159	......	986,372
Victoria	161,636	174,805	92,867	415,048	......	844,356
Queensland	131,346		......	141,895	*90,257	363,498
South Australia	104,028	55,589	105,024	114,720	......	379,361
Western Australia	8,952	53,500	......	......	†127,607	190,059
Tasmania	6,980	27,364	41,862	11,863	†3,081	91,150
Commonwealth	1,197,309		553,857	882,685	220,945	2,854,796
New Zealand	118,003	237,172	296,062	200,684	......	851,921
Australasia	1,552,484		849,919	1,083,369	220,945	3,706,717

* Includes £10,002 from Totalisator Tax. † From Companies' Tax.

Land Revenue.

The practice of treating as ordinary revenue money derived from the sale and occupation of Crown lands obtains in all the states, and the money so raised forms in several states a large item of income. The propriety of so doing is open to grave doubt, but the argument used in its justification is that the sums so obtained have enabled the Government either to construct works, which both enhance the value of the remaining public lands and facilitate settlement, or to endow municipalities, and thus enable them to carry out local works. The revenue from land sales is declining year by year, both absolutely and as compared with population. In New South Wales and South Australia the falling-off has been most noticeable; in the former state the revenue from this source is now some £1,377,000 less than was the case in 1881, while in South Australia the revenue from land sales is under £37,000.

Adopting the division of land revenue into receipts from sales and receipts from occupation, the following table shows the income for 1881:—

State.	Total Land Revenue, 1881.			Land Revenue per head.		
	From Auction and other classes of sales.	Occupation, &c., of Crown lands.	Total.	From Auction and other classes of sales.	Occupation, &c., of Crown lands.	Total.
	£	£	£	£ s. d.	£ s. d.	£ s. d.
New South Wales	2,483,338	337,651	2,820,989	3 4 11	0 8 10	3 13 9
Victoria	701,276	135,194	836,470	0 16 4	0 3 2	0 19 6
Queensland	435,664	186,893	622,557	2 0 6	0 17 5	2 17 11
South Australia	651,914	97,042	748,956	2 8 9	0 7 3	2 16 0
Western Australia	5,750	34,695	40,445	0 3 11	1 3 6	1 7 5
Tasmania	37,269	39,487	76,756	0 6 5	0 6 9	0 13 2
Commonwealth	4,315,211	830,962	5,146,173	1 17 10	0 7 3	2 5 1
New Zealand	376,461	174,479	550,940	0 15 4	0 7 1	1 2 5
Australasia	4,691,672	1,005,441	5,697,113	1 14 2	0 7 4	2 1 6

Compared with 1881, the land revenue for 1902–3 shows a large decline, amounting to £1,877,431 for the states included in the Commonwealth, and to £2,176,093 for the whole of Australasia. The falling-off is found entirely in the amount of revenue from sales, that derived from rents having largely increased in all the states except Victoria and Tasmania. However, general remarks applicable to all the states can scarcely be made. New South Wales obtained £2,483,338 from land sales in 1881, out of a total of £4,691,672 for all the states, or more than one-half; while from occupation its revenue was £337,651 out of £1,005,441, or little more than one-third. In 1902–3 the revenue of the state from sales amounted to £1,106,408—still a large amount, but £1,376,930 short of the receipts of 1881. In regard to occupation, a different condition of things is disclosed. The receipts in New South Wales during 1902–3 totalled £698,819, or an increase of £361,168 as compared with 1881, and amounting to 45·18 per cent. of the total of the states comprising the

Commonwealth, or to 39·82 per cent. of the total for Australasia. The following are the figures for 1902–3:—

State.	Total Land Revenue, 1902–3.			Land Revenue per head.								
	From Auction and other classes of sales.	Occupation, &c., of Crown lands.	Total.	From Auction and other classes of sales.			Occupation, &c., of Crown lands.			Total.		
	£	£	£	£	s.	d.	£	s.	d.	£	s.	d.
New South Wales	1,106,408	698,819	1,805,227	0	15	9	0	9	11	1	5	8
Victoria	250,433	97,775	348,208	0	4	2	0	1	7	0	5	9
Queensland	258,760	351,520	610,280	0	10	0	0	13	8	1	3	8
South Australia	36,723	123,127	159,850	0	2	0	0	6	9	0	8	9
Western Australia	28,399	244,850	273,249	0	2	8	1	2	9	1	5	5
Tasmania	41,319	30,609	71,928	0	4	8	0	3	6	0	8	2
Commonwealth	1,722,042	1,546,700	3,268,742	0	8	10	0	8	0	0	16	10
New Zealand	44,148	208,130	252,278	0	1	1	0	5	2	0	6	3
Australasia	1,766,190	1,754,830	3,521,020	0	7	6	0	7	6	0	15	0

In all the states, New South Wales and Victoria excepted, a general sinking fund is established to assist in the redemption of public loans on maturity, and in New South Wales and Victoria special sinking funds have been inaugurated in connection with portions of the local funded stocks. The desirableness of establishing a general sinking fund is on all sides admitted, and a portion of the proceeds of land sales could with advantage be set apart from the general revenue and devoted to this purpose. Victoria deals with a portion of the proceeds from the sale of Crown lands apart from the general revenue, and at the close of the financial year 1890–1 a sum of £578,740 derived from that source had been placed to the credit of the Railway Construction Account; while since that year various sums amounting to £705,526 have been appropriated on account of the "Land Sales by Auction Fund" for expenditure on public works, and a total of £375,332 has been received from sales, &c., leaving a debit balance of £330,194 on the 30th June, 1903.

Heads of Expenditure.

The amount disbursed by the Government of New South Wales is far larger than that expended by any other state of the group; in the last financial year it exceeded the expenditure of Victoria by £4,693,151, was nearly twice as great as that of New Zealand, and was over one million and a half more than the united expenditure of Queensland, South Australia, and Western Australia. This is chiefly owing to the absence of a complete system of local government in New South Wales, and the system of centralisation already referred to. The following is a statement of the expenditure of each state during the financial year 1902-3 :—

State.	Railways and Tramways.	Posts and Telegraphs.	Public Instruction.	Interest and charges on Public Debt.	All other Services.	Total Expenditure.
	£	£	£	£	£	£
New South Wales	2,954,554	......	899,918	2,989,178	4,623,585	11,467,235
Victoria	1,860,493	......	631,968	1,990,132	2,291,491	6,774,084
Queensland	861,749	......	317,266	1,569,188	1,029,508	3,777,711
South Australia	643,871	......	178,059	1,089,511	730,348	2,641,789
Western Australia.........	1,275,565	......	120,305	692,692	1,433,201	3,521,763
Tasmania	173,151	......	67,186	355,464	254,883	850,684
Commonwealth	7,769,383	......	2,214,802	8,626,160	10,363,016	28,973,361
New Zealand	1,357,385	485,860	566,568	1,900,979	1,903,227	6,214,019
Australasia	9,126,768	485,860	2,781,370	10,527,139	12,266,243	35,187,380

It will be seen from the foregoing figures that for the states of the Commonwealth 26·8 per cent. of the whole expenditure is for working the railways—a service not undertaken by the Government in the United Kingdom and the United States. Public instruction accounts for 7·6 per cent., and interest on the public debt, 29·8 per cent. For the whole of Australasia the corresponding percentages are :—Railways, 25·9; public instruction, 7·9; and interest on the public debt, 29·9 per cent.

Adopting the classification of expenditure used in the preceding table, the amounts per inhabitant of each province are given below. It may be here mentioned that in New South Wales, and to some extent in South Australia and Western Australia, the tramways are the property of the state, and are under the same management as the railways, with which they are included in the various statements in this sub-chapter relating to revenue and expenditure :—

State.	Railways and Tramways.	Posts and Telegraphs.	Public Instruction.	Interest and charges on Public Debt.	All other Services.	Total Expenditure.
	£ s. d.	£ s. d.	£ s. d.	£ s. d.	£ s. d.	£ s. d.
New South Wales..	2 2 0	......	0 12 10	2 2 6	3 5 10	8 3 2
Victoria	1 10 10	......	0 10 6	1 13 0	1 18 0	5 12 4
Queensland	1 13 5	......	0 12 4	2 18 8	2 0 0	7 4 5
South Australia.....	1 15 2	......	0 9 9	2 19 7	1 19 11	7 4 5
Western Australia..	5 16 8	......	0 11 2	3 4 5	6 13 2	16 7 5
Tasmania	0 19 8	......	0 7 8	2 0 6	1 9 0	4 16 10
Commonwealth	2 0 0	......	0 11 5	2 4 5	2 13 5	7 9 3
New Zealand.........	1 13 7	0 12 0	0 14 0	2 7 1	2 7 2	7 18 10
Australasia......	1 18 11	0 2 1	0 11 10	2 4 11	2 12 4	7 10 1

The most remarkable feature in the general expenditure of the Australasian states is the largeness of the amount required to pay interest and charges on the public debt, both in regard to the rate per head and the proportion of total revenue thus hypothecated. The proportion for the states of the Commonwealth is 29·8 per cent. of the total expenditure, or £2 4s. 5d. per head of population, and for the whole of Australasia 29·9 per cent., or £2 4s. 11d. per head. The actual expenditure for each state during 1902–3 was as shown below. The amounts given are actual payments made during the financial year, and do not represent the interest liabilities of that period, the amounts of which will be found on page 831 :—

State.	Interest and Charges on Public Debt.		
	Total.	Per head of Population.	Proportion of Total Expenditure.
	£	£ s. d.	per cent.
New South Wales	2,989,178	2 2 6	26·06
Victoria	1,990,132	1 13 0	29·38
Queensland	1,509,183	2 18 8	40·59
South Australia	1,089,511	2 19 7	41·24
Western Australia	692,692	3 4 5	19·67
Tasmania	355,464	2 0 6	41·78
Commonwealth	8,626,160	2 4 5	29·77
New Zealand	1,900,979	2 7 1	30·59
Australasia	10,527,139	2 4 11	29·92

A casual glance at the figures quoted will lend colour to the suggestion sometimes hazarded that the states are too rapidly mortgaging their resources, and that the expense of the public debt will prove a greater burthen than can easily be borne. However true this may be so far as any individual state is concerned, it is certainly erroneous as regards the whole of Australasia. Out of the sum of £8,626,160 required to pay interest and charges on the public debt by the states of the Commonwealth during 1902–3, £3,507,442 was directly recouped by the net revenue from public railways. Water supply and sewerage yielded a sum of £526,722, the net revenue from harbour and river improvements was £141,673, and the interest on advances to settlers, local bodies, and on the purchase of lands for settlement yielded a further sum of £100,763, making a total of £4,276,600. Including New Zealand, the sum required to pay interest and charges on the public debt was £10,527,139, but of this £5,155,258 was directly recouped, viz., £4,132,608 by the net revenue from railways, £526,722 by water supply and sewerage, together with £495,928, representing the net revenue from harbour and river improvements, interest on advances to settlers and local bodies, and on the purchase of land for settlement. Besides this, there is a large indirect revenue obtained by each of the states from the opening-up of its public lands, and from the construction of breakwaters, wharves, bridges, and other works of public utility. But even these advantages might have been bought at too high a price if production had not correspondingly advanced. Fortunately such has been the case, as will be seen from the chapters in this volume which deal with the leading items of Australasian production.

Adjusted Revenue and Expenditure.

The form in which the public accounts of the states are presented has led to a great deal of misconception regarding the actual requirements of the various Governments for public purposes. Nor has it been possible to do other than follow that form in the foregoing pages, as otherwise the figures quoted would differ from the various Treasury statements, and add another element of confusion; nevertheless, it would be well before closing the remarks on this branch of public finance to make a separation of the items of revenue and expenditure according to the principles which should govern the presentation of the public accounts. This is effected by treating the services which are generally regarded as outside the functions of the central Government, namely, railways and tramways, and water supply and sewerage, as matters apart from the general receipts and expenditure, and only crediting the state with the surplus from, or debiting it with the cost of these services, after deducting working expenses and making allowance for the estimated interest on the invested capital. Posts and telegraphs have not been excluded in the case of New Zealand, but the exclusion has been made from the returns of the six states of the Commonwealth as the administration is now with the Federal Government. The adjusted revenue for the year 1902-3 will be found below:—

State.	Revenue, excluding Services.*	Net Revenue from Services.*	Total adjusted Revenue.	Per head of Population.
	£	£	£	£ s. d.
New South Wales	6,807,607	....	6,807,607	4 16 10
Victoria	3,893,851	....	3,893,851	3 4 7
Queensland	2,280,550	....	2,280,550	4 8 7
South Australia	1,330,100	....	1,330,100	3 12 8
Western Australia	2,002,167	....	2,002,167	9 6 1
Tasmania	501,919	....	501,919	2 17 2
Commonwealth	16,816,194	....	16,816,194	4 6 7
New Zealand	4,460,653	....	4,460,653	5 10 5
Australasia	21,276,847	....	21,276,847	4 10 8

* Railways, tramways, water supply and sewerage.

It will be seen that none of the states obtained a revenue from its services during 1902–3, after working expenses and interest on capital had been allowed for, a result brought about chiefly by the decrease in the revenue of most of the states, due to the prolonged drought. The next table shows the adjusted expenditure:—

State.	Expenditure, excluding Services.*	Net Expenditure on Services.*	Total adjusted Expenditure.	Per head of Population.
	£	£	£	£ s. d.
New South Wales	6,338,219	640,554	6,978,773	4 19 4
Victoria	3,153,047	546,837	3,699,884	3 1 5
Queensland	1,953,917	517,974	2,471,891	4 16 0
South Australia	1,272,474	167,872	1,440,346	3 18 9
Western Australia	1,862,562	31,130	1,893,692	8 16 0
Tasmania	529,384	88,556	617,940	3 10 3
Commonwealth	15,109,603	1,992,923	17,102,526	4 9 1
New Zealand	4,110,058	117,179	4,227,237	5 4 8
Australasia	19,219,661	2,110,102	21,329,763	4 10 11

* Railways, tramways, water supply and sewerage.

The figures just given show that the actual cost of government is materially less in the states than would appear from the returns of ordinary revenue and expenditure.

Position of Revenue Accounts.

The following table has been compiled with the view of showing the position of the Revenue Account of each state at the close of the last financial year. It will be seen that five of the states have large overdrafts, partly cash and partly in the form of Treasury bills, and that to establish the necessary equilibrium between income and outgo a restricted expenditure by future administrations will be absolutely necessary. For Tasmania the figures refer to the end of the year 1902; for New Zealand, to the 31st March, 1903; and for the other five states, to the 30th June, 1903. The figures given in the last column of the table represent the total debit balances at these dates. It is very necessary that this fact should be borne in mind, as it often happens that the official returns of the states show only the cash overdraft, the amount represented by outstanding Treasury bills being omitted from consideration:—

State.	Cr. Balance.	Dr. Balance.		
		Overdraft represented by Treasury Bills.	Cash Overdraft.	Total Dr. Balance.
	£	£	£	£
New South Wales	....	2,227,626	484,356	2,711,982
Victoria	....	100,000	1,971,644	2,071,644
Queensland	....	1,130,000	23,281	1,153,281
South Australia	....	1,088,950	225,036	1,313,986
Western Australia	231,660	....	....	....
Tasmania	....	....	212,856	212,856
Commonwealth	231,660	4,546,576	2,917,173	7,463,749
New Zealand	519,279	....	....	....
Australasia	750,939	4,546,576	2,917,173	7,463,749

It will be seen that for the state of New South Wales the table shows an overdraft of £2,227,626 which has been liquidated by Treasury bills, and a cash overdraft on 30th June, 1903, of £484,356, inclusive of £236,781 brought forward from the previous year. In reference to the South Australian cash overdraft of £225,036, it should be pointed out that it represents the debit balance for the Northern Territory, while the overdraft liquidated by Treasury bills belongs both to South Australia proper and the Northern Territory. During the year ended 30th June, 1903, the Government issued Treasury bills liquidating the cash overdraft on the 30th June, 1902, for the state proper.

The condition of the revenue accounts of New South Wales, Victoria, and New Zealand needs further explanation. In New South Wales land was resumed in 1889 for the purpose of facilitating certain improvements in connection with a street facing the General Post-office, Sydney, and it was determined that the sum paid for resumption should not be treated as a matter of ordinary expenditure, but be held in suspense pending the sale of the land resumed, or so much of it as was not needed for the formation of the Post-office street. Another resumption of land by the Government of New South Wales was authorised by the Centenary Celebration Act of 1887, which provided for the acquisition of a large area of land, close to Sydney, for the formation of a public park to commemorate the centenary of the state. Of the area so acquired, 640 acres were to be set aside for the park, and the remainder was to be sold, and the proceeds placed against the expenditure. So far no sales have been effected, and in 1894 the payments on account of the formation of the park were transferred from the Consolidated Revenue Fund Account to a special Suspense Account. On the 30th June, 1901, the debit balance of the Centennial Park Account was £228,417, and of the General Post-office New Street Resumption Account, £376,762, neither of which amounts is included in the above table. Legislation has been passed, and Treasury bills have been issued covering the liability under the Suspense Accounts referred to, and the replacing of £150,000 to the credit of the sinking fund for Railway Loan, 53 Vic. No. 24, which was applied to the redemption of the balance of Railway Loan, 31 Vic. No. 11. The authority was for the issue of Treasury bills to the amount of £755,179, which will cover all deficiencies to 30th June, 1902, with the exception of the debit balance of the Consolidated Revenue Fund. Provision was made that on the 31st December, 1902, and on the same day in each year thereafter, until all the payments provided for have been made, the sum of £100,000 was to be paid from the Consolidated Revenue Fund to the credit of the respective accounts mentioned. Such annual sums are in the first place to be paid to the credit of a special Trust Account. In addition to the annual sum of £100,000, the net proceeds of the sales of the unsold portions of the land resumed under the General Post Office (Approaches Improvement) Act of 1889, and the net proceeds of the sale of the unsold portions of the land referred to in the Centenary Celebration Act of 1887 (Centennial Park), are to be paid to the credit of the account. The moneys at credit of such account are to be applied to the purpose of redeeming the bills issued under the Treasury Bills Deficiency Acts of 1901 and 1902, and when all such bills have been redeemed the account is to be closed. The appropriation of £100,000 is, however, to continue to redeem bills issued under the Deficiency Act of 1889, and on the redemption of these bills, the same annual appropriation is to be applied to redeem bills issued under the Deficiency Act of 1895. When this has been effected the appropriation is to lapse. The annual appropriation of £150,000 under the Deficiency Act of 1889 continues, so that the total annual appropriation for the liquidation of the unfunded debt for revenue purposes will be £250,000.

In Victoria certain public works to the amount of £678,624 were undertaken on the understanding that the cost should be defrayed from the proceeds of the sale of certain lands specifically set apart for the purpose. These works have been constructed, but the sales have fallen short to the extent of £330,194, and this sum has been placed to a Suspense Account, which is likewise excluded from the debit balance given above. In the credit balance of New Zealand, shown on page 825, allowance has been made for the transactions of several Suspense Accounts, viz., the State Forests Account, the Local Bodies Account, the Deposits Account, and the State Coal Mines Account; but in order to place the revenue and expenditure of that colony on the same footing as those of the other provinces, the operations on the accounts referred to have not been taken into consideration in the table on page 792. The credit balance of the Consolidated Revenue Fund proper amounted to £303,906.

The practice of issuing Treasury bills for the purpose of liquidating an overdraft, which is illustrated by the above table, obtains in all the states. The bills have been sometimes compared to the exchequer bills issued by the British Treasury. There is, however, only a slight resemblance between the two. The British exchequer bills bear interest at a rate which is fixed from year to year, and at the end of every twelve months the holder has the option of retaining them or presenting them at the Treasury for payment. They are, therefore, readily saleable, and are used with great freedom in commercial transactions, for, as will be seen, they combine the two advantages of ready money and money bearing interest. The Treasury bills of these states, on the other hand, are only payable at the Treasury on the expiry of the period for which they are issued, and they carry interest at a fixed rate during the whole term of currency; consequently they are not used to any extent in commerce. The nearest approach to the British system is that prevailing in New Zealand, where Treasury bills to the amount of £700,000 are outstanding at the close of the financial year, but are redeemed early in the following year. With the exception of these New Zealand bills, Treasury bills are regarded as unfunded or floating debt, and until wiped off form part of the public debt.

Trust Funds.

It may be pointed out here that all the Governments in Australasia hold sums in trust, either directly or indirectly. In some instances these sums are considerable, and are found extremely useful in adjusting the finances, forming a strong reserve which a Government is able to use in tiding over temporary difficulties. It is, however, very questionable whether the existence of a large balance, out of which a necessitous Treasurer can make advances to an overdrawn Revenue or Loans Account, is desirable. In past years it has led to much extravagance that a Treasurer forced to rely on the legitimate revenue of the country would have been compelled to avoid. Several states have seen this, and in Victoria, New Zealand, and South Australia, public trustees have been appointed to control Trust Funds in the hands of the Government; but in the other states these funds are directly subject to the Treasury. The following are the balances of the Trust Funds at the close of the financial year, exclusive of the Funds now dealt with by the Federal Government. The figures for New South Wales, Victoria, Queensland, South Australia, and Western Australia, are for the year ended 30th June, 1903; for

Tasmania, for the year ended 31st December, 1902; and for New Zealand, for the year ended 31st March, 1903 :—

State.	Invested.	Uninvested.	Total.
	£	£	£
New South Wales	6,456,865	4,107,161	10,564,026
Victoria	4,283,534	4,139,038	8,422,572
Queensland	3,210,973	467,505	3,678,478
South Australia	....	525,206	525,206
Western Australia	1,979,146	673,143	2,652,289
Tasmania	596,901	32,425	629,326
Commonwealth	16,527,419	9,944,478	26,471,897
New Zealand	8,745,095	1,025,375	9,770,470
Australasia	25,272,514	10,969,853	36,242,367

The New Zealand figures include £2,706,785 in the hands of the Public Trustees.

Growth of Public Debt.

The practice of raising money for state purposes by means of public loans was begun in 1842, when New South Wales issued debentures redeemable in two years and bearing interest at the rate of 8 per cent. per annum. The sum raised—£45,900—was devoted to immigration purposes. This, as well as the succeeding loans, nine in number, raised prior to 1855, was obtained locally; in the year named, however, New South Wales placed on the London market the first instalment of a 5 per cent. loan for £683,300, which was the first external loan raised, and may be rightly said to mark the commencement of the present Australasian indebtedness.

So far as most of the states are concerned, their public debts date from about the time of their assuming the control of their own affairs; but Western Australia, which obtained responsible government in 1890, incurred liabilities in London as far back as 1872. In the case of that state, however, the granting of Parliamentary government was unduly delayed. The following table is interesting as showing the liabilities of each of the provinces at the date of its taking charge of its own affairs:—

State.	Date of obtaining Responsible Government.	Amount of Debt Liability at that date.
		£
New South Wales	1855	1,386,770
Victoria	1855	480,000
Queensland	1859	Nil
South Australia	1856	294,900
Western Australia	1890	1,367,444
Tasmania	1855	Nil
New Zealand	1856	Nil

No feature of Australasian finance is so astonishing as the growth of the public indebtedness, and this fact has formed the gravamen of the many indictments which have been urged against the states during recent years. The debts have undoubtedly grown at a much more rapid pace than the population; but as the states were in an entirely undeveloped state when public borrowing first came into favour, the more rapid growth of their indebtedness as compared with the population was in a sense the corollary of the position taken up by the various Governments—that the state should reserve to itself the construction of railways and similar undertakings which in other countries are prosecuted by private enterprise. Even with this explanation, however, the figures in the following statement are sufficiently striking:—

State.	1861.	1871.	1881.	1891.	1901-2.	1902-3
	£	£	£	£	£	£
New South Wales	4,017,630	10,614,339	16,924,019	52,950,733	71,592,485	77,[illegible]
Victoria	6,345,060	11,994,800	22,426,502	43,638,897	50,933,957	51,447,906
Queensland	70,000	4,047,859	13,245,150	29,457,134	39,338,427	41,031,247
South Australia	866,509	2,167,700	11,196,800	20,347,125	27,272,545	27,843,870
Western Australia	1,750	Nil	511,000	1,613,594	14,942,310	15,627,298
Tasmania	Nil	1,315,200	2,003,000	7,110,290	9,095,735	9,228,966
Commonwealth	11,300,940	30,139,889	66,306,471	155,117,773	213,175,459	222,871,765
New Zealand..............	600,761	8,900,991	29,659,111	38,844,914	52,966,447	55,899,019
Australasia	11,901.701	39,040,871	95,965,582	193,962,687	266,141,906	278,770,784

The Queensland figures are inclusive of £1,082,020 for Savings Bank Inscribed Stock.

The amounts for the year 1902–3 represent both funded and unfunded debt. In round figures the increase for the states of the Commonwealth from 1861 to 1871 was 19 millions; from 1871 to 1881, 36 millions; from 1881 to 1891, 89 millions; and from 1891 to 1902–3, 67 millions; or for the whole of Australasia, from 1861 to 1871, 27 millions; from 1871 to 1881, 57 millions; from 1881 to 1891, 98 millions; and from 1891 to 1902–3, 85 millions. It must be pointed out that the figures in the last column show the public indebtedness as represented by outstanding debentures or stock; but the real sum is less by the amount of sinking funds in the case of all the states viz., New South Wales, £775,208; Victoria, £241,170; Queensland, £8,079; South Australia, £117,338; Western Australia, £655,069; Tasmania, £242,127; and New Zealand, £2,313,239. In New South Wales, sinking funds have been established in connection with some of the recent loans for the purpose of extinguishing portions of the expenditure on works of an unproductive character, the total amount accrued to 30th June, 1903, being £250,208. There are also annual payments on account of one of the railway loans and the Treasury bills in aid of revenue, but the instalments in the latter case are deducted annually, and the net indebtedness is shown in the statement of the public debt, while for the redemption of the railway loan an amount of £525,000 was in hand at the same date.

The figures showing the total amount of the debt of each state would be incomplete without corresponding information respecting the debt per head of population. In 1861 the public debt of the states included in the Commonwealth stood at £9 13s. 8d. per inhabitant; in 1871, at £17 13s. 11d.; in 1881, at £28 10s. 9d.; in 1891, at £47 14s. 1d.; in 1901–2 it was £55 3s. 10d., while in 1902-3 it was £57 1s. 5d. The corresponding figures for Australasia were: in 1861, £9 8s.; in 1871, £19 16s. 4d.; in 1881, £34 0s. 2d.; in 1891, £49 18s. 4d.; in 1901–2, £57 4s. 8d., and in 1902-3, £59 1s. 3d. For each state the figures are as follows:—

State.	1861.	1871.	1881.	1891.	1901-2.	1902-3.
	£ s. d.	£ s. d.	£ s. d.	£ s. d.	£ s. d.	d.
New South Wales	11 4 5	20 10 0	21 14 8	45 10 8	51 6 0	11
Victoria	11 14 3	16 0 11	25 9 7	37 14 4	42 4 2	8
Queensland	2 0 9	32 6 11	58 7 2	73 12 5	76 8 6	10
South Australia	6 16 8	11 13 7	39 2 1	62 9 11	75 2 10	5
Western Australia	0 2 3	Nil.	17 0 6	30 5 8	71 14 6	6
Tasmania	Nil.	12 18 5	16 16 10	46 11 10	52 4 1	[illegible] 13 4
Commonwealth	9 13 8	17 13 11	28 10 9	47 14 1	55 3 10	57 1 5
New Zealand	6 1 4	33 6 9	59 4 2	61 5 3	67 4 11	68 12 0
Australasia	9 8 0	19 16 4	34 0 2	49 18 4	57 4 8	59 1 3

Of the £222,871,765 which constituted the debt of the states of the Commonwealth in 1902–3, £212,028,414 represented funded debt raised either as debentures or as funded or inscribed stock, and £10,843,351 unfunded or floating debt. For the whole of Australasia, the total debt of £278,770,784 was divided into £267,927,433 of funded debt and £10,843,351 of unfunded debt. The particulars for each state will be found below:—

State.	Date.	Debenture Bonds.	Inscribed and Funded Stock.	Treasury Bills. For Works.	Treasury Bills. In aid of Revenue.	Total.
		£	£	£	£	£
New South Wales	30 June, 1903	*8,367,950	62,118,411	†4,979,000	2,227,626	77,692,987
Victoria	30 June, 1903	17,565,495	32,832,405	950,000	100,000	51,447,900
Queensland	30 June, 1903	13,980,980	25,920,267	....	1,130,000	41,031,247
South Australia	30 June, 1903	9,274,300	17,112,345	367,775	1,088,950	27,843,370
Western Australia	30 June, 1903	221,500	15,405,798	....	....	15,627,298
Tasmania	31 Dec., 1902	3,102,300	6,126,663	....	....	9,228,963
Commonwealth	....	52,512,525	159,515,889	6,296,775	4,546,576	222,871,765
New Zealand	31 Mar., 1903	10,601,997	45,297,022	....	....	55,899,019
Australasia	....	63,114,522	204,812,911	6,296,775	4,546,576	278,770,784

* £1,650 overdue. † £4,000 overdue.

The relative burthen of the public debt of the various states is not to be determined only by comparing the gross amounts with the population, for the rate of interest payable must also be taken into consideration. Thus the general average interest payable by Western Australia is 3·38 per cent., while South Australia pays 3·74 per cent., so that a debt of £100 in the former is not more burthensome than £90 7s. 6d. in the latter state. A more exact basis of comparison is obtained by taking the interest liability, which is shown below. The interest given is on the supposition that the debt is outstanding for the whole of the year following the day on which the amounts are made up. The whole debt, funded and unfunded, has been included :—

State.	Average rate of Interest.			Amount of Interest.			
	Funded Debt.	Unfunded Debt.	Total.	Amount on Outstanding Liabilities.	Per Inhabitant.		
	per cent.	per cent.	per cent.	£	£	s.	d.
New South Wales	3·53	3·55	3·54	2,746,765	1	18	9
Victoria	3·73	3·44	3·72	1,916,175	1	11	10
Queensland	3·69	4·00	3·70	1,518,718	2	18	10
South Australia	3·75	3·50	3·74	1,042,291	2	17	3
Western Australia	3·38	......	3·38	528,609	2	7	2
Tasmania	3·66	......	3·66	338,230	1	19	0
Commonwealth	3·63	3·58	3·63	8,090,788	2	1	5
New Zealand	3·71	......	3·71	2,075,065	2	11	0
Australasia	3·65	3·58	3·65	10,165,853	2	3	1

In 1884 the nominal rate of interest on New South Wales loans floated in London was reduced to 3½ per cent., at which rate stock to the amount of £29,326,200 and Treasury bills for £2,000,000 had been sold to June, 1903. This example was not followed by any of the other states until 1888, when Queensland successfully floated a loan of £2,520,000 at the reduced rate; and in 1889 Victoria, South Australia, Tasmania, and New Zealand, in the order named, were successful in issuing stock at a similar nominal rate. Through the pressure of the financial crisis, the nominal rate for those states which issued in 1893 was increased to 4 per cent. Early in the following year, however, South Australia and Tasmania again placed loans on the market at the lower rate. New Zealand, in May, 1895, was the first colony to issue a 3 per cent. loan —an example which was followed by New South Wales in October of the same year, and by all the states since that date. Tasmania, however, did not place a 3 per cent. loan in London till 1901, but local inscribed stocks had been previously sold at the rate mentioned. Hereunder will be found the amount of the total debt under each rate of interest. For Tasmania the figures refer to the 31st December, 1902; for New Zealand, to the 31st March, 1903; and for all the other states to the 30th June, 1903 :—

Rate of Interest.	New South Wales.	Victoria.	Queensland.	South Australia.	Western Australia.	Tasmania.	Commonwealth.	New Zealand.	Australasia.
				FUNDED DEBT.					
₩ cent.	£	£	£	£	£	£	£	£	£
Nil.	1,650	....	....	....	....	....	1,650	500,000	501,650
6	2,300	....	....	468,900	....	....	471,200	55,200	526,400
5	60,700	....	....	290,000	17,600	100	368,400	557,400	925,800
4½	3,700	5,000,000	....	....	71,400	....	5,075,100	52,900	5,128,000
4	21,665,440	23,310,795	21,384,300	16,302,400	3,485,068	4,101,890	89,649,503	34,504,352	124,153,855
3¾	1,500,000	....	....	....	....	....	1,500,000	349,000	1,849,000
3½	30,567,499	12,001,800	12,527,564	3,363,000	4,703,230	4,054,076	67,216,369	10,367,170	77,583,539
3¼	....	....	....	....	....	29,418	29,418	....	29,418
3	17,285,072	10,686,165	5,989,383	5,962,345	7,350,000	1,043,869	47,716,774	9,512,997	57,229,771
Total	70,486,361	50,397,900	39,901,247	26,386,645	15,627,298	9,228,968	212,028,414	55,899,019	267,927,433
		UNFUNDED DEBT. *(Treasury Bills for Works and Deficiencies in Revenue.)*							
Nil.	4,000	....	....	....	....	....	4,000	....	4,000
4	3,006,500	....	1,130,000	....	....	....	4,136,500	....	4,136,500
3½	2,000,000	800,000	....	1,456,725	....	....	4,256,725	....	4,256,725
3¼	....	250,000	....	....	....	....	250,000	....	250,000
3	2,196,126	....	....	....	....	....	2,196,126	....	2,196,126
Total	7,206,626	1,050,000	1,130,000	1,456,725	....	....	10,843,351	....	10,843,351
Total Debt	77,692,987	51,447,900	41,031,247	27,843,370	15,627,298	9,228,968	222,871,765	55,899,019	278,770,784

The Treasury Bills of New Zealand do not rightly form part of the public debt, and such of these as were outstanding have therefore been excluded from the foregoing statement.

Redemption of Loans.

Loans are either redeemed or renewed. In the former case, the amount of the obligations of the state to its public creditors is reduced : in the latter case, the liability remains the same or is only slightly altered. Repayments, however, are chiefly effected under the head of renewals, the amount of loans redeemed from revenue—by sinking fund, annual drawings, or directly from the general account—being small. The principle of extinguishing public debt by the operation of sinking funds or by annual drawings does not extend to the whole of the public debt of Australasia, and the loans affected do not amount to a large sum. In the case of sinking funds, the money is held until the date of redemption; but exactly the opposite course is followed where annual drawings are provided, for in such cases the Government retire a certain amount of their debentures yearly, and thus effect a gradual extinction of the loan. As already explained, all the states have sinking funds in operation, the amounts to the credit of which will be found on page 829. The system of annual drawings has been adopted to a very limited extent only by New Zealand, New South Wales, and Western Australia; the only loan so issued by New South Wales has, however, been redeemed.

With the exception of one or two small amounts of perpetual or interminable stock, all the Australasian loans are redeemable at prescribed dates; hence the Governments frequently find themselves at the mercy of an adverse market when they are compelled to raise a loan to pay off stock falling due. Within the last few years, however, practical steps have been taken by Victoria, Queensland, South Australia, Western Australia, and Tasmania to avoid this disability, the Governments of those states, in their late issues, having reserved to themselves the option of redeeming at a minimum or a maximum date, or any intervening period, on giving the necessary six or twelve months' notice. Canada was the first of the British possessions to introduce this principle.

Dates of Maturity.

Australasian loans have been issued for fixed periods, and the amount maturing in each year is given in the following statement. No combined action is taken to regulate the raising of loans, each state acting according to the exigencies of its Government, regardless of the financial condition of its neighbours. The placing of a loan on the London market, especially if it be for a large amount, generally results in an all round fall in the prices of Australasian stocks, and subsequent issues of other states are placed at a disadvantage if the market is approached before it has recovered its tone; in fact, the states have in this respect all the evils of disintegration and all the liabilities of federation, without any of the advantages which federation would give. The evil effects of this lack of consultation between the Australian Treasurers will be seen from the table on the opposite page. In ten years only of the next fifty is there no loan to be renewed or to be paid off, and the amounts to be met range as high as £34,878,774. Happily, the amounts to be redeemed during the next decade are moderate, and the fact of heavy obligations requiring to be met in any remote year may prove of advantage, as it will simplify negotiations when the time is ripe for the conversion of Australasian loans into one consolidated stock. Only one colony—New Zealand—is at present systematically working with this end in view, but so far it has treated the question from a provincial standpoint only. The principle of adopting a minimum and a maximum date for repayment has been so recently introduced that, in the table now given, no attempt has been made to show specially the amounts to which it is applicable, the period of redemption in each case being assumed to be the more remote date.

Due Dates.	New South Wales.	Victoria.	Queensland.	South Australia.	Western Australia.	Tasmania.	Commonwealth.	New Zealand.	Australasia
					FUNDED DEBT.				
	£	£	£	£	£	£	£	£	£
Overdue..	1,650	1,000	....	....	....	....	2,650	....	2,650
1903	1,003,700	....	....	....	....	167,994	1,171,694	680,000	1,851,694
1904	58,000	5,457,000	....	62,500	....	24,840	5,602,340	1,698,950	7,301,290
1905	903,800	....	....	72,500	17,600	179,986	1,173,886	1,640,100	2,813,986
1906	224,900	....	....	37,500	....	235,811	498,211	1,799,766	2,297,977
1907	....	4,000,000	....	1,037,500	....	177,046	5,214,546	1,811,800	7,026,346
1908	2,865,500	2,000,000	....	1,951,100	....	382,441	7,199,041	562,338	7,761,379
1909	384,000	....	....	3,122,700	....	117,866	3,624,566	801,000	4,425,566
1910	2,863,700	....	....	60,300	1,573,180	53,048	4,550,178	497,556	5,047,734
1911	....	2,107,000	....	68,300	....	1,024,661	3,199,961	2,843	3,202,804
1912	9,350,351	63,000	....	85,000	....	2,125	9,500,476	....	9,500,476
1913	....	4,746,795	1,466,500	46,300	....	547,650	6,807,245	496,300	7,303,545
1914	....	....	....	35,000	....	800,000	835,000	331,800	1,166,800
1915	....	....	11,728,800	35,000	100	....	11,763,900	3,000	11,766,900
1916	....	....	....	9,486,045	....	100	9,486,145	12,700	9,498,845
1917	...	3,196,933	....	3,546,200	....	....	6,743,133	....	6,743,133
1918	12,826,200	....	....	1,474,400	....	....	14,300,600	....	14,300,600
1919	365,050	4,000,000	....	26,000	....	....	4,391,050	....	4,391,050
1920	....	6,000,000	....	336,300	....	300,000	6,636,300	....	6,636,300
1921	....	6,000,000	....	....	....	228,493	6,228,493	500,000	6,728,493
1922	....	....	....	....	....	8,252	8,252	....	8,252
1923	....	7,297,700	....	....	483,215	....	7,780,915	....	7,780,915
1924	16,698,065	...	12,973,834	1,651,300	....	....	31,323,199	....	31,323,199
1925	222,255	....	....	....	....	4,550	226,805	....	226,805
1926	....	....	....	....	....	67,600	67,600	....	67,600
1927	....	....	....	....	2,500,000	....	2,500,000	....	2,500,000
1928	....	5,528,472	....	200,000	....	....	5,728,472	29,150,302	34,878,774
1930	....	....	3,704,800	....	....	....	3,704,800	....	3,704,800
1931	....	....	....	....	1,876,000	....	1,876,000	....	1,876,000
1933	9,686,300	....	....	....	....	....	9,686,300	....	9,686,300
1934	....	....	....	....	993,353	....	993,353	....	993,353
1935	12,500,000	....	....	....	6,880,000	....	19,380,000	....	19,380,000
1936	....	....	....	332,900	1,100,000	....	1,432,900	....	1,432,900
1939	....	....	....	2,719,800	....	....	2,719,800	....	2,719,800
1940	....	....	....	....	....	4,906,500	4,906,500	6,161,167	11,067,667
1945	....	....	2,000,000	....	....	....	2,000,000	9,512,997	11,512,997
1947	....	....	4,498,693	....	....	....	4,498,693	....	4,498,693
1950	....	....	946,600	....	....	....	946,600	....	946,600
1951	....	....	1,000,000	....	....	....	1,000,000	....	1,000,000
Interminable..	532,890	....	....	....	....	....	532,890	....	532,890
Annual Drawings...	...	....	....	....	203,900	....	203,900	236,400	440,300
Undefined	....	....	1,582,020	....	....	....	1,582,020	....	1,582,020
Total	70,486,361	50,397,900	39,901,247	26 386,645	15,627,298	9,228,963	212,028,414	55,899,019	267,927,433

Due Dates.	New South Wales.	Victoria.	Queensland.	South Australia.	Western Australia.	Tasmania.	Commonwealth.	New-Zealand.	Australasia.
UNFUNDED DEBT. *(Treasury Bills for Works and Deficiencies in Revenue.)*									
	£	£	£	£	£	£	£	£	£
Over-due..	4,000	....	....	....	....	....	4,000	....	4,000
1904	....	50,000	....	361,500	....	....	411,500	....	411,500
1905	2,000,000	50,000	....	710,775	....	....	2,760,775	....	2,760,775
1906	1,000,000	50,000	....	183,700	....	....	1,233,700	....	1,233,700
1907	1,875,000	750,000	....	92,200	....	....	2,717,200	....	2,717,200
1908	100,000	25,000	....	47,575	....	....	172,575	....	172,575
1909	....	25,000	....	60,975	....	....	85,975	....	85,975
1910	....	25,000	....	....	....	....	25,000	....	25,000
1911	....	25,000	....	....	....	....	25,000	....	25,000
1912	....	25,000	530,000	....	....	....	555,000	....	555,000
1913	....	25,000	600,000	....	....	....	625,000	....	625,000
Annual Drawings...	2,227,626	....	....	....	....	....	2,227,626	....	2,227,62
Total	7,206,626	1,050,000	1,130,000	1,456,725	....	....	10,843,351	....	10,843,351
Total Debt	77,692,987	51,447,900	41,081,247	27,843,870	15,627,298	9,228,963	222,871,765	55,899,019	278,770,784

EXPENSES OF NEGOTIATION.

From 1855, when the first New South Wales loan was placed on the London market, until the present time, the Australasian states have obtained from the same source a large proportion of the money which they have borrowed.

The following table shows the amounts raised locally, and in London, but small sums raised in states other than those incurring the debt have been included with the London flotations :—

State.	Raised Locally.			Raised in London.			Total Debt.	Percentage of Loans raised Locally to Total Debt.
	Debentures, Inscribed and Funded Stock.	Treasury Bills for Public Works and in aid of Revenue.	Total.	Debentures, Inscribed and Funded Stock.	Treasury Bills for Public Works and in aid of Revenue.	Total.		
	£	£	£	£	£	£	£	£
New South Wales ..	10,835,911	4,405,126	15,241,037	59,650,450	2,801,500	62,451,950	77,692,987	19·62
Victoria	5,305,428	1,050,000	6,355,428	45,092,472	....	45,092,472	51,447,900	14·09
Queensland	5,242,900	1,130,000	6,372,900	34,658,347	....	34,658,347	41,081,247	15 53
South Australia	3,475,295	1,256,725	4,732,020	22,911,850	200,000	23,111,350	27,848,370	16·99
Western Australia ..	2,056,445	....	2,056,445	13,570,853	....	13,570,853	15,627,298	13·16
Tasmania	1,398,713	....	1,398,713	7,830,250	....	7,830,250	9,228,963	15.15
Commonwealth	28,314,692	7,841,851	36,156,543	183,713,722	3,001,500	186,715,222	222,871,765	16.22
New Zealand	8,006,653	....	8,006,653	47,892,366	....	47,892,366	55,899,019	14·32
Australasia	36,321,345	7,841,851	44,163,196	231,606,088	3,001,500	234,607,588	278,770,784	15·88

The dependence on the English market was originally due to lack of local capital; but even in late years, when such capital has been fairly abundant, the Governments have still turned to London, and, strange to say, have offered the London investor a higher rate than that at which they have been able to place the small loans raised locally.

The charges incidental to the floating of an inscribed stock loan in England are heavy. The chief expense is the stamp duty of 12s. 6d. per cent. imposed by the British Government on inscribed stock, the other charges being for services rendered. New South Wales, Queensland, and New Zealand issue their stock through the Bank of England; the London and Westminster Bank acts for Victoria and Western Australia; South Australia issues its loans through its Agent-General in London; while in the case of Tasmania also the Agent-General is the channel through whom the loans are placed, but he has the assistance of the London and Westminster Bank.

The cost of negotiation by the Bank of England is ½ per cent. commission; and by the London and Westminster Bank, ¼ per cent. Brokerage costs ¼ per cent. In addition to these charges and the stamp duty referred to above, there has usually to be added 4d. or 5d. per £100 for incidental expenses. The charges annually made by the Bank of England for the inscription and management of stock and the payment of the half-yearly dividends were formerly £600 per million for the first ten millions, £550 for the next five, and £500 per million for all subsequent amounts. In 1895, however, these rates were reduced by £100 per million to the three states employing the Bank; while from May, 1899, all amounts raised through the agency of the Bank of England, on behalf of New South Wales, are charged £200 per million. The charges of the London and Westminster Bank were £500 per million for the first ten millions, £450 for a second like sum, and £400 per million for any subsequent amount to the end of 1897, when the Victorian Government arranged with the Bank to reduce its rates for inscription of stock to £250 per million, without regard to the total amount inscribed.

On the old form of debenture the stamp duty imposed is 2s. 6d. per cent., or £1,250 per million. The expenditure per £100 debentures or inscribed stock floated in London of those states for which information is obtainable is given in the subjoined table. The debenture loans shown are some of the last issued. It will be seen that the cost of floating inscribed stock loans is much greater than that under the debenture system, but the extra outlay is inappreciable when compared with the advantages gained :—

State.	Year of Negotiation.	Principal.		Expenses per £100 Debenture and Stock.	Class of Stock.
		Rate of Interest.	Amount.		
			£	£ s. d.	
New South Wales......	1883	4	2,000,000	0 11 5	Debentures.
	1889	3½	3,500,000	1 7 10	Inscribed.
	1891	3½	4,500,000	1 7 9	do.
	1893	4	2,500,000	1 8 0	do.
	1894	3½	832,000	1 9 5	do.
	1895	3	4,000,000	1 7 10	do.
	1898	3	1,500,000	1 8 5	do.
	1901	3	4,000,000	*2 12 8	do.
	1902	3	3,000,000	*2 12 11	do.

* Including underwriting commission.

State.	Year of Negotiation.	Principal.		Expenses per £100 Debenture and Stock.	Class of Stock.
		Rate of Interest.	Amount.		
			£	£ s. d.	
Victoria	1880	4½	2,000,000	0 17 9½	Debentures.
	1891	3½	3,000,000	1 2 9	Inscribed.
	1892	3½	2,000,000	1 3 0	do.
	1893	4	2,107,000	1 3 0	do.
	1899	3	1,600,000	1 2 11	do.
	1901	3	3,000,000	2 8 0	do.
Queensland	1881	4	1,089,500	0 15 9	Debentures
	1890	3½	2,264,734	1 8 0	Inscribed.
	1891	3½	2,500,000	1 8 2	do.
	1893	3½	1,182,400	2 18 8	do.
	1895	3½	1,250,000	1 11 7	do.
	1896	3	1,500,000	1 9 4	do.
	1900	3	1,400,000	2 15 0	do.
	1901	3	1,374,213	2 15 0	do.
South Australia	1883	4	1,438,500	0 9 0	Debentures.
	1889	3½	1,317,800	0 19 1	Inscribed.
	1892	3½	932,300	1 1 2	do.
	1893	3½	125,000	....	do.
	1894	3½	475,600	....	do.
	1894	3½	200,000	....	do.
	1896	3	839,500	1 2 5	do.
	1897	3	500,000	1 0 11	do.
	1899	3	1,500,000	2 4 5	do.
	1900	3	1,000,000	2 7 7	do.
Western Australia	1891	4	250,000	1 3 6	do.
	1892	4	400,000	1 3 7	do.
	1894	4	540,000	1 5 6	do.
	1895	3½	750,000	1 3 7	do.
	1896	3	750,000	1 3 8	do.
	1897	3	1,000,000	1 3 7	do.
	1898	3	1,000,000	1 3 11	do.
	1898	3	1,000,000	1 3 11	do.
	1909	3	1,000,000	2 9 0	do.
	1900	3½	880,000	2 12 3	do.
Tasmania	1886	4	1,000,000	0 18 0	Debentures.
	1889	3½	1,000,000	1 3 6	Inscribed.
	1893	3½	600,000	1 3 5	do.
	1894	4	1,000,000	1 3 8	do.
	1895	3½	750,000	1 4 5	do.
	1901	3	450,000	.. ..	do.
New Zealand	1895	3	1,500,000	2 2 8	do.
	1899	3	1,000,000	1 13 0	do.
	1901	3	1,000,000	....	do.
	1903	3	1,250,000	....	do.

The loan of £3,000,000 raised by Victoria in 1901 was for the purpose of redeeming a similar amount floated in 1876 and falling due on 1st July, 1901.

Against several loans the expenses have not been stated, as the information has not been published by the state interested. The high rate of expenses on the 1893 Queensland loan is accounted for partly by the fact that the amount was underwritten at the rate of 1 per cent. The latest loans issued by all the states and New Zealand have also been burdened with a charge for underwriting.

Quotations of Stock.

In another chapter the growth of Australasian indebtedness on private account has been traced over a period of about thirty-two years, and it has been shown that during that time nearly the whole of the advances made to the various state governments, and one hundred and eighteen millions of private advances, have been obtained in Great Britain. This condition of dependence on external capital for the development of the country has on more than one occasion proved a great danger to Australasia, but never to the same extent as during the crisis of 1892–93. The withdrawal of confidence on the part of the British investor at that time caused widespread confusion in almost every department of industry, with intense financial unrest, from which some of the states have not yet recovered, although, as will be seen from the appended table, Australasian stocks are now quoted at satisfactory prices.

The quotations for Colonial stocks in the London markets at the close of June, 1892, 1893, 1894, and 1903 are given below, the price in every instance being "cum dividend." With one exception—India—the quotations are for loans raised on the security of the local revenues of the country borrowing; in the case of India there is an Imperial guarantee. This advantage has also been extended to some Canadian, Mauritius, and New Zealand loans, but these are not quoted in the following list. In passing, it may be mentioned that the guarantee of the British Government is certainly to the advantage of the dependencies to which it has been extended, as in addition to the absolute security afforded, it carries the right of trustees in the United Kingdom to invest trust funds in the stock—a privilege which was not extended to Australasian securities till September, 1901:—

Country.	Class of Stock.	Selling Price, "cum dividend."			
		June, 1892.	June, 1893.	June, 1894.	June, 1903.
Australasia—					
New South Wales	$3\frac{1}{2}$ per cent. Inscribed	$96\frac{7}{8}$	93	$98\frac{7}{8}$	$99\frac{1}{16}$
Victoria	$3\frac{1}{2}$ do do	97	$88\frac{1}{2}$	$97\frac{1}{2}$	$97\frac{11}{16}$
Queensland	4 do do	$103\frac{1}{2}$	99	104	$104\frac{1}{16}$
South Australia	4 do do	106	103	$106\frac{1}{2}$	$103\frac{7}{16}$
Western Australia	4 do do	$103\frac{1}{2}$	104	108	$103\frac{1}{8}$
Tasmania	4 do do	103	$98\frac{1}{2}$	103	$100\frac{13}{16}$
New Zealand	4 do do	$104\frac{1}{2}$	$104\frac{1}{2}$	$108\frac{7}{8}$	$107\frac{13}{16}$
Canada	3 do do	$94\frac{1}{2}$	96	97	$101\frac{3}{8}$
Cape Colony	4 do do	106	108	112	$105\frac{3}{8}$
Natal	4 do do	103	108	109	$111\frac{11}{16}$
India	3 do Stocks	$97\frac{1}{4}$	$98\frac{1}{2}$	$99\frac{1}{4}$	$97\frac{1}{16}$

In order to make the comparison between different stocks quite fair, other things than bare quotations on a given date—chiefly the accrued interest and the unexpired currency of the scrip—have to be considered. A uniform date for the payment of interest on loans has not been adopted, so that the amount of interest accrued at the above-quoted dates varies with each loan; while the date on which the loan is repayable is a factor not to be neglected in estimating the price of a stock. The return obtained by investors from the inscribed stock of each colony on the basis of previous quotations, allowing for interest accrued and redemption at par on maturity, is given below:—

Country.	Nominal rate of Interest.	Selling Price, "ex dividend."	Currency.	Effective annual Rate of Interest per £100 sterling. — If no allowance is made for redemption at par on maturity.	Effective annual Rate of Interest per £100 sterling. — Rate if Stock is held till date of maturity.
	℔ cent.	£	Years.	£ s. d.	£ s. d.
June, 1892.					
Australasia—					
New South Wales	3½	96·19	32	3 13 5	3 14 2¾
Victoria	3½	95·45	31	3 13 11¾	3 15 0
Queensland	4	101·72	32	3 19 5	3 19 1¼
South Australia	4	105·22	44	3 16 9½	3 16 4
Western Australia	4	101·72	42	3 19 5	3 19 3
Tasmania	4	101·22	16	3 19 10	3 19 0
New Zealand	4	104·05	37	3 17 8	3 17 1¼
Canada	3	93·17	46	3 4 10½	3 5 7½
Cape Colony	4	105·89	31	3 16 3¾	3 15 1½
Natal	4	102·55	34	3 18 9½	3 18 4½
India	3	96·69	56	3 2 6¼	3 2 9
June, 1893.					
Australasia—					
New South Wales	3½	92·33	31	3 16 5½	3 18 2¼
Victoria	3½	86·97	30	4 1 2¼	4 4 3¼
Queensland	4	97·25	31	4 3 1	4 3 7½
South Australia	4	102·23	43	3 19 0¼	3 18 10
Western Australia	4	102·25	41	3 19 0¼	3 18 9½
Tasmania	4	96·75	15	4 3 6	4 6 0¼
New Zealand	4	104·06	36	3 17 8	3 17 1
Canada	3	94·68	45	3 3 10	3 4 5½
Cape Colony	4	107·90	30	3 14 10½	3 13 2¼
Natal	4	107·56	33	3 15 1½	3 13 9¾
India	3	97·92	55	3 1 8¾	3 1 0¼

Country.	Nominal rate of Interest.	Selling Price, "ex dividend."	Currency.	Effective annual Rate of Interest per £100 sterling. If no allowance is made for redemption at par on maturity.	Rate if Stock is held till date of maturity.
	℔ cent.	£	Years.	£ s. d.	£ s. d.
June, 1894.					
Australasia—					
New South Wales	3½	98·21	30	3 11 10¾	3 12 4
Victoria	3½	95·92	29	3 13 7¼	3 14 8
Queensland	4	102·25	30	3 19 0¼	3 18 6½
South Australia	4	105·74	42	3 16 5	3 15 10½
Western Australia	4	106·25	40	3 16 0½	3 15 4½
Tasmania	4	101·25	14	3 19 9½	3 18 9
New Zealand	4	108·45	35	3 14 6	3 13 2¼
Canada	3	95·68	44	3 3 2¼	3 3 8
Cape Colony	4	111·91	29	3 12 2½	3 9 5
Natal	4	108·57	32	3 14 5	3 12 9¾
India	3	98·68	54	3 1 3	3 1 4¼
June, 1903.					
Australasia—					
New South Wales	3½	99·30	21	3 11 1¼	3 11 5¼
Victoria	3½	97·44	23	3 12 5½	3 15 6
Queensland	4	104·21	21	3 17 6¼	3 15 8½
South Australia	4	103·70	33	3 17 11	3 17 3¼
Western Australia	4	103·20	28	3 18 3½	3 17 6
Tasmania	4	100·71	5	4 0 2¾	3 17 9½
New Zealand	4	107·53	26	3 15 1¾	3 12 11½
Canada	3	101·66	35	2 19 5½	2 19 1¼
Cape Colony	4	105·87	20	3 16 4	3 13 6¾
Natal	4	111·53	23	3 12 5¼	3 8 3
India	3	97·90	45	3 2 0	3 2 2¾

The figures given in the last column of the table show the relative positions of the various stocks quoted. As will be seen, the credit of each division of Australasia was somewhat better in 1894 than in 1892, notwithstanding the financial panic which occurred between those dates. In 1893 there was naturally a heavy fall, as compared with the preceding year, in all Australasian securities except those of New Zealand and Western Australia. Victorian stock showed the largest fall—which was only to be expected in view of the fact that the panic originated in that state. The quotation for New Zealand stock at the middle of 1893 was the same as that of the preceding year, which seemed to point to the conclusion that the London market did not consider the interests of New Zealand to be bound up with those of the states on the mainland. In 1895 a great improvement took place in the prices of stock of all the states, and the rise has since been well maintained. To illustrate the fluctuations in the prices of colonial securities, the rates obtained during 1892, 1893, 1894, and 1903 are given below in a simpler form than in the preceding table. It is probable that the price of Victorian securities would have been higher were it not for the large sum falling due this year.

Country.	1892.	1893.	1894.	1903.
Australasia—	£ s. d.	£ s. d.	£ s. d.	£ s. d.
New South Wales	3 14 2¾	3 18 2¼	3 12 4	3 11 5¼
Victoria	3 15 0	4 4 3¼	3 14 8	3 15 6
Queensland	3 19 1¼	4 3 7½	3 18 6½	3 15 8½
South Australia	3 16 4	3 18 10	3 15 10½	3 17 3¼
Western Australia	3 19 3	3 18 9½	3 15 4¼	3 17 6
Tasmania	3 19 0	4 6 0¼	3 18 9	3 17 9½
New Zealand	3 17 1¼	3 17 1	3 13 2½	3 12 11½
Canada	3 5 7½	3 4 5½	3 3 8	2 19 1¼
Cape Colony	3 15 1½	3 13 2¼	3 9 5	3 13 6¾
Natal	3 18 4½	3 13 9¾	3 12 9¾	3 8 3
India	3 2 9	3 1 0¼	3 1 4¼	3 2 2¾

So far, only the return yielded to the investor has been considered. The following table shows the average prices obtained by the Australasian Governments for some of their last issues, and the quotations for the same stocks in June, 1903, the latter prices being, of course, "ex dividend":—

State.	Date of Negotiation.	Rate per cent.	Amount of Issue.	Net average price realised.	Quotation, ex-dividend, June, 1903.
			£	£	£
New South Wales.........	1895	3	4,000,000	95·14	89·90
Do	1898	3	1,500,000	98·65	89·90
Do	1901	3	4,000,000	91·12	89·90
Do	1902	3	3,000,000	90·90	89·90
Victoria	1893	4	2,107,000	96·00	99·21
Do	1899	3	1,600,000	93·21	88·41
Do	1901	3	3,000,000	89·36	88·41
Queensland	1897	3	1,500,000	95·61	91·16
Do	1900	3	1,400,000	91·26	91·16
Do	1900	3	1,374,213	91·50	91·16
South Australia............	1896	3	839,500	95·34	92·00
Do	1897	3	500,000	96·05	92·00
Do	1899	3	1,500,000	92·67	92·00
Do	1900	3	1,000,000	90·81	92·00
Western Australia	1897	3	1,000,000	93·45	91·65
Do	1898	3	1,000,000	94·76	91·65
Do	1898	3	1,000,000	91·96	91·65
Do	1900	3	1,000,000	89·66	91·65
Do	1900	3½	880,000	97·39	99·59
Tasmania	1895	3½	750,000	98·30	100·44
Do	1895	3	450,000	....	*
New Zealand..............	1895	3	1,500,000	93·73	91·90
Do	1899	3	1,000,000	96·55	91·90
Do	1901	3	1,000,000	....	91·90
Do	1903	3	1,250,000	....	*

* No quotation.

Character of Stock Issued.

By far the larger part of Australasian loans is inscribed, and the outstanding issues under the debenture system are being converted into inscribed stock as quickly as circumstances permit. New Zealand was the first colony to introduce inscription in 1877, in which year was passed the Consolidated Stock Act, a measure made necessary by the abolition of the Provincial Councils. Under this Act the liabilities of the various provinces were merged into the general debt of the colony; and under the same Act and its amendment of 1884 the Government has worked systematically to consolidate the debt by conversion and inscription, so that in March, 1903, the whole of the public liabilities were inscribed, with the exception of £10,601,997 represented by debentures. The Consolidated Stock Act of New Zealand was assented to in December, 1877; and in August of that year the Imperial Parliament passed the Colonial Stock Act, which provided for the inscription and transfer of Colonial stock raised in the United Kingdom. Certain steps were required to be taken before a colony could take advantage o the provisions of the Imperial Act. As already mentioned, New Zealand passed the necessary legislation at the end of 1877; but nothing was done by the other states until 1882, when Victoria and South Australia passed Inscribed Stock Acts; New South Wales and Queensland passed similar legislation in the following year, Western Australia in 1884, and Tasmania in 1889. It will thus be seen that a gradual change in the mode of floating loans for public purposes has been going on since 1877, and the time cannot be far distant when the whole debt of each state will be represented by one class of stock. In 1879, or two years after passing the Consolidated Stock Act, New Zealand placed on the market a 5 per cent. loan of £5,000,000 at 97½ in the form of debentures, the subscribers having the option up to March, 1881, of exchanging for 4 per cent. inscribed stock, at the rate of £120 of stock for each £100 of debentures. The loan was successfully floated, and within the stated period £4,476,000 of the £5,000,000 debentures were exchanged for £5,371,200 inscribed stock at 4 per cent. The other states issued inscribed stock loans shortly after passing the respective Acts.

The Imperial Colonial Stock Act, 1877, as previously mentioned, provides for the inscription and transfer of stock raised in the United Kingdom and for stamp duty to be levied thereon. It also defines the position of the British Government as regards Colonial indebtedness, and provides that every document connected with stock transactions shall have printed upon it a distinct intimation that no liability, direct or indirect, is incurred by the British Government in respect of such stock, unless the loan is under Imperial guarantee.

Under the provisions of the Colonial Stock Act, 1900, trustees are empowered to invest in Australasian securities after certain conditions have been complied with, and these conditions were proclaimed in the *London Gazette* of 6th September, 1901.

The difference between registered and inscribed stock is practically small. Transactions under the former head are confined to a few old funded stock loans. Debentures and inscribed stock form the principal classes of securities, and, as previously pointed out, the debenture form is rapidly giving way to inscription. Debenture coupons are, like ordinary scrip, negotiable by bearer, and are liable to the risk of forgery. By inscription the possibilities of fraud in transfer are minimised, as the stock is inscribed in the books of the bank, and transferable therein by the stock-holders personally or by their attorneys, without the issue of certificates of stock. In the case of registered stock, certificates are issued transferable by deed.

The practice of issuing Treasury bills, either in anticipation of or to make good deficiencies in revenue, obtains in each state, and, as previously explained, is an old-established custom; but Treasury bills have been made to serve another purpose, and money has been raised by their sale to meet certain obligations for public works. This is an innovation which could not well be avoided in the disturbed markets of the last few years.

The bills are in reality ordinary loans with short currencies, and carry generally a higher rate of interest than issues of the funded debt. The unsatisfactory state of Australasian finance does not allow of the absolute redemption of these bills; consequently they will either have to be renewed or converted into stock, an operation which will entail an additional expenditure to the charges of first negotiation. The New Zealand Treasury bills are issued direct by the Treasury at par, and the expenses of negotiation are small. The bills are usually redeemed during the year of issue, and for this reason they have not been included with or considered as part of the public debt of New Zealand, though in the case of the other states Treasury bills have been so included.

CONVERSION AND CONSOLIDATION OF LOANS.

Conversion and consolidation as applied to loans are not interchangeable terms, but represent two distinct transactions in so far related that without conversion consolidation would be impracticable. All the states are systematically converting their old loans into inscribed stock, and by so doing they are taking a step towards consolidation. Since the Consolidated Stock Act was passed in 1877, New Zealand has been engaged in converting its old loans into inscribed stock, and consolidating the whole debt by adopting three uniform interest rates of 4, 3½, and 3 per cent., and fixing the dates of maturity at 1929, 1940, and 1945 respectively. The transactions in conversion and consolidation in New Zealand from 1877 to 31st March, 1903, were as stated below. In addition to the transactions shown, old debentures to the amount of £6,225,500 were converted into short-dated debentures under the 1884 Consolidated Stock Act, pending subsequent conversion into inscribed stock; of these short-dated debentures, £4,257,700 have since been converted into 4 per cent. stock, and are included in the £19,724,400 shown below. The amount of these debentures outstanding on 31st March, 1903, was £1,967,800:—

Amount of Old Debentures Converted or Redeemed.	Additional Capital added to Principal by Conversion or Consolidation.	New Stock Issued.		
		Nominal Rate of Interest.	Amount.	Date of Maturity.
£	£		£	
19,724,400	1,600,902	4 per cent.	21,325,302	1929
5,720,550	440,617	3½ „	6,161,167	1940
3,919,332	68,665	3 „	3,987,997	1945

The loading of the principal by conversion appears heavy; but New Zealand was saddled with a number of small loans, much after the type of municipal borrowings, which it was most desirable should be consolidated without delay, and some sacrifice was made to accomplish this; besides, the compensation obtained in a lower rate of interest must be set against the increased capital. The annual saving in interest on the amount converted to the 31st March, 1903, is stated as £203,658, viz., £102,114 on the 4 per cent., £59,262 on the 3½ per cent., and £42,282 on the 3 per cent. stock. All conversions into short-dated debentures took place at par, the saving in interest thereby amounting to £7,990 annually, in addition to the £203,658 shown above. The subject of the New Zealand conversion is a large one, and inquirers should consult the publications of the Government of that colony, which give details that would hardly be in place in a volume such as this.

In Victoria the 4 per cent. stock floated in Melbourne to the amount of £2,089,613 was converted during 1898-9 into 3 per cent. stock, with the exception of £120,062 subsequently redeemed. The saving in interest by the conversion is £19,696.

Late Issues of Loans and Treasury Bills.

As late as the year 1890 the states could borrow in London on very favourable terms, but in the year named the conditions were no longer satisfactory. This change had for its immediate cause a condition of things not of Australasia's own creation, the Baring failure and the Argentine crisis being primarily responsible for the stoppage of Australasian credit; but there is no reasonable ground for supposing that if the Baring failure had not taken place the London markets would have been much longer open to the Australasian states. The Treasurers of the various provinces were entirely unprepared for this revulsion in credit. They were committed to engagements for the construction of public works which they could not terminate; contracts had been entered into for large sums on the assumption that funds would be available; besides this, no preparations had been made to meet debentures falling due in a short time. The sudden stoppage of credit greatly embarrassed the Governments, and most of the states had recourse to Treasury bills to enable them to adjust their finances to the altered circumstances. The amounts received from the sale of these bills were devoted to meeting loans maturing, and providing funds for public works already contracted for. Pressing necessities and the improved condition of the London market encouraged several of the states during 1893 and 1894 to place ordinary loan issues, which were successfully negotiated; and the proceeds of these loans relieved the liabilities on matured Treasury bills and current obligations. In 1895 the credit of the Australasian states was fully re-established in London.

New South Wales.—In 1892 and 1893 the Treasury had authority to issue £3,000,000 of 4 per cent. funded stock at a minimum price of par. Up to the 30th June, 1902, £2,549,350 had been disposed of, leaving stock to the amount of £450,650 yet to be raised, the cost of the issue being practically nil.

The Loan Acts 58 Vic. No. 14, 59 Vic. No. 6, 60 Vic. No. 32, 61 Vic. No. 43, 62 Vic No. 36, and 63 Vic. No. 42, passed in 1894, 1895, 1896, 1897, 1898, and 1899 respectively, provided for the establishment of other local stocks. The stocks under the first-mentioned Act are known as New South Wales 1924 Stock and Funded Stock, the latter running *pari passu* with the stock floated under 56 Vic. No. 1, the amounts outstanding on 30th June, 1903, being £198,065 and £863,947 respectively; the stocks under the 1895 Act are known as New South Wales 1925 Stock and Funded Stock, the latter also being subject to the same conditions as that floated under 56 Vic. No. 1 (Funded Stock Act of 1892). The amounts outstanding on the 30th June, 1903, were £222,255 and £1,332,945 respectively. The stocks under the 1896 Act are known as New South Wales 1927 Stock and Funded Stock, and are subject to conditions similar to those imposed in respect of the issues under the 1894 and 1895 Acts. Up to the 30th June, 1903, sales of funded stock had been effected to the extent of £1,802,810. The rate of interest on the stock is 3 per cent., and the date of maturity, 1912. The stocks under the 1897 Act are known as New South Wales 1928 Stock and Funded Stock, and are issued under the same conditions as those already referred to. The amount of funded stock sold to 30th June, 1903, was £1,241,299, the rate being 3½ per cent., and the date of maturity, 1912. The only expense attached to the issues was a small amount for brokerage. The stocks under the 1898 Act are known as New South Wales 1929 Stock and Funded Stock, and are issued under similar conditions to those already adverted to. The amount of funded stock sold to 30th June, 1903, was £1,500,000, the rate being 3¾ per cent., and the date of maturity 1912. No expense was attached to the issue. Provision has been made for sinking funds to liquidate certain portions of the loans expended on works of an unproductive character. With regard to the loan authorised under the Loan Act 1899, it must be mentioned that no sales have yet taken place under that Act, but the annual instalment for the Sinking Fund has been appropriated each year.

The Loan Act of 1899 gave authority for the local issue of £500,000 inscribed stock at 3 per cent., and maturing in 1919, for the purpose of making advances to settlers. Under the Advances to Settlers (Amendment) Act, No. 106 of 1902, the issue was increased to £1,000,000. Of this stock, £365,050 were issued to the 30th June, 1903. As in the case of the 4 per cent. funded stock, the only expense in connection with the later local issues of funded and inscribed stock was a small amount of brokerage.

In October, 1893, an inscribed stock loan of £2,500,000 was floated in London, the rate of interest being 4 per cent., and the currency forty years. The minimum price was fixed at 98½, and the average price realised was £100 11s. 10½d. The rate paid by the Government, allowing for redemption at par on maturity, was £4 3s. 0¼d.; while the return to investors was £4 1s. 8½d.

During 1894 several small 5 per cent. loans matured, amounting in the aggregate to £832,000. In September of that year a 3½ per cent. covering loan was successfully issued, the average price realised on the gross proceeds being £101 15s., which is reduced to £99 13s. 6d. if allowance be made for accrued interest and charges. The rate paid by the Government is £3 10s. 11d. per cent., and the interest yielded to investors, £3 9s. 4¼d. The loan was subscribed over five-fold, the amount tendered being £4,268,000.

In October, 1895, an inscribed stock loan for £4,000,000 was floated, the rate of interest being 3 per cent., and the currency forty years. The minimum price was fixed at 94, and the gross proceeds averaged £96 18s. 3d. The next flotation on the London market took place in January, 1898, when a loan of £1,500,000, bearing interest at 3 per cent., with a minimum of 99, was successfully floated, the gross proceeds being £1,506,269. The actual rate paid by the Government was £3 1s. 6d., and the yield to investors, allowing for redemption at par, was £3 0s. 4½d.

In September, 1901, stock to the amount of £4,000,000 was authorised to be raised for the purpose of resuming wharfs and other premises and services generally. The loan was negotiated at 94, the nominal rate being 3 per cent., and the due date 1935. The actual cost to the Government was £3 9s. per cent., while the yield to investors was £3 5s. 10d. In May, 1902, a 3 per cent. loan of £3,000,000 was placed in London at a fixed price of 94½, the total applications being £35,420,000. The gross proceeds amounted to £2,835,000, and the net proceeds available for expenditure, after allowing for accrued interest, underwriting, and other expenses, were £2,727,191, or £90 18s. 1½d. per £100. The actual rate per cent. payable by the Government, allowing for redemption at par on maturity, is £3 8s. 7d. per £100, and the yield to investors £3 6s. 1¼d.

In 1895 authority was given to issue Treasury bills to the amount of £1,174,700 to cover the accumulated deficiencies in revenue on the 30th June of that year. The rate of interest allowed is 3 per cent., and a sum of £150,000 is set aside annually for the repayment of the debt, together with the Treasury bills issued under the Act of 1889.

In 1899 the London market was practically closed to the state government, chiefly on account of the South African war; and, as money was urgently required to complete existing contracts, and to provide for urgent works, authority was obtained under Act 63 Vic. No. 46 for the issue of short-dated Treasury bills to the amount of £4,000,000. The first instalment, viz., £1,000,000 at 4 per cent. was negotiated in London, the net proceeds realising £99 12s. per £100—the cost to the Government being £4 9s. 11¾d., and the yield to investors £4 6s. 0¼d. The second instalment, amounting to £500,000, was placed locally at 3½ per cent., the net average price realised being 100·14 per £100. The actual cost to the Government was £3 10s. 7½d., and the yield to investors £3 9s. 6d. During 1900-1 three instalments of £500,000 each at 3½ per cent. were sold at the Treasury in Sydney. The net averages per £100 were 99·92, 99·71, and 99·37 respectively, and the corresponding amounts paid by the Government were £3 10s. 11¾d., £3 11s. 9¾d., and £3 13s. 3¼d., the yield to investors being £3 10s. 3¼d., £3 11s. 4½d., and £3 12s. 9d. respectively. The balance, viz., £1,000,000, was floated in London at 4 per cent., the net price per £100 being 98·63—the cost to Government, £4 8s. 1d., and the actual yield to investors, £4 6s. 1d. During 1901 Treasury bills to the amount of £755,179 were issued to cover deficiencies in revenue to the 30th June, 1902, exclusive of the debit balance of the Consolidated Revenue Fund. The rate allowed is 3 per cent., and the bills are repayable by annual instalments of £100,000. During the year ended 30th June, 1903, Treasury bills for public works were issued in London, under the authority of 2. Edw. VII No. 94 for £1,000,000, £600,000 and £200,000, carrying interest at the rate of 4 per cent., redeemable in 1907. After allowing for charges of negotiation, the net amount raised in each case was £996,250, £597,750, and £197,750, or a net price per £100 in relation of the first two of 99·63, and in the last 98·88. Under the same authority Treasury bills were issued locally to the amount of £175,000 with interest at the rate of 4 per cent., £75,000 being redeemable in 1907, and £100,000 in 1909; no expense was attached to these issues.

Victoria.—An inscribed stock loan of £2,107,000 was floated in London in October, 1893, the rate of interest being 4 per cent., and the date of maturity between 1911 and 1926, at the option of the Government on due notice being given. A 3 per cent. inscribed stock loan of £1,600,000 was floated in London in February, 1899—the minimum price fixed being £95. The gross proceeds amounted to £1,522,835, and the net proceeds to £1,491,355, or to £93 4s. 2d. per £100. The date of maturity is from 1929 to 1949. Four per cent. debentures were also disposed of locally from March, 1893, to June, 1903, to the amount of £746,795, and 3 per cent. debentures, amounting to £1,063,000, had been sold in Melbourne to the same date.

During 1896 an Act was passed providing for the conversion of the 4 per cent. stocks on the Melbourne register into a 3 per cent. stock. The amount of 4 per cent. stock sold from January, 1895, to June, 1903, was £249,130, holders of which have availed themselves of the privilege of conversion. The amount of new 3 per cent. stock sold under the Conversion Act to 30th June, 1903, was £2,290,482.

In December, 1898, and December, 1901, Acts were passed providing for the issue of local inscribed stock at 3 per cent. to the amount of £400,000, and on the 30th June, 1903, the total sales amounted to £206,285. Another Act for the same purpose became law in November, 1899, the amount authorised being £500,000 at 3 per cent., of which £247,174 had been sold to 30th June, 1903.

An issue of 4 per cent. Treasury bills in aid of revenue to the amount of £1,250,000 was authorised in 1893; in 1898, however, the amount was reduced to £250,000. The amount sold to 30th June, 1903, was £250,000, of which £150,000 have been redeemed.

In September, 1896, authority was given for the issue of £375,000 Treasury bills for public works and services. The amount sold to the 30th June, 1903, was £375,000, bearing interest at 3¼ per cent., and repayable in annual instalments of £25,000 each. The total amount of Treasury bills outstanding under this Act on the 30th June, 1903, was £250,000.

A further issue of £1,000,000 Treasury bills was authorised in December, 1898, and, to the 30th, June, 1903, bills to the amount of £500,000 were sold locally at 3½ per cent. interest, and to the amount of £500,000 at 4 per cent. interest in London. These bills were converted into stock in January, 1903, carrying interest at the rate of 3 per cent. The total amount of Treasury bills outstanding on 30th June, 1903, was £1,050,000.

On the 22nd March, 1901, a loan of £3,000,000 at 3 per cent. was floated in London for conversion purposes, the price being fixed at 93½. The expenses were increased by a charge of 1¼ per cent. for underwriting, and, consequently, the net proceeds realised only £89 17s. 3d. per £100. Debentures to the amount of £500,000 at 3 per cent. were disposed of locally on the 21st August, 1900, realising £96 10s. 5d. per £100, and a further instalment of £500,000, sold on 4th June, 1901, realised £96 8s. 1d. per £100. Local 3 per cent. inscribed stock, amounting to £86,833, was also taken up during 1900–1, at par or a slight premium.

To meet £5,000,000 debentures at 4½ per cent., falling due on 1st January, 1904, arrangements were made in London during October, 1903, for their conversion. The present holders of the maturing debentures were offered the following options, viz.:—(1) £108 of 3½ per cent. inscribed stock, due 1929-49, at the Government's option, acceptors to retain the interest coupons on the 4½ per cent. debentures due on 1st January, 1904, and equal to 2¼ per cent., while the new 3½ per cents. will carry interest as from 1st October, 1903; (2) for every £100 of 4½ per cent. debentures, £100 in Treasury bills, bearing interest at 4 per cent. and maturing on 1st July, 1906, acceptors to be paid 25s. per cent. in cash, and have the option, up to 31st December, 1905, of converting into 3½ per cent. inscribed stock, due 1929-49, at par, six months' interest to be paid on the Treasury bills on 1st July, 1904. At latest advices about £3,500,000 were converted on the terms. The balance of £1,598,000 was offered to the public, with the option of taking 3½ per cent. stock at £92 12s. 6d., or 4 per cent. Treasury bonds at £98 15s. On the date on which the applications were opened (14th November), about £250,000 were taken up by the public, the balance, £1,350,000, being taken by the underwriters.

Queensland, in January, 1893, placed a 3½ per cent. loan of £1,182,400 on the London market, the average price obtained being £88 14s. 0½d. The charges were heavier than usual, as the loan was underwritten at the rate of 1 per cent.

In June, 1895, another 3½ per cent. loan for £1,250,000, with a currency of fifty years, was placed on the market. The gross price obtained was £101 12s. 7d., and deducting accrued interest the Government received about £100 0s. 2d. In addition, stock to the amount of £750,000 was sold locally, the net proceeds being £743,750, or £99 3s. 4d. per £100.

In June, 1897, a 3 per cent. loan for £1,500,000, repayable in 1947, was floated in London, the average price realised being £97 1s. 5d. Local sales of 3 per cent. stock were also negotiated during the year, the total issued being £124,480, which was sold at the average price obtained in London.

In July, 1898, an amount of £100,000 at 3 per cent. was sold locally at £97 1s. 5d. per £100, and in December, 1899, further sales to the extent of £750,000, also at 3 per cent., took place at an average of 97. In July, 1900, loans amounting to £150,000 at 3 per cent., and £1,400,000 at the same rate, were floated in Brisbane and London respectively, the average prices realised being £97 for the former issue, and £94 0s. 2d. for the latter. The expenses of the London issue were largely increased owing to an underwriting commission of 1¼ per cent. In 1900, further sales to the amount of £2,374,213 took place, £1,000,000 of which bearing interest at 3½ per cent. was sold locally, and the balance, which carries 3 per cent., in London. The former realised £99 7s. 7¾d. (net) per £100, and the latter, £88 12s. 4d. per £100.

Another class of stock was authorised in 1895, viz., Government Savings Bank Stock. The object of the establishment of this class of security was to enable depositors of over £200 to earn interest on such excess. On the 30th June, 1903, the amount outstanding was £1,082,020, of which £991,330 is bearing interest at 3½ per cent., and £90,690 at 3 per cent.

During 1893 three issues of Treasury bills were placed locally, viz., £222,500 in January, £5,000 in April, and £11,000 in December. The rate of interest was 4 per cent., and the bills have been redeemed. In January, 1894, bills to the amount of £1,000 were also disposed of locally, the rate being the same as for the previous issues, and the date of redemption, 1903. Bills to the amount of £286,000, which were issued during 1897–8, under the 1893 Act, have been purchased with the proceeds of the Savings Bank Stock. Under the Treasury Bills Act of 1901, authority was given for the issue of bills to the amount of £530,000 to cover deficiencies in revenue. The rate of interest was fixed at 4 per cent., and the due date is 1912. The total amount realised, less expenses, was £535,119, or £100 19s. 5d. per £100.

Under the Treasury Bills Act of 1902, authority was given for the issue of bills to the amount of £600,000 to cover deficiencies in revenue. The rate of interest was determined at 4 per cent., and the due date is 1913. The total amount realised, less expenses, was £603,826, or £100 12s. 9d. per £100.

South Australia.—In 1893 a small loan of £125,000, being portion of the 1890 loan of £1,532,900, was floated in London. The rate of interest is 3½ per cent., and the loan is redeemable in 1939. An instalment of the £1,013,279 loan of 1892 was placed in Adelaide in February, 1894. The amount of the issue was £200,000, the price realised per £100 being £92. The rate of interest is 3½ per cent. In June, 1895, a further issue of £311,000 was floated in Adelaide. In February, 1896, a loan of £839,500 was issued in London, bearing interest at 3 per cent., and redeemable in 1926. The net proceeds, after allowing for charges and accrued interest, amounted to £800,406, or £95 6s. 10d. per cent. In May, 1897, the first of a number of loans under the "Consolidated Stock Act" was floated in London, amounting to £500,000. Further issues took place in Adelaide for £295,835 and £606,800 ; in London and Adelaide, for £1,500,000 ; and in Adelaide, for £249,075. Of the last issue, £36,000 were sold at par, on condition of being placed on the London register, while the balance realised £98 17s. 3d. per cent. The first issue of £500,000 was sold for £94 7s. 4d. ; the £295,835 for £99 18s. 8d. ; the £606,800, for £98 3s. 9d. ; and the £1,500,000, for £94 17s. 10½d. per cent. The total issues under the "Consolidated Stock Act" to the 30th June, 1903, amounted to £5,094,245. All these loans bear interest at the rate of 3 per cent., and mature in 1916. On the 4th April, 1900, an issue of £1,000,000 at 3 per cent. was floated in London, being part of the loan authorised under the "Public Purposes Loan Act of 1898," the minimum price being fixed at 94½. The net proceeds, after allowing for charges, amounted to £92 3s. 1½d. per £100. During 1899–1900, stock to the amount of £518,970 was disposed of in Adelaide, the net price realised being £95 7s. 11d., while in 1900–1, further local sales, amounting to £384,325, were effected at an average price of £94 7s. 6¼d. These issues bear the same rate, and are redeemable on the same date, as the former consolidated stock loans. During 1901–2, a small parcel of £64,240 was sold locally at £95 6s. 10d., and in 1902–3 £3,600 at about £92.

In June, 1892, Treasury bills were issued to the amount of £349,225 with interest at the rate of £4 11s. 3d. per cent., and payable in five years; and in March and July, 1893, further issues of £250,000 each were made bearing the same rate; the bills have all been redeemed.

In order to liquidate the debt due by the Northern Territory to South Australia proper, authority was obtained in 1901 to issue Treasury bills to the amount of £849,500 at 3½ per cent. The whole of the bills were floated at par, and, with the exception of £200,000 sold in London, were negotiated locally.

During the year ended 30th June, 1903, it became necessary to issue Treasury bills to liquidate the deficit of the previous year, and to provide funds for carrying on works in progress without appealing to the London money market, which was not in a favourable condition. An issue of Treasury bills, in aid of revenue, to the amount of £238,950 was made, the expenses in connection with which totalled £607. The bills were for periods extending from two to seven years, carrying interest at the rate of 3½ per cent. Other bills, to aid the loan fund, were issued to the extent of £367,775, the total expense attached to which was £2,568. The bills have a currency of from two to five years, and carry interest at the rate of 3½ per cent.

Western Australia.—In June, 1894, a loan of £540,000, at 4 per cent., was floated in London at a minimum of 102, the average price realised being £103 6s. 1d. In May, 1895, the state floated a 3½ per cent. loan of £750,000, having a forty years' currency, but redeemable from 1915 on twelve months' notice being given. The minimum price was fixed at 99, and the average obtained was £103 1s. 5d., or, deducting accrued interest, £101 9s. 2d.

In May, 1896, Western Australia, following the example of New Zealand and New South Wales, placed on the market a 3 per cent. loan for £750,000, having a currency until 1935, but redeemable from 1915 on twelve months' notice being given. A sinking fund is to be established in connection with this loan, commencing three years after flotation, the contribution being 1 per cent. per annum. The gross price obtained was £100 16s. 8d., and the accrued interest amounted to about 7s. 6d., so that the Government obtained £100 9s. 2d. This is the cheapest loan yet floated by any of the Australasian states.

In May, 1897, an issue of £1,000,000 was floated in London, the minimum price being fixed at 95, and the rate of interest 3 per cent. The loan is redeemable in 1935, and the net proceeds per £100, after allowing for charges and accrued interest, amounted to £93 8s. 11d.

In January, 1898, an issue of £1,000,000 was placed in London, being the first instalment under the Coolgardie Gold-fields Water Supply Loan Act, the minimum price being fixed at £95, and the rate of interest 3 per cent. For this, applications to the amount of £2,891,250 were received. The loan matures in 1927, and the net proceeds were £94 15s. 3d. per £100.

In July, 1898, a further issue of £1,000,000 was floated in London, being the second instalment under the Loans Act of 1896, the minimum price being fixed at £94, and the rate of interest 3 per cent. At the public tendering only £550,000 were offered, which brought an average price of £94 3s. 4d. The balance was sold afterwards at the minimum, which brought the average down to £94 1s. 10d. per cent. The loan is redeemable in 1935, and the net proceeds per £100 amounted to £91 19s. 4d.

In March, 1900, another issue of £1,000,000 was floated in London, the minimum price being fixed at £93½, and the rate of interest 3 per cent. The amount offered was £1,570,000, and the average price obtained was £93 12s. 9¾d. per cent., while the net proceeds per £100, after deducting accrued interest and expenses, came to £89 13s. 2d. In November, 1900, loans to the amount of £880,000 were negotiated, the rate of interest being raised to 3½ per cent. The net proceeds per £100 were £96 8s. 3d. and the rate paid by the Government, allowing for redemption at par at the latest date of maturity (1935) was £3 13s. 8d., while the corresponding yield to original investors was £3 11s.

During the year ended 30th June, 1903, loans aggregating £722,389 were floated locally, but no particulars in connection with them are yet avail ble.

The Government has authority to issue Treasury bills, but there were no bills outstanding on the 30th June, 1903.

Tasmania, in March, 1893, issued a 3½-per cent. loan of £800,000, which was part of the £2,100,000 authorised in December, 1892. The loan was only a partial success, £600,000 being taken up and the balance withdrawn. The average price realised per £100 was £92 2s. 2d. In 1894 a loan of £1,000,000 was negotiated in London, the rate of interest being 4 per cent., and the date of maturity between 1920 and 1940, at the option of the Government on 12 months' notice being given. The average amount realised per £100 was £101 4s. 3d. In February, 1895, a 3½ per cent. loan of £750,000 was floated, redeemable in 1940, or from 1920 on 12 months' notice being given. The price realised was £98 6s. 1d. In 1901, stock to the amount of £450,000 was sold in London, being the first 3 per cent. loan placed there. The amount realised averaged 92 per £100, but no other particulars are available.

In 1895 authority was given for the issue of £250,000 "local inscribed stock" to cover deficiencies in revenue, and in 1896 and 1897 further sums of £250,000 in each year, and a sum of £100,000 in 1898, were authorised. Prior to the passing of the Appropriation Act of 1899 the whole of the local inscribed stock hitherto raised in the state was placed in the Treasury books to an account for stock raised temporarily in aid of Consolidated Revenue; but as the amount raised was far in excess of revenue requirements, and was largely being used to meet expenditure on loans and public works accounts, which had not otherwise been provided for, a transfer of the whole of the local inscribed stock then issued, and maturing subsequently to the year 1900, was effected by that enactment, and was marked as an addition to the funded debt of the state. The amount so treated was £510,747, leaving a sum outstanding on the 31st December, 1899, of £91,727, which has been duly paid off.

Local inscribed stock for general purposes was sold during 1900 to the amount of £270,258, the rate of interest being 3 per cent., while during 1901, £136,000 was sold at 3 per cent., £25,000 at 3¼ per cent., and £252,000 at 3½ per cent. During 1902, local inscribed stock to to the amount of £302,719 was sold, but no particulars are available in respect of it.

During 1894, Treasury bills to the amount of £96,900 were negotiated in the state, viz., £40,500 at 4 per cent. and £56,400 at 4½ per cent., the bills having a currency until 1899 and 1900 respectively. The total amount of Treasury bills floated was £215,000, and they have been all redeemed.

New Zealand.—Under the amending Consolidation Act of 1884, short-dated debentures are issued pending the sale of inscribed stock under the Act of 1877. In May, 1895, New Zealand placed a loan for £1,500,000 on the market. With the exception of some New South Wales Treasury bills, this was the first 3 per cent. loan floated by any of the Australasian colonies. The loan has a currency of fifty years, and the minimum price was fixed at 90. The average gross price obtained was £94 8s. 9d., so that, after deducting accrued interest, the Government obtained £93 14s. 6d.

In February, 1899, a further issue of £1,000,000 was placed in London, the minimum price being fixed at £96, and the rate of interest 3 per cent. For this stock applications to the amount of £3,027,500 were received. The loan is redeemable in 1945, and the average price secured was £96 11s. per cent. This was the last flotation in London till November, 1901, when a loan of £1,000,000 was floated at 3 per cent. The price of issue was £94 per £100, and the loan was underwritten at a fee of £1 per cent. No further particulars are yet available. Debentures and stocks have been sold locally, £500,000 being disposed of in 1900–1, bearing interest at 4 per cent., and £250,000 in 1901–2 at the same rate of interest. Authority was given to raise £1,750,000 under "The Aid to Public Works and Land Settlement Act of 1902," and £1,000,000 of the loan so authorised, together with £250,000 authorised by "The Government Advances to Settlers Extension Act, 1901," was placed upon the London market in February 1903, the loan carrying 3 per cent. interest. Complete particulars are not yet available, but it would appear that the net result is about £91·15 per cent. During the year ended 31st March, 1903, under the authority of "The Aid to Public Works and Land Settlement Act, 1902," an amount of £750,000, and a sum of £338,700 under "The Land for Settlements Consolidation Act, 1900," were raised locally; these amounts carry interest at the rate of 4 per cent.

The amount of Treasury bills outstanding on the 31st March, 1902, was £700,000; the issue during the ensuing twelve months amounted to £1,400,000, while bills representing £1,400,000 were paid off, leaving the amount outstanding on the 31st March, 1903, at £700,000. As, however, allowance is made for these at the end of the financial year when carrying forward the balance of the Revenue Account, the liability is practically wiped out.

The particulars of the latest issues of the Funded Debts negotiated in London for which information is available are as follow :—

State.	Year of Issue.	Year of Maturity.	Nominal— Interest.	Nominal— Amount of Loan.	Net Proceeds, less charges and accrued Interest. Total.	Net Proceeds, less charges and accrued Interest. Per cent.	Effective annual Interest per £100 sterling, paid by Government. Nominal Interest on net Proceeds.	Effective annual Interest per £100 sterling, paid by Government. Rate paid, allowing for redemption at par on maturity.
			per cent.	£	£	£	£ s. d.	£ s. d.
New South Wales......	1893	1933	4	2,500,000	2,440,549	97·62	4 2 9½	4 3 0½
,, ...	1894	1918	3½	832,000	829,551	99·70	3 10 10	3 10 11
,, ...	1895	1935	3	4,000,000	3,804,573	95·14	3 3 6¼	3 4 3½
,, ...	1898	1935	3	1,500,000	1,479,746	98·65	3 1 3¼	3 1 6
,, ...	1901	1935	3	4,000,000	3,644,918	91·12	3 6 4	3 9 0
,, ...	1902	1935	3	3,000,000	2,727,191	90·91	3 6 6	3 8 7
Victoria..............	1892	1921-26	3½	2,000,000	1,810,696	90·53	3 18 0	3 19 8¾
,, ...	1893	1911-26	4	2,107,000	1,999,733	94·91	4 5 1½	4 6 0
,, ...	1899	1926-49	3	1,600,000	1,491,355	93·21	3 4 4	3 5 7
,, ...	1901	1926-49	3	3,000,000	2,695,875	89·86	3 7 3½	3 8 3
Queensland	1893	1930	3½	1,182,400	1,014,162	85·77	4 2 4	4 4 4½
,, ...	1895	1945	3½	1,250,000	1,230,274	98·42	3 11 9	3 11 10½
,, ...	1896	1947	3	1,500 000	1,434,122	95·61	3 2¾	3 7½
,, ...	1900	1950	3	1,400 000	1,277,590	91·26	6 3	7 0
,, ...	1901	1947	3	1,374 213	1,217,790	88·61	8 2½	9 4½
South Australia	1890-4	1939	3½	1,532,900	1,417,457	92·47	3 16 4½	3 17 0
,, ...	1892-4	1939	3½	513,200	497,052	96·85	3 12 11	3 13 2½
,, ...	1896	1926	3	839,500	800,406	95·34	3 5	4 8¾
,, ...	1897	1916	3	500,000	480,246	96·05	2 11½	5 4½
,, ...	1899	1916	3	1,500,000	1,390,084	92·67	5 2¾	10 2½
,, ...	1900	1916	3	1,000,000	908,125	90·81	6 6¾	14 1
Western Australia....	1892	1911-31	4	400,000	393,211	98·30	4 2 2½	4 2 4½
,, ...	1894	1911-31	4	540,000	544,964	100·92	3 0 0¾	3 0 6
,, ...	1895	1915-35	3½	750,000	760,934	101·46	9 7	9
,, ...	1896	1915-35	3	750,000	744,542	99·27	0 10¾	1
,, ...	1897	1915-35	3	1,000 000	934,465	93·45	4 8½	5 9¾
,, ...	1898	1927	3	1,000 000	947,610	94·76	3 4	5 3
,, ...	1898	1915-35	3	1,000 000	919,648	91·96	5 8	7 6
,, ...	1900	1915-35	3	1,000 000	896,583	89·66	7 5	9
,, ...	1900	1920-35	3½	880 000	848,426	96·41	12 7	11
Tasmania	1893	1920-40	4	1,000,000	994,912	99·49	4 1 2½	4 1 3
,, ...	1895	1920-40	3½	750,000	737,308	98·31	3 11 10	3 12 0
,, ...	1901	......	3	450,000	......	....	......	......
New Zealand	1896	1945	3	1,500,000	1,394,117	92·94	3 5 0½	3 5 9¾
,, ...	1899	1945	3	1,000,000	*933,375	93·34	3 4 9	3 5 6
,, ...	1901	1945	3	1,000,000	......	....	......	......
,, ...	1903	....	3	1,250,000	......	...	......	......

* Approximate.

The Treasury bills outstanding on the 30th June, 1903, were issued to cover deficiencies in revenue, with the exception of £4,979,000 in New South Wales, of which a sum of £4,000 is overdue, £950,000 in Victoria, and £367,775 in South Australia. The expenses incurred in these issues were practically nil—except for the flotations by New South Wales in London, the usual charges being made for brokerage, commission, and stamp duty—as the bills were sold at par, or a very small discount, and in some cases even at a premium. Particulars of the cost of Treasury bills negotiated prior to 1896 will be found in previous editions of this work.

Expenditure from Loans.

In the foregoing pages the chief points dwelt upon have been the amount of the public indebtedness and the credit enjoyed by each state as tested by the selling price of its loans. Before closing this chapter it would be well to consider for what purpose the debts were incurred. The services upon which the proceeds of the public loans were expended are various, but the bulk of the expenditure may be placed to the account of the construction of railways, water supply and sewerage, and electric telegraphs. In the early stages of Australasian borrowing the expenditure was moderate, loans being difficult to raise and interest high, but latterly, as the conditions under which loans could be contracted became favourable, especially since 1881, few of the states have set any bounds to their requirements. It was a repetition of the old experience—the opportunity engendered the desire, and the open purses of the investors tempted the states to undue borrowing and lavish expenditure. What is termed a "vigorous public works policy" was the order of the day, and works were pressed forward which under other circumstances would either not have been undertaken, or have been held back until the growth of population warranted their construction. The plethora of money has been harmful in many ways, the most apparent being the construction of not a few branch railways, in outlying and sparsely-settled districts, which do not pay even their working expenses. But when every allowance is made for unwise or improvident expenditure, it will be found that by far the larger portion of the proceeds of loans has been well expended. In some instances it will be years, taking a most hopeful view of the situation, before many of the revenue-producing works will yield a sum sufficient to pay working expenses and interest; nevertheless, a practical consideration of the conditions which surround Australasian settlement will demonstrate that in some instances the construction of these works was justifiable, for apart from the consideration that they will ultimately be self-supporting, they have already materially assisted in developing the country's resources, and have largely enhanced the value of the public estate. Whether their cost in all cases should have been charged against the loans account is a different matter, seeing that the rents obtained from public lands, and proceeds of sales, invariably go into the ordinary revenue of the states.

The following statement gives, under a convenient classification, the loan expenditure of each state during 1902–3 :—

Service.	New South Wales.	Victoria.	Queensland.	South Australia.	Western Australia.
	£	£	£	£	£
Railways and Tramways	1,683,755	347,612	695,632	141,335	1,059,418
Telegraphs and Telephones	......	......	33,288	......	......
Water Supply and Sewerage	554,581	115,405	11,822	175,909	413,435
Harbours, Rivers, and Navigation	2,014,565	2,999	1,632	27,640	138,422
Roads and Bridges	75,679	......	1,333	200	......
Public Works and Buildings	213,188	263,901	62,436	117,480	53,698
Defence	......	......	12,931	3,393	......
Immigration	......	......	10,901	......	928
Advances to Settlers	158,938	......	......	......	......
Land for Settlement	......	1,189	......	......	......
Loans to Local Bodies	......	......	192,430	......	......
Total	4,700,701	781,106	1,022,405	465,957	1,665,901

Service.	Tasmania.	Commonwealth.	New Zealand.	Australasia.
	£	£	£	£
Railways and Tramways	56,616	3,984,368	759,753	4,744,121
Telegraphs and Telephones	693	33,981	68,578	102,559
Water Supply and Sewerage	......	1,271,152	24,213	1,295,365
Harbours, Rivers, and Navigation	16,579	2,201,837	13,581	2,215,418
Roads and Bridges	54,862	132,074	300,617	432,691
Public Works and Buildings	53,643	764,346	225,741	990,087
Defence	346	16,670	37,004	53,674
Immigration	......	11,829	142	11,971
Advances to Settlers	......	158,933	249,714	408,647
Land for Settlement	......	1,189	368,984	370,173
Loans to Local Bodies	56,052	248,482	234,870	483,352
Total	238,791	8,824,861	2,283,197	11,108,058

The expenditure of the Commonwealth states during 1902–3 from funds derived from the proceeds of loans was £8,824,861. Of this amount, the sum of £7,696,317 was spent on services, the net revenue from which, during the financial year ended 30th June, 1903, amounted to £4,276,600, and the remainder was chiefly devoted to works such as the construction of roads and bridges, the erection of schools and public buildings, less obviously a proper charge against loan votes. The loan expenditure of the six Commonwealth states and New Zealand during 1902–3 was £11,108,058, of which amount £9,309,638 was spent on works from which a net return of £5,155,200 was received during the year ended 30th June, 1903.

In most of the states the expenditure from loans was greatly reduced during the years 1893 to 1896. In some cases this was to be attributed to a settled policy of retrenchment; but in others, the difficulty of raising a loan in London affords a more probable explanation. The expenditure, however, since 1897–8, shows a tendency to increase, the figures for the last financial year being largely in excess of the previous five years in the states of New South Wales, Tasmania, and New Zealand. The expenditure was chiefly on account of revenue-producing works; and in the case of New Zealand and Queensland large advances from loans were also made to local bodies. The expenditure of each state during the last five years is given in the following table:—

State.	1898-9.	1899-1900.	1900-1.	1901-2.	1902-3.
	£	£	£	£	£
New South Wales	2,025,944	2,400,943	2,788,120	4,938,212	4,700,701
Victoria	775,841	1,033,588	939,890	889,331	731,106
Queensland	1,054,787	1,182,668	1,212,020	1,161,689	1,022,405
South Australia	581,577	602,650	422,343	566,081	465,957
Western Australia	1,032,690	878,329	1,495,292	1,545,823	1,665,901
Tasmania	130,257	176,257	283,537	341,994	238,791
Commonwealth	5,601,096	6,274,435	7,141,202	9,443,130	8,824,861
New Zealand	1,836,863	2,051,899	2,246,221	3,284,932	2,283,197
Australasia	7,437,959	8,326,334	9,387,423	12,728,062	11,108,058

The total expenditure of the proceeds of loans from the commencement of borrowing to the end of the financial year 1902–3 for the six Commonwealth states was £215,503,505, and for the whole of Australasia £269,642,180. Of these sums, £179,705,787, or over eighty-three per cent., was spent by the Commonwealth states, and £207,604,204, or seventy-seven per cent., by the six states of Australia and New Zealand in the construction of railways, water supply and sewerage works, electric telegraphs, the improvement of harbours and rivers, advances to settlers, purchase of estates for the purpose of settlement, and in advances to local bodies, from which a net revenue of £4,300,000 was received during the last financial year in the case of the Commonwealth states, and in that of the whole of Australasia a net return of £5,089,000. The balance was expended on services which, though non-productive, were claimed by their proposers as being necessary in the interests of national development. The expenditure on defence and the payments made to meet deficiency in revenue are the exceptions to the rule which has governed the expenditure of the proceeds of loan issues. The expenditure to cover deficiency in revenue has not been large, and is looked upon as but a temporary charge on the loan funds, while the expenditure on defence has been extremely small in all the states except New South Wales and New

Zealand. The following table shows the total loan expenditure of each state up to the close of the last financial year :—

Service.	New South Wales.	Victoria.	Queensland.	South Australia.	Western Australia.
	£	£	£	£	£
Railways and Tramways	47,098,238	38,037,773	23,180,491	13,592,828	8,607,368
Telegraphs and Telephones	1,294,882	8,366	1,048,510	991,812	269,308
Water Supply and Sewerage......	10,919,619	8,684,923	1,251,679	4,913,455	2,742,799
Harbours, Rivers, and Navigation	9,313,740	614,058	2,597,485	1,371,752	1,973,633
Roads and Bridges	1,608,807	106,259	900,221	1,464,658	142,588
Public Works and Buildings......	4,700,987	3,125,377	3,111,404	3,397,456	1,333,585
Defence	1,421,976	149,324	377,097	292,683	...
Immigration	194,430	....	2,943,963	....	28,625
Advances to Settlers	427,835	....	....	....	....
Land for Settlement	....	205,675	....	235,708	....
Loans to Local Bodies...........	....	....	1,992,285	....	....
Total..................	76,980,464	50,984,755	37,353,135	26,260,352	15,097,856

Service.	Tasmania.	Common-wealth.	New Zealand.	Australasia.
	£	£	£	£
Railways and Tramways	4,047,793	134,564,491	19,261,749	153,826,240
Telegraphs and Telephones	142,410	3,755,288	1,006,466	4,761,754
Water Supply and Sewerage......	....	28,512,475	725,892	29,238,367
Harbours, Rivers, and Navigation	440,839	16,311,507	991,353	17,302,800
Roads and Bridges	2,175,746	6,398,220	6,248,243	12,646,477
Public Works and Buildings......	1,367,068	17,038,827	16,118,818	33,157,645
Defence	128,180	2,369,260	733,839	3,103,099
Immigration	235,000	3,402,018	2,148,000	5,550,018
Advances to Settlers	....	427,835	3,323,399	3,751,234
Land for Settlement	...	441,383	1,999,013	2,440,396
Loans to Local Bodies	289,907	2,282,192	1,581,898	3,864,090
Total..................	8,826,943	215,503,505	54,138,675	269,642,180

In the New Zealand returns, old provincial debts contracted prior to 1876, amounting to £11,535,469, have been included under the head "Public works and buildings," as there is no available record of the services upon which the loans of the old Provincial Governments were expended, except for the construction of railways. There is, however, no doubt that a very large proportion of this expenditure was incurred for war purposes, the cost of suppressing the Maori risings between 1860 and 1870 being charged to loan votes. The figures given for New South Wales, South Australia, Western Australia, and Tasmania under the head of "Railways" include loan expenditure on state tramways, but, except in the case of the first-mentioned state, the amount thus expended is unimportant, as this service in the other states is generally in the hands of municipal authorities or private companies. The Governments of New South Wales and New Zealand have borrowed money for the purpose of making advances to settlers for the improvement of their holdings, such advances being interest bearing and repayable by instalments. The sums advanced by the respective Governments named were—New South Wales, £427,835, to the 30th June, 1903, and New Zealand, £3,323,399, to 31st March, 1903.

In the case of New South Wales a sum of £724,733 was spent on immigration before the inauguration of the General Loan Account, but it is not included in the above table. The total expenditure on immigration in the states comprising the Commonwealth was, therefore, £4,126,751, and for Australasia, £6,274,751.

The subjoined table shows the expenditure per inhabitant on the basis of the figures given in the table on page 859 :—

Service.	New South Wales.	Victoria.	Queensland.	South Australia.	Western Australia.	Tasmania.	Commonwealth.	New Zealand.	Australasia.
	£ s. d.	£ s. d.	£ s. d.	£ s. d.	£ s. d.	£ s. d.	£ s. d.	£ s. d.	£ s. d.
Railways and Tramways.	33 10 8	31 11 11	44 18 7	37 8 2	40 0 2	28 0 11	34 13 2	23 16 10	32 15 11
Telegraphs and Telephones.	0 18 5	0 0 2	2 0 9	2 14 8	1 5 0	0 16 2	0 19 4	1 4 11	1 0 4
Water Supply and Sewerage.	7 15 5	7 4 1	2 8 7	13 8 8	12 15 0	....	7 6 11	0 17 11	6 4 8
Harbours, Rivers, and Navigation.	6 12 6	0 10 2	5 0 11	3 15 0	2 3 6	2 10 2	4 4 0	1 4 6	3 13 9
Roads and Bridges.	1 2 11	0 1 9	1 14 11	4 0 1	0 13 8	12 7 9	1 12 11	7 14 8	2 13 11
Public Works and Buildings.	3 6 10	2 11 11	6 0 10	9 5 10	6 4 0	7 15 8	4 7 10	19 19 0	7 1 5
Defence	1 0 3	0 2 6	0 14 8	0 16 0	....	0 14 7	0 12 3	0 18 2	0 13 3
Immigration. ..	0 2 9	....	5 14 4	....	0 2 8	1 6 9	0 17 6	2 13 2	1 3 8
Advances to Settlers	0 6 1	....	....	....	....	....	0 2 2	4 2 3	0 16 0
Land for Settlement	....	0 3 5	....	0 12 10	....	....	0 2 3	2 9 5	0 10 5
Loans to Local Bodies.	....	....	3 17 5	....	....	1 13 0	0 11 10	1 19 2	0 16 5
Total..........	54 15 5	42 5 11	72 11 0	71 15 10	70 3 7	50 5 0	55 10 2	67 0 0	57 9 9

A perusal of the previous pages indicates that while the public debt of the states of the Commonwealth, on the 30th June, 1903, aggregated £222,871,765, there has been an expenditure of £215,503,505 on public works; and that as a set off against the public debt of the six states of Australia and New Zealand, which amounted to £278,770,784 at the same date an expenditure totalling £269,642,180 has been incurred for public works. An attempt has been made in the previous pages to classify this expenditure under such specific headings as would admit of the amount being ascertained on which there is a net return, that is to say, a margin left after the payment of working expenses to meet interest on capital cost. In the subjoined table the receipts, expenditure, and the amount available to meet the interest on capital expenditure in connection with the services are set forth, and it will be observed that so far as the Commonwealth states are concerned, the net revenue shows a return of 1·92 per cent. on the public debt of the states, and for the whole of Australasia, 1·85 per cent. In the consideration of these figures, the fact must not be overlooked that the transactions of the past twelve months can by no means be considered normal, inasmuch as the greater part of Australia, and certainly that portion involving the most vital interests has lain under the incubus of a severe drought, and as a consequence not only were avenues of revenue under the different headings restricted, but the working expenditure necessary to obtain the results secured was unduly increased.

Service.	New South Wales.			Victoria.		
	Receipts.	Expenditure.	Amount available to meet interest on capital cost.	Receipts.	Expenditure.	Amount available to meet interest on capital cost.
	£	£	£	£	£	£
Railways and Tramways	4,079,788	2,954,554	1,125,234	3,033,597	1,860,493	1,173,104
Water Supply and Sewerage	427,588	139,932	287,656	156,952	31,687	125,265
Harbours, Rivers, and Navigation	398,769	305,030	93,739	74,694	33,892	40,802
Advances to Settlers	7,139	4,016	3,123	......	......	......
Loans to Local Bodies	......	......	......	......	......	......
Land for Settlement	......	......	......	......	......	......
Total	4,913,284	3,403,532	1,509,752	3,265,243	1,926,072	1,339,171

Service.	Queensland.			South Australia.		
	Receipts.	Expenditure.	Amount available to meet interest on capital cost.	Receipts.	Expenditure.	Amount available to meet interest on capital cost.
	£	£	£	£	£	£
Railways and Tramways	1,245,915	861,749	384,166	1,086,758	643,871	442,887
Water Supply and Sewerage	......	......	......	151,016	43,685	107,331
Harbours, Rivers, and Navigation	......	......	......	18,220	11,088	7,132
Advances to Settlers	......	......	......	......	......	......
Loans to Local Bodies	76,525	......	76,525	......	......	......
Land for Settlement	......	......	......	12,813	106	12,707
Total	1,322,440	861,749	460,691	1,268,807	698,750	570,057

Service.	Western Australia.			Tasmania.		
	Receipts.	Expenditure.	Amount available to meet interest on capital cost.	Receipts.	Expenditure.	Amount available to meet interest on capital cost.
	£	£	£	£	£	£
Railways and Tramways	1,598,023	1,275,565	322,458	232,744	173,151	59,593
Water Supply and Sewerage	30,048	23,578	6,470	......	......	......
Harbours, Rivers, and Navigation	......	......	......	......	......	......
Advances to Settlers	......	......	......	......	......	......
Loans to Local Bodies	......	......	......	8,408	......	8,408
Land for Settlement	......	......	......	......	......	......
Total	1,628,071	1,299,143	328,928	241,152	173,151	68,001

Service.	Commonwealth.			New Zealand.		
	Receipts.	Expenditure.	Amount available to meet interest on capital cost.	Receipts.	Expenditure.	Amount available to meet interest on capital cost.
	£	£	£	£	£	£
Railways and Tramways	11,276,825	7,769,383	3,507,442	1,962,551	1,357,385	625,166
Water Supply and Sewerage	765,604	238,882	526,722	......	......	......
Harbours, Rivers, and Navigation	491,683	350,010	141,673	......	......	......
Advances to Settlers	7,139	4,016	3,123	89,700	......	89,700
Loans to Local Bodies	84,933	......	84,933	57,713	......	57,713
Land for Settlement	12,813	106	12,707	109,820	3,741	106,079
Total	12,638,997	8,362,397	4,276,600	2,239,784	1,361,126	878,658

Service.	Australasia.		
	Receipts.	Expenditure.	Amount available to meet interest on capital cost.
	£	£	£
Railways and Tramways	13,259,376	9,126,768	4,132,608
Water Supply and Sewerage	765,604	238,882	526,722
Harbours, Rivers, and Navigation	491,683	350,010	141,673
Advances to Settlers	96,839	4,016	92,823
Loans to Local Bodies	142,646	......	142,646
Land for Settlement	122,633	3,847	118,786
Total	14,878,781	9,723,523	5,155,258

Expenditure by the Government and Local Bodies.

The question of Local Government is dealt with in another chapter. It is well, however, to give here a statement of the total amount which passed through the hands of the general and local governments. The sum can in no sense, however, be taken as the cost of governing the various states; as will appear from page 824, this may be taken as £17,102,526 for the six Commonwealth states, and £21,329,763 for the whole of Australasia.

The total sum expended by the general and local governments of the Commonwealth states during the year 1902-3 was £40,994,473, or £10 11s. 4d. per head, and for Australasia £50,900,369, or £10 17s. 5d. per head. Of these large sums, £28,973,361, or £7 9s. 3d. per inhabitant, was spent by the general governments of the six Commonwealth states from their revenues, and £8,824,861, or £2 5s. 5d. per inhabitant, from loans; the local expenditure—exclusive, of course, of a sum equal to the Government endowment—was £3,196,251, or 16s. 8d. per inhabitant. For the six Commonwealth states and New Zealand the expenditure by the general government from revenue was £35,187,380 or £7 10s. 1d. per inhabitant, and from loans £11,108,058, or £2 7s. 5d. per inhabitant; while the local expenditure, exclusive of government endowment, amounted to £4,604,931, or 19s. 11d. per inhabitant.

The following table shows the general, loan, and local expenditure for each state:—

State.	General Government.		Local Government.	Total.
	From Revenue.	From Loans.		
	£	£	£	£
New South Wales	11,467,235	4,700,701	807,210	16,975,146
Victoria	6,774,084	731,106	1,400,271	8,905,461
Queensland	3,717,806	1,022,405	437,414	5,177,625
South Australia	2,641,789	465,957	257,652	3,365,398
Western Australia	3,521,763	1,665,901	147,555	5,335,219
Tasmania	850,684	238,791	146,149	1,235,624
Commonwealth	28,973,361	8,824,861	3,196,251	40,994,473
New Zealand	6,214,019	2,283,197	1,408,680	9,905,896
Australasia	35,187,380	11,108,058	4,604,931	50,900,369

The expenditure per inhabitant, under the same classification, will be found below. The distribution of the expenditure for New South Wales, between general and local government, is to some extent misleading, as a little over 36 per cent. of the population lives outside the boundaries of the municipalities:—

State.	General Government.		Local Government.	Total.
	From Revenue.	From Loans.		
	£ s. d.	£ s. d.	£ s. d.	£ s. d.
New South Wales	8 3 2	3 6 11	0 11 5	12 1 6
Victoria	5 12 4	0 12 2	1 3 2	7 7 8
Queensland	7 4 5	1 19 8	0 17 2	10 1 3
South Australia	7 4 5	1 5 6	0 14 2	9 4 1
Western Australia	16 7 5	7 14 10	0 15 2	24 17 5
Tasmania	4 16 10	1 7 2	0 16 9	7 0 9
Commonwealth	7 9 3	2 5 5	0 16 8	10 11 4
New Zealand	7 13 10	2 16 6	1 15 9	12 6 1
Australasia	7 10 1	2 7 5	0 19 11	10 17 5

COMMERCE.

IT is reasonable to expect that the trade of the states which now form the Commonwealth of Australia, and the colony of New Zealand would increase as quickly as the population; but as a matter of fact its growth for many years was much more rapid, and at the present time under normal conditions the total commerce of Australasia per head of population is exceeded by that of no country except Belgium, half of whose trade consists of goods in course of transit to and from the north-western and central parts of the continent of Europe. Below will be found a statement of the trade of Australasia for various periods since the year 1825, prior to which date no information is available:—

Year.	Trade of Australasia.	
	Total Value.	Value per head.
	£	£ s. d.
1825	511,998	10 13 11
1841	5,573,000	22 4 0
1851	8,957,610	18 10 7
1861	52,228,207	41 19 10
1871	69,435,524	35 17 10
1881	101,710,967	36 12 7
1891	144,766,285	37 14 11
1901	167,663,713	36 11 8
1902	163,442,664	34 16 4

It will be seen that the average value of trade per inhabitant increased by £1 17s. 1d. during the twenty years extending from 1871 to 1891, of which the period from 1881 to 1891 accounted for no less than £1 2s. 4d. This, however, does not show the full extent of the growth in trade, for the prices of produce—especially of wool, which has been the staple product since very early years—had fallen heavily during the same period. From 1891 till 1894, the trade of Australasia seriously declined, viz., from £37 14s. 11d. to £26 17s. 10d. per inhabitant, a state of affairs partly brought about by the continued fall in prices and partly resulting from the financial crisis of 1893. Since 1894, however, the value has steadily increased, reaching its maximum in 1901 with a sum of £167,663,713, the largest total yet recorded, and thus proving that the states have shaken off to a great extent the ill effects of the period of depression. The figures for 1902 show some falling off as compared with those of the preceding two years, the decline being due chiefly to the adverse effect of the bad season, but regard must also be paid to the fact that there were some importations in 1900 and 1901 in anticipation of the imposition of the federal tariff, while the exports underwent considerable expansion through the demand for produce created by the South African war.

The following series of tables shows the distribution of the total trade of Australasia, and also of the Australian Commonwealth, for the years 1881, 1891, and 1902, with the average value per head of population. The first table represents the imports:—

State.	Total Value of Imports.			Value per Inhabitant.		
	1881.	1891.	1902.	1881.	1891.	1902.
	£	£	£	£ s. d.	£ s. d.	£ s. d.
New South Wales	17,587,012	25,383,397	25,974,210	23 2 7	22 4 5	18 9 0
Victoria	16,718,521	21,711,608	13,270,245	19 4 8	18 19 2	15 3 1
Queensland	4,063,625	5,079,004	7,352,538	13 5 8	12 16 2	14 5 7
South Australia	5,320,549	10,051,123	6,130,064	19 4 8	31 3 4	16 15 2
Western Australia	404,831	1,280,093	7,218,352	13 14 8	25 14 3	33 11 0
Tasmania	1,431,144	2,051,964	2,442,745	12 5 0	13 15 6	13 15 10
Commonwealth	45,525,682	65,557,189	67,388,144	19 18 7	20 9 1	17 6 9
New Zealand	7,457,045	6,503,849	11,326,723	15 2 7	10 6 5	14 0 4
Australasia	52,982,727	72,061,038	78,714,867	19 1 7	18 15 9	16 15 4

The values of the total exports for the same years were as given below:—

State.	Total Value of Exports.			Value per Inhabitant.		
	1881.	1891.	1902.	1881.	1891.	1902.
	£	£	£	£ s. d.	£ s. d.	£ s. d.
New South Wales	16,307,305	25,944,020	23,544,051	21 9 0	22 14 8	16 14 6
Victoria	16,252,103	16,006,743	18,210,523	18 13 6	13 19 7	15 2 1
Queensland	3,540,336	8,306,387	9,171,023	15 18 6	20 18 11	17 16 8
South Australia	4,508,754	10,642,416	7,861,357	16 5 7	33 0 0	21 9 10
Western Australia	502,770	799,466	9,051,358	17 0 8	16 1 2	42 1 5
Tasmania	1,555,576	1,440,818	3,244,508	13 6 3	9 13 6	18 6 6
Commonwealth	42,667,374	63,138,850	71,082,820	18 13 6	19 13 11	18 5 10
New Zealand	6,060,866	9,566,397	13,644,977	12 5 11	15 3 8	16 17 9
Australasia	48,728,240	72,705,247	84,727,797	17 11 0	18 19 2	18 1 0

The total trade, similarly classified, was as follows:—

State.	Value of Total Trade.			Value per Inhabitant.		
	1881.	1891.	1902.	1881.	1891.	1902.
	£	£	£	£ s. d.	£ s. d.	£ s. d.
New South Wales	33,894,817	51,327,417	49,518,261	44 11 7	44 18 8	35 3 6
Victoria	32,970,624	37,718,351	36,480,768	37 17 9	32 18 9	30 5 2
Queensland	7,603,991	13,384,391	16,523,561	34 4 2	33 15 1	32 1 10
South Australia	9,829,303	20,093,539	13,991,411	35 9 10	64 3 4	38 5 0
Western Australia	907,601	2,079,559	16,269,710	30 14 11	41 15 5	75 12 5
Tasmania	2,986,720	3,492,782	5,687,258	25 11 3	23 9 0	32 2 4
Commonwealth	88,193,056	128,696,039	138,470,964	38 12 1	40 3 0	35 12 7
New Zealand..............	13,517,911	16,070,246	24,971,700	27 8 6	25 10 1	30 18 1
Australasia	101,710,967	144,766,285	163,442,664	36 12 7	37 14 11	34 16 4

The point most notable in this series of tables is the very marked impetus which the trade of South Australia received during the period 1881–91—a trade of £64 3s. 4d. per inhabitant, the value transacted by that state during 1891, being almost without parallel in any important country. This huge trade was, however, not drawn altogether from its own territory, for in 1891 more than £5,731,000, or about £17 15s. per inhabitant, and in 1902, £1,986,700, or £5 8s. 7d. per inhabitant, was due to the Barrier District of New South Wales, of which South Australia is the natural outlet; and it must also be remembered that considerable quantities of goods on their way to Broken Hill are entered as imports in South Australia when they arrive in that state, and as exports to New South Wales when they cross the border. Of the total shrinkage of £25 18s. 4d. per head from 1891 to 1902, £8 15s. 1d. must be attributed to the falling-off in the Barrier trade. The large and increasing production of the gold-fields is the chief cause of the remarkable development in the trade of Western Australia, which will be noticed when comparing the years 1891 and 1902.

The trade of New South Wales in 1891 was valued at no less than £51,327,417. Five years later, owing in great measure to the same influences as affected the trade of Australia generally, the total had fallen to £43,571,859; but for 1901 the value stood at £54,279,342, the largest amount yet recorded. In 1902, owing to causes which have already been alluded to, there was a decline to £49,518,261. If the figures for the years 1902 and 1891 be compared for the states comprising the Commonwealth, it will be found that, there is an increase of upwards of £1,830,000 in the total value of imports, and of £7,944,000 in the exports, while the value of the total trade advanced during the period in question from £128,696,039 to £138,470,964, representing an expansion of upwards of £9,774,000.

Interstate Trade.

The trade shown in the above series of tables represents, not only the business transacted with countries outside Australasia, but the trade maintained by the states of the Commonwealth with one another.

This interstate trade forms a considerable proportion of the total which has just been dealt with, and reached an amount of £54,088,459 in 1902; this however, in proportion to population, is lower than that for any previous year shown in the table.

The following figures represent the value of the interstate trade, excluding that of New Zealand, as well as the value per inhabitant. It is obvious that the total interstate trade which is shown by the table represents in reality twice the actual value of goods passing from one state to another, the same merchandise figuring in one place as exports, and in another as imports. The value of goods passing through a state on their way to foreign countries, as well as of goods imported from abroad and re-exported, is, of course, also included in the figures. The actual movement is therefore less than half of the values given below :—

Year.	Total.	Value per Inhabitant of Australia.
1861	£14,912,688	£12 18 5
1871	25,431,948	15 4 10
1881	34,166,233	15 3 4
1891	57,395,687	18 0 7
1901	54,088,459	14 6 10

Extra-Australasian Trade.

If Australasia be regarded as a whole, and an elimination made of the real trade which the provinces carry on with each other, as well as the value of the goods which pass through one state on their way to another, as shown under the heading of Interstate Trade, the total and average amounts will, of course, be greatly reduced. Such an elimination has been made in the following table, which shows the growth since 1861 of what may be called the external trade—that is, trade transacted with all countries outside of Australasia :—

Year.	External Trade.	
	Total Value.	Value per head.
	£	£ s. d.
1861	35,061,282	28 3 10
1871	39,729,016	20 10 10
1881	64,554,678	23 6 3
1891	84,651,488	22 0 8
1902	105,165,516	22 8 1

Trade with the United Kingdom.

In order to make a useful comparison of the value of the Australasian trade to the United Kingdom, it is necessary to refer to the British Board of Trade returns, and these returns have been used in the ensuing comparisons. The figures relating to Australasia, especially for late years, approximate very closely to the local Customs statistics. From the table it will be observed that while in 1881 the produce of the Commonwealth of Australia and the colony of New Zealand formed 29·5 per cent. of the imports of the United Kingdom from her possessions, in 1891 the proportion was 31·4 per cent., while in 1902 it declined to 28·7 per cent.

The year 1902 was, however, an unfortunate one for some of the mainland states, and the diminished production was reflected in the decreased body of exports. In the preceding year the proportion of imports into the United Kingdom from Australia was 23 per cent., and from New Zealand 10 per cent., making a total of 33 per cent :—

Year.	As returned by British Customs.				Proportion of Imports from Australasia to total from British Possessions.		
	Total Imports from British Possessions.	Imports from Australasia.					
		Commonwealth of Australia.	New Zealand.	Total.	Commonwealth of Australia.	New Zealand.	Total.
	£	£	£	£	per cent.	per cent.	per cent.
1881	91,539,660	21,837,709	5,125,859	26,963,568	23·9	5·6	29·5
1891	99,464,718	23,068,972	8,192,594	31,261,566	23·2	8·2	31·4
1901	105,573,706	24,217,669	10,594,587	34,812,256	23·0	10·0	33·0
1902	106,793,033	19,734,017	10,883,648	30,617,665	18·5	10·2	28·7

Although it is very little more than a century since the commencement of Australasian settlement, an examination of the trade statistics of the mother country with her numerous dependencies shows that the total trade of the Commonwealth and New Zealand with the United Kingdom is more than one and a half times that of Canada, and in a larger degree exceeds the trade of any other British possession, with the exception of India. In normal years the Australasian trade is even in excess of that of India, the amount of such excess in 1901 being considerably over a million sterling. The following table, which is also compiled from the returns of the Board of Trade, shows the total trade of the United Kingdom exclusive of specie and diamonds for the three years 1881, 1891, and 1902, with the most important of British possessions :—

Country.	1881.	1891.	1902.	Proportion of Trade of United Kingdom with British possessions.		
				1881.	1891.	1902.
	£	£	£	per cent	per cent	per cent
India	63,682,398	64,783,605	62,215,041	35·7	33·6	27·7
British North America	20,608,159	20,906,357	36,048,950	11·6	10·8	16·1
Cape Colony and Natal	13,105,264	14,892,965	32,096,628	7·4	7·7	14·3
Straits Settlements	6,527,675	7,946,127	8,857,246	3·7	4·1	3·9
Hongkong	4,815,905	3,833,859	2,884,615	2·7	2·0	1·3
Australasia—						
Commonwealth of Australia	41,662,820	47,522,331	41,263,423	23·4	24·7	18·4
New Zealand	9,206,331	11,970,988	17,042,533	5·2	6·2	7·6
Total, Australasia	50,869,151	59,493,319	58,305,956	28·6	30·9	26·0

If, again, a comparison be made of the total trade transacted by the United Kingdom with all countries during the year 1902, it will be found that the trade with Australasia, amounting to £58,305,956, was only exceeded by that carried on with three countries, namely, the United States, with a total of £170,042,674; France, with £72,918,649; and Germany, with £66,728,521. The amounts taken by other countries will be found below, and it must be noted that the values given do not include specie:—

Country.	1881.	1891.	1902.	Proportion to Total Trad of United Kingdom		
				1881.	1891.	1902.
	£	£	£	per cent	per cent	per cent
France	70,069,848	69,114,136	72,918,649	10·1	9·8	8·3
Germany	52,927,199	56,976,104	66,728,521	7·6	7·7	7·6
Belgium	25,047,333	30,525,737	39,158,510	3·6	4·1	4·5
Holland	38,295,414	42,290,587	47,913,659	5·5	5·7	5·4
Spain	14,421,326	16,050,036	19,652,029	2·1	2·2	2·3
Italy	10,792,015	10,272,329	11,675,995	1·6	1·2	1·3
United States	139,990,876	145,475,197	170,042,674	20·2	19·5	19·4
Argentine Republic	4,000,090	7,817,256	20,144,348	0·6	1·0	2·3
Chili	5,417,363	5,916,225	7,587,142	0·8	0·8	0·9
Brazil	13,254,733	12,855,202	11,857,831	1·9	1·7	1·3
Uruguay	1,881,522	1,568,891	2,233,936	0·3	0·2	0·2
Australasia—						
Commonwealth of Australia	41,662,820	47,522,331	41,263,423	6·0	6·4	4·7
New Zealand	9,206,331	11,970,988	17,042,533	1·3	1·6	1·9
Total, Australasia	50,869,151	59,493,319	58,305,956	7·3	8·0	6·6

Trade with Foreign Countries.

Every year steamers of greater tonnage and higher speed are visiting the Commonwealth of Australia and the colony of New Zealand from Europe, and a considerable expansion of commerce must of necessity take place, owing to the new outlets for trade which have been opened up thereby. The values of the imports into the Commonwealth from the principal foreign countries during the period 1861–1902 were as shown below:—

Country.	1861.	1871.	1881.	1891.	1901.	1902.
	£	£	£	£	£	£
Belgium	......	......	26,687	314,434	567,808	352,447
France and New Caledonia	136,053	158,573	321,238	359,951	486,175	547,617
Germany	90,686	3,899	219,893	1,707,175	2,800,342	2,658,060
Netherlands and Java	110,179	194,519	464,503	652,517	993,778	813,565
Italy	......	......	7,874	56,617	156,389	163,797
Sweden and Norway	22,666	106,720	259,147	459,046	506,457	479,798
China	827,847	842,087	1,281,765	680,328	159,485	226,207
Japan	......	......	23,150	52,887	288,216	354,327
South Sea Islands	35,973	84,913	104,932	12,792	73,966	128,795
United States	1,053,883	557,280	1,249,443	2,558,320	5,854,239	4,989,812
Other Foreign Countries	884,101	139,639	93,389	73,874	525,486	730,350
Total	3,160,888	2,087,630	4,052,021	6,927,941	12,412.336	11,444,775

For the same period the exports from the Commonwealth to the countries mentioned in the preceding table were as appended:—

Country.	1861.	1871.	1881.	1891.	1901.	1902.
	£	£	£	£	£	£
Belgium	......	......	100,437	1,484,073	1,506,635	1,435,965
France and New Caledonia	26,793	101,618	281,544	1,807,905	2,475,406	2,753,830
Germany	......	......	70,422	859,557	2,552,458	2,543,260
Netherlands and Java	3,907	39,517	52,192	92,645	322,970	282,451
Italy	......	......	152,914	27,956	139,166	142,311
Sweden and Norway	......	......	......	......	4,040	1,001
China	112,969	26,636	67,501	30,185	128,976	107,071
Japan	1,805	9,470	6,872	16,485	123,355	414,533
South Sea Islands	31,319	111,715	108,758	55,963	107,857	120,123
United States	66,602	271,800	943,118	2,754,053	3,373,876	2,714,424
Other Foreign Countries	483,457	3,133,350	363,453	581,286	1,758,333	978,215
Total	726,852	3,694,106	2,147,216	7,710,108	12,492,072	11,492,862

SUMMARY.

Summary.	1861.	1871.	1881.	1891.	1901.	1902.
	£	£	£	£	£	£
Imports and Exports	3,887,740	5,781,736	6,199,237	14,638,049	24,904,408	22,937,637

Similar information regarding the trade of New Zealand with foreign countries will be found in the succeeding tables. The first table gives the imports:—

Country.	1861.	1871.	1881.	1891.	1901.	1902.
	£	£	£	£	£	£
Belgium	......	......	26	6,591	68,083	86,236
France and New Caledonia	71	419	19,512	9,084	27,714	35,595
Germany	18,486	......	5,779	66,102	198,521	210,560
Netherlands and Java	4,125	......	1,941	2,148	100,730	65,368
Italy	......	......	......	1,867	9,211	11,129
Sweden and Norway	......	......	9	368	11,963	19,543
China	......	32,838	149,228	18,815	15,324	12,509
Japan	......	......	95	8,399	45,465	56,067
South Sea Islands	4,227	50,147	19,515	65,493	68,733	41,042
United States	26,790	59,345	343,645	361,796	1,415,260	1,318,937
Other Foreign Countries	2,151	14,745	11,555	21,826	62,214	48,769
Total	55,850	157,494	551,305	562,483	2,018,218	1,905,766

The next table shows the exports from New Zealand to foreign countries during the same period :—

Country.	1861.	1871.	1881.	1891.	1901.	1902.
	£	£	£	£	£	£
Belgium	......	......	......	1,658	14	394
France and New Caledonia	......	140	54,954	27,879	1,771	2,026
Germany	......	......	......	4,258	10,470	9,359
Netherlands and Java	......	......	......	......	100	82
Italy	......	......	......	43	......	32
Sweden and Norway	......	......	......	......	692	169
China	1,180	2,501	11,098	564	15,407	42
Japan	......	......	......	93	1,640	3,780
South Sea Islands	4,811	41,853	31,541	93,407	109,460	93,963
United States	9,552	95,561	355,787	515,208	519,079	489,964
Other Foreign Countries	4,095	9,809	9,993	19,506	20,004	16,658
Total	19,638	149,864	463,373	662,616	678,637	616,499

SUMMARY.

Summary.	1861.	1871.	1881.	1891.	1901.	1902.
	£	£	£	£	£	£
Imports and Exports	75,488	307,358	1,014,678	1,225,099	2,696,855	2,522,265

Combining the results obtained in the previous series of tables, the following figures will show the trade of Australasia with foreign countries at intervals since 1861. The first table represents the imports :—

Country.	1861.	1871.	1881.	1891.	1901.	1902.
	£	£	£	£	£	£
Belgium	......	......	26,713	321,025	630,886	438,683
France and New Caledonia	136,124	158,992	340,750	369,035	513,889	583,212
Germany	109,172	3,899	225,672	1,773,277	2,998,863	2,868,620
Netherlands and Java	114,304	194,519	466,444	654,660	1,094,508	878,933
Italy	......	......	7,874	58,484	165,600	174,926
Sweden and Norway	22,666	106,720	259,156	459,414	518,420	499,341
China	827,347	874,925	1,430,903	699,143	174,809	238,707
Japan	......	......	23,245	61,286	333,681	410,414
South Sea Islands	40,200	135,060	124,447	78,285	142,699	139,837
United States	1,080,678	616,625	1,593,068	2,920,115	7,269,499	6,308,749
Other foreign Countries	886,252	154,384	104,944	95,700	587,700	779,119
Total	3,216,738	2,245,124	4,603,326	7,490,424	14,430,554	13,350,541

The following table shows the exports from Australasia to foreign countries during the years 1861–1902 :—

Country.	1861.	1871.	1881.	1891.	1901.	1902.
	£	£	£	£	£	£
Belgium	......	......	100,487	1,485,731	1,505,649	1,435,657
France and New Caledonia	26,793	101,758	336,498	1,835,784	2,477,177	2,755,846
Germany	......	......	70,422	863,815	2,561,928	2,552,749
Netherlands and Java	3,907	39,517	52,192	92,645	823,070	282,588
Italy	......	......	152,914	27,999	139,166	142,343
Sweden and Norway	......	......	......	......	4,732	1,170
China	114,149	29,137	73,599	30,749	144,388	167,113
Japan	1,805	9,470	6,872	16,578	124,995	418,608
South Sea Islands	36,130	153,568	140,299	149,370	217,317	214,085
United States	76,154	367,861	1,298,905	3,269,261	3,892,955	3,20[illegible]
Other foreign Countries	487,552	3,143,159	373,451	600,792	1,778,337	994,873
Total	746,490	3,843,970	2,610,589	8,372,724	13,170,709	12,109,361

SUMMARY.

Summary.	1861.	1871.	1881.	1891.	1901.	1902.
	£	£	£	£	£	£
Imports and Exports	3,963,228	6,089,094	7,213,915	15,863,148	27,601,263	25,459,992

The commerce with foreign countries from the commencement of the period under review exhibits very satisfactory progress; the imports have increased by over ten millions sterling, and the exports by considerably over eleven millions, while the expansion in the total trade was as much as 542 per cent. This remarkable growth is chiefly due to the development of the European continental trade, consequent on the diversion of part of the wool business from London, which was largely brought about by the display of local resources at the Sydney and Melbourne International Exhibitions of 1879 and 1880. The annual increase per cent. of the trade of Australasia with the four principal foreign countries with which it has commercial relations is shown below, the period covered being the twenty-one years extending from 1881 to 1902 :—

Country.	Imports.	Exports.	Total Trade.
	per cent.	per cent.	per cent.
Belgium	14·26	13·50	13·67
France	2·59	10·53	7·97
Germany	12·87	18·65	14·58
United States	6·77	4·39	5·83

It will be seen from the table on the previous page that trade with these countries has now reached a fairly large volume, but its beginnings were small, hence the large percentage of increase just shown. Turning to individual countries, Germany exhibits the greatest progress, and Belgium ranks second. From Antwerp, in the latter country, a great portion of German and French manufactures is shipped. This port is also the distributing centre for a considerable part of the wool destined for the Continent, and large quantities of this product landed there ultimately find their way to Germany, France, and other countries. The French, early in 1883, were the first to establish direct commercial relations with Australia, the steamers of the Messageries Maritimes, a subsidised line, making their appearance for the first time in Australian waters in the year named. In 1887 the vessels of the Norddeutscher Lloyd Company, of Bremen, commenced trading with Australasia; and in the latter part of 1888 a line of German cargo-boats opened up further communication between the great wool-exporting cities of Sydney, Melbourne, and Adelaide and the ports of Antwerp, Hamburg, and Dunkirk. Belgium has also established a line of steamships; and the latest foreign testimony to the growing importance of Australasia is the regular running of the Nippon Yusen Kaisha's steamers between Japanese ports and Sydney, and a line of steamers which run between San Francisco and Sydney, calling at New Zealand. In addition to the companies mentioned, some British lines run their vessels direct to Continental ports.

The result of these efforts to establish commercial relations is evident from the increase of trade which the foregoing table discloses, and from the diversion, now rapidly being effected, in the channel by which the wool required for Europe reaches the market. The example of the South American Republics, the bulk of whose produce now finds a market at the ports of Antwerp, Hamburg, Havre, and Dunkirk without passing through London, was not lost on Continental buyers. It was manifest that direct shipments of wool to Europe could as readily be made from Sydney or Melbourne as from Buenos Ayres or Monte Video; hence the presence in the local markets, in increasing numbers, of buyers representing Continental firms.

Australasia has for many years maintained important commercial relations with the United States of America, and in 1902 America's share of the trade of Australasia with foreign countries was 37·4 per cent. The greater part of this trade was carried on with the states of New South Wales, Victoria and Tasmania, and the colony of New Zealand. The main exports to the United States are specie, copper, wool, coal, kauri gum, and New Zealand flax—chiefly the two first mentioned; so that, though large in its nominal amount, the trade is less valuable than would at first sight appear. The total exports to the United States from New South Wales were valued at £2,092,000, but this sum included gold coin to the amount of £1,601,000. Tasmania's export to America in 1902 reached a value of £464,000, practically the whole of which was made up by the export of blister copper, copper matte, and copper ore. If to these figures there be added the value of coal and coke exported from New South Wales, £103,444, and of marsupial skins, £242,096, a total of £2,410,000 is reached out of the entire Commonwealth export to the United States of £2,714,000. Of the balance, the principal item was wool, the export of which was valued at £198,588, of which Victoria contributed £108,688. The wool trade with the United States has fallen away considerably since 1891, when the export amounted to £514,243, while the export from the whole of Australia in 1902 was only £198,588. The export from New Zealand to the United States in 1902 was valued at £490,000, and included kauri gum to the value of £323,000, and phormium £64,000.

Under present tariff conditions little extension of commercial relations with the United States can be looked forward to; but trade with the East gives good promise for the future, especially with India, China, Japan, and the East Indian Archipelago, where markets for Australasian wool will possibly in time be found, little in that direction having been accomplished up to the present time. As mentioned above, Japan has established a national line of steamers to foster the trade between that country and Australasia; and with the abolition of the duty on wool, and the benefits to be derived from wearing woollen clothing impressed upon the people, there ought to be a good opening in that country for the staple product of these states. The foundation of such a trade has already been laid down, the exports of wool from New South Wales ports to Japan in 1902 being valued at £34,000, and from Victoria at £17,000. Western Australia in 1902 showed an export to Japan of £250,000, but the whole of this amount was made up of specie.

A large volume of business is already transacted with India and Ceylon, and this trade bids fair to increase, particularly in the tea of those places, which now strongly competes with the Chinese leaf in public estimation. The value of the direct import of Indian teas increased from £280,780 in 1890 to £766,616 in 1902; while the imports of this article from China decreased from £788,943 in 1890 to £83,913 in 1902. The following table shows the direct import of tea by each of the Commonwealth states and New Zealand from India and Ceylon, and from China, during the year 1902:—

State.	Imports of tea from—		Total.
	India and Ceylon.	China (including Hongkong).	
	£	£	£
New South Wales	203,560	25,584	229,144
Victoria	257,820	42,144	299,964
Queensland	34,401	5,598	39,999
South Australia	53,250	2,091	55,341
Western Australia	63,225	6,431	69,656
Tasmania	3,140	1,394	4,534
Commonwealth	615,396	83,242	698,638
New Zealand	151,220	671	151,891
Australasia	766,616	83,913	850,529

The total import into Australasia from India and Ceylon was valued at £1,735,201, and of this amount the value of tea imported was equal to 44 per cent. Of the remaining imports the chief items were jute and canvas goods and castor oil. The exports from Australasia to India in 1902 were valued at £3,881,932, but this amount included £2,822,000 worth of specie. In addition, New South Wales exported coal to the value of £25,000, and horses valued at £16,000, while Victoria and Queensland exported horses to the value of £36,000 and £28,000 respectively,

For 1902 the total of the Australasian exports to China was recorded as £107,113. The Customs returns, however, do not represent the whole amount of the trade with China, as a considerable portion of the commerce with Hongkong is in reality transacted with the Chinese Empire, Hongkong being to a large extent a distributing centre for the Empire. In view of this fact, the following table, showing the trade with the Chinese Empire and Hongkong, has been compiled :—

Country.		Commonwealth of Australia.		New Zealand.		Australasia.	
		1891.	1902.	1891.	1902.	1891.	1902.
Chinese Empire ..	Imports....	680,328	226,207	18,815	12,500	699,143	238,707
	Exports....	30,185	107 071	564	42	30,749	107,113
Hongkong	Imports ...	626,882	320,429	21,903	18,670	648,785	339,099
	Exports....	484,363	390,178	7,408	66,354	491,771	456,532
Total	Imports....	1,307,210	546,636	40,718	31,170	1,347,928	577,806
	Exports....	514,548	497,249	7,972	66,396	522,520	563,645
	Total Trade	1,821,758	1,043,885	48,690	97,566	1,870,448	1,141,451

Trade with Java has assumed considerable proportions, the total for Australasia in 1902 being £975,000, of which imports represented £803,000, and exports £172,000. Kapok and sugar are the chief articles imported, the import into Australasia of the former being valued in 1902 at £68,000, and of the latter at £726,000. The export trade was confined to the four states New South Wales, Victoria, Queensland and South Australia, New South Wales exporting coal to the value of £51,000, Victoria butter to the value of £20,000, Queensland preserved meat to the value of £22,000 and South Australia flour to the value of £52,000.

Trade with the South Pacific Islands is increasing, and consists mostly of the importation of raw articles in exchange for Australasian produce. The bulk of the trade is done with Fiji and New Caledonia, the French colony dealing principally with New South Wales, as Sydney is the terminal port in Australia for the mail-steamers of the Messageries line. But owing to the enforcement of the new French Customs tariff, which is highly protective in its character, in the colonies of that country as well as in France itself, the New Caledonian trade bids fair to be lost to Sydney; for while the exports from New South Wales to New Caledonia in 1892 amounted to £184,128, they had fallen in 1902 to £147,858, or by more than 19 per cent. The Commonwealth trade with Fiji was valued in 1902 at £294,000 and was practically confined to New South Wales whose share came to £285,000. The chief article of import is copra, the value of the quantity taken by New South Wales in 1902 being £59,000. New Zealand transacts a considerable trade with the group the value for 1902 being £388,000. The principal article of import was unrefined sugar, the quantity imported being 26,000 tons valued at £286,000. The trade with New Guinea is at present but small, though when the resources of that prolific island come to be developed a large increase may be expected. Besides the countries mentioned, Australasia maintains a not inconsiderable trade with Norway and Sweden, but it consists mainly of imports.

In the following table will be found some interesting information respecting the nature of the goods imported into the Commonwealth from foreign countries during the year 1901. This statement was prepared by the Board of Trade and it is unfortunate that the different classifications adopted in the Customs returns of the various states do not permit of a more detailed tabulation.

Article.	Value.	Article.	Value.
	£		£
Agricultural Implements	146,000	Iron and Steel, and manufactures thereof.	2,116,000
Apparel and Slops	164,000	Leather	157,000
Arms, Ammunition, and Explosives	234,000	Matches	68,000
Beer and Ale	53,000	Milk, Condensed	111,000
Bicycles, &c., including parts	50,000	Oil, Kerosene	687,000
Boots and Shoes	277,000	,, all other kinds	171,000
Carriages, Carts, Waggons, including materials.	77,000	Paper and Stationery	526,000
Cement and Plaster of Paris	158,000	Spirits and Liqueurs	173,000
China and Earthenware	56,000	Sugar	1,072,000
Copra	62,000	Tea	[illegible]
Drapery (Textiles in general)	581,000	Telegraphic materials	72,000
Drugs and Chemicals	393,000	Timber, rough	383,000
Fancy Goods	87,000	,, manufactured	[illegible]
Fish (dried or preserved)	126,000	Tobacco, unmanufactured	201,000
Fruit of all kinds	198,000	,, manufactured	337,000
Furniture (including kapok and materials).	204,000	Tools	174,000
Glass and Glassware (including bottles).	209,000	Turpentine	56,000
Grain—Rice	127,000	Watches and Clocks	71,000
Hats and Caps	65,000	Wax	24,000
Instruments, musical	754,000	Wines	[illegible]
,, scientific	73,000	Other articles	1,[illegible]
		Total foreign imports	£12,412,000

A classification of the goods imported into New Zealand from foreign countries during the year 1901 will be found below:—

Article.	Value.	Article.	Value.
	£		£
Apparel and Slops	20,000	Instruments, musical	68,000
Arms and Ammunition	20,000	Iron and Steel, and manufactures thereof.	603,000
Bicycles, Tricycles, &c.	25,000	Manure, Guano	11,000
Boots and Shoes	62,000	Oil, Kerosene	122,000
Carriages, Carts, &c.	16,000	Paper, Books, and Stationery	88,000
Chinaware, Earthenware, Glassware	31,000	Seeds	14,000
Clocks and Watches	16,000	Sugar	99,000
Drapery	51,000	Tobacco, manufactured	165,000
Drugs, Chemicals, &c.	48,000	Tools	54,000
Fancy Goods	82,000	Other articles	315,000
Fish, dried and preserved	20,000		
Fruit, fresh or preserved	104,000		
Furniture and Upholstery	21,000		
Grain, Rice	18,000	Total foreign imports	£2,018,000

The figures relating to the trade of each state with countries outside Australasia would be extremely interesting if they could be given with exactness. Unfortunately this is impossible, as the destination of goods exported overland cannot be traced beyond the state to which they are in the first instance despatched—all that can be given is the trade by sea, which the following series of tables shows. The imports during 1902 from countries outside Australia for the states comprised in the Commonwealth, together with the total for Australasia were as follows:—

State.	Value of Imports.	Value per Inhabitant.		
	£	£	s.	d.
New South Wales	15,024,535	10	13	6
Victoria	12,857,725	10	13	4
Queensland	3,734,212	7	5	1
South Australia	3,157,500	8	12	8
Western Australia	5,171,651	24	0	9
Tasmania	732,616	4	2	9
Commonwealth	40,678,239	10	9	4
New Zealand	9,611,428	11	17	11
Australasia	50,289,667	10	14	3

The values of the external exports for 1902 were as shown below:—

State.	Value of Exports.	Value per Inhabitant.		
	£	£	s.	d.
New South Wales	15,975,129	11	7	0
Victoria	10,369,335	8	12	0
Queensland	4,108,269	7	19	7
South Australia	3,766,206	10	5	11
Western Australia	8,252,608	38	7	2
Tasmania	1,443,675	8	3	0
Commonwealth	43,915,222	11	6	0
New Zealand	10,960,627	13	11	4
Australasia	54,875,849	11	13	10

The total extra Australian trade for the year 1902 was therefore as follows:—

State.	Total Extra Australian Trade.	Value per Inhabitant.		
	£	£	s.	d.
New South Wales	30,999,664	22	0	6
Victoria	23,227,060	19	5	4
Queensland	7,842,481	15	4	8
South Australia	6,923,706	18	18	7
Western Australia............	13,424,259	62	7	11
Tasmania........................	2,176,291	12	5	9
Commonwealth	84,593,461	21	15	
New Zealand	20,572,055	25	9	3
Australasia	105,165,516	22	8	1

It will be seen from the above table that the total value of the external trade of Australasia in 1902 was £105,165,516, equal to £22 8s. 1d. per head of population. The effects of the adverse season experienced over a great portion of the continent are reflected in these figures, which show a serious decline on the returns for 1901, when the total trade was valued at nearly 117 millions, and averaged £25 9s. 11d. per inhabitant. Turning to individual states, it will be found that in proportion to population, the trade of Western Australia is far in excess of that of any of the other Commonwealth states or of New Zealand. This of course is only to be expected in a rich gold-producing state with a comparatively small population. New Zealand, which had a remarkably favourable season, comes next with an average of £25 9s. 3d. per head, followed by New South Wales with £22 0s. 6d., and Victoria with £19 5s. 4d., Tasmania occupying the lowest position with £12 5s. 9d. per inhabitant. Comparisons of this description are, however, not quite fair, since states like Queensland and Tasmania, possessing but a small direct trade, appear at a disadvantage.

The foregoing represent the figures as returned by the statistical branches of the various Customs departments. Somewhat different and slightly smaller figures will be given later on as representing the goods valued for purposes of duty. The difference is in no case very great and may be accounted for partly by the difference in the year, the trade year coinciding with the calendar year and the fiscal year ending on June 30th following, partly by the amount of goods imported and placed in bond, while the totals are also modified by the fact that certain ship's stores pay duty but are not included in the Customs statements of imports.

A comparison of the external trade of the Commonwealth and of New Zealand with the latest returns of other countries is given below:—

Country.	Total Trade.			Per Inhabitant.		
	Merchandise.	Specie and Bullion.	Total.			
	£	£	£	£	s.	d.
United Kingdom	877,630,000	57,519,000	935,149,000	22	5	9
France	433,036,000	34,188,000	467,224,000	11	19	11
Germany	523,550,000	18,515,000	542,065,000	9	10	8
Italy	125,755,000	1,125,000	126,880,000	3	18	2
Belgium......	275,204,000	13,387,000	288,591,000	42	8	9
Spain...............	69,358,000	1,182,000	70,540,000	3	15	10
Canada	78,368,000	1,133,000	79,501,000	14	15	1
United States ...	481,445,000	45,814,000	527,259,000	6	18	2
Commonwealth of Australia...	67,701,948	16,891,513	84,593,461	21	15	4
New Zealand.....	22,642,071	2,329,629	24,971,700	30	18	2
Australasia	90,344,019	19,221,142	109,565,161	23	6	10

The trade of Australasia per head of population exceeds that of any country appearing in the list with the exception of Belgium.

An excess in the value of imports over exports was for many years a prominent feature of the trade of Australasia taken as a whole, although in some states the reverse was the case. The surplus of imports was due to two causes: (1) the importation, by the Governments and local bodies of the various states, of money to cover the cost of construction of public works; and (2) the private capital sent to Australasia for investment. Taking the states as a whole, these two items combined exceeded the payments made for interest on past loans, both public and private, and the sums drawn from the country by absentees; but as some of the states have ceased to borrow, and the amount borrowed by the others has fallen below their yearly payments for interest, the whole of Australasia now shows an excess of exports, and the same fact is also exhibited in the trade returns for 1902 for all the states with the exception of New South Wales and Victoria. The present excess of exports and its cause come more properly within the parts of this work dealing with Public and Private Finance, and are dealt with at some length there.

COMPARISON OF TRADE WITH BRITISH POSSESSIONS AND FOREIGN STATES

The external trade of the Commonwealth amounts to £84,593,461, and of this trade more than half still remains with Great Britain, as the following statement shows :—

	Total trade (Imports and Exports).	Proportion of total.
United Kingdom............	44,073,053.........	52·1 per cent.
British Possessions.........	17,582,771.........	20·8 ,,
Foreign Countries	22,937,637.........	27·1 ,,
=	84,593,461.........	100 ,,

The figures just given refer to the direct trade, but a considerable amount of goods is sent from foreign countries to Great Britain and thence exported to Australia. There are no means of ascertaining with exactitude the value of this trade, but a measure of it may be obtained from the British Board of Trade returns, which show an average export of foreign and colonial produce to Australia, during the last five years, of £1,966,730 per annum, while a somewhat larger quantity of Australian produce is exported from Great Britain to foreign countries. Neglecting this indirect trade, the following is a statement of the direction of the external trade of the Commonwealth in 1891 and in 1902.

Trade with—	Imports.		Exports.		Total trade.	
	1891.	1902.	1891.	1902.	1891.	1902.
British Empire—	£	£	£	£	£	£
United Kingdom	26,453,841	23,848,562	25,498,010	20,224,491	51,951,851	44,073,053
New Zealand	1,793,038	2,749,958	660,213	1,396,211	2,453,251	4,146,169
India and Ceylon	982,824	1,323,249	998,320	3,879,771	1,981,144	5,203,020
Canadian Dominion	149,786	846,276	40	33,372	149,826	879,648
Cape Colony	873	6,153	171,312	3,781,261	171,685	3,787,414
Natal	......	815	......	2,187,795	......	2,188,110
Fiji	155,067	89,059	122,430	204,793	277,497	293,852
Mauritius	388,529	280,731	107,147	64,176	495,676	344,907
Hongkong	626,882	320,429	484,363	390,178	1,111,245	710,607
Straits Settlements	178,516	118,456	151,143	118,555	329,659	237,011
Other Possessions	54,256	150,276	139,464	141,757	193,720	292,033
Total	30,783,112	29,233,464	28,332,442	32,422,360	59,115,554	61,655,824
Foreign Countries—						
France	359,951	525,937	1,807,905	2,603,336	2,167,856	3,129,273
Germany	1,707,175	2,658,060	859,557	2,543,360	2,566,732	5,201,420
Italy	56,617	163,797	27,956	142,311	84,573	306,108
Belgium	314,434	352,447	1,484,073	1,435,263	1,798,507	1,787,710
Sweden and Norway........	459,046	479,798	......	1,001	459,046	480,799
United States	2,558,320	4,989,812	2,754,053	2,714,424	5,312,373	7,704,236
Netherlands and Java	652,517	813,565	92,645	282,451	745,162	1,096,016
South Sea Islands	12,792	128,795	55,963	120,123	68,755	248,918
China	680,328	226,207	30,185	107,071	710,513	333,278
Japan	52,887	354,327	16,485	414,823	69,372	769,150
Other Countries............	73,874	752,030	581,286	1,128,699	655,160	1,880,729
Total	6,927,941	11,444,775	7,710,108	11,492,862	14,638,049	22,937,637
Total, British and Foreign	37,711,053	40,678,239	36,042,550	43,915,222	73,753,603	84,593,461

The foregoing table shows that a considerable change is taking place in the direction of the Australian trade. The United Kingdom, though still the greatest factor in the trade of the Commonwealth, has diminished in importance both actually and relatively. Amongst British Possessions the most notable increase appears in the trade of Cape Colony, which advanced from £171,685 in 1891 to £3,787,414 in 1902. Natal appears in the returns for 1902 with a total of £2,188,110, a trade due, as in the case of Cape Colony, almost wholly to the war in South Africa, which created a large demand for Australian produce. Trade with India and Ceylon advanced during the period from £1,981,144 to £5,203,020; the increased popularity of India and Ceylon tea accounts for some portion of this growth; but in 1902 there was a considerable export of specie and bullion, Western Australia sending £1,895,000 and Victoria £1,063,000. Amongst foreign countries the most notable increase observable is in the trade with Germany, which more than doubled during the period, the total trade in 1902 being £5,201,420 as compared with £2,566,732 in 1891. The exports also show a remarkable advance during this period, the value rising from £859,557 to £2,543,360. Trade with the United States showed a total of £7,704,236 in 1902, the value in 1891 being £5,312,373; the increase of trade was, however, wholly on the import side, the exports showing a fall of £39,629, while the imports showed an increase of £2,431,492. The exports for 1891, however, included gold bullion and specie to the value of £1,710,670, the corresponding figure for 1902 being £1,601,000. Extending the period reviewed back to 1861, the importance of the change taking place will be more clearly apprehended. The following statement shows the volume of trade in quinquennial periods, commencing with 1861, and distinguishing the trade with the United Kingdom, British Possessions, and foreign countries.

Years.	Imports from—			Total Imports.
	United Kingdom.	British Possessions.	Foreign Countries.	
	£	£	£	£
1861–65	69,824,585	13,284,813	16,931,345	100,040,743
1866–70	60,392,217	18,068,939	14,537,213	92,998,369
1871–75	75,568,020	19,924,188	13,491,699	108,983,907
1876–80	89,020,970	18,327,973	15,766,484	123,115,427
1881–85	128,073,941	22,491,217	24,066,365	174,631,523
1886–90	122,729,684	21,329,451	28,849,366	172,908,501
1891–95	97,408,111	15,915,497	23,352,095	136,675,703
1896–1900	109,024,399	18,709,125	41,090,263	168,823,787
*1901–1902	49,085,594	10,169,381	23,857,111	83,112,086

* Two Years.

Stating the foregoing figures as percentages of the total imports in each quinquennium, the following results are obtained :—

Years.	Imports from—		
	United Kingdom.	British Possessions.	Foreign Countries.
	per cent.	per cent.	per cent.
1861–65	69·80	13·28	16·92
1866–70	64·94	19·43	15·63
1871–75	69·34	18·28	12·38
1876–80	72·30	14·89	12·81
1881–85	73·34	12·88	13·78
1886–90	70·98	12·34	16·68
1891–95	71·27	11·64	17·09
1896–1900	64·58	11·08	24·34
1901-2	59·06	12·24	28·70

These figures show a remarkable diversion of trade, especially in recent years, from the United Kingdom to foreign countries. An explanation has been hazarded that the diversion is more apparent than real, being due to the carriage of goods direct from foreign countries to Australia, whereas such goods were formerly sent via London, but this explanation only partly accounts for the change. Making allowance for foreign goods reaching Australia by way of London, the following would appear to be the percentages of foreign goods to total goods imported in the years named. It is unfortunately impossible to give the information for an earlier period :—

1886–90	23·5
1891–95	23·4
1896–1900	30·0
1901-2	33·6

One-third of all goods now imported into Australia may be said to be of non-British origin as compared with one-fourth ten years ago. The chief factor in bringing about this change is undoubtedly the establishment of direct and rapid communication between Germany, France, Belgium, Japan, the United States, and the Commonwealth. Twenty years ago it was difficult, if not impossible, to obtain goods direct from the continent of Europe or the eastern sea-board of the United States, now there is fortnightly communication with Hamburg and Bremerhaven by a line subsidised by the German Imperial Government, and with Marseilles, Havre, and Dunkirk by the Messageries Maritimes—a line heavily subsidised by the French Republic. Turning to the exports to the same countries it will be found that a change of a somewhat similar character has taken place.

Year.	Exports to—			
	United Kingdom.	British Possessions.	Foreign Countries.	Total Exports.
	£	£	£	£
1861	11,643,598	5,030,311	725,747	17,399,656
1871	15,754,990	5,055,926	609,032	21,419,948
1881	19,866,821	5,516,610	2,105,644	27,489,075
1891	25,498,010	2,834,432	7,710,108	36,042,550
1901	25,194,923	12,028,463	12,492,072	49,715,458
1902	20,224,491	12,197,869	11,492,862	43,915,222
	PERCENTAGE OF TOTAL.			
1861	66·9	28.9	4·2	100·0
1871	73·6	23·6	2·8	100·0
1881	72·3	20·0	7·7	100·0
1891	70·7	7·9	21·4	100·0
1901	50·7	24·2	25·1	100·0
1902	46·1	27 8	26·1	100·0

As the table shows there was a remarkable falling off in the percentage of exports to British Possessions in 1891 as compared with 1881. Investigation of the returns discloses the fact that the Victorian exports to British Possessions dropped from £3,863,760 in 1881 to £968,550 in 1901, and this was brought about by a decline in the exports to Ceylon of gold bullion and specie from £2,784,046 in 1881 to £58,074 in 1891; the exports of specie have been since resumed.

From the above figures it is apparent that, as in the case of the imports, there has been a considerable modification in the direction of the export trade. The causes of the great advance in the proportion of trade taken by foreign countries have already been discussed. It will be observed that the percentage of exports to the British Possessions advanced considerably in 1901 and 1902, the increase being chiefly due to the demand for the produce of the Commonwealth occasioned by the war in South Africa.

TRADE OF NEW ZEALAND.

The trade of New Zealand during the years 1891 and 1902 will be found below :—

Trade with—	Imports.		Exports.		Total Trade.	
	1891.	1902.	1891.	1902.	1891.	1902.
British Empire—	£	£	£	£	£	£
Commonwealth of Australia	1,013,549	1,715,295	1,705,561	2,684,350	2,719,110	4,399,645
United Kingdom	4,369,633	6,851,452	7,140,831	9,450,648	11,510,464	16,302,100
India and Ceylon	275,248	411,952	2,551	2,161	277,799	414,113
Canadian Dominion	1,941	33,516	......	3,018	1,941	36,534
Cape Colony	9	848	100	79,213	109	80,056
Natal......................	......	135	......	674,708	......	674,843
Fiji	177,707	327,972	43,896	59,690	221,603	387,662
Mauritius..................	70,650	......	4	......	70,654	......
Hongkong	21,903	18,670	7,408	66,354	29,311	85,024
Straits Settlements	10,055	23,113	100	284	10,155	23,397
Other Possessions..........	671	38,009	3,330	8,052	4,001	46,061
Total..........	5,941,366	9,420,957	8,903,781	13,028,478	14,845,147	22,449,435
Foreign Countries—	£	£	£	£	£	£
France	9,084	35,572	27,879	15	36,963	35,587
Germany	66,102	210,560	4,258	9,389	70,360	219,949
Italy	1,867	11,129	43	32	1,910	11,161
Belgium	6,591	86,236	1,658	394	8,249	86,630
Sweden and Norway	368	19,543	......	169	368	19,712
United States..............	361,795	1,318,937	515,208	489,964	877,003	1,808,901
Netherlands and Java	2,143	65,368	......	82	2,143	65,450
South Sea Islands..........	65,493	41,042	93,407	93,963	158,900	135,005
China	18,815	12,500	564	42	19,379	12,542
Japan	8,399	56,087	93	3,780	8,492	59,867
Other Countries...........	21,826	48,792	19,506	18,669	41,332	67,461
Total	562,483	1,905,766	662,616	616,499	1,225,099	2,522,265
Total, British and Foreign	6,503,849	11,326,723	9,566,397	13,644,977	16,070,246	24,971,700

The following table shows the volume and percentage of New Zealand trade at intervals since 1881, distinguishing the trade with United Kingdom, British possessions, and foreign countries :—

Year.	Imports from—			Total.
	United Kingdom.	British Possessions.	Foreign Countries.	
	£	£	£	£
1881	4,530,316	2,489,839	436,890	7,457,045
1891	4,369,633	1,571,733	562,483	6,503,849
1901	6,885,831	2,913,866	2,018,218	11,817,915
1902	6,851,452	2,569,505	1,905,766	11,326,723
PERCENTAGE OF TOTAL.				
1881	60·8	33·4	5·8	100·0
1891	67·2	24·2	8·6	100·0
1901	58·3	24·6	17·1	100·0
1902	60·5	22·7	16·8	100·0

In spite of fluctuations in individual years, trade with the United Kingdom still comprises more than three-fifths of the total, but the greatest increase in imports has taken place in the trade with foreign countries, which doubled itself during the period from 1891 to 1902. Amongst the chief countries contributing to this advance were the United States, the imports from which rose from £362,000 in 1891 to £1,319,000 in 1902, and Germany, from which the imports increased from £66,000 in 1891 to £211,000 in 1902.

A similar statement regarding the exports for the same years is given below:—

Year.	Exports to—			Total.
	United Kingdom.	British Possessions.	Foreign Countries.	
	£	£	£	£
1881	4,475,601	1,116,948	468,317	6,060,866
1891	7,140,831	1,762,950	662,616	9,566,397
1901	9,295,375	2,907,412	678,637	12,881,424
1902	9,450,648	3,577,830	616,499	13,644,977
	Percentage of total—			
1881	73·9	18·4	7·7	100·0
1891	74·7	18·4	6·9	100·0
1901	72·2	22·5	5·3	100·0
1902	69·3	26·2	4·5	100·0

As the table shows, the percentage of exports to the United Kingdom and foreign countries declined during the period 1881–1902, while the rate of export to the other British possessions shows an increase. Under British Possessions it must be noted that the States of the Commonwealth are included. The figures for 1901 and 1902 are, however, swollen by reason of the heavy exports of New Zealand produce to South Africa to supply the demand created by the war; the export of oats alone in 1901 being valued at £716,000, and in 1902 at £512,000. Of the foreign countries New Zealand's chief customer in 1902 was the United States, the value of the export thereto being £490,000, the export of kauri gum being £323,000, and phormium £64,000.

Exports of Domestic Produce.

The values of the exports of Australasia and of its various provinces have been given in the previous pages without respect to the countries where the articles were produced. It is important to find to what extent the exports have been the produce of each of the states whence they were shipped. The following table shows the value of the exports of domestic produce of each state as returned by the Customs for the years 1891, 1901, and 1902, and the value thereof per inhabitant :—

State.	Total Value.			Value per Inhabitant.		
	1891.	1901.	1902.	1891.	1901.	1902.
	£	£	£	£ s. d.	£ s. d.	£ s. d.
New South Wales	21,065,712	19,915,884	17,248,494	18 8 9	14 10 3	12 5 1
Victoria	13,026,426	14,134,028	18,823,989	11 7 6	11 14 11	11 9 4
Queensland	7,979,080	9,009,696	8,732,058	19 17 4	17 17 3	16 19 2
South Australia	4,810,512	4,392,364	4,935,529	14 17 10	12 1 11	13 9 11
Western Australia	788,873	8,216,718	8,871,676	15 9 7	43 16 4	41 4 9
Tasmania	1,367,927	2,938,878	3,227,777	9 3 8	10 18 0	18 4 7
Commonwealth..........	49,058,530	58,602,568	56,839,473	15 16 1	15 8 2	14 12 6
New Zealand.............	9,400,094	12,690,460	13,498,599	14 18 6	16 5 9	16 14 2
Australasia	58,458,624	71,293,028	70,338,072	15 4 4	15 11 1	14 19 8

The figures, prior to 1901, must be regarded as approximate, for it is difficult to ascertain with exactitude the domestic exports of some of the states, chiefly New South Wales, South Australia, and Victoria. In the last-mentioned state, a large proportion of the domestic export of wool consisted, in former years, of New South Wales produce, but in 1902 the amount of Victorian wool was found to be largely under-stated and the figures in the following table have therefore been amended. There is also an export by South Australia, as local produce, of wool grown in New South Wales, but the value thereof is inconsiderable, and, in fact, as regards the total export of South Australian wool, the figures for 1902 were somewhat under-estimated. Wool, chiefly from Queensland, has in some years been exported as domestic produce by New South Wales, but in 1902 no such over-statement took place. Also, as regards New South Wales, tin and copper ore, the former chiefly from Queensland and Tasmania and the latter from South Australia, which are imported for the purpose of being refined, are exported as domestic produce. An attempt has been made to remove these elements of error from the returns as they are presented by the

Customs, and the amounts shown in the following table may be accepted as the true values of domestic produce exported by each state during 1902:—

State.	Domestic Exports.		
	Total Value.	Proportion to Total.	Value per Inhabitant.
	£	per cent.	£ s. d.
New South Wales	17,140,316	24·1	12 3 6
Victoria	14,554,922	20·5	12 1 6
Queensland	8,732,058	12·3	16 19 2
South Australia	4,959,949	7·0	13 11 2
Western Australia	8,871,676	12·5	41 4 9
Tasmania	3,227,777	4·6	18 4 7
Commonwealth	57,486,698	81·0	14 15 10
New Zealand	13,498,599	19·0	16 14 2
Australasia	70,985,297	100·0	15 2 5

As the table shows, the largest values per inhabitant were returned by Western Australia and Tasmania, with £41 4s. 9d. and £18 4s. 7d. respectively per head of population. The growth of the domestic exports of Western Australia has been extremely rapid, the total value rising from £1,273,638 at the end of 1895 to £8,871,676 for the year 1902, an increase of over 596 per cent. Of course, this great expansion is in the main due to the export of gold, the value of the total export of the precious metal being returned at £3,318,958 in 1902 as against £879,748 in 1895. Tasmania also shows a large increase both in actual and comparative value of domestic export trade, the returns for 1902 showing a total value of £3,227,777, with £18 4s. 7d. per head of population, as against £1,473,283 and £9 0s. 3d. in 1896 The phenomenal mineral export of Tasmania for the year 1902, when the gross total reached the sum of £1,526,000, is chiefly accountable for the expansion, and, so far as can be seen, there is every prospect of this being sustained.

Placing the values of the external exports of domestic production of Australasia side by side with those of some of the more important countries of the world, a useful comparison is afforded, and from whatever standpoint the matter be viewed these states appear in a very favourable light. The following table shows the value of the domestic exports, exclusive of coin and bullion, of some of the principal countries of the world, the figures referring to the year 1901. The figures for Australasia only represent the external exports of domestic produce in

1902; in the preceding table the values include the domestic produce of each state consumed in the other provinces :—

Country.	Exports of Domestic Produce (exclusive of Coin and Bullion).	Value per Inhabitant.
United Kingdom	£283,424,000	£6 16 9
France	160,516,000	4 2 5
Germany	221,570,000	3 17 11
Austria-Hungary	78,561,000	1 13 7
Italy	54,978,000	1 7 8
Belgium	73,129,000	10 17 1
Canada	36,472,000	6 15 5
Argentine Republic	33,543,000	7 5 0
United States	304,263,000	3 19 9
Australasia	33,897,000	7 4 5

The extent to which the geographical position of a state enables it to benefit by the production of its neighbours is illustrated by the proportion which the non-domestic bear to the total exports. The following table shows the value of the total re-export trade and the proportion which it bears to the total export trade of each state in 1902; and it would appear that South Australia, New South Wales, and Victoria, in the order named, benefit largely by their position, the re-export trade of the other states being insignificant :—

State.	Total Re-exports.	Proportion to Total Exports.
New South Wales	£6,295,557	26·74 per cent.
Victoria	4,386,584	24·09 ,,
Queensland	438,965	4·79 ,,
South Australia	2,926,113	37·22 ,,
Western Australia	179,682	1·99 ,,
Tasmania	16,731	0·51 ,,
Commonwealth	£14,243,632	20·04 ,,
New Zealand	146,378	1·07 ,,
Australasia	£14,390,010	16·98 ,,

More than one-half of this re-export trade is external, the amount for the Commonwealth states being £8,500,459, as compared with £5,743,173 of interstate trade.

The Wool Trade.

The following table shows the destination of the wool exported by the Commonwealth and New Zealand to countries outside Australasia, with the proportion of the total amount taken by each during the period 1881–1902:—

Country.	Value.				Proportion.			
	1881.	1891.	1901.	1902.	1881.	1891.	1901.	1902.
	£	£	£	£	per cent	per cent	per cent	per cent
United Kingdom.....	15,777,827	19,891,218	13,497,871	10,947,298	97·8	82·7	71·3	68·0
Belgium	96,557	1,453,755	1,146,349	924,447	0 6	6·0	6·0	5·8
Germany	53,809	782,676	1,852,053	1,755,053	0·3	3·3	9·8	10·9
France	26,965	1,386,768	2,003,197	2,133,975	0·2	5·8	10·6	13·2
United States	132,699	514,551	273,983	212,960	0·8	2·1	1·5	1·4
Other Countries....	48,725	34,259	147,460	128,807	0·3	0·1	0·8	0·7
Total	16,136,082	24,063,227	18,920,863	16,102,540	100·0	100·0	100·0	100·0

The total under the heading of "Other Countries" included for 1902 wool to the value of £55,367 sent to Italy, and £55,802 taken by Japan.

The table shows that, while the trade increased considerably during the period from 1881 to 1891, since the latter year there has been a heavy decline, the value of the external export in 1902 being slightly less than that of 1881. The decrease is accounted for by the series of unfavourable seasons experienced since 1891. In 1891, the sheep depastured in the Commonwealth of Australia and New Zealand numbered 124,548,000, but at the end of 1902, the total had fallen to 74,348,000; a decrease of over 50 millions. It will be observed that since 1881 the wool exported to the United Kingdom has decreased in value to the extent of £4,830,000, or from 97·8 to 68 per cent. France and Germany both show proportionate increases throughout the whole period, the proportion for France rising from 0·2 per cent. in 1881 to 13·3 per cent. in 1902, while the percentage for Germany rose from 0·3 per cent. in 1881 to 10·9 per cent. in 1902.

It is necessary to point out here that all the figures in the present chapter dealing with the export of wool are based on the Customs returns of the different states, and represent the values placed on the wool by the exporters. The figures relating to the value of the wool clip which are given in the chapter on the pastoral industry are less than those just given, the difference being made up in the cost of carriage and other charges from the sheep-runs to the ship's side.

The following table shows the total and proportionate value of the wool shipped direct to countries outside Australasia by each state:—

State.	Value.			Proportion.		
	1881.	1891.	1902.	1881.	1891.	1902.
	£	£	£	per cent	per cent	per cent
New South Wales	4,485,295	7,917,587	6,704,424	27·8	32·9	41·6
Victoria	5,327,934	7,070,661	3,458,548	33·0	29·4	21·5
Queensland	996,047	2,438,321	868,842	6·2	10·1	5·4
South Australia	1,747,696	1,888,107	1,059,146	10·8	7·8	6·6
Western Australia	256,689	311,925	454,995	1·6	1·3	2·8
Tasmania	416,572	313,422	205,029	2·6	1·3	1·3
New Zealand	2,905,849	4,123,204	3,351,556	18·0	17·2	20·8
Australasia	16,136,082	24,063,227	16,102,540	100·0	100·0	100·0

It will be seen from the table just given that Victoria was credited in 1881 with exporting wool to a considerable value in excess of that of New South Wales. In 1891 and 1902, however, the positions were reversed. The change is mainly due to the extension of railways, especially noticeable in New South Wales, where some lines are expressly designed to bring trade to Sydney.

In connection with this subject, a statement of the value of wool of its own production which each state exports direct and by way of the other states may not be without interest. The figures, which are given below, relate to the year 1902:—

State.	Domestic Wool Exported.			Proportion of Export of Australasia.
	Direct.	By way of the other states.	Total.	
	£	£	£	per cent.
New South Wales	6,370,531	936,279	7,306,810	45·4
Victoria	2,309,804	23,356	2,333,160	14·5
Queensland	868,842	435,358	1,304,200	8·1
South Australia	923,629	144,391	1,068,020	6·6
Western Australia	454,995	3,083	458,078	2·9
Tasmania	205,029	58,222	263,251	1·6
New Zealand	3,351,556	3,007	3,354,563	20·9
Australasia	14,484,386	1,603,696	16,088,082	100·0

In the table given on the preceding page the value of the direct export of wool is quoted at £16,102,540. The apparent discrepancy, however, is of no moment when it is remembered that about one-fifth of the clip of Australasia is subject to valuation first at the border of the state in which it is produced, and again at the port from which it is finally shipped to Europe or America. In the amount of £16,088,082 shown above is, besides, included the value of such wool as was exported during 1902 to one of the adjacent states, and there held over for the sales in January of the following year.

The following figures serve to illustrate the development of the local wool sales in those states where such sales are held, viz., in New South Wales, Victoria, Queensland, South Australia, and New Zealand, for the ten seasons from 1892-93 to 1902-1903. The seasons are taken as extending from the 1st July to the 30th June. The number of bales sold during each period shown was as follows:—

Season.	New South Wales.	Victoria.	Queensland.	South Australia.	New Zealand.	Total.
	bales.	bales.	bales.	bales.	bales.	bales.
1892-93	362,688	310,828	....	54,285	85,505	813,306
1893-94	401,185	305,700	....	65,000	82,547	854,432
1894-95	425,135	328,142	... .	64,056	82,547	899,880
1895-96	415,538	315,543	....	80,234	82,965	894,280
1896-97	401,048	310,835	....	63,804	82,515	858,202
1897-98	444,808	286,625	....	51,287	100,514	883,234
1898-99	447,517	278,482	10,925	60,531	90,806	888,261
1899-1900 ...	399,893	312,571	27,015	70,717	108,846	919,042
1900-1901 ...	388,946	273,641	13,453	42,637	90,235	808,912
1901-1902 ...	522,003	321,482	25,936	65,239	100,860	1,035,520
1902-1903 ...	383,506	270,107	14,754	60,782	115,553	844,702

The importance of the pastoral industry to Australasia will be made clear in another part of this volume. Its value to each state varies considerably, as the statement of the exports of pastoral produce on the next page will show. In no state, however, Western Australia and Tasmania excepted, does the proportion of exports of this class fall below one-fourth of the total value of domestic produce exported. In the case of New South Wales it reaches 62 per cent., while in New Zealand it is 56 per cent., and in Queensland 47 per cent. On account of the unfavourable season in 1902 the proportion for Australasia was nearly 3 per cent. below that of the preceding year, but it is anticipated that the results for 1903 will show a considerable increase.

State.	Wool.	Other Pastoral Products.	Total.	Proportion of Exports of Pastoral Produce to Total Exports of Domestic Products.
	£	£	£	per cent.
New South Wales	7,306,810	3,385,817	10,692,627	62·0
Victoria..................	2,333,160	1,622,245	3,955,405	23·6
Queensland	1,304,200	2,771,419	4,075,619	46·7
South Australia	1,068,020	634,983	1,703,003	34·5
Western Australia	458,078	131,710	589,788	6·6
Tasmania	263,251	157,974	421,225	13·1
New Zealand	3,354,563	4,149,965	7,504,528	55·6
Australasia— All Domestic	16,088,082	12,854,113	28,942,195	41·1
External Domestic.	14,484,386	9,411,255	23,895,641	49·7

It will be observed that the figures given in this table are not those furnished by the various Customs Departments; they have been corrected in the manner already explained in order to allow for the incorrect information furnished by shippers in regard to the state of origin.

Movements of Gold.

Since the discovery of gold in the year 1851 large quantities of the metal—in the form of coin as well as of bullion—have been exported from the Australasian states every year. In the figures given below, showing the excess of exports of gold of each state, no attempt has been made to exclude the interstate trade. The largest exporters, it will be found, are also the largest producers, namely, Victoria, New Zealand, and Queensland. The other states, except Western Australia, now produce very little more than what suffices to meet their requirements. It will be understood, of course, that the production is considerably in excess of the exports shown hereunder :—

State.	1851-60.	1861-70.	1871-80.	1881-90.
	£	£	£	£
New South Wales	8,337,067	13,656,650	5,248,994	277,509
Victoria	86,342,134	62,609,042	37,222,632	23,106,371
Queensland	......	1,768,575	9,430,137	11,540,245
South Australia	1,900,955	*395,633	*1,100,309	*673,548
Western Australia	......	19,586	*38,000	*44,320
Tasmania	843,029	*34,255	165,040	872,754
Commonwealth	97,423,185	77,623,965	50,928,494	35,079,011
New Zealand	48,981	20,294,822	14,215,143	7,637,381
Total Excess of Exports	97,472,166	97,918,787	65,143,637	42,716,392
Average per annum	9,747,217	9,791,879	6,514,364	4,271,639

State.	1891-1900.	1901.	1902.	1851-1902.
	£	£	£	£
New South Wales	7,478,424	381,055	*49,389	35,330,310
Victoria	21,903,262	3,104,911	2,945,511	237,233,863
Queensland	21,672,494	2,008,774	2,602,438	49,022,663
South Australia	1,206,945	33,286	145,822	1,117,518
Western Australia	19,266,987	6,749,717	7,451,487	33,405,457
Tasmania	1,599,258	192,164	*34,438	3,603,552
Commonwealth	73,127,370	12,469,907	13,061,431	359,713,363
New Zealand	9,433,361	1,324,141	1,609,114	54,562,943
Total Excess of Exports	82,560,731	13,794,048	14,670,545	414,276,306
Average per annum	8,256,073	13,794,048	14,670,545	7,966,852

* Excess of Imports.

Dutiable and Free Goods.

Very interesting results are obtained from a classification of the imports for home consumption into dutiable and free goods. In this connection, however, the fact must not be lost sight of that under the terms of the Commonwealth Constitution Act, Western Australia may continue to levy duties on interstate imports, for a period of five years after the imposition of the federal tariff, subject to the following restrictions :—For the first year the duties to be at the rates in force in the state at the time when the uniform federal tariff was imposed; for the second year at four-fifths of those rates; for the third year, three-fifths; for the fourth year, two-fifths; and for the fifth year, one-fifth; these special rates thereafter ceasing. During the same five years the state is also authorised to levy on goods imported from beyond the Commonwealth a rate equal to the excess of the Western Australian tariff over the Commonwealth tariff where such existed at the time the Commonwealth tariff was instituted, *i.e.*, the 8th October, 1901. Under this special tariff Western Australia collected in 1902 £265,185. The state levied duties on foreign goods valued at £379,956; and on Australian goods to the value of £1,304,266, both free under the federal tariff; and on stimulants to the value of £133,232. In addition, duties were collected on other goods to the value of £387,701, taxable under the federal tariff, but in regard to which the Western Australian rates were higher.

The following statement shows the dutiable and free imports into the Commonwealth from places outside its boundaries, together with the amount of duty collected, exclusive of sums collected under the special tariff of Western Australia. In addition to the non-dutiable goods shown, merchandise to the value of £16,798,122, the produce of Australia, passed from one state to another free of duty.

With respect to the information contained in the following statement, it must be understood that interstate adjustments have not been taken into consideration. Thus the values of goods entered for home consumption in New South Wales and Victoria are in excess of those actually ascribable to these states, the former being debited with about £39,300, and the latter with £174,600 in connection with imports which paid duty in these states, but which were consumed in other portions of the Commonwealth. Information as to the declared value of the goods in question is not available, and they have, therefore, been allowed to remain in the totals of the states into which they were originally imported both in this and the succeeding statements: the total for the Commonwealth is, of course, correct.

State.	Dutiable Goods.				Free Goods.	Total.
	Narcotics.	Stimulants.	Other Merchandise.	Total Dutiable.	Value.	
	£	£	£	£	£	£
New South Wales	178,595	507,670	8,339,900	9,086,165	3,487,030	12,573,195
Victoria	120,527	321,534	7,322,403	7,764,464	4,320,860	12,085,324
Queensland	95,467	219,575	2,620,626	2,935,668	1,359,801	4,295,469
South Australia ...	47,340	91,071	1,830,595	1,969,006	757,959	2,726,965
Western Australia	101,982	247,155	3,727,157	4,076,294	988,855	5,065,149
Tasmania	33,341	44,011	815,806	893,158	540,717	1,433,875
Commonwealth ...	577,252	1,431,016	24,716,487	26,724,755	11,455,222	38,179,977

The duties collected, distributed under the foregoing headings, were as follows :—

State.	Duties Collected on—			
	Narcotics.	Stimulants.	Other Merchandise.	* Total.
	£	£	£	£
New South Wales............	271,265	845,416	1,649,196	2,765,877
Victoria	193,238	428,399	1,448,318	2,069,955
Queensland	155,224	305,896	523,945	985,065
South Australia	60,511	104,294	450,662	615,467
Western Australia	154,298	270,749	668,531	1,093,578
Tasmania	37,048	66,105	131,561	234,714
Commonwealth	871,584	2,020,859	4,872,213	7,764,656

* Excluding interstate adjustments.

A comparison of the amount of duty realised, with the value of the goods on which the taxes were imposed, gives the following results :—

	Value of Imports for Home Consumption.	Duty.	Average Rate of Duty.
	£	£	per cent.
Stimulants	1,431,016	2,020,859	141·2
Narcotics	577,252	871,584	151·0
Other dutiable goods......	24,716,487	4,872,213	19·7
Free goods	11,455,222	....	....

As shown above the total value of British and foreign goods imported for home consumption into Australia during the year ending December, 1902, was £38,179,977. Excluding stimulants and narcotics the imports were £36,171,709, and as the duties collected were £4,872,213, the average rate of duty on merchandise, including free goods, was therefore 13·5 per cent.

Although the duties are uniform throughout the Commonwealth, the collections do not work out as equal percentages for all the states. This of course is only to be expected, seeing that the different states are unequal consumers of dutiable goods, while the proportion of free goods also varies. Excluding stimulants and narcotics, the following statement shows the percentage of free goods to total imports, together with the average rate of duty on dutiable goods, as well as on all goods for each state of the Commonwealth.

State.	Percentage of Free to Total Imports..	Rate of Duty—	
		On Dutiable Merchandise.	On all Merchandise Free and Dutiable.
	per cent.	per cent.	per cent.
New South Wales	29·3	19·6	13·9
Victoria	37·1	19·8	12·4
Queensland	34·2	20·0	13·2
South Australia	29·3	24·6	17·4
Western Australia	21·0	17·9	14·2
Tasmania	39·9	16·1	9·7
Commonwealth	31·7	19·7	13·5

The variations in the percentage of duty are capable of simple explanation. For South Australia it appears that the average *ad valorem* on dutiable goods is 24·6 per cent. as compared with 20 per cent. in Queensland. The latter state, however, is not an importer of foreign sugar, and consequently receives little or no duty on that article, whereas the collections from sugar alone raise the *ad valorem* percentage by 5·4, that is to say, under like conditions as in Queensland the South Australian duties would average 19·2 per cent. Tasmania collects very little duty on sugar, as most of that consumed in the state is grown in Queensland or New South Wales. On this account the Customs revenue of the state suffers to the extent of £33,800 a year, while if it obtained an equivalent amount of duty the Tasmanian collections would be raised to an *ad valorem* of 20·2 per cent. The variations in the percentage results for some of the other states are susceptible of analogous explanation.

It will be seen from the foregoing that, taking the Commonwealth as a whole, the percentage of free goods is 31·7 per cent. of all goods imported, excluding narcotics and stimulants. As the following table shows, this is somewhat lower than the free list obtaining in the states prior to the imposition of the uniform duties of Customs; in fact, the only state with a smaller free list than the Commonwealth was Tasmania. As regards the average burthen of duties, the Commonwealth tariff was lower than that of any of the states with the exception of Western Australia and New South Wales. For the year 1902 the average of the Commonwealth was 13·5 per cent. on all goods imported other than narcotics and stimulants, and 19·7 per cent. *ad valorem* on dutiable goods. The averages for the six states separately for the year 1900 were as shown :—

State.	Free List—Proportion of Goods on.	Average Rate of Duty, *ad valorem*.	
		On Dutiable Goods, Merchandise.	On all Merchandise other than Narcotics and Stimulants.
	Per cent.	Per cent.	Per cent.
New South Wales	89·8	10·3	1·1
Victoria	53·4	36·2	17·0
Queensland	39·5	20·4	12·4
South Australia	35·7	21·8	14·0
Western Australia	37·1	14 8	9·3
Tasmania	9·0	24·2	22·0

The operation of the Commonwealth tariff affords an interesting study, and it will probably be found that the percentage of free goods to dutiable will gradually increase. There is already evidence of this, for the percentage of free goods in the first year of the tariff's operation was 26·6 per cent., and in the second year, 31·7 per cent.

It is impossible at the present time to determine, with any degree of definiteness, the effect which the tariff has had or is likely to have on the trade of the different states, but a measure of that effect may be obtained by comparing the volume of the trade before the imposition of uniform duties and subsequent thereto. The period shown in the following table is five years; but of these five years only one, viz., 1902, represents a full year under the Commonwealth tariff; 1901 was partly under Commonwealth tariff, partly under state tariffs. The preceding years were wholly under the state tariffs. It is also to be borne in mind that it has been claimed that there was considerable loading-up of goods in anticipation of the imposition of the federal tariff. It is, however, difficult to discover evidence of such loading-up in the trade returns of any of the states except New South Wales, and to a less extent in Victoria. In some of the states it is probable that the loading-up was purely imaginary, as the federal tariff as it now exists is on an average less in all the states, except New South Wales and Western Australia, than the tariff which existed prior to the 8th October, 1901.

It will be understood that the actual consumption is less than the net import in the distributing states, as goods imported into such states were distributed amongst the other states on interstate certificates, and their import does not appear in the returns of the states where such goods were ultimately consumed.

State.	Gross Import.	Re-export.	Net Import.
1898.			
	£	£	£
New South Wales	12,732,527	911,059	11,821,468
Victoria	9,509,952	273,256	9,236,696
Queensland	3,274,940	24,921	3,250,019
South Australia	2,901,680	12,918	2,888,762
Western Australia	2,507,305	7,607	2,499,698
Tasmania	555,114	889	554,225
Total £	31,481,518	1,230,650	30,250,868
1899.			
New South Wales	14,725,878	1,063,472	13,662,406
Victoria	9,902,375	248,028	9,654,347
Queensland	3,816,546	27,750	3,788,796
South Australia	3,138,202	14,428	3,123,774
Western Australia	2,169,688	13,916	2,155,772
Tasmania	577,546	646	576,900
Total £	34,330,235	1,368,240	32,961,995
1900.			
New South Wales	17,396,991	1,082,376	16,314,615
Victoria	11,937,644	267,200	11,670,444
Queensland	4,116,834	49,948	4,066,886
South Australia	3,948,349	6,136	3,942,213
Western Australia	3,287,022	11,218	3,275,804
Tasmania	701,105	214	700,891
Total £	41,387,945	1,417,092	39,970,853
1901.			
New South Wales	17,560,207	900,321	16,659,886
Victoria	12,686,880	243,633	12,443,247
Queensland	3,515,667	38,628	3,477,039
South Australia	3,964,745	10,736	3,954,009
Western Australia	3,895,151	21,343	3,873,808
Tasmania	811,198	756	810,442
Total £	42,433,848	1,215,417	41,218,431
1902.			
New South Wales	15,024,535	1,996,694	13,027,841
Victoria	13,503,517	1,986,737	11,516,780
Queensland	4,902,052	183,531	4,718,521
South Australia	3,157,499	500,028	2,657,471
Western Australia	5,171,651	65,145	5,106,506
Tasmania	1,728,925	16,095	1,712,830
Total £	43,488,179	4,748,230	38,739,949

The following tables show the revenue received from Customs and Excise, the cost of collecting the duties, and the proportion which such cost bears to the total revenue received in each of the Commonwealth states during the last six years. In the first table will be found the revenue from duties since 1898.

CUSTOMS AND EXCISE COLLECTIONS.

Year.	New South Wales.	Victoria.	Queensland.	South Australia.	Western Australia.	‡Tasmania.	Commonwealth.
1898-9	1,608,859	2,234,442	1,504,968	629,229	867,520	427,963	7,272,981
1899-1900	1,736,377	2,267,131	1,602,985	645,074	933,717	448,120	7,633,404
*1900	939,336	1,202,191	787,695	337,371	500,845	490,916	4,258,354
†1901	1,019,008	1,356,099	710,830	351,953	491,371	†221,328	4,150,589
1901-2	2,812,731	2,376,525	1,297,662	698,647	1,335,614	‖373,140	8,894,319
1902-3	3,478,742	2,499,014	1,261,066	689,727	1,395,997	‖360,607	9,685,153

* Half year ended 31st December, except Tasmania. † Half year ended 30th June. ‡ Year ended 31st December previous. ‖ Year ended 30th June.

In the following statement will be found the cost of collecting the Customs and Excise duties during each year of the period, together with the proportion which such cost bears to the total receipts in each state and in the Commonwealth.

Year.	New South Wales.	Victoria.	Queensland.	South Australia.	Western Australia.	‡Tasmania.	Commonwealth.
1898-9	53,774	66,290	58,104	26,418	29,734	8,423	242,743
1899-1900	54,241	68,782	59,608	26,712	28,765	8,851	246,959
*1900	26,995	35,147	31,814	15,277	17,261	9,732	136,226
†1901	29,318	32,915	28,056	11,742	15,377	†4,898	122,306
1901-2	65,318	65,454	64,911	27,012	32,256	‖10,564	265,515
1902-3	73,324	67,175	67,284	26,583	35,201	‖11,019	280,586
PERCENTAGE OF COST OF COLLECTION TO TOTAL RECEIPTS.							
1898-9	3·3	3·0	3·8	4·2	3·4	2·0	3·3
1899-1900	3·1	3·0	3·7	4·1	3·1	2·0	3·2
*1900	2·9	2·9	4·0	4·5	3·4	2·0	3·2
†1901	2·9	2·4	3·9	3·3	3·1	†2·2	2·9
1901-2	2·3	2·8	5·0	3·9	2·4	‖2·8	3·0
1902-3	2·1	2·7	5·3	3·9	2·5	‖3·0	2·9

* Half year ended 31st December, except Tasmania. † Half year ended 30th June. Year ended 31st December previous. ‖ Year ended 30th June.

It will be seen that under federal administration in the Commonwealth as a whole and in the various states, with the exception of Queensland and Tasmania, the cost of collection of the duties has greatly declined. The greatest proportional decrease has taken place in New South Wales, the percentage falling from 3·3 in 1898-9 to 2·1 in 1902-3.

EMPLOYMENT AND PRODUCTION.

TO obtain a fair approximation of the number of persons engaged in the various walks of life in Australasia was impossible before the census of 1891 was taken, for although at the Census enumerations of 1881 and previous years the occupations of the people were made a feature of the inquiry, the classification, which followed closely that originally devised by the late Dr. Farr for the English Census, was unsatisfactory, as it completely failed to distinguish between makers and modifiers, and distributors. To avoid a repetition of this defect the Census Conference, held at Hobart in March, 1890, abandoned the English system and adopted a scheme of classification more in accordance with sound principles. This classification was reviewed at the conference of Statisticians held in Sydney in February, 1900, and was adopted, with very slight modification, for use at the decennial Census of 1901. Under this classification the population is divided into two broad sections—bread-winners and dependents—and the bread-winners are arranged in their natural classes of primary producers, makers and distributors, with their various orders and sub-orders. The classes may be briefly defined as follows:—

Section A.—Bread-winners.

Class 1 ... Professional.
2 ... Domestic.
3 ... Commercial.
4 ... Transport and Communication.
5 ... Industrial.
6 ... Agricultural, Pastoral, Mineral, and other Primary producers.
7 ... Indefinite.

Section B.—Dependents: Non-Breadwinners.

Class 8 ... Dependents.

The information relating to the various classes and orders in each state has been arranged and presented in as concise a manner as practicable, as it is impossible to enter minutely into details in a work such as this, and those who desire to pursue the subject further are referred to the Census Reports of the various states.

Bread-winners and Dependents.

Of the total population of Australasia whose occupations were ascertained at the Census of 1901, the bread-winners numbered 1,979,484, and comprised 43·67 per cent., and the dependents 2,553,819, or 56·33 per cent. The number in each state and their proportion to the total population are shown below :—

Sex.	New South Wales.	Victoria.	Queensland.	South Australia.	Western Australia.	Tasmania.	Commonwealth.	New Zealand	Australasia.
				NUMBER OF BREAD-WINNERS.					
Males	451,408	389,381	182,146	120,328	85,382	57,585	1,286,225	272,077	1,558,302
Females	113,396	144,668	36,022	32,968	13,489	15,909	356,452	64,730	421,182
Persons	564,799	534,049	218,168	153,296	98,871	73,494	1,642,677	336,807	1,979,484
				PROPORTION PER CENT. OF BREAD-WINNERS.					
Males	63·75	64·86	65·94	65·25	75·82	64·25	65·25	67·47	65·63
Females	17·59	24·27	16·35	18·50	18·98	19·20	19·88	17·70	19·51
Persons	41·76	44·64	43·93	42·28	53·83	42·61	43·64	43·80	43·67
				NUMBER OF DEPENDENTS.					
Males	256,634	210,980	94,084	64,094	27,229	32,089	685,060	131,164	816,224
Females	531,164	451,375	184,344	145,214	57,571	66,942	1,436,610	300,985	1,737,595
Persons	787,798	662,355	278,428	209,308	84,800	98,981	2,121,670	432,149	2,553,819
				PROPORTION PER CENT. OF DEPENDENTS.					
Males	36·25	35·14	34·06	34·75	24·18	35·75	34·75	32·53	34·37
Females	82·41	75·73	83·65	81·50	81·02	80·80	80·12	82·30	80·49
Persons	58·24	55·36	56·07	57·72	46·17	57·39	56·36	56·20	56·33

The largest proportion of bread-winners is found in Western Australia, where this class comprises more than three-fourths of the male and nearly one-fifth of the female population. The striking feature of the table is the large number of bread-winners in the female population of Victoria, the proportion in that state being 24·27 per cent., while the corresponding figure for the Commonwealth is only 19·88 per cent. The number and proportion per cent. of bread-winners and dependents in each state at the Census of 1891 were as follows :—

CENSUS OF 1891.

Sex.	New South Wales.	Victoria.	Queensland.	South Australia.	Western Australia.	Tasmania.	New Zealand.	Australasia.
				NUMBER OF BREAD-WINNERS.				
Males	382,385	387,684	146,611	99,109	21,375	48,833	205,956	1,291,953
Females	89,502	114,270	31,651	24,253	3,092	12,578	43,589	318,935
Persons	471,887	501,954	178,262	123,362	24,467	61,411	249,545	1,610,888
				PROPORTION PER CENT. OF BREAD-WINNERS.				
Males	63·09	65·43	65·84	61·57	71·91	62·96	62·11	63·92
Females	17·36	21·15	18·66	15·97	16·53	18·20	14·86	18·13
Persons	42·07	44·31	45·44	39·44	49·30	41·87	39·98	42·61

Sex.	New South Wales.	Victoria.	Queensland.	South Australia.	Western Australia.	Tasmania.	New Zealand.	Australasia.
				NUMBER OF DEPENDENTS.				
Males	223,711	204,922	76,064	61,870	8,351	28,727	125,633	729,278
Females	425,950	426,060	137,934	127,582	16,814	56,529	249,772	1,440,641
Persons	649,661	630,982	213,998	189,452	25,165	85,256	375,405	2,169,919
				PROPORTION PER CENT. OF DEPENDENTS.				
Males	36·91	34·58	34·16	38·43	28·09	37·04	37·39	36·08
Females	82·64	78·85	81·34	84·08	84·47	81·80	85·14	81·67
Persons	57·93	55·69	54·56	60·56	50·70	58·13	60·07	57·39

An examination of the figures for the two census periods will show that the proportions have undergone no great change, nevertheless there has been a general tendency in each state and in Australasia as a whole towards an increase in the proportion of bread-winners, both male and female. In all the states, with the single exception of Queensland, there is evidence of the increased employment of females.

The number of bread-winners, male and female, in each of the various classes at the Census of 1901 was as follows:—

Sex.	New South Wales.	Victoria.	Queensland.	South Australia.	Western Australia.	Tasmania.	Commonwealth.	New Zealand	Australasia.
				CLASS I.—PROFESSIONAL.					
Males	26,855	20,383	9,122	5,372	5,103	3,067	69,902	14,549	84,451
Females	14,529	14,841	4,486	3,485	1,964	1,930	41,235	8,960	50,195
Persons	41,384	35,224	13,608	8,857	7,067	4,997	111,137	23,509	134,646
				CLASS II.—DOMESTIC.					
Males	20,128	13,129	7,790	3,452	4,873	1,463	50,335	6,542	56,877
Females	52,690	53,686	16,402	14,529	6,930	6,474	150,711	27,852	178,563
Persons	72,818	66,815	24,192	17,981	11,803	7,937	201,046	34,394	235,440
				CLASS III.—COMMERCIAL.					
Males	67,097	64,633	22,950	17,080	10,280	6,097	188,137	34,409	222,546
Females	10,567	14,415	3,524	3,085	1,528	1,400	34,514	5,528	40,042
Persons	77,664	79,048	26,474	20,165	11,808	7,497	222,651	39,937	262,588
				CLASS IV.—TRANSPORT AND COMMUNICATION.					
Males	42,822	30,318	17,745	12,591	10,736	4,518	118,730	21,265	139,995
Females	1,045	1,198	341	259	256	330	3,429	485	3,914
Persons	43,867	31,516	18,086	12,850	10,992	4,848	122,159	21,750	143,909
				CLASS V.—INDUSTRIAL.					
Males	122,692	113,527	44,082	34,255	19,602	16,475	350,633	84,874	435,507
Females	23,996	32,706	7,407	6,978	2,208	2,275	75,570	16,310	91,880
Persons	146,688	146,233	51,489	41,233	21,810	18,750	426,203	101,184	527,387

Sex.	New South Wales.	Victoria.	Queensland.	South Australia.	Western Australia.	Tasmania.	Commonwealth.	New Zealand	Australasia.
CLASS VI.—AGRICULTURAL, PASTORAL, MINING, AND OTHER PRIMARY PRODUCERS.									
Males	168,212	140,149	79,413	45,898	35,081	25,439	494,192	108,007	602,199
Females	4,642	24,998	3,090	3,263	491	2,460	38,944	3,914	42,858
Persons	172,854	165,147	82,503	49,161	35,572	27,899	533,136	111,921	645,057
CLASS VII.—INDEFINITE.									
Males	3,597	7,242	1,044	1,680	207	526	14,296	2,431	16,727
Females	5,927	2,824	772	1,369	117	1,040	12,049	1,681	13,730
Persons	9,524	10,066	1,816	3,049	324	1,566	26,345	4,112	30,457
TOTAL NUMBER OF BREAD-WINNERS.									
Males	451,403	389,381	182,146	120,328	85,382	57,585	1,286,225	272,077	1,558,302
Females	113,396	144,668	36,022	32,968	13,489	15,909	356,452	64,730	421,182
Persons	564,799	534,049	218,168	153,296	98,871	73,494	1,642,677	336,807	1,979,484

PRIMARY PRODUCERS.

From the foregoing table it will be apparent that the principal source of employment in Australasia is in its primary producing industries, no less than 645,047 persons being engaged therein. These persons were distributed as follows :—

Sex.	New South Wales.	Victoria.	Queensland.	South Australia.	Western Australia.	Tasmania.	Commonwealth.	New Zealand	Australasia.
PERSONS ENGAGED IN AGRICULTURAL PURSUITS.									
Males	75,884	78,539	38,260	33,039	8,322	17,348	251,392	65,723	317,115
Females	1,735	17,381	2,081	1,147	285	2,074	24,703	2,089	26,792
Persons	77,619	95,920	40,341	34,186	8,607	19,422	276,095	67,812	343,907
PERSONS ENGAGED IN PASTORAL PURSUITS.									
Males	31,312	11,650	15,576	4,112	1,633	957	65,240	16,377	81,617
Females	595	1,692	174	81	52	26	2,620	495	3,115
Persons	31,907	13,342	15,750	4,193	1,685	983	67,860	16,872	84,732
PERSONS ENGAGED IN DAIRY FARMING AND POULTRY FARMING.									
Males	15,850	11,701	3,154	839	350	561	32,455	3,223	35,678
Females	2,285	5,877	825	2,029	144	337	11,497	1,315	12,812
Persons	18,135	17,578	3,979	2,868	494	898	43,952	4,538	48,490
PERSONS ENGAGED IN THE CAPTURE OF WILD ANIMALS OR THE ACQUISITION OF PRODUCTS THEREFROM.									
Males	949	1,436	762	296	85	399	3,927	970	4,897
Females	17	23	2	4	2	15	63	3	66
Persons	966	1,459	764	300	87	414	3,990	973	4,963

Sex.	New South Wales.	Victoria.	Queensland.	South Australia.	Western Australia.	Tasmania.	Commonwealth.	New Zealand	Australasia.
PERSONS ENGAGED IN FISHERIES.									
Males	1,238	916	2,211	558	1,503	158	6,579	718	7,297
Females	3	2	4	....	4	4	17	2	19
Persons	1,241	918	2,215	558	1,507	162	6,596	720	7,316
PERSONS ENGAGED IN FORESTRY, ETC.									
Males	2,451	3,824	2,041	109	2,177	525	11,107	2,941	14,048
Females	1	3	....	2	....	3	9	2	11
Persons	2,452	3,827	2,041	111	2,177	528	11,116	2,943	14,059
PERSONS ENGAGED IN THE CONSERVATION AND SUPPLY OF WATER.									
Males	2,170	655	557	649	1,176	25	5,232	247	5,479
Females	2	1	2	....	1	....	6	....	6
Persons	2,172	656	559	649	1,177	25	5,238	247	5,485
PERSONS ENGAGED IN MINES AND QUARRIES, OR IN THE ACQUISITION OF MINERAL PRODUCTS.									
Males	38,378	31,428	16,852	6,301	19,885	5,466	118,260	17,808	136,068
Females	4	19	2	....	3	1	29	8	37
Persons	38,382	31,447	16,854	6,301	19,888	5,467	118,289	17,816	136,105
ALL PRIMARY PRODUCERS.									
Males	168,212	140,149	79,413	45,898	85,081	25,439	494,192	108,007	602,199
Females	4,642	24,998	3,090	3,263	491	2,460	38,944	3,914	42,858
Persons	172,854	165,147	82,503	49,161	85,572	27,899	533,136	111,921	645,057

Of the primary producers by far the largest proportion is engaged in agricultural pursuits, and, in fact, persons so employed outnumber those in any other calling. The persons engaged therein numbered 343,907, and as the total area under cultivation in Australasia at 31st March, 1901, was 10,456,538 acres, this would give an average of 30·4 acres to each person engaged. The number of persons engaged in agricultural pursuits and the area under cultivation in each state on the 31st March, 1901, was as follows:—

State.	Area under Cultivation.	Number of Persons engaged in Agricultural Pursuits.	Average No. of Acres per Person engaged.
	acres.		acres.
New South Wales	2,446,767	77,619	31·5
Victoria	3,114,132	95,920	32·5
Queensland	457,397	40,341	11·3
South Australia	2,369,680	34,186	69·3
Western Australia	201,338	8,607	23·4
Tasmania	224,352	19,422	11·6
Commonwealth	8,813,666	276,095	31·9
New Zealand	1,642,872	67,812	24·2
Australasia	10,456,538	343,907	30·4

The number of females engaged in agricultural pursuits is large in Victoria in comparison with the other states, as in that state a number of females, relatives of the farmers, who were partly engaged in agriculture and partly in domestic duties, have [illegible]

Commonwealth	173,037,215	67,860	2,550
New Zealand	36,647,659	16,872	2,172
Australasia	209,684,874	84,732	2,475

In Western Australia the number of primary producers was 35,572, and of these no less than 19,838 were engaged in mining pursuits.

The timber industry has not been specially dealt with in this volume. The interests involved, however, are somewhat large, especially in New Zealand and in the states of Western Australia, Queensland, and New South Wales. The total annual value of the timber industry of the Commonwealth is £2,080,000, and of New Zealand £971,000. This represents the value of the rough timber as it leaves the forest saw-mills, the value added by further treatment in the saw-mills and joinery yards is included in the manufacturing industries. Amongst the states of the Commonwealth, Western Australia stands first as regards timber production. In the year 1902 the value was £828,000, for New South Wales the return was £526,000 during the same period, and for Queensland £458,000. The other states show much smaller amounts, viz., Victoria, £143,000; Tasmania, £95,000; and South Australia about £30,000. The figures for South Australia, Tasmania,

Sex.	New South Wales.	Victoria.	Queensland.	South Australia.	Western Australia.	Tasmania.	Commonwealth.	New Zealand	Australasia.

ERRATA.

On page 905, lines 9 and 10, the figures for 1851 have inadvertently been used in place of those for 1901. The corrected figures are as follows:—

For Sheep, *instead of* 17,326,021, *read* 92,358,824
„ Cattle, „ 1,921,963, „ 9,827,433
„ Horses, „ 166,421, „ 1,905,172
„ Swine „ 121,035, „ 1,171,381

The total in terms of sheep, 209,684,874, is correct.

agricultural pursuits, and, in fact, persons so employed outnumber those in any other calling. The persons engaged therein numbered 343,907, and as the total area under cultivation in Australasia at 31st March, 1901, was 10,456,538 acres, this would give an average of 30·4 acres to each person engaged. The number of persons engaged in agricultural pursuits and the area under cultivation in each state on the 31st March, 1901, was as follows:—

State.	Area under Cultivation.	Number of Persons engaged in Agricultural Pursuits.	Average No. of Acres per Person engaged.
	acres.		acres.
New South Wales	2,446,767	77,619	31·5
Victoria	3,114,132	95,920	32·5
Queensland	457,397	40,341	11·3
South Australia	2,369,680	34,186	69·3
Western Australia	201,338	8,607	23·4
Tasmania	224,352	19,422	11·6
Commonwealth	8,813,666	276,095	31·9
New Zealand	1,642,872	67,812	24·2
Australasia	10,456,538	343,907	30·4

The number of females engaged in agricultural pursuits is large in Victoria in comparison with the other states, as in that state a number of females, relatives of the farmers, who were partly engaged in agriculture and partly in domestic duties, have been counted as engaged in agricultural pursuits, while in the other states they were classified as performing domestic duties, and, consequently, as dependents.

Persons engaged in pastoral pursuits numbered 84,732, and of those in the Commonwealth nearly one-half were in New South Wales. The live stock in Australasia at the end of 1901 consisted of 17,326,021 sheep, 1,921,963 cattle, 166,421 horses, and 121,035 swine, the total being equal to 209,684,874 sheep, or an average of 2,475 sheep to each person. The number of live stock in each state, expressed in terms of sheep, and the number of persons engaged in pastoral pursuits during 1901 are shown below:—

State.	Live Stock expressed in terms of Sheep.	Persons engaged in Pastoral Pursuits.	Average Number of Sheep per Person.
New South Wales	67,196,799	31,907	2,106
Victoria	30,788,000	13,342	2,308
Queensland	52,379,231	15,750	3,326
South Australia	11,641,160	4,193	2,776
Western Australia	7,226,944	1,685	4,289
Tasmania	3,803,081	983	3,869
Commonwealth	173,037,215	67,860	2,550
New Zealand	36,647,659	16,872	2,172
Australasia	209,684,874	84,732	2,475

In Western Australia the number of primary producers was 35,572, and of these no less than 19,838 were engaged in mining pursuits.

The timber industry has not been specially dealt with in this volume. The interests involved, however, are somewhat large, especially in New Zealand and in the states of Western Australia, Queensland, and New South Wales. The total annual value of the timber industry of the Commonwealth is £2,080,000, and of New Zealand £971,000. This represents the value of the rough timber as it leaves the forest saw-mills, the value added by further treatment in the saw-mills and joinery yards is included in the manufacturing industries. Amongst the states of the Commonwealth, Western Australia stands first as regards timber production. In the year 1902 the value was £828,000, for New South Wales the return was £526,000 during the same period, and for Queensland £458,000. The other states show much smaller amounts, viz., Victoria, £143,000; Tasmania, £95,000; and South Australia about £30,000. The figures for South Australia, Tasmania, and New Zealand refer to the year 1901, as no later information is available.

The fisheries of Australia comprise the ordinary coast and river fisheries, and the pearl-fishing industry of Queensland and Western and Northern Australia; while there is a small export of whale oil from Tasmania. The pearl-shell fisheries of Queensland show an export of nearly £130,000 per annum, and of bêche-de-mer the value exported is, in round figures, £10,000. From Western Australia the export of pearl-shell is about £137,000, and of pearls £40,000. Reckoning the home fisheries of all the states and New Zealand, as well as the pearl fisheries, the total production of the industry may be set down at £967,000.

The Industrial Class.

The persons engaged in industrial pursuits numbered 527,387, being only exceeded by those engaged in the primary producing industries. The largest proportionate number is to be found in Victoria, where 146,233 persons were engaged, being only 455 less than in New South Wales. Of the total number engaged in industrial pursuits 328,545 were employed in the manufacturing industry, and the following table has been prepared so as to show the number of persons engaged in the different branches thereof:—

Sex.	New South Wales.	Victoria.	Queensland.	South Australia.	Western Australia.	Tasmania.	Commonwealth.	New Zealand.	Australasia.
Persons working in Art and Mechanic Productions.									
Males	26,346	20,676	9,401	5,849	3,636	2,368	68,276	18,479	86,755
Females	1,157	1,748	334	303	95	76	3,713	946	4,659
Persons	27,503	22,424	9,735	6,152	3,731	2,444	71,989	19,425	91,414
Persons working in Textile Fabrics, Dress, and Fibrous Materials.									
Males	9,451	10,664	3,146	2,492	1,088	1,269	28,110	8,173	36,283
Females	21,644	28,450	6,606	6,243	2,024	2,099	67,066	14,237	81,303
Persons	31,095	39,114	9,752	8,735	3,112	3,368	95,176	22,410	117,586
Persons working in Food, Drinks, Narcotics, and Stimulants.									
Males	11,638	10,251	5,308	2,762	1,638	1,133	32,730	7,302	40,032
Females	875	1,402	283	201	74	84	2,919	357	3,276
Persons	12,513	11,653	5,591	2,963	1,712	1,217	35,649	7,659	43,308
Persons working in Animal and Vegetable Substances.									
Males	5,546	5,281	2,050	762	1,356	575	15,570	2,431	18,001
Females	50	85	3	3	1	7	149	18	167
Person	5,596	5,366	2,053	765	1,357	582	15,719	2,449	18,168

Sex.	New South Wales.	Victoria.	Queensland.	South Australia.	Western Australia.	Tasmania.	Commonwealth.	New Zealand.	Australasia.
PERSONS WORKING IN MINERALS AND METALS.									
Males	15,336	14,315	4,710	6,059	2,583	2,051	45,054	8,280	53,334
Females	60	88	6	11	2	1	168	13	181
Persons	15,396	14,403	4,716	6,070	2,585	2,052	45,222	8,293	53,515
PERSONS WORKING IN FUEL, LIGHT, AND OTHER FORMS OF ENERGY.									
Males	2,012	1,035	286	239	237	120	3,929	580	4,509
Females	4	37	1	....	....	....	42	3	45
Persons	2,016	1,072	287	239	237	120	3,971	583	4,554
ALL PERSONS ENGAGED IN MANUFACTURING INDUSTRIES.									
Males	70,329	62,222	24,901	18,163	10,538	7,516	193,669	45,245	238,914
Females	23,790	31,810	7,233	6,761	2,196	2,267	74,057	15,574	89,631
Persons	94,119	94,032	32,134	24,924	12,734	9,783	267,726	60,819	328,545

The number shown above as employed in manufacturing industrics exceeds that given in the chapter dealing with manufactories, since the factory returns relate to employment in industries coming under the provisions of the Factories Act, and take no account of places where less than four hands are employed, unless machinery is used. In the Census figures also are included casual workers and all single workers engaged on their own account, both of which classes are omitted from the factories returns. The case of New South Wales may be cited as an example to show the difference between the two returns in the number of female workers. According to the Census there were 18,000 dressmakers and tailoresses, many of them on their own account. According to the factories returns there were under 7,000.

At the census of 1891 the persons engaged in the manufacturing industries of the states which comprise the Commonwealth numbered 214,220, so that there has been an increase of 53,506 persons or nearly 25 per cent. during the ten years. The largest increase was in New South Wales, where the total was 74,559 in 1891, and 94,119 in 1901, an addition of 19,560 persons or more than 26 per cent.

The number of persons engaged in the other branches of the industrial class is shown in the following table:—

Sex	New South Wales.	Victoria.	Queensland.	South Australia.	Western Australia.	Tasmania.	Commonwealth.	New Zealand.	Australasia.
PERSONS ENGAGED IN MANUFACTURING INDUSTRIES.									
Males	70,329	62,222	24,901	18,163	10,538	7,516	193,669	45,245	238,914
Females	23,790	31,810	7,233	6,761	2,196	2,267	74,057	15,574	89,681
Persons	94,119	94,032	32,134	24,924	12,734	9,783	267,726	60,819	328,545

Sex.	New South Wales.	Victoria.	Queensland.	South Australia.	Western Australia.	Tasmania.	Commonwealth.	New Zealand.	Australasia.
Persons engaged in the Construction or Repair of Buildings, Railways, Roads, &c.									
Males	36,898	27,392	9,878	8,652	5,827	3,924	92,571	22,879	115,450
Females	11	17	....	....	1	2	31	13	44
Persons	36,909	27,409	9,878	8,652	5,828	3,926	92,602	22,892	115,494
Persons engaged in the Disposal of the Dead, or of Refuse.									
Males	1,278	1,260	276	183	222	86	3,305	181	3,486
Females	15	24	2	1	....	1	43	2	45
Persons	1,293	1,284	278	184	222	87	3,348	183	3,531
Persons engaged in imperfectly defined Industrial Pursuits.									
Males	14,187	22,653	9,027	7,257	3,015	4,949	61,088	16,569	77,657
Females	180	855	172	216	11	5	1,439	721	2,160
Persons	14,367	23,508	9,199	7,473	3,026	4,954	62,527	17,290	79,817
All Industrial Workers.									
Males	122,692	113,527	44,082	34,255	19,602	16,475	350,633	84,874	435,507
Females	23,996	32,706	7,407	6,978	2,208	2,275	75,570	16,310	91,880
Persons	146,688	146,233	51,489	41,233	21,810	18,750	426,203	101,184	527,387

The Commercial Class.

The persons engaged in commercial pursuits in Australasia numbered 262,588, and of these 220,757 were engaged in trade. The following table shows the number of persons engaged in the various branches of trade :—

Sex.	New South Wales.	Victoria.	Queensland.	South Australia.	Western Australia.	Tasmania.	Commonwealth.	New Zealand.	Australasia.
Persons dealing in Art and Mechanic Productions.									
Males	4,144	3,720	1,543	810	728	305	11,250	1,956	13,206
Females	564	934	216	168	131	54	2,067	334	2,401
Persons	4,708	4,654	1,759	978	859	359	13,317	2,290	15,607
Persons dealing in Textile Fabrics, Dress, and Fibrous Materials.									
Males	6,957	6,374	2,291	1,654	969	707	18,952	4,175	23,127
Females	2,269	2,452	868	739	376	250	6,954	1,376	8,330
Persons	9,226	8,826	3,159	2,393	1,345	957	25,906	5,551	31,457
Persons dealing in Food, Drink, Narcotics, and Stimulants.									
Males	19,522	18,217	6,643	4,460	2,596	1,301	52,739	8,521	61,260
Females	2,581	3,428	705	374	294	229	7,611	878	8,489
Persons	22,103	21,645	7,348	4,834	2,890	1,530	60,350	9,399	69,749

Sex.	New South Wales.	Victoria.*	Queensland.	South Australia.	Western Australia.	Tasmania.	Commonwealth.	New Zealand.	Australasia.
PERSONS DEALING IN ANIMAL AND VEGETABLE MATTERS.									
Males	5,984	3,977	1,540	958	730	329	13,518	2,592	16,110
Females	154	198	34	30	14	16	446	55	501
Persons	6,138	4,175	1,574	988	744	345	13,964	2,647	16,611
PERSONS DEALING IN FUEL AND LIGHT.									
Males	2,084	2,794	911	591	476	255	7,111	748	7,859
Females	25	34	5	3	2	4	73	11	84
Persons	2,109	2,828	916	594	478	259	7,184	759	7,943
PERSONS DEALING IN MINERALS AND METALS.									
Males	2,136	2,044	709	636	543	195	6,263	1,519	7,782
Females	60	162	11	4	13	10	260	38	298
Persons	2,196	2,206	720	640	556	205	6,523	1,557	8,080
GENERAL AND UNSPECIFIED DEALERS.									
Males	16,689	16,091	6,173	5,668	2,647	1,960	49,228	8,948	58,176
Females	3,130	4,446	1,139	1,266	433	477	10,891	2,243	13,134
Persons	19,819	20,537	7,312	6,934	3,080	2,437	60,119	11,191	71,310
TOTAL PERSONS ENGAGED IN TRADE.									
Males	57,516	53,217	19,810	14,777	8,689	5,052	159,061	28,459	187,520
Females	8,783	11,654	2,978	2,584	1,263	1,040	28,302	4,935	33,237
Persons	66,299	64,871	22,788	17,361	9,952	6,092	187,363	33,394	220,757

The largest number of persons in the above class is found in the division which relates to those dealing in foods, drinks, and stimulants, the total being 69,749. The number of females employed in trade has increased nearly four fold in the Commonwealth since 1891. A classification of the persons engaged in other branches of commercial pursuits will be found below :—

Sex.	New South Wales.	Victoria.	Queensland.	South Australia.	Western Australia.	Tasmania.	Commonwealth.	New Zealand.	Australasia.
PERSONS ENGAGED IN FINANCE AND REAL PROPERTY.									
Males	8,985	10,039	3,004	2,267	1,482	1,008	26,785	5,046	31,831
Females	1,783	2,760	533	496	254	356	6,182	585	6,767
Persons	10,768	12,799	3,537	2,763	1,736	1,364	32,967	5,631	38,598
PERSONS ENGAGED IN TRADE.									
Males	57,516	53,217	19,810	14,777	8,689	5,052	159,061	28,459	187,520
Females	8,783	11,654	2,978	2,584	1,263	1,040	28,302	4,935	33,237
Persons	66,299	64,871	22,788	17,361	9,952	6,092	187,363	33,394	220,757

Sex.	New South Wales.	Victoria.	Queensland.	South Australia.	Western Australia.	Tasmania.	Commonwealth.	New Zealand	Australasia.
Speculators on Chance Events.									
Males	424	284	42	18	38	35	836	41	877
Females	....	1	13	5	6	4	29	3	32
Persons	424	285	55	18	44	39	865	44	909
Persons engaged in Storage.									
Males	172	1,093	94	23	71	2	1,455	863	2,318
Females	1	....	....	....	....	....	1	5	6
Persons	173	1,093	94	23	71	2	1,456	868	2,324
Total, Commercial Class.									
Males	67,097	64,633	22,950	17,080	10,280	6,097	188,137	34,409	222,546
Females	10,567	14,415	3,524	3,085	1,523	1,400	34,514	5,528	40,042
Persons	77,664	79,048	26,474	20,165	11,803	7,497	222,651	39,937	262,588

The Domestic Class.

The domestic class embraces all persons engaged in the supply of board and lodging, and in rendering personal services for which remuneration is usually paid. The numbers in each state were as follows :—

Sex.	New South Wales.	Victoria.	Queensland.	South Australia.	Western Australia.	Tasmania.	Commonwealth.	New Zealand	Australasia.
Persons engaged in providing Board and Lodging.									
Males	8,258	6,984	3,056	1,482	2,474	701	22,955	3,893	26,848
Females	15,622	14,850	4,502	1,202	3,278	788	40,242	6,749	46,991
Persons	23,880	21,834	7,558	2,684	5,752	1,489	63,197	10,642	73,839
Persons engaged in Domestic Service and Attendance.									
Males	11,870	6,145	4,734	1,970	1,899	762	27,380	2,649	30,029
Females	37,068	38,836	11,900	13,327	3,652	5,686	110,469	21,103	131,572
Persons	48,938	44,981	16,634	15,297	5,551	6,448	137,849	23,752	161,601
Total, Domestic Class.									
Males	20,128	13,129	7,790	3,452	4,373	1,463	50,335	6,542	56,877
Females	52,690	53,686	16,402	14,529	6,930	6,474	150,711	27,852	178,563
Persons	72,818	66,815	24,192	17,981	11,303	7,937	201,046	34,394	235,440

Of all the females employed it will be seen that over 40 per cent. are in the Domestic class. The females shown above as employed in domestic service, perform similar duties to those classed as dependents, but they receive remuneration for their services.

THE PROFESSIONAL CLASS.

The persons in this class numbered 134,646 and were distributed amongst the various states as follows :—

Sex.	New South Wales.	Victoria.	Queensland.	South Australia.	Western Australia.	Tasmania.	Commonwealth.	New Zealand.	Australasia.
PERSONS ENGAGED IN GENERAL GOVERNMENT.									
Males [1]	1,545	1,427	847	660	539	288	5,306	1,043	6,349.
Females	31	91	15	6	12	9	164	47	211
Persons	1,576	1,518	862	666	551	297	5,470	1,090	6,560
PERSONS ENGAGED IN LOCAL GOVERNMENT.									
Males	349	856	365	174	95	88	1,922	396	2,318
Females	5	19	7	3	1	....	35	11	46
Persons	354	875	372	177	96	88	1,957	407	2,364
PERSONS ENGAGED IN DEFENCE.									
Males	3,511	689	777	237	312	317	5,843	1,033	6,876
Females	....	....	....	....	....	....	....	....	....
Persons	3,511	689	777	237	312	317	5,843	1,033	6,876
PERSONS ENGAGED IN LAW AND IN THE PRESERVATION OF ORDER.									
Males	5,404	3,747	1,826	892	1,040	624	13,533	2,341	15,874
Females	74	55	24	20	21	8	202	71	273
Persons	5,478	3,802	1,850	912	1,061	632	13,735	2,412	16,147
PERSONS MINISTERING TO RELIGION, CHARITY, HEALTH, EDUCATION, ART, AND SCIENCE.									
Males	16,046	13,664	5,307	3,409	3,117	1,755	43,298	9,736	53,034
Females	14,419	14,676	4,440	3,456	1,930	1,913	40,834	8,831	49,665
Persons	30,465	28,340	9,747	6,865	5,047	3,668	84,132	18,567	102,699
TOTAL, PROFESSIONAL CLASS.									
Males	26,855	20,383	9,122	5,372	5,103	3,067	69,902	14,549	84,451
Females	14,529	14,841	4,486	3,485	1,964	1,930	41,235	8,960	50,195
Persons	41,384	35,224	13,608	8,857	7,067	4,997	111,137	23,509	134,646

The number shown above as engaged in general government does not represent the total persons employed by the state, as the government officers have been included in the sections to which the nature of their work is most closely allied. It is not possible to give the total number of government employees for any state, except New South Wales, where they numbered 32,000 at the census of 1901.

GRADES OF WORKERS.

In all the states except Queensland a distribution of bread-winners was made into the characteristic divisions, viz., employers, workers on their own account, relatives assisting, wage earners, other persons to whom the grades are not applicable, and unemployed. The figures for the various states and New Zealand were as shown below :—

Sex.	New South Wales.	Victoria.	South Australia.	Western Australia.	Tasmania.	New Zealand.
			EMPLOYERS.			
Males	48,911	43,157	14,259	7,714	6,205	34,002
Females	4,933	4,997	1,089	633	462	2,010
Persons	53,844	48,154	15,348	8,347	6,667	36,012
PERSONS ENGAGED ON THEIR OWN ACCOUNT BUT NOT EMPLOYERS OF LABOUR.						
Males	65,561	71,384	15,959	10,219	9,388	47,313
Females	16,779	22,879	3,547	1,766	2,790	8,750
Persons	82,340	94,263	19,506	11,985	12,178	56,063
			RELATIVES ASSISTING.			
Males	17,635	26,842	5,493	1,904	4,090	17,052
Females	6,077	26,748	2,240	931	2,070	4,523
Persons	23,712	53,590	7,733	2,835	6,160	21,575
			WAGE-EARNERS.			
Males	290,239	234,203	78,879	61,840	36,093	166,431
Females	72,238	87,397	23,366	9,277	10,231	48,088
Persons	362,477	321,600	102,245	71,117	46,324	214,519
OTHERS TO WHOM THESE GRADES ARE NOT APPLICABLE.						
Males	8,276	......	2,381	565	......	......
Females	9,747	......	2,038	433	......	......
Persons	18,023	......	4,419	998	......	......
			UNEMPLOYED.			
Males	20,781	13,795	3,357	3,140	1,809	7,279
Females	3,622	2,647	688	449	356	1,359
Persons	24,403	16,442	4,045	3,589	2,165	8,638
			TOTAL WORKERS.			
Males	451,403	389,381	120,328	85,382	57,585	272,077
Females	113,396	144,668	32,968	13,489	15,909	64,730
Persons	564,799	534,049	153,296	98,871	73,494	336,807

Value of Production from all Industries.

Under the various chapters devoted to the discussion of agriculture, dairying, grazing, mining, &c., particulars regarding the value of the production of the great primary industries have been given at some length; combining the results there shown with the value of manufactures, the total value of production during the year 1902 was £139,809,000, of which amount the total of each state and the value per inhabitant were as follow:—

State.	Value of Production.	Value per Inhabitant.
	£	£ s. d.
New South Wales	36,922,000	26 9 11
Victoria	29,987,000	24 16 10
Queensland	13,541,000	26 8 3
South Australia	9,721,000	26 12 3
Western Australia	13,781,000	67 4 5
Tasmania	5,663,000	32 4 9
Commonwealth	109,615,000	28 8 0
New Zealand	30,194,000	37 16 11
Australasia	139,809,000	30 0 5

The distribution of the production of the states under the various branches of primary and other productive industries was as follows:—

State.	Agriculture.	Pastoral Industries.	Dairying, Poultry, and Bee Farming	Mining Industries.	Forestry and Fisheries.	Manufactories.
	£	£	£	£	£	£
New South Wales	5,568,000	10,731,000	3,408,000	5,078,000	695,000	11,452,000
Victoria	7,216,000	4,348,000	4,181,000	3,289,000	[illegible]	10,734,000
Queensland	1,876,000	3,187,000	1,252,000	3,311,000	678,000	3,237,000
South Australia	3,287,000	1,909,000	948,000	576,000	127,000	2,883,000
Western Australia	759,000	1,036,000	422,000	8,096,000	1,046,000	2,423,000
Tasmania	1,506,000	611,000	652,000	1,383,000	122,000	1,389,000
Commonwealth	20,207,000	21,813,000	10,808,000	21,732,000	2,987,000	32,118,000
New Zealand	8,619,000	6,876,000	3,466,000	*3,222,000	1,081,000	6,930,000
Australasia	28,826,000	28,689,000	14,274,000	24,954,000	4,018,000	39,048,000

* Including value of production of Kauri gum.

In the following statement the total value of production in each state in 1902 is compared with that of each decennial period since 1871. In 1901 the value per head was £31 4s. 3d., being greater than in 1891, and nearly equal to that of 1881, although the year could not be called a favourable one to Australia. In 1902 the value per head was only £30 0s. 5d., a decrease of £1 3s. 10d., but that year was one of the most disastrous ever experienced, especially as regards the primary producing industries. If the prices of 1870-4, shown on page 545, had been maintained, the following would have been the value of production in the years indicated; for purposes of comparison the actual results are also quoted:—

Year.	Average value of Production per Inhabitant.	Average value of Production if 1870-4 prices had been obtained in each year.
	£ s. d.	£ s. d.
1871	29 3 8	29 3 8
1881	31 9 10	35 2 2
1891	30 13 5	44 10 4
1901	31 4 3	47 7 3
1902	30 0 5	42 17 7

During the interval of eleven years between 1891 and 1902 the sheep depastured in Australasia declined in number from 124 millions to 74 millions, the decrease in 1902 alone numbering 18,000,000, while there was also a large decline in other classes of stock. The total value of production for each of the years named was as follows:—

State.	1871.	1881.	1891.	1901.	1902.
	£	£	£	£	£
New South Wales	15,379,000	25,180,000	36,739,760	38,954,000	36,922,000
Victoria	19,260,000	22,750,000	30,319,610	30,807,000	29,987,000
Queensland	3,995,000	10,200,000	14,273,660	16,933,000	13,541,000
South Australia	5,228,000	8,457,000	9,025,675	10,314,000	9,721,000
Western Australia	707,000	943,000	1,806,340	12,544,000	13,781,000
Tasmania	2,131,000	3,586,000	3,920,940	5,033,000	5,663,000
Commonwealth	46,700,000	71,116,000	96,085,985	114,585,000	109,615,000
New Zealand	9,739,000	16,490,000	21,518,915	28,452,000	30,194,000
Australasia	56,439,000	87,606,000	117,604,900	143,037,000	139,809,000

The results per inhabitant for the same years were as follow :—

State.	1871.			1881.			1891.			1901.			1902.		
	£	s.	d.	£	s.	d.	£	s.	d.	£	s.	d.	£	s.	d.
New South Wales	30	5	3	32	18	3	32	3	5	28	7	9	26	9	11
Victoria	26	2	8	26	3	0	26	9	3	25	12	2	24	16	10
Queensland	33	3	10	45	0	7	35	19	11	33	11	5	26	8	3
South Australia	28	7	7	29	19	11	28	1	1	28	8	2	26	12	3
Western Australia	28	0	9	31	19	0	36	5	8	66	17	11	67	4	5
Tasmania	21	0	10	30	16	0	26	8	9	28	19	10	32	4	9
Commonwealth	27	17	2	31	1	3	29	19	9	30	2	6	28	8	0
New Zealand	37	15	10	33	9	8	34	3	1	36	10	4	37	16	11
Australasia	29	3	8	31	9	10	30	13	5	31	4	3	30	0	5

Taking the figures for the ten year periods it will be seen that since 1871 the value of production per head of population increased in all the states of the Commonwealth with the exception of Victoria and New South Wales, while the decrease in those states was more than counterbalanced by the increased production in the other states, so that the net total for the Commonwealth showed an increase. For the period of ten years, 1891–1901, South Australia, Western Australia, Tasmania, and New Zealand show increases, but the average for Australasia also increased slightly, and this must be regarded as satisfactory when it is considered that the year 1901 was by no means a favourable one as regards the pastoral and agricultural industries.

Compared with the older countries of the world, the amounts stated in the table given above are by no means insignificant, and in production per head Australasia exceeds any other country for which records are available. Although the data on which an exact statement can be founded are incomplete, there is sufficient information to warrant the assertion that from primary industries alone, in an ordinary year, Australasia produces more per inhabitant than is produced from the combined industries of any other country, and a consideration of this fact will, perhaps, explain the ease with which these states bear their apparently great indebtedness, and the general prosperity they enjoyed until the disturbances incident to the banking crisis unsettled general business. The following figures, giving the value of production from primary industries in the principal countries of the world, are, with the exception of those for the Australasian states, taken from Mulhall's *Dictionary of Statistics* :—

Country.	Total Production in Primary Industries.	Per head of Population.		
	£	£	s.	d.
United Kingdom	317,000,000	7	18	6
France	451,000,000	11	11	6
Germany	465,000,000	8	18	4
Russia	594,000,000	4	19	8
Austria	347,000,000	8	7	11
Italy	212,000,000	6	17	1
Spain	143,000,000	8	4	3
Portugal	28,000,000	5	10	2
Sweden	50,000,000	10	1	11
Norway	15,000,000	7	6	2
Denmark	36,000,000	10	4	0
Holland	37,000,000	7	17	5
Belgium	55,000,000	8	16	6
Switzerland	21,000,000	7	2	1
United States	1,037,000,000	14	14	0
Canada	83,000,000	16	5	8
Australasia (1902)	100,761,000	21	12	9
New South Wales	25,470,000	18	5	6
Victoria	19,253,000	15	19	0
Queensland	10,304,000	20	1	0
South Australia	6,838,000	18	14	5
Western Australia	11,358,000	55	8	0
Tasmania	4,274,000	24	6	8
New Zealand	23,264,000	29	3	2

Judged by the aggregate production, New South Wales stands above the other Commonwealth states, a position which it owes to the largeness of its pastoral interests. The value of the return from the pastoral industry was £10,731,000, a sum almost equal to the combined total of all the other Commonwealth states. In value of primary production per inhabitant, Western Australia stands easily first with the very high production of £55 8s. 0d. per head. New Zealand comes next, followed by Tasmania. The high position occupied by Western Australia is due to its great production of gold, and to its large timber industries.

A comparison of the production of the states from primary industries per head of population, however, is liable to give an undue importance to those which have large territories and scanty population; for it is but a natural expectation that where the population of a country is dense a large proportion of the inhabitants will be engaged in other than primary industries. If the value of primary production, therefore, be compared with the extent of territory enjoyed by each state, it will be found that the positions of several of the provinces are reversed. Thus, of the Commonwealth states, Victoria occupies first position with an average primary production of £219 1s. 6d. per square mile, while Western Australia has the second lowest return with £11 12s. 9d. The following, as well as the preceding table, bears testimony to the great natural resources of New Zealand, which has an average production per head of £29 3s. 2d., and per square mile of £222 13s. 8d. :—

State.	Production of Primary Industries per square mile.		
	£	s.	d.
New South Wales	81	19	6
Victoria	219	1	6
Queensland	15	8	3
South Australia	7	11	4
Western Australia	11	12	9
Tasmania	163	0	9
Commonwealth	26	1	4
New Zealand	222	13	8
Australasia	32	14	10

If the value of production in all the industries be related to the area of territory possessed by each state, which is a favourite comparison with some statisticians, the following results are obtained. There is, however, no necessary connection between the production of the manufacturing industries of a country and the area of its territory, the development of manufactures depending upon entirely different considerations :—

State.	Total production per square mile.		
	£	s.	d.
New South Wales	118	16	8
Victoria	341	4	3
Queensland	20	5	1
South Australia	10	15	2
Western Australia	14	2	5
Tasmania	216	0	5
Commonwealth	36	17	5
New Zealand	289	0	4
Australasia	45	8	7

THE MANUFACTURING INDUSTRY.

THE progress of the manufacturing industry in Australasia has been somewhat irregular, even in the most advanced states; and although the tabular statement given below shows an increase since 1885 of 94,752 hands in the Commonwealth and 26,623 in New Zealand, a growth proportionately much greater than that of the population, by far the greater part of this extension has taken place during the last seven years. The population of the continent at the present time is not sufficient to maintain industries on an extensive scale, and in past years the field was still further limited by intercolonial tariffs. Now that these barriers have been swept away, and the Australian market secured to a certain extent to the local manufacturer, more rapid progress may reasonably be expected in the manufacturing industry.

The majority of the manufactories of Australasia may be classified as domestic industries—that is to say, industries naturally arising from the circumstances of the population, or connected with the treatment of perishable products; but there are nevertheless a fair number of firmly established industries of a more complex character. A statement of the number of establishments and of the hands employed in Australasia is given below for various years since 1885. The information is obtained annually in the states of the Commonwealth, but only once in every five years in New Zealand:—

Year.	Establishments.		Hands employed.	
	Commonwealth.	New Zealand.	Commonwealth.	New Zealand.
	No.	No.	No.	No.
1885	8,632	1,946	105,265	22,095
1890	8,903	2,254	133,147	25,633
1895	8,247	2,459	133,631	27,389
1900	10,040	3,663	184,160	48,718
1902	11,696	3,668	200,017	48,718

It is interesting to note the extent to which the employment of female labour has increased during late years. In 1897, the females engaged in the manufactories of the states which comprise the Commonwealth numbered only 26,837 and represented 17·7 per cent. of the total hands employed; in 1902 their number had increased to 45,242 and the proportion to 22·6 per cent. In New Zealand the experience has been similar, from 4,391 in 1895 the number of females increased to 10,624 in 1900, and their proportion to the total hands employed rose from 16·1 per cent. to 21·8 per cent. The increase may have been slightly prejudiced by the fact that the returns for the states were not all compiled on the same basis; still there is sufficient evidence that the employment of female labour is extending, a result borne out also by the information obtained at the Census of 1901 and published in part "Employment and Production" of this volume. The proportion of females employed is largest in Victoria, where there were 23,405 out of a total of 73,063 persons, equal to 32 per cent.; South Australia followed with 19·20 per cent., and Western Australia had the lowest proportion with 11·11 per cent. The following table shows the number of males and females employed in the Commonwealth in each year since 1897:—

Year.	Hands Employed.	
	Males.	Females.
1897	124,938	26,837
1898	130,389	28,221
1899	139,755	31,707
1900	147,652	36,508
1901	154,000	39,664
1902	154,775	45,242

Manufactories of Victoria.

Victoria was the state which first displayed activity in the manufacturing industries. In 1885 there were employed in factories, properly so called, 49,297 hands, and in 1889 there were 57,432 hands; but the number fell away to 41,729 in 1893. Since that year there has been an increase to the extent of 31,334 hands. Of the 73,063 workers employed in 1902, 3,711 may be said to have found occupation in connection with domestic industries for the treatment of perishable produce for immediate use; 32,617 in other industries dependent upon the natural resources of the country, and 36,735 in industries the production from which comes into competition with imported goods:—

Year.	Establishments.	Males.	Females.	Total Hands employed.
1885	2,813	41,542	7,755	49,297
1886	2,770	39,453	6,320	45,773
1887	2,854	42,019	7,665	49,684
1888	2,975	47,335	7,153	54,488
1889	3,137	49,105	8,327	57,432
1890	3,104	47,596	8,773	56,369
1891	3,128	43,627	10,786	54,413
1892	2,984	35,726	9,689	45,415
1893	2,659	32,209	9,520	41,729
1894	2,614	32,638	10,681	43,319
1895	2,724	35,406	12,240	47,646
1896	2,809	37,728	12,669	50,397
1897	2,759	38,620	14,030	52,650
1898	2,869	40,631	14,147	54,778
1899	3,027	44,041	16,029	60,070
1900	3,097	45,794	18,413	64,207
1901	3,249	47,059	19,470	66,529
1902	4,003	49,658	23,405	73,063

The number of factories and industrial establishments of various sizes, with the number of hands employed in each class, during 1902, will be found below:—

Number of Hands employed by each Establishment.	Number of Establishments.	Total number of Hands.
Under 4 hands	525	*1,647
4 hands	398	1,592
5 to 10 hands	1,629	11,303
11 to 20 „	726	10,562
21 to 50 „	467	14,361
51 to 100 „	148	10,238
101 hands and upwards	110	23,360
Total........................	4,003	73,063

* Includes 380 hands employed in creameries.

Manufactories of New South Wales.

The manufacturing industries of New South Wales do not cover so wide a field as those of Victoria, nor do they afford employment for as many persons. For the year 1902 the two states compare as follows:—

State.	Establishments.	Hands employed.		Total.
		Males.	Females.	
Victoria	4,003	49,658	23,405	73,063
New South Wales	3,396	54,326	11,943	66,269

In Victoria, therefore, there were employed 11,462 females more than in New South Wales, and 4,668 fewer males. In order to trace the progress of the manufacturing industry in New South Wales during the last eleven years, it is necessary to adjust the figures for the five years 1891–95, because in 1896 a change was made in the scope of the returns by the inclusion of dressmakers and milliners who were not previously counted as factory hands. Certain other small changes were made, the object of which was to secure uniformity with Victoria. Making the necessary adjustments, the figures since 1891 are as follows:—

Year.	Establishments.	Males.	Females.	Total Hands employed.
1891	3,056	43,203	7,676	50,879
1892	2,657	42,909	5,007	47,916
1893	2,428	37,832	4,225	42,057
1894	3,070	41,070	5,432	46,502
1895	2,723	41,546	6,484	48,030
1896	2,928	42,908	6,932	49,840
1897	2,826	44,333	7,106	51,439
1898	2,839	44,673	7,845	52,518
1899	2,912	47,063	8,583	55,646
1900	3,077	50,516	10,263	60,779
1901	3,367	54,556	11,674	66,230
1902	3,396	54,326	11,943	66,269

Up to the year 1891 there had been a fairly regular increase in the employment afforded by the factories of the state; in the following year, owing to causes already discussed in another part of this volume, there was a decrease in the number of persons employed, and, from 50,879 in 1891, the number had fallen to 42,057 in 1893—the year of the bank failures. In the following years there was a rapid recovery, so that the employment in 1897 was greater than in 1891, and the year 1902 showed an improvement of 15,390 during the eleven years since 1891, and an increase of 24,212 over the figures of 1893.

Of the 66,269 workers employed in 1902, 31,693 found employment in connection with industries the products from which come into competition with imported goods, 3,855 were engaged in domestic industries for the treatment of perishable produce required for immediate use, and 30,721 in other industries called into existence by the natural resources of the state.

The number of factories and industrial establishments of various sizes, with the number of hands employed in each class during 1902, were as follows:—

Number of Hands employed by each Establishment.	Number of Establishments.	Total number of Hands.
Under 4 hands	574	1,429
4 hands	335	1,340
5 to 10 hands	1,228	8,465
11 to 20 ,,	593	8,794
21 to 50 ,,	438	13,948
51 to 100 ,,	123	8,859
101 hands and upwards	105	23,434
Total	3,396	66,269

Manufactories of Queensland.

In Queensland systematic statistics relating to manufactories have been taken only since 1892. Until the year 1900, no details were available with reference to the employment of males and females, and the numbers for previous years have therefore been estimated. The figures for the last ten years are as follows:—

Year.	Establishments.	Persons employed.		
		Males.	Females.	Total.
1893	1,391	12,434	2,000	14,434
1894	1,323	13,124	2,100	15,224
1895	1,397	16,128	2,600	18,728
1896	1,332	17,013	2,720	19,733
1897	1,682	19,100	3,060	22,160
1898	1,864	20,830	3,340	24,170
1899	2,172	23,440	3,760	27,200
1900	2,019	23,138	3,766	26,904
1901	2,062	23,431	3,692	27,123
1902	1,977	17,595	3,363	20,958

The value of materials used in Queensland industries in 1902 was £4,180,000, the wages paid £1,598,400, and the value of production £7,417,000; the value added to materials in the process of manufacture was therefore £3,237,000. Owing to the adversity of the season and from other causes the year 1902 was by no means a favourable one, and taking this fact into consideration in conjunction with the smallness of the population and the large inflow of imported goods, the output of the factories must appear large. Queensland possesses important sugar-refining and meat-preserving industries, the combined output of which amounts to slightly over £3,093,000, or more than 40 per cent. of the total production of all the manufacturing industries of the state. The figures relating to these two industries are worthy of special attention, and are dealt with at some length in another place.

Manufactories of South Australia.

In South Australia returns were obtained from manufactories in 1892, but in the following three years no information was obtained; since 1895, however, the returns have been collected annually. The following are the available figures:—

Year.	Establishments.	Males.	Females.	Total Hands employed.
1892	815	9,642	1,847	11,489
1896	767	10,974	1,811	12,785
1897	768	10,930	2,027	12,957
1898	766	12,296	2,085	14,381
1899	841	12,941	2,214	15,155
1900	1,036	14,800	2,859	17,659
1901	1,129	14,881	3,442	18,323
1902	1,325	16,595	3,943	20,538

Manufactories of Western Australia.

In Western Australia, the manufacturing industry has advanced very rapidly in importance, and the number of hands employed now exceeds eleven thousand. The following are the figures for the last six years:—

Year.	Establishments.	Males.	Females.	Total Hands employed.
1897	413	8,683	408	9,091
1898	485	8,521	613	9,134
1899	476	8,641	766	9,407
1900	507	9,440	880	10,320
1901	537	10,238	1,062	11,300
1902	575	10,420	1,303	11,723

MANUFACTORIES OF TASMANIA.

Tasmania has several long-established industries, but until 1902 little information was available concerning them. In that year, however, a systematic attempt to gather complete statistics was made, and this accounts for the apparently large increase in the number of hands shown to be employed as compared with those for previous years given in former issues of this volume :—

Establishments	420
Hands—Males	6,181
Females	1,285
Total	7,466

MANUFACTORIES OF NEW ZEALAND.

In New Zealand, information regarding the manufacturing industry is obtained only at the quinquennial census. The following statement shows the progress made since 1886 :—

Year.	Establishments.	Hands employed.		
		Males.	Females.	Total.
1886	1,946	19,601	2,494	22,095
1891	2,254	22,664	2,969	25,633
1896	2,440	22,945	4,391	27,336
1901	3,668	38,094	10,624	48,718

The foregoing figures show very marked progress during the last five years, and from an analysis of the returns it appears that this progress has been general amongst all classes of industries.

VALUE ADDED BY PROCESSES OF MANUFACTURE OR TREATMENT.

Statistics of a more or less exhaustive character are taken annually in all the states in order to show the condition and progress of the manufacturing industry ; but it is only at certain periods, usually on the occasion of a general census, that details of the output of factories are obtained. In New South Wales for the year 1901, and in New Zealand for the previous year, elaborate returns were obtained of the output of all branches of manufacturing industries, the value of materials operated on, wages paid, and other particulars. From the information gathered some interesting deductions may be made. As regards New Zealand, it may be remarked that the totals do not agree in all cases with those shown in the New Zealand Year Book, additional information having been supplied by the Statistician of that colony to complete the values of raw materials, wages and output. The following are some of the salient features of the returns :—

	New South Wales.	New Zealand.
	£	£
Raw materials and other materials worked up	12,587,982	9,166,787
Fuel	492,428	243,000
Wages	4,867,917	3,511,590
Value of goods manufactured and work done (including custom work and repairing)	22,820,839	16,339,450

These figures do not take into consideration the returns from butter and cheese factories, the production from which is included elsewhere. From the figures just given the following values are obtained :—

	New South Wales.	New Zealand.
	£	£
Value added to materials and fuel during the process of production	9,740,429	6,929,663
Percentage added to value of materials and fuel	74·5	73·6
Value added to materials, fuel, and wages	4,872,512	3,418,073
Percentage added to materials, fuel, and wages	27·1	26·5

A close examination of the returns of the two countries would probably disclose some discrepancies in details, but these are unavoidable in a general statistical review of the manufacturing operations of separate countries compiled by different persons. Taken as a whole, however, the returns of New South Wales and New Zealand are in very close agreement. The margin above the cost of materials, fuel, and wages includes the interest on land and buildings where these are the property of the manufacturer ; repairs and renewals to buildings and fixtures ; rent, where the buildings, etc., are not the property of the manufacturer ; interest on capital represented by machinery ; renewals and depreciation in machinery and conveyance plant ; advertising ; and insurance, rates, and taxes not in the nature of excise duty or income tax. These, from a close analysis of the returns for New South Wales were found to be represented during the year 1901 by a total sum of £1,492,000. Assuming that approximately the same proportion of expenses obtains in New Zealand, and taking the two countries together, the following results are arrived at:—

	£
Value of Materials Used	21,764,769
Fuel	725,428
Wages	8,379,507
Miscellaneous Expenses	2,472,367
	33,342,071

As the total output was valued at £39,160,289 there remained, when the foregoing charges were met, the sum of £5,818,218, which provides for the interest on capital embarked in the business, and trade losses and profits. This latter figure represents 17·5 per cent. of all the items included in cost of production, or 14·9 per cent. of the value of the production itself. In other words, for every hundred pounds worth of goods produced in the factories of the two countries, the following were the proportions of the various elements included in the price of the goods as they left the manufactories:—

Materials and Fuel	57·4
Wages	21·4
Miscellaneous Expenses	6·3
Interest, Provision for Trade Losses, Profits, &c.	14·9
	100·0

The voluminous returns of the industrial census of the United States for 1900 give some very interesting figures relating to the manufacturing industries of that country:—

	Million Dollars.
Value of Materials used, including Fuel	7,345·4
Wages	2,726·0
Miscellaneous Expenses	1,027·7
Interest, Provision for Trade Losses, Profits, &c.	1,905·3
Total Output	13,004·4

The proportion of total output borne by each of the above items is given below:—

Value of Materials used, including Fuel	56·5
Wages	21·0
Miscellaneous Expenses	7·9
Interest, Provision for Trade Losses, Profits, &c.	14·6
	100·0

It will be seen that the Australian figures are in close agreement with those of America, nor is this agreement a matter of mere coincidence, for it is characteristic of the great majority of the industries making up the total, and shows that the business of manufacturing tends everywhere to fall into the same lines.

Interesting statistics were obtained in 1891, and again in 1901, of the value of materials used, and of the output by the manufactories of Victoria. The following are the official figures for the two periods, excluding the returns from butter and cheese factories:—

1890–1.

	£
Value of output	22,227,909
Value of materials used or operated on	11,902,089
Value added in process of treatment or of manufacture	£10,325,820

1900.

	£
Value of output	16,948,951
Value of materials used or operated on	10,104,131
Value added in process of treatment or of manufacture	£6,844,820

It will be seen that there has been an apparent decline in the value of production of not less than £3,481,000. There are, however, omissions to be allowed for. Taking these into consideration, there is still a difference in favour of 1890 to the extent of about £3,000,000.

In order to make a comparison of the returns for the two years on the same basis, the figures relating to those industries not common to each have been excluded from the statement given in the following pages. From the figures thus obtained it is found that as regards industries of a precisely similar character there was a net increase for the ten years in the number of persons employed of 853—there being an increase of 3,211 in the female workers and a decrease of 2,358 in the males. The horse-power employed in the factories of the state increased from 26,307 to 26,921 during the same period. These increases, taken in conjunction with the fact that there has not been any great decline in the value of materials used or operated on, would seem to point to the necessity of considerable caution in dealing with the Victorian official figures. For the year 1890, it is impossible to review the returns except in regard to a few omissions from the value of materials operated on, but these can be supplied with a fair approximation to the truth. Another important omission is that of the value of fuel. Fuel is of course a considerable item in the value of materials consumed in production, and in the following figures an estimate of the value of fuel used has been made. The figures for 1900 also require attention. On analysing them, and comparing the results with the extremely comprehensive statistics of New Zealand and New South Wales, as will be hereafter explained, the author came to the conclusion that the output of certain large classes of industries was greatly understated. In justice to the Victorian office it must be stated that the correctness of the published figures is strongly maintained, and, since no appeal can be made to the original documents, as these have been destroyed, the question can be argued only on the probabilities of the case. Allowing reasonable rates for wages and fuel in 1890 and 1900, the following totals and percentages are obtained :—

	1890–1.	1900.
Materials used	£10,760,110	£9,749,549
Fuel	289,000	262,000
Wages	3,980,000	3,884,362
Value of output	20,218,070	16,315,171
Do added to materials and fuel during the process of production	9,168,960	6,303,622
Percentage added to value of materials and fuel	82·98	62·96
Value added to materials, fuel and wages	5,188,960	2,419,260
Percentage added to value of materials, fuel, and wages	34·53	17·41

If these percentages be compared with those obtained for the United States, New South Wales and New Zealand, the figures will stand as follows :—

	Victoria.		United States.	New South Wales.	New Zealand.
	1890–1	1900			
Percentage added to value of materials and fuel	82·98	62·96	77·04	74·5	73·6
Percentage added to value of materials, fuel, and wages	34·53	17·41	29·12	27·1	26·5

The miscellaneous expenses of production in New Zealand and New South Wales average about 8 per cent. of the cost of materials, fuel, and wages, and in America they amount to 10 per cent. ; if the lower of these figures be allowed in the case of Victorian factories, the following would represent the margin for interest, provision for trade losses, profits, etc. :—

	per cent.
Victoria, 1890–1	24·6
Do. 1900	8·7
New South Wales	17·4
New Zealand	17·5
United States	17·2

It does not appear at all probable that in comparison with the other states the margin for profit, etc., in Victoria for the year 1900 was so small as the foregoing figures would make it appear, and the author has therefore ventured to substitute his own figures for the Victorian official compilation. The new figures will bear comparison with those obtained in the state ten years previously, and will show that the additional labour employed and the vast improvement in machinery effected in the ten years have not been without satisfactory results.

It has been considered necessary to raise the gross output shown in the official figures from £16,948,951 to £19,210,100, and the net output —that is to say, the excess of gross output over the value of materials, fuel, and labour—from £6,844,820 to £8,169,809, or by £1,324,989. The figures for the two years, which include all industries except butter and cheese factories, and not merely those shown on the preceding page, would then be as follows:—

	1890–1.	1900.
	No.	No.
Number of establishments	3,104	3,097
Horse-power	29,174	33,410
Persons employed—Males	47,596	45,794
Females	8,773	18,413
Total	56,369	64,207
	£	£
Value of materials treated, including fuel	13,077,089	11,040,291
Amount of wages paid	*4,240,000	*4,233,000
Total value of output	22,227,909	19,210,100
Value added to materials during process of manufacture	9,150,820	8,169,809

* Approximate.

As the author has not had the advantage of being able to use the original returns, the figures just given are advanced with considerable diffidence, and it is open to anyone who prefers the authority of the Victorian office to use its figures in place of the approximate estimates herein given. The estimated value added in the process of manufacture and treatment for each state will be found on page 956.

Classes of Industry.

The information in regard to industrial establishments is not given by the various statistical departments in precisely the same form, but the following classification which was agreed upon at a conference of statisticians held in 1901, is observed in the majority of the states. The table shows the number of hands, male and female, employed in 1902:—

Class of Industry.	Commonwealth.		New Zealand.		Australasia.	
	Males.	Females.	Males.	Females.	Males.	Females.
Treating Raw Materials, the Product of Pastoral Pursuits, &c.	7,661	54	2,357	7	10,018	61
Oils and Fats, Animal, Vegetable, &c.	1,681	72	239	8	1,930	80
Processes in Stone, Clay, Glass, &c.	8,039	88	1,146	1	9,185	89
Working in Wood	16,278	32	7,104	10	23,382	42
Metal Works, Machinery, &c.	38,323	91	6,404	13	44,727	104
Connected with Food and Drink, etc.	28,772	4,932	6,760	679	35,532	5,611
Clothing and Textile Fabrics and Materials	16,876	34,714	5,874	8,546	22,750	43,260
Books, Paper, Printing, and Engraving	14,076	3,408	2,960	662	17,036	4,065
Musical Instruments	199	13	11	......	210	13
Arms and Explosives	145	151	21	84	166	235
Vehicles and Fittings, Saddlery, and Harness, etc.	7,660	67	2,197	40	9,857	107
Ship and Boat Building, etc.	2,014	12	393	81	2,407	93
Furniture, Bedding, and Upholstery	5,031	399	1,382	73	6,413	472
Drugs, Chemicals, and By-products	1,711	484	174	33	1,885	517
Surgical and other Scientific Instruments	105	21	......	......	105	21
Jewellery, Timepieces, and Plated Ware	1,082	39	19	......	1,101	39
Heat, Light, and Power	3,440	86	657	150	4,097	236
Leatherware, not elsewhere included	353	70	19	3	372	73
Minor Wares, not elsewhere included	1,329	514	377	234	1,706	748
Total	154,775	45,242	33,094	10,624	192,869	55,866

Distributing the above total for the Commonwealth amongst the various states, the results shown in the following table are obtained. A comparison of the information now published in regard to Tasmania with that of former years would convey the idea that a large increase of employment had occurred, but the apparent increase is due to the fact that in 1902, for the first time, exhaustive information was obtained as to the development of the manufacturing industries.

Class of Industry.	New South Wales.	Victoria.	Queensland.	South Australia.	Western Australia.	Tasmania.
Treating Raw Materials, the Product of Pastoral Pursuits, &c.	3,187	2,887	488	876	68	309
Oils and Fats, Animal, Vegetable, &c.	533	618	148	317	75	67
Processes in Stone, Clay, Glass, &c.	3,293	2,934	466	526	595	313
Working in Wood	5,175	3,714	2,354	417	3,631	1,019
Metal Works, Machinery, &c.	13,724	9,872	3,589	7,334	2,175	1,720
Connected with Food and Drink, &c.	11,244	11,325	5,917	2,642	1,233	1,298
Clothing and Textile Fabrics and Materials	14,357	25,589	3,840	4,568	1,647	1,589
Books, Paper, Printing, and Engraving	5,936	6,551	2,001	1,600	908	48[illegible]
Musical Instruments	202	....	1	9	....	....
Arms and Explosives	12	284	....	....	....	....
Vehicles and Fittings, Saddlery, and Harness, &c.	2,135	2,[illegible]91	877	858	537	22[illegible]
Ship and Boat Building, &c.	1,474	174	163	114	76	25
Furniture, Bedding, and Upholstery	2,019	1,871	542	528	283	187
Drugs, Chemicals, and By-products	636	1,256	56	142	67	39
Surgical and other Scientific Instruments	65	44	17	....	....	....
Jewellery, Timepieces, and Plated Ware	243	616	34	139	47	42
Heat, Light, and Power	1,545	1,067	354	187	298	75
Leatherware, not elsewhere included	97	276	38	....	12	....
Minor wares, not elsewhere included	392	949	124	281	21	76
Total	66,269	73,063	20,958	20,538	11,723	7,466

INDUSTRIES TREATING RAW MATERIALS THE PRODUCT OF PASTORAL PURSUITS.

A consideration of the details relating to the various classes of industry discloses some very interesting features. The hands employed in the industries treating raw material, the product of pastoral pursuits, arranged according to the principal groups, were as follow :—

Class of Industry.	Commonwealth.		New Zealand.		Australasia.	
	Males.	Females.	Males.	Females.	Males.	Females.
Boiling-down and Tallow Refining	341	7	75	....	416	7
Tanneries .... Wool-scouring and Fellmongering	5,282	17	1,957	6	7,239	23
Chaff-cutting	1,978	30	265	1	2,243	31
Grass-seed Dressing	....	....	60	....	60	....
Compressed Forage..............	60	....	....	....	60	....
Total	7,661	54	2,357	7	10,018	61

The horse-power of the machinery in use in the Commonwealth was 6,933, and in New Zealand 2,099, the value of the machinery and plant being £532,803 and £128,988 respectively.

It is difficult to say if the figures for all the states are compiled upon the same basis. In New South Wales and Victoria wool-scouring works on sheep stations are not included, as the hands are employed in such works only during the shearing season, and frequently for not more than a few weeks. In Queensland there are no establishments classed as tallow-refineries, tallow being incidentally extracted in the process of meat-preserving, and the persons engaged therein are included in the latter industry.

The number of hands employed in treating raw material, the product of the pastoral industries, varies greatly from year to year, and, owing to the decrease in the number of live stock depastured, is much less than in former years. The following is a distribution of the total persons employed in the various states of the Commonwealth :—

Class of Industry.	New South Wales.	Victoria.	Queensland.	South Australia.	Western Australia.	Tasmania.
Boiling-down and Tallow Refining	207	99	4	38	....	....
Tanneries	1,115	1,685 (Tanneries and Wool-scouring combined)	218	298	43	101
Wool-scouring and Fellmongering	1,610		200	79	....	....
Chaff-cutting	255	1,103	16	401	25	208
Compressed Forage	....	....	....	60	....	...
Total	3,187	2,887	438	876	68	309

Tanning, fellmongering, and wool-scouring afford the largest amount of employment amongst industries of this class, and the details show the goods treated or manufactured in tanneries during the latest year available.

State.	Number Tanned.			
	Hides.	Skins.		
		Calf.	Sheep.	Other.
New South Wales	433,299	41,565	3,282,600	32,040
Victoria	422,224	177,480	247,333	65,833
Queensland	167,000	......	132,221	......
Western Australia	10,730	......	6,100	......
Tasmania	*108,720	......	......	......
New Zealand	178,075	.....	272,775	......

* Includes skins.

The foregoing information is somewhat imperfect, but will serve to convey an idea of the development of the industry in each state.

The quantity of wool washed in ordinary wool-scouring establishments cannot be stated with exactitude, but the following figures will give some idea of the extent of the industry. The figures represent the weight of clean wool exported from each state or locally consumed, in accordance with the latest annual returns; the amount of wool washed in Victoria appears small, but it is given on the authority of the Customs returns of that state.

	lb.
New South Wales	30,014,656
Victoria	2,620,877
Queensland	12,219,040
South Australia	2,626,327
Western Australia	447,910
New Zealand	23,366,416

Oils and Fats, &c.

There were 2,000 persons employed in factories dealing with oils and fats, the numbers in each industry being as follows:—

Class of Industry.	Commonwealth.		New Zealand.		Australasia.	
	Males.	Females.	Males.	Females.	Males.	Females.
Oil and grease	233	10	10	......	243	10
Soap and candles	1,424	62	224	8	1,648	70
Glue	24	......	5	......	29	......
Total	1,681	72	239	8	1,920	80

The horse-power of the machinery used in the Commonwealth was 1,812, and in New Zealand 428, and the value of the machinery and plant was £467,904 and £44,203 respectively.

Of the 1,753 hands employed in the Commonwealth, 1,486 were engaged in soap and candle factories. The employment afforded by other industries was but small, as will be seen from the next table.

Class of Industry.	New South Wales.	Victoria.	Queensland.	South Australia.	Western Australia.	Tasmania.
Oil and grease	108	127	8	......	......	......
Soap and candles	425	486	140	293	75	67
Glue	......	......	......	24	......	......
Total	533	613	148	317	75	67

In view of the important dimensions attained by the soap and candle-making industry in the several states, the following information regarding the output during the year 1902 may be interesting; no information is available as to the production of candles in Queensland:—

State.	Soap manufactured.	Candles manufactured.
	cwt.	lb.
New South Wales	175,822	2,965,766
Victoria	150,698	5,533,472
Queensland	63,522	......
Western Australia	22,782	1,866,725
Tasmania	15,020	1,081,920
New Zealand	92,321	2,989,280

Stone, Clay, Glass, &c.

The industries which are comprised in this class deal with the various processes in stone, clay, and glass, and are each year assuming larger proportions. Brick and tile-making is far the most important, sixty-one out of every hundred employed being engaged therein.

Class of Industry.	Commonwealth.		New Zealand.		Australasia.	
	Males.	Females.	Males.	Females.	Males.	Females.
Asphalt	48	......	......	......	48	......
Bricks and Tiles	4,740	75	838	......	5,578	75
Glass (including Bottles)	948	5	9	......	957	5
Glass (Ornamental)	309	1	7	......	316	1
Lime, Plaster, and Cement	890	1	184	......	1,074	1
Marble and Slate	217	1	......	......	217	1
Modelling, &c.	116	......	......	......	116	......
Pottery and Earthenware	189	......	......	......	189	......
Stone-dressing	549	5	81	......	630	5
Other Industries	33	......	27	1	60	1
Total	8,039	88	1,146	1	9,185	89

The horse-power of machinery employed in the Commonwealth was 5,784, and in New Zealand 1,166, the value of the machinery and plant being £674,678 and £68,952 respectively.

The hands employed in each industry for the different states are shown below. Those engaged in the manufacture of pottery and earthenware can be given only for New South Wales and South Australia; in the other states they are included with brick and tile makers.

Class of Industry.	New South Wales.	Victoria.	Queensland.	South Australia.	Western Australia.	Tasmania
Asphalt	48	......	......	......	......	......
Bricks and Tiles	1,973	1,451	329	298	455	279
Glass (including Bottles)	280	610	......	63	......	......
Glass (Ornamental)	145	165	......	......	......	......
Lime, Plaster, and Cement	396	265	37	67	00	26
Marble and Slate	148	......	70	......	......	......
Modelling, &c.	45	61	......	......	10	......
Pottery and Eartheuware	155	......	......	34	......	......
Other Industries	......	......	30	......	......	3
Stone Dressing	103	382	......	64	......	5
Total	3,293	2,934	466	526	595	313

The term "asphalt" is popularly applied to tarred stone and screenings, but the asphalt workers referred to in the foregoing table are engaged in processes connected with the preparation for market of Trinidad and other asphalts.

The manufacture of pottery is generally associated with brick-making, and in the following table the products of brickyards and potteries for the year 1902 are shown together.

State.	Number of bricks and fire-bricks made.	Value of—	
		Pipes and tiles made.	Pottery, &c., made.
		£	£
New South Wales	180,727,000	77,626	*
Victoria	90,545,280	71,074	27,289
Queensland	15,241,165	13,471	*
Western Australia	37,721,897	....	....
Tasmania	6,873,936	4,212	*
New Zealand	41,290,316	27,335	7,475

* Included with Pipes and Tiles.

Working in Wood.

The persons employed in these industries numbered 23,424, the largest employment being afforded by saw-mills. Owing to the lack of uniformity in the statistics of the various states it is impossible to state the strength of the hands in the various industries, but this has been done as far as practicable.

Class of Industry.	Commonwealth.		New Zealand.		Australasia.	
	Males.	Females.	Males.	Females.	Males.	Females.
Boxes and Cases	183	......	......	......	183	......
Cooperage			137	1		
Joinery	15,664	30	5	......	22,611	38
Saw-mills			6,805	7		
Wood Turning and Cork Cutting	266	2	157	2	423	4
Other Industries	165	......	......	......	165	......
Total	16,278	32	7,104	10	23,382	42

Machinery is largely used in these industries, although not of a very valuable character. The horse-power of that employed in the Commonwealth was 18,717 and in New Zealand 9,097, the values being £1,524,662 and £425,695 respectively.

The succeeding table shows the distribution of employment in the various states of the Commonwealth. The figures relating to saw-mills and joinery appear slightly misleading; this is due to the fact that the returns for the different states are not compiled on the same basis. In Western Australia the joiners are included with workers in saw-mills, and in New South Wales a number of them are also included with the saw-mill employees. In South Australia no information is given concerning them, although there must be a considerable number. Apparently New South Wales is the only state where establishments are engaged exclusively in the manufacture of boxes and packing-cases, in the remaining states this industry is combined with some other branch of wood-working.

Class of Industry.	New South Wales.	Victoria.	Queensland.	South Australia.	Western Australia.	Tasmania.
Boxes and Cases	183	......	......	......	......	......
Cooperage	210	90	53	56		3
Joinery	777	1,949	416	......	3,631	58
Saw-mills	3,930	1,467	1,855	270		929
Wood Turning and Cork Cutting	75	173	......	20	......	......
Other Industries	......	35	30	71	......	29
Total	5,175	3,714	2,354	417	3,631	1,019

There is no uniformity in the details published by the various states regarding saw-mills; but the information as to the quantity of timber roughly sawn for the latest year available is given below.

	Square feet, 1 inch thick.
New South Wales	90,308,834
Victoria	40,494,660
Queensland	72,478,971
Western Australia	124,005,005
New Zealand	261,583,518

The figures for New South Wales show a great falling off compared with those for 1900, when the quantity operated on was returned as 168,440,000 feet.

Metal Works, Machinery, &c.

Works connected with the treatment of metals, manufacture of machinery, agricultural implements, and railway rolling stock form a large and growing class of industry. The grouping given below is not by any means satisfactory. Persons engaged in the various processes connected with the extraction of gold from gold-bearing stone are in a sense just as much entitled to be classified in the following tables as those concerned in the reduction of silver, lead, or copper ores. The determination of what constitutes an establishment classifiable as a work or factory is by no means clear. As regards works for the extraction of metals from their ores, the determining factor seems to be the degree of intricacy involved in the process of reduction; and whereas a quartz battery would not be called a factory or work, an establishment using a cyanide plant might be so classified. The distinction is not very logical, but as it has long obtained in these states it is retained here.

Class of Industry.	Commonwealth.		New Zealand.		Australasia.	
	Males.	Females.	Males.	Females.	Males.	Females.
Agricultural Implements	1,522	9	584	2	2,106	11
Brass and Copper	676	2	......	......	676	2
Cutlery	76	1	2	......	78	1
Galvanized Iron	1,276	9	261	......	1,537	9
Engineering, Ironworks and Foundries	17,915	30	3,392	10	21,307	40
Lead Mills	69	1	......	......	69	1
Railway Carriages	365	1	......	......	365	1
Railway and Tramway Workshops	7,614	21	1,626	......	9,240	21
Smelting	6,656	......	......	......	6,656	......
Stoves, Ovens, and Ranges	267	1	193	......	460	1
Tinsmithing	1,014	2	336	1	1,350	3
Wireworking	439	7	......	......	439	7
Other Metal Works	434	7	10	......	444	7
Total	38,323	91	6,404	13	44,727	104

In these industries machinery is very extensively used. The horse-power of the machinery in use in the Commonwealth was 21,192 and in New Zealand 2,780, the values being £3,394,973 and £317,07[illegible] respectively.

In considering this and the subsequent tables, several difficulties in making comparisons will be met with. In Queensland, for example, all metal works, except smelting, are grouped in the one line, which is also the case in Western Australia. In Queensland and Tasmania no hands are shown as being employed in the manufacture and repairs of rolling stock; this, of course, is incorrect, for though little manufacturing may be carried on, all the states make their own repairs. In Victoria 1,351 hands are shown as employed in railway carriage and rolling-stock manufacture and repairs as compared with 4,050 in New South Wales. The employment afforded in railway workshops is chiefly in the nature of repairs, but locomotives, passenger carriages, and goods waggons are built in each state, and it is evident that the repairs in the former state are not on such an extensive scale as in the latter. The number of hands set down as employed in the manufacture of agricultural implements in New South Wales is only 82, few establishments devoting themselves entirely to this business, the manufacture of implements being usually associated with ironworking generally. Included in the 610 workers in tinsmithing in South Australia are a number of plumbers and persons engaged in the manufacture of stoves and ovens. New South Wales and South Australia possess smelting works on a large scale, affording employment to 2,558 hands in the first-named state, and to 1,768 in the latter. The chief smelting works of New South Wales are situated at Cockle Creek, near Newcastle, and at Dapto, in close proximity to the coal-fields. The chief ores treated are copper, tin, silver, and lead, partly the production of the state itself, and partly of Tasmania, South Australia, Western Australia, Queensland, and New Caledonia. The smelting works of South Australia are situated at Port Pirie, and deal with silver and lead ore from Broken Hill. The number of hands employed in each state is shown in the following table :—

Class of Industry.	New South Wales.	Victoria.	Queensland.	South Australia.	Western Australia.	Tasmania.
Agricultural Implements	82	789	......	559	40	61
Brass and Copper	162	516	......	......	......	......
Cutlery	17	60	......	......	......	......
Galvanized Iron	379	823	......	83	......	......
Engineering, Ironworks and Foundries	5,547	4,975	3,254	2,809	1,040	320
Lead-mills	14	56	......	......	......	......
Railway Carriages	366	......	......	......	......	......
Railway and Tramway Workshops	3,684	1,351	......	1,505	1,095	......
Smelting	2,558	732	335	1,768	......	1,263
Stoves and Ovens	148	120	......	......	......	......
Tinsmithing	333	......	......	610	......	73
Wireworking	258	188	......	......	......	......
Other Metal Works	176	262	......	......	......	3
Total	13,724	9,872	3,589	7,334	2,175	1,720

Industries connected with Food and Drink.

The industries connected with food and drink afford employment for a large number of hands, the distribution into detailed groups being as shown in the following table. The figures for the most part afford their own explanation. Included under the head of cornflour, oatmeal, and arrowroot are, in the case of Victoria, a small number of hands making macaroni, and some starch makers; these last are few in number, and it was not found possible to exclude them from the persons employed in making farinaceous foods, otherwise they could have been classed elsewhere. Owing to an arrangement between the statistical offices of New South Wales and Victoria, factories dealing with milk products have been included in the list of manufactories, although they cannot rightly be considered as such.

Class of Industry.	Commonwealth.		New Zealand.		Australasia.	
	Males.	Females.	Males.	Females.	Males.	Females
Bacon Curing	675	7	185	11	860	18
Butter Factories Cheese Factories	2,782	96	1,165	23	3,947	119
Condensed Milk	31	6	17	16	48	22
Meat Preserving	2,937	131	2,369	51	5,306	182
Biscuits	3,073	1,387	454	213	3,685	1,747
Confectionery			158	147		
Cornflour, Oatmeal, &c.	546	296	19	10	565	306
Flour Mills	2,404	25	513	2	2,917	27
Jam and Fruit Canning	2,375	1,153	88	84	2,553	1,298
Pickles, Sauces, and Vinegar			90	61		
Sugar Mills	2,296	....	....	....	2,296	....
Sugar Refineries	955	5	256	....	1,211	5
Aerated Waters, Cordials, &c.	3,478	160	437	15	3,915	175
Breweries	3,512	9	677	5	4,189	14
Condiments, Coffee, Spices &c.	563	260	63	15	626	275
Distilleries	207	....	....	....	207	....
Ice and Refrigerating	390	13	5	....	395	13
Malting	208	....	145	....	353	....
Tobacco, Cigars, &c.	1,514	1,380	12	26	1,526	1,406
Salt	263	....	....	....	263	....
Other Industries	63	4	107	....	170	4
Total	28,772	4,932	6,760	679	35,532	5,611

In the preparation of foods and drinks machinery enters largely into use; the capital invested in machinery in the Commonwealth was £7,617,338, and in New Zealand £1,035,939 the average horse-power used being 52,021 and 14,792 respectively

Distributing the persons shown above as employed in the Commonwealth amongst the various states, the most noticeable point is the strong position of Queensland, due entirely to the development of the sugar and meat-preserving industries.

Class of Industry.	New South Wales.	Victoria.	Queensland.	South Australia.	Western Australia.	Tasmania.
Bacon Curing	128	285	26	226	....	22
Butter Factories	824	} 1,407	{ 328	....	3	82
Cheese Factories	62			167	....	....
Condensed Milk	37	....	....	....	....	....
Meat-preserving	919	596	1,544	....	....	7
Biscuits	894	957	237	....	} 148	{ 111
Confectionery	808	808	284	218		....
Cornflour, Oatmeal, &c.	378	442	22	....	....	....
Flour Mills	812	664	194	527	94	138
Jam, and Fruit Canning	679	} 1,638	243	155	} 54	661
Pickles, Sauces and Vinegar	58		....	11		9
Sugar Mills	633	....	1,663	....	....	....
Sugar Refineries	531	324	....	105	....	....
Aerated Waters, Cordials, &c.	1,348	1,053	632	199	346	65
Breweries	1,088	1,112	419	342	445	170
Condiments, Coffee, Spices, &c.	368	259	65	106	22	8
Distilleries	10	78	58	71	....	....
Ice and Refrigerating	598	139	73	32	66	....
Malting	45	163	....	....	....	....
Tobacco, Cigars, &c.	1,104	1,298	129	263	106	....
Salt	....	59	....	204	....	....
Other Industries	....	51	....	16	....	....
Total	11,244	11,325	5,917	2,642	1,283	1,293

There are many important industries in this class the details of which would prove interesting, but only for a limited number is the necessary information available. The most important of these is perhaps the meat-preserving and refrigerating industry, and the following table will give some idea of its development in the various states. The figures show the latest annual output, those for New South Wales are exclusive of 1,264,743 lb. of tongues preserved during the year.

State.	Sheep and lambs, frozen.	Beef, frozen and chilled.	Rabbits frozen.	Meat Preserved.		
				Beef.	Mutton.	Rabbits.
	carcases.	lb.	No.	lb.	lb.	lb.
New South Wales	963,614	8,138,144	*	5,703,701	7,678,960	......
Victoria	375,178	702,450	6,218,422	862,960	1,670,256	1,852,144
Queensland	117,729	85,743,229	......	23,023,137	5,374,696	......
New Zealand	3,348,123	34,285,328	6,040,047	7,867,440		......

* Value £6,233.

The sugar industry has attained considerable dimensions in New South Wales and Queensland. Some details of the industry for the year 1902 are given below, but more extended information is given on this subject in the chapter dealing with "Agriculture."

State.	Sugar cane crushed.	Sugar manufactured.	Molasses manufactured.
	tons.	tons.	gallons.
New South Wales	222,276	21,544	1,073,640
Queensland	641,927	76,626	2,217,738

Detailed information regarding flour-mills is available for each state excepting South Australia, and the following items have been selected as being of most value in showing the progress made. The quantity of flour made compared with the wheat ground seems a little inconsistent in some of the states, but the figures are given as they appear in the official records.

State.	Wheat ground.	Other grain ground.	Flour made.
	bushels.	bushels.	tons.
New South Wales	8,853,048	....	185,147
Victoria	8,491,224	126,765	170,696
Queensland	1,338,346	84,833	26,579
Western Australia	576,781	....	11,840
Tasmania	903,298	97,259	18,620
New Zealand	4,004,789	762,340	83,017

Breweries afford a large amount of employment, and those of Victoria have attained the most importance and have the largest annual output, as the following figures show :—

State.	Beer and Porter made.	Materials used—		
		Sugar.	Malt.	Hops.
	gallons.	cwt.	bushels.	lb.
New South Wales	15,074,794	89,332	606,160	756,770
Victoria	17,160,408	115,240	625,441	677,262
Queensland	5,073,164	....	....	....
Western Australia	4,780,058	28,680	181,955	300,350
Tasmania	1,814,077	....	....	....
New Zealand	7,379,581	21,647	455,035	562,245

Clothing and Textile Fabrics.

Industries connected with the manufacture of clothing and textile fabrics afford more employment than any other class. The females employed largely outnumber the males, and the excess would be still greater if all persons working in their own homes, or in dwelling-houses not classed as factories, had been included. The following table shows the number of males and females employed in this class of industry:—

Class of Industry.	Commonwealth.		New Zealand.		Australasia.	
	Males.	Females.	Males.	Females.	Males.	Females.
Woollen Mills	995	884	769	924	1,764	1,808
Boots and Shoes	8,612	3,582	1,906	790	10,518	4,372
Slop Clothing and Tailoring	4,763	11,878	1,153	2,980	5,916	14,858
Dressmaking and Millinery	517	12,021	24	2,889	541	14,910
Underclothing	177	3,362	......	......	177	3,362
Dyeworks and Cleaning	87	101	28	23	115	124
Furriers	47	67	......	......	47	67
Hats and Caps	745	1,079	37	80	782	1,159
Waterproof and Oilskin	147	556	22	92	169	648
Shirts, Ties, and Scarfs	49	604	28	503	77	1,107
Rope and Cordage	563	177	192	......	755	177
Tents and Tarpaulins	139	99	......	......	139	99
Flax Mills	......	......	1,698	......	1,698	......
Hosiery	35	304	17	265	52	569
Total	16,876	34,714	5,874	8,546	22,750	43,260

The use of machinery is not extensive in this class, as compared with the number of hands engaged. The value in the Commonwealth was only £800,197, and in New Zealand £340,933, the average horse-power used being 4,932 and 3,644 respectively.

Victoria shows the greatest development in these industries, and employs more hands than any other state in almost every branch of them. The only exceptions are waterproof clothing, where New South Wales employs more hands, and textiles, in which it is surpassed by New Zealand. The colony last named has 1,693 hands employed in woollen mills compared with 1,122 in Victoria and 276 in New South Wales. New Zealand has also 1,698 hands in flax mills; in no other state has this industry been established. The classification of the minor industries is a matter of some difficulty as in many cases two or more branches are combined; this will account for the variations in such industries as shirt-making, underclothing, &c. The following table shows the distribution of employment in the various states of the Commonwealth :—

Class of Industry.	New South Wales.	Victoria.	Queensland.	South Australia.	Western Australia.	Tasmania.
Woollen Mills	276	1,122	129	142	......	210
Boots and Shoes	4,098	5,101	1,045	1,368	284	298
Slop Clothing and Tailoring	5,439	7,040	1,527	1,744	891	......
Dressmaking and Millinery	2,593	6,550	*950	962	458	1,025
Underclothing	†......	8,825	......	190	......	24
Dyeworks and Cleaning	58	116	......	14	......	......
Furriers	41	67	......	......	......	6
Hats and Caps	474	1,170	125	55	......	......
Waterproof and Oilskin	454	249	......	......	......	......
Shirts, Ties, and Scarfs	658	†......	......	......	......	......
Rope and Cordage, Mats, &c.	141	477	64	58	......	......
Tents and Tarpaulins	130	59	......	35	14	......
Hosiery	†......	313	......	......	......	26
Total	14,357	25,559	3,840	4,568	1,647	1,589

* Estimated. † Included elsewhere.

There are important boot and shoe factories in each of the states, and the output is attaining considerable proportions, as will be seen from the figures given below. No output of uppers is recorded from New South Wales or Victoria, although there are some establishments solely devoted to upper making; but the great bulk of the uppers is made in the ordinary boot factories.

State.	Articles manufactured.			Value of Output.
	Boots and Shoes.	Slippers.	Uppers.	
	pairs.	pairs.	pairs.	£
New South Wales	3,052,914	451,588	....	....
Victoria	3,613,487	216,483	....	....
Queensland	687,667	....	17,721	179,687
Western Australia	212,768	....	....	....
Tasmania	187,584	....	....	59,610
New Zealand	1,161,873	104,583	166,027	529,254

The manufacture of textile fabrics is becoming an important industry, especially in New Zealand, where the hands employed in woollen mills are nearly equal in number to those in the whole of the Commonwealth. Of the Commonwealth states Victoria is the most important, as may be judged by its consumption of wool, which is five times that of New South Wales. The following information shows the output from woollen mills in the various states :—

State.	Wool used.	Articles manufactured.				Value of Output.
		Tweed and Cloth.	Flannel.	Blankets.	Shawls and Rugs.	
	lb.	yds.	yds.	pairs.	No.	£
New South Wales ...	693,328	566,296	14,500	6,340	800	...
Victoria	3,473,835	708,749	2,612,343	67,609	5,718	...
Tasmania	913,828	.....	......	.....	......	...
New Zealand...........	3,257,319	1,445,867	1,191,234	49,523	26,806	359,382

Books, Paper, Printing, &c.

The different industries connected with printing, bookbinding, paper-making, &c., afford work to 21,101 persons. The great bulk of these is employed in the various processes of printing, actual manufacturers being comparatively few in number. Australia and New Zealand produce many excellent paper-making materials; nevertheless, only 300 persons are employed in paper-making, and a large proportion of the output of the mills consists of ordinary brown or wrapping papers.

Class of Industry.	Commonwealth.		New Zealand.		Australasia.	
	Males.	Females.	Males.	Females.	Males.	Females.
Electrotyping and stereotyping ..	77	5	......	......	77	5
Paper, Paper bags, boxes, &c.....	632	705	103	76	735	781
Photo-engraving	62	23	......	......	62	23
Printing and bookbinding	13,140	2,669	2,852	586	15,992	3,255
Printing materials	58	1	5	......	63	1
Engraving	107	......	......	......	107	......
Total	14,076	3,403	2,960	662	17,036	4,065

The machinery employed in the above had a value of £1,765,582 in the Commonwealth, and £381,958 in New Zealand. The average horse-power used was 4,811 and 1,762 respectively.

There are several difficulties in the way of making comparisons regarding these industries. Under the headings of electrotyping and stereotyping and photo-engraving there are no returns for any state but New South Wales. It must be presumed, therefore, that persons employed in these pursuits in the other states are included with printing, bookbinding, &c. Under the head of printing are included the composing and mechanical staff of the newspaper offices—persons whom it takes a very wide definition to bring in under the term "manufacturers." The following table shows the employment afforded in the various states :—

Class of Industry.	New South Wales.	Victoria.	Queensland.	South Australia.	Western Australia.	Tasmania.
Electrotyping and stereotyping ..	82	......	......	......	......	......
Paper, Paper bags, boxes, &c.	522	531	85	171	28	......
Photo-engraving	57	......	......	......	28	......
Printing and bookbinding	5,275	5,864	1,906	1,429	852	483
Printing materials	......	49	10	......	......	......
Engraving	......	107	......	......	......	......
Total	5,936	6,551	2,001	1,600	908	483

Musical Instruments.

The manufacture of musical instruments is not yet firmly established in Australasia, and until recently the employment afforded was mainly in the direction of fitting and repairs.

Class of Industry.	Commonwealth.		New Zealand.		Australasia.	
	Males.	Females.	Males.	Females.	Males.	Females.
Musical Instruments	199	13	11	..	210	13

In New Zealand no machinery was employed, and in the Commonwealth the average horse-power used was only 33, and the value £3,325.

New South Wales is the only state which shows much development, 202 persons out of a total for the Commonwealth of 212 being engaged in that state. The greater part of this employment is afforded by one establishment.

Arms and Explosives.

The manufacture of small arms and explosives is of great importance in connection with the defence of these shores, but so far little attention has been devoted to the industry, only 401 hands being employed, these being occupied exclusively in the manufacture of explosives.

Class of Industry.	Commonwealth.		New Zealand.		Australasia.	
	Males.	Females.	Males.	Females.	Males.	Females.
Explosives	145	151	21	84	166	235

The horse-power of the machinery used in the Commonwealth was 92, and in New Zealand 39, the value of the plant being £47,458 and £10,650 respectively.

Of the Commonwealth states Victoria alone shows much development in this industry, and 284 hands are engaged in the manufacture of explosives, the remaining 12 hands being employed in New South Wales.

Vehicles, Saddlery, and Harness.

In connection with the manufacture and repair of vehicles, saddlery, harness, &c., there are 9,964 hands employed. The great bulk of the work done in connection with coaches and waggons consists of repairing; but there are establishments in all the states where vehicles of all classes are manufactured.

Class of Industry.	Commonwealth.		New Zealand.		Australasia.	
	Males.	Females.	Males.	Females.	Males.	Females.
Coach and Waggon Building	5,245	13	1,185	......	6,430	13
Cycles	613	6	378	17	991	23
Perambulators	62	6	......	......	62	6
Saddlery and Harness	1,650	42	629	23	2,309	65
Spokes, &c.	33	......	......	......	33	......
Whips	27	......	5	......	32	......
Total	7,660	67	2,197	40	9,857	107

The employment of machinery in this class is mainly in tyre-setting. The horse-power of the machinery used in the Commonwealth was 758, and in New Zealand 226, the values being £178,726 and £38,868 respectively.

Victoria shows by far the greatest progress in this class, no less than 3,091 hands being employed in that state.

Class of Industry.	New South Wales.	Victoria.	Queensland.	South Australia.	Western Australia.	Tasmania.
Coach and Waggon Building ...	1,566	2,302	476	395	372	147
Cycles	77	301	......	153	41	47
Perambulators	27	41	......	......	......	......
Saddlery and Harness	491	431	401	310	124	35
Spokes, &c.	33	......	......	......	......	......
Whips	11	16	......	......	......	......
Total	2,185	3,091	877	858	537	229

Ship and Boat-building and Repairing.

The industries depending upon shipping have not attained large dimensions in any of the states, and as regards ship-building itself, the use of iron instead of wood for the frames and hulls of vessels has injuriously affected a promising industry, as the woods of Australia are eminently fitted for ship-building purposes. The following is a statement of the persons employed :—

Class of Industry.	Commonwealth.		New Zealand.		Australasia.	
	Males.	Females.	Males.	Females.	Males.	Females.
Docks and Slips	} 2,014	......	32	......	} 2,407	93
Sails, Tents, and Tarpaulins		12	150	81		
Ship and boat-building and repairs		......	211	......		
Total	2,014	12	393	81	2,407	93

The use of machinery of a powerful character is necessary for the purpose of quickly emptying docks, although it is not in constant requisition. The value in the Commonwealth was £385,201, and in New Zealand £209,878, the average horse-power in use being 1,505 and 484 respectively.

In industries connected with ship-building and repairing, New South Wales has a far larger number of hands employed than any other state, mainly due to the fact that Sydney is the terminal port of most of the great lines of steamers trading with Australia. The chief portion of the business is in connection with the docking and repairing of ships, although there are several establishments engaged exclusively in ship and boat building.

Class of Industry.	New South Wales.	Victoria.	Queensland.	South Australia.	Western Australia.	Tasmania
Docks and Slips	1,042	} 174	} 163	} 114	} 76	......
Sails, Tents, and Tarpaulins......	40					15
Ship and boat-building and repairs	392					10
Total	1,474	174	163	114	76	25

Furniture, Bedding, &c.

Although Australia and New Zealand produce various kinds of wood admirably adapted to the requirements of the furniture trades, it can hardly be said that the industry has attained a development equal to its opportunities. As showing the possibilities of the industry, it may be mentioned that the value of furniture, bedding, flock, and upholstery imported into the Commonwealth during 1902 was £262,400, and into

New Zealand £62,840. The employment afforded by the industry was :—

Class of Industry.	Commonwealth.		New Zealand.		Australasia.	
	Males.	Females.	Males.	Females.	Males.	Females.
Bedding, Flock, and Upholstery..	820	268	64	1	884	269
Billiard Tables	29	......	7	......	36	......
Chair-making	45	......	......	......	45	......
Furniture and Cabinet-making ..	3,830	46	1,243	67	5,073	113
Picture Frames	219	84	19	3	238	87
Window Blinds..................	88	1	49	2	137	3
Total	5,081	399	1,382	73	6,413	472

The value of the machinery employed in the Commonwealth was £91,672, and in New Zealand £28,249, the average horse-power used being 960 and 464 respectively.

The manufacture of furniture, bedding, &c., in the Commonwealth affords employment to 5,430 persons, of whom 2,019 are in New South Wales and 1,871 in Victoria. The distribution in the various states is as follows :—

Class of Industry.	New South Wales.	Victoria.	Queensland.	South Australia.	Western Australia.	Tasmania.
Bedding, Flock, and Upholstery..	492	436	126	12	......	22
Billiard Tables	29	......	......	......	......	......
Chair-making	45	......	......	......	......	......
Furniture and Cabinet-making ..	1,808	1,276	416	441	283	157
Picture Frames	118	107	......	75	......	8
Window Blinds..................	37	52	......	......	......	......
Total	2,019	1,871	542	528	283	187

The manufacture of billiard tables is an established industry in Victoria, but the number of hands employed cannot be given separately, as they are included amongst those shown in furniture and cabinet-making.

Drugs and Chemicals and By-Products.

In all the states there are establishments engaged in making chemicals or medicines of some description, while the manufacture of fertilisers is also an established industry in every state.

Class of Iudustry.	Commonwealth.		New Zealand.		Australasia.	
	Males.	Females.	Males.	Females.	Males.	Females.
Chemicals, Drugs, and Medicine..	1,205	423	96	33	1,301	456
Fertilisers	308	5	47	......	355	5
Paints and Varnishes............	198	56	31	......	229	56
Total	1,711	484	174	33	1,885	517

The horse-power of the machinery used in the Commonwealth was 2,132, and in New Zealand 319, the values of the plant being £257,876 and £32,963 respectively.

The classification for individual states will be found below :—

Class of Industry.	New South Wales.	Victoria.	Queensland.	South Australia.	Western Australia.	Tasmania.
Chemicals, Drugs, and Medicines..	437	1,072	33	32	31	23
Fertilisers	37	136	22	96	7	16
Paints and Varnishes	162	48	......	15	29	......
Total	636	1,256	55	142	67	39

The information regarding Victoria is misleading; included in the workers engaged in chemicals, &c., are a number of persons engaged in the manufacture of rubber goods, the two returns having been combined so that the particulars regarding an individual establishment might not be disclosed.

Surgical and Scientific Appliances.

The employment afforded in these industries is not great, and the major portion of the work is in connection with the manufacture of spectacles, etc.

Class of Industry.	Commonwealth.		New Zealand.		Australasia.	
	Males.	Females.	Males.	Females.	Males.	Females.
Surgical, Optical, and other Scientific Instruments	105	21	......	......	05	1

The machinery employed was valued at £4,975, and the average horse-power used was 25.

In only three of the Commonwealth states are these industries established, and in none of them have they attained any important dimensions.

Class of Industry.	New South Wales.	Victoria.	Queensland.	South Australia.	Western Australia.	Tasmania.
Surgical, Optical, and other Scientific Instruments	65	44	17	......	......	......

Timepieces, Jewellery, and Plated Ware.

There are 1,140 hands engaged in this class, mostly employed in connection with jewellery.

Class of Industry.	Commonwealth.		New Zealand.		Tasmania.	
	Males.	Females.	Males.	Females.	Males.	Females.
Electro-plating	97	3	11	......	108	3
Manufacturing Jewellery	985	36	8	......	993	36
Total	1,082	39	19	......	1,101	39

The horse-power of the machinery employed in the Commonwealth was 91, and in New Zealand 14, the values of the plant being £24,348 and £3,822 respectively.

In each of the states certain persons are returned as being engaged in the manufacture of jewellery, but it is extremely doubtful if as many as are set down are employed solely in this industry. It is more than probable that the numbers include some hands principally engaged in the repair of watches and clocks.

Class of Industry.	New South Wales.	Victoria.	Queensland.	South Australia.	Western Australia.	Tasmania.
Electro-plating	75	......	} 34 {	25	......	......
Manufacturing Jewellery	168	616		114	47	42
Total	243	616	34	139	47	42

Industries connected with the Production of Light.

Industries connected with the production of fuel, heat, and light do not afford employment to many hands. The following table shows 4,333 hands, of whom 2,545 are employed in gas-works, 1,034 in electric-lighting works, 283 in coke-making, and 183 in manufacturing matches. Gas-supply gives employment to far more persons than the table shows—possibly to twice as many—but the additional hands are not employed in gas making, but in laying down pipes and other work connected with gas supply.

Industry.	Commonwealth.		New Zealand.		Australasia.	
	Males.	Females.	Males.	Females.	Males.	Females.
Coke-works	283	......	......	......	283	......
Electric Apparatus	119	1	......	......	119	1
Electric Light and Power	979	3	52	......	1,031	3
Gas-works and Kerosene	1,973	......	568	4	2,541	4
Lamps and Fittings, &c.	37	35	......	......	37	35
Hydraulic Power	49	47	......	......	49	47
Matches	......	......	37	146	37	146
Total	3,440	86	657	150	4,097	236

Machinery of a very powerful and valuable character is required in these industries, as will be seen from the fact that the value of the plant in the Commonwealth was £2,733,872, and in New Zealand £871,653, the average horse-power used being 30,457 and 2,419 respectively.

Only in New South Wales is the number of hands employed in each industry specified. The coke-workers in Victoria are included with hands employed in gas-works, while the hands employed in establishments other than gas-works are grouped together in Queensland. The number of hands employed in manufacturing candles is not included in the following table. The soap and candle industries are usually worked together, so that it is not possible to separate the hands employed which are accordingly classified under the heading of soap and candle workers, in the second group of the series. The manufacture of matches is carried on in Victoria, but the number of hands employed is not disclosed in the official statistics.

Industry.	New South Wales.	Victoria.	Queensland.	South Australia.	Western Australia.	Tasmania.
Coke-works	283	......	......	......	......	......
Electric Apparatus	44	76	} 106	} 91	} 216	......
Electric Light and Power	413	147				9
Gas-works and Kerosene	723	758	248	96	82	66
Lamps and Fittings, &c.	72	......	......	......	......	......
Hydraulic Power, &c.	10	86	......	......	......	......
Total	1,545	1,067	354	187	298	75

In view of the magnitude attained by gas-works in the various states, the following particulars as to the quantity of coal used and gas made during 1902, may prove interesting :—

State.	Coal used.	Cubic feet of gas produced.
	tons.	
New South Wales	196,460	2,304,814,000
Victoria	169,356	1,642,652,799
Queensland	36,709	339,023,600
Western Australia	....	52,423,870
Tasmania	....	69,686,979
New Zealand	....	786,531,150

Leatherware.

In view of the fact that the tanning industry has assumed such important dimensions, it is unsatisfactory to find that only 445 hands are employed in connection with the manufacture of leatherware.

Class of Industry.	Commonwealth.		New Zealand.		Australasia.	
	Males.	Females.	Males.	Females.	Males.	Females.
Leather Belting, Fancy Leather, Portmanteaux, and Bags.	353	70	19	3	372	73

The machinery employed in the Commonwealth was valued at £10,941, and the average horse-power in use was 70.

The largest development of the industry is in Victoria, where 276 hands are employed, the majority of them, 123 males and 47 females, being engaged in the manufacture of fancy leather.

Class of Industry.	New South Wales.	Victoria.	Queensland.	South Australia.	Western Australia.	Tasmania.
Leather Belting, Fancy Leather, Portmanteaux, and Bags.	97	276	38	......	12	......

MINOR WARES.

All industries which could not properly be brought under the foregoing classification are included here. The more important of the industries are shown separately, but owing to their varied nature it is impossible to show them all, so that a number of separate industries have been brought together under the comprehensive title of "Other Industries."

Class of Industry.	Commonwealth.		New Zealand.		Australasia.	
	Males.	Females.	Males.	Females.	Males.	Females.
Baskets and Wickerware, Mats, &c.	96	7	116	19	212	26
Brooms and Brushware	585	217	86	42	671	259
Rubber Goods	62	2	3	......	65	2
Toys	11	......	......	......	11	......
Umbrellas	72	157	......	......	72	157
Other Industries	503	131	172	173	675	304
Total	1,329	514	377	234	1,706	748

The horse-power of the machinery employed in the Commonwealth was 417, and in New Zealand 206, the values of the plant being £54,995 and £22,028 respectively.

The returns of the various states are each compiled on a different basis, so that it is impossible to give accurate information regarding the several industries. The manufacture of brooms and brushware is, however, the most important, while umbrella-making also employs a considerable number of hands. In Victoria the hands employed in the manufacture of rubber goods are included with those engaged in the preparation of chemicals, &c.

Class of Industry.	New South Wales.	Victoria.	Queensland.	South Australia.	Western Australia.	Tasmania.
Baskets and Wickerware Mats, &c.	25	57	} 124	} 199	21	......
Brooms and Brushware	233	294			......	76
Rubber Goods	49	......		15	......	......
Toys	11	......		......	......	......
Umbrellas	43	172		14	......	......
Other Industries	31	426		53	......	......
Total	392	949	124	281	21	76

The relative development of the industries of the states may be measured by the information shown in the following table, in which the industries are arranged in three classes, viz.:—First, those connected with the treatment of perishable products for domestic consumption; second, those dependent upon the natural resources of the country; and, third, those the production from which comes into competition with imported goods:—

State.	Employed in domestic industries for the treatment of perishable products for immediate use.		Employed in industries dependent upon the natural resources of the country.		Employed in industries the production from which comes into competition with imported goods.	
	Males.	Females.	Males.	Females.	Males.	Females.
New South Wales	3,790	65	25,786	4,935	24,750	6,943
Victoria	3,652	59	19,504	13,113	26,502	10,233
Queensland	1,363	94	8,290	1,841	7,942	1,428
South Australia	726	14	6,710	2,784	9,159	1,145
Western Australia	854	6	6,461	1,067	3,105	230
Tasmania	277	40	4,133	728	1,771	517
Commonwealth	10,662	278	70,884	24,468	73,229	20,496
New Zealand	2,446	59	20,155	4,496	15,493	6,069
Australasia	13,108	337	91,039	28,964	88,722	26,565

Plant Employed in Manufactories.

The character of the industry chiefly determines the horse-power required and the value of the plant. Thus, in the clothing and allied industries, the average number of persons per 100 horse-power is 770; in industries connected with the preparation of food and drink, the average is only 62. The value of the plant, compared with the horse-power, also varies greatly as between the different industries. In industries working in wood, the value of plant is only about £70 per horse-power; in furniture trades, £85; while in gas-making it is about £1,200. The following is a statement of the amount of horse-power and value of plant employed in the various groups of industries, according to the classification used in the foregoing pages :—

Class of Industry.	Commonwealth.		New Zealand.	
	Horse-power.	Value of plant.	Horse-power.	Value of plant.
	No.	£	No.	£
Treating raw materials, &c.	6,933	532,808	2,099	123,983
Oils and fats, &c.	1,812	467,904	428	44,203
Processes in stone, clay, glass, &c.	5,784	674,678	1,166	68,952
Working in wood	18,717	1,524,662	9,097	425,695
Metal works, machinery, &c.	21,192	3,394,973	2,780	317,072
Connected with food and drink, &c.	52,021	7,617,838	14,792	1,035,989
Clothing and textile fabrics, &c.	4,932	800,197	3,644	340,933
Books, paper, printing, &c.	4,811	1,765,582	1,762	381,958
Musical instruments	33	3,325	......	......
Arms and explosives	92	47,458	39	10,650
Vehicles, saddlery, and harness	758	178,726	226	38,868
Ship and boat building, &c.	1,505	885,201	484	209,878
Furniture, bedding, and upholstery	960	91,672	464	28,249
Drugs, chemicals, and by-products	2,132	257,876	319	32,963
Surgical and other scientific instruments	25	4,975	......	......
Jewellery, platedware, &c.	91	24,348	14	3,822
Heat, light, and power	30,457	2,783,872	2,419	871,658
Leatherware not elsewhere included	70	10,941	......	670
Minor wares not elsewhere included	417	54,995	206	22,028
Total	152,742	20,571,526	39,989	3,962,521

There is a slight inaccuracy in the returns that it is well should be pointed out. The horse-power quoted represents the average power actually used, while the value of machinery and plant represents that of all the usable machinery that the establishments contain.

Similar information for each state of the Commonwealth is given below :

HORSE POWER.

Class of Industry.	New South Wales.	Victoria.	Queensland.	South Australia.	Western Australia.	Tasmania.
	No	No.	No.	No.	No.	No.
Treating raw materials, &c.	2,535	2,634	591	842	43	288
Oils and fats, &c.	525	376	95	683	82	51
Processes in stone, clay, glass, &c.	2,961	1,822	256	287	292	166
Working in wood	5,699	3,923	3,990	483	3,317	1,305
Metal works, machinery, &c.	8,020	4,784	2,520	2,392	742	2,734
Connected with food and drink, &c.	13,711	12,996	18,502	4,068	1,374	1,375
Clothing and textile fabrics, &c.	829	3,480	225	263	39	146
Books, paper, printing, &c.	1,456	2,061	420	475	305	94
Musical instruments	83	......	......	......	......	......
Arms and explosives	2	90	......	......	......	......
Vehicles, saddlery, and harness	147	298	62	170	61	20
Ship and boat building, &c.	978	258	135	116	22	6
Furniture, bedding, & upholstery	269	529	85	2	29	46
Drugs, chemicals, and by-products	280	1,427	153	169	57	46
Surgical and other scientific instruments	10	6	5	......	4	......
Jewellery, platedware, &c.	13	74	......	4	......	......
Heat, light, and power	15,248	8,908	682	1,186	2,790	1,634
Leatherware not elsewhere included	24	42	......	......	4	......
Minor wares not elsewhere included	78	168	46	120	......	5
Total	52,813	43,821	27,767	11,255	9,170	7,916

VALUE OF PLANT.

Class of Industry.	New South Wales.	Victoria.	Queensland.	South Australia.	Western Australia.	Tasmania.
	£	£	£	£	£	£
Treating raw material, &c.	197,136	166,824	76 752	64,420	5,571	22,100
Oils and fats, &c.	187,287	99,055	31,342	183,560	8,260	8,400
Processes in stone, clay, glass, &c.	379,016	153,415	60,226	38,750	33,363	14,908
Working in wood	340,160	189,716	269,267	28,360	613.364	83,295
Metal works, machinery, &c.	1,140,127	851,972	338,965	363,870	218,985	481,054
Connected with food and drink, &c.	2,280,679	1,413,407	2,988,037	600,560	204,850	129,806
Clothing and textile fabrics, &c.	197,310	438,116	72,015	41,490	14,751	36,515
Books, paper, printing, &c.	594 939	637,720	197,162	172,510	122,514	40,737
Musical instruments	3,325	......	......	......	......	......
Arms and explosives	286	47,172	......	......	......	......
Vehicles, saddlery, and harness, &c.	39,310	61,194	18,496	39,900	16,993	2,833
Ship and boat building, &c.	270,430	52,935	27,691	29,920	3,975	250
Furniture, bedding, and upholstery	31,655	42,587	11,117	190	3,912	2,211
Drugs, chemicals, and by-products	67,526	148,697	14,391	20,950	4,112	2,200
Surgical and other scientific instruments	1,900	770	663	......	1,642	......
Jewellery, plated ware, &c.	6,675	13,618	1,500	1,000	905	650
Heat, light, and power	1,094,962	735,230	410,927	107,010	149,094	256,649
Leatherware not elsewhere included	3,390	5,459	450	......	1,642	......
Minor wares not elsewhere included	9,730	24,136	2,709	15,030	......	3,390
Total	6,795,843	5,082,023	4,521,710	1,702,510	1,404,442	1,064,998

The average value of plant per horse-power of machinery employed ranges from £99 in the case of New Zealand to £163 for Queensland, the average for Australasia being £127. The average for each state was as follows:—New South Wales £129, Victoria £116, Queensland £163, South Australia £151, Western Australia £153, and Tasmania £135. A mere statement of values, however, has no special meaning, since the difference in the figures is compatible with two opposite conditions—either the same plant is put to greatest use in the case of New Zealand, or it is of superior character in the case of Queensland.

VALUE OF PRODUCTION OF MANUFACTORIES.

The value of the articles produced in the manufactories has been carefully estimated for each of the states and is given below. For New South Wales and Queensland the information is now obtained annually; but although this is not the case in the other states, there is no difficulty in arriving at a satisfactory estimate, owing to the ample data at command. The production from butter, cheese, and bacon factories and creameries has not been taken into consideration, as it has already been included under the pastoral and dairying industries. The figures refer to the year 1902, except in the case of New Zealand, where the census returns of 1901 are the latest figures available, and have accordingly been used. The total value of the output of all factories was £92,032,000, of which £52,984,000 represents the value of materials and fuel used, and £39,048,000 the value added in the processes of treatment. Of the latter sum, £18,611,000 was paid in wages, leaving a balance of £20,437,000, which accrued to the proprietors, and out of which rent, insurance, depreciation, &c., had to be paid, the remainder representing profits on the business. The difference between the value of materials and fuel used and the total output is the real value of production from manufactories; this sum has been stated above as £39,048,000, and the amount in each state was as follows :—

State.	Value of Production.	Value per Inhabitant.
	£	£ s. d.
New South Wales	11,452,000	8 4 4
Victoria	10,734,000	8 17 10
Queensland	3,237,000	6 6 3
South Australia	2,883,000	7 17 10
Western Australia	2,423,000	11 16 5
Tasmania	1,389,000	7 18 2
Commonwealth	32,118,000	8 6 5
New Zealand	6,930,000	9 1 6
Australasia	39,048,000	8 7 8

The above table would seem to indicate that, in proportion to population, Western Australia holds the premier position; but the position occupied by that state is due to the higher prices obtained for the products rather than from any great development of the manufacturing industries. New Zealand stands second, and its position is ample evidence of the great expansion that has occurred in the manufacturing industries of the colony during the last few years. The added value for Victoria has been set down at £10,734,000, which is £4,330,000 higher than that shown by the latest official returns. On the basis of these returns the production per inhabitant would be £5 5s. 3d., or £2 18s. 10d. below the average of the other Commonwealth states, a condition of things far removed from the bounds of probability.

Wages paid in Manufactories.

A comparison of the wages paid in the manufactories of the various states would be decidedly interesting, but unfortunately the figures are available only for New South Wales, Victoria, and New Zealand, and even in these states they are not compiled on the same basis. What information is available has, however, been prepared and is presented in the form of a table showing the average weekly wages paid in the various industries where a sufficient number of hands is employed to enable a fair average rate to be stated. The figures refer to the year 1901; those for New South Wales were compiled from the returns furnished under the Factories and Shops' Act; those for Victoria were obtained from the report of the Chief Inspector of Factories and Shops; while the New Zealand figures were obtained from the census returns published by the Government Statistician.

Industry.	Average Weekly Wages.					
	Males.			Females.		
	New South Wales.	Victoria.	New Zealand.	New South Wales.	Victoria.	New Zealand.
	£ s. d.	£ s. d.	£ s. d.	£ s. d.	£ s. d.	£ s d.
Boiling-down and tallow refineries	2 6 10	......	......	......	......	......
Tanneries	1 16 6	1 15 2	} 1 11 3	......	......	......
Wool scouring and fellmongery	1 19 2	1 17 2	}	......	......	......
Chaff cutting	1 14 7	1 12 3	......	......	......	......
Oil and grease	2 0 9	......	......	......	......	......
Soap and candles	1 13 6	1 8 6	1 12 8	0 10 1	......	......
Bricks and tiles	2 3 5	2 4 9	1 9 0	......	......	......
Glass (including bottles)	1 8 9	1 10 10	......	......	......	......
Glass (ornamental)	1 18 2	1 15 10	......	......	......	......
Lime, plaster, and cement	1 19 11	1 16 3	1 14 9	......	......	......
Marble and slate	1 13 9	......	......	......	......	......
Pottery and earthenware	1 14 2	1 15 6	......	......	......	......
Boxes and cases	1 12 7	......	......	......	......	......
Cooperage	1 13 0	2 4 7	1 10 7	......	......	......
Joinery	2 6 0	......	......	......	......	......
Saw-mills	1 14 2	2 3 2	1 9 0	......	......	......
Wood-turning	......	1 16 11	1 9 5	......	......	......
Agricultural implements	......	......	1 15 6	......	......	......
Brass and copper	1 7 2	1 9 6	}	......	......	......
Galvanised iron	1 12 4	......	} 1 12 0	......	......	......
Ironworks and foundries	1 18 4	1 16 5	}	......	......	......
Engineering	1 16 6	......	1 13 0	......	......	......
Railway carriage works	1 16 8	......	......	......	......	......
Smelting	2 9 7	1 19 9	......	......	......	......
Stoves and ovens	1 12 7	1 11 6	1 13 9	......	......	......
Tinsmithing, sheet ironworks	1 8 7	1 4 0	1 6 5	......	......	......
Other metal works	1 19 7	1 10 8	1 10 4	......	......	......
Wire working	1 12 1	1 5 1	......	......	......	......
Bacon curing	1 19 3	1 18 9	1 8 11	......	......	......
Butter factories	1 2 6	1 7 9	1 11 6	......	0 10 10	0 16 3
Meat preserving	1 14 1	2 0 8	1 15 1	0 11 0	......	0 11 2
Biscuits	1 2 8	1 2 8	1 9 0	0 11 5	0 13 4	0 8 2
Confectionery	1 4 0	1 9 6	1 7 1	0 8 6	0 12 8	0 9 5
Cornflour, oatmeal, &c.	1 14 5	......	......	0 11 9	......	......
Flour-mills	1 17 11	1 19 3	1 17 0	......	......	......
Jam and fruit canning	1 2 2	} 1 5 10	1 8 7	0 11 2	} 0 14 5	0 8 3
Pickles, sauces, and vinegar	1 9 2	}	1 3 1	0 9 0	}	0 13 3
Sugar refineries	2 2 10	1 18 0	......	......	......	......
Aerated waters, cordials, &c.	1 8 9	1 8 8	1 8 0	0 12 5	......	......
Breweries	1 12 7	1 15 5	2 7 5	......	......	......
Condiments, coffee, and spices	1 6 6	1 6 8	......	0 9 6	0 11 2	......
Distilleries	......	2 2 5	......	......	......	......
Ice and refrigerating	2 10 5	......	......	......	......	......
Malting	......	......	1 19 9	......	......	......
Tobacco, cigars, &c.	1 10 7	1 15 5	......	0 17 3	0 17 7	......
Fish-curing and preserving	......	......	1 1 2	......	......	......
Woollen mills	1 2 6	1 3 10	1 15 9	0 15 3	0 16 5	0 16 11
Boots and shoes	1 10 7	1 14 6	1 13 4	0 13 1	0 15 3	0 13 3
Slop clothing	1 16 3	......	......	0 13 2	......	......

Industry.	Average Weekly Wages.					
	Males.			Females.		
	New South Wales.	Victoria.	New Zealand.	New South Wales.	Victoria.	New Zealand.
	£ s. d.	£ s. d.	£ s. d.	£ s. d.	£ s. d.	£ s. d.
Clothing (tailoring)	2 2 0	2 0 5	1 15 0	0 18 4	0 18 3	11
Dressmaking and millinery	1 15 2	2 0 6	1 17 5	0 10 9	0 11 5	3
Hats and caps	1 11 2	1 19 7	1 7 5	0 13 10	0 17 0	3
Waterproof and oilskin	1 18 0	1 12 6	1 6 9	0 12 11	0 15 6	0 15 6
Shirts, ties, and scarfs	1 14 1	1 12 9	1 6 3	0 11 1	0 14 3	0 [illegible]
Rope and cordage	1 4 7	1 5 0	1 6 4	......	0 11 9	......
Tents and tarpaulins	1 7 2	......	......	0 13 6	......	......
Paper bags, boxes, &c.	1 0 4	1 9 0	......	0 10 5	0 10 3	......
Printing and bookbinding	1 19 7	1 15 4	1 19 3	0 11 7	0 11 11	0 12 7
Musical instruments	1 18 2	2 0 4	......	......	......	......
Explosives	......	1 13 4	......	......	0 12 3	......
Coach and wagon building	1 12 5	1 11 1	1 7 1	......	......	......
Cycles	......	1 7 0	1 1 3	......	0 19 6	......
Docks and slips	2 4 7	......	......	......	......	......
Ship and boat building	2 4 10	......	1 4 7	......	......	......
Bedding, flock and upholstery	1 12 5	1 18 11	......	0 16 0	0 16 8	......
Iron bedsteads	......	1 12 4	......	......	......	......
Furniture and cabinetmaking	1 13 6	2 0 2	1 7 6	0 15 0	......	0 13 0
Picture frames	1 10 5	1 0 11	......	0 15 2	0 16 4	......
Chemicals, drugs, and medicines	1 8 4	1 9 0	......	0 11 3	0 15 11	......
Manufacturing jewellery	1 19 1	2 0 11	......	......	0 16 1	......
Electric light and power	1 15 1	2 3 6	......	......	......	......
Gas works	2 3 9	......	2 7 8	......	......	......
Leather belting	1 12 5	1 6 8	......	......	......	......
Fancy leather, portmanteaux, and bags	1 7 0	1 3 9	......	0 12 10	0 12 5	......
Brooms and brushware	1 7 3	1 9 5	1 6 8	......	0 13 1	0 10 11
Saddlery and harness	1 12 5	1 14 5	1 4 11	1 3 0	0 17 2	0 17 2
Basket and perambulator factories	......	......	1 3 5	......	......	......
Flax mills	......	......	1 3 0	......	......	......

These figures must be accepted with a certain degree of caution. In each state a considerable number of juvenile workers is employed, but only in Victoria is their actual strength ascertained, and as the average weekly wage paid in any establishment would depend to a large extent on the proportion of juvenile labour employed, a fair comparison is impossible while that information is lacking.

INDEX.

Sydney: William Applegate Gullick, Government Printer.—1904.

Lightning Source UK Ltd.
Milton Keynes UK
UKHW021329170119
335636UK00009B/939/P